Childhood and Adolescence

Voyages in Development

THIRD EDITION

Spencer A. Rathus

New York University

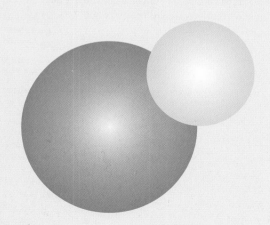

THOMSON

WADSWORTH

Australia • Brazil • Canada • Mexico • Singapore
• Spain • United Kingdom • United States

THOMSON

WADSWORTH

Publisher: Michele Sordi
Development Editor: Kate Barnes
Assistant Editor: Rachel Guzman
Editorial Assistant: Erin Miskelly
Technology Project Manager: Amy Cohen
Marketing Manager: Sara Swangard
Marketing Assistant: Melanie Cregger
Marketing Communications Manager: Linda Yip
Project Manager, Editorial Production: Mary Noel
Creative Director: Rob Hugel

Art Director: Vernon T. Boes
Print Buyer: Judy Inouye
Permissions Editor: Bob Kauser
Production Service: Joan Keyes, Dovetail Publishing Services/G&S
Text Designer: Cheryl Carrington
Photo Researcher: Eric Schrader
Copy Editor: Kathleen Lafferty
Cover Designer: Cheryl Carrington
Cover Image: Digital Vision/Getty Images
Compositor: G&S Book Services

Printed in Canada
1 2 3 4 5 6 7 11 10 09 08 07

For more information about our products, contact us at:
Thomson Learning Academic Resource Center
1-800-423-0563
For permission to use material from this text or product, submit a request online at http://www.thomsonrights.com.
Any additional questions about permissions can be submitted by e-mail to thomsonrights@thomson.com.

Library of Congress Control Number: 2007939602

Student Edition:
ISBN-13: 978-0-495-50390-3
ISBN-10: 0-495-50390-8

Loose-leaf Edition:
ISBN-13: 978-0-495-50458-0
ISBN-10: 0-495-50458-0

Thomson Higher Education
10 Davis Drive
Belmont, CA 94002-3098
USA

Credits:

A Closer Look: Glowimages/Getty Images; Active review chapters 1–7: © PhotoDisc/Getty Images; Active review chapters 8–10: © Maya Barnes/The Image Works; Active review chapters 11–13: © Royalty-Free/CORBIS; Active review chapters 14–16: © Image 100/Royalty-Free/CORBIS; Developing in a World of Diversity, left: Camille Tokerud/Getty Images; Developing in a World of Diversity, middle: Peter Cade/Getty Images; Developing in a World of Diversity, right: Russell Underwood/Getty Images; Lessons in Observation, Video Camera: Paul Tearle/Getty Images; Lessons in Observation, Book: Siede Preis/Getty Images; Lessons in Observation, screen shots: From *Childhood and Adolescence, Voyages in Development* 2nd edition by RATHUS, 2006. Reprinted with permission of Wadsworth, a division of Thomson Learning: www.thomsonrights.com. Fax 800-730-2215.

For Lois

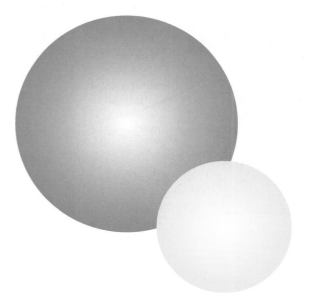

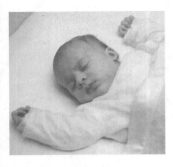

Numerous personal experiences enter into Rathus's textbooks. For example, he was the first member of his family to go to college. He found college textbooks to be cold and intimidating, and when his opportunity came to write college textbooks, he wanted them to be different—warm and encouraging, especially to students who were also the first generation in their families to be entering college.

Rathus's first professional experience was teaching high school English. Part of the task of the high school teacher is to motivate students and make learning fun. Through this experience he learned the importance of humor, and personal stories, which later became part of his textbook approach. Rathus wrote poetry and novels while he was an English teacher—and some of the poetry was published in poetry journals. The novels never saw the light of day (which is just as well, Rathus admits).

Rathus earned his Ph.D. in psychology and then entered clinical practice and teaching. He has published research articles in journals such as *Adolescence, Behavior Therapy, Journal of Clinical Psychology, Behaviour Research and Therapy, Journal of Behavior Therapy and Experimental Psychiatry*, and *Criminology*. His research interests lie in the areas of human growth and development, psychological disorders, methods of therapy, and psychological assessment.

Foremost among his research publications is the Rathus Assertiveness Schedule, which remains widely used in research and clinical practice. Rathus has since poured his energies into writing textbooks, while teaching at Northeastern University, St. John's University, and, currently, New York University. His introductory psychology textbook, *Psychology: Concepts and Connections,* is in its ninth edition.

Rathus is proud of his family. His wife Lois is a successful author and a professor of art at The College of New Jersey. His daughter Allyn graduated New York University's Tisch School of the Arts and is in theater management. His daughter Jordan also graduated from NYU's Tisch School of the Arts and is a production coordinator in film/video. Rathus's youngest daughter, Taylor, an eleventh grader, can dance the pants off of both of them. Rathus's eldest daughter, Jill, is a psychologist and teaches at C. W. Post College of Long Island University.

The author is shown at various stages of development in the four photos on this page.

Brief CONTENTS

1 | What Is Child Development?

Chapter 1   History, Theories, and Methods 3

2 | Beginnings

Chapter 2   Heredity and Conception 47

Chapter 3   Prenatal Development 77

Chapter 4   Birth and the Newborn Baby: In the New World 111

3 | Infancy

Chapter 5   Infancy: Physical Development 151

Chapter 6   Infancy: Cognitive Development 187

Chapter 7   Infancy: Social and Emotional Development 221

4 | Early Childhood

Chapter 8   Early Childhood: Physical Development 265

Chapter 9   Early Childhood: Cognitive Development 295

Chapter 10   Early Childhood: Social and Emotional
             Development 331

5 | Middle Childhood

Chapter 11   Middle Childhood: Physical Development 371

Chapter 12   Middle Childhood: Cognitive Development 395

Chapter 13   Middle Childhood: Social and Emotional
             Development 441

6 | Adolescence

Chapter 14   Adolescence: Physical Development 477

Chapter 15   Adolescence: Cognitive Development 517

Chapter 16   Adolescence: Social and Emotional Development 545

Answers to Active Reviews A-1

Glossary G-1

References R-1

Credits C-1

Name Index I-1

Subject Index I-13

CONTENTS

Part 1 | What is Child Development?

1 History, Theories, and Methods

Truth or Fiction? 3

Preview 3

What Is Child Development?
Coming to Terms with Terms 4

    Why Do We Study Child Development? 5
    The Development of Child Development 6

Theories of Child Development 8

    What Are Theories of Child Development?
        Why Do We Have Them? 8
    The Psychoanalytic Perspective 9
    Concept Review 1.1: *Comparison of Freud's and*
              Erikson's Stages of Development 12
    The Learning Perspective: Behavioral and
        Social Cognitive Theories 13
A CLOSER LOOK | Operant Conditioning of Vocalizations in Infants 15
    The Cognitive Perspective 18
    Concept Review 1.2: *Jean Piaget's Stages of*
              Cognitive Development 20
    The Biological Perspective 21
    The Ecological Perspective 22
    The Sociocultural Perspective 24
Developing in a World of Diversity | Influence of the Macrosystem on the
              Development of Independence 24
    Concept Review 1.3: *Perspectives on Child Development* 28

Controversies in Child Development 30

    The Nature–Nurture Controversy 30
    The Continuity–Discontinuity Controversy 31
    The Active–Passive Controversy 31

How Do We Study Child Development? 32

    The Scientific Method 32
    Gathering Information 34
    Correlation: Putting Things Together 35
    The Experiment: Trying Things Out 36

Longitudinal Research: Studying Development over Time   37
Concept Review 1.4: *Comparison of Cross-Sectional and
Longitudinal Research   38*

Ethical Considerations   39

Recite: An Active Summary   41

Key Terms   43

Active Learning Resources   44

Part 2 | Beginnings

2 Heredity and Conception

Truth or Fiction?   47

Preview   47

**The Influence of Heredity on Development:
The Nature of Nature**   48

Chromosomes and Genes   48
Mitosis and Meiosis   49
Identical and Fraternal Twins   50
Dominant and Recessive Traits   51
Chromosomal Abnormalities   53
Concept Review 2.1: *Chromosomal and Genetic
Disorders   54*
Genetic Abnormalities   56
Genetic Counseling and Prenatal Testing   57
Lessons in Observation | Prenatal Assessment   60

Heredity and the Environment: Nature versus Nurture   61

Kinship Studies: Are the Traits of Relatives Related?   62
Twin Studies: Looking in the Genetic Mirror   62
Adoption Studies   63

Conception: Against All Odds   64

Ova   64
Sperm Cells   65
Infertility and Other Ways of Becoming Parents   66
Selecting the Sex of Your Child: Fantasy or Reality?   69
Developing in a World of Diversity | Where Are the Missing Chinese Girls?   70

Recite: An Active Summary   72

Key Terms   74

Active Learning Resources   75

3 Prenatal Development

Truth or Fiction?   77

Preview   77

The Germinal Stage: Wanderings   78

    Without Visible Means of Support . . .   79

The Embryonic Stage   80

    Sexual Differentiation   82

    The Amniotic Sac: A Shock Absorber   84

    The Placenta: A Filtration System   84

The Fetal Stage   85

    Fetal Perception: Bach at Breakfast and
        Beethoven at Brunch?   87

    Fetal Movements   88

    Concept Review 3.1: *Highlights of Prenatal
          Development*   88

Developing in a World of Diversity **|** Birth Rates Around the World   90

Environmental Influences on Prenatal Development   93

    Nutrition   93

    Teratogens and Health Problems of the Mother   94

    Drugs Taken by the Parents   97

A CLOSER LOOK **|** Preventing One's Baby from Being Infected with HIV   97

    Environmental Hazards   102

    Maternal Stress   104

    Parents' Age   104

    Concept Review 3.2: *Risks of Various Agents to the Embryo and Fetus*   105

Recite: An Active Summary   106

Key Terms   109

Active Learning Resources   109

4 Birth and the Newborn Baby: In the New World

Truth or Fiction?   111

Preview   111

Countdown . . .   112

The Stages of Childbirth   113

    The First Stage   113

    The Second Stage   114

Lessons in Observation | Birth   115
    The Third Stage   116

Methods of Childbirth   117

    Anesthesia   117
    Prepared Childbirth   118
    Cesarean Section   119
    Laboring Through the Birthing Options   120

Birth Problems   122

    Oxygen Deprivation   122
    Preterm and Low-Birth-Weight Infants   122
Developing in a World of Diversity | Maternal and Infant Mortality
                Around the World   124

The Postpartum Period   127

    Maternal Depression   128
    Bonding   129
A CLOSER LOOK | Have We Found the Daddy Hormones?   129

Characteristics of Neonates   130

    Assessing the Health of Neonates   130
    Reflexes   131
    Sensory Capabilities   134
A CLOSER LOOK | Studying Visual Acuity in Neonates:
        How Well Can They See?   135
    Learning: Really Early Childhood "Education"   139
    Sleeping and Waking   139
    Sudden Infant Death Syndrome (SIDS)   143

Recite: An Active Summary   146

Key Terms   148

Active Learning Resources   149

Part 3 | Infancy

5 Infancy: Physical Development

Truth or Fiction?   151

Preview   151

Physical Growth and Development   151

    Sequences of Physical Development: Head First?   151
    Growth Patterns in Height and Weight: Heading
        Toward the Greek Ideal?   153
    Concept Review 5.1: *Sequences of Physical Development*   154
    Failure to Thrive   156
    Nutrition: Fueling Development   157

Breast Feeding versus Bottle Feeding: Pros and Cons,
Biological and Political 158
Developing in a World of Diversity | Alleviating Protein-Energy
Malnutrition (PEM) 160

Development of the Brain and Nervous System 162
Development of Neurons 162
Development of the Brain 164
Nature and Nuture in the Development
of the Brain 165

Motor Development: How Moving 166
Lifting and Holding the Torso and Head:
Heads Up 167
Control of the Hands: Getting a
Grip on Things 167
Locomotion: Getting a Move On 167
Nature and Nurture in Motor Development 169

**Sensory and Perceptual Development:
Taking in the World 171**
Development of Vision: The Better to See You With 171
Development of Hearing: The Better to Hear You With 175
A CLOSER LOOK | Strategies for Studying the Development of
Shape Constancy 175
Development of Coordination of the Senses:
If I See It, Can I Touch It? 177
A CLOSER LOOK | Effects of Early Exposure to Garlic, Alcohol,
and—Gulp—Veggies 177
The Active–Passive Controversy in Perceptual Development 178
Lessons in Observation | Sensation and Perception in Infancy 179
Nature and Nurture in Perceptual Development 180

Recite: An Active Summary 182
Key Terms 183
Active Learning Resources 184

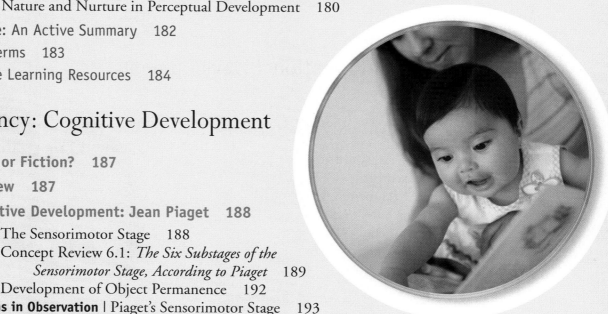

6 Infancy: Cognitive Development

Truth or Fiction? 187

Preview 187

Cognitive Development: Jean Piaget 188
The Sensorimotor Stage 188
Concept Review 6.1: *The Six Substages of the
Sensorimotor Stage, According to Piaget* 189
Development of Object Permanence 192
Lessons in Observation | Piaget's Sensorimotor Stage 193
Evaluation of Piaget's Theory 195

A Closer Look | Orangutans, Chimps, Magpies, and Object
Permanence 196
A Closer Look | Counting in the Crib? Findings from a
"Mickey-Mouse Experiment" 197

Information Processing 198
Infants' Memory 198
Imitation: Infant See, Infant Do? 198

Individual Differences in Intelligence among Infants 200

Testing Infants: Why and with What? 201

Instability of Intelligence Scores Attained in Infancy 201

**Use of Visual Recognition Memory:
An Effort to Enhance Predictability 201**

Language Development 203
Developing in a World of Diversity | Babbling Here, There, and Everywhere 203
Early Vocalizations 204
Development of Vocabulary 205
A Closer Look | Teaching Sign Language to Infants 206
Development of Sentences: Telegraphing Ideas 208
Theories of Language Development:
Can You Make a Houseplant Talk? 209
Views That Emphasize Nurture 210
Developing in a World of Diversity | Two-Word Sentences Here,
There, and . . . 211
A Closer Look | "Motherese" 212
Views That Emphasize Nature 213

Recite: An Active Summary 217
Key Terms 218
Active Learning Resources 219

7 | Infancy: Social and Emotional Development

Truth or Fiction? 221

Preview 221

Attachment: Bonds That Endure 222
Patterns of Attachment 222
Establishing Attachment 224
Stability of Attachment 225
Stages of Attachment 226
Theories of Attachment 226

When Attachment Fails 229
Concept Review 7.1: *Theories of Attachment* 230
Social Deprivation 231
Child Abuse and Neglect 233
A Closer Look | Prevention of Sexual Abuse of Children 235

A Closer Look | How Child Abuse May Set the Stage for
Psychological Disorders   237
A Closer Look | What to Do If You Think a Child Has Been the Victim of
Sexual Abuse   239
Autism Spectrum Disorders: Alone among the Crowd   240

Day Care   244
How Does Day Care Affect Bonds of Attachment?   244
How Does Day Care Influence Social and Cognitive
Development?   244
A Closer Look | The Latest Shoe to Drop from The NICHD   245
A Closer Look | Finding Day Care You (and Your Child) Can Live With   247

Emotional Development   248
Theories of the Development of Emotions   248
Fear of Strangers   250
Social Referencing: What Should I Do Now?   251
Emotional Regulation: Keeping on an Even Keel   251

Personality Development   252
The Self-Concept   253
Temperament: Easy, Difficult, or Slow to Warm Up?   254
Sex Differences   256
Lessons in Observation | Gender   257

Recite: An Active Summary   259

Key Terms   262

Active Learning Resources   262

Part 4 | Early Childhood

8 Early Childhood: Physical Development

Truth or Fiction?   265

Preview   265

Growth Patterns   266
Height and Weight   266
Development of the Brain   266

Motor Development   269
Gross Motor Skills   269
Physical Activity   270
Fine Motor Skills   272
Developing in a World of Diversity | Sex Differences
in Motor Activity   272
Children's Drawings   273
Handedness   274
Lessons in Observation | Gross and Fine Motor Skills   275

Nutrition   276

    Nutritional Needs   276

    Patterns of Eating   277

Health and Illness   278

A CLOSER LOOK | Ten Things You Need to Know about Immunizations   279

    Minor Illnesses   280

    Major Illnesses   280

    Accidents   281

A CLOSER LOOK | Assessing and Minimizing the Risk of Lead Poisoning   282

Sleep   283

    Sleep Disorders   284

Developing in a World of Diversity | Cross-Cultural Differences in
                Sleeping Arrangements   285

Elimination Disorders   287

    Enuresis   287

A CLOSER LOOK | What To Do About Bed-Wetting   288

    Encopresis   288

Recite: An Active Summary   290

Key Terms   291

Active Learning Resources   292

9 Early Childhood: Cognitive Development

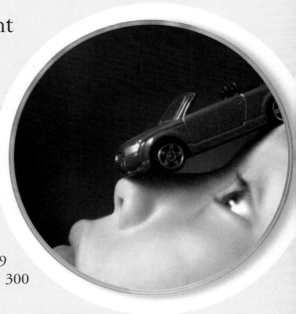

Truth or Fiction?   295

Preview   295

Jean Piaget's Preoperational Stage   296

    Symbolic Thought   296

    Symbolic or Pretend Play:
        "We Could Make Believe"   296

    Operations: "Transformers" of the Mind   297

    Egocentrism: It's All About Me   298

    Causality: Why? Because.   298

    Confusion of Mental and Physical Events:
        On "Galaprocks" and Dreams That Are Real   299

    Focus on One Dimension at a Time: Mental Blinders   300

    Evaluation of Piaget   302

Lessons in Observation | Piaget's Preoperational Stage   302

Developing in a World of Diversity | Cognitive Development and
                Concepts of Ethnicity and Race   303

    Concept Review 9.1: *Features of Preoperational Cognition,*
        According to Piaget   305

Factors in Cognitive Development   306

    Scaffolding and the Zone of Proximal Development   306

    Being at HOME: The Effect of the Home Environment   306

Effects of Early Childhood Education: Does It Give
Preschoolers a Head Start?   308
Television: Window on the World or Prison
Within a False World?   309
A CLOSER LOOK | Helping Children Use Television Wisely   311

Theory of Mind: What Is the Mind? How Does It Work?   312

False Beliefs: Just Where Are Those Crayons?   313
Origins of Knowledge: Where Does It Come From?   314
The Appearance–Reality Distinction: Appearances
Are More Deceiving at Some Ages Than at Others   314

**Development of Memory: Creating "Documents,"
Storing Them, and Retrieving Them   315**

Memory Tasks: Recognition and Recall   315
Competence of Memory in Early Childhood   316
Factors Influencing Memory   317
Memory Strategies: Remembering to Remember   318

Language Development: Why "Daddy Goed Away"   319

Development of Vocabulary: Words, Words, and More Words   319
Development of Grammar: Toward More Complex Language   321
Pragmatics: Preschoolers Can Be Practical   323
Language and Cognition   324

Recite: An Active Summary   326

Key Terms   327

Active Learning Resources   328

10 Early Childhood: Social and Emotional Development

Truth or Fiction?   331

Preview   331

Influences on Development: Parents,
Siblings, and Peers   332

Dimensions of Child Rearing   332
Parenting Styles: How Parents Transmit
Values and Standards   334
Effects of the Situation and the Child on
Parenting Styles   336
Influence of Siblings   336
Developing in a World of Diversity | Individualism, Collectivism, and
Patterns of Child Rearing   338
Birth Order: Not Just Where in the World But Also
Where in the Family   340
Peer Relationships   341
Developing in a World of Diversity | Where Are the Missing American Fathers?   342

Social Behaviors: In the World, among Others 344

  Play—Child's Play, That Is 344
  Prosocial Behavior: It Could Happen, and Does 347
  Development of Aggression:
      The Dark Side of Social Interaction 349
  Theories of Aggression 358
A CLOSER LOOK | When *Doom* Leads to . . . Doom: What Children Learn
              from Violent Video Games 353

Personality and Emotional Development 355

  The Self 355
  Initiative versus Guilt 356
  Fears: The Horrors of Early Childhood 356
A CLOSER LOOK | Helping Children Cope with Fears 357

Development of Gender Roles and Sex Differences 358

  Sex Differences 359
  Theories of the Development of Sex Differences 359
Lessons in Observation | Gender 361
  Concept Review 10.1: *Theories of the Development of Sex
                      Differences* 363
  Psychological Androgyny 365

Recite: An Active Summary 367

Key Terms 369

Active Learning Resources 369

Part 5 | Middle Childhood

11 Middle Childhood: Physical Development

Truth or Fiction? 371

Preview 371

Growth Patterns 372

  Height and Weight 372
  Nutrition and Growth 372
  Sex Similarities and Differences in
      Physical Growth 373
  Overweight in Children 374
A CLOSER LOOK | Helping Overweight Children Manage
              Their Weight 376

Motor Development 378

  Gross Motor Skills 378
  Fine Motor Skills 379
  Concept Review 11.1: *Development of Motor Skills during
                      Middle Childhood* 375

Sex Similarities and Differences in Motor Development   380
Exercise and Fitness   380

Children with Disabilities   382

Attention-Deficit/Hyperactivity Disorder (ADHD)   382
Developing in a World of Diversity | African American Youth and ADHD   385
Learning Disabilities   386
Concept Review 11.2: *Types of Learning Disabilities*   387
Educating Children with Disabilities   389

Recite: An Active Summary   391

Key Terms   392

Active Learning Resources   393

12 Middle Childhood: Cognitive Development

Truth or Fiction?   395

Preview   395

Piaget: The Concrete-Operational Stage   396

Conservation   396
Lessons in Observation | Piaget's Concrete-
        Operational Stage   397
Transitivity   398
Class Inclusion   399
Applications of Piaget's Theory to
        Education   399
Concept Review 12.1: *Aspects of Concrete-
        Operational Thinking*   400
Evaluation of Piaget's Theory   401

Moral Development: The Child as Juror   401

Piaget's Theory of Moral Development   402
Kohlberg's Theory of Moral Development   403

**Information Processing: Learning,
Remembering, Problem Solving**   406

Development of Selective Attention   407
Developments in the Storage and Retrieval of Information   407
Development of Recall Memory   410
Development of Metacognition and Metamemory   410
A CLOSER LOOK | Children's Eyewitness Testimony   412

Intellectual Development, Creativity, and Achievement   413

Theories of Intelligence   413
Concept Review 12.2: *Theories of Intelligence*   416
Measurement of Intellectual Development   416
A CLOSER LOOK | Emotional Intelligence and Social Intelligence?   417
Patterns of Intellectual Development   422
Differences in Intellectual Development   424

Creativity and Intellectual Development   425

Developing in a World of Diversity | Socioeconomic and Ethnic
Differences in IQ   426

Determinants of Intellectual Development   428

Language Development and Literacy   431

Vocabulary and Grammar   431

Reading Skills and Literacy   431

Methods of Teaching Reading   432

Diversity of Children's Linguistic Experiences in the United States:
Ebonics and Bilingualism   433

Recite: An Active Summary   436

Key Terms   438

Active Learning Resources   439

13 Middle Childhood: Social and Emotional Development

Truth or Fiction?   441

Preview   441

**Theories of Social and Emotional
Development in Middle Childhood   442**

Psychoanalytic Theory   443

Social Cognitive Theory   443

Cognitive-Developmental Theory and Social Cognition   443

Development of the Self-Concept in Middle Childhood   445

Lessons in Observation | Self-Concept   447

The Family   448

Parent–Child Relationships   448

Lesbian and Gay Parents   449

A CLOSER LOOK | How to Answer a 7-Year-Olds Questions about—
Gulp—Sex   449

Generation X or Generation Ex? What Happens
to Children Whose Parents Get Divorced?   450

The Effects of Maternal Employment   454

Peer Relationships   456

Peers as Socialization Influences   456

Peer Acceptance and Rejection   456

Development of Friendships   457

The School   459

Entry into School: Getting to Know You   459

The School Environment: Setting the Stage for Success, or . . .   460

A CLOSER LOOK | Bullying: An Epidemic of Misbehavior and Fear   460

Teachers: Setting Limits, Making Demands,
　　　Communicating Values, and—Oh, Yes—Teaching 461

Social and Emotional Problems 464

Conduct Disorders 464
Childhood Depression 465
Concept Review 13.1: *Social and Emotional Problems That*
　　　　　　May Emerge during Middle Childhood 468
Childhood Anxiety 468
Developing in a World of Diversity | Problems? No Problem. (For Some
　　　　　Children) 472

Recite: An Active Summary 473

Key Terms 475

Active Learning Resources 475

Part 6　Adolescence

14 Adolescence: Physical Development

Truth or Fiction? 477

Preview 477

Puberty: The Biological Eruption 479

The Adolescent Growth Spurt: Changed
　　Forever 479
Pubertal Changes in Boys 482
Concept Review 14.1: *Stages of Pubertal*
　　　　　　Development in
　　　　　　Males 483
Pubertal Changes in Girls 484
Concept Review 14.2: *Stages of Pubertal*
　　　　　　Development in Females 486
Early versus Late Maturers: Does It Matter
　　When You Arrive, as Long as You Do? 487
Body Image in Adolescence 489

**Emerging Sexuality and the Risks of
Sexually Transmitted Infections 490**

HIV/AIDS 491
Risk Factors 492
Prevention of Sexually Transmitted Infections 492
A CLOSER LOOK | Preventing HIV/AIDS and Other STIs:
　　　　　It's More than Safe(r) Sex 493

Health in Adolescence 496

Risk Taking in Adolescence 496
Nutrition: An Abundance of Food 497

An Abundance of Eating Disorders:
When Dieting Turns Deadly   498
Substance Abuse and Dependence:
Where Does It Begin? Where Does It End?   503
Developing in a World of Diversity | Sex, Education, and Substance
Abuse   509

Recite: An Active Summary   513

Key Terms   515

Active Learning Resources   515

15 Adolescence: Cognitive Development

Truth or Fiction?   517

Preview   517

**The Adolescent in Thought: My, My,
How "Formal"**   518

Piaget's Stage of Formal Operations   518
Lessons in Observation | Piaget's Formal Operational
Stage: Abstraction and
Hypothetical Propositions   519
A CLOSER LOOK | The Puzzle and the Pendulum   521
Adolescent Egocentrism: Center Stage   522
Sex Differences in Cognitive Abilities   523

The Adolescent in Judgment: Moral Development   528

The Postconventional Level   528
Moral Behavior and Moral Reasoning:
Is There a Relationship?   529
Developing in a World of Diversity | Cross-Cultural and Sex Differences in
Moral Development   531

The Adolescent in School   532

Making the Transition from Elementary School   532
Dropping Out of School   533
A CLOSER LOOK | Beyond the Classroom: How Parents Can
Help Teenagers Improve Their Academic
Performance   535

**The Adolescent at Work: Career
Development and Work Experience**   536

Career Development   537
Adolescents in the Workforce   538
Developing in a World of Diversity | Ethnic Identity and Gender in Career
Self-Efficacy Expectancies   538

Recite: An Active Summary   541

Key Terms   542

Active Learning Resources   543

16 Adolescence: Social and Emotional Development

Truth or Fiction?   545

Preview   545

**Development of Identity and the Self-Concept:
"Who Am I?" (and Who Else?)**   546

Erikson's View of Identity Development   547
"Identity Statuses": Searching for the Self,
   Making a Commitment   547
Concept Review 16.1: *The Four Identity
               Statuses of James Marcia*   548
Ethnicity and Development of Identity   549
Sex and Development of Identity   551
Development of the Self-Concept in Adolescence   552
Self-Esteem in Adolescence: Bottoming? Rising?   552

Relationships with Parents and Peers   553

Relationships with Parents   553
Relationships with Peers   555

**Sexuality: When? What? (How?) Who? Where?
and Why?—Not to Mention, "Should I?"**   559

Masturbation   560
Sexual Orientation   560
Male–Female Sexual Behavior   562
Teenage Pregnancy   564
A CLOSER LOOK | What Parents Want from Sex
               Education Courses   566

Juvenile Delinquency   568

Ethnicity, Sex, and Juvenile Delinquency   569
Who Are the Delinquents? What Are They Like?   570
Prevention and Treatment of Juvenile Delinquency   571

**Suicide: When the Adolescent Has Nothing—
Except Everything—to Lose**   572

Risk Factors for Suicide   572
Ethnicity, Sex, and Suicide   573
A CLOSER LOOK | Warning Signs of Suicide   574

**Epilogue: Emerging Adulthood—Bridging
Adolescence and the Life Beyond**   575

Recite: An Active Summary   578
Key Terms   580
Active Learning Resources   581

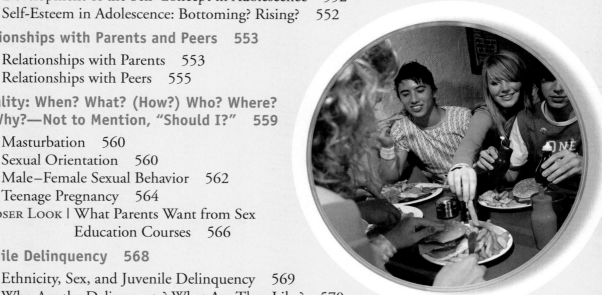

Answers to Active Reviews A-1

Glossary G-1

References R-1

Credits C-1

Name Index I-1

Subject Index I-13

Preface

These are our children.
These are our selves.

In children, we have the making of ourselves. In children, parents have the most impetuous, comical, ingratiating, delightful, and—at times—frustrating versions of themselves. It is hard to believe, but true, that the babies we hold in our hands at birth may someday be larger and stronger, more talented, and more insightful than we are.

Portraying the Fascination of Children: Personal and Scientific

My goal in writing this book has been to capture the wonder of child and adolescent development, while portraying the field of development as the rigorous science it is. My approach is designed to help motivate students by showing them the joy of observing children and adolescents. How can one hope to convey a true sense of development if one is blind to its marvels?

Childhood and Adolescence: Voyages in Development evolved from my scientific interest and research in human growth and development and also from my experiences with my own developing family. While my intention is to keep the tone of this text engaging and accessible, this book is rigorous in its reporting of research methods and science. On the other hand, the book is also "hands on"; it contains many applications, ranging from preventing protein-energy malnutrition (PEM) and what to know about immunizations to helping children overcome enuresis and handling bullying in school.

Key Features

The third edition of *Childhood and Adolescence: Voyages in Development* contains the following key features:

- A thorough and rigorous update
- **Lessons in Observation**—a video feature that allows students to observe different stages of development
- **Concept Reviews**—visual presentations of complex developmental concepts
- **Developing in a World of Diversity**—interesting and timely topics covering the many aspects of diversity in child and adolescent development
- **A Closer Look**—highlight expanded coverage of important research, present issues of currency or high interest, and allow readers to "take this book home with them"—that is, to apply what they are learning with children and adults in their own lives
- An enhanced pedagogical package: PQ4R

A Thorough Update

This is an exciting time to be studying child and adolescent development: Every day new research and new insights help us to better understand the mysteries and marvels of the many aspects of development. There are nearly 1,000 new references that refer to research studies and broader issues, such as the most recent research on the (probable) causes of SIDS, the most recent "Recommended Immunization Schedule for Persons Aged 0–6," the most recent research from the University of Michigan Monitoring the Future Study, the most recent information on teenage pregnancy, and the most recent HIV/AIDS Surveillance studies published by the Centers for Disease Control and Prevention.

Chapter-by-Chapter Updates

In addition to containing new research, every chapter has undergone updating in terms of the coverage of topics and pedagogy. Following is a sampling of what is new in each chapter:

Chapter 1—History, Theories, and Methods

- The history and theories section has been updated and edited to make it more manageable and streamlined.

Chapter 2—Heredity and Conception

- New research on psychological traits that are heritable
- New updates on the number of genes
- Update on numbers of multiple births
- Update on problems of children with Down syndrome
- Updates on Klinefelter syndrome and Turner syndrome
- Update on amniocentesis versus chorionic villus sampling
- Updates on results of twin studies and heritability of psychological preferences (coffee versus tea, marriage versus single life)
- Update on causes of infertility
- New "Developing in a World of Diversity" feature: *Where Are the Missing Chinese Girls?*

Chapter 3—Prenatal Development

- New Truth-or-Fiction item about parents in wealthy nations
- Update on possible effects of fetal learning on attachment
- Updates on effects of maternal malnutrition and obesity during pregnancy
- Updates on effects of maternal use of marijuana, cocaine, alcohol, and caffeine
- New "Developing in a World of Diversity" feature: *Birth Rates around the World*

Chapter 4—Birth and the Newborn Baby: In the New World

- Updates on the frequency of use of episiotomy
- Update on the effects on the baby of anesthesia during childbirth
- Update on the effects of having a doula present during childbirth
- Updated statistics on the frequency of C-sections
- Update on the effects of hypoxia
- Update on the risks of prematurity and VLBW babies
- Update on parental response to preterm babies
- Update on the use of music as part of intervention for preterm babies
- Expanded coverage of (very early) parent–infant bonding
- Update on the hearing of neonates
- Revised information on the sensitivity of neonates to pain
- Revision of section on SIDS to include the Children's Hospital Boston Study, which focuses on relatively lower responsiveness of the medulla of SIDS babies to the neurotransmitter serotonin
- New "A Closer Look" feature: *Have We Found the Daddy Hormones?*

Chapter 5—Infancy: Physical Development

- Updated research on failure to thrive
- Update on breast-feeding versus bottle-feeding: advantages and disadvantages for the health of the child, politics, and trends.
- Updated research on the effects of myelination of the brain
- Updated research on the effects of fetal malnutrition on brain development
- Updated research on infant preferences for human faces
- Updated research on development of coordination of the senses

Chapter 6—Infancy: Cognitive Development

- Updated research on the priming of infants' memory
- Update on the possibility that newborns have "memory neurons" that facilitate imitation and bonding
- A revised critical look at testing intelligence in infancy
- Updated research on a "sensitive period" for language development

Chapter 7—Infancy: Social and Emotional Development

- New "A Closer Look" feature: *Prevention of Sexual Abuse of Children*
- New "A Closer Look" feature: *The Latest Shoe to Drop on Day Care from the NICHD* (results of research reported in 2007)
- Updated research on secure attachment and stability of attachment
- Updated research on incidence and biological correlates of autism spectrum disorders
- Updated research on social referencing
- Updated research on sex differences in infant's behavior

Chapter 8—Early Childhood: Physical Development

- Update on nutritional needs in early childhood
- New table on a diet that avoids excess sugar and excess fats for a 4-year-old
- Updated (2007) CDC version of "Ten Things You Need To Know About Immunizations"
- Updated figure: "Recommended Immunization Schedule for Persons Aged 0–6 Years, United States, 2007"
- Revised "A Closer Look" feature: *Assessing and Minimizing the Risk of Lead Poisoning*
- New table on leading causes of death for children aged 2 to 6
- Updated "Developing in a World of Diversity" feature: *Cross-Cultural Differences in Sleeping Arrangements*

Chapter 9—Early Childhood: Cognitive Development

- Updated information on the effects of Head Start
- Updated information on the effects of educational television
- Updated information on the "couch-potato" effect

Chapter 10—Early Childhood: Social and Emotional Development

- Updates on dimensions of child rearing
- Updates on the correlates of birth order
- Updates in evolutionary and hormonal factors in aggression
- New "A Closer Look" feature: *When* Doom *Leads to . . . Doom—What Children Learn from Violent Video Games*
- New "Developing in a World of Diversity" feature: *Where Are the Missing American Fathers?*
- Revised "A Closer Look" feature: *Helping Children Cope with Fears*

Chapter 11—Middle Childhood: Physical Development

- Complete revision of section on childhood obesity, "re-emerging" as a section on "Overweight in Children"
- New coverage of ethnicity and percent of children and adolescents who are overweight
- Updating of "A Closer Look" feature: *Helping Overweight Children Manage Their Weight*
- New coverage of the "Traffic Light Diet"
- New case description on attention-deficit/hyperactivity disorder
- Updating of literature on causes of attention-deficit/hyperactivity disorder, with emphasis on role of dopamine
- Updating of literature on dyslexia, including focus on the double-deficit hypothesis

Chapter 12—Middle Childhood: Cognitive Development

- New discussion of "social intelligence"
- Revised discussion of ethnic differences in intelligence
- New coverage of languages other than English spoken in the home in the United States, and how well people who speak another language in the home speak English

Chapter 13—Middle Childhood: Social and Emotional Development

- New "A Closer Look" feature: *How to Answer a 7-Year-Old's Questions about—Gulp—Sex*
- New coverage of Japanese research on factors in life satisfaction among mothers in the workplace
- New coverage of cyberbullying

Chapter 14—Adolescence: Physical Development

- Revised section: "Emerging Sexuality and Risks of Sexually Transmitted Infections"
- New table highlighting the ways in which adolescents and adults become infected with HIV
- New table showing percentage of adolescents who have initiated sexual intercourse at various ages
- New discussion of ethnicity and causes of death among adolescents
- New coverage of death among adolescents from the Centers for Disease Control and Prevention
- Updated information on nutritional needs of adolescents
- Updated information on eating disorders
- Updated information on the addictiveness of various drugs
- Updated information on ethnicity and substance abuse

Chapter 15—Adolescence: Cognitive Development

- New "Developing in a World of Diversity" feature: *Ethnic Identity and Gender in Career Self-Efficacy Expectancies*
- Revised section: "Sex Differences in Cognitive Abilities"
- New discussion of adolescent girls' vulnerability to stereotypes concerning female math ability
- New coverage of women as a percentage of college students receiving Bachelor's degrees in the sciences, and women in professions once populated almost exclusively by men
- New statistics on dropout rates of students in grades 10–12

- Revised evaluation of Kohlberg's theory
- Revised discussion of Carol Gilligan's views concerning Kohlberg
- New discussion of the social cognitive theory of adolescent career exploration and decision making

Chapter 16—Adolescence: Social and Emotional Development

- New recognition in the "Formation of Identity" section that inner city adolescent girls of color are unlikely to have the choices available that Erik Erikson theorized about
- Updated information on the formation of ethnic identity
- Updated information on ethnic differences in amount of time spent on homework
- Updated information on factors that influence the incidence of masturbation
- Revised information on the development of sexual orientation and the development of an adolescent's sexual identity vis-á-vis sexual orientation
- Updated information on parental and peer influences on the initiation of sexual activity
- Updated information on teenage pregnancy
- Completely revised "A Closer Look" feature: *What Parents Want from Sex Education*
- Completely revised section on juvenile delinquency highlighting delinquency rates for adolescents from different racial backgrounds. Topics include the percentage of adolescents of various racial backgrounds who live in poverty, percentage of children living with one or both of their parents according to race and ethnicity, and sex differences in delinquent behavior.
- New information on social and technological factors that contribute to a hypothesized new stage of development: emerging adulthood

New! Annotated Instructor's Edition

Child and adolescent development has many applications to teaching, everyday life, and different careers. As such, we have created a new Annotated Instructors Edition designed to help instructors identify and teach these important areas of development. Written by Debra Schwiesow of Creighton University, the new annotated instructor's edition contains the following Teaching Tips:

- Teaching Tip (for general development students)
- Teaching Tip: Parenting & Family Studies
- Teaching Tip: Education
- Teaching Tip: Social Work & Helping Professions
- Teaching Tip: Nursing & Health
- Technology Tip (suggestions for useful websites that relate to the chapter topics)

New Pedagogical Features

Reflect Items in "A Closer Look" and "Diversity" Features

Each "A Closer Look" and "Developing in a World of Diversity" feature now ends with at least one **Reflect** item. As used elsewhere in the text, **Reflect** items help students learn more effectively because they encourage students to think more deeply about the subject matter. Psychologists refer to reflection on subject matter as *elaborative rehearsal,* which helps students both understand and remember the subject matter.

Reflect: How closely did your parents pay attention to your height and weight? Did they chart it? When did you begin to think that you were average or above or below average in height and weight? What effect did your size have on your self-concept and self-esteem?

Page Numbers Accompany "Truth or Fiction" Items
In the third edition, you will find page numbers alongside the Truth or Fiction items at the beginning of each chapter. The page numbers indicate where in the text students will be able to check whether the item is, in fact, truth or fiction.

Truth or Fiction?

T F The head of the newborn child doubles in length by adulthood, but the legs increase in length by about five times. p. 153

T F Infants triple their birth weight within a year. p. 153

T F Breast feeding helps prevent obesity later in life. p. 161

Question: What patterns of growth occur in infancy? During the first year after birth, gains in height and weight are also dramatic, although not by the standards of prenatal gains. Infants usually double their birth weight in about 5 months and triple it by the first birthday (Kuczmarski et al., 2000). Their height increases by about 50% in the first year, so that a child whose length at birth was 20 inches is likely to be about 30 inches tall at 12 months. **Truth or Fiction Revisited:** Thus, it is true that infants triple their birth weight within a year. The gain sounds dramatic, but keep in mind that their weight increases more than a billionfold in the 9 months between conception and birth.

What Carries through from Edition to Edition

The third edition of *Childhood and Adolescence: Voyages in Development* continues to present cutting-edge topic coverage, emphasizing the latest findings and research in key areas. The text is organized chronologically beginning with introductory theoretical material followed by the developmental sequences.

"Lessons in Observation" Feature

One of the themes of this text is how children learn by observation. College students and other adults also learn by observation. One of the best ways to learn about child development is to observe the behavior of children. Unfortunately, many students do not have everyday access to children and therefore cannot observe for themselves how the many concepts and theories discussed in this textbook evidence themselves in the everyday lives of children.

Fortunately, all users of *Childhood and Adolescence: Voyages in Development* will find the "Lessons in Observation" feature integrated throughout the book. This feature showcases a series of observational videos that are available through the student website. These observational videos illustrate a wide range of topics, such as:

• Chapter 2: Prenatal Assessment
• Chapter 8: Gross and Fine Motor Skills

- Chapter 9: Piaget's Preoperational Stages
- Chapter 10: Gender
- Chapter 12: Piaget's Concrete-Operational Stage

Each video is discussed in an interactive format in the text. Each "Lessons in Observation" box includes **Learning Objectives, Applied Lessons**, and **Critical Thinking Questions**. This format makes the observation experience more meaningful and encourages higher-order thinking. The videos are available through the Student Companion Website where students can email their responses to their instructors, making this feature easily assignable.

Concept Reviews

Concept Reviews are more than simple summaries. They take complex developmental concepts—such as theories of intelligence—and present them in dynamic layouts that readily communicate the key concepts and the relationships among concepts. Many of them have photographs and figures as well as text. Here is a sampling of the *Concept Reviews* found in *Childhood and Adolescence: Voyages in Development*:

- Concept Review 1.3: Perspectives on Child Development
- Concept Review 6.1: The Six Substages of the Sensorimotor Stage, According to Piaget
- Concept Review 14.2: Stages of Pubertal Development in Females

"Developing in a World of Diversity" Feature

This feature is inclusive. We address the challenging issues of how children and adolescents are influenced by their ethnic backgrounds and gender roles in areas ranging from intellectual development to substance abuse. In many cases, cultural and ethnic factors affect the very survival of the child. This coverage helps students understand why parents of different backgrounds and sexes rear their children and adolescents in certain ways, why children and adolescents from various backgrounds behave and think in different ways, and how the study of child and adolescent development is enriched by addressing those differences.

Examples of "Developing in a World of Diversity" topics include:

- *New* Chapter 2: *Where Are the Missing Chinese Girls?*
- *New* Chapter 3: *Birth Rates around the World*
- Chapter 4: *Maternal and Infant Mortality Around the World*
- Chapter 8: *Cross-Cultural Differences in Sleeping Arrangements*
- *New* Chapter 15: *Ethnic Identity and Gender in Career Self-Efficacy Expectancies*

"A Closer Look" Feature

The "A Closer Look" features in this edition allow expanded treatment of a number of topics that serve a strong pedagogical purpose, present issues of high currency or interest, and allow readers to "take this book home with them"—that is, to apply what they are learning with children and adults in their own lives.

The following are examples of "A Closer Look" features that explain how researchers carry out their work:

- Chapter 1: *Operant Conditioning of Vocalizations in Infants*
- Chapter 4: *Studying Visual Acuity in Neonates: How Well Can They See?*
- Chapter 5: *Strategies for Studying the Development of Shape Constancy*
- Chapter 6: *Counting in the Crib? Findings from a "Mickey-Mouse Experiment"*

The following features allow readers to apply what they are learning with their own children, in their own lives:

- Chapter 3: *Preventing One's Baby from Being Infected with HIV*
- Chapter 7: *Finding Day Care You (and Your Child) Can Live With*
- Chapter 8: *Ten Things You Need To Know About Immunizations*
- Chapter 9: *Helping Children Use Television Wisely* (including teaching children *not* to imitate the violence they observe in the media)
- Chapter 10: *Helping Children Cope with Fears*

The following features share developmental information especially related to those studying to be child educators:

- Chapter 6: *Teaching Sign Language to Infants*
- Chapter 7: *What to Do If You Think a Child Has Been the Victim of Sexual Abuse*
- Chapter 10: *Helping Children Cope with Fears*
- Chapter 13: *Bullying—An Epidemic of Misbehavior and Fear*
- Chapter 16: *What Parents Want from Sex Education Courses*

An Enhanced Pedagogical Package: PQ4R

PQ4R discourages students from believing that they are sponges who will automatically soak up the subject matter in the same way that sponges soak up water. The PQ4R method stimulates students to *actively* engage the subject matter. Students are encouraged to become *proactive* rather than *reactive*.

PQ4R is the acronym for Preview, Question, Read, Reflect, Review, and Recite, a method that is related to the work of educational psychologist Francis P. Robinson. PQ4R is more than the standard built-in study guide. It goes well beyond a few pages of questions and exercises that are found at the ends of the chapters of many textbooks. It is an integral part of every chapter. It flows throughout every chapter. It begins and ends every chapter, and it accompanies the student page by page.

Preview

Chapter previews are provided in the form of chapter outlines intended to help shape students' expectations. It enables them to create mental templates or "advance organizers" into which they categorize the subject matter. Each chapter of *Childhood and Adolescence: Voyages in Development* previews the subject matter with a "Truth or Fiction" section and a chapter "Preview." The "Truth or Fiction" items stimulate students to delve into the subject matter by challenging folklore and common sense (which is often common *non*sense). "Truth-or-Fiction Revisited" sections in the chapter inform students as to whether or not they were correct in their assumptions. The *Preview* outlines the material in the chapter, creating mental categories that guide students' reading.

Following is a sample of challenging "Truth or Fiction" items from various chapters:

T F You can carry the genes for a deadly illness and not become sick yourself.

T F More children die from sudden infant death syndrome (SIDS) than from cancer, heart disease, pneumonia, child abuse, AIDS, cystic fibrosis and muscular dystrophy combined.

T F Infants need to have experience crawling before they develop fear of heights.

T F It is dangerous to awaken a sleepwalker.

T F Three-year-olds usually say "Daddy goed away" instead of "Daddy went away" because they *do* understand rules of grammar.

T F Children who watch 2 to 4 hours of TV a day will see 8,000 murders and another 100,000 acts of violence *by the time they have finished elementary school.*

Question

Devising questions about the subject matter before reading it in detail is another feature of the PQ4R method. Writing questions gives students goals: They attend class or read the text *in order to answer the questions.* Questions are placed in all primary sections of the text to help students use the PQ4R method most effectively. They are printed in **blue**. When students see a question, they can read the following material in order to answer that question. If they wish, they can also write the questions and answers in their notebooks, as recommended by Robinson.

Read

Reading is the first "R" in the PQ4R method. Although students will have to read for themselves, they are not alone. The text helps by providing:

- Previews of the chapter that help students organize the material
- "Truth or Fiction" sections that stimulate students by challenging common knowledge and folklore
- Presentation of the subject matter in clear, stimulating prose
- A running glossary that defines key terms in the margin of the text, near where the terms appear
- Development of concepts in an orderly fashion so that new concepts build on previously presented concepts

I have chosen a writing style that is "personal." It speaks directly to the student and employs humor and personal anecdotes designed to motivate and stimulate students.

Review

The second "R" in PQ4R stands for review. Regular reviews of the subject matter help students learn. There are two types of review features in *Childhood and Adolescence: Voyages in Development.* The first review feature is the "Concept Review." Because reviewing the subject matter is so important, and because of the value of visual cues in learning, "Concept Reviews" are found throughout the text (see page xxix of this preface). The second type of review feature is the "Active Review." These features follow each major section in the text.

"Active Reviews" contain two types of items that foster active learning, retention, and critical thinking. Fill-in-the-blanks are the first type of item. The fill-in-the-blank format challenges students to *produce,* not simply *recognize,* the answer. Items are numbered and answers are found at the end of each chapter. For example, an "Active Review" from the chapter on "Heredity and Conception" has the following fill-in-the-blanks items:

13. The sets of traits that we inherit are referred to as our (Genotypes or Phenotypes?).
14. The actual traits that we display at any point in time are the product of genetic and environmental influences and are called our (Geno- types or Phenotypes?).
15. Parents and children have a _____ percent overlap in their genetic endowments.
16. _____ (MZ) twins share 100% of their genes.
17. _____ (DZ) twins have a 50% overlap, as do other siblings.

Reflect & Relate

Students learn more effectively when they *reflect* (the third "R" in PQ4R), on or *relate* to the subject matter. Psychologists who study learning and memory refer to reflection on subject matter as *elaborative rehearsal.* One way of reflecting on a subject is to *relate* it to things they already know about, whether it be academic material or events in their own lives. Reflecting and relating to the material makes it meaningful and easier to remember. It also makes it more likely that students will be able to *apply* the information to their own lives. Through effective reflection, students can embed material firmly in their memory so that rote repetition is unnecessary.

Because reflecting on the material is intertwined with relating to it, the second kind of item in each "Active Review" section is termed *Reflect & Relate*. Here is the *Reflect & Relate* item from Chapter 13's "Active Review" following the section on social and emotional development in middle childhood:

> *Reflect & Relate:* Are you "responsible" for your own self-esteem, or does your self-esteem pretty much vary with the opinion that others have of you? Why is this an important question?

Recite

The PQ4R method recommends that students recite (the fourth "R" in PQ4R) the answers to the questions aloud. Reciting answers aloud helps students remember them by means of repetition, by stimulating students to produce concepts and ideas they have learned, and by associating them with spoken words and gestures.

Recite sections are found at the end of each chapter. They help students summarize the material, but they are active summaries. For this reason, the sections are called "Recite: An Active Summary." They are written in question-and-answer format. To provide a sense of closure, the active summaries repeat the questions found within the chapters. The answers are concise but include most of the key terms found in the text.

The "Recite: An Active Summary" sections are designed in two columns so that students can cover the second column (the answers) as they read the questions. Students can recite the answers as they remember or reconstruct them, and then check what they have recited against the answers they had covered. Students should not feel that they are incorrect if they have not produced the exact answer written in the second column; their individual approach might be slightly different, even more inclusive. The answers provided in the second column are intended to be a guide, to provide a check on students' learning. They are not carved in stone.

Themes

Childhood and Adolescence: Voyages in Development also continues its emphasis on a number of themes:

- human diversity in development
- biology: neuroscience, evolution, genes, hormones, and behavior
- applications

Coverage of these themes is summarized in the following Theme Indexes.

Human Diversity in Development
- Ecological circumstances that affect development (pp. 22–23)
- Study of Mexican American students and their environments in relationship to their happiness (p. 23)
- Influence of the macrosystem on the development of independence (p. 24)
- The sociocultural perspective and human diversity (pp. 25–27)
- Naturalistic observations in children of different cultures (p. 34)
- Ethnic differences in incidence of bearing fraternal twins (p. 51)
- Ethnic differences in chromosomal and genetic disorders (p. 57)
- Birth rates around the world (pp. 90–92)
- Cross-cultural differences when using a doula during delivery (p. 119)

- Maternal and infant mortality around the world (p. 124)
- Socioeconomic status and nutrition (pp. 157–158)
- Differences in preference for breastfeeding (pp. 158–159)
- Ethnic differences in infant capacity to walk (pp. 169–170)
- Differences in babbling across cultures (p. 203)
- Two-word sentence development across different languages (p. 211)
- Low-income families and levels of child attachment (pp. 224–225)
- Attachment of Ugandan and Scottish infants (p. 226)
- Social deprivation in a Guatemalan tribe (p. 233)
- Stranger anxiety across cultures (pp. 250–251)
- Sex differences in personality (pp. 256–258)
- Cultural differences in rough-and-tumble play (p. 271)
- Sex differences in motor activity (p. 272)
- Cultural differences in the perception of handedness (pp. 274–275)
- Ethnicity and immunization (p. 280–281)
- Differences in accidental death rate (p. 281–283)
- Cross-cultural differences in sleeping arrangements (p. 285)
- Development of concepts of ethnicity and race (p. 303)
- Cross-cultural differences in effects of parental styles (p. 333)
- Cultural and gender differences in authoritarian parenting and the results on children (p. 335)
- Individualism, collectivism, and patterns of child rearing (p. 338)
- Fathers in America (p. 342)
- Differences in the presence of a father (p. 342)
- Sex differences in play (pp. 346–347)
- Cultural differences in empathy (p. 348)
- Aggressiveness in sons of criminal and noncriminal fathers (p. 350)
- Sex differences in effects of TV violence (pp. 352–354)
- Development of gender roles and sex differences (pp. 358–359)
- Possible sex differences in organization of the brain (pp. 360–361)
- Cross-cultural differences in gender identity, stability, and constancy (p. 364)
- Psychological androgyny (pp. 365–366)
- Ethnicity and percent of children and adolescents who are overweight (p. 374)
- Sex differences and motor skills (p. 380)
- Education for disabled children (pp. 389–390)
- Discrimination in standardized testing (pp. 420–422)
- Testing bias and culture-free tests (p. 422)
- Mental retardation and giftedness (pp. 424–425)
- Socioeconomic and ethnic differences in IQ (pp. 426–427)
- Sex differences in self-esteem (p. 446)
- Sex differences in learned helplessness (p. 447)
- Sex differences in self-concept (p. 447)
- Effects of divorce across cultures (p. 452)
- Sex differences in coping with divorce (p. 452)
- Japanese research on factors in life satisfaction among mothers in the workplace (p. 455)
- Sex differences in development of friendships (p. 457)
- Differences in preparedness for school (p. 459)
- Sexism in the classroom (p. 463)
- Gender differences in social impact of acne (p. 482)
- Cultural impact of menarche (pp. 484–485)
- Ethnicity and causes of death among adolescents (p. 496–497)
- Sex differences in anorexia nervosa (p. 500)

- Sex, college plans, ethnicity, and substance abuse (p. 509)
- Differences in formal-operational thought (p. 522)
- Sex differences in verbal ability (p. 524)
- Sex differences in visual-spatial ability (p. 524)
- Sex differences in mathematical ability (pp. 525–527)
- Adolescent girls' vulnerability to stereotypes concerning female math ability (pp. 526–527)
- Differences in postconventional thought (p. 530)
- Cross-cultural differences in moral development (p. 531)
- Sex differences in moral development (p. 531)
- Ethnic identity and gender in career self-efficacy expectancies (p. 538)
- Ethnicity and development of identity (pp. 549–550)
- Sex and development of identity (pp. 551–552)
- Ethnicity, sex, and adolescent friendships (pp. 556–557)
- Differences in sexual orientation (p. 560)
- The origins of sexual orientation (p. 561)
- Percentage of adolescents of various racial backgrounds who live in poverty (p. 570)
- Percentage of children living with one or both of their parents according to race and ethnicity (p. 570)
- Ethnicity, sex, and juvenile delinquency (pp. 569–570)
- Sex differences in delinquent behavior (p. 571)
- Ethnicity, sex, and suicide (p. 573)

Biology: Neuroscience, Evolution, Genes, Hormones, and Behavior

- Ethology (pp. 21–22)
- The nature-nurture controversy (pp. 30–31)
- Frequency of fraternal twins (pp. 50–51)
- Chromosomal and genetic disorders (pp. 53–58)
- Ethnic differences in chromosomal and genetic disorders (p. 57)
- The possible evolution of reflexes (p. 132)
- Pain as adaptive (p. 139)
- Nature and nurture in the development of the brain (pp. 165–166)
- Nature and nurture in motor development (pp. 169–170)
- Are humans prewired to prefer human stimuli to other stimuli? (p. 172)
- Nature and nurture in perceptual development (pp. 180–181)
- Imitation as adaptive (p. 199)
- Nature and nurture in language development (pp. 209–216)
- The nativist view of language development (p. 213)
- Nature and nurture in theories of attachment development (pp. 226–229)
- Genetic factors in handedness (pp. 275–276)
- Evolutionary theory of aggression (p. 350)
- Genetic/hormonal factors in aggression (p. 350)
- The possible roles of evolution and heredity in sex differences (pp. 359–360)
- Organization of the brain (pp. 360–361)
- Genetic factors in obesity (p. 375)
- Genetic factors in dyslexia (pp. 388–389)
- Genetic influences on intelligence (pp. 428–429)
- The possible role of evolution in step-families (p. 453)
- Possible genetic factors in conduct disorder (p. 465)

- Depression and serotonin (p. 467)
- The biology of puberty (p. 479)
- Hormonal regulation of the menstrual cycle (p. 485)
- Serotonin and eating disorders (p. 502)
- Genetic factors in eating disorders (p. 502)
- Biological factors in substance abuse (p. 511)
- Possible evolutionary factors in visual–spatial ability (p. 524)
- The origins of sexual orientation (pp. 561–562)
- Biological effects of puberty (p. 563)

Applications

- Problems associated with use of punishment (pp. 14–15)
- Ways of reversing infertility (p. 68)
- Choosing the sex of one's child (p. 69)
- Maternal nutrition during pregnancy (pp. 93–94)
- Effects of maternal health problems on the embryo and fetus (pp. 94–97)
- Effects of environmental hazards on the embryo and the fetus (pp. 102–104)
- Using the Lamaze method to decrease fear and pain during delivery (pp. 118–119)
- Using C-section to avoid disease transmission from mother to infant (pp. 119–120)
- How interaction, talking, and stimulation can help preterm infants develop (p. 126)
- How a woman can work to get beyond postpartum depression (pp. 128–129)
- Understanding visual accommodation (p. 136)
- How to soothe an infant and ease crying (p. 143)
- How to introduce infants to new food (p. 158)
- Where women can go to learn more about breast-feeding (p. 161)
- Teaching sign language to infants (pp. 206–207)
- "Motherese" (pp. 212–213)
- Establishing attachment (p. 224)
- How child abuse may lead to psychological disorders in adulthood (p. 237)
- What to do if you think a child has been the victim of sexual abuse (p. 239)
- Neurological differences in autistic children (p. 242)
- Finding day care you and your child can live with (p. 247)
- How to comfort a child who doesn't know you (p. 251)
- Brain development and visual skills (pp. 267–268)
- Right brain/left brain (p. 268)
- Plasticity of the brain (p. 268)
- Teaching a child to enjoy healthy food (pp. 276–278)
- Ten things you need to know about immunizations (p. 279)
- Assessing and minimizing the risk of lead poisoning (p. 282)
- What to do about bed-wetting (p. 288)
- Watching how children show (or don't show) conservation (pp. 300–301)
- Memory strategies (pp. 318–319)
- Techniques for restricting children's behavior (pp. 333–334)
- Techniques parents can use to help control their children's behavior (p. 336)
- Helping children cope with fears (p. 357)
- Piaget's theory applied to education (pp. 399, 401)
- Rehearsal strategies for memory (pp. 410–411)
- How to ask children questions that elicit truthful answers (p. 412)
- How teachers can help motivate students (pp. 462–463)

- How to help children with conduct disorders (p. 465)
- How parents and teachers can help children with mild depression (p. 467)
- How parents and teachers can help children with school phobia (p. 471)
- Prevention of HIV/AIDS and other STIs (pp. 492–493)
- Treatment and prevention of eating disorders (pp. 502–513)
- Using different parenting styles to combat adolescent substance abuse (p. 511)
- Treatment and prevention of substance abuse (pp. 511–512)
- How parents can help teenagers improve their academic performance (p. 535)

The Package

Childhood and Adolescence: Voyages in Development is accompanied by a wide array of supplements prepared for both the instructor and student.

For the Instructor

Instructor's Manual (0-495-51029-7)

By Gwynn Morris of North Carolina State University. Available to adopters of Rathus' text, this comprehensive manual offers learning objectives, chapter outlines, chapter summaries, lecture topics, student exercises (such as Internet activities), film and videotape suggestions, activities for the Observing Children video series, and the Resource Integration Guide.

Test Bank (0-495-51030-0)

By Kimberly Dechman of George Mason University. For each chapter of the text, this Test Bank includes 130 multiple-choice questions, 20 matching questions, 15 true/false questions, 10 fill-in-the-blank questions, and 5 essay questions with model answers.

Observation Worksheets (0-495-51047-5)

By Debra Schwiesow of Creighton University. Perfect for homework or small group assignments, these Observation Worksheets encourage students to directly apply their knowledge and experience to their work as parents, counselors, caretakers, and teachers. The easy-to-complete, hands-on activities guide students through the process of observing, recording, and analyzing the behavior of children they encounter in the real world. For each chapter of the text, there is one individual activity and one small group activity.

PowerLecture with *JoinIn*™ and *ExamView*® CD-ROM (0-495-51031-9)

This one-stop lecture and class preparation tool contains ready-to-use Microsoft® PowerPoint® slides by Robin Musselman of LeHigh Carbon Community College, and allows you to assemble, edit, publish, and present custom lectures for your course. PowerLecture lets you bring together text-specific lecture outlines along with videos or your own materials, culminating in a powerful, personalized, media-enhanced presentation. The CD-ROM also includes JoinIn™, an interactive tool that lets you pose book-specific questions and display students' answers seamlessly within the Microsoft® PowerPoint® slides of your own lecture, in conjunction with the "clicker" hardware of your choice, as well as the ExamView® assessment and tutorial system, which guides you step by step through the process of creating tests.

ThomsonNow™ (0-495-51050-5)

ThomsonNow can be packaged with this text at no additional cost to your students. This dynamic, online personalized study system saves time for students and instructors. Through a series of diagnostic pre- and post-tests written by Vivian Baglien of Green River Community College, and personalized study plans with learning modules, eBook files and other media, students discover those areas of the text where they need to focus their efforts.

ThomsonNow for *Childhood and Adolescence: Voyages in Development* also includes access to hundreds of up-to-date articles from nearly 5,000 top journals and popular publications through InfoTrac® College Edition.

New! Careers in Developmental Psychology Module (0-495-59488-1)

By Gwynn Morris, North Carolina State University
The "Careers in Developmental Psychology Module" can be ordered with any Wadsworth psychology textbook. From education to jobs shaping public policy, developmental psychology offers many opportunities for career advancement. This helpful resource provides students with practical information about the range of careers informed by the field of developmental psychology, addressing questions such as: What is Developmental Psychology? What Does a Developmental Psychologist Do? How Does One Become a Developmental Psychologist? The module includes information about professional organizations and additional resources.

Observing Children and Adolescents Videos on CD-ROM and Workbook
(0-534-62272-0)
by Michie O. Swartwood and Kathy H. Trotter
This program includes nearly four hours of video segments featuring the highlights of infant, child, and adolescent development. Designed to deepen your students' understanding of major developmental milestones, the program focuses on concrete and observable behavior, and features segments of children interacting with peers, parents, and teachers in a variety of settings. The video also examines the ways in which major developmental theories are exhibited in everyday behavior. The accompanying workbook offers students concept overviews, key terms, and definitions, and a variety of critical-thinking applications, many of which ask you to approach the same video segment from more than one theoretical perspective.

Current Perspectives: Readings from InfoTrac College Edition, with InfoTrac®
(0-495-00762-5)
By Debra Schwiesow from Creighton University. For each chapter, this reader includes a full text article from the InfoTrac College Edition Online library and critical thinking questions about that article.

WebTutor Toolbox on WebCT® and Blackboard®
For ordering information, please contact your Wadsworth publishing representative.

Preloaded with content, and available at no extra charge via access code when packaged with this text, WebTutor pairs all the content of this text's Book Companion Website with course management functionality. You can assign materials (including online quizzes) and have the results flow automatically to your grade book. It is ready to use as soon as you log on, or you can customize its preloaded content by uploading images and other resources, adding web links, or creating your own practice materials.

For the Student:

Audio Study Tools

Audio Study Tools provide audio reinforcement of key concepts your student can listen to from their personal computer or MP3 player. Created specifically for Rathus's *Childhood and Adolescence: Voyages in Development,* 3e, Audio Study Tools provide approximately ten minutes of audio content per chapter, giving your students a quick and convenient way to master key concepts. Audio content allows students to test their knowledge with quiz questions as well as listen to a brief overview reflecting the major themes and key terms for each chapter.

Study Guide (0-495-50751-2)
By Randall Osborne and Shirley Ogletree,
both of Texas State University–San Marcos
For each chapter of Rathus's text, this comprehensive student guide includes a chapter summary, critical thinking exercises, internet activities, and a quiz.

Lecture Outlines with Note-Taking (0-495-51048-3)
By Robin Musselman of Lehigh Carbon Community College
Designed for convenient note-taking and review, this resource features printed Microsoft® PowerPoint® slides. The slides match those featured in PowerLecture. By taking notes alongside lecture outlines, students save time and stay focused, making them better able to listen and participate in class.

Acknowledgments

This book is about human development. This section is about the development of this book. The book may have a single author, but its existence reflects the input and aid of a significant cast of characters.

First among these are my professional academic colleagues—the people who teach the course, the people who conduct the research. They know better than anyone else what's going on "out there"—out there in the world of children and adolescents, out there in the classroom. The book you hold in your hands would not be what it is without their valuable insights and suggestions. Thank you to reviewers of this edition:

Vivian G. Baglien, Green River Community College, Central Washington University, Auburn Mountainview High School
Stephen Burgess, Southwestern Oklahoma State University
Ann Englert, California State Polytechnic University

Patricia Kyle, Ph.D., Southern Oregon University
Ashley Maynard, University of Hawaii
Whitney Scott, California State University Northridge
Naomi Wagner, San Jose State University

Many thanks also to the reviewers of the previous two editions, who helped shape this book through its earlier incarnations:

Vivian Baglien, Green River Community College

D. Bruce Carter, Syracuse University

Tim Croy, Eastern Illinois University

Kimberly Dechman, George Mason University

Roberta Dihoff, Rowan University

Ruth Doyle, Casper College

Kim Fordham, North Idaho College

Betsy Jennings, Chaffey College

Sara Lawrence, California State University–Northridge

Karin Levine, Creighton University

Frank Manis, University of Southern California

Ashley E. Maynard, University of Hawaii–Manoa

Cathleen McGreal, Michigan State University

Martha Mendez-Baldwin, Manhattan College

George Meyer, Suffolk County Community College

Robin Musselman, Lehigh Carbon Community College

Judy Payne, Murray State University

Sandra Portko, Grand Valley State University

Carol D. Raupp, California State University–Bakersfield

Debra L. Schwiesow, Creighton University

Muriel Singer, Kean University

Elayne Thompson, Harper College

David N. Yarbrough, University of Louisiana at Lafayette

Priscilla Wright, Colorado Christian University

Glenna Zeak, Penn State University

Jackie L. Adamson, California State University–Fresno

Frank R. Asbury, Valdosta State University

Daniel R. Bellack, Trident Technical College

Pearl Susan Berman, Indiana University of Pennsylvania

Elizabeth Cauffman, Stanford Center on Adolescence

Margaret Sutton Edmands, University of Massachusetts–Boston

JoAnn Farver, University of Southern California

William Franklin, California State University–Los Angeles

Hulda Goddy Goodson, Palomar College

Tresmaine R. Grimes, Iona College

Jane Hovland, University of Minnesota–Duluth

Charles LaBounty, Hamline University

Richard Langford, California State University–Humboldt

Dennis A. Lichty, Wayne State College

Rebecca K. Loehrer, Blinn College

Patricia M. Martin, Onondaga Community College

Laura Massey, Montana State University–Bozeman

John Prange, Irvine Valley College

Mary Ann Ringquist, University of Massachusetts–Boston

Lee B. Ross, Frostburg State University

Julia Rux, Georgia Perimeter College

Alice A. Scharf-Matlick, Iona College

Debra Grote Schwiesow, Creighton University

Linda Sperry, Indiana State University

With a group like this looking over your shoulder, it's difficult to make a mistake. But if any remain, I am solely responsible.

I said that the book you hold in your hands would not be what it is without the insights and suggestions of my academic colleagues. It also owes much to the fine editorial and production team at Wadsworth and assembled by Wadsworth. This book would not exist without Kate Barnes and Michele Sordi. They are essential pleasures and tough taskmasters. I am grateful to Eve Howard, vice president/editor-in-chief, and dinner companion once upon a time in a border town; Michele Sordi, publisher; Kate Barnes, senior developmental editor; Mary Noel, production project manager; Joan Keyes, production service; Amy Cohen, managing technology project manager; Rachel Guzman, assistant editor; Erin Miskelly, senior editorial assistant; Eric Schrader, photo researcher; Sara Swangard, marketing manager; and Vernon Boes, creative director. And thanks always to Sean Wakely, president, and former CEO, Susan Badger.

Finally, I acknowledge the loving assistance of my family. My wife, Lois Fichner-Rathus, continues in her supportive role of author's "widow" and critical reviewer. As shown in experiments with the visual cliff, infants will not usually go off the deep end. As a textbook author herself, and as an academic, Lois often prevents me from going off the deep end. My children I thank as the sources of stories—and stories and more stories. But mostly I thank them for being what they are: sources of delight and fancy, occasional annoyances, and perpetual goads. They are in the world as it is now, and they keep me in the world as it is now.

Childhood and Adolescence

1

History, Theories, and Methods

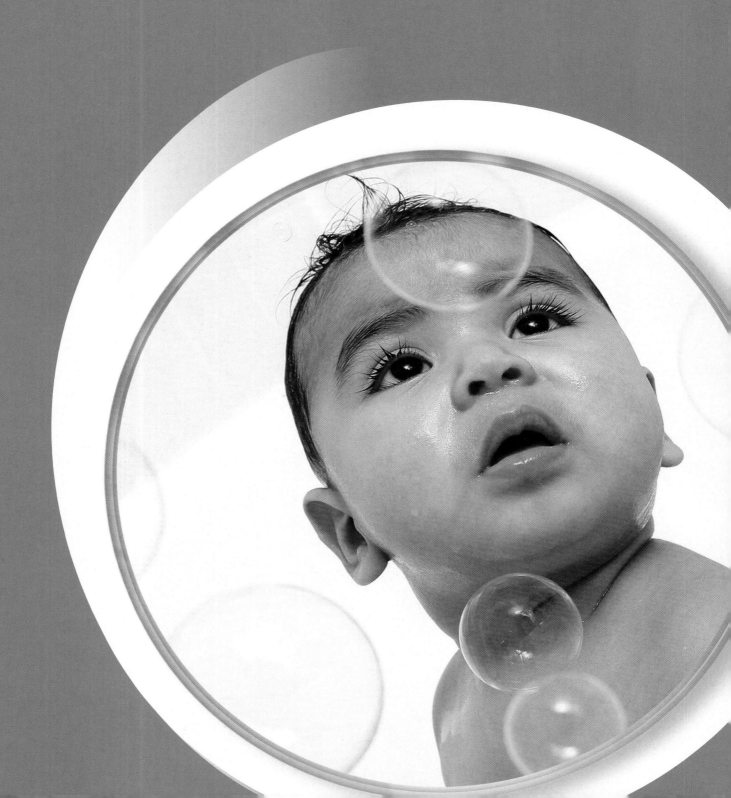

Truth or Fiction?

T F During the Middle Ages, children were often treated as miniature adults. p. 6

T F Children come into the world as "blank tablets," without inborn differences in intelligence and talents. p. 6

T F Nail biting and smoking cigarettes are signs of conflict experienced during early childhood. p. 10

T F Some theorists contend that children actively strive to understand and take charge of their worlds, whereas other theorists argue that children respond passively to environmental stimulation. p. 17

T F Research with monkeys has helped psychologists understand the formation of attachment in humans. p. 37

T F To learn how a person develops over a lifetime, researchers have tracked some individuals for more than 50 years. p. 37

Preview

What Is Child Development? Coming to Terms with Terms
    Why Do We Study Child Development?
    The Development of Child Development

Theories of Child Development
    What Are Theories of Child Development?
    Why Do We Have Them?
    The Psychoanalytic Perspective
    The Learning Perspective: Behavioral and Social
    Cognitive Theories

    A Closer Look: Operant Conditioning of
    Vocalizations in Infants

    The Cognitive Perspective
    The Biological Perspective
    The Ecological Perspective
    The Sociocultural Perspective

    Developing in a World of Diversity: Influence
    of the Macrosystem on the Development of
    Independence

Controversies in Child Development
    The Nature–Nurture Controversy
    The Continuity–Discontinuity Controversy
    The Active–Passive Controversy

How Do We Study Child Development?
    The Scientific Method
    Gathering Information
    Correlation: Putting Things Together
    The Experiment: Trying Things Out
    Longitudinal Research: Studying Development
    over Time
    Ethical Considerations

Go to
http://www.thomsonedu.com/psychology/rathus
for an interactive version of this "Truth or Fiction" feature.

This book has a story to tell. An important story. A remarkable story. It is your story. It is about the remarkable journey you have already taken through childhood. It is about the unfolding of your adult life. Billions of people have made this journey before. You have much in common with them. Yet you are unique, and things will happen to you, and because of you, that have never happened before.

Development of children is what this book is about. In a very real sense, we cannot hope to understand ourselves as adults—we cannot catch a glimpse of the remarkable journeys we have taken—without understanding children.

In this chapter, we explore some of the reasons for studying child development. We then take a brief tour of the history of child development. It may surprise you that until relatively recent times, people were not particularly sensitive to the ways in which children differ from adults. Next, we examine some controversies in child development, such as whether there are distinct stages of development. We see how theories help illuminate our observations and how theories help point the way toward new observations. Then we consider methods for the study of child development. Scientists have devised sophisticated methods for studying children, and ethics helps to determine the types of research that are deemed proper and improper. But first, let us embark on our search for ourselves by considering a basic question. ***Question: What is child development?***

What Is Child Development? Coming to Terms with Terms

You have heard the word *child* all your life, so why bother to define it? We do so because words in common usage are frequently used inexactly. A **child** is a person undergoing the period of development from *infancy* to *puberty*, two more familiar words that are frequently used inexactly. The term **infancy** derives from Latin roots meaning "not speaking," and infancy is usually defined as the first 2 years of life, or the period of life before the development of *complex* speech. We stress the word *complex* because many children have a large vocabulary and use simple sentences before their second birthday.

Researchers commonly speak of two other periods of development that lie between infancy and adolescence: early childhood and middle childhood. Early childhood encompasses the ages from 2 to 5 years. Middle childhood generally is defined as the years from 6 to 12. In Western society, the beginning of this period usually is marked by the child's entry into first grade. To study development, we must also look further back to the origin of sperm and ova (egg cells), the process of **conception**, and the **prenatal period**. Yet even that is not far enough to satisfy scientists. We also describe the mechanisms of heredity that give rise to traits in both humans and other animals.

Development is the orderly appearance of physical structures, psychological traits, behaviors, and ways of adapting to the demands of life over time. The changes brought on by development are both *qualitative* and *quantitative.* Qualitative changes are changes in type or kind. Consider **motor development**. As we develop, we gain the abilities to lift our heads, sit up, crawl, stand, and walk. These changes are qualitative. However, within each of these qualitative changes are quantitative developments, or changes in *amount*. After babies begin to lift their heads, they lift them higher and higher. Soon after children walk, they begin to run. Then they gain the capacity to run faster.

Development occurs across many dimensions: physiological, cognitive, social, emotional, and behavioral. Development is spurred by internal factors, such as genetics, and it is shaped by external factors, such as nutrition and culture.

child A person undergoing the period of development from infancy through puberty.

infancy The period of very early childhood, characterized by lack of complex speech; the first 2 years after birth.

conception The process of becoming pregnant; the process by which a sperm cell joins with an ovum to begin a new life.

prenatal period The period of development from conception to birth. (From roots meaning "prior to birth.")

development The processes by which organisms unfold features and traits, grow, and become more complex and specialized in structure and function.

motor development The development of the capacity for movement, particularly that made possible by changes in the nervous system and the muscles.

growth The processes by which organisms increase in size, weight, strength, and other traits as they develop.

4 •••

The terms *growth* and *development* are not synonymous, although many people use them interchangeably. **Growth** is usually used to refer to changes in size or quantity, whereas development also refers to changes in quality. During the early days following conception in the fallopian tube, the fertilized egg cell develops rapidly. It divides repeatedly, and cells begin to take on specialized forms, yet it does not "grow" in that there is no gain in mass. Why? Because the developing mass of cells has not yet become implanted in the uterus and therefore is without any external source of nourishment. Language development refers to the process by which the child's use of language becomes progressively more sophisticated and complex during the first few years of life. Vocabulary growth, by contrast, refers to the simple accumulation of new words and their meanings.

Child development, then, is a field of study that tries to understand the processes that govern the appearance and growth of children's biological structures, psychological traits, behavior, understanding, and ways of adapting to the demands of life.

Professionals from many fields are interested in child development. They include psychologists, educators, anthropologists, sociologists, nurses, and medical researchers. Each brings his or her own brand of expertise to the quest for knowledge. Intellectual cross-fertilization enhances the skills of developmentalists and enriches the lives of children.

© Photodisc/First Light

Motor Development
This infant has just mastered the ability to pull herself up to a standing position. Soon she will be able to stand alone, and then she will begin to walk.

Why Do We Study Child Development?

Question: Why do researchers study child development? An important motive for studying child development is curiosity and the desire to learn about children. Curiosity may be driven by the desire to answer questions about development that remain unresolved. It may also be driven by the desire to have fun. (Yes, children and the study of children can be fun.) There are other motives described below.

To Gain Insight into Human Nature
For centuries, philosophers, scientists, and educators have argued over whether children are aggressive or loving, whether children are conscious and self-aware, whether they have a natural curiosity that demands to unravel the mysteries of the universe, or whether they merely react mechanically to environmental stimulation. The quest for answers has an effect on the lives of children, parents, educators, and others who interact with children.

To Gain Insight into the Origins of Adult Behavior
How do we explain the origins of empathy in adults? Of antisocial behavior? How do we explain the assumption of "feminine" and "masculine" behavior patterns? The origins of special talents in writing, music, athletics, and math?

To Gain Insight into the Origins of Sex Differences and Gender Roles, and the Effects of Culture on Development
How do **gender roles**—that is, culturally induced expectations for stereotypical feminine and masculine behavior—develop? Are there sex differences in cognition and behavior? If so, how do they develop?

To Gain Insight into the Origins, Prevention, and Treatment of Developmental Problems
Fetal alcohol syndrome, **PKU**, **SIDS**, Down syndrome, autism, hyperactivity, dyslexia, and child abuse are but a handful of the buzzwords that stir fear in parents and parents-to-be. A major focus in child development research is the search for the causes of such problems so that they can be prevented and, when possible, treated.

gender roles Complex clusters of behavior that are considered stereotypical of females and males.

PKU Phenylketonuria. A genetic abnormality in which a child cannot metabolize phenylalanine, an amino acid, which consequently builds up in the body and causes mental retardation. If treated with a special diet, retardation is prevented.

SIDS Sudden infant death syndrome (discussed in Chapter 5).

To Optimize Conditions of Development

Most parents want to provide the best in nutrition and medical care so that their children will develop strong and healthy bodies. Parents want their infants to feel secure with them. They want to ensure that major transitions, such as the transition from the home to the school, will be as stress-free as possible. Developmentalists therefore undertake research to learn about issues such as:

- The effects of various foods and chemicals on the development of the embryo
- The effects of parent–infant interaction immediately following birth on bonds of attachment
- The effects of bottle feeding versus breast feeding on mother–infant attachment and the baby's health
- The effects of day-care programs on parent–child bonds of attachment and on children's social and intellectual development
- The effects of various patterns of child rearing on development of independence, competence, and social adjustment

The Development of Child Development

Child development as a field of scientific inquiry has existed for little more than a century.

Question: What views of children do we find throughout history? In ancient times and in the Middle Ages, children often were viewed as innately evil and discipline was harsh. Legally, medieval children were treated as property and servants. They could be sent to the monastery, married without consultation, or convicted of crimes. Children were nurtured until they were 7 years old, which was considered the "age of reason." Then they were expected to work alongside adults in the home and in the field. They ate, drank, and dressed as miniature adults. **Truth or Fiction Revisited:** Children were also treated as miniature adults throughout most of the Middle Ages. (For much of the Middle Ages, artists depicted children as small adults.) However, that means more was expected of them, not that they were given more privileges.

The transition to the study of development in modern times is marked by the thinking of philosophers such as John Locke and Jean-Jacques Rousseau. **Truth or Fiction Revisited:** Englishman John Locke (1632–1704) believed that the child came into the world as a *tabula rasa*—a "blank tablet" or clean slate—that was written on by experience. Locke did not believe that inborn predispositions toward good

A View of Children as Perceived in the 1600s
Centuries ago, children were viewed as miniature adults. In this 17th-century painting, notice how the body proportions of the young princess (in the middle) are similar to those of her adult attendants.

© Erich Lessing/Art Resource, NY

or evil played an important role in the conduct of the child. Instead, he focused on the role of the environment or of experience. Locke believed that social approval and disapproval are powerful shapers of behavior. Jean-Jacques Rousseau (1712–1778), a Swiss–French philosopher, reversed Locke's stance. Rousseau argued that children are inherently good and that, if allowed to express their natural impulses, they will develop into generous and moral individuals.

During the Industrial Revolution, family life came to be defined in terms of the nuclear unit of mother, father, and children rather than the extended family. Children became more visible, fostering awareness of childhood as a special time of life. Still, children often labored in factories from dawn to dusk through the early years of the 20th century.

In the 20th century, laws were passed to protect children from strenuous labor, to require that they attend school until a certain age, and to prevent them from getting married or being sexually exploited. Whereas children were once considered the property of parents to do with as they wished, laws now protect children from the abuse and neglect of parents and other caretakers. Juvenile courts see that children who break the law receive fair and appropriate treatment in the criminal justice system.

Pioneers in the Study of Child Development

Various thoughts about child development coalesced into a field of scientific study in the 19th and early 20th centuries. Many individuals, including Charles Darwin, G. Stanley Hall, and Alfred Binet, contributed to the emerging field.

Charles Darwin (1809–1882) is perhaps best known as the originator of the theory of evolution, but he was also one of the first observers to keep a *baby biography* in which he described his infant son's behaviors in great detail. G. Stanley Hall (1844–1924) is credited with founding child development as an academic discipline. He adapted the questionnaire method for use with large groups of children so that he could study the "contents of children's minds." The Frenchman Alfred Binet (1857–1911), along with Theodore Simon, developed the first standardized intelligence test near the beginning of the 20th century. Binet's purpose was to identify public school children who were at risk of falling behind their peers in academic achievement. By the start of the 20th century, child development had emerged as a scientific field of study. Within a short time, major theoretical views of the developing child had begun to emerge, proposed by such developmentalists as Arnold Gesell, Sigmund Freud, John B. Watson, and Jean Piaget. We next describe their theories of child development and those of others.

A Young Child Laborer
Children often worked long days in factories up through the early years of the 20th century. A number of cultures in the world today still use child labor.

Active Review

1. A child is a person undergoing the period of development from *infancy* to _____.
2. _____ is the orderly appearance of structures, traits, and behaviors over time.
3. The word *growth* is usually used to refer to changes in size or quantity, whereas the term _____ also refers to changes in quality.

Reflect & Relate: Do you believe that children are "wild"? Do you believe that children must be "tamed"? Do you see dangers (to children) in answering yes to either question? Explain.

Go to

http://www.thomsonedu.com/psychology/rathus
for an interactive version of this review.

Theories of Child Development

"Give me a dozen healthy infants, well-formed, and my own specified world to bring them up in, and I'll guarantee to train them to become any type of specialist I might suggest—doctor, lawyer, merchant, chief, and, yes, even beggar and thief, regardless of their talents, penchants, tendencies, abilities, vocations, and the race of their ancestors" (Watson, 1924, p. 82).

John B. Watson, the founder of American **behaviorism**, viewed development in terms of learning. He generally agreed with Locke's idea that children's ideas, preferences, and skills are shaped by experience. There has been a long-standing nature–nurture debate in the study of children. In his theoretical approach to understanding children, Watson came down on the side of nurture—the importance of the physical and social environments—as found, for example, in parental training and approval. Watson's view turned upside down the history of approaches to understanding children. Nature, or the inherited, genetic characteristics of the child, had long been the more popular explanation of how children get to be what they are.

Four years after Watson sounded his call for the behavioral view, Arnold Gesell expressed the opposing idea that biological **maturation** was the main principle of development: "All things considered, the inevitability and surety of maturation are the most impressive characteristics of early development. It is the hereditary ballast which conserves and stabilizes growth of each individual infant" (Gesell, 1928, p. 378). Watson was talking largely about the behavior patterns that children develop, whereas Gesell was focusing mainly on physical aspects of growth and development. Still, the behavioral and maturational perspectives lie at opposite ends of the continuum of theories of development. Many scientists fall into the trap of overemphasizing the importance of either nature or nurture at the risk of overlooking the ways in which nature and nurture interact. Just as a child's environments and experiences influence the development of his or her biological endowment, children often place themselves in environments that are harmonious with their personal characteristics. Children, for example, are influenced by teachers and other students. Nevertheless, because of the traits they bring to school with them, some children may prefer to socialize with other children and others with teachers. Still other children may prefer solitude.

What Are Theories of Child Development? Why Do We Have Them?

Child development is a scientific enterprise. Like other scientists, developmentalists seek to describe, explain, predict, and influence the events they study.

Developmentalists attempt to describe and explain behavior in terms of concepts such as heredity, perception, language, learning, cognition, emotion, socialization, and gender roles. For example, we may describe learning as a process in which behavior changes as a result of experience. We can be more specific and describe instances of learning in which children memorize the alphabet through repetition or acquire gymnastic skills through practice. We may explain how learning occurs in terms of rules or principles that govern learning. Thus, we might explain the trainer's use of the words "fine" and "good" as *reinforcers* that provide the gymnast with positive feedback.

Questions: What are theories? Why do we have them? **Theories** are related sets of statements about events. When possible, descriptive terms and concepts are interwoven into theories. Theories are based on certain assumptions about behavior, such as Watson's assumption that training outweighs talents and abilities or Gesell's assumption that the unfolding of maturational tendencies holds sway. Theories allow us to derive explanations and predictions. Many developmental theories combine statements about psychological concepts (such as learning and motivation), behavior

behaviorism John B. Watson's view that a science or theory of development must study observable behavior only and investigate relationships between stimuli and responses.

maturation The unfolding of genetically determined traits, structures, and functions.

theory A formulation of relationships underlying observed events. A theory involves assumptions and logically derived explanations and predictions.

(such as reading or problem solving), and anatomical structures or biological processes (such as maturation of the nervous system). For instance, a child's ability to learn to read is influenced by her or his motivation, attention span, and perceptual development, and also by biological processes in the brain.

A useful theory allows us to make predictions. For instance, a theory concerning the development of gender roles should allow us to predict how—and whether—children will acquire stereotypical feminine or masculine gender-typed behavior patterns. A broad theory of the development of gender roles might apply to children from different cultural and racial backgrounds and, perhaps, to children with gay male or lesbian sexual orientations as well as to children with a heterosexual orientation. If observations cannot be explained by or predicted from a theory, we may need to revise or replace the theory.

Useful theories also enable researchers to influence events, as in better working with parents, teachers, nurses, and children themselves to promote the welfare of children. Psychologists may summarize and interpret theory and research on the effects of day care to help day-care workers provide an optimal child-care environment. Teachers may use learning theory to help children learn to read and write. Let us consider various theoretical approaches to child development.

The Psychoanalytic Perspective

A number of theories fall within the psychoanalytic perspective. Each owes its origin to Sigmund Freud and views children—and adults—as caught in conflict. Early in development the conflict is between the child and the world outside. The expression of basic drives, such as sex and aggression, conflict with parental expectations, social rules, moral codes, even laws. However, the external limits—parental demands and social rules—are brought inside. That is, they are *internalized*. Once this internalization happens, the conflict takes place between opposing *inner* forces. The child's observable behavior, thoughts, and feelings reflect the outcomes of these hidden battles.

In this section, we explore Freud's theory of **psychosexual development** and Erik Erikson's theory of psychosocial development. Each is a **stage theory** that sees children as developing through distinct periods of life. Each suggests that the child's experiences during early stages affect the child's emotional and social life at the time and later on.

Question: What is Freud's psychoanalytic theory of child development?

Sigmund Freud's Theory of Psychosexual Development

Sigmund Freud (1856–1939) was a mass of contradictions. He has been praised as the greatest thinker of the 20th century and criticized as overrated. He preached liberal views on sexuality but was himself a model of sexual restraint. He invented a popular form of psychotherapy but experienced lifelong emotional problems including migraine headaches, fainting under stress, hatred of the telephone, and an addiction to cigars. He smoked 20 cigars a day and could not or would not break the habit, even after he developed cancer of the jaw.

Freud focused on the emotional and social development of children and on the origins of psychological traits such as dependence, obsessive neatness, and vanity. Let us dive into Freud's theory. Diving is a good metaphor because Freud believed that most of the human mind lies beneath consciousness like an iceberg. The children you observe do and say many things—cry, crawl, run, talk, build, play—but all that is the tip of the iceberg. And the tip of an iceberg—even the tip of the giant iceberg that sank the Titanic—is only the smaller part of the iceberg. Its greater part lies below the surface. Freud theorized that people, because of their childhood experiences, are only vaguely aware of the ideas and impulses that occupy the greater depths of their minds.

psychosexual development In psychoanalytic theory, the process by which libidinal energy is expressed through different erogenous zones during different stages of development.

stage theory A theory of development characterized by hypothesizing the existence of distinct periods of life. Stages follow one another in an orderly sequence.

Sigmund Freud
Freud is the originator of psychoanalytic theory. He proposed five stages of psychosexual development and emphasized the importance of biological factors in the development of personality.

Freud theorized three parts of the personality: *the id, ego,* and *superego.* The id is present at birth and while **unconscious**. It represents biological drives and demands instant gratification, as suggested by a baby's wailing. The ego, or the conscious sense of self, begins to develop when children learn to obtain gratification for themselves, without screaming or crying. The ego curbs the appetites of the id and makes plans that are in keeping with social conventions so that a person can find gratification yet avoid the disapproval of others. The superego develops throughout infancy and early childhood. It brings inward the wishes and morals of the child's caregivers and other members of the community. Throughout the remainder of the child's life, the superego will monitor the intentions and behavior of the ego and hand down judgments of right and wrong. If the child misbehaves, the superego will flood him or her with guilt and shame.

According to Freud, childhood has five stages of psychosexual development: *oral, anal, phallic, latency,* and *genital.* If a child receives too little or too much gratification during a stage, the child can become *fixated* in that stage. For example, during the first year of life, which Freud termed the *oral stage,* "oral" activities such as sucking and biting bring pleasure and gratification. If the child is weaned early or breast-fed too long, the child may become fixated on oral activities such as nail biting or smoking, or even show a "biting wit." **Truth or Fiction Revisited:** There is actually no research evidence that nail biting and smoking cigarettes are signs of conflict experienced during early childhood, even though these beliefs are consistent with Freudian theory.

In the second, or anal, stage, gratification is obtained through control and elimination of waste products. Excessively strict or permissive toilet training can lead to the development of anal-retentive traits, such as perfectionism and neatness, or anal-expulsive traits, such as sloppiness and carelessness. In the third stage, the *phallic stage,* parent–child conflict may develop over masturbation, which many parents treat with punishment and threats. It is normal for children to develop strong sexual attachments to the parent of the other sex during the phallic stage and to begin to view the parent of the same sex as a rival. Girls in this stage may express the wish to marry their fathers when they grow up. Boys are likely to have similar designs on their mothers.

By age 5 or 6, Freud believed, children enter a *latency stage* during which sexual feelings remain unconscious, children turn to schoolwork, and they typically prefer playmates of their own sex. The final stage of psychosexual development, the *genital stage,* begins with the biological changes that usher in adolescence. Adolescents generally desire sexual gratification through intercourse with a member of the other sex. Freud believed that oral or anal stimulation, masturbation, and male–male or female–female sexual activity are immature forms of sexual conduct that reflect fixations at early stages of development.

Evaluation   Freud's theory has had much appeal and was a major contribution to modern thought. It is a rich theory of development, explaining the childhood origins of many traits, and stimulating research on attachment, development of gender roles, and moral development. Freud's views about the anal stage have influenced child-care workers to recommend that toilet training not be started too early or handled punitively. His emphasis on the emotional needs of children has influenced educators to be more sensitive to the possible emotional reasons behind a child's misbehavior.

Yet Freud's work has been criticized on many grounds. For one thing, Freud developed his theory on the basis of contacts with patients (mostly women) who were experiencing emotional problems (Schultz & Schultz, 2008). He also concluded that most of his patients' problems originated in childhood conflicts. It is possible that he might have found less evidence of childhood conflict had his sample consisted of people drawn at random from the population. He was also dealing with recollections of

unconscious   In psychoanalytic theory, not available to awareness by simple focusing of attention.

psychosocial development   Erikson's theory, which emphasizes the importance of social relationships and conscious choice throughout the eight stages of development.

his patients' pasts rather than observing children directly. Such recollections are subject to errors in memory. Freud may also have inadvertently guided patients into expressing ideas that confirmed his views.

Some of Freud's own disciples, including Erik Erikson and Karen Horney, believe that Freud placed too much emphasis on basic instincts and unconscious motives. They argue that people are motivated not only by drives such as sex and aggression but also by social relationships and conscious desires to achieve, to have aesthetic experiences, and to help others.

Once we have catalogued our criticisms of Freud's views, what is left? A number of things are. Freud pointed out that childhood experiences can have far-reaching effects. He noted that our mental processes can be distorted by our efforts to defend ourselves against anxiety and guilt. If these ideas no longer impress us as unusual, perhaps it is because they have been widely accepted since Freud gave voice to them.

Karen Horney
Horney, a follower of Freud, argued that Freud placed too much emphasis on sexual and biological determinants of behavior while neglecting the importance of social factors.

Erik Erikson's Theory of Psychosocial Development

Question: How does Erikson's theory differ from Freud's? Erik Erikson (1902–1994) modified and expanded Freud's theory. Erikson's theory, like Freud's, focuses on the development of the emotional life and psychological traits. But Erikson also focuses on the development of self-identity. Out of the chaos of his own identity problems, Erikson forged a personally meaningful life pattern, and Erikson's social relationships had been more important than sexual or aggressive instincts in his development. Therefore, Erikson speaks of **psychosocial development** rather than of *psychosexual development*. Furthermore, it seemed to Erikson that he had developed his own personality through a series of conscious and purposeful acts. Consequently, he places greater emphasis on the ego, or the sense of self.

Erikson (1963) extended Freud's five developmental stages to eight to include the changing concerns throughout adulthood. Rather than label his stages after parts of the body, Erikson labeled stages after the **life crises** that the child (and then the adult) might encounter during that stage. Erikson's stages are compared with Freud's in Concept Review 1.1.

Erikson proposed that our social relationships and physical maturation give each stage its character. For example, the parent–child relationship and the infant's utter dependence and helplessness are responsible for the nature of the earliest stages of development. The 6-year-old's capacity to profit from the school setting reflects the cognitive capacities to learn to read and to understand the basics of math, and even the ability to sit still long enough to focus on schoolwork.

According to Erikson, early experiences affect future developments. With proper parental support early on, most children resolve early life crises productively. Successful resolution of each crisis bolsters their sense of identity—of who they are and what they stand for—and their expectation of future success.

Erik Erikson with his wife, Joan Erikson

Stages of Psychosocial Development Each stage in Erikson's theory carries a specific developmental task. Successful completion of this task depends heavily on the nature of the child's social relationships at each stage (see Concept Review 1.1).

Erikson's views, like Freud's, have influenced child rearing, early childhood education, and child therapy. For example, Erikson's views about an adolescent **identity crisis** have entered the popular culture and have affected the way many parents and teachers deal with teenagers. Some schools help students master the crisis by means of life-adjustment courses and study units on self-understanding in social studies and literature classes.

Evaluation Erikson's views have received much praise and much criticism. They are appealing in that they emphasize the importance of human consciousness and choice and minimize the role—and the threat—of dark, poorly perceived urges. They

life crisis An internal conflict that attends each stage of psychosocial development. Positive resolution of early life crises sets the stage for positive resolution of subsequent life crises.

identity crisis According to Erikson, a period of inner conflict during which one examines one's values and makes decisions about one's life roles.

Concept Review 1.1 Comparison of Freud's and Erikson's Stages of Development

Age	Freud's Stages of Psychosexual Development	Erikson's Stages of Psychosocial Development
Birth to 1 year	**Oral Stage.** Gratification derives from oral activities, such as sucking. Fixation leads to development of oral traits, such as dependence, depression, and gullibility.	**Trust versus Mistrust.** The developmental task is to come to trust the key caregivers, primarily the mother, and the environment. It is desirable for the infant to connect its environment with inner feelings of satisfaction and contentment.
About 1 to 3 years	**Anal Stage.** Gratification derives from anal activities involving elimination. Fixation leads to development of anal-retentive traits (e.g., excessive neatness) or anal-expulsive traits (e.g., sloppiness).	**Autonomy versus Shame and Doubt.** The developmental task is to develop the desire to make choices and the self-control to regulate one's behavior so that choices can be actualized.
About 3 to 6 years	**Phallic Stage.** Gratification derives from stimulation of the genital region. Oedipal and Electra complexes emerge and are resolved. Fixation leads to development of phallic traits, such as vanity.	**Initiative versus Guilt.** The developmental task is to add initiative, planning and attacking to choice. The preschooler is on the move and becomes proactive.
About 6 to 12 years	**Latency Stage.** Sexual impulses are suppressed, allowing the child to focus on development of social and technological skills.	**Industry versus Inferiority.** The developmental task is to become absorbed in the development and implementation of skills, to master the basics of technology, and to become productive.
Adolescence	**Genital Stage.** Reappearance of sexual impulses, with gratification sought through sexual relations with an adult of the other sex.	**Identity versus Role Diffusion.** The developmental task is to associate one's skills and social roles with the development of career goals. More broadly, the development of identity refers to a sense of who one is and what one believes in.
Young adulthood		**Intimacy versus Isolation.** The developmental task is to commit oneself to another person and to engage in a mature sexual love.
Middle adulthood		**Generativity versus Stagnation.** The developmental task is to appreciate the opportunity to "give back." Not only are generative people creative, but they also give encouragement and guidance to the younger generation, which may include their own children.
Late adulthood		**Ego Integrity versus Despair.** The developmental task is to achieve wisdom and dignity in the face of declining physical abilities. Ego integrity also means accepting the time and place of one's own life cycle.

are also appealing in that they portray us as prosocial and helpful, whereas Freud portrayed us as selfish and needing to be forced into compliance with social rules.

There is also some empirical support for the Eriksonian view that positive outcomes of early life crises help put children on the path to positive development. For example, infants who come to trust in their parents are more likely to achieve autonomy and ego identity later in their lives (Hoegh & Bourgeois, 2002).

The Learning Perspective: Behavioral and Social Cognitive Theories

During the 1930s, psychologists derived an ingenious method for helping 5- and 6-year-old children overcome bed-wetting from the behavioral perspective. Most children at this age wake up and go to the bathroom when their bladders are full. But bed wetters sleep through bladder tension and reflexively urinate in bed. The psychologists' objective was to teach sleeping children with full bladders to wake up rather than wet their beds.

The psychologists placed a special pad beneath the sleeping child. When the pad was wet, an electrical circuit was closed, causing a bell to ring and the sleeping child to waken. After several repetitions, most children learned to wake up before they wet the pad. How? They learned through a technique called *classical conditioning*, which I explain in this section.

The so-called bell-and-pad method for bed-wetting is an exotic example of the application of learning theory in child development. However, most applications of learning theory to development are found in everyday events. For example, children are not born knowing what the letters A and B sound like or how to tie their shoes. They learn these things. They are not born knowing how to do gymnastics. Nor are they born understanding the meanings of abstract concepts such as big, blue, decency, and justice. All these skills and knowledge are learned.

In this section, we discuss learning theories and see how they are involved in child development. We see how two types of learning—classical conditioning and operant conditioning—have contributed to behaviorism and the understanding of development. We also see how the principles of learning have been used in **behavior modification** to help children overcome behavior disorders or cope with adjustment problems. Then we consider a more recent theory of learning that deals with children's cognitive processes and their overt behavior, social cognitive theory. We begin with John B. Watson's theory of behaviorism.

Behaviorism

Question: What is behaviorism? John B. Watson argued that a scientific approach to development must focus on the observable behavior only and not on things like thoughts, fantasies, and other mental images.

Classical conditioning is a simple form of learning in which an originally neutral **stimulus** comes to bring forth, or **elicit**, the response usually brought forth by a second stimulus as a result of being paired repeatedly with the second stimulus. In the bell-and-pad method for bed-wetting, psychologists repeatedly pair tension in the children's bladders with a stimulus that wakes them up (the bell). The children learn to respond to the bladder tension as if it were a bell; that is, they wake up (see ● Figure 1.1).

The bell is an unlearned or **unconditioned stimulus (UCS)**. Waking up in response to the bell is an unlearned or **unconditioned response (UCR)**. Bladder tension is at first a meaningless, or neutral stimulus (see Figure 1.1). Then, through repeated association with the bell, bladder tension becomes a learned or **conditioned stimulus (CS)** for waking up. Waking up in response to bladder tension (the CS) is a learned or **conditioned response (CR)**. Behaviorists argue that a good

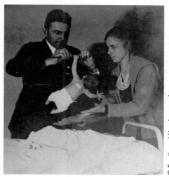

John B. Watson
Watson is shown here testing the grasping reflex of an infant. As a behaviorist, Watson believed that the environment is all-important in shaping development.

behavior modification The systematic application of principles of learning to change problem behaviors or encourage desired behaviors.

classical conditioning A simple form of learning in which one stimulus comes to bring forth the response usually brought forth by a second stimulus by being paired repeatedly with the second stimulus.

stimulus A change in the environment that leads to a change in behavior.

elicit (ee-LISS-it) To bring forth; to evoke.

unconditioned stimulus (UCS) A stimulus that elicits a response from an organism without learning.

unconditioned response (UCR) An unlearned response. A response to an unconditioned stimulus.

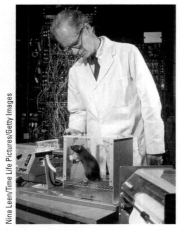

B. F. Skinner
Skinner, a behaviorist, developed principles of operant conditioning and focused on the role of reinforcement of behavior.

conditioned stimulus (CS)
A previously neutral stimulus that elicits a response because it has been paired repeatedly with a stimulus that already elicited that response.

conditioned response (CR)
A learned response to a previously neutral stimulus.

operant conditioning A simple form of learning in which an organism learns to engage in behavior that is reinforced.

reinforcement The process of providing stimuli following a response, which has the effect of increasing the frequency of the response.

positive reinforcer A reinforcer that, when applied, increases the frequency of a response.

negative reinforcer A reinforcer that, when removed, increases the frequency of a response.

extinction The cessation of a response that is performed in the absence of reinforcement.

punishment An unpleasant stimulus that suppresses behavior.

deal of emotional learning is acquired through classical conditioning. For example, touching a hot stove is painful, and one or two incidents may elicit a fear response when a child looks at a stove or considers touching it again.

In classical conditioning, children learn to associate stimuli so that a response made to one is then made in response to the other. But in **operant conditioning** (a different kind of conditioning), children learn to do something because of its effects. B. F. Skinner introduced the key concept of **reinforcement**. Reinforcers are stimuli that increase the frequency of the behavior they follow. Most children learn to adjust their behavior to conform to social codes and rules to earn reinforcers such as the attention and approval of their parents and teachers. Other children, ironically, may learn to misbehave because misbehavior also draws attention. Any stimulus that increases the frequency of the responses preceding it serves as a reinforcer. Most of the time, food, social approval, and attention serve as reinforcers.

Skinner distinguished between positive and negative reinforcers. **Positive reinforcers** increase the frequency of behaviors when they are *applied*. Food and approval usually serve as positive reinforcers. **Negative reinforcers** increase the frequency of behaviors when they are *removed*. Fear acts as a negative reinforcer in that its removal increases the frequency of the behaviors preceding it. For example, fear of failure is removed when students study for a quiz. ● Figure 1.2 compares positive and negative reinforcers.

Extinction results from repeated performance of operant behavior without reinforcement. After a number of trials, the operant behavior is no longer shown. In many cases, children's temper tantrums and crying at bedtime can be extinguished within a few days by simply having parents remain out of the bedroom after the children have been put to bed. Previously, parental attention and company had reinforced the tantrums and crying. When the reinforcement of the problem behavior was removed, the behavior was eliminated.

Punishments are aversive events that suppress or *decrease* the frequency of the behavior they follow. (● Figure 1.3 on page 16 compares negative reinforcers with punishments.) Punishments can be physical (such as spanking) or verbal (e.g., scolding or criticizing) or the removal of privileges. Punishments can rapidly suppress undesirable behavior and may be warranted in emergencies, such as when a child tries to

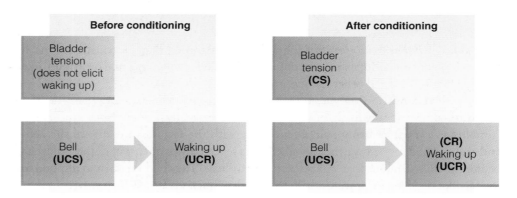

● Figure 1.1 Schematic Representation of Classical Conditioning

Before conditioning, the bell elicits waking up. Bladder tension, a neutral stimulus, does not elicit waking up. During conditioning, bladder tension always precedes urination, which in turn causes the bell to ring. After conditioning, bladder tension has become a conditional stimulus (CS) that elicits waking up, which is the conditioned response (CR).

Procedure	Behavior	Consequence	Change in behavior
Use of positive reinforcement	Behavior (studying) →	Positive reinforcer (teacher approval) is **presented** when student studies →	Frequency of behavior **increases** (student studies more)
Use of negative reinforcement	Behavior (studying) →	Negative reinforcer (teacher disapproval) is **removed** when student studies →	Frequency of behavior **increases** (student studies more)

● **Figure 1.2** Positive versus Negative Reinforcers

All reinforcers *increase* the frequency of behavior. In these examples, teacher approval functions as a positive reinforcer when students study harder because of it. Teacher *disapproval* functions as a negative reinforcer when its *removal* increases the frequency of studying.

A Closer Look

Operant Conditioning of Vocalizations in Infants

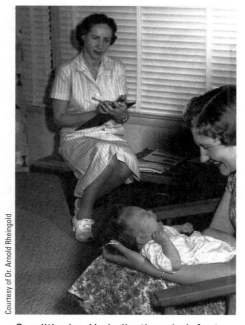

A classic study by psychologist Harriet Rheingold and her colleagues (1959) demonstrated how reinforcement and extinction can influence the behavior—in this case, vocalization—of infants. A researcher first observed the subjects, 3-month-old infants, for about half an hour to record baseline (preexperimental) measures of the frequency of their vocalizing. Infants averaged 13–15 vocalizations each. During the conditioning phase of the study, the researcher reinforced the vocalizations with social stimuli, such as encouraging sounds, smiles, and gentle touches. There was a significant increase in the frequency of vocalizing throughout this phase. By the end of an hour of conditioning spread over a 2-day period, the average incidence of vocalizations had nearly doubled to 24–25 within a half-hour. During the extinction phase, as during the baseline period, the researcher passively observed each infant, no longer reinforcing vocalization. After two half-hour extinction periods, average vocalizing had returned to near baseline, 13–16 per half hour.

Reflect: Rheingold changed the frequency of vocalizations of infants. In what other kinds of learning do infants engage?

Courtesy of Dr. Arnold Rheingold

Conditioning Verbalizations in Infants
In this historic photo, Harriet Rheingold observes as a mother attempts to condition verbalizing in her infant.

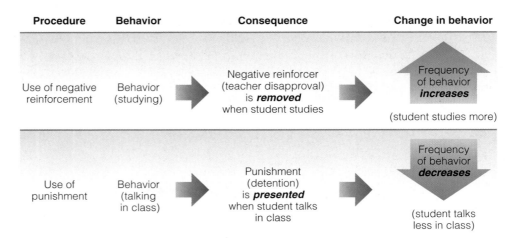

● **Figure 1.3** **Negative Reinforcers versus Punishments**

Both negative reinforcers and punishments tend to be aversive stimuli. However, reinforcers *increase* the frequency of behavior. Punishments *decrease* the frequency of behavior. Negative reinforcers increase the frequency of behavior when they are *removed*.

run out into the street. But many learning theorists agree that punishment is usually undesirable, especially in rearing children, for reasons such as the following.

- Punishment does not in itself suggest an alternative, acceptable form of behavior.
- Punishment tends to suppress undesirable behavior only when its delivery is guaranteed. It does not take children long to learn that they can "get away with murder" with one parent or one teacher but not with another.
- Punished children may withdraw from the situation. Severely punished children may run away, cut class, or drop out of school.
- Punishment can create anger and hostility. After being spanked by their parents, children may hit smaller siblings or destroy objects in the home.
- Punishment may generalize too far. The child who is punished severely for bad table manners may stop eating altogether. Such overgeneralization is more likely to occur when children do not know why they are being punished.
- Punishment may be imitated as a way of solving problems or coping with stress. Children learn by observing others. For example, children who are physically punished by their parents may act aggressively toward other children (Sim & Ong, 2005) or toward their own children when they become parents (Huesmann et al., 2006).

It is usually preferable to reward children for desirable behavior than to punish them for unwanted behavior. By ignoring their misbehavior or by using **time out** from positive reinforcement, we can consistently avoid reinforcing children for misbehavior.

We can teach children complex behaviors by **shaping**, or at first reinforcing small steps toward the behavioral goals. In teaching a 2-year-old child to put on her own coat, it helps first to praise her for trying to stick her arm into a sleeve on a couple of occasions, then praise her for actually getting her arm into the sleeve, and so on.

Operant conditioning is used every day in the **socialization** of young children. For example, parents and peers influence children to acquire gender-appropriate behaviors through the elaborate use of rewards and punishments. Thus, boys may ignore other boys when they play with dolls and housekeeping toys but play with boys when they use transportation toys.

Research suggests that when teachers praise and attend to appropriate behavior and ignore misbehavior, studying and classroom behavior improve while disruptive

time out A behavior-modification technique in which a child who misbehaves is temporarily placed in a drab, restrictive environment in which reinforcement is unavailable.

shaping A procedure for teaching complex behavior patterns by means of reinforcing small steps toward the target behavior.

socialization A process in which children are encouraged to adopt socially desirable behavior patterns through a system of guidance, rewards, and punishments.

and aggressive behaviors decrease (McIlvane & Dube, 2003; Takahashi & Sugiyama, 2003). Teachers frequently use time out from positive reinforcement to discourage misbehavior. In this method, children are placed in drab, restrictive environments for a specified time period such as 10 minutes when they behave disruptively. When isolated, they cannot earn the attention of peers or teachers, and no reinforcing activities are present.

Social Cognitive Theory

Behaviorists tend to limit their view of learning to the classical and operant conditioning of observable behavior. *Question: How does social cognitive theory differ from behaviorism?* **Social cognitive theorists** such as Albert Bandura (1986, 2006a, 2006b; *American Psychologist*, 2006) have shown that much of children's learning also occurs by observing parents, teachers, other children, and characters in the media. Children may need practice to refine their skills, but they can acquire the basic know-how through observation. Children can also let these skills *lie latent*. For example, children (and adults) are not likely to imitate aggressive behavior unless they are provoked and believe that they are more likely to be rewarded than punished for aggressive behavior.

In the view of behaviorists, learning occurs by mechanical conditioning. There is no reference to thought processes. In social cognitive theory, by contrast, cognition plays a central role. For social cognitive theorists, learning alters children's mental representation of the environment and affects their belief in their ability to change the environment. Children choose whether or not to engage in the behaviors they have learned. Their values and expectations of reinforcement affect whether they will imitate the behavior they observe.

Social cognitive theorists see children as active. They intentionally seek out or create environments in which reinforcers are available. As an example of how a child's behavior and characteristics create a reinforcing environment, consider the child who has artistic ability. The child may develop this skill by taking art lessons and by imitating her art teacher. In doing so, she creates an environment of social reinforcement in the form of praise from others. This reinforcement, in turn, influences the child's view of herself as a good artist.

Observational learning accounts for much human learning. It occurs when children observe how parents cook, clean, or repair a broken appliance. It takes place when children watch teachers solve problems on the blackboard or hear them speak a foreign language. Observational learning does not occur because of direct reinforcement. It occurs as long as children pay attention to the behavior of others. Once children are a few years old, observational learning becomes intentional. Children appear to select models for imitation who show certain positive characteristics. In social cognitive theory, the people after whom children pattern their own behavior are termed *models*.

Truth or Fiction Revisited: Yes, some theorists, including social cognitive theorists, contend that children actively strive to understand and take charge of their worlds. Other theorists, including behaviorists, argue that children respond passively to environmental stimulation. We will see that cognitive-development theorists side with social cognitive theorists on this matter.

Evaluation of Learning Theories

Learning theories have done a fine job of allowing us to describe, explain, predict, and influence many aspects of children's behavior. Psychologists and educators have developed many applications of conditioning and social cognitive theory. The use of the bell-and-pad method for bed-wetting is an example of behavior modification that probably would not have been derived from any other theoretical approach. Behavior modification has been used to help deal with autistic children, self-injurious children, and children showing temper tantrums and conduct disorders. Many of the teaching approaches used in educational TV shows are based on learning theory.

John Brenneis/Time Life Pictures/Getty Images

Albert Bandura
Bandura and other social cognitive theorists have shown that one way children learn is by observing others. Whereas behaviorists like John Watson and B. F. Skinner portrayed children as reactive to environmental stimuli, social cognitive theorists depict children as active learners who are capable of fashioning new environments.

social cognitive theory A cognitively oriented learning theory that emphasizes observational learning in the determining of behavior.

observational learning The acquisition of expectations and skills by means of observing others.

Jean Piaget

Piaget's cognitive-developmental theory is a stage theory that focuses on the ways children adapt to the environment by mentally representing the world and solving problems. Piaget's early training as a biologist led him to view children as mentally assimilating and accommodating aspects of their environment.

Despite the demonstrated effectiveness of behavior modification, learning-theory approaches to child development have been criticized in several ways. First, there is the theoretical question of whether the conditioning process in children is mechanical or whether it changes the ways that children mentally represent the environment. In addition, learning theorists may underestimate the importance of maturational factors (Schultz & Schultz, 2008). Social cognitive theorists seem to be working on these issues. For example, they place more value on cognition and view children as being active, not as merely reacting mechanically to stimuli. Now let us turn to theories that place cognition at the heart of development.

The Cognitive Perspective

Cognitive theorists focus on children's mental processes. They investigate the ways in which children perceive and mentally represent the world, how they develop thinking, logic, and problem-solving ability. One cognitive perspective is **cognitive-developmental theory** advanced by Swiss biologist Jean Piaget (1896–1980). Another is information-processing theory.

Jean Piaget's Cognitive-Developmental Theory

During adolescence, Piaget studied philosophy, logic, and mathematics, but years later he took his Ph.D. in biology. In 1920, he obtained a job at the Binet Institute in Paris, where research on intelligence tests was being conducted. Piaget tried out items on children in various age groups. The task became boring, but then Piaget became interested in children's *wrong* answers. Someone else might have shrugged them off and forgotten them, but Piaget realized that there were methods to the children's madness. Their wrong answers reflected consistent—although illogical—mental processes. Piaget looked into the patterns of thought that led to the wrong answers.

Piaget wrote dozens of books and articles on these patterns, but his work was almost unknown in English-speaking countries until the 1950s. For one thing, Piaget's writing is difficult to understand, even to native speakers of French. (Piaget joked that he had the advantage of *not* having to read Piaget.) For another, Piaget's views differed from those of other theorists. Psychology in England and the United States was dominated by behaviorism and psychoanalysis, and Piaget's ideas had a biological-cognitive flavor. But today they are quite popular.

Behaviorists, such as John B. Watson, focus on learning observable behavior. They see children as "blank slates" that are written upon by experience. Freud's psychoanalytic theory focuses on personality and emotional development. It portrays children as largely irrational and at the mercy of instinctive impulses. ***Question: What are Jean Piaget's views on development?*** Piaget, by contrast, was concerned with how children form concepts or mental representations of the world and how they work with concepts to plan changes in the external world. But, like the behaviorists, he recognized that thoughts cannot be measured directly, so he tried to link his views on children's mental processes to observable behavior.

Piaget believed that that cognitive development largely depends on the maturation of the brain. He regarded maturing children as natural physicists who actively intend to learn about and take intellectual charge of their worlds. In the Piagetian view, children who squish their food and laugh enthusiastically are often acting as budding scientists. In addition to enjoying a response from parents, they are studying the texture and consistency of their food. (Parents, of course, often prefer that their children practice these experiments in the laboratory, not the dining room.)

cognitive-developmental theory The stage theory that holds that the child's abilities to mentally represent the world and solve problems unfold as a result of the interaction of experience and the maturation of neurological structures.

scheme According to Piaget, an action pattern or mental structure that is involved in the acquisition and organization of knowledge.

Piaget's Basic Concepts Piaget used concepts such as *schemes, adaptation, assimilation, accommodation*, and *equilibration* to describe and explain cognitive development. Piaget defines the **scheme** as a pattern of action or a mental structure that is involved in acquiring or organizing knowledge. Babies are said to have sucking schemes, grasping schemes, and looking schemes. (Others call these *reflexes*.) Newborn babies suck things that are placed in their mouths, grasp objects placed in their hands, and visually track moving objects. Piaget would say that infants' schemes give meaning to objects. Infants are responding to objects as "things I can suck" versus "things I can't suck" and as "things I can grasp" versus "things I can't grasp." Among older children, a scheme may be the inclusion of an object in a class. For example, the mammal class, or concept, includes a group of animals that are warm-blooded and nurse their young. The inclusion of cats, apes, whales, and people in the mammal class involves schemes that expand the child's knowledge of the natural world.

Adaptation refers to the interaction between the organism and the environment. According to Piaget, all organisms adapt to their environment; it is a biological tendency. Adaptation consists of assimilation and accommodation, which occur throughout life. In biology, assimilation is the process by which food is digested and converted into the tissues that compose an animal. Cognitive **assimilation** refers to the process by which someone responds to new objects or events according to existing schemes or ways of organizing knowledge. Infants, for example, usually try to place new objects in their mouths to suck, feel, or explore them. Piaget would say that the child is assimilating (fitting) a new toy or object into the sucking-an-object scheme. Similarly, 2-year-olds who refer to sheep and cows as "doggies" or "bowwows" can be said to be assimilating these new animals into the doggy (or bowwow) scheme.

Sometimes, a novel object or event cannot be made to fit (i.e., it cannot be assimilated into an existing scheme). In that case, the scheme may be changed or a new scheme may be created to incorporate the new event. This process is called **accommodation**. Consider the sucking reflex. Within the first month of life, infants modify sucking behavior as a result of experience sucking various objects. The nipple on the bottle is sucked one way, the thumb in a different way. Infants accommodate further by rejecting objects that are too large, that taste bad, or that are of the wrong texture or temperature.

Piaget theorized that when children can assimilate new events to existing schemes, they are in a state of cognitive harmony, or equilibrium. When something that does not fit happens along, their state of equilibrium is disturbed and they may try to accommodate. The process of restoring equilibrium is termed **equilibration**. Piaget believed that the attempt to restore equilibrium is the source of intellectual motivation and lies at the heart of the natural curiosity of the child.

Piaget's Stages of Cognitive Development

Piaget (1963) hypothesized that children's cognitive processes develop in an orderly sequence, or series, of stages. As with motor development, some children may be more advanced than others at particular ages, but the developmental sequence remains the same. Piaget identified four major stages of cognitive development: sensorimotor, preoperational, concrete operational, and formal operational. These stages are described in Concept Review 1.2 and are discussed in subsequent chapters.

Because Piaget's theory focuses on cognitive development, its applications are primarily in educational settings. Teachers following Piaget's views would engage the child actively in solving problems. They would gear instruction to the child's developmental level and offer activities that challenge the child to advance to the next level. For example, 5-year-olds learn primarily through play and direct sensory contact with the environment. Early formal instruction using workbooks and paper may be less effective than other methods in this age group (Crain, 2000).

Evaluation

Many researchers, using a variety of methods, have found that Piaget may have underestimated the ages when children are capable of doing certain things. It also appears that cognitive skills may develop more gradually than Piaget thought and not in distinct stages. Here, let us simply note that Piaget presented a view of

adaptation According to Piaget, the interaction between the organism and the environment. It consists of two processes: assimilation and accommodation.

assimilation According to Piaget, the incorporation of new events or knowledge into existing schemes.

accommodation According to Piaget, the modification of existing schemes to permit the incorporation of new events or knowledge.

equilibration The creation of an equilibrium, or balance, between assimilation and accommodation as a way of incorporating new events or knowledge.

Concept Review 1.2   Jean Piaget's Stages of Cognitive Development

Stage	Approximate Age	Comments	
Sensorimotor	Birth to 2 years	At first, the child lacks language and does not use symbols or mental representations of objects. In time, reflexive responding ends, and intentional behavior—as in making interesting stimulation last—begins. The child develops the object concept and acquires the basics of language.	
Preoperational	2 to 7 years	The child begins to represent the world mentally, but thought is egocentric. The child does not focus on two aspects of a situation at once and therefore lacks conservation. The child shows animism, artificialism, and objective responsibility for wrongdoing.	
Concrete operational	7 to 12 years	Logical mental actions—called operations—begin. The child develops conservation concepts, can adopt the viewpoint of others, can classify objects in series, and shows comprehension of basic relational concepts (such as one object being larger or heavier than another).	
Formal operational	12 years and older	Mature, adult thought emerges. Thinking is characterized by consideration of various possibilities (mental trial and error), abstract thought, and the formation and testing of hypotheses.	

©Doug Goodman/Photo Researchers Inc.

children that is different from the psychoanalytic and behaviorist views, and he provided a strong theoretical foundation for researchers concerned with sequences in children's cognitive development.

Information-Processing Theory

Another face of the cognitive perspective is information processing (Flavell et al., 2002; Siegler & Alabali, 2005). *Question: What is information-processing theory?* Psychological thought has long been influenced by the status of the physical sciences of the day. For example, Freud's psychoanalytic theory was related to the development of the steam engine—which can explode when too much steam builds up—in the 19th century. Many of today's cognitive psychologists are influenced by computer science. Computers process information to solve problems. Information is encoded so that it can be accepted as input and then fed ("inputted") into the computer. Then it is placed in working memory (RAM) while it is manipulated. The information can be stored more permanently on a storage device, such as a hard drive. Many psychologists also speak of people as having working or short-term memory and a more permanent long-term memory (storage). If information has been placed in long-term memory, it must be retrieved before we can work on it again. To retrieve information from computer storage, we must know the code or name for the data file and the rules for retrieving data files. Similarly, note psychologists, without the cues to retrieve information from our own long-term memories, the information may be lost.

Thus, many cognitive psychologists focus on information processing in people—the processes by which information is encoded (input), stored (in long-term memory), retrieved (placed in short-term memory), and manipulated to solve problems (output). Our strategies for solving problems are sometimes referred to as our "mental programs" or "software." In this computer metaphor, our brains are the "hardware" that runs our mental programs. Our brains—containing billions of brain cells called *neurons*—become our most "personal" computers.

When psychologists who study information processing contemplate the cognitive development of children, they are likely to talk in terms of the *size* of the child's short-term memory at a given age and of the *number of programs* a child can run simultaneously.

The most obvious applications of information processing occur in teaching. For example, information-processing models alert teachers to the sequence of steps by which children acquire information, commit it to memory, and retrieve it to solve problems. By understanding this sequence, teachers can provide experiences that give students practice with each stage.

We now see that the brain is a sort of biological computer. Let us next see what other aspects of biology can be connected with child development.

The Biological Perspective

Question: What is the scope of the biological perspective? The biological perspective directly relates to physical development: to gains in height and weight; development of the brain; and developments connected with hormones, reproduction, and heredity. Here we consider one biologically oriented theory of development, *ethology*.

Ethology: "Doing What Comes Naturally"

Ethology was heavily influenced by the 19th-century work of Charles Darwin and by the work of 20th-century ethologists Konrad Lorenz and Niko Tinbergen (Washburn, 2007). *Question: What is ethology?* Ethology is concerned with instinctive, or inborn, behavior patterns.

The nervous systems of most, and perhaps all, animals are "prewired" or "preprogrammed" to respond to some situations in specific ways. For example, birds raised in isolation from other birds build nests during the mating season even if they have never seen a nest or seen another bird building one. Nest-building could not have been learned. Birds raised in isolation also sing the songs typical of their species. Salmon spawned in particular rivers swim out into the vast oceans and then, when mature, return to their own river to spawn. These behaviors are "built in," or instinctive. They are also referred to as inborn **fixed action patterns (FAPs)**.

During prenatal development, genes and sex hormones are responsible for the physical development of female and male sex organs. Most theorists also believe that

ethology The study of behaviors that are specific to a species.

fixed action pattern (FAP) A stereotyped pattern of behavior that is evoked by a "releasing stimulus." An instinct.

in many species, including humans, sex hormones can "masculinize" or "feminize" the embryonic brain by creating tendencies to behave in stereotypical masculine or feminine ways. Testosterone, the male sex hormone, seems to be connected with feelings of self-confidence, high activity levels, and—the negative side—aggressiveness (Archer, 2006; Davis et al., 2005; Geary, 2006).

Evaluation   Most theorists with an ethological perspective do not maintain that human behaviors are as mechanical as those of lower animals. Moreover, they tend to assume that instinctive behaviors can be modified through learning. Research into the ethological perspective suggests, however, that instinct may play a role in human behavior. Two questions that research seeks to answer are, What areas of human behavior and development, if any, involve instincts? and How powerful are instincts in people?

The Ecological Perspective

Ecology is the branch of biology that deals with the relationships between living organisms and their environment. *Question: What is the ecological systems theory of child development?* The **ecological systems theory** of child development addresses aspects of psychological, social, and emotional development as well as aspects of biological development. Ecological systems theorists explain child development in terms of the interaction between children and the settings in which they live (Bronfenbrenner & Morris, 2006).

According to Urie Bronfenbrenner (1917–2005), we need to focus on the two-way interactions between the child and the parents, not just maturational forces (nature) or parental child-rearing approaches (nurture). For example, some parents may choose to feed newborns on demand, whereas others may decide to stick to feedings that occur 4 hours apart. Some babies, however, will be more accepting than others, and some will never be comfortable with a strict schedule. That is the point: Parents are a key part of the child's environment and have a major influence on the child, but even babies have inborn temperaments that affect the parents.

Bronfenbrenner (Bronfenbrenner & Morris, 2006) suggested that we can view the setting or contexts of human development as consisting of multiple systems, each embedded within the next larger context. From narrowest to widest, these systems are the microsystem, the mesosystem, the exosystem, the macrosystem, and the chronosystem (● Figure 1.4).

The **microsystem** involves the interactions of the child and other people in the immediate setting, such as the home, the school, or the peer group. Initially, the microsystem is small, involving care-giving interactions with the parents or others, usually at home. As children get older, they do more, with more people, in more places.

The **mesosystem** involves the interactions of the various settings within the microsystem. For instance, the home and the school interact during parent–teacher conferences. The school and the larger community interact when children are taken on field trips. The ecological systems approach addresses the joint effect of two or more settings on the child.

The **exosystem** involves the institutions in which the child does not directly participate but which exert an indirect influence on the child. For example, the school board is part of the child's exosystem because board members put together programs for the child's education, determine what textbooks will be acceptable, and so forth. In similar fashion, the parents' workplaces and economic situations determine the hours during which they will be available to the child, what mood they will be in when they are with the child, and so on. For example, poverty and unemployment cause psychological distress in parents, which affects their parenting (Kaminski & Stormshak, 2007). As a result, children may misbehave at home and in school. Studies that

ecology The branch of biology that deals with the relationships between living organisms and their environment.

ecological systems theory The view that explains child development in terms of the reciprocal influences between children and the settings that make up their environment.

microsystem The immediate settings with which the child interacts, such as the home, the school, and one's peers (from the Greek *mikros*, meaning "small").

mesosystem The interlocking settings that influence the child, such as the interaction of the school and the larger community when children are taken on field trips (from the Greek *mesos*, meaning "middle").

exosystem Community institutions and settings that indirectly influence the child, such as the school board and the parents' workplaces (from the Greek *exo*, meaning "outside").

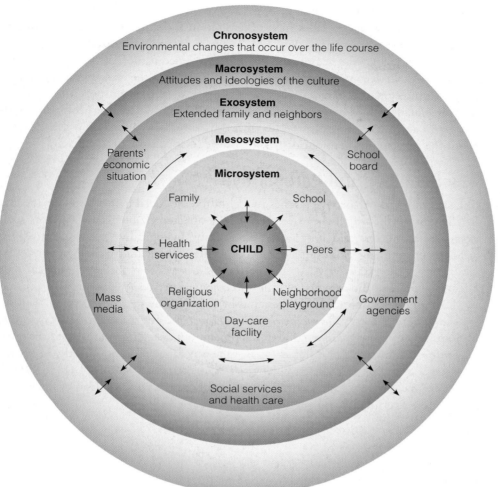

● **Figure 1.4**
The Contexts of Human Development

According to ecological systems theory, the systems within which children develop are embedded within larger systems. Children and these systems reciprocally influence each other.

address the effects of housing, health care, TV programs, church attendance, government agencies, or even iPods on children examine the interactions of the exosystem with the child (Kaminski & Stormshak, 2007).

The **macrosystem** involves the interaction of children with the beliefs, values, expectations, and lifestyles of their cultural settings. Cross-cultural studies examine children's interactions with their macrosystem. Macrosystems exist within a particular culture as well. For example, in the United States, the two-wage-earner family, the low-income single-parent household, and the family with father as sole breadwinner describe three different macrosystems. Each has its lifestyle, set of values, and expectations (Bronfenbrenner & Morris, 2006; Silbereisen, 2006). One issue affecting children is multiculturalism. A study of 258 Mexican American eighth- to eleventh-graders found that those who perceived their environment to be multicultural found school to be easier, obtained higher grades, and were more likely to stay in school (Tan, 1999).

The **chronosystem** considers the changes that occur over time. For example, the effects of divorce peak about a year after the event, and then children begin to recover (see Chapter 13). The breakup has more of an effect on boys than on girls. The ecological approach broadens the strategies for intervention in problems such as prevention of teenage pregnancy, child abuse, and juvenile offending, including substance abuse (Kaminski & Stormshak, 2007).

macrosystem The basic institutions and ideologies that influence the child, such as the American ideals of freedom of expression and equality under the law (from the Greek *makros*, meaning "long" or "enlarged").

chronosystem The environmental changes that occur over time and have an effect on the child (from the Greek *chronos*, meaning "time").

Evaluation

Ecological systems theory helps focus attention on the shifting systems with which children interact as they as they develop. The health of the infant requires relationships between parents and the health-care system, and the education of the child requires relationships between parents and schools. At the level of the exosystem, researchers look into the effects of parents' work lives, welfare agencies, transportation systems, shopping facilities, and so on. At the level of the macrosystem, we may compare child-rearing practices in the United States with those in other countries. We learn more about the role of culture in our discussion of the sociocultural perspective.

The Sociocultural Perspective

The sociocultural perspective teaches that children are social beings who are affected by the cultures in which they live. Yes, we are affected by biochemical forces such as neurotransmitters and hormones. We may be biologically "prewired" to form attachments and engage in other behaviors. Perhaps there are psychological tendencies to learn in certain ways, or maybe there are ways that the psychological past affects the present. But as noted within the ecological perspective, we are also affected by the customs, traditions, languages, and heritages of the societies in which we live.

Question: What is the sociocultural perspective? The sociocultural perspective overlaps other perspectives on child development, but developmentalists use the term *sociocultural* in a couple of different ways. One way refers quite specifically to the *sociocultural theory* of Russian psychologist Lev Semenovich Vygotsky (1896–1934). The other way broadly addresses the effect on children of human diversity, including such factors as ethnicity and gender.

Developing in a World of Diversity

Influence of the Macrosystem on the Development of Independence

Cross-cultural studies provide interesting insights into the way children interact with their macrosystems. Consider the development of independence. Among the !Kung people of Namibia, babies are kept in close contact with their mothers during the first year (Konner, 1977). !Kung infants are frequently carried in slings across their mothers' hips that allow the mothers to nurse at will, literally all day long. The !Kung seem to follow the commandment "The infant shall not go hungry," not even for 5 seconds. In every way, !Kung mothers try to respond at once to their babies' cries and whims. By Western standards, !Kung babies are "spoiled." However, overindulgence does not appear to make !Kung babies overly dependent on their mothers. By the time the babies are capable of walking, they do. They do not cling to their mothers. In comparison to Western children of the same age, !Kung children spend less time with their mothers and more time with their peers.

Also compare Urie Bronfenbrenner's (1973) observations of child rearing in the United States and Russia. Russian babies, as a group, are more likely than U.S. babies to be cuddled, kissed, and hugged. Russian mothers are not quite so solicitous as their !Kung counterparts, but they are highly protective compared with U.S. mothers. However, Russian children are taught to take care of themselves at younger ages than U.S. children. By 18 months of age, Russian children are usually learning to dress themselves and are largely toilet trained.

Vygotsky's Sociocultural Theory

Whereas genetics is concerned with the biological transmission of traits from generation to generation, Vygotsky's (1978) theory is concerned with the transmission of information and cognitive skills from generation to generation. The transmission of skills involves teaching and learning, but Vygotsky does not view learning in terms of the conditioning of behavior. Rather, he focuses on how the child's social interaction with adults, largely in the home, organizes a child's learning experiences in such a way that the child can obtain cognitive skills—such as computation or reading skills—and use them to acquire information. Like Piaget, Vygotsky sees the child's functioning as adaptive (Kanevsky & Geake, 2004), and the child adapts to his or her social and cultural interactions.

Question: What are the key concepts of Vygotsky's sociocultural theory? Key concepts in Vygotsky's theory include the *zone of proximal development* and *scaffolding*. The word *proximal* means "nearby" or "close," as in the words *approximate* and *proximity*. The **zone of proximal development (ZPD)** refers to a range of tasks that a child can carry out with the help of someone who is more skilled. It is similar to an apprenticeship. Many developmentalists find that observing how a child learns when working with others provides more information about that child's cognitive abilities than does a simple inventory of knowledge (Meijer & Elshout, 2001). When learning with other people, the child tends to internalize— or bring inward—the conversations and explanations that help him or her gain the necessary skills (Ash, 2004; Umek et al., 2005; Vygotsky, 1962). In other words, children not only learn the meanings of words from teachers but also learn ways of talking to themselves about solving problems within a cultural context (Murata & Fuson, 2006). Outer speech becomes inner speech. What was the teacher's becomes the child's. What was a social and cultural context becomes embedded within the child.

A *scaffold* is a temporary skeletal structure that enables workers to fabricate a building, bridge, or other more permanent structure. In Vygotsky's theory, teachers and parents provide children with problem-solving methods that serve as cognitive **scaffolding** while the child gains the ability to function independently. For example, a child's instructors may offer advice on sounding out letters and words that provide a temporary support until reading "clicks" and the child no longer needs the device. Children may be offered scaffolding that enables them to use their fingers or their toes to do simple calculations. Eventually, the scaffolding is removed and the cognitive structures stand alone. A Puerto Rican study found that students also use scaffolding when they are explaining to one another how they can improve school projects, such as essay assignments (Guerrero & Villamil, 2000). Vygotsky's theory points out that children's attitudes toward schooling are embedded within the parent–child relationship.

The Sociocultural Perspective and Human Diversity

The field of child development focuses mainly on individuals and is committed to the dignity of the individual child. *Question: What is the connection between the sociocultural perspective and human diversity?* The sociocultural perspective asserts that we cannot understand individual children without awareness of the richness of their diversity (Fouad & Arredondo, 2007). For example, children diverge or differ in their ethnicity, gender, and socioeconomic status.

Children's **ethnic groups** involve their cultural heritage, their race, their language, and their common history. ● Figures 1.5 and ● 1.6 highlight the population shifts under way in the United States as a result of reproductive patterns and immigration. The numbers of African Americans and Latino and Latina Americans (who

Lev Semonovich Vygotsky
Vygotsky is known for showing how social speech becomes inner speech and how "scaffolding" by others assists children in developing the cognitive skills to succeed.

zone of proximal development (ZPD) Vygotsky's term for the situation in which a child carries out tasks with the help of someone who is more skilled, frequently an adult who represents the culture in which the child develops.

scaffolding Vygotsky's term for temporary cognitive structures or methods of solving problems that help the child as he or she learns to function independently.

ethnic groups Groups of people distinguished by cultural heritage, race, language, and common history.

● **Figure 1.5**

Numbers of Various Racial and Ethnic Groups in the United States, Year 2000 versus Year 2050 (in millions)

The numbers of each of the various racial and ethnic groups in the United States will grow over the next half-century, with the numbers of Latino and Latina Americans and Asian Americans and Pacific Islanders growing most rapidly.

Source: U.S. Bureau of the Census (2004).

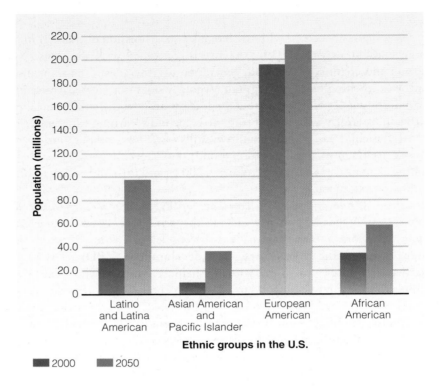

● **Figure 1.6**

Percentages of Various Racial and Ethnic Groups in the United States, Year 2000 versus Year 2050

Although European Americans are projected to remain the most populous ethnic group in the United States in the year 2050, the group's percentage of the population will diminish from 72% to 53%. But because of general population growth, there will still be more European Americans in the United States in 2050 than there are today.

Source: U.S. Bureau of the Census (2004).

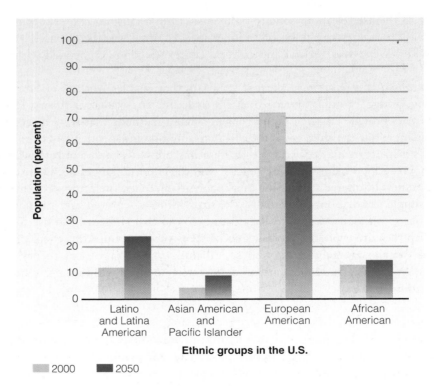

may be White, Black, or Native American in racial origin) are growing more rapidly than those of European Americans (U.S. Bureau of the Census, 2006). The cultural heritages, languages, and histories of ethnic minority groups are thus likely to have an increasing effect on the cultural life of the United States. Yet it turns out that the dominant culture in the United States has often disparaged the traditions and languages of people from ethnic minority groups. For example, it has been considered harmful to rear children bilingually, although research suggests that bilingualism broadens children, as we see in Chapter 12.

Studying diversity is also important so that children have appropriate educational experiences. To teach children and guide their learning, educators need to understand children's family values and cultural expectations. Many professionals—psychologists, teachers, social workers, psychiatrists, and others—are called on to help children and families who are having problems in school or in the community. Professionals may need special training to identify the problems of children and families from ethnic minority groups and to treat them in culturally sensitive ways (Constantine, 2007; Fu et al., 2007; Torres & Rollock, 2007).

Throughout the text, we consider many issues that affect children from various ethnic groups. A handful of them include bilingualism, ethnic differences in intelligence test scores, the prevalence of suicide among members of different ethnic minority groups, and patterns of child rearing among parents of various ethnic minority groups.

Gender is another aspect of human diversity. Gender is the psychological state of being male or being female, as influenced by cultural concepts of gender-appropriate behavior. The French have a saying, *Vive la différence* ("Long live the difference!"), which celebrates the difference between females and males. The French expression exudes the excitement people may feel when they are interacting with individuals of the other sex, but, unfortunately, it also alludes to the problem that females and males are often polarized by cultural expectations. That is, the differences may be exaggerated, as in the case of intellectual abilities. Put it this way: Males may very well differ from females in some respects, but history has created more burdens for women than men as a result. Gender-role expectations affect children's self-esteem and limit their hopes and dreams for the future.

Historically, girls have been discouraged from careers in the sciences, politics, and business. Women today are making inroads into academic and vocational spheres—such as medicine, law, engineering, and the military—that were traditionally male preserves. Today, most college students in the United States are female, but it is worth noting that girls were not considered qualified for education until relatively recent times. Who, for example, is Lucinda Foote? She was a brilliant young woman who is known to us only because of her rejection letter from Yale University in 1792, which confirmed that she was qualified for Yale in every way *except* for her sex (Leon, 2001). It may surprise you to learn that women were not admitted to college in the United States until 1833, the year that Oberlin College opened its doors to women. Even today, however, there remain many—many!—parts of the world in which women are prevented from obtaining an education.

Opportunities for women are crucial to the development of girls. Opportunities for adults give children their sense of what is possible for them. Just as many children from ethnic minority groups wonder whether they can experience the rewards and opportunities they see in the dominant culture, so do girls wonder whether the career and social roles they admire are available to them. I was surprised to learn that my daughters once thought that the presidency of the United States was open only to men. The effects of cultural expectations on girls' self-concepts and motivation are clear and compelling.

In this book, the focus on human diversity extends beyond ethnicity and gender to include children with various sexual orientations and disabilities. This approach broadens our understanding of all children as they experience the developmental changes brought about by quite different influences of heredity and experience.

Concept Review 1.3 summarizes similarities and differences among the perspectives on child development.

gender The psychological state of being female or male, as influenced by cultural concepts of gender-appropriate behavior. Compare and contrast the concept of gender with *anatomic sex*, which is based on the physical differences between females and males.

Concept Review 1.3 Perspectives on Child Development

Perspective or Theory	Core Concepts	Is Nature or Nurture More Important?	Is Development Viewed as Being Continuous or Discontinuous	Is the Child Viewed as Being Active or Passive?
The Psychoanalytic Perspective				
Theory of psycho-sexual development (Sigmund Freud)	Instinctive impulses are channeled via social codes, but conflict develops as a result. Much of the mind is unconscious.	Interaction of nature and nurture: Biological maturation sets the stage for reaction to social influences.	Discontinuous: There are five stages of development, each of which involves the expression of sexual impulses.	Passive: The child is largely at the mercy of older people and cultural modes of conduct.
Theory of psycho-social development (Erik Erikson)	Child (and adult) experiences life crises that are largely based on social relationships, opportunities, and expectations.	Interaction of nature and nurture: Biological maturation sets the stage for reaction to social influences and opportunities.	Discontinuous: There are eight stages of development, each of which involves a particular kind of life crisis.	Active: The child (and adult) makes conscious decisions about formation of his or her own personality and behavior.
The Learning Perspective: Behavioral and Social Cognitive Theories				
Behaviorism (John B. Watson, Ivan Pavlov, B. F. Skinner)	Behavior is learned by association; two key types of learning are classical conditioning and operant conditioning.	Nurture: Children are seen almost as blank tablets.	Continuous: Behavior reflects the summation of conditioned responses.	Passive: Responses are learned by association, and behavior is maintained due to its effects.
Social cognitive theory (Albert Bandura and others)	Conditioning occurs, but children also learn purposefully by observing others, and they choose whether to display learned responses.	Emphasizes nurture but allows for expression of natural tendencies.	Continuous.	Active: Principle of reciprocal determinism states that children influence the environment even as the environment influences them.
The Cognitive Perspective				
Cognitive-developmental theory (Jean Piaget)	Children adapt to the environment via processes of assimilation to existing mental structures (schemes) or by changing these structures (accommodation).	Emphasizes nature but allows for influences of experience.	Discontinuous: Cognitive development follows an invariant sequence of four stages.	Active: Children are budding scientists who seek to understand and manipulate their worlds.

© Hulton Archive/ Getty Images

Sarah Putnam/Index Stock/PhotoLibrary

Nina Leen/Time Life Pictures/Getty Images

John Brenneis/Time Life Pictures/Getty Images

© Farrell Grehan/ CORBIS

Perspective or Theory	Core Concepts	Is Nature or Nurture More Important?	Is Development Viewed as Being Continuous or Discontinuous	Is the Child Viewed as Being Active or Passive?
Information-processing theory (numerous theorists)	Children's cognitive functioning is compared to that of computers, involving the inputting, manipulation, storage, and output of information.	Interaction of nature and nurture.	Continuous: Development facilitates the child's storage capacity and ability to run multiple "programs" simultaneously; cognitive skills are cumulative.	Active: Children seek to obtain and manipulate information.

The Biological Perspective

Ethology (Charles Darwin, Konrad Lorenz, Niko Tinbergen)	Organisms are biologically "prewired" to show inborn fixed action patterns (FAPs) in response to species-specific releasing stimuli.	Emphasizes nature but experience is also critical; for example, imprinting occurs at a given point in development, but *what* an organism is imprinted on is determined by experience.	Discontinuous: Certain kinds of learning, for example, are said to occur during *critical periods*, which are biologically determined.	Not indicated, although organisms are depicted as responding automatically (passively) to FAPs.

The Ecological Perspective

Ecological systems theory (Urie Bronfenbrenner)	Children's development occurs within interlocking systems. Development is enhanced by intervening at the levels of various systems.	Interaction of nature and nurture: Children's personalities and skills contribute to their development.	Not specifically indicated.	Active: Influences are bidirectional—Systems influence the child, and vice versa.

The Sociocultural Perspective

Sociocultural theory (Lev Vygotsky) University of Akron	Addresses the ways in which children internalize sociocultural dialogues as ways of guiding their own behavior and developing problem-solving skills.	Interaction of nature and nurture; nurture is discussed in social and cultural terms.	Continuous: Learning in the presence of experienced members of a culture enables the child to accumulate knowledge and skills.	Both: Children seek to develop problem-solving abilities by internalizing cultural dialogues, but the dialogues originate within society, not within the individual.
Sociocultural perspective and human diversity (numerous theorists)	Focuses on the influences of sociocultural factors, such as ethnic background and sex on development.	Nurture.	Not specifically indicated.	Not indicated.

Active Review

4. _____ are intended to allow us to explain, predict, and control events.
5. _____ hypothesized five stages of psychosexual development.
6. Erikson extended Freud's five stages of development to _____.
7. Behaviorism sees children's learning as mechanical and relies on classical and _____ conditioning.
8. According to _____, children assimilate new events to existing schemes or accommodate schemes to incorporate novel events.
9. Information-_____ theory focuses on the processes by which information is encoded, stored, retrieved, and manipulated.

10. The _____ systems theory explains child development in terms of the interaction between children and the settings in which they live.
11. Vygotsky's _____ theory is concerned with the transmission of information and cognitive skills from generation to generation.

Reflect & Relate: How have your ethnic background and your sex influenced your development? Consider factors such as race, country of origin, language, nutrition, values, and the dominant culture's reaction to people of your background.

Go to

http://www.thomsonedu.com/psychology/rathus

for an interactive version of this review.

Controversies in Child Development

The discussion of theories of development reveals that developmentalists can see things in very different ways. Let us consider how they react to three of the most important debates in the field.

The Nature–Nurture Controversy

Question: Which exerts the greater influence on children, nature or nurture? Think about your friends for a moment. Some may be tall and lanky, others short and stocky. Some are outgoing and sociable, others more reserved and quiet. One may be a good athlete, another a fine musician. What made them this way? How much does inheritance have to do with it, and how much does the environment play a role?

Researchers are continually trying to sort out the extent to which human behavior is the result of **nature** (heredity) and of **nurture** (environmental influences). What aspects of behavior originate in our **genes** and are biologically programmed to unfold in the child as time goes on, as long as minimal nutrition and social experience are provided? What aspects of behavior can be traced largely to such environmental influences as nutrition and learning?

Scientists seek the natural causes of development in children's genetic heritage, the functioning of the nervous system, and in maturation. Scientists seek the environmental causes of development in children's nutrition, cultural and family backgrounds, and opportunities to learn about the world, including cognitive stimulation during early childhood and formal education.

Some theorists (e.g., cognitive-developmental and biological theorists) lean heavily toward natural explanations of development, whereas others (e.g., learning the-

nature The processes within an organism that guide that organism to develop according to its genetic code.

nurture The processes external to an organism that nourish it as it develops according to its genetic code or that cause it to swerve from its genetically programmed course. Environmental factors that influence development.

genes The basic building blocks of heredity.

orists) lean more heavily toward environmental explanations. But today nearly all researchers agree that nature and nurture play important roles in nearly every area of child development. Consider the development of language. Language is based in structures found in certain areas of the brain. Thus, biology (nature) plays a vital role in language development. But children also come to speak the languages spoken by their caretakers. Parent–child similarities in accent and vocabulary provide additional evidence for the role of learning (nurture) in language development.

The Continuity–Discontinuity Controversy

Question: Is development continuous or discontinuous? Do developmental changes occur gradually (continuously), the way a seedling becomes a tree? Or do changes occur in major qualitative leaps (discontinuously) that dramatically alter our bodies and behavior, the way a caterpillar turns into a butterfly?

Some developmentalists view human development as a continuous process in which the effects of learning mount gradually, with no major sudden qualitative changes. In contrast, other theorists believe that a number of rapid qualitative changes usher in new stages of development. Maturational theorists point out that the environment, even when enriched, profits us little until we are ready, or mature enough, to develop in a certain way. For example, newborn babies will not imitate their parents' speech, even when parents speak clearly and deliberately. Nor does aided practice in "walking" during the first few months after birth significantly accelerate the emergence of independent walking. They are not ready to do these things.

Stage theorists such as Sigmund Freud and Jean Piaget saw development as discontinuous. They saw biological changes as providing the potential for psychological changes. Freud focused on the ways in which biological developments might provide the basis for personality development. Piaget believed maturation of the nervous system allowed cognitive development.

Certain aspects of physical development do occur in stages. For example, from the age of 2 years to the onset of puberty, children gradually grow larger. Then the adolescent growth spurt occurs as rushes of hormones cause rapid biological changes in structure and function (as in the development of the sex organs) and in size. Psychologists disagree on whether developments in cognition occur in stages.

The Active–Passive Controversy

Question: Are children active (prewired to act on the world) or passive (shaped by experience)? Broadly speaking, all animals are active. But in the field of child development, the issue has a more specific meaning.

Historical views of children as willful and unruly suggest that people have generally seen children as active, even if mischievous (at best) or evil (at worst). John Locke introduced a view of children as passive beings (blank tablets); experience "wrote" features of personality and moral virtue on them.

At one extreme, educators who view children as passive may assume that they must be motivated to learn by their instructors. Such educators are likely to provide a traditional curriculum with rigorous exercises in spelling, music, and math to promote absorption of the subject matter. They are also likely to apply a powerful system of rewards and punishments to keep children on the straight and narrow.

© Mark Richards/PhotoEdit

Stages of Physical Development
Certain aspects of physical development seem to occur in stages. Girls usually spurt in growth before boys. The girl and boy who are dancing are the same age.

At the other extreme, educators who view children as active may assume that they have a natural love of learning. Such educators are likely to argue for open education and encourage children to explore an environment rich with learning materials. Such educators are likely to listen to the children to learn about their unique likes and talents and then support children as they pursue their own agendas.

These examples are extremes. Most educators probably agree that children show individual differences and that some children require more guidance and external motivation than others. In addition, children can be active in some subjects and passive in others. Whether children who do not actively seek to master certain subjects are coerced tends to depend on how important the subject is to functioning in today's society, the age of the child, the attitudes of the parents, and many other factors.

Urie Bronfenbrenner (Bronfenbrenner & Morris, 2006) argued that we miss the point when we assume that children are entirely active or passive. Children are influenced by the environment, but children also influence the environment. The challenge is to observe the ways in which children interact with their settings. Albert Bandura (2006a, 2006b) also refers to the two-way influences between children and the environment.

These debates are theoretical. Scientists value theory for its ability to tie together observations and suggest new areas of investigation, but they also follow an **empirical** approach. That is, they engage in research methods, such as those described in the next section, to find evidence for or against various theoretical positions.

empirical Based on observation and experimentation.

Active Review

12. Researchers in child development try to sort out the effects of _____ (heredity) and nurture (environmental influences).
13. Learning theorists tend to see development as continuous, whereas stage theorists see development as _____.

Reflect & Relate: Consider the active–passive controversy. Do you see yourself as being active or passive? Explain.

Go to

http://www.thomsonedu.com/psychology/rathus

for an interactive version of this review.

How Do We Study Child Development?

What is the relationship between children's intelligence and their achievement? What are the effects of maternal use of aspirin and alcohol on the fetus? How can you rear children to become competent and independent? What are the effects of parental divorce on children? We may have expressed opinions on such questions at one time or another. But scientists insist that such questions be answered by research. Strong arguments or reference to authority figures are not evidence. Scientific evidence is obtained only by the scientific method. ***Question: What is the scientific method?***

The Scientific Method

The scientific method is a systematic way of forming and answering research questions. It allows scientists to test the theories discussed in the previous section. The scientific method has five steps.

Step 1: Forming a Research Question

Our daily experiences, theory, and even folklore help generate questions for research. Daily experience in using day-care centers may stimulate us to wonder whether day care affects children's intellectual or social development or the bonds of attachment between children and parents. Reading about observational learning may suggest research into the effects of TV violence.

Step 2: Developing a Hypothesis

The second step is the development of a hypothesis. A **hypothesis** is a specific statement about behavior that is tested through research. One hypothesis about day care might be that preschool children placed in day care will acquire better skills in getting along with other children than will preschoolers who are cared for in the home. A hypothesis about TV violence might be that elementary school children who watch more violent TV shows will behave more aggressively toward other children.

Step 3: Testing the Hypothesis

The third step is testing the hypothesis. Psychologists test the hypothesis through carefully controlled information-gathering techniques and research methods, such as **naturalistic observation**, the case study, correlation, and the experiment.

For example, we could introduce two groups of children—children who are in day care and children who are not in day care—to a new child in a college child-research center and see how each group acts toward the new child. Concerning the effects of TV violence, we could have parents help us tally which TV shows their children watch and rate the shows for violent content. Then we could ask the children's teachers to report how aggressively the children act toward classmates. We could do some math to determine whether more aggressive children also watch more violence on TV. We describe research methods such as these later in the chapter.

© M. Plantec/First Light

The Scientific Method
What is the cause of this girl's aggression? Would she behave differently if the other child reacted to her with anger instead of fear? How does the scientific method help us answer this type of question?

Step 4: Drawing Conclusions about the Hypothesis

The fourth step is drawing conclusions. Psychologists draw conclusions about the accuracy of their hypotheses from their research results. When research does not bear out their hypotheses, the researchers may modify the theories from which the hypotheses were derived. Research findings often suggest new hypotheses and new studies.

In our research on the effects of day care, we would probably find that children in day care show somewhat greater social skills than children cared for in the home (see Chapter 7). We would probably also find that more aggressive children spend more time watching TV violence, as we shall see in Chapter 10. But we will also see in the following pages that it might be wrong to conclude from this kind of evidence that TV violence *causes* aggressive behavior.

Step 5: Publishing Findings

Scientists publish their research findings in professional journals and make their data available to scientists and the public at large for scrutiny. Thus, they give other scientists the opportunity to review their data and conclusions to help determine the accuracy of the research.

hypothesis (high-POTH-uh-sis) A Greek word meaning "groundwork" or "foundation" that has come to mean a specific statement about behavior that is tested by research.

naturalistic observation A method of scientific observation in which children (and others) are observed in their natural environments.

Now let us consider the information-gathering techniques and the research methods used by developmentalists. Then we will discuss ethical issues concerning research in child development.

Gathering Information

Developmentalists use various methods to gather information. For example, they may ask children to keep diaries of their behavior, ask teachers or parents to report on the behavior of their children, or use interviews or questionnaires with children themselves. They also directly observe children in the laboratory or in the natural setting. Let us discuss two ways of gathering information: the naturalistic-observation method and the case-study method.

Naturalistic Observation

Question: What is naturalistic observation? Naturalistic-observation studies of children are conducted in "the field," that is, in the natural, or real-life, settings in which they happen. In field studies, investigators observe the natural behavior of children in settings such as homes, playgrounds, and classrooms and try not to interfere with it. Interference could affect or "bias" the results. Researchers may try to "blend into the woodwork" by sitting quietly in the back of a classroom or by observing the class through a one-way mirror.

A number of naturalistic-observation studies have been done with children of different cultures. For example, researchers have observed the motor behavior of Native American Hopi children who are strapped to cradle boards during the first year. They have observed language development in the United States, Mexico, Turkey, Kenya, and China—seeking universals that might suggest a major role for maturation in the acquisition of language skills. They have also observed the ways in which children are socialized in Russia, Israel, Japan, and other nations in an effort to determine what patterns of child rearing are associated with development of behaviors such as attachment and independence.

The Case Study

Another way of gathering information about children is the case-study method. *Question: What is the case study?* The **case study** is a carefully drawn account of the behavior of an individual. Parents who keep diaries of their children's activities

case study A carefully drawn biography of the life of an individual.

standardized test A test of some ability or trait in which an individual's score is compared to the scores of a group of similar individuals.

What Is the Relationship Between Intelligence and Achievement?
Does the correlational method allow us to say that intelligence causes or is responsible for academic achievement? Why or why not?

© Bob Daemmrich/The Image Works

are involved in informal case studies. Case studies themselves often use a number of different kinds of information about children. In addition to direct observation, case studies may include questionnaires, **standardized tests**, and interviews with the child and his or her parents, teachers, and friends. Information gleaned from school and other records may be included. Scientists who use the case-study method take great pains to record all the relevant factors in a child's behavior, and they are cautious in drawing conclusions about what leads to what.

Jean Piaget used the case-study method in carefully observing and recording the behavior of children, including his own (see Chapter 6). Sigmund Freud developed his psychoanalytic theory largely on the basis of case studies. Freud studied his patients in great depth and followed some of them for many years.

Correlation: Putting Things Together

*Question: **What does it mean to correlate information?*** Correlation is a mathematical method that researchers use to determine whether one behavior or trait being studied is related to, or correlated with, another. Consider, for example, the **variables** of intelligence and achievement. These variables are assigned numbers such as intelligence test scores and academic grade averages. Then the numbers or scores are mathematically related and expressed as a correlation coefficient. A **correlation coefficient** is a number that varies between +1.00 and −1.00.

Numerous studies report **positive correlations** between intelligence and achievement. In general, the higher children score on intelligence tests, the better their academic performance is likely to be. The scores attained on intelligence tests are positively correlated (about +0.60 to +0.70) with overall academic achievement.[1]

There is a **negative correlation** between children's school grades and their commission of delinquent acts. The higher a child's grades in school, the less likely the child is to engage in criminal behavior. ● Figure 1.7 illustrates positive and negative correlations.

Limitations of Correlational Information

Correlational information can reveal relationships between variables, but they do not show cause and effect. For example, children who watch TV shows with a lot of violence are more likely to show aggressive behavior at home and in school. It may seem logical to assume that exposure to TV violence makes children more aggressive. But it may be that children who are more aggressive to begin with prefer violent TV shows. The relationship between viewing violence and behaving aggressively may not be so clear-cut.

Similarly, studies in locations as far-flung as the United States and China report that children (especially boys) in divorced families sometimes show more problems than do children in intact families (Greene et al., 2006; Lansford et al., 2006). However, these studies do not show that divorce causes these adjustment problems. It could be that the factors that led to divorce (such as parental disorganization or conflict) also led to adjustment problems among the children (Hetherington, 2006). Or it may be that having a child with problems might put a strain on the parents' marriage and ultimately be a factor contributing to divorce.

Positive correlation	Negative correlation
As one variable increases, the other variable increases.	As one variable increases, the other variable decreases.
A	B
Time spent studying — Grades in school	Frequency of delinquent acts — Grades in school

● **Figure 1.7**
Examples of Positive and Negative Correlations

When two variables are correlated *positively*, one increases as the other increases. There is a positive correlation between the amount of time spent studying and grades, as shown in Part A. When two variables are correlated *negatively*, one increases as the other decreases. There is a negative correlation between the frequency of a child's delinquent acts and his or her grades, as shown in Part B. As one's delinquent behavior increases, grades tend to decline.

variables Quantities that can vary from child to child or from occasion to occasion, such as height, weight, intelligence, and attention span.

correlation coefficient A number ranging from +1.00 to −1.00 that expresses the direction (positive or negative) and strength of the relationship between two variables.

positive correlation A relationship between two variables in which one variable increases as the other variable increases.

negative correlation A relationship between two variables in which one variable increases as the other variable decreases.

---

[1]Of course, +0.60 is the same as +.60. We insert the zeros to help prevent the decimal points from getting lost.

When we study patterns of child rearing, we must also ask why parents choose to rear their children in certain ways. It is possible that the factors that lead parents to make these choices, such as the cultural environment, also influence the behavior of the children. Thus, correlational research does not allow us to place clear "cause" and "effect" labels on variables. To investigate cause and effect, researchers turn to the experimental method.

The Experiment: Trying Things Out

The experiment is the preferred method for investigating questions of cause and effect. *Question: What is an experiment?* An **experiment** is a research method in which a group of subjects receives a **treatment** and another group does not. The subjects are then observed to determine whether the treatment makes a difference in their behavior.

Experiments are used when possible because they allow researchers to control the experiences of children and other subjects to determine the outcomes of a treatment. Experiments, like other research methods, are usually undertaken to test a hypothesis. For example, a researcher might hypothesize that TV violence will cause aggressive behavior in children. To test this hypothesis, she might devise an experiment in which some children are purposely exposed to TV violence and others are not. Remember that it is not enough to demonstrate that children who choose to watch more violent shows behave more aggressively; such evidence is only correlational. We review this research—correlational and experimental—in Chapter 10.

Independent and Dependent Variables

In an experiment to determine whether TV violence causes aggressive behavior, subjects in the experimental group would be shown a TV program containing violence and its effects on behavior would be measured. TV violence would be considered an **independent variable**, a variable whose presence is manipulated by the experimenters so that its effects can be determined. The measured result—in this case, the child's behavior—is called a **dependent variable**. Its presence or level presumably depends on the independent variables.

Experimental and Control Groups

Experiments use experimental and control groups. Subjects in the **experimental group** receive the treatment, whereas subjects in the **control group** do not. Every effort is made to ensure that all other conditions are held constant for both groups of subjects. By doing so, we can have confidence that experimental outcomes reflect the treatments and not chance factors. In a study on the effects of TV violence on children's behavior, children in the experimental group would be shown TV programs containing violence and children in the control group would be shown programs that do not contain violence.

Random Assignment

Subjects should be assigned to experimental or control groups on a chance or random basis. We could not conclude much from an experiment on the effects of TV violence if the children were allowed to choose whether they would be in a group that watched a lot of TV violence or in a group that watched TV shows without violence. Children who chose to watch TV violence might have more aggressive tendencies to begin with! In an experiment on the effects of TV violence, we would therefore have to assign children randomly to view TV shows with or without violence, regardless of their personal preferences. As you can imagine, that would be difficult, if not impossible, to do in the child's own home. But such studies can be performed in laboratory settings, as we see in Chapter 10.

experiment A method of scientific investigation that seeks to discover cause-and-effect relationships by introducing independent variables and observing their effects on dependent variables.

treatment In an experiment, a condition received by subjects so that its effects may be observed.

independent variable A condition in a scientific study that is manipulated (changed) so that its effects can be observed.

dependent variable A measure of an assumed effect of an independent variable.

experimental group A group made up of subjects who receive a treatment in an experiment.

control group A group made up of subjects in an experiment who do not receive the treatment but for whom all other conditions are comparable to those of subjects in the experimental group.

Ethical and practical considerations also prevent researchers from doing experiments on the effects of many significant life circumstances, such as divorce or different patterns of child rearing. We cannot randomly assign some families to divorce or conflict and assign other families to "bliss." Nor can we randomly assign authoritarian parents to raising their children in a permissive manner, or vice versa. In some areas of investigation, we must be relatively satisfied with correlational evidence.

When experiments cannot ethically be performed on humans, researchers sometimes carry out experiments with animals and then generalize the findings to humans. For example, no researcher would separate human infants from their parents to study the effects of isolation on development, yet experimenters have deprived monkeys of early social experience. Such research has helped psychologists investigate the formation of parent–child bonds of attachment (see Chapter 7). **Truth or Fiction Revisited:** Although it is true that research with monkeys has helped psychologists understand the formation of attachment in humans, ethics would prevent investigators from carrying out this type of research with humans.

Longitudinal Research: Studying Development over Time

The processes of development occur over time, and researchers have devised different strategies for comparing children of one age with children (or adults) of other ages. *Question: How do researchers study development over time?* In **longitudinal research**, the same children are observed repeatedly over time, and changes in development, such as gains in height or changes in approach to problem solving, are recorded. In **cross-sectional research**, children of different ages are observed and compared. It is assumed that when a large number of children are chosen at random, the differences found in the older age groups are a reflection of how the younger children will develop, given time. Concept Review 1.4 summarizes the major features of cross-sectional and longitudinal research.

Longitudinal Studies

Some ambitious longitudinal studies have followed the development of children and adults for more than half a century. One, the Fels Longitudinal Study, began in 1929. Children were observed twice a year in their homes and twice a year in the Fels Institute nursery school. From time to time, younger investigators dipped into the Fels pool of subjects, further testing, interviewing, and observing these individuals as they grew into adults. In this way, researchers have been able to observe, for example, the development of intelligence and of patterns of independence and dependence.

The Terman Studies of Genius, also begun in the 1920s, tracked children with high IQ scores for more than half a century. **Truth or Fiction Revisited:** It is true that researchers have followed some subjects in developmental research for more than 50 years. Male subjects, but not female subjects, went on to high achievements in the professional world (see Chapter 12). Why? Contemporary studies of women show that women with high intelligence generally match the achievements of men and suggest that women of the earlier era were held back by traditional gender-role expectations.

Most longitudinal studies span months or a few years, not decades. In Chapter 13, for example, we see that briefer longitudinal studies have found that the children of divorced parents undergo the most severe adjustment problems within a few months of the divorce. By 2 or 3 years afterward, many children regain their equilibrium, as indicated by improved academic performance, social behavior, and other measures (Hetherington et al., 1992).

Longitudinal studies have drawbacks. For example, it can be difficult to enlist volunteers to participate in a study that will last a lifetime. Many subjects fall out of

longitudinal research The study of developmental processes by taking repeated measures of the same group of children at various stages of development.

cross-sectional research The study of developmental processes by taking measures of children of different age groups at the same time.

Concept Review 1.4 Comparison of Cross-Sectional and Longitudinal Research

	Cross-Sectional Research	Longitudinal Research
Description	• Studies children of different ages at the same point in time	• Studies the same children repeatedly over time
Advantages	• Can be completed in short period of time • No drop-out or practice effects	• Allows researchers to follow development over time • Studies the relationships between behavior at earlier and later ages
Disadvantages	• Does not study development across time • Cannot study relationship between behavior displayed at earlier and later ages • Is prey to cohort effect (subjects from different age groups may not be comparable)	• Expensive • Takes a long time to complete • Subjects drop out • Subjects who drop out may differ systematically from those who remain in the study • Practice effects may occur

© Johnny Crawford/The Image Works

Is Surfing the Internet an Activity That Illustrates the Cohort Effect?
Children and adults of different ages experience cultural and other events unique to their age group. Such experience is known as the cohort effect. For example, today's children—unlike their parents—are growing up taking video games, the Internet, and rap stars for granted.

touch as the years pass; others die. Also, those who remain in the study tend to be more motivated than those who drop out. The researchers must be patient. To compare 3-year-olds with 6-year-olds, they must wait 3 years. In the early stages of such a study, the idea of comparing 3-year-olds with 21-year-olds remains a distant dream. When the researchers themselves are middle-aged or older, they must hope that the candle of yearning for knowledge will be kept lit by a new generation of researchers.

Cross-Sectional Studies

Because of the drawbacks of longitudinal studies, most research that compares children of different ages is cross-sectional. In other words, most investigators gather data on what the "typical" 6-month-old is doing by finding children who are 6 months old today. When they expand their research to the behavior of typical 12-month-olds, they seek another group of children, and so on.

A major challenge to cross-sectional research is the **cohort effect**. A cohort is a group of people born at about the same time. As a result, they experience cultural and other events unique to their age group. In other words, children and adults of different ages are not likely to have shared similar cultural backgrounds. People who are 70 years old today, for example, grew up without TV. (Really, there was a time when television did not exist.) People who are 60 years old today grew up before people landed on the Moon. Nor did today's 50-year-olds spend their earliest years with *Sesame Street*. And today's children are growing up taking iPods and the Internet for granted. In fact, for today's children, Jennifer Lopez is an older woman.

Children of past generations also grew up with different expectations about gender roles and appropriate social behavior. Women in the Terman study generally chose motherhood over careers because of the times. Today's girls are growing up with female role models who are astronauts, government officials, and athletes. More-

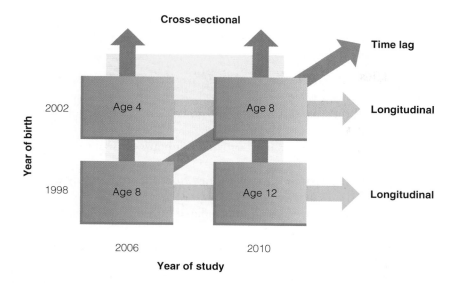

Example of Cross-Sequential Research

Cross-sequential research combines three methods: cross-sectional, longitudinal, and time lag. The child's age at the time of testing appears in the boxes. Vertical columns represent cross-sectional comparisons. Horizontal rows represent longitudinal comparisons. Diagonals represent time-lag comparisons.

over, today the great majority of mothers are in the workforce, and their attitudes about women's roles have changed.

In other words, today's 75-year-olds are not today's 5-year-olds as seen 70 years later. The times change, and their influence on children changes also. In longitudinal studies, we know that we have the same individuals as they have developed over 5, 25, even 50 years or more. In cross-sectional research, we can only hope that they will be comparable.

Cross-Sequential Research

Cross-sequential research combines the longitudinal and cross-sectional methods so that many of their individual drawbacks are overcome. In the cross-sequential study, the full span of the ideal longitudinal study is broken up into convenient segments (see ● Figure 1.8). Assume that we wish to follow the attitudes of children toward gender roles from the age of 4 through the age of 12. The typical longitudinal study would take 8 years. However, we can divide this 8-year span in half by obtaining two samples of children (a cross-section) instead of one: 4-year-olds and 8-year-olds. We would then interview, test, and observe each group at the beginning of the study (2006) and 4 years later (2010). By the time of the second observation period, the 4-year-olds would have become 8 years old and the 8-year-olds would have become 12.

An obvious advantage to this collapsed method is that the study is completed in 4 years rather than 8 years. Still, the testing and retesting of samples provides some of the continuity of the longitudinal study. By observing both samples at the age of 8 (a **time-lag** comparison), we can also determine whether they are, in fact, comparable or whether the 4-year difference in their birthdates is associated with a cohort effect, that is, cultural and other environmental changes that lead to different attitudes.

Ethical Considerations

Researchers adhere to ethical standards that are intended to promote the dignity of the individual, foster human welfare, and maintain scientific integrity. These standards also ensure that they do not use methods or treatments that harm subjects. *Question: What ethical guidelines are involved in research in child development?*

Various professional groups, such as the American Psychological Association and the Society for Research in Child Development, and government review

cohort effect Similarities in behavior among a group of peers that stem from the fact that group members are approximately of the same age. (A possible source of misleading information in cross-sectional research.)

cross-sequential research An approach that combines the longitudinal and cross-sectional methods by following individuals of different ages for abbreviated periods of time.

time lag The study of developmental processes by taking measures of children of the same age group at different times.

boards have proposed guidelines for research with children. The overriding purpose of these guidelines is to protect children from harm. These guidelines include the following:

- Researchers are not to use methods that may do physical or psychological harm.
- Children and their parents must be informed of the purposes of the research and about the research methods.
- Children and their parents must provide voluntary consent to participate in the study.
- Children and their parents may withdraw from the study at any time, for any reason.
- Children and their parents should be offered information about the results of the study.
- The identities of the children participating in a study are to remain confidential.
- Researchers should present their research plans to a committee of their colleagues and gain the committee's approval before proceeding.

These guidelines present researchers with a number of hurdles to overcome before proceeding with and while conducting research. But because they protect the welfare of children, the guidelines are valuable.

Active Review

14. The steps of the scientific method include formulating a research question, developing a _____, testing the hypothesis, drawing conclusions, and publishing results.

15. _____ observation studies are conducted in the real-life setting.

16. The _____ study is a carefully drawn account or biography of an individual child.

17. A correlational study describes relationships but does not reveal _____ and effect.

18. In an experiment, members of an experimental group receive a treatment, whereas members of a _____ group do not.

19. _____ research observes the same children repeatedly over time.

20. In cross-_____ research, children of different ages are observed and compared.

Reflect & Relate: How do you gather information about the behavior and mental processes of other people? Which of the methods described in this section come closest to your own? Are your methods adequately scientific? Explain.

Go to

http://www.thomsonedu.com/psychology/rathus
for an interactive version of this review.

1. **What is child development?**

   The field of child development attempts to advance knowledge of the processes that govern the development of children's physical structures, traits, behaviors, and cognitions. *Growth* usually refers to changes in size or quantity, whereas *development* also refers to changes in quality.

2. **Why do researchers study child development?**

   Researchers study child development to gain insight into human nature, the origins of adult behavior, the origins of developmental problems, ways of optimizing development, and the effects of culture on development.

3. **What views of children do we find throughout history?**

   Locke focused on the role of the environment or experience in development. Rousseau argued that children are good by nature, and if allowed to express their natural impulses, they would develop into moral and giving people. Darwin originated the modern theory of evolution and was one of the first observers to keep a baby biography. Hall founded child development as an academic discipline. Binet developed the first modern standardized intelligence test.

4. **What are theories? Why do we have them?**

   Theories are related sets of statements about events. Theories of development help us describe, explain, and predict, and they influence development.

5. **What is Freud's psychoanalytic theory of child development?**

   Freud viewed children as caught in conflict. He believed that people undergo *oral, anal, phallic, latency*, and *genital* stages of psychosexual development. Too little or too much gratification in a stage can lead to fixation.

6. **How does Erikson's theory differ from Freud's?**

   Erikson's psychosocial theory sees social relationships as more important than sexual or aggressive impulses. Erikson extended Freud's five developmental stages to eight (to include adulthood) and labeled stages after life crises.

7. **What is the theory of behaviorism?**

   Watson argued that scientists must address observable behavior only, not mental activity. Behaviorism relies on two types of learning: classical conditioning and operant conditioning. In classical conditioning, one stimulus comes to signal another by being paired repeatedly with it. In operant conditioning, children learn to engage in or to discontinue behavior because of its effects (reinforcement or lack of reinforcement).

8. **How does social cognitive theory differ from behaviorism?**

   Social cognitive theorists, such as Bandura, argue that much learning occurs by observing models and that children choose whether or not to engage in behaviors they have learned.

9. **What are Jean Piaget's views on development?**

   Piaget saw children as actors on the environment, not reactors. He studied how children form mental representations of the world and manipulate them. Piaget's theory uses the concepts of *schemes, adaptation, assimilation, accommodation*, and *equilibration*. He hypothesized that children's cognitive processes develop in an invariant series of stages: *sensorimotor, preoperational, concrete operational*, and *formal operational*.

10. **What is information-processing theory?**

    Information-processing theory deals with the ways in which children encode information, transfer it to working memory (short-term memory), manipulate it, place information in storage (long-term memory), and retrieve it from storage.

11. What is the scope of the biological perspective?	The biological perspective refers to heredity and to developments such as formation of sperm and ova, gains in height and weight, maturation of the nervous system, and the way hormones spur the changes of puberty.
12. What is ethology?	Ethology involves instinctive, or inborn, behavior patterns, termed *fixed action patterns (FAPs)*. Many FAPs, such as those involved in attachment, occur during a *critical period* of life.
13. What is the ecological systems theory of child development?	Bronfenbrenner's ecological theory explains development in terms of the *reciprocal interaction* between children and the settings in which development occurs. These settings are the *microsystem, mesosystem, exosystem, macrosystem*, and *chronosystem*.
14. What is meant by the sociocultural perspective?	The sociocultural perspective emphasizes that children are social beings who are influenced by their cultural backgrounds.
15. What are the key concepts of Vygotsky's sociocultural theory?	Vygotsky's key concepts are the *zone of proximal development (ZPD)* and *scaffolding*. Children internalize conversations and explanations that help them gain skills. Children learn ways of solving problems within a cultural context.
16. What is the connection between the sociocultural perspective and human diversity?	The sociocultural perspective addresses the richness of children's diversity, as in their ethnicity and sex. Understanding the cultural heritages and historical problems of children from various ethnic groups is necessary for education and psychological intervention.
17. Which exerts the greater influence on children, nature or nurture?	Development would appear to reflect the interaction of nature (genetics) and nurture (nutrition, cultural and family backgrounds, and opportunities to learn about the world).
18. Is development continuous or discontinuous?	Maturational, psychoanalytic, and cognitive-developmental theorists see development as discontinuous (occurring in stages). Aspects of physical development, such as the adolescent growth spurt, do occur in stages. Learning theorists tend to see development as more continuous.
19. Are children active ("prewired" to act on the world), or are they passive (shaped by experience)?	Bronfenbrenner and Bandura do not see children as entirely active or entirely passive. They believe that children are influenced by the environment but that the influence is reciprocal.
20. What is the scientific method?	The scientific method is a systematic way of formulating and answering research questions that includes formulating a research question, developing a hypothesis, testing the hypothesis, drawing conclusions, and publishing results.
21. What is naturalistic observation?	Naturalistic observation is conducted in "the field," in the actual settings in which children develop.

22. What is the case study?

The case study is a carefully drawn account or biography of the behavior of a child. Information may be derived from diaries, observation, questionnaires, standardized tests, interviews, and public records.

23. What does it mean to correlate information?

Correlation enables researchers to determine whether one behavior or trait is related to another. A correlation coefficient can vary between +1.00 and −1.00. Correlational studies reveal relationships but not cause and effect.

24. What is an experiment?

In an experiment, an experimental group receives a treatment (independent variable), whereas another group (a control group) does not. Subjects are observed to determine whether the treatment has an effect.

25. How do researchers study development over time?

Longitudinal research studies the same children repeatedly over time. Cross-sectional research observes and compares children of different ages. A drawback to cross-sectional research is the cohort effect. Cross-sequential research combines the longitudinal and cross-sectional methods by breaking down the full span of the ideal longitudinal study into convenient segments.

26. What ethical guidelines are involved in research in child development?

Ethical standards promote the dignity of the individual, foster human welfare, and maintain scientific integrity. Researchers are not to use treatments that may do harm. Subjects must participate voluntarily.

Key Terms

child, 4
infancy, 4
conception, 4
prenatal period, 4
development, 4
motor development, 4
growth, 4
gender roles, 5
PKU, 5
SIDS, 5
behaviorism, 8
maturation, 8
theory, 8
psychosexual development, 9
stage theory, 9
unconscious, 10
psychosocial development, 10
life crisis, 11
identity crisis, 11
behavior modification, 13
classical conditioning, 13
stimulus, 13

elicit, 13
unconditioned stimulus (UCS), 13
unconditioned response (UCR), 13
conditioned stimulus (CS), 14
conditioned response (CR), 14
operant conditioning, 14
reinforcement, 14
positive reinforcer, 14
negative reinforcer, 14
extinction, 14
punishment, 14
time out, 16
shaping, 16
socialization, 16
social cognitive theory, 17
observational learning, 17
cognitive-developmental theory, 18
scheme, 18
adaptation, 19
assimilation, 19
accommodation, 19

equilibration, 19
ethology, 21
fixed action pattern (FAP), 21
ecology, 22
ecological systems theory, 22
microsystem, 22
mesosystem, 22
exosystem, 22
macrosystem, 23
chronosystem, 23
zone of proximal development (ZPD), 25
scaffolding, 25
ethnic groups, 25
gender, 27
nature, 30
nurture, 30
genes, 30
empirical, 32
hypothesis, 33
naturalistic observation, 33
case study, 34

standardized test, 35
variables, 35
correlation coefficient, 35
positive correlation, 35
negative correlation, 35
experiment, 36

treatment, 36
independent variable, 36
dependent variable, 36
experimental group, 36
control group, 36
longitudinal research, 37

cross-sectional research, 37
cohort effect, 38
cross-sequential research, 39
time lag, 39

Active Learning Resources

Childhood & Adolescence Book Companion Website

http://www.thomsonedu.com/psychology/rathus

Visit your book companion website, where you will find more resources to help you study. There you will find interactive versions of your book features, including the Lessons in Observation video, Active Review sections, and the Truth or Fiction feature. In addition, the companion website contains quizzing, flash cards, and a pronunciation glossary.

Thomson NOW! is an easy-to-use online resource that helps you study in less time to get the grade you want, NOW.

http://www.thomsonedu.com/login

Need help studying? This site is your one-stop study shop. Take a Pre-Test and ThomsonNOW will generate a Personalized Study Plan based on your test results. The Study Plan will identify the topics you need to review and direct you to online resources to help you master those topics. You can then take a Post-Test to determine the concepts you have mastered and what you still need to work on.

2 Heredity and Conception

Truth or Fiction?

T F Your father determined whether you are female or male. p. 49

T F Brown eyes are dominant over blue eyes. p. 51

T F You can carry the genes for a deadly illness and not become sick yourself. p. 52

T F Girls are born with all the egg cells they will ever have. p. 64

T F Approximately 120 to 150 boys are conceived for every 100 girls. p. 65

T F Sperm travel about at random inside the woman's reproductive tract, so reaching the ovum is a matter of luck. p. 65

T F Extensive athletic activity may contribute to infertility in the male. p. 67

T F "Test-tube" babies are grown in a laboratory dish throughout their 9-month gestation period. p. 68

Preview

The Influence of Heredity on Development: The Nature of Nature
    Chromosomes and Genes
    Mitosis and Meiosis
    Identical and Fraternal Twins
    Dominant and Recessive Traits
    Chromosomal Abnormalities
    Genetic Abnormalities
    Genetic Counseling and Prenatal Testing
    Lessons in Observation: Prenatal Assessment

Heredity and the Environment: Nature versus Nurture
    Kinship Studies: Are the Traits of Relatives Related?
    Twin Studies: Looking in the Genetic Mirror
    Adoption Studies

Conception: Against All Odds
    Ova
    Sperm Cells
    Infertility and Other Ways of Becoming Parents
    Selecting the Sex of Your Child: Fantasy or Reality?
    Developing in a World of Diversity: Where Are the Missing Chinese Girls?

Go to

http://www.thomsonedu.com/psychology/rathus
for an interactive version of this "Truth or Fiction" feature.

et's talk about the facts of life. Here are a few of them:

- People cannot breathe underwater (without special equipment).
- People cannot fly (without special equipment).
- Fish cannot learn to speak French or dance an Irish jig, even if you raise them in enriched environments and send them to finishing school.

We cannot breathe underwater or fly because we have not inherited gills or wings. Fish are similarly limited by their heredity. *Question: What is meant by heredity?* **Heredity** defines one's nature, which is based on the biological transmission of traits and characteristics from one generation to another. Because of their heredity, fish cannot speak French or do a jig.

In this chapter, we explore heredity and conception. We could say that development begins long before conception. Development involves the origins of the genetic structures that determine that human embryos will grow arms rather than wings, lungs rather than gills, and hair rather than scales. Our discussion thus begins with an examination of the building blocks of heredity: genes and chromosomes. Then, we describe the process of conception and find that the odds against any one sperm uniting with an ovum are quite literally astronomical.

The Influence of Heredity on Development: The Nature of Nature

Heredity makes possible all things human. The structures we inherit make our behavior possible and place limits on it. The field within the science of biology that studies heredity is called **genetics**.

Genetic (inherited) influences are fundamental in the transmission of physical traits, such as height, hair texture, and eye color. Genetics also appears to play a role in intelligence and in traits such as activity level, sociability, shyness, anxiety, empathy, effectiveness as a parent, happiness, even interest in arts and crafts (Johnson & Krueger, 2006; Knafo & Plomin, 2006; Leonardo & Hen, 2006). Genetic factors are also involved in psychological problems such as schizophrenia, depression, and dependence on nicotine, alcohol, and other substances (Farmer et al., 2007; Hill et al., 2007; Metzger et al., 2007; Riley & Kendler, 2005).

Chromosomes and Genes

Heredity is made possible by microscopic structures called chromosomes and genes. *Question: What are chromosomes and genes?* **Chromosomes** are rod-shaped structures found in cells. A normal human cell contains 46 chromosomes organized into 23 pairs. Each chromosome contains thousands of segments called genes. **Genes** are the biochemical materials that regulate the development of traits. Some traits, such as blood type, appear to be transmitted by a single pair of genes, one of which is derived from each parent. Other traits, referred to as **polygenic**, are determined by combinations of pairs of genes.

We have 20,000 to 25,000 genes in every cell of our bodies (International Human Genome Sequencing Consortium, 2006). Genes are segments of large strands of **deoxyribonucleic acid (DNA)**. DNA takes the form of a double spiral, or helix, similar in appearance to a twisting ladder (see ● Figure 2.1). In all living things, from one-celled animals to fish to people, the sides of the "ladder" consist of alternating segments of phosphate (P) and simple sugar (S). The "rungs" of the ladder are attached to the sugars and consist of one of two pairs of bases, either adenine with thymine

heredity The transmission of traits and characteristics from parent to child by means of genes.

genetics The branch of biology that studies heredity.

chromosomes Rod-shaped structures composed of genes that are found within the nuclei of cells.

gene The basic unit of heredity. Genes are composed of deoxyribonucleic acid (DNA).

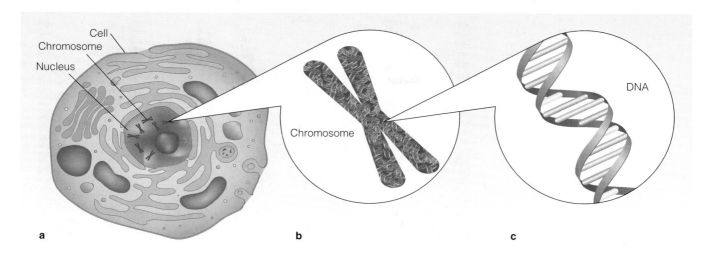

a   b   c

● **Figure 2.1**   The Double Helix of DNA

DNA consists of phosphate, sugar, and a number of bases. It takes the form of a double spiral, or helix.

(A with T) or cytosine with guanine (C with G). The sequence of the rungs is the genetic code that will cause the developing organism to grow arms or wings, skin or scales.

Mitosis and Meiosis

We begin life as a single cell, or zygote, that divides again and again. ***Question: What happens during cell division?*** There are two types of cell division: mitosis and meiosis. **Mitosis** is the cell-division process by which growth occurs and tissues are replaced. Through mitosis, our genetic code is carried into new cells in our bodies. In mitosis, strands of DNA break apart, or "unzip" (see ● Figure 2.2). The double helix then duplicates. The DNA forms two camps on either side of the cell, and then the cell divides. Each incomplete rung combines with the appropriate "partner" element (i.e., G combines with C, A with T, and so on) to form a new complete ladder. The two resulting identical copies of the DNA strand move apart when the cell divides, each becoming a member of one of the newly formed cells. As a consequence, the genetic code is identical in new cells unless **mutations** occur through radiation or other environmental influences. Mutations are also believed to occur by chance, but not often.

Sperm and ova ("egg cells") are produced through **meiosis**, or *reduction division*. In meiosis, the 46 chromosomes within the cell nucleus first line up into 23 pairs. The DNA ladders then unzip, leaving unpaired chromosome halves. When the cell divides, one member of each pair goes to each newly formed cell. As a consequence, each new cell nucleus contains only 23 chromosomes, not 46. Thus, a cell that results from meiosis has half the genetic material of a cell that results from mitosis.

When a sperm cell fertilizes an ovum, we receive 23 chromosomes from our father's sperm cell and 23 from our mother's ovum, and the combined chromosomes form 23 pairs (● Figure 2.3). Twenty-two of the pairs are **autosomes**, that is, pairs that look alike and possess genetic information concerning the same set of traits. The 23rd pair consists of the **sex chromosomes**, which look different from other chromosomes and determine our sex. We all receive an X sex chromosome (so called because of its X shape) from our mothers. **Truth or Fiction Revisited:** It is true that your father determined whether you are female or male, either by supplying a Y or an X sex

polygenic Resulting from many genes.

deoxyribonucleic acid (DNA) Genetic material that takes the form of a double helix composed of phosphates, sugars, and bases.

mitosis The form of cell division in which each chromosome splits lengthwise to double in number. Half of each chromosome combines with chemicals to retake its original form and then moves to the new cell.

mutation A sudden variation in a heritable characteristic, as by an accident that affects the composition of genes.

meiosis The form of cell division in which each pair of chromosomes splits so that one member of each pair moves to the new cell. As a result, each new cell has 23 chromosomes.

● **Figure 2.2**
Mitosis

(a) A segment of a strand of DNA before mitosis. (b) During mitosis, chromosomal strands of DNA "unzip." (c) The double helix is rebuilt in the cell as each incomplete "rung" combines with appropriate molecules. The resulting identical copies of the DNA strand move apart when the cell divides, each joining one of the new cells.

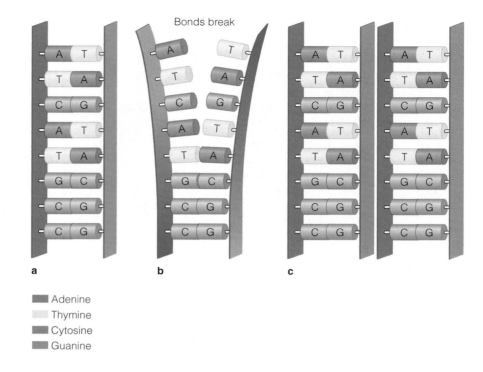

a   b   c

■ Adenine
■ Thymine
■ Cytosine
■ Guanine

● **Figure 2.3**
The 23 Pairs of Human Chromosomes

People normally have 23 pairs of chromosomes. Females have two X chromosomes, whereas males have an X and a Y sex chromosome.

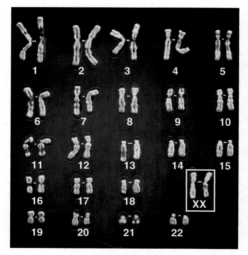

Female

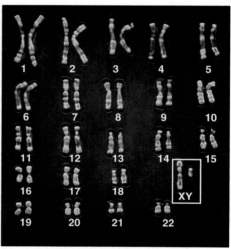

Male

Both: © CNRI/SPL/Photo Researchers, Inc.

autosome A member of a pair of chromosomes (with the exception of sex chromosomes).

sex chromosome A chromosome in the shape of a Y (male) or X (female) that determines the sex of the child.

monozygotic (MZ) twins Twins that derive from a single zygote that has split into two; identical twins. Each MZ twin carries the same genetic code.

dizygotic (DZ) twins Twins that derive from two zygotes; fraternal twins.

chromosome. If we receive another X sex chromosome from our fathers, we develop into females. If we receive a Y sex chromosome (named after its Y shape) from our fathers, we develop into males.

Identical and Fraternal Twins

Question: How are twins formed? Now and then, a zygote divides into two cells that separate so that each subsequently develops into an individual with the same genetic makeup. These individuals are known as identical twins, or **monozygotic (MZ) twins**. If the woman produces two ova in the same month and they are each fertilized by a different sperm cell, they develop into fraternal twins, or **dizygotic (DZ) twins**.

There are 14 to 15 singleton pregnancies for each twin pregnancy, and of these, about two thirds are of DZ twins (Office of National Statistics, 2006). MZ twins occur with equal frequency in all ethnic groups, but Black people are most likely to have DZ twins and Asians are least likely to do so.

DZ twins run in families. If a woman is a twin, if her mother was a twin, or if she has previously borne twins, the chances rise that she will bear twins (Office of National Statistics, 2006). Similarly, women who have borne several children have an increased likelihood of twins in subsequent pregnancies.

As women reach the end of their child-bearing years, **ovulation** becomes less regular, resulting in a number of months when more than one ovum is released. Thus, the chances of twins increase with parental age (National Guideline Clearinghouse, 2007). Fertility drugs also enhance the chances of multiple births by causing more than one ovum to ripen and be released during a woman's cycle (National Guideline Clearinghouse, 2007).

Dominant and Recessive Traits

Question: How do genes determine traits? Traits are determined by pairs of genes. Each member of a pair of genes is referred to as an **allele**. When both of the alleles for a trait, such as hair color, are the same, the person is said to be **homozygous** for that trait. (*Homo*, in this usage, derives from the Greek root meaning "same," not the Latin root meaning "man.") When the alleles for a trait differ, the person is **heterozygous** for that trait.

Gregor Mendel (1822–1884), an Austrian monk, established a number of laws of heredity through his work with pea plants. Mendel realized that some traits result from an "averaging" of the genetic instructions carried by the parents. When the effects of both alleles are shown, there is said to be incomplete dominance or codominance.

Mendel also discovered the "law of dominance." When a *dominant* allele is paired with a *recessive* allele, the trait determined by the dominant allele appears in the off-spring. For example, the offspring from the crossing of purebred tall peas and pure-bred dwarf peas were tall, suggesting that tallness is dominant over dwarfism. We now know that many genes determine **dominant traits** or **recessive traits**.

Truth or Fiction Revisited: Brown eyes, for instance, are dominant over blue eyes. If one parent carried genes for only brown eyes and if the other parent carried genes for only blue eyes, the children would invariably have brown eyes. But brown-eyed parents can also carry recessive genes for blue eyes, as shown in ● Figure 2.4. Similarly, the offspring of Mendel's crossing of purebred tall and purebred dwarf peas were not pure. They carried recessive genes for dwarfism.

If the recessive gene from one parent combines with the recessive gene from the other parent, the recessive trait will be shown. As suggested by Figure 2.4, approximately 25% of the offspring of brown-eyed parents who carry recessive blue eye color will have blue eyes. Mendel found that 25% of the offspring of parent peas that carried recessive dwarfism would be dwarfs. ■ Table 2.1 shows a number of dominant and recessive traits in humans.

Our discussion of eye color has been simplified. The percentages are not always perfect because other genes can alter the expression of the genes for brown and blue eyes, producing hazel, or greenish, eyes. Some genes also switch other genes "on" or "off" at various times during development. For example, we normally reach reproductive capacity in the teens and not earlier, and men who go bald usually do so during adulthood. Similarly, the heart and the limbs develop at different times in the embryo, again because of the switching on or off of certain genes by other genes.

People who bear one dominant gene and one recessive gene for a trait are said to be **carriers** of the recessive gene. In the cases of recessive genes that give rise to serious

ovulation The releasing of an ovum from an ovary.

allele A member of a pair of genes.

homozygous Having two identical alleles.

heterozygous Having two different alleles.

dominant trait A trait that is expressed.

recessive trait A trait that is not expressed when the gene or genes involved have been paired with dominant genes. Recessive traits are transmitted to future generations and expressed if they are paired with other recessive genes.

carrier A person who carries and transmits characteristics but does not exhibit them.

● **Figure 2.4**
Transmission of Dominant and Recessive Traits

Two brown-eyed parents each carry a gene for blue eyes. Their children have an equal opportunity of receiving genes for brown eyes and blue eyes.

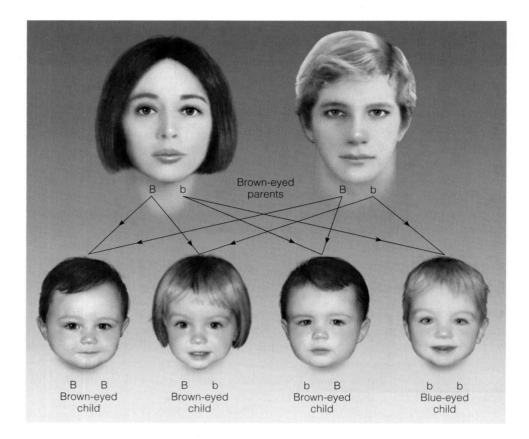

illnesses, carriers of those genes are fortunate to have dominant genes that cancel their effects. **Truth or Fiction Revisited:** Therefore, it is true that you can carry the genes for a deadly illness and not become sick yourself. This situation occurs when genes are recessive and dominant genes cancel their effects.

Chromosomal or genetic abnormalities can cause health problems. Some chromosomal disorders reflect abnormalities in the 22 pairs of autosomes (such as Down syn-

■ **Table 2.1** Examples of Dominant and Recessive Traits

Dominant Trait	Recessive Trait
Dark hair	Blond hair
Dark hair	Red hair
Curly hair	Straight hair
Normal color vision	Red–green color blindness
Normal vision	Myopia (nearsightedness)
Farsightedness	Normal vision
Normal pigmentation	Deficiency of pigmentation in skin, hair, and retina (albinism)
Normal sensitivity to touch	Extremely fragile skin
Normal hearing	Some forms of deafness
Dimples	Lack of dimpling
Type A blood	Type O blood
Type B blood	Type O blood
Tolerance of lactose	Lactose intolerance

drome); others reflect abnormalities in the 23rd pair, the sex chromosomes (e.g., XYY syndrome). Some genetic abnormalities, such as cystic fibrosis, are caused by a single pair of genes; others are caused by combinations of genes. Diabetes mellitus, epilepsy, and peptic ulcers are **multifactorial problems**; that is, they reflect both a genetic predisposition and environmental contributors. Chromosomal and genetic abnormalities are discussed in the following sections and are summarized in Concept Review 2.1.

Chromosomal Abnormalities

People normally have 46 chromosomes. Children with more or fewer chromosomes usually experience health problems or behavioral abnormalities. The risk of chromosomal abnormalities rises with the age of the parents (American Fertility Association, 2007). *Question: What kinds of disorders are caused by chromosomal abnormalities?*

Down Syndrome

Down syndrome is usually caused by an extra chromosome on the 21st pair, resulting in 47 chromosomes. The probability of having a child with Down syndrome varies positively with the age of the parents: Older parents are more likely to bear children with the syndrome (see ■ Table 2.2 on page 56).

Children with Down syndrome have characteristic facial features that include a rounded face, a protruding tongue, a broad, flat nose, and a sloping fold of skin over the inner corners of the eyes (● Figure 2.5). Children with Down syndrome usually die from cardiovascular problems by middle age, although modern medicine has extended life appreciably. The children show deficits in cognitive development, including language development (Rondal & Ling, 2006), and in motor development (Virji-Babul et al., 2006). They encounter frequent disorders of the ear, nose, and throat, which also contribute to academic problems (Virji-Babul et al., 2006).

As you can imagine, children with Down syndrome have adjustment problems in school and in the community at large (King et al., 2000). Other children are not always sensitive to their needs and feelings and may poke fun at them. Children with Down syndrome and other problems also tend to need more attention from their parents. Parental response is variable; some parents are overwhelmed and a few are abusive, but many parents report that the special needs of their children have contributed to their own self-esteem and self-worth (Gowers & Bryan, 2005). We can make the generalization that parents who want their children usually do a better job of parenting, and this same principle applies when their children have special needs.

Sex-Linked Chromosomal Abnormalities

A number of disorders stem from an abnormal number of sex chromosomes and are therefore said to be **sex-linked chromosomal abnormalities**. Most individuals with an abnormal number of sex chromosomes are infertile. Beyond that common finding, there are many differences, some of them associated with "maleness" or "femaleness" (Wodrich, 2006).

Approximately 1 male in 700–1,000 has an extra Y chromosome. The Y chromosome is associated with maleness, and the extra Y sex chromosome apparently heightens male secondary sex characteristics. For example, XYY males are somewhat taller than average and develop heavier beards. For these kinds of reasons, males with XYY sex chromosomal structure were once referred to as "supermales." But the prefix *super-* often implies superior, and it turns out that XYY males tend to have more problems than XY males. For example, they are often mildly delayed, particularly in language development. As part of their "excessive maleness," it was once thought that XYY males were given to aggressive criminal behavior. When we examine prison populations, we find that the number of XYY males is "overrepresented" relative to their number in the population. However, it may be that the number of XYY males in

multifactorial problems Problems that stem from the interaction of heredity and environmental factors.

Down syndrome A chromosomal abnormality characterized by mental retardation and caused by an extra chromosome in the 21st pair.

sex-linked chromosomal abnormalities Abnormalities that are transmitted from generation to generation, carried by a sex chromosome, usually an X sex chromosome.

Concept Review 2.1 Chromosome and Genetic Disorders

Health Problem	Incidence	Comments	Treatment
Chromosomal Disorders			
Down syndrome **www.ndss.org**	1 birth in 700–800 overall; risk increases with parental age.	A condition characterized by a third chromosome on the 21st pair. A child with Down syndrome has a characteristic fold of skin over the eye and mental retardation.	No treatment, but educational programs are effective; usually fatal as a result of complications by middle age.
Klinefelter syndrome **www.klinefelter syndrome.org**	1 male in 500–900	A disorder affecting males that is characterized by an extra X sex chromosome and that is connected with underdeveloped male secondary sex characteristics, gynecomastia, and mild mental retardation, particularly in language skills.	Hormone (testosterone) replacement therapy; special education.
Turner syndrome **www.turner-syndrome-us.org**	1 girl in 2,500	A disorder that affects females, characterized by single X-sex-chromosomal structure and associated with infertility, poorly developed ovaries, underdevelopment of female secondary sex characteristics, and problems in visual-spatial skills and mathematics.	Hormone (estrogen) replacement therapy; special education.
XXX syndrome **www.triplo-x.org**	1 girl in 1,000	A sex-chromosomal disorder that affects females and that is connected with mild mental retardation.	Special education.
XYY syndrome **http://www.aaa .dk/turner/ engelsk/index .htm**	1 male in 700–1,000	A sex-chromosomal disorder that affect males—sometimes referred to as "supermale syndrome"—and that is connected with heavy beards, tallness, and mild mental retardation, particularly in language development.	None.
Genetic Disorders			
Cystic fibrosis **www.cff.org**	1 birth in 2,000 among European Americans; 1 birth in 16,000 among African Americans.	A genetic disease caused by a recessive gene in which the pancreas and lungs become clogged with mucus, impairing the processes of respiration and digestion.	Physical therapy to loosen mucus and prompt bronchial drainage; antibiotics for infections of respiratory tract; management of diet.

Health Problem	Incidence	Comments	Treatment
Duchenne muscular dystrophy **www.mdausa.org**	1 male birth in 3,000–5,000	A fatal sex-linked degenerative muscle disease caused by a recessive gene, usually found in males and characterized by loss of ability to walk during middle childhood or early adolescence.	None; usually fatal by adolescence because of respiratory infection or cardiovascular damage.
Hemophilia **www.hemophilia.org**	1 male in 4,000–10,000	A sex-linked disorder in which blood does not clot properly.	Transfusion of blood to introduce clotting factors; proactive avoidance of injury.
Huntington's disease **www.hdsa.org**	1 birth in 18,000	A fatal neurological disorder caused by a dominant gene; onset occurs in middle adulthood.	None; usually fatal within 20 years of onset of symptoms.
Neural tube defects **ibis-birthdefects .org/start/ntdfact .htm**	1 birth in 1,000	Disorders of the brain or spine, such as *anencephaly*, in which part of the brain is missing, and *spina bifida*, in which part of the spine is exposed or missing. Some individuals with spina bifida survive for years, albeit with handicaps.	None for anencephaly, which is fatal; surgery to close spinal canal in spina bifida.
Phenylketonuria (PKU) **www .pkunetwork.org**	1 birth in 8,000–10,000	A disorder caused by a recessive gene in which children cannot metabolize the amino acid phenylalanine, which builds up in the form of phenylpyruvic acid and causes mental retardation. PKU is diagnosable at birth.	Controlled by special diet, which can prevent mental retardation.
Sickle-cell anemia **www.ascaa.org**	1 African American in 500	A blood disorder caused by a recessive gene that mostly afflicts African Americans; deformed blood cells obstruct small blood vessels, decreasing their capacity to carry oxygen and heightening the risk of occasionally fatal infections.	Transfusions to treat anemia and prevent strokes; antibiotics for infections; anesthetics; fatal to about half of those with disorder before adulthood.
Tay-Sachs disease **www.ntsad.org**	1 Jewish American of Eastern European origin in 3,000–3,600	A fatal neurological disorder caused by a recessive gene that primarily afflicts Jews of Eastern European origin.	None; usually fatal by age 3–4.
Thalassemia (Cooley's anemia) **www .thalassemia.org**	1 birth in 400–500 among Mediterranean American children	A disorder caused by a recessive gene that primarily afflicts people of Mediterranean origin and causes weakness and susceptibility to infections; usually fatal in adolescence or young adulthood.	Frequent blood transfusions; usually fatal by adolescence.

■ **Table 2.2** Risk of Giving Birth to an Infant with Down Syndrome, According to Age of the Mother

Age of Mother	Probability of Down Syndrome in the Child
20	1 in 1,667
30	1 in 953
40	1 in 106
49	1 in 11

Sources: American Fertility Association (2007) and Centers for Disease Control and Prevention (2002b).

● **Figure 2.5**
Down Syndrome

The development and adjustment of children with Down syndrome are related to their acceptance by their families. Children with Down syndrome who are reared at home develop more rapidly and achieve higher levels of functioning than those who are reared in institutions.

Klinefelter syndrome A chromosomal disorder found among males that is caused by an extra X sex chromosome and that is characterized by infertility and mild mental retardation.

testosterone A male sex hormone produced mainly by the testes.

Turner syndrome A chromosomal disorder found among females that is caused by having a single X sex chromosome and is characterized by infertility.

estrogen A female sex hormone produced mainly by the ovaries.

prisons reflects their level of intelligence rather than aggressiveness. Most XYY males in prison have committed crimes against property (e.g., stealing) rather than crimes against persons (e.g., assault and battery). And when we examine XYY individuals in the general population, most do not have records of aggressive criminal behavior (Wodrich, 2006).

Approximately 1 male in 500 has **Klinefelter syndrome**, which is caused by an extra X sex chromosome (an XXY sex chromosomal pattern). XXY males produce less of the male sex hormone—**testosterone**—than normal males. As a result, male primary and secondary sex characteristics—such as the testes, deepening of the voice, musculature, and the male pattern of body hair—do not develop properly. XXY males usually have enlarged breasts (*gynecomastia*) and are usually mildly mentally retarded, particularly in language skills (van Rijn et al., 2006). XXY males are typically treated with testosterone replacement therapy, which can foster growth of sex characteristics and elevate the mood, but the therapy does not reverse infertility.

Approximately 1 girl in 2,500 has a single X sex chromosome and as a result develops what is called **Turner syndrome**. The external genitals of girls with Turner syndrome are normal, but their ovaries are poorly developed and they produce little of the female sex hormone **estrogen**. Girls with this problem are shorter than average and infertile. Because of low estrogen production, they do not develop breasts or menstruate. Researchers have connected a specific pattern of cognitive deficits with low estrogen levels: problems in visual–spatial skills, mathematics, and nonverbal memory (Hart et al., 2006). Some studies find them to be more extroverted and more interested in seeking novel stimulation than other girls (e.g., Boman et al., 2006).

Approximately 1 girl in 1,000 has an XXX sex chromosomal structure, *Triple X syndrome*. Such girls are normal in appearance, but they tend to show lower-than-average language skills and poorer memory for recent events. Development of external sexual organs appears normal enough, although there is increased incidence of infertility (Wodrich, 2006).

Genetic Abnormalities

A number of disorders have been attributed to defective genes. *Question: What kinds of disorders are caused by genetic abnormalities?*

Phenylketonuria

The enzyme disorder **phenylketonuria (PKU)** is transmitted by a recessive gene, and affects about 1 child in 8,000. Therefore, if both parents possess the gene, PKU will be transmitted to one child in four (as in Figure 2.4). Two children in four will possess the gene but will not develop the disorder. These two, like their parents, will be carriers of the disease. One child in four will not receive the recessive gene. Therefore, he or she will not be a carrier.

Children with PKU cannot metabolize an amino acid called phenylalanine. As a consequence, the substance builds up in their bodies and impairs the functioning of the central nervous system. The results are serious: mental retardation, psychological disorders, and physical problems. There is no cure for PKU, but PKU can be detected in newborn children through analysis of the blood or urine. Children with PKU who are placed on diets low in phenylalanine within three to six weeks after birth develop normally. The diet prohibits all meat, poultry, fish, dairy products, beans, and nuts. Fruits, vegetables, and some starchy foods are allowed (Brazier & Rowlands, 2006). Pediatricians recommend staying on the diet at least until adolescence, and some encourage staying on it for life.

Huntington's Disease

Huntington's disease (HD) is a fatal, progressive degenerative disorder and is a dominant trait. Physical symptoms include uncontrollable muscle movements (Jacobs et al., 2006). Psychological symptoms include loss of intellectual functioning and personality change (Robins Wahlin et al., 2007). Because the onset of HD is delayed until middle adulthood, many individuals with the defect have borne children only to discover years later that they and possibly half their offspring will inevitably develop it. Fortunately, the disorder is rare, affecting approximately 1 American in 18,000. Medicines are helpful with some of the symptoms of HD, but they do not cure it.

Sickle-Cell Anemia

Sickle-cell anemia is caused by a recessive gene. Sickle-cell anemia is most common among African Americans but also occurs in people from Central and South America, the Caribbean, Mediterranean countries, and the Middle East. Nearly 1 African American in 10 and 1 Latino or Latina American in 20 is a carrier. In sickle-cell anemia, red blood cells take on the shape of a sickle and clump together, obstructing small blood vessels and decreasing the oxygen supply. The lessened oxygen supply can impair cognitive skills and academic performance (Hogan et al., 2005; Ogunfowora et al., 2005). Physical problems include painful and swollen joints, jaundice, and potentially fatal conditions such as pneumonia, stroke, and heart and kidney failure.

Tay-Sachs Disease

Tay-Sachs disease is also caused by a recessive gene. It causes the central nervous system to degenerate, resulting in death. The disorder is most commonly found among children in Jewish families of Eastern European background. Approximately 1 in 30 Jewish Americans from this background carries the recessive gene for Tay-Sachs. Children with the disorder progressively lose control over their muscles. They experience visual and auditory sensory losses, develop mental retardation, become paralyzed, and die toward the end of early childhood, by about the age of 5.

Cystic Fibrosis

Cystic fibrosis, also caused by a recessive gene, is the most common fatal hereditary disease among European Americans. Approximately 30,000 Americans have the disorder, but another 10 million (1 in every 31 people) are carriers (Cystic Fibrosis Foundation, 2007). Children with the disease suffer from excessive production of thick mucus that clogs the pancreas and lungs. Most victims die of respiratory infections in their 20s.

Sex-Linked Genetic Abnormalities

Some genetic defects, such as **hemophilia**, are carried on only the X sex chromosome. For this reason, they are referred to as **sex-linked genetic abnormalities**. These defects also involve recessive genes. Females, who have two X sex chromosomes, are less likely than males to show sex-linked disorders because the genes that cause the

phenylketonuria (PKU) (fee-nill-key-toe-NOOR-ee-uh) A genetic abnormality in which phenylalanine builds up and causes mental retardation.

Huntington's disease A fatal genetic neurologic disorder whose onset is in middle age.

sickle-cell anemia A genetic disorder that decreases the blood's capacity to carry oxygen.

Tay-Sachs disease A fatal genetic neurological disorder.

cystic fibrosis A fatal genetic disorder in which mucus obstructs the lungs and pancreas.

hemophilia (he-moe-FEEL-yuh) A genetic disorder in which blood does not clot properly.

sex-linked genetic abnormalities Abnormalities resulting from genes that are found on the X sex chromosome. They are more likely to be shown by male offspring (who do not have an opposing gene from a second X chromosome) than by female offspring.

disorder would have to be present on both of a female's sex chromosomes for the disorder to be expressed. Sex-linked diseases are more likely to afflict sons of female carriers because males have only one X sex chromosome, which they inherit from their mothers. Queen Victoria was a carrier of hemophilia and transmitted the blood disorder to many of her children, who in turn carried it into a number of the ruling houses of Europe. For this reason, hemophilia has been dubbed the "royal disease."

One form of **muscular dystrophy**, Duchenne muscular dystrophy, is sex-linked. Muscular dystrophy is characterized by a weakening of the of the muscles, which can lead to wasting away, inability to walk, and sometimes death. Other sex-linked abnormalities include diabetes, color blindness, and some types of night blindness.

Genetic Counseling and Prenatal Testing

It is now possible to detect the genetic abnormalities that are responsible for hundreds of diseases. *Question: How do health professionals determine whether children will have genetic or chromosomal abnormalities?*

In an effort to help parents avert these predictable tragedies, **genetic counseling** is becoming widely used. Genetic counselors compile information about a couple's genetic heritage to explore whether their children might develop genetic abnormalities. Couples who face a high risk of passing along genetic defects to their children sometimes elect to adopt or not have children rather than conceive their own.

In addition, **prenatal** testing can indicate whether the embryo or fetus is carrying genetic abnormalities. Prenatal testing includes amniocentesis, chorionic villus sampling, ultrasound, and blood tests.

Amniocentesis

Amniocentesis is usually performed on the mother at about 14–16 weeks after conception, although many physicians now perform the procedure earlier ("early amniocentesis"). In this method, the health professional uses a syringe (needle) to withdraw fluid from the amniotic sac (● Figure 2.6). The fluid contains cells that are sloughed off by the fetus. The cells are separated from the amniotic fluid, grown in a culture, and then examined microscopically for genetic and chromosomal abnormalities.

Amniocentesis has become routine among American women who become pregnant past the age of 35 because the chances of Down syndrome increase dramatically as women approach or pass the age of 40. But women carrying the children of aging fathers may also wish to have amniocentesis. Amniocentesis can detect the presence of well over 100 chromosomal and genetic abnormalities, including sickle-cell anemia, Tay-Sachs disease, **spina bifida**, muscular dystrophy, and Rh incompatibility in the fetus. Women (or their partners) who carry or have a family history of any of these disorders are advised to have amniocentesis performed. If the test reveals the presence of a serious disorder, the parents may decide to abort the fetus. Or, they may decide to continue the pregnancy and prepare themselves to raise a child who has special needs.

Amniocentesis also permits parents to learn the sex of their unborn child through examination of the sex chromosomes, but most parents learn the sex of their baby earlier by means of ultrasound. Amniocentesis carries some risk of miscarriage (approximately 1 woman in 100 who undergo the procedure will miscarry), so health professionals would not conduct it to learn the sex of the child.

Chorionic Villus Sampling

Chorionic villus sampling (CVS) is similar to amniocentesis but offers the advantage of diagnosing fetal abnormalities earlier in pregnancy. CVS is carried out between the 9th and 12th week of pregnancy. A small syringe is inserted through the vagina into the **uterus**. The syringe gently sucks out a few of the threadlike projections (villi) from the outer membrane that envelops the amniotic sac and fetus. Re-

muscular dystrophy (DIS-truh-fee) A chronic disease characterized by a progressive wasting away of the muscles.

genetic counseling Advice concerning the probabilities that a couple's children will show genetic abnormalities.

prenatal Before birth.

amniocentesis (AM-nee-oh-sent-TEE-sis) A procedure for drawing and examining fetal cells sloughed off into amniotic fluid to determine the presence of various disorders.

spina bifida A neural tube defect that causes abnormalities of the brain and spine.

chorionic villus sampling (CORE-ee-AH-nick VILL-us) A method for the prenatal detection of genetic abnormalities that samples the membrane enveloping the amniotic sac and fetus.

uterus The hollow organ within females in which the embryo and fetus develop.

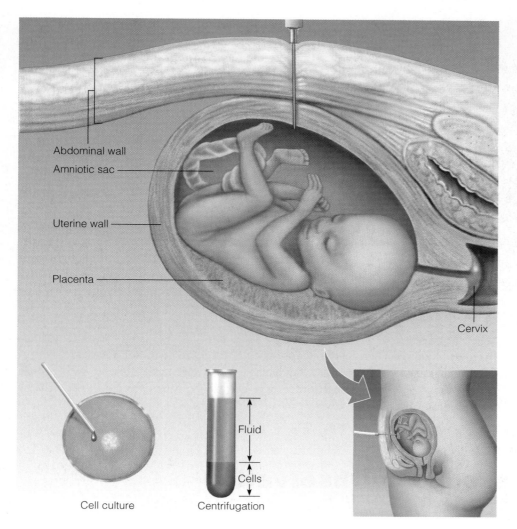

● **Figure 2.6**
Amniocentesis

Amniocentesis allows prenatal identification of certain genetic and chromosomal disorders by examining genetic material sloughed off by the fetus into amniotic fluid. Amniocentesis also allows parents to learn the sex of their unborn child. Would you want to know?

Abdominal wall

Amniotic sac

Uterine wall

Placenta

Cervix

Fluid

Cells

Cell culture

Centrifugation

sults are available within days of the procedure. CVS has not been used as frequently as amniocentesis because many studies have shown that CVS carries a slightly greater risk of spontaneous abortion.

Consideration of the relative risks of amniocentesis and CVS is a highly controversial issue. Some studies have suggested that the risks of the procedures are about equivalent (Simpson, 2000). However, there are two types of amniocentesis—"late" and "early"—and there are also different types of CVS. More recent studies suggest that both amniocentesis and CVS increase the risk of miscarriage and that the risks might *not* be equal (Alfirevic et al., 2003; Philip et al., 2004). Another factor to consider, sad to say, is that some practitioners are better at carrying out these procedures than others. If you are considering having CVS or amniocentesis, ask your doctor for the latest information about the risks of each procedure. Also ask around to make sure that your doctor is the right doctor to carry out the procedure.

Ultrasound

For more than half a century, the military has been using sonar to locate enemy submarines. Sonar sends high-frequency sound waves into the depths of the ocean, and the waves bounce back from objects such as submarines (and whales and schools of fish and the ocean floor) to reveal their presence. Within the past generation, health professionals have also innovated the use of (very!) high-frequency sound waves to obtain information about the fetus. The sounds waves are too high in frequency to be heard by the human ear and are called **ultrasound**. However, they are reflected by

ultrasound Sound waves too high in pitch to be sensed by the human ear.

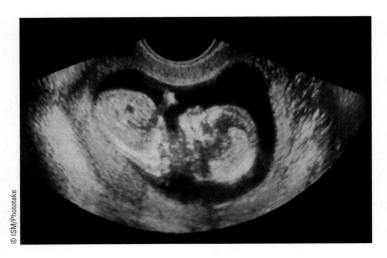

● **Figure 2.7**
Sonogram of a 5-Month-Old Fetus

In the ultrasound technique, sound waves are bounced off the fetus and provide a picture, called a sonogram, that enables professionals to detect various abnormalities.

the fetus, and a computer can use the information to generate a picture (visual) of the fetus. The picture is referred to as a **sonogram**, from roots meaning "written with sound" (see ● Figure 2.7).

Ultrasound is used in amniocentesis and CVS to better determine the position of the fetus. It helps the physician to make sure that the needle enters the sac surrounding the fetus and not the fetus itself, although a mistake will *not* be lethal to the fetus. Ultrasound is also used to locate fetal structures when intrauterine transfusions are necessary for the survival of a fetus with Rh disease.

Ultrasound also is used to track the growth of the fetus, to determine fetal age and sex, and to detect multiple pregnancies and structural abnormalities. Although ultrasound is beneficial for pregnant women whose fetuses are at risk of serious medical problems, it may not improve birth outcomes for women with low-risk pregnancies.

Blood Tests

Parental blood tests can reveal the presence of recessive genes for a variety of disorders, such as sickle-cell anemia, Tay-Sachs disease, and cystic fibrosis. When both parents carry genes for these disorders, the disorders can be detected in the fetus by means of amniocentesis or CVS.

Lessons in Observation
Prenatal Assessment

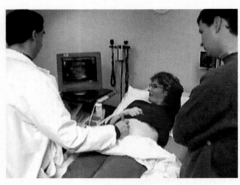

During a routine prenatal visit, Dr. Cohen performs a detailed ultrasound on Eleanor Walsh, who is in her fourth month of pregnancy.

 To watch this video, visit the book companion website. You can also answer the questions and email your responses to your professor.

Learning Objectives

- What is the purpose of a prenatal ultrasound?
- What does an ultrasound look like?
- What does an ultrasound tell doctors and parents about the fetus?
- What is amniocentesis?
- Why would a pregnant woman choose to have amniocentesis?
- What is the most common chromosomal disorder seen in live-born babies?

Applied Lesson

Describe the ultrasound procedure. What structures does Dr. Cohen identify, and what does their appearance tell him about the health of the baby? Describe the reasons that Dr. Cohen does not recommend an amniocentesis for Eleanor.

Critical Thinking

For what reasons might a doctor recommend that a woman under age 35 have an amniocentesis? What are the risks involved in this procedure? How might the doctor and mother determine whether amniocentesis is the right choice during the course of the pregnancy? What are some ethical considerations in the use of prenatal monitoring?

Another kind of blood test, the **alpha-fetoprotein (AFP) assay**, is used to detect neural tube defects such as spina bifida and certain chromosomal abnormalities. Neural tube defects cause an elevation in the AFP level in the mother's blood. Elevated AFP levels also are associated with increased risk of fetal death. However, the mother's AFP level also varies with other factors. For this reason, the diagnosis of a neural tube defect is confirmed by other methods of observation, such as amniocentesis or ultrasound.

In the next section, we see that our development is affected not only by genes but also by environmental influences.

Active Review

1. A normal human cell contains 46 _____, which are organized into 23 pairs.
2. Each chromosome contains thousands of genes, which are segments of _____ acid (DNA), which takes the form of a twisting ladder.
3. _____ is the cell-division process by which growth occurs and tissues are replaced.
4. Sperm and ova are produced through _____.
5. When a zygote divides into two cells that separate so that each develops into an individual, we have _____ (MZ) twins.
6. If two ova are fertilized by different sperm cells, they develop into _____ (DZ) twins.
7. People who bear one dominant gene and one recessive gene for a trait are said to be _____ of the recessive gene.
8. In _____, the 21st pair of chromosomes has an extra, or third, chromosome.
9. Phenylketonuria (PKU) is transmitted by a _____ (Dominant or Recessive?) gene.

10. _____ anemia is caused by a recessive gene and is most common among African Americans.
11. In the prenatal testing method of _____, fetal cells found in amniotic fluid are examined for genetic abnormalities.
12. The use of _____ can form a picture ("sonogram") of the fetus.

Reflect & Relate: Many methods of prenatal testing, including amniocentesis, some blood tests, and ultrasound, can allow parents to learn the sex of their fetus. If you were having such testing, would you want to know the sex of your fetus or would you prefer to wait? Explain.

Go to

http://www.thomsonedu.com/psychology/rathus
for an interactive version of this review.

Heredity and the Environment: Nature versus Nurture

Now that we have studied heredity, we know why we have arms rather than wings and hairy skin rather than feathers (well, perhaps not so hairy for many of us). But none of us is the result of heredity alone.

Question: What is the difference between our genotypes and our phenotypes? Heredity provides the biological basis for a **reaction range** in the expression of traits. Our inherited traits can vary in expression, depending on environmental conditions. In addition to inheritance, the development of our traits is also influenced by nutrition, learning, exercise, and—unfortunately—accident and illness. A

sonogram A procedure for using ultrasonic sound waves to create a picture of an embryo or fetus.

alpha-fetoprotein (AFP) assay A blood test that assesses the mother's blood level of alpha-fetoprotein, a substance that is linked with fetal neural tube defects.

reaction range The variability in the expression of inherited traits as they are influenced by environmental factors.

potential Shakespeare who is reared in poverty and never taught to read or write will not create a *Hamlet*. Our traits and behaviors represent the interaction of heredity and environment. The sets of traits that we inherit from our parents are referred to as our **genotypes**. Our actual sets of traits are called our **phenotypes**. Our phenotypes develop because of both genetic and environmental influences.

Researchers have developed a number of strategies to help sort out the effects of heredity and the environment on development. *Question: What kinds of research strategies do researchers use to sort out the effects of genetics and environmental influences on development?*

Kinship Studies: Are the Traits of Relatives Related?

Researchers study the distribution of a particular behavior pattern among relatives who differ in degree of genetic closeness. The more closely people are related, the more genes they have in common. Parents and children have a 50% overlap in their genetic endowments, and so do siblings (brothers and sisters), on average. Aunts and uncles have a 25% overlap with nieces and nephews, and so do grandparents with their grandchildren. First cousins share 12.5% of their genetic endowment. So, if genes are implicated in a physical trait or behavior pattern, people who are more closely related should be more likely to share the pattern. You probably look more like a parent or brother or sister than like a cousin, and you probably look very little like a stranger.

Twin Studies: Looking in the Genetic Mirror

Monozygotic (MZ) twins share 100% of their genes, whereas dizygotic (DZ) twins have a 50% overlap, just as other siblings do. If MZ twins show greater similarity on some trait or behavior than DZ twins do, a genetic basis for the trait or behavior is indicated.

MZ twins resemble each other more closely than DZ twins on a number of physical and psychological traits. MZ twins are more likely to look alike and to be similar in height, and they may even have more similar cholesterol levels than DZ twins (Plomin, 2002). This finding holds even when the MZ twins are reared apart and the DZ twins are reared together (Bouchard & Loehlin, 2001). Other physical similarities between pairs of MZ twins may be more subtle, but they are also strong. For example, research shows that MZ twin sisters begin to menstruate about 1 to 2 months apart, whereas DZ twins begin to menstruate about 1 year apart. MZ twins are more alike than DZ twins in their blood pressure, brain wave patterns, their speech patterns, gestures, and mannerisms (Plomin, 2002; Bouchard & Loehlin, 2001). Heredity even has an effect on their preference for coffee or tea (Luciano et al., 2005).

MZ twins resemble one another more strongly than DZ twins in intelligence and in personality traits such as sociability, anxiety, friendliness, conformity, and even happiness and the tendency to choose marriage over the single life (Hur, 2005; Johnson et al., 2004; McCrae et al., 2000). David Lykken and Mike Csikszentmihalyi (2001) suggested that we inherit a tendency toward a certain level of happiness. Despite the ups and downs of life, we tend to drift back to our usual levels of cheerfulness or irritability. It seems that our bank accounts, our levels of education, and our marital status are less influential than genes as contributors to happiness. Heredity is also a key contributor to psychological developmental factors such as cognitive functioning, and early signs of attachment (e.g., smiling, cuddling, and expression of fear of strangers) (Plomin, 2002). MZ twins are more likely than DZ twins to share psychological disorders such as **autism**, depression, schizophrenia, and even vulnerability to alcoholism (Belmonte & Carper, 2006; Plomin, 2002; Ronald et al., 2006).

genotype The genetic form or constitution of a person as determined by heredity.

phenotype The actual form or constitution of a person as determined by heredity and environmental factors.

autism A developmental disorder characterized by failure to relate to others, communication problems, intolerance of change, and ritualistic behavior.

Of course, twin studies are not perfect. MZ twins may resemble each other more closely than DZ twins partly because they are treated more similarly. MZ twins frequently are dressed identically, and parents sometimes have difficulty telling them apart.

One way to get around this difficulty is to find and compare MZ twins who were reared in different homes. Any similarities between MZ twins reared apart cannot be explained by a shared home environment and would appear to be largely a result of heredity. In the fascinating Minnesota Study of Twins Reared Apart (T. J. Bouchard et al., 1990; DiLalla et al., 1999; Lykken, 2006), researchers have been measuring the physiological and psychological characteristics of 56 sets of MZ adult twins who were separated in infancy and reared in different homes. The MZ twins reared apart are about as similar as MZ twins reared together on a variety of measures of intelligence, personality, temperament, occupational and leisure-time interests, and social attitudes. These traits thus would appear to have a genetic underpinning.

Adoption Studies

Adoption studies in which children are separated from their natural parents at an early age and reared by adoptive parents provide special opportunities for sorting out nature and nurture. As we see in discussions of the origins of intelligence (Chapter 12) and of various problem behaviors (Chapters 10 and 13), psychologists look for the relative similarities between children and their adoptive and natural parents. When children who are reared by adoptive parents are nonetheless more similar to their natural parents in a trait, a powerful argument is made for a genetic role in the appearance of that trait.

Traits are determined by pairs of genes. One member of each pair comes from each parent. *Question: **What process brings together the genes from each parent?*** That process is called conception. In the following section, we talk about the birds and the bees and the microscope to understand how conception works.

Active Review

13. The sets of traits that we inherit are referred to as our (Genotype or Phenotype?).

14. The actual traits that we display at any point in time are the product of genetic and environmental influences and are called our (Genotypes or Phenotypes?).

15. Parents and children have a _____% overlap in their genetic endowments.

16. _____ (MZ) twins share 100% of their genes.

17. _____ (DZ) twins have a 50% overlap, as do other siblings.

Reflect & Relate: Do you know sets of twins? Are they monozygotic or dizygotic? How are they alike? How do they differ?

Go to

http://www.thomsonedu.com/psychology/rathus

for an interactive version of this review.

Conception: Against All Odds

On a balmy day in October, Marta and her partner, Jorge, rush to catch the train to their jobs in the city. Marta's workday is outwardly the same as any other. Within her body, however, a drama is unfolding. Yesterday, hormones had caused an ovarian follicle to rupture, releasing its egg cell, or ovum. Like all women, Marta possessed all the ova she would ever have at birth, each encased in a follicle. How this particular follicle was selected to ripen and release its ovum this month remains a mystery. But for the next day or so, Marta will be capable of conceiving.

The previous morning, Marta had used her ovulation-timing kit, which showed that she was about to ovulate. So later that night, Marta and Jorge had made love, hoping that Marta would conceive. Jorge ejaculated hundreds of millions of sperm within Marta's vagina. Only a few thousand survived the journey through the cervix and uterus to the fallopian tube that contained the ovum, released just hours earlier. Of these, a few hundred remained to bombard the ovum. One succeeded in penetrating the ovum's covering, resulting in conception. From a single cell formed by the union of sperm and ovum, a new life begins to form. The **zygote** is but 1/175 of an inch across, a tiny beginning for the drama about to take place.

Marta is age 37. Four months into her pregnancy, Marta obtains amniocentesis to check for the presence of chromosomal abnormalities, such as Down syndrome. (Down syndrome is more common among children born to women in their late 30s and older.) Amniocentesis also indicates the sex of the fetus. Although many parents prefer to know the sex of their baby before it is born, Marta and Jorge ask their doctor not to inform them. "Why ruin the surprise?" Jorge tells his friends. So Marta and Jorge are left to debate boys' names and girls' names for the next few months.

Conception is the union of an ovum and a sperm cell. Conception, from one perspective, is the beginning of a new human life. From another perspective, though, conception is also the end of a fantastic voyage in which one of several hundred thousand ova produced by the woman unites with one of hundreds of million sperm produced by the man in the average ejaculate.

Ova

Truth or Fiction Revisited: At birth, women already have all the ova they will ever have: some 400,000. However, the ova are immature in form. The ovaries also produce the female hormones estrogen and progesterone. At puberty, in response to hormonal command, some ova begin to mature (● Figure 2.8). Each month, one egg (occasionally more than one) is released from its ovarian follicle about midway through the menstrual cycle and enters a nearby **fallopian tube**. It might take 3 to 4 days for an egg to be propelled by small, hairlike structures called cilia and, perhaps, by contractions in the wall of the tube, along the few inches of the fallopian tube to the uterus. Unlike sperm, eggs do not propel themselves.

If the egg is not fertilized, it is discharged through the uterus and the vagina along with the **endometrium** that had formed to support an embryo, in the menstrual flow. During a woman's reproductive years, only about 400 ova (i.e., 1 in 1,000) will ripen and be released.

In an early stage of development, egg cells contain 46 chromosomes. Each developing egg cell contains two X sex chromosomes. After meiosis, each ovum contains 23 chromosomes, one of which is an X sex chromosome.

Ova are much larger than sperm. The chicken egg and the 6-inch ostrich egg are each just one cell, although the sperm of these birds are microscopic. Human ova are barely visible to the eye, but their bulk is still thousands of times larger than that of sperm cells.

zygote A new cell formed from the union of a sperm and an ovum (egg cell); a fertilized egg.

conception The union of a sperm cell and an ovum that occurs when the chromosomes of each of these cells combine to form 23 new pairs.

fallopian tube A tube through which ova travel from an ovary to the uterus.

endometrium The inner lining of the uterus.

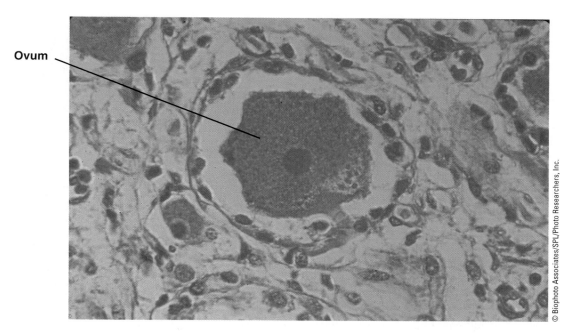

Ovum

● **Figure 2.8** A Ripening Ovum in an Ovarian Follicle

At puberty, some ova begin to mature. Each month one egg (occasionally more than one) is released from its ovarian follicle and enters a fallopian tube.

Sperm Cells

Sperm cells develop through several stages. Like ova, in one early stage they each contain 46 chromosomes, including one X and one Y sex chromosome. After meiosis, each sperm has 23 chromosomes. Half have X sex chromosomes, and the other half have Y sex chromosomes. Each sperm cell is about 1/500th of an inch long, one of the smallest types of cells in the body. Sperm with Y sex chromosomes appear to swim faster than sperm with X sex chromosomes. **Truth or Fiction Revisited:** One reason that 120 to 150 boys are conceived for every 100 girls is because of this difference. Male fetuses suffer a higher rate of **spontaneous abortion** than females, however, often during the first month of pregnancy. At birth, boys outnumber girls by a ratio of only 106 to 100. Boys also have a higher incidence of infant mortality, which further equalizes the numbers of girls and boys.

The 150 million or so sperm in the ejaculate may seem to be a wasteful investment because only one sperm can fertilize an ovum, but only 1 in 1,000 sperm will ever approach an ovum. Millions deposited in the vagina flow out of the woman's body because of gravity. Normal vaginal acidity kills many more sperm. Many surviving sperm then have to swim against the current of fluid coming from the cervix (see ● Figure 2.9).

Sperm that survive these initial obstacles may reach the fallopian tubes 60 to 90 minutes after ejaculation. About half the sperm enter the wrong tube, that is, the tube without the egg. Perhaps 2,000 enter the correct tube. Fewer still manage to swim the final 2 inches against the currents generated by the cilia that line the tube.

Although the journey of sperm is literally blind, it is apparently not random. **Truth or Fiction Revisited:** It is not true that sperm travel about at random inside the woman's reproductive tract so that reaching the ovum is a matter of luck. Sperm cells are apparently "egged on" (pardon the pun) by a change in calcium ions that occurs when an ovum is released by a follicle (Angier, 2007).

spontaneous abortion Unplanned, accidental abortion.

● Figure 2.9
Female Reproductive Organs

Conception is something of an obstacle course. Sperm must survive the pull of gravity and vaginal acidity, risk winding up in the wrong fallopian tube, and surmount other hurdles before they reach the ovum.

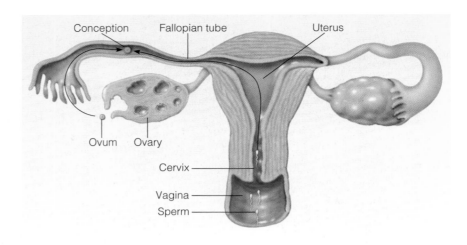

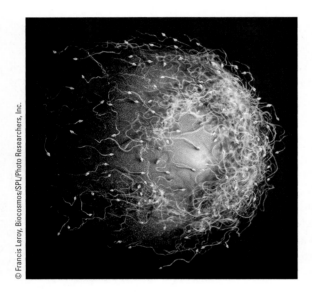

● Figure 2.10
Human Sperm Swarming Around an Ovum in a Fallopian Tube

Fertilization normally occurs in a fallopian tube, not in the uterus. Thousands of sperm may wind up in the vicinity of an ovum, but only one fertilizes it. How this sperm cell is "selected" remains one of the mysteries of nature.

zona pellucida (pell-LOOSE-see-duh) A gelatinous layer that surrounds an ovum. (From roots referring to a "zone through which light can shine.")

Of all the sperm swarming around the egg, only one enters (see ● Figure 2.10). Ova are surrounded by a gelatinous layer called the **zona pellucida**, which is the layer that must be penetrated if fertilization is to occur. Many of the sperm that have completed their journey to the ovum secrete an enzyme called **hyaluronidase**. The group bombardment of hyaluronidase briefly thins the zona pellucida, but it enables only one sperm to penetrate. Once a sperm cell has entered, the zona pellucida thickens, locking other sperm out. How this one sperm cell is "selected" is another biological mystery. Nevertheless, other sperm are unable to enter.

The chromosomes from the sperm cell line up across from the corresponding chromosomes in the egg cell. Conception finally occurs as the chromosomes combine to form 23 new pairs with a unique set of genetic instructions.

For couples who want children, few problems are more frustrating than the inability to conceive. Physicians often recommend that couples try to conceive on their own for 6 months before seeking medical assistance. The term *infertility* usually is not applied until the couple has failed to conceive for 1 year. We consider the problem of infertility next.

Infertility and Other Ways of Becoming Parents

Approximately one American couple in six or seven has fertility problems (Rebar & DeCherney, 2004). Infertility was once viewed as a problem of the woman, but it turns out that the problem lies with the man in about 40% of cases.

Causes of Infertility

Question: What are the causes of infertility? The following fertility problems are found in men (American Fertility Association, 2007):

- Low sperm count
- Deformed sperm
- Poor ability of the sperm to swim to the ovum ("low sperm motility")
- Infectious diseases, such as sexually transmitted infections
- Chronic diseases, such as diabetes

- Injury of the testes
- An "autoimmune" response, in which the man's body attacks his own sperm as foreign agents

A low sperm count—or lack of sperm—is the most common infertility problem found in men. Men's fertility problems have a variety of causes: genetic factors, environmental poisons, diabetes, sexually transmitted infections (STIs), overheating of the testes (which happens now and then among athletes, such as long-distance runners), pressure (which can be caused by certain bicycle seats; have your doctor recommend a more comfortable and less harmful seat), aging, and certain prescription and illicit drugs (Hatcher et al., 2007; Shevell et al., 2005).

Truth or Fiction Revisited: Yes, extensive athletic activity can contribute to infertility in the male. Sometimes the sperm count is adequate, but other factors such as prostate or hormonal problems deform sperm or deprive them of their **motility**. Motility can also be impaired by the scar tissue from infections, such as STIs.

Women encounter the following major fertility problems (Focus on Fertility, 2007):

- Irregular ovulation, including failure to ovulate
- Declining hormone levels of estrogen and progesterone that occur with aging and that may prevent the ovum from becoming fertilized or remaining implanted in the uterus
- Inflammation of the tissue that is sloughed off during menstruation ("endometriosis")
- Obstructions or malfunctions of the reproductive tract, which are often caused by infections or diseases involving the reproductive tract

The most common problem in women is irregular ovulation or lack of ovulation. This problem can have many causes, including irregularities among the hormones that govern ovulation, stress, and malnutrition. So-called fertility drugs (e.g., *clomiphene* and *pergonal*) are made up of hormones that cause women to ovulate. These drugs may cause multiple births by stimulating more than one ovum to ripen during a month (Legro et al., 2007).

Infections may scar the fallopian tubes and other organs, impeding the passage of sperm or ova. Such infections include **pelvic inflammatory disease (PID)**. PID can result from any of a number of bacterial or viral infections, including the STIs gonorrhea and chlamydia. Antibiotics are usually helpful in treating bacterial infections, but infertility can be irreversible if the infection has gone without treatment for too long.

Endometriosis can obstruct the fallopian tubes, where conception normally takes place. This problem is clear enough. But endometriosis is also believed to somehow dampen the "climate" for conception; the mechanisms involved in this effect are not as well understood. Endometriosis has become a fairly frequent cause of infertility today because so many women are delaying childbearing. What apparently happens is that each month, tissue develops to line the uterus in case the woman conceives. This tissue, called the endometrium, is then normally sloughed off during menstruation. However, some of it backs up into the abdomen through the same fallopian tubes that would provide a duct for an ovum. Endometrial tissue then collects in the abdomen, where it can cause abdominal pain and lessen the chances of conception. Physicians may treat endometriosis through hormone treatments that temporarily prevent menstruation or through surgery. These treatments are often successful, but they are not reliable.

Let us now consider some of the methods that have been developed in recent years to help infertile couples bear children. *Question: How are couples helped to have children?*

hyaluronidase (high-al-you-RON-uh-dace) An enzyme that briefly thins the zona pellucida, enabling a single sperm cell to penetrate. (From roots referring to a "substance that breaks down a glasslike fluid.")

motility Self-propulsion.

pelvic inflammatory disease (PID) An infection of the abdominal region that may have various causes and that may impair fertility.

endometriosis (end-oh-me-tree-OH-sis) Inflammation of endometrial tissue sloughed off into the abdominal cavity rather than out of the body during menstruation; the condition is characterized by abdominal pain and sometimes infertility.

Artificial Insemination

Multiple ejaculations of men with low sperm counts can be collected and quick-frozen. The sperm can then be injected into the woman's uterus at the time of ovulation. This method is one **artificial insemination** procedure. Sperm from men with low sperm motility can also be injected into their partners' uteruses so that the sperm can begin their journey closer to the fallopian tubes. When a man has no sperm or an extremely low sperm count, his partner can be artificially inseminated with the sperm of a donor who resembles the man in physical traits. Women who want a baby but do not have a partner may also have artificial insemination. So may lesbian couples. The child then bears the genes of one of the parents, the mother.

In Vitro Fertilization

Have you heard the expression "test-tube baby"? Does it sound as though a baby develops in a test tube? **Truth or Fiction Revisited:** It is not true that test-tube babies are grown in a test tube. Does it sound as though a baby is conceived in a test tube? That's not so, but it's close. In this method, which is more technically known as **in vitro fertilization** (IVF), ripened ova are removed surgically from the mother and placed in a laboratory dish. The father's sperm are also placed in the dish. One or more ova are fertilized and then injected into the mother's uterus to become implanted.

In vitro fertilization may be used when the fallopian tubes are blocked because the ova need not travel through them. If the father's sperm are low in motility, they are sometimes injected directly into the ovum. A variation known as donor IVF can be used when the intended mother does not produce ova. An ovum from another woman is fertilized and injected into the uterus of the mother-to-be.

Because only a minority of attempts lead to births, it can take several tries to achieve a pregnancy. Several embryos may be injected into the uterus at once, however, heightening the odds. IVF remains costly but is otherwise routine, if not guaranteed.

Donor IVF

Donor IVF is used when a woman does not produce ova of her own but when her uterus is apparently capable of providing an adequate environment to bring a baby to term. An ovum is harvested from another woman, the donor. It is fertilized in vitro, often by sperm from the partner of the recipient. Then, as in other cases of IVF, the fertilized ovum is placed directly into the uterus of the recipient. The embryo becomes implanted and undergoes the remainder of prenatal development in the recipient's uterus. This procedure is known as an **embryonic transplant.**

Surrogate Mothers

In recent years, stories about **surrogate mothers** have filled the headlines. Surrogate mothers bring babies to term for other women who are infertile. (The word *surrogate* means "substitute.") Surrogate mothers may be artificially inseminated by the partners of infertile women, in which case the baby thus carries the genes of the father. But sometimes—as with 53-year-old singer-songwriter James Taylor and his 47-year-old wife—ova are surgically extracted from the biological mother, fertilized in vitro by the biological father, and then implanted in another woman's uterus, where the baby is brought to term. Surrogate mothers are usually paid fees and sign agreements to surrender the baby. (These contracts have been annulled in some states, however, so that surrogate mothers cannot be forced to hand over their babies.) In the case of Taylor and his wife, the surrogate mother was a friend of the family and she delivered twins.

artificial insemination Injection of sperm into the uterus to fertilize an ovum.

in vitro fertilization (VEE-tro) Fertilization of an ovum in a laboratory dish.

donor IVF The transfer of a donor's ovum, fertilized in a laboratory dish, to the uterus of another woman.

embryonic transplant The transfer of an embryo from the uterus of one woman to that of another.

surrogate mother A woman who is artificially inseminated and carries to term a child who is then given to another woman, typically the spouse of the sperm donor.

Biologically, surrogate motherhood might seem the mirror image of the more common artificial insemination technique in which a fertile woman is artificially inseminated with sperm from a donor. But the methods are psychologically very different. For example, sperm donors usually do not know the identity of the women who have received their sperm, nor do they follow the child's prenatal development. Surrogate mothers, however, are involved throughout the course of prenatal development.

Ethical and legal dilemmas revolve around the issue of artificially inseminated surrogate mothers having a genetic link to their babies. If the surrogate mothers change their minds and do not want to hand the babies over to the contractual parents, there can be legal struggles.

Adoption

Adoption is another way for people to obtain children. Despite occasional conflicts that pit adoptive parents against biological parents who change their minds about giving up their children, most adoptions result in the formation of loving new families. Many Americans find it easier to adopt infants from other countries or with special needs.

Adoption
Many couples choose to adopt children whether or not they are capable of bearing children on their own.

Selecting the Sex of Your Child: Fantasy or Reality?

Folklore is replete with methods—and non-methods—of sex selection. Some cultures advised coitus under the full moon to conceive boys. The Greek philosopher Aristotle suggested that making love during a north wind would beget sons and that a south wind would produce daughters. Sour foods were once suggested for parents desirous of having boys. Those who wanted girls were advised to consume sweets. Husbands who yearned to have boys might be advised to wear their boots to bed. It goes without saying that none of these methods worked (but we will say it anyhow).

These methods, or nonmethods, would supposedly lead to the conception of children of the desired sex. However, methods after conception—such as the abortion of fetuses because of their sex—have also been used. There are also many cultures in which infanticide has been used. See the nearby "Developing—or Not—in a World of Diversity."

Today, there is a reliable method for selecting the sex of your child prior to implantation: preimplantation genetic diagnosis (PGD). PGD was developed to detect genetic disorders, but it also allows health professionals to learn of the sex of the embryo. In PGD, ova are fertilized in vitro, leading to conception of perhaps six to eight embryos. After a few days of cell division, a cell is extracted from each. The sex chromosomal structure of the cell is examined microscopically to determine whether the embryo is female or male. Embryos of the desired sex are implanted in the woman's uterus, where one or more can grow to term. PGD is a fool-proof sex-selection method, but it is medically invasive, it is expensive, and implantation cannot be guaranteed. Yet when implantation does occur the sex of the embryo is known.

In most of the next chapter, we deal with issues on a smaller scale. We begin with the division of the single cell formed by the union of sperm cell and ovum into two cells, then four, and so on.

Where Are the Missing Chinese Girls?

It is no secret that most people in most cultures would prefer that their child, or at least their first child, be a boy. According to traditional gender roles, boys carry on the business of the family and represent continuity of a family's lineage (Ding & Hesketh, 2006; Sullum, 2007). They also pass on the family name. In less developed nations such as China and India, especially in rural areas, sons also represent protection from neglect and poverty in the later years. These attitudes are reflected in verses from the ancient Chinese *Book of Songs*, written some three thousand years ago:

> When a son is born,
> Let him sleep on the bed,
> Clothe him with fine clothes,
> And give him jade with which to
>   play. . . .
> When a daughter is born,
> Let her sleep on the ground,
> Wrap her in common wrappings,
> And give her broken tiles with
>   which to play. . . .

When Mao Zedong took power in 1949, his Communist government replaced family support in old age with state support and also rejected male superiority. There remained a balance in the numbers of males and females in the population throughout most of the 1970s. But beginning in 1979, China attempted to gain control of its mushrooming population of more than one billion by enforcing strict limits on family size. One child per family is allowed in urban areas. A second child is usually allowed in rural areas after 5 years have passed, especially if the first child is a girl (Li, 2004). Because Chinese families, like the families of old, continue to prefer boys,

the ratio of boys to girls began to change with the limitations on family size (Ding & Hesketh, 2006).

As noted in ■ Table 2.3, the desirability of having small families has generally caught on in the Chinese population. That is, the great majority of women interviewed in a recent survey expressed the desire to have either one or two children. However, there were some differences according to the woman's age, her area of residence, and her level of education. How would you account for such differences?

Because more boys than girls die in infancy, a "normal" ratio of boys to girls is about 106 to 100, which characterized China in the 1970s. The ratio was about 108.5 boys to 100 girls in the early 1980s, 111 to 100 in 1990, and 117 to 100 in 2000, and it is now at least 120 boys for every 100 girls and as high as 123 to 100 by some estimates (Ding & Hesketh, 2006).

Therefore, a great shortage of Chinese women is being created, which may not be much of a problem for parents but which will certainly be a problem for men seeking mates in future years. Chinese officials are concerned that the shortfall will result in millions of men with no prospect of getting married and thereby settling down when they are of age. Thus, they fear that this shortfall of women will result in an increased likelihood of social unrest, which can become political dissent as well as ordinary crime (Festini et al., 2006; Potts, 2006).

Prenatal Sex Selection

How do the Chinese have so many more sons than daughters? Once upon a time in places

like China and India, much of the answer lay in infanticide, that is, in the killing of unwanted female babies. More recently, according to the International Planned Parenthood Federation (Hesketh & Xing, 2006), the main answer is the selective abortion of female fetuses, as identified by inexpensive, portable ultrasound scanners and backstreet abortion clinics. It is estimated that some seven million abortions are performed in China each year and that 70% percent of them are of female fetuses (Hesketh & Xing, 2006).

The director of China's National Population and Family Planning Commission admitted that the gender gap created by the country's population policy has created a very serious challenge for the country (Festini et al., 2006; Sullum, 2007). China, however, does not intend to loosen its constraints on population growth. Instead, the government will experiment with educational campaigns, penalties for sex-selective abortions, and bonuses for parents who have girls (Sullum, 2007; Zhu, 2003).

Reflect:

- *Do you believe that there are any circumstances under which a government such as China's has the right to limit family size? Why or why not?*
- *How would you explain the relationship between the number of children a Chinese woman desires and her age? Her area of residence (urban or rural)? Her level of education?*
- *What sources of error might distort the results in Table 2.3?*

■ **Table 2.3** Preferred Number of Children among Chinese Women
(Percent Expressing Preference)

	No children	1 child	2 children	3 or more children
Age of woman				
15–19	2.1	49	45	1.9
20–29	1.3	47	48	2.1
30–39	0.8	32	60	6.1
40–49	1.0	27	62	11
Area of residence				
Urban	3.1	52	43	1.5
Rural	0.4	30	61	7.5
Level of Education				
Illiterate or semi-literate	0.4	17	67	14
Primary school	0.3	25	65	8.5
Secondary school	2.1	46	47	2.5
College	4.0	49	44	2.2

Source: National Family Planning and Reproductive Health Survey, reported in Q. J. Ding & T. Hesketh (2006), Family size, fertility preferences, and sex ratio in China in the era of the one child family policy: Results from National Family Planning and Reproductive Health Survey, *British Medical Journal, 333*(7564), 371–373.

Note: Number of women interviewed: 39,344

Active Review

18. The union of an ovum and a sperm cell is called _____ .

19. Each month, an ovum is released from its follicle and enters a nearby _____ tube.

20. Low _____ count is the most common infertility problem in the male.

21. Failure to _____ is the most frequent infertility problem in women.

Reflect & Relate: What methods do people use to try to select the sex of their children? Do you believe that it is right or proper to attempt to select the sex of one's child? Support your point of view.

Go to

http://www.thomsonedu.com/psychology/rathus

for an interactive version of this review.

1. What is meant by heredity?	Heredity defines one's nature, as determined by the biological transmission of traits and characteristics from one generation to another. Heredity is fundamental in the transmission of physical traits and is also involved in psychological traits, including psychological disorders.
2. What are chromosomes and genes?	Chromosomes are rod-shaped structures found in cell nuclei. People normally have 46 chromosomes organized into 23 pairs. Each chromosome contains thousands of genes, the biochemical materials that regulate the development of traits. Genes are segments of strands of DNA, which takes the form of a twisting ladder.
3. What happens during cell division?	In mitosis, strands of DNA break apart and are rebuilt in the new cell. Sperm and ova are produced by meiosis—or reduction division—and have 23 rather than 46 chromosomes.
4. How are twins formed?	If a zygote divides into two cells that separate and each develops into an individual, monozygotic (MZ) twins, which are identical, develop. If two ova are each fertilized by a different sperm cell, they develop into dizygotic (DZ) twins, which are fraternal twins. DZ twins run in families.
5. How do genes determine traits?	Traits are determined by pairs of genes. Mendel established laws of heredity and realized that some traits result from an "averaging" of the genetic instructions carried by the parents. However, genes can also be dominant (as in the case of brown eyes) or recessive (blue eyes). When recessive genes from both parent combine, the recessive trait is shown. People who bear one dominant gene and one recessive gene for a trait are carriers of the recessive gene. Some genetic abnormalities are caused by a single pair of genes, others by combinations of genes.
6. What kinds of disorders are caused by chromosomal abnormalities?	Chromosomal abnormalities become more likely as parents age. Mental retardation is common in many such disorders. Down syndrome is caused by an extra chromosome on the 21st pair. Children with Down syndrome have characteristic facial features, including a downward-sloping fold of skin at the inner corners of the eyes, and various physical health problems. Disorders that arise from abnormal numbers of sex chromosomes are called sex-linked. They include XYY males and girls with a single X sex chromosome.
7. What kinds of disorders are caused by genetic abnormalities?	Phenylketonuria (PKU) is a metabolic disorder transmitted by a recessive gene. Huntington's disease is a fatal progressive degenerative disorder and a dominant trait. Sickle-cell anemia is caused by a recessive gene and is most common among African Americans. Tay-Sachs disease is a fatal disease of the nervous system that is caused by a recessive gene and is most common among children in Jewish families of Eastern European origin. Cystic fibrosis is caused by a recessive gene and is the most common fatal hereditary disease among European Americans. Sex-linked genetic abnormalities are carried only on the X sex chromosome and include hemophilia, Duchenne muscular dystrophy, diabetes, and color blindness.

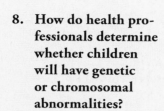

8. How do health professionals determine whether children will have genetic or chromosomal abnormalities?

Prenatal testing procedures can determine the presence of various genetic and chromosomal abnormalities. Such tests include amniocentesis, chorionic villus sampling, ultrasound, and parental blood tests.

9. What is the difference between our genotypes and our phenotypes?

Our genotypes are the sets of traits that we inherit. However, inherited traits vary in expression, depending on environmental conditions. One's actual set of traits at a given point in time is one's phenotype.

10. What research strategies do researchers use to sort out the effects of genetics and environmental influences on development?

Researchers can study the distribution of a trait among relatives who differ in degree of genetic closeness. Parents and children have a 50% overlap in genes, as do brothers and sisters, with the exception of MZ twins, who have 100% overlap. MZ twins resemble each other more closely than DZ twins on physical and psychological traits, even when reared apart. If adopted children are closer to their natural than to their adoptive parents on a physical or psychological trait, that trait is likely to have a strong genetic basis.

11. What process brings together the genes from each parent?

The process is the union of a sperm and an ovum, or conception. Fertilization normally occurs in a fallopian tube. If the egg is not fertilized, it is discharged. Men typically ejaculate hundreds of millions of sperm. More boys are conceived than girls, but male fetuses have a higher rate of spontaneous abortion. Chromosomes from the sperm cell align with chromosomes in the egg cell, combining to form 23 new pairs.

12. What are the causes of infertility?

Male fertility problems include low sperm count and motility, infections, and trauma to the testes. Female fertility problems include failure to ovulate, infections such as PID, endometriosis, and obstructions.

13. How are couples helped to have children?

Fertility drugs help regulate ovulation. Artificial insemination can be done with the sperm from multiple ejaculations of a man with a low sperm count or with the sperm of a donor. In vitro fertilization (IVF) can be used when the fallopian tubes are blocked. An embryo can also be transferred into a host uterus, as when the mother cannot produce ova.

14. How do people attempt to select the sex of their children?

The only reliable method for prenatal sex selection of a child is preimplantation genetic diagnosis.

Key Terms

heredity, 48
genetics, 48
chromosomes, 48
gene, 48
polygenic, 49
deoxyribonucleic acid
    (DNA), 49
mitosis, 49
mutation, 49
meiosis, 49
autosome, 50
sex chromosome, 50
monozygotic (MZ) twins, 50
dizygotic (DZ) twins, 50
ovulation, 51
allele, 51
homozygous, 51
heterozygous, 51
dominant trait, 51
recessive trait, 51
carrier, 51
multifactorial problems, 53
Down syndrome, 53

sex-linked chromosomal
    abnormalities, 53
Klinefelter syndrome, 56
testosterone, 56
Turner syndrome, 56
estrogen, 56
phenylketonuria (PKU), 57
Huntington's disease, 57
sickle-cell anemia, 57
Tay-Sachs disease, 57
cystic fibrosis, 57
hemophilia, 57
sex-linked genetic
    abnormalities, 57
muscular dystrophy, 58
genetic counseling, 58
prenatal, 58
amniocentesis, 58
spina bifida, 58
chorionic villus
    sampling, 58
uterus, 58
ultrasound, 59

sonogram, 61
alpha-fetoprotein (AFP)
    assay, 61
reaction range, 61
genotype, 62
phenotype, 62
autism, 62
zygote, 64
conception, 64
fallopian tube, 64
endometrium, 64
spontaneous abortion, 65
zona pellucida, 66
hyaluronidase, 67
motility, 67
pelvic inflammatory disease
    (PID), 67
endometriosis, 67
artificial insemination, 68
in vitro fertilization, 68
donor IVF, 68
embryonic transplant, 68
surrogate mother, 68

Active Learning Resources

Childhood & Adolescence Book Companion Website
http://www.thomsonedu.com/psychology/rathus

Visit your book companion website, where you will find more resources to help you study. There you will find interactive versions of your book features, including the Lessons in Observation videos, Active Review sections, and the Truth or Fiction feature. In addition, the companion website contains quizzing, flash cards, and a pronunciation glossary.

 **is an easy-to-use online resource that helps you study in less time to get the grade you want, NOW.**

http://www.thomsonedu.com/login

Need help studying? This site is your one-stop study shop. Take a Pre-Test and ThomsonNOW will generate a Personalized Study Plan based on your test results. The Study Plan will identify the topics you need to review and direct you to online resources to help you master those topics. You can then take a Post-Test to determine the concepts you have mastered and what you still need to work on.

3 Prenatal Development

Truth or Fiction?

T F Newly fertilized egg cells survive without any nourishment from the mother for more than a week. p. 79

T F Your heart started beating when you were only one-fourth of an inch long and weighed a fraction of an ounce. p. 81

T F If it were not for the secretion of male sex hormones a few weeks after conception, we would all develop external sex organs that look like those of females. p. 82

T F Fetuses hiccup, sometimes for hours on end. p. 86

T F Parents in wealthy nations have more children. p. 90

T F The same disease organism or chemical agent that can do serious damage to a 6-week-old embryo may have no effect on a 4-month-old fetus. p. 94

T F Babies can be born addicted to narcotics and other drugs. p. 98

T F It is harmless to the embryo and fetus for a pregnant woman to have a couple of glasses of wine in the evening. p. 100

Preview

The Germinal Stage: Wanderings
Without Visible Means of Support . . .

The Embryonic Stage
Sexual Differentiation
The Amniotic Sac: A Shock Absorber
The Placenta: A Filtration System

The Fetal Stage
Fetal Perception: Bach at Breakfast and Beethoven at Brunch?
Fetal Movements

Developing in a World of Diversity: Birth Rates around the World

Environmental Influences on Prenatal Development
Nutrition
Teratogens and Health Problems of the Mother
Drugs Taken by the Parents

A Closer Look: Preventing One's Baby from Being Infected with HIV

Environmental Hazards
Maternal Stress
Parents' Age

Andrew O' Toole/Getty Images

 Go to

http://www.thomsonedu.com/psychology/rathus
for an interactive version of this "Truth or Fiction" feature.

ack in 1938, when rapping was still something that hurt the knuckles, L. W. Sontag and T. W. Richards reported the results of a study in fetal behavior. They stimulated pregnant women with methods such as ringing a bell and measured the results on the heart rate of the fetus, as assessed by an instrument on the mother's abdomen. Many of the mothers smoked, and the researchers assessed the effects of smoking on the fetal heart rate. They also got the fetus all shook up by placing a vibrator against the mother's abdomen.

Sontag and Richards learned that powerful vibrations usually induced faster heart rates in the fetus (big surprise?), but maternal smoking had less predictable effects on the fetus. Cigarette smoke contains nicotine, which is a stimulant, but smoke also reduces the supply of oxygen in the bloodstream, and oxygen is needed to fuel bursts of activity. How could the researchers spend their time assessing the effects of maternal smoking rather than warning the mothers that their smoking was placing their fetuses at risk for low birth weight, prematurity, short attention span, academic problems, or hyperactivity? It was 1938, and little was known of the harmful effects of smoking.

In any event, Sontag and Richards also discovered that fetuses are sensitive to sound waves during the last months of pregnancy, which has led to a wave of more recent research, including research into whether **neonates** are "loyal" and prefer their mothers' voices to those of strangers and whether listening to classical rather than heavy metal music during pregnancy has noticeable effects (on the neonate's brain as well as heart rate). Stay tuned. Researchers are finding that the most rapid and dramatic human developments are literally "out of sight" and take place in the uterus. Within 9 months, a fetus develops from a nearly microscopic cell to a neonate about 20 inches long. Its weight increases a billionfold.

We can date pregnancy from the onset of the last menstrual period before conception, which makes the normal gestation period 280 days. We can also date pregnancy from the assumed date of fertilization, which normally occurs 2 weeks after the beginning of the woman's last menstrual cycle. With this accounting method, the gestation period is 266 days.

Soon after conception, the single cell formed by the union of sperm and egg begins to multiply, becoming two cells, then four, then eight, and so on. During the weeks and months that follow, tissues, organs, and structures begin to form, and the fetus gradually takes on the unmistakable shape of a human being. By the time a fetus is born, it consists of hundreds of billions of cells, more cells than there are stars in the Milky Way galaxy. Prenatal development is divided into three periods: the germinal stage (approximately the first 2 weeks), the embryonic stage (the third through the eighth weeks), and the fetal stage (the third month through birth). Health professionals also commonly speak of prenatal development in terms of three trimesters of 3 months each.

The Germinal Stage: Wanderings

Question: What happens during the germinal stage of prenatal development?
Within 36 hours after conception, the zygote divides into two cells. It then divides repeatedly as it proceeds on its journey to the uterus. Within another 36 hours, it has become 32 cells. It takes the zygote 3 to 4 days to reach the uterus. The mass of dividing cells wanders about the uterus for another 3 to 4 days before it begins to become implanted in the uterine wall. Implantation takes another week or so. The period from conception to implantation is called the **germinal stage** (see ● Figure 3.1).

A few days into the germinal stage, the dividing cell mass takes the form of a fluid-filled ball of cells called a **blastocyst**. A blastocyst already shows cell differentiation.

neonate A newborn baby.

germinal stage The period of development between conception and the implantation of the embryo.

blastocyst A stage within the germinal period of prenatal development in which the zygote has the form of a sphere of cells surrounding a cavity of fluid.

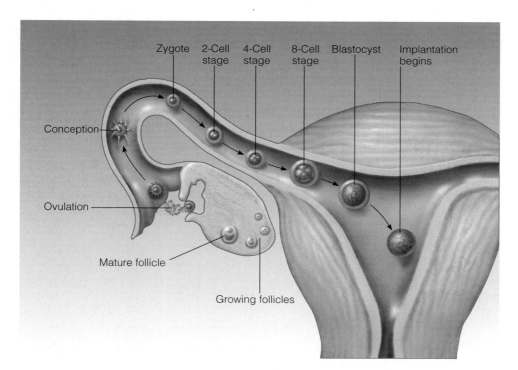

See your student companion website for an interactive version of Figure 3.1.

● **Figure 3.1**   The Ovarian Cycle, Conception, and the Early Days of the Germinal Stage

The zygote first divides approximately 36 hours after conception. Continuing division creates the hollow sphere of cells termed the blastocyst. The blastocyst normally becomes implanted in the wall of the uterus.

Cells begin to separate into groups that will eventually become different structures. The inner part of the blastocyst has two distinct layers of cells that form a thickened mass of cells called the **embryonic disk**. These cells will become the embryo and eventually the fetus.

The outer part of the blastocyst, or **trophoblast**, at first consists of a single layer of cells, but it rapidly differentiates into four membranes that will protect and nourish the embryo. One membrane produces blood cells until the embryo's liver develops and takes over this function. Then that membrane disappears. Another membrane develops into the **umbilical cord** and the blood vessels of the **placenta**. A third develops into the amniotic sac, and the fourth becomes the chorion, which will line the placenta.

Without Visible Means of Support . . .

Question: If the dividing mass of cells is moving through a fallopian tube and then "wandering" through the uterus for another few days, how does it obtain any nourishment?

Although people are not chickens, the dividing cluster of cells that will become the embryo and then the fetus is at first nourished only by the yolk of the egg cell, just like a chick developing in an egg. **Truth or Fiction Revisited:** It is true that newly fertilized egg cells survive without any nourishment from the mother for more than a week. They are nourished by the yolk of the ovum until they implant in the wall of the uterus. Therefore, they make no gains in mass. A blastocyst gains mass only when it receives nourishment from the outside. For that to happen, it must be implanted in the wall of the uterus.

embryonic disk The platelike inner part of the blastocyst that differentiates into the ectoderm, mesoderm, and endoderm of the embryo.

trophoblast The outer part of the blastocyst from which the amniotic sac, placenta, and umbilical cord develop.

umbilical cord A tube that connects the fetus to the placenta.

placenta (pluh-SEN-tuh) An organ connected to the uterine wall and to the fetus by the umbilical cord. The placenta serves as a relay station between mother and fetus for the exchange of nutrients and wastes.

Implantation may be accompanied by some bleeding, which is usually normal and results from the rupturing of small blood vessels that line the uterus.

Bleeding can also be a sign of miscarriage (which is also called spontaneous abortion). However, most women who experience implantation bleeding do not miscarry, but go on to have normal pregnancies and normal babies. Miscarriage usually stems from abnormalities in the developmental process. Many women miscarry early in pregnancy, but their menstrual flow appears about on schedule so that they may not even realize they had conceived. Nearly one-third of all pregnancies result in miscarriage, with most miscarriages occurring in the first 3 months (Miscarriage, 2007). Women who have miscarriages tend to experience a good deal of anxiety for several months afterward and especially during the early months of subsequent pregnancies (Geller et al., 2004).

Active Review

1. A few days into the germinal stage, the dividing cell mass becomes a fluid-filled ball of cells that is called a _____.
2. The outer part of the blastocyst—called the _____—differentiates into membranes that will protect and nourish the embryo.
3. The dividing cluster of cells is nourished by the yolk of the ovum before _____.

Reflect & Relate: Most of us have known—or have been—pregnant women. What early signs made the women suspect that they were pregnant? How do these signs fit with what was happening in their bodies?

Go to

http://www.thomsonedu.com/psychology/rathus

for an interactive version of this review.

---

embryonic stage The stage of prenatal development that lasts from implantation through the eighth week of pregnancy; it is characterized by the development of the major organ systems.

cephalocaudal From head to tail.

proximodistal From the inner part (or axis) of the body outward.

ectoderm The outermost cell layer of the newly formed embryo from which the skin and nervous system develop.

neural tube A hollowed-out area in the blastocyst from which the nervous system develops.

endoderm The inner layer of the embryo from which the lungs and digestive system develop.

The Embryonic Stage

The **embryonic stage** begins with implantation and covers the first 2 months during which the major organ systems differentiate. *Question: What happens during the embryonic stage of prenatal development?* Development follows two general trends: **cephalocaudal** (Latin for "head to tail") and **proximodistal** (Latin for "near to far"). The apparently oversized heads of embryos and fetuses at various stages of prenatal development show that growth of the head takes precedence over growth of the lower parts of the body (see ● Figure 3.2). You can also think of the body as containing a central axis that coincides with the spinal cord. The growth of the organ systems close to this axis (i.e., in close proximity to the axis) occurs earlier than the growth of the extremities, which are farther away (i.e., distant from the axis). Relatively early maturation of the brain and organ systems that lie near the central axis allows these organs to play important roles in the subsequent development of the embryo and fetus.

During the embryonic stage, the outer layer of cells of the embryonic disk, or **ectoderm**, develops into the nervous system, sensory organs, nails, hair, teeth, and outer layer of skin. At approximately 21 days, two ridges appear in the embryo and fold to compose the **neural tube**, from which the nervous system will develop. The inner layer, or **endoderm**, forms the digestive and respiratory systems, the liver, and the pancreas. A bit later during the embryonic stage, the mesoderm, a middle

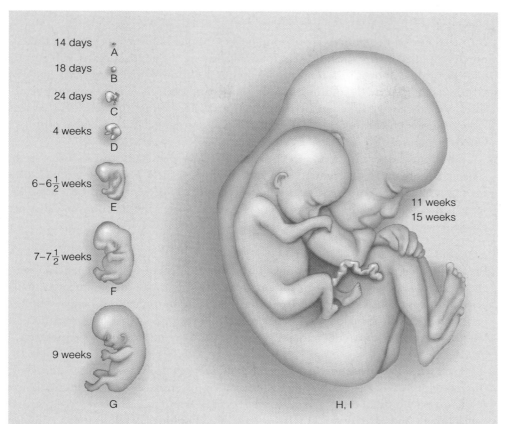

● **Figure 3.2**
Human Embryos and Fetuses at Various Stages of Development

Development proceeds in cephalocaudal and proximodistal directions. Development of the head takes precedence over development of the lower parts of the body, enabling the brain to be involved in subsequent developments.

layer of cells, becomes differentiated. The **mesoderm** develops into the excretory, reproductive, and circulatory systems, the muscles, the skeleton, and the inner layer of the skin.

During the third week after conception, the head and blood vessels begin to form. *Question: When does the heart begin to beat?* **Truth or Fiction Revisited:** It is true that your heart started beating when you were only one-fourth of an inch long and weighed a fraction of an ounce. The major organ systems develop within the first 2 months of pregnancy. The heart will continue to beat without rest every minute of every day for perhaps 80 or 90 years.

Question: What else happens during the embryonic stage? Arm buds and leg buds begin to appear toward the end of the first month. Eyes, ears, nose, and mouth begin to take shape. By this time, the nervous system, including the brain, has also begun to develop. In accord with the principle of proximodistal development, the upper arms and legs develop before the forearms and lower legs. Next come hands and feet, followed at 6 to 8 weeks by webbed fingers and toes. By the end of the second month, the limbs are elongating and separated, and the webbing is gone. By this time, the embryo is looking quite human. The head has the lovely, round shape of your own, and the facial features have become quite distinct. Bear in mind that all this detail is inscribed on an embryo that is only approximately 1 inch long and weighs only about 1/30th of an ounce. During the second month of embryonic development, the cells in the nervous system begins to "fire"; that is, they send messages among themselves. Most likely, it is random cell firing, and the "content" of such "messages" is anybody's guess. (No, the embryo isn't contemplating Toni Morrison or Einstein.) By the end of the embryonic period, teeth buds have formed. The embryo's kidneys are filtering acid from the blood, and its liver is producing red blood cells.

mesoderm The central layer of the embryo from which the bones and muscles develop.

Sexual Differentiation

By 5 to 6 weeks, the embryo is only one-quarter to one-half inch long. Nevertheless, nondescript sex organs, including the internal and external genital organs, will already have formed, as shown in ● Figures 3.3 and ● 3.4. Both female and male embryos possess a pair of sexually undifferentiated gonads and two sets of primitive duct structures, the so-called Müllerian (female) ducts and the Wolffian (male) ducts. At this stage of development, both the internal and the external genitals resemble primitive female structures.

By about the seventh week, the genetic code (XY or XX) begins to assert itself, causing sex organs to differentiate. Genetic activity on the Y sex chromosome causes the testes to begin to differentiate. The ovaries begin to differentiate if the Y chromosome is *absent*. By about 4 months after conception, males and females show distinct external genital structures.

Sex Hormones and Sexual Differentiation

Prenatal sexual differentiation requires hormonal influences as well as genetic influences. Male sex hormones—**androgens**—are critical in the development of male genital organs. **Truth or Fiction Revisited:** Without androgens, all people whether genetically female or male would develop external sex organs that look like those of females. However, apparent "females" with an XY sex chromosomal structure would be infertile.

Once the testes have developed in the embryo, they begin to produce androgens, the most important of which is **testosterone**. Testosterone spurs the differentiation of the male (Wolffian) duct system (see ● Figure 3.3) and remains involved in sexual development and activity for a lifetime. Each Wolffian duct develops into a complex

androgens Male sex hormones (from roots meaning "giving birth to men").

testosterone A male sex hormone—a steroid—that is produced by the testes and that promotes growth of male sexual characteristics and sperm.

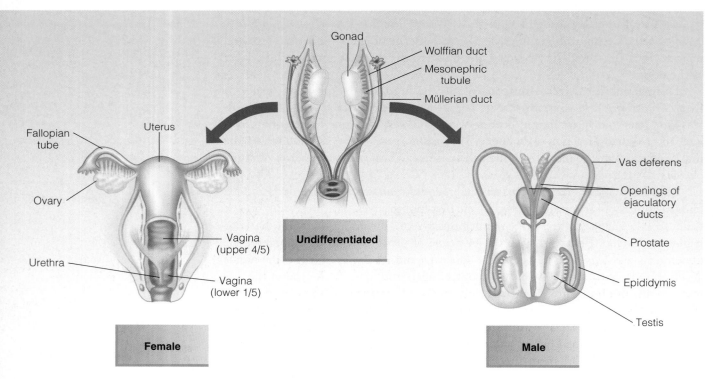

 *See your student companion website for an interactive version of Figure 3.3.*

● **Figure 3.3** Development of the Internal Genital Organs from an Age of 5–6 Weeks Following Conception

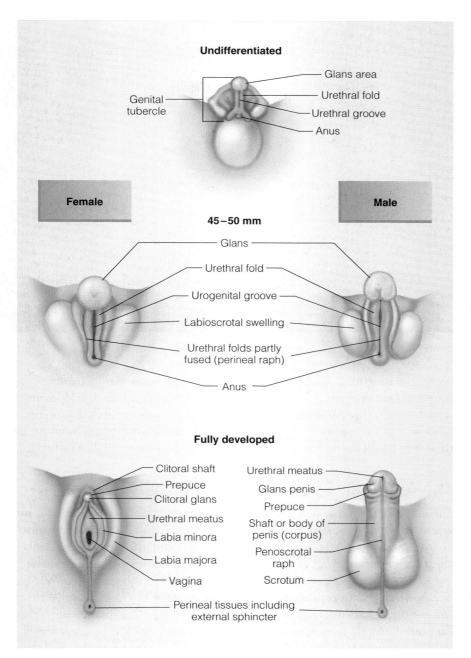

See your student companion website for an interactive version of Figure 3.4.

● **Figure 3.4** Development of the External Genital Organs from an Undifferentiated Stage at 5–6 Weeks Following Conception

maze of ducts and storage facilities for sperm. At about the eighth week of prenatal development, another androgen, dihydrotestosterone (DHT), spurs the formation of the external male genital organs, including the penis. Yet another testicular hormone, secreted somewhat later, prevents the Müllerian ducts from developing into the female duct system. That hormone is labeled Müllerian inhibiting substance (MIS).

Female embryos and fetuses do produce small amounts of androgens, but they are usually not enough to cause sexual differentiation along male lines. However, they do play important roles in the development of some secondary sexual characteristics in adolescence, such as the appearance of pubic hair and underarm hair. Androgens are also important in the sex drive of females for a lifetime (Morley & Perry, 2003;

A Human Embryo at 7 Weeks
At this late part of the embryonic stage, the major organ systems except for the sex organs have already become differentiated.

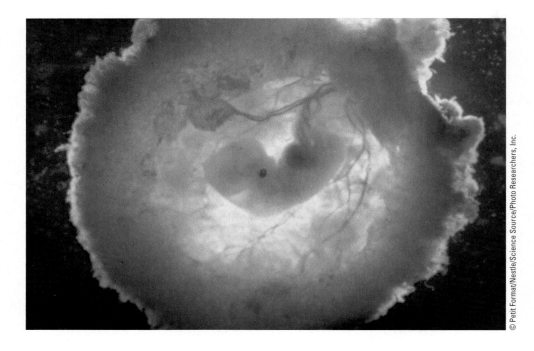

Nyunt, et al., 2005). But in the female embryo and fetus, low levels of androgens are connected with degeneration of the Wolffian ducts and further development of female sexual organs. The Müllerian ducts develop into fallopian tubes, the uterus, and the inner part of the vagina. The presence of the female sex hormones is not necessary for these developments to occur, although they will become crucial in puberty.

The Amniotic Sac: A Shock Absorber

The embryo and fetus develop suspended within a protective **amniotic sac** in the uterus. This sac is surrounded by a clear membrane and contains **amniotic fluid**. The fluid serves as a kind of natural air bag, allowing the embryo and fetus to move around without injury. It also helps maintain an even temperature in the sac.

Questions: How does the embryo get nourishment from its mother? How does it eliminate waste products? The answers to these questions involve the placenta and the umbilical cord. The placenta is a mass of tissue that permits the embryo (and, later on, the fetus) to exchange nutrients and wastes with the mother. The placenta is unique in origin. It grows from material supplied by both the mother and the embryo. The fetus is connected to the placenta by the umbilical cord. The mother is connected to the placenta by the system of blood vessels in the uterine wall.

The Placenta: A Filtration System

Question: Do germs or drugs in the mother pass through the placenta and affect the embryo? In one of the more fascinating feats of prenatal engineering, it turns out that the mother and embryo have separate circulatory systems. The mother's bloodstream is hers, and the embryo's bloodstream is the embryo's. The pancake-shaped placenta contains a membrane that acts as a filter, and only certain substances can pass through it. The membrane permits oxygen and nutrients to reach the embryo from the mother. It also permits carbon dioxide (which is the gas you breathe out and plants "breathe" in) and waste products to pass to the mother from the embryo. Once the mother has them, she eliminates them through her lungs and kidneys. That is the good part. It also happens that a number of harmful substances can sneak through

amniotic sac The sac containing the fetus.

amniotic fluid Fluid within the amniotic sac that suspends and protects the fetus.

the placenta, including various "germs" (microscopic disease-causing organisms), such as the ones that cause syphilis (a bacterium called *Treponema pallidum*), German measles, and, to some degree, AIDS. The good news here is that most pregnant women who are infected with HIV (the virus that causes AIDS) do not transmit it to the embryo through the placenta. HIV is more likely to be transmitted through childbirth. But some drugs—aspirin, narcotics, alcohol, tranquilizers, and others—do cross the placenta and can affect the fetus in one way or another.

The placenta also secretes hormones that preserve the pregnancy, prepare the breasts for nursing, and stimulate the uterine contractions that prompt childbirth. Ultimately, the placenta passes from the woman's body after the child is delivered. For this reason, it is also called the afterbirth.

Active Review

4. The embryo and fetus develop within an _____ sac, which functions as a shock absorber among other things.
5. Development follows two general trends: cephalocaudal and _____.
6. The (Inner or Outer?) layer of cells of the ectoderm develops into the nervous system, sensory organs, and the outer layer of skin.
7. Without sex hormones, all embryos would develop the appearance of being (Males or Females?).

8. The _____ permits the embryo to exchange nutrients and wastes with the mother.
9. The embryo and fetus are connected to the placenta by the _____.

Reflect & Relate: Are you surprised at how early the heart begins to beat and at the size of the embryo at the time? Explain.

Go to

http://www.thomsonedu.com/psychology/rathus

for an interactive version of this review.

The Fetal Stage

The **fetal stage** lasts from the beginning of the third month until birth. *Question: What happens during the fetal stage of prenatal development?* The fetus begins to turn and respond to external stimulation at about the ninth or tenth week. By the end of the first trimester, all the major organ systems have been formed. The fingers and toes are fully formed. The eyes can be clearly distinguished, and the sex of the fetus can be determined visually.

The second trimester is characterized by further maturation of fetal organ systems and dramatic gains in size. The brain continues to mature, contributing to the fetus's ability to regulate its own basic body functions. During the second trimester, the fetus advances from 1 ounce to 2 pounds in weight and grows four to five times in length, from about 3 inches to 14 inches. Soft, downy hair grows above the eyes and on the scalp. The skin turns ruddy because of blood vessels that show through the surface. (During the third trimester, fatty layers will give the skin a pinkish hue.)

By the end of the second trimester, the fetus opens and shuts its eyes, sucks its thumb, alternates between periods of wakefulness and sleep, and perceives light and

fetal stage The stage of development that lasts from the beginning of the ninth week of pregnancy through birth; it is characterized by gains in size and weight and by maturation of the organ systems.

A Human Fetus at 12 Weeks

By the end of the first trimester, formation of all the major organ systems is complete. Fingers and toes are fully formed, and the sex of the fetus can be determined visually.

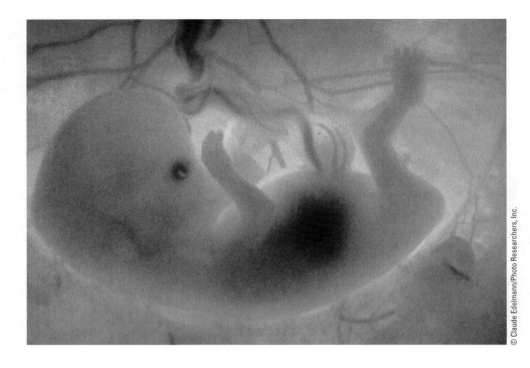

© Claude Edelmann/Photo Researchers, Inc.

sounds. **Truth or Fiction Revisited:** There are also sharp spasms of the diaphragm, or fetal hiccups, which may last for hours (ask a weary pregnant woman).

About half of babies who are born at 22 to 25 weeks of gestation will survive, and the survival rate is connected with the quality of the medical care they receive (Rogowski et al., 2004).

During the third trimester, the organ systems of the fetus continue to mature. The heart and lungs become increasingly capable of sustaining independent life. The fetus gains about 5½ pounds and doubles in length. Newborn boys average about 7½ pounds and newborn girls about 7 pounds.

During the seventh month, the fetus normally turns upside down in the uterus so that delivery will be head first. By the end of the seventh month, the fetus will have almost doubled in weight, gaining another 1 pound, 12 ounces, and will have increased another 2 inches in length. If born now, chances of survival are nearly

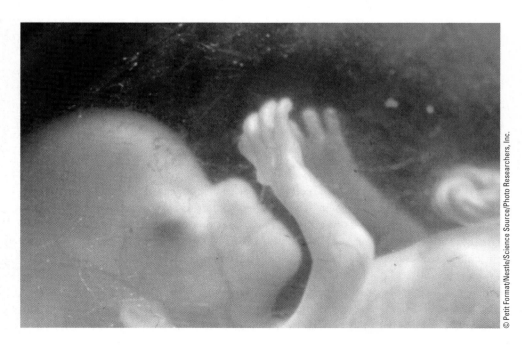

A Human Fetus at 4½ Months

At this midway point between conception and birth, the fetus is covered with fine, downy hair, called lanugo.

© Petit Format/Nestle/Science Source/Photo Researchers, Inc.

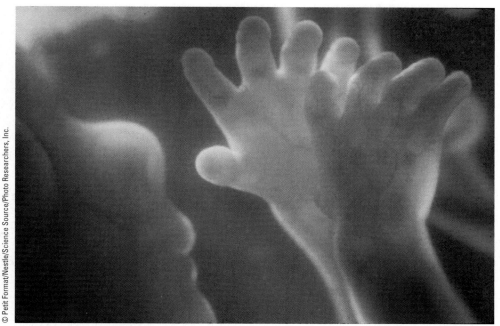

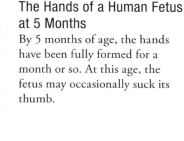

The Hands of a Human Fetus at 5 Months
By 5 months of age, the hands have been fully formed for a month or so. At this age, the fetus may occasionally suck its thumb.

90%. If born at the end of the eighth month, the odds are overwhelmingly in favor of survival.

Fetal Perception: Bach at Breakfast and Beethoven at Brunch?

Question: Why did my Aunt Margaret play classical music (and put the speakers near her abdomen) when she was 7 months pregnant? I never met your Aunt Margaret, so I can't be sure about the answer, but I'll share something with you. When I was a beginning graduate student and thought I knew everything, I was astounded by what I thought was the naïveté of parents-to-be who listened to Bach or Beethoven or who read Shakespeare aloud to promote the cultural development of their fetuses. But in more recent years, I admit that my wife and I have made more of an effort to expose our fetuses to good music as well.

Why? Classic research shows that by the 13th week of pregnancy, the fetus responds to sound waves. In research cited at the beginning of the chapter—and repeated here so that you cannot complain I sent you searching—Sontag and Richards (1938) rang a bell near the mother, and the fetus responded with movements similar to those of the startle reflex shown after birth. During the third trimester, fetuses respond to sounds of different frequencies through a variety of movements and changes in heart rate, suggesting that by this time they can discriminate pitch (Lecanuet et al., 2000).

An experiment by Anthony DeCasper and William Fifer (1980) is even more intriguing. In this study, women read the Dr. Seuss book *The Cat in the Hat* out loud twice daily during the final month and a half of pregnancy. After birth, their babies were given special pacifiers. Sucking on these pacifiers in one way would activate recordings of their mothers reading *The Cat in the Hat*, and sucking on them in another way would activate their mothers' readings of another book—*The King, the Mice, and the Cheese*—which was written in very different rhythms. The newborns "chose" to hear *The Cat in the Hat*. Using similar research methods, DeCasper and his colleagues also found that newborns prefer the mother's voice to that of their father or an unfamiliar woman (DeCasper & Prescott, 1984; DeCasper & Spence, 1986, 1991). Fetal learning may be one basis for the development of attachment to the mother (Krueger et al., 2004; Lecanuet, et al., 2005; Roth et al., 2004).

Perhaps Bach at breakfast and Beethoven at brunch may not be a bad idea during the later days of pregnancy. It might do more than help the food go down.

Fetal Movements

Now we know that the fetus can hear toward the end of the pregnancy. *Question: When does the mother begin to detect fetal movements?* The mother usually feels the first fetal movements in the middle of the fourth month (Adolph & Berger, 2005). By 29–30 weeks, the mother gets her kicks—that is, the fetus moves its limbs so vigorously that the mother may complain of being kicked—often at 4 a.m. The fetus also turns somersaults, which are clearly felt by the mother. The umbilical cord will not break or become dangerously wrapped around the fetus, no matter how many acrobatic feats the fetus performs.

Concept Review 3.1   Highlights of Prenatal Development

First Trimester

Period of the Ovum
First 2 weeks

- Dividing cluster of cells enters and moves around the uterus, living off the yolk of the egg cell.
- Blastocyst becomes implanted in the wall of uterus, possibly accompanied by implantation bleeding.

© David M. Phillips/Photo Researchers, Inc.

Embryonic Stage
3 weeks

- Head and blood vessels form.
- Brain begins to develop.

4 weeks

- Heart begins to beat and pump blood.
- Arm buds and leg buds appear.
- Eyes, ears, nose, and mouth form.
- Nerves begin to develop.
- Umbilical cord is functional.
- Embryo weighs a fraction of an ounce and is half an inch long.

© Petit Format/Nestle/Science Source/Photo Researchers, Inc.

5–8 weeks

- Hands and feet develop with webbed fingers and toes.
- Undifferentiated sex organs appear.
- Teeth buds develop.
- Kidneys filter uric acid from the blood; liver produces blood cells.
- Bone cells appear.
- Head is half the length of the entire body.
- Embryo weighs about 1/13th of an ounce and is 1 inch long.

Fetal Stage
9–12 weeks

- All major organ systems are formed.
- Fingers and toes are fully formed.
- Eyes can be clearly distinguished.
- Sex of fetus can be determined visually (e.g., by ultrasound).
- Mouth opens and closes; fetus swallows.
- Fetus responds to external stimulation.
- Fetus weighs 1 ounce and is 3 inches long.
- Mother detects fetal movement.

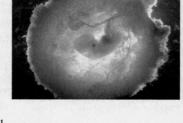

© Claude Edelmann/Photo Researchers, Inc.

Fetuses show different patterns of prenatal activity (de Vries & Hopkins, 2005). Slow squirming movements begin at about 5 or 6 months. Sharp jabbing or kicking movements begin at about the same time and increase in intensity until shortly before birth. As the fetus grows, it becomes cramped in the uterus, and its movement is constricted. Many women become concerned that their fetuses are markedly less active during the ninth month than previously, but most of the time this change is normal.

Although there are individual differences in level of fetal activity, a Dutch study found no sex differences in fetal movement (Robles de Medina et al., 2003). Moreover, prenatal activity predicts activity levels after birth. For instance, highly active fetuses show more advanced motor development after birth than do their more lethargic counterparts (de Vries & Hopkins, 2005).

Concept Review 3.1 highlights key events during prenatal development.

Second Trimester

13–16 weeks
- Many reflexes are present.
- Fingernails and toenails form.
- Head is about one-fourth the length of the body.

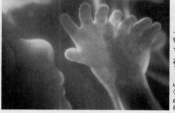

17–20 weeks
- Hair develops on head.
- Fine, downy hair (lanugo) covers body.
- Fetus sucks its thumb and hiccups.
- Heartbeat can be heard when listener presses head against mother's abdomen.

© Petit Format/Nestle/Science Source/Photo Researchers, Inc.

21–24 weeks
- Eyes open and shut.
- Light and sounds can be perceived.
- Fetus alternates between periods of wakefulness and sleep.
- Skin looks ruddy because blood vessels show through the surface.
- Survival rate is low if fetus is born.
- Fetus weighs about 2 pounds and is 14 inches long; growth rate is slowing down.

Third Trimester

25–28 weeks
- Organ systems continue to mature.
- Fatty layer begins to develop beneath the skin.
- Fetus turns head down in the uterus.
- Fetus cries, swallows, and sucks its thumb.
- Chances of survival are good if born.
- Fetus weighs 3 to 4 pounds and is 16 inches long.

© Ansell Horn/Phototake

29 to 36–38 weeks
- Organ systems function well.
- Fatty layer continues to develop.
- Fetal activity level decreases in the weeks before birth as a result of crowding.
- Weight increases to an average of 7–7½ pounds; boys are about half a pound heavier than girls; length increases to about 20 inches.

Developing in a World of Diversity

Let's have a look at some history and some pre-history—that is, some guesstimates of events that might have occurred before records were made. According to the U.S. Census Bureau[1] (http://www.census .gov/ipc/www/worldhis.html), which was *not* distributing questionnaires at the time, some 5 million humans walked the Earth about 10,000 years ago. It took another 5,000 years for that number to expand to 14 million. Skipping ahead 3,000 years to the year 1, humans gained a stronger foothold on the planet, and the number increased tenfold, to some 170 million. By 1900 the number increased ten- to twentyfold

(continued, page 92)

■ **Table 3.1** Fertility Rates and Related Factors Around the World

Nation	Fertility Rates	Rate of Usage of Modern Methods of Contraception (%)	Literacy Rates (%) Men	Literacy Rates (%) Women	Years of Education Men	Years of Education Women
Afghanistan	7.48	3.6	43	13	9	4
Algeria	2.53	50.1	80	60	13	13
Angola	6.75	4.5	83	54	4	3
Argentina	2.35	a	97	97	15	16
Australia	1.75	72.2	a	a	20	20
Bolivia	3.96	34.9	93	81	a	a
Brazil	2.35	70.3	88	89	14	14
Cambodia	4.14	18.5	85	64	11	9
Canada	1.51	73.3	a	a	15	16
Chile	2.00	a	96	96	14	14
China	1.70	83.3	95	87	11	11
Colombia	2.62	67.6	93	93	11	12
Congo	6.70	4.4	81	54	4[b]	4[b]
Costa Rica	2.28	70.7	93	93	a	a
Cuba	1.61	72.1	100	100	14	14
Denmark	1.75	72.0	a	a	16	17
Dominican Republic	2.73	65.8	87	87	12	13
Equador	2.82	50.1	92	90	a	a
Egypt	3.29	56.5	83	59	12[b]	12[b]
France	1.87	69.3	a	a	15	16
Germany	1.32	71.8	a	a	16	16
Ghana	4.39	18.7	66	50	8	7
Greece	1.25	a	98	94	15	16
Guatemala	4.60	34.4	75	63	10	9
Honduras	3.72	50.8	80	80	11	12
India	3.07	42.8	73	48	11	9
Indonesia	2.37	56.7	94	87	12	12

(continued on page 91)

■ Table 3.1 (continued)

Nation	Fertility Rates	Rate of Usage of Modern Methods of Contraception (%)	Literacy Rates (%)		Years of Education	
			Men	Women	Men	Women
Iran	2.12	56.0	84	70	13	12
Iraq	4.83	10.4	84	64	11	8
Ireland	1.94	a	a	a	18	18
Israel	2.85	51.9	98	96	15	16
Italy	1.28	38.9	99	98	16	16
Jamaica	2.44	62.6	74	86	11	12
Japan	1.33	51.0	a	a	15	15
Jordan	3.53	41.2	95	85	13	13
Kenya	5.00	31.5	78	70	10	10
Lithuania	1.28	30.5	100	100	15	16
Mali	6.92	5.7	27	12	6	5
Mexico	2.40	59.5	92	90	13	13
Morocco	2.76	54.8	66	40	11	9
Nicaragua	3.30	66.1	77	77	11	11
Pakistan	4.27	20.2	63	36	7	5
Palestinian Territories	5.57	37.1	97	88	13	14
Peru	2.86	50.4	93	82	14	14
Philippines	3.22	33.4	93	93	12	12
Russia	1.33		100	99	13	14
Saudi Arabia	4.09	28.5	87	69	10	10
Spain	1.27	67.4	a	a	16	17
Syria	3.47	28.3	86	74	a	a
Thailand	1.93	69.8	95	91	13	13
Turkey	2.46	37.7	95	80	12	10
Viet Nam	2.32		94	87	11	10
United Kingdom	1.66	81.0	a	a	16	17
United States of America	2.04	70.5	a	a	15	16

Sources: United Nations Department of Economic and Social Affairs, Demographic and Social Statistics, Social Indicators. Available at http://unstats.un.org/unsd/demographic/products/socind/default.htm (accessed April 1, 2007). Total fertility rate estimates from Population Division of the United Nations Secretariat, *World Population Prospects: Various Editions* (United Nations, Department of Economic and Social Affairs, Population Division, 2005), *World Contraceptive Use 2005, CD-ROM Edition*; data in digital form (POP/DB/CP/Rev. 2005); supplemented by contraceptive use data published by ORC Macro, available at http://www.measuredhs.com (accessed July 17, 2006). UNESCO Institute for Statistics, Table 8: School life expectancy (approximation method). Data on school life expectancy (years) from primary to tertiary by country and sex, available from UIS website, http://www.uis.unesco.org (last updated June 20, 2006).

[a]Data missing or unavailable at the United Nations website. It is not possible to draw conclusions of any kind.

[b]Number of years is for males and females combined because the numbers provided by the nation did not permit categorization by sex.

Developing in a World of Diversity

Birth Rates around the World (*continued*)

again, to more than 1.7 billion. In 1950 estimates place the number at about 2.5 billion, and today—with the increase in the food supply, sanitary water supplies, and vaccinations—the number is estimated to be at about 6.7 billion.

Therefore, we are in the middle of a population explosion, are we not? The answer would seem to depend on where one happens to be. **Truth or Fiction Revisited:** For example, if you check out ■ Table 3.1, you will readily see that it is not true that parents in wealthy nations have more children. Parents need to have slightly in excess of two children to reproduce themselves because some children are lost to illness, accidents, or violence. The table will show you that in countries such as Spain, Greece, Italy, Japan, Canada, Russia, and the United Kingdom, parents are not coming close to reproducing themselves. In some cases,

the national birth rates mask major differences within a country. In Israel, for example, the minorities of Orthodox Jews and Arabs out-reproduce the majority of less religious or non-religious Jews, providing an overall somewhat inflated birth rate.

Also consider factors related to birth rates, such as use of modern means of contraception, literacy rates, and education, as measured by numbers of years spent in school. Consider the extremes. How do the birth rates of countries where 30% or fewer of the population use modern means of contraception compare with those where 60% or more use modern means? Similarly, what are the relationships between literacy and birth rate? Between education and birth rate?

I will now ask you to reflect upon some questions but I will not "spoon feed" you the answers. You

can develop your own views on the basis of your moral values or research.

[1]U.S. Census Bureau. Historical estimates of world population. http://www.census.gov/ipc/www/worldhis.html. Accessed 2 April, 2007.

Reflect:

- *How would you judge whether a particular birth rate in a particular nation is a good thing or a bad thing? If it is a bad thing, what can be done about it? Explain your views.*
- *Why do parents in wealthier nations tend to have fewer children? What are your feelings about this? Explain your views.*
- *Does the information in Table 3.1 show cause and effect? Why or why not?*

Active Review

10. The fetal stage is characterized by _____ of organ systems and gains in size and weight.
11. Research shows that fetuses respond to sound waves by about the _____ week of pregnancy.
12. Mothers usually detect fetal movements during the _____ month of pregnancy.

Reflect & Relate: During the fourth month, when the fetus's movements can be detected, many women have the feeling that their babies are "alive." What is your view on when the baby is alive? What standard or standards are you using to form your opinion?

Go to

http://www.thomsonedu.com/psychology/rathus
for an interactive version of this review.

Environmental Influences on Prenatal Development

Yes, the fetus develops in a protective "bubble," the amniotic sac. Nevertheless, the developing fetus is subject to many environmental hazards. Scientific advances have made us keenly aware of the types of things that can go wrong and what we can do to prevent these problems. In this section, we consider some environmental factors that can affect prenatal development.

Nutrition

Question: How does the nutrition of the mother affect prenatal development? We quickly bring nutrition inside, but nutrition originates outside. Therefore, it is one environmental factor in prenatal (and subsequent) development.

It is a common misconception that fetuses "take what they need" from their mothers. If that were true, pregnant women would not have to be highly concerned about their diets, but malnutrition in the mother, especially during the last trimester when the fetus should be making rapid gains in weight, has been linked to low birth weight, prematurity, stunted growth, retardation of brain development, cognitive deficiencies, behavioral problems, and even cardiovascular disease (Giussani, 2006; Guerrini et al., 2007; Morton, 2006).

Fortunately, the effects of fetal malnutrition can sometimes be overcome by a supportive, care-giving environment. Experiments with children who suffered from fetal malnutrition show that enriched day-care programs enhance intellectual and social skills by 5 years of age (Ramey et al., 1999). Supplementing the diets of pregnant women who might otherwise be deficient in their intake of calories and protein also shows modest positive effects on the motor development of the women's infants (Morton, 2006).

On the other hand, maternal obesity is linked with a higher risk of **stillbirth** (Fernandez-Twinn & Ozanne, 2006). Obesity during pregnancy also increases the likelihood of neural tube defects. In a study reported in the *Journal of the American Medical Association*, women who weighed 176 to 195 pounds before pregnancy were about twice as likely as women who weighed 100 to 130 pounds to bear children with neural tube defects; women who weighed 242 pounds or more were four times as likely to have children with neural tube defects (Shaw et al., 1996). Note that these findings were for obese women only. Very tall women normally weigh more than shorter women, so the study's findings must be considered in terms of women's desirable weights for a given height. In Shaw's study, folic acid supplements did not appear to prevent neural tube defects in the babies of women who weighed more than 154 pounds.

What Should a Pregnant Woman Eat?

Pregnant women require the following food elements to maintain themselves and to give birth to healthy babies: protein, which is heavily concentrated in red meat, fish, poultry, eggs, beans, milk, and cheese; vitamin A, which is found in milk and vegetables; vitamin B, which is found in wheat germ, whole grain breads, and liver; vitamin C, which is found in citrus fruits; vitamin D, which is derived from sunshine, fish-liver oil, and vitamin D–fortified milk; vitamin E, which is found in whole grains, some vegetables, eggs, and peanuts; iron, which is concentrated heavily in meat (especially liver), egg yolks, fish, and raisins; the trace minerals zinc and cobalt, which are found in seafood; calcium, which is found in dairy products; and, yes, calories. Research also demonstrates the importance of consuming folic acid, which is found in leafy green vegetables. Women who eat a well-rounded diet do not require food

stillbirth The birth of a dead fetus.

supplements, but most doctors recommend them to be safe (Balluz et al., 2000). Pregnant women who take folic acid supplements reduce the risk of giving birth to babies with neural tube defects, which can cause paralysis and death (Honein et al., 2001; Lawrence et al., 2003).

How Much Weight Should a Pregnant Woman Gain?

Women can expect to gain quite a bit of weight during pregnancy because of the growth of the placenta, amniotic fluid, and the fetus itself. Women who do not restrict their diet during pregnancy normally will gain 25 to 35 pounds. Overweight women may gain less, and slender women may gain more. Regular weight gains of about 0.5 pound per week during the first half of pregnancy and 1 pound per week during the second half are most desirable. Sudden large gains or losses in weight should be discussed with the doctor.

Over the years, the pendulum has swung back and forth between views of ideal weight gains during pregnancy. Early in the 20th century, it was believed that greater weight gains would ensure proper nutrition for both the mother and the fetus. During the 1960s and part of the 1970s, pregnant women were advised to watch their weight. It was believed that excess weight posed risks for the mother and might be hard to take off following pregnancy, concerns with some basis in fact. But now the pendulum has swung back again. It is now known that inadequate weight gain in pregnancy increases the chances of having a premature or low-birth-weight baby (Bhutta et al., 2002; Christian et al., 2003; Hynes et al., 2002). Women who gain 25 to 35 pounds during pregnancy are more likely to have healthy babies than those who gain less. But a woman in the seventh or eighth month who finds herself overshooting a weight-gain target of, say, 25–30 pounds, should avoid a crash diet, especially when the fetus is making its most dramatic gains in weight.

Teratogens and Health Problems of the Mother

Most of what the mother does for the embryo is not only remarkable but also healthful. There are exceptions, however. Consider the case of teratogens. **Teratogens** (the word derives from frightening roots meaning "giving birth to monsters") are environmental agents that can harm the embryo or fetus. Teratogens include drugs that the mother ingests, such as thalidomide (connected with birth deformities) and alcohol, and substances that the mother's body produces, such as Rh-positive antibodies. Another class of teratogens is the heavy metals, such as lead and mercury, which are toxic to the embryo. Hormones are healthful in countless ways—for example, they help maintain pregnancy. However, excessive quantities of hormones are harmful to the embryo. If the mother is exposed to radiation, that radiation can harm the embryo. Then, of course, disease-causing organisms—also called pathogens—such as bacteria and viruses are also teratogens. When it comes to pathogens, bigger is better for the embryo. That is, larger pathogens are less likely to pass through the placenta and affect the embryo, but smaller pathogens sneak through, including those that cause mumps, syphilis, measles, and chicken pox. Some disorders, such as toxemia, are not transmitted to the embryo or fetus, but instead they adversely affect the environment in which it develops.

Critical Periods of Vulnerability

Question: Does it matter when, during pregnancy, a woman is exposed to a teratogen? Exposure to particular teratogens is most harmful during **critical periods** that correspond to the times when organs are developing. **Truth or Fiction Revisited:** Therefore, the same disease organism or chemical agent that can do serious damage to a 6-week-old embryo may have no effect on a 4-month-old fetus. For example, the heart develops rapidly in the third to fifth weeks after conception. As you can see

teratogens Environmental influences or agents that can damage the embryo or fetus (from the Greek teras, meaning "monster").

critical period In this usage, a period during which an embryo is particularly vulnerable to a certain teratogen.

in ● Figure 3.5, the heart is most vulnerable to certain teratogens at this time. The arms and legs, which develop later, are most vulnerable in the fourth through eighth weeks. Because the major organ systems differentiate during the embryonic stage, the embryo is generally more vulnerable to teratogens than the fetus. Even so, many teratogens are harmful throughout the entire course of prenatal development.

Question: What are the effects of maternal health problems? Let us consider the effects of various health problems of the mother. We begin with sexually transmitted infections (STIs).

Sexually Transmitted Infections

The **syphilis** bacterium can cause miscarriage, stillbirth, or **congenital** syphilis. Routine blood tests early in pregnancy can diagnose syphilis. The syphilis bacterium is vulnerable to antibiotics, and rates of syphilis are currently low in Western nations. In addition, the bacterium does not readily cross the placental membrane early in pregnancy. The fetus will probably not contract syphilis if an infected mother is treated with antibiotics before the fourth month of pregnancy. However, an infected woman has about a 40% chance of having a child who is stillborn or dies shortly after birth (Centers for Disease Control and Prevention, 2006a). If the mother is not treated, the baby has a 40% to 70% chance of being infected in utero and of developing congenital syphilis. Approximately 12% of those infected die.

syphilis A sexually transmitted infection that, in advanced stages, can attack major organ systems.

congenital Present at birth; resulting from the prenatal environment.

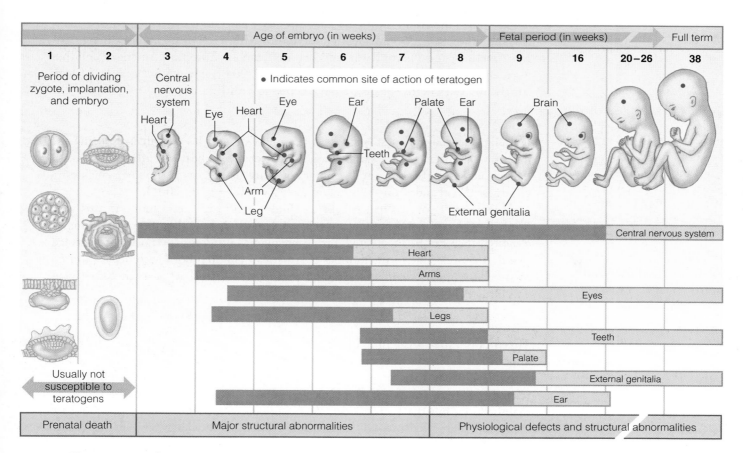

● **Figure 3.5** Critical Periods in Prenatal Development

Knowledge of the sequences of prenatal development allows one to understand why specific teratogens are most harmful during certain periods of prenatal development. Major structural abnormalities are most likely to occur when teratogens strike during the embryonic period.

Infected babies may show no symptoms when they are born, but they may develop symptoms within a few weeks if they are not treated. The symptoms of congenital syphilis include skin sores, a sometimes bloody (and infectious) runny nose, slimy patches in the mouth, inflamed bones in the arms and legs, a swollen liver, jaundice, anemia, and a small head. Congenital syphilis can impair vision and hearing, damage the liver, or deform the bones and teeth. Untreated babies may develop mental retardation or have seizures.

HIV/AIDS (human immunodeficiency virus/acquired immunodeficiency syndrome) disables the body's immune system and leaves victims prey to a variety of fatal illnesses, including respiratory disorders and cancer. HIV/AIDS is lethal unless treated with a combination of antiviral drugs. Even then, the drugs do not work for everyone, and the eventual outcome remains in doubt (Rathus et al., 2008).

HIV can be transmitted by sexual relations, blood transfusions, sharing hypodermic needles while shooting up drugs, childbirth, and breast feeding. About one-fourth of babies born to HIV-infected mothers become infected themselves (Coovadia, 2004). During childbirth, blood vessels in the mother and baby rupture, enabling an exchange of blood and transmission of HIV. HIV is also found in breast milk. An African study found that the probability of transmission of HIV through breast milk was about 1 in 6 (16.2%) (Nduati et al., 2000).

Children from ethnic and racial minority groups are at greater risk of being infected with HIV. African Americans account for more than half of the pediatric cases of HIV/AIDS, and Latino and Latina Americans (especially those of Puerto Rican origin) account for almost one-fourth. Inner-city neighborhoods, where there is widespread intravenous drug use, are especially hard hit (Centers for Disease Control and Prevention, 2006a). Death rates resulting from AIDS are higher among African American and Puerto Rican children than among European American children (Centers for Disease Control and Prevention, 2004), apparently because African Americans and Puerto Ricans have less access to health care.

Rubella

Rubella (German measles) is a viral infection. Women who are infected during the first 20 weeks of pregnancy stand at least a 20% chance of bearing children with birth defects such as deafness, mental retardation, heart disease, or eye problems, including blindness (Food and Drug Administration, 2004; Reef et al., 2004).

Many adult women had rubella as children and became immune in this way. Women who are not immune are best vaccinated before they become pregnant, although they can be inoculated during pregnancy, if necessary. Inoculation has led to a dramatic decline in the number of American children born with defects caused by rubella, from approximately 2,000 cases in 1964–1965 to 21 cases in 2001 (Food and Drug Administration, 2004; Reef et al., 2004).

Toxemia

Toxemia is a life-threatening disease characterized by high blood pressure that may afflict women late in the second or early in the third trimester. Women with toxemia often have **premature** or undersized babies. Toxemia is also a cause of pregnancy-related maternal deaths (Rumbold et al., 2006). Toxemia appears to be linked to malnutrition, but the causes are unclear. Women who do not receive prenatal care are much more likely to die from toxemia than those who receive prenatal care (Scott, 2006).

Rh Incompatibility

In **Rh incompatibility**, antibodies produced by the mother are transmitted to a fetus or newborn infant and cause brain damage or death. Rh is a blood protein found in the red blood cells of some individuals. Rh incompatibility occurs when a woman

HIV/AIDS HIV stands for a virus, the human immuno-deficiency virus, which cripples the body's immune system. AIDS stands for acquired immunodeficiency syndrome. HIV is a sexually transmitted infection that can also be transmitted in other ways, such as sharing needles when shooting up drugs. AIDS is caused by HIV and describes the body's state when the immune system is weakened to the point where it is vulnerable to a variety of diseases that would otherwise be fought off.

rubella A viral infection that can cause retardation and heart disease in the embryo. Also called German measles.

toxemia A life-threatening disease that can afflict pregnant women; it is characterized by high blood pressure.

premature Born before the full term of gestation. Also referred to as preterm.

Rh incompatibility A condition in which antibodies produced by the mother are transmitted to the child, possibly causing brain damage or death.

who does not have this factor—and is thus Rh negative—is carrying an Rh-positive fetus, which can happen if the father is Rh positive. The negative–positive combination occurs in approximately 10% of American couples and becomes a problem in some resulting pregnancies. Rh incompatibility does not affect a first child because women will not have formed Rh antibodies. The chances of an exchange of blood are greatest during childbirth. If an exchange occurs, the mother produces Rh-positive antibodies to the baby's Rh-positive blood. These antibodies can enter the fetal bloodstream during subsequent deliveries, causing anemia, mental deficiency, or death.

If an Rh-negative mother is injected with Rh immunoglobulin within 72 hours after delivery of an Rh-positive baby, she will not develop the antibodies. A fetus or newborn child at risk of Rh disease may receive a blood transfusion to remove the mother's antibodies.

Drugs Taken by the Parents

Rh antibodies can be lethal to children, but many other substances can have harmful effects. *Question: What are the effects of drugs taken by the mother on prenatal development?* In this section, we discuss the effects of various drugs—prescription drugs, over-the-counter drugs, and illegal drugs—on the unborn child. Even commonly used medications, such as aspirin, can be harmful to the fetus. If a woman is pregnant or thinks she may be, it is advisable for her to consult her obstetrician before taking any drugs, not just prescription medications. A physician usually can recommend a safe and effective substitute for a drug that could potentially harm a developing fetus.

A CLOSER LOOK

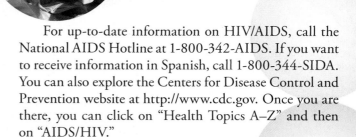

Preventing One's Baby from Being Infected with HIV

Pregnant women who are infected with HIV or any other sexually transmitted disease should discuss this issue with their physicians. Measures can be taken that will help prevent their babies from being infected. Current recommendations concerning transmission of HIV from mother to baby include highly active antiretroviral therapy (HAART), a combination of three drugs that decrease the amount of HIV in the bloodstream; cesarean section (C-section); and formula feeding. C-sections help prevent transmission of HIV to the fetus because it is not exposed to the mother's blood during vaginal delivery, when blood vessels rupture. HIV is also found in breast milk (hence the recommendation for formula feeding). All in all, the combination of HAART, C-section, and formula feeding has reduced mother-to-infant transmission of HIV from about 25% to 1–2% (Coovadia, 2004).

For up-to-date information on HIV/AIDS, call the National AIDS Hotline at 1-800-342-AIDS. If you want to receive information in Spanish, call 1-800-344-SIDA. You can also explore the Centers for Disease Control and Prevention website at http://www.cdc.gov. Once you are there, you can click on "Health Topics A–Z" and then on "AIDS/HIV."

Reflect: What have you done—or what will you do—to try to protect your babies from being infected with HIV and any other disease organism?

Thalidomide

Thalidomide was marketed in the 1960s as a treatment for insomnia and nausea. It was available in Germany and England without prescription. Within a few years, more than 10,000 babies with missing or stunted limbs were born in these countries and elsewhere as a result of their mothers using thalidomide during pregnancy (Ances, 2002). Thalidomide is still in use today and is used to treat disorders as various as dermatological problems and Kaposi's sarcoma, a form of cancer that affects many people with HIV/AIDS (Chaudhry et al., 2002).

Thalidomide provides a dramatic example of critical periods of vulnerability to various teratogens. A fetus's extremities undergo rapid development during the second month of pregnancy (see Figure 3.5). Thalidomide taken during this period almost invariably causes birth defects.

Antibiotics

Several antibiotics may be harmful to the fetus. Tetracycline, which is frequently prescribed for bacterial infections, can lead to yellowed teeth and bone abnormalities. Other antibiotics are implicated in hearing loss.

Hormones

Women at risk for miscarriages have been prescribed hormones to help maintain their pregnancies. For example, **progestin** is chemically similar to male sex hormones and can masculinize the external sex organs of female embryos. Prenatal progestin has also been linked to aggressive behavior and masculine-typed behaviors in females (Keenan & Soleymani, 2001; Molenda-Figueira et al., 2006).

DES (short for diethylstilbestrol), a powerful estrogen, was given to many women during the 1940s and 1950s to help prevent miscarriage, but it has caused cervical and testicular cancer in some of the offspring. Among daughters of DES users, about 1 in 1,000 will develop cancer in the reproductive tract. Daughters are also more likely to have babies who are premature or low in birth weight. Daughters and sons of mothers who took DES have high rates of infertility and immune system disorders (Centers for Disease Control and Prevention, 2005).

Vitamins

Although pregnant women are often prescribed multivitamins to maintain their own health and to promote the development of their fetuses, too much of a good thing can be dangerous. High doses of vitamins A and D have been associated with central nervous system damage, small head size, and heart defects (National Institutes of Health, 2002).

Heroin and Methadone

Maternal addiction to heroin or methadone is linked to low birth weight, prematurity, and toxemia. Narcotics such as heroin and methadone readily cross the placental membrane, and the fetuses of women who use them regularly can become addicted (Lejeune et al., 2006). **Truth or Fiction Revisited:** It is true that babies can be born addicted to narcotics and other substances used regularly by their mothers.

Addicted newborns may be given the narcotic or a substitute shortly after birth so that they will not suffer serious withdrawal symptoms. The drug is then withdrawn gradually. Addicted newborns may also have behavioral effects. For example, infants exposed to heroin in utero show delays in motor and language development at the age of 12 months (Bunikowski et al., 1998).

Marijuana (Cannabis)

Smoking marijuana during pregnancy apparently poses a number of risks for the fetus, including slower fetal growth (Hurd et al., 2005) and low birth weight (Visscher et al., 2003). These and the following risks are all proportional to the amount of

thalidomide A sedative used in the 1960s that has been linked to birth defects, especially deformed or absent limbs.

progestin A hormone used to maintain pregnancy that can cause masculinization of the fetus.

DES Abbreviation for diethylstilbestrol, a powerful estrogen that has been linked to cancer in the reproductive organs of children of women who used the hormone when pregnant.

marijuana smoked; that is, women who smoke more, or who inhale more secondary smoke (that is, smoke from others who are smoking), place their fetuses at relatively greater risk. The babies of women who regularly used marijuana show increased tremors and startling, suggesting immature development of the nervous system (Huestis et al., 2002).

Research into the cognitive effects of maternal prenatal use of marijuana shows mixed results. Some studies suggest that there may be no impairment (Fried & Smith, 2001). Others suggest that cognitive skills, including learning and memory, may be impaired (Huizink & Mulder, 2006). One study assessed the behavior of 10-year-olds who had been exposed prenatally to maternal use of marijuana (Goldschmidt et al., 2000). The study included the children of 635 mothers, age 18 to 42. Prenatal use of marijuana was significantly related to increased hyperactivity, impulsivity, and problems in paying attention (as measured by the Swanson, Noland, and Pelham checklist); increased delinquency (as measured by the Child Behavior Checklist); and increased delinquency and aggressive behavior (as measured by teacher report). The researchers hypothesized that the pathway between prenatal marijuana exposure and delinquency involves the effects of marijuana on attention, impairing the abilities to learn in school and to conform to social rules and norms. A Swedish study also suggests that fetal exposure to marijuana may impair systems in the brain that regulate emotional behavior (Wang et al., 2004).

Researchers have also found that maternal use of marijuana predisposes offspring to dependence on opiates (narcotics derived from the opium poppy). The fetal brain, like the adult brain, has cannabinoid receptors—called CB-1 receptors—and other structures that are altered by exposure to marijuana. The alterations make the individual more sensitive to the reinforcing properties of opiates, even in adulthood (Moreno et al., 2003). In any event, longitudinal research with 763 women recruited in the fourth month of pregnancy found that prenatal exposure to maternal marijuana smoking is a reasonably good predictor of whether or not the child will smoke marijuana at the age of 14 (Day et al., 2006).

Cocaine

There is little doubt that prenatal exposure to cocaine can harm the child. Pregnant women who abuse cocaine increase the risk of stillbirth, low birth weight, and birth defects. The infants are often excitable and irritable, or lethargic. The more heavily exposed to cocaine they are in utero, the more problems they have with jitteriness, concentration, and sleep (Schuetze et al., 2006). There are suggestions of delays in cognitive development even at 12 months of age (Singer et al., 2005).

Children who are exposed to cocaine prenatally also show problems at later ages. One study compared 189 children at 4 years of age who had been exposed to cocaine in utero with 185 other 4-year-olds who had not on the Clinical Evaluation of Language Fundamentals—Preschool (CELF-P) test (Lewis et al., 2004). The children exposed to cocaine had much lower expressive language scores and somewhat lower receptive language scores than those not exposed to cocaine. That is, the relative ability of children exposed to cocaine to express themselves was affected more than their ability to understand language. The study controlled for prenatal exposure to cigarette smoke, alcohol, and marijuana.

A study of 473 children who were 6 years old compared children who were exposed to cocaine in utero (204) with those who were not (Delaney-Black et al., 2004). The study found effects for the amount of cocaine used by the mother and the sex of the child. Boys, first of all, were more likely to be affected than girls. According to teacher reports, boys whose mothers used cocaine regularly were likely to be rated as hyperactive and indifferent to their environment and to show deficits in cognitive skills. The study controlled for maternal use of alcohol and illegal drugs other than cocaine while pregnant.

The studies with humans are correlational. That is, mothers are not randomly assigned to use cocaine; instead, they make the choice themselves. This problem is technically termed a selection factor. Thus, it may be that the same factors that lead mothers to use cocaine also affect their children. To overcome the selection factor, numerous experiments have been conducted with laboratory animals (Buxhoeveden et al., 2006; Chelonis et al., 2003). In one study, randomly selected pregnant rats were given cocaine during days 12–21 of gestation, whereas control rats received no cocaine (Huber et al., 2001). The rat pups were then exposed to stressors such as cold-water swimming and tail flicks. The pups exposed to cocaine showed less tolerance of the stressors—as measured by behaviors such as tail twitches and convulsions—than the control subjects. Another study found that such group differences in response to stressors endure into rat adulthood, that is, 90–120 days of age (Campbell et al., 2000).

Some investigators have also exposed rabbit embryos to cocaine during various periods of prenatal brain development (Gabriel et al., 2003; Stanwood et al., 2001; Thompson et al., 2005). The researchers found deficiencies in learning in the offspring and that a structure in the brain called the anterior cingulate cortex (ACC) shows changes in development. The ACC is involved in attention and self-control.

Alcohol

No drug has meant so much to so many as alcohol. Alcohol is our dinnertime relaxant, our bedtime sedative, our cocktail-party social lubricant. We use alcohol to celebrate holy days, applaud our accomplishments, and express joyous wishes. Millions of adolescents assert their maturity with alcohol. Alcohol is used at least occasionally by the majority of high school and college students (Johnston et al., 2006). Alcohol even kills germs on surface wounds.

Because alcohol passes through the placenta, however, drinking by a pregnant woman poses risks for the embryo and fetus. Heavy drinking can be lethal to the fetus and neonate. It is also connected with deficiencies and deformities in growth. Some children of heavy drinkers develop **fetal alcohol syndrome (FAS)** (Floyd et al., 2005; Connor et al., 2006). Babies with FAS are often smaller than normal, and so are their brains. Such babies have distinct facial features: widely spaced eyes, an underdeveloped upper jaw, a flattened nose. There may be malformation of the limbs, poor coordination, and cardiovascular problems. A number of psychological characteristics are connected with FAS and appear to reflect dysfunction of the brain: mental retardation, hyperactivity, distractibility, lessened verbal fluency, and learning disabilities (Guerrini et al., 2007; Connor et al., 2006). There are deficits in speech and hearing, practical reasoning, and visual–motor coordination (Connor et al., 2006).

The facial deformities of FAS diminish as the child moves into adolescence, and most children catch up in height and weight, but the intellectual, academic, and behavioral deficits of individuals with FAS persist. Academic and intellectual problems relative to peers range from verbal difficulties to deficiency in spatial memory (Guerrini et al., 2007). Studies find that the average academic functioning of adolescents and young adults with FAS was at the second- to fourth-grade level. Maladaptive behaviors such as poor judgment, distractibility, and difficulty perceiving social cues are common (Schonfeld et al., 2005).

FAS is part of a broader group of fetal alcohol–related problems referred to as fetal alcohol spectrum disorders (Connor et al., 2006). **Truth or Fiction Revisited:** It cannot be guaranteed that one glass of wine a day is harmless to the embryo and

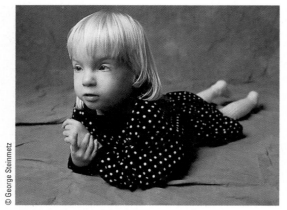
© George Steinmetz

Fetal Alcohol Syndrome (FAS)
The children of many mothers who drank alcohol during pregnancy exhibit FAS. This syndrome is characterized by developmental lags and such facial features as an underdeveloped upper jaw, a flattened nose, and widely spaced eyes.

fetal alcohol syndrome (FAS) A cluster of symptoms shown by children of women who drank heavily during pregnancy, including characteristic facial features and mental retardation.

fetus. Although some health professionals allow pregnant women a glass of wine with dinner, research suggests that even moderate drinkers place their offspring at increased risk for a less severe set of effects known as **fetal alcohol effect (FAE)**. Pregnant women who have as few as one or two drinks a day may be more likely to miscarry and have growth-delayed babies than pregnant women who do not drink alcohol (Newburn-Cook et al., 2002; Ornoy, 2002).

The reported effects of maternal alcohol use, as with the effects of maternal use of cocaine, are based on correlational evidence. No researcher would randomly assign some pregnant women to drinking and others to abstention. However, researchers have randomly assigned experimental animals to intake of alcohol, and the results support the correlational evidence with humans. For example, research with animals finds that exposure to alcohol during gestation is connected with retarded growth, facial malformations characteristic of FAS, deficiencies in the immune system, and structural and chemical differences in the central nervous system (Lugo et al., 2006; Ponnappa & Rubin, 2000).

Caffeine

Many pregnant women consume caffeine in the form of coffee, tea, soft drinks, chocolate, and nonprescription drugs. Research findings on caffeine's effects on the developing fetus have been inconsistent. Some studies report no adverse findings, but other studies (e.g., Cnattingius et al., 2000) suggest that pregnant women who take in a good deal of caffeine may be more likely than nonusers of caffeine to have a miscarriage or a low-birth-weight baby. Because of such findings, many obstetricians recommend that pregnant women are well advised to be moderate in their caffeine intake.

Perhaps the best review of the literature to date is by Lisa Signorello and Joseph McLaughlin (2004). They carefully reviewed—perhaps I should say "ripped apart"— 15 epidemiologic studies on caffeine and miscarriage, paying specific attention to the kinds of methodological problems that can lead to inaccurate results, such as selection factors in the sampling, problems in women's recall of exactly how much caffeine they used or in the measurement of exposure to caffeine, and the timing of the loss of the embryo or the fetus. They concluded that (1) each study was flawed and (2) there was no way to compare the results of the studies to one another, even though most studies reported a link between the intake of caffeine by the mother and the risk of miscarriage.

The evidence, apparently, is a train wreck, so what can I advise? Simply that until we have better evidence, pregnant women are well advised to be moderate in their caffeine intake.

Cigarettes

Cigarette smoke contains many ingredients, including the stimulant nicotine, the gas carbon monoxide, and hydrocarbons ("tars"), which are carcinogens. Fortunately, only the first two, the nicotine and the carbon monoxide, pass through the placenta and reach the fetus. That's the end of the fortunate news. Nicotine stimulates the fetus, but its long-term effects are uncertain. Carbon monoxide is toxic; it decreases the amount of oxygen available to the fetus. Oxygen deprivation is connected with cognitive and behavioral problems, including impaired motor development. The cognitive difficulties include academic delays, learning disabilities, and mental retardation. Not all children of smokers develop these problems, but many do not function as well as they would have if they had not been exposed to maternal smoking.

Pregnant women who smoke are likely to deliver smaller babies than nonsmokers (Bernstein et al., 2005). In addition, their babies are more likely to be stillborn or to die soon after birth (Cnattingius, 2004). The combination of smoking and drinking

fetal alcohol effect (FAE)
A cluster of symptoms less severe than those of fetal alcohol syndrome shown by children of women who drank moderately during pregnancy.

Smoking during pregnancy hurts the fetus. The only question is, "How much?"

alcohol places the child at greater risk of low birth weight than either practice alone (Spencer, 2006).

Maternal smoking may also have long-term negative effects on development. Children whose mothers smoke during pregnancy are more likely to show short attention spans, hyperactivity, lower cognitive and language scores, and poor grades (Secker-Walker & Vacek, 2003).

Smoking during pregnancy obviously poses significant threats to the fetus. So why do pregnant women do it? Are they ignorant of the risks to their children? Perhaps. Despite decades of public education efforts, some women remain unaware that smoking will hurt the fetus. But most American women are aware of the threat, yet they say that they can't quit or that they can't suspend smoking until the baby is born. Why? Some claim that they are under too much stress to stop smoking, although cigarette smoking actually contributes to stress; it's not a one-way ticket to relaxation. Others smoke to fight feelings of depression (nicotine is a stimulant and depression is, well, depressing), because "everybody" around them smokes (often, "everybody" translates to "partner"), or because they just don't have the willpower (or perhaps I should say, the "won't power") to deal with the withdrawal symptoms of quitting (Cnattingius, 2004; Spencer, 2006). Some parents simply deny that their smoking is likely to harm their children, despite knowledge to the contrary. They reason: Why worry about quitting smoking? I could be run over by a truck tomorrow. (Yes, dear reader, one could be run over by a truck, but one can also look both ways before crossing the street, and one can choose to act as if one is in control of one's life.)

Secondhand smoke also holds dangers. Men who smoke are more likely to produce abnormal sperm. Babies of fathers who smoke have higher rates of birth defects, infant mortality, lower birth weights, and cardiovascular problems (Goel et al., 2004).

Environmental Hazards

Mothers know when they are ingesting drugs, but there are many other substances in the environment they may take in unknowingly. These substances are environmental hazards to which we are all exposed, and we refer to them collectively as pollution. *Question: What are the effects of environmental hazards during pregnancy?*

Prenatal exposure to heavy metals such as lead, mercury, and zinc threatens the development of children. Longitudinal research finds that newborns who have mildly elevated levels of lead in their umbilical cord blood show delayed mental development at 1 and 2 years of age (Heindel & Lawler, 2006). However, their cognitive functioning can improve if there is no longer lead in the home.

One study of the effects of prenatal exposure to lead recruited 442 children in Yugoslavia (Wasserman et al., 2000). Some of the children lived in a town with a smelter, and the others did not. (Smelting, or the melting of lead-bearing scrap metal into metallic lead, is a major source of lead fume emissions.) The children received intelligence testing at the ages of 3, 4, 5, and 7, using Wechsler and other scales. The researchers found that the children from the town with the smelter obtained somewhat lower intelligence test scores. It is conceivable, of course, that people who choose to live in a town without a smelter differ from those who live near one.

Experiments with rodents support the correlational findings with humans. For example, mice exposed to lead in utero do not form memories as well as those who are free of prenatal exposure to lead (de Oliveira et al., 2001). Research with rats has found that prenatal exposure to lead decreases the levels of neurotransmitters (the chemical messengers of the brain) in all areas of the brain, but especially in the hippocampus. The hippocampus is involved in memory formation.

The devastating effects of mercury on the fetus were first recognized among the Japanese who lived around Minimata Bay. Industrial waste containing mercury was dumped into the bay and accumulated in local fish, which were a major food source for local residents. Children born to women who had eaten the fish during pregnancy often were profoundly retarded and neurologically damaged (Vorhees & Mollnow, 1987). Prenatal exposure to even small amounts of mercury and other heavy metals such as cadmium and chromium can produce subtle deficits in cognitive functioning and physical health (Heindel & Lawler, 2006).

Polychlorinated biphenyls (PCBs) are chemicals used in many industrial products. Like mercury, they accumulate in fish that feed in polluted waters. Newborns whose mothers had consumed PCB-contaminated fish from Lake Michigan were smaller and showed poorer motor functioning and less responsiveness than newborns whose mothers had not eaten these fish. Furthermore, even those PCB-exposed infants who appeared normal at birth showed deficits in memory at 7 months and at 4 years of age (Jacobson et al., 1992).

An unfortunate natural experiment in the effects of prenatal exposure to PCBs took place in Taiwan during the late 1970s, when a group of people accidentally ingested contaminated rice. Children born to mothers who ate the rice had characteristic signs of PCB poisoning, including hyperpigmented skin. The researchers (Lai et al., 2001) had the opportunity to compare the cognitive development of 118 children born to exposed mothers with other children in the community. The children were all followed through the age of 12 and were tested with instruments that included the Bayley Scale for Infant Development, the Chinese version of the Stanford–Binet IQ Test, and two nonverbal intelligence tests. The children of mothers who ate the contaminated rice scored lower than the control children on each of these methods of measurement throughout the observation period. It appears that prenatal exposure to PCBs has long-term harmful effects on cognitive development.

Experiments with mice show that fetal exposure to radiation in high doses can cause defects in a number of organs, including the eyes, central nervous system, and skeleton (e.g., Hossain et al., 2005). Pregnant women who were exposed to atomic radiation during the bombings of Hiroshima and Nagasaki in World War II gave birth to babies who were more likely to be mentally retarded in addition to being physically deformed (Sadler, 2005). Pregnant women are advised to avoid unnecessary exposure to x-rays. (Ultrasound, which is not an x-ray, has not been shown to be harmful to the fetus, but women may question what appears to them to be excessive use of ultrasound.)

Research suggests that men exposed to heavy metals and radiation can also produce children with abnormalities. For example, children of fathers employed in jobs with high exposure to lead had three times more kidney tumors than children whose fathers were not exposed (Davis, 1991). Another study found a higher incidence of leukemia among children whose fathers worked in nuclear plants, where they were exposed to high levels of radiation before the children's conception ("British Study Finds," 1990).

The risks of radiation and other environmental agents to the embryo and fetus are summarized in Concept Review 3.2.

Maternal Stress

Although pregnancy can be a time of immense gratification for women, it can also be a time of stress. The baby might be unplanned and unwanted. Parents might not have the financial resources or the room for the child. The mother might be experiencing physical discomforts because of the pregnancy. *Question: What, then, are the apparent effects of maternal stress on the child?*

How does a mother's emotional state affect her fetus? Emotions are psychological feeling states, but they also have physiological components. For example, they are linked to the secretion of hormones such as adrenaline. **Adrenaline** stimulates the mother's heart rate, respiratory rate, and other bodily functions. Hormones pass through the placenta and also have an effect on the fetus.

Parents' Age

Question: Is the parents' age connected with the outcome of pregnancy?

Older fathers are more likely to produce abnormal sperm. The mother's age also matters. From a biological vantage point, the 20s may be the ideal age for women to bear children. Teenage mothers have a higher incidence of infant mortality and children with low birth weight (Phipps et al., 2002; Save the Children, 2004b). Girls who become pregnant in their early teens may place a burden on bodies that may not have adequately matured to facilitate pregnancy and childbirth. Teenage mothers also are less educated and less likely to obtain prenatal care than older mothers. These factors are associated with high-risk pregnancy (Berg et al., 2003).

What about women older than 30? Women's fertility declines gradually until the mid-30s, after which it declines more rapidly. Women beyond their middle 30s may have passed the point at which their reproductive systems function most efficiently. Women possess all their ova in immature form at birth. Over 30 years, these cells are exposed to the slings and arrows of an outrageous environment of toxic wastes, chemical pollutants, and radiation, thus increasing the risk of chromosomal abnormalities such as Down syndrome (Behrman et al., 2000). Women who wait until their 30s or 40s to have children also increase the likelihood of having stillborn or preterm babies (Berg et al., 2003). However, with adequate prenatal care, the risk of bearing a premature or unhealthy baby still is relatively small, even for older first-time mothers (Berg et al., 2003). This news should be encouraging for women who have delayed, or plan to delay, bearing children until their 30s or 40s.

Whatever the age of the mother, the events of childbirth provide some of the most memorable moments in the lives of parents. In Chapter 4, we continue our voyage with the process of birth and the characteristics of the newborn child.

adrenaline A hormone that generally arouses the body, increasing the heart and respiration rates.

Concept Review 3.2   Risks of Various Agents to the Embryo and Fetus

Agent	Risks
Prescription Drugs[a]	
Accutane (used to treat acne; repeated blood tests required to show that one is not pregnant or encountering drug-related problems)	Stillbirth, malformation of limbs and organs
Bendectin	Cleft palate, malformation of the heart
Carbamazepine (and other anticonvulsant drugs)	Spina bifida
Diethylstilbestrol (DES; once used to help maintain pregnancy)	Cancer of the cervix or testes
Strong general anesthesia during labor (sedation that goes beyond normal medical practice)	Anoxia, asphyxiation, brain damage
Progestin (a synthetic version of the natural hormone progesterone, which is sometimes used to help maintain pregnancy)	Masculinization of the sex organs of female embryos, possible development of "masculine" aggressiveness
Streptomycin (an antibiotic)	Deafness
Tetracycline (an antibiotic)	Malformed bones, yellow teeth
Thalidomide (several uses, including sedation)	Malformed or missing limbs
Other Drugs	
Alcohol	Fetal death, low birth weight, addiction, academic and intellectual problems, hyperactivity, distractibility, fetal alcohol syndrome (FAS, including characteristic facial features)
Aspirin (high doses)	Bleeding, respiratory problems
Caffeine (the stimulant found in coffee, tea, colas, chocolate)	Stimulates fetus (not necessarily a problem in itself), miscarriage, low birth weight
Cigarette smoke (the stimulant nicotine and carbon monoxide are transmitted through the placenta)	Stimulates fetus (not necessarily a problem in itself), premature birth, low birth weight, fetal death, academic problems, hyperactivity and shirt attention span
Opiates (heroin, morphine, others)	Low birth weight, premature birth, addiction, toxemia
Marijuana	Tremors, startling, premature birth, birth defects, neurological problems
Vitamins[b]	
Vitamin A (high doses)	Cleft palate, damage to the eyes
Vitamin D (high doses)	Mental retardation
Pathogens (disease-causing agents)	
HIV (the virus that causes AIDS)	Physical deformity, mental retardation
Rubella (German measles)	Neurological impairment involving sensation and perception (vision, hearing), mental retardation, heart problems, cataracts
Syphilis (a sexually transmitted infection caused by the *Treponema pallidum* bacterium)	Infant mortality, seizures, mental retardation, sensory impairment (vision, hearing), liver damage, malformation of bones and teeth
Environmental Hazards	
Heavy metals (lead, mercury, zinc)	Mental retardation, hyperactivity, stillbirth, problems in memory formation
Paint fumes (heavy exposure)	Mental retardation
PCBs (polychlorinated biphenyls), dioxin, other insecticides and herbicides	Stillbirth, low birth weight, cognitive impairment, motor impairment
X-rays	Deformation of organs
Biochemical Incompatibility with Mother	
Rh antibodies	Infant mortality, brain damage

[a]Normally healthful, even life-saving drugs can be harmful to the embryo and fetus. Women should inform their physicians when they are pregnant, may be pregnant, or are planning to become pregnant.

[b]Adequate intake of vitamins is essential to the well-being of the mother and the embryo and fetus. Most obstetricians advise pregnant women to take vitamin supplements, but too much of a good thing can be harmful. In brief, don't do "megavitamins" and, when in doubt, ask your obstetrician.

Active Review

13. Mothers who ingest folic acid reduce the risk of giving birth to babies with _____ tube defects.

14. _____ are environmental agents that can harm the developing embryo or fetus.

15. Women (Can or Cannot?) be successfully treated for syphilis during pregnancy.

16. Toxemia is mainly characterized by high _____ pressure.

17. In _____ incompatibility, antibodies produced by the mother are transmitted to a fetus or newborn infant and cause brain damage or death to the infant.

18. _____ was prescribed to help women maintain their pregnancies, but it caused cervical and testicular cancer in some of their children.

19. The babies of women who regularly used _____ during pregnancy have been found to show increased tremors and startling.

20. Heavy maternal use of alcohol is linked to _____ alcohol syndrome (FAS).

21. Women who smoke during pregnancy deprive their fetuses of _____, sometimes resulting in stillbirth and persistent academic problems.

22. Fetal exposure to the heavy metals lead and mercury can (Slow or Accelerate?) mental development.

Reflect & Relate: How will your knowledge of critical periods of prenatal development allow you to predict— and possibly prevent—the effects of various agents on the embryo and fetus? How difficult do you think it would be for you or someone you know to give up drinking alcohol or smoking during pregnancy? Would looking on the "sacrifice" as temporary make it easier?

Go to

http://www.thomsonedu.com/psychology/rathus

for an interactive version of this review.

RECITE: *An Active Summary*

1. **What happens during the germinal stage of prenatal development?**

   During the germinal stage, the zygote divides repeatedly, but it does not gain in mass. It travels through a fallopian tube to the uterus, where it implants. It then takes the form of a blastocyst. Layers of cells form within the embryonic disk. The outer part of the blastocyst differentiates into membranes that will protect and nourish the embryo.

2. **If the dividing mass of cells is moving through a fallopian tube and then "wandering" through the uterus for another few days, how does it obtain any nourishment?**

   Before implantation, the dividing cluster of cells is nourished by the yolk of the original egg cell. Once implanted in the uterine wall, it obtains nourishment from the mother.

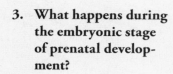

3. **What happens during the embryonic stage of prenatal development?**

The embryonic stage lasts from implantation until the eighth week of development, during which the major organ systems differentiate. Development follows cephalocaudal and proximodistal trends. The outer layer of the embryonic disk develops into the nervous system, sensory organs, nails, hair, teeth, and skin. Two ridges form the neural tube, from which the nervous system develops. The inner layer forms the digestive and respiratory systems, liver, and pancreas. The middle layer becomes the excretory, reproductive, and circulatory systems, the muscles, the skeleton, and the inner layer of the skin.

4. **When does the heart begin to beat?**

The heart begins to beat during the fourth week.

5. **What else happens during the embryonic stage?**

Toward the end of the first month, arm and leg buds appear and the face takes shape. The nervous system has also begun to develop. By the end of the second month, limbs are elongating, facial features are becoming distinct, teeth buds have formed, the kidneys are working, and the liver is producing red blood cells.

6. **How do some babies develop into girls and others into boys?**

By 5 to 6 weeks, the embryo has undifferentiated sex organs that resemble female structures. Testes produce male sex hormones that spur development of male genital organs and the male duct system.

7. **How does the embryo get nourishment from its mother? How does it eliminate waste products?**

The embryo and fetus exchange nutrients and wastes with the mother through a mass of tissue called the placenta. The umbilical cord connects the fetus to the placenta.

8. **Do germs or drugs in the mother pass through the placenta and affect the baby?**

Many do, including the germs that cause syphilis and rubella. Some drugs also pass through, including aspirin, narcotics, and alcohol.

9. **What happens during the fetal stage of prenatal development?**

The fetal stage lasts from the end of the embryonic stage until birth. The fetus begins to turn in the ninth or tenth week. The second trimester is characterized by maturation of organs and gains in size. By the end of the second trimester, the fetus opens and shuts its eyes, sucks its thumb, alternates between wakefulness and sleep, and responds to light and sounds. During the third trimester, the heart and lungs become increasingly capable of sustaining independent life.

10. **Why did my Aunt Margaret play classical music (and put the speakers near her abdomen) when she was 7 months pregnant?**

I can't explain exactly why your Aunt Margaret played classical music, but the fetus responds to sound waves by the 13th week of pregnancy. Newborn babies prefer their mother's voice to that of other women, apparently because of prenatal exposure.

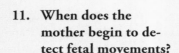

11.	**When does the mother begin to detect fetal movements?**	The mother usually detects fetal movements during the fourth month. By the end of the second trimester, the fetus turns somersaults.
12.	**How does the nutrition of the mother affect prenatal development?**	Malnutrition in the mother has been linked to low birth weight, prematurity, stunted growth, retardation of brain development, cognitive deficiencies, and behavioral problems. Folic acid reduces the risk of neural tube defects.
13.	**Does it matter when, during pregnancy, a woman is exposed to a teratogen?**	Yes. Exposure to particular teratogens is most harmful during critical periods, the times when certain organs are developing. The embryo is generally more vulnerable than the fetus because the major organ systems are differentiating.
14.	**What are the effects of maternal health problems?**	Women who contract rubella may bear children who suffer from deafness, mental retardation, heart disease, or cataracts. Syphilis can cause miscarriage, stillbirth, or congenital syphilis. Babies can be infected with HIV in utero, during childbirth, or by breast feeding. Toxemia is characterized by high blood pressure and is connected with preterm or undersized babies. In Rh incompatibility, antibodies produced by the mother are transmitted to a fetus or newborn infant and cause brain damage or death.
15.	**What are the effects of drugs taken by the mother on prenatal development?**	Thalidomide causes missing or stunted limbs in babies. Tetracycline can cause yellowed teeth and bone problems. DES leads to high risk of cervical and testicular cancer. High doses of vitamins A and D are associated with nervous system damage and heart defects. Maternal addiction to narcotics is linked to low birth weight, prematurity, and toxemia, and fetuses can be born addicted themselves. Marijuana may cause tremors and startling in babies. Cocaine increases the risk of stillbirth, low birth weight, and birth defects. Maternal use of alcohol is linked to death of the fetus and neonate, malformations, growth deficiencies, and fetal alcohol syndrome (FAS). Caffeine is connected with miscarriage and low birth weight. Maternal cigarette smoking is linked with low birth weight, stillbirth, and mental retardation.
16.	**What are the effects of environmental hazards during pregnancy?**	Prenatal exposure to heavy metals threatens cognitive development. Prenatal exposure to mercury is connected with neurological damage. Prenatal exposure to PCBs is connected with babies that are smaller, less responsive, and more likely to develop cognitive deficits. Fetal exposure to radiation can cause neural and skeletal problems.
17.	**What are the apparent effects of maternal stress on the child?**	Maternal stress is linked to the secretion of hormones such as adrenaline, which pass through the placenta and affect the baby. Maternal stress may be connected with complications during pregnancy and labor, preterm or low-birth-weight babies, and irritable babies.
18.	**Is the parents' age connected with the outcome of pregnancy?**	Yes. Teenage mothers have a higher incidence of infant mortality and children with low birth weight. Women older than the age of 30 run an increasing risk of chromosomal abnormalities and of having stillborn or preterm babies.

Key Terms

neonate, 78
germinal stage, 78
blastocyst, 78
embryonic disk, 79
trophoblast, 78
umbilical cord, 78
placenta, 78
embryonic stage, 80
cephalocaudal, 80
proximodistal, 80
ectoderm, 80
neural tube, 80

endoderm, 80
mesoderm, 81
androgens, 82
testosterone, 82
amniotic sac, 84
amniotic fluid, 84
fetal stage, 85
stillbirth, 93
teratogens, 94
critical period, 94
syphilis, 95
congenital, 95

HIV/AIDS, 96
rubella, 96
toxemia, 96
premature, 96
Rh incompatibility, 96
thalidomide, 98
progestin, 98
diethylstilbestrol (DES), 98
fetal alcohol syndrome (FAS), 100
fetal alcohol effect (FAE), 101
adrenaline, 104

Active Learning Resources

Childhood & Adolescence Book Companion Website
http://www.thomsonedu.com/psychology/rathus

Visit your book companion website, where you will find more resources to help you study. There you will find interactive versions of your book features, including the Lessons in Observation video, Active Review sections, and the Truth or Fiction feature. In addition, the companion website contains quizzing, flash cards, and a pronunciation glossary.

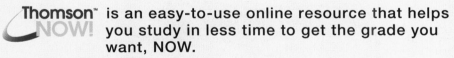

Thomson NOW! is an easy-to-use online resource that helps you study in less time to get the grade you want, NOW.

http://www.thomsonedu.com/login

Need help studying? This site is your one-stop study shop. Take a Pre-Test and ThomsonNOW will generate a Personalized Study Plan based on your test results. The Study Plan will identify the topics you need to review and direct you to online resources to help you master those topics. You can then take a Post-Test to determine the concepts you have mastered and what you still need to work on.

4

Birth and the Newborn Baby:
In the New World

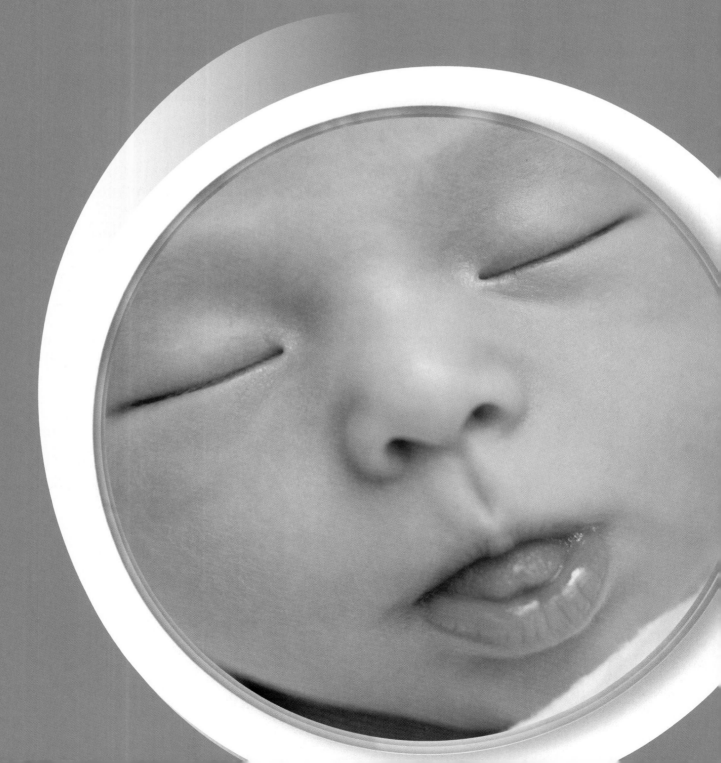

Truth or Fiction?

T F The fetus signals its mother when it is ready to be born. p. 113

T F After birth, babies are held upside down and slapped on the buttocks to stimulate independent breathing. p. 116

T F The way the umbilical cord is cut determines whether the baby's "belly button" will be an "innie" or an "outie." p. 116

T F Women who give birth according to the Lamaze method do not experience pain. p. 119

T F In the United States, nearly 3 of every 10 births are by cesarean section. p. 120

T F It is abnormal to feel depressed following childbirth. p. 128

T F Parents must have extended early contact with their newborn children if adequate bonding is to take place. p. 129

T F More children die from sudden infant death syndrome (SIDS) than from cancer, heart disease, pneumonia, child abuse, AIDS, cystic fibrosis, and muscular dystrophy combined. p. 143

Preview

Countdown …

The Stages of Childbirth
The First Stage
The Second Stage

Lessons in Observation: Birth
The Third Stage

Methods of Childbirth
Anesthesia
Prepared Childbirth
Cesarean Section
Laboring Through the Birthing Options

Birth Problems
Oxygen Deprivation
Preterm and Low-Birth-Weight Infants

Developing in a World of Diversity: Maternal and Infant Mortality Around the World

The Postpartum Period
Maternal Depression
Bonding

A Closer Look: Have We Found the Daddy Hormones?

Characteristics of Neonates
Assessing the Health of Neonates
Reflexes
Sensory Capabilities

A Closer Look: Studying Visual Acuity in Neonates: How Well Can They See?

Learning: Really Early Childhood "Education"
Sleeping and Waking
Sudden Infant Death Syndrome (SIDS)

Go to

http://www.thomsonedu.com/psychology/rathus
for an interactive version of this "Truth or Fiction" feature.

During the last few weeks before she gave birth, Michele explained: "I couldn't get my mind off the pregnancy—what it was going to be like when I finally delivered Lisa. I'd had the amniocentesis, so I knew it was a girl. I'd had the ultrasounds, so all her fingers and toes had been counted, but I was still hoping and praying that everything would turn out all right. To be honest, I was also worried about the delivery. I had always been an A student, and I guess I wanted to earn an A in childbirth as well. Matt was understanding, and he was even helpful, but, you know, it wasn't him.

"My obstetrician was bending over backwards—she could bend, I couldn't—being politically correct and kept on talking about how *we* had gotten pregnant and about how we were going to have the baby. Toward the end there, I would have been thrilled if it had really been we. Or I would even have allowed Matt to do it all by himself. But the fact is it was me, and I was worrying about how I could even reach the steering wheel of the car in those days, much less deliver a perfect healthy child. On TV, of course, they do it without even disturbing their mascara, but I was living in the real world. And waiting, waiting, waiting. And, oh yes, did I mention waiting?"

Nearly all first-time mothers struggle through the last weeks of pregnancy and worry about the mechanics of delivery. Childbirth is a natural function, of course, but so many of them have gone to classes to learn how to do what comes naturally! They worry about whether they'll get to the hospital or birthing center on time ("Is there gas in the car?" "Is it snowing?"). They worry about whether the baby will start breathing on its own properly. They may wonder if they'll do it on their own or need a C-section. They may also worry about whether it will hurt, and how much, and when they should ask for anesthetics, and, well, how to earn that A.

Close to full **term**, Michele and other women are sort of front-loaded and feel bent out of shape, and guess what? They are. The weight of the fetus may also be causing backaches. Will they deliver the baby, or will the baby—by being born—deliver them from discomfort? "Hanging in and having Lisa was a wonderful experience," Michele said. "I think Matt should have had it."

term A set period of time, such as the typical period of time between conception and the birth of a baby.

Braxton-Hicks contractions The first, usually painless, contractions of childbirth.

prostaglandins (pross-tuh-GLAN-dins) Hormones that stimulate uterine contractions.

oxytocin (ok-see-TOE-sin) A pituitary hormone that stimulates labor contractions (from the Greek *oxys*, meaning "quick," and *tokos*, meaning "birth").

neonate A newborn child (from the Greek *neos*, meaning "new," and the Latin *natus*, meaning "born").

Countdown . . .

Question: What events occur just before the beginning of childbirth? Early in the last month of pregnancy, the head of the fetus settles in the pelvis. This process is called dropping or lightening. Because lightening decreases pressure on the diaphragm, the mother may, in fact, feel lighter.

The first uterine contractions are called **Braxton-Hicks contractions**, or false labor contractions. They are relatively painless and may be experienced as early as the sixth month of pregnancy. They tend to increase in frequency as the pregnancy progresses and may serve to tone the muscles that will be used in delivery. Although Braxton-Hicks contractions may be confused with actual labor contractions, real labor contractions are more painful and regular and are also usually intensified by walking.

A day or so before labor begins, increased pelvic pressure from the fetus may rupture superficial blood vessels in the birth canal so that blood appears in vaginal secretions. The mucous tissue that had plugged the cervix and protected the uterus from infection becomes dislodged. At about this time, about 1 woman in 10 has a rush of warm liquid from the vagina. This liquid is amniotic fluid, and its discharge means that the amniotic sac has burst. The amniotic sac usually does not burst until the end of the first stage of childbirth, as described later. Indigestion, diarrhea, an ache in the small of the back, and abdominal cramps are also common signs that labor is beginning.

Truth or Fiction Revisited: The fetus may actually signal the mother when it is "ready" to be born, that is, when it is mature enough to sustain life outside the uterus. The adrenal and pituitary glands of the fetus may trigger labor by secreting hormones (Snegovskikh et al., 2006).

Fetal hormones stimulate the placenta (which is a gland as well as a relay station for nutrition and wastes between mother and fetus) and the uterus to secrete **prostaglandins**. Prostaglandins are the main culprits when women experience uncomfortable cramping before or during menstruation; they also serve the function of exciting the muscles of the uterus to engage in labor contractions. As labor progresses, the pituitary gland releases **oxytocin**, another hormone. Oxytocin stimulates contractions that are powerful enough to expel the baby.

In this chapter, we discuss the events of childbirth and the characteristics of the **neonate**. Arriving in the new world may be a bit more complex than you had thought, and it may also be that neonates can do a bit more than you had imagined.

The Stages of Childbirth

Regular uterine contractions signal the beginning of childbirth. Developmentalists speak of childbirth as occurring in three stages.

The First Stage

Question: What happens during the first stage of childbirth? In the first stage of childbirth, uterine contractions **efface** and **dilate** the cervix. This passageway needs to widen to about 4 inches (10 centimeters) to allow the baby to pass. Dilation of the cervix is responsible for most of the pain during childbirth. If the cervix dilates rapidly and easily, there may be little or no discomfort.

The first stage is the long stage. Among women undergoing their first deliveries, this stage may last from a few hours to more than a day. One-half a day to one day is about average, but some long stages are much briefer and some last up to a couple of days. Subsequent pregnancies take less time and may be surprisingly rapid, sometimes between 1 and 2 hours. The first contractions are not usually all that painful and are spaced 10 to 20 minutes apart. They may last from 20 to 40 seconds each.

As the process continues, the contractions become more powerful, frequent, and regular. Women are usually advised to go to the hospital or birthing center when the contractions are 4 to 5 minutes apart. Until the end of the first stage of labor, the mother is usually in a labor room with her partner or another companion.

If the woman is to be "prepped"—that is, if her pubic hair is to be shaved—it takes place now. The prep is intended to lower the chances of infection during delivery and to facilitate the performance of an **episiotomy** (described later). A woman may be given an enema to prevent an involuntary bowel movement during labor. However, many women find prepping and enemas degrading and seek obstetricians who do not perform them routinely.

During the first stage of childbirth, **fetal monitoring** may be used. One kind of monitoring is an electronic sensing device strapped around the woman's abdomen. It can measure the fetal heart rate as well as the frequency, strength, and duration of the mother's contractions. An abnormal heart rate alerts the medical staff to possible fetal distress so that appropriate steps can be taken, such as speeding up the delivery by **forceps**, a **vacuum extraction tube**, or other means. The forceps is a curved instrument that fits around the baby's head and allows the baby to be pulled out of the mother's body. The vacuum extraction tube relies on suction to pull the baby through the birth canal.

efface To rub out or wipe out; to become thin.

dilate To make wider or larger.

episiotomy (ih-pee-zee-AH-tuh-mee) A surgical incision in the area between the birth canal and the anus that widens the vaginal opening, preventing random tearing during childbirth.

fetal monitoring The use of instruments to track the heart rate and oxygen levels of the fetus during childbirth.

forceps A curved instrument that fits around the head of the baby and permits it to be pulled through the birth canal.

vacuum extraction tube An instrument that uses suction to pull the baby through the birth canal.

When the cervix is nearly fully dilated, the head of the fetus begins to move into the vagina, or birth canal. This process is called **transition**. During transition, which lasts about 30 minutes or less, contractions usually are frequent and strong.

The Second Stage

The second stage of childbirth follows transition. *Question: What occurs during the second stage of childbirth?* The second stage begins when the baby appears at the opening of the vagina (now referred to as the "birth canal"; see ● Figure 4.1). The second stage is briefer than the first stage. It may last minutes or a few hours and culminates in the birth of the baby. The woman may be taken to a delivery room for the second stage of childbirth.

transition The initial movement of the head of the fetus into the birth canal.

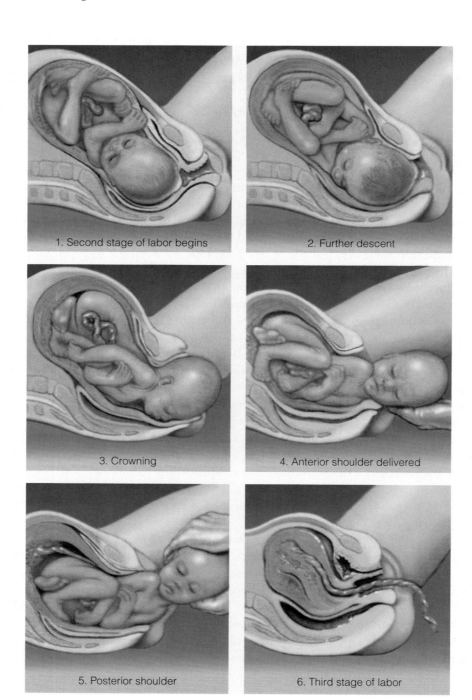

1. Second stage of labor begins

2. Further descent

3. Crowning

4. Anterior shoulder delivered

5. Posterior shoulder

6. Third stage of labor

● **Figure 4.1**
The Stages of Childbirth

In the first stage, uterine contractions efface and dilate the cervix to about 4 inches so that the baby may pass. The second stage begins with movement of the baby into the birth canal and ends with birth of the baby. During the third stage, the placenta separates from the uterine wall and is expelled through the birth canal.

The contractions of the second stage stretch the skin surrounding the birth canal farther and propel the baby farther along. The baby's head is said to have crowned when it begins to emerge from the birth canal. Once crowning has occurred, the baby normally emerges completely within minutes.

The physician, nurse, or midwife may perform an episiotomy once crowning takes place. The purpose of the episiotomy is to prevent random tearing when the area between the birth canal and the anus becomes severely stretched. Women are unlikely to feel the incision of the episiotomy because the pressure of the crowning head tends to numb the region between the vagina and the anus. The episiotomy, like prepping and the enema, is controversial and is not practiced in Europe. The incision may cause itching and discomfort as it heals. The incidence of the use of episiotomy in the United States dropped from about 70% in 1983 to 19% in 2000 (Goldberg et al., 2002). Many health professionals believe that an episiotomy is warranted when the baby's shoulders are quite wide or if the baby's heart rate declines for a long period of time. The strongest predictor of whether a practitioner will choose to use episiotomy is not the condition of the mother or the baby, but rather whether the physician normally performs an episiotomy.

Whether or not the physician performs an episiotomy, the passageway into the world outside is a tight fit, and the baby squeezes through. Mothers may be alarmed at

Lessons in Observation
Birth

 To watch this video, visit your book companion website. You can also answer the questions and e-mail your responses to your professor.

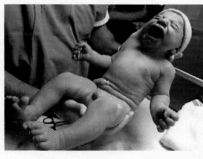

Lee delivers a healthy baby boy named Carter after laboring for more than 9 hours. The appearance of a newborn does not fit most people's definition of a "cute baby."

Learning Objectives

- What are the different birthing options available to expectant mothers?
- What are the different stages of birth?
- What does a newborn baby look like?
- What does a newborn baby act like?
- What does the Apgar scale test for in newborn babies?
- Why do health-care providers use the Apgar scale?

Applied Lesson

Describe the stages of birth. What stage is highlighted in the video?

Critical Thinking

If a baby scores low on the Apgar scale, what treatment options do parents and health-care providers have? Does the Apgar score predict the future health of a baby?

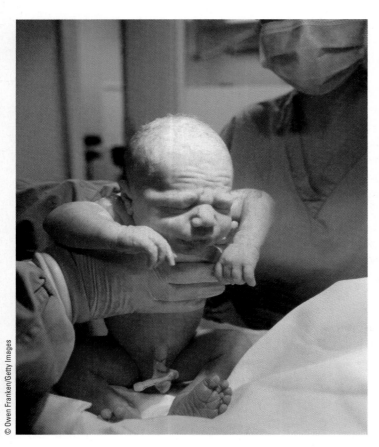

© Owen Franken/Getty Images

● **Figure 4.2** A Clamped and Severed Umbilical Cord

The stump of the cord dries and falls off in about 10 days.

the visual results of the tight fit. Sometimes the baby's head and facial features are quite bent out of shape. The baby's head can wind up elongated, its nose can be flattened or pushed to the side, and the ears can be contorted, as though this little thing had gotten caught up in a vicious prizefight. My wife and I sometimes joke that our second child was born with her nose apparently coming out the side of her cheek. Parents understandably wonder whether their baby's features will "pop up" properly or return to a more normal shape. Usually they need not worry.

Don't wait for the baby to be held upside down and slapped on the buttocks to spur breathing on its own. That happens in old movies but not in today's hospitals and birthing centers. Today, to clear the passageway for breathing from any obstructions, mucus is suctioned from the baby's mouth as soon as the head emerges from the birth canal. The procedure may be repeated when the baby has fully emerged. **Truth or Fiction Revisited:** It is not true that newborn babies are held upside down and slapped on the buttocks to stimulate independent breathing.

When the baby is breathing adequately on its own, the umbilical cord is clamped and severed about 3 inches from the baby's body (● Figure 4.2). At approximately 266 days after conception, mother and infant have finally become separate beings. The stump of the umbilical cord will dry and fall off on its own in about 7 to 10 days. There are exceptions. My daughter Allyn, nearly 2 at the time, yanked off the umbilical cord of her newborn sister Jordan, causing a crisis in the family but no particular harm to Jordan.

Truth or Fiction Revisited: It is not true that the way the umbilical cord is cut determines whether the baby's "belly button" will be an "innie" or an "outie." Your belly-button status—that is, whether you have an outie or an innie—is unrelated to the methods of your obstetrician.

You might think that it would be nice for mother and baby to hang out together for a while at this juncture, but the baby is frequently whisked away by a nurse, who will perform various procedures, including footprinting the baby, supplying an ID bracelet, putting antibiotic ointment (erythromycin) or drops of silver nitrate into the baby's eyes to prevent bacterial infections, and giving the baby a vitamin K injection to help its blood clot properly if it bleeds (newborn babies do not manufacture vitamin K). While these procedures go on, the mother is in the third stage of labor.

The Third Stage

The third stage of labor is also referred to as the placental stage. It lasts from minutes to an hour or more. *Question: What happens during the third stage of childbirth?* During the third stage, the placenta separates from the wall of the uterus and is expelled through the birth canal along with fetal membranes. Bleeding is normal at this time. The uterus begins to shrink, although it will take some weeks for it to approximate its prepregnancy size. The obstetrician now sews the episiotomy, if one has been performed.

Active Review

1. The first uterine contractions are "false" and are called _____ contractions.
2. A day or so before delivery, about 1 woman in 10 has a rush of _____ fluid from the vagina.
3. In the first stage of childbirth, uterine contractions cause the cervix to become effaced and _____.
4. _____ occurs when the cervix is nearly fully dilated and the head of the fetus begins to move into the birth canal.
5. When the baby is breathing adequately, the _____ cord is clamped and severed.
6. During the third stage, the _____ separates from the uterine wall and is expelled.

Reflect & Relate: How do you feel about the routine performance of "prepping" and episiotomy? Why are these issues often controversial and personal?

Go to

http://www.thomsonedu.com/psychology/rathus

for an interactive version of this review.

Methods of Childbirth

Think of old movies in which a woman is giving birth in her home on the prairie and a helpful neighbor emerges from the bedroom, heralding the good news to the anxious father and members of the community. Perhaps prairies have not hosted the majority of childbirths over the millennia, but childbirth was once a more intimate procedure that usually took place in the woman's home and involved her, perhaps a **midwife**, and family. This pattern is followed in many less developed nations today, but only rarely in the United States and other developed nations. Contemporary American childbirths usually take place in hospitals, where physicians who use sophisticated instruments and **anesthetics** to protect mother and child from complications and discomfort oversee the birth. There is no question that modern medicine has saved lives, but childbearing has also become more impersonal. Some argue that modern methods wrest control from women over their own bodies. They even argue that anesthetics have denied many women the experience of giving birth, although many or most women admit that they appreciate having the experience "muted."

In the next section, we consider a number of contemporary methods for facilitating childbirth.

Anesthesia

Painful childbirth has historically been seen as the standard for women, but the development of modern medicine and effective anesthetics has led many people to believe that women need not experience discomfort during childbirth. Today, at least some anesthesia is used in most American deliveries. *Questions: How is anesthesia used in childbirth? What are its effects on the baby?*

General anesthesia achieves its anesthetic effect by putting the woman to sleep by means of a barbiturate that is injected into a vein in the hand or arm. Other drugs in common use are **tranquilizers**, oral barbiturates, and narcotics. These drugs are not anesthetics per se, but they may reduce anxiety and the perception of pain without causing sleep.

midwife An individual who helps women in childbirth (from Old English roots meaning "with woman").

anesthetics Agents that produce partial or total loss of the sense of pain (from Greek roots meaning "without feeling").

general anesthesia The process of eliminating pain by putting the person to sleep.

tranquilizer A drug that reduces feelings of anxiety and tension.

General anesthesia can have negative effects on the infant, including abnormal patterns of sleep and wakefulness and decreased attention and social responsiveness shortly after birth (Caton et al., 2002). The higher the dosage of anesthesia, the greater the effect. But there is little evidence that these anesthetics have long-term effects on the child (Caton et al., 2002).

Regional or **local anesthetics** deaden pain without putting the mother to sleep. With a pudendal block, the mother's external genitals are numbed by local injection. With an epidural block and the spinal block, anesthesia is injected into the spinal canal or spinal cord, temporarily numbing the body below the waist. Local anesthesia has minor depressive effects on the strength and activity levels of neonates shortly after birth, but when administered properly, the effects have not been shown to linger (Caton et al., 2002; Eltzschig et al., 2003).

In contrast to the use of anesthesia is a trend toward **natural childbirth**. In natural childbirth, a woman uses no anesthesia. Instead, a woman is educated about the biological aspects of reproduction and delivery, encouraged to maintain physical fitness, and taught relaxation and breathing exercises.

Prepared Childbirth

Question: What is prepared childbirth? Most women who are pregnant for the first time expect pain and discomfort during childbirth. Certainly the popular media image of childbirth is one in which the woman sweats profusely and screams and thrashes in pain. When French obstetrician Fernand Lamaze visited Russia, he discovered that many Russian women bore babies without anesthetics or pain. He studied their relaxation techniques and brought these techniques to Western Europe and the United States, where they became known as the **Lamaze method**, or pre-

local anesthetic A method that reduces pain in an area of the body.

natural childbirth A method of childbirth in which women use no anesthesia and are educated about childbirth and strategies for coping with discomfort.

Lamaze method A childbirth method in which women are educated about childbirth, learn to relax and breathe in patterns that conserve energy and lessen pain, and have a coach (usually the father) present during childbirth. Also called prepared childbirth.

© Masterfile

An Exercise Class for Pregnant Women
Years ago, the rule of thumb was that pregnant women were not to exert themselves. Today, it is recognized that exercise is healthful for pregnant women because it promotes cardiovascular fitness and increases muscle strength. Fitness and strength are assets during childbirth, and at other times.

pared childbirth. Lamaze (1981) contended that women could engage in breathing and relaxation exercises that would lessen fear and pain by giving them something to do and distracting them from discomfort.

In the Lamaze method, women do not go it alone. The mother-to-be attends Lamaze classes with a "coach"—most often, her partner—who will aid her in the delivery room by doing things such as massaging her, timing the contractions, offering social support, and coaching her in patterns of breathing and relaxation. The woman is taught to breathe in a specific way during contractions. She is taught how to contract specific muscles in her body while remaining generally relaxed. The idea is that she will be able to transfer this training to the process of childbirth by remaining generally at ease while her uterine muscles contract. The training procedure tones muscles that will be helpful in childbirth (such as leg muscles) and enables a woman to minimize tension, conserve energy, and experience less anxiety.

The woman is also educated about the process of childbirth, and the father-to-be or another coach is integrated into the process. As a result, the woman receives more social support than pregnant women who do not go through Lamaze training. **Truth or Fiction Revisited:** It is not true that women who give birth according to the Lamaze method do not experience pain. They do, however, apparently report less pain and ask for less medication when others, such as their partner, are present (Meldrum, 2003).

Social support during labor can be provided by individuals other than a woman's partner. A mother, sibling, or friend also can serve as a coach. Studies also demonstrate the benefit of continuous emotional support during labor by an experienced but non-professional female companion known as a doula (Guzikowski, 2006). Women with doulas present during the birth appear to have shorter labors than women without doulas (Campbell et al., 2006).

Cesarean Section

There are many controversies about the **cesarean section**. The first that comes to my mind is the proper spelling. Years ago, the term was spelled *Caesarean* section, after the Roman emperor Julius Caesar, who was thought to have been delivered in this

cesarean section A method of childbirth in which the neonate is delivered through a surgical incision in the mother's abdomen. (Also spelled Caesarean.)

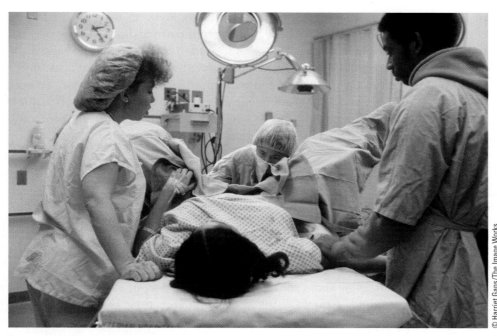

© Harriet Gans/The Image Works

Partner in the Delivery Room
Today, the woman's partner is usually integrated into the process of childbirth. In this case, the father and mother take pride in "their" accomplishment of childbirth.

manner. Now, however, the more common spelling is *cesarean*. In any event, the term is usually abbreviated C-section.

Questions: What is a C-section? Why is it so common? In a C-section, the physician delivers the baby by abdominal surgery. The physician cuts through the mother's abdomen and the uterus and physically removes the baby. The incisions are then sewn up. Most health professionals encourage the mother to get up and walk around on the same day as the surgery, but doing so is usually painful. When the C-section first came into common practice, it left visible scars on the abdomen. Physicians usually perform C-sections today so that the incision is more or less hidden by the upper edge of the woman's pubic hair. This method is referred to as a "bikini cut," meaning that it is below the area normally exposed when a woman wears that type of brief swimsuit.

Truth or Fiction Revisited: Nearly 3 of every 10 births (29%) in the United States are currently by C-section (Bakalar, 2005). To gain some perspective, note that C-sections accounted for only 1 in 20 births (5%) in 1965. Why the upsurge? Some of the increase is due to advances in medicine. For example, fetal monitors now allow physicians to more readily detect fetal distress. Other factors, though, are less "medical." Physicians also perform C-sections because they are concerned about the possibility of malpractice suits if something goes wrong during a vaginal delivery and also, frankly, because so many physicians are trained to perform them whenever they suspect that there might be a reason for them (Maternity Center Association, 2004).

Physicians prefer C-sections to vaginal delivery when they believe that normal delivery may threaten the mother or child or may simply be more difficult than desired. Typical indications of the C-section are a small pelvis in the mother, maternal weakness or fatigue (e.g., if labor has been prolonged), multiple babies, or a baby that is very large or in apparent distress. C-sections are also performed when the physician wants to prevent the circulatory systems of the mother and baby from mixing, as might occur when there is bleeding during vaginal delivery. C-sections in such cases help prevent transmission of genital herpes or HIV, the virus that causes AIDS (see the "Closer Look" feature "Preventing One's Baby from Being Infected with HIV" in Chapter 3). The combination of anti-HIV drugs and C-section cuts the chance that an HIV-infected mother will transmit HIV to her baby to less than 1 in 50 from an original chance of 1 in 4 (Coovadia, 2004). The physician may also perform a C-section when it appears that the baby is facing in the wrong direction. It is normal, and safest, for babies to be born head first. A C-section is indicated if the baby is going to be born sideways or "backward," that is, feet first. Some women also ask for C-sections (Cohen & Feig, 2003). Some want to avoid the pain of vaginal delivery (Nerum et al., 2006), and some want to control exactly when the baby will be born (Lo, 2003). Women who have C-sections tend to be less satisfied with the procedure than women who have vaginal deliveries (East et al., 2006).

Laboring Through the Birthing Options

We have considered some of the kinds of childbirth available today. Now we consider some other issues. *Question: How can a woman decide where to deliver her baby?* Women in the developed world have never had so many choices in childbirth. They have the option to labor in a pool of warm water or at home in bed, in a cozy hospital "birthing suite" or in a traditional labor room. They can choose between an obstetrician or midwife, or both. How about some aromatherapy or acupuncture, yoga or Yanni to help ease the pain and discomfort? Whatever your desire, those in the baby-delivery business want to make sure that a woman's birthing experience is all it can be.

There is an increasing demand for nurse-midwives. These trained professionals, usually women, stay with a woman throughout her labor, supporting her and working with techniques such as massage to avoid surgery, forceps, and other interventions.

More women also seek a family atmosphere for their deliveries, inviting relatives, friends, and their other children to witness the event. And, unhappy with the days when obstetricians dictated every step of the way, today's mothers-to-be want control, many working through every detail of their "birth plan" with their providers.

"State-of the Art" Birthing

In a traditional hospital birth, labor and delivery take place in separate rooms or in the same room, after which a woman may be transferred to a recovery room and then to a hospital room for the duration of her stay. Today's all-in-one labor, delivery, recovery, and postpartum (LDRP) rooms aim to reduce problems for both mother and medical staff.

LDRP rooms resemble high-class hotel suites, but they are equipped with all the medical necessities for an uncomplicated birth and emergency facilities are generally just down the hall. Many doctors worry about delivering babies at freestanding birthing centers because there are no surgical facilities at such centers; if complications arise, a woman would need to be transferred elsewhere.

The Home Birth Debate

The overwhelming majority of U.S. women give birth in hospitals. In the United States, there is approximately 1 maternal death for every 2,500 live births. In developing countries, where medical resources are scarce, as many as 1 woman in 6 will die in childbirth (Save the Children, 2004b). Although these impressive numbers may be partly explained as a result of women giving birth in hospitals, home delivery can be a fairly safe option for healthy women with little risk of complications, especially if they have given birth before. A certified nurse-midwife will typically assess a woman's risk for complications and her proximity to emergency medical care before agreeing to assist with a home birth.

With all these options available, obstetricians encourage women to be informed of the risks and benefits of each before making a decision.

Active Review

7. _____ anesthesia achieves its anesthetic effect during childbirth by putting the woman to sleep.

8. In a(n) _____ block, anesthesia is injected into the spine, numbing the body below the waist.

9. _____ argued that women can learn to dissociate uterine contractions from pain and fear through breathing exercises and muscle-relaxation techniques.

10. A _____ is performed for various reasons, including when a baby is too large to pass through the woman's pelvis, when the mother or baby is in

distress, and when striving to prevent transmission of genital herpes or HIV.

Reflect & Relate: If you were delivering a child, would you want to use anesthetic medication? Would you use the Lamaze method? Why or why not? If you were a prospective father, what would your thoughts be? What are the pros and cons of both methods?

Go to

http://www.thomsonedu.com/psychology/rathus

for an interactive version of this review.

Birth Problems

Although most deliveries are unremarkable from a medical standpoint, perhaps every delivery is most remarkable from the parents' point of view. Still, a number of problems can and do occur. In this section, we discuss the effects of oxygen deprivation and the problems of preterm and low-birth-weight neonates.

Oxygen Deprivation

Question: What are the effects of oxygen deprivation at birth? Researchers use two terms to discuss oxygen deprivation: anoxia and hypoxia. **Anoxia** derives from roots meaning "without oxygen." **Hypoxia** derives from roots meaning "under" and "oxygen," the point again being that the baby does not receive enough oxygen throughout pregnancy to develop properly. Prenatal oxygen deprivation can impair the development of the fetus's central nervous system, leading to a host of problems, including cognitive and motor problems and even psychological disorders (Golan & Huleihel, 2006; Hogan et al., 2006). Much research has focused on the effects of oxygen deprivation on the hippocampus, a brain structure that is vital in memory formation. Children who were deprived of oxygen at birth often show the predicted problems in learning and memory, and also in motor development and spatial relations (Hopkins-Golightly et al., 2003).

Prolonged cutoff of the baby's oxygen supply during delivery can also cause psychological and physical health problems, such as early-onset **schizophrenia** and cerebral palsy (Rees et al., 2006). Most researchers now consider schizophrenia a disease of the brain, and oxygen deprivation is believed to impair the development of neural connections in the brain. And, of course, severe, prolonged oxygen deprivation is lethal.

Oxygen deprivation can be caused by maternal disorders such as diabetes, by immaturity of the baby's respiratory system, and by accidents, some of which involve pressure against the umbilical cord during birth. The fetus and emerging baby receive oxygen through the umbilical cord. Passage through the birth canal is tight, and the umbilical cord is usually squeezed during the process. If the squeezing is temporary, the effect is like holding one's breath for a moment and no problems are likely to ensue. (In fact, slight oxygen deprivation at birth is not unusual because the baby's transition from receiving oxygen through the umbilical cord to breathing on its own may not take place immediately after it is born.) But if constriction of the umbilical cord is prolonged, developmental problems can result. Prolonged constriction is more likely during a **breech** (bottom-first) **presentation**, when the baby's body may press the umbilical cord against the birth canal.

Fetal monitoring can help detect anoxia before it causes damage. A C-section can be performed if the fetus seems to be in distress.

Preterm and Low-Birth-Weight Infants

Because the fetus makes dramatic gains in weight during the last weeks of pregnancy, prematurity and low birth weight usually go hand in hand. *Question: What is meant by the terms prematurity and low birth weight?* A baby is considered premature or **preterm** when birth occurs at or before 37 weeks of gestation compared with the normal 40 weeks. A baby is considered to have a low birth weight when it weighs less than 5 pounds (about 2,500 grams). When a baby is low in birth weight, even though it is born at full term, it is referred to as being **small for dates**. As described in Chapter 3, mothers who smoke, abuse drugs, or fail to receive proper nutrition place their babies at risk of being small for dates. Small-for-dates babies tend to remain shorter and lighter than their age-mates and show slight delays in

anoxia A condition characterized by lack of oxygen.

hypoxia A condition characterized by less oxygen than is required.

schizophrenia A severe psychological disorder characterized by disturbances in thought and language, perception and attention, motor activity, and mood and by withdrawal and absorption in daydreams or fantasy.

breech presentation A position in which the fetus enters the birth canal buttocks first.

preterm Born at or before completion of 37 weeks of gestation.

small for dates Descriptive of neonates who are unusually small for their age.

learning and problems in attention when compared with their age-mates (O'Keeffe et al., 2003). Preterm babies who survive are more likely than small-for-dates babies to achieve normal heights and weights.

Approximately 7% of children are born preterm or low in birth weight, although the incidence varies in different racial and ethnic groups. But in the case of multiple births—even twins—the risk of having a preterm child rises to at least 50% (Kogan et al., 2000).

Risks Associated with Prematurity and Low Birth Weight

Question: *What risks are connected with being born prematurely or low in birth weight?* Neonates weighing between 3.25 and 5.5 pounds are 7 times more likely to die than infants of normal birth weight, whereas those weighing less than 3.3 pounds are nearly 100 times as likely to die (Nadeau et al., 2003). But physical survival is only one issue connected with prematurity and low birth weight.

By and large, the lower a child's birth weight, the more poorly he or she fares on measures of neurological development and cognitive functioning throughout the school years (Dorling et al., 2006; Nadeau et al., 2003; Wocadlo & Rieger, 2006). Children whose birth weight is less than 750 grams (1.65 pounds) fare less well at middle-school age than children whose birth weight was 750–1,499 grams (1.65–3.30 pounds) (Taylor et al., 2004). Both low-birth-weight groups perform more poorly than children whose birth weight was normal. There also seem to be sex differences. The cognitive functioning and school achievement of girls with low birth weight seem to improve more rapidly than those of boys with low birth weight (Hindmarsh et al., 2000).

There are also risks for motor development. One study compared 96 very low birth weight (VLBW) children with normal-term children at 6, 9, 12, and 18 months, correcting for age according to the expected date of delivery (Jeng et al., 2000). The median age at which the full-term infants began to walk was 12 months, compared with 14 months for the VLBW infants. By 18 months of age, all full-term infants were walking, whereas 11% of the VLBW infants had not yet begun to walk.

The outcomes for low-birth-weight children are variable. One research group followed a group of 1,338 Dutch individuals who were born in 1983 with either a gestational age of less than 32 weeks or a birth weight of less than 3.3 pounds (Walther et al., 2000). The children were assessed at the age of 2 years by their pediatricians, and at the ages of 5 and 9–14 years by teams of investigators, including teachers and parents. All in all, only 10% of the group could be characterized as having a severe disability at ages 9–14. However, many more children appeared to have mild to moderate problems in learning or behavior.

Preschool experience appears to foster the cognitive and social development of VLBW children. Hoy and McClure (2000) compared a group of VLBW children who attended preschool with a group who did not and also with a group of normal-birth-weight children of the same age. The VLBW children who attended preschool outperformed the VLBW children who did not on measures of cognitive functioning and teacher ratings. They earned higher grades, worked harder, were more likely to participate in social interactions, and were more likely to be rated as "learns a lot." However, their performance on all measures was still exceeded somewhat by the normal-birth-weight children.

Signs of Prematurity

Preterm babies show characteristic signs of immaturity. They are relatively thin because they have not yet formed the layer of fat that gives so many full-term children their round, robust appearance. They often have fine, downy hair, referred to as **lanugo**, and an oily white substance on the skin known as **vernix**. Lanugo and

lanugo (luh-NOO-go) Fine, downy hair that covers much of the body of the neonate, especially preterm babies.

vernix An oily white substance that coats the skin of the neonate, especially preterm babies.

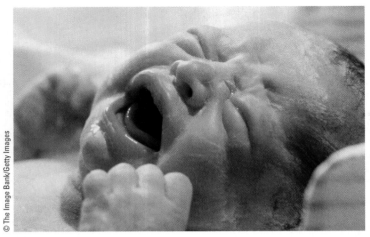

A Newborn Baby
This newborn shows lanugo and vernix, both characteristics of prematurity.

vernix disappear within a few days or weeks after birth. If the babies are born 6 weeks or more before full term, their nipples will not yet have emerged. The testicles of boys born this early will not yet have descended into the scrotum. However, the nipples develop further and the testes descend after birth.

The muscles of preterm babies are immature. As a result, the babies' vital sucking and breathing reflexes are weak. The muscles of preterm babies may not be mature enough to sustain independent breathing. In addition, the walls of the tiny air sacs in their lungs may tend to stick together because the babies do not yet secrete substances that lubricate the walls of the sacs. As a result, babies born more than a month before full term may breathe irregularly or may suddenly stop breathing, evidence of a cluster of problems known as **respiratory distress syndrome**. About one baby in seven born 1 month early shows the syndrome, and it is found more fre-

Developing in a World of Diversity

Maternal and Infant Mortality Around the World

Modern medicine has made vast strides in decreasing the rates of maternal and infant mortality, but the advances are not equally spread throughout the world. Save the Children, a nonprofit relief and development organization that helps children in more than 40 countries, has been tracking the likelihood that a woman will die in childbirth and that an infant will die during its first year.

As shown in ■ Table 4.1, the likelihood of maternal mortality and infant mortality is connected with factors such as the percentage of births that are attended by trained people, the literacy rate of adult women (which is one measure of the level of education of women), and the participation of women in national government (which is one measure of the extent to which a society empowers women). The safest

place for a woman to deliver and for her baby to survive is Sweden, where the chances of the woman dying are about 1 in 30,000 and where only 3 infants in 1,000 die during the first year. Perhaps it is no coincidence that Sweden also has nearly a 100% adult female literacy rate, attends all recorded births with trained personnel, and has the highest participation rate (45%) by women in national government. Afghanistan may have the world's most frightening statistics. As the result of a pregnancy, 1 woman in 6 will die, and 165 children of 1,000 will die during their first year. In Afghan society, the literacy rate for women is only 21%. There is little, if any, professional assistance during childbirth (12%). And, in this male-dominated society, women have virtually no role in government. There is also little, if any,

prenatal care in Afghanistan and other nations with high infant mortality rates.

Americans who view charts such as Table 4.1 wonder why the United States is not closer to the top of the list. One answer is that the United States is made up of nations within the nation. States with above-average poverty rates, large rural populations, and less-than-average levels of education have the highest maternal mortality and infant mortality rates. Among these states are Texas, Mississippi, Arkansas, Arizona, and New Mexico.

Reflect: *How can you make certain that you—or those you care about— receive the proper health care needed during pregnancy and during childbirth?*

quently among infants born still earlier. Respiratory distress syndrome causes a large percentage of U.S. neonatal deaths. Preterm infants with severe respiratory stress syndrome show poorer development in cognitive, language, and motor skills and show more persistent neurological abnormalities over the first 2 years of development than infants with less severe respiratory distress and full-term infants. Injecting pregnant women at risk for delivering preterm babies with corticosteroids, however, increases the babies' chances of survival (Crowther et al., 2006). Babies of these women are less likely to have respiratory distress syndrome or severe lung disease and are less likely to need treatment with oxygen or mechanical help breathing.

Major strides have been made in helping low-birth-weight children survive. Still, low-birth-weight children who do survive often have problems, including below-average verbal ability and academic achievement and various physical, motor, perceptual, neurological, and behavioral impairments (Saigal et al., 2006).

Preterm infants with very low birth weights (less than 3.3 pounds) are likely to show the greatest cognitive deficits and developmental delays. Medical advances in recent years, though, have reduced the severity and incidence of handicaps among babies with very low birth weights.

respiratory distress syndrome A cluster of breathing problems, including weak and irregular breathing, to which preterm babies are particularly prone.

■ **Table 4.1** Maternal Mortality and Infant Mortality Around the World as Related to Access to Medical Assistance and Empowerment of Women

Country	Lifetime Risk of Maternal Mortality	Percentage of Births Attended by Trained Personnel	Adult Female Literacy Rate (%)	Participation of Women in National Government (% of Seats Held by Women)	Infant Mortality Rate (per 1,000 Live Births)
1 in 29,800	100	99	45	3	
1 in 16,000	100	99	34	6	
1 in 9,800	100	99	38	4	
1 in 3,800	99	99	18	5	
1 in 2,800	100	96	6	5	
1 in 2,500	99	99	18	5	
1 in 1,800	99	93	15	6	
1 in 1,000	99	99	8	18	
1 in 830	76	78	22	31	
1 in 590	97	96	20	42	
1 in 480	81	77	4	36	
1 in 370	90	69	4	35	
1 in 370	86	89	23	24	
1 in 310	61	44	2	35	
1 in 140	88	87	9	30	
1 in 65	72	23	8	102	
1 in 48	43	45	9	67	
1 in 31	20	28	22	83	
1 in 19	43	72	12	108	
1 in 6	12	21	—	165	

Treatment of Preterm Babies

Question: How are preterm infants treated following birth? Because of their physical frailty, preterm infants usually remain in the hospital and are placed in **incubators**, which maintain a temperature-controlled environment and afford some protection from disease. The babies may be given oxygen, although excessive oxygen can cause permanent eye injury.

Parents and Preterm Neonates

One might assume that parents would be more concerned about preterm babies than babies who have gone to full term and thus would treat them better. Ironically, that is not the case. Parents often do not treat preterm neonates as well as they treat full-term neonates. For one thing, preterm neonates are less attractive than full-term babies. Preterm infants usually do not have the robust, appealing appearance of many full-term babies. Their cries are more high pitched and grating, and they are more irritable (Bugental & Happaney, 2004; Eckerman et al., 1999). The demands of caring for preterm babies can be depressing to mothers (Davis et al., 2003; Drewett et al., 2004). Mothers of preterm babies frequently report that they feel alienated from their babies and harbor feelings of failure, guilt, and low self-esteem. They respond less sensitively to their infants' behavior than mothers of full-term babies (Bugental & Happaney, 2004). Mothers of preterm infants also touch and talk to their infants less and hold them at a greater distance during feeding. Fear of hurting preterm babies can further discourage parents from handling them, but encouraging mothers to massage their preterm infants can help them cope with fear of handling their babies and with feelings of helplessness and hopelessness (Feijó et al., 2006).

Once they come home from the hospital, preterm infants remain more passive and less sociable than full-term infants (Larroque et al., 2005; McGrath et al., 2005), so they demand less interaction with parents. However, when their parents do interact with them during the first year, the parents are more likely to poke at preterm babies, caress them, and talk to them, perhaps in an effort to prod them out of their passivity. Mothers of preterm babies report feeling overprotective toward them, which may in part explain why 1-year-old preterm infants explore less and stay closer to their mothers than do full-term babies of the same age.

Preterm infants fare better when they have responsive and caring parents. Longitudinal research shows that preterm children who are reared in attentive and responsive environments attain higher intelligence test scores, have higher self-esteem, show more positive social skills, and have fewer behavioral and emotional problems in childhood than do preterm children reared in less responsive homes (Dieterich et al., 2004; Lawson & Ruff, 2004).

Intervention Programs

A generation ago, preterm babies were left as undisturbed as possible. For one thing, concern was aroused by the prospect of handling such a tiny, frail creature. For another, preterm babies would not normally experience interpersonal contact or other sources of external stimulation until full term. However, experiments carried out over the past two decades have suggested that preterm infants profit from early stimulation just as full-term babies do. Preterm babies benefit from being cuddled, rocked, talked to, and sung to, being exposed to recordings of their mothers' voices, and having mobiles placed within view. Recent studies have shown the value of live and recorded music in the preterm infant's environment (Arnon et al., 2006; Hunter & Sahler, 2006; Lai et al., 2006). Other forms of stimulation include massage (Field et al., 2006) and "kangaroo care" (Lai et al., 2006), in which the baby spends several hours a day lying skin to skin, chest to chest, with one of its parents. By and large, preterm infants exposed to stimulation tend to gain weight more rapidly, show fewer

incubator A heated, protective container in which premature infants are kept.

respiratory problems, and make greater advances in motor, intellectual, and neurological development than control infants (Caulfield, 2000; Dombrowski et al., 2000)(see ● Figure 4.3).

Other intervention programs help parents adjust to the birth and care of a low-birth-weight infant. One such program involved 92 preterm infants at three sites (Als et al., 2003). The following factors contributed to superior cognitive and motor development in the infants and better adjustment in the parents: early discontinuation of intravenous feeding, hospitalization with intensive care for digestive and other problems, and individualized counseling to foster appreciation of the infant.

As we see in the nearby "Developing in a World of Diversity" feature, maternal and infant mortality remain serious problems in many—perhaps most—parts of the world.

Louie Psihoyos/Getty Images

● **Figure 4.3**
Stimulating a Preterm Infant

It was once believed that preterm infants should be left as undisturbed as possible. Today, however, it is recognized that preterm infants usually profit from various kinds of stimulation.

Active Review

11. Prenatal _____ deprivation can impair the development of the fetus's central nervous system, leading to cognitive and motor problems and even psychological disorders.
12. A baby is considered to be _____ when birth occurs at or before 37 weeks of gestation.
13. A baby has a low _____ when it weighs less than 5.5 pounds (about 2,500 grams).

14. Research suggests that it is (Helpful or Harmful?) to stimulate preterm infants.

Reflect & Relate: If you had a preterm infant, do you think you would want to handle him or her as much as possible or would you tend to leave him or her alone? Explain.

Go to

http://www.thomsonedu.com/psychology/rathus

for an interactive version of this review.

The Postpartum Period

Postpartum derives from roots meaning "after" and "birth." The **postpartum period** refers to the weeks following delivery, but there is no specific limit. "Parting is such sweet sorrow," Shakespeare has Juliet tell Romeo. The "parting" from the baby is also frequently a happy experience. The family's long wait is over. Concerns about pregnancy and labor are over, fingers and toes have been counted, and despite some local discomfort, the mother finds her "load" to be lightened, most literally. However, according to the American Psychiatric Association (2000, p. 423), about 70% of new mothers have periods of tearfulness, sadness, and irritability that the association refers to as the "baby blues." In this section, we discuss two issues of the postpartum period: maternal depression and bonding.

postpartum period The period that immediately follows childbirth.

Maternal Depression

*Question: **What kinds of problems in mood do women experience during the postpartum period?*** These problems include the "baby blues" and more serious mood disorders ("postpartum-onset mood episodes"), which occasionally include "psychotic features" (American Psychiatric Association, 2000).

Truth or Fiction Revisited: Actually, it is normal to feel depressed following childbirth. The baby blues affect most women in the weeks after delivery (American Psychiatric Association, 2000). Baby blues and other postpartum mood problems are so common that they are statistically normal (Gavin et al., 2005). These problems are not limited to the United States or even to developed nations. They are far-flung, and researchers find them in China, Turkey, Guyana, Australia, and South Africa with similar frequency (Bloch et al., 2006; Cohen et al., 2006). Researchers believe that the baby blues are common because of hormonal changes that follow delivery (Kohl, 2004).

The baby blues last about 10 days and are generally not severe enough to impair the mother's functioning. Don't misunderstand; the baby blues are seriously discomforting and not to be ignored as in, "Oh, you're just experiencing what most women experience." The point is that most women can handle the baby blues, even though they are awful at times, partly because the women know that they are transient.

A minority of women but perhaps as many as one in five encounter the more serious mood disorder frequently referred to as **postpartum depression (PPD)**. PPD begins about a month after delivery and may linger for weeks, even months. PPD is technically referred to as a major depressive disorder with postpartum onset. As in other major depressive disorders, it is characterized by serious sadness, feelings of hopelessness and helplessness, feelings of worthlessness, difficulty concentrating, and major changes in appetite (usually loss of appetite) and sleep patterns (frequently insomnia). There can also be severe fluctuations in mood, with women sometimes feeling elated. Some women show obsessive concern with the well-being of their babies at this time. PPD can also interfere with the mother–baby relationship in the short term (Stanley et al., 2004).

Many researchers have suggested that PPD is caused by the interactions of physiological (mainly hormonal) and psychological factors, including a sudden drop in estrogen (Kohl, 2004). Feelings of depression before getting pregnant or during pregnancy are a risk factor for PPD, as are concerns about all the life changes that motherhood creates, marital problems, and having a sick or unwanted baby. But today the focus is on physiological factors because of the major changes in body chemistry during and after pregnancy and because women around the world seem to experience similar disturbances in mood, even when their life experiences and support systems are radically different from those found in the United States (Cohen et al., 2006).

According to the American Psychiatric Association (2000), postpartum mood episodes are accompanied by "psychotic features" in as many as 1 woman in 500. A psychotic feature may mean a break with reality. Mothers with these features may have delusional thoughts about the infant that place the infant at risk of injury of death. Some women experience delusions that the infant is possessed by the devil. Some women have "command hallucinations" to kill the infant and experience a command to kill the infant as though it is coming from the outside—perhaps from a commanding person or some kind of divine or evil spirit—even though the idea originates from within. Because these women may not be able to tell the difference between hallucinations and reality, the infant may be in serious jeopardy. Remember that these psychotic features are rather rare, however, and that when they occur, they need not always place the baby at risk.

Women who experience PPD usually profit from social support and a general history of high self-esteem. They may profit from counseling even if it does little more

postpartum depression (PPD) Severe, prolonged depression that afflicts 10–20% of women after delivery and that is characterized by sadness, apathy, and feelings of worthlessness.

than explain that many women encounter PPD and it usually eases and ends as time goes on. Drugs that increase estrogen levels or act as antidepressants may help. Most women will resolve PPD without professional help. At the very least, women should know that the problem is common and does not necessarily mean that something is wrong with them or that they are failing to live up to their obligations.

Bonding

Bonding—that is, the formation of bonds of attachment between parents and their children—is essential to the survival and well-being of children. Since the publication of controversial research by Marshall Klaus and John Kennell in the 1970s, many have wondered about the importance of bonding. *Question: How critical is parental interaction with neonates in the formation of bonds of attachment?*

Klaus and Kennell (1978) argued that the first hours postpartum provided a special—even a necessary—opportunity for bonding between parents and neonates. They labeled these hours a "maternal-sensitive" period during which the mother is particularly disposed, largely because of hormone levels, to form a bond with the neonate. In their study, one group of mothers was randomly assigned to standard hospital procedure in which their babies were whisked away to the nursery shortly after birth. Throughout the remainder of the hospital stay, the babies visited their mothers during

bonding The process of forming bonds of attachment between parent and child.

A Closer Look

Have We Found the Daddy Hormones?

Are oxytocin and vasopressin the "Daddy hormones"? Perhaps so, at least in meadow voles, which are a kind of tailless mouse, and sheep. These hormones are connected with the creation of mother–infant bonds in sheep, pair bonds in monogamous voles, and bonds of attachment between vole fathers and their young. **Truth or Fiction Revisited:** Experimental research shows that increasing vasopressin levels transforms an indifferent male into a caring, monogamous, and protective mate and father (Lim et al., 2004; Lim & Young, 2006).

Oxytocin and vasopressin are secreted by the pituitary gland, which secretes many hormones that are involved in reproduction and the nurturing of young. For example, prolactin regulates maternal behavior in lower mammals and stimulates the production of milk in women. Oxytocin stimulates labor but is also involved in social recognition and bonding. Vasopressin enables the body to conserve water by inhibiting urine production when fluid levels are low; however, it is also connected with paternal behavior patterns in some mammals. For example, male

prairie voles form pair-bonds with female prairie voles after mating with them (Lim et al., 2004; Lim & Young, 2006). Mating stimulates secretion of vasopressin, and vasopressin causes the previously promiscuous male to sing "I only have eyes for you."

Given their effects on voles, we may wonder how oxytocin and vasopressin may be connected with the formation of bonds between men and women, and men and children. Will perfume makers be lacing new scents with these hormones?

Reflect: In your own experience and in the portrayals of men and women you see in the media, what are the apparent sex differences in "cuddling," parenting, and tendencies toward monogamy? To what extent do you think that these differences may be the result of cultural influences or the result of chemistry, that is, chemicals such as oxytocin and vasopressin? Explain.

feeding. The other group of mothers spent 5 hours a day with their infants during the hospital stay. The hospital staff encouraged and reassured the group of mothers who had extended contact. Follow-ups over 2 years suggested that extended contact benefited both the mothers and their children. Mothers with extended contact were more likely than control mothers to cuddle their babies, soothe them when they cried, and interact with them.

Critics note that the Klaus and Kennell studies are fraught with methodological problems. For example, we cannot separate the benefits of extended contact from benefits attributable to parents' knowledge that they were in a special group and from the extra attention of the hospital staff. In short, the evidence that the hours after birth are critical is tainted. Consider the millions of solid adoptive parent–child relationships in which parents did not have early access to their children.

Parent–child bonding has been shown to be a complex process involving desire to have the child; parent–child familiarity with one another's sounds, odors, and tastes; and caring. On the other hand, serious maternal depression can delay bonding with newborns (Klier, 2006), and a history of rejection by parents can interfere with women's bonding with their own children (Leerkes & Crockenberg, 2006).

Truth or Fiction Revisited: Despite the Klaus and Kennell studies, which made a brief splash a generation ago, it is not true that parents must have extended early contact with their newborn children if adequate bonding is to take place. Researchers now view the hours after birth as only one element—and not even an essential element—in a complex and prolonged bonding process.

Active Review

15. Research suggests that the (Majority or Minority?) of new mothers experience periods of depression.
16. Postpartum depression has been connected with a precipitous decline in the hormone _____.
17. Research (Does or Does not?) show that early parental interaction with neonates is critical in the formation of bonds of attachment.

Reflect & Relate: Pretend for a minute that you visit a friend who has just had a baby. She is weepy and listless and worries that she doesn't have the "right" feelings for a new mother. What would you say to her? Why?

Go to

http://www.thomsonedu.com/psychology/rathus
for an interactive version of this review.

Characteristics of Neonates

Many neonates come into the world looking a bit fuzzy, but even though they are utterly dependent on others, they are probably more aware of their surroundings than you had imagined. Neonates make rapid adaptations to the world around them. In this section, we see how health professionals assess the health of neonates and describe the characteristics of neonates.

Assessing the Health of Neonates

Apgar scale A measure of a newborn's health that assesses appearance, pulse, grimace, activity level, and respiratory effort.

Question: How do health professionals assess the health of neonates? The neonate's overall level of health is usually evaluated at birth according to the **Apgar scale**, developed by Virginia Apgar in 1953. Apgar scores are based on five signs of health, as shown in ■ Table 4.2. The neonate can receive a score of 0, 1, or 2 on each sign. The total Apgar score can therefore vary from 0 to 10. A score of 7 or above usually indicates that the baby is not in danger. A score below 4 suggests that the baby is in critical condition and requires medical attention. By 1 minute after birth, most normal babies attain scores of 8 to 10 (Clayton & Crosby, 2006).

The acronym APGAR is commonly used as an aid to remember the five criteria of the Apgar scale:

A: the general **a**ppearance or color of the neonate
P: the **p**ulse or heart rate
G: **g**rimace (the 1-point indicator of reflex irritability)
A: general **a**ctivity level or muscle tone
R: **r**espiratory effort, or rate of breathing

The **Brazelton Neonatal Behavioral Assessment Scale**, developed by pediatrician T. Berry Brazelton, measures neonates' reflexes and other behavior patterns. This test screens neonates for behavioral and neurological problems by assessing four areas of behavior: motor behavior, including muscle tone and most **reflexes**; response to stress; adaptive behavior; and control over physiological state.

Reflexes

If soon after birth you had been held gently for a few moments with your face down in comfortably warm water, you would not have drowned. Instead of breathing the water in, you would have exhaled slowly through your mouth and engaged in swimming motions. (We urge readers not to test babies for this reflex. The hazards are obvious.) This swimming response is "prewired"—innate or inborn—and is just one of the many reflexes shown by neonates. *Questions: What are reflexes? What kinds of reflexes are shown by neonates?*

Reflexes are simple, unlearned, stereotypical responses that are elicited by certain types of stimulation. They do not require higher brain functions; they occur automatically, without thinking. Reflexes are the most complicated motor activities displayed by neonates. Neonates cannot roll over, sit up, reach for an object they see, or raise their heads.

Brazelton Neonatal Behavioral Assessment Scale A measure of a newborn's motor behavior, response to stress, adaptive behavior, and control over physiological state.

reflex An unlearned, stereotypical response to a stimulus.

■ **Table 4.2** The Apgar Scale

Points	0	1	2
Appearance:			
Color	Blue, pale	Body pink, extremities blue	Entirely pink
Pulse:			
Heart rate	Absent (not detectable)	Slow—below 100 beats/minute	Rapid—100–140 beats/minute
Grimace:			
Reflex irritability	No response	Grimace	Crying, coughing, sneezing
Activity level:			
Muscle tone	Completely flaccid, limp	Weak, inactive	Flexed arms and legs; resists extension
Respiratory effort:			
Breathing	Absent (infant is apneic)	Shallow, irregular, slow	Regular breathing; lusty crying

● **Figure 4.4**
The Rooting Reflex

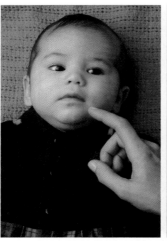

● **Figure 4.5** Testing the Sucking Reflex

● **Figure 4.6** The Moro Reflex

neural Of the nervous system.

rooting reflex A reflex in which infants turn their mouths and heads in the direction of a stroking of their cheek or the corner of their mouth.

Let us return to our early venture into the water. If you had been placed into the water not a few moments but several months after birth, the results might have been very different and disastrous. After a few months, the swimming reflex, like many others, ceases to exist. However, at 6 to 12 months of age infants can learn how to swim voluntarily. In fact, with careful guided practice, the transition from reflexive swimming to learned swimming can be reasonably smooth.

Many reflexes have survival value. Adults and neonates, for example, will reflexively close their eyes when assaulted with a puff of air or sudden bright light. Other reflexes seem to reflect interesting facets of the evolution of the nervous system. The swimming reflex seems to suggest that there was a time when our ancestors profited from being born able to swim.

Pediatricians learn a good deal about the adequacy of a neonate's **neural** functioning by testing a baby's reflexes. The absence or weakness of a reflex may indicate immaturity (as in prematurity), slowed responsiveness (which can result from anesthetics used during childbirth), brain injury, or retardation. Let us examine some of the reflexes shown by neonates.

The rooting and sucking reflexes are basic to survival. In the **rooting reflex**, the baby turns the head and mouth toward a stimulus that strokes the cheek, chin, or corner of the mouth (● Figure 4.4). The rooting reflex facilitates finding the mother's nipple in preparation for sucking. Babies will suck almost any object that touches their lips. The sucking reflex grows stronger during the first days after birth and can be lost if not stimulated (● Figure 4.5). As the months go on, reflexive sucking becomes replaced by voluntary sucking.

In the startle or **Moro reflex**, the back arches and the legs and arms are flung out and then brought back toward the chest, with the arms in a hugging motion (● Figure 4.6). The Moro reflex occurs when a baby's position is suddenly changed or when support for the head and neck is suddenly lost. It can also be elicited by

● **Figure 4.7**
The Grasping Reflex

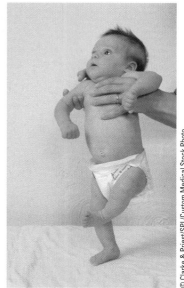

● **Figure 4.8**
The Stepping Reflex

loud noises, bumping the baby's crib, or jerking the baby's blanket. The Moro reflex is usually lost within 6 to 7 months after birth, although similar movements can be found in adults who suddenly lose support. Absence of the Moro reflex can indicate immaturity or brain damage.

During the first few weeks following birth, babies show an increasing tendency to reflexively grasp fingers or other objects pressed against the palms of their hands (● Figure 4.7). In this **grasping reflex**, or palmar reflex, they use four fingers only (the thumbs are not included). The grasping reflex is stronger when babies are simultaneously startled. Most babies can support their own weight in this way. They can be literally lifted into the air as they reflexively cling with two hands. Some babies can actually support their weight with only one hand. (Please do not try this experiment, however!) Absence of the grasping reflex may indicate depressed activity of the nervous system, which can stem from use of anesthetics during childbirth. The grasping reflex is usually lost within 3 to 4 months of age, and babies generally show voluntary grasping within 5 to 6 months.

Within 1 or 2 days after birth, babies show a reflex that mimics walking. When held under the arms and tilted forward so that the feet press against a solid surface, a baby will show a **stepping reflex** in which the feet advance one after the other (● Figure 4.8). A full-term baby "walks" heel to toe, whereas a preterm infant is more likely to remain on tiptoe. The stepping reflex usually disappears by about 3 or 4 months of age.

In the **Babinski reflex**, the neonate fans or spreads the toes in response to stroking of the underside of the foot from heel to toes. The Babinski reflex normally disappears toward the end of the first year, to be replaced by curling downward of the toes. Persistence of the Babinski reflex may suggest defects of the lower spinal cord, lagging development of nerve cells, or other disorders.

The **tonic-neck reflex** is observed when the baby is lying on its back and turns its head to one side (● Figure 4.9). The arm and leg on that side extend, while the limbs on the opposite side flex. You can see why this reflex sometimes is known as the "fencing position."

Moro reflex A reflex in which infants arch their back, fling out their arms and legs, and draw them back toward the chest in response to a sudden change in position.

grasping reflex A reflex in which infants grasp objects that cause pressure against the palms.

stepping reflex A reflex in which infants take steps when held under the arms and leaned forward so that the feet press against the ground.

Babinski reflex A reflex in which infants fan their toes when the undersides of their feet are stroked.

tonic-neck reflex A reflex in which infants turn their head to one side, extend their arm and leg on that side, and flex their limbs on the opposite side. Also known as the "fencing position."

● **Figure 4.9**
The Tonic-Neck Reflex

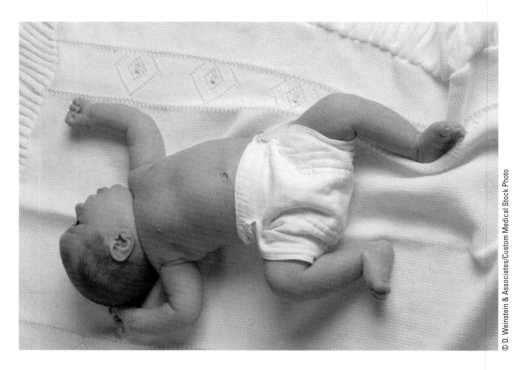

Some reflexes, such as breathing regularly and blinking the eye in response to a puff of air, remain with us for life. Others, such as the sucking and grasping reflexes, are gradually replaced after a number of months by voluntary sucking and graspings. Still others, such as the Moro and Babinski reflexes, disappear, indicating that the nervous system is maturing on schedule.

Sensory Capabilities

In 1890, William James (1890), a founder of modern psychology, wrote that the neonate must sense the world "as one great blooming, buzzing confusion." The neonate emerges from being literally suspended in a temperature-controlled environment to being—again, in James's words—"assailed by eyes, ears, nose, skin, and entrails at once." *Question: How well do neonates see, hear, and so on?* In this section, we describe the sensory capabilities of neonates and see that James, for all his eloquence, probably exaggerated their disorganization.

Vision

Neonates can see, but they do not possess great sharpness of vision, or **visual acuity**. Visual acuity is expressed in numbers such as 20/20 or 20/200. Think for a moment of the big E on the Snellen chart (● Figure 4.10), which you have probably seen during many eye examinations. If you were to stand 20 feet from the Snellen chart and could see only the E, we would say that your vision is

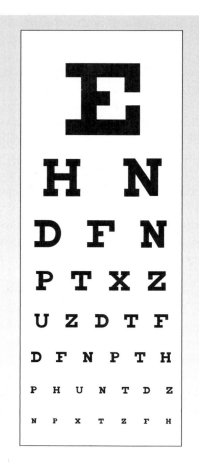

● **Figure 4.10**
The Snellen Chart

The Snellen chart is used in eye examinations to provide an approximate measure of visual acuity.

20/200, which would mean that you can see from a distance of 20 feet what a person with normal vision can discriminate from a distance of 200 feet. In such a case, you would be quite nearsighted and would have to be unusually close to an object to discriminate its details.

Expressed in these terms, investigators estimate that neonates are nearsighted, with visual acuity in the neighborhood of 20/600 (Kellman & Arterberry, 2006). Neonates can best see objects that are about 7 to 9 inches away from their eyes. Neonates also see best through the centers of their eyes. They do not have the peripheral vision of older children (Candy et al., 1998). To learn how psychologists measure the visual acuity of infants, check the nearby "A Closer Look" feature.

Neonates can visually detect movement, and many neonates can **track** movement the first day after birth. In fact, they appear to prefer (i.e., they spend more time looking at) moving objects to stationary objects (Kellman & Arterberry, 2006).

visual acuity Keenness or sharpness of vision.

track Follow.

A CLOSER LOOK

Studying Visual Acuity in Neonates: How Well Can They See?

How do psychologists determine the visual acuity of neonates? Naturally, psychologists cannot ask babies to report how well they see, but they can determine what babies are looking at and draw conclusions from this information.

One method of observing what a baby is looking at is by using a "looking chamber" of the sort used in research by Robert Fantz and his colleagues (1975) (see ● Figure 4.11). In this chamber, the baby lies on its back, with two panels above. Each panel contains a visual stimulus. The researcher observes the baby's eye movements and records how much time is spent looking at each panel. A similar strategy can be carried out in the baby's natural environment. Filtered lights and a movie or TV camera can be trained on the baby's eyes. Reflections from objects in the environment can then be recorded to show what the baby is looking at.

Neonates will stare at almost any nearby object for minutes, be it a golf ball, wheel, checkerboard, bull's-eye, circle, triangle, or even a line (Maurer & Maurer, 1976), but babies have their preferences, as measured by the amount of time they spend fixating on (looking at) certain objects. For example, they will spend more time looking at black-and-white stripes than at gray blobs. This fact suggests one strategy for measuring visual acuity in the neonate. As black-and-white stripes become narrower, they eventually take on the appearance of that gray blob. And, as the stripes are progressively narrowed, we can assume that babies continue to discriminate them as stripes only as long as they spend more time looking at them than at blobs.

Such studies suggest that neonates are very nearsighted. But we should remember that they, unlike adults

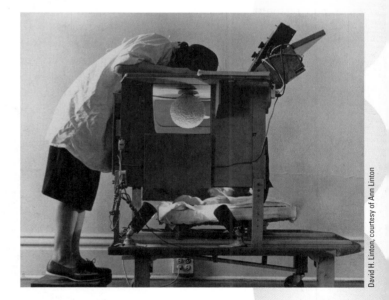

● **Figure 4.11** The Looking Chamber

This chamber makes it easier for a researcher to observe a baby's eye movements and record how much time the baby spends looking at a visual stimulus.

or older children, are not motivated to "perform" in such experiments. If they were, they might show somewhat greater acuity.

Reflect: What are the problems in studying the "preferences" of newborn children? How do researchers "get around" these problems? Are you confident that they are studying the preferences of newborns? Explain.

In classic research (Haith, 1966), 1- to 4-day-old neonates were exposed to moving or nonmoving lights while they sucked on a pacifier. The frequency of their sucking decreased significantly when moving lights were presented, suggesting that they preferred this visual stimulus.

Visual accommodation refers to the self-adjustments made by the eye's lens to bring objects into focus. If you hold your finger at arm's length and bring it gradually nearer, you will feel tension in your eyes as your lenses automatically foreshorten and thicken in an effort to maintain the image in focus. When you move your finger away, the lens accommodates by lengthening and flattening to keep your finger in focus. Neonates show little or none of this visual accommodation; rather, they see as if through a fixed-focus camera. Objects placed about 7–9 inches away are in clearest focus for most neonates, although this range can be somewhat expanded when lighting conditions are bright. Interestingly, this distance is about the same distance from a neonate to the face of the adult who is cradling the baby. It has been speculated that this sensory capacity for gazing into others' eyes may promote attachment between neonates and caregivers. Visual accommodation improves dramatically during a baby's first 2 months (Kellman & Arterberry, 2006).

Now bring your finger toward your eyes and try to maintain a single image of the approaching finger. If you do so, it is because your eyes turn inward, or converge on the finger, resulting in a crossed-eyed look and feelings of tension in the eye muscles (see ● Figure 4.12). **Convergence** is made possible by the coordination of the eye muscles. Neonates do not have the muscular control to converge their eyes on an object that is close to them. For this reason, one eye may be staring off to the side while the other fixates on an object straight ahead. Convergence does not occur until 7 or 8 weeks of age for near objects, although neonates show some convergence for objects at intermediate distances (Kellman & Arterberry, 2006).

The degree to which neonates perceive color remains an open question. The research problem is that colors vary in **intensity** (i.e., brightness), **saturation** (richness), and **hue**. For this reason, we cannot be certain that babies are responding to the hue when they appear to show preference for one color over another. They may be responding to the difference in brightness or saturation. So, you say, simply change hues and keep intensity and saturation constant. That's a marvelous idea, but it is easier said than done, unfortunately.

Physiological observations also cast doubt on a neonate's capacity to have highly developed color vision. There are two types of cells in the retina of the eye sensitive

visual accommodation The automatic adjustments made by the lenses of the eyes to bring objects into focus.

convergence The inward movement of the eyes as they focus on an object that is drawing nearer.

intensity Brightness.

saturation Richness or purity of a color.

hue Color.

● **Figure 4.12**
Convergence of the Eyes

Neonates do not have the muscular control to converge their eyes on an object that is close to them, but they do show some convergence for objects at intermediate viewing distances.

© Elizabeth Crews

to light: rods and cones. **Rods** transmit sensations of light and dark. **Cones** transmit sensations of color. At birth, cones are less well developed than rods in structure.

Infants younger than 1 month of age do not show the ability to discriminate stimuli that differ in color. Two-month-olds can do so, but they require large color differences. By 4 months, infants can see most of, if not all, the colors of the visible spectrum (Franklin et al., 2005).

Even at birth, babies do not just passively respond to visual stimuli. Babies placed in absolute darkness open their eyes wide and actively search the visual field (Kellman & Arterberry, 2006).

Hearing

Fetuses respond to sound months before they are born. Although myelination of the auditory pathways is not complete before birth, fetuses' middle and inner ears normally reach their mature shapes and sizes before birth. Normal neonates hear well unless their middle ears are clogged with amniotic fluid (Priner et al., 2003). Most neonates turn their heads toward unusual sounds, such as the shaking of a rattle.

Neonates have the capacity to respond to sounds of different **amplitude** and **pitch**. They are more likely to respond to high-pitched sounds than to low-pitched sounds (Trehub & Hannon, 2006). By contrast, speaking or singing to infants softly, in a relatively low-pitched voice, can have a soothing effect (Volkova et al., 2006). That may explain the widespread practice in many cultures of singing lullabies to infants to promote sleep (Volkova et al., 2006).

The sense of hearing may play a role in the formation of affectional bonds between neonates and their mothers that goes well beyond the soothing potential of the mothers' voices. Research indicates that neonates prefer their mothers' voices to those of other women, but they do not show similar preferences for the voices of their fathers (DeCasper & Prescott, 1984; Freeman et al., 1993). It may seem tempting to conclude that the human nervous system is prewired to respond positively to the voice of one's biological mother. However, neonates have already had several months of experience in the uterus, and, for a good part of this time, they have been capable of sensing sounds. Because they are predominantly exposed to prenatal sounds produced by their mothers, learning appears to play a role in neonatal preferences.

There is fascinating evidence that neonates are particularly responsive to the sounds and rhythms of speech, although they do not show preferences for specific languages. Neonates can discriminate between different speech sounds (Dehaene-Lambertz et al., 2004), and they can discriminate between new sounds of speech and those sounds they have heard before (Brody et al., 1984).

Smell: The Nose Knows—Early

Neonates can definitely discriminate distinct odors, such as those of onions and anise (licorice). They show more rapid breathing patterns and increased bodily movement in response to powerful odors. They also turn away from unpleasant odors, such as ammonia and vinegar, as early as the first day after birth (Werner & Bernstein, 2001).

The nasal preferences of neonates are quite similar to those of older children and adults (Werner & Bernstein, 2001). When a cotton swab saturated with the odor of rotten eggs was passed beneath their noses, neonate infants spat, stuck out their tongues, wrinkled their noses, and blinked their eyes. However, they showed smiles and licking motions when presented with the odors of chocolate, strawberry, vanilla, butter, bananas, and honey.

Classic research by Aidan Macfarlane (1975, 1977) and others suggests that the sense of smell, like hearing, may provide a vehicle for mother–infant recognition and attachment. Macfarlane suspected that neonates may be sensitive to the smell of milk because, when held by the mother, they tend to turn toward her nipple before they

rods In the eye, rod-shaped receptors of light that are sensitive to intensity only. Rods permit black-and-white vision.

cones In the eye, cone-shaped receptors of light that transmit sensations of color.

amplitude Height. The higher the amplitude of sound waves, the louder they are.

pitch The highness or lowness of a sound, as determined by the frequency of sound waves.

have had a chance to see or touch it. In one experiment, Macfarlane placed nursing pads above and to the sides of neonates' heads. One pad had absorbed milk from the mother, the other was clean. Neonates less than 1 week old spent more time turning to look at their mothers' pads than at the new pads.

Neonates will also turn toward preferred odors. In the second phase of this research, Macfarlane suspended pads with milk from the neonates' mothers and from strangers to the sides of babies' heads. For the first few days following birth, the infants did not turn toward their mothers' pads. However, by the time they were 1 week old, they turned toward their mothers' pads and spent more time looking at them than at the strangers' pads. It appears that the babies learned to respond positively to the odor of their mothers' milk during the first few days. Afterward, a source of this odor received preferential treatment even when the infants were not nursing.

Breast-fed 15-day-old infants also prefer their mother's axillary (underarm) odor to odors produced by other lactating (milk-producing) women and by nonlactating women. Bottle-fed infants do not show this preference (Cernoch & Porter, 1985; Porter et al., 1992). Investigators of such practices explain this difference by suggesting that breast-fed infants may be more likely than bottle-fed infants to be exposed to their mother's axillary odor. That is, mothers of bottle-fed infants usually remain clothed when feeding their babies. Axillary odor, along with odors from breast secretions, might contribute to the early development of recognition and attachment.

Taste

Neonates are sensitive to different tastes, and their preferences, as suggested by their facial expressions in response to various fluids, appear to be similar to those of adults (Werner & Bernstein, 2001). Neonates swallow without showing any facial expression suggestive of a positive or negative response when distilled water is placed on their tongues. Sweet solutions are met with smiles, licking, and eager sucking, as in ● Figure 4.13a (Rosenstein & Oster, 1988). Neonates discriminate among solutions with salty, sour, and bitter tastes, as suggested by reactions in the lower part of the face (Rosenstein & Oster, 1988). Sour fluids (Figure 4.13b) elicit pursing of the lips, nose wrinkling, and eye blinking. Bitter solutions (Figure 4.13c) stimulate spitting, gagging, and sticking out the tongue.

Sweet solutions have a calming effect on neonates (Blass & Camp, 2003). One study found that sweeter solutions increase the heart rate, suggesting heightened arousal, but also slow down the rate of sucking (Crook & Lipsitt, 1976). Researchers interpret this finding to suggest an effort to savor the sweeter solution, to make the flavor last. Although we do not know why infants ingest sweet foods more slowly than other foods, this difference could be adaptive in the sense of preventing overeating. Sweet foods tend to be high in calories; eating them slowly gives infants' brains more time to respond to bodily signals that they have eaten enough and thus to stop eating. Ah, to have the wisdom of a neonate!

a–c: Rosenstein, D.S. & Oster, H. (1988). Differential facial responses to four basic tastes in newborns. *Child Development,* 59, 1555–1568.

● **Figure 4.13**
Facial Expressions Elicited by Sweet, Sour, and Bitter Solutions

Neonates are sensitive to different tastes, as shown by their facial expressions when tasting (a) sweet, (b) sour, and (c) bitter solutions.

Touch and Pain

The sense of touch is an extremely important avenue of learning and communication for babies. Not only do the skin senses provide information about the external world, but the sensations of skin against skin also appear to provide feelings of comfort and security that may be major factors in the formation of bonds of attachment between infants and their caregivers, as we see in Chapter 7.

Neonates are sensitive to touch. As noted earlier in this chapter, many reflexes—including the rooting, sucking, Babinski, and grasping reflexes, to name a few—are activated by pressure against the skin.

It has been widely believed for many years that neonates are not as sensitive to pain as older babies are. Considering the squeezing that takes place during childbirth, relative insensitivity to pain would seem to be adaptive. However, this belief has recently been challenged by health professionals (e.g., Royal Australasian College of Physicians, 2006). What would appear to be accurate enough is that neonates are not cognitively equipped to fret about pain that may be coming or to ruminate about pain they have experienced. But they are certainly conditionable, meaning that if they perceive themselves to be in a situation that has brought them pain in the past, we should not be surprised if they shriek—and shriek and shriek. Health professionals now recommend that neonates and older infants be given anesthetics if they are going to undergo uncomfortable procedures, such as circumcision.

Learning: Really Early Childhood "Education"

Question: Can neonates learn? The somewhat limited sensory capabilities of neonates suggest that they may not learn as rapidly as older children do. After all, we must sense clearly those things we are to learn about. However, neonates do seem capable of at least two basic forms of learning: classical conditioning and operant conditioning.

Classical Conditioning of Neonates

In classical conditioning of neonates, involuntary responses are conditioned to new stimuli. In a typical study (Lipsitt, 2002), neonates were taught to blink in response to a tone. Blinking (the unconditioned response) was elicited by a puff of air directed toward the infant's eye (the unconditioned stimulus). A tone was sounded (the conditioned stimulus) as the puff of air was delivered. After repeated pairings, sounding the tone caused the neonate to blink (the conditioned response). Thus, neonates are equipped to learn that events peculiar to their own environments (touches or other conditioned stimuli) may mean that a meal is at hand (more accurately, at mouth). One neonate may learn that a light switched on overhead precedes a meal. Another may learn that feeding is preceded by the rustling of a carpet of thatched leaves. The conditioned stimuli are culture specific; the capacity to learn is universal.

Operant Conditioning of Neonates

Operant conditioning, like classical conditioning, can take place in neonates. In Chapter 3, we described an experiment in which neonates learned to suck on a pacifier in such a way as to activate a recording of their mothers reading *The Cat in the Hat* (DeCasper & Fifer, 1980; DeCasper & Spence, 1991) (● Figure 4.14), which the mothers had read aloud during their final weeks of pregnancy. In this example, the infants' sucking reflexes were modified through the reinforcement of hearing their mothers read a familiar story.

The younger the child, the more important it is that reinforcers be administered rapidly. Among neonates, it seems that reinforcers must be administered within 1 second after the desired behavior is performed if learning is to occur. Infants of age 6–8 months can learn if the reinforcer is delayed by 2 seconds, but if the delay is 3 seconds or more, learning does not take place (Millar, 1990). Although there are individual differences in conditionability in neonates, these differences do not correspond to differences in the complex cognitive abilities we later refer to as intelligence.

Sleeping and Waking

As adults, we spend about one-third of our time sleeping. *Question: What patterns of sleep are found among neonates?* Neonates greatly outdo us, spending two-thirds of their time, or about 16 hours per day, in sleep. And, in one of life's basic challenges to parents, neonates do not sleep their 16 hours consecutively.

● **Figure 4.14**
A Neonate Sucking to Hear
Her Mother's Voice

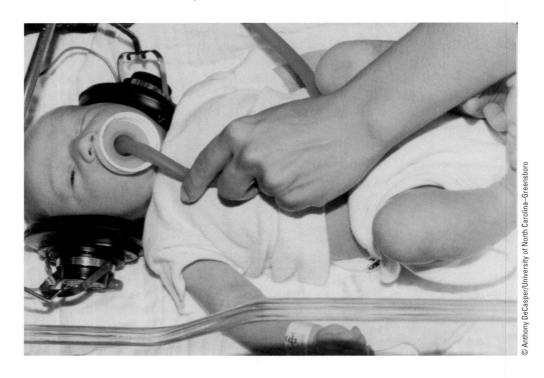

A number of different states of sleep and wakefulness have been identified in neo-nates and infants, as shown in ■ Table 4.3 (Cornwell & Feigenbaum, 2006; Salza-rulo & Ficca, 2002; Wulff & Siegmund, 2001). Although individual babies differ in the amount of time they spend in each of these states, sleep clearly predominates over wakefulness in the early days and weeks of life.

Different infants require different amounts of sleep and follow different patterns of sleep, but virtually all infants distribute their sleeping throughout the day and night through a series of naps. The typical infant has about six cycles of waking and sleeping in a 24-hour period. The longest nap typically approaches 4½ hours, and the neonate is usually awake for a little more than 1 hour during each cycle.

This pattern of waking and sleeping changes rapidly and dramatically over the course of the years. Even after a month or so, the infant has fewer but longer sleep pe-riods and will usually take longer naps during the night. Parents whose babies do not know the difference between night and day usually teach the babies the difference by playing with them during daytime hours, once feeding and caretaking chores have been carried out, and by putting them back to sleep as soon as possible when they awaken hungry during the night. Most parents do not require professional instruc-tion in this method. At 3:00 A.M., parents are not likely to feel playful.

By the ages of about 6 months to 1 year, many infants begin to sleep through the night. Some infants start sleeping through the night even earlier (Salzarulo & Ficca, 2002). A number of infants begin to sleep through the night for a week or so and then revert to their wakeful ways again for a while.

REM and Non-REM Sleep

Sleep is not a consistent state. It can be divided into **rapid-eye-movement (REM) sleep** and **non-rapid-eye-movement (non-REM) sleep** (● Figure 4.15). Studies with the **electroencephalograph (EEG)** show that we can subdivide non-REM sleep into four additional stages of sleep, each with its characteristic brain waves, but our discussion will be limited to REM and non-REM sleep. REM sleep is characterized by rapid eye movements that can be observed beneath closed lids. The EEG patterns

rapid-eye-movement (REM) sleep A period of sleep during which we are likely to dream, as indicated by rapid eye movements.

non-rapid-eye-movement (non-REM) sleep Periods of sleep during which we are unlikely to dream.

electroencephalograph (EEG) An instrument that measures electrical activity of the brain.

■ **Table 4.3** States of Sleep and Wakefulness in Infancy

State	Comments
Quiet sleep (non-REM)	Regular breathing, eyes closed, no movement
Active sleep (REM)	Irregular breathing, eyes closed, rapid eye movement, muscle twitches
Drowsiness	Regular or irregular breathing, eyes open or closed, little movement
Alert inactivity	Regular breathing, eyes open, looking around, little body movement
Alert activity	Irregular breathing, eyes open, active body movement
Crying	Irregular breathing, eyes open or closed, thrashing of arms and legs, crying

produced during REM sleep resemble those of the waking state. For this reason, REM sleep is also called paradoxical sleep. However, we are difficult to awaken during REM sleep. Adults who are roused during REM sleep report that they have been dreaming about 80% of the time. Is the same true of neonates?

Note from Figure 4.15 that neonates spend about half their time sleeping in REM sleep. As they develop, the percentage of sleeping time spent in REM sleep declines. By 6 months or so, REM sleep accounts for only about 30% of the baby's sleep. By 2 to 3 years, REM sleep drops off to about 20–25% (Salzarulo & Ficca, 2002). There is a dramatic falling-off in the total number of hours spent in sleep as we develop (Salzarulo & Ficca, 2002). ● Figure 4.15 shows that the major portion of the drop-off can be attributed to lessened REM sleep.

What is the function of REM sleep in neonates? Research with humans and other animals, including kittens and rat pups, suggests that the brain requires a cer-

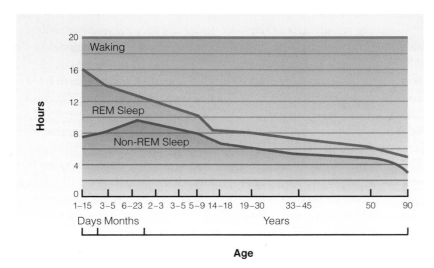

● **Figure 4.15**   REM Sleep and Non-REM Sleep

Neonates spend nearly 50% of their time sleeping in rapid-eye movement (REM) sleep. The percentage of time spent in REM sleep drops off to 20–25% for 2- to 3-year-olds.

Source: Roffwarg et al. (1966).

tain amount of activity for the creation of proteins that are involved in the development of neurons and synapses (Dang-Vu et al., 2006). Brain activity can be stimulated by internal or external sources. In older children and adults, external sources of stimulation are provided by activity, a vast and shifting array of sensory impressions, and, perhaps, thought processes during the waking state. The neonate, however, spends its brief waking periods largely isolated from the kaleidoscope of events of the world outside and is not likely to be lost in deep thought. Thus, in the waking state, the brain may not be provided with the needed stimulation. Perhaps the neonate compensates by spending relatively more time in REM sleep, which most closely parallels the waking state in terms of brain waves. While infants are in REM sleep, internal stimulation spurs the brain on to appropriate development. Preterm babies spend an even greater proportion of their time in REM sleep than full-term babies, perhaps—goes the argument—because they require relatively greater stimulation of the brain.

Crying

No discussion of the sleeping and waking states of the neonate would be complete without mentioning crying, a comment that parents will view as an understatement. I have known first-time parents who have attempted to follow an imaginary 11th commandment: "The baby shall not cry." ***Question: Why do babies cry?***

The main reason babies cry seems to be simple enough. Studies suggest that a one-word answer often suffices: pain (Gormally et al., 2001; Zeifman, 2004).

Some parents have entered into conflict with hospital nurses who tell them not to worry when their babies are crying on the other side of the nursery's glass partition. Nurses often tell the parents that their babies must cry because crying helps clear their respiratory systems of fluids that linger from the amniotic sac and also stimulates the circulatory system.

Whether crying is healthful and necessary remains an open question, but at least some crying among babies seems to be universal. Some scholars have suggested that crying may be a primitive language, but it is not. Languages contain units and groupings of sounds that symbolize objects and events, and crying does not. Still, crying appears to be both expressive and functional. It serves as an infant's expressive response to unpleasant feelings and also stimulates caretakers to do something to help. Crying thus communicates something, even though it is not a form of language. Crying may also communicate the identity of the crier across distance. Cries have multiple markers of individuality, and they may signal parents and other caretakers as to the location of their infant in a group.

Before parenthood, many people wonder whether they will be able to recognize the meaning of their babies' cries, but it usually does not take them long. Parents typically learn to distinguish cries that signify hunger, anger, and pain. A sudden, loud, insistent cry associated with flexing and kicking of the legs may indicate colic, that is, pain resulting from gas or other sources of distress in the digestive tract. The baby may seem to hold its breath for a few moments, then gasp and begin to cry again. Crying from colic can be severe and persistent; it may last for hours, although cries generally seem to settle into a pattern after a while (Barr et al., 2005). Much to the relief of parents, colic tends to disappear by the third to sixth month, as a baby's digestive system matures.

Parents and other people, including children, have similar bodily responses to infant crying, such as increases in heart rate, blood pressure, and sweating (Reijneveld et al., 2004). Infant crying makes others feel irritated and anxious and motivates them to run to the baby to try to relieve the distress. The pitch of an infant's cries appears to provide information (Zeifman, 2004). Adults perceive high-pitched crying to be more urgent, distressing, and sick sounding than low-pitched crying (Zeifman, 2004).

Certain high-pitched cries, when prolonged, may signify health problems. For example, the cries of chronically distressed infants differ from those of nondistressed infants in both rhythm and pitch. Patterns of crying may be indicative of such problems as chromosomal abnormalities, infections, fetal malnutrition, and exposure to narcotics (Zeifman, 2004). A striking example of the link between crying and a health problem is the syndrome called cri du chat, French for "cry of the cat." This genetic disorder produces abnormalities in the brain, atypical facial features, and a high-pitched, squeaky cry.

There are certain patterns of crying. For example, peaks of crying appear to be concentrated in the late afternoon and early evening (McGlaughlin & Grayson, 2001). Although some cries may seem extreme and random at first, they tend to settle into a pattern that is recognizable to most parents. Infants seem to produce about the same number of crying bouts during the first 9 months or so, but the duration of the bouts grows briefer, by half, during this period (Ijzendoorn & Hubbard, 2000). The response of the mother apparently influences infants' crying. It turns out that the more frequently mothers ignore their infants' crying bouts in the first 9 weeks, the less frequently their infants cry in the following 9-week period (Ijzendoorn & Hubbard, 2000). This finding should certainly not be interpreted to mean that infant crying is best ignored. At least at first, crying communicates pain and hunger, and these are conditions that it is advisable to correct. Persistent crying can strain the mother–infant relationship (Reijneveld et al., 2004).

Soothing

Question: What will stop an infant from crying? For one thing, sucking seems to function as a built-in tranquilizer. Sucking on a **pacifier** decreases crying and agitated movement in neonates who have not yet had the opportunity to feed (Field, 1999). Therefore, the soothing function of sucking need not be learned through experience. Sucking (drinking) a sweet solution also appears to have a soothing effect (Stevens et al., 2005). (Can it be that even babies are programmed to enjoy "comfort food"?)

Parents find many other ways to soothe infants: picking them up, patting them, caressing and rocking them, swaddling them, and speaking to them in a low voice. Parents then usually try to find the specific cause of the distress by offering a bottle or pacifier or checking the diaper. These responses to a crying infant are shown by parents in many cultures, including those of the United States, France, and Japan.

Learning occurs quickly during the soothing process. Parents learn by trial and error what types of embraces and movements are likely to soothe their infants, and infants learn quickly that crying is followed by being picked up or other forms of intervention. Parents sometimes worry that if they pick up the crying baby quickly, they are reinforcing the baby for crying. In this way, they believe, the child may become spoiled and find it progressively more difficult to engage in self-soothing to get to sleep.

Fortunately, as infants mature and learn, crying tends to become replaced by less upsetting verbal requests for intervention. Among adults, of course, soothing techniques take very different forms—a bouquet of flowers or admission that one started the argument.

© Photodisc/First Light

Soothing
How can a crying baby be soothed? Picking the baby up, talking to it quietly, patting, stroking, and rocking all seem to have calming effects.

Sudden Infant Death Syndrome (SIDS)

Truth or Fiction Revisited: It is true that more children die from sudden infant death syndrome (SIDS) than die from cancer, heart disease, pneumonia, child abuse, AIDS, cystic fibrosis, and muscular dystrophy combined (Lipsitt, 2003). ***Questions: What is SIDS? What are the risk factors for SIDS?***

pacifier An artificial nipple, teething ring, or similar device that, when sucked, soothes babies.

Sudden infant death syndrome (SIDS)—also known as crib death—is a disorder of infancy that apparently strikes while a baby is sleeping. In the typical case, a baby goes to sleep, apparently in perfect health, and is found dead the next morning. There is no sign that the baby struggled or was in pain.

SIDS is more common among the following (Hunt & Hauck, 2006; Paterson et al., 2006):

- Babies age 2–4 months
- Babies who are put to sleep in the prone position (on their stomachs) or their sides
- Premature and low-birth-weight infants
- Male babies
- Babies in families of lower socioeconomic status
- Babies in African American families (African American babies are twice as likely as European American babies to die of SIDS)
- Babies of teenage mothers
- Babies whose mothers smoked during or after pregnancy or whose mothers used narcotics during pregnancy

Studies have found a higher risk of SIDS among babies who sleep on their stomachs (Lipsitt, 2003). These findings led the American Academy of Pediatrics to recommend putting babies down to sleep on their back. A recent national survey revealed that before the recommendation, 43% of infants were usually placed to sleep on their stomachs (prone) and 27% on their back. By 2000, however, only 17% were placed in the prone position, and 56% were placed on their back (Willinger et al., 2000).

Home monitoring systems to alert parents to episodes of apnea and to give them time to intervene—for example, by using artificial respiration—have been developed. However, there is little evidence that SIDS rates have been reduced as a result of using monitors (SIDS Network, 2001).

The incidence of SIDS has been declining, but some 2,000–3,000 infants in the United States still die each year of SIDS. It is the most common cause of death in infants between the ages of 1 month and 1 year, and most of these deaths occur between 2 and 5 months of age (Paterson et al., 2006). New parents frequently live in dread of SIDS and check regularly through the night to see if their babies are breathing. It is not abnormal, by the way, for babies occasionally to suspend breathing for a moment. The intermittent suspension of respiration is called **apnea**, and the buildup of carbon dioxide usually spurs a return to breathing. Lewis Lipsitt (2003) noted that any theory of the causes of SIDS must include that it tends to occur between the second and fourth months, when reflexive behavior is weakening. He suggests that babies who are less likely to move reflexively and vigorously to obtain air when their air passageways are occluded are at higher risk of SIDS. Although it is known that SIDS does not result from suffocation or from choking on regurgitated food, its causes have remained largely obscure.

The Children's Hospital Boston Study

Perhaps the most compelling study to date about the causes of SIDS was led by health professionals at the Children's Hospital Boston and published in the *Journal of the American Medical Association* (Paterson et al., 2006). The study focused on an area in the brainstem called the **medulla** (● Figure 4.16), which is involved in basic functions such as breathing and sleep-and-wake cycles. Among other things, the medulla causes us to breathe if we are in need of oxygen. Researchers compared the medullas of babies who had died from SIDS with those of babies who had died at the same ages

---

sudden infant death syndrome (SIDS) The death, while sleeping, of apparently healthy babies who stop breathing for unknown medical reasons. Also called crib death.

apnea (AP-nee-uh) Temporary suspension of breathing (from the Greek *a-*, meaning "without," and *pnoie*, meaning "wind").

medulla A part of the brain stem that regulates vital and automatic functions such as breathing and the sleep–wake cycle.

serotonin A naturally occurring brain chemical that is involved in transmission of messages from one brain cell to another, the responsiveness of the medulla, emotional responses such as depression, and motivational responses such as hunger.

from other causes. They found that the medullas of the babies who died from SIDS were less sensitive to the brain chemical **serotonin**, a chemical that helps keep the medulla responsive. The problem was particularly striking in the brains of the boys, which could account for the sex difference in the incidence of SIDS.

What should *you* do about SIDS? Bear in mind that the prevention of SIDS begins during pregnancy. Smoking and using other drugs during pregnancy increase the risk of SIDS. Obtain adequate nutrition and health care during pregnancy. Place your baby to sleep in the supine position (on its back). Keep current with research data on SIDS by checking with your pediatrician and exploring websites such as those of the Centers for Disease Control and Prevention (http://www.cdc.gov/) and the SIDS Network (http://www.sids-network .org/). Perhaps within a few years we will have a screening test for SIDS and a method for preventing or controlling it.

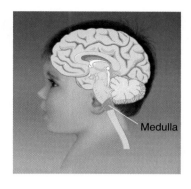

● **Figure 4.16**
The Medulla

Research by a team at the Children's Hospital Boston suggests that sudden infant death syndrome (SIDS) may be caused by a relatively low level of sensitivity of the medulla to the brain chemical serotonin.

Active Review

18. In the United States today, the neonate's overall level of health is usually evaluated at birth according to the _____ scale.

19. In the _____ reflex, the baby turns the head and mouth toward a stimulus that strokes the cheek, chin, or corner of the mouth.

20. Neonates are rather (Nearsighted or Farsighted?).

21. Neonates (Do or Do not?) prefer their mothers' voices to those of other women.

22. As babies mature, they spend a (Greater or Smaller?) percentage of their time sleeping in REM sleep.

23. _____ is the most common cause of death in infants between the ages of 1 month and 1 year.

Reflect & Relate: Have you or a family member had to adjust to the waking and sleeping patterns of a baby? Do you think that it is normal to occasionally resent being awakened repeatedly through the night? Explain.

Go to

http://www.thomsonedu.com/psychology/rathus

for an interactive version of this review.

1. **What events occur just before the beginning of childbirth?**

   The first uterine contractions are called Braxton-Hicks contractions, or false labor contractions. A day or so before labor begins, some blood spotting can occur in vaginal secretions. At about this time, 1 woman in 10 has a rush of amniotic fluid from the vagina. The initiation of labor may be triggered by secretion of hormones by the fetus. Maternal hormones stimulate contractions strong enough to expel the baby.

2. **What happens during the first stage of childbirth?**

   Childbirth begins with the onset of regular contractions of the uterus, which cause the cervix to become effaced and dilated. The first stage may last from a few hours to more than a day. During transition, the cervix is nearly fully dilated and the head of the fetus moves into the birth canal.

3. **What occurs during the second stage of childbirth?**

   The second stage begins when the baby appears at the opening of the birth canal. It ends with the birth of the baby. Once the baby's head emerges from the mother's body, mucus is suctioned from its mouth so that breathing is not obstructed. When the baby is breathing on its own, the umbilical cord is clamped and severed.

4. **What happens during the third stage of childbirth?**

   During this stage, the placenta separates from the uterine wall and is expelled along with fetal membranes.

5. **How is anesthesia used in childbirth? What are its effects on the baby?**

   General anesthesia puts the woman to sleep, but it decreases the strength of uterine contractions and lowers the responsiveness of the neonate. Regional or local anesthetics deaden pain in parts of the body without putting the mother to sleep.

6. **What is prepared childbirth?**

   Prepared childbirth teaches women to dissociate uterine contractions from pain and fear by associating other responses, such as relaxation, with contractions. A coach aids the mother in the delivery room.

7. **What is a C-section? Why is it so common?**

   A cesarean section (C-section) delivers a baby surgically through the abdomen. C-sections are most likely to be advised if the baby is large or in distress or if the mother's pelvis is small or she is tired or weak. Herpes and HIV infections in the birth canal can be bypassed by C-section.

8. **How can a woman decide where to deliver her baby?**

   Women have choices in childbirth, such as home delivery, birthing suites, or traditional labor rooms. Birthing suites provide homelike surroundings with immediate hospital backup available.

9. **What are the effects of oxygen deprivation at birth?**

   Prenatal oxygen deprivation can be fatal if prolonged; it can also impair development of the nervous system, leading to cognitive and motor problems.

10. **What is meant by the terms *prematurity* and *low birth weight*?**

    A baby is preterm when birth occurs at or before 37 weeks of gestation. A baby has a low birth weight when it weighs less than 5½ pounds (about 2,500 grams). A baby who is low in birth weight but born at full term is said to be small for dates. The risk of having preterm babies rises with multiple births.

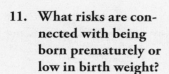

11. **What risks are connected with being born prematurely or low in birth weight?**

Risks include infant mortality and delayed neurological and motor development. Preterm babies are relatively thin and often have vernix on the skin and lanugo. Sucking and breathing reflexes may be weak. The walls of air sacs in the lungs may stick together, leading to respiratory distress.

12. **How are preterm infants treated following birth?**

Preterm babies usually remain in the hospital in incubators. Preterm infants profit from early stimulation just as full-term babies do. Parents often do not treat preterm neonates as well as they treat full-term neonates, perhaps because preterm infants are less attractive and have irritating, high-pitched cries.

13. **What kinds of problems in mood do women experience during the postpartum period?**

Women may encounter the baby blues, postpartum depression, and postpartum psychosis. These problems are found around the world and probably reflect hormonal changes following birth, although stress can play a role. High self-esteem and social support help women manage these adjustment problems.

14. **How critical is parental interaction with neonates in the formation of bonds of attachment?**

It may not be critical. Research by Klaus and Kennell suggested that the first few hours after birth present a "maternal-sensitive" period during which the mother's hormone levels particularly dispose her to "bond" with her neonates. The study confounded the effects of extra time with their babies with special attention from health professionals, however.

15. **How do health professionals assess the health of neonates?**

The neonate's overall health is usually evaluated according to the Apgar scale. The Brazelton Neonatal Behavioral Assessment Scale also screens neonates for behavioral and neurological problems.

16. **What are reflexes? What kinds of reflexes are shown by neonates?**

Reflexes are simple, unlearned, stereotypical responses that are elicited by specific stimuli. The rooting and sucking reflexes are basic to survival. Other key reflexes include the startle reflex, the grasping reflex, the stepping reflex, the Babinski reflex, and the tonic-neck reflex. Most reflexes disappear or are replaced by voluntary behavior within months.

17. **How well do neonates see, hear, and so on?**

Neonates are nearsighted. They visually detect movement, and many track movement. Fetuses respond to sound months before they are born. Neonates are particularly responsive to the sounds and rhythms of speech. The nasal preferences of neonates are similar to those of older children and adults. Neonates prefer the taste of sweet solutions and find them soothing. The sensations of skin against skin are also soothing and may contribute to formation of bonds of attachment.

18. **Can neonates learn?**

Yes. Neonates are capable of classical and operant conditioning. For example, they can be conditioned to blink their eyes in response to a tone.

19. **What patterns of sleep are found among neonates?**

Neonates spend two-thirds of their time in sleep. Nearly all neonates distribute sleep through naps. Neonates spend about half their time sleeping in REM sleep, but as time goes on, REM sleep accounts for less of their sleep. REM sleep may be connected with brain development.

20. Why do babies cry?

Babies cry mainly because of pain and discomfort. Crying may communicate the identity of the crier across distance, as well as hunger, anger, pain, and the presence of health problems.

21. What will stop an infant from crying?

Pacifiers help because sucking is soothing. Parents also try picking babies up, patting them, caressing and rocking them, and speaking to them in a low voice.

22. What is SIDS? What are the risk factors for SIDS?

SIDS is a disorder of infancy that apparently strikes while a baby is sleeping. It is the most common cause of death in infants between the ages of 1 month and 1 year. SIDS is more common among babies who are put to sleep in the prone position, preterm and low-birth-weight infants, male infants, and infants whose mothers smoked during or after pregnancy or whose mothers used narcotics during pregnancy.

Key Terms

term, 112
Braxton-Hicks contractions, 112
prostaglandins, 112
oxytocin, 112
neonate, 112
efface, 113
dilate, 113
episiotomy, 113
fetal monitoring, 113
forceps, 113
vacuum extraction tube, 113
transition, 114
midwife, 117
anesthetics, 117
general anesthesia, 117
tranquilizer, 117
local anesthetic, 118
natural childbirth, 118
Lamaze method, 118
cesarean section, 119
anoxia, 122
hypoxia, 122

schizophrenia, 122
breech presentation, 122
preterm, 122
small for dates, 122
lanugo, 123
vernix, 123
respiratory distress syndrome, 125
incubator, 126
postpartum period, 127
postpartum depression (PPD), 128
bonding, 129
Apgar scale, 130
Brazelton Neonatal Behavioral Assessment Scale, 131
reflex, 131
neural, 132
rooting reflex, 132
Moro reflex, 133
grasping reflex, 133
stepping reflex, 133
Babinski reflex, 133
tonic-neck reflex, 133

visual acuity, 135
track, 135
visual accommodation, 136
convergence, 136
intensity, 136
saturation, 136
hue, 136
rods, 137
cones, 137
amplitude, 137
pitch, 137
rapid-eye-movement (REM) sleep, 140
non-rapid-eye-movement (non-REM) sleep, 140
electroencephalograph (EEG), 140
pacifier, 143
sudden infant death syndrome (SIDS), 144
apnea, 144
medulla, 144
serotonin, 144

Active Learning Resources

Childhood & Adolescence Book Companion Website
http://www.thomsonedu.com/psychology/rathus .

Visit your book companion website, where you will find more resources to help you study. There you will find interactive versions of your book features, including the Lessons in Observation video, Active Review sections, and the Truth or Fiction feature. In addition, the companion website contains quizzing, flash cards, and a pronunciation glossary.

Thomson™ NOW! is an easy-to-use online resource that helps you study in less time to get the grade you want, NOW.

http://www.thomsonedu.com/login

Need help studying? This site is your one-stop study shop. Take a Pre-Test and ThomsonNOW will generate a Personalized Study Plan based on your test results. The Study Plan will identify the topics you need to review and direct you to online resources to help you master those topics. You can then take a Post-Test to determine the concepts you have mastered and what you still need to work on.

5

Infancy: Physical Development

Truth or Fiction?

T F The head of the newborn child doubles in length by adulthood, but the legs increase in length by about five times. p. 153

T F Infants triple their birth weight within a year. p. 153

T F Breast feeding helps prevent obesity later in life. p. 161

T F A child's brain reaches half its adult weight by the age of 2 years. p. 164

T F The cerebral cortex—the outer layer of the brain that is vital to human thought and reasoning—is only one-eighth of an inch thick. p. 165

T F Native American Hopi infants spend the first year of life strapped to a board, yet they begin to walk at about the same time as children who are reared in other cultures. p. 169

T F Infants need to have experience crawling before they develop fear of heights. p. 174

Preview

Physical Growth and Development
Sequences of Physical Development: Head First?
Growth Patterns in Height and Weight: Heading Toward the Greek Ideal?
Failure to Thrive
Nutrition: Fueling Development
Breast Feeding versus Bottle Feeding: Pros and Cons, Biological and Political

Developing in a World of Diversity: Alleviating Protein-Energy Malnutrition (PEM)

Development of the Brain and Nervous System
Development of Neurons
Development of the Brain
Nature and Nurture in the Development of the Brain

Motor Development: How Moving
Lifting and Holding the Torso and Head: Heads Up
Control of the Hands: Getting a Grip on Things
Locomotion: Getting a Move On
Nature and Nurture in Motor Development

Sensory and Perceptual Development: Taking in the World
Development of Vision: The Better to See You With
Development of Hearing: The Better to Hear You With

A Closer Look: Strategies for Studying the Development of Shape Constancy

Development of Coordination of the Senses: If I See It, Can I Touch It?

A Closer Look: Effects of Early Exposure to Garlic, Alcohol, and—Gulp—Veggies

The Active–Passive Controversy in Perceptual Development

Lessons in Observation: Sensation and Perception in Infancy

Nature and Nurture in Perceptual Development

Go to

http://www.thomsonedu.com/psychology/rathus

for an interactive version of this "Truth or Fiction" feature.

© IndexStock

am a keen observer of children—of my own, that is. From my experiences, I have derived the following basic principles of physical development:

- Just when you think your child has finally begun to make regular gains in weight, she or he will begin to lose weight or go for months without gaining an ounce.
- No matter how early your child sits up or starts to walk, your neighbor's child will do it earlier.
- Children first roll over when one parent is watching but will steadfastly refuse to repeat it when the other parent is called in.
- Children begin to get into everything before you get childproof latches on the cabinets.
- Every advance in locomotor ability provides your child with new ways to get hurt.
- Children will display their most exciting developmental milestones when you can't find the camera or forget how to use the video function on the cell phone.

More seriously, in this chapter we discuss various aspects of physical development during the first 2 years. We examine changes in physical growth, the development of the brain and the nervous system, motor development, and the development and coordination of sensory and perceptual capabilities, such as vision and hearing.

Physical Growth and Development

What a fascinating creature the newborn is: tiny, seemingly helpless, apparently oblivious to its surroundings, yet perfectly formed and fully capable of letting its caregivers know when it is hungry, thirsty, or uncomfortable. And what a fascinating creature is this same child 2 years later: running, climbing, playing, talking, hugging, and kissing.

It is hard to believe that only 2 short years can bring about such remarkable changes. It seems that nearly every day brings a new accomplishment. But as we will see, not all infants share equally in the explosion of positive developments. Therefore, we will also be enumerating some developmental problems and what can be done about them.

Sequences of Physical Development: Head First?

Question: What are the sequences of physical development? During the first 2 years, children make enormous strides in physical growth and development. In this section, we explore sequences of physical development, changes in height and weight, and nutrition. Three key sequences of physical development are cephalocaudal development, proximodistal development, and differentiation (see Concept Review 5.1).

Cephalocaudal Development

Development proceeds from the upper part of the head to the lower parts of the body. When we consider the central role of the brain, which is contained within the skull, the cephalocaudal sequence appears quite logical. The brain regulates essential functions, such as heartbeat. Through the secretion of hormones, the brain also regulates the growth and development of the body and influences basic drives, such as hunger and thirst.

The head develops more rapidly than the rest of the body during the embryonic stage. By 8 weeks after conception, the head constitutes half the entire length of the embryo. The brain develops more rapidly than the spinal cord. Arm buds form before leg buds. Most newborn babies have a strong, well-defined sucking reflex, although their legs are spindly and their limbs move back and forth only in diffuse excitement or agitation. Infants can hold up their heads before they gain control over their arms, their torsos, and, finally, their legs. They can sit up before they can crawl and walk. When they first walk, they use their hands to hold on to a person or object for support.

The lower parts of the body, because they get off to a later start, must do more growing to reach adult size. **Truth or Fiction Revisited:** The head does double in length between birth and maturity, but the torso triples in length. The arms increase their length by about four times, but the legs and feet do so by about five times.

Proximodistal Development

Growth and development also proceed from the trunk outward, from the body's central axis toward the periphery. The proximodistal principle, too, makes sense. The brain and spinal cord follow a central axis down through the body, and it is essential that the nerves be in place before the infant can gain control over the arms and legs. Consider also that the life functions of the newborn baby—heartbeat, respiration, digestion, and elimination of wastes—are all carried out by organ systems close to the central axis. These functions must be in operation or ready to operate when the child is born.

In terms of motor development, infants gain control over their trunks and their shoulders before they can control their arms, hands, and fingers. They make clumsy swipes at objects with their arms before they can voluntarily grasp them with their hands. Infants can grab large objects before picking up tiny things with their fingers. Similarly, infants gain control over their hips and upper legs before they can direct their lower legs, feet, and toes.

Differentiation

As children mature, their physical reactions become less global and more specific. The tendency of behavior to become more specific and distinct is called **differentiation**. If a neonate's finger is pricked or burned, he or she may withdraw the finger but also thrash about, cry, and show general signs of distress. Toddlers may also cry, show distress, and withdraw the finger, but they are less likely to thrash about wildly. Thus, the response to pain has become more specific. An older child or adult is also likely to withdraw the finger, but less likely to wail (sometimes) and show general distress.

Growth Patterns in Height and Weight: Heading Toward the Greek Ideal?

The most dramatic gains in height and weight occur during prenatal development. Within a span of 9 months, children develop from a zygote that is about 1/175 of an inch long to a neonate that is about 20 inches in length. Weight increases by a factor of billions.

Question: What patterns of growth occur in infancy? During the first year after birth, gains in height and weight are also dramatic, although not by the standards of prenatal gains. Infants usually double their birth weight in about 5 months and triple it by the first birthday (Kuczmarski et al., 2000). Their height increases by about 50% in the first year, so that a child whose length at birth was 20 inches is likely to be about 30 inches tall at 12 months. **Truth or Fiction Revisited:** Thus, it is true that infants triple their birth weight within a year. The gain sounds dramatic, but keep in mind that their weight increases more than a billionfold in the 9 months between conception and birth.

Growth in infancy has long been viewed as a slow and steady process. Growth charts in pediatricians' offices resemble the smooth, continuous curves shown in

differentiation The processes by which behaviors and physical structures become more specialized.

Concept Review 5.1   Sequences of Physical Development

Cephalocaudal Development

Cephalocaudal means that development proceeds from the "head" to the "tail," or, in the case of humans, to the lower parts of the body. Cephalocaudal development gives the brain an opportunity to participate more fully in subsequent developments.

This photo shows that infants gain control over their hands and upper body before they gain control over their lower body.

Proximodistal Development

Proximodistal means that development proceeds from the trunk or central axis of the body outward. The brain and spine make up the central nervous system along the central axis of the body and are functional before the infant can control the arms and legs.

In this photo you can see that the infant's arm is only slightly longer than her head. Compare this to the length of your own head and arm.

Differentiation

As children mature, physical reactions become less global and more specific. This infant engages in diffuse motor activity. Within a few months, he will be grasping for objects and holding onto them with a more and more sophisticated kind of grasp.

This photo shows that infants engage in diffuse motion before they begin to reach and grasp.

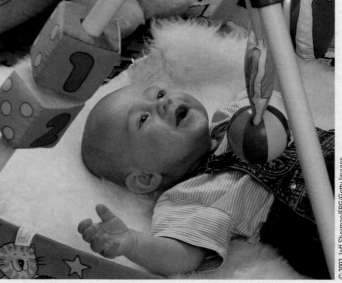

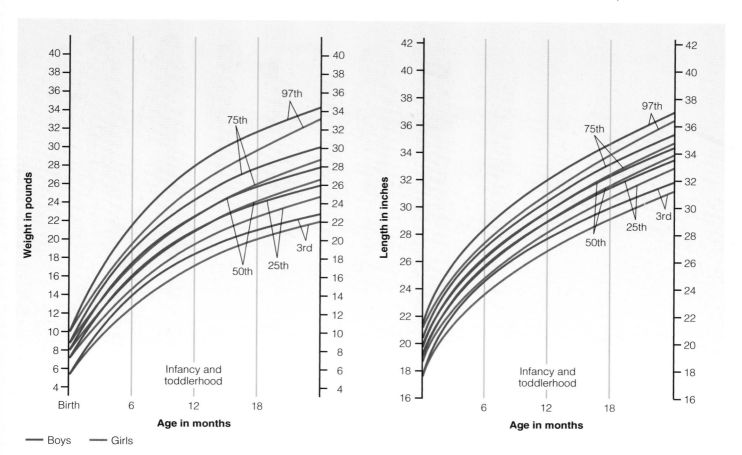

● **Figure 5.1**   Growth Curves for Weight and Height (Length) from Birth to Age 2 Years

The curves indicate the percentiles for weight and length at different ages. Lines labeled 97th show the height and weight of children who are taller and heavier than 97% of children of a particular age. Lines marked 50th indicate the height and weight of the average child of a given age: Half their agemates are shorter and lighter, and half are heavier and taller. Lines labeled 3rd designate children who are taller and heavier than only 3% of children their age, and so on.

Source: Kuczmarski et al. (2000, Figures 1–4).

● Figure 5.1, but research suggests that infants actually grow in spurts. About 90%–95% of the time, they are not growing at all. One study measured the height of infants throughout their first 21 months (Lampl et al., 1992). The researchers found that the infants would remain the same size for 2 to 63 days and then would shoot up in length from one-fifth of an inch (0.5 centimeter) to a full inch (2.5 centimeters) in less than 24 hours. Parents who swear that their infants sometimes consume enormous amounts of food and grow overnight may not be exaggerating.

Infants grow another 4 to 6 inches during the second year and gain another 4 to 7 pounds. Boys generally reach half their adult height by their second birthday. Girls, however, mature more quickly than boys and are likely to reach half their adult height at the age of 18 months (Tanner, 1989). The growth rates of taller-than-average infants, as a group, tend to slow down. Those of shorter-than-average infants, as a group, tend to speed up. I am not suggesting that there is no relationship between infant and adult heights or that we all wind up in an average range. Tall infants, as a group, wind up taller than short infants, but in most cases not by as much as seemed likely during infancy.

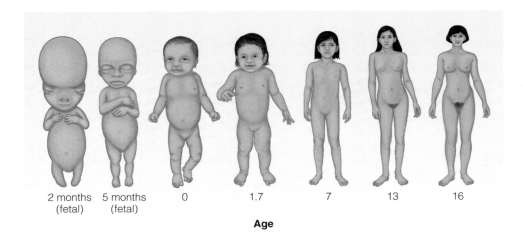

2 months (fetal)	5 months (fetal)	0	1.7	7	13	16

Age

● **Figure 5.2** Changes in the Proportions of the Body

Development proceeds in a cephalocaudal direction. The head is proportionately larger among younger children.

Changes in Body Proportions

In rendering the human form, Greek classical sculptors followed the rule of the "golden section": The length of the head must equal one-eighth of the height of the body (including the head). The ideal of human beauty may be so, but the reality is that, among adults, the length of the head actually varies from about one-eighth to one-tenth of the entire body. Among children, the head is proportionately larger (see ● Figure 5.2).

Development proceeds in a cephalocaudal manner. A few weeks after conception, an embryo is almost all head. At the beginning of the fetal stage, the head is about half the length of the unborn child. In the neonate, it is about one-fourth the length of the body. The head gradually diminishes in proportion to the rest of the body, even though it doubles in size by adulthood.

Among adults, the arms are nearly three times the length of the head. The legs are about four times as long, nearly half the length of the body. Among neonates, the arms and legs are about equal in length. Each is only about one and a half times the length of the head. By the first birthday, the neck has begun to lengthen visibly, as have the arms and legs. The arms grow more rapidly than the legs do at first (an example of the cephalocaudal trend); by the second birthday, the arms are actually longer than the legs. The legs then grow more rapidly, soon catching up with and surpassing the arms in length.

We have described typical growth patterns. Most infants follow these patterns and thrive. Some do not. *Question: What is failure to thrive?*

Failure to Thrive

failure to thrive (FTT) A disorder of impaired growth in infancy and early childhood characterized by failure to gain weight within normal limits.

Haley is 4 months old. Her mother, as she puts it, is breast-feeding Haley "all the time" because she is not gaining weight. Not gaining weight for a while is normal enough, but Haley is also irritable, and she feeds fitfully, sometimes refusing the breast entirely. Her pediatrician is evaluating her for a syndrome called **failure to thrive (FTT)**.

We live in one of the world's most bountiful nations, and few have trouble accessing food. Nevertheless, a number of infants, such as Haley, show FTT, which is a serious disorder that impairs growth in infancy and early childhood (Simonelli et al., 2005). FTT is sometimes a fuzzy diagnosis. Historically, researchers have spoken of biologically based (or "organic") FTT versus nonbiologically based ("nonorganic") FTT. The idea is that in organic FTT an underlying health problem accounts for the failure to obtain or make use of adequate nutrition. Nonorganic FTT (abbreviated NOFTT in the research literature) apparently has psychological roots, social roots, or both. In any case, the infant does not make normal gains in weight and size (Simonelli et al., 2005).

Regardless of the cause or causes, feeding problems are central. Research has shown that infants with FTT tend to be introduced to solid and finger foods later than other children. As in Haley's case, they are more likely to be described as variable eaters and less often as being hungry (Wright & Birks, 2000). FTT is linked not only to slow physical growth but also to cognitive, behavioral, and emotional problems (Corbett & Drewett, 2004; Culebras, 2005; Simonelli et al., 2005). For example, at the age of 2 to 12 months, infants with FTT express more negative feelings, vocalize less, and often refuse to make eye contact with adults (Steward, 2001). Another study found that at the age of 8½, children who had been diagnosed with FTT at the median age of 20 months remained smaller, were less cognitively advanced, and were more emotionally and behaviorally disturbed than normal children (Dykman et al., 2001). They wind up shorter and lighter than their peers at the age of 12 but apparently do not enter puberty later (Drewett et al., 2006).

Many investigators believe that deficiencies in caregiver–child interaction play a key role in FTT (Benoit & Coolbear, 2004). For example, compared with mothers of healthy infants, mothers of infants with FTT show fewer adaptive social interactions (they are less likely to "go with the flow") and fewer positive feelings toward their infants. The mothers also terminate feedings more arbitrarily (Robinson et al., 2001). Perhaps as a consequence, children with FTT are less likely than other children to be securely attached to their mothers (Benoit & Coolbear, 2004). Why are the mothers of children with FTT less likely to help their children to feel secure? Many have a large number of children, an unstable home environment, or psychological problems of their own (Mackner et al., 2003).

Because FTT often results from a combination of factors, treatment may not be easy. Children with FTT need both nutritional support and attention to possible adjustment problems (Simonelli et al., 2005). It turns out that Haley's parents will profit from both personal counseling and advice on relating to Haley.

Catch-Up Growth

A child's growth can be slowed from its genetically predetermined course by many organic factors, including illness and dietary deficiency. If the problem is alleviated, the child's rate of growth frequently accelerates to approximate its normal course (Harding & McCowan, 2003; IJzendoorn & Juffer, 2006). The tendency to return to one's genetically determined pattern of growth is referred to as **canalization**. Once Haley's parents receive counseling and once Haley's FTT is overcome, Haley will put on weight rapidly and catch up to the norms for her age.

Nutrition: Fueling Development

The overall nutritional status of children in the United States is good compared with that of children in most countries (Arija et al., 2006). The nutritional status of poor American children has improved through federal programs such as the Food Stamp Program, the Supplemental Food Program for Women, Infants, and Children (WIC), the Child and Adult Care Food Program, and the National School Breakfast and Lunch programs. Even so, infants and young children from low-income families

canalization The tendency of growth rates to return to genetically determined patterns after undergoing environmentally induced change.

are more likely than other children to display signs of poor nutrition, such as anemia and FTT (National Center for Children in Poverty, 2004). For more information on children in poverty, go to www.nccp.org. *Question: What are the nutritional needs of infants?*

From birth, infants should be fed either breast milk or an iron-fortified infant formula. The introduction of solid foods is not recommended until the infant can indicate hunger by leaning forward and fullness by turning away from food. These behaviors normally occur at 4 to 6 months of age, although the American Academy of Pediatrics recommends that infants be fed breast milk throughout the first year and longer if possible (American Academy of Pediatrics, 2007). For more information, go to the website of the American Academy of Pediatrics at www.aap.org. The first solid food is usually iron-enriched cereal, followed by strained fruits, then vegetables, and finally meats, poultry, and fish. Whole cow's milk is normally delayed until the infant is 9 to 12 months old. Finger foods such as teething biscuits are introduced in the latter part of the first year.

Here are some useful guidelines for infant nutrition (Infant and Toddler Nutrition, 2007):

- Build up to a variety of foods. Introduce new foods one at a time, if possible, to determine whether they make a difference in the infant's behavior. (The infant may be allergic to a new food, and introducing foods one at a time helps isolate a new food's possible effects on the infant.)
- In general, pay attention to the infant's appetite to help avoid overfeeding or underfeeding. (If the infant seems to have a poor appetite, discuss it with the pediatrician.)
- Do not restrict fat and cholesterol too much. (For example, do not substitute skim milk for whole milk.) Infants need calories and some fat.
- Do not overdo high-fiber foods.
- In general, avoid items with added sugar and salt.
- Encourage eating of high-iron foods; infants need more iron, pound for pound, than adults do.

When in doubt, parents should check with a pediatrician. What is good for adults is not good for infants. Parents who are on low-fat, high-fiber diets to ward off cardiovascular problems, cancer, and other health problems should not assume that the same diet is healthful for infants.

Breast Feeding versus Bottle Feeding: Pros and Cons, Biological and Political

In many developing nations, women have no choice: If their infants are going to be nourished, mothers will have to breast-feed. Even in developed nations, where formula is readily available, breast milk today is considered by most health professionals to be the "medical gold standard" and by many, perhaps most, mothers to be the "moral gold standard" (Knaak, 2005). Perhaps for this reason, popular magazines in the United States, including magazines that aim at African American mothers, tend to carry more articles on breast feeding than on bottle feeding (Frerichs et al., 2006).

Breast feeding, of course, is the "natural" way to nourish a baby. Infant formulas were developed in the 1930s. Over the next several decades, breast feeding declined because women were entering the workforce, bottle feeding was seen as "scientific," and the women's movement encouraged women to become liberated from traditional roles (Sloan et al., 2006). Breast feeding thus has political and social aspects as well as nutritional aspects (Knaak, 2005). *Question: How do women decide to bottle-*

feed or to breast-feed their children? Much of the decision of whether or not to breast-feed has to do with domestic and occupational arrangements, day care, social support, reactions to public breast feeding, and beliefs about mother–infant bonding (Sloan et al., 2006).

A survey of 35 African American and Latina American mothers or pregnant adolescents (age 12 to 19) found that those who recognized the benefits of breast feeding were more likely to do it (Hannon et al., 2000). They reported benefits such as promoting mother–infant bonding and the infant's health. Barriers to breast feeding include fear of pain, embarrassment by public exposure, and unease with the act itself. An influential person, such as the woman's partner or mother, often successfully encourages the mother to breast-feed, however (Sloan et al., 2006). Community support through volunteer workers and visiting nurses also encourages women to breast-feed (Fetrick et al., 2003; Graffy et al., 2004). Better-educated women are more likely to breast-feed, even among low-income women (Sloan et al., 2006).

In any event, breast feeding has become more popular during the past generation, largely because of increased knowledge of its health benefits, even among women at the lower end of the socioeconomic spectrum (Sloan et al., 2006). Today, most American mothers—more than 70%—breast-feed their children for at least a while, but only about two women in five continue to breast-feed after 6 months, and only one in five is still breast feeding after 1 year (Breastfeeding, 2006). The American Academy of Pediatrics (2007) recommends that women breast-feed for 1 year or more.

Many women bottle-feed because they return to work after childbirth and therefore are unavailable to breast-feed. Their partners, extended families, nannies, or child-care workers give their children bottles during the day. Some mothers pump their milk and bottle it for their children's use when they are away. Some parents bottle-feed because it permits both parents to share in feeding, around the clock. The father may not be equipped to breast-feed, but he can bottle-feed. Even though bottle feeding requires preparing formulas, many women find it to be less troublesome than breast feeding.

Question: What are the advantages and disadvantages of breast milk? Let us begin with the positive (American Academy of Pediatrics, 2007):

- Breast milk conforms to human digestion processes (i.e., it is unlikely to upset the infant's stomach).
- Breast milk alone is adequate for the first 6 months after birth. Water, juice, and other foods are generally unnecessary. Even if babies enjoy discovering new tastes and textures, solid foods should not replace breast feeding, but merely supplement breast milk through the first year (Breastfeeding, 2006).
- As the infant matures, the composition of breast milk changes to help meet the infant's changing needs.
- Breast milk contains the mother's antibodies; when they are transmitted to the infant, they help to prevent problems ranging from ear infections, pneumonia, wheezing, bronchiolitis, and tetanus to chicken pox, bacterial meningitis, and typhoid fever.
- Breast milk helps protect against the form of cancer known as childhood lymphoma (a cancer of the lymph glands).
- Diarrhea can be a persistent and deadly disease for millions of infants in developing countries, and breast milk decreases the likelihood of developing serious and lingering cases of diarrhea.
- Infants who are nourished by breast milk are less likely to develop allergic responses and constipation than infants who are bottle-fed.

Developing in a World of Diversity

Alleviating Protein-Energy Malnutrition (PEM)

Protein-energy malnutrition (PEM) is the most severe form of malnutrition. Protein is essential for growth, and food energy translates as calories. Here are a few facts about PEM from the World Health Organization (2004):

- PEM affects one child in four around the world. One-hundred-fifty million children (27%) are underweight, and 182 million (33%) have stunted growth.
- More than 70% of children with PEM live in Asia, 26% live in Africa, and about 4% live in Latin America and the Caribbean.
- Children may encounter PEM before birth if their mother is malnourished.
- Malnutrition, also known as "the silent emergency," has contributed to about 60% of the 11 million deaths of children each year.
- Infants and young children are most vulnerable to growth impairment as a result of PEM because of their high protein and energy needs and their susceptibility to infection.
- Children with PEM suffer up to 160 days of illness per year.

The World Health Organization (2003) produced guidelines on the treatment of children with PEM in the clinical setting. The guidelines are being promoted for use worldwide by physicians, nurses, and all other frontline health workers. The guidelines for instruction include:

- Educating health workers on the extent and severity of PEM
- Identifying children with severe malnutrition. Symptoms include hypoglycemia (shakiness resulting from low blood sugar levels), hypothermia, shock, dehydration, and severe anemia.
- Preparing appropriate feeding formulas and food supplements
- Using antibiotics and other medicines to treat disease
- Monitoring the child's intake of food and the child's waste products; preparing and using a weight chart
- Monitoring the child's vital signs—pulse, respiration rate, and temperature—and being aware of signs of danger
- Bathing the child
- Involving mothers in care so that they can continue care at home, including feeding and play activities (for purposes of stimulation); providing mothers with comprehensive instructions at discharge

The mortality rate of children with PEM can be as high as 50%, but with adequate care, the rate can be reduced to less than 5%. For more information, contact the Department of Nutrition for Health and Development, World Health Organization, 1211 Geneva 27, Switzerland (phone: 141-22-791-2624/4342; fax: 141-22-791-4156).

Reflect: *What can you do to help alleviate PEM in developing nations?*

Fighting Malnutrition through Aid and Education

This doctor, who works for the Medecins sans Frontieres organization, tends a severely malnourished child in Maradi, Niger. Medecins sans Frontieres is an independent organization that is committed to providing medical aid wherever necessary and raising awareness of the plight of the people they help.

© Per-Anders Pettersson/Getty Images

- Breast-fed infants are less likely than bottle-fed infants to develop obesity later in life.
- Breast feeding is associated with better neural and behavioral organization in the infant, at least in the short term.

Truth or Fiction Revisited: Therefore, it is true that drinking breast milk is connected with a better chance of avoiding obesity later in life. Perhaps it is because breast milk is lower in fat than whole milk.

Breast feeding also has health benefits for the mother: It reduces the risk of early breast cancer and ovarian cancer, and it builds the strength of bones, which can reduce the likelihood of the hip fractures that result from osteoporosis following menopause. Breast feeding also helps shrink the uterus after delivery.

Human newborns also prefer human milk to formula. An interesting study recruited breast-fed and bottle-fed four-day-old infants as subjects and presented them with the odors of human milk or formula (Marlier & Schaal, 2005). Those who were breast-fed were presented with the odors of unfamiliar human milk, that is, milk from strangers. Preference was measured in terms of the direction in which the infants turned their heads and the intensity of sucking movements. Although the responses of the infants were somewhat more complex than I am presenting here, they generally showed a preference for human milk. Should this finding influence parents? Perhaps, but the truth of the matter is that few formula-fed infants have been shown to refuse to eat (or develop a sour disposition) because of the type of food.

Breast feeding has also been shown to help mothers respond more calmly to stress, as defined by stress-related bodily responses when presented with demanding mental arithmetic problems (Mezzacappa et al., 2005), but don't decide to breast-feed your baby purely on this basis. If breast feeding doesn't fit in with your life, it could be another source of stress—for you.

There are downsides to breast feeding. For example, one of the bodily fluids that transmits HIV (the virus that causes AIDS) is breast milk. Researchers estimate that as many as one-third of the world's infants who have HIV/AIDS were infected in this manner (UNAIDS, 2006). Alcohol, many drugs taken by the mother, and environmental hazards such as polychlorinated biphenyls (PCBs) can also be transmitted to infants through breast milk. Therefore, breast milk is not always as pure as it would seem to be. Moreover, for breast milk to contain the necessary nutrients, the mother must be adequately nourished herself. In many cases, mothers in developing countries do not eat sufficiently well enough to pass along proper nutrition to their infants.

Other negatives to breast feeding include the mother's assumptions of the sole responsibility for nighttime feedings. She also encounters the physical demands of producing and expelling milk, a tendency for soreness in the breasts, and the inconvenience of being continually available to meet the infant's feeding needs.

Question: Should mothers who smoke breast-feed? Breast milk remains the ideal food for a baby even if the mother smokes (Breastfeeding, 2006). Although nicotine may be present in breast milk, harmful effects on the infant have not been noted.

The hormones prolactin and oxytocin are involved in breast feeding. Prolactin means in favor of ("pro") producing milk. By a few days after delivery, prolactin stimulates the mammary glands to produce milk. Oxytocin is secreted in response to suckling and stimulates the breasts to eject milk. When breast feeding is discontinued, prolactin and oxytocin are no longer secreted, and lactation ends.

Readers who are seeking help with or want more information about breast feeding can visit www.BreastfeedingTaskForLA.org, www.breastfeeding.org, www.breastfeeding.com, www.lalecheleague.org, or www.ILCA.org.

Active Review

1. Cephalocaudal development describes the processes by which development proceeds from the _____ to the lower parts of the body.
2. The _____ principle means that development proceeds from the trunk outward.
3. Infants usually double their birth weight in about _____ months and triple it by the first birthday.
4. Mothers of infants with failure to thrive, compared with mothers of healthy infants, show fewer (Positive or Negative?) feelings toward their infants.
5. After illness or dietary deficiency, children show _____, which is a tendency to return to their genetically determined pattern of growth.
6. Breast milk contains _____ that can prevent problems such as ear infections, meningitis, tetanus, and chicken pox.

Reflect & Relate: How closely did your parents pay attention to your height and weight? Did they chart it? When did you begin to think that you were average or above or below average in height and weight? What effect did your size have on your self-concept and self-esteem?

Go to

http://www.thomsonedu.com/psychology/rathus
for an interactive version of this review.

Development of the Brain and Nervous System

When I was a child, I did not think that it was a good idea to have a nervous system. Who, after all, wants to be nervous? But then I learned that the nervous system is a system of **nerves** involved in heartbeat, visual–motor coordination, thought and language, and so on. The human nervous system is more complex than that of other animals. Although elephants and whales have heavier brains, our brains make up a larger proportion of our body weight.

Development of Neurons

The basic units of the nervous system are **neurons**. *Questions: What are neurons? How do they develop?* Neurons are cells that receive and transmit messages from one part of the body to another. The messages transmitted by neurons account for phenomena as varied as reflexes, the perception of an itch from a mosquito bite, the visual–motor coordination of a skier, the composition of a concerto, and the solution of a math problem.

People are born with about 100 billion neurons, most of which are in the brain. Neurons vary according to their functions and locations in the body. Some neurons in the brain are only a fraction of an inch in length, whereas neurons in the leg can grow several feet long. Each neuron possesses a cell body, dendrites, and an axon (see ● Figure 5.3). **Dendrites** are short fibers that extend from the cell body and receive incoming messages from up to 1,000 adjoining transmitting neurons. The **axon** extends trunklike from the cell body and accounts for much of the difference in length in neurons. An axon can be up to several feet in length if it is carrying messages from the toes upward. Messages are released from axon terminals in the form

nerves Bundles of axons from many neurons.

neurons Nerve cells; cells found in the nervous system that transmit messages.

dendrites The rootlike parts of a neuron that receive impulses from other neurons (from the Greek *dendron*, meaning "tree" and referring to the branching appearance of dendrites).

axon A long, thin part of a neuron that transmits impulses to other neurons through small branching structures called axon terminals.

See your student companion website for an interactive version of Figure 5.3.

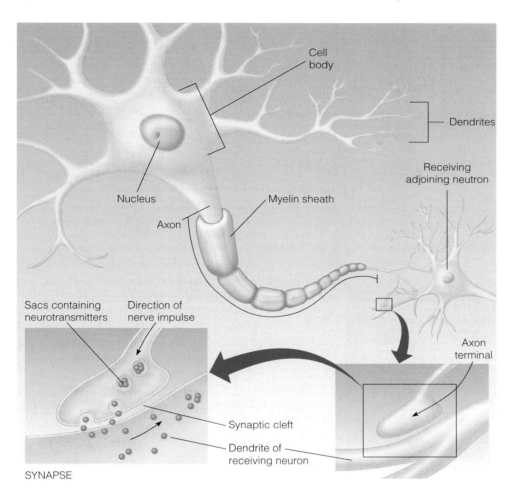

Cell body

Dendrites

Receiving adjoining neutron

Nucleus

Myelin sheath

Axon

Sacs containing neurotransmitters

Direction of nerve impulse

Axon terminal

Synaptic cleft

Dendrite of receiving neuron

SYNAPSE

● **Figure 5.3**   Anatomy of a Neuron

"Messages" enter neurons through dendrites, are transmitted along the axon, and then are sent through axon terminals to muscles, glands, and other neurons. Neurons develop by means of proliferation of dendrites and axon terminals and through myelination.

of chemicals called **neurotransmitters**. These messages are then received by the dendrites of adjoining neurons, muscles, or glands. As the child matures, the axons of neurons grow in length, and the dendrites and axon terminals proliferate, creating vast interconnected networks for the transmission of complex messages.

Myelin

Many neurons are tightly wrapped with white, fatty **myelin sheaths** that give them the appearance of a string of white sausages. The high fat content of the myelin sheath insulates the neuron from electrically charged atoms in the fluids that encase the nervous system. In this way, leakage of the electric current being carried along the axon is minimized, and messages are conducted more efficiently.

The term **myelination** refers to the process by which axons are coated with myelin. Myelination is not complete at birth, but rather is part of the maturation process that leads to the abilities to crawl and walk during the first year after birth. Incomplete myelination accounts for some of the helplessness of neonates. Myelination of the brain's prefrontal matter continues into the second decade of life and is connected with advances in working memory and language ability (Aslin & Schlaggar, 2006; Pujol et al., 2006). Breakdown of myelin is believed to be associated with Alzheimer's disease, a source of cognitive decline that usually begins in middle to late adulthood (Bartzokis, 2004; Connor, 2004).

neurotransmitter A chemical substance that enables the transmission of neural impulses from one neuron to another.

myelin sheath (MY-uh-lin) A fatty, whitish substance that encases and insulates neurons, permitting more rapid transmission of neural impulses.

myelination The process by which axons are coated with myelin.

● **Figure 5.4**
Growth of Body Systems as a Percentage of Total Postnatal Growth

The brain of the neonate weighs about one-fourth of its adult weight. In keeping with the principle of cephalocaudal growth, the brain will triple in weight by the infant's first birthday, reaching nearly 70% of its adult weight.

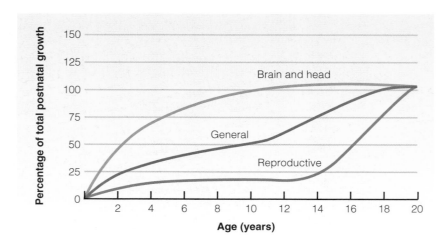

● **Figure 5.5**
Structures of the Brain

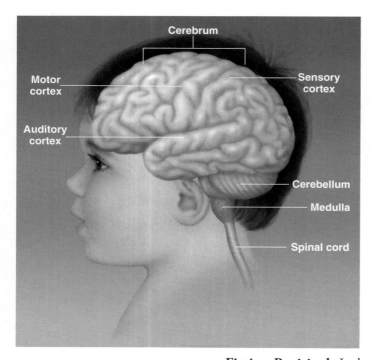

The convolutions of the cortex increase its surface area and, apparently, its intellectual capacity. (In this case, wrinkles are good.) The medulla is involved in vital functions such as respiration and heartbeat; the cerebellum is involved in balance and coordination.

See your student companion website for an interactive version of Figure 5.5.

In the disease **multiple sclerosis,** myelin is replaced by a hard, fibrous tissue that disrupts the timing of neural transmission, thus interfering with muscle control (Stankoff et al., 2006). The disorder phenylketonuria (PKU; see Chapter 2) leads to mental retardation by inhibiting the formation of myelin in the brain (Sirrs et al., 2007). Congenital infection with HIV has been shown to be connected with abnormalities in the formation of myelin and with cognitive and motor impairment (Blanchette et al., 2001; Thierry et al., 2005).

Development of the Brain

Questions: What is the brain? How does the brain develop? The brain is the command center of the developing organism. (If you like computer analogies, think of the brain as the central processing unit.) It contains neurons and provides the basis for physical, cognitive, and personal and social development.

The brain of the neonate weighs a little less than a pound, or nearly one-fourth its adult weight. **Truth or Fiction Revisited:** In keeping with the principles of cephalocaudal growth, an infant's brain reaches about 50% of its adult weight by the second birthday (see ● Figure 5.4). Let us look at the brain, as shown in ● Figure 5.5, and discuss the development of the structures within.

Structures of the Brain

Many nerves that connect the spinal cord to higher levels of the brain pass through the **medulla**. The medulla is vital in the control of basic functions, such as heartbeat and respiration. The medulla is part of an area called the brain stem, which may be implicated in sudden infant death syndrome (SIDS; see Chapter 4).

Above the medulla lies the **cerebellum**, which is Latin for "little brain." The cerebellum helps the child maintain balance, control motor behavior, and coordinate eye movements with bodily sensations.

The **cerebrum** is the crowning glory of the brain. It makes possible the breadth and depth of human learning, thought, memory, and language. Only in human beings does the cerebrum constitute such a large proportion of the brain. The surface of the cerebrum consists of two hemispheres—left and right—that become increasingly wrinkled as the child develops, coming to show ridges and valleys called fissures. This surface is the cerebral cortex. The wrinkles allow a great deal of surface area to be packed into the brain. **Truth or Fiction Revisited:** Yes, the cerebral cortex is only one-eighth of an inch thick, yet it is here that thought and reasoning occur. It is here that we display sensory information from the world outside and command muscles to move.

Growth Spurts of the Brain

The brain makes gains in size and weight in different ways. One way is in the formation of neurons, a process completed by birth. The first major growth spurt of the brain occurs during the fourth and fifth months of prenatal development, when neurons proliferate. A second growth spurt in the brain occurs between the 25th week of prenatal development and the end of the second year after birth. Whereas the first growth spurt of the brain is due to the formation of neurons, the second growth spurt is due primarily to the proliferation of dendrites and axon terminals (see ● Figure 5.6).

Brain Development in Infancy

There is a clear link between what infants can do and the myelination of areas within the brain. At birth, the parts of the brain involved in heartbeat and respiration, sleeping and arousal, and reflex activity are fairly well myelinated and functional.

Myelination of motor pathways allows neonates to show stereotyped reflexes, but otherwise neonates' physical activity tends to be random and ill-organized. Myelination of the motor area of the cerebral cortex begins at about the fourth month of prenatal development. Myelin develops rapidly along the major motor pathways from the cerebral cortex during the last month of pregnancy and continues after birth. The development of intentional physical activity coincides with myelination as the unorganized movements of the neonate come under increasing control. Myelination of the nerves to muscles is largely developed by the age of 2 years, although research using magnetic resonance imaging, or MRI, suggests that myelination continues to some degree into adolescence (Wozniak & Lim, 2006).

Although neonates respond to touch and can see and hear quite well, the areas of the cortex that are involved in vision, hearing, and the skin senses are less well myelinated at birth. As myelination progresses and the interconnections between the various areas of the cortex thicken, children become increasingly capable of complex and integrated sensorimotor activities (Wozniak & Lim, 2006).

Neonates whose mothers read *The Cat in the Hat* aloud during the last few weeks of pregnancy show a preference for this story (see Chapter 3). It turns out that myelination of the neurons involved in the sense of hearing begins at about the sixth month of pregnancy, coinciding with the period in which fetuses begin to respond to sound. Myelination of these pathways is developing rapidly at term and continues until about the age of 4 years.

Although the fetus shows some response to light during the third trimester, it is hard to imagine what use the fetus could have for vision. It turns out that the neurons involved in vision begin to myelinate only shortly before full term, but then they complete the process of myelination rapidly. Within a short 5 to 6 months after birth, vision has become the dominant sense.

Nature and Nurture in the Development of the Brain

Development of the areas of the brain that control sensation and movement begins as a result of maturation, but sensory stimulation and physical activity during early infancy also spur the development of these areas. *Question: How do nature and nurture affect the development of the brain?* Experience interacts with the unfolding of the genetic code to produce the brain—and intellectual functioning—as seen by a snapshot at a given point in time (Güntürkün, 2006; Posner & Rothbart, 2007).

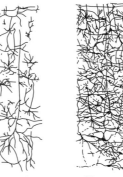

Neonate   **Six months**   **Two years**

● **Figure 5.6**
Increase in Neural Connections in the Brain

A major growth spurt in the brain occurs between the 25th week of prenatal development and the end of the second year after birth. This growth spurt is due primarily to the proliferation of dendrites and axon terminals.

Source: Conel (1959).

multiple sclerosis A disorder in which myelin is replaced by hard fibrous tissue that impedes neural transmission.

medulla (muh-DUH-luh) An oblong-shaped area of the hindbrain involved in heartbeat and respiration.

cerebellum (ser-uh-BEH-lum) The part of the hindbrain involved in muscle coordination and balance.

cerebrum (seh-REE-brum) The large mass of the forebrain, which consists of two hemispheres.

Research with animals shows how sensory stimulation sparks growth of the cortex. Researchers have been given complex environmental exposure, in some cases rat "amusement parks" with toys such as ladders, platforms, and boxes to demonstrate the effects of enriched environments. In these studies, rats exposed to more complex environments develop heavier brains than control animals. The weight differences in part reflect more synapses per neuron than other rats (Briones et al., 2004). On the other hand, animals reared in darkness show shrinkage of the visual cortex, impaired vision, and impaired visual–motor coordination (Klintsova & Greenough, 1999). If they don't use it, they lose it?

Human brains also are affected by experience. Infants actually have more connections among neurons than adults do. Connections that are activated by experience survive; the others do not (Tsuneishi & Casaer, 2000; Weinberg, 2004).

The great adaptability of the brain appears to be a double-edged sword. Adaptability allows us to develop different patterns of neural connections to meet the demands of different environments, but lack of stimulation—especially during critical early periods of development (as we will see later)—can impair adaptability.

Brain nourishment, like early experience, plays a role in the brain achieving what is permitted by the child's genes. Inadequate fetal nutrition, especially during the prenatal growth spurt of the brain, has several negative effects such as smallness in the size of the brain, the formation of fewer neurons, and less myelination (Guerrini et al., 2007; Massaro et al., 2006).

Active Review

7. _____ are the basic units of the nervous system.
8. Each neuron possesses a cell body, dendrites, and a(n) _____.
9. The brain reaches nearly _____% of its adult weight by the first birthday.
10. The wrinkled part of the brain, called the _____, enables the child to maintain balance and to control physical behavior.

Reflect & Relate: Are you surprised that there is such a close connection between experience and development of the brain? How does the information presented in this section fit with the adage "Use it or lose it"?

Go to

http://www.thomsonedu.com/psychology/rathus

for an interactive version of this review.

Motor Development: How Moving

"Allyn couldn't walk yet at 10 months, but she zoomed after me in her walker, giggling her head off." "Anthony was walking forward and backward by the age of 13 months."

These are some of the types of comments parents make about their children's motor development. *Questions: What is motor development? How does it occur?* Motor development involves the activity of muscles, leading to changes in posture, movement, and coordination of movement with the infant's developing sensory apparatus. Motor development provides some of the most fascinating changes in infants, in part because so much seems to happen so fast, and so much of it during the first year.

Like physical development, motor development follows cephalocaudal and proximodistal patterns and differentiation. Infants gain control of their heads and upper torsos before they can effectively use their arms. This trend illustrates cephalocaudal development. Infants also can control their trunks and shoulders before they can use their hands and fingers, demonstrating the proximodistal trend.

Lifting and Holding the Torso and Head: Heads Up

Neonates can move their heads slightly to the side. They can thus avoid suffocation if they are lying face down and their noses or mouths are obstructed by bedding. At about 1 month, infants can raise their heads. By about 2 months, they can also lift their chests while lying on their stomachs.

When neonates are held, their heads must be supported. But by 3 to 6 months of age, infants generally manage to hold their heads quite well so supporting the head is no longer necessary. Unfortunately, infants who can normally support their heads cannot do so when they are lifted or moved about in a jerky manner; infants who are handled carelessly can thus develop neck injuries.

Control of the Hands: Getting a Grip on Things

The development of hand skills is a clear example of proximodistal development. Infants will track (follow) slowly moving objects with their eyes shortly after birth, but they will not generally reach for them. They show a grasp reflex but do not reliably reach for the objects that appear to interest them. Voluntary reaching and grasping require visual–motor coordination. By about the age of 3 months, infants will make clumsy swipes at objects, failing to grasp them, because their aim is poor or they close their hands too soon or too late.

Between the ages of 4 and 6 months, infants become more successful at grasping objects (Piek, 2006; Santos et al., 2000). However, they may not know how to let go and may hold an object indefinitely, until their attention is diverted and the hand opens accidentally. Four to 6 months is a good age for giving children rattles, large plastic spoons, mobiles, and other brightly colored hanging toys that can be grasped but are harmless when they wind up in the mouth.

Grasping is reflexive at first. Voluntary grasping (holding) replaces reflexive grasping by the age of 3 to 4 months. Infants first use an **ulnar grasp**, in which they hold objects clumsily between their fingers and their palm (Butterworth et al., 1997). By the age of 4 to 6 months, they can transfer objects back and forth between hands. The oppositional thumb comes into play at about the age of 9 to 12 months. Use of the thumb gives infants the ability to pick up tiny objects in a **pincer grasp** (● Figure 5.7). By about 11 months of age, infants can hold objects in each hand and inspect them in turn.

Between the ages of 5 and 11 months, infants adjust their hands in anticipation of grasping moving targets. They also gather information from the objects' movements to predict their future location and catch them (Wentworth et al., 2000). Think of the complex concepts it requires to explain this behavior and how well infants perform it, without any explanation at all! Of course, I am not suggesting that infants solve problems in geometry and physics to grasp moving objects; that interpretation, as developmental psychologist Marshall M. Haith (1998) would describe it, would put a "cog in infant cognition."

Another aspect of visual–motor coordination is stacking blocks. On average, children can stack two blocks at 15 months, three blocks at 18 months, and five blocks at 24 months (Wentworth et al., 2000). At about 24 months of age, children can also copy horizontal and vertical lines.

Locomotion: Getting a Move On

Locomotion is movement from one place to another. Children gain the capacity to move their bodies through a sequence of activities that includes rolling over, sitting up, crawling, creeping, walking, and running (see ● Figure 5.8). There is much variation in the ages at which infants first engage in these activities. Although the sequence

© Masterfile

● **Figure 5.7**
Pincer Grasp

Infants first hold objects between their fingers and palm. Once the oppositional thumb comes into play at about 9 to 12 months of age, infants are able to pick up tiny objects using what is termed a pincer grasp.

ulnar grasp A method of grasping objects in which the fingers close somewhat clumsily against the palm.

pincer grasp The use of the opposing thumb to grasp objects between the thumb and other fingers.

locomotion Movement from one place to another.

mostly remains the same, some children will skip a step. For example, an infant may creep without ever having crawled.

Most infants can roll over, from back to stomach and from stomach to back, by about the age of 6 months. They can also sit (and support their upper bodies, necks, and heads) for extended periods if they are aided by a person or placed in a seat with a strap, such as a high chair. By about 7 months of age, infants usually begin to sit up by themselves.

At about 8 to 9 months, most infants begin to crawl, a motor activity in which they lie prone and use their arms to pull themselves along, dragging their bellies and feet behind. Creeping, a more sophisticated form of locomotion in which infants move themselves along up on their hands and knees, requires a good deal more coordination and usually appears a month or so after crawling (● Figure 5.9).

There are fascinating alternatives to creeping. Some infants travel from one place to another by rolling over and over. Some lift themselves and swing their arms while in a sitting position, in effect dragging along on their buttocks. Still others do a "bear walk" in which they move on their hands and feet, without allowing their elbows and knees to touch the floor. And some, as noted, just crawl until they are ready to stand and walk from place to place while holding onto chairs, other objects, and people.

Standing overlaps with crawling and creeping. Most infants can remain in a standing position by holding on to something at the age of 8 or 9 months. At this age, they may also be able to walk a bit when supported by adults. Such walking is voluntary and does not have the stereotyped appearance of the walking reflex described in Chapter 4. About 2 months later, they can pull themselves to a standing position by holding on to the sides of their cribs or other objects and can stand briefly without holding on. Soon afterward, they walk about unsteadily while holding on. By 12 to 15 months or so, they walk by themselves, earning them the name **toddler** (● Figure 5.10). Attempts to master these new motor skills are often accompanied by signs of pleasure such as smiling, laughing, and babbling.

Toddlers soon run about, supporting their relatively heavy heads and torsos by spreading their legs in bowlegged fashion. Because they are top-heavy and inexperienced, they fall frequently. Some toddlers require consoling when they fall. Others spring right up and run on again with barely an interruption. Many toddlers are skillful at navigating steep and shallow slopes (Adolph & Berger, 2005). They walk down shallow slopes but prudently choose to slide or crawl down steep ones. Walking lends children new freedom. It allows them to get about rapidly and to grasp objects that were formerly out of reach. Give toddlers a large ball to toss and run after; it is about the least expensive and most enjoyable toy they can be given.

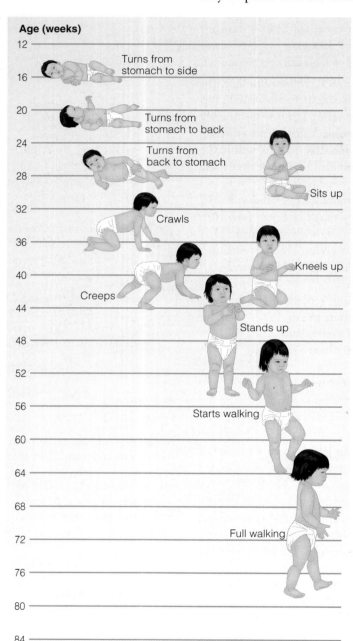

Age (weeks)

12
16 — Turns from stomach to side
20 — Turns from stomach to back
24 — Turns from back to stomach
28 — Sits up
32 — Crawls
36 — Kneels up
40
Creeps
44 — Stands up
48
52
56 — Starts walking
60
64
68
72 — Full walking
76
80
84

● **Figure 5.8**   Motor Development in Infancy

Motor development proceeds in an orderly sequence, but there is considerable variation in the timing of the marker events shown in this figure. An infant who is a bit behind will most likely develop without problems, and a precocious infant will not necessarily become a rocket scientist (or gymnast).

As children mature, their muscle strength, the density of their bones, and their balance and coordination improve (Metcalfe et al., 2005). By the age of 2 years, they can climb steps one at a time, placing both feet on each step. They can run well, walk backward, kick a large ball, and jump several inches.

Black African and African American infants generally reach such motor milestones as sitting, walking, and running before European and European American infants do (Allen & Alexander, 1990; Garcia-Coll, 1990; Kelly et al., 2006). Although genetic factors may be involved in the earlier motor development of Black African and African American infants, environmental factors also appear to play a role. African infants excel in areas of motor development in which they have received considerable stimulation and practice. For example, parents in Africa and in cultures of African origin, such as Jamaica, stress the development of sitting and walking and provide experiences, including stretching and massage, from birth that stimulate the development of these behaviors. From the second or third months, other activities are added, such as propping infants in a sitting position, bouncing them on their feet, and exercising the stepping reflex.

● **Figure 5.9**
Crawling

In crawling, infants lie prone and pull themselves along, dragging the bellies and feet behind. Creeping requires more coordination of arm and leg movements and usually appears a month or so after crawling. In creeping, infants move themselves elevated on their hands and knees.

Nature and Nurture in Motor Development

Question: What are the roles of nature and nurture in motor development?
Research with humans and other species leaves little doubt that both maturation (nature) and experience (nurture) are involved in motor development (Muir, 2000; Pryce et al., 2001; Roncesvalles et al., 2005). Certain voluntary motor activities are not possible until the brain has matured in terms of myelination and the differentiation of the motor areas of the cortex. Although the neonate shows stepping and swimming reflexes, these behaviors are controlled by more primitive parts of the brain. They disappear when cortical development inhibits some functions of the lower parts of the brain, and, when they reappear, they differ in quality.

Infants also need some opportunity to experiment before they can engage in milestones such as sitting up and walking. Even so, many of these advances can apparently be attributed to maturation. **Truth or Fiction Revisited:** It is true that Native American Hopi infants spend the first year strapped to a board yet begin to walk at about the same time as children who are reared in other cultures. In classic research, Wayne Dennis and Marsena Dennis (1940) reported on the motor development of Native American Hopi children who spent their first year strapped to a cradle board. Although denied a full year of experience in locomotion, the Hopi infants gained the capacity to walk early in their second year, about when other children do. Classic cross-cultural research (Hindley et al., 1966) reported that infants in five European cities began to walk at about the same time (generally, between 12 and 15 months) despite cultural differences in encouragement to walk.

On the other hand, evidence is mixed on whether specific training can accelerate the appearance of motor skills. For example, in a classic study with identical twins, Arnold Gesell (1929) gave one twin extensive training in hand coordination, block

● **Figure 5.10**
Walking

By 12 to 15 months or so, babies walk by themselves, earning them the name toddler.

toddler A child who walks with short, uncertain steps. Toddlerhood lasts from about 18 to 30 months of age, thereby bridging infancy and early childhood.

© Mike Greenlar/The Image Works

A Native American Hopi Infant Strapped to a Cradle Board

Researchers have studied Hopi children who are strapped to cradle boards during their first year to see whether their motor development is delayed significantly. Once released from their boards, Hopi children make rapid advances in motor development, suggesting the importance of maturation in motor development.

building, and stair climbing from early infancy. The other twin was allowed to develop on his own. At first, the trained twin had better skills, but as time passed, the untrained twin became just as skilled.

Although the appearance of motor skills can be accelerated by training (Adolph & Berger, 2005; Zelazo, 1998), the effect seems slight. Practice in the absence of neural readiness has limited results. There is also little evidence that early training leads to superior motor skills.

Although being strapped to a cradle board did not permanently prevent the motor development of Hopi infants, Wayne Dennis (1960) reported that infants in an Iranian orphanage were significantly retarded in their motor development. In contrast to the Hopi infants, the institutionalized infants were exposed to extreme social and physical deprivation. Under these conditions, they grew apathetic, and all aspects of development suffered. But there is also a bright side to this tale of deprivation. The motor development of similar infants in a Lebanese orphanage accelerated dramatically in response to such minimal intervention as being propped up in their cribs and being given a few colorful toys (Dennis & Sayegh, 1965).

Nature provides the limits—the "reaction range"—for the expression of inherited traits. Nurture determines whether the child will develop skills that reach the upper limits of the range. Even as fundamental a skill as locomotion is determined by a complex interplay of maturational and environmental factors (Adolph & Berger, 2005). There may be little purpose in trying to train children to enhance motor skills before they are ready. Once they are ready, however, teaching and practice do make a difference. One does not become an Olympic athlete without "good genes," but one also usually does not become an Olympic athlete without high-quality training. And because motor skills are important to the self-concepts of children, good teaching is important.

Active Review

11. Infants can first raise their heads at about the age of _____ month(s).

12. Infants first use a(n) (Ulnar or Pincer?) grasp for holding objects.

13. Developmentalists assess infants' ability to stack blocks as a measure of their _____–motor coordination.

14. Infants (Sit up or Crawl?) before they (Sit up or Crawl?).

15. As children mature, their bones (Increase or Decrease?) in density.

16. Research reveals that both maturation and _____ play indispensable roles in motor development.

17. Arnold Gesell (Did or Did not?) find that extensive training in hand coordination, block building, and stair climbing gave infants enduring advantages over untrained infants in these skills.

Reflect & Relate: "When did your baby first sit up?" "When did he walk?" Why are people so concerned about when infants do what? Imagine that you are speaking to a parent who is concerned that her child is not yet walking at 14 months. What would you say to the parent? When should there be cause for concern?

Go to

http://www.thomsonedu.com/psychology/rathus
for an interactive version of this review.

Sensory and Perceptual Development: Taking in the World

What a world we live in: green hills and reddish skies; rumbling trucks, murmuring brooks, and voices; the sweet and the sour; the acrid and the perfumed; the metallic and the fuzzy. What an ever-changing display of sights, sounds, tastes, smells, and touches. The pleasures of the world, and its miseries, are known to us through sensory impressions and the organization of these impressions into personal inner maps of reality. Our eyes, our ears, the sensory receptors in our noses and our mouths, our skin senses—these are our tickets of admission to the world.

In Chapter 4, we examined the sensory capabilities of the neonate. ***Question: How do sensation and perception develop in the infant?*** In this section, we see how infants develop the ability to integrate disjointed **sensations** into meaningful patterns of events termed **perceptions**. We see what captures the attention of infants, and we see how young children develop into purposeful seekers of information selecting the sensory impressions they choose to capture. We focus on the development of vision and hearing, because most of the research on sensory and perceptual development in infancy has been done in these areas.

We will see that many things that are obvious to us are not so obvious to infants. You may know that a coffee cup is the same whether you see it from above or from the side, but make no such assumptions about the infant's knowledge. You may know that an infant's mother is the same size whether she is standing next to the infant or approaching from two blocks away, but do not assume that the infant agrees with you.

We cannot ask infants to explain why they look at some things and not at others. Nor can we ask them if their mother appears to be the same size whether she is standing close to them or far away. But investigators of childhood sensation and perception have devised clever methods to answer these questions, and their findings provide us with fascinating insights into the perceptual processes of even the neonate. They reveal that many basic perceptual competencies are present early in life.

Development of Vision: The Better to See You With

Development of vision involves development of visual acuity or sharpness, development of peripheral vision (seeing things off to the sides while looking straight ahead), visual preferences, depth perception, and perceptual constancies, such as knowing that an object remains the same object even though it may look different when seen from a different angle. (You knew that, didn't you?)

Development of Visual Acuity and Peripheral Vision

Newborns are extremely nearsighted, with vision beginning at about 20/600. The most dramatic gains in visual acuity are made between birth and 6 months of age, with acuity reaching about 20/50 (Cavallini et al., 2002; Haith, 1990; Skoczenski, 2002). Gains in visual acuity then become more gradual, approximating adult levels (20/20 in the best cases) by about 3 to 5 years of age.

Neonates also have poor peripheral vision (Cavallini et al., 2002; Skoczenski, 2002). Adults can perceive objects that are nearly 90 degrees off to the side (i.e., directly to the left or right), although objects at these extremes are unclear. Neonates cannot perceive visual stimuli that are off to the side by an angle of more than 30 degrees, but their peripheral vision expands to an angle of about 45 degrees by the age of 7 weeks. By 6 months of age, their peripheral vision is about equal to that of an adult.

Let us now consider the development of visual perception. In so doing, we will see that infants frequently prefer the strange to the familiar and will avoid going off the deep end—sometimes.

sensation The stimulation of sensory organs such as the eyes, ears, and skin and the transmission of sensory information to the brain.

perception The process by which sensations are organized into a mental map of the world.

Visual Preferences: How Do You Capture an Infant's Attention?

Questions: What captures the attention of infants? How do visual preferences develop? Neonates look at stripes longer than at blobs. This finding has been used in much of the research on visual acuity. Classic research found that by the age of 8 to 12 weeks, most infants also show distinct preferences for curved lines over straight ones (Fantz et al., 1975).

Robert Fantz (1961) also wondered whether there was something intrinsically interesting about the human face that drew the attention of infants. To investigate this question, he showed 2-month-old infants the six disks illustrated in ● Figure 5.11. One disk contained a caricature of human features, another contained newsprint, and still another contained a bull's-eye. The remaining three disks were featureless but were colored red, white, and yellow. In this study, the infants fixated significantly longer on the human face.

Some studies suggest that the infants in Fantz's (1961) study may have preferred the human face because it had a complex, intriguing pattern of dots (eyes) within an outline and not because it was a face. But theorists such as Michelle de Haan and Margrite Groen (2006) assert that "reading" faces is particularly important to infants because they do not understand verbal information as communicated through language. Thus, it would make evolutionary sense for infants to orient toward the human face and perceive the difference between some facial expressions at very early ages.

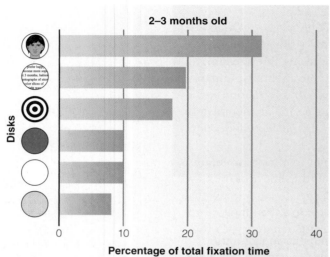
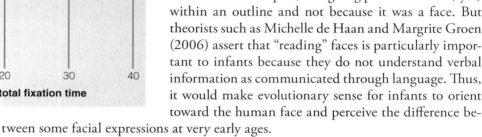
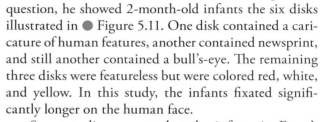

● Figure 5.11
Preferences for Visual Stimuli in 2-Month-Olds

Infants appear to prefer complex to simple visual stimuli. By the time they are 2 months old, they also tend to show a preference for the human face. Researchers continue to debate whether the face draws attention because of its content (i.e., being a face) or because of its stimulus characteristics (complexity, arrangement, etc.).

Researchers therefore continue to investigate infants' preferences for the human face. They ask whether humans come into the world "prewired" to prefer human stimuli to other stimuli that are just as complex, and—if so—just what it is about human stimuli that draws attention. Some researchers—unlike de Haan and Groen—argue that neonates do not "prefer" faces because they are faces per se but because of the structure of their immature visual systems (Simion et al., 2001). A supportive study of 34 neonates found that the longer fixations on facelike stimuli resulted from a larger number of brief fixations (looks) rather than from a few prolonged fixations (Cassia et al., 2001). The infants' gaze, then, was sort of bouncing around from feature to feature rather than "staring" at the face in general. The researchers interpreted the finding to show that the stimulus properties of the visual object are more important than the fact that it represents a human face. Even so, of course, the "immature visual system" would be providing some "prewired" basis for attending to the face.

Learning clearly plays a role. Neonates can discriminate their mother's face from a stranger's after 8 hours of mother–infant contact spread over 4 days (Bushnell, 2001). By 3 to 5 months of age, infants respond differently to happy, surprised, and sad faces (Muir & Hains, 1993). Moreover, infants as young as 2 months prefer attractive faces to unattractive faces (Ramsey et al., 2004). This preference is more deeply ingrained by 6 months of age (Ramsey et al., 2004). Do standards of attractiveness have an inborn component, or are they learned (very!) early?

Neonates appear to direct their attention to the edges of objects. This pattern persists for the first several weeks (Bronson, 1991). When they are given the opportunity to look at human faces, 1-month-old infants tend to pay most attention to the "edges," that is, the chin, an ear, or the hairline. The eye movements of two-month-old infants move in from the edge, as shown in ● Figure 5.12. The infants focus particularly on the eyes, although they also inspect other inner features, such as the mouth and nose (Nelson & Ludemann, 1989).

Some researchers (e.g., Haith, 1979) explain infants' tendencies to scan from the edges of objects inward by noting that for the first several weeks of life, infants seem to be essentially concerned with *where* things are. Their attention is captured by movement and sharp contrasts in brightness and shape, such as those found where the edges of objects stand out against their backgrounds. But by about 2 months of age, infants tend to focus on the *what* of things. They may locate objects by looking at their edges, but now they scan systematically within the boundaries of objects (Bronson, 1990, 1997).

Development of Depth Perception: On *Not* Going Off the Deep End

Infants generally respond to cues for depth by the time they are able to crawl (6 to 8 months of age or so), and most have the good sense to avoid "going off the deep end," that is, crawling off ledges and tabletops into open space (Campos et al., 1978). ***Question: How do researchers determine whether infants will "go off the deep end"?***

In a classic study on depth perception, Eleanor Gibson and Richard Walk (1960) placed infants of various ages on a fabric-covered runway that ran across the center of a clever device called a visual cliff (see ● Figure 5.13). The visual cliff is a sheet of Plexiglas that covers a cloth with a high-contrast checkerboard pattern. On one side, the cloth is placed immediately beneath the Plexiglas; on the other, it is dropped about 4 feet below. Because the Plexiglas alone would easily support the infant, it is a visual cliff rather than an actual cliff. In the Gibson and Walk study, 8 out of 10 infants who had begun to crawl refused to venture onto the seemingly unsupported surface, even when their mothers beckoned encouragingly from the other side.

Psychologists can assess infants' emotional responses to the visual cliff long before infants can crawl. For example, Joseph Campos and his colleagues (1970) found that 1-month-old infants showed no change in heart rate when placed face down on the "cliff." They apparently did not perceive the depth of the cliff. At 2 months, infants showed decreases in heart rate when so placed, which psychologists interpret as a sign of interest. But the heart rates of 9-month-olds accelerated on the cliff, which is interpreted as a fear response. The study appears to suggest that infants profit from some experience crawling about (and, perhaps, accumulating some bumps) before they develop fear of heights. The 9-month-olds but not the 2-month-olds had had such experience. Other studies support the view that infants usually do not develop fear of heights until they can move around (Bertenthal & Campos, 1990). Newly walking infants are highly reluctant to venture out onto the visual cliff, even when their mothers signal them to do so (Sorce et al., 2000; Witherington et al., 2005).

Infants' tendencies to avoid falling off a cliff are apparently connected with their body positions at the time (Adolph, 2000; Adolph & Berger, 2005). Infants generally sit before they crawl, and by 9 months of age, we can think of most of them as experienced sitters. Crawling enters the picture at about 9 months. Karen Adolph

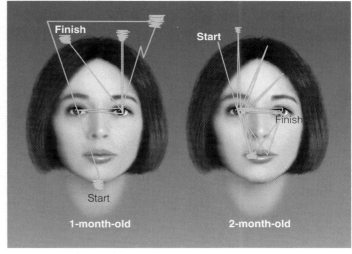

1-month-old   **2-month-old**

● **Figure 5.12**
Eye Movements of
1- and 2-Month-Olds

One-month-olds direct their attention to the edges of objects. Two-month-olds "move in from the edge." When looking at a face, for example, they focus on the eyes and other inner features. How do researchers explain this change?

Source: Salapatek (1975).

● **Figure 5.13**
The Visual Cliff

This young explorer has the good sense not to crawl out onto an apparently unsupported surface, even when mother beckons from the other side. Do infants have to experience some of life's "bumps" before they avoid "going off the deep end"?

(2000) examined the behavior of nineteen 9-month-old infants who were on the edge of crawling as well as on the edge of a visual cliff. The infants were placed in a sitting or crawling position and enticed to reach out for an object over the cliff. The infants were more likely to avoid the cliff when they were sitting, which suggests that different postures involve the brain in different ways and that infants' avoidance of the cliff is connected with their posture. Adolph's findings bring into question the view that avoidance of the cliff depends on general knowledge, such as fear of heights, associations between perceived depth and falling, or awareness that the body cannot be supported in empty space.

Truth or Fiction Revisited: Actually, evidence is mixed as to whether infants need to have experience crawling before they develop fear of heights. Some do not. This would appear to be a case in which survival might be wrapped up in not having to learn from experience.

Development of Perceptual Constancies

Questions: What are perceptual constancies? How do they develop? It may not surprise you that a 12-inch ruler is the same length whether it is 2 feet or 6 feet away or that a door across the room is a rectangle whether closed or ajar. Awareness of these facts depends not on sensation alone but on the development of perceptual constancies. **Perceptual constancy** is the tendency to perceive an object to be the same, even though the sensations produced by the object may differ under various conditions.

Consider again the example of the ruler. When it is 2 feet away, its image, as focused on the retina, is a certain length. This length is the image's "retinal size." From 6 feet away, the 12-inch ruler is only one-third as long in terms of retinal size, but we perceive it as being the same size because of size constancy. **Size constancy** is the tendency to perceive the same objects as being of the same size even though their retinal sizes vary as a function of their distance. From 6 feet away, a 36-inch yardstick casts an image equal in retinal size to the 12-inch ruler at 2 feet, but—if recognized as a yardstick—it is perceived as longer, again because of size constancy.

In a classic study of the development of size constancy, Thomas Bower (1974) conditioned 2½- to 3-month-old infants to turn their heads to the left when shown a 12-inch cube from a distance of 3 feet. He then presented them with three experimental stimuli: (1) a 12-inch cube 9 feet away, whose retinal size was smaller than that of the original cube; (2) a 36-inch cube 3 feet away, whose retinal size was larger than that of the original cube; and (3) a 36-inch cube 9 feet away, whose retinal size was the same as that of the original cube. The infants turned their heads most frequently in response to the first experimental cube, although its retinal image was only one-third the length of that to which they had been conditioned, suggesting that they had achieved size constancy. Later studies have confirmed Bower's finding that size constancy is present in early infancy. Some research suggests that even neonates possess rudimentary size constancy (Slater, 2000; Slater et al., 1990).

Shape constancy is the tendency to perceive an object as having the same shape even though, when perceived from another angle, the shape projected onto the retina may change dramatically. When the top of a cup or a glass is seen from above, the visual sensations are in the shape of a circle. When seen from a slight angle, the sensations are elliptical, and when seen from the side, the retinal image is the same as that of a straight line. However, because of our familiarity with the object, we still perceive the rim of the cup or glass as being a circle. In the first few months after birth, infants see the features of their caregivers, bottles, cribs, and toys from all different angles so that by the time they are 4 or 5 months old, a broad grasp of shape constancy seems to be established, at least under certain conditions (Slater, 2000). Strategies for studying the development of shape constancy are described in the nearby "A Closer Look" feature.

perceptual constancy The tendency to perceive objects as the same even though sensations produced by them may differ when, for example, they differ in position or distance.

size constancy The tendency to perceive objects as being the same size even though the sizes of their retinal images may differ as a result of distance.

shape constancy The tendency to perceive objects as being the same shape even though the shapes of their retinal images may differ when the objects are viewed from different positions.

Development of Hearing:
The Better to Hear You With

Question: How does the sense of hearing develop in infancy? Neonates can crudely orient their heads in the direction of a sound (Saffran et al., 2006). By 18 months of age, the accuracy of sound-localizing ability approaches that of adults. Sensitivity to sounds increases in the first few months of life (Saffran et al., 2006). As infants mature, the range of the pitch of the sounds they can sense gradually expands to include the adult's range of 20 to 20,000 cycles per second. The ability to detect differences in the pitch and loudness of sounds improves considerably throughout the preschool years. Auditory acuity also improves gradually over the first several years (Saffran et al., 2006), although infants' hearing can be so acute that many parents complain their napping infants will awaken at the slightest sound. This is especially true if parents have been overprotective in attempting to keep their rooms as silent as

A CLOSER LOOK

Strategies for Studying the Development of Shape Constancy

People are said to show shape constancy when they perceive an object as having the same shape even though, when viewed from another angle, the shape projected onto the retina may be very different. We can determine whether infants have developed shape constancy through the process of *habituation*, which involves paying less attention to a repeated stimulus.

Neonates tend to show a preference for familiar objects (Barrile et al., 1999), but once they are a few months old, infants show a preference for novel objects. They have become habituated to familiar objects, and—if we can take the liberty of describing their responses in adult terms—they are apparently bored by them. Certain bodily responses indicate interest in an object, including a slower heart rate (as with 2-month-old infants placed face down on a visual cliff) and concentrated gazing. Therefore, when infants have become habituated to an object, their heart rates speed up moderately and they no longer show concentrated gazing.

Here, then, is the research strategy. Show an infant Stimulus A for a prolonged period of time. At first, the heart rate will slow, and the infant will focus on the object. But as time goes on the heart rate will again rise to prestimulated levels and the infant's gaze will wander. Now show the infant Stimulus B. If the heart rate again slows and the gaze again becomes concentrated, we can infer that Stimulus B is perceived as a novel (different) object. But if the heart rate and pattern of gazing does not change, we can infer that the infant does not perceive a difference between Stimuli A and B.

If Stimuli A and B are actually the same object but seen from different angles, what does it mean when the infant's heart rate and pattern of gazing do not change? We can assume that lack of change means that the infant perceives Stimuli A and B to be the same (in this case, the same object). Therefore, we can conclude that the infant has developed shape constancy.

Using a strategy similar to that just described, Caron and his colleagues (1979) first habituated 3-month-old infants to a square shown at different angles. The infants were then presented with one of two test stimuli: (1) the identical square shown at an entirely new angle or (2) a novel figure (a trapezoid) shown at the new angle. The two test stimuli projected identical trapezoidal images on the retina, even though their real shapes were different. Infants who were shown the square at the new angle showed little change in response, but infants shown the trapezoid did show different responses. Therefore, it seems that infants perceived the trapezoid as novel, even though it cast the same retinal image as the square. But the infants were able to recognize the "real" shape of the square even though it cast a trapezoidal image on the retina. In other words, they showed shape constancy.

Reflect: Can you think of examples of habituation in your own life?

Infants typically prefer the sound of their mother's voice and can discriminate the sounds of their parents' voices by the age of 3½ months.

possible. Infants who are normally exposed to a backdrop of moderate noise levels become habituated to them and are not likely to awaken unless there is a sudden, sharp noise.

By the age of 1 month, infants perceive differences between speech sounds that are highly similar. In a classic study relying on the **habituation** method, infants of this age could activate a recording of "bah" by sucking on a nipple (Eimas et al., 1971). As time went on, habituation occurred, as shown by decreased sucking so as to hear the "bah" sound. Then the researchers switched from "bah" to "pah." If the sounds had seemed the same to the infants, their lethargic sucking patterns would have continued, but they immediately sucked harder, suggesting that they perceived the difference. Other researchers have found that within another month or two, infants reliably discriminate three-syllable words such as *marana* and *malana* (Kuhl et al., 2006).

Infants can discriminate the sounds of their parent's voices by 3½ months of age. In classic research, infants of this age were oriented toward their parents as they reclined in infant seats. The experimenters (Spelke & Owsley, 1979) played recordings of the mother's or father's voice while the parents themselves remained inactive. The infants reliably looked at the parent whose voice was being played.

Young infants are capable of perceiving most of the speech sounds present in the world's languages. But after exposure to one's native language, infants gradually lose the capacity to discriminate those sounds that are not found in the native language (Werker et al., 2007). Before 6 months of age, for example, infants reared in an English-speaking environment could discriminate sounds found in Hindi (a language of India) and Salish (a Native American language). But by 10 to 12 months of age, they had lost the ability to do so, as shown in ● Figure 5.14 (Werker, 1989).

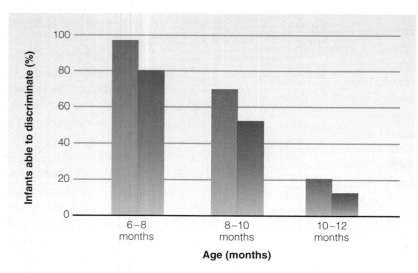

● **Figure 5.14** Declining Ability to Discriminate the Sounds of Foreign Languages

Infants show a decline in the ability to discriminate sounds not found in their native language. Before 6 months of age, infants from English-speaking families could discriminate sounds found in Hindi (red bars) and Salish, a Native American language (blue bars). By 10 to 12 months of age, they could no longer do so.
Source: Werker (1989).

Infants also learn at an early age to ignore small, meaningless variations in the sounds of their native language. Adults do this routinely. For example, if someone speaking your language has a head cold or a slight accent, you ignore the minor variations in the person's pronunciation and hear these variations as the same sound. But when you hear slight variations in the sounds of a foreign language, you might assume that each variation carries a different meaning and so you hear the sounds as different.

Infants can screen out meaningless sounds as early as 6 months of age (Kuhl et al., 2006). Patricia Kuhl and her colleagues (1997) presented American and Swedish infants with pairs of sounds in either their own language or the other one. The infants were trained to look over their shoulder when they heard a difference in the sounds and to ignore sound pairs that seemed to be the same. The infants routinely ignored variations in sounds that were part of their language, because they apparently perceived them as the same sound. But the infants noticed slight variations in the sounds of the other language. Another study demonstrated the same ability in infants as young as 2 months (Marean et al., 1992). By their first birthday, many infants understand many words, and some may even say a word or two of their own.

Development of Coordination of the Senses: If I See It, Can I Touch It?

Neonates crudely orient their heads toward sounds and pleasant odors. In this way, they increase the probability that the sources of the sounds and odors will also be sensed through visual scanning. Young infants can also recognize that objects experienced by one sense (e.g., vision) are the same as those experienced through another sense (e.g., touch). This ability has been demonstrated in infants as young as

habituation A process in which one becomes used to and therefore pays less attention to a repeated stimulus.

A CLOSER LOOK

Effects of Early Exposure to Garlic, Alcohol, and—Gulp—Veggies

Research shows that infants begin to learn about the flavors found in their cultures through breast milk, possibly even through amniotic fluid. For example, psychologist Julie A. Mennella found that when women eat garlic, their infants suckle longer (Azar, 1998). It is not that the infants ingest more milk. Instead, they seem to be spending the extra time analyzing what they are tasting. They keep the milk in their mouths, pause, and perceive the flavors. Vanilla flavoring has a similar effect on suckling: enhancing the duration.

Infants ingest amniotic fluid while they are still in the womb, and this fluid also acquires a distinct smell after a woman eats garlic, according to Mennella. It would appear that the fetus detects this change in its environment.

Mennella and her colleagues (Mennella & Beauchamp, 2002; Mennella et al., 2006) also studied the effects of introducing various flavors to infants' formulas and juices. For example, infants fed soy-based formula, which has something of a bitter taste to it, were more likely to prefer eating broccoli, which has a bitter flavor, later on. A protein hydrolysate formula is quite bitter tasting to adults but bears some similarity in flavor to broccoli. Sure enough, infants fed this formula show a preference for broccoli years later (Mennela et al., 2006).

No Direct Road to Alcohol Abuse

Does exposure to alcohol in the breast milk of mothers who drink create a disposition toward alcohol abuse in the infant? Mennella's research suggests that the truth

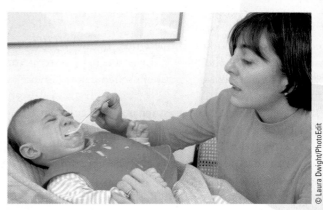

How Do You Encourage Children To Eat Their Veggies?

Do you want to talk about cruel experimental treatments that skirt the edges of the ethical limits of the researchers? Try this one on for size. Leann Birch and her colleagues repeatedly exposed 4- to 7-month-old infants to baby food consisting of vegetables. Actually, the "treatment" apparently had the effect of teaching the infants to like vegetables. In terms of what the experimenters measured, they found that the infants exposed to vegetables ate more of them during test trials.

may lie in the opposite direction. First of all, infants appear not to like the taste of alcohol in breast milk. Mennella (2001) found that infants of age 2 to 5 months drink less breast milk when the mother has

(*continued on page 178*)

1 month of age (Bushnell, 1993). One experiment demonstrating such understanding in 5-month-olds takes advantage of the fact that infants of this age tend to look longer at novel rather than familiar sources of stimulation. Julie Féron and her colleagues (2006) first allowed 5-month-old infants to handle (become manually familiar with) groups of either two or three objects, when they were presented one by one, to their right hand. The infants were then shown visual displays of either two or three objects. The infants looked significantly longer at the group of objects that differed from the one they had become manually familiar with, showing a transfer of information from the sense of touch to the sense of vision.

The Active–Passive Controversy in Perceptual Development

Question: Do children play an active or a passive role in perceptual development? Newborn children may have more sophisticated sensory capabilities than you expected. Still, their ways of perceiving the world are largely mechanical, or passive. The description of a stimulus capturing an infant's attention seems quite appropriate. Neonates seem to be generally at the mercy of external stimuli. When a bright light

A CLOSER LOOK

Effects of Early Exposure to Garlic, Alcohol, and—Gulp—Veggies *(continued)*

recently drunk alcohol. In fact, they ingest more breast milk once the alcohol is out of the mother's system, apparently to compensate for the lessened calorie intake at the previous feeding.

A related study by Mennella and a colleague, Pamela Garcia (2000), showed that early exposure to the odor of alcohol may also be something of a turnoff to infants. In this study, Mennella and Garcia compared the preferences of children who had been exposed to alcohol around the house during infancy with those of children who had not. All the children were about 4 to 6 years of age at the time of testing. Children who had been exposed to alcohol early were significantly more likely than the other children to dislike the odor of a bottle containing alcohol.

I would not suggest that parents drink alcohol to discourage their children from drinking later on, but the findings do seem to contradict what one might have expected.

And What About Encouraging Children to Eat Their Veggies during Infancy?

Many parents in the United States understand the benefits of eating vegetables and bring out the jars of vegetable baby food when they are feeding their infants. Does early exposure to these foods encourage or discourage the infants to eat them?

Early exposure generally seems to have a positive effect on children's appetites for vegetables. Consider a study of 4- to 7-month-old infants by Leann Birch and her colleagues (1998). The investigators repeatedly exposed infants to vegetables such as peas and green beans in the form of baby food to see whether they would subsequently eat more or less of them. Thirty-nine infants were fed the target foods once a day for 10 consecutive days. During that period, their consumption of the vegetables doubled from an average of 35 grams to an average of 72 grams. Moreover, the infants became more likely to eat similar foods, that is, other vegetables. Julie Mennella and her colleagues have also found that the infants of mothers who eat more diverse diets are more willing to eat a variety of foods (cited in Azar, 1998). Moreover, studies of rodents, pigs, and sheep show that once they are weaned, young animals prefer the flavors to which they were exposed through their mothers' milk. Early exposure to the foods that are traditional within a culture may be a key to shaping an infant's food preferences.

Reflect: Do you have any "ethnic" food preferences? Can you trace them to early experiences in the home or the neighborhood?

strikes, they attend to it. If the light moves slowly across the plane of their vision, they track it.

As time passes, broad changes occur in the perceptual processes of children, and the child's role in perception appears to become decidedly more active. Developmental psychologist Eleanor Gibson (1969, 1991) noted a number of these changes:

1. Intentional action replaces "capture" (automatic responses to stimulation). As infants mature and gain experience, purposeful scanning and exploration of the environment take the place of mechanical movements and passive responses to potent stimulation.

   Consider the scanning "strategies" of neonates. In a lighted room, neonates move their eyes mostly from left to right and back again. Mechanically, they sweep a horizontal plane. If they encounter an object that contrasts sharply with the background, their eye movements bounce back and forth against the edges. Even when neonates awaken in a dark room, they show the stereotypical horizontal scanning pattern, with about two eye movements per second (Haith, 1990).

   The stereotypical quality of these initial scanning movements suggests that they are inborn. They provide strong evidence that the neonate is neurologically prewired to gather and seek visual information. They do not reflect what we would consider a purposeful, or intentional, effort to learn about the environment.

2. Systematic search replaces unsystematic search. Over the first few years of life, children become more active as they develop systematic ways of exploring the environment. They come to pay progressively more attention to details of objects and people and to make finer and finer discriminations.

3. Attention becomes selective. Older children become capable of selecting the information they need from the welter of confusion in the environment.

Lessons in Observation

Sensation and Perception in Infancy

Vision is the least mature of a newborn's senses, but infants have a strong preference for patterns with strong contrasts and prefer human faces above all else. Here, 2-month-old Giuseppina fixates on a drawing of a face.

 To watch this video, visit the book companion website. You can also answer the questions and e-mail your responses to your professor.

Learning Objectives

- What types of tests do doctors perform to test newborn and infant senses?
- What visual preferences do newborns have?
- Do visual preferences change as a newborn becomes an infant?

Applied Lesson

Describe the different tests doctors use to check the senses in newborns and infants.

Critical Thinking

How can a newborn's capacities for vision and hearing be considered adaptive? Hint: Think about Carter's initial interaction with his mother in this video.

For example, when older children are separated from their parents in a department store, they have the capacity to systematically scan for people of their parents' height, hair color, vocal characteristics, and so on. They are also more capable of discriminating the spot where the parent was last seen. A younger child is more likely to be confused by the welter of voices and faces and aisles and to be unable to extract essential information from this backdrop.

4. Irrelevant information becomes ignored. Older children gain the capacity to screen out or deploy their attention away from stimuli that are irrelevant to the task at hand. That might mean shutting out the noise of cars in the street or radios in the neighborhood so as to focus on a book.

In short, children develop from passive, mechanical reactors to the world about them into active, purposeful seekers and organizers of sensory information. They develop from beings whose attention is diffuse and "captured" into people who make decisions about what they will attend to. This process, as with so many others, appears to depend on both maturation and experience.

Let us now screen out distractions and turn our attention to consideration of the importance of maturation (the development of nature) and experience (nurture) in perceptual development.

Nature and Nurture in Perceptual Development

The nature–nurture issue is found in perceptual development, just as it is in other dimensions of development. *Question: What is the evidence for the roles of nature and nurture in perceptual development?*

Evidence for the Role of Nature

Compelling evidence supports the idea that our inborn sensory capacities play a crucial role in our perceptual development. For one thing, neonates have already come into the world with a good number of perceptual skills. They can see nearby objects quite well, and their hearing is usually fine. They are also born with tendencies to track moving objects, to systematically scan the horizon, and to prefer certain kinds of stimuli. Preferences for different kinds of visual stimuli appear to unfold on schedule as the first months wear on. Sensory changes, as with motor changes, appear to be linked to maturation of the nervous system.

For these reasons, it seems clear that we do have certain inborn ways of responding to sensory input—certain "categories" and built-in limits—that allow us to perceive certain aspects of the world of physical reality.

Evidence for the Role of Nurture

Evidence that experience plays a crucial role in perceptual development is also compelling. We could use any of hundreds of studies with children and other species to make the point, but let us limit our discussion to a couple of examples of research with kittens and human infants.

Children and lower animals have critical periods in their perceptual development. Failure to receive adequate sensory stimulation during these critical periods can result in permanent sensory deficits (Greenough et al., 2002). For example, newborn kittens raised with a patch over one eye wind up with few or no cells in the visual area of the cerebral cortex that would normally be stimulated by light that enters that eye. In effect, that eye becomes blind, even though sensory receptors in the eye itself may fire in response to light. On the other hand, if the eye of an adult cat is patched for the same amount of time, the animal will not lose vision in that eye. The critical period apparently will have passed. Similarly, if health problems require that a child's eye must be patched for an extensive period of time during the first year, the child's visual acuity in that eye may be impaired.

Consider a study of visual acuity among 28 human infants who had been deprived of all patterned visual input by cataracts in one or both eyes until they were treated at 1 week to 9 months of age (Maurer et al., 1999). Immediately following treatment, their visual acuity was no better than that of normal neonates, suggesting that their lack of visual experience has impaired their visual development. However, their visual acuity improved rapidly over the month following treatment. They showed some improvement in as little as 1 hour following visual input.

So, with perceptual development as with other dimensions of development, nature and nurture play indispensable roles. Today, few developmentalists would subscribe to either extreme. Most would agree that nature and nurture interact to shape perceptual development. Nature continues to guide the unfolding of the child's physical systems. Yet nurture continues to interact with nature in the development of these systems. We know that inborn physical structures, such as the nature of the cortex of the brain, place limits on our abilities to respond to the world. But we also know that experience continues to help shape our most basic physical structures. For example, sensorimotor experiences thicken the cortex of the brain. Sensory experiences are linked to the very development of neurons in the cortex, causing dendrites to proliferate and affecting myelination.

In the next chapter, we see how nature and nurture influence the development of thought and language in infants.

Active Review

18. At 2 months of age, infants tend to fixate longer on a (Scrambled or Real?) face.
19. Neonates direct their attention to the (Center or Edges?) of objects.
20. Researchers have studied depth perception in infants through use of the visual _____.
21. Research suggests that infants have developed size constancy by about _____ months.
22. As infants develop, they have (Greater or Lesser?) ability to screen out meaningless sounds in their native languages.
23. As time passes during infancy, one change in perceptual development is that intentional action replaces _____ (automatic responses to stimulation).
24. Research shows that both nature and _____ are essential to perceptual development.

Reflect & Relate: What do you think it would mean if infants came into the world "prewired" to prefer the human face to other equally complex visual stimulation? Can you explain the evolutionary advantage that such prewiring would provide?

Go to

http://www.thomsonedu.com/psychology/rathus
for an interactive version of this review.

1. **What are the sequences of physical development?**

   Three key sequences of physical development are cephalocaudal development, proximodistal development, and differentiation.

2. **What patterns of growth occur in infancy?**

   Infants usually double their birth weight in 5 months and triple it by their first birthday. Height increases by about half in the first year. Infants grow another 4 to 6 inches and gain another 4 to 7 pounds in their second year. The head gradually diminishes in proportion to the rest of the body.

3. **What is failure to thrive?**

   Failure to thrive (FTT) is a serious disorder that impairs growth in infancy and early childhood. FTT can have organic causes or nonorganic causes. Deficiencies in caregiver–child interaction may play a major role in FTT.

4. **What are the nutritional needs of infants?**

   Infants require breast milk or an iron-fortified infant formula. Introduction of solid foods is recommended at 4 –6 months. Caregivers are advised to build up to an infant eating a variety of foods.

5. **Why do women bottle-feed or breast-feed their children?**

   Breast feeding is connected with factors such as the mother's availability (most women work), knowledge of the advantages of breast feeding, and availability of alternatives to breast milk.

6. **What are the advantages and disadvantages of breast milk?**

   Breast milk is tailored to human digestion, contains essential nutrients, contains the mothers' antibodies, helps protect against infant diarrhea, and is less likely than formula to cause allergies. Yet some environmental toxins are found in breast milk.

7. **What are neurons? How do they develop?**

   Neurons are cells that receive and transmit messages in the form of chemicals called neurotransmitters. As the child matures, axons grow in length, dendrites and axon terminals proliferate, and many neurons become wrapped in myelin, enabling them to function more efficiently.

8. **What is the brain? How does the brain develop?**

   The brain is the command center of the developing organism. The brain triples in weight by the first birthday, reaching nearly 70% of its adult weight. There are two major prenatal growth spurts: Neurons proliferate during the first growth spurt, and the second spurt is due mainly to the proliferation of dendrites and axon terminals.

9. **How do nature and nurture affect the development of the brain?**

   Sensory and motor areas of the brain begin to develop because of maturation, but sensory stimulation and motor activity also spur development. Rats raised in enriched environments develop more dendrites and axon terminals. Malnutrition is connected with a small brain, fewer neurons, and less myelination.

10. **What is motor development? How does it occur?**

    Motor development refers to developments in the activity of muscles and is connected with changes in posture, movement, and coordination. Children gain the ability to move their bodies through a sequence of activities that includes rolling over, sitting up, crawling, creeping, walking, and running. The sequence remains stable, but some children skip a step.

11. **What are the roles of nature and nurture in motor development?**

    Both maturation (nature) and experience (nurture) play indispensable roles in motor development. Infants need some opportunity for experimentation before they can engage in milestones such as sitting up and walking. Development of motor skills can be accelerated by training, but the effect is generally slight.

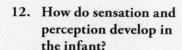

| 12. | How do sensation and perception develop in the infant? | Neonates are nearsighted and have poor peripheral vision. Acuity and peripheral vision approximate adult levels by the age of 6 months. |

| 13. | What captures the attention of infants? How do visual preferences develop? | Neonates attend longer to stripes than blobs, and by 8 to 12 weeks of age they prefer curved lines to straight ones. Two-month-old infants fixate longer on the human face than on other stimuli. Some researchers argue that neonates do not prefer faces because they are faces but because they are complex images. Infants can discriminate their mother's face from a stranger's after about 8 hours of contact. Neonates direct their attention to the edges of objects, but 2-month-olds scan objects from the edges inward. |

| 14. | How do researchers determine whether infants will "go off the deep end"? | Many researchers use the classic visual cliff apparatus. Most infants refuse to venture out over the visual cliff by the time they can crawl. Researchers have speculated that infants may need some experience crawling before they can develop fear of heights. |

| 15. | What are perceptual constancies? How do they develop? | A perceptual constancy is a tendency to perceive an object to be the same, even though it produces different sensations under different conditions. Size constancy appears to be present by 2½ to 3 months of age; shape constancy develops by age 4 to 5 months. |

| 16. | How does the sense of hearing develop in infancy? | Neonates reflexively orient their heads toward a sound. By 18 months of age, infants locate sounds about as well as adults. Infants discriminate caregivers' voices by 3½ months of age. Early infants can perceive most of the speech sounds throughout the languages of the world, but by 10–12 months of age, this ability lessens. |

| 17. | Do children play an active or a passive role in perceptual development? | Neonates seem to be at the mercy of external stimuli, but later on, intentional action replaces capture. Systematic search replaces unsystematic search, attention becomes selective, and irrelevant information gets ignored. |

| 18. | What is the evidence for the roles of nature and nurture in perceptual development? | Evidence shows that sensory changes are linked to maturation of the nervous system (nature) but that experience also plays a crucial role in perceptual development (nurture). For one thing, there are critical periods in the perceptual development of children and lower animals such that sensory experience is required to optimize—or maintain—sensory capacities. |

Key Terms

differentiation, 153
failure to thrive (FTT), 156
canalization, 157
nerves, 162
neurons, 162
dendrites, 162
axon, 162
neurotransmitter, 163

myelin sheath, 163
myelination, 163
multiple sclerosis, 165
medulla, 165
cerebellum, 165
cerebrum, 165
ulnar grasp, 167
pincer grasp, 167

locomotion, 167
toddler, 169
sensation, 171
perception, 171
perceptual constancy, 174
size constancy, 174
shape constancy, 174
habituation, 177

Active Learning Resources

Childhood & Adolescence Book Companion Website

http://www.thomsonedu.com/psychology/rathus

Visit your book companion website where you will find more resources to help you study. There you will find interactive versions of your book features, including the Lessons in Observation video, Active Review sections, and the Truth or Fiction feature. In addition, the companion website contains quizzing, flash cards, and a pronunciation glossary.

Thomson™ NOW! is an easy-to-use online resource that helps you study in less time to get the grade you want—NOW.

http://www.thomsonedu.com/login

Need help studying? This site is your one-stop study shop. Take a Pre-Test and ThomsonNOW will generate a Personalized Study Plan based on your test results. The Study Plan will identify the topics you need to review and direct you to online resources to help you master those topics. You can then take a Post-Test to determine the concepts you have mastered and what you still need to work on.

6

Infancy: Cognitive Development

Truth or Fiction?

T F For 2-month-old infants, "out of sight" is "out of mind." p. 193

T F A 1-hour-old infant may imitate an adult who sticks out his or her tongue. p. 199

T F Psychologists can begin to measure intelligence in infancy. p. 201

T F Infant crying is a primitive form of language. p. 204

T F You can advance children's development of pronunciation by correcting their errors. p. 211

T F Children are "prewired" to listen to language in such a way that they come to understand rules of grammar. p. 214

Preview

Cognitive Development: Jean Piaget
The Sensorimotor Stage
Development of Object Permanence

Lessons in Observation: Piaget's Sensorimotor Stage

Evaluation of Piaget's Theory

A Closer Look: Orangutans, Chimps, Magpies, and Object Permanence

A Closer Look: Counting in the Crib? Findings from a "Mickey Mouse Experiment"

Information Processing
Infants' Memory
Imitation: Infant See, Infant Do?

Individual Differences in Intelligence among Infants
Testing Infants: Why and with What?
Instability of Intelligence Scores Attained in Infancy
Use of Visual Recognition Memory: An Effort to Enhance Predictability

Language Development
Developing in a World of Diversity: Babbling Here, There, and Everywhere

Early Vocalizations
Development of Vocabulary

A Closer Look: Teaching Sign Language to Infants

Development of Sentences: Telegraphing Ideas
Theories of Language Development: Can You Make a Houseplant Talk?
Views That Emphasize Nurture

Developing in a World of Diversity: Two-Word Sentences Here, There, and . . .

A Closer Look: "Motherese"
Views That Emphasize Nature

Go to

http://www.thomsonedu.com/psychology/rathus
for an interactive version of this "Truth or Fiction" feature.

Victoria Snowber/Getty Images

aurent . . . resumes his experiments of the day before. He grabs in succession a celluloid swan, a box, etc., stretches out his arm and lets them fall. He distinctly varies the position of the fall. Sometimes he stretches out his arm vertically, sometimes he holds it obliquely, in front of or behind his eyes, etc. When the object falls in a new position, he lets it fall two or three times more on the same place, as though to study the spatial relation; then he modifies the situation.

Is this description one of a scientist at work? In a way, it is. Although Swiss psychologist Jean Piaget (1963 [1936]) was describing his 11-month-old son Laurent, children of this age frequently act like scientists, performing what Piaget called "experiments in order to see."

In this chapter, we chronicle the developing thought processes of infants and toddlers—that is, their cognitive development. We focus on the sensorimotor stage of cognitive development hypothesized by Piaget. Then, we examine infant memory and imitation. We next explore individual differences in infant intelligence. Finally, we turn our attention to a remarkable aspect of cognitive development: language.

Cognitive Development: Jean Piaget

Cognitive development focuses on the development of children's ways of perceiving and mentally representing the world. Piaget labeled children's concepts of the world **schemes**. He hypothesized that children try to use **assimilation** to absorb new events into existing schemes, and when assimilation does not allow the child to make sense of novel events, children try to modify existing schemes through **accommodation**.

Piaget (1963 [1936]) hypothesized that children's cognitive processes develop in an orderly sequence, or series, of stages. As with motor and perceptual development, some children may be more advanced than others at particular ages, but the developmental sequence does not normally vary (Flavell et al., 2002; Siegler & Alibali, 2005). Piaget identified four major stages of cognitive development: sensorimotor, preoperational, concrete operational, and formal operational. In this chapter, we discuss the sensorimotor stage.

The Sensorimotor Stage

Question: What is the sensorimotor stage of cognitive development? Piaget's sensorimotor stage refers to the first 2 years of cognitive development, a time when these developments are demonstrated by means of sensory and motor activity. Although it may be difficult for us to imagine how we can develop and use cognitive processes in the absence of language, children do so in many ways.

During the sensorimotor stage, infants progress from responding to events with reflexes, or ready-made schemes, to goal-oriented behavior that involves awareness of past events. During this stage, they come to form mental representations of objects and events, to hold complex pictures of past events in mind, and to solve problems by mental trial and error.

Question: What are the parts or substages of the sensorimotor stage? Piaget divided the sensorimotor stage into six substages, each of which is characterized by more complex behavior than the preceding substage. But there is also continuity from substage to substage. Each substage can be characterized as a variation on a theme in which earlier forms of behavior are repeated, varied, and coordinated. The approximate time periods of the substages and some characteristics of each are summarized in Concept Review 6.1.

scheme Within Piaget's cognitive view of development, an action pattern (such as a reflex) or a mental structure that is involved in the acquisition or organization of knowledge.

assimilation According to Piaget, the incorporation of new events or knowledge into existing schemes.

accommodation According to Piaget, the modification of existing schemes so as to incorporate new events or knowledge.

Concept Review 6.1   The Six Substages of the Sensorimotor Stage, According to Piaget

Substage	Comments

1. Simple reflexes (0–1 month)

Assimilation of new objects into reflexive responses. Infants "look and see." Inborn reflexes can be modified by experience.

2. Primary circular reactions (1–4 months)

Repetition of actions that may have initially occurred by chance but that have satisfying or interesting results. Infants "look in order to see." The focus is on the infant's body. Infants do not yet distinguish between themselves and the external world.

3. Secondary circular reactions (4–8 months)

Repetition of schemes that have interesting effects on the environment. The focus shifts to external objects and events. There is initial cognitive awareness that schemes influence the external world.

4. Coordination of secondary schemes (8–12 months)

Coordination of secondary schemes, such as looking and grasping to attain specific goals. There is the beginning of intentionality and means–end differentiation. We find imitation of actions not already in infants' repertoires.

5. Tertiary circular reactions (12–18 months)

Purposeful adaptation of established schemes to specific situations. Behavior takes on an experimental quality. There is overt trial and error in problem solving.

6. Invention of new means through mental combinations (18–24 months)

Mental trial and error in problem solving. Infants take "mental detours" based on cognitive maps. Infants engage in deferred imitation and symbolic play. Infants' cognitive advances are made possible by mental representations of objects and events and the beginnings of symbolic thought.

Simple Reflexes

At birth, neonates assimilate objects into reflexive responses. But even within hours after birth, neonates begin to modify reflexes as a result of experience. For example, they adapt sucking patterns to the shape of the nipple. (But don't be too impressed; porpoises are born swimming and "know" to rise to the surface of the ocean to breathe.)

Simple Reflexes

The first substage covers the first month after birth. It is dominated by the assimilation of sources of stimulation into inborn reflexes such as grasping, visual tracking, crying, sucking, and crudely turning the head toward a sound.

At birth, reflexes have a stereotypical, inflexible quality. But even within the first few hours, neonates begin to modify reflexes as a result of experience. For example, infants will adapt (accommodate) patterns of sucking to the shape of the nipple and the rate of flow of fluid.

During the first month or so, infants apparently make no connection between stimulation perceived through different sensory modalities. They make no effort to grasp objects that they visually track. Crude turning toward sources of sounds and smells has a mechanical look about it that cannot be considered purposeful searching.

Primary Circular Reactions

The second substage, primary circular reactions, lasts from about 1 to 4 months of age and is characterized by the beginnings of the ability to coordinate various sensorimotor schemes. In this substage, infants tend to repeat stimulating actions that first occurred by chance. For example, they may lift their arm repeatedly to bring it into view. A circular reaction is a behavior that is repeated. **Primary circular reactions** focus on the infant's own body rather than on the external environment. Piaget noticed the following primary circular reaction in his son Laurent:

> At 2 months 4 days, Laurent by chance discovers his right index finger and looks at it briefly. At 2 months 11 days, he inspects for a moment his open right hand, perceived by chance. At 2 months 17 days, he follows its spontaneous movement for a moment, then examines it several times while it searches for his nose or rubs his eye.
>
> At 2 months 21 days, he holds his two fists in the air and looks at the left one, after which he slowly brings it toward his face and rubs his nose with it, then his eye. A moment later the left hand again approaches his face; he looks at it and touches his nose. He recommences and laughs five or six times in succession while moving the left hand to his face. . . . He laughs beforehand but begins to smile again on seeing the hand.
>
> —Piaget (1963 [1936], pp. 96–97)

Primary Circular Reactions

In the substage of primary circular reactions, infants repeat actions that involve their bodies. The 3-month-old in this picture is also beginning to coordinate visual and sensorimotor schemes; that is, looking at the hand is becoming coordinated with holding it in the field of vision.

Thus, Laurent, early in the third month, visually tracks the behavior of his hand, but his visual observations do not seem to influence their movement. At about 2 months 21 days, Laurent can apparently exert some control over his hands because he seems to know when a hand is about to move (and entertain him), but the link between looking at and moving the hands remains weak. A few days later, however, his looking "acts" on the hands, causing them to remain in his field of vision. Sensorimotor coordination has been achieved. An action is repeated because it stimulates the infant.

In terms of assimilation and accommodation, the child is attempting to assimilate the motor scheme (moving the hand) into the sensory scheme (looking at it). But the schemes do not automatically fit. Several days of apparent trial and error pass, during which the infant seems to be trying to make accommodations so that they will fit.

Goal-directed behavior makes significant advances during the second substage. During the month after birth, infants visually track objects that contrast with their backgrounds, especially moving objects. But this ready-made behavior is largely automatic, so that the infant is "looking and seeing." But by the third month, infants may examine objects repeatedly and intensely, as Laurent did. It seems clear that the infant is no longer simply looking and seeing but is now "looking in order to see." And by the end of the third month, Laurent seems to be moving his hands just to look at them.

Because Laurent (and other infants) will repeat actions that allow them to see, cognitive-developmental psychologists consider sensorimotor coordination self-reinforcing. Laurent does not seem to be looking or moving his hands because these acts allow him to satisfy a more basic drive such as hunger or thirst. The desire to prolong stimulation may be just as basic.

Secondary Circular Reactions

The third substage lasts from about 4 to 8 months and is characterized by **secondary circular reactions**, in which patterns of activity are repeated because of their effect on the environment. In the second substage (primary circular reactions), infants are focused on their own bodies, as in the example given with Laurent. In the third substage (secondary circular reactions), the focus shifts to objects and environmental events. Infants may now learn to pull strings in order to make a plastic face appear or to shake an object in order to hear it rattle.

Although infants in this substage track the trajectory of moving objects, they abandon their searches when the objects disappear from view. As we see later in this chapter, the object concepts of infants are quite limited at these ages, especially the age at which the third substage begins.

Coordination of Secondary Schemes

In the fourth substage, infants no longer act simply to prolong interesting occurrences. Now they can coordinate schemes to attain specific goals. Infants begin to show intentional, goal-directed behavior in which they differentiate between the means of achieving a goal and the goal or end itself. For example, they may lift a piece of cloth to reach a toy that they had seen a parent place under the cloth earlier. In this example, the scheme of picking up the cloth (the means) is coordinated with the scheme of reaching for the toy (the goal or end).

This example indicates that the infant has mentally represented the toy placed under the cloth. Consider another example. At the age of 5 months, one of Piaget's daughters, Lucienne, was reaching across her crib for a toy. As she did so, Piaget obscured the toy with his hand. Lucienne pushed her father's hand aside but, in doing so, became distracted and began to play with the hand. A few months later, Lucienne did not allow her father's hand to distract her from the goal of reaching the toy. She moved the hand firmly to the side and then grabbed the toy. The mental representation of the object appears to have become more persistent. The intention of reaching the object was also maintained, and so the hand was perceived as a barrier and not as another interesting stimulus.

During the fourth substage, infants also gain the capacity to copy actions that are not in their own repertoires. Infants can now imitate many gestures and sounds that they had previously ignored. The imitation of a new facial gesture implies that infants have mentally represented their own faces and can tell what parts of their faces they are moving through feedback from facial muscles. For example, when a girl imitates her mother sticking out her tongue, it would appear that she has coordinated moving her own tongue with feedback from muscles in the tongue and mouth. In this way, imitation suggests a great deal about the child's emerging self-concept.

Tertiary Circular Reactions

In the fifth substage, which lasts from about 12 to 18 months of age, Piaget looked on the behavior of infants as characteristic of budding scientists. Infants now engage in **tertiary circular reactions**, or purposeful adaptations of established schemes to specific situations. Behavior takes on a new experimental quality, and infants may vary their actions dozens of times in a deliberate trial-and-error fashion to learn how things work.

Piaget reported an example of tertiary circular reactions by his daughter Jacqueline. The episode was an experiment in which Piaget placed a stick outside Jacqueline's playpen, which had wooden bars (Piaget, 1963 [1936]). At first, Jacqueline grasped the stick and tried to pull it sideways into the playpen. The stick was too long and could not fit through the bars. Over a number of days of trial and error, however, Jacqueline

Secondary Circular Reactions
In the substage of secondary circular reactions, patterns of activity are repeated because of their effect on the environment. This infant shakes a rattle to produce an interesting sound.

Coordination of Secondary Schemes
During this substage, infants coordinate their behaviors to attain specific goals. This infant lifts a piece of cloth to retrieve a toy that has been placed under the cloth.

primary circular reactions
The repetition of actions that first occurred by chance and that focus on the infant's own body.

secondary circular reactions
The repetition of actions that produce an effect on the environment.

tertiary circular reactions
The purposeful adaptation of established schemes to new situations.

Tertiary Circular Reactions
In this substage, infants vary their actions in a trial-and-error fashion to learn how things work. This child is fascinated by what happens when he pulls the toilet paper from the toilet paper holder.

discovered that she could bring the stick between the bars by turning it upright. In future presentations, she would immediately turn the stick upright and bring it in.

Jacqueline's eventual success with the stick was the result of overt trial and error. In the sixth substage, described next, the solution to problems is often more sudden, suggesting that children have manipulated the elements of the problems in their minds and engaged in mental trial and error before displaying the correct overt response.

Invention of New Means through Mental Combinations

The sixth substage lasts from about 18 to 24 months of age. It serves as a transition between sensorimotor development and the development of symbolic thought. External exploration is replaced by mental exploration.

Recall Jacqueline's trials with the stick. Piaget waited until his other children, Lucienne and Laurent, were 18 months old, and then he presented them with the playpen and stick problem. By waiting until 18 months, he could attribute differences in their performance to the age change instead of a possible warm-up effect from earlier tests. Rather than engage in overt trial and error, the 18-month-old children sat and studied the situation for a few moments. Then they grasped the stick, turned it upright, and brought it into the playpen with little overt effort.

Jacqueline had at first failed with the stick. She then turned it every which way, happening on a solution almost by chance. Lucienne and Laurent solved the problem fairly rapidly, suggesting that they mentally represented the stick and the bars of the playpen and perceived that the stick would not fit through as it was. They must then have rotated the mental image of the stick until they perceived a position that would allow the stick to pass between the bars.

At about 18 months, children may also use imitation to symbolize or stand for a plan of action. Consider how Lucienne goes about retrieving a watch chain her father placed in a matchbox. It seems that symbolic imitation serves her as a way of thinking out loud.

> I put the chain back into the box and reduce the opening. [Lucienne] is not aware of [how to open and close] the match box. [She] possesses two preceding schemes: turning the box over in order to empty it of its contents, and sliding her fingers into the slit to make the chain come out. [She] puts her finger inside and gropes to reach the chain, but fails. A pause follows during which Lucienne manifests a very curious reaction. . . .
>
> She looks at the slit with great attention. Then, several times in succession, she opens and shuts her mouth, at first slightly, then wider and wider! Apparently Lucienne understands the existence of a cavity. . . . [Lucienne then] puts her finger in the slit, and, instead of trying as before to reach the chain, she pulls so as to enlarge the opening. She succeeds and grasps the chain.
>
> —Piaget (1963 [1936], pp. 337–338)

Development of Object Permanence

The appearance of **object permanence** is an important aspect of sensorimotor development. *Questions: What is object permanence? How does it develop?* Object permanence is the recognition that an object or person continues to exist when out of sight. Your child development textbook continues to exist when you accidentally leave it in the library after studying for the big test, and an infant's mother continues to exist even when she is in another room. Your realization that your book exists, although out of view, is an example of object permanence. If an infant acts as though its mother no longer exists when she is out of sight, the infant does not have the concept of object permanence. The development of object permanence is tied into the development of infants' working memory and reasoning ability (Aguiar & Baillargeon, 2002; Barth & Call, 2006; Fiset & Doré, 2006; Saiki & Miyatsuji, 2007).

object permanence Recognition that objects continue to exist even when they are not seen.

Neonates show no tendency to respond to objects that are not within their immediate sensory grasp. By the age of 2 months, infants may show some surprise if an object (such as a toy duck) is placed behind a screen and then taken away so that when the screen is lifted, it is absent. However, they make no effort to search for the missing object. Through the first 6 months or so, when the screen is placed between the object and the infant, the infant behaves as though the object is no longer there (see ● Figure 6.1). **Truth or Fiction Revisited:** It is true that "out of sight" is "out of mind" for 2-month-old infants. Apparently, they do not yet reliably mentally represent objects they see.

There are some interesting advances in the development of the object concept by about the sixth month (Piaget's substage 3). For example, an infant at this age will tend to look for an object that has been dropped, behavior that suggests some form of object permanence. By this age, there is also reason to believe that the infant perceives a mental representation (image) of an object, such as a favorite toy, in response to sensory impressions of part of the object. This perception is shown by the infant's reaching for an object that is partly hidden.

By 8 to 12 months of age (Piaget's substage 4), infants will seek to retrieve objects that have been completely hidden. But in observing his own children, Piaget (1963 [1936]) noted an interesting error known as the A not B error. Piaget repeatedly hid a toy behind a screen (A), and each time, his infant removed the screen and retrieved the toy. Then, as the infant watched, Piaget hid the toy behind another screen (B) in a different place. Still, the infant tried to recover the toy by pushing aside the first screen (A). It is as though the child had learned that a certain motor activity would reinstate the missing toy. The child's concept of the object did not, at this age, extend to recognition that objects usually remain in the place where they have been most recently mentally represented.

But under certain conditions, 9- to 10-month-old infants do not show the A not B error (Bremner & Bryant, 2001; Marcovitch et al., 2002; Marcovitch & Zelazo,

Lessons in Observation
Piaget's Sensorimotor Stage

 To watch this video, visit the book companion website. You can also answer the questions and e-mail your responses to your professor.

Nine-month-old Hayden has learned that he can use one secondary circular reaction in service of another. That is, he moves the large toy (obstacle) to retrieve the more desirable toy underneath.

Learning Objectives

■ What is Piaget's sensorimotor stage?
■ What is a primary circular reaction?
■ What is a secondary circular reaction?
■ In terms of Piaget's stages, what is a scheme?
■ How do infants display object permanence?

Applied Lesson

Describe the substages of the sensorimotor period in terms of each of the children you see in the video. How do sensory and motor activities affect the development of cognitive skills?

Critical Thinking

Which of the infants illustrates a tertiary circular reaction? How have the other stages of the sensorimotor period helped this child reach this level?

● **Figure 6.1**
Development of Object Permanence

To the infant who is in the early part of the sensorimotor stage, out of sight is truly out of mind. Once a sheet of paper is placed between the infant and the toy monkey (top two photos), the infant loses all interest in the toy. From evidence of this sort, Piaget concluded that the toy is not mentally represented. The bottom series of photos shows a child in a later part of the sensorimotor stage. This child does mentally represent objects and pushes through a towel to reach an object that has been screened from sight.

2006). For example, if infants are allowed to search for the object immediately after seeing it hidden, the error often does not occur. But if they are forced to wait 5 or more seconds before looking, they are likely to commit the A not B error (Wellman et al., 1986).

In the next chapter, we see that most children develop object permanence before they develop emotional bonds to specific caregivers. It seems logical that infants must have permanent representations of their mothers before they will show distress at being separated from them. But wait, you say. Don't even 3- or 4-month-old infants cry when mother leaves and then stop crying when she returns and picks them up? Doesn't this behavior pattern show object permanence? Not necessarily. Infants appear to appreciate the comforts provided by their mothers and to express displeasure when they end (as when their mothers depart). The expression of displeasure frequently results in the reinstatement of pleasure (being held, fed, and spoken to). Therefore, infants may learn to engage in these protests when their mothers leave because of the positive consequences of protesting, and not because they have developed object permanence.

Nevertheless, studies by Renee Baillargeon and her colleagues (Aguiar & Baillargeon, 1999; Wang et al., 2005) show that some rudimentary knowledge of object permanence may be present as early as 2½–3½ months. In one study, Baillargeon (1987) first showed 3½- and 4½-month-olds the event illustrated in the top part of ● Figure 6.2. A screen rotated back and forth through a 180-degree arc like a drawbridge. After several trials, the infants showed habituation; that is, they spent less time looking at the screen. Next, a box was placed in the path of the screen, as shown in the middle drawing of Figure 6.2. The infant could see the box at the beginning of each trial, but could no longer see it when the screen reached the box. In one condition, labeled the "possible event," the screen stopped when it reached the box. In another condition, labeled the "impossible event," the screen rotated through a full 180-degree arc, as though the box were no longer behind it. (How could this happen? Unknown to the infant, a trapdoor was released, causing the box to drop out of the way.) The infants looked longer at the "impossible event" than at the "possible" one. (Infants look longer at unexpected events.) So it seems they were surprised that the screen did not stop when it reached the box. Therefore, children as young as 3½ months of age realized that the box continued to exist when it was hidden. But why, then, do infants not actively look for hidden objects until about 8 months of age? Perhaps, as Piaget suggested, *coordination of acts* (such as removing a barrier so as to reach a toy) does not occur until the later age.

Evaluation of Piaget's Theory

Question: What are the strengths and limitations of Piaget's theory of sensorimotor development? Piaget's theory remains a comprehensive model of infant cognition. Many of his observations of his own infants have been confirmed by others. The pattern and sequence of events he described have been observed among American, European, African, and Asian infants (Werner, 1988). Still, research has raised questions about the validity of many of Piaget's claims (Siegler & Alibali, 2005).

First, most researchers now agree that cognitive development is not as tied to discrete stages as Piaget suggested (Krojgaard, 2005; Siegler & Alibali, 2005). Although later developments seem to build on earlier ones, the process appears to be more gradual than discontinuous.

Second, Piaget emphasized the role of maturation, almost to the point of excluding adult and peer influences on cognitive development. However, these interpersonal influences have been shown to play important roles in cognitive development (Kuhn, 2007; Maratsos, 2007).

Third, Piaget appears to have underestimated infants' competence (Siegler & Alibali, 2005). For example, infants display object permanence earlier than he believed (Wang et al., 2005). Also consider studies on **deferred imitation** (imitation of an action that may have occurred hours, days, or even weeks earlier). The presence of deferred imitation suggests that children have mentally represented behavior patterns. Piaget believed that deferred imitation appears at about 18 months, but others have found that infants show deferred imitation as early as 9 months (Meltzoff, 1988, 2002). In Meltzoff's (1988) study, 9-month-old infants watched an adult perform behaviors such as pushing a button to produce a beep. When given a chance to play with the same objects a day later, many infants imitated the actions they had witnessed.

Let me mention a final example of infant competence that occurs earlier than Piaget predicted. Five-month-old infants may be able to grasp some basic computational concepts, more and less (see the nearby "A Closer Look" feature). In Piaget's view, this ability does not emerge until approximately 2 years of age.

Psychologists Andrew Meltzoff and M. Keith Moore (1998) asserted bluntly that "the sensorimotor theory of infancy has been overthrown," but they admitted that

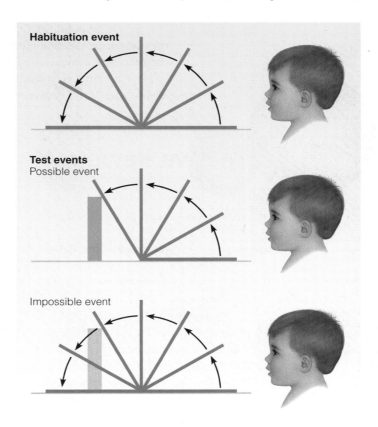

● **Figure 6.2** Object Permanence Before 4 Months of Age?

Renee Baillargeon (1987) used the technique shown here to demonstrate that knowledge of object permanence may exist before 4 months of age. She first showed infants a screen rotated back and forth like a drawbridge (top drawing). After infants showed habituation, a box was placed in the path of the screen. The middle drawing shows a possible event: The screen stops when it reaches the box. The bottom drawing shows an impossible event: The screen rotes through a full 180-degree arc as though the box were no longer behind it. (The experimenter had removed it, unknown to the infant.) Infants looked longer at the impossible event, indicating that they realized that the box still existed even when hidden behind the screen.

 *See your student companion website for an interactive version of Figure 6.2.*

deferred imitation The imitation of people and events that occurred hours, days, or weeks in the past.

"there is little consensus on a replacement." In an interview with a staff writer for the American Psychological Association's *Monitor*, Meltzoff remarked that "Piaget's theories were critical for getting the field of [cognitive development] off the ground, . . . but it's time to move on" (Meltzoff, 1997, p. 9). But move on to what exactly? Again, there is no consensus.

Active Review

1. Piaget labeled children's concepts of the world as _____.

2. Children try to _____ new events into existing schemes.

3. Piaget's _____ stage spans the first 2 years of cognitive development.

4. Primary _____ reactions are characterized by repeating stimulating actions that occur by chance.

5. In _____ circular reactions, activity is repeated because of its effect on the environment.

6. _____ circular reactions are purposeful adaptations of established schemes to specific situations.

7. Object _____ is recognition that an object or person continues to exist when out of sight.

Reflect & Relate: How might an outside observer gather evidence that you and a friend or family member have mentally represented each other? How are you asked to demonstrate that you have mentally represented the subject matter in this textbook and in this course?

Go to

http://www.thomsonedu.com/psychology/rathus

for an interactive version of this review.

A CLOSER LOOK

Orangutans, Chimps, Magpies, and Object Permanence

Let us not limit our discussion of the development of object permanence to humans. Comparative psychologists have also studied the development of object permanence in nonhuman species, including dogs and cats, primates, and even magpies. Animal boosters will be quite intrigued by the findings reported in articles such as these two:

• "Object Permanence in Orangutans (*Pongo pygmaeus*), Chimpanzees (*Pan troglodytes*), and Children (*Homo sapiens*)" (Call, 2001)

• "Tracking the Displacement of Objects: A Series of Tasks with Great Apes (*Pan troglodytes, Pan paniscus, Gorilla gorilla,* and *Pongo pygmaeus*) and Young Children (*Homo sapiens*)" (Barth & Call, 2006)

Despite the conclusion of most researchers that primates such as chimpanzees and gorillas do not make use of language—even sign language—in the sophisticated way that humans do, Josep Call (2001) found that the three species—orangutan, chimp, and human—

performed at the same intellectual level in tasks used to assess object permanence. The key caveat is that orangutans and chimpanzees mature more rapidly than humans, and Call was comparing juvenile and adult orangutans with 19–26-month-old human infants. (Go, *Homo sapiens!*)

Now what about the magpies? Magpies are notorious thieves in the bird world, and they also hide their food to keep it safe from other animals—especially other magpies. Bettina Pollock and her colleagues (2000) found that magpies develop object permanence before they begin to hide food. Think about it: Magpies would not profit from secreting away their food if out of sight meant the same thing as "out of existence."

Reflect: Why do you think scientists study the development of object permanence in nonhuman species? Can you provide at least two possible reasons?

A Closer Look

Counting in the Crib? Findings from a "Mickey Mouse Experiment"

Even during the first year, infants may have some ability to add and subtract (McCrink & Wynn, 2004; Wynn, 2002). Karen Wynn (1992) showed this ability with infants at 5 months of age. Her research method was based on the fact that infants look longer at unexpected (novel) events than at expected (familiar) events. If infants are able to engage in some basic addition and subtraction, then they should look longer at a "wrong answer"—that is, at an unexpected answer—than at an expected "correct answer."

In her research, Wynn showed infants 4-inch-tall Mickey Mouse dolls. (Yes, this was a "Mickey Mouse experiment," literally.) One group of infants saw a single doll. Then a screen was raised, blocking the infants' view. Some behind-the-scenes manipulation occurred so that when the screen was removed, the infants were either presented with two dolls (the unexpected or "wrong answer") or only one doll (the expected or "right answer"). The infants looked longer at the wrong answer. Another group of infants was initially shown two dolls. The screen was raised, and the infants observed while one doll was removed. But some manipulation took place behind the scenes again, so that when the screen was removed, the infants were shown either one doll (the right answer) or two dolls (the wrong answer). The infants consistently looked longer at the two dolls, that is, at the wrong answer.

These results suggest that infants were responsive to some change in quantity—perhaps they showed some rudimentary sense of "more" or "less." But how do we know that the infants were aware of a difference in the *number* of objects? Can infants somehow calculate the change in number that was produced in the experiment?

To gain some insight into infants' abilities to "count," Wynn first presented a third group of infants with a single doll. She raised the screen and added one doll as the infants observed. Again, some behind-the-scenes manipulation took place so that when the screen was removed, the infants would be presented with either two Mickeys

Photo by David Sanders, The Arizona Daily Star

● **Figure 6.3** Counting in the Crib?

Research by Karen Wynn suggests that 5-month-old infants may know when simple computations—or demonstrations involving concepts of more and less—are done correctly. The research is made possible by the fact that infants stare longer at unexpected (novel) stimuli—in this case, at a "wrong answer." Wynn conducted her research by exposing infants to Mickey Mouse dolls. She then added or removed one or more dolls behind a screen as the infant watched her, removed the screen, and observed how long the infants gazed at "right" or "wrong" answers.

(the right answer) or three Mickeys (the wrong answer) (see ● Figure 6.3). In this phase of the research, the infants stared longer at the three Mickeys than the two, suggesting that they might have somehow calculated the number of Mickeys that should have resulted from the researcher's manipulations. But again, we cannot say that the infants are adding per se. Other researchers suggest that the infants are more likely to be sensitive to simpler concepts of *more* and *less* (Gao et al., 2000).

Reflect: Can you relate Wynn's methodology to the concept of *habituation*?

Information Processing

The information-processing approach to cognitive development focuses on how children manipulate or process information coming in from the environment or already stored in the mind (Siegler & Alibali, 2005). *Question: What are infants' tools for processing information?* One is memory. Another is imitation.

Infants' Memory

Many of the cognitive capabilities of infants—recognizing the faces of familiar people, developing object permanence, and, in fact, learning in any form—depend on one critical aspect of cognitive development: their memory (Daman-Wasserman et al., 2006; Hayne & Fagen, 2003; Pascual-Leone, 2000). Even neonates demonstrate memory for stimuli to which they have been exposed previously. For example, neonates adjust their rate of sucking to hear a recording of their mother reading a story she had read aloud during the last weeks of pregnancy (DeCasper & Fifer, 1980; DeCasper & Spence, 1991). Remember, too, that neonates who are breast-fed are able to remember and show recognition of their mother's unique odor (Cernoch & Porter, 1985).

Memory improves dramatically between 2 and 6 months of age and then again by 12 months (Pelphrey et al., 2004; Rose et al., 2001). The improvement may indicate that older infants are more capable than younger ones of encoding (i.e., storing) information, retrieving information already stored, or both (Hayne & Fagen, 2003).

A fascinating series of studies by Carolyn Rovee-Collier and her colleagues (Rovee-Collier, 1993) illustrates some of these developmental changes in infant memory (see ● Figure 6.4). One end of a ribbon was tied to a brightly colored mobile suspended above the infant's crib. The other end was tied to the infant's ankle, so that when the infant kicked, the mobile moved. Infants quickly learned to increase their rate of kicking. To measure memory, the infant's ankle was again fastened to the mobile after a period of 1 or more days had elapsed. In one study, 2-month-olds remembered how to make the mobile move after delays of up to 3 days, and 3-month-olds remembered for more than a week (Greco et al., 1986).

Infant memory can be improved if infants receive a reminder before they are given the memory test (Bearce et al., 2006). In one study that used a reminder ("priming"), infants were shown the moving mobile on the day before the memory test, but they were not allowed to activate it. Under these conditions, 3-month-olds remembered how to move the mobile after a 28-day delay (Rovee-Collier, 1993).

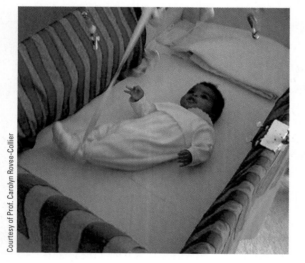

● **Figure 6.4**
Investigating Infant Memory

In this technique, developed by Carolyn Rovee-Collier, the infant's ankle is connected to a mobile by a ribbon. Infants quickly learn to kick to make the mobile move. Two- and 3-month-olds remember how to perform this feat after a delay of a few days. If given a reminder of simply viewing the mobile, their memory lasts for 2 to 4 weeks.

Courtesy of Prof. Carolyn Rovee-Collier

Imitation: Infant See, Infant Do?

Imitation is the basis for much of human learning. Deferred imitation—that is, the imitation of actions after a time delay—occurs as early as 6 months of age (Barr et al., 2005; Campanella & Rovee-Collier, 2005). To help them remember the imitated act, infants are usually permitted to practice it when they learn it. But in one study, 12-month-old infants were prevented from practicing the behavior they imitated. Yet they were able to demonstrate it 4 weeks later, suggesting that they had mentally represented the act (Klein & Meltzoff, 1999).

But infants can imitate certain actions at a much earlier age. Neonates only 0.7 to 71 hours old have been found to imitate adults who open their mouths or stick out their tongues (Meltzoff & Prinz, 2002; Rizzolatti et al., 2002) (see ● Figure 6.5).

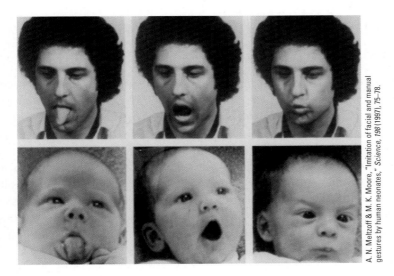

A. N. Meltzoff & M. K. Moore, "Imitation of facial and manual gestures by human neonates," *Science, 198* (1997), 75–78.

● **Figure 6.5**
Imitation in Infants
These 2- to 3-week-old infants are imitating the facial gestures of an adult experimenter. How are we to interpret these findings? Can we say that the infants "knew" what the experimenter was doing and "chose" to imitate the behavior, or is there an another explanation?

Before you become too impressed with this early imitative ability of neonates, you should know that some studies have not found imitation in early infancy (Abravanel & DeYong, 1991). One key factor may be the infants' age. The studies that find imitation generally have been done with very young infants—up to 2 weeks old—whereas the studies that do not find imitation have tended to use older infants. Therefore, the imitation of neonates is likely to be reflexive. Thus, imitation might disappear when reflexes are "dropping out" and re-emerge when it has a firmer cognitive footing. **Truth or Fiction Revisited:** It is true that a 1-hour-old infant may imitate an adult who sticks out his or her tongue, but such imitation is reflexive. That is, the infant is not observing the adult and then deciding to stick out his or her tongue.

Why might newborns possess some sort of imitation reflex? Answers lie in the realm of speculation. One possibility is that such a built-in response would contribute to the formation of caregiver–infant bonding and the survival of the newborn (Meltzoff & Prinz, 2002). Some theorists speculate that the imitation reflex is made possible by "mirror neurons" that are found in human brains. Such neurons are maintained by evolutionary forces because they enhance the probability of survival as a result of caregiving (Oztop et al., 2006; Rizzolatti et al., 2002).

Active Review

8. The _____-processing approach to cognitive development focuses on how children manipulate or process information.

9. _____ improves dramatically between the ages of 2 and 6 months.

10. The imitation of actions after a time delay is called _____ imitation.

Reflect & Relate: Why do adolescents and adults stick their tongues out at infants? (Why not ask a few—a few adolescents and adults, that is?)

Go to

http://www.thomsonedu.com/psychology/rathus

for an interactive version of this review.

Individual Differences in Intelligence among Infants

Cognitive development does not proceed in the same way or at the same pace for all infants (Newman et al., 2006; Rose et al., 2001, 2005). *Question: How do we measure individual differences in the development of cognitive functioning?* Efforts to understand the development of infant differences in cognitive development have relied on so-called scales of infant development or infant intelligence.

Measuring cognition or intelligence in infants is quite different from measuring it in adults. Infants cannot, of course, be assessed by asking them to explain the meanings of words, the similarity between concepts, or the rationales for social rules. One of the most important tests of intellectual development among infants—the Bayley Scales of Infant Development, constructed in 1933 by psychologist Nancy Bayley and revised since—contains very different kinds of items.

The Bayley test currently consists of 178 mental-scale items and 111 motor-scale items. The mental scale assesses verbal communication, perceptual skills, learning and memory, and problem-solving skills. The motor scale assesses gross motor skills, such as standing, walking, and climbing, and fine motor skills, as shown by the ability to manipulate the hands and fingers. A behavior rating scale based on examiner observation of the child during the test is also used. The behavior rating scale assesses attention span, goal directedness, persistence, and aspects of social and emotional development. ■ Table 6.1 contains sample items from the mental and motor scales

■ **Table 6.1** Items from the Bayley Scales of Infant Development (BSID–II)

Age	Mental-Scale Items	Motor-Scale Items
1 month	The infant quiets when picked up.	The infant makes a postural adjustment when put to examiner's shoulder.
2 months	When examiner presents two objects (bell and rattle) above the infant in a crib, the infant glances back and forth from one to the other.	The infant holds his or her head steady when being carried about in a vertical position.
5 months	The infant is observed to transfer an object from one hand to the other during play.	When seated at a feeding-type table and presented with a sugar pill that is out of reach, the infant attempts to pick it up.
8 months	When an object (toy) in plain view of the infant (i.e., on a table) is covered by a cup, the infant removes the cup to retrieve the object.	The infant raises herself or himself into a sitting position.
12 months	The infant imitates words that are spoken by the examiner.	When requested by the examiner, the infant stands up from a position in which she or he had been lying on her or his back on the floor.
14–16 months	The infant builds a tower with two cubes (blocks) after the examiner demonstrates the behavior.	The infant walks alone with good coordination.

and shows the ages at which 50% of the infants taking the test passed the items.

Truth or Fiction Revisited: It is true that psychologists can begin to measure intelligence in infancy, but they use items that differ from the kinds of items used with older children and adults. It remains unclear how well results obtained in infancy predict intellectual functioning at later ages.

Testing Infants: Why and with What?

As you can imagine, it is no easy matter to test an infant. The items must be administered on a one-to-one basis by a patient tester, and it can be difficult to judge whether the infant is showing the targeted response. Why, then, do we test infants?

One reason is to screen infants for handicaps. A highly trained tester may be able to detect early signs of sensory or neurological problems, as suggested by development of visual–motor coordination. In addition to the Bayley scales, a number of tests have been developed to screen infants for such difficulties, including the Brazelton Neonatal Behavioral Assessment Scale (see Chapter 4) and the Denver Developmental Screening Test.

The Bayley Scales of Infant Development
The Bayley scales measure an infant's mental and motor development.

Instability of Intelligence Scores Attained in Infancy

Researchers have also tried to use infant scales to predict development, but this effort has been less than successful. *Question: How well do infant scales predict later intellectual performance?* The answer is somewhat less than clear. One study found that scores obtained during the first year of life correlated moderately at best with scores obtained a year later (Harris et al., 2005). Certain items on the Bayley scales appear to predict related intellectual skills later in childhood. For example, Bayley items measuring infant motor skills predict subsequent fine motor and visual–spatial skills at 6 to 8 years of age (Siegel, 1992). Bayley language items also predict language skills at the same age (Siegel, 1992).

One study found that the Bayley scales and socioeconomic status were able to predict cognitive development among low-birth-weight children from 18 months to 4 years of age (Dezoete et al., 2003). But overall scores on the Bayley and other infant scales apparently do not predict school grades or IQ scores among schoolchildren very well (Colombo, 1993). Why do infant tests fail to do a good job of predicting IQ scores among school-age children? Aside from the possibility that intellectual functioning fluctuates between the preschool and school years, it may be that the sensorimotor test items used during infancy are not that strongly related to the verbal and symbolic items used to assess intelligence at later ages.

The overall conclusion seems to be that the Bayley scales can identify gross lags in development and relative strengths and weaknesses. However, they are only moderate predictors of intelligences scores even one year later, and are still poorer predictors of scores taken beyond longer stretches of time.

Use of Visual Recognition Memory: An Effort to Enhance Predictability

In a continuing effort to find aspects of intelligence and cognition that might remain consistent from infancy through later childhood, a number of researchers have recently focused on visual recognition memory (Courage et al., 2004). *Questions: What is visual recognition memory? How is it used?* **Visual recognition memory** is the ability to discriminate previously seen objects from novel objects. How is it

visual recognition memory
The kind of memory shown in an infant's ability to discriminate previously seen objects from novel objects.

used? This procedure is based on habituation, as are many of the methods for assessing perceptual development (see Chapter 5).

Let us consider longitudinal studies of this type. Susan Rose and her colleagues (Rose et al., 1992) showed 7-month-old infants pictures of two identical faces. After 20 seconds, the pictures were replaced with one picture of a new face and a second picture of the familiar face. The amount of time the infants spent looking at each face in the second set of pictures was recorded. Some infants spent more time looking at the new face than at the older face, suggesting that they had better memory for visual stimulation. The children were given standard IQ tests yearly from ages 1 through 6. It was found that the children with greater visual recognition memory later attained higher IQ scores.

Rose and her colleagues (2001) also showed that, from age to age, individual differences in capacity for visual recognition memory are stable. This finding is important because intelligence—the quality that many researchers seek to predict from visual recognition memory—is also theorized to be a reasonably stable trait. Similarly, items on intelligence tests are age graded; that is, older children perform better than younger children, even as developing intelligence remains constant. So, too, with visual recognition memory. Capacity for visual recognition memory increases over the first year after birth (Rose et al., 2001).

A number of other studies have examined the relationship between either infant visual recognition memory or preference for novel stimulation (which is a related measure) and later IQ scores. In general, they show good predictive validity for broad cognitive abilities throughout childhood, including measures of intelligence and language ability (Heiman et al., 2006; S. A. Rose et al., 2004).

In sum, scales of infant development may provide useful data as screening devices, as research instruments, or simply as a way to describe the things that infants do and do not do, but their predictive power as intelligence tests has been disappointing. Tests of visual recognition hold better promise as predictors of intelligence at older ages.

Many parents today spend a good deal of time trying to teach their children skills that will enhance their intelligence testing scores. Any number of commercial products prey on parents' fears that their children might not measure up. These products are found on the shelves of stores such as Toys "R" Us. Although these products themselves probably do no harm, parents might better spend their time reading to children, playing with them, and taking them on stimulating excursions. Even a supermarket provides ample opportunities for parents to talk about shapes and colors and temperatures and kinds of foods with their young children.

Now let us turn our attention to a fascinating aspect of cognitive development, the development of language.

Active Review

11. The Bayley Scales of Infant Development contain mental-scale items and _____-scale items.
12. The Brazelton Neonatal Behavioral Assessment Scale is used to screen for sensory or _____ problems.
13. _____ recognition memory refers to an infant's ability to discriminate previously seen objects from novel objects.

Reflect & Relate: When you have observed infants, what kinds of behaviors have led you to think that one is "brilliant" or another one "dull"? How do your "methods" correspond to those used by researchers who attempt to assess intellectual functioning among infants?

Go to

http://www.thomsonedu.com/psychology/rathus

for an interactive version of this review.

Language Development

"The time has come," the Walrus said,
"To talk of many things
Of shoes—and ships—and sealing wax—
Of cabbages—and kings—
And why the sea is boiling hot—
And whether pigs have wings."

— Lewis Carroll, *Through the Looking-Glass*

No, in his well-known children's book, Lewis Carroll wasn't quite telling the truth: The sea is not boiling hot—at least in most places and at most times. Nor do walruses speak. At the risk of alienating walrus aficionados, I will assert that walruses neither speak nor use other forms of language to communicate. But children do. Children come "to talk of many things," perhaps only rarely of sealing wax and cabbages, but certainly about the things more closely connected with their environments and their needs. Children may be unlikely to debate "whether pigs have wings," unless they are reared on an unusual farm, but they do develop the language skills that will eventually enable them to do just that. Lewis Carroll enjoyed playing with language, and we will see that children also join in that game. In physical development, the most dramatic developments come early—fast and furious—long before the child is born. Language does not come quite as early, and its development may not seem quite so fast and furious. Nevertheless, during the years of infancy, most children develop from creatures without language to little people who understand nearly all the things that are said to them and who relentlessly sputter words and simple sentences for all the world to hear. If much of the world might think that children do not yet have much of value to say, most parents find their utterances to be just priceless.

In this section, we trace language development from early crying and cooing through the production of two-word sentences. We then consider theoretical views of language development.

Developing in a World of Diversity

Babbling Here, There, and Everywhere

Babbling, like crying and cooing, appears to be inborn. Children from different cultures, where languages sound very different, all seem to babble the same sounds, including many they could not have heard (Oller, 2000). Deaf children whose parents use sign language babble with their hands and fingers, using repetitive gestures that resemble the vocal babbling of infants who can hear (Bloom, 1998; Koopmans-van Beinum et al., 2001).

Even though babbling is innate, it is readily modified by the child's language environment. One study followed infants growing up in French-, Chinese-, and Arabic-speaking households (de Boysson-Bardies & Halle, 1994). At 4 to 7 months of age, the infants began to use more of the sounds in their language environment, and foreign phonemes began to drop out. The role that experience plays in language development is further indicated by the fact that the babbling of deaf infants never begins to approximate the sounds of the parents' language.

Reflect: *We say that babbling is innate, yet as infants develop through the first year, they begin to babble sounds heard in the home and foreign sounds begin to drop out. Why?*

Early Vocalizations

prelinguistic Referring to vocalizations made by the infant before the development of language. (In language, words symbolize objects and events.)

Children develop language according to an invariant sequence of steps, or stages, as outlined in ■ Table 6.2. We begin with the **prelinguistic** vocalizations. *Question: What are prelinguistic vocalizations?* True words are symbols of objects and events. Prelinguistic vocalizations, such as cooing and babbling, do not represent objects or events. **Truth or Fiction Revisited:** Actually, infant crying is not a primitive form of language. Cries do not represent objects or events.

■ **Table 6.2** Milestones in Language Development in Infancy

Approximate Age	Vocalization and Language
Birth	• Cries.
12 weeks	• Cries less.
	• Smiles when talked to and nodded at.
	• Engages in squealing and gurgling sounds (cooing).
	• Sustains cooing for 15–20 seconds.
16 weeks	• Responds to human sounds more definitely.
	• Turns head, searching for the speaker.
	• Chuckles occasionally.
20 weeks	• Cooing becomes interspersed with consonant-like sounds.
	• Vocalizations differ from the sounds of mature language.
6 months	• Cooing changes to single-syllable babbling.
	• Neither vowels nor consonants have fixed pattern of recurrence.
	• Common utterances sound somewhat like *ma, mu, da,* or *di.*
8 months	• Continuous repetition (reduplication) enters into babbling.
	• Patterns of intonation become distinct.
	• Utterances can signal emphasis and emotion.
10 months	• Vocalizations mixed with sound play, such as gurgling, bubble blowing.
	• Makes effort to imitate sounds made by older people with mixed success.
12 months	• Identical sound sequences replicated more often.
	• Words (e.g., *mamma* or *dadda*) emerge.
	• Many words and requests understood (e.g., "Show me your eyes").
18 months	• Repertoire of 3–50 words.
	• Explosive vocabulary growth.
	• Babbling consists of several syllables with intricate intonation.
	• Little effort to communicate information.
	• Little joining of words into spontaneous two-word utterances.
	• Understands nearly everything spoken.
24 months	• Vocabulary more than 50 words, naming everything in the environment.
	• Spontaneous creation of two-word sentences.
	• Clear efforts to communicate.

Source: Table items adapted from Lenneberg (1967, pp. 128–130).

Note: Ages are approximations. Slower development does not necessarily indicate language problems. Albert Einstein did not talk until the age of 3.

Newborn children, as parents are well aware, have an unlearned but highly effective form of verbal expression: crying and more crying. Crying is accomplished by blowing air through the vocal tract. There are no distinct well-formed sounds. Crying is about the only sound that infants make during the first month.

During the second month, infants begin **cooing**. Infants use their tongues when they coo. For this reason, coos are more articulated than cries. Coos are often vowel-like and may resemble extended "oohs" and "ahs." Cooing appears linked to feelings of pleasure or positive excitement. Infants tend not to coo when they are hungry, tired, or in pain.

Cries and coos are innate but can be modified by experience (Volterra et al., 2004). When parents respond positively to cooing by talking to their infants, smiling at them, and imitating them, cooing increases. Early parent–child "conversations," in which parents respond to coos and then pause as the infant coos, may foster infant awareness of taking turns as a way of verbally relating to other people.

By about 8 months of age, cooing decreases markedly. Somewhere between 6 and 9 months, children begin to babble. **Babbling** is the first vocalizing that sounds like human speech. In babbling, infants frequently combine consonants and vowels, as in *ba*, *ga*, and, sometimes, the much valued *dada* (Stoel-Gammon, 2002). At first, *dada* is purely coincidental (sorry, you dads), despite the family's jubilation over its appearance.

In verbal interactions between infants and adults, the adults frequently repeat the syllables produced by their infants. They are likely to say "dadada" or "bababa" instead of simply "da" or "ba." Such redundancy apparently helps infants discriminate these sounds from others and further encourages them to imitate their parents (Elkind, 2007; Tamis-LeMonda et al., 2006).

After infants have been babbling for a few months, parents often believe that their children are having conversations with themselves. At 10 to 12 months, infants tend to repeat syllables, showing what linguists refer to as **echolalia**. Parents overhear them going on and on, repeating consonant–vowel combinations ("ah-bah-bah-bah-bah"), pausing, and then switching to other combinations.

Toward the end of the first year, infants are also using patterns of rising and falling **intonation** that resemble the sounds of adult speech. It may sound as though the infant is trying to speak the parents' language. Parents may think that their children are babbling in English or in whatever tongue is spoken in the home.

Development of Vocabulary

Question: How does vocabulary develop? Vocabulary development refers to the child's learning the meanings of words. In general, children's **receptive vocabulary** development outpaces their **expressive vocabulary** development (Lickliter, 2001; Ouellette, 2006). In other words, at any given time, they can understand more words than they can use. One study, for example, found that 12-month-olds could speak an average of 13 words but could comprehend the meaning of 84 (Tamis-LeMonda et al., 2006). Infants usually understand much of what others are saying well before they themselves utter any words at all. Their ability to segment speech sounds into meaningful units—or words—before 12 months is a good predictor of their vocabulary at 24 months (Newman et al., 2006).

The Child's First Words

Ah, that long-awaited first word! What a milestone! Sad to say, many parents miss it. They are not quite sure when their infants utter their first word, often because the first word is not pronounced clearly or because pronunciation varies from usage to usage.

A child's first word typically is spoken between the ages of 11 and 13 months, but a range of 8 to 18 months is considered normal (Hoff, 2006; Tamis-LeMonda et al.,

cooing Prelinguistic, articulated vowel-like sounds that appear to reflect feelings of positive excitement.

babbling The child's first vocalizations that have the sounds of speech.

echolalia The automatic repetition of sounds or words.

intonation The use of pitches of varying levels to help communicate meaning.

receptive vocabulary The sum total of the words whose meanings one understands.

expressive vocabulary The sum total of the words that one can use in the production of language.

2006). First words tend to be brief, consisting of one or two syllables. Each syllable is likely to consist of a consonant followed by a vowel. Vocabulary acquisition is slow at first. It may take children 3 or 4 months to achieve a vocabulary of 10 to 30 words after the first word is spoken (de Villiers & de Villiers, 1999).

By about 18 months of age, children may be producing up to 50 words. Many of them are quite familiar, such as *no, cookie, mama, hi*, and *eat*. Others, such as *all gone* and *bye-bye*, may not be found in the dictionary, but they function as words. That is, they are used consistently to symbolize the same meaning.

More than half (65%) of children's first words make up "general nominals" and "specific nominals" (Hoff, 2006; Nelson, 1973). General nominals are similar to nouns in that they include the names of classes of objects (*car, ball*), animals (*doggy, cat*), and people (*boy, girl*), but they also include both personal and relative pronouns

A CLOSER LOOK

Teaching Sign Language to Infants

When Jacqueline Turner's daughter Riley was only 8 months old, she could let her mother know she was thirsty for milk by pumping her fingers against her palm. Or that she wanted more cereal by touching her fingertips together. Or ask for a ball, or her stuffed dog, or a book—all without saying a word. She used hand gestures taught to her by her mother.

Why teach signs to a baby who is not deaf? Mrs. Turner, a Spanish-language interpreter from Beaverton, said she bought a book and video about teaching signs to babies to help eliminate the frustration Riley had in not being able to communicate, as well as Mrs. Turner's own frustration in not understanding her. "It makes her feel that she's more in control of a situation and has choices," Mrs. Turner said.

For hearing and deaf children, the ability to gesture tends to develop ahead of words. Babies can wave bye-bye to Grandma months before they can talk, for instance.

In interviews in 2003, Dr. Elizabeth Bates, one of the leading researchers in the field and the director of the Center for Research in Language at the University of California at San Diego, talked about the development of this type of communication.

"It has to do with how easily one can imitate and reproduce something with a great big fat hand as opposed to the mini, delicate hundreds of muscles that control the tongue," Dr. Bates said in the interview. "You can also see somebody using a hand, which you can't do with a tongue." The areas in the brain that control the mouth and speech and the areas that control the hands and ges-

Signs of the Times?

Infants are apparently capable of learning some signs before they can speak. Does teaching infants sign language stimulate intellectual development, as some researchers suggest, or is it too early to sign off on this form of cognitive enrichment?

tures overlap a great deal and develop together, Dr. Bates added.

Teaching simple gestures, or signs, to babies before they can talk is a way to jump-start the language and communication process, and stimulate intellectual development. It can also confer a host of related benefits, including increased vocabulary, a deeper parent–child

(*continued*)

(*she, that*). Specific nominals are proper nouns, such as *Daddy* and *Rover*. The attention of infants seems to be captured by movement. Words expressing movement are frequently found in early speech. Of children's first 50 words, the most common were names for people, animals, and objects that move (*Mommy, car, doggy*) or that can be moved (*dolly, milky*), action words (*bye-bye*), a number of modifiers (*big, hot*), and expressive words (*no, hi, oh*) (Tamis-LeMonda et al., 2006).

At about 18 to 22 months of age, there is a rapid burst in vocabulary (Tamis-LeMonda et al., 2006). The child's vocabulary may increase from 50 to more than 300 words in only a few months. This vocabulary spurt could also be called a naming explosion because almost 75% of the words added during this time are nouns. The rapid pace of vocabulary growth continues through the preschool years, with children acquiring an average of nine new words per day (Hoff, 2006).

bond, enhanced self-esteem, and decreased tantrums during the "Terrible 2's," proponents say.

Research by Dr. Linda Acredolo and Dr. Susan W. Goodwyn has perhaps drawn the most interest. They found that second-graders who had been encouraged to use their signing system during the second year had an advantage of 12 IQ points higher than children who did not use any such system.

Also intriguing has been the work of Joseph Garcia, the author of the book and video series *Sign with Your Baby: How to Communicate with Infants Before They Can Speak*. Mr. Garcia, an American Sign Language and early child development researcher, noticed that the hearing babies of deaf parents could communicate their needs and desires at a much earlier age than children of hearing parents. His research found that through signs, parent–infant communication could begin at 8 months, rather than waiting for comprehensible speech to develop at 16 to 18 months.

Parents who sign with their babies may be learning as much about communicating as their children. "Research shows huge individual differences in how much adults communicate with children," Dr. Bates said. "The studies out there show significant effects probably because a subset of the parents in the studies were not communicating with their kids as much as they start to when they enter these programs."

Many parents wonder whether signing will get in the way of their babies' learning how to talk. According to Mrs. Turner, who continued to sign with Riley

for several months after she began speaking, what happened was just the opposite. "Once she started saying her first words, the more I used signs, the more she answered back with words," she said. Riley, now 20 months old, is very verbal and says cogent three-word sentences.

Signing can also ease a toddler's transition to speaking by reducing the frustration of trying to pronounce words like *toothbrush*, or to express concepts like needing a diaper changed. For instance, even before Riley could speak, she was able to show her mother that something hurt by making the sign for pain and pointing to a part of her body. And according to Mrs. Turner, Riley understood that the word *please* would get her a favorite toy or a drink of milk more quickly, but it was difficult for her to say because of the l's. Instead, she did the sign for "please."

For Mrs. Turner, signing with a child is as much about empowerment as about communication. It provided Riley, and would provide other children, with another tool to get their needs met.

Reflect: The article notes that teaching 1-year-olds to sign before they can speak "jump-starts" the communication process. Do you believe that it is important to accelerate language development at such an early age? Why or why not?

Source: From Judith Berck, "Before Baby Talk, Signs and Signals," *New York Times* online, January 5, 2004. Copyright © 2004 by the New York Times Co. Reprinted by permission.

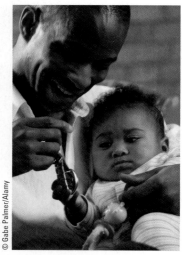

Fostering Language Development

Language growth in young children is enhanced when parents and caregivers engage the infant "in conversation" about activities and objects in the environment.

referential language style
Use of language primarily as a means for labeling objects.

expressive language style
Use of language primarily as a means for engaging in social interaction.

overextension Use of words in situations in which their meanings become extended or inappropriate.

telegraphic speech Type of speech in which only the essential words are used.

mean length of utterance (MLU) The average number of morphemes used in an utterance.

morpheme The smallest unit of meaning in a language.

Referential and Expressive Styles in Language Development

Some children prefer a referential approach in their language development, whereas others take a more expressive approach (Hoff, 2006; Nelson, 1981). Children who show the **referential language style** use language primarily to label objects in their environments. Their early vocabularies consist mainly of nominals. Children who use an **expressive language style** use language primarily as a means for engaging in social interactions. Children with an expressive style use more pronouns and many words involved in social routines, such as *stop, more,* and *all gone.* More children use an expressive style than a referential style (Tamis-LeMonda et al., 2006), but most use a combination of the styles.

Why do some children prefer a referential style and others an expressive style? It may be that some children are naturally oriented toward objects, whereas others are primarily interested in social relationships. Nelson (1981) also found that the parents' ways of teaching children play a role. Some parents focus on labeling objects for children as soon as they notice their vocabularies expanding. Others are more oriented toward social interactions themselves, teaching their children to say "hi," "please," and "thank you."

Overextension

Young children try to talk about more objects than they have words for (not so surprising; so do adults, now and then). To accomplish their linguistic feats, children often extend the meaning of one word to refer to things and actions for which they do not have words (McDonough, 2002). This process is called **overextension**. In classic research, Eve Clark (1973, 1975) studied diaries of infants' language development and found that overextensions are generally based on perceived similarities in function or form between the original object or action and the new one to which the first word is being extended. She provides the example of the word *mooi,* which one child originally used to designate the moon. The child then overextended *mooi* to designate all round objects, including the letter *o* and cookies and cakes.

Overextensions gradually pull back to their proper references as the child's vocabulary and ability to classify objects develop (McDonough, 2002). Consider the example of a child who first refers to a dog as a "bowwow." The word *bowwow* then becomes overextended to also refer to horses, cats, and cows. In effect, bowwow comes to mean something akin to "familiar animal." Next, the child learns to use the word *moo* to refer to cows. But *bowwow* still remains extended to horses and cats. As the child's vocabulary develops, she acquires the word *doggy.* So dogs and cats may now be referred to with either *bowwow* or *doggy.* Eventually, each animal has one or more correct names.

Development of Sentences: Telegraphing Ideas

Question: How do infants create sentences? The infant's first sentences are typically one-word utterances, but these utterances appear to express complete ideas and therefore can be thought of as sentences. Roger Brown (1973) called brief expressions that have the meanings of sentences **telegraphic speech**. Adults who write telegrams use principles of syntax to cut out all the unnecessary words. "Home Tuesday" might stand for "I expect to be home on Tuesday." Similarly, only the essential words are used in children's telegraphic speech—in particular, nouns, verbs, and some modifiers.

Mean Length of Utterance

The **mean length of utterance (MLU)** is the average number of **morphemes** that communicators use in their sentences (Pancsofar & Vernon-Feagans, 2006; Saaristo-Helin et al., 2006). Morphemes are the smallest units of meaning in a language. A morpheme may be a whole word or part of a word, such as a prefix or suffix. For example, the word *walked* consists of two morphemes: the verb *walk* and the suffix *ed*, which changes the verb to the past tense. In ● Figure 6.6, we see the relationship between chronological age and MLU for three children tracked by Roger Brown (1973, 1977): Lin, Victor, and Sarah.

The patterns of growth in MLU are similar for each child, showing swift upward movement, broken by intermittent and brief regressions. Figure 6.6 also shows us something about individual differences. Lin was precocious compared with Victor and Sarah, extending her MLU at much earlier ages. But as suggested earlier, the receptive language of all three children would have exceeded their expressive language at any given time. Also, Lin's earlier extension of MLU does not guarantee that she will show more complex expressive language than Victor and Sarah at maturity.

Let us now consider the features of two types of telegraphic speech: the holophrase and two-word utterances.

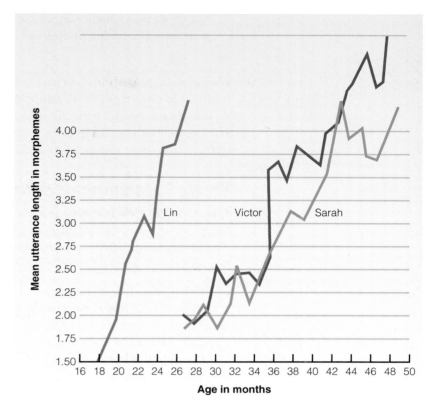

● **Figure 6.6**
Mean Length of Utterance for Three Children

Some children begin speaking earlier than others. However, the mean length of utterance (MLU) increases rapidly once speech begins.

Holophrases

Holophrases are single words that are used to express complex meanings. For example, Mama may be used by the child to signify meanings as varied as "There goes Mama," "Come here, Mama," and "You are Mama." Most children readily teach their parents what they intend by augmenting their holophrases with gestures, intonations, and reinforcers. That is, they act delighted when parents do as requested and howl when they do not.

Infants are likely to combine single words with gestures as they undertake the transition from holophrases to two-word utterances (Tamis-LeMonda et al., 2006). For example, pointing can signify "there" before the word is used.

Two-Word Sentences

When the child's vocabulary consists of 50 to 100 words (usually somewhere between 18 and 24 months of age), telegraphic two-word sentences begin to appear (Tamis-LeMonda et al., 2006). In the sentence "That ball," the words *is* and *a* are implied.

Two-word sentences, although brief and telegraphic, show understanding of **syntax** (Slobin, 2001). The child will say "Sit chair," not "Chair sit," to tell a parent to sit in a chair. The child will say "My shoe," not "Shoe my," to show possession. "Mommy go" means Mommy is leaving, whereas "Go Mommy" expresses the wish for Mommy to go away.

Theories of Language Development: Can You Make a Houseplant Talk?

Since all normal humans talk but no house pets or house plants do, no matter how pampered, heredity must be involved in language. But since a child growing up in Japan speaks Japanese whereas the same child brought up in California would speak English, the environment is also crucial. Thus, there is no question about whether heredity or environment is involved in lan-

holophrase A single word that is used to express complex meanings.

syntax The rules in a language for placing words in proper order to form meaningful sentences (from the Latin *syntaxis*, meaning "joining together").

guage, or even whether one or the other is "more important." Instead, . . . our best hope [might be] finding out how they interact.

—Steven Pinker

Countless billions of children have learned the languages spoken by their parents and have passed them down, with minor changes, from generation to generation. But how do they do so? In discussing this question—and so many others—we refer to the possible roles of nature and nurture. Learning theorists have come down on the side of nurture, and those who point to a basic role for nature are said to hold a nativist view.

Views That Emphasize Nurture

Question: How do learning theorists account for language development? Learning plays an obvious role in language development. Children who are reared in English-speaking homes learn English, not Japanese or Russian. Learning theorists usually explain language development in terms of imitation and reinforcement.

The Role of Imitation

From a social cognitive perspective, parents serve as **models**. Children learn language, at least in part, by observation and imitation. It seems likely that many vocabulary words, especially nouns and verbs (including irregular verbs), are learned by imitation.

But imitative learning does not explain why children spontaneously utter phrases and sentences that they have not observed (Tamis-LeMonda et al., 2006). Parents, for example, are unlikely to model utterances such as "Bye-bye sock" and "All gone Daddy," but children do say them.

And children sometimes steadfastly avoid imitating certain language forms suggested by adults, even when the adults are insistent. Note the following exchange between 2-year-old Ben and a (very frustrated) adult (Kuczaj, 1982, p. 48):

> Ben: I like these candy. I like they.
> Adult: You like them?
> Ben: Yes, I like they.
> Adult: Say them.
> Ben: Them.
> Adult: Say "I like them."
> Ben: I like them.
> Adult: Good.
> Ben: I'm good. These candy good too.
> Adult: Are they good?
> Ben: Yes. I like they. You like they?

Ben is not resisting the adult because of obstinacy. He does repeat "I like them" when asked to do so. But when given the opportunity afterward to construct the object *them*, he reverts to using the subjective form *they*. Ben is likely at this period in his development to use his (erroneous) understanding of syntax spontaneously to actively produce his own language, rather than just imitate a model.

The Role of Reinforcement

B. F. Skinner (1957) allowed that prelinguistic vocalizations such as cooing and babbling may be inborn. But parents reinforce children for babbling that approximates the form of real words, such as *da*, which, in English, resembles *dog* or *daddy*. Children, in fact, do increase their babbling when it results in adults smiling at them, stroking them, and talking back to them. We have seen that as the first year progresses, children babble the sounds of their native tongues with increasing frequency; foreign sounds tend to drop out. The behaviorist explains this pattern of changing frequencies in terms of reinforcement (of the sounds of the adults' language) and

models In learning theory, those whose behaviors are imitated by others.

extinction (of foreign sounds). Another (nonbehavioral) explanation is that children actively attend to the sounds in their linguistic environments and are intrinsically motivated to utter them.

From Skinner's perspective, children acquire their early vocabularies through **shaping**. That is, parents require that children's utterances be progressively closer to actual words before they are reinforced. In support of Skinner's position, research has shown that reinforcement accelerates the growth of vocabulary in children, especially children with learning disabilities (August et al., 2005; Kroeger & Nelson, 2006). Skinner viewed multiword utterances as complex stimulus–response chains that are also taught by shaping. As children's utterances increase in length, parents foster correct word order by uttering sentences to their children and reinforcing imitation. As with Ben, when children make grammatical errors, parents recast their utterances correctly. They reinforce the children for repeating them.

But recall Ben's refusal to be shaped into correct syntax. If the reinforcement explanation of language development were sufficient, parents' reinforcement would facilitate children's learning of syntax and pronunciation. We do not have such evidence. For one thing, parents are more likely to reinforce their children for the accuracy, or "truth value," of their utterances than for their grammatical correctness (Brown, 1973). Parents, in other words, generally accept the syntax of their children's vocal efforts. The child who points down and says "The grass is purple" is not likely to be reinforced, despite correct syntax. But the enthusiastic child who shows her empty plate and blurts out "I eated it all up" is likely to be reinforced, despite the grammatical incorrectness of "eated." Research confirms that, although parents do expand and rephrase their children's ungrammatical utterances more than their grammatically correct ones, they do not overtly correct their children's language mistakes (Bohannon & Stanowicz, 1988; Coley, 1993).

Selective reinforcement of children's pronunciation can also backfire. Children whose parents reward proper pronunciation but correct poor pronunciation develop vocabulary more slowly than children whose parents are more tolerant about pronunciation (Nelson, 1973). **Truth or Fiction Revisited:** Actually, the evidence suggests that correcting children's pronunciation may slow their vocabulary development.

Learning theory also cannot account for the invariant sequences of language development and for children's spurts in acquisition. Even the types of two-word utterances emerge in a consistent pattern in diverse cultures. Although timing differs from

extinction The decrease and eventual disappearance of a response in the absence of reinforcement.

shaping In learning theory, the gradual building of complex behavior patterns through reinforcement of successive approximations of the target behavior.

Developing in a World of Diversity

Two-Word Sentences Here, There, and . . .

Two-word sentences appear at about the same time in the development of all languages (Slobin, 2001). Also, the sequence of emergence of the types of two-word utterances—for example, first, subject–verb ("Mommy go"), then verb–object ("Hit ball"), location ("Ball here"), and possession ("My ball")—is the same in lan-

guages as diverse as English, Luo (an African tongue), German, Russian, and Turkish. This example illustrations the point that language develops in a series of steps that appear to be invariant. Dan Slobin interprets his findings to mean that the construction of sentences serves specific functions of communication in various languages. Slobin does not

argue that there is an innate linguistic structure but rather that basic human processes of cognition, communication, and information processing are found across cultures (Slobin, 2001).

Reflect: *Which theory of language do Slobin's findings appear to support?*

child to child, the types of questions used, passive versus active sentences, and so on all emerge in the same order. It is unlikely that parents around the world teach language skills in the same sequence.

On the other hand, there is ample evidence that aspects of the child's language environment influence the development of language. Much of the research in this area has focused on the ways in which adults—especially mothers—interact with their children.

Studies show that language growth in young children is enhanced when mothers and other adults do the following things (Tamis-LeMonda et al., 2006):

- Use a simplified form of speech known as "Motherese."
- Use questions that engage the child in conversation.
- Respond to the child's expressive language efforts in a way that is "attuned"; for example, adults relate their speech to the child's utterance by saying "Yes, your doll is pretty" in response to the child's statement "My doll."

A Closer Look

"Motherese"

One fascinating way that adults influence the language development of young children is through the use of baby talk or "Motherese," known more technically as child-directed speech or infant-directed speech. But "Motherese" is a limiting term, because grandparents, fathers, siblings, and unrelated people, including older children, also use Motherese when talking to infants (Kidd & Bavin, 2007; Snedeker et al., 2007). Moreover, at least one study found that women (but not men) often talk to their pets in Motherese (Prato-Previde et al., 2006). Motherese occurs in languages as different as Arabic, English, Comanche, Italian, French, German, Xhosa (an African language), Japanese, Mandarin Chinese, and even a Thai sign language (Masataka, 1998; Nonaka, 2004; Trainor & Desjardins, 2002).

Researchers find that Motherese has several characteristics (Gogate et al., 2000; Trevarthen, 2003; Weppelman et al., 2003):

1. Motherese is spoken more slowly than speech addressed to adults. Motherese is spoken at a higher pitch, and there are distinct pauses between ideas.
2. Sentences are brief, and adults make the effort to speak in a grammatically correct manner.
3. Sentences are simple in syntax. The focus is on nouns, verbs, and only a few modifiers.
4. Key words are put at the ends of sentences and are spoken in a higher and louder voice.
5. The diminutive morpheme *y* is frequently added to nouns. *Dad* becomes *Daddy* and *horse* becomes *horsey*.

6. Motherese is repetitive. Adults repeat sentences several times, sometimes using minor variations, as in "Show me your nose." "Where is your nose?" "Can you touch your nose?" Adults also repeat children's utterances, often rephrasing them in an effort to expand children's awareness of their expressive opportunities. If the child says, "Baby shoe," the mother may reply, "Yes, that's your shoe. Shall Mommy put the shoe on baby's foot?"
7. Motherese includes a type of repetition called reduplication. *Yummy* becomes *yummy-yummy*. *Daddy* may alternate with *Da-da*.
8. Vocabulary is concrete, referring, when possible, to objects that are in the immediate environment. For example, stuffed lions may be referred to as "kitties." Purposeful overextension is intended to avoid confusing the child by adding too many new labels.
9. Objects may be overdescribed by being given compound labels. Rabbits may become "bunny rabbits," and cats may become "kitty cats." In this way, parents may try to be sure that they are connecting with the child by using at least one label that the child will recognize.
10. Parents speak for the children, as in "Is baby tired?" "Oh, we're so tired." "We want to take our nap now, don't we?" This parent is pretending to have a two-way conversation with the child. In this way, parents seem to be trying to help their children express themselves by offering children models of sentences they can use later on.

- Join the child in paying attention to a particular activity or toy.
- Gesture to help the child understand what they are saying.
- Describe aspects of the environment occupying the infant's current focus of attention.
- Read to the child.
- Talk to the child a great deal.

Views That Emphasize Nature

Question: What is the nativist view of language development? The nativist view holds that innate or inborn factors cause children to attend to and acquire language in certain ways. From this perspective, children bring an inborn tendency in the form of neurological "prewiring" to language learning (Clancy & Finlay, 2001; Pinker, 1994; Werker & Desjardins, 2001).

11. Users of Motherese stay a step ahead of the child. As children's vocabularies grow and their syntax develops, adults step up their own language levels, remaining just ahead of the child. In this way, adults seem to be encouraging the child to continue to play catch-up.

So adults and older children use a variety of strategies to communicate with young children and to draw them out. Does it work? Does Motherese foster language development? Research on the effects of Motherese supports its use. Infants as young as 2 days old prefer baby talk to adult talk (Trevarthen, 2003; Weppelman et al., 2003). The short, simple sentences and high pitch used in Motherese are more likely to produce a response from the child and enhance vocabulary development than are complex sentences and those spoken in a lower pitch.

Children who hear their utterances repeated and recast do seem to learn from the adults who are modeling the new expressions (Tamis-LeMonda et al., 2001; Trevarthen, 2003). Repetition of children's vocalizations also appears to be one method of reinforcing vocalizing. In sum, Motherese may be of significant help in fostering children's language development.

Reflect:
- How would you explain the finding that Motherese is apparently found in all cultures throughout the world?
- Why do you believe that women are more likely than men to use Motherese?

For Better or For Worse®   **by Lynn Johnston**

FOR BETTER OR FOR WORSE © 1991 Lynn Johnston Productions. Dist. by Universal Press Syndicate. Reprinted with permission. All rights reserved.

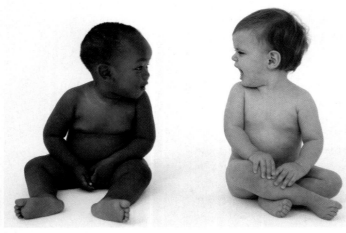

According to psycholinguistic theory, humans have in inborn "language acquisition device" that leads to commonalities in language development in all cultures. Babbling, for example, emerges at about the same time everywhere, and, at about the same time, infants begin to sound as if they are babbling the sounds in the language spoken in the home. Chomsky also hypothesizes that all languages have a universal grammar regardless of how different they might seem.

According to Steven Pinker and Ray Jackendoff (2005), the structures that enable humans to perceive and produce language evolved in bits and pieces. Those individuals who possessed these "bits" and "pieces" were more likely to reach maturity and transmit their genes from generation to generation because communication ability increased their chances of survival.

Psycholinguistic Theory

According to **psycholinguistic theory**, language acquisition involves an interaction between environmental influences—such as exposure to parental speech and reinforcement—and an inborn tendency to acquire language (Clancy & Finlay, 2001). Noam Chomsky (1988, 1990) and some others labeled this innate tendency a **language acquisition device (LAD)**. Evidence for an inborn tendency is found in the universality of human language abilities; in the regularity of the early production of sounds, even among deaf children; and in the invariant sequences of language development, regardless of which language the child is learning (Bloom, 1998; Volterra et al., 2004).

The inborn tendency primes the nervous system to learn grammar. On the surface, languages differ a great deal in their vocabulary and grammar. Chomsky refers to these elements as the **surface structure** of language. However, the LAD serves children all over the world because languages share what Chomsky refers to as a "universal grammar": an underlying **deep structure** or set of rules for transforming ideas into sentences. From Chomsky's perspective, children are genetically prewired to attend to language and to deduce the rules for constructing sentences from ideas. Consider an analogy with computers: According to psycholinguistic theory, the universal grammar that resides in the LAD is the basic operating system of the computer, whereas the particular language a child learns to use is the word-processing program. **Truth or Fiction Revisited:** It is apparently true that children are prewired to listen to language in such a way that they come to understand rules of grammar.

Brain Structures Involved in Language

Question: What parts of the brain are involved in language development? Research shows that many parts of the brain are involved in language development and that each person may have a unique pattern of organization for language ability (Rosen et al., 2000; Schwartz et al., 2000). However, some of the key biological structures that may provide the basis for the functions of the LAD appear to be based in the left hemisphere of the cerebral cortex for nearly all right-handed people and for two out of three left-handed people (Pinker, 1994).

Although both hemispheres of the brain are involved in perception of speech (Dehaene-Lambertz et al., 2004), the sounds of speech elicit greater electrical activity in the left hemisphere of newborns than in the right hemisphere, as indicated by the activity of brain waves. In the left hemisphere of the cortex, the two areas most involved in speech are Broca's area and Wernicke's area (Dogil et al., 2002) (see ● Figure 6.7). Even in the human fetus, Wernicke's area is usually larger in the left hemisphere than in the right. Damage to either area is likely to cause an **aphasia**, that is, a disruption in the ability to understand or produce language.

Broca's area is located near the section of the motor cortex that controls the muscles of the tongue and throat and other areas of the face that are used when

psycholinguistic theory The view that language learning involves an interaction between environmental influences and an inborn tendency to acquire language. The emphasis is on the inborn tendency.

language acquisition device (LAD) In psycholinguistic theory, neural "prewiring" that facilitates the child's learning of grammar.

surface structure The superficial grammatical construction of a sentence.

deep structure The underlying meaning of a sentence.

aphasia A disruption in the ability to understand or produce language.

speaking. When Broca's area is damaged, people speak slowly and laboriously, with simple sentences, in a pattern known as **Broca's aphasia**. Their ability to understand the speech of others is relatively unaffected, however. Wernicke's area lies near the auditory cortex and is connected to Broca's area by nerve fibers. People with damage to Wernicke's area may show **Wernicke's aphasia**. Although they usually speak freely and with proper syntax, their abilities to comprehend other people's speech and to think of the words to express their own thoughts are impaired. Thus, Wernicke's area seems to be essential to understanding the relationships between words and their meanings.

A part of the brain called the angular gyrus lies between the visual cortex and Wernicke's area. The angular gyrus "translates" visual information, such as written words, into auditory information (sounds) and sends it on to Wernicke's area. It appears that problems in the angular gyrus can give rise to dyslexia, or serious impairment in reading, because it becomes difficult for the reader to segment words into sounds (Pugh et al., 2000).

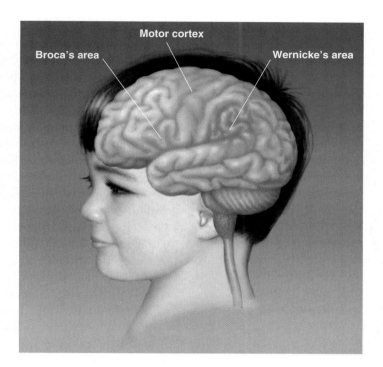

● **Figure 6.7** Broca's and Wernicke's Areas of the Cerebral Cortex

Broca's area and Wernicke's area of the (usually left) hemisphere are most involved in speech. Damage to either area can produce an aphasia, an impairment in the ability to understand or produce language.

The Sensitive Period

Numerous researchers have suggested that language learning occurs during one or more **sensitive periods**, which begin at about 18 to 24 months and last until puberty (Clancy & Finlay, 2001; Uylings, 2006). *Question: What is meant by a sensitive period for language development?* During these sensitive periods, neural development (as in the differentiating of brain structures) provides plasticity that facilitates language learning. Experience with language also alters the structure of the brain, although the exact relationships have not been discovered (Uylings, 2006).

Evidence for a sensitive period is found in recovery from brain injuries in some people. Injuries to the hemisphere that controls language (usually the left hemisphere) can impair or destroy the ability to speak (Werker & Tees, 2005). But before puberty, children suffering left-hemisphere injuries frequently recover a good deal of speaking ability. In young children, left-hemisphere damage may encourage the development of language functions in the right hemisphere. But adaptation ability wanes in adolescence, when brain tissue has reached adult levels of differentiation (Snow, 2006).

The best way to determine whether people are capable of acquiring language once they have passed puberty would be to run an experiment in which one or more children were reared in such severe isolation that they were not exposed to language until puberty. Of course, such an experiment could not be run because of ethical and legal barriers.

However, the disturbing case history of Genie offers insights into the issue of whether there is a sensitive period for language development (Fromkin et al., 2004; LaPointe, 2005). Genie's father locked her in a small room at the age of 20 months and kept her there until she was 13 years old. Her social contacts during this period were limited to her mother, who entered the room only to feed Genie, and to beatings by her father. When Genie was rescued, she weighed only about 60 pounds, did not speak, was not toilet trained, and could barely stand. Genie was placed in a foster home, where she was exposed to English for the first time in nearly 12 years. Her language development followed the normal sequence of much younger children in a number of ways, but she never acquired the proficiency of children reared un-

Broca's aphasia A form of aphasia caused by damage to Broca's area and characterized by slow, laborious speech.

Wernicke's aphasia A form of aphasia caused by damage to Wernicke's area and characterized by impaired comprehension of speech and difficulty in attempting to produce the right word.

sensitive period In linguistic theory, the period from about 18 months to puberty when the brain is thought to be especially capable of learning language because of its plasticity.

der normal circumstances. Five years after her liberation, Genie's language remained largely telegraphic. She still showed significant problems with syntax, such as failing to reverse subjects and verbs to phrase spontaneous questions. She showed confusion concerning the use of the past tense (adding *ed* to words) and had difficulty using negative helping verbs such as *isn't* and *haven't*.

Genie's language development provides some support for the sensitive-period hypothesis, although her language problems might also be partly attributed to her years of malnutrition and abuse. She may also have been mentally retarded to begin with. Her efforts to acquire English after puberty were clearly laborious, and the results were substandard compared even with the language of many 2- and 3-year-olds.

Further evidence for the sensitive-period hypothesis is provided by a study of a deaf boy named Simon, who was observed from the age of 2½ to 9 years (Newport, 1992). Researchers reported that Simon signed in **American Sign Language (ASL)** with correct grammar, even though he had been exposed only to grammatically incorrect ASL by his parents and their friends, who also were deaf. Simon's parents and their friends had not learned to sign until they were teenagers. At that age, people often learn languages imperfectly. But Simon showed early mastery of grammatical rules that his parents used incorrectly or not at all. Simon's deduction of these rules on his own supports the view that the tendency to acquire language is inborn, and it also provides evidence that such learning occurs most readily during a sensitive period early in life.

In sum, the development of language in infancy represents the interaction of environmental and biological factors. The child brings a built-in readiness to the task of language acquisition, whereas houseplants and other organisms do not. The child must also have the opportunity to hear spoken language and to interact verbally with others. In the next chapter, we see how interaction with others affects the social development of the infant.

American Sign Language (ASL) The communication of meaning through the use of symbols that are formed by moving the hands and arms. The language used by some deaf people.

Active Review

14. _____ is the first vocalizing that sounds like human speech.
15. Children with a(n) _____ language style use language mainly to label objects.
16. Children try to talk about more objects than they have words for, often resulting in _____ of the meanings of words.
17. _____ are single words that are used to express complex meanings.
18. The sequence of emergence of types of two-word utterances is (The same or Different?) in diverse languages.
19. _____ theorists explain language development in terms of imitation and reinforcement.
20. According to _____ theory, language acquisition involves an interaction between environmental influences and an inborn tendency to acquire language.
21. Chomsky refers to this inborn tendency as a language _____ device (LAD).
22. Key biological structures that provide a basis for language are based in the (Left or Right?) hemisphere of the cerebral cortex for most people.
23. The brain areas most involved in speech are Broca's area and _____ area.

Reflect & Relate: Why are so many parents concerned with exactly when their children learn to talk?

Go to

http://www.thomsonedu.com/psychology/rathus

for an interactive version of this review.

1. **What is the sensorimotor stage of cognitive development?**

Piaget's sensorimotor stage refers to the first 2 years of cognitive development, during which changes are shown by means of sensory and motor activity.

2. **What are the parts or substages of the sensorimotor stage?**

The first substage is dominated by the assimilation of stimulation into reflexes. In the second substage, primary circular reactions, infants repeat stimulating actions that occur by chance. In the third substage, secondary circular reactions, patterns of activity are repeated because of their effects. In the fourth substage, infants intentionally coordinate schemes to attain goals. In the fifth substage, tertiary circular reactions, infants purposefully adapt established schemes to specific situations. In the sixth substage, external exploration is replaced by mental exploration.

3. **What is object permanence? How does it develop?**

Object permanence is recognition that an object or person continues to exist when out of sight. Through the first 6 months or so, when a screen is placed between an object and an infant, the infant behaves as if the object is no longer there.

4. **What are the strengths and limitations of Piaget's theory of sensorimotor development?**

Evidence supports the pattern and sequence of events described by Piaget, but cognitive development may not be tied to discrete stages as Piaget believed. Piaget also appears to have been incorrect about the ages at which infants develop various concepts.

5. **What are infants' tools for processing information?**

The tools include memory and imitation. Older infants are more capable of encoding and retrieving information than younger infants. Neonates reflexively imitate certain behaviors, such as sticking out the tongue. Infants later show deferred imitation, suggesting that they have mentally represented actions.

6. **How do we measure individual differences in the development of cognitive functioning?**

Some infants develop cognitive functioning more rapidly than others. The Bayley Scales of Infant Development (BSID) consist of mental-scale and motor-scale items. A tester may be able to detect early signs of sensory or neurological problems.

7. **How well do infant scales predict later intellectual performance?**

Certain BSID items predict intellectual skills later in childhood, but overall scores on such scales do not predict school grades accurately.

8. **What is visual recognition memory? How is it used?**

Visual recognition memory is the ability to discriminate previously seen objects from novel objects. Visual recognition memory moderately predicts IQ scores in later childhood.

9. **What are prelinguistic vocalizations?**

Prelinguistic vocalizations do not represent objects or events and include crying, cooing, and babbling. Children from different cultures initially babble the same sounds.

10. **How does vocabulary develop?**

Receptive vocabulary development outpaces expressive vocabulary. The first word typically is spoken between 11 and 13 months of age. It may take another 3 or 4

months to achieve a vocabulary of 10 to 30 words. Children's first words are mostly nominals. Children with a referential language style use language mainly to label objects. Those with an expressive language style mainly seek social interactions. Infants often extend the meaning of a word to refer to things and actions for which they do not have words.

11. How do infants create sentences?

Infants' early sentences are telegraphic. Two-word sentences show understanding of syntax. The kinds of two-word sentences are the same among children from diverse linguistic environments.

12. How do learning theorists account for language development?

Learning theorists explain language development in terms of imitation and reinforcement, but children resist imitating sentences that do not fit with their awareness of grammar.

13. What is the nativist view of language development?

The nativist view holds that innate or inborn prewiring causes children to attend to and acquire language in certain ways. Psycholinguistic theory considers that language acquisition involves the interaction between environmental influences and prewiring. Chomsky argues that languages share a "universal grammar" that children are prewired to perceive and use.

14. What parts of the brain are involved in language development?

Key biological structures are based in the left hemisphere for most people: Broca's area and Wernicke's area. Damage to either area may cause a characteristic aphasia.

15. What is meant by a *sensitive period* for language development?

This theory proposes that plasticity of the brain provides a sensitive period for learning language that begins at about 18 to 24 months and lasts until puberty.

Key Terms

scheme, 188
assimilation, 188
accommodation, 188
primary circular reactions, 191
secondary circular
    reactions, 191
tertiary circular reactions, 191
object permanence, 192
deferred imitation, 195
visual recognition
    memory, 201
prelinguistic, 204
cooing, 205
babbling, 205

echolalia, 205
intonation, 205
receptive vocabulary, 205
expressive vocabulary, 205
referential language
    style, 208
expressive language style, 208
overextension, 208
telegraphic speech, 208
mean length of utterance
    (MLU), 208
morpheme, 208
holophrase, 209
syntax, 209

models, 210
extinction, 211
shaping, 211
psycholinguistic theory, 214
language acquisition device
    (LAD), 214
surface structure, 214
deep structure, 214
aphasia, 214
Broca's aphasia, 215
Wernicke's aphasia, 215
sensitive period, 215
American Sign Language
    (ASL), 216

Active Learning Resources

Childhood & Adolescence Book Companion Website

http://www.thomsonedu.com/psychology/rathus

Visit your book companion website where you will find more resources to help you study. There you will find interactive versions of your book features, including the Lessons in Observation video, Active Review sections, and the Truth or Fiction feature. In addition, the companion website contains quizzing, flash cards, and a pronunciation glossary.

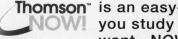 **is an easy-to-use online resource that helps you study in less time to get the grade you want—NOW.**

http://www.thomsonedu.com/login

Need help studying? This site is your one-stop study shop. Take a Pre-Test and ThomsonNOW will generate a Personalized Study Plan based on your test results. The Study Plan will identify the topics you need to review and direct you to online resources to help you master those topics. You can then take a Post-Test to determine the concepts you have mastered and what you still need to work on.

7

Infancy:
Social and Emotional Development

Truth or Fiction?

T F Infants who are securely attached to their mothers do not like to stray from them. p. 224

T F You can estimate how strongly infants are attached to their fathers if you know how many diapers per week their fathers change. p. 225

T F Child abusers have frequently been the victims of child abuse themselves. p. 236

T F Autism is caused by the mercury in measles-mumps-rubella vaccine. p. 242

T F Autistic children may respond to people as though they were pieces of furniture. p. 242

T F Children placed in day care are more aggressive than children who are cared for in the home. p. 246

T F Fear of strangers is abnormal among infants. p. 250

T F All children are "born" with the same temperament. Treatment by caregivers determines whether they are difficult or easygoing. p. 255

T F Girls prefer dolls and toy animals, and boys prefer toy trucks and sports equipment only after they have become aware of the gender roles assigned to them by society. p. 257

Preview

Attachment: Bonds That Endure
Patterns of Attachment
Establishing Attachment
Stability of Attachment
Stages of Attachment
Theories of Attachment

When Attachment Fails
Social Deprivation
Child Abuse and Neglect

A Closer Look: Prevention of Sexual Abuse of Children

A Closer Look: How Child Abuse May Set the Stage for Psychological Disorders in Adulthood

A Closer Look: What to Do If You Think a Child Has Been the Victim of Sexual Abuse

Autism Spectrum Disorders: Alone among the Crowd

Day Care
How Does Day Care Affect Bonds of Attachment?
How Does Day Care Influence Social and Cognitive Development?

A Closer Look: The Latest Shoe to Drop on Day Care from the NICHD

A Closer Look: Finding Child Care You (and Your Child) Can Live With

Emotional Development
Theories of the Development of Emotions
Fear of Strangers
Social Referencing: What Should I Do Now?
Emotional Regulation: Keeping on an Even Keel

Personality Development
The Self-Concept
Temperament: Easy, Difficult, or Slow to Warm Up?
Sex Differences

Lessons in Observation: Gender

Go to

http://www.thomsonedu.com/psychology/rathus
for an interactive version of this "Truth or Fiction" feature.

© Masterfile

At the age of 2, my daughter Allyn almost succeeded at preventing publication of a book on which I was working. When I locked myself into my study, she positioned herself outside the door and called, "Daddy, oh Daddy." At other times she would bang on the door or cry. When I would give in (several times a day) and open the door, she would run in and say, "I want you to pick up me," and hold out her arms or climb into my lap. How would I ever finish the book? Being a psychologist, solutions came easily. For example, I could write outside the home, but this solution had the drawback of distancing me from my family. Another solution was to ignore my daughter and let her cry. If I refused to reinforce crying, crying might become extinguished. (And research does suggest that ignoring crying discourages it [IJzendoorn & Hubbard, 2000].) There was only one problem with this solution: I didn't want to extinguish her efforts to get to me. **Attachment**, you see, is a two-way street.

Attachment is one of the key issues in the social and personality development of the infant. If this chapter had been written by the poet John Donne, it might have begun, "No children are islands unto themselves." Children come into this world fully dependent on others for their survival and well-being.

This chapter is about some of the consequences of that absolute dependency. It is about the social relationships between infants and caregivers and about the development of the bonds of attachment that usually—but not always—bind them. It is about the behaviors of infants that prompt social and emotional responses from adults and about the behaviors of adults that prompt social and emotional responses from infants. It is also about infants' unique and different ways of reacting socially and emotionally.

Let us first consider the issue of attachment and the factors that contribute to its development. Next, we examine some circumstances that interfere with the development of attachment: social deprivation, child abuse, and autism. Then, we turn to a discussion of day care. Finally, we look at the development of emotions and personality in infancy, including the self-concept, temperament, and sex differences.

Attachment: Bonds That Endure

Question: What is meant by "attachment"? Attachment is what most people refer to as affection or love. Mary Ainsworth (1989), one of the preeminent researchers on attachment, defines attachment as an emotional tie formed between one animal or person and another specific individual. Attachment keeps organisms together and tends to endure. John Bowlby believes that attachment is essential to the very survival of the infant (Bowlby, 1988; Ainsworth & Bowlby, 1991). He argues that babies are born with behaviors—crying, smiling, clinging—that elicit caregiving from parents.

Babies and children try to maintain contact with caregivers to whom they are attached. They engage in eye contact, pull and tug at them, and ask to be picked up. When they cannot maintain contact, infants show behaviors suggestive of **separation anxiety**. They may thrash about, fuss, cry, screech, or whine. Parents who are seeking a few minutes to attend to their own needs sometimes see these behaviors as manipulative, and, in a sense, they are. That is, children learn that the behaviors achieve desired ends. But what is wrong with "manipulating"—or influencing—a loved one to end distress?

Patterns of Attachment

Mary Ainsworth and her colleagues (1978) identified various patterns of attachment. Broadly, infants show either **secure attachment** or insecure attachment. Ainsworth and other investigators have found that most infants, older children, and adults in the United States are securely attached (Belsky, 2006a; McCartney et al., 2004).

© Robert Marvin

Mary D. Salter Ainsworth

attachment An affectional bond between individuals characterized by a seeking of closeness or contact and a show of distress upon separation.

separation anxiety Fear of being separated from a target of attachment, usually a primary caregiver.

secure attachment A type of attachment characterized by mild distress at leave-takings, seeking nearness to an attachment figure, and being readily soothed by the figure.

Question: What does it mean for a child to be "secure"? Think of security in terms of what infants do. Ainsworth developed the strange-situation method as a way of measuring the development of attachment (● Figure 7.1). In this method, an infant is exposed to a series of separations and reunions with a caregiver (usually the mother) and a stranger who is a confederate of the researchers. In the strange situation, securely attached infants mildly protest their mother's departure, seek interaction upon reunion, and are readily comforted by her.

Question: What, then, is "insecurity"? There are two major types of insecurity, or "insecure attachment": They are **avoidant attachment** and **ambivalent/resistant attachment**. Babies who show avoidant attachment are least distressed by their mothers' departure. They play without fuss when alone and ignore their mothers upon reunion. Ambivalent/resistant babies are the most emotional infants. They show severe signs of distress when their mothers leave and show ambivalence upon reunion by alternately clinging to and pushing away their mothers. Additional categories of insecure attachment have been proposed, including **disorganized–disoriented attachment**. Babies showing this pattern appear dazed, confused, or disoriented. They may show contradictory behaviors, such as moving toward the mother while looking away from her.

Question: Is it better for an infant to be securely attached to its caregivers? Sure it is. Securely attached infants and toddlers are happier, more sociable with unfamiliar adults, and more cooperative with parents, get along better with peers, and are better adjusted in school than insecurely attached children (Belsky, 2006a; McCartney et al., 2004; Spieker et al., 2003). Insecure attachment at the age of 1 year predicts psychological disorders at the age of 17 (Sroufe, 1998; Steele, 2005). Infants use the mother as a secure base from which to venture out and explore the environment (Belsky, 2006a). Secure attachment is also connected with the experiencing of fewer negative emotions toward members of out-groups (Mikulincer & Shaver, 2001). Thus, security encourages children to explore interactions with unfamiliar

avoidant attachment A type of insecure attachment characterized by apparent indifference to the leave-takings of and reunions with an attachment figure.

ambivalent/resistant attachment A type of insecure attachment characterized by severe distress at the leave-takings of and ambivalent behavior at reunions with an attachment figure.

disorganized–disoriented attachment A type of insecure attachment characterized by dazed and contradictory behaviors toward an attachment figure.

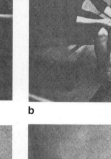

a   b   c   d

© Mary D. S. Ainsworth

● **Figure 7.1**
The Strange Situation

These historic photos show a 12-month-old child in the strange situation. In (a), the child plays with toys, glancing occasionally at mother. In (b), the stranger approaches with a toy. While the child is distracted, mother leaves the room. In (c), mother returns after a brief absence. The child crawls to her quickly and clings to her when picked up. In (d), the child cries when mother again leaves the room. What pattern of attachment is this child showing?

people, broadening their horizons. **Truth or Fiction Revisited:** Thus, infants who are securely attached to their mothers are likely to "stray" from them in the sense that they use them as a secure base for exploration of the environment.

Securely attached toddlers also have longer attention spans, are less impulsive, and are better at solving problems than insecurely attached toddlers (Granot & Mayseless, 2001; Spieker et al., 2003). At ages 5 and 6, securely attached children are better liked by peers and teachers, are more competent, are less aggressive, and have fewer behavior problems than insecurely attached children (Belsky, 2006a; Coleman, 2003).

Question: What are the roles of the parents in the formation of bonds of attachment?

Establishing Attachment

Attachment is one measure of the quality of care that infants receive (Belsky, 2006a; Coleman, 2003). The parents of securely attached infants are more affectionate, cooperative, and predictable in their caregiving than parents of insecurely attached infants. These parents respond more sensitively to their infants' smiles, cries, and other social behaviors (Harel & Scher, 2003).

A Japanese study found evidence for the "intergenerational transmission of attachment" from mother to child (Kazui et al., 2000). For example, the children of secure mothers showed the most secure patterns of attachment themselves, as assessed by various means. The children of secure mothers interacted positively both with their mothers and with strangers, so their pattern of attachment provided a secure base for exploration.

Providing economically stressed families with support services can enhance their involvement with their infants and increase secure attachment. In one study, low-income women received child-care information and social support from home visitors during pregnancy and through the child's third year (Spieker et al., 2005). The visitors first worked with the mothers on how they conceptualized their fetuses. Following childbirth, the home visitors helped the mothers accurately interpret their babies' cues and respond to them. They also encouraged mother–infant interaction and play, by and large resulting in appropriate maternal responsiveness and secure attachment between infant and mother.

Insecure attachment occurs more often among infants whose mothers are mentally ill or abusive (Cicchetti et al., 2006; McCartney et al., 2004). It is found more often among infants whose mothers are slow to meet their needs or meet them coldly (Steele et al., 2003).

Research by Marinus van IJzendoorn and his colleagues (2000) suggests that siblings tend to develop similar attachment relationships with their mother. The study pooled data on sibling attachment from research groups in the United States, the Netherlands, and Canada to form 138 pairs of siblings. Children's security of attachment was assessed with the strange-situation procedure at 12 to 14 months. Maternal sensitivity to infants' needs was also observed. Broad sibling attachment relationships (secure or insecure, but not necessarily the kinds of insecurity) with the mother were found to be significantly alike. It was also found that siblings of the same sex are more likely to form similar attachment relationships with their mother than are girl–boy pairs. Mothers, that is, may behave differently with daughters and sons.

Although it is tempting to seek the sources of attachment in caregivers' behavior and personalities, that is not the whole story. Security is also connected with the baby's temperament (Belsky, 2006a; Kerns et al., 2007). Babies who are more active and irritable and who display more negative emotion are more likely to develop insecure attachment. Such babies may elicit parental behaviors that are not conducive to the development of secure attachment. For example, mothers of "difficult" children are less responsive to their children and report that they feel less emotionally close to them (Morrell & Steele, 2003; Stams et al., 2002). Caregivers respond to babies' behavior, just as the babies respond to caregivers' behavior. The process of attachment is a two-way street.

Involvement of Fathers

Truth or Fiction Revisited: It is true that you can predict how well babies are attached to their fathers if you know how many diapers the fathers change each week. Gail Ross and her colleagues (1975) found that the more diapers the father changed, the stronger the attachment. There is no magical connection between diapers and love, but the number of diapers the father changes roughly reflects his involvement in child rearing.

How involved is the average father with his children? The brief answer, in developed nations, is more so than in the past. Gender roles are blurring to some degree, and fathers, as well as mothers, can rear infants competently and sensitively (Grossmann et al., 2002). But studies of parents in the United States show that father–child interactions differ qualitatively and quantitatively from mother–child interactions (Laflamme et al., 2002). Mothers engage in far more interactions with their infants. Most fathers spend much less time on basic child-care tasks, such as feeding and diaper changing, than mothers do. Fathers are more likely to play with their children than to feed or clean them (Laflamme et al., 2002). Fathers more often than mothers engage in physical rough-and-tumble play, such as tossing their babies into the air and poking them. Mothers are more likely to play games like patty-cake and peekaboo and to play games involving toys (Laflamme et al., 2002).

How strongly, then, do infants become attached to their fathers? The answer depends on the quality of the time that the father spends with the baby (R. A. Thompson et al., 2003). The more affectionate the interaction between father and infant, the stronger the attachment (R. A. Thompson et al., 2003). Infants under stress still seek out mothers more than fathers (Lamb et al., 1992b). But when observed at their natural activities in the home and other familiar settings, infants seek to be near to and touch their fathers about as often as their mothers.

© Laura Dwight/Photo Edit

Fathers and Attachment: The "Diaper Index"
The number of diapers a father changes reflects his involvement in child rearing. Children develop strong attachments to fathers as well as mothers, especially if the father interacts positively and affectionately with the child.

Stability of Attachment

Patterns of attachment tend to persist when care-giving conditions remain consistent (Ammaniti et al., 2005; Karavasilis et al., 2003). But attachment patterns can change when child care changes. Byron Egeland and Alan Sroufe (1981) followed a number of infants who were severely neglected and others who received high-quality care from 12 to 18 months of age. Attachment patterns remained stable (secure) for infants receiving fine care. However, many neglected infants changed from insecurely to securely attached over the 6-month period, sometimes because of a relationship with a supportive family member, sometimes because home life grew less tense. Children can also become less securely attached to caregivers when the quality of home life deteriorates (Belsky, 2006a).

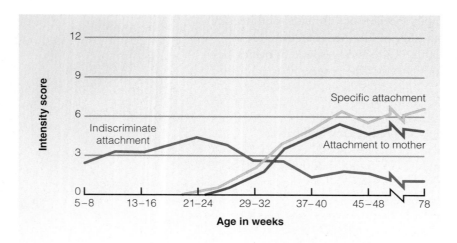

● Figure 7.2
The Development of Attachment

During the first 6 months, infants tend to show indiscriminate attachment. Indiscriminate attachment then wanes while specific attachments grow intense and remain at high levels. Fear of strangers develops a month or so after the intensity of specific attachments begins to blossom.

Children adopted at various ages can become securely attached to their adoptive parents (Veríssimo & Salvaterra, 2006). Children show resilience in their social and emotional development. Early insecurities can be overcome.

Early attachment patterns tend to endure into middle childhood, adolescence, and even adulthood (Ammaniti et al., 2005; Karavasilis et al., 2003). As Erik Erikson (1963) argued in *Childhood and Society*, positive relationships with caregivers may set the stage for positive relationships throughout life.

Stages of Attachment

Cross-cultural studies by Mary Ainsworth (1967) and others have led to a theory of stages of attachment. In one study, Ainsworth tracked the attachment behaviors of Ugandan infants. Over a 9-month period, she noted their efforts to maintain contact with the mother, their protests when separated, and their use of the mother as a base for exploring the environment. *Question: What did Ainsworth learn about the stages of attachment?* At first, the Ugandan infants showed **indiscriminate attachment**. That is, they showed no particular preferences for the mother or another familiar caregiver. Specific attachment to the mother, as evidenced by separation anxiety and other behaviors, began to develop at about 4 months of age and grew intensely by about 7 months. Fear of strangers developed 1 or 2 months later.

In another study, shown in ● Figure 7.2, Scottish infants showed indiscriminate attachment during the first 6 months or so after birth (Schaffer & Emerson, 1964). Then, indiscriminate attachment waned. Specific attachments to the mother and other familiar caregivers intensified, as demonstrated by the appearance of separation anxiety, and remained at high levels through the age of 18 months. Fear of strangers occurred a month or so after the intensity of specific attachments began to mushroom. Thus, in both this study and the Ugandan study, fear of strangers followed separation anxiety and the development of specific attachments by a number of weeks.

From such studies, Ainsworth and her colleagues (1978) identified the following three phases of attachment:

1. The **initial-preattachment phase** lasts from birth to about 3 months and is characterized by indiscriminate attachment.
2. The **attachment-in-the-making phase** occurs at about 3 or 4 months and is characterized by preference for familiar figures.
3. The **clear-cut-attachment phase** occurs at about 6 or 7 months and is characterized by intensified dependence on the primary caregiver, usually the mother.
4. Most infants have more than one adult caregiver, however, and are likely to form multiple attachments: to the father, day-care providers, grandparents, and other caregivers, as well as to the mother. In most cultures, single attachments are the exception, not the rule.

Theories of Attachment

Attachment, as with so many other behavior patterns, seems to develop as a result of the interaction of nature and nurture. *Question: How do different theorists emphasize nature or nurture in their explanation of the development of attachment?*

indiscriminate attachment The display of attachment behaviors toward any person.

initial-preattachment phase The first phase in the formation of bonds of attachment, lasting from birth to about 3 months of age and characterized by indiscriminate attachment.

attachment-in-the-making phase The second phase in the development of attachment, occurring at 3 or 4 months of age and characterized by preference for familiar figures.

Cognitive View of Attachment

The cognitive view of attachment focuses on the contention that an infant must have developed some concept of object permanence before specific attachment becomes possible. In other words, if caregivers are to be missed when absent, the infant must perceive that they continue to exist. We have seen that infants tend to develop specific attachments at about the age of 6 to 7 months. In support of the cognitive view, recall that rudimentary object permanence concerning physical objects develops somewhat earlier (see Chapter 6).

Behavioral View of Attachment: Caregiver as Reinforcer

Early in the twentieth century, behaviorists argued that attachment behaviors are learned through conditioning. Caregivers feed their infants and tend to their other physiological needs. Thus, infants associate their caregivers with gratification and learn to approach them to meet their needs. From this perspective, a caregiver becomes a conditioned reinforcer.

Psychoanalytic Views of Attachment: Caregiver as Love Object

Psychoanalytic theorists view the development of attachment somewhat differently from behaviorists. The caregiver, usually the mother, becomes not just a "reinforcer" but also a love object who forms the basis for all later attachments.

In both the psychoanalytic and behaviorist views, the caregiver's role in gratifying the child's needs is crucial. Sigmund Freud emphasized the importance of oral activities, such as eating, in the first year. Freud believed that the infant becomes emotionally attached to the mother during this time because she is the primary satisfier of the infant's needs for food and sucking.

Erik Erikson believed that the first year is critical for developing a sense of trust in the mother, which fosters attachment. Erikson wrote that the mother's general sensitivity to the child's needs, not just the need for food, fosters the development of trust and attachment.

The Harlows' View of Attachment: The Caregiver as a Source of Contact Comfort

Harry and Margaret Harlow conducted a series of classic experiments to demonstrate that feeding is not as critical to the attachment process as Freud suggested (Harlow & Harlow, 1966). In one study, the Harlows placed rhesus monkey infants in cages with two surrogate mothers (see ● Figure 7.3). One "mother" was made from wire mesh, from which a baby bottle was extended. The other surrogate mother was made of soft, cuddly terry cloth. Infant monkeys spent most of their time clinging to the cloth mother, even though she did not offer food. The Harlows concluded that monkeys—and perhaps humans—have a need for **contact comfort** that is as basic as the need for food.

Ethological View of Attachment: Smiling and Imprinting

Ethologists note that for many animals, attachment is an inborn **fixed action pattern (FAP)**. The FAP of attachment, as with other FAPs, is theorized to occur in the presence of a species-specific **releasing stimulus**. According to John Bowlby, one component of the FAP of attachment in humans—and its releasing stimulus—is a baby's smile in response to a human voice or face (Ainsworth & Bowlby, 1991; Bowlby, 1988). Bowlby proposed that the baby's smile helps ensure survival by eliciting affection from caregivers. By 2 to 3 months of age, the human face begins to elicit a **social smile** in infants (Emde et al., 1976). When her infant looks at her, the mother's social response can reliably produce infant smiling by 8 months of age (Jones & Hong, 2005). The development of smiling seems to follow the same sequence throughout the world (Werner, 1988).

clear-cut-attachment phase The third phase in the development of attachment, occurring at 6 or 7 months of age and characterized by intensified dependence on the primary caregiver.

contact comfort The pleasure derived from physical contact with another; a hypothesized need or drive for physical contact with another.

ethologist A scientist who studies the behavior patterns that are characteristic of various species.

fixed action pattern (FAP) An instinct; a stereotyped behavior pattern that is characteristic of a species and is triggered by a releasing stimulus.

releasing stimulus A stimulus that elicits a fixed action pattern (FAP).

social smile A smile that occurs in response to a human voice or face.

● **Figure 7.3** Contact Comfort: The Source of Attachment in Infant Monkeys

As shown in this classic series of photos, although this rhesus monkey infant is fed by the "wire-mesh mother," it spends most of its time clinging to a soft, cuddly "terry-cloth mother." It knows where to get a meal, but contact comfort is apparently more central to attachment than feeding in infant monkeys (and infant humans?).

In many nonhuman animals, the FAP of attachment apparently occurs during a **critical period** of life. If it does not occur then, it may never do so. During this period, young animals can form an instinctive attachment to caregivers if the releasing stimuli are present. Waterfowl become attached during this period to the first moving object they encounter. The image of the moving object seems to become "imprinted" on the young animal, so this process is termed **imprinting**.

Ethologist Konrad Lorenz (1962, 1981) became well known when pictures of his "family" of goslings were made public (see ● Figure 7.4). How did Lorenz acquire his family? He was present when the goslings hatched and during their critical period, and he allowed them to follow him. The critical period for geese and ducks begins when they first engage in locomotion and ends when they develop fear of strangers. The goslings followed Lorenz persistently, ran to him when frightened, honked with distress at his departure, and tried to overcome barriers placed between them. If you substitute crying for honking, it all sounds rather human.

Ethology, Ainsworth, and Bowlby

Now let us return full circle to Mary D. Salter Ainsworth and John Bowlby (1991). At the beginning of a major retrospective article, they wrote that "the distinguishing characteristic of the theory of attachment that we have jointly developed is that it is an ethological approach to personality development." The theoretical aspects of their work developed almost by accident and have a broad base in the psychological and biological perspectives of their day (Ainsworth & Bowlby, 1991):

> Bowlby intended his contribution as an up-to-date version of psychoanalytic object-relations theory [developed largely by Margaret Mahler], compatible with contemporary ethology [e.g., Lorenz] and evolution theory [e.g., Charles Darwin], supported by research, and helpful to clinicians in understanding and treating child and adult patients. Nevertheless, it was developmental psychologists rather than clinicians who first adopted attachment theory.

critical period A period of development during which a releasing stimulus can elicit a fixed action pattern (FAP).

imprinting The process by which some animals exhibit the fixed action pattern (FAP) of attachment in response to a releasing stimulus. The FAP occurs during a critical period and is difficult to modify.

But theirs is not the attachment theory of Konrad Lorenz. Yes, they, like Lorenz, refer to "releasing stimuli," such as the human face and the crying, smiling, and clinging of infants. But caregiving in humans is largely learned and not inborn. Ainsworth and Bowlby's ethological perspective is also informed by Bowlby's observations of rhesus monkeys (Suomi, 2005). Children and infants of many other species also try to maintain contact with caregivers to whom they have grown attached. When they cannot maintain contact, they show signs of distress: honking and flapping about in geese, whining and barking in dogs, crying and fussing in children.

The critical period for attachment in humans is extended for months or years (Ainsworth & Bowlby, 1991; Verissimo & Salvaterra, 2006). It involves learning and perceptual and cognitive processes. The type of attachment that develops is related to the quality of the caregiver–infant relationship. Caregiving itself and infant responsiveness, such as infant smiling, appear to spur the development of attachment. Theories of attachment are reviewed in Concept Review 7.1 (page 230).

● **Figure 7.4** Imprinting: A Source of Attachment in Etiological Theory

Quite a following? Konrad Lorenz may not look like Mommy to you, but these goslings became attached to him because he was the first moving object they perceived and followed. This type of attachment process is referred to as imprinting.

Active Review

1. Ainsworth defines _____ as an emotional tie that is formed between one animal or person and another specific individual.
2. One of Ainsworth's contributions to the field of child development is the innovation of the _____ method of measuring attachment.
3. Broadly, infants have either secure attachment or _____ attachment.
4. Securely attached infants use the caregiver as a secure base from which to _____ the environment.
5. Ainsworth's study of Ugandan infants found that they at first show _____ attachment.

6. From the _____ perspective, a caregiver becomes a conditioned reinforcer.
7. The Harlows' research with monkeys suggests that _____ comfort is a key source of attachment.
8. Lorenz believed that attachment is an inborn _____ action pattern (FAP).

Reflect & Relate: To which caregiver are you most attached? Why?

Go to

http://www.thomsonedu.com/psychology/rathus
for an interactive version of this review.

When Attachment Fails

We have glimpsed the effects of rearing children in a group setting (a kibbutz) on attachment, but children in a kibbutz continue to have contact with their parents. What happens when children are reared in group settings, such as some orphanages, where they have little or no contact with parents or other caregivers? What happens when parents neglect or abuse their children? In both cases, children's attachments may be impaired. Attachment may fail in some children because of the development of autism spectrum disorders (ASDs). In this section, we consider the effect of social deprivation, child abuse, and ASDs on the development of attachment.

Concept Review 7.1 Theories of Attachment

Theory	Characteristics
Cognitive theory (proponent: Alan Sroufe)	• Emotional development is connected with and relies on cognitive development. • Infant must have developed object permanence before attachment to a specific other becomes possible. • Infant must be able to discriminate familiar people from strangers to develop fear of strangers.
Behaviorism (proponent: John B. Watson)	• Caregiver is a conditioned reinforcer; attachment behaviors are learned through conditioning. • Caregivers meet infants' physiological needs; thus, infants associate caregivers with gratification. • Feelings of gratification associated with meeting needs generalize into feelings of security when the caregiver is present.
Psychoanalytic theory (proponents: Sigmund Freud, Erik Erikson, Margaret Mahler)	• Caregiver is a love object who forms the basis for future attachments. • Infant becomes attached to the mother during infancy because she primarily satisfies the infant's needs for food and sucking (Freud). • First year is critical in developing a sense of trust in the mother, which, in turn, fosters feelings of attachment (Erikson).
Contact comfort (proponents: Harry and Margaret Harlow)	• Caregiver is a source of contact comfort. • Experiments with rhesus monkeys suggest that contact comfort is more crucial than feeding to attachment.

Ethological theory (proponents: Konrad Lorenz, Mary Ainsworth, John Bowlby)	• Attachment is an inborn fixed action pattern (FAP) that occurs in the presence of a species-specific releasing stimulus during a critical period of development (Lorenz).
	 • Waterfowl become attached to the first moving object they encounter (Lorenz).
	 • The image of the moving object becomes "imprinted" on the young animal (Lorenz).
	 • Caregiving in humans is elicited by infants' cries of distress (Bowlby).
	 • The human face is a releasing stimulus that elicits a baby's smile (Bowlby).
	 • Smiling helps ensure survival by eliciting caregiving and feelings of affection (Bowlby).
	 • Attachment in humans is a complex process that continues for months or years (Ainsworth).
	 • The quality of attachment is related to the quality of the caregiver–infant relationship (Ainsworth).
	 • Attachment in humans occurs in stages or phases (Ainsworth):
	   1. The initial-preattachment phase: birth to about 3 months; indiscriminate attachment
	   2. The attachment-in-the-making phase: 3 or 4 months; preference for familiar figures
	   3. The clear-cut-attachment phase; 6 or 7 months; intensified dependence on the primary caregiver.

Social Deprivation

Studies of children reared in institutions where they receive little social stimulation from caregivers are limited in that they are correlational. In other words, family factors that led to the children's placement in institutions may also have contributed to their developmental problems. Ethical considerations prevent us from conducting experiments in which we randomly assign children to social deprivation. However, experiments of this kind have been undertaken with rhesus monkeys, and the results are consistent with those of the correlational studies of children. Let us first examine these animal experiments and then turn to the correlational research involving children.

Experiments with Monkeys

The Harlows and their colleagues conducted studies of rhesus monkeys that were "reared by" wire-mesh and terry-cloth surrogate mothers. In later studies, rhesus monkeys were reared without even this questionable "social" support. They were reared without seeing any other animal, whether monkey or human.

Question: What are the findings of the Harlows' studies on the effects of social deprivation on monkeys? The Harlows (Harlow et al., 1971) found that rhesus infants reared in this most solitary confinement later avoided contact with other monkeys. They did not engage in the characteristic playful chasing and romping. Instead, they cowered in the presence of others and failed to respond to them. Nor did they attempt to fend off attacks by other monkeys. Rather, they sat in the corner, clutching themselves and rocking back and forth. Females who later bore children tended to ignore or abuse them.

Can the damage done by social deprivation be overcome? When monkeys deprived for 6 months or more are placed with younger, 3- to 4-month-old females for a couple of hours a day, the younger monkeys make efforts to initiate social interaction with their deprived elders (see ● Figure 7.5). Many of the deprived monkeys begin to play with the youngsters after a few weeks, and many of them eventually expand their social contacts to other rhesus monkeys of various ages (Suomi et al., 1972). Perhaps of greater interest is the related finding that socially withdrawn 4- and 5-year-old children make gains in their social and emotional development when they are provided with younger playmates (Furman et al., 1979).

Question: What do we know about the effects of social deprivation on humans?

Studies with Children

Institutionalized children whose material needs are met but who receive little social stimulation from caregivers encounter problems in their physical, intellectual, social, and emotional development (Ganesh & Magdalin, 2007; Rutter, 2006a). René A. Spitz (1965) noted that many institutionalized children appear to develop a syndrome

 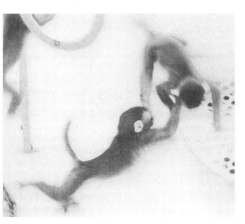

Harlow Primate Laboratory, University of Wisconsin

● **Figure 7.5**
Monkey Therapists

In the left-hand photo, a 3- to 4-month-old rhesus monkey "therapist" tries to soothe a monkey who was reared in social isolation. The deprived monkey remains withdrawn. She clutches herself into a ball and rocks back and forth. The right-hand photo was taken several weeks later and shows that deprived monkeys given young "therapists" can learn to play and adjust to community life. Socially withdrawn preschoolers have similarly profited from exposure to younger peers.

characterized by withdrawal and depression. They show progressively less interest in their world and become progressively inactive. Some of them die.

In one institution, infants were maintained in separate cubicles for most of their first year to ward off infectious diseases (Provence & Lipton, 1962). Adults tended to them only to feed and change their diapers. As a rule, baby bottles were propped up in the infants' cribs. Attendants rarely responded to the babies' cries, and the infants were rarely played with or spoken to. By the age of 4 months, the infants in this institution showed little interest in adults. They rarely tried to gain the adults' attention, even when in distress. A few months later, some of them sat withdrawn in their cribs and rocked back and forth, almost like the Harlows' monkeys. Language deficiencies were striking. As the first year progressed, little babbling was heard within the infants' cubicles. None were speaking even one word at 12 months.

Why do children whose material needs are met show such dramatic deficiencies? Is it because they do not receive the love and affection of a human? Or is it because they do not receive adequate sensory or social stimulation?

The answer may depend, in part, on the age of the child. Classic studies by Leon Yarrow and his colleagues (Yarrow et al., 1971; Yarrow & Goodwin, 1973) suggest that deficiencies in sensory stimulation and social interaction may cause more problems than lack of love in infants who are too young to have developed specific attachments. But once infants have developed specific attachments, separation from their primary caregivers can lead to problems.

In the first study, the development of 53 adopted children was followed over a 10-year period (Yarrow et al., 1971). The researchers compared the development of three subgroups: (1) children who were transferred to their permanent adoptive homes almost immediately after birth, (2) children who were given temporary foster mothers and then transferred to permanent adoptive homes before they were 6 months old, and (3) children who were transferred from temporary foster mothers to their permanent adoptive homes after they were 6 months old. At the age of 10, children in the first two groups showed no differences in social and emotional development. However, children in the third group showed significantly less ability to relate to other people. Perhaps their deficits resulted from being separated from their initial foster mothers after they had become attached to them.

In the second study, Yarrow and Goodwin (1973) followed the development of 70 adopted children who were separated from temporary foster parents between birth and the age of 16 months. The researchers found strong correlations between the age at which the children were separated and feeding and sleeping problems, decreased social responsiveness, and extremes in attachment behaviors (see ● Figure 7.6). Disturbed attachment behaviors included excessive clinging to the new mother and violent rejection of her. None of the children who were separated from the initial foster mothers before the age of 3 months showed moderate or severe disturbances. All the children who were separated at 9 months or older did show such disturbances. Forty percent to ninety percent of the children separated between the ages of 3 and 9 months showed moderate to severe disturbances. The incidence of problems increased as the age advanced.

The Yarrow studies suggest that babies in institutions, at least up to the age of 3 months or so, may require general sensory and social stimulation more than a

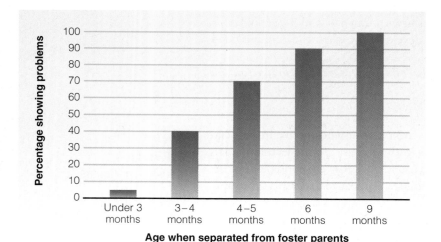

Age when separated from foster parents

● **Figure 7.6**

The Development of Adopted Children Separated from Temporary Foster Parents

The older the child at the time of separation, the more likely it is that behavioral disturbances will occur.

Source: Yarrow & Goodwin (1973).

specific relationship with a primary caregiver. After the age of 3 months, some disturbance is likely if there is instability in the care-giving staff. By the ages of 6 to 9 months, disturbance seems to be guaranteed if there is instability in the position of primary caregiver. Fortunately, there is also evidence that children show some capacity to recover from early social deprivation.

The Capacity to Recover from Social Deprivation

Studies with animals and children show that early social deprivation is linked to developmental deficits. But the research also suggests that infants also have powerful capacities to recover from deprivation.

One study showed how many children may be able to recover fully from 13 or 14 months of deprivation (Kagan & Klein, 1973). The natives in an isolated Guatemalan village believe that fresh air and sunshine will make children ill. Thus, children are kept in windowless huts until they can walk. They are played with infrequently. During their isolation, the infants behave apathetically; they are physically and socially retarded when they start to walk. But by 11 years of age they are alert, active, and as intellectually able as American children of the same age.

A classic longitudinal study of orphanage children also offers evidence of the ability of children to recover from social deprivation (Skeels, 1966). In this study, a group of 19-month-old apparently retarded children were placed in the care of older institutionalized girls. The girls spent a great deal of time playing with, talking to, and nurturing them. Four years after being placed with the girls, the "retarded" children made dramatic gains in intelligence test scores, whereas children remaining in the orphanage showed declines in IQ.

The children placed in the care of the older girls also appeared to be generally well adjusted. By the time Skeels reported on their progress in 1966, most were married and were rearing children of their own who showed no intellectual or social deficits. Unfortunately, many of the children who had been left in the orphanage were still in some type of institutional setting. Few of them showed normal social and emotional development. Few were functioning as independent adults.

The good news is that many children who have been exposed to early social deprivation can catch up in their social and emotional development and lead normal adult lives if they receive individual attention and environmental stimulation (Rutter, 2006a). The bad news is that society has not yet allocated the resources to give all children the opportunity to do so.

Child Abuse and Neglect

We have considered the results of rearing children in settings in which contact with parents is reduced or absent. Yet living with one's parents does not guarantee that a child will receive tender loving care. Sadly, sometimes there's no place like home—for violence. *Questions: What are the incidences of child abuse and neglect? What are their effects?* Consider the following statistics from national surveys by Straus and his colleagues (Straus & Field, 2003; Straus & Stewart, 1999):

- By the time a child is 2 years of age, 90% of parents have engaged in some sort of psychological or emotional abuse.
- 55% of parents have slapped or spanked their children.
- 31% of parents have pushed, grabbed, or shoved their children.
- 10% have hit their children with an object.
- 3% have thrown something at their children.
- 1% or less of parents have kicked or bitten their children or hit them with their fists, threatened their children with a knife or a gun, or actually used a knife or a gun on their children.

Mexican University Students Protest against Child Abuse

Nearly 3 million American children are neglected or abused each year by their parents or caregivers (U.S. Department of Health and Human Services, 2004). About one in six of these children experiences serious injury. Thousands die. Physical abuse is more prevalent among poor and among southern parents (Straus & Stewart, 1999). Boys are more likely than girls to be hit, and the mother is more likely than the father to be the aggressor, perhaps because she spends more time than the father with the children (Straus & Stewart, 1999). More than 150,000 of the 3 million are sexually abused (Letourneau et al., 2004; U.S. Department of Health and Human Services, 2004). But researchers believe that 50–60% of cases of child abuse and neglect go unreported, so the actual incidences are higher (U.S. Department of Health and Human Services, 2004).

The U.S. Department of Health and Human Services recognizes six types of maltreatment of children:

- Physical abuse: actions causing pain and physical injury
- Sexual abuse: sexual molestation, exploitation, and intercourse
- Emotional abuse: actions impairing the child's emotional, social, or intellectual functioning
- Physical neglect: failure to provide adequate food, shelter, clothing, or medical care
- Emotional neglect: failure to provide adequate nurturance and emotional support
- Educational neglect: permitting or forcing the child to be truant

Physical neglect is more common (38%) than active physical abuse (30%) (U.S. Department of Health and Human Services, 2004). Although blatant abuse is more horrifying, more injuries, illnesses, and deaths result from neglect (U.S. Department of Health and Human Services, 2004).

Sexual Abuse of Children

No one knows how many children are sexually abused (Hines & Finkelhor, 2007; Finkelhor et al., 2005a, 2005b). Although most sexually abused children are girls, one quarter to one third are boys (Edwards et al., 2003). Interviews with 8,667 adult members of an HMO suggest that the prevalence of sexual abuse among boys is about 18% and among girls it is 25% (Edwards et al., 2003). These estimates may underrepresent the actual prevalence because people may fail to report incidents due to faulty memory, shame, or embarrassment.

Sexual abuse of children ranges from exhibitionism, kissing, fondling, and sexual touching to oral sex and anal intercourse and, with girls, vaginal intercourse. Acts such as touching children's sexual organs while changing or bathing them, sleeping with children, or appearing nude before them are open to interpretation and are often innocent (Haugaard, 2000).

Effects of Child Abuse

Abused children show a high incidence of personal and social problems and psychological disorders (Letourneau et al., 2004). In general, abused children are less securely attached to their parents. They are less intimate with their peers and are more aggressive, angry, and noncompliant than other children (Joshi et al., 2006). They rarely express positive emotions, have lower self-esteem, and show impaired cognitive functioning, leading to poorer performance in school (Shonk & Cicchetti, 2001). When they reach adulthood, they are more likely to act aggressively toward their intimate partners (Malinosky-Rummell & Hansen, 1993). As they mature, maltreated children are at greater risk for delinquency, academic failure, and substance abuse (Eckenrode et al., 1993; Haapasalo & Moilanen, 2004).

There is no single concrete identifiable syndrome—cluster of symptoms—that indicates a history of physical abuse or neglect or sexual abuse (Saywitz et al., 2000). More generally, however, there seems to be little doubt that victims of child sexual abuse develop a higher incidence of psychological and physical health problems than other children (Saywitz et al., 2000). Child sexual abuse, as with physical abuse, also appears to have lingering effects on children's relationships in adulthood. For one thing, sexually abused children are more likely to engage in risky sexual behavior later in life (Letourneau et al., 2004; Noll et al., 2000). Abusive experiences at the hands of adults also color children's expectation of other adults.

Causes of Child Abuse

A number of factors contribute to the probability that parents will abuse their children. These factors include situational stress, a history of child abuse in at least one of the parents' families of origin, lack of adequate coping and problem-solving skills, de-

A CLOSER LOOK

Prevention of Sexual Abuse of Children

Many of us were taught by our parents never to accept a ride or an offer of candy from a stranger. Unfortunately, many instances of sexual abuse are perpetrated by familiar adults, often a family member or friend (Ullman, 2007). Prevention programs help children understand what sexual abuse is and how they can avoid it. In addition to learning to avoid strangers, children need to recognize the differences between acceptable touching, as in an affectionate embrace or pat on the head, and unacceptable or "bad" touching. Even elementary-school-age children can learn the distinction between good touching and bad touching. School-based programs can help prepare children handle an actual encounter with a molester. Children who receive training are more likely to use strategies such as running away, yelling, or saying no if they are threatened by an abuser. They are also more likely to report incidents to adults.

Researchers recognize that children can easily be intimidated or overpowered by adults or older children (Miller, 2005). Children may be unable to say no in a sexually abusive situation, even though they want to and know it is the right thing to do. Although children may not always be able to prevent abuse, they can be encouraged to tell someone about it. Most prevention programs emphasize teaching children messages such as: it's not

your fault; never keep a bad or scary secret; and always tell your parents about this, especially if someone says you shouldn't tell them.

Children also need to be alerted to the types of threats they might receive for disclosing the abuse. They are more likely to resist threats if they are reassured that they will be believed if they disclose the abuse, that their parents will continue to love them, and that they and their families will be protected from the molester.

School-based prevention programs focus on protecting the child. In most states, teachers and helping professionals are required to report suspected abuse to authorities. Tighter controls and better screening are needed to monitor the hiring of day-care employees. Administrators and teachers in preschool and day-care facilities also need to be educated to recognize the signs of sexual abuse and to report suspected cases. Treatment programs to help people who are sexually attracted to children *before* they commit abusive acts would also be of use.

Reflect: How would you attempt to teach a child the difference between good touching and bad touching?

ficiency in child-rearing skills, unrealistic expectations of what a child should be able to do at a given developmental level, and substance abuse (Maluccio & Ainsworth, 2003; Merrill et al., 2004).

Stress has many sources, including such life changes as parental conflict and divorce or separation, the loss of a job, moving, and the birth of a new family member. Unemployment seems to be a particularly predisposing life change. Child abuse increases among the unemployed (Joshi et al., 2006).

Stress is created by crying infants themselves (Green et al., 1987). Ironically, infants who are already in pain of some kind and relatively difficult to soothe may be more likely to be abused (Frodi, 1985). Abusive parents may find the cries of their infants to be particularly aversive and so the infants' crying may precipitate abusive behavior (Schuetze & Zeskind, 2001; Schuetze et al., 2003). Ironically, mothers who are deeply depressed or using cocaine may neglect crying infants because they perceive the cries to be less aversive (Schuetze & Zeskind, 2001; Schuetze et al., 2003). Children who act disobediently, inappropriately, or unresponsively also are at greater risk of abuse (Bugental & Happaney, 2004). Why? Because parents tend to become frustrated and irritated when their children show prolonged signs of distress or misbehavior. Abusive mothers are more likely than nonabusive mothers to assume that their children's misbehavior is intentional, even when it is not (Bugental & Happaney, 2004). Within the American culture, intentional misconduct is seen as more deserving of punishment than incidental misconduct. Abusive mothers also tend to believe that they have little control over their child's misbehavior (Bugental & Happaney, 2004).

What of the role of failure of attachment in abuse? The parents of preterm children have more difficulty becoming attached to them (see Chapter 4). One reason may be that the early parent–infant relationship is interrupted by hospital procedures. Preterm children are more likely than their full-term counterparts to be abused (Crittenden & Ainsworth, 1989). With prematurity, of course, we are not only dealing with possible failures in attachment. Preterm children are also more likely to develop illnesses and other problems. As a consequence, they may cry more frequently and generally make more demands on their parents.

Truth or Fiction Revisited: It is true that child abusers have frequently been the victims of child abuse themselves (Ertem et al., 2000; White & Smith, 2004). Nevertheless, most people who were abused as children do not abuse their own children (Kaufman & Zigler, 1992). Still, many adults who were victims of child abuse worry that they are destined to abuse their own children. One study found that abused mothers who broke the cycle were more likely to have received emotional support from a nonabusive adult during childhood, to have participated in therapy at some point, and to have had a supportive mate (Egeland et al., 1988).

Question: Why does child abuse run in families? There are a number of reasons child abuse runs in families (White & Smith, 2004). One is that parents serve as role models for their children. As noted by Murray Straus (1995), spanking teaches children that when people are doing something one does not like and won't stop, the thing to do is to hit them. If children grow up observing their parents using violence as a means of coping with stress and feelings of anger, they are less likely to learn to diffuse anger through techniques such as humor, verbal expression of feelings, reasoning, or even counting to 10 to let the anger pass.

Exposure to violence in their own homes may lead some children to accept family violence as a norm. They may see nothing wrong with it. Certainly, parents can find any number of "justifications" for violence, if they seek them. One is the adage, "Spare the rod, spoil the child." Another is the belief that they are hurting their children "for their own good," that is, to discourage behavior that is likely to get them into trouble.

Still another "justification" of child abuse is the sometimes cloudy distinction between the occasional swat on the rear end and spanking. Child abusers may argue that all parents hit their children (which is not true), and they may claim not to understand why outsiders are making such a fuss about private family behavior. Child abusers who were subjected to abuse also may harbor the (incorrect) belief that "everyone does it."

A CLOSER LOOK

How Child Abuse May Set the Stage for Psychological Disorders in Adulthood

There is a significant correlation between child abuse and psychological disorders in adulthood, but the causal connections have remained somewhat clouded. But now two bodily systems likely pave the route from child abuse to psychological disorders in adulthood (e.g., Newport et al., 2004; Penza et al., 2006). One is the autonomic nervous system (ANS), which is intimately involved in stress reactions and negative emotions such as anxiety and fear. The other system is the endocrine system, which consists of ductless glands that release hormones directly into the bloodstream. The sex hormones estrogen and testosterone stoke the development of the sexual organs, and estrogen and progesterone regulate the menstrual cycle. The pituitary hormones oxytocin and prolactin are involved in childbirth and breast feeding. Other hormones—so-called stress hormones—are released when the body is under stress. And child abuse is a most prominent stressor.

Researchers assess the individual's responses to stress by measuring the quantities of stress hormones in bodily fluids, such as blood or saliva. One such hormone is the pituitary hormone ACTH, which, in a sort of domino effect, stimulates the cortex (outer layer) of the adrenal glands to release corticosteroids, such as cortisol. Corticosteroids increase resistance to stress in ways such as promoting muscle development and causing the liver to release stored sugar, which makes more energy available in emergencies. The sympathetic division of the ANS goes into overdrive under stress, as can be measured by the heart rate, the blood pressure, muscle tension, and sweating.

A study conducted by Christine Heim and her colleagues (2000) recruited 49 women (mean age = 35 years). The sample was selected to have a high number of women who had suffered child abuse and who were currently depressed. In interviews, 27 of the recruits reported that they had experienced physical and/or sexual abuse in childhood, whereas the other 22 had not. In addition, 23 of the group members were experiencing major depressive episodes at the time of the study, compared with 26 who were not. All the participants in the experiment were exposed to a stressor that other studies had shown to stimulate reactions of the endocrine system and the ANS. The women were given the task of making a speech in front of strangers; moreover, the speech would entail doing mental arithmetic. The women's levels of stress hormones and heart rates were measured while the women anticipated and made the speeches.

Results of the experiment are shown in ■ Table 7.1 on page 238, which reports the participants' blood levels of ACTH and cortisol and their heart rates. When we consider women who did not experience child abuse (Groups A and B), the presence of depression did not make a significant difference. Now consider the two groups of women who had been abused as children (Groups C and D). When they were subjected to the stressor, they were significantly more likely to show high blood levels of ACTH and cortisol than women who had not been abused as children (women in Groups A and B). The women in Group D showed the greatest hormonal and cardiac responses to the stressor, and they were women who (1) had been abused as children and (2) were undergoing a major depressive episode. The researchers concluded that child abuse leads to more reactive endocrine and autonomic nervous systems and that a combination of abuse and depression makes the body most reactive to stress.

These stress reactions exhaust the body. Women who were abused as children are apparently carrying a historic burden that makes current burdens all the more unbearable.

Reflect: What does biology contribute to our understanding of psychology? How can biological changes in childhood set the stage for psychological reactions in adulthood?

■ Table 7.1 Responses of Women With or Without a History of Child Abuse to a Stressor

History of Child Abuse	Women Who Are Not Experiencing a Major Depressive Episode	Women Who Are Experiencing a Major Depressive Episode
Women with no history of child abuse	*Group A: 12 Women* Endocrine system • ACTH peak: 4.7 parts/liter • Cortisol peak: 339 parts/liter Autonomic nervous system • Heart rate: 78.4/minute	*Group B: 10 Women* Endocrine system • ACTH peak: 5.3 parts/liter • Cortisol peak: 337 parts/liter Autonomic nervous system • Heart rate: 83.8/minute
Women with a history of child abuse	*Group C: 14 Women* Endocrine system • ACTH peak: 9.3 parts/liter • Cortisol peak: 359 parts/liter Autonomic nervous system • Heart rate: 82.2/minute	*Group D: 13 Women* Endocrine system • ACTH peak: 12.1 parts/liter • Cortisol peak: 527 parts/liter Autonomic nervous system • Heart rate: 89.7/minute

The patterns of attachment of the perpetrators of child abuse have also been studied. One study, for example, found that nonfamilial perpetrators of sexual child abuse were significantly less likely to have a secure attachment style in their relationships (Jamieson & Marshall, 2000).

In any event, child abuse must be conceptualized and dealt with as a crime of violence. Whether or not child abusers happen to be victims of abuse themselves, child abusers are criminals and children must be protected from them.

What to Do

Dealing with child abuse is a frustrating task. Social agencies and the courts can find it as difficult to distinguish between spanking and abuse, as many abusers do. Because of the belief in the United States that parents have the right to rear their children as they wish, police and the courts have also historically tried to avoid involvement in domestic quarrels and family disputes. However, the alarming incidence of child abuse has spawned new efforts at detection and prevention. Many states require helping professionals such as psychologists and physicians to report any suspicion of child abuse. Many states legally require *anyone* who suspects child abuse to report it to authorities.

A number of techniques have been developed to help prevent child abuse. One approach focuses on strengthening parenting skills among the general population (Joshi et al., 2006). Parent-education classes in high school are an example of this approach.

Another approach targets groups at high risk for abuse, such as poor, single teen mothers (Joshi et al., 2006). In some programs, for example, home visitors help new parents develop skills in caregiving and home management (Duggan et al., 2004).

A third technique focuses on presenting information about abuse and providing support to families. For instance, many locales have child abuse hotlines. Private citizens who suspect child abuse may call for advice. Parents who are having difficulty controlling aggressive impulses toward their children are encouraged to call. Some hotlines are serviced by groups such as Parents Anonymous, whose members have had similar difficulties and can help callers diffuse feelings of anger in less harmful ways.

Another helpful measure is increased publicity on the dimensions of the child abuse problem. The public may also need more education about where an occasional swat on the behind ends and child abuse begins. Perhaps the format for such education could be something like, "If you are doing such and such, make no mistake about it: You are abusing your child."

A Closer Look

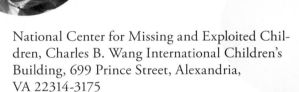

What to Do If You Think a Child Has Been the Victim of Sexual Abuse

What can you do if you suspect that a child has been victimized by sexual abuse? The American Psychological Association (APA) suggests the following guidelines:

- Give the child a safe environment in which to talk to you or another trusted adult. Encourage the child to talk about what he or she has experienced, but be careful to not suggest events to him or her that may not have happened. Guard against displaying emotions that would influence the child's telling of the information.
- Reassure the child that he or she did nothing wrong.
- Seek mental health assistance for the child.
- Arrange for a medical examination for the child. Select a medical provider who has experience in examining children and identifying sexual and physical trauma. It may be necessary to explain to the child the difference between a medical examination and the abuse incident.
- Be aware that many states have laws requiring that persons who know or have a reason to suspect that a child has been sexually abused must report that abuse to either local law enforcement officials or child protection officials. In all 50 states, medical personnel, mental health professionals, teachers, and law enforcement personnel are required by law to report suspected abuse.

The American Psychological Association also lists the following resources:

American Professional Society on the Abuse of Children, 407 South Dearborn, Suite 1300, Chicago, IL 60605 (312) 554-0166
www.apsac.org

National Center for Missing and Exploited Children, Charles B. Wang International Children's Building, 699 Prince Street, Alexandria, VA 22314-3175
24-hour hotline: 1-800-THE-LOST
www.missingkids.com

Child Help USA, 15757 North 78th Street, Scottsdale, AZ 85260
1-800-4-A-CHILD
www.childhelpusa.org

National Clearinghouse on Child Abuse and Neglect Information, U.S. Department of Health and Human Services, P.O. Box 1182, Washington, DC 20013
1-800-FYI-3366
www.calib.com/nccanch

Prevent Child Abuse America, 332 S. Michigan Ave., Suite 1600, Chicago, IL 60604-4357
1-800-CHILDREN
www.preventchildabuse.org

Reflect: In most states, helping professionals are required by law to report suspected cases of child abuse to authorities. Do you think that all adults should be required by law to reported suspected cases of child abuse to authorities? Why or why not?

Guidelines from Office of Public Communications, American Psychological Association, 750 First Street, NE, Washington DC 20002-4242.
(202) 336-5700. www.apa.org/releases/sexabuse/todo.html.
Copyright © American Psychological Association.
Reprinted by permission.

Autism Spectrum Disorders: Alone among the Crowd

Question: What are autism spectrum disorders? **Autism spectrum disorders (ASDs)** are characterized by impairment in communication skills, social interactions, and repetitive, stereotyped behavior (Strock, 2004) (■ Table 7.2). They tend to become evident by the age of 3 years and sometimes before the end of the first year. A CDC study of 407,578 children from 14 different areas in the United States found that about one in every 152 children was identified as having an ASD (Rice et al., 2007). There are several variations of ASDs, but autism is the major type and is the focus here. Other forms of ASDs include the following:

- *Asperger's disorder.* An ASD characterized by social deficits and stereotyped behavior but without the significant cognitive or language delays associated with autism.
- *Rett's disorder.* An ASD characterized by a range of physical, behavioral, motor, and cognitive abnormalities that begins after a few months of apparently normal development.
- *Childhood disintegrative disorder.* An ASD involving abnormal functioning and loss of previously acquired skills that begins after about 2 years of apparently normal development.

autism spectrum disorders (ASDs) Developmental disorders—including autism, Asperger's syndrome, Rett's disorder, and childhood disintegrative disorder—that are characterized by impairment in communication skills, social interactions, and repetitive, stereotyped behavior. Also referred to as pervasive developmental disorders.

Autism

Peter nursed eagerly, sat and walked at the expected ages. Yet some of his behavior made us vaguely uneasy. He never put anything in his mouth. Not his fingers nor his toys—nothing. . . .

More troubling was the fact that Peter didn't look at us, or smile, and wouldn't play the games that seemed as much a part of babyhood as diapers. He rarely laughed, and when he did, it was at things that didn't seem funny to us. He didn't cuddle, but sat upright in my lap, even when I rocked him. But children differ and we were content to let Peter be himself. We thought it hilarious when my brother, visiting us when Peter was 8 months old, observed, "That kid has no social instincts, whatsoever." Although Peter was a

■ **Table 7.2** Characteristics of Autism Spectrum Disorders (ASDs)

Key Indicators
• Does not babble, point, or make meaningful gestures by 1 year of age
• Does not speak one word by 16 months
• Does not combine two words by 2 years
• Does not respond to name
• Loses language or social skills

Other Indicators
• Poor eye contact
• Doesn't seem to know how to play with toys
• Excessively lines up toys or other objects
• Is attached to one particular toy or object
• Doesn't smile
• At times seems to be hearing impaired

Source: Adapted from Strock (2004).

first child, he was not isolated. I frequently put him in his playpen in front of the house, where the schoolchildren stopped to play with him as they passed. He ignored them, too.

It was Kitty, a personality kid, born two years later, whose responsiveness emphasized the degree of Peter's difference. When I went into her room for the late feeding, her little head bobbed up and she greeted me with a smile that reached from her head to her toes. And the realization of that difference chilled me more than the wintry bedroom.

Peter's babbling had not turned into speech by the time he was 3. His play was solitary and repetitious. He tore paper into long thin strips, bushel baskets of it every day. He spun the lids from my canning jars and became upset if we tried to divert him. Only rarely could I catch his eye, and then saw his focus change from me to the reflection in my glasses. . . .

[Peter's] adventures into our suburban neighborhood had been unhappy. He had disregarded the universal rule that sand is to be kept in sandboxes, and the children themselves had punished him. He walked around a sad and solitary figure, always carrying a toy airplane, a toy he never played with. At that time, I had not heard the word that was to dominate our lives, to hover over every conversation, to sit through every meal beside us. That word was autism.

—Adapted from Eberhardy (1967)

Peter, the boy with "no social instincts," was autistic. *Question: What is autism?* The word *autism* derives from the Greek *autos*, meaning "self." (An automobile is a self-driven method of moving from place to place.) **Autism** is four to five times more common among boys than girls. Perhaps the most poignant feature of autism is the child's utter aloneness (Constantino et al., 2006). Autistic children do not show interest in social interaction and may avoid eye contact. Attachment to others is weak or absent.

Other features of autism include communication problems, intolerance of change, and ritualistic or stereotypical behavior (Georgiades et al., 2007). Parents of autistic children frequently report that they were "good babies," which usually means that they made few demands. But as autistic children develop, they tend to shun affectionate contacts such as hugging, cuddling, and kissing.

Development of speech lags in autistic children (Mackic-Magyar & McCracken, 2004). There is little babbling and communicative gesturing during the first year. Autistic children may show **mutism, echolalia**, and pronoun reversal, referring to themselves as "you" or "he." About half use language by middle childhood, but their speech is unusual and troubled (Dobbinson et al., 2003).

Autistic children become bound by ritual (Georgiades et al., 2007). Even slight changes in routines or the environment may cause distress. The teacher of a 5-year-old autistic girl would greet her each morning with, "Good morning, Lily, I am very, very glad to see you." Lily would ignore the greeting, but she would shriek if the teacher omitted even one of the *verys*. This feature of autism is termed "preservation of sameness." When familiar objects are moved from their usual places, children with autism may throw tantrums or cry until they are restored. They may insist on eating the same food every day. Autistic children show deficits in peer play, imaginative play, imitation, and emotional expression. Many sleep less than their age-mates (Georgiades et al., 2007).

Some autistic children mutilate themselves, even as they cry out in pain. They may bang their heads, slap their faces, bite their hands and shoulders, or pull out their hair.

Question: What are the origins of autism spectrum disorders?

Autism

The most poignant feature of autism is the child's utter aloneness. Autism is rather rare, but it is more common in boys than in girls. Symptoms include communication problems, intolerance of any change, and ritualistic or stereotypical behavior.

autism An autism spectrum disorder characterized by extreme aloneness, communication problems, intolerance of change, and ritualistic behavior.

mutism Inability or refusal to speak.

echolalia The automatic repetition of sounds or words.

Causes of Autism Spectrum Disorders

Some theorists argue that children develop ASDs in response to parental rejection. From this viewpoint, autistic behavior shuts out the cold outside world. But research evidence shows that the parents of autistic children are not deficient in child rearing (Mackic-Magyar & McCracken, 2004).

Various lines of evidence suggest a key role for biological factors in autism. For example, very low birth weight and advanced maternal age may heighten the risk of autism (Maimburg & Væth, 2006). A role for genetic mechanisms is suggested by kinship studies (Constantino et al., 2006; Gutknecht, 2001; Plomin, 2001). For example, the concordance (agreement) rates for ASDs are about 60% among pairs of identical (monozygotic) twins, who fully share their genetic heritage, compared with about 10% for pairs of fraternal (dizygotic) twins, whose genetic codes overlap by only 50% (Plomin et al., 1994). Twin status appears to increase susceptibility to the symptoms of autism, especially among males (Ho et al., 2005). Researchers suspect that multiple genes are involved in ASDs and interact with other factors, environmental, biological, or a combination of the two.

Biological factors focus on neurological involvement. Many children with ASDs have abnormal brain wave patterns or seizures (Canitano, 2007; Roulet-Perez & Deonna; 2006). Other researchers have found that, compared with others, the brains of children with ASDs have abnormal sensitivities to neurotransmitters such as serotonin, dopamine, acetylcholine, and norepinephrine (Bauman et al., 2006). Other researchers note unusual activity in the motor region of the cerebral cortex (R. Mueller et al., 2001) and less activity in some other areas of the brain, including the frontal and temporal lobes and the limbic system (Lam et al., 2006; Penn, 2006). Still other researchers link autism to disorders of the immune system that they believe originate during prenatal development (Zimmerman et al., 2006).

Truth or Fiction Revisited: While we are discussing biological factors in causation, let us delete one. It has been widely believed—it is almost something of a myth—that vaccines or the mercury preservative used in a number of vaccines is a cause of autism. But let us note, rather strongly, that there is *no* scientific evidence for this view, regardless of whether or not it is widely held (Richler et al., 2006; Taylor, 2006).

All in all, it seems rather clear that we can consider autism to be a disease of the brain and that parents of children with autism should not be blaming themselves. Moreover, although researchers have found many biological abnormalities among children with autism, not every child has every abnormality. Although it appears that heredity creates a vulnerability to autism, the other conditions that interact with heredity to produce autistic behavior and various neurobiological signs of autism remain unknown.

Treatment of Autism Spectrum Disorders

Question: What can be done to help children with autism spectrum disorders? Treatment for ASDs is mainly based on principles of learning, although investigation of biological approaches is also under way (Strock, 2004). Behavior modification has been used to increase the child's ability to attend to others, to play with other children, and to discourage self-mutilation. Brief bursts of mild, harmless electric shock rapidly eliminate self-mutilation (Lovaas, 1977). The use of electric shock raises serious moral, ethical, and legal concerns, but O. Ivar Lovaas has countered that failure to eliminate self-injurious behavior places the child at yet greater risk.

Because children with ASDs show behavioral deficits, behavior modification is used to help them develop new behavior. **Truth or Fiction Revisited:** For example, many autistic children do respond to people as though they were furniture. They run around them rather than relate to them as people. But many autistic children can be taught to accept people as reinforcers, for example, by pairing praise with food treats (Drasgow et al., 2001). Praise can then be used to encourage speech and social play.

The most effective treatment programs focus on individualized instruction to correct behavioral, educational, and communication deficits (Rapin, 1997). In a classic study conducted by Lovaas at UCLA (Lovaas et al., 1989), autistic children received more than 40 hours of one-to-one behavior modification a week for at least 2 years. Significant intellectual and educational gains were reported for 9 of the 19 children (47%) in the program. The children who improved achieved normal scores on intelligence tests and succeeded in first grade. Only 2% of an untreated control group achieved similar gains. Treatment gains were maintained at a follow-up at the age of 11 (McEachin et al., 1993). Somewhat less intensive educational programs have also yielded positive results with many autistic toddlers (Stahmer et al., 2004).

Biological approaches for the treatment of ASDs are under study. Drugs that enhance serotonin activity (selective serotonin reuptake inhibitors, or SSRIs, such as those used to treat depression) can help prevent self-injury, aggressive outbursts, depression and anxiety, and repetitive behavior (Kwok, 2003). Drugs that are usually used to treat schizophrenia—the "major tranquilizers"—are helpful with stereotyped behavior, hyperactivity, and self-injury but not with cognitive and language problems (Kwok, 2003; McClellan & Werry, 2003; Volkmar, 2001).

Autistic behavior generally continues into adulthood to one degree or another. Nevertheless, some autistic children go on to achieve college degrees and function independently (Rapin, 1997). Others need continuous treatment, which may include institutionalized care.

We have been examining the development of attachment and some of the circumstances that may interfere with its development. In recent years, a lively debate has sprung up concerning the effects of day care on children's attachment and on their social and cognitive development. Let us turn now to a consideration of these issues.

Active Review

9. The Harlows found that rhesus infants reared in isolation later (Sought or Avoided?) contact with other monkeys.
10. Spitz noted that many institutionalized children appear to develop a syndrome characterized by _____ and depression.
11. Relatively more deaths occur from (Physical abuse or Neglect?).
12. Children with _____ do not show interest in social interaction, have communication problems, are intolerant of change, and display repetitive behavior.

Reflect & Relate: What would you do if you learned that the child of a neighbor was being abused? What would you do if you were a teacher and learned that a child in your class was being abused?

Go to

http://www.thomsonedu.com/psychology/rathus

for an interactive version of this review.

Day Care

Looking for a phrase that can strike fear in the hearts of millions of American parents? Try day care. Only a relatively small percentage of American families still fits the conventional model where the father works and the mother stays at home and cares for the children. Nowadays, most mothers, including those with infants, are in the workforce (Carey, 2007a). As a result, millions of American parents are obsessed with trying to find proper day care.

When both parents spend the day on the job, the children—at least young children—must be taken care of by others. What happens to them? According to the Children's Defense Fund (in Carey, 2007), of the more than 10 million American children under the age of 5, more than 20% are cared for in day-care centers.

Questions: Does day care affect children's bonds of attachment with their parents? Does it affect their social and cognitive development?

How Does Day Care Affect Bonds of Attachment?

Many parents wonder whether day care will affect their children's attachment to them. Are such concerns valid? This issue has been hotly debated. Some studies have found that infants who are in full-time day care are more likely than children in part-time day care or children cared for in the home to show insecure attachment (Brandtjen & Verny, 2001). Some developmentalists conclude that a mother who works full time puts her infant at risk for developing emotional insecurity (Belsky, 1990a, 1990b). Others note that infants whose mothers work may become less distressed by her departure and less likely to seek her out when she returns as time goes on, thus providing the appearance of being less attached. Also keep in mind that the likelihood of insecure attachment is not much greater in infants placed in day care than in those cared for in the home. Most infants in both groups are securely attached (Timmerman, 2006).

How Does Day Care Influence Social and Cognitive Development?

Day care has mixed effects on children's social and cognitive development. Infants with day-care experience are more peer oriented and play at higher developmental levels than do home-reared infants. Children in good quality day care are more likely to share their toys. They are more independent, self-confident, outgoing, and affectionate as well as more helpful and cooperative with peers and adults (Lamb & Ahnert, 2006; Pierce & Vandell, 2006). Participation in day care also is associated with better school performance during the elementary school years (Belsky, 2006b).

The National Institute on Child Health and Human Development Study

An ongoing study funded by the National Institute on Child Health and Human Development (NICHD) compared the development of children in "high-quality" day care with that of children in low-quality day care and with that of children reared in the home by their mothers. The quality of the day care was defined in terms of the richness of the learning environment (availability of toys, books, and other materials), the ratio of caregivers to children (high quality meant more caregivers), the amount of individual attention received by the child (more was better), and the extent to which caregivers talked to the children and asked them questions (again, more was better). The researchers found that high-quality day care resulted in scores on tests of language and cognitive skills that rivaled or exceeded those of the children reared in the home by their mothers (Belsky, 2006b; Belsky et al., 2007).

A Closer Look

The Latest Shoe to Drop on Day Care from the NICHD

Just when parents were sort of forgetting about the NICHD study reported in 2001, which indicated that 17% of children who were in child care for more than 30 hours a week behaved more aggressively in school than children cared for in the home, along came the 2007 report that underscored the idea. In the more recent report, teacher ratings found that once children who were in day care are in school, they are significantly more likely than children cared for in the home by parents or relatives to interrupt in class and tease or bully other children (Belsky et al., 2007). As in the study reported in 2001 (Belsky et al., 2001), the degree of disturbance generally remained "within normal limits." That is, the children who had been in day care could not be labeled criminals and were not being expelled or spending their days in the principal's office. Nevertheless, their conduct—as a group—was measurably different.

A striking finding was that *the quality of the day-care center made no difference* in the more current data: Children from high-quality day-care centers were also more likely to be disruptive than children cared for in the home. Moreover, the study tracked the children through the sixth grade and found that the measurable difference in disturbing behavior lasted throughout primary school.

Noting that the findings held even for so-called high-quality day-care centers, where there was a low ratio of well-trained staff to children and academic instruction, Jay Belsky (in Carey, 2007a), the first author of the study, raised a troubling **Question: "*So what happens in classrooms, schools, playgrounds and communities when more and more children, at younger and younger ages, spend more and more time in centers, many that are indisputably of limited quality?*"**

Now that we have probably frightened many readers who are parents or who will be parents, let us list some limitations of the study, or at least factors to be considered, along with the results:

- Although the differences in disruptive behavior between children in full time day care and those cared for in the home are statistically significant—meaning that they are unlikely to be due to chance—they are not large. The disruptiveness of the great majority of children from day-care programs was "within normal limits."

- The study implies cause and effect—that day care causes the disruptive behavior of concern later on—but there is no control group (Harris, 2007). Children are not assigned at random to day care or care in the home. Parents or other guardians make that choice. Therefore, as noted by Taylor (2007), it is possible that children placed in day care are those whose parents are also most stressed by their work and who continue to be most stressed through their children's primary school years.

- Or, as suggested by Harris (2007), parents not only select day care for their children, but also the program that seems best suited for their children. Thus, it might be that parents of quiet, timid children are reluctant to place their children in noisy, busy centers and that the placement of bold, extroverted children in such centers is responsible for the slight but measurable effect noted in the study.

- And, as suggested by Lederman (2007), it is also possible that children placed in the open play space of the day-care environment learn coping skills that ill suit them later on for the restricted spaces they are allotted within the classroom.

- Then, too, as Kulp (2007) suggests, who says that so-called disruptive children—especially those who remain within normal limits—become "less productive and successful adults"? She wonders if they are destined, rather, to become "assertive and entrepreneurial," especially, we might add, because their cognitive skills and other social skills are apparently intact.

Reflect:

- Does it seem reasonable to you that even high-quality day care can have some "negative effects" on the child's social development? Why or why not?

- Why might high-quality day care have "negative effects" on social development at the same time it has positive effects on cognitive development?

- Would you place your child in day care? Why or why not? What alternatives are available to you?

Children in Day Care
High-quality day care often has a positive influence on children's cognitive development.

Yet the findings of the National Institute on Child Health and Human Development study also reveal that children placed in day care may be less cooperative and more aggressive toward peers and adults than children who are reared in the home. For example, the more time preschoolers spent in child care, the more likely they were to display behavioral problems in kindergarten (Belsky et al., 2001). The more time spent away from their mothers, the more likely these children were to be rated as defiant, aggressive, and disobedient once they got to kindergarten. **Truth or Fiction Revisited:** It therefore appears to be true that children who attend day-care programs behave more aggressively than children who do not.

Seventeen percent of children who were in child care for more than 30 hours a week received higher scores on rating items such as "gets in lots of fights," "cruelty," "talking too much," "explosive behavior," "argues a lot," and "demands a lot of attention." Only 6% of children who were in child care for fewer than 10 hours a week had these problems. Children who were cared for in traditional day-care settings—by a grandmother, by a nanny, even by their fathers—received the troublesome ratings. Was Mom the only answer?

The study also held some good news. For example, it found that children who are enrolled in high-quality day care show cognitive benefits compared with children who are in lower-quality day care or who spend more time in the home with their mothers.

Although the study found a connection between time spent away from mothers and aggression, disobedience, and defiance in kindergarten, the reasons for these problems were not clear. For example, was it the time spent away from mothers that brought on the problems, or did the problems stem from other factors, such as the stresses encountered by families who need two incomes?

A number of the researchers on the team added that if other information yielded by the study had been presented, the reaction might have been different. Note the following:

- Although 17% of kindergartners who had been in child care acted more assertively and aggressively, that percentage is actually the norm for the general population of children. (In addition, 9% of the children who spent most of their time with their mothers were also rated by teachers as showing the more troubling behaviors.)
- The nature of family–child interactions had a greater effect on children's behavior than the number of hours spent in child care.
- Some aspects of aggressiveness—and the fact that infants in day care may demand more attention as kindergartners—may be adaptive responses to being placed in a situation where many children are competing for limited resources.

In addition, the researchers admitted that the statistics are modest: Yes, 17% of the children in day care acted aggressively and assertively, but only a few of them exhibited above-average behavior problems. Moreover, the problems were not that serious.

In any case, millions of parents do not have the option of deciding whether to place their children in day care; their only choice is where to do so. (Some parents, given their financial and geographic circumstances, might not even have such a choice.) The "A Closer Look" feature on page 247 may help you make the choice that is right for you.

A CLOSER LOOK

It is normal to be anxious. You are thinking about selecting a day-care center or a private home for your precious child, and there are risks. So be a little anxious, but it may not be necessary to be overwhelmed. You can go about the task with a checklist that can guide your considerations. Above all, don't be afraid to open your mouth and ask questions, even pointed, challenging questions. If the day-care provider does not like questions or if the provider does not answer them satisfactorily, you want your child someplace else. So much for the preamble. Here's the checklist.

1. Does the day-care center have a license? Who issued the license? What did the day-care center have to do to acquire the license? (You can also call the licensing agency to obtain the answer to the last question.)

2. How many children are cared for by the center? How many caregivers are there? Remember this nursery rhyme: There was an old woman who lived in a shoe. She had so many children she didn't know what to do. All right, the rhyme is sexist and ageist and maybe even shoe-ist, but it suggests that it is important for caregivers not to be overburdened by too many children, especially infants. It is desirable to have at least one caregiver for every four infants, although fewer workers are required for older children.

3. How were the caregivers hired? How were they trained? Did the center check references? What were the minimum educational credentials? Did the center check the references and credentials? Do the caregivers have any education or training in the behavior and needs of children? Do the caregivers seem to be proactive and attempt to engage the children in activities and educational experiences, or are they inactive unless a child cries or screams? Sometimes it is impossible to find qualified day-care workers, because they tend to be paid poorly (often the minimum wage, and sometimes less).

4. Is the environment child-proofed and secure? Can children stick their fingers in electric sockets? Are toys and outdoor equipment in good condition? Are sharp objects within children's reach? Can anybody walk in off the street? What is the history of children being injured or otherwise victimized in this day-care center? Is the day-care provider hesitant about answering any of these questions? When are meals served? Snacks? What do they consist of? Will your child find them appetizing or go hungry? Some babies are placed in day care at 6 months or younger, and parents will need to know what formulas are used.

5. Is it possible for you to meet the caregivers who will be taking care of your child? If not, why not?

6. With what children will your child interact and play?

7. Does the center seem to have an enriching environment? Do you see books, toys, games, and educational objects strewn about?

8. Are there facilities and objects such as swings and tricycles that will enhance your child's physical and motor development? Are children supervised when they play with these things, or are they often left on their own?

9. Does the center's schedule coincide with your needs?

10. Is the center located conveniently for you? Does it appear to be in a safe location or to have adequate security arrangements? (Let me emphasize that you have a right to ask whether neighborhood or other people can walk in unannounced to where the children are. It's a fair question. You can also ask what they would do if a stranger broke into the place.)

11. Are parents permitted to visit unannounced?

12. Do you like the overall environment and feel of the center or home? Listen to your "gut."

Reflect: Which of the considerations in selecting a day-care center are most important to you? Why?

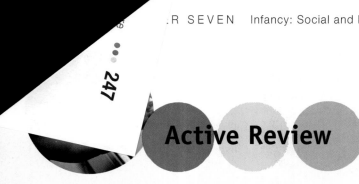

Active Review

13. The (Minority or Majority?) of mothers in the United States work outside the home.
14. Infants with day-care experience play at (Higher or Lower?) developmental levels than do home-reared babies.
15. Belsky and his colleagues found that once children are in school, those who had spent more time in day care were rated by teachers, caregivers, and mothers as being (More or Less?) aggressive toward other children.

Reflect & Relate: What are your concerns about placing children in day care? How do your concerns fit with the evidence on the effects of day care?

Go to

http://www.thomsonedu.com/psychology/rathus

for an interactive version of this review.

Emotional Development

Emotions color our lives. We are green with envy, red with anger, blue with sorrow. Positive emotions such as love can fill our days with pleasure. Negative emotions such as fear, depression, and anger can fill us with dread and make each day a chore.

Question: What are emotions? An **emotion** is a state of feeling that has physiological, situational, and cognitive components. Physiologically, when emotions are strong, our hearts may beat more rapidly and our muscles may tense. Situationally, we may feel fear in the presence of a threat and joy or relief in the presence of a loved one. Cognitively, fear is accompanied by the idea that we are in danger.

Theories of the Development of Emotions

Question: How do emotions develop? A number of theories concerning the development of emotions have been offered. They break down into two basic camps. The first, proposed originally by Katherine Bridges (1932), holds that we are born with a single emotion and that other emotions become differentiated as time passes. The second, Carroll Izard's **differential emotions theory** (2004), holds that the major emotions are present and differentiated at birth. But they are not shown all at once. Instead, they emerge in response to the child's developing needs and maturational sequences.

Bridges's and Sroufe's Theory

On the basis of her observations of babies, Bridges proposed that newborns experience one emotion—diffuse excitement. By the age of 3 months, two other emotions have differentiated from this general state of excitement—a negative emotion, distress, and a positive emotion, delight. By 6 months of age, fear, disgust, and anger will have developed from distress. By 12 months, elation and affection will have differentiated from delight. Jealousy develops from distress, and joy develops from delight—both during the second year.

Alan Sroufe (1979, 2005) has advanced Bridges's theory by focusing on the ways in which cognitive development provides a basis for emotional development. Jealousy, for example, could not become differentiated without some understanding of object

emotion A state of feeling that has physiological, situational, and cognitive components.

differential emotions theory Izard's view that the major emotions are distinct at birth but emerge gradually in accord with maturation and the child's developing needs

permanence (the continuing existence of people and objects) and possession. Similarly, infants usually show distress at the mother's departure after they have developed object permanence. Fear of strangers cannot occur without the perceptual ability to discriminate familiar people from others.

Izard's Theory

Carroll Izard's (2004; Izard et al., 2006) differential emotions theory proposes that infants are born with discrete emotional states, but the timing of their appearance is linked to the child's cognitive development and social experiences. For example, Izard and his colleagues (1987) reported that 2-month-old babies receiving inoculations showed distress, whereas older infants showed anger.

Izard's view may sound similar to Sroufe's. Both suggest an orderly unfolding of emotions such that they become more specific as time passes. But in keeping with Izard's view, researchers have found that a number of different emotions appear to be shown by infants at ages earlier than those suggested by Bridges and Sroufe (Bennett et al., 2004). In one study of emotions shown by babies during the first 3 months, 95% of the mothers interviewed reported observing joy; 84%, anger; 74%, surprise; and 58%, fear (Johnson et al., 1982).

Izard claimed to have found many discrete emotions at the age of 1 month by using his Maximally Discriminative Facial Movement Scoring System. ● Figure 7.7 shows some infant facial expressions that Izard believes are associated with the basic emotions of anger/rage, enjoyment/joy, fear/terror, and interest/excitement. Izard and his colleagues reported that facial expressions indicating interest, disgust, and pain are present at birth. They and others have observed expressions of anger and sadness at 2 months of age, expressions of surprise at 4 months, and expressions of fear at 7 months (Izard & Malatesta, 1987). However, some researchers believe that this type of research has many problems. First, observers cannot always accurately identify the emotions shown in slides or drawings of infant facial expressions. Second, we cannot know the exact relationship between a facial expression and an infant's inner feelings, which, of course, are private events. Even if the drawings accurately represent young infants' facial expressions, we cannot be certain that they express the specific emotions they would suggest if they were exhibited by older children and adults.

In sum, researchers agree that infants show only a few emotions during the first few months. They agree that other emotions develop in an orderly manner. They agree that emotional development is linked to cognitive development and social experience. They do not agree on exactly when specific emotions are first shown or whether discrete emotions are present at birth.

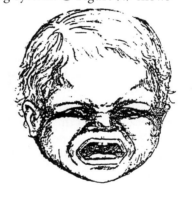

● **Figure 7.7**
Illustrations from Izard's Maximally Discriminative Facial Movement Scoring System

What emotion do you think is being experienced by each of these infants?

Source: Izard (1983).

Emotional Development and Patterns of Attachment

Emotional development has been linked with various histories of attachment. In a longitudinal study of 112 children at ages 9, 14, 22, and 33 months, Kochanska (2001) studied the development of fear, anger, and joy using laboratory situations designed to evoke these emotions. Patterns of attachment were assessed using the strange-situation method. Differences in emotional development could first be related to attachment at the age of 14 months. Resistant children were most fearful and least joyful. Fear was their most powerful emotion. They frequently responded with distress even in episodes designed to evoke joy. When they were assessed repeatedly over time, it became apparent that securely attached children were becoming significantly less angry. By contrast, the negative emotions of insecurely attached children rose: Avoidant children grew more fearful, and resistant children became less joyful. At 33 months of age, securely attached children were less likely to show fear and anger, even when they were exposed to situations designed to elicit these emotions.

Enough disagreement. Let us focus on an emotion that we can all agree is little fun: fear. We focus on a common fear of infants: the fear of strangers.

Fear of Strangers

When my daughter Jordan was 1 year old, her mother and I decided that we had to get a nanny for a few hours a day so that we could teach, write, breathe, and engage in other life activities. We hired a graduate student in social work who had a mild, engaging way about her. She nurtured Jordan and played with her for about 4 months, during which time Jordan came to somewhat grudgingly accept her, most of the time. Even so, Jordan was never completely comfortable with her. Jordan frequently let out a yowl as if buildings were collapsing around her, although the nanny did nothing except attempt to soothe her in a calm, consistent manner.

Jordan had a nanny and she had fear of strangers. Unfortunately, she met the nanny during the period when she had developed fear of strangers. The fear was eventually to subside, as these fears do, but during her entire encounter with the nanny, the nanny wondered what she was doing wrong. The answer, of course, was simple: She was existing, within sight of Jordan. Worse yet, Jordan's parents were not there to protect her from this vicious foe.

Was Jordan's response to her nanny "normal"? ***Question: Is fear of strangers normal?*** **Truth or Fiction Revisited:** Development of fear of strangers—sometimes termed **stranger anxiety**—is normal. Most infants develop it. Stranger anxiety appears at about 6 to 9 months of age in many different cultures, including those of the United States, Great Britain, Guatemala, and Zambia (Smith, 1979). By 4 or 5

stranger anxiety A fear of unfamiliar people that emerges between 6 and 9 months of age. Also called fear of strangers.

Stranger Anxiety
Infants in many cultures develop a fear of strangers, known as stranger anxiety, at about 6 to 9 months of age. This infant shows clear signs of distress when held by a stranger even though mother is close by. How would you behave around an infant who does not know you to try to minimize her or his stranger anxiety?

months of age, infants smile more in response to their mothers than to strangers. At this age, infants may compare the faces of strangers and their mothers, looking back and forth. Somewhat older infants show marked distress by crying, whimpering, gazing fearfully, and crawling away. Fear of strangers may peak between 9 and 12 months of age and decline in the second year or reach a second peak between the ages of 18 and 24 months and then decline in the third year (Thompson & Limber, 1990).

Children who have developed fear of strangers show less distress in response to strangers when their mothers are present. Babies are less likely to show fear of strangers when they are held by their mothers than when they are placed a few feet away (Thompson & Limber, 1990). Children also are less likely to show fear of strangers when they are in familiar surroundings, such as their homes, than when they are in the laboratory (Sroufe et al., 1974).

In terms of proximity, the fear response to strangers is the mirror image of attachment. Children attempt to remain near people to whom they are attached. But the closer they are to strangers, the greater their signs of distress (Boccia & Campos, 1989). They are most distressed when the strangers touch them. For this reason, if you find yourself in a situation in which you are trying to comfort an infant who does not know you, it may be more effective to talk in a friendly and soothing manner from a distance. Reconsider rushing in and picking up the child. Your behavior with an unfamiliar child also can make a difference. Studies have found that adults who are active and friendly—who gesture, smile, and offer toys—receive more positive response from 6- to 18-month-olds than do strangers who are quiet and passive (Bretherton et al., 1981; Mangelsdorf, 1992).

Social Referencing: What Should I Do Now?

Social referencing is the seeking out of another person's perception of a situation to help us form our own view of it (Hertenstein & Campos, 2004). In novel situations, adolescents and adults frequently observe how others behave and pattern their behavior after them. For example, people who are not afraid may help children reduce their fears. Essentially, the models provide information about how to act in a frightening situation.

Question: When does social referencing develop? Infants also display social referencing, as early as 6 months of age. They use caregivers' facial expressions or tone of voice to provide clues on how to respond (Hertenstein & Campos, 2004). In one study, for example, 8-month-old infants were friendlier to a stranger when their mothers exhibited a friendly facial expression in the stranger's presence than when she displayed a worried expression (Boccia & Campos, 1989).

Leslie Carver and Brenda Vaccaro (2007) suggest that social referencing requires three components: (1) looking at another, usually older individual in a novel, ambiguous situation; (2) associating that individual's emotional response with the unfamiliar situation; and (3) regulating their own emotional response in accord with the response of the older individual. In an experiment, Carver and Vaccaro (2007) found that 12-month-old infants were quicker to mold their responses to those of an adult who displayed a negative emotion rather than a neutral or a positive emotion. Perhaps we are wired to respond to danger first and pleasure later.

Emotional Regulation: Keeping on an Even Keel

Infants use emotional signals from an adult to help them cope with uncertainty. Another important feature of early emotional development is emotional regulation (Rothbart & Sheese, 2007). *Question: What is emotional regulation?* **Emotional regulation** refers to the ways in which young children control their own emotions. Even young infants display certain behaviors to control unpleasant emotional states.

social referencing Using another person's reaction to a situation to form one's own assessment of it.

emotional regulation Techniques for controlling one's emotional states.

They may look away from a disturbing event or suck their thumbs (Rothbart & Sheese, 2007). Caregivers play an important role in helping infants learn to regulate their emotions. Early in life, a two-way communication system develops in which the infant signals the caregiver that help is needed and the caregiver responds. Claire Kopp (1989, p. 347) gave an example of how this system works:

> A 13-month-old, playing with a large plastic bottle, attempted to unscrew the cover, but could not. Fretting for a short time, she initiated eye contact with her mother and held out the jar. As her mother took it to unscrew the cover, the infant ceased fretting.

Research evidence suggests that the children of secure mothers are not only likely to be securely attached themselves but also are likely to regulate their own emotions in a positive manner (Grolnick et al., 2006; Thompson & Meyer, 2007). A German longitudinal study (Zimmermann et al., 2001) related emotional regulation in adolescence with patterns of attachment during infancy, as assessed using the strange-situation method. Forty-one adolescents, age 16 and 17 years, were placed in complex problem-solving situations with friends. It turned out that those adolescents who were secure as infants were most capable of regulating their emotions to interact cooperatively with their friends. Another study (Volling, 2001) addressed the relationship between attachment in infancy and emotional regulation in an interaction with a distressed sibling at the age of 4. Of 45 preschoolers in the study, those who had an insecure-resistant infant–mother attachment at the age of 1 year engaged in more conflict with their siblings and showed greater hostility at the age of 4.

Active Review

16. Bridges proposed that we are born with a single emotion: diffuse _____.
17. The (Majority or Minority?) of infants develop fear of strangers.
18. Social _____ is the seeking out of another person's perception of a situation to help us form our own view of it.
19. Emotional _____ refers to the ways in which young children control their own emotions.

Reflect & Relate: Have you ever been in a novel situation and been uncertain about what to do? How about when you entered adolescence or began your first college class? Did you observe other people's reactions to the situation in an effort to determine what to do? This behavior is called *social referencing*. At what age do humans begin to use social referencing?

Go to

http://www.thomsonedu.com/psychology/rathus
for an interactive version of this review.

Personality Development

An individual's **personality** refers to his or her distinctive ways of responding to people and events. In this section, we examine important aspects of personality development in the infant years. First, we look at the emergence of the self-concept. We then turn to a discussion of temperament. Finally, we consider sex differences in behavior.

personality An individual's distinctive ways of responding to people and events.

The Self-Concept

At birth, we may find the world to be a confusing blur of sights, sounds, and inner sensations—yet the "we" may be missing, at least for a while. When our hands first come into view, there is little evidence we realize that the hands "belong" to us and that we are somehow separate and distinct from the world outside.

Questions: What is the self-concept? How does it develop? The **self-concept** is the sense of self. It appears to emerge gradually during infancy. At some point, infants understand that the hand they are moving in and out of sight is "their" hand. At some point, they understand that their own bodies extend only so far and that at a certain point, external objects and the bodies of others begin.

Development of the Self-Concept

Psychologists have devised ingenious methods to assess the development of the self-concept among infants. One of these is the mirror technique, which involves the use of a mirror and a dot of rouge. Before the experiment begins, the researcher observes the infant for baseline data on how frequently the infant touches his or her nose. Then the mother places rouge on the infant's nose, and the infant is placed before a mirror. Not until about the age of 18 months do infants begin to touch their own noses upon looking in the mirror (Campbell et al., 2000; Keller et al., 2005).

Nose touching suggests that children recognize themselves and that they have a mental picture of themselves that allows them to perceive that the dot of rouge is an abnormality. Most 2-year-olds can point to pictures of themselves, and they begin to use "I" or their own name spontaneously (Smiley & Johnson, 2006).

Self-awareness affects the infant's social and emotional development (Foley, 2006). Knowledge of the self permits the infant and child to develop notions of sharing and cooperation. In one study, for example, 2-year-olds who had a better developed sense of self were more likely to cooperate with other children (Brownell & Carriger, 1990).

Self-awareness also makes possible the development of "self-conscious" emotions such as embarrassment, envy, empathy, pride, guilt, and shame (Foley, 2006). One illustration of the development of these "self-conscious" emotions comes from a study by Deborah Stipek and her colleagues (1992). They found that children older than 21 months often seek their mother's attention and approval when they have successfully completed a task, whereas younger toddlers do not.

Psychoanalytic Views of the Self-Concept

Margaret Mahler, a psychoanalyst, has proposed that development of self-concept comes about through a process of **separation–individuation**, which lasts from about 5 months until 3 years of age (Mahler et al., 1975). Separation involves the child's growing perception that her mother is separate from herself. Individuation refers to the child's increasing sense of independence and autonomy.

The word *autonomy* may remind you of a similar view proposed by Erik Erikson that was discussed in Chapter 1. Erikson states that the major developmental task of the child from ages 2 to 3 is acquiring a sense of autonomy and independence from parents. Remember that Freud, too, believed that children of this age are gaining greater independence and control. His focus, however, was primarily on such bodily functions as toileting behavior.

One of the ways toddlers demonstrate their growing autonomy, much to the dismay of their parents, is by refusing to comply with parental requests or commands. Studies of toddlers and preschoolers between the ages of 1½ and 5 years have found that as children grow older, they adopt more skillful ways of expressing resistance to

Self-Awareness
In the middle of the second year, infants begin to develop self-awareness, which has a powerful effect on social and emotional development.

self-concept One's impression of oneself; self-awareness.

separation–individuation The child's increasing sense of becoming separate from and independent of the mother.

parental requests (Smith et al., 2004; Stifter & Wiggins, 2004). For example, young toddlers are more likely to ignore a parent's request or defy it ("No, I won't," accompanied by foot stamping). Older toddlers and preschoolers are more likely to make excuses ("I'm not hungry") or engage in negotiations ("Can I just eat some of my vegetables?").

Temperament: Easy, Difficult, or Slow to Warm Up?

Question: What is meant by the temperament of a child? Each child has a characteristic way of reacting and adapting to the world. The term **temperament** refers to stable individual differences in styles of reaction that are present early in life (Wachs, 2006). Many researchers believe that temperament forms the basic core of personality and that there is a strong genetic component to temperament (e.g., Goldsmith et al., 2003; Plomin, 2000; Wachs, 2006).

The child's temperament includes many aspects of behavior. Alexander Thomas and Stella Chess, in their well-known New York Longitudinal Study, followed the development of temperament in 133 girls and boys from birth to young adulthood (Chess & Thomas, 1991; Thomas & Chess, 1989) and identified nine characteristics of temperament. Other researchers have identified other characteristics (e.g., Gartstein et al., 2003). They include the following:

1. Activity level
2. Smiling/laughter
3. Regularity in child's biological functions, such as eating and sleeping
4. Approach or withdrawal from new situations and people
5. Adaptability to new situations
6. Sensitivity to sensory stimulation
7. Intensity of responsiveness
8. Quality of mood—generally cheerful or unpleasant
9. Distractibility
10. Attention span and persistence
11. Soothability
12. Distress at limitations

Questions: What types of temperament do we find among children? How do they develop?

Types of Temperament

Thomas and Chess (1989) found that from the first days of life, many of the children in their study could be classified into one of three types of temperament: "easy" (40% of their sample), "difficult" (10%), and "slow to warm up" (15%). Only 65% of the children studied by Chess and Thomas fit into one of the three types of temperament. Some of the differences among these three types of children are shown in ■ Table 7.3. As you can see, the easy child has regular sleep and feeding schedules, approaches new situations (such as a new food, a new school, or a stranger) with enthusiasm and adapts easily to them, and is generally cheerful. It is obvious why such a child would be relatively easy for parents to raise. Some children are more inconsistent and show a mixture of temperament traits. For example, a toddler may have a pleasant disposition but be frightened of new situations.

The difficult child, on the other hand, has irregular sleep and feeding schedules, is slow to accept new people and situations, takes a long time to adjust to new routines, and responds to frustrations with tantrums and loud crying. Parents find this type of child more difficult to deal with. The slow-to-warm-up child falls somewhere between the other two. These children have somewhat irregular feeding and sleeping

temperament Individual differences in styles of reaction that are present early in life.

■ **Table 7.3** Types of Temperament

Temperament Category	Easy	Difficult	Slow to warm up
• Regularity of biological functioning	Regular	Irregular	Somewhat irregular
• Response to new stimuli	Positive approach	Negative withdrawal	Negative withdrawal
• Adaptability to new situations	Adapts readily	Adapts slowly or not at all	Adapts slowly
• Intensity of reaction	Mild or moderate	Intense	Mild
• Quality of mood	Positive	Negative	Initially negative; gradually more positive

Sources: Chess & Thomas (1991) and Thomas & Chess (1989).

patterns and do not react as strongly as difficult children. They initially respond negatively to new experiences and adapt slowly only after repeated exposure.

Stability of Temperament

How stable is temperament? **Truth or Fiction Revisited:** Children are not all "born" with the same temperament. Thomas and Chess found that many children have one of three kinds of temperament from the first days of life. Evidence also indicates that there is at least moderate consistency in the development of temperament from infancy onward (Wachs, 2006). The infant who is highly active and cries in novel situations often becomes a fearful toddler. An anxious, unhappy toddler tends to become an anxious, unhappy adolescent. The child who refuses to accept new foods during infancy may scream when getting the first haircut, refuse to leave a parent's side during the first day of kindergarten, and have difficulty adjusting to college as a young adult. Difficult children in general are at greater risk for developing psychological disorders and adjustment problems later in life (Pauli-Pott et al., 2003; Rothbart et al., 2004). A longitudinal study tracked the progress of infants with a difficult temperament from 1½ through 12 years of age (Guerin et al., 1997). Temperament during infancy was assessed by the mother. Behavior patterns were assessed both by parents during the third year through the age of 12 and by teachers from the ages of 6 to 11. A difficult temperament correlated significantly with parental reports of behavioral problems from ages 3 to 12, including problems with attention span and aggression. Teachers concurred that children who had shown difficult temperaments during infancy were more likely to be aggressive later on and to have shorter attention spans.

Goodness of Fit: The Role of the Environment

The environment also affects the development of temperament. An initial biological predisposition to a certain temperament may be strengthened or weakened by the parents' reaction to the child. Consider the following: Parents may react to a difficult child by becoming less available and less responsive (Schoppe-Sullivan et al., 2007). They may insist on imposing rigid care-giving schedules, which in turn can cause the child to become even more difficult to handle (Schoppe-Sullivan et al., 2007). This example illustrates a discrepancy, or poor fit, between the child's behavior style and the parents' expectations and behaviors.

Differences in Temperament

Differences in temperament emerge in early infancy. The photo on the left shows the positive reactions of a 5-month-old girl being fed a new food for the first time. The photo on the right shows the very different response of another girl of about the same age when she is introduced to a new food.

On the other hand, parents may respond in such a way as to modify a child's initial temperament in a more positive direction. Take the case of Carl, who in early life was one of the most difficult children in the New York Longitudinal Study:

> Whether it was the first solid foods in infancy, the beginning of nursery and elementary school, first birthday parties, or the first shopping trip, each experience evoked stormy responses, with loud crying and struggling to get away. However, his parents learned to anticipate Carl's reactions, knew that if they were patient, presented only one or a few new situations at a time, and gave him the opportunity for repeated exposure, Carl would finally adapt positively. Furthermore, once he adapted, his intensity of responses gave him a zestful enthusiastic involvement, just as it gave his initial negative reactions a loud and stormy character. His parents became fully aware that the difficulties in raising Carl were due to his temperament and not to their being "bad parents." The father even looked on his son's shrieking and turmoil as a sign of lustiness. As a result of this positive parent–child interaction, Carl never became a behavior problem.
>
> —Chess & Thomas (1984, p. 263)

This example demonstrates **goodness of fit** between the behaviors of child and parent. A key factor is the parents' realization that their youngster's behavior does not mean that the child is weak or deliberately disobedient, or that they are bad parents. This realization helps parents modify their attitudes and behaviors toward the child, whose behavior may in turn change in the desired direction (Bird et al., 2006; Schoppe-Sullivan et al., 2007).

Sex Differences

goodness of fit Agreement between the parents' expectations of or demands on the child and the child's temperamental characteristics.

All cultures make a distinction between females and males and have beliefs and expectations about how they ought to behave. For this reason, a child's sex is a key factor in shaping its personality and other aspects of development. *Questions: How do girls and boys differ in their social, emotional, and other behaviors?*

Behaviors of Infant Girls and Boys

Girls tend to advance more rapidly in their motor development in infancy: They sit, crawl, and walk earlier than boys do (Matlin, 2008). Female and male infants are quite similar in their responses to sights, sounds, tastes, smells, and touch. Although a few studies have found that infant boys are more active and irritable than girls, others have not (Matlin, 2008). Girls and boys also are similar in their social behaviors. They are equally likely to smile at people's faces, for example, and do not differ in their dependency on adults (Maccoby & Jacklin, 1974; Matlin, 2008). One area in which girls and boys begin to differ early in life is their preference for certain toys and play activities. By 12 to 18 months of age, girls prefer to play with dolls, doll furniture, dishes, and toy animals, whereas boys prefer transportation toys (trucks, cars, airplanes, and the like), tools, and sports equipment as early as 9 to 18 months of age (Campbell et al., 2000; Serbin et al., 2001). On the other hand, sex differences that appear to show up later, such as differences in spatial relations skills, are not necessarily evident in infancy (Örnkloo & von Hofsten, 2007). By 24 months, both girls and boys appear to be quite aware of which behaviors are considered gender-consistent and gender-inconsistent, as measured in terms of time spent looking at the "novel" (in this case, "gender-inconsistent," as dictated by cultural stereotypes) behavior (Hill & Flom, 2007).

Truth or Fiction Revisited: Thus, it appears to be fiction that children play with gender-typed toys only after they have become aware of the gender roles assigned to them by society. It may well be the case that (most) girls prefer dolls and toy animals and that (most) boys prefer toy trucks and sports equipment before they have been socialized, even before they fully understand whether they themselves are female or

Lessons in Observation
Gender

 To watch this video, visit the book companion website. You can also answer the questions and e-mail your responses to your professor.

Learning Objectives

- What are gender roles?
- Why do children seem to engage in gender-typed behavior?
- How do adults encourage gender-typed behavior through expectations and gifts?
- Do children show preference for same-sex playmates, or do they play with others regardless of sex?

Applied Lesson

Describe how parental expectations and gifts can influence gender-typed behavior in children.

Critical Thinking

How might parents try to raise their children in a more "gender-free" environment? Do you think a child raised in a relatively gender-free environment will develop differently from other children?

Researchers believe that children may be born with gender-typed preferences but that peers and adults also encourage these behaviors. Does this toddler girl's desire to feed her doll reflect her genetic code, learning from peers or adults, or all three?

© Graham Light/Alamy

Adults Treat Infant Girls and Boys Differently

Perhaps the most obvious way in which parents treat their baby girls and boys differently is in their choice of clothing, toys, and room furnishings. If you were to meet this infant, would you have any doubt as to his or her sex?

male. Researchers continue to try to sort out the effects of nature and nurture in children's gender-related preferences.

Adults' Behaviors toward Infant Girls and Boys

Adults respond differently to girls and boys. For example, in some studies adults are presented with an unfamiliar infant who is dressed in boy's clothes and has a boy's name, whereas other adults are introduced to a baby who is dressed in girl's clothing and has a girl's name. (In reality, it is the same baby who simply is given different names and clothing.) When adults believe they are playing with a girl, they are more likely to offer "her" a doll; when they think the child is a boy, they are more likely to offer a football or a hammer. "Boys" also are encouraged to engage in more physical activity than are "girls" (Worell & Goodheart, 2006). Perhaps it is no wonder that infants labeled as "girls" are perceived as littler and softer (as well as nicer and more beautiful) than infants labeled as "boys."

Parents' Behaviors toward Sons and Daughters

Do parents treat infant sons and daughters differently? Yes, as did the adults with the unfamiliar babies, parents are more likely to encourage rough-and-tumble play in their sons than in their daughters. Fathers are especially likely to do so (Eccles et al., 2000; Fagot et al., 2000). On the other hand, parents talk more to infant daughters than to infant sons. They smile more at daughters, are more emotionally expressive toward them, and focus more on feelings when talking to them (Matlin, 2008; Powlishta et al., 2001).

Perhaps the most obvious way in which parents treat their baby girls and boys differently is in their choice of clothing, room furnishings, and toys. Infant girls are likely to be decked out in a pink or yellow dress, embellished with ruffles and lace, whereas infant boys wear blue or red (Eccles et al., 2000; Powlishta et al., 2001). Parents provide baby girls and boys with different bedroom decorations and toys. Examination of the contents of rooms of children from 5 months to 6 years of age found that boys' rooms were often decorated with animal themes and with blue bedding and curtains. Girls' rooms featured flowers, lace, ruffles, and pastels. Girls owned more dolls; boys had more vehicles, military toys, and sports equipment.

Other studies find that parents react favorably when their preschool daughters play with "toys for girls" and their sons play with "toys for boys." Parents and other adults show more negative reactions when girls play with toys for boys and boys play with toys for girls (Martin et al., 2002; Worell & Goodheart, 2006). In general, fathers are more concerned than mothers that their children engage in activities viewed as "appropriate" for their sex.

Parents thus attempt to influence their children's behavior during infancy and lay the foundation for development in early childhood. It is to that period of life that we turn next, in Chapter 8.

Active Review

20. Psychologists devised the mirror technique to assess development of the self-_____.
21. The child's _____ refers to the stable individual differences in styles of reaction that are present very early in life.
22. The three basic types of temperament are easy, difficult, and _____ to warm up.
23. Girls prefer to play with dolls, whereas boys show a preference to play with transportation toys as early as _____ months of age.

Reflect & Relate: Have you known infants who were easygoing or difficult? How did their temperaments affect their relationships with their parents?

Go to

http://www.thomsonedu.com/psychology/rathus

for an interactive version of this review.

RECITE: *An Active Summary*

1. **What is meant by "attachment"?**

An attachment is an enduring emotional tie between one animal or person and another specific individual. Children try to maintain contact with persons to whom they are attached.

2. **What does it mean for a child to be "secure"?**

Most infants in the United States are securely attached. In the strange situation, securely attached infants mildly protest mother's departure and are readily comforted by her.

3. **What, then, is "insecurity"?**

The two major types of insecure attachment are avoidant attachment and ambivalent/resistant attachment. Infants with avoidant attachment are least distressed by their mothers' departure. Infants with ambivalent/resistant attachment show severe distress when their mothers leave but are ambivalent upon reunion.

4. **Is it better for an infant to be securely attached to its caregivers?**

Yes, securely attached infants are happier, more sociable, and more cooperative. They use the mother as a secure base from which to explore the environment. At ages 5 and 6, securely attached children are preferred by peers and teachers and more competent.

5. **What are the roles of the parents in the formation of bonds of attachment?**

High-quality care contributes to security. Parents of securely attached infants are more likely to be affectionate and sensitive to their needs. Security of attachment is related to the infant's temperament as well as to caregivers' behavior.

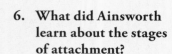

6.	**What did Ainsworth learn about the stages of attachment?**	The initial-preattachment phase lasts from birth to about 3 months and is characterized by indiscriminate attachment. The attachment-in-the-making phase occurs at about 3 or 4 months and is characterized by preference for familiar figures. The clear-cut-attachment phase occurs at about 6 or 7 months and is characterized by dependence on the primary caregiver.
7.	**How do different theorists emphasize nature or nurture in their explanation of the development of attachment?**	Cognitive theorists suggest that an infant must develop object permanence before specific attachment is possible. Behaviorists suggest that infants become attached to caregivers because caregivers meet their bodily needs. Psychoanalysts suggest that the primary caregiver becomes a love object. The Harlows' experiments with monkeys suggest that contact comfort is a key to attachment. Ethologists view attachment as an inborn fixed action pattern (FAP) that occurs during a critical period in response to a releasing stimulus.
8.	**What are the findings of the Harlows' studies on the effects of social deprivation on monkeys?**	The Harlows found that rhesus infants reared in isolation confinement later avoided contact with other monkeys. Females who later had offspring tended to ignore or abuse them.
9.	**What do we know about the effects of social deprivation on humans?**	Institutionalized children who receive little social stimulation encounter problems in development. Many develop withdrawal and depression. Deficiencies in sensory stimulation and social interaction may cause more problems than lack of love per se. Infants have much capacity to recover from deprivation.
10.	**What are the incidences of child abuse and neglect? What are their effects?**	Nearly 3 million American children are neglected or abused each year, and neglect results in more serious harm than abuse. About 150,000 children are sexually abused each year. Maltreated children are less intimate with peers and are more aggressive, angry, and noncompliant than other children.
11.	**Why does child abuse run in families?**	Abusive parents serve as role models. Exposure to violence in the home may lead children to accept family violence as the norm. Some parents rationalize that they are hurting their children "for their own good" to discourage problematic behavior.
12.	**What are autism spectrum disorders?**	Autism spectrum disorders (ASDs) are characterized by impairment in communication skills and social interactions, and repetitive, stereotyped behavior.
13.	**What is autism?**	The most striking feature of autism is the child's aloneness. Other features include communication problems, intolerance of change, stereotypical behavior, mutism, echolalia, and self-mutilation.
14.	**What are the origins of autism spectrum disorders?**	Evidence suggests a role for biological factors in autism. Genetic studies find higher concordance rates for autism among monozygotic than dizygotic twins. Researchers also suspect neurological involvement.
15.	**What can be done to help children with autism spectrum disorders?**	Behavior modification has been used to increase the child's attention to others and social play and to decrease self-mutilation. Aversive stimulation has been used to curtail self-injury. Researchers are studying the use of SSRIs and major tranquilizers.

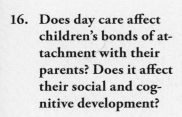

16. Does day care affect children's bonds of attachment with their parents? Does it affect their social and cognitive development?	Infants with day-care experience are more independent, self-confident, outgoing, affectionate, and more cooperative with peers and adults than infants who are not in day care. Children in high-quality day care outperform children who remain in the home in terms of cognitive development. Children in day care are more aggressive than other children, but a small degree of aggression may indicate independence, not maladjustment.
17. What are emotions?	Emotions are states of feeling that have physiological, situational, and cognitive components.
18. How do emotions develop?	Bridges proposed that we are born with one emotion—diffuse excitement—and that other emotions differentiate over time. Sroufe focused on the ways in which cognitive development can provide the basis for emotional development. Izard proposed that infants are born with several emotional states but that their appearance is linked to cognitive development and social experiences.
19. Is fear of strangers normal?	Fear of strangers is normal in that most infants develop it at about the age of 6 to 9 months.
20. When does social referencing develop?	Infants display social referencing as early as 6 months of age, when they use caregivers' facial expressions or tones of voice for information on how to respond in novel situations.
21. What is emotional regulation?	Emotional regulation is emotional self-control. Caregivers help infants learn to regulate their emotions. The children of secure mothers are more likely to regulate their emotions positively.
22. What is the self-concept? How does it develop?	The self-concept is the sense of self. Findings using the mirror technique suggest that the self-concept develops by about 18 months of age. Self-awareness enables the child to develop concepts of sharing and cooperation and "self-conscious" emotions such as embarrassment, envy, empathy, pride, guilt, and shame.
23. What is meant by the temperament of a child?	The term *temperament* refers to stable individual differences in styles of reaction to the world that are present early in life. These reactions include activity level, regularity, approach or withdrawal, adaptability, response threshold, response intensity, quality of mood, distractibility, attention span, and persistence.
24. What types of temperament do we find among children? How do they develop?	Thomas and Chess found that most infants can be classified as having easy, difficult, or slow-to-warm-up temperaments. Temperament remains moderately consistent from infancy through young adulthood.
25. How do girls and boys differ in their social, emotional, and other behaviors?	Female infants sit, crawl, and walk earlier than boys do. By 12 to 18 months of age, girls prefer to play with dolls and similar toys, whereas boys prefer transportation toys and gear.

Key Terms

attachment, 222

separation anxiety, 222

secure attachment, 222

avoidant attachment, 223

ambivalent/resistant attachment, 223

disorganized–disoriented attachment, 223

indiscriminate attachment, 226

initial-preattachment phase, 226

attachment-in-the-making phase, 226

clear-cut-attachment phase, 227

contact comfort, 227

ethologist, 227

fixed action pattern (FAP), 227

releasing stimulus, 227

social smile, 227

critical period, 228

imprinting, 228

autism spectrum disorders (ASDs), 240

autism, 241

mutism, 241

echolalia, 241

emotion, 248

differential emotions theory, 248

stranger anxiety, 250

social referencing, 251

emotional regulation, 251

personality, 252

self-concept, 253

separation–individuation, 253

temperament, 254

goodness of fit, 256

Active Learning Resources

Childhood & Adolescence Book Companion Website

http://www.thomsonedu.com/psychology/rathus

Visit your book companion website where you will find more resources to help you study. There you will find interactive versions of your book features, including the Lessons in Observation video, Active Review sections, and the Truth or Fiction feature. In addition, the companion website contains quizzing, flash cards, and a pronunciation glossary.

Thomson NOW! is an easy-to-use online resource that helps you study in less time to get the grade you want—NOW.

http://www.thomsonedu.com/login

Need help studying? This site is your one-stop study shop. Take a Pre-Test and ThomsonNOW will generate a Personalized Study Plan based on your test results. The Study Plan will identify the topics you need to review and direct you to online resources to help you master those topics. You can then take a Post-Test to determine the concepts you have mastered and what you still need to work on.

8

Early Childhood
Physical Development

Truth or Fiction?

T F Some children are left-brained, and others are right-brained. p. 268

T F Children's levels of motor activity increase during the preschool years. p. 270

T F Sedentary parents are more likely to have "couch potatoes" for children than are active parents. p. 271

T F Julius Caesar, Michelangelo, Tom Cruise, and Oprah have something in common. (Hint: They don't all have book clubs.) p. 274

T F A disproportionately high percentage of math whizzes are left-handed. p. 274

T F Some diseases are normal. p. 280

T F Infections are the most common cause of death among children in the United States. p. 281

T F It is dangerous to awaken a sleepwalker. p. 286

T F Parents who are more competent than other parents toilet train their children by the child's second birthday. p. 287

Preview

Growth Patterns
Height and Weight
Development of the Brain

Motor Development
Gross Motor Skills
Physical Activity
Fine Motor Skills

Developing in a World of Diversity: Sex Differences in Motor Activity

Children's Drawings
Handedness

Lessons in Observation: Gross and Fine Motor Skills

Nutrition
Nutritional Needs
Patterns of Eating

Health and Illness
A Closer Look: Ten Things You Need To Know About Immunizations
Minor Illnesses
Major Illnesses
Accidents

A Closer Look: Assessing and Minimizing the Risk of Lead Poisoning

Sleep
Sleep Disorders

Developing in a World of Diversity: Cross-Cultural Differences in Sleeping Arrangements

Elimination Disorders
Enuresis

A Closer Look: What to Do about Bed-Wetting
Encopresis

Go to

http://www.thomsonedu.com/psychology/rathus
for an interactive version of this "Truth or Fiction" feature.

ark is a 2-year-old boy having lunch in his high chair. He is not without ambition. He begins by shoving fistfuls of hamburger into his mouth. He picks up his cup with both hands and drinks milk. Then he starts banging his spoon on his tray and his cup. He kicks his feet against the chair. He throws hamburger on the floor. Compare Mark's behavior with that of Larry, age 3½, who is getting ready for bed. Larry carefully pulls his plastic train track apart and places each piece in the box. Then he walks to the bathroom, brings his stool over to the sink, and stands on it. He takes down his toothbrush and toothpaste, opens the cap, squeezes toothpaste on the brush, and begins to brush his teeth (Rowen, 1973).

Mark and Larry are in early childhood, the years from 2 to 6, which are also known as the preschool period. During early childhood, physical growth is slower than it was in infancy. Children become taller and leaner, and by the end of early childhood they look more like adults than infants. An explosion of motor skills occurs as children become stronger, faster, and better coordinated.

Language improves enormously, and children can carry on conversations with others. As cognitive skills develop, a new world of make believe or "pretend" play emerges. Curiosity and eagerness to learn are hallmarks of the preschool years.

Increased physical and cognitive capabilities enable the child to emerge from total dependence on parents and caregivers to become part of the broader world outside the family. Peers take on an increasingly important role in the life of the preschooler. Children begin to acquire a sense of their own abilities and shortcomings.

We learn about all these developments of early childhood—physical, cognitive, social, and emotional—in Chapters 8, 9, and 10.

Growth Patterns

During the preschool years, physical and motor development proceeds, literally, by leaps and bounds. While toddlers like Mark are occupied with grasping, banging, and throwing things, 3-year-olds like Larry are busy manipulating objects and exercising their newly developing fine motor skills. *Question: What changes occur in height and weight during early childhood?*

Height and Weight

Following the dramatic gains in height in a child's first 2 years, the growth rate slows down during the preschool years (Kuczmarski et al., 2000). Girls and boys tend to gain about 2 to 3 inches in height per year throughout early childhood. Weight gains also remain fairly even, at about 4 to 6 pounds per year (see Figure 8.1). Children become increasingly slender during early childhood, as they gain in height and lose some of their "baby fat." Boys as a group are only slightly taller and heavier than girls in early childhood (■ Figure 8.1). Noticeable variations in growth patterns also occur from child to child.

Development of the Brain

Question: How does the brain develop during early childhood? The brain develops more quickly than any other organ in early childhood. At 2 years of age, for example, the brain already has attained 75% of its adult weight. By the age of 5, the brain has reached 90% of its adult weight, even though the total body weight of the 5-year-old is barely one-third of what it will be as an adult (Tanner, 1989).

The increase in brain size is due in part to the continuing process of myelination of nerve fibers (see Chapter 5). Completion of the myelination of the neural path-

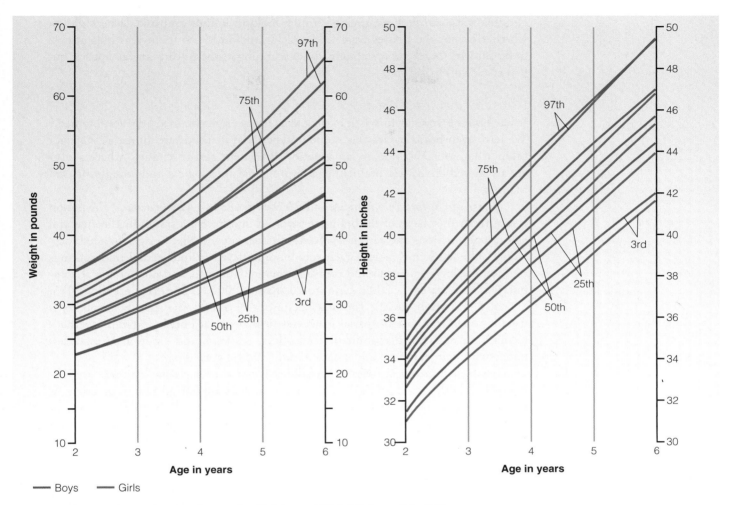

— Boys   — Girls

● **Figure 8.1** Growth Curves for Height and Weight, Ages 2 to 6 Years

The numbers on the curves indicate the percentiles for height and weight at different ages. The growth rate slows down during early childhood. As in infancy, boys are only slightly taller and heavier than girls. Variations in growth patterns from child to child are evident.

Source: Kuczmarski et al. (2000, Figures 9–12).

ways that link the cerebellum to the cerebral cortex facilitates the development of fine motor skills (Nelson & Luciana, 2001; Paus et al., 1999). The cerebellum is involved in balance and coordination, and the young child's balancing abilities increase dramatically as myelination of these pathways nears completion.

Brain Development and Visual Skills

Brain development is also linked to improvements in the ability to attend to and process visual information (Yamada et al., 2000). These skills are critical in learning to read. The parts of the brain that enable the child to sustain attention and screen out distractions become increasingly myelinated between the ages of about 4 and 7 (Nelson & Luciana, 2001). As a result, most children are ready to focus on schoolwork between these ages.

The speed with which children process visual information improves throughout childhood, reaching adult levels at the beginning of adolescence (Chou et al., 2006; Paus et al., 1999). The child's ability to systematically scan visual material also improves in early childhood. For example, researchers in one classic study presented children with pairs of pictures of similar-looking houses and asked the children whether or not the houses were identical (Vurpillot, 1968). Four-year-olds almost never showed thorough, systematic visual scanning of the features of the houses, but 9-year-olds often did so.

Right Brain, Left Brain?

It has become popular to speak of people as being "right-brained" or "left-brained." We have even heard it said that some instructional methods are aimed at the right brain (they are presented in an emotionally laden, aesthetic way), whereas others are aimed at the left brain (they are presented in a logical and straightforward manner).

Question: What does it mean to be left-brained or right-brained? The notion is that the hemispheres of the brain are involved in different kinds of intellectual and emotional functions and responses. Research does suggest that in right-handed individuals, the left hemisphere is relatively more involved in intellectual undertakings that require logical analysis and problem solving, language, and mathematical computation (Cabeza et al., 2003; Grindrod & Baum, 2005; O'Shea & Corballis, 2005; Shenal & Harrison, 2003). The other hemisphere (usually the right hemisphere) is usually superior in visual–spatial functions (it is better at putting puzzles together), recognition of faces, discrimination of colors, aesthetic and emotional responses, understanding metaphors, and creative mathematical reasoning.

Truth or Fiction Revisited: Actually, it is not true that some children are left-brained and others are right-brained. Brain functions are not split up so precisely, as has been popularly believed. The functions of the left and right hemispheres overlap to some degree, and the hemispheres also tend to respond simultaneously when we focus our attention on one thing or another. They are aided in "cooperation" by the myelination of the **corpus callosum**, a thick bundle of nerve fibers that connects the hemispheres (Kinsbourne, 2003). Myelination of the corpus callosum proceeds rapidly during early and middle childhood and is largely complete by the age of 8. By that time, children can better integrate logical and emotional functioning.

Plasticity of the Brain

Many parts of the brain have specialized functions. Specialization allows our behavior to be more complex, but it also means that injuries to certain parts of the brain can result in loss of these functions.

Fortunately, the brain also shows **plasticity** (Kolb & Gibb, 2007). *Question: What is meant by "plasticity of the brain"?* "Plasticity" means that the brain frequently can compensate for injuries to particular areas. This compensatory ability is greatest at about 1–2 years of age and then gradually declines, although it may not be completely gone, even in adulthood (Kolb & Gibb, 2007; Nelson et al., 2006). When we suffer damage to the areas of the brain that control language, we may lose the ability to speak or understand language. However, other areas of the brain may assume these functions in young children who suffer such damage. As a result, they may dramatically regain the ability to speak or comprehend language (Nelson et al., 2006). In adolescence and adulthood, regaining such functions is much more difficult and may be all but impossible.

Various factors are involved in the brain's plasticity (Nelson et al., 2006; Szaflarski et al., 2006). The first is "sprouting," or the growth of new dendrites. To some degree, new dendrites can allow for the rearrangement of neural circuits. The second factor is the redundancy of neural connections. In some cases, similar functions are found at two or more sites in the brain, although they are developed to different degrees. If one site is damaged, the other may be able to develop to perform the function.

corpus callosum The thick bundle of nerve fibers that connects the left and right hemispheres of the brain.

plasticity The tendency of new parts of the brain to take up the functions of injured parts.

Active Review

1. Children gain about _____ inches in height per year throughout early childhood.
2. Weight gains are about _____ pounds per year.
3. The _____ develops more rapidly than any other organ in early childhood.
4. _____ of the neural pathways that link the cerebellum to the cerebral cortex facilitates the development of fine motor skills.
5. The _____ is involved in balance and coordination.
6. Research suggests that in _____-handed individuals, the left hemisphere is relatively more involved in logical analysis and problem solving, language, and mathematical computation.

7. The _____ hemisphere of the cerebral cortex is usually superior in visual–spatial functions and emotional responses.
8. The brain can often compensate for injuries to particular areas because of its _____.

Reflect & Relate: Have you ever compared the growth of a child to the norms on a growth chart? What were you looking for? What were your concerns?

Go to

http://www.thomsonedu.com/psychology/rathus

for an interactive version of this review.

Motor Development

The preschool years witness an explosion of motor skills, as children's nervous systems mature and their movements become more precise and coordinated. *Question: How do motor skills develop in early childhood?*

Gross Motor Skills

During the preschool years, children make great strides in the development of **gross motor skills**, which involve the large muscles used in locomotion (see ■ Table 8.1). At about the age of 3, children can balance on one foot. By age 3 or 4, they can walk up stairs as adults do, by placing a foot on each step. By age 4 or 5, they can skip and pedal a tricycle (McDevitt & Ormrod, 2002). Older preschoolers are better able to coordinate two tasks, such as singing and running at the same time, than are younger preschoolers. In general, preschool children appear to acquire motor skills by teaching themselves and observing the behavior of other children. The opportunity to play with other children seems more important than adult instruction at this age.

Throughout early childhood, girls and boys are not far apart in their motor skills. Girls are somewhat better at tasks requiring balance and precision of movement. Boys, on the other hand, show some advantage in throwing and kicking (McDevitt & Ormrod, 2002).

Individual differences are more impressive than sex differences throughout early and middle childhood. Some children develop motor skills earlier than others. Some are genetically predisposed to developing better coordination or more strength than others. Motivation and practice also are important in children's acquisition of motor skills. Motor experiences in infancy may affect the development of motor skills in

gross motor skills Skills employing the large muscles used in locomotion.

■ **Table 8.1** Development of Gross Motor Skills in Early Childhood

2 Years (24–35 Months)	3 Years (36–47 Months)	4 Years (48–59 Months)	5 Years (60–71 Months)
• Runs well straight ahead	• Goes around obstacles while running	• Turns sharp corners while running	• Runs lightly on toes
• Walks up stairs, two feet to a step	• Walks up stairs, one foot to a step	• Walks down stairs, one foot to a step	• Jumps a distance of 3 feet
• Kicks a large ball	• Kicks a large ball easily	• Jumps from a height of 12 inches	• Catches a small ball, using hands only
• Jumps a distance of 4–14 inches	• Jumps from the bottom step	• Throws a ball overhand	• Hops 2 to 3 yards forward on each foot
• Throws a small ball without falling	• Catches a bounced ball, using torso and arms to form a basket	• Turns sharp corners while pushing and pulling toys	• Stands on one foot for 8–10 seconds
• Pushes and pulls large toys	• Goes around obstacles while pushing and pulling toys	• Hops on one foot, four to six hops	• Climbs actively and skillfully
• Hops on one foot, two or more hops	• Hops on one foot, up to three hops	• Stands on one foot for 3–8 seconds	• Skips on alternate feet
• Tries to stand on one foot	• Stands on one foot	• Climbs ladders	• Rides a bicycle with training wheels
• Climbs on furniture to look out of window	• Climbs nursery-school apparatus	• Skips on one foot	
		• Rides a tricycle well	

Note: The ages are averages; there are individual variations.

early childhood. For example, children with early crawling experience perform better than those who do not on tests of motor skills in the preschool years (McEwan et al., 1991).

Physical Activity

Preschool children spend quite a bit of time in physical activity. One study found that preschoolers spend an average of more than 25 hours a week in large muscle activity (D. W. Campbell et al., 2002). Younger preschoolers are more likely than older preschoolers to engage in physically oriented play, such as grasping, banging, and mouthing objects (D. W. Campbell et al., 2002). Consequently, they need more space and less furniture in a preschool or day-care setting.

Truth or Fiction Revisited: It is not true that motor activity increases during the preschool years. Motor activity level begins to decline after 2 or 3 years of age. Children become less restless and are able to sit still longer (D. W. Campbell et al., 2002; Eaton et al., 2001). Between the ages of 2 and 4, children in free play show an increase in sustained, focused attention.

Gross Motor Skills
During the preschool years, children make great strides in the development of gross motor skills. By age 4 or 5, they can pedal a tricycle quite skillfully.

Rough-and-Tumble Play

One form of physical and social activity often observed in young children is known as **rough-and-tumble play**. Rough-and-tumble play consists of running, chasing, fleeing, wrestling, hitting with an open hand, laughing, and making faces. Rough-and-tumble play is not the same as aggressive behavior. Aggression involves hitting with fists, pushing, taking, grabbing, and angry looks. Unlike aggression, rough-and-tumble play helps develop both physical and social skills in children (Fry, 2005; Colwell & Lindsey, 2005; Smith, 2005).

Play fighting and chasing activities are found among young children in societies around the world (Whiting & Edwards, 1988). But the particular form that rough-and-tumble play takes is influenced by culture and environment. For example, rough-and-tumble play among girls is quite common among the Pilaga Indians and the !Kung of Botswana but less common among girls in the United States. In the United States, rough-and-tumble play usually occurs in groups made up of the same sex. However, !Kung girls and boys engage in rough-and-tumble play together, and among the Pilaga, girls often are matched against the boys.

Rough-and-Tumble Play
Play fighting and chasing activities—known as rough-and-tumble play—are found among young children in societies around the world.

Individual Differences in Activity Level

Children differ widely in their activity levels. Some children are much more active than others.

Truth or Fiction Revisited: It is true that sedentary parents are more likely to have "couch potatoes" for children. Physically active children are more likely to have physically active parents. In a study of 4- to 7-year-olds (Moore et al., 1991), children of active mothers were twice as likely to be active as children of inactive mothers. Children of active fathers were 3.5 times as likely to be active as children of inactive fathers.

Several reasons may explain this relationship. First, active parents may serve as role models for activity. Second, sharing of activities by family members may be responsible. Parents who are avid tennis players may involve their children in games of tennis from an early age. By the same token, couch-potato parents who prefer to view tennis on television rather than play it may be more likely to share this sedentary activity with their children. A third factor is that active parents may encourage and

rough-and-tumble play Play fighting and chasing.

■ Table 8.2 Development of Fine Motor Skills in Early Childhood

2 Years (24–35 Months)	3 Years (36–47 Months)	4 Years (48–59 Months)	5 Years (60–71 Months)
• Builds tower of 6 cubes • Copies vertical and horizontal lines • Imitates folding of paper • Prints on easel with a brush • Places simple shapes in correct holes	• Builds tower of 9 cubes • Copies circle and cross • Copies letters • Holds crayons with fingers, not fist • Strings 4 beads using a large needle	• Builds tower of 10 or more cubes • Copies square • Prints simple words • Imitates folding paper three times • Uses pencil with correct hand grip • Strings 10 beads	• Builds 3 steps from 6 blocks, using a model • Copies triangle and star • Prints first name and numbers • Imitates folding of piece of square paper into a triangle • Traces around a diamond drawn on paper • Laces shoes

Note: The ages are averages; there are individual variations.

fine motor skills Skills employing the small muscles used in manipulation, such as those in the fingers.

placement stage An early stage in drawing, usually found among 2-year-olds, in which children place their scribbles in various locations on the page (such as in the middle or near a border).

support their child's participation in physical activity. Finally, a tendency to be active or inactive may be transmitted genetically, as shown by evidence from twin studies (see Chapter 2) (Saudino & Eaton, 1993; Stevenson, 1992). Genetic and environmental factors apparently interact to determine a child's activity level.

Fine Motor Skills

In yet another example of the proximodistal trend in development, (see Chapters 3 and 5) **fine motor skills** develop gradually and lag gross motor skills. Fine motor skills involve the small muscles used in manipulation and coordination. Control over the wrists and fingers enables children to hold a pencil properly, dress themselves, and stack blocks (see ■ Table 8.2). Preschoolers can labor endlessly in attempting to tie their shoelaces and get their jackets zipped. There are terribly frustrating (and funny)

Developing in a
World of Diversity

Sex Differences in Motor Activity

Question: *Do girls and boys differ in their activity levels during early childhood?* During early childhood, boys tend to be more active than girls, at least in some settings (Campbell & Eaton, 1999; D. W. Campbell et al., 2002). Boys spend more time than girls in large muscle activities. Boys tend to be more fidgety and distractible than girls and to spend less time focusing on tasks (McGuinness, 1990).

Why are boys more active and restless than girls? One theory is that boys of a given age are less mature physically than girls of the same age. Children tend to become less active as they develop (Eaton & Yu, 1989).

Boys also are more likely than girls to engage in rough-and-tumble play (Moller et al., 1992; Pellegrini, 1990). What might account for this sex difference? Some psychologists suggest that the reasons might be

partly based in biology (Maccoby, 1990a, 1991). Others argue that the socializing influences of the family and culture at large promote play differences among girls and boys (Caplan & Larkin, 1991; Meyer et al., 1991).

Reflect: *Why is it useful to know about sex differences in motor activity?*

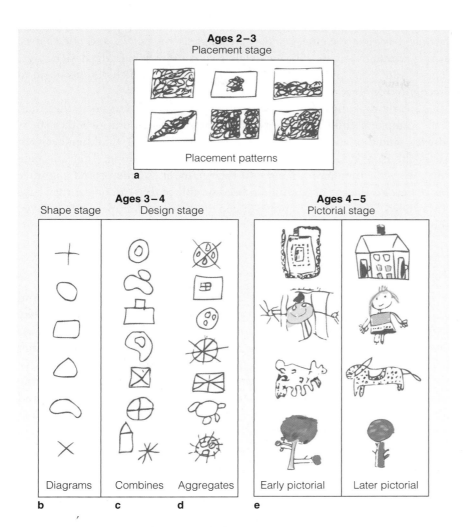

Ages 2–3
Placement stage

Placement patterns

a

Ages 3–4

Shape stage | Design stage

Ages 4–5
Pictorial stage

Diagrams | Combines | Aggregates

b | c | d

Early pictorial | Later pictorial

e

● **Figure 8.3** Four Stages in Children's Drawings

Children go through four stages in drawing pictures. (a) They first place their scribbles in various locations on the page. They then (b) draw basic shapes and (c, d) combine shapes into designs. Finally, (e) they draw recognizable objects.

Source: Kellogg (1970).

● **Figure 8.2**
The Twenty Basic
Scribbles (Really)

By the age of 2, children can scribble. Rhoda Kellogg has identified these 20 basic scribbles as the building blocks of the young child's drawings.

Source: Kellogg (1970).

Fine Motor Skills
Control over the wrists and fingers enables children to hold a pencil, play a musical instrument, and, as shown in this photograph, play with clay.

scenes of children alternating between steadfastly refusing to allow a parent to intervene and requesting the parent's help.

Children's Drawings

The development of drawing in young children is closely linked to the development of both motor and cognitive skills. Children first begin to scribble during the second year of life. Initially, they seem to make marks for the sheer joy of it (Eisner, 1990).

Question: Are children's scribbles the result of random motor activity? Rhoda Kellogg (1959, 1970) studied more than 1 million drawings made by children. She found a meaningful pattern in the scribbles. She identified 20 basic scribbles that she considered the building blocks of all art including vertical, horizontal, diagonal, circular, curving, waving or zigzagging lines, and dots (see ● Figure 8.2).

Children go through four stages as they progress from making scribbles to drawing pictures. These are the **placement, shape, design**, and **pictorial stages** (see ● Figure 8.3). Two-year-olds place their scribbles in various locations on the page

shape stage A stage in drawing, attained by age 3, in which children draw basic shapes such as circles, squares, triangles, crosses, X's and odd shapes.

design stage A stage in drawing in which children begin to combine shapes.

(e.g., in the middle of the page or near one of the borders). By age 3, children are starting to draw basic shapes: circles, squares, triangles, crosses, X's, and odd shapes. As soon as they can draw shapes, children begin to combine them in the design stage. Between ages 4 and 5, the child reaches the pictorial stage, in which designs begin to resemble recognizable objects.

Children's early drawings tend to be symbolic of a broad category rather than specific. For example, a child might draw the same simple building whether she is asked to draw a school or a house (Tallandini & Valentini, 1991). Children between 3 and 5 years old usually do not start out to draw a particular thing. They are more likely to first see what they have drawn and then name it. As motor and cognitive skills improve beyond the age of 5, children become able to draw an object they have in mind (Matthews, 1990). They improve at copying figures (Karapetsas & Kantas, 1991; Pemberton, 1990).

Handedness

Truth or Fiction Revisited: Yes, Julius Caesar, Michelangelo, Tom Cruise, and Oprah do have something in common. They are all left-handed. *Questions: When does handedness emerge? How many children are left-handed?* **Handedness** emerges during infancy. By the age of 2 to 3 months, a rattle placed in an infant's hand is held longer with the right hand than with the left (Fitzgerald et al., 1991). By 4 months of age, most infants show a clear-cut right-hand preference in exploring objects using the sense of touch (Streri, 2002). Preference for grasping with one hand or the other increases markedly between the ages of 7 and 11 months (Hinojosa et al., 2003). Handedness becomes more strongly established during the early childhood years (McManus et al., 1988). Most people are right-handed, although studies vary as to how many are left-handed.

Left-Handedness: Is It Gauche To Be Left-Handed? Myths and Realities

Question: Are there problems connected with being left-handed? Being a "lefty" was once regarded as a deficiency. The language still swarms with slurs on lefties. We speak of "left-handed compliments," of having "two left feet," of strange events as "coming out of left field." The word *sinister* means "left-hand or unlucky side" in Latin. *Gauche* is a French word that literally means "left," although in English it is used to mean awkward or ill-mannered. The English word *adroit*, meaning "skillful," derives from the French *à droit*, literally translated as "to the right." Also consider positive usages such as "being righteous" or "being on one's right side."

Being left-handed is not gauche or sinister, but left-handedness may matter because it appears to be connected with language problems, such as dyslexia and stuttering, and with health problems, such as high blood pressure and epilepsy (Andreou et al., 2002; Bryden et al., 2005; Ostatnikova et al., 2002). Left-handedness is also apparently connected with psychological disorders, including schizophrenia and depression (Annett & Moran, 2006; Dollfus et al., 2005).

There may be advantages to being left-handed. **Truth or Fiction Revisited:** A disproportionately high percentage of math whizzes are in fact left-handed. In a series of studies, Camilla Benbow (O'Boyle & Benbow, 1990) related handedness to scores on the math part of the Scholastic Assessment Test (SAT) among 12- and 13-year-olds. Twenty percent of the highest-scoring group was left-handed. Only 10% of the general population is left-handed, so it appears that left-handed children are more than adequately represented among the most academically gifted in mathematics.

pictorial stage A stage in drawing attained between ages 4 and 5 in which designs begin to resemble recognizable objects.

handedness The tendency to prefer using the left or right hand in writing and other activities.

Left-handedness (or use of both hands) also has been associated with success in athletic activities such as handball, fencing, boxing, basketball, and baseball (Coren, 1992; Dane & Erzurumluoglu, 2003). Higher frequencies of left-handedness also are found among musicians, architects, and artists (Natsopoulos et al., 1992; O'Boyle & Benbow, 1990). Two of the greatest artists in history—Leonardo da Vinci and Michelangelo—were left-handed.

In the next section, we consider how it can be that left-handedness is associated with both talent and giftedness on the one hand (excuse the pun!) and with problems and deficits on the other. What are the origins of handedness?

Theories of Handedness

The origins of handedness apparently have a genetic component (Geschwind, 2000; McManus, 2003). Left-handedness runs in families. In the English royal family, the Queen Mother was left-handed as are Queen Elizabeth II, Prince Charles, and Prince William (Rosenbaum, 2000). If both of your parents are right-handed, your chances of being right-handed are about 92%. If one of your parents is left-handed, your chances of being right-handed drop to about 80%. And if both of your parents are left-handed, your chances of also being left-handed are about 50% (Annett, 1999; Clode, 2006).

Lessons in Observation
Gross and Fine Motor Skills

To watch this video, visit the book companion website. You can also answer the questions and e-mail your responses to your professor.

Although 3-year-old Olivia can kick a ball, she has to use her torso and arms formed into a basket to catch a ball.

Learning Objectives

- What is the difference between gross motor skills and fine motor skills?
- How do gross motor skills improve as children age?
- How does Olivia's attempt to catch a ball illustrate the proximodistal trend in motor development?
- What activities help prepare children for writing and drawing?

Applied Lesson

Describe the different stages of climbing and how each stage represents an advancement in gross motor skills.

Critical Thinking

How might parents help their child improve fine motor development? At what stage(s) should a parent introduce new toys and activities?

Fine motor activities, such as building things with blocks, help children improve their skills and prepare them for drawing and writing.

On the other hand, identical (monozygotic) twins frequently are different in handedness (Sommer et al., 2002). One explanation is that monozygotic twins are sometimes mirror opposites (Sommer et al., 2002). If that were so, the disagreement on handedness among monozygotic twins would not contradict a role for genetics in handedness.

In any case, handedness develops early. An ultrasound study found that about 95% of fetuses suck their right thumbs rather than their left (Hepper et al., 1990).

Interestingly, handedness is also found in species other than humans, for example, chimpanzees and parrots (yes, parrots). It appears that hand preferences in chimpanzees are heritable, as they are in humans, but that environmental factors can modify inborn preferences, in chimps as well as in humans (Hopkins et al., 2001).

In sum, left-handed children are not necessarily clumsier than right-handed children. They are somewhat more prone to allergies. Academically, left-handedness is associated with positive as well as negative outcomes. Because handedness may reflect the differential development of the hemispheres of the cortex, there is no point in struggling to write with the nondominant hand. After all, would training right-handed children to write with their left hands help them in math?

Active Review

9. (Girls or Boys?) are somewhat better at tasks requiring balance and precision of movement.
10. (Girls or Boys?) show some advantage in throwing and kicking.
11. Motor activity begins to (Increase or Decrease?) after 2 or 3 years of age.
12. During early childhood, (Girls or Boys?) tend to be more active.
13. Left-handed people have a (Higher or Lower?) incidence of language problems and psychological disorders compared with right-handed people.

Reflect & Relate: Think of left-handed people you know (perhaps including yourself). Do they seem to be awkward in any activities? Explain. Do you know anyone who was "changed" from a lefty to a righty? Why was the change made? How was it done? Was it successful? Explain.

Go to

http://www.thomsonedu.com/psychology/rathus

for an interactive version of this review.

Nutrition

Nutrition affects both physical and behavioral development. *Question: What are children's nutritional needs and their eating behavior like in early childhood?*

Nutritional Needs

As children move from infancy into the preschool years, their nutritional needs change. True, they still need to consume the basic foodstuffs—proteins, fats, carbohydrates, minerals, and vitamins—but more calories are required as children get older. For example, the average 4- to 6-year-old needs about 1,400 calories, compared with about 1,000 to 1,300 calories for the average 1- to 3-year-old (American Academy of Family Physicians, 2006). However, preschoolers grow at a slower rate than infants, so preschoolers need fewer calories per pound of body weight.

Patterns of Eating

During the second and third years, a child's appetite typically decreases and becomes erratic, often causing parents great worry. But it must be remembered that because the child is growing more slowly now, he or she needs fewer calories than before. Also, young children who eat less at one meal typically compensate by eating more at another. Children may develop strong (and strange) preferences for certain foods (Cooke et al., 2003). At one time during her third year, my daughter Allyn wanted to eat nothing but Spaghetti-O's.

Many children (and adults) consume excessive amounts of sugar and salt, which can be harmful to their health. Infants seem to be born liking the taste of sugar, although they are fairly indifferent to salty tastes. But preference for both sweet and salty foods increases if children are repeatedly exposed to them during childhood. Parents also serve as role models in the development of food preferences. If a parent—especially the parent who usually prepares meals—displays an obvious dislike for vegetables, children may develop a similar dislike (Hannon et al., 2003). The message to parents is clear: The eating habits you help create will probably last.

What is the best way to get children to eat their green peas or spinach or other healthful foods they may dislike? (Notice that it is rarely dessert that the child refuses to eat.) One method is to encourage the child to taste tiny amounts of the food 8 or 10 times within a period of a few weeks so that it becomes more familiar. Perhaps familiarity with food becomes content and not contempt.

■ Table 8.3 shows a healthful 1-day diet for a 4-year-old girl, a diet too high in sugar, and another too high in fat. Both the unhealthful diets are excessively high in calories, which can lead to the child's being overweight. Overweight children have a way of becoming overweight adults (American Academy of Family Physicians, 2006).

"He just learned in school that potato chips are vegetables."

© WM Hoest Enterprises, Inc. Reprinted with special permission of King Features Syndicate.

Food Aversions
Strong preferences—and aversions—for certain foods may develop in early childhood.

■ **Table 8.3** Sample Meal Patterns for a Four-Year-Old Girl

Meal	Recommended	Excessive sugar	Excessive fat*
Breakfast	1/2 cup oatmeal 4 oz of 2 percent milk 1 orange	1 package of oatmeal with "dinosaur bones" 4 oz of 2 percent milk 4 oz orange juice	1 store-bought blueberry muffin with 1/2 Tbsp butter 4 oz of 2 percent milk 1 orange
Snack	1 apple, quartered 1 oz cheese	8 oz fruit punch drink 10 animal crackers	1 peanut butter granola bar with chocolate coating
Lunch	1/2 egg salad sandwich (1 boiled egg, 1 Tbsp mayonnaise, 1 slice wheat bread) 4 oz of 2 percent milk 10 baby carrots 1/2 banana	1/2 egg salad sandwich (1 boiled egg, 1 Tbsp mayonnaise, 2 slices wheat bread) 4 oz orange juice 10 baby carrots	1/2 egg salad sandwich (1 boiled egg, 2 Tbsp mayonnaise, 1/2 Tbsp butter, 1 slice wheat bread) 1/2 cup chocolate pudding 1/2 banana
Snack	1/2 raisin bagel 1 Tbsp peanut butter	1/2 plain bagel 1 Tbsp strawberry jam	1/4 bag (8 oz) plain potato chips *(continued)*

■ **Table 8.3** Sample Meal Patterns for a Four-Year-Old Girl (*continued*)

Meal	Recommended	Excessive sugar	Excessive fat*
Supper	1/2 chicken breast, grilled	1/2 chicken breast, grilled	6 chicken nuggets
	1/2 cup cooked peas	1/2 cup cooked peas	Medium order of French fries
	1/2 cup cauliflower	1/2 cup cauliflower	4 oz of 2 percent milk
	1/2 cup cooked long-grain rice	1/2 cup cooked long-grain rice	Chocolate-covered ice cream bar
	4 oz of 2 percent milk	4 oz apple juice	
	1/4 cantaloupe, cubed	2 fruit-flavored wraps	
Snack	2 slices Black Forest ham	1 store-bought blueberry muffin	2 slices Black Forest ham
	6 saltine crackers	1 Tbsp raspberry jam	6 saltine crackers
Nutritional information			
Calories	1,393	1,945	2,526
Fat (% calories)	43 g (28%)	39 g (18%)	130.6 g (47%)
Protein (g per kg)	70.2 g (4.4)	59.4 g (3.7)	65.7 g (4.1)
Fiber	25 g	21.8 g	18.9 g

Source: American Academy of Family Physicians (2006).

Note: Child's length is 39.5 inches (100 cm), and weight is 16 kg (35 lb, 3 oz).

*The high-fat meal pattern has adequate protein intake but almost no fruits or vegetables.

Active Review

14. During the second and third years, a child's appetite typically (Increases or Decreases?).

Reflect & Relate: Did you ever try to convince a 2- or 3-year-old to eat something? What did you do? What were the consequences?

Go to

http://www.thomsonedu.com/psychology/rathus

for an interactive version of this review.

Health and Illness

Almost all children get ill now and then. Some seem to be ill every other week or so. Most of these illnesses are minor, and children seem to eventually outgrow many of them, including ear infections. However, some illnesses are more serious. Fortunately, we have ways of preventing or curing a great many of them.

Questions: How healthy are children in the United States and in other countries? What are some of the illnesses and environmental hazards encountered during early childhood?

A CLOSER LOOK

Ten Things You Need to Know about Immunizations

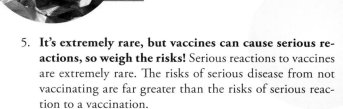

1. **Why your child should be immunized.** Children need immunizations (shots) to protect them from dangerous childhood diseases. These diseases can have serious complications and even kill children.

2. **Diseases that childhood vaccines prevent:**
   • Diphtheria
   • *Haemophilus influenzae* type b (Hib disease, a major cause of bacterial meningitis)
   • Hepatitis A
   • Hepatitis B
   • Measles
   • Meningococcal
   • Mumps
   • Pertussis (whooping cough)
   • Pneumococcal (causes bacterial meningitis and blood infections)
   • Polio
   • Rotavirus
   • Rubella (German measles)
   • Tetanus (lockjaw)
   • Varicella (chickenpox)

   Audio, text-only, and other language versions of the Vaccine Information Sheets are available on the Centers for Disease Control website.

3. **Number of doses your child needs:** The following vaccinations are recommended by age two and can be given over five visits to a doctor or clinic:
   • 4 doses of diphtheria, tetanus & pertussis vaccine (DTaP)
   • 3–4 doses of Hib vaccine (depending on the brand used)
   • 4 doses of pneumococcal vaccine
   • 3 doses of polio vaccine
   • 2 doses of hepatitis A vaccine
   • 3 doses of hepatitis B vaccine
   • 1 dose of measles, mumps, and rubella vaccine (MMR)
   • 3 doses of rotavirus vaccine
   • 1 dose of varicella vaccine
   • 2–3 doses of influenza vaccine (6 months and older) (number of doses depends on child's birthday)

4. **Like any medicine, there may be minor side effects.** Side effects can occur with any medicine, including vaccines. Depending on the vaccine, the side effects can include slight fever, rash, and soreness at the site of injection. Slight discomfort is normal and should not be a cause for alarm. Your health-care provider can give you additional information.

5. **It's extremely rare, but vaccines can cause serious reactions, so weigh the risks!** Serious reactions to vaccines are extremely rare. The risks of serious disease from not vaccinating are far greater than the risks of serious reaction to a vaccination.

6. **What to do if your child has a serious reaction.** If you think your child is experiencing a persistent or severe reaction, call your doctor or get the child to a doctor right away. Write down what happened and the date and time it happened. Ask your doctor, nurse, or health department to file a Vaccine Adverse Event Report form or call 1-800-338-2382 to file this form yourself.

7. **Why you should not wait to vaccinate.** Children under 5 are especially susceptible to disease because their immune systems have not built up the necessary defenses to fight infection. By immunizing on time (by age 2), you can protect your child from disease and also protect others at school or in day care.

8. **Be sure to track your shots via a health record.** A vaccination health record helps you and your health-care provider keep your child's vaccinations on schedule. If you move or change providers, having an accurate record might prevent your child from repeating vaccinations he or she has already had. A shot record should be started when your child receives his or her first vaccination and updated with each vaccination visit.

9. **Some are eligible for free vaccinations.** A federal program called Vaccines for Children provides free vaccines to eligible children, including those without health insurance coverage, all those who are enrolled in Medicaid, American Indians, and Alaskan Natives.

10. **More information is available.** General immunization questions can be answered by the CDC Contact Center at 1-800-CDC-INFO (1-800-232-4636); English and Español.

Source: Centers for Disease Control and Prevention (2007b).

Reflect:
• Are you unclear about the meaning of any of the diseases these vaccinations protect against?
• Do you know whether or not the children in your life have gotten every recommended vaccine?
• Do you know what to do if a child has missed a vaccination?
• Do you know what to do if you are unsure of the answer to any of these questions?

Minor Illnesses

Minor illnesses refer to respiratory infections, such as colds, and to gastrointestinal upsets, such as nausea, vomiting, and diarrhea. **Truth or Fiction Revisited:** These diseases are normal—statistically speaking—in the sense that most children come down with them. They typically last a few days or less and are not life threatening. Although diarrheal illness in the United States is usually mild, it is a leading killer of children in developing countries (UNICEF, 2006).

American children between the ages of 1 and 3 generally average eight to nine minor illnesses a year. Between the ages of 4 and 10, the incidence drops to about four to six illnesses a year. You may be surprised to learn that illness can have some beneficial effects on development. It can lead to the creation of antibodies that may prevent children from coming down with the same illnesses later, say, in adulthood, when the illnesses can be more harmful.

Major Illnesses

Advances in immunization along with the development of antibiotics and other medications have dramatically reduced the incidence of serious and potentially fatal childhood diseases in the United States. Because most preschoolers and schoolchildren have been inoculated against major childhood illnesses such as rubella (German measles), measles, tetanus, mumps, whooping cough, diphtheria, and polio, these diseases no longer pose the threat they once did. Still, as you can see in ■ Table 8.4, immunization in the United States is not universal. The recommended immunization schedule of the American Academy of Pediatrics and the American Academy of Family Physicians is given in Figure ● 8.4.

Nearly one-third of the children in the United States younger than 18 years of age—about 20 million children—suffer from some type of chronic illness (Agency for Healthcare Research and Quality, 2004). These illnesses include such major disorders as arthritis, diabetes, cerebral palsy, and cystic fibrosis. Other chronic medical problems such as asthma and migraine headaches are less serious but still require extensive health supervision.

Although many major childhood diseases have been largely eradicated in the United States and other industrialized nations, they remain fearsome killers of children in developing countries. Around the world, more than 13 million children die each year. Two-thirds of these children die of just six diseases: pneumonia, diarrhea, measles, tetanus, whooping cough, and tuberculosis (UNICEF, 2006). Air pollution from the combustion of fossil fuels for heating and cooking gives rise to many respiratory infections, which are responsible for nearly one death in five among children

■ **Table 8.4** Coverage Estimates for School Entry Vaccinations, 2005–2006 School Year

| National Estimate (U.S. States and District of Columbia) | |
Vaccine	Percent of children vaccinated
Polio	95.47%
DTaP	95.23%
Measles	95.22%
Mumps	95.90%
Rubella	95.88%
Hep B	96.03%
Varicella	96.04%

Source: Centers for Disease Control and Prevention (2007a).

Vaccine ▼ Age ▶	Birth	1 month	2 months	4 months	6 months	12 months	15 months	18 months	19–23 months	2–3 years	4–6 years
Hepatitis B	HepB	HepB			HepB				HepB Series		
Rotavirus		Rota	Rota	Rota							
Diphtheria, Tetanus, Pertussis		DTaP	DTaP	DTaP		DTaP					DTaP
Haemophilus influenzae type b		Hib	Hib	Hib	Hib		Hib				
Pneumococcal		PCV	PCV	PCV	PCV					PCV / PPV	
Inactivated Poliovirus		IPV	IPV		IPV						IPV
Influenza					Influenza (Yearly)						
Measles, Mumps, Rubella						MMR					MMR
Varicella						Varicella					Varicella
Hepatitis A						HepA (2 doses)				HepA Series	
Meningococcal										MPSV4	

▢ Range of recommended ages   ▉ Catch-up immunization   ▉ Certain high-risk groups

The schedule indicates the recommended ages for routine administration of currently licensed childhood vaccines, as of December 1, 2006, for children aged 0–6 years. Additional information is available at http://wwwcdc.gov/nip/recs/child-schedule.htm. Any dose not administered at the recommended age should be administered at any subsequent visit, when indicated and feasible. Additional vaccines may be licensed and recommended during the year. Licensed combination vaccines may be used whenever any components of the combination are indicated and other components of the vaccine are not contraindicated and if approved by the Food and Drug Administration for that dose of the series. Providers should consult the respective Advisory Committee on Immunization Practices statement for detailed recommendations. Clinically significant adverse events that follow immunization should be reported to the Vaccine Adverse Event Reporting System (VAERS). Guidence about how to obtain and complete a VAERS form is available at **http://www.vaers, hhs.gov** or by telephone, **800-822-7967** The recommended Immunization Schedules for Persons Aged 0–18 Years are approved by the Advisory Committee on Immunization Practices (http://www.cdc.gov/nip/acip), the American Academy of Pediatrics (http://www.aap.org), and the American Academy of Family Physicians (http://www.aafp.org).

● **Figure 8.4**   Recommended Immunization Schedule for Persons Aged 0–6 Years, United States, 2007

who are younger than 5 years of age (UNICEF, 2006). Around the world, diarrhea kills nearly 2 million children under the age of 5. Diarrheal diseases are almost completely related to unsafe drinking water and a general lack of sanitation and hygiene. Children's immune systems and detoxification mechanisms are not as strong as those of adults, and they are thus more vulnerable to chemical, physical, and biological hazards in the water, soil, and air (UNICEF, 2006).

Lead is a particularly harmful pollutant. Many youngsters are exposed to lead in early childhood, often by eating chips of lead paint from their homes or by breathing in dust from the paint. Infants fed formula made with tap water also are at risk of lead poisoning, because the pipes that carry water into homes sometimes contain lead. Lead causes neurological damage and may result in lowered cognitive functioning and other developmental delays in early childhood. To help assess and minimize the risks of lead poisoning in children younger than 6 years of age, see the nearby "A Closer Look" feature.

Low-cost measures such as vaccines, antibiotics, and a technique called **oral rehydration therapy** could prevent most deaths due to diarrhea. Oral rehydration therapy involves giving a simple homemade salt and sugar solution to a child who is dehydrated from diarrhea. Most children in developing countries are also now immunized against tuberculosis, measles, polio, diphtheria, tetanus, and whooping cough (UNICEF, 2006).

Accidents

Truth or Fiction Revisited: Infections are not the most common cause of death in early childhood in the United States (see ▉ Table 8.5). Accidents are. Accidents cause more deaths in early childhood than the next six most frequent causes combined

oral rehydration therapy
A treatment involving administration of a salt and sugar solution to a child who is dehydrated from diarrhea.

■ **Table 8.5** Ten Leading Causes of Death in Early Childhood, United States, 2004, All Races, Both Sexes

Rank	Age Group 2–6
1	Unintentional Injury
2	Malignant neoplasms (cancer)
3	Congenital anomalies (malformations, deformations, and chromosomal abnormalities with which the child is born)
4	Homicide
5	Heart disease
6	Influenza and pneumonia
7	Benign neoplasms (usually nonfatal cancers)
8	Septicemia (blood poisoning)
9	Chronic respiratory disease
10	Cerebrovascular problems (e.g., stroke)

Source: Adapted from National Center for Injury Prevention and Control, Centers for Disease Control and Prevention (2007).

A CLOSER LOOK

Assessing and Minimizing the Risk of Lead Poisoning

People can get lead in their body if they put their hands or other objects covered with lead dust in their mouths, eat paint chips or soil that contains lead, or breathe in lead dust (especially during renovations that disturb painted surfaces). If not detected early, children with high levels of lead in their bodies can suffer from damage to the brain and nervous system, behavior and learning problems (such as hyperactivity), slowed growth, hearing problems, and headaches.

Lead is found mainly in paint. Many homes built before 1978 have lead-based paint. The federal government banned lead-based paint from housing in 1978. Some states stopped its use even earlier. Lead can also be found in homes in the city, country, or suburbs; in apartments, single-family homes, and both private and public housing; in soil inside and outside of a house; in household dust; and in drinking water. Your home might have plumbing with lead or lead solder. Call your local health department or water supplier to find out about testing your water. Use only cold water for drinking and cooking, and run water for 15 to 30 seconds before drinking it, especially if you have not used your water for a few hours. Lead is also found on some jobs, on old painted toys and furniture, on food and liquids stored in lead crystal or lead-glazed pottery or porcelain, and near lead smelters or other industries that release lead into the air.

Peeling, chipping, chalking, or cracking lead-based paint is a hazard and needs immediate attention. Lead-based paint may also be a hazard when found on surfaces that children can chew or that get a lot of wear-and-tear. Lead-based paint that is in good condition is usually not a hazard.

Consult your doctor for advice on testing your children. A simple blood test can detect high levels of lead. You can get your home checked in one of two ways, or both: A paint inspection tells you the lead content of every different type of painted surface in your home. A risk assessment tells you if there are any sources of serious lead exposure (such as peeling paint and lead dust). It also tells you what actions to take to address these hazards. Have qualified professionals do the work.

Contact the National Lead Information Center for more information:

By phone: 1-800-424-LEAD [5323].
By e-mail: http://www.epa.gov/lead/pubs/nlic.htm

Reflect: Have you checked your residence for the risk of lead poisoning? If not, why not? (Will you? When?)

Source: Abridged from the Environmental Protection Agency (2007).

(National Center for Injury Prevention and Control, 2007). The single most common cause of death in early childhood is motor vehicle accidents, followed by drowning and fires.

Accidents also are the major killer of children in most countries of the world, except for those developing nations still racked by high rates of malnutrition and disease. Injuries are responsible for nearly half the deaths of children 2 to 6 years of age and for more than half the deaths of children through the age of 14. Boys are more likely than girls to incur accidental injuries at all ages and in all socioeconomic groups.

Accidental injuries occur most often among low-income children. Poor children are five times as likely to die from fires and more than twice as likely to die in motor vehicle accidents than are children who are not poor (National Center for Injury Prevention and Control, 2007). The high accident rate of low-income children may result partly from living in dangerous housing and neighborhoods. Poor parents also are less likely than higher-income parents to take such preventive measures as using infant safety seats, fastening children's seat belts, installing smoke detectors, or having the telephone number of a poison control center. The families of children who are injured frequently may be more disorganized and under more stress than other families. Injuries often occur when family members are distracted and children are under minimal supervision.

Prevention of Accidental Injury

Legislation has helped reduce certain injuries in children (National Center for Injury Prevention and Control, 2007). All 50 states and the District of Columbia now require child safety seats in automobiles, and their use has decreased deaths resulting from automobile injuries. Most large cities in the United States also now have laws requiring installation of window guards in high-rise apartment buildings. In a number of countries, the risks of injury to children have been reduced because of legislation requiring manufacturers to meet safety standards for such items as toys and flammable clothing.

Automobile Safety
Automobile accidents are the most common cause of death in young children in the United States. All 50 states and the District of Columbia now require child-restraint seats in automobiles. These laws have contributed to a reduction in child deaths and injuries.

Active Review

15. The most frequent cause of death of children in the United States is _____.
16. Many children are exposed to the poisonous metal _____ by eating chips of paint.

Reflect & Relate: What pollutants in your area are harmful to children? What can you do about them?

Go to

http://www.thomsonedu.com/psychology/rathus

for an interactive version of this review.

Sleep

Question: How much sleep is needed in early childhood? Children in the early years do not need as much sleep as infants. Most preschoolers sleep 10 to 11 hours in a 24-hour period (National Sleep Foundation, 2007) (see ■ Table 8.6). A common pattern includes 9 to 10 hours at night and a nap of 1 to 2 hours. In the United States,

■ **Table 8.6** Sleep Obtained by Children during a 24-Hour Period

	Infancy	Preschoolers	Younger School-Age Children	Older School-Age Children
Bottom 25%	11 hours or less	9.9 hours or less	9 hours or less	8.9 hours or less
Middle 50%	11.1–14.9 hours	10–11 hours	9.1–10 hours	9–9.9 hours
Upper 25%	15 hours or more	11.1 hours or more	10.1 hours or more	10 hours or more

Source: National Sleep Foundation (2007).

the young child's bedtime routine typically includes putting on pajamas, brushing teeth, and being read a story. Many young children also take a so-called **transitional object**—such as a favored blanket or a stuffed animal—to bed with them (Morelli et al., 1992). Such objects apparently help children make the transition to greater independence and separation from their parents.

But we're not ending the topic here, because it sounds much too easy. As too many parents know, getting children to sleep can be a major challenge of parenthood. Many children resist going to bed or going to sleep (Christophersen & Mortweet, 2003). A Japanese study suggests that getting to sleep late can be a problem, because preschoolers tend not to make up fully for lost sleep (Kohyama et al., 2002). But resisting sleep is a run-of-the-mill problem. In the next section we focus on more serious problems, called sleep disorders.

Sleep Disorders

Question: What kinds of problems or disorders disrupt sleep during early childhood? In this section, we focus on the sleep disorders of sleep terrors, nightmares, and sleep walking.

Sleep Terrors and Nightmares

First, a few words about terms. **Sleep terrors** are more severe than the anxiety dreams we refer to as nightmares. For one thing, sleep terrors usually occur during deep sleep. **Nightmares** take place during lighter rapid-eye-movement (REM) sleep, when about 80% of normal dreams occur. In fact, nightmares sort of qualify as "normal" dreams because of their frequency, not because of their desirability!

Deep sleep alternates with lighter REM sleep. Sleep terrors tend to occur early during the night, when periods of deep sleep are longest. Nightmares tend to occur more often in the morning hours, when periods of REM sleep tend to lengthen (National Sleep Foundation, 2007). Children have several periods of REM sleep a night and may dream in each one of them. Don't be confused by the fact that sleep terrors are sometimes referred to as *night terrors*. "Night terrors" always refer to sleep terrors and never to nightmares.

Sleep terrors usually begin in childhood or early adolescence and are outgrown by late adolescence. They are often but not always associated with stress, such as moving to a new neighborhood, attending school for the first time, adjusting to parental divorce, or being caught up in a war zone (Krippner & McIntyre, 2003). (Children are also more likely to experience nightmares during stressful periods.) Children with sleep terrors may wake up suddenly with a surge in heart and respiration rates, talk incoherently, and thrash about. Children are not completely awake during sleep terrors and may fall back into more restful sleep. Fortunately, the incidence of sleep terrors wanes as children develop and spend less time in deep sleep. Sleep terrors are all but absent among adults.

transitional object A soft, cuddly object often carried to bed by a child to ease the separation from parents.

sleep terrors Frightening dreamlike experiences that occur during the deepest stage of non-REM sleep, shortly after the child has gone to sleep.

nightmares Frightening dreams that occur during REM sleep, often in the morning hours.

Developing in a World of Diversity

Cross-Cultural Differences in Sleeping Arrangements

The commonly accepted practice in middle-class American families is for infants and children to sleep in separate beds and, when finances permit, in separate rooms from their parents. Child-care experts in the United States have generally endorsed this practice. Sleeping in the same room, they have sometimes warned, can lead to problems such as the development of overdependence, the difficulty of breaking the habit when the child gets older, and even accidental sexual stimulation of the child (Morelli et al., 1992).

Nevertheless, bed-sharing has more recently been promoted as a means for facilitating breast feeding (McCoy et al., 2004). In fact, co-sleeping or bed-sharing is the most common sleeping arrangement throughout the world for mothers who are breast feeding (Young, 2006). Although some are concerned that bed-sharing can be dangerous for an infant, with parents rolling onto them and crushing or suffocating them (Mesich, 2005), observational evidence suggests that such dangers are more likely to emanate from fathers than mothers and are least likely to derive from mothers who are breast feeding (Ball, 2006).

In many other cultures, as noted, children sleep with their mothers for the first few years of life, often in the same bed (Javo et al., 2004; Young, 2006). Co-sleeping occurs in cultures that are technologically advanced, such as Austria (Rothrauff et al., 2004) and Japan (Takahashi, 1990), as well as in those that are less technologically sophisticated, such as among the indigenous Sami people of Norway (Javo et al., 2004).

Resistance to going to bed occurs regularly in 20% to 40% of American infants and preschoolers

© Jose Luis Pelaez, Inc./CORBIS

Getting Their Z's

In the United States, most parents believe that it is harmful or at least inappropriate for parents to sleep with their children. Parents in many other cultures are more relaxed about sleeping arrangements.

(Johnson, 1991), but it seldom occurs in cultures that practice co-sleeping. Some psychologists believe that the resistance shown by some young American children at bedtime is caused by the stress of separating from parents. This view is supported by the finding that young children who sleep with or near their parents are less likely to use transitional objects or to suck their thumbs at night than are children who sleep alone (Morelli et al., 1992; Wolf & Lozoff, 1989). Bed-sharing has also been shown to help children settle down and sleep better through the night especially children with developmental disabilities (Cotton & Richdale, 2006).

Research does not reveal harmful effects for co-sleeping. For example, an Austrian study found no significant differences between children's sleeping arrangements and their subsequent social development (Rothrauff et al., 2004). Among the Norwegian Sami, children not only slept with their parents but—also unlike other Norwegians—regulated their own sleeping and eating schedules. Sami parents were less tolerant of aggressive behavior in their children than Norwegian parents were. The outcome of all these cultural approaches was connected with relatively greater social independence among Sami children.

Reflect: *Would you (do you) allow your child to share your bed with you? Why or why not? Is your decision based on the scientific literature related to bed-sharing? (Should it be?)*

Children who have frequent nightmares or sleep terrors may come to fear going to sleep. They may show distress at bedtime, refuse to get into their pajamas, and insist that the lights be kept on during the night. As a result, they can develop **insomnia**. Children with frequent nightmares or sleep terrors need their parents' understanding and affection. They also profit from a regular routine in which they are expected to get to sleep at the same time each night (Christophersen & Mortweet, 2003). Yelling at them over their "immature" refusal to have the lights out and return to sleep will not alleviate their anxieties.

Sleep Walking

Sleep walking, or **somnambulism**, is much more common among children than adults. As with sleep terrors, sleep walking tends to occur during deep sleep (Stores & Wiggs, 2001). Onset is usually between the ages of 3 and 8.

During medieval times, people believed that sleep walking was a sign of possession by evil spirits. Psychoanalytic theory suggests that sleep walking allows people the chance to express feelings and impulses they would inhibit while awake. But children who sleepwalk have not been shown to have any more trouble controlling impulses than other children do. Moreover, what children do when they sleepwalk is usually too boring to suggest exotic motivation. They may rearrange toys, go to the bathroom, or go to the refrigerator and have a glass of milk. Then they return to their rooms and go back to bed. Their lack of recall in the morning is consistent with sleep terrors, which also occur during deep sleep. Sleep-walking episodes are brief; most tend to last no longer than half an hour.

There are some myths about sleep walking, such as that sleepwalkers' eyes are closed, that they will avoid harm, and that they will become violently agitated if they are awakened during an episode. All these notions are false. Sleepwalkers' eyes are usually open, although they may respond to onlooking parents as furniture to be walked around and not as people. Children may incur injury when sleep walking, just as they may when awake. **Truth or Fiction Revisited:** It is also not true that it is dangerous to awaken a sleepwalker. Children may be difficult to rouse when they are sleep walking, just as during sleep terrors, but if they are awakened, they are more likely to show confusion and disorientation (again, as during sleep terrors) than violence.

Today, sleep walking in children is assumed to reflect immaturity of the nervous system, not acting out of dreams or psychological conflicts. As with sleep terrors, the incidence of sleep walking drops as children develop. It may help to discuss a child's persistent sleep terrors or sleep walking with a health professional.

insomnia   One or more sleep problems including falling asleep, difficulty remaining asleep during the night, and waking early.

somnambulism   Sleep walking (from the Latin *somnus,* meaning "sleep," and *ambulare*, meaning "to walk").

Active Review

17. Most 2–3-year-olds sleep about _____ hours at night and also have one nap during the day.
18. (Nightmares or Sleep terrors?) usually occur during deep sleep.
19. _____ is also referred to as somnambulism.

Reflect & Relate: Critical thinkers insist on evidence before they will accept beliefs, even widely held cultural beliefs. What are your attitudes toward children sleeping with their parents? Are your attitudes supported by research evidence? Explain.

Go to

http://www.thomsonedu.com/psychology/rathus

for an interactive version of this review.

Elimination Disorders

The elimination of waste products occurs reflexively in neonates. As children develop, their task is to learn to inhibit the reflexes that govern urination and bowel movements. The process by which parents teach their children to inhibit these reflexes is referred to as toilet training. The inhibition of eliminatory reflexes makes polite conversation possible. *Questions: When are children considered to be gaining control over elimination too slowly? What can be done to help them gain control?*

Truth or Fiction Revisited: It is not true that more competent parents toilet train their children by the child's second birthday. Most American children are toilet trained between the ages of 3 and 4 (Scheres & Castellanos, 2003). They may have accidents at night for another year or so.

In toilet training, as in so many other areas of physical growth and development, maturation plays a crucial role. During the first year, only an exceptional child can be toilet trained, even when parents devote a great deal of time and energy to the task. If parents wait until the third year to begin toilet training, the process usually runs smoothly.

An end to diaper changing is not the only reason parents are motivated to toilet train their children. Parents often experience pressure from grandparents, other relatives, and friends who point out that so-and-so's children were all toilet trained before the age of _____. (You fill it in. Choose a number that will make most of us feel like inadequate parents.) Parents, in turn, may pressure their children to become toilet trained, and toilet training can become a major arena for parent–child conflict. Children who do not become toilet trained within reasonable time frames are said to have enuresis, encopresis, or both.

Toilet Training
If parents wait until the third year to begin toilet training, the process usually goes relatively rapidly and smoothly.

Enuresis

Give it a name like **enuresis** (en-you-REE-sis), and suddenly it looms like a serious medical problem rather than a bit of an annoyance. Enuresis is the failure to control the bladder (urination) once the "normal" age for achieving control of the bladder has been reached. Conceptions as to the normal age vary. The American Psychiatric Association (2000) is reasonably lenient on the issue and places the cutoff age at 5 years. The frequency of "accidents" is also an issue. The American Psychiatric Association does not consider such accidents enuresis unless the incidents occur at least twice a month for 5- and 6-year-olds or once a month for children who are older.

A nighttime accident is referred to as **bed-wetting**. Nighttime control is more difficult to achieve than daytime control. At night, children must first wake up when their bladders are full. Only then can they go to the bathroom.

Overall, 8% to 10% of American children wet their beds (Mellon & Houts, 2006), with the problem about twice as common among boys as girls. The incidence drops as age increases. A study of 3,344 Chinese children found that these children appeared to attain control a bit earlier: 7.7% obtained nocturnal urinary control by the age of 2, 53% by the age of 3, and 93% by the age of 5 (Liu et al., 2000b). As with American studies, girls achieved control earlier than boys.

Causes of Enuresis

It is believed that enuresis might have organic causes, such as infections of the urinary tract or kidney problems, or immaturity in development of the motor cortex of the brain (von Gontard, 2006; von Gontard et al., 2006). If so, cases with different causes might clear up at different rates or profit from different kinds of treatment. In the case of immaturity of parts of the brain, no treatment at all might be in order.

Numerous psychological explanations of enuresis have also been advanced. Psychoanalytic theory suggests that enuresis is a way of expressing hostility toward

enuresis (en-you-REE-sis) Failure to control the bladder (urination) once the normal age for control has been reached.

bed-wetting Failure to control the bladder during the night. (Frequently used interchangeably with enuresis, although bed-wetting refers to the behavior itself and enuresis is a diagnostic category, related to the age of the child.)

A Closer Look

What to Do about Bed-Wetting

Parents are understandably disturbed when their children continue to wet their beds long after most children are dry through the night. Cleaning up is a hassle, and parents also often wonder what their child's bed-wetting "means," about the child and about their own adequacy as parents.

Bed-wetting may only "mean" that the child is slower than most children to keep his or her bed dry through the night. Bed-wetting may mean nothing at all about the child's intelligence or personality or about the parents' capabilities (von Gontard et al., 2006). Certainly a number of devices (alarms) can be used to teach the child to awaken in response to bladder pressure (Ikeda et al., 2006). Medications also can be used to help the child retain fluids through the night (Sumner et al., 2006). Before turning to these methods, however, methods such as the following may be of help.

- **Limit fluid intake late in the day.** Less pressure on the bladder makes it easier to control urinating, but do not risk depriving the child of liquids. On the other hand, it makes sense to limit fluid intake in the evening, especially at bedtime. Because drinks with caffeine, such as colas, coffee, and tea, act as diuretics, making it more difficult to control urination, it is helpful to cut down on them after lunch.
- **Wake the child during the night.** Waking the child at midnight or 1:00 in the morning may make it possible for him or her to go to the bathroom and urinate. Children may complain and say that they don't have to go, but often they will. Praise the child for making the effort.
- **Try a night-light.** Many children fear getting up in the dark and trying to find their way to the bathroom. A night-light can make the difference. If the bathroom is far from the child's bedroom, it may be helpful to place a chamber pot in the bedroom. The child can empty the pot in the morning.
- **Maintain a consistent schedule so that the child can form helpful bedtime and nighttime habits.** Having a regular bedtime not only helps ensure that your child gets enough sleep but also enables the child to get into a routine of urinating before going to bed and keeps the child's internal clock in sync with the clock on the wall. Habits can be made to work for the child rather than against the child.
- **Use a "sandwich" bed.** A sandwich bed is simply a plastic sheet, covered with a cloth sheet, covered with yet another plastic sheet, and then still another cloth sheet. If the child wets his or her bed, the top wet sheet and plastic sheet can be pulled off, and the child can get back into a comfortable dry bed. In this way, the child develops the habit of sleeping in a dry bed. Moreover, the child learns how to handle his or her "own mess" by removing the wet sheets.
- **Have the child help clean up.** The child can throw the sheets into the wash and, perhaps, operate the washing machine. The child can make the bed or at least participate. These behaviors are not punishments; they help connect the child to the reality of what is going on and what needs to be done to clean things up.
- **Reward the child's successes.** Parents risk becoming overly punitive when they pay attention only to the child's failures. Ignoring successes also allows them to go unreinforced. When the child has a dry night, or half of a dry night, make a note of it. Track successes on a calendar. Connect them with small treats, such as more TV time or time with you. Make a "fuss," that is, a positive fuss. Also consider rewarding partial successes, such as the child getting up after beginning to urinate so that there is less urine in the bed.
- **Show a positive attitude.** ("Accentuate the positive.") Talk with your child about "staying dry" rather than "not wetting." Communicate the idea that you have confidence that things will get better. (They almost always do.)

Reflect:

- Why do so many parents "take it personally" when their children wet their beds?
- What do we mean when we say that children "outgrow" bed-wetting?
- How do you feel about giving a preschool child medicine to help curb bed-wetting? Explain.

parents (because of their harshness in toilet training) or a form of symbolic masturbation. These views are largely unsubstantiated. Learning theorists point out that enuresis is most common among children whose parents attempted to train them early. Early failures might have conditioned anxiety over attempts to control the bladder. Conditioned anxiety, then, prompts rather than inhibits urination.

Situational stresses seem to play a role. Children are more likely to wet their beds when they are entering school for the first time, when a sibling is born, or when they are ill. There may also be a genetic component in that there is a strong family history in the majority of cases (Bayoumi et al., 2006).

It has also been noted that bed-wetting tends to occur during the deepest stage of sleep. That is also the stage when sleep terrors and sleep walking take place. For this reason, bed-wetting could be considered a sleep disorder. Like sleep walking, bed-wetting could reflect immaturity of certain parts of the nervous system (von Gontard, 2006). Just as children outgrow sleep terrors and sleep walking, they tend to outgrow bed-wetting (Mellon & Houts, 2006). In most cases, bed-wetting resolves itself by adolescence, and usually by the age of 8.

Encopresis

Soiling, or **encopresis**, is lack of control over the bowels. Soiling, like enuresis, is more common among boys than among girls, but the overall incidence of soiling is lower than that of enuresis. About 1% to 2% of children at the ages of 7 and 8 have continuing problems controlling their bowels (Mellon, 2006; von Gontard, 2006).

Soiling, in contrast to enuresis, is more likely to occur during the day. Thus, it can be acutely embarrassing to the child, especially in school.

Encopresis stems from both physical causes, such as chronic constipation, and psychological factors (Mellon, 2006; Needlman, 2001; von Gontard, 2006). Soiling may follow harsh punishment of toileting accidents, especially in children who are already anxious or under stress. Punishment may cause the child to tense up on the toilet, when moving one's bowels requires that one relax the anal sphincter muscles. Harsh punishment also focuses the child's attention on soiling. The child then begins to ruminate about soiling so that soiling, punishment, and worrying about future soiling become a vicious cycle.

We now leave our exploration of physical development in early childhood and begin an examination of cognitive development.

encopresis Failure to control the bowels once the normal age for bowel control has been reached. Also called soiling.

Active Review

20. In toilet training, maturation (Does or Does not?) play a crucial role.
21. Bed-wetting is more common among (Girls or Boys?).
22. A common physical cause of encopresis is _____.

Reflect & Relate: Why do you think so many parents become upset when their children are a bit behind others in toilet training? Do you think it is bad if it takes 3 or 4 years for a child to learn to use the toilet reliably? If so, why?

Go to

http://www.thomsonedu.com/psychology/rathus
for an interactive version of this review.

1. **What changes occur in height and weight during early childhood?**

Children gain about 2 to 3 inches in height and 4 to 6 pounds in weight per year in early childhood. Boys are slightly larger than girls.

2. **How does the brain develop during early childhood?**

The brain develops more quickly than any other organ in early childhood, in part because of myelination. Myelination enhances children's ability to attend to and process visual information, enabling them to read and to screen out distractions.

3. **What does it mean to be left-brained or right-brained?**

The left hemisphere is relatively more involved in logical analysis and problem solving, language, and mathematical computation. The right hemisphere is usually superior in visual–spatial functions, aesthetic and emotional responses, and creative mathematical reasoning. Nevertheless, the functions of the left and right hemispheres are not independent.

4. **What is meant by "plasticity of the brain"?**

Plasticity means that the brain compensates for injuries to particular areas. Two factors involved in the brain's plasticity are the growth of new dendrites and the redundancy of neural connections.

5. **How do motor skills develop in early childhood?**

In the preschool years, children make great strides in the development of gross motor skills, which involve the large muscles. Girls are somewhat better at tasks requiring balance and precision; boys have some advantage in throwing and kicking. Fine motor skills develop gradually. The most active children generally show less well developed motor skills. After 2 or 3 years of age, children become less restless and are more able to sustain attention during play.

6. **Do girls and boys differ in their activity levels during early childhood?**

Boys tend to be more active than girls in large muscle activities. Boys are more fidgety and distractible, perhaps because they are less mature physically.

7. **Are children's scribbles the result of random motor activity?**

Apparently not. Kellogg identified 20 scribbles that she considers the building blocks of art. She theorizes that children undergo four stages of progressing from scribbles to drawing pictures.

8. **When does handedness emerge? How many children are left-handed?**

By 6 months, most infants show clear-cut hand preferences, which become still more established during early childhood. More than 90% of children are right-handed.

9. **Are there problems connected with being left-handed?**

Left-handedness may be connected with language problems and some health problems, yet a disproportionately large number of artists, musicians, and mathematicians are left-handed.

10. **What are children's nutritional needs and their eating behavior like in early childhood?**

The typical 4- to 6-year-old needs 1,800 calories a day, compared with 1,300 for the average 1- to 3-year-old. During the second and third years, children's appetites typically wane and grow erratic. Many children eat too much sugar and salt, which can harm their health.

11. **How healthy are children in the United States and in other countries? What are some of the illnesses and environmental hazards encountered during early childhood?**

The incidence of minor illnesses, such as colds, nausea and vomiting, and diarrhea, is high. Although diarrheal illness is usually mild in the United States, it is a leading killer of children in developing countries. Immunization and antibiotics reduce the incidence of serious childhood diseases. Air pollution contributes to respiratory infections. Diarrheal diseases are almost completely related to unsafe drinking water and lack of sanitation. Lead poisoning causes neurological damage.

12. **How much sleep is needed during early childhood?**

Most 2- and 3-year-olds sleep about 10 hours at night and nap during the day.

13. **What kinds of problems or disorders disrupt sleep during early childhood?**

Sleep terrors are more severe than nightmares. Sleep terrors and sleep walking usually occur during deep sleep. Sleepwalkers' eyes are usually open, and if they are awakened, they may show confusion and disorientation but are unlikely to be violent.

14. **When are children considered to be gaining control over elimination too slowly? What can be done to help them gain control?**

Most American children are toilet trained by about age 3 or 4 but continue to have "accidents" at night for another year or so. Enuresis is the failure to control the bladder once a child has reached the "normal" age for doing so, placed at 5 years of age by the American Psychiatric Association. Encopresis (soiling) is lack of control over the bowels. Enuresis is apparently connected with physical immaturity and stress. Encopresis can stem from physical causes, such as constipation, and psychological factors.

Key Terms

corpus callosum, 268
plasticity, 268
gross motor skills, 269
rough-and-tumble play, 271
fine motor skills, 272
placement stage, 272
shape stage, 273

design stage, 273
pictorial stage, 274
handedness, 274
oral rehydration therapy, 281
transitional object, 284
sleep terrors, 284
nightmares, 284

insomnia, 286
somnambulism, 286
enuresis, 287
bed-wetting, 287
encopresis, 289

Active Learning Resources

Childhood & Adolescence Book Companion Website

http://www.thomsonedu.com/psychology/rathus

Visit your book companion website where you will find more resources to help you study. There you will find interactive versions of your book features, including the Lessons in Observation video, Active Review sections, and the Truth or Fiction feature. In addition, the companion website contains quizzing, flash cards, and a pronunciation glossary.

 **is an easy-to-use online resource that helps you study in less time to get the grade you want—NOW.**

http://www.thomsonedu.com/login

Need help studying? This site is your one-stop study shop. Take a Pre-Test and ThomsonNOW will generate a Personalized Study Plan based on your test results. The Study Plan will identify the topics you need to review and direct you to online resources to help you master those topics. You can then take a Post-Test to determine the concepts you have mastered and what you still need to work on.

9

Early Childhood:
Cognitive Development

Truth or Fiction?

T F A preschooler's having imaginary playmates is a sign of loneliness or psychological problems. p. 297

T F Two-year-olds tend to assume that their parents are aware of everything that is happening to them, even when their parents are not present. p. 298

T F "Because Mommy wants me to" may be a perfectly good explanation, for a 3-year-old. p. 298

T F Children's levels of intelligence—not just their knowledge—are influenced by early learning experiences. p. 307

T F A highly academic preschool education provides children with advantages in school later on. p. 308

T F One- and 2-year-olds are too young to remember past events. p. 316

T F During her third year, a girl explained that she and her mother had finished singing a song by saying, "We singed it all up." p. 322

T F Three-year-olds usually say "Daddy goed away" instead of "Daddy went away" because they do understand rules of grammar. p. 322

Preview

Jean Piaget's Preoperational Stage
Symbolic Thought
Symbolic or Pretend Play: "We Could Make Believe"
Operations: "Transformers" of the Mind
Egocentrism: It's All About Me
Causality: Why? Because.
Confusion of Mental and Physical Events:
    On "Galaprocks" and Dreams That Are Real
Focus on One Dimension at a Time: Mental Blinders
Evaluation of Piaget

Lessons in Observation: Piaget's Preoperational Stage

Developing in a World of Diversity: Development of Concepts of Ethnicity and Race

Factors in Cognitive Development
Scaffolding and the Zone of Proximal Development
Being at HOME: The Effect of the Home Environment
Effects of Early Childhood Education: Does It Give Preschoolers a Head Start?
Television: Window on the World or Prison within a False World?

A Closer Look: Helping Children Use Television Wisely

Theory of Mind: What Is the Mind?
How Does It Work?
False Beliefs: Just Where Are Those Crayons?
Origins of Knowledge: Where Does It Come From?
The Appearance–Reality Distinction: Appearances Are More Deceiving at Some Ages than at Others

Development of Memory: Creating "Documents," Storing Them, Retrieving Them
Memory Tasks: Recognition and Recall
Competence of Memory in Early Childhood
Factors Influencing Memory
Memory Strategies: Remembering to Remember

Language Development: Why "Daddy Goed Away"
Development of Vocabulary: Words, Words, and More Words
Development of Grammar: Toward More Complex Language
Pragmatics: Preschoolers Can Be Practical
Language and Cognition

Go to

http://www.thomsonedu.com/psychology/rathus
for an interactive version of this "Truth or Fiction" feature.

Brian Summers/First Light

was confused when my daughter Allyn, at the age of 2 ½, insisted that I continue to play "Billy Joel" on the stereo. Put aside the question of her taste in music. My problem was that when Allyn asked for Billy Joel, the name of the singer, she could be satisfied only by my playing the song "Moving Out." When "Moving Out" had ended and the next song, "The Stranger," had begun to play, she would insist that I play "Billy Joel" again. "That is Billy Joel," I would protest. "No, no," she would insist, "I want Billy Joel!"

Finally, it dawned on me that, for her, "Billy Joel" symbolized the song "Moving Out," not the name of the singer. Of course my insistence that the second song was also "Billy Joel" could not satisfy her! She was conceptualizing Billy Joel as a property of a particular song, not as the name of a person who could sing many songs.

Children between the ages of 2 and 4 tend to show confusion between symbols and the objects they represent. They do not yet recognize that words are arbitrary symbols for objects and events and that people can use different words. They tend to think of words as inherent properties of objects and events.

In this chapter, we discuss cognitive development during early childhood. First, we examine Jean Piaget's preoperational stage of cognitive development. Piaget largely viewed cognitive development in terms of maturation; however, in the section on factors in cognitive development, we will see that social and other factors foster cognitive development by placing children in "the zone," as Lev Vygotsky might have put it. Next, we consider other aspects of cognitive development, such as how children acquire a "theory of mind" and develop memory. Finally, we continue our exploration of language development.

Jean Piaget's Preoperational Stage

According to Piaget, the **preoperational stage** of cognitive development lasts from about age 2 to age 7. Be warned: Any resemblance between the logic of a preschooler and your own may be purely coincidental.

Symbolic Thought

Question: How do children in the preoperational stage think and behave? Preoperational thought is characterized by the use of symbols to represent objects and relationships among them. Perhaps the most important kind of symbolic activity of young children is language, but we will see that children's early use of language leaves something to be desired in the realm of logic.

Children begin to scribble and draw pictures in their early years. These drawings are symbols of objects, people, and events in children's lives. Symbolism is also expressed as symbolic or pretend play, which emerges during these years.

Symbolic or Pretend Play: "We Could Make Believe"

Children's **symbolic play**—the "let's pretend" type of play—may seem immature to busy adults meeting the realistic demands of the business world, but it requires cognitive sophistication (Feldman & Masalha, 2007; Keen et al., 2007; Lytle, 2003).

Piaget (1962 [1946]) wrote that pretend play usually begins in the second year, when the child begins to symbolize objects. The ability to engage in pretend play is based on the use and recollection of symbols, that is, on mental representations of things children have experienced or heard about. At 19 months, Allyn picked up a pinecone and looked it over. Her babysitter said, "That's a pinecone." Allyn pretended to lick it, as if it were an ice-cream cone.

preoperational stage The second stage in Piaget's scheme, characterized by inflexible and irreversible mental manipulation of symbols.

symbolic play Play in which children make believe that objects and toys are other than what they are. Also called pretend play.

Children first engage in pretend play at about 12 or 13 months of age. They make believe that they are performing familiar activities, such as sleeping or feeding themselves. By age 15 to 20 months, they can shift their focus from themselves to others. A child may thus pretend to feed her doll. By 30 months, she or he can make believe that the other object takes an active role. The child may now pretend that the doll is feeding itself (McCune, 1993; Paavola et al., 2006; Thyssen, 2003).

The quality of preschoolers' pretend play has implications for subsequent development. For example, preschoolers who engage in violent pretend play are less empathic, less likely to help other children, and more likely to engage in anti-social behavior later on (Dunn & Hughes, 2001). Preschoolers who engage in more elaborate pretend play are also more likely to do well in school later on (Stagnitti et al., 2000). The quality of pretend play is also connected with preschoolers' creativity and their ability to relate to peers (Russ, 2006).

Imaginary friends are one example of pretend play. At age 2, Allyn acquired an imaginary playmate named Loveliness. He told Allyn to do lots of things, such as move things from here to there and get food for him. At times, Allyn was overheard talking to Loveliness in her room. As many as 65% of preschoolers have such friends; they are more common among firstborn and only children than among children with siblings (Gleason et al., 2003).

Truth or Fiction Revisited: It is not true that having imaginary playmates is a sign of loneliness or psychological problems. Having an imaginary playmate does not mean that the child is having difficulty in real relationships (Gleason, 2004; Hoff, 2005). In fact, children with imaginary companions are less aggressive, more cooperative—they often nurture the imaginary friend (Gleason, 2002)—and more creative than children without such companions. They have more real friends, show greater ability to concentrate, and are more advanced in language development (Taylor, 1999).

As long as we are talking about play, let's note that some toys are called Transformers. In the following section, we see that the mental processes of children are also "transformers." (Clever transition from one section to another?)

Symbolic Play

Symbolic play—also called pretend play—usually begins in the second year, when the child begins to form mental representations of objects. This 2½-year-old may engage in a sequence of play acts such as making a doll sit down at the table and offering it a make-believe cup of tea.

Operations: "Transformers" of the Mind

Any resemblance between the logic of children ages 2 to 7 and your own may be purely coincidental. *Question: How do we characterize the logic of the preoperational child?* **Operations** are mental acts (or schemes) in which objects are changed or transformed and then can be returned to their original states. Mental operations are flexible and reversible.

Consider the example of planning a move in checkers. A move requires knowledge of the rules of the game. The child who plays the game well (as opposed to simply making moves) is able to picture the results of the move: how, in its new position, the piece will support or be threatened by other pieces and how other pieces might

operations Flexible, reversible mental manipulations of objects, in which objects can be mentally transformed and then returned to their original states.

be left undefended by the move. Playing checkers well requires that the child be able to picture, or focus on, different parts of the board and on relationships between pieces at the same time. By considering several moves, the child shows flexibility. By picturing the board as it would be after a move and then as it is, the child shows reversibility.

Having said all that, let us return to preoperational children, children who cannot yet engage in flexible and reversible mental operations. Young children's logic reflects that their ability to perform operations is "under construction." The preoperational stage is thus characterized by features such as egocentrism, immature notions about what causes what, confusion between mental and physical events, and the ability to focus on only one dimension at a time.

Egocentrism: It's All About Me

Sometimes the attitude "It's all about me" is a sign of early childhood, not of selfishness. One consequence of one-dimensional thinking is **egocentrism**. *Question: What is egocentrism?* Egocentrism, in Piaget's use of the term, does not mean that preoperational children are selfish (although, of course, they may be). Rather, it means that they do not understand that other people may have different perspectives on the world.

Truth or Fiction Revisited: Two-year-olds may, in fact, assume that their parents are aware of everything that is happening to them, even when their parents are not present. They may view the world as a stage that has been erected to meet their needs and amuse them. When I asked Allyn—still at the age of 2½—to tell me about a trip to the store with her mother, she answered, "You tell me." It did not occur to her that I could not see the world through her eyes.

Piaget used the "three-mountains test" (see ● Figure 9.1) to show that egocentrism literally prevents young children from taking the viewpoints of others. In this demonstration, the child sits at a table before a model of three mountains, which differ in color. One has a house on it, and another has a cross at the summit.

Piaget then placed a doll elsewhere on the table and asked the child what the doll sees. The language abilities of very young children do not permit them to provide verbal descriptions of what can be seen from where the doll is situated, so they can answer in one of two ways. They can either select a photograph taken from the proper vantage point, or they can construct another model of the mountains as they would be seen by the doll. The results of a classic experiment with the three-mountains test suggest that 5- and 6-year-olds usually select photos or build models that correspond to their own viewpoints (Laurendeau & Pinard, 1970).

Causality: Why? Because.

Preoperational children's responses to questions such as "Why does the sun shine?" show other facets of egocentrism. At the age of 2 or so, they may answer that they do not know or change the subject. **Truth or Fiction Revisited:** Three-year-olds may report themselves as doing things because they want to do them or "Because Mommy wants me to." In egocentric fashion, this explanation of behavior is extended to inanimate objects. The sun may thus be thought of as shining because it wants to shine or because someone (or something) else wants it to shine. In this case, the sun's behavior is thought of as being caused by will, perhaps the sun's wish to bathe the child in its rays or the child's wish to remain warm. In either case, the answer puts the child at the center of the conceptual universe. The sun becomes an instrument similar to a lightbulb.

Piaget labels this type of structuring of cause and effect **precausal**. *Question: What is precausal thinking?* Preoperational children believe that things happen for reasons and not by accident. However, unless preoperational children know the

egocentrism Putting oneself at the center of things such that one is unable to perceive the world from another person's point of view. Egocentrism is normal in early childhood but is a matter of choice, and rather intolerable, in adults. (Okay, I sneaked an editorial comment into a definition. Dr. Samuel Johnson also did that.)

precausal A type of thought in which natural cause-and-effect relationships are attributed to will and other preoperational concepts. (For example, the sun sets because it is tired.)

natural causes of an event, their reasons are likely to have an egocentric flavor and not be based on science. Consider the question, "Why does it get dark outside?" The preoperational child usually does not have knowledge of Earth's rotation and is likely to answer something like, "So I can go to sleep."

Another example of precausal thinking is **transductive reasoning.** In transductive reasoning, children reason by going from one specific isolated event to another. For example, a 3-year-old may argue that she should go on her swings in the backyard because it is light outside or that she should go to sleep because it is dark outside. That is, separate specific events, daylight and going on the swings (or being awake), are thought of as having cause-and-effect relationships.

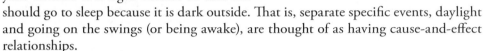

Piaget used the three-mountains test to learn whether children at certain ages are egocentric or can take the viewpoints of others.

Preoperational children also show **animism** and **artificialism** in their attributions of causality. In animistic thinking, they attribute life and intentions to inanimate objects, such as the sun and the moon. ("Why is the moon gone during the day?" "It is afraid of the sun.") Artificialism assumes that environmental features such as rain and thunder have been designed and made by people. In *Six Psychological Studies,* Piaget (1967 [1964], p. 28) wrote: "Mountains 'grow' because stones have been manufactured and then planted. Lakes have been hollowed out, and for a long time the child believes that cities are built [before] the lakes adjacent to them." ■ Table 9.1 shows other examples of egocentrism, animism, and artificialism.

Confusion of Mental and Physical Events: On "Galaprocks" and Dreams That Are Real

What would you do if someone asked you to pretend you were a galaprock? Chances are, you might inquire what a galaprock is and how it behaves. So might a 5-year-old child. But a 3-year-old might not think that such information is necessary (Gottfried et al., 2003). Have you seen horror movies in which people's dreams become real? It could be said that preoperational children tend to live in such worlds, although, for them, that world is normal and not horrible.

Question: Why do young children think that they can pretend to be galaprocks without knowing what galaprocks are? According to Piaget, the preoperational child has difficulty making distinctions between mental and physical phenomena. Children between the ages of 2 and 4 show confusion between symbols and the things that they represent. Egocentrism contributes to the assumption that their thoughts exactly reflect external reality. They do not recognize that words are arbitrary and that people can use different words to refer to things. In *Play, Dreams, and Imitation in Childhood,* Piaget (1962 [1946]) asked a 4-year-old child, "Could you call this table a cup and that cup a table?" "No," the child responded. "Why not?" "Because," explained the child, "you can't drink out of a table!"

Another example of the preoperational child's confusion of the mental and the physical is the tendency to believe that dreams are real. Dreams are cognitive events that originate within the dreamer but seem to be perceived through the dreamer's senses. These facts are understood by 7-year-olds, but many 4-year-olds believe that dreams are real (Meyer & Shore, 2001). They think that their dreams are visible to others and that dreams come from the outside. It is as though they were watching a movie (Crain, 2000).

transductive reasoning Reasoning from the specific to the specific. (In deductive reasoning, one reasons from the general to the specific; in inductive reasoning, one reasons from the specific to the general.)

animism The attribution of life and intentionality to inanimate objects.

artificialism The belief that environmental features were made by people.

■ **Table 9.1** Highlights of Preoperational Thought

Type of Thought	Sample Questions	Typical Answers
Egocentrism (placing oneself at the center of things such that one is unable to perceive the world from another's point of view)	Why does it get dark out?	So I can go to sleep.
	Why does the sun shine?	To keep me warm.
	Why is there snow?	For me to play in.
	Why is grass green?	Because that's my favorite color.
	What are TV sets for?	To watch my favorite shows and cartoons.
Animism (attributing life and consciousness to physical objects)	Why do trees have leaves?	To keep them warm.
	Why do stars twinkle?	Because they're happy and cheerful.
	Why does the sun move in the sky?	To follow children and hear what they say.
	Where do boats go at night?	They sleep like we do.
Artificialism (assuming that environmental events are human inventions)	What makes it rain?	Someone emptying a watering can.
	Why is the sky blue?	Somebody painted it.
	What is the wind?	A man blowing.
	What causes thunder?	A man grumbling.
	How does a baby get in Mommy's tummy?	Just make it first. (How?) You put some eyes on it, then put on the head.

Focus on One Dimension at a Time: Mental Blinders

To gain further insight into preoperational thinking, consider these two problems. First, imagine that you pour water from a low, wide glass into a tall, thin glass, as in ● Figure 9.2(b). Now, does the tall, thin glass contain more than, less than, or the same amount of water as in the low, wide glass? We won't keep you in suspense. If you said the same amount (with possible minor exceptions for spillage and evaporation), you were correct.

Now that you're on a roll, here's another problem. If you flatten a ball of clay into a pancake, do you wind up with more, less, or the same amount of clay? If you said the same amount, you are correct once more.

To arrive at the correct answers to these questions, you must understand the law of **conservation**. *Question: What is conservation (in cognitive development)?* The law of conservation holds that properties of substances such as volume, mass, and number remain the same—or are conserved—even if you change their shape or arrangement.

Now, preoperational children are not conservationists. I don't mean that they throw out half-eaten meals (although they do so often enough); I mean that they tend to focus on only one aspect of a problem at a time.

Conservation requires the ability to focus on two aspects of a situation at once, such as height and width. The preoperational boy in Figure 9.2(c) focuses or centers on only one dimension at a time, a characteristic of thought that Piaget called **centration**. First, the boy is shown two tall, thin glasses of water and agrees that they have the same amount of water. Then, as he watches, water is poured from one tall glass

conservation In cognitive psychology, the principle that properties of substances such as weight and mass remain the same (are conserved) when superficial characteristics such as their shapes or arrangement are changed.

centration Focusing on one dimension of a situation while ignoring others.

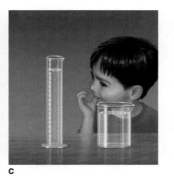

● **Figure 9.2** Conservation

(a) The boy in this illustration agreed that the amount of water in two identical containers is equal. (b) He then watched as water from one container was poured into a tall, thin container. (c) When asked whether the amounts of water in the two containers are now the same, he says no.

into a squat glass. Asked which glass has more water, he points to the tall glass. Why? When he looks at the glasses, he is swayed by the fact that the thinner glass is taller.

The preoperational child's failure to show conservation also comes about because of a characteristic of thought known as **irreversibility.** That is, the child does not realize that pouring water from the tall glass to the squat glass can be reversed, restoring things to their original condition.

If all this sounds rather illogical, it is because it is illogical or, to be precise, preoperational. But if you have any doubts concerning its accuracy, borrow a 3-year-old and try the water experiment for yourself or check the "Lessons in Observation" video feature on page 302.

After you have tried the experiment with the water, try this experiment on conservation of number. Make two rows with four pennies in each, about one-half inch apart. As the 3-year-old child is watching, move the pennies in the second row to about 1 inch apart, as in ● Figure 9.3. Then ask the child which row has more pennies. What do you think the child will say? Why?

Class Inclusion

Class inclusion, as we are using it here, does not refer to whether a class is open to children from diverse backgrounds. We are talking about an aspect of conceptual thinking that you most likely take for granted: including new objects or categories in broader mental classes or categories.

Class inclusion also requires children to focus on two aspects of a situation at once. Class inclusion means that one category or class of things includes other subclasses. For example, the class "animals" includes the subclasses of dogs and cats.

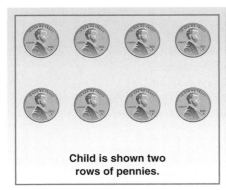

Child is shown two rows of pennies.

Experimenter moves pennies in one row.

● **Figure 9.3** Conservation of Number

In this demonstration, we begin with two rows of pennies that are spread out equally, as shown in the left-hand part of the drawing. Then one row of pennies is spread out more, as shown in the drawing on the right-hand side. We then ask the child, "Do the two rows still have the same number of pennies?" Do you think that a preoperational child will conserve the number of pennies or focus on the length of the longer row in arriving at an answer?

irreversibility Lack of recognition that actions can be reversed.

class inclusion The principle that one category or class of things can include several subclasses.

● **Figure 9.4**
Class Inclusion

A typical 4-year-old child will say that there are more dogs than animals in the example.

In one of Piaget's class-inclusion tasks, the child is shown several objects from two subclasses of a larger class (see ● Figure 9.4). For example, a 4-year-old child is shown pictures of four cats and six dogs. She is asked whether there are more dogs or more animals. Now, she knows what dogs and cats are. She also knows that they are both animals. What do you think she will say? Preoperational children typically answer that there are more dogs than animals (Piaget, 1963 [1936]). That is, they do not show class inclusion.

Why do children make this error? According to Piaget, the preoperational child cannot think about the two subclasses and the larger class at the same time. Therefore, he or she cannot easily compare them. The child views dogs as dogs, or as animals, but finds it difficult to see them as both dogs and animals at once (Branco & Lourenço, 2004; Rabinowitz et al., 2002).

Evaluation of Piaget

Piaget was an astute observer of the cognitive processes of young children. But more recent research questions the accuracy of his age estimates concerning children's failures (or apparent failures) to display certain cognitive skills. For example, Donaldson (1979) argues that the difficulty young children have with the three-mountains test may not be due to egocentrism. Instead, she attributes much of the problem to the demands that this method makes on the child. The three-mountains test presents a

Lessons in Observation
Piaget's Preoperational Stage

 To watch this video, visit the book companion website. You can also answer the questions and e-mail your responses to your professor.

Preoperational children, such as this young girl, fail to conserve volume. She believes that there is more liquid in the taller glass because she is focusing on height alone.

Learning Objectives

- How do pretend play and symbolic representation illustrate Piaget's preoperational stage of development?
- How do children show egocentrism?
- What is the meaning of conservation in Piaget's theory?
- How do children show failure to conserve?

Applied Lesson

How do preoperational inflexibility and irreversibility affect the children's failure to conserve in this video?

Critical Thinking

How did Piaget's experimental procedures and task demands influence the responses of children in conservation tasks?

Developing in a World of Diversity

Development of Concepts of Ethnicity and Race

Americans are encouraged to be "colorblind" in matters of employment, housing, and other areas in which discrimination has historically occurred (Quintana et al., 2006). However, children, like adults, are not literally colorblind. Therefore, it is fascinating to see how children's concepts of race and ethnicity develop. Knowledge of the connection between cognitive development and the development of concepts about people from different ethnic and racial backgrounds suggests when it might be most useful to intervene to help children develop open attitudes toward people from different backgrounds.

From interviews of 500 African American, Asian American, Latino and Latina American, and Native American children, psychologist Stephen Quintana (1998) concluded that children undergo four levels of understanding of ethnicity and race. Between the ages of 3 and 6, children generally think about racial differences in physical terms. They do not necessarily see race as a fixed or stable attribute. They may think that a person could change his or her race by means of surgery or tanning in the sun.

From age 6 to age 10, children generally understand that race is a matter of ancestry that affects not only physical appearance but also one's language, diet, and leisure activities. But understanding at this stage is literal, or concrete. For example, children believe that being Mexican American means that one speaks Spanish and eats Mexican-style food. Interethnic friendships are likely to develop among children of this age group.

From the age of about 10 to age 14, children tend to link ethnicity with social class. They become aware of connections between race and income, race and neighborhood, and race and affirmative action. During adolescence, many individuals begin to take pride in their ethnic heritage and experience a sense of belonging to their ethnic group. They are less open to intergroup relationships than younger children are.

Quintana's research found that middle childhood and early adolescence (ages 6 to 14) are probably the best times to fend off the development of prejudice by teaching children about people from different cultural backgrounds. "That's when [children are] able to go beyond the literal meaning of the words and address their own observations about race and ethnicity," he noted (cited in Rabasca, 2000). Children at these ages also tend to be more open to forming relationships with children from different backgrounds than they are during adolescence.

Reflect: *Why does Quintana suggest that early childhood might be too soon to try to prevent the development of prejudice? Do you agree? Explain.*

© Bonnie Kamin/PhotoEdit

If You Are Born White, Do You Remain White? If You Are Born Asian, Do You Remain Asian? If You Are Born . . .
According to research by Quintana, children between the ages of 3 and 6 tend to think about racial differences in physical terms. They do not necessarily see race as a fixed or stable attribute. They may think that people can change their race by means of surgery or sun tanning.

lifeless scene, one devoid of people and human motives. By contrast, she has found that when children are asked to place a boy doll behind tabletop screens so that it cannot be "seen" by police dolls, 3½-year-olds succeed most of the time.

Language development may also play a role in tests of children's egocentrism and other aspects of cognitive development. Young children may not quite understand what is being asked of them in the three-mountains test, even though they may proceed to select the (wrong) photograph rather quickly. Let me give you an example. I was interested in knowing whether Allyn, at age 2 years 9 months, thought that her mother could see her from another room. "Can Mommy see you now?" I asked. "Sure," said Allyn, "if she wants to." Allyn thought I was asking whether her mother could have permission to see her, not whether her mother had the capacity to see Allyn from behind a wall.

Newer studies indicate that the young child's understanding of causality is somewhat more sophisticated than Piaget believed (Hickling & Wellman, 2001). Again, much depends on how the task is presented. When 4- to 7-year-olds are asked the kind of open-ended questions that Piaget used (e.g., "Where did the ocean come from?"), they give artificialistic responses, such as "The ocean comes from sinks." But when asked direct questions ("Do you think people made the oceans?"), most will correctly respond that people do not make natural things such as oceans or flowers. However, 4- to 7-year-olds will say that people do make objects such as cups and TVs (Gelman & Kremer, 1991).

The demands of the standard conservation task may also present a misleading picture of the child's knowledge. Piaget and other experimenters filled identical beakers with the same amount of water and then poured water from one beaker into a beaker of another shape. Before pouring the water, the experimenter typically asked the child whether both beakers have the same amount of water and instructed the child to watch the pouring carefully. In doing so, perhaps the experimenter is "leading the witness," that is, leading the child to expect a change.

Active Review

1. According to Piaget, _____ play is based on the use of symbols.
2. _____ are mental acts in which objects are changed or transformed and can then be returned to their original states.
3. Piaget used the three-mountains test to show that preoperational children are _____.
4. The type of thinking in which children attribute will to inanimate objects is termed _____ thinking.
5. In _____ reasoning, children reason from one specific event to another.
6. The law of _____ holds that properties of substances such as volume, mass, and number remain the same even when their shape or arrangement changes.

7. Preoperational children focus on (How many?) dimension(s) of a problem at once.

Reflect & Relate: Preoperational children focus on one dimension of a problem at a time. Do we as adults sometimes focus on one dimension of a situation at a time? If you injure someone in an accident, should you be held responsible? (Note the two elements: the injury and the fact that it is accidental.) Most people would probably say "An accident is an accident." But what if a utility company injures 8 million people in a nuclear accident? Should the utility company be held responsible? (That is, does the enormity of the damage affect responsibility?)

Go to

http://www.thomsonedu.com/psychology/rathus

for an interactive version of this review.

Concept Review 9.1   Features of Preoperational Cognition, According to Piaget

Symbolic thought

- Child uses symbols to represent objects and relationships.
- Child engages in symbolic play.
- Symbolic play grows more frequent and complex.
- Child may have imaginary friend(s).
- Mental operations are inflexible and irreversible.

Egocentrism

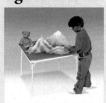

- Child does not take viewpoint of others.
- Child may be lacking in empathy for others.
- Piaget used three-mountains test to assess egocentrism.

Precausal thinking

- Child believes things happen for a reason.
- Child engages in transductive reasoning ("Should sleep because it's dark outside").
- Child shows animism (attributes life and will to inanimate objects).
- Child shows artificialism (assumes environmental features are made by people).

Confusion of mental and physical events

- Child assumes thoughts reflect external reality.
- Child believes dreams are real.

Focus on one dimension at a time

- Child does not understand law of conservation.
- Child centers on one dimension at a time.
- Child does not show appropriate class inclusion (may not include dogs as animals).

Note: Researchers find that the demand characteristics of testing and young children's developments in language and counting ability may lead to an underestimate of their general cognitive abilities.

Factors in Cognitive Development

Question: What are some of the factors that influence cognitive development in early childhood? Two factors are Vygotsky's concepts of scaffolding and the zone of proximal development. Other factors include social and family factors: family income, parents' educational level, family size, parents' mental health, and stressful family events such as divorce, job loss, and illness (Bradley, 2006). In this section, we consider Vygotsky's theory, the home environment, preschool education, and television.

Scaffolding and the Zone of Proximal Development

Parental responsiveness and interaction with the child are key ingredients in the child's cognitive development. One component of this social interaction is **scaffolding** (see Chapter 1). A scaffold is a temporary structure used for holding workers during building construction. Similarly, cognitive scaffolding refers to temporary support provided by a parent or teacher to a learning child. The guidance provided by the adult decreases as the child gains skill and becomes capable of carrying out the task on her or his own (Lengua et al., 2007; Sylva et al., 2007).

A related concept is Vygotsky's **zone of proximal development (ZPD)**. The zone refers to the gap between what the child is capable of doing now and what she or he could do with help from others. Adults or older children can best guide the child through this zone by gearing their assistance to the child's capabilities (Lantolf & Thorne, 2007; Wennergren & Rönnerman, 2006). These researchers recognize that human neurobiology underlies cognitive development in early childhood. However, they argue that the key forms of children's cognitive activities develop through interaction with older, more experienced individuals who teach and guide them within appropriate learning environments such as schools and shops.

In a related study, K. Alison Clarke-Stewart and Robert Beck (1999) had 31 children, all 5-year-olds, observe a videotaped film segment with their mothers, talk about it with their mothers, and then retell the story to an experimenter. The researchers found that the quality of the stories, as retold by the children, was related to the scaffolding strategies the mothers had used with them. Children whose mothers focused the children's attention on the tape, asked their children to talk about it, and discussed the feelings of the characters told better stories than children whose mothers did not use such scaffolding strategies and children in a control group who did not discuss the story at all. Children's understanding of the characters' emotional states was most strongly connected with the number of questions the mother asked and her correction of the child's misunderstandings of what he or she saw.

Researchers observed 21 mother–child pairs as they engaged in specially constructed tasks when the children were 30, 36, and 42 months of age (Haden et al., 2001). They analyzed the children's recall of their performance 1 and 3 days afterward at all three ages. It turned out that the children best recalled those aspects of the tasks they had both worked on and discussed with their mothers. Recall under these circumstances exceeded recall when the activities were (1) handled jointly but talked about only by the mother or (2) handled jointly but not discussed.

In sum, scaffolding within a zone of proximal development helps children learn.

Being at HOME: The Effect of the Home Environment

Bettye Caldwell and her colleagues (e.g., Bradley, Caldwell, & Corwyn, 2003) developed a measure for evaluating children's home environments labeled, appropriately enough, HOME, an acronym for Home Observation for the Measurement of the Environment. With this method, researchers directly observe parent–child interaction

scaffolding Vygotsky's term for temporary cognitive structures or methods of solving problems that help the child as he or she learns to function independently.

zone of proximal development (ZPD) Vygotsky's term for the situation in which a child carries out tasks with the help of someone who is more skilled, frequently an adult who represents the culture in which the child develops.

■ Table 9.2 Scales of the HOME Inventory

Scale	Sample Items
Parental emotional and verbal responsiveness	• The parent spontaneously vocalizes to the child during the visit. • The parent responds to the child's vocalizations with vocal or other verbal responses.
Avoidance of restriction and punishment	• The parent does not shout at the child. • The parent does not interfere with the child's actions or restrict the child's movements more than three times during the visit.
Organization of the physical environment	• The child's play environment seems to be safe and free from hazards.
Provision of appropriate play materials	• The child has a push or a pull toy. • The child has one or more toys or pieces of equipment that promote muscle activity. • The family provides appropriate equipment to foster learning.
Parental involvement with child	• The parent structures the child's play periods. • The parent tends to keep the child within her or his visual range and looks at the child frequently.
Opportunities for variety in daily stimulation	• The child gets out of the house at least four times a week. • The parent reads stories to the child at least three times a week.

in the home. The HOME inventory contains six subscales, as shown in ■ Table 9.2. The HOME inventory items are better predictors of young children's later IQ scores than social class, mother's IQ, or infant IQ scores (Bradley, 2006; Luster & Dubow, 1992). Longitudinal research also shows that the home environment is connected with occupational success as an adult (Huesmann et al., 2006).

Truth or Fiction Revisited: It is true that early learning experiences affect children's levels of intellectual functioning. In a longitudinal study, Caldwell and her colleagues observed children from poor and working-class families over a period of years, starting at 6 months of age. The HOME inventory was used at the early ages, and standard IQ tests were given at ages 3 and 4. The children of mothers who were emotionally and verbally responsive, who were involved with their children, and who provided appropriate play materials and a variety of daily experiences during the early years showed advanced social and language development even at 6 months of age (Parks & Bradley, 1991). These children also attained higher IQ scores at ages 3 and 4 and higher achievement test scores at age 7. Other studies support the view that being responsive to preschoolers, stimulating them, and encouraging independence is connected with higher IQ scores and greater school achievement later on (Bradley, 2006; Bradley & Corwyn, 2006; Molfese et al., 1997). Victoria Molfese and her colleagues (1997) found that the home environment was the single most important predictor of scores on IQ tests among children aged 3 to 8.

The Home Environment

The home environment of the young child is linked to intellectual development and later academic achievement. Key aspects of the home environment include the parents' involvement and encouragement of the child, the availability of toys and learning materials, and the variety of experiences to which the child is exposed.

© Syd Johnson/The Image Works

Effects of Early Childhood Education: Does It Give Preschoolers a Head Start?

How important are academic experiences in early childhood? Do they facilitate cognitive development? Research suggests that preschool education enables children to get an early start on achievement in school.

Preschool Education for Economically Disadvantaged Children

Children growing up in poverty generally perform less well on standardized intelligence tests than children of higher socioeconomic status, and they are at greater risk for school failure (Stipek & Hakuta, 2007; Whitehouse, 2006). As a result, preschool programs were begun in the 1960s and 1970s to enhance the cognitive development and academic skills of poor children to increase their readiness for elementary school. Some, such as the federally funded Head Start program, also provide health care to children and social services to their families. Children in these programs typically are exposed to letters and words, numbers, books, exercises in drawing, pegs and pegboards, puzzles, and toy animals and dolls in addition to other materials and activities that middle-class children can usually take for granted. Many programs encourage parental involvement in the program itself.

Truth or Fiction Revisited: It is true that an academic preschool can provide children with advantages in school. Studies of Head Start and other intervention programs show that environmental enrichment can enhance the cognitive development of economically disadvantaged children (Stipek & Hakuta, 2007; Wilson, 2004). The initial effects can be dramatic. In the Milwaukee Project, poor children of low-IQ mothers were provided with enriched day care from the age of 6 months. By the late preschool years, the children's IQ scores averaged about 121, compared with an average of 95 for children from similar backgrounds who did not receive day care (Garber, 1988). In addition to positively influencing IQ scores, Head Start and other programs also lead to gains in school readiness tests and achievement tests (Stipek & Hakuta, 2007; Wilson, 2004). Programs that involve and educate parents are particularly beneficial (Stipek & Hakuta, 2007).

Preschool intervention programs can have long-term effects on life outcomes for poor children (Stipek & Hakuta, 2007). During the elementary and high school years, graduates of preschool programs are less likely to have been left back or placed in classes for slow learners than peers who did not have the benefit of such programs. They are more likely to graduate from high school, go on to college, and earn higher incomes. They are also less likely to become involved in substance abuse or other areas of delinquent behavior, or be unemployed or on welfare in adulthood (Stipek & Hakuta, 2007; Webster-Stratton & Reid, 2007; Zigler & Styfco, 2001).

A contributor to the cycle of poverty is the incidence of pregnancy among single teenage girls. Pregnancy in these cases usually means that formal education comes to an end, so these children are destined to be reared by poorly educated mothers. Some researchers have found that preschool education programs decrease the probability of single motherhood (Schweinhart & Weikart, 1993). Girls who attended preschool intervention programs became pregnant as frequently as matched controls but were more likely to return to school after giving birth.

Educators recognize that academic environments in the preschool years will benefit advantaged as well as disadvantaged children (Hyson et al., 2006). On the other hand, excessive pressures to achieve during the preschool years, especially on the part of middle-class parents, may impair children's learning and social–emotional development.

Head Start

Preschoolers enrolled in Head Start programs have made dramatic increases in readiness for elementary school and in intelligence test scores. Head Start and similar programs also can have long-term effects on educational and employment outcomes.

© Masterfile

Television: Window on the World or Prison within a False World?

American children spend more time watching television than they do in school. By the time he or she turns 3, the average child already watches 2 to 3 hours of television a day (Palmer, 2003).

Television has great potential for teaching a variety of cognitive skills, social behaviors, and attitudes. In Chapter 10, we explore the effects of television on children's social behaviors and attitudes (uh-oh). Here, we focus on television's effect on cognitive development in early childhood. In many ways, television provides children with an important window on the outside world and on the cognitive skills required to succeed in that world.

Educational Television

"At its best, educational television can provide children with a window to new experiences, enrich academic knowledge, enhance attitudes and motivation, and nurture social skills" (Fisch, 2004). The Children's Television Act requires that networks devote a number of hours per week to educational television. Many but not all the resultant programs have been shown to have mild to moderate positive effects on preschoolers' cognitive development, more so with girls than with boys (Calvert & Kotler, 2003).

Sesame Street, which began broadcasting in 1969, is the most successful children's educational TV program. The goal of *Sesame Street* is to promote the intellectual growth of preschoolers, particularly those of lower socioeconomic status. Large-scale evaluations of the effects of the program have concluded that regular viewing

Sesame Street

Sesame Street is viewed regularly by an estimated 50% to 60% of children in the United States between the ages of 2 and 3 years. Research shows that regular viewing of the program improves children's cognitive and language skills.

increases children's learning of numbers, letters, and cognitive skills such as sorting and classification (Fisch, 2004). These effects are found for African American and European American children, girls and boys, and urban, suburban, and rural children.

Other researchers (e.g., Linebarger & Walker, 2005) reviewed the effects of watching a potpourri of children's TV shows, including *Sesame Street, Dora the Explorer, Blue's Clues, Arthur, Barney & Friends, Clifford, Teletubbies,* and *Dragon Tales.* Of these shows, watching *Dora the Explorer, Blue's Clues, Arthur, Clifford,* or *Dragon Tales* was associated with better vocabulary and expressive language scores on standardized tests for 30-month-old children. *Teletubbies* was associated with poorer vocabularies. *Sesame Street* yielded only a slight positive effect on expressive language. *Barney & Friends* had mixed effects, if any.

What about the effects of television on other aspects of cognitive behavior in the young child? Characters on *Sesame Street* talk out differences and do not fight with one another. Therefore, it is not surprising that most research indicates that exposure to such educational programs as *Sesame Street* may increase impulse control and concentration among preschoolers (Cole et al., 2003). In fact, a joint project by Israelis and Palestinians is under way to bring a Middle Eastern version of *Sesame Street* to the region in the hope that it may contribute to a more peaceful interaction between the groups (Lampel & Honig, 2006).

We can argue about just how much good a program like *Sesame Street* does, but few would argue that it does any harm. However, television programs—even those that target children—differ widely. Readers may profit from reviewing the suggested guidelines for helping children use television wisely in the nearby "A Closer Look" feature.

Commercials

Critics are concerned that the cognitive limitations of young children make them particularly susceptible to commercial messages, which can be potentially misleading and even harmful. Preschoolers do not understand the selling intent of advertising, and they often are unable to tell the difference between commercials and program content (Kundanis & Massaro, 2004; Palmer, 2003). Exposure to commercials does not make the child a sophisticated consumer. In fact, children who are heavy TV viewers are more likely than light viewers to believe commercial claims.

Commercials that encourage children to choose nutritionally inadequate foods—such as sugared breakfast cereals, candy, and fast foods—are harmful to children's nutritional beliefs and diets. Young children do not understand that sugary foods are detrimental to health, nor do they understand disclaimers in ads that, for example, state that sugared cereals should be part of a balanced breakfast (Palmer, 2003; Pine & Nash, 2002).

The Couch-Potato Effect

Watching television, of course, is also a sedentary activity. Parents might prefer that children spend more time exercising, but television also functions as an engrossing babysitter. However, research in the United States, England, and even China shows that preschool children who watch more television are more likely to be overweight than peers who watch less television (Hawkins & Law, 2006; Jago et al., 2006; Jiang et al., 2006). The American study in this case (Jago et al., 2006) found that the number of hours watching television was a stronger predictor of being overweight than diet!

A Closer Look

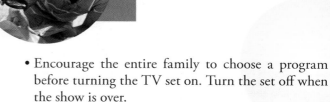

Helping Children Use Television Wisely

Overall, television appears to have some positive effects on cognitive development. But there is more to life than television. Let me share some ideas on how parents can help their children reap the benefits of television without allowing it to take over their lives.

General Suggestions

- Encourage children to watch educational programming.
- Help them choose among cartoon shows. Not all are filled with violence. *It's a Big, Big World* and *Rugrats* may help foster intellectual and social development.
- Encourage your children to sit with you when you are watching educational programming.
- If your child is spending too much time in front of the tube, keep a chart with the child of his or her total activities, including TV, homework, and play with friends. Discuss what to eliminate and what to substitute.
- Set a weekly viewing limit.
- Rule out TV at certain times, such as before breakfast or on school nights.
- Make a list of alternative activities, such as riding a bicycle, reading a book, working on a hobby.

TV, TV Everywhere: How Do We Teach Children to Stop to Think?
Parents can have a positive effect on children's cognitive processing of the information they glean from TV programs and commercials.

- Encourage the entire family to choose a program before turning the TV set on. Turn the set off when the show is over.

Coping with Violence

- Watch at least one episode of programs the child watches to see how violent they are.
- When viewing TV together, discuss the violence with the child. Talk about why the violence happened and how painful it is. Discuss how conflict can be resolved without violence.
- Explain to the child how violence on TV shows is faked.
- Encourage children to watch programs with characters who cooperate, help, and care for one another. Such programs can influence children in a positive way.

Applying TV to Real Life

- Ask children to compare what they see on the screen with people, places, and events they know firsthand, have read about, or have studied in school.
- Tell children what is real and what is make-believe on TV, such as the use of stunt people, dream sequences, and animation.
- Explain to the child your values with regard to sex, alcohol, and drugs.

Understanding Advertising

- Explain to children that the purpose of advertising is to sell products.
- On shopping trips, let children see that toys that look big, fast, and exciting on the screen are disappointingly small and slow close up.
- Talk to the child about nutrition. If the child can read package labels, allow her or him to choose a breakfast cereal from those in which sugar levels are low.

Reflect: Do you know parents who use television as a babysitter? What risks do they run?

This research is correlational, to be sure; that is, children choose (or are allowed) to watch more or less television. They are not randomly assigned to view various amounts of television. Thus, it may be that the same factors that lead them to choose more television also lead them to put on more body fat. On the other hand, there may be little harm (and much good!) in encouraging children to spend more time in physical activity.

Active Review

8. Cognitive _____ refers to temporary support provided by a parent or teacher to a child who is learning to perform a task.

9. Caldwell and her colleagues found that the children of parents who are emotionally and verbally _____ show advanced social and language development.

10. Molfese and her colleagues found that the _____ was the single most important predictor of scores on IQ tests among children.

11. Head Start programs (Can or Cannot?) significantly enhance the cognitive development of economically disadvantaged children.

12. During the elementary and high school years, graduates of preschool programs are (More or Less?) likely to have been left back or placed in classes for slow learners.

13. American children spend (More or Less?) time watching television than they do in school.

Reflect & Relate: What was your early home environment like? How do you think it would have appeared in terms of the factors described in Table 9.2? How can you use the information in this section to create a home environment for your own children?

How much television did you watch as a child? Can you think of things you learned by watching television? Can you imagine developing in a world without television? Explain.

Go to

http://www.thomsonedu.com/psychology/rathus
for an interactive version of this review.

Theory of Mind: What Is the Mind? How Does It Work?

Adults appear to have a commonsense understanding of how the mind works. This understanding, known as a **theory of mind,** allows us to explain and predict behavior by referring to mental processes. For example, we understand that we can acquire knowledge through our senses or through hearsay. We understand the distinction between external and mental events and between how things appear and how they really are. We are able to infer the perceptions, thoughts, and feelings of others. We understand that mental states affect behavior.

Question: What are children's ideas about how the mind works? Piaget might have predicted that preoperational children are too egocentric and too focused on misleading external appearances to have a theory of mind, but research has shown

theory of mind A common-sense understanding of how the mind works.

that even preschool-age children can accurately predict and explain human action and emotion in terms of mental states. They are beginning to understand where knowledge comes from. In addition, they have a rudimentary ability to distinguish appearance from reality (Wellman et al., 2006). Let us consider these developments.

False Beliefs: Just Where Are Those Crayons?

One important indication of the young child's understanding that mental states affect behavior is the ability to understand false beliefs. This concept involves children's ability to separate their beliefs from those of another person who has false knowledge of a situation. It is illustrated in a study of 3-year-olds by Louis Moses and John Flavell (1990). The children were shown a videotape in which a girl named Cathy found some crayons in a bag. When Cathy left the room briefly, a clown entered the room. The clown removed the crayons from the bag, hid them in a drawer, and put rocks in the bag instead. When Cathy returned, the children were asked whether Cathy thought there would be rocks or crayons in the bag. Most of the 3-year-olds incorrectly answered "rocks," demonstrating their difficulty in understanding that the other person's belief would be different from their own (see ● Figure 9.5). But by the age of 4 to 5 years, children do not have trouble with this concept and correctly answer "crayons" (Flavell, 1993). By the ages of 4 and 5, children are also starting to understand that beliefs may be held with differing degrees of certainty (Tardif et al., 2005).

Another intriguing demonstration of the false belief concept comes from studies of children's ability to deceive others. For example, Beate Sodian and her colleagues (1991) asked children to hide a toy truck driver in one of five cups in a sandbox so that another person could not find it. The child was given the opportunity to deceive the other person by removing real trails in the sand and creating false ones. Once again, 4-year-olds acted in ways that were likely to mislead the other person. Younger children did not.

a　　　　　　　　　　b　　　　　　　　　　c

● Figure 9.5   False Beliefs

Flavell and his colleagues showed preschoolers a videotape in which a girl named Cathy found crayons in a bag (a). When Cathy left the room, a clown entered, removed the crayons from the bag, hid them in a drawer (b), and filled the bag with rocks (c). When asked whether Cathy thought there would be rocks or crayons in the bag, most 3-year-olds said "rocks." Most 4-year-olds correctly answered "crayons," showing the ability to separate their own beliefs from someone who has erroneous knowledge of a situation.

The ability to understand false beliefs is related to the development of executive functioning, including working memory, ability to pay sustained attention to problems, and self-control (Flynn et al., 2004; Hala et al., 2003; Ziv & Frye, 2003).

Origins of Knowledge: Where Does It Come From?

Another aspect of theory of mind is how we acquire knowledge. *Questions: Do children understand where their knowledge comes from? If so, how early do they show this ability?*

By age 3, most children begin to realize that people gain knowledge about something by looking at it (Pratt & Bryant, 1990). By age 4, children understand that particular senses provide information about only certain qualities of an object; for example, we come to know an object's color through our eyes, but we learn about its weight by feeling it (O'Neill & Chong, 2001). In a study by Daniela O'Neill and Alison Gopnik (1991), 3-, 4-, and 5-year-olds learned about the contents of a toy tunnel in three different ways: They saw the contents, were told about them, or felt them. The children were then asked to state what was in the tunnel and also how they knew what was in the tunnel. Although 4- and 5-year-olds had no trouble identifying the sources of their knowledge, the 3-year-olds did. For example, after feeling but not seeing a ball in the tunnel, a number of 3-year-olds told the experimenter that they could tell it was a blue ball. The children apparently did not realize that it was impossible to discover the ball's color simply by feeling it.

The Appearance–Reality Distinction: Appearances Are More Deceiving at Some Ages than at Others

Questions: Is seeing believing? What do preoperational children have to say about that? One of the most important things children must acquire in developing a theory of mind is a clear understanding of the difference between real events, on the one hand, and mental events, fantasies, and misleading appearances, on the other hand (Bialystock & Senman, 2004; Flavell et al., 2002). This understanding is known as the **appearance–reality distinction.**

Piaget's view was that children do not differentiate reality from appearances or mental events until the age of 7 or 8. But more recent studies have found that children's ability to distinguish between the two emerges in the preschool years. Children as young as age 3 can distinguish between pretend actions and real actions, between pictures of objects and the actual objects, and between toy versions of an object and the real object (Cohen, 2006; Wellman, 2002). By the age of 4, children make a clear distinction between real items (such as a cup) and imagined items (such as an imagined cup or an imagined monster) (Harris et al., 1991).

Despite these accomplishments, preoperational children still show some difficulties in recognizing the difference between reality and appearances, perhaps because children of this age still have only a limited understanding of **mental representations.** They have trouble understanding that a real object or event can take many forms in our minds (Abelev & Markman, 2006). In a study by Marjorie Taylor and Barbara Hort (1990), children aged 3 to 5 were shown a variety of objects that had misleading appearances, such as an eraser that looked like a cookie. The children initially reported that the eraser looked like a cookie. However, once they learned that it was actually an eraser, they tended to report that it looked like an eraser, ignoring its cookie-like appearance. Apparently, the children could not mentally represent the eraser as both being an eraser and looking like a cookie.

Three-year-olds also apparently cannot understand changes in their mental states. In one study (Gopnik & Slaughter, 1991), 3-year-olds were shown a crayon box. They

appearance–reality distinction The difference between real events on the one hand and mental events, fantasies, and misleading appearances on the other hand.

mental representations The mental forms that a real object or event can take, which may differ from one another. (Successful problem solving is aided by accurate mental representation of the elements of the problem.)

consistently said they thought crayons were inside. The box was opened, revealing birthday candles, not crayons. When the children were asked what they had thought was in the box before it was opened, they now said "candles."

Two-and-a-half- to 3-year-olds also find it difficult to understand the relationship between a scale model and the larger object or space that it represents (Sharon & DeLoache, 2002; Ware et al., 2006). Perhaps it is because the child cannot conceive that the model can be two things at once: both a representation of something else and an object in its own right.

Active Review

14. Moses and Flavell used crayons and a clown to learn whether preschoolers can understand _____ beliefs.
15. By age 3, most children begin to realize that people gain knowledge about things through the _____.

Reflect & Relate: Think of research on the origins of knowledge, on where knowledge comes from. Can you relate this area of research to arguments we might find among adults about sources of knowledge such as experience versus revelation?

Go to

http://www.thomsonedu.com/psychology/rathus
for an interactive version of this review.

Development of Memory: Creating "Documents," Storing Them, Retrieving Them

Even newborns have some memory skills, and memory improves substantially throughout the first 2 years of life. *Question: What sorts of memory skills do children possess in early childhood?*

Memory Tasks: Recognition and Recall

Two of the basic tasks used in the study of memory are recognition and recall. Recognition is the easiest type of memory task. For this reason, multiple-choice tests are easier than fill-in-the-blank or essay tests. In a **recognition** test, one simply indicates whether a presented item has been seen before or which of a number of items is paired with a stimulus (as in a multiple-choice test). Children are capable of simple recognition during early infancy; they recognize their mother's nursing pads, her voice, and her face. To test recognition memory in a preschooler, you might show the child some objects and then present those objects along with some new ones. The child is then asked which objects you showed her the first time.

Recall is more difficult than recognition. In a **recall** task, children must reproduce material from memory without any cues. If I ask you to name the capital of Wyoming, that is a test of recall. A recall task for a preschooler might consist of showing her some objects, taking them away, and asking her to name the objects from memory.

recognition A memory task in which the individual indicates whether presented information has been experienced previously.

recall A memory task in which the individual must reproduce material from memory without any cues.

● **Figure 9.6** Recognition and Recall Memory

Preschoolers can recognize previously seen objects (a) better than they can recall them (b). They also are better at recalling their activities (c) than at recalling objects (b). Older preschoolers (green bars) have better memories than younger ones (gold bars).

Source: Jones et al. (1988).

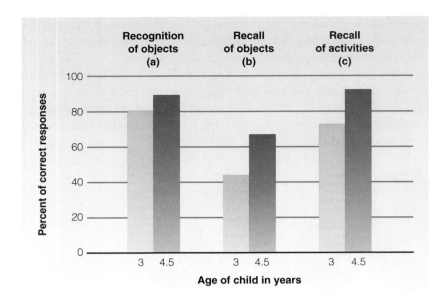

When preschoolers are presented with objects, words, or TV shows, they typically recognize more later on than they can recall (Holliday, 2003; Valkenburg & Buijzen, 2005). In fact, younger preschoolers are almost as good as older ones in recognizing objects they have seen, but they are not nearly as good at recall (Holliday, 2003). In ● Figure 9.6, compare the ability of 3- and 4-year-olds to recognize and recall various objects from a life-size playhouse (Jones et al., 1988). (We discuss the "activities" part of this figure later.)

Competence of Memory in Early Childhood

Until recently, most studies of children's memory were conducted in laboratory settings. The tasks had little meaning for the children. The results appeared to show that the memories of young children are deficient relative to those of older children. But parents often tell you that their children have excellent memories for events. It turns out that they are correct. Children, like adults, frequently remember what they *want* to remember. More recently, psychologists have focused their research on children's memory for meaningful events and activities.

Truth or Fiction Revisited: It is not true that 1- and 2-year-olds are too young to remember past events. Children as young as 11½ months of age can remember organized sequences of events they have just experienced (Bauer & Mandler, 1992). Even after a delay of 6 weeks, 16-month-old children can reenact a sequence of events they experienced only one time, such as placing a ball in a cup, covering it with another cup, and shaking the resulting "rattle" (Bauer & Mandler, 1990). By the age of 4 years, children can remember events that occurred at least 1½ years earlier (Fivush & Hammond, 1990).

Katherine Nelson (1990, 1993) interviewed children aged 2 to 5 to study their memory for recurring events in their lives, such as having dinner, playing with friends, and going to birthday parties. She found that even 3-year-olds can present coherent, orderly accounts of familiar events. Furthermore, young children seem to form **scripts**, which are abstract, generalized accounts of these repeated events. For example, in describing what happens during a birthday party, a child might say, "You play games, open presents, and eat cake" (Fivush, 2002). Details of particular events often are omitted. However, an unusual experience, such as a devastating hurricane, may be remembered in detail for many years (Fivush et al., 2004).

scripts Abstract generalized accounts of familiar repeated events.

Young children begin forming scripts after experiencing an event only once. The script becomes more elaborate with repeated experiences. As might be expected, older preschoolers form detailed scripts more quickly than younger preschoolers (Fivush, 2002).

Even though children as young as 1 and 2 years of age clearly can remember events, these memories seldom last into adulthood. This memory of specific events— known as **autobiographical memory** or *episodic memory*—appears to be linked to the development of language skills. It is facilitated by children talking with their parents and others about past events (Nelson & Fivush, 2004).

Factors Influencing Memory

Question: What factors affect memory in early childhood? The factors that affect memory include what the child is asked to remember, the interest level of the child, the availability of retrieval cues or reminders, and what memory measure we are using. Let us discuss each factor in turn.

Types of Memory

Preschoolers' memories for activities are better than their memories for objects. Return to Figure 9.6. Compare children's accuracy in recalling the activities they engaged in while in the playhouse with their accuracy in recalling the objects they used. You will see that children were much better at recalling their activities (e.g., washing a shirt, chopping ice) than they were at recalling specific objects, such as shirts and ice picks (Jones et al., 1988).

Children also find it easier to remember events that follow a logical order than events that do not occur in a particular order. For instance, 3- and 5-year-olds have a better memory for the activities involved in making pretend cookies out of Play-Doh (you put the ingredients in the bowl, then mix the ingredients, then roll out the dough, and so on) than they do for the activities involved in sand play, which can occur in any order (Fivush et al., 1992).

Childhood Memory
Despite his youth, this boy will most likely remember traumatic experiences in detail for years to come.

Interest Level

There is nothing new about the idea that we pay more attention to the things that interest us. The world is abuzz with signals, and we tend to remember those to which we pay attention. Attention opens the door to memory.

Interest level and motivation also contribute to memory among young children (Ghetti & Alexander, 2004; Sales et al., 2003). Research consistently shows that (most) preschool boys are more interested in playing with toys such as cars and weapons, whereas (most) preschool girls are more interested in playing with dolls, dishes, and teddy bears. Later, the children typically show better recognition and recall for the toys in which they were interested (Martin & Ruble, 2004).

Retrieval Cues

To retrieve information (a file) from your computer's storage, you have to remember its name or some part of it. Then you can use a Find routine. The name is the retrieval cue. In the same way, we need retrieval cues to find things in our own memories.

Although young children can remember a great deal, they depend more than older children do on cues provided by adults to help them retrieve their memories.

autobiographical memory
The memory of specific episodes or events.

Consider the following interchange between a mother and her 2-year-old child (Hudson, 1990, p. 186):

Mother:	What did we look for in the grass and in the bushes?
Child:	Easter bunny.
Mother:	Did we hide candy eggs outside in the grass?
Child:	(nods)
Mother:	Remember looking for them? Who found two? Your brother?
Child:	Yes, brother.

Preschoolers whose parents elaborate on the child's experiences and ask questions that encourage the child to contribute information to the narrative remember an episode better than children whose parents simply provide reminders (Nelson & Fivush, 2004). Parental assistance is more important under some conditions than others. For example, when 4-year-olds were internally motivated to remember items needed to prepare their own sack lunches, they did equally well with or without parental coaching. But when the task was simply to recall a series of items, they did better with parental assistance (Rogoff & Mistry, 1990).

Types of Measurement

What we find is in part determined by how we measure it. Children's memory is often measured or assessed by asking them to say what they remember. But verbal reports, especially from preschoolers, appear to underestimate children's memory (Mandler, 1990). In one longitudinal study, children's memory for certain events was tested at age 2½ and again at age 4. Most of the information recalled at age 4 had not been mentioned at age 2½, indicating that when they were younger, the children remembered much more than they reported (Fivush & Hammond, 1990).

What measures might be more accurate than verbal report? One study found that when young children were allowed to use dolls to reenact an event, their recall was much better than when they gave a verbal report of the event (Goodman et al., 1990).

Memory Strategies: Remembering to Remember

Question: How do we remember to remember? When adults and older children are trying to remember things, they use strategies to help their memory. One common strategy is mental repetition, or **rehearsal**. If you are trying to remember a new friend's phone number, for example, you might repeat it several times. Another strategy is to organize things to be remembered into categories. Many students outline textbook chapters to prepare for an exam. Organizing information in a meaningful way makes it easier to learn and remember. Similarly, if you are going to buy some things at the grocery store, you might mentally group together items that belong to the same category: dairy items, produce, household cleaners, and so on.

Preschool children, though, generally do not appear to use memory strategies on their own initiative. Most young children do not spontaneously engage in rehearsal until about 5 years of age (Labrell & Ubersfeld, 2004). They also rarely group objects into related categories to help them remember. By about age 5, many children have learned to verbalize information silently to themselves by counting mentally, for example, rather than aloud.

Even very young children are capable of using some simple and concrete memory aids to help them remember. They engage in behaviors such as looking, pointing, and touching when trying to remember. For example, in a study by Judith DeLoache and her colleagues (1985), 18- to 24-month-old children observed as the experimenter hid a Big Bird doll under a pillow. Then they were given attractive toys to play with and, after a short period of time, were asked to find the hidden object. During the play

rehearsal Repetition.

interval, the children frequently looked or pointed at the hiding place or repeated the name of the hidden object. These behaviors suggest the beginning of the use of strategies to prompt the memory.

Young children also can be taught to successfully use strategies they might not use on their own. For example, 6-year-old children who are trained to rehearse show improvement in their ability to recall items on a memory test (Small, 1990). Similarly, having preschoolers sort objects into categories enhances memory (Howe, 2006; Lange & Pierce, 1992). Even 3- and 4-year-olds will use rehearsal and labeling if they are instructed to try to remember something (DeMarie et al., 2004; Fabricius & Cavalier, 1989).

The preschooler's use of memory strategies is not nearly as sophisticated as that of the school-age child. Children's use of memory strategies and understanding of how memory works advance greatly in middle childhood.

© Brad Wrobleski/Masterfile

Helping Young Children Remember
Memory functioning in early childhood—and at other ages— is aided when adults provide cues to help children remember. Adults can help by elaborating on the child's experiences and asking questions that encourage the child to contribute information.

Active Review

16. Children are capable of simple (Recognition or Recall?) during infancy.
17. Memory for events in one's life is referred to as _____ memory.
18. Preschoolers' memories for activities are (Better or Worse?) than their memories for objects.
19. Interest level is (Positively or Negatively?) connected with ability to remember.
20. Using mental repetition to remember is termed _____.

Reflect & Relate: How do you prepare for a test? How do you remember lists of new vocabulary words, for example? What strategies does your textbook author (that's me!) use to help you remember the subject matter in this course?

Go to

http://www.thomsonedu.com/psychology/rathus
for an interactive version of this review.

Language Development: Why "Daddy Goed Away"

Children's language skills grow dramatically during the preschool years. By the fourth year, children are asking adults and each other questions, taking turns talking, and engaging in lengthy conversations. *Question: What language developments occur during early childhood?* Some milestones of language development that occur during early childhood are shown in ■ Table 9.3. Let us consider a number of them.

Development of Vocabulary: Words, Words, and More Words

The development of vocabulary proceeds at an extraordinary pace during early childhood. Preschoolers learn an average of nine new words per day (Tamis-LaMonda et al., 2006). But how can that be possible when each new word has so many potential meanings? Consider the following example. A toddler observes a small, black dog

■ **Table 9.3** Development of Language Skills in Early Childhood

Age	Characteristics	Typical Sentences
2½ years	• There is rapid increase in vocabulary, with new additions each day. • There is no babbling. • Intelligibility is still not very good. • Child uses 2–3 words in sentences. • Child uses plurals. • Child uses possessives. • Child uses past tense. • Child uses some prepositions.	Two cups. Sarah's car. It broke. Keisha in bed
3 years	• Child has vocabulary of some 1,000 words. • Speech nears 100% intelligibility. • Articulation of *l* and *r* is frequently faulty. • Child uses 3–4 words in sentences. • Child uses yes–no questions. • Child uses *wh* questions. • Child uses negatives. • Child embeds one sentence within another.	Will I go? Where is the doggy? I not eat yucky peas. That's the book Mommy buyed me.
4 years	• Child has vocabulary of 1,500–1,600 words. • Speech is fluent. • Articulation is good except for *sh, z, ch,* and *j* sounds. • Child uses 5–6 words in sentences. • Child coordinates two sentences.	I went to Allie's and I had cookies.

running through the park. His older sister points to the animal and says, "Doggy." The word *doggy* could mean this particular dog, or all dogs, or all animals. It could refer to one part of the dog (e.g., its tail) or to its behavior (running, barking) or to its characteristics (small, black) (Waxman & Lidz, 2006). Does the child consider all these possibilities before determining what doggy actually means?

Studies have generally shown that word learning, in fact, does not occur gradually but is better characterized as a **fast-mapping** process in which the child quickly attaches a new word to its appropriate concept (Homer & Nelson, 2005; Waxman & Lidz, 2006). The key to fast mapping seems to be that children are equipped with early cognitive biases or constraints that lead them to prefer certain meanings over others (Waxman & Lidz, 2006).

One bias that children have is assuming that words refer to whole objects and not to their component parts or their characteristics, such as color, size, or texture (Bloom, 2002). This inclination is known as the **whole-object assumption.** In the example given at the beginning of the section, this bias would lead the young child to assume that the word *doggy* refers to the dog rather than to its tail, its color, or its barking.

fast mapping A process of quickly determining a word's meaning, which facilitates children's vocabulary development.

whole-object assumption The assumption that words refer to whole objects and not to their component parts or characteristics.

Lawrence Migdale/Stock Boston

Vocabulary Development
When this adult points to the goat and says "goat," the child assumes that "goat" refers to the whole animal, rather than to its horns, fur, size, or color. This bias, known as the whole-object assumption, helps children acquire a large vocabulary in a relatively short period of time.

Children also seem to hold the bias that objects have only one label. Therefore, novel terms must refer to unfamiliar objects and not to familiar objects that already have labels. This concept is the **contrast assumption**, which is also known as the mutual exclusivity assumption (Bloom, 2002; Waxman & Lidz, 2006). How might this bias help children figure out the meaning of a new word? Suppose that a child is shown two objects, one of which has a known label ("doggy") and one of which is an unknown object. Let us further suppose that an adult now says, "Look at the lemur." If the child assumes that "doggy" and "lemur" each can refer to only one object, the child would correctly figure out that "lemur" refers to the other object and is not just another name for "doggy." This bias facilitates children's learning of words (Homer & Nelson, 2005; Waxman & Lidz, 2006).

Development of Grammar:
Toward More Complex Language

Somewhat similar to the naming explosion in the second year is a "grammar explosion," which occurs during the third year (Tamis-LeMonda et al., 2006). Children's sentence structure expands to include the words missing in telegraphic speech. During the third year, children usually add to their vocabulary an impressive array of articles (*a, an, the*), conjunctions (*and, but, or*), possessive adjectives (*your, her*), pronouns (*she, him, one*), and prepositions (*in, on, over, around, under, through*). Usually between the ages of 3 and 4, children show knowledge of rules for combining phrases and clauses into complex sentences. An early example of a complex sentence is "You goed and Mommy goed, too." ■ Table 9.4 shows some interesting examples of one child's use of language during the third year. (All right! I'm prejudiced. It's my child.)

Overregularization

The apparent basis of one of the more intriguing language developments—**overregularization**—is that children acquire grammatical rules as they learn language. At young ages they tend to apply these rules rather strictly, even in cases that call for exceptions (Jacobson & Schwartz, 2005; Stemberger, 2004). Consider the formation of the past tense and plurals in English. We add *d* or *ed* to regular verbs and *s* to regular nouns. Thus, *walk* becomes *walked* and *doggy* becomes *doggies*. But then there are irregular verbs and irregular nouns. For example, *sit* becomes *sat* and *go* becomes *went*. *Sheep* remains *sheep* (plural) and *child* becomes *children*.

contrast assumption The assumption that objects have only one label. Also known as the mutual exclusivity assumption (if a word means one thing, it cannot mean another).

overregularization The application of regular grammatical rules for forming inflections (e.g., past tense and plurals) to irregular verbs and nouns.

■ **Table 9.4** Examples of Allyn's Speech during the Third Year

- Objecting to something said to her: "No, that is not a good talk to say. I don't like that."
- Describing her younger sister: "Jordan is very laughy today."
- On the second floor of her home: "This is not home. This is upstairs."
- Objecting to her father's departure: "Stay here for a couple of whiles."
- Directing her father to turn up the stereo: "Make it a big louder, not a small louder."
- Use of the plural number: "I see two policemans."
- Use of the past tense: "I goed on the choo-choo."
- Requesting a nickel: "Give me another money."
- Explaining that she and her mother are finished singing a song: "We singed it all up."
- Requesting an empty cup: "Give me that. I need it to drink nothing."
- Use of the possessive case: "That car is blue, just like us's."
- When she wants her father to hold her: "I want you to pick up me."
- Directing her father to turn on the stereo: "Push the button and make it too loud." (A minute later): "Make it more louder."
- Refusing to answer a question: "I don't want you to ask that to me."
- Confessing what she did with several coins: "I taked those money and put it on the shelf."

Allyn, age 2½

Courtesy of author

At first, children learn a small number of these irregular constructions by imitating their parents. Two-year-olds tend to form them correctly temporarily. Then children become aware of the syntactic rules for forming the past tense and plurals in English. As a result, they tend to make charming errors (Stemberger, 2004). **Truth or Fiction Revisited:** It is true that a 2½-year-old girl—mine—said "We singed it all up" after she and her mother had finished singing a song. Some 3- to 5-year-olds are more likely to say "Mommy sitted down" than "Mommy sat down." They are likely to talk about the "sheeps" they "seed" on the farm and about all the "childs" they ran into at the playground. **Truth or Fiction Revisited:** It is also true that a 3-year-old is likely to say "Daddy goed away" rather than "Daddy went away" because the child does understand rules of grammar. The child is correctly applying a rule for forming the past tense of regular verbs to an irregular verb.

Some parents recognize that their children were forming the past tense of irregular verbs correctly and that they then began to make errors. And some of these parents become concerned that their children are "slipping" in their language development and attempt to correct them. However, overregularization reflects accurate knowledge of grammar, not faulty language development. (Really.) In another year or two, *mouses* will be boringly transformed into *mice*, and Mommy will no longer have sitted down. Parents might as well enjoy overregularization while they can.

In a classic experiment designed to show that preschool children are not simply clever mimics in their formation of plurals but have actually grasped rules of

This is a wug.   **Now there are two of them.**   **There are two _____.**

● **Figure 9.7** Wugs

Wugs? Why not? Many bright, sophisticated college students have not heard of "wugs." What a pity. Here are several wugs, actually make-believe animals used in a study to learn whether preschool children can use rules of grammar to form the plurals of unfamiliar nouns.

grammar, Jean Berko (1958) showed children pictures of nonexistent animals (see ● Figure 9.7). She first showed them a single animal and said, "This is a wug." Then she showed them a picture of two animals and said, "Now there are two of them. There are two _____," asking the children to finish the sentence. Ninety-one percent of the children said "wugs," providing the proper plural of the bogus word.

Asking Questions

Children's first questions are telegraphic and characterized by a rising pitch (which signifies a question mark in English) at the end. Depending on the context, "More milky?" for example, can be translated into "May I have more milk?" "Would you like more milk?" or "Is there more milk?" It is usually toward the latter part of the third year that the *wh* questions appear. Consistent with the child's general cognitive development, certain *wh* questions (*what, who,* and *where*) appear earlier than others (*why, when, which,* and *how*) (Tamis-LeMonda et al., 2006). *Why* is usually too philosophical for a 2-year-old, and *how* is too involved. Two-year-olds are also likely to be now-oriented, so *when* is of less than immediate concern. By the fourth year, most children are spontaneously producing *why, when,* and *how* questions. These *wh* words are initially tacked on to the beginnings of sentences. "Where Mommy go?" can stand for "Where is Mommy going?" "Where did Mommy go?" or "Where will Mommy go?", and its meaning must be derived from context. Later on, the child will add the auxiliary verbs *is, did,* and *will* to indicate whether the question concerns the present, past, or future.

Passive Sentences

Passive sentences, such as "The food is eaten by the dog," are difficult for 2- and 3-year-olds to understand, and so young preschoolers almost never produce them. In a fascinating study of children's comprehension (Strohner & Nelson, 1974), 2- to 5-year-olds used puppets and toys to act out a number of sentences that were read to them. Two- and 3-year-olds in the study made errors in acting out passive sentences (e.g., "The car was hit by the truck") 70% of the time. Older children had less difficulty interpreting the meanings of passive sentences correctly. However, most children usually do not produce passive sentences spontaneously even at the ages of 5 and 6.

Pragmatics: Preschoolers Can Be Practical

Pragmatics in language development refers to the practical aspects of communication. Children are showing pragmatism when they adjust their speech to fit the social situation (Nelson, 2006). For example, children show greater formality in their choice of words and syntax when they are role-playing high-status figures, such as teachers or physicians, in their games. They also say "please" more often when making requests of high-status people. Children also show pragmatism in their adoption of Motherese when they are addressing a younger child.

Pragmatism provides another example of the ways in which cognitive and language development are intertwined. Preschoolers tend to be egocentric; therefore, a 2-year-old telling another child "Gimme my book," without specifying which book,

pragmatics The practical aspects of communication, such as adaptation of language to fit the social situation.

may be assuming that the other child knows what she herself knows. She is also probably overestimating the clearness of her communication and how well she is understood. Once children can perceive the world through the eyes of others, however, they advance in their abilities to make themselves understood to others. Now the child recognizes that the other child will require a description of the book or of its location to carry out the request. Between the ages of 3 and 5, egocentric speech gradually disappears and there is rapid development of pragmatic skills. The child's conversation shows increasing sensitivity to the listener, as, for example, by taking turns talking and listening.

Language and Cognition

Language and cognitive development are strongly interwoven (Homer & Nelson, 2005; Waxman & Lidz, 2006). For example, the child gradually gains the capacity to discriminate between animals on the basis of distinct features, such as size, patterns of movement, and the sounds they make. At the same time, the child also is acquiring words that represent broader categories, such as mammal and animal.

But it's chicken-and-egg time. Which comes first? ***Question: What is the relationship between language and cognition?*** Does the child first develop concepts and then acquire the language to describe them, or does the child's increasing language ability lead to the development of new concepts?

Does Cognitive Development Precede Language Development?

Piaget (1976) believed that cognitive development precedes language development. He argued that children must first understand concepts before they can use words that describe the concepts. Object permanence emerges toward the end of the first year. Piaget believed that words that relate to the disappearance and appearance of people and objects (such as *all gone* and *bye-bye*) are used only after the emergence of object permanence.

From Piaget's perspective, children learn words to describe classes or categories that they have already created (Nelson, 2005). Children can learn the word *doggy* because they have perceived the characteristics that distinguish dogs from other things.

Some studies support the notion that cognitive concepts may precede language. For example, the vocabulary explosion that occurs at about 18 months of age is related to the child's ability to group a set of objects into two categories, such as "dolls" and "cars" (Gopnik & Meltzoff, 1992). Other research suggests that young children need to experience an action themselves or by observation to learn the meaning of a verb (Pulverman et al., 2006).

Does Language Development Precede Cognitive Development?

Although many theorists argue that cognitive development precedes language development, others reverse the causal relationship and claim that children create cognitive classes to understand things that are labeled by words (Clark, 1983). When children hear the word *dog,* they try to understand it by searching for characteristics that separate dogs from other things. Research with 4-year-olds shows that descriptions of events can prompt children to create categories in which to classify occurrences (Nazzi & Gopnik, 2000).

The Interactionist View: Outer Speech and Inner Speech

Today, most developmentalists find something of value in each of these cognitive views (Rakison & Oakes, 2003; Waxman & Lidz, 2006). In the early stages of language development, concepts often precede words, and many of the infant's words describe classes that have already developed. Later, however, language is not merely the servant of thought; language influences thought.

Vygotsky also made key contributions to our understanding of the relationships between concepts and words. Vygotsky believed that during most of the first year, vocalizations and thought are separate. But during the second year, thought and speech—cognition and language—usually combine forces. "Speech begins to serve intellect and thoughts begin to be spoken" (Vygotsky, 1962, p. 43). Usually during the second year, children discover that objects have labels. Learning labels becomes more active, more self-directed. At some point, children ask what new words mean. Learning new words clearly fosters the creation of new categories and classes. An interaction develops in which classes are filled with labels for new things, and labels nourish the blossoming of new classes.

Vygotsky's concept of **inner speech** is a key feature of his position. At first, according to Vygotsky, children's thoughts are spoken aloud. You can overhear the 3-year-old giving herself instructions as she plays with toys. At this age, her vocalizations may serve to regulate her behavior. But language gradually becomes internalized. What was spoken aloud at 4 and 5 becomes an internal dialogue by 6 or 7. This internal dialogue, or inner speech, is the ultimate binding of language and thought. Inner speech is involved in the development of planning and self-regulation, and facilitates learning. Vygotsky's ideas about the self-regulative function of language have inspired psychological treatment approaches for children with problems in self-control. For example, hyperactive children can be taught to use self-directed speech to increase self-control (Crain, 2000).

Language is thus connected not only with thought but also with the social and emotional development of the young child. We turn to these areas of development in Chapter 10.

inner speech Vygotsky's concept of the ultimate binding of language and thought. Inner speech originates in vocalizations that may regulate the child's behavior and become internalized by age 6 or 7.

Active Review

21. Word learning does not occur gradually but is better characterized as a fast-_____ process.
22. The _____-object assumption refers to young children assuming that words refer to whole objects and not to their component parts or to their characteristics, such as color or texture.
23. Young children also tend to assume that objects have (How many?) label(s).
24. Therefore, they have the _____ assumption, which holds that novel terms must refer to unfamiliar objects and not to familiar objects that already have labels.
25. Vygotsky's concept of _____ speech refers to what was spoken aloud at 4 and 5 becoming an internal dialogue by 6 or 7.

Reflect & Relate: What are some of the new words you are learning by reading this book? Do the words you chose to list have a single meaning or multiple meanings? How does their number of meanings affect your acquisition of these words? (Consider the examples of conservation, scaffold, and mapping.)

Go to

http://www.thomsonedu.com/psychology/rathus

for an interactive version of this review.

1. **How do children in the preoperational stage think and behave?**

   Piaget's preoperational stage lasts from about age 2 to 7 and is characterized by the use of symbols to represent objects and relationships. Pretend play is based on the use and recollection of symbols or on mental representations of things. By 30 months, children can pretend that objects are active.

2. **How do we characterize the logic of the preoperational child?**

   Preoperational thinking is characterized by egocentrism, precausal thinking, confusion between mental and physical events, and ability to focus on only one dimension at a time.

3. **What is egocentrism?**

   Egocentrism is inability to see the world from the perspective of others. Young children often view the world as a stage that is meant to meet their needs.

4. **What is precausal thinking?**

   Young children's thinking is egocentric, animistic, and artificialistic. In transductive reasoning, children reason by going from one instance of an event to another.

5. **Why do young children think that they can pretend to be galaprocks without knowing what galaprocks are?**

   Preoperational children have difficulty distinguishing between mental and physical events. Egocentrism contributes to their belief that their thoughts reflect reality.

6. **What is conservation (i.e., in terms of the cognitive development of the child)?**

   The law of conservation holds that properties of substances such as volume, mass, and number stay the same (are conserved) even if their shape or arrangement changes. Conservation requires focusing on two aspects of a situation at once.

7. **What are some of the factors that influence cognitive development in early childhood?**

   Two of the most important factors are scaffolding and the zone of proximal development, as envisioned by Vygotsky. Others include social and family factors such as family income, parents' educational level, family size, and the presence of stressful family events such as divorce, job loss, or illness. The children of responsive parents who provide appropriate play materials and stimulating experiences show gains in social and language development. Head Start programs enhance economically disadvantaged children's cognitive development, academic skills, and readiness for school.

8. **What are children's ideas about how the mind works?**

   As children's theory of mind develops, children come to understand that there are distinctions between external and mental events and between appearances and realities.

9. **Do children understand where their knowledge comes from? If so, how early do they show this ability?**

   By age 3, most children begin to realize that people gain knowledge through the senses. By age 4, children understand which sense is required to provide information about qualities such as color (vision) and weight (touch).

10. **Is seeing believing? What do preoperational children have to say about that?**

Although Piaget believed that children do not differentiate reality from appearances or mental events until the age of 7 or 8, research finds that preschoolers can do so.

11. **What sorts of memory skills do children possess in early childhood?**

Preschoolers recognize more items than they can recall. Autobiographical memory is linked to language skills. By the age of 4, children can remember events that occurred 1½ years earlier. Young children seem to form scripts, which are abstract, generalized accounts of events.

12. **What factors affect memory in early childhood?**

Factors affecting memory include what the child is asked to remember, interest level and motivation, the availability of retrieval cues, and the memory measure being used.

13. **How do we remember to remember?**

Preschoolers engage in behaviors such as looking, pointing, and touching when trying to remember. Preschoolers can be taught to use strategies such as rehearsal and grouping of items that they might not use on their own.

14. **What language developments occur during early childhood?**

Preschoolers acquire about nine new words per day. Word learning often occurs rapidly through fast mapping. During the third year, children usually add articles, conjunctions, possessive adjectives, pronouns, and prepositions. Between the ages of 3 and 4, children combine phrases and clauses into complex sentences. Preschoolers tend to overregularize irregular verbs and noun forms as they acquire rules of grammar.

15. **What is the relationship between language and cognition?**

Piaget believed that children learn words to describe classes or categories they have created. Other theorists argue that children create classes to understand things that are labeled by words. Vygotsky believed that during most of the first year, vocalizations and thought are separate, but usually during the second year, cognition and language combine forces. To Vygotsky, inner speech is the ultimate binding of language and thought.

Key Terms

preoperational stage, 296
symbolic play, 296
operations, 297
egocentrism, 298
precausal, 298
transductive reasoning, 299
animism, 299
artificialism, 299
conservation, 300
centration, 300

irreversibility, 301
class inclusion, 301
scaffolding, 306
zone of proximal development (ZPD), 306
theory of mind, 312
appearance–reality distinction, 314
mental representations, 314
recognition, 315
recall, 315

scripts, 316
autobiographical memory, 317
rehearsal, 318
fast mapping, 320
whole-object assumption, 320
contrast assumption, 321
overregularization, 321
pragmatics, 323
inner speech, 325

Active Learning Resources

Childhood & Adolescence Book Companion Website

http://www.thomsonedu.com/psychology/rathus

Visit your book companion website where you will find more resources to help you study. There you will find interactive versions of your book features, including the Lessons in Observation video, Active Review sections, and the Truth or Fiction feature. In addition, the companion website contains quizzing, flash cards, and a pronunciation glossary.

 is an easy-to-use online resource that helps you study in less time to get the grade you want—NOW.

http://www.thomsonedu.com/login

Need help studying? This site is your one-stop study shop. Take a Pre-Test and ThomsonNOW will generate a Personalized Study Plan based on your test results. The Study Plan will identify the topics you need to review and direct you to online resources to help you master those topics. You can then take a Post-Test to determine the concepts you have mastered and what you still need to work on.

10

Early Childhood
Social and Emotional Development

Truth or Fiction?

T F Parents who are restrictive and demand mature behavior wind up with rebellious children, not mature children. p. 333

T F There is no point in trying to reason with a 4-year-old. p. 334

T F Firstborn children are more highly motivated to achieve than later-born children. p. 340

T F Children who are physically punished are more likely to be aggressive than children who are not. p. 351

T F Children who watch 2 to 4 hours of TV a day will see 8,000 murders and another 100,000 acts of violence by the time they have finished elementary school. p. 351

T F Children mechanically imitate the aggressive behavior they view in the media. p. 354

T F The most common fear among preschoolers is fear of social disapproval. p. 356

T F A 2½-year-old may know that she is a girl but still think that she can grow up to be a daddy. p. 364

© Rommel/Masterfile

Preview

Influences on Development: Parents, Siblings, and Peers
Dimensions of Child Rearing
Parenting Styles: How Parents Transmit Values and Standards
Effects of the Situation and the Child on Parenting Styles
Influence of Siblings

Developing in a World of Diversity: Individualism, Collectivism, and Patterns of Child Rearing

Birth Order: Not Just Where in the World but Also Where in the Family
Peer Relationships

Developing in a World of Diversity: Where Are the Missing American Fathers?

Social Behaviors: In the World, among Others
Play—Child's Play, That Is
Prosocial Behavior: It Could Happen, and Does
Development of Aggression: The Dark Side of Social Interaction
Theories of Aggression

A Closer Look: When *Doom* Leads to . . . Doom: What Children Learn from Violent Video Games

Personality and Emotional Development
The Self
Initiative versus Guilt
Fears: The Horrors of Early Childhood

A Closer Look: Helping Children Cope with Fears

Development of Gender Roles and Sex Differences
Sex Differences
Theories of the Development of Sex Differences

Lessons in Observation: Gender

Psychological Androgyny

 Go to

http://www.thomsonedu.com/psychology/rathus
for an interactive version of this "Truth or Fiction" feature.

eremy and Jessica are both 2½ years old. They are standing at the water table in the preschool classroom. Jessica is filling a plastic container with water and spilling it out. She watches the water splash down the drain. Jeremy watches and then goes to get another container. He, too, fills his container with water and spills it out. The children stand side by side. They empty and refill their plastic pails; they glance at each other and exchange a few words. They continue to play like this for several minutes, until Jessica drops her pail and runs off to ride the tricycle. Soon after, Jeremy also loses interest and finds something else to do.

Meanwhile, 4½-year-olds Melissa and Mike are building in the block corner, making a huge, rambling structure that they have decided is a spaceship. They talk animatedly as they work, negotiating who should be captain of the ship and who should be the space alien. Mike and Melissa take turns adding blocks. They continue to build, working together and talking as they play (Campbell, 1990).

These observations illustrate some of the changes that occur in social development during early childhood. Toddlers often spend time watching and imitating each other, but they do not interact very much. Older preschoolers are more likely to take turns, work cooperatively toward a goal, and share. They often engage in fantasy play that involves adopting adult roles.

In this chapter, we explore social and emotional development in early childhood. We consider the roles played by parents, siblings, and peers. We examine child's play, helping and sharing, and aggression. Then we look at personality and emotional development. We begin with the development of the self-concept, move on to Erikson's stage of initiative versus guilt, and explore the changing nature of children's fears. Finally, we discuss the development of gender roles and sex differences in behavior.

Influences on Development: Parents, Siblings, and Peers

Young children usually spend most of their time within the family. Most parents attempt to foster certain behaviors in their children. They want their children to develop a sense of responsibility and conform to family routines. They want them to develop into well-adjusted individuals. They want them to acquire social skills. In other words, they want to ensure their children's healthy social and emotional development. How do parents go about trying to achieve these goals? What part do siblings play? How do children's peers influence social and emotional development?

Dimensions of Child Rearing

Parents have different approaches to rearing their children. *Question: What are the dimensions of child rearing?* Investigators of parental patterns of child rearing have found it useful to classify them according to two broad dimensions: warmth–coldness and restrictiveness–permissiveness (Baumrind, 1989, 1991a, 1991b, 2005). Warm parents and cold parents can be either restrictive or permissive.

Warmth–Coldness

Warm parents are affectionate toward their children. They tend to hug and kiss them and smile at them frequently. Warm parents are caring and supportive of their children. They generally behave in ways that communicate their enjoyment in being with the children. Warm parents are less likely than cold parents to use physical discipline (Bender et al., 2007).

Cold parents may not enjoy being with their children and may have few feelings of affection for them. They are likely to complain about their children's behavior, saying that they are naughty or have "minds of their own." Warm parents may also say that their children have "minds of their own," but they are frequently proud of and entertained by their children's stubborn behavior. Even when they are irked by it, they usually focus on attempting to change it, instead of rejecting the children.

It requires no stretch of the imagination to conclude that it is better to be warm than cold toward children. The children of parents who are warm and accepting are more likely to develop internalized standards of conduct, a moral sense or conscience (Bender et al., 2007; Lau et al., 2006). Parental warmth also is related to the child's social and emotional well-being (Kerr et al., 2004; Lau et al., 2006; Leung et al., 2004).

Where does parental warmth come from? Some of it reflects parental beliefs about how to best rear children, and some reflects parents' tendencies to imitate the behavior of their own parents. But research by E. Mavis Hetherington and her colleagues (Feinberg et al., 2001) suggests that genetic factors may be involved as well.

Restrictiveness–Permissiveness

Parents must generally decide how restrictive they will be. How will they respond when children make excessive noise, play with dangerous objects, damage property, mess up their rooms, hurt others, go nude, or masturbate? Parents who are restrictive tend to impose rules and to watch their children closely.

Truth or Fiction Revisited: It is not true that parents who are strict and demand mature behavior wind up with rebellious children. Consistent control and firm enforcement of rules can have positive consequences for the child, particularly when combined with strong support and affection (Grusec, 2006). This parenting style is termed the *authoritative style.* On the other hand, if "restrictiveness" means physical punishment, interference, or intrusiveness, it can have negative effects such as disobedience, rebelliousness, and lower levels of cognitive development (Paulussen-Hoogeboom et al., 2007; Rudy & Grusec, 2006).

Permissive parents impose few if any rules and supervise their children less closely than restrictive parents do. Permissive parents allow their children to do what is "natural," such as make noise, treat toys carelessly (although they may also extensively child-proof their homes to protect their children and the furniture), and experiment with their own bodies. They may also allow their children to show some aggression, intervening only when another child is in danger. Parents may be permissive for different reasons. Some parents believe that children need the freedom to express their natural urges. Others may simply be uninterested and uninvolved.

Research in Spain and Brazil suggests that the permissive parenting style is connected with higher self-esteem and adjustment compared with other parenting styles (Martínez et al., 2003). The investigators suggested that these cultures may be somewhat more "laid back" than "Anglo-Saxon" cultures and that there is a better fit between indulgence of children and their adjustment in Latino/Latina cultures.

How Parents Enforce Restrictions

Regardless of their general approaches to child rearing, most if not all parents are restrictive now and then, even if only when they are teaching their children not to run into the street or to touch a hot stove. *Question: What techniques do parents use to restrict their children's behavior?* Parents tend to use the methods of induction, power assertion, and withdrawal of love.

Inductive Techniques

Inductive methods aim to impart knowledge that will enable children to generate desirable behavior in similar situations. The main inductive technique is "reasoning," or explaining why one kind of behavior is good and another is not. Reasoning with a 1- or 2-year-old can be basic. "Don't do that—it hurts!" qualifies as reasoning

inductive Characteristic of disciplinary methods, such as reasoning, that attempt to foster an understanding of the principles behind parental demands.

Inductive Reasoning
Inductive methods for enforcing restrictions attempt to teach children the principles they should use in guiding their own behavior. This mother is using the inductive technique of reasoning.

with toddlers. "It hurts!" is an explanation, although a brief one. **Truth or Fiction Revisited:** Thus, there is a point in trying to reason with a 4-year-old. The inductive approach helps the child understand moral behavior and fosters prosocial behavior such as helping and sharing (Paulussen-Hoogeboom et al., 2007).

Power-Assertive Methods

Power-assertive methods include physical punishment and denial of privileges. Parents often justify physical punishment with sayings such as "Spare the rod, spoil the child." Parents may insist that power assertion is necessary because their children are noncompliant. However, the use of power-assertive methods is related to parental authoritarianism as well as to children's behavior (Roopnarine et al., 2006; Rudy & Grusec, 2006). Parental power assertion is associated with lower acceptance by peers, poorer grades, and higher rates of antisocial behavior in children (Roopnarine et al., 2006). The more parents use power-assertive techniques, the less children appear to develop internal standards of moral conduct. Parental punishment and rejection are often linked with aggression and delinquency (Rudy & Grusec, 2006).

Withdrawal of Love

Some parents control children by threatening them with withdrawal of love. They isolate or ignore misbehaving children. Because most children need parental approval and contact, loss of love can be more threatening to a child than physical punishment. Withdrawal of love may foster compliance, but it may also instill guilt and anxiety (Grusec, 2002).

Preschoolers more readily comply when asked to do something than when asked to stop doing something (Kochanska et al., 2001). One way to manage children who are doing something wrong or bad is to involve them in something else.

Parenting Styles: How Parents Transmit Values and Standards

Traditional views of the ways in which children acquire values and standards for behavior focus on parenting styles (Grusec, 2006). However, many other factors are involved, including the characteristics of a particular child, the child's situation, and other aspects of parental behavior.

Psychologist Diana Baumrind (1989, 1991b) focused on the relationship between parenting styles and the development of competent behavior in young children. She used the dimensions of warmth–coldness and restrictiveness–permissiveness to develop a grid of four parenting styles based on whether parents are high or low on each of the two dimensions, as seen in ■ Table 10.1. *Question: What are the parenting styles involved in the transmission of values and standards?*

Authoritative Parents

The parents of the most capable children are rated as high on both dimensions of behavior (see Table 10.1). They make strong efforts to control their children (i.e., they are highly restrictive), and they make strong demands for maturity. However, they also reason with their children and show them strong support and feelings of love. Baumrind applies the label **authoritative** to these parents not only to suggest that they have a clear vision of what they want their children to do, but also to suggest that they respect their children and provide them with warmth.

Compared with other children, the children of authoritative parents tend to show self-reliance and independence, high self-esteem, high levels of activity and exploratory behavior, and social competence. They are highly motivated to achieve and do well in school (Baumrind, 1989, 1991b; Grusec, 2006).

authoritative A child-rearing style in which parents are restrictive and demanding yet communicative and warm.

■ Table 10.1 Baumrind's Patterns of Parenting

Parental Style	Parental Behavior Patterns	
	Restrictiveness and Control	Warmth and Responsiveness
Authoritative	High	High
Authoritarian	High	Low
Permissive–indulgent	Low	High
Rejecting–neglecting	Low	Low

© Masterfile

Permissive Parents

Some parents are considered permissive and demand little of their children in terms of mature behavior or control. Permissive–indulgent parents still provide plenty of warmth and support for their children, whereas rejecting–neglecting parents tend to neglect or ignore their children.

Authoritarian Parents

"Because I say so" could be the motto of parents that Baumrind labels **authoritarian.** These parents tend to value obedience regardless of the situation. Authoritarian parents have strict guidelines for right and wrong. They demand that their children accept these guidelines without question. Like authoritative parents, they are controlling. But unlike authoritative parents, their enforcement methods rely on force. Moreover, authoritarian parents do not communicate well with their children. They do not show respect for their children's viewpoints, and most researchers find them to be generally cold and rejecting. But among some ethnic groups—such as Egyptians—authoritarianism reflects cultural values, and these authoritarian parents may also be warm and reasonably flexible (Grusec, 2002; Rudy & Grusec, 2006).

In Baumrind's research, the sons of authoritarian parents were relatively hostile and defiant and the daughters were low in independence and dominance (Baumrind, 1989). Other researchers have found that children of authoritarian parents are less competent socially and academically than children of authoritative parents. Children of authoritarian parents also tend to be conflicted, anxious, and irritable. They are less friendly and spontaneous in their social interactions (Grusec, 2002). As adolescents, they may be conforming and obedient but have lower self-reliance and self-esteem.

Permissive Parents

Baumrind found two types of parents who are permissive as opposed to restrictive. One type is labeled permissive–indulgent and the other rejecting–neglecting. **Permissive–indulgent** parents are rated low in their attempts to control their children and in their demands for mature behavior. They are easygoing and unconventional. Their brand of permissiveness is accompanied by high nurturance (warmth and support).

Rejecting–neglecting parents also are rated low in their demands for mature behavior and their attempts to control their children. But unlike indulgent parents, they are low in support and responsiveness.

The neglectful parenting style is associated with poor outcomes for children. By and large, the children of neglectful parents are the least competent, responsible, and mature and the most prone to problem behaviors. Children of permissive–indulgent parents, like those of neglectful parents, show less competence in school and more deviant behavior (e.g., misconduct and substance abuse) than children of more restrictive, controlling parents. But children from permissive–indulgent homes, unlike those from neglectful homes, are fairly high in social competence and self-confidence (Baumrind, 1991a).

authoritarian A child-rearing style in which parents demand submission and obedience from their children but are not very communicative and warm.

permissive–indulgent A child-rearing style in which parents are not controlling and restrictive but are warm.

rejecting–neglecting A child-rearing style in which parents are neither restrictive and controlling nor supportive and responsive.

■ **Table 10.2** Advice for Parents in Guiding Young Children's Behavior

Do . . .	Don't . . .
• Reward good behavior with praises, smiles, and hugs.	• Pay attention only to a child's misbehavior.
• Give clear, simple, realistic rules appropriate to the child's age.	• Issue too many rules or enforce them haphazardly.
• Enforce rules with reasonable consequences.	• Try to control behavior solely in the child's domain, such as thumb sucking, which can lead to frustrating power struggles.
• Ignore annoying behavior such as whining and tantrums.	• Nag, lecture, shame, or induce guilt.
• Childproof the house, putting dangerous and breakable items out of reach. Then establish limits.	• Yell or spank.
• Be consistent.	• Be overly permissive.

Effects of the Situation and the Child on Parenting Styles

Parenting styles are not only a one-way street, from parent to child. Parenting styles also depend partly on the situation and partly on the characteristics of the child (Grusec, 2006; Grusec et al., 2000). *Question: How do the situation and the child influence parenting styles?*

One example of how the situation affects the parenting style is that parents are more likely to use power-assertive techniques for dealing with aggressive behavior than social withdrawal (Casas et al., 2006; Lipman et al., 2006). Parents prefer power assertion to induction when they believe that children understand the rules they have violated, are capable of acting appropriately, and are responsible for their bad behavior. Stressful life events, marital discord, and emotional problems all contribute to parental use of power assertion.

Baumrind's research suggests that we can make an effort to avoid some of the pitfalls of being authoritarian or overly permissive. Some recommended techniques that parents can use to help control and guide their children's behavior are listed in ■ Table 10.2.

Influence of Siblings

Our neighbor—who will deny this story (but don't believe her)—admits that when she was 5, she would carefully walk her younger sister, then 2, into the middle of the street. And then leave her there! Fortunately, both survived. They are quite close now. They literally lived to laugh about it.

Of American families with children, most have at least two children. In many cases, children spend more time with their siblings in the early years than they spend with their parents. *Question: How do siblings influence social and emotional development in early childhood?*

Siblings make a unique contribution to one another's social, emotional, and cognitive development (McHale et al., 2006). They serve many functions, including giving physical care, providing emotional support and nurturance, offering advice and direction, serving as role models, providing social interaction that helps develop social skills, and making demands and imposing restrictions (McHale et al., 2006; Parke & Buriel, 2006). They also advance each other's cognitive development, as shown in research concerning false beliefs and the theory of mind (see Chapter 9).

In early childhood, when siblings spend a great deal of time together, their interactions are often emotionally loaded and marked by both positive aspects (cooperation, teaching, nurturance) and negative aspects (conflict, control, competition) (Parke & Buriel, 2006). By and large, older siblings are more caring but also more dominating than younger siblings. Younger siblings are more likely to imitate older siblings and to accept their direction.

Siblings
Siblings make a unique contribution to one another's social, emotional, and cognitive development.

However, older siblings may also imitate younger siblings, especially when parents remark "how cute" the baby is being in front of the older child. At the age of 2 years 5 months, my daughter Allyn would pretend that she could not talk every once in a while, just like her 5-month-old sister, Jordan.

In many cultures (including this one, laments my wife, a firstborn child), older girls are given the chore of caring for younger siblings (Clark, 2005). Younger siblings frequently turn to older sisters when the mother is unavailable. ("They still do," notes my wife.)

Parents often urge their children to stop fighting among themselves, and there are times when these conflicts look deadly (and occasionally they are). It is important to note, however, that garden-variety conflict among siblings can have positive outcomes. (Really.) It appears that conflict between siblings enhances their social competence, their development of self-identity (who they are and what they stand for), and their ability to rear their own children in a healthful manner (Ross et al., 2006). When adults look back on their childhood conflicts with their siblings, their memories of them are often positive.

As siblings move from early childhood through middle childhood and into adolescence, their relationships change in at least two ways (Scharf et al., 2005). First, as siblings grow more competent and their developmental statuses become similar, their relationship becomes more egalitarian. In other words, as later-born siblings grow older and become more self-sufficient, they need and accept less nurturance and direction from older siblings. Second, sibling relationships become less intense as children grow older. The exercise of power and the amount of conflict declines. The extent of warmth and closeness diminishes somewhat as well, although the attachment between siblings remains fairly strong throughout adolescence.

Other factors also affect the development of sibling relationships. For example, there is more conflict between siblings in families in which the parents treat the children differently than in families in which they are treated in the same way (Scharf et al., 2005). Conflict between siblings also is greater when the relationship between the parents or between the parents and children is not harmonious (Kim et al., 2006; Volling, 2003).

Adjusting to the Birth of a Sibling

The birth of a sister or brother is often a source of stress for young children because of changes in family relationships and the environment (Volling, 2003). When a new baby comes into the home, the mother pays relatively more attention to that child and spends much less time in playful activities with the older child. No wonder the older

Developing in a World of Diversity

Individualism, Collectivism, and Patterns of Child Rearing

Much of the research on parenting styles has been done with middle-class European American families. But parenting styles must be viewed within the context of particular cultures (Lins-Dyer at el., 2007; Suizzo, 2004). Socialization methods that appear authoritarian or punitive by middle-class standards may be used more frequently among poor families from ethnic minority groups to prepare children to cope with the hazards of daily life. Placing a high value on unquestioned obedience might be considered overly restrictive in a quiet middle-class neighborhood but warranted now and then in a more dangerous inner-city environment (Keller et al., 2006). Poor families in other countries also tend to use authoritarian child-rearing styles.

One study compared child-rearing practices of middle-class Japanese and American parents whose children ranged in age from 4 to 7 (Kobayashi-Winata & Power, 1989). In both groups of families, the most compliant children had parents who provided opportunities for appropriate behavior and who used relatively little punishment. But American parents were more likely to rely on external punishments such as sending children to their room, whereas Japanese parents more often used verbal commands, reprimands, and explanations (see ■ Table 10.3).

These differences in disciplinary practices apparently reflect cultural differences. Cross-cultural research reveals that people in the United States and many northern European nations tend to be individualistic (Ayyash-Abdo, 2001; French et al., 2001). On the other hand, many people from cultures in Africa, Asia, and Central and South America tend to be collectivistic (Abe-Kim et al., 2001; Keller et al., 2006).

Individualists tend to define themselves in terms of their personal identities and to give priority to their personal goals (Berry & Triandis, 2006; Triandis, 2005). When asked to complete the statement "I am . . ." they are likely to respond in terms of their personality traits ("I am outgoing," "I am artistic") or their occupations ("I am a nurse," "I am a systems analyst"). In contrast, **collectivists** tend to define themselves in terms of the groups to which they belong and to give priority to the group's goals (Berry & Triandis, 2006; Triandis, 2005). They feel complete in terms of their relationships with others (see ● Figure 10.1). They are more likely than individualists to conform to group norms and judgments (Berry & Triandis, 2006; Triandis, 2005). When asked to complete the statement "I am . . ." they are more likely to respond in terms of their families, sex, or nation ("I am a father," "I am a Buddhist," "I am Japanese").

It must be mentioned, however, that individuals from within the same country can belong to different "cultures" in terms of individualistic and collectivist tendencies. A Lebanese researcher found that college students who spoke French or English were more likely to be individualistic than those who spoke mainly Arabic (Ayyash-Abdo, 2001). Moreover, traditional Islamic values were also connected with collectivism.

Other studies reveal additional differences in the child-rearing techniques of American and Japanese parents that appear to foster the American emphasis on early socialization and independence and the Japanese focus on group harmony and dependence on others. For example, in one study, American mothers of preschoolers expected their children to follow more rules but also were more likely to listen to their children's opinions. Japanese mothers, in contrast, made fewer demands on their children and were more indulgent (Power et al., 1992).

Reflect:

• *Do you think that it is better to raise a child to be individualistic or to be collectivistic? Explain.*

• *We all belong to subcultures within the United States. Would you characterize your subculture as mainly individualistic or collectivistic? Explain.*

• *The culture of the United States is said to value the "rugged individual." Is that always true? Explain.*

• *Can you make the case that a culture or subculture is individualistic in some ways but collectivistic in others? Explain.*

■ **Table 10.3** Cultural Values and Child-Rearing Techniques in the United States and Japan

Culture	Parental Value	Child-Rearing Practices
United States middle class	• Early socialization • Independence • Individualism	• Expect child to follow more rules • Listen to child's opinion • Use external punishment (e.g., send child to his or her room)
Japanese middle class	• Group harmony • Dependence on others • Conformity	• Make fewer demands • Be more indulgent • Use verbal commands • Use reprimands and explanations

child may feel displaced and resentful of the affection lavished on the newborn. These feelings are illustrated by the comments of a 3-year-old who worried that his new sister would take all his mother's love and not leave enough for him (Campbell, 1990).

Children show a mixture of negative and positive reactions to the birth of a sibling. They include **regression** to babyish behaviors, such as increased clinging, crying, and toilet accidents. Anger and naughtiness may increase as well. But the same children will often show increased independence and maturity, insisting on feeding or dressing themselves and helping to take care of the baby (Volling, 2003).

What can parents do to help a young child cope with the arrival of a new baby? For one thing, they can prepare the child by explaining in advance what is to come. In one study, preschoolers who attended a sibling preparation class with their mothers showed fewer signs of **sibling rivalry** (Fortier et al., 1991). Parental support is extremely important as well. Children show less distress following the birth of a sibling when the parents spend time with them, encourage them, and praise them (Kavcic & Zupancic, 2005).

individualist A person who defines herself or himself in terms of personal traits and gives priority to her or his own goals.

collectivist A person who defines herself or himself in terms of relationships to other people and groups and gives priority to group goals.

regression A return to behaviors characteristic of earlier stages of development.

sibling rivalry Jealousy or rivalry among brothers and sisters.

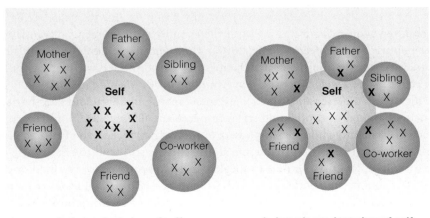

a. Independent view of self   b. Interdependent view of self

● **Figure 10.1**
The Self in Relation to Others from the Individualist and Collectivist Perspectives

(a) To an individualist, the self is separate from other people. (b) To a collectivist, the self is complete only in terms of relationships to other people. (Based on Markus & Kitayama, 1991.) Are there differences in the ways in which people in individualist and collectivist cultures rear their children?

Birth Order: Not Just Where in the World but Also Where in the Family

Let me confess at the beginning of this section that I am an only child. As I was developing, I experienced what I imagine are most of the rewards and, yes, punishments of being an only child. First and perhaps foremost, I was the little king in my household in the Bronx. A petty tyrant at best, and at worst. I enjoyed all the resources my family had to offer: a relatively good allowance (with which I bought a comic book a day; Superman did nothing that escaped my young attention) and lots of parental attention. Because I got most of what I wanted, I never knew that we were poor.

On the other hand, for many years I was more comfortable relating to adults than to other children. And many times I was lonely in the home and wished that I had a sister or a brother. But these are the experiences of one person, and it is difficult to know how accurately they are recalled. So let's be more scientific about it. *Question: What does the research say about the effects of being a firstborn or an only child?*

Many differences in personality and achievement have been observed among firstborn and only children compared with later-born children. **Truth or Fiction Revisited:** It is true that firstborn children, as a group, are more highly motivated to achieve than later-born children (Latham & Budworth, 2007). As a group, firstborn and only children perform better academically (that's me) and are more cooperative (not so sure that was me) (Healy & Ellis, 2007). They are also helpful (not so sure), are adult-oriented (that's me), and are less aggressive than later-born children (I guess that was me; not easy to recall) (Beck et al., 2006; Braza et al., 2000; Zajonc, 2001). They also obtain higher standardized test scores, including intelligence and SAT scores (Kristensen & Bjerkedal, 2007; Sulloway, 2007; Zajonc & Mullally, 1997). An adoptee study found that first-reared children, regardless of their biological birth order, were more conscientious than later-reared children (Beer & Horn, 2000). As part of their achievement orientation, firstborn children also see themselves as being more in control of their successes (Phillips & Phillips, 2000). On the negative side, firstborn and only children show greater anxiety (that's me) and are less self-reliant (hmmm . . . I wonder) than later-born children.

Interviews with the parents of 478 children ranging in age from 3 to 9 years found that firstborn children are more likely than later-born children to have imaginary playmates (Bouldin & Pratt, 1999). It is Allyn, our firstborn, who had the imaginary playmate Loveliness. Our second-born (Jordan) and our third-born (Taylor) may have been too busy coping with older siblings to have imaginary playmates.

Later-born children may learn to act aggressively to compete for the attention of their parents and older siblings (Carey, 2007b). They must also deal with the fact that they do not come first (Downey, 2001). Perhaps for that reason, their self-concepts tend to be lower than those of firstborn or only children. But the social skills later-born children acquire from dealing with their family position seem to translate into greater popularity with peers (Carey, 2007). They tend to be more rebellious, liberal, and agreeable than firstborn children, factors that are connected with their popularity (Beck et al., 2006; Zweigenhaft & Von Ammon, 2000).

Differences in personality and achievement among firstborn and later-born children may be linked to contrasting styles in parenting (Carey, 2007). Firstborn children start life as only children. For a year or more, they receive the full attention of parents. Even after other children come along, parents still tend to relate more often to the first child. Parents continue to speak at levels appropriate for the firstborn. Parents impose tougher restrictions on firstborn children and make greater demands of them. Parents are more highly involved in the activities of their firstborn child. Firstborn children are often recruited to help teach younger siblings (Zajonc, 2001). As

I can testify, being asked to teach something (often) prompts one to learn something about it.

By and large, parents are more relaxed and flexible with later-born children. A firstborn child is aware of the greater permissiveness often given to later-born children and may complain about it. (Endlessly). Why are parents more indulgent with later-born children? They have probably gained some self-confidence in child rearing. They see that the firstborn child is turning out just fine. (All right, the firstborn child usually turns out to be just fine, and sometimes "just fine" needs to be qualified as "just fine much of the time.") Parents may therefore assume that later-born children will also turn out, well, just fine. In any event, my wife and I were more relaxed with Jordan and with Taylor than we were with Allyn.

There is a more negative interpretation of parents' relative "relaxation" in rearing later-born children. Parents have only so many resources, in terms of time, energy, and, yes, money. As new children come along, they dilute the resources so that not as much can be devoted to each child (Downey, 2001).

All right, then, siblings hold key places in child development. *Question: How do peers influence social and emotional development in early childhood?*

Peer Relationships

The importance of **peers** in the development of the young child is widely recognized. As children move into the preschool years, they spend more time in the company of other children. Peer interactions serve many functions. Children develop social skills—sharing, helping, taking turns, dealing with conflict—in the peer group. They learn how to lead and how to follow. Physical and cognitive skills develop through peer interactions. Peers also provide emotional support (Dishion & Stormshak, 2007; Grusec, 2006).

Infants first show positive interest in one another at about 6 months. If they are placed on the floor facing one another, they will smile, occasionally imitate one another, and often touch one another. Social interaction increases over the next few months, but during the first year, contacts between infants tend to be brief. In the second year, children show more interest in other children and interact by playing with one another's toys. But they still show relatively little social interaction (Gevers Deynoot-Schaub & Riksen-Walraven, 2006; Valentino et al., 2006). But by about 2 years of age, children imitate one another's play and engage in social games such as follow the leader (Fontaine, 2005; Kavanaugh, 2006). By the age of 2, children show preferences for a few particular playmates.

The preference of a toddler for certain other children is an early sign of friendship (Gleason & Hohmann, 2006; Sherwin-White, 2005). Friendship extends beyond casual interactions. It is characterized by shared positive experiences and feelings of attachment (Grusec, 2002; Park et al., 1993). Even early friendships can be fairly stable. One- to 6-year-olds tend to maintain their friendships from one year to the next, some for as long as 3 years (Rubin et al., 2006). On the other hand, parental conflict can spill over into peer conflict. Children of fighting parents are less tolerant of the bumps and bruises of peer relationships than children of more agreeable parents (Du Rocher Schudlich et al., 2004).

Tom Prettyman/PhotoEdit

Friendship
Friendship takes on different meanings as children develop. Preschoolers focus on sharing toys and activities. Five- to 7-year-olds report that friends are children with whom they have "fun." Sharing confidences becomes important in late childhood and in adolescence.

peers Children of the same age. (More generally, people of similar background and social standing.)

Developing in a World of Diversity

Where Are the Missing American Fathers?

In Chapter 2 we posed the question, Where are the missing Chinese girls? In this chapter, we turn to another question, one that is much closer to home: Where are the missing American fathers?

Over the past two centuries, forces such as urbanization, industrialization, and government-funded child-support programs have contributed, indirectly to be sure, to illegitimacy and fathers' abandonment of families. So, too, has the divorce rate. And within minority communities in the United States, forces such as substance abuse and unemployment have also played key roles (Waller & Swisher, 2006). Social scientists believe that fathers play a significant role in children's development and conceptualize responsible fatherhood as providing children with financial support, caregiving (feeding and bathing children, tucking them in, reading to them, spending time with them), and emotional support (McMahon & Spector, 2007).

Yet it's not happening, at least not for many children in the United States today. And the numbers break down into noticeable patterns according to ethnicity (see ■ Table 10.4). For example, among European Americans, 76% of children live with two married parents. Among African Americans, only 35% of children live with two married parents, and among Latino and Latina Americans, 65% do so. Looking at it from another point of view,

among European Americans, 16% of children live with single mothers compared with 50% of African American children and 25% of Latino and Latina American children.

For African American families, the legacy of slavery, with family members being bought and sold without regard for family structure, has apparently contributed to a multigenerational legacy of family instability (Canton, 2005). Many single fathers give lip service to intending to support and care for their children, but studies show that the majority drop out as their children develop through early childhood. Yet the figures in Table 10.4 do not reveal the complex interactions of mothers who may voluntarily separate from fathers of children who engage in physical abuse or substance abuse (Waller & Swisher, 2006). Nor do they indicate the "custom" in the African American community—more common than in the European American community—for committed couples to live together permanently without benefit of a marriage ceremony. For many European American couples, living together—also known as cohabitation—has become another stage of courtship, one that occurs between dating and marriage (Bramlett & Mosher, 2002). Yet for about 5 million couples today (that's 10 million Americans, dear readers!), cohabitation is a way of life, and it is more popular as a permanent fixture

among African Americans (Whitehead & Popenoe, 2006).

Although the numbers in Table 10.4 do not tell the whole story, the problem of father absence in the African American community is a real one for children who would profit from having a father and for single mothers (Connor, 2006). Even so, in those cases in which a father is absent from the household, the children may nevertheless have a father figure. Maternal partners, relatives, and friends often engage in fathering, especially among low-income families and African Americans (Centers for Disease Control and Prevention, 2006a; Snyder & Sickmund, 2006). One-third to one-half of single African American mothers report that father figures are involved with their preschoolers. But for the rest, fathers and father figures alike are missing.

Reflect:

- *How do the percentages in Table 10.4 fail to represent the full story of the households in which American children live?*
- *Of children living with two married parents, are they necessarily always the children's biological parents? Explain.*
- *What types of "father figures," other than your biological father, did you have when you were a child? What type of influence did these father figures have on you?*

■ **Table 10.4** Children's Living Arrangements: Percentage of American Children Younger than Age 18, 2005

Ethnicity	Percentage Living with Two Married Parents	Percentage Living with a Single Mother*	Percentage Living with a Single Father*
European American	76	16	5
African American	35	50	5
Latino and Latina American	65	25	5

Source: Centers for Disease Control and Prevention. National Center for Health Statistics. (2006), *America's Children in Brief: Key National Indicators of Well-Being, 2006.* www.childstats.gov/americaschildren/tables/pop6a.asp (accessed May 11, 2007).

*Might be living with cohabiting (unmarried) parents.

Preschool children behave somewhat differently toward their friends than toward ordinary playmates. Friends, compared with other children, show higher levels of interaction, helpful behavior, smiling and laughing, and more frequent cooperation and collaboration (Rubin et al., 2006). Conflicts between young friends are less intense and are resolved more readily than other conflicts.

What are children's conceptions of friendships? When preschoolers are asked what they like about their friends, they typically mention the toys and activities they share (Gleason & Hohmann, 2006). Primary schoolchildren usually report that their friends are the children with whom they do things and have fun (Gleason & Hohmann, 2006). Not until late childhood and adolescence do friends' traits and notions of trust, communication, and intimacy become key aspects of friendship.

Active Review

1. Investigators of child rearing find it useful to classify parents according to two dimensions: warmth–coldness and _____.
2. _____ methods of enforcing restrictions attempt to give children knowledge that will enable them to generate desirable behavior patterns in similar situations.
3. _____ parents are both warm and restrictive.
4. _____ parents believe that obedience is a virtue for its own sake.
5. (Firstborn? Later-born?) children are most highly motivated to achieve.

Reflect & Relate: Where do you fit into your family of origin? Are you a firstborn or only child? Were you born later in the family? How does your own development and personality fit in with the stereotypes discussed in this section?

Go to

http://www.thomsonedu.com/psychology/rathus

for an interactive version of this review.

Social Behaviors: In the World, among Others

During the early childhood years, children make tremendous strides in the development of social skills and behavior. Their play activities increasingly involve other children. They learn how to share, cooperate, and comfort others. But young children, like adults, are complex beings. They can be aggressive at times as well as loving and helpful. We turn now to the development of social behaviors in the early years.

Play—Child's Play, That Is

Question: What do developmentalists know about child's play? While children play, developmentalists work to understand just how they do so. Researchers have found that play has many characteristics. It is meaningful, pleasurable, voluntary, and internally motivated (Elkind, 2007). Play is fun! But play also serves many important functions in the life of the young child (Elkind, 2007). Play helps children develop motor skills and coordination. It contributes to social development, because children learn to share play materials, take turns, and try on new roles through **dramatic play.** It supports the development of such cognitive qualities as curiosity, exploration, symbolic thinking, and problem solving. Play may even help children learn to control impulses (Elkind, 2007).

Play and Cognitive Development

Play contributes to and expresses milestones in cognitive development. Jean Piaget (1962 [1946]) identified kinds of play, each characterized by increasing cognitive complexity:

- *Functional play.* Beginning in the sensorimotor stage, the first kind of play involves repetitive motor activity, such as rolling a ball or running and laughing.
- *Symbolic play.* Also called pretend play, imaginative play, or dramatic play, symbolic play emerges toward the end of the sensorimotor stage and increases during early childhood. In symbolic play, children create settings and characters and scripts (Kavanaugh, 2006).
- *Constructive play.* Constructive play is common in early childhood. Children use objects or materials to draw something or make something, such as a tower of blocks.
- *Formal games.* The most complex form of play, according to Piaget, involves formal games with rules. Formal games include board games, which are sometimes enhanced or invented by children, and games involving motor skills, such as marbles and hopscotch, ball games involving sides or teams, and video games. Such games may involve social interaction as well as physical activity and rules. People play such games for a lifetime.

Mildred Parten, whom we discuss next, focused on the social dimensions of play.

Parten's Types of Play

In classic research on children's play, Mildred Parten (1932) observed the development of six types of play among 2- to 5-year-old nursery school children: unoccupied play, solitary play, onlooker play, parallel play, associative play, and cooperative play (see ■ Table 10.5). Solitary play and onlooker play are considered types of **nonsocial play,** that is, play in which children do not interact socially. Nonsocial play occurs more often in 2- and 3-year-olds than in older preschoolers. Parallel play, associative play,

dramatic play Play in which children enact social roles; made possible by the attainment of symbolic thought. A form of pretend play.

nonsocial play Forms of play (solitary play or onlooker play) in which play is not influenced by the play of nearby children.

■ Table 10.5 Parten's Categories of Play

Category	Nonsocial or Social?	Description
Unoccupied play	Nonsocial	Children do not appear to be playing. They may engage in random movements that seem to be without a goal. Unoccupied play appears to be the least frequent kind of play in nursery schools.
Solitary play	Nonsocial	Children play with toys by themselves, independently of the children around them. Solitary players do not appear to be influenced by children around them. They make no effort to approach them.
Onlooker play	Nonsocial	Children observe other children who are at play. Onlookers frequently talk to the children they are observing and may make suggestions, but they do not overtly join in.
Parallel play	Social	Children play with toys similar to those of surrounding children. However, they treat the toys as they choose and do not directly interact with other children.
Associative play	Social	Children interact and share toys. However, they do not seem to share group goals. Although they interact, individuals still treat toys as they choose. The association with the other children appears to be more important than the nature of the activity. They seem to enjoy each other's company.
Cooperative play	Social	Children interact to achieve common, group goals. The play of each child is subordinated to the purposes of the group. One or two group members direct the activities of others. There is also a division of labor, with different children taking different roles. Children may pretend to be members of a family, animals, space monsters, and all sorts of creatures.

and cooperative play are considered **social play.** In each case, children are influenced by other children as they play. Parten found that associative play and cooperative play become common by age 5. They are more likely to be found among older and more experienced preschoolers (Dyer & Moneta, 2006). Girls are somewhat more likely than boys to engage in social play (Zheng & Colombo, 1989).

But there are exceptions to these age trends in social play. Nonsocial play can involve educational activities that foster cognitive development. In fact, many 4- and

social play Play in which children interact with and are influenced by the play of others. Examples are parallel play, associative play, and cooperative play.

Associative Play
Associative play is a form of social play in which children interact and share toys.

5-year-olds spend a good deal of time in parallel constructive play. For instance, they may work on puzzles or build with blocks near other children. Parallel constructive players are frequently perceived by teachers to be socially skillful and are popular with their peers (Coplan et al., 1994). Some toddlers are also more capable of social play than one might expect, given their age. Two-year-olds with older siblings or with a great deal of group experience may engage in advanced forms of social play.

Lisa Serbin and her colleagues (2001) explored infants' visual preferences for gender-stereotyped toys using the time-honored assumption that infants spend more time looking at objects that are of greater interest to them. They found that both girls and boys showed significant preferences for gender-stereotyped toys by 18 months of age. Although preferences for gender-typed toys are well developed by the ages of 15 to 36 months, girls are more likely to stray from the stereotypes (Bussey & Bandura, 1999). Girls ask for and play with "boys' toys" such as cars and trucks more often than boys choose dolls and other "girls' toys." "Cross-role" activities may reflect the greater prestige of "masculine" activities and traits in American culture. Therefore, a boy's playing with "girls' toys" might be seen as taking on an inferior role. A girl's playing with "boys' toys" might be interpreted as having an understandable desire for power or esteem.

Sex Differences in Play

Question: Are there boys' toys and girls' toys? It appears that there are. The reasons are a bit harder to pin down.

Girls and boys differ not only in toy preferences but also in their choice of play environments and activities. During the preschool and early elementary school years, boys prefer vigorous physical outdoor activities such as climbing, playing with large vehicles, and rough-and-tumble play (Else-Quest et al., 2006). In middle childhood, boys spend more time than girls in large play groups of five or more children and spend more time in competitive play (Crombie & Desjardins, 1993; Else-Quest et al., 2006). Girls are more likely than boys to engage in arts and crafts and domestic play. Girls' activities are more closely directed and more structured by adults than are boys' activities (A. Campbell et al., 2002). Girls spend more time than boys playing with only one other child or with a small group of children (Crombie & Desjardins, 1993).

Why do children show these early preferences for gender-stereotyped toys and activities? Although one cannot rule out the possibility of biological factors, such as boys' slightly greater strength and activity levels and girls' slightly greater physical maturity and coordination, note that these differences are simply that—slight. On the other hand, parents and other adults treat girls and boys differently from birth onward. They consistently provide gender-stereotyped toys and room furnishings and encourage gender typing in children's play activities and even household chores (Leaper, 2002). Children, moreover, tend to seek out information on which kinds of toys and play are "masculine" or "feminine" and then conform to the label (Martin & Ruble, 2004).

© Philip James Corwin / CORBIS

A Girl Enjoying a Game of Baseball
Although preferences for gender-typed toys are well established by the age of 3, girls are more likely to stray from the stereotypes, as in this photograph of a girl playing the masculine-typed game of baseball.

Whom Do You Want to Play With?
During early and middle childhood, children tend to prefer the company of children of their own sex. Why?

Some studies find that children who "cross the line" by exhibiting an interest in toys or activities considered appropriate for the other sex are often teased, ridiculed, rejected, or ignored by their parents, teachers, other adults, and peers. Boys are more likely to be criticized than girls (Fagot & Hagan, 1991; Garvey, 1990). On the other hand, one study of 50 preschoolers—25 girls and 25 boys—found that most children believed that their peers should not be excluded from gender-typed play on the basis of sex (Theimer et al., 2001). That is, most believed that it was unfair to prevent girls from playing with trucks and boys from playing with dolls. Perhaps the inconsistency in research findings has something to do with the difference between what preschoolers are observed to do and what they say. (Why should children be more consistent than the rest of us?)

Another well-documented fact involving sex and play is that girls prefer the company of girls, whereas boys prefer to play with boys. This phenomenon is found in a wide variety of cultures and ethnic groups, and it appears early in life. Children begin to prefer playmates of the same sex by the age of 2, with girls developing this preference somewhat earlier than boys (Fagot, 1990; Hay et al., 2004; Strayer, 1990). The tendency to associate with peers of the same sex becomes stronger during middle childhood (Bukowski et al., 1993a; Crombie & Desjardins, 1993). Do you remember a period during your childhood when you and your friends found members of the other sex to be loathsome and wanted nothing to do with them?

Question: Why do children choose to associate with peers of their own sex? Eleanor Maccoby (1990b) believed that two factors are involved. One is that boys' play is more oriented toward dominance, aggression, and rough play than girls' play is. The second is that boys are not very responsive to girls' polite suggestions. Maccoby suggested that girls avoid boys because they want to protect themselves from boys' aggression and because they find it unpleasant to interact with unresponsive people. Boys may avoid the company of girls because they see girls as inferior (Caplan & Larkin, 1991).

Another view is that children "like" peers of their own sex more than peers of the other sex (Bukowski et al., 1993a). But "liking" is usually based on similarity in interests. Children who prefer dolls to transportation toys may prefer to associate with children who share their preference.

Prosocial Behavior: It Could Happen, and Does

My wife recalls always trying to help others in early childhood. She remembers sharing her toys, often at her own expense. She had many sad times when toys or favors she gave were not returned or when toys were broken by others.

Prosocial behavior, sometimes known as *altruism,* is behavior intended to benefit another without expectation of reward. Prosocial behavior includes helping and

prosocial behavior Behavior intended to benefit another without expectation of reward.

comforting others in distress, sharing, and cooperating (Strayer & Roberts, 2004). *Question: How does prosocial behavior develop?*

Even in the first year, children begin to share. They spontaneously offer food and objects to others (Markova & Legerstee, 2006). In the second year, children continue to share objects, and they also begin to comfort distressed companions and help others with tasks and chores (Knafo & Plomin, 2006a).

By the preschool and early school years, children frequently engage in prosocial behavior. Some types of prosocial behavior occur more often than others. One study observed 4- and 7-year-olds at home and found that helping occurred more often than sharing, affection, and reassuring (Grusec, 1991). Research suggests that the development of prosocial behavior is linked to the development of other capabilities in the young child, such as empathy and perspective taking.

Empathy: "I Feel Your Pain"

Empathy is sensitivity to the feelings of others. It is the ability to understand and share another person's feelings and is connected with sharing and cooperation. A survey of American and Japanese mothers of preschoolers found that both groups reported that cooperativeness and interpersonal sensitivity were the most desirable characteristics in young children (Olson et al., 2001).

Children respond emotionally from infancy when others are in distress (Strayer & Roberts, 2004). Infants frequently begin to cry when they hear other children crying, although this early agitated response may be largely reflexive. Even so, crying might signal an early development in empathy.

Empathy appears to promote prosocial behavior and to decrease aggressive behavior, and these links are evident by the second year (Hastings et al., 2000; Strayer & Roberts, 2004). During the second year, many children approach other children and adults who are in distress and try to help them. They may hug a crying child or tell the child not to cry. Toddlers who are rated as emotionally unresponsive to the feelings of others are more likely to behave aggressively throughout the school years (Olson et al., 2000).

There is evidence that girls show more empathy than boys (Eisenberg et al., 1992; Strayer & Roberts, 2004). The difference may arise because girls are socialized to be more attuned to others' emotions than boys are (Strayer & Roberts, 2004), but genetic factors may also play a role in the sex difference.

Perspective Taking: Standing in Someone Else's Shoes

According to Piaget, children in the preoperational stage tend to be egocentric. That is, they tend not to be able to see things from the vantage points of others. It turns out that various cognitive abilities, such as being able to take another person's perspective, are related to knowing when someone is in need or distress (Carlo et al., 1991). Perspective-taking skills improve with age, and so do prosocial skills. Among children of the same age, those with better developed perspective-taking ability also show more prosocial behavior and less aggressive behavior (Hastings et al., 2000).

Influences on Prosocial Behavior

Yes, altruistic behavior is usually defined as prosocial behavior that occurs in the absence of rewards or the expectations of rewards. Nevertheless, prosocial behavior is influenced by rewards and punishments.[1] Observations of nursery school children

---

[1] It reminds me of these lines from Walt Whitman's "Song of Myself":

> Do I contradict myself?
> Very well then I contradict myself.
> (I am large, I contain multitudes.)

Be tolerant of contradictions. You will find them all around you for the rest of your life.

empathy Ability to share another person's feelings.

show that the peers of children who are cooperative, friendly, and generous respond more positively to them than they do to children whose behavior is self-centered (Hartup, 1983). Children who are rewarded in this way for acting prosocially are likely to continue these behaviors (Knafo & Plomin, 2006a).

Some children at early ages are made responsible for doing household chores and caring for younger siblings. They are taught helping and nurturance skills, and their performances are selectively reinforced by other children and adults. Whiting and Edwards (1988) reported that children who are given such tasks are more likely to show prosocial behaviors than children who are not.

There is evidence that children can acquire sharing behavior by observing models who help and share. In one experiment in sharing, 29- to 36-month-olds were more likely to share toys with playmates who first shared toys with them (Levitt et al., 1985). The children appeared to model—and reciprocate—the sharing behavior of their peers.

It also appears that children's prosocial behavior is influenced by the kinds of interactions they have with their parents. For example, prosocial behavior and empathy are enhanced in children who are securely attached to their parents and in children whose mothers show a high degree of empathy (Clark & Ladd, 2000; Strayer & Roberts, 2004).

Parenting styles also affect the development of prosocial behavior. Prosocial behavior is fostered when parents use inductive techniques such as explaining how behavior affects others: "You made Josh cry. It's not nice to hit." Parents of prosocial children are more likely to expect mature behavior from their children. They are less likely to use power-assertive techniques of discipline (Strayer & Roberts, 2004).

Development of Aggression: The Dark Side of Social Interaction

Children, like adults, are complex beings. Not only can they be loving and altruistic, they can also be aggressive. Some children, of course, are more aggressive than others. Aggression refers to behavior intended to cause pain or hurt to another person.

Question: How does aggression develop? Aggressive behaviors, as with other social behaviors, seem to follow developmental patterns. For one thing, the aggression of preschoolers is frequently instrumental or possession oriented (Persson, 2005). That is, young children tend to use aggression to obtain the toys and things they want, such as a favored seat at the table or in the car. But older preschoolers are more likely to resolve their conflicts over toys by sharing rather than fighting (Caplan et al., 1991). Anger and aggressive behavior in preschoolers usually causes other preschoolers to reject them (Henry et al., 2000; Walter & LaFreniere, 2000).

By age 6 or 7, aggression becomes hostile and person oriented. Children taunt and criticize one another and call one another names; they also attack one another physically.

Aggressive behavior appears to be generally stable and predictive of a wide variety of social and emotional difficulties in adulthood (Mesman et al., 2001; Nagin & Tremblay, 2001). Boys are more likely than girls to show aggression from childhood through adulthood, a finding that has been documented in many cultures (Nagin & Tremblay, 2001; Tapper & Boulton, 2004). Toddlers who were perceived as difficult and defiant were more likely to behave aggressively throughout the school years (Olson et al., 2000). A longitudinal study of more than 600 children found that aggressive 8-year-olds tended to remain more aggressive than their peers 22 years later, at age 30 (Eron et al., 1991). Aggressive children of both sexes were more likely to have criminal convictions as adults, to abuse their spouses, and to drive while drunk.

Theories of Aggression

Question: What causes aggression in children? What causes some children to be more aggressive than others? Aggression in childhood appears to result from a complex interplay of biological factors and environmental factors such as reinforcement and modeling.

Evolutionary Theory

Is aggression "natural"? According to evolutionary theory, more individuals are produced than can find food and survive into adulthood. Therefore, there is a struggle for survival. Individuals who possess characteristics that give them an advantage in this struggle are more likely to reach reproductive maturity and contribute their genes to the next generation. In many species, then, whatever genes are linked to aggressive behavior are more likely to be transmitted to new generations (Buss & Duntley, 2006; Vitaro et al., 2006).

Biological Factors

Evidence suggests that genetic factors may be involved in aggressive behavior, including criminal and antisocial behavior (Hicks et al., 2007; Lykken, 2006a; E. O. Wilson, 2004). Jasmine Tehrani and Sarnoff Mednick (2000) report that there is a greater concordance (agreement) rate for criminal behavior between monozygotic (MZ) twins, who fully share their genetic code, than dizygotic (DZ) twins, who, like other brothers and sisters, share only half of their genetic code.

If genetics is involved in aggression, genes may do their work at least in part through the male sex hormone testosterone. Testosterone is apparently connected with feelings of self-confidence, high activity levels, and—the negative side—aggressiveness (Archer, 2006; Cunningham & McGinnis, 2007; Popma et al., 2007). Males are more aggressive than females, and males have higher levels of testosterone than females (Pope et al., 2000). Studies show, for example, that 9- to 11-year-old boys with conduct disorders are likely to have higher testosterone levels than their less aggressive peers (A. Booth et al., 2003; Chance et al., 2000). Research with same-sex female DZ twins and opposite-sex female DZ twins suggests that fetal exposure to male sex hormones (in this case from a male fraternal twin) may heighten aggressiveness (Cohen-Bendahan et al., 2005).

Cognitive Factors

Aggressive boys are more likely than nonaggressive boys to incorrectly interpret the behavior of other children as potentially harmful (Dodge et al., 2002). This bias may make the aggressive child quick to respond aggressively in social situations. Research with primary schoolchildren finds that children who believe in the legitimacy of aggression are more likely to behave aggressively when they are presented with social provocations (Tapper & Boulton, 2004).

Aggressive children are also often found to be lacking in empathy and the ability to see things from the perspective of other people (Hastings et al., 2000). They fail to conceptualize the experiences of their victims, and so they are less likely to inhibit their aggressive impulses.

Social Learning

Social-cognitive explanations of aggression focus on the role of environmental factors such as reinforcement and observational learning. Children, like adults, are most likely to be aggressive when they are frustrated in attempts to gain something they want, such as attention or a toy. When children repeatedly push, shove, and hit to grab toys or break into line, other children usually let them have their way (Kempes et al., 2005). Children who are thus rewarded for acting aggressively are likely to continue to use aggressive means, especially if they do not have alternative means to achieving their ends.

Aggressive children may associate with peers who value their aggression and encourage it (Cairns & Cairns, 1991; Stauffacher & DeHart; 2006). Aggressive children have often been rejected by less aggressive peers, which decreases their motivation to please less aggressive children and reduces their opportunity to learn social skills (Henry et al., 2000; Walter & LaFreniere, 2000).

Parents may also encourage aggressive behavior, sometimes inadvertently. Gerald Patterson (2005) studied families in which parents use coercion as the primary means for controlling children's behavior. In a typical pattern, parents threaten, criticize, and punish a "difficult" or "impossible" child. The child then responds by whining, yelling, and refusing to comply until the parents give in. Both parents and child are relieved when the cycle ends. Thus, when the child misbehaves again, the parents become yet more coercive and the child yet more defiant, until parents or child gives in. A study with 407 children, all 5-year-olds, found that the Patterson model predicts aggressive behavior in both sexes (Eddy et al., 2001).

Children learn not only from the effects of their own behavior but also from observing the behavior of others. They may model the aggressive behavior of their peers, their parents, or their communities at large (Thomas et al., 2006). Children are more apt to imitate what their parents do than to heed what they say. If adults say they disapprove of aggression but smash furniture or hit each other when frustrated, children are likely to develop the notion that aggression is the way to handle frustration.

Truth or Fiction Revisited: It is true that children who are physically punished are more likely to be aggressive themselves than children who are not physically punished (Patterson, 2005). Physically aggressive parents serve as models for aggression and also stoke their children's anger.

Media Influences

Real people are not the only models of aggressive behavior in children's lives. A classic study by Albert Bandura and his colleagues (1963) suggested that televised models had a powerful influence on children's aggressive behavior. One group of preschool children observed a film of an adult model hitting and kicking an inflated Bobo doll, whereas a control group saw an aggression-free film. The experimental and control children were then left alone in a room with the same doll as hidden observers recorded their behavior. The children who had observed the aggressive model showed significantly more aggressive behavior toward the doll themselves (see ● Figure 10.2). Many children imitated bizarre attack behaviors devised for the model in this experiment, behaviors that they would not have thought up themselves.

The children exposed to the aggressive model also showed aggressive behavior patterns that had not been modeled. Therefore, observing the model not only led to imitation of modeled behavior patterns but also apparently **disinhibited** previously learned aggressive responses. The results were similar whether children observed human or cartoon models on film.

The Bandura study was a setup; it was an experimental setup, to be sure, but still a setup. It turns out that television is one of children's major sources of informal observational learning. It also turns out that television is a fertile source of aggressive models throughout much of the world (Villani, 2001). Children are routinely exposed to scenes of murder, beating, and sexual assault simply by turning on the TV set. **Truth or Fiction Revisited:** It is true that children who watch 2 to 4 hours of TV a day will see 8,000 murders and another 100,000 acts of violence by the time they have finished elementary school (Eron, 1993). Are children less likely to be exposed to violence by watching only G-rated movies? No. One study found that virtually all

disinhibit To stimulate a response that has been suppressed (inhibited) by showing a model engaging in that response without aversive consequences.

Albert Bandura / Dept. of Psychology, Stanford University

● **Figure 10.2**   Photos from Albert Bandura's Classic Experiment in the Imitation of Aggressive Models

Research by Albert Bandura and his colleagues has shown that children frequently imitate the aggressive behavior they observe. In the top row, an adult model strikes a clown doll. The second and third rows show a boy and a girl imitating the aggressive behavior.

G-rated animated films have scenes of violence, with a mean duration of 9 to 10 minutes per film (Yokota & Thompson, 2000). Other media that contain violence include movies, rock music and music videos, advertising, video games, and the Internet (Villani, 2001).

In any event, most organizations of health professionals agree that media violence does contribute to aggression (Holland, 2000; Villani, 2001). This relationship has been found for girls and boys of different ages, social classes, ethnic groups, and cultures. Consider a number of ways in which depictions of violence make such a contribution:

- *Observational learning.* Children learn from observation (Holland, 2000). TV violence supplies models of aggressive "skills," which children may acquire. Classic experiments show that children tend to imitate the aggressive behavior they see in the media (Bandura et al., 1963) (see Figure 10.2).
- *Disinhibition.* Punishment inhibits behavior. Conversely, media violence may disinhibit aggressive behavior, especially when media characters "get away" with violence or are rewarded for it.
- *Increased arousal.* Media violence and aggressive video games increase viewers' level of arousal. That is, television "works them up." We are more likely to be aggressive under high levels of arousal.
- *Priming of aggressive thoughts and memories.* Media violence "primes" or arouses aggressive ideas and memories (Bushman, 1998; Meier et al., 2006).

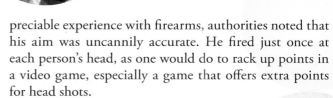

A CLOSER LOOK

When Doom *Leads to . . .* Doom: *What Children Learn from Violent Video Games*

Dylan Klebold and Eric Harris were engrossed in violent video games for hours at a time. They were particularly keen on a game named *Doom.* Harris had managed to reprogram *Doom* so that he, the player, became invulnerable and had an endless supply of weapons. He would "mow down" all the other characters in the game. His program caused some of the characters to ask God why they had been shot as they lay dying. Later on, Klebold and Harris asked some of their shooting victims at Columbine High School in Colorado whether they believed in God. One of the killers also referred to his shotgun as Arlene, the name of a character in *Doom* (Saunders, 2003).

In the small rural town of Bethel, Alaska, Evan Ramsey would play *Doom, Die Hard,* and *Resident Evil* for endless hours. Ramsey shot four people, killing two and wounding two. Afterward, he said the video games taught him that being shot would reduce a player's "health factor," but probably would not be lethal.

Michael Carneal was also a fan of *Doom* and another video game, *Redneck Revenge.* He showed up at school one morning with a semiautomatic pistol, two shotguns, and two rifles. He aimed them at people in a prayer group. Before he was finished, three people lay dead and five were wounded. Although Carneal had had no ap-

preciable experience with firearms, authorities noted that his aim was uncannily accurate. He fired just once at each person's head, as one would do to rack up points in a video game, especially a game that offers extra points for head shots.

The debate as to whether violence in media such as films, television, and video games fuel violence in the real world has been going on for many years. However, research strongly suggests that media violence is a risk factor for increasing emotional arousal, aggressive behavior, and violent thoughts (Arriaga et al., 2006; Buckley & Anderson, 2006; Sherry et al., 2006; Weber et al., 2006).

One reason to be particularly concerned about violent video games is that they require audience participation (Buckley & Anderson, 2006). Players don't just watch; they *participate.* Violent games like *Grand Theft Auto* have grown increasingly popular. Some games reward players for killing police, prostitutes, and bystanders. Virtual weapons include guns, knives, flamethrowers, swords, clubs, cars, hands, and feet. Sometimes the player assumes the role of a hero, but it is also common for the player to assume the role of a criminal.

What do we *learn* from violent video games and violence in other media, such as television, films, and books? The research suggests that we learn a great deal, not only aggressive skills, but also the idea that violence is the normal state of affairs.

© David Young-Wolff/Photo Edit

Reflect:
• Why is it that some, but not all, children react violently to violent video games?
• For debate: Should violent video games be censored?
• Have you ever played a violent video game? What were its effects on you?
• Why do you think that violent video games are more appealing to boys than girls?

- *Habituation.* We become "habituated to," or used to, repeated stimuli. Repeated exposure to TV violence may decrease viewers' sensitivity to real violence (Holland, 2000).

A joint statement issued by the American Medical Association, the American Academy of Pediatrics, the American Psychological Association, and the American Academy of Child and Adolescent Psychiatry (Holland, 2000) made some additional points:

- Children who see a lot of violence are more likely to view violence as an effective way of settling conflicts. Children exposed to violence are more likely to assume that violence is acceptable.
- Viewing violence can decrease the likelihood that one will take action on behalf of a victim when violence occurs.
- Viewing violence may lead to real-life violence. Children exposed to violent programming at a young age are more likely to be violent themselves later on in life.

There is no simple one-to-one connection between media violence and violence in real life. **Truth or Fiction Revisited:** Therefore, it is not true that children mechanically imitate the aggressive behavior they view in the media. But exposure to violence in the media increases the probability of violence in viewers in several ways.

There is apparently a circular relationship between exposure to media violence and aggressive behavior (Anderson & Dill, 2000; Eron, 1982; Funk et al., 2000). Yes, media violence contributes to aggressive behavior, but aggressive youngsters are also more likely to seek out this kind of "entertainment."

The family constellation also affects the likelihood that children will imitate the violence they see on TV. Studies find that parental substance abuse, physical punishments, and father absence contribute to the likelihood of aggression in early childhood (Bendersky et al., 2006; Chang et al., 2003; Roelofs et al., 2006). Parental rejection further increases the likelihood of aggression in children (Eron, 1982). These family factors suggest that the parents of aggressive children are absent or unlikely to help young children understand that the kinds of socially inappropriate behaviors they see in the media are not for them. A harsh home life may also confirm the TV viewer's vision of the world as a violent place and further encourage reliance on television for companionship. In Chapter 9, we saw how parents can help children understand that the violence they view in the media is not real and not to be imitated.

Active Review

6. In _____ play, children play with toys by themselves.
7. In _____ play, children interact and share toys.
8. Preschoolers tend to prefer to play with children of the (Other or Same?) sex.
9. _____ is another term for prosocial behavior.

10. Preschoolers tend to (Admire or Reject?) aggressive peers.
11. Aggressive behavior is linked with the hormone _____.
12. _____ theorists explain aggressive behavior in terms of reinforcement and observational learning.

13. The observation of aggression in the media tends to (Inhibit or Disinhibit?) aggressive behavior in children.

Reflect & Relate: Do you believe that violence in the media causes aggression? (What does the word *cause* mean?) Media violence is everywhere, not only in R-rated films but also in G-rated films and in video games. There are connections between media violence and aggression, but not everyone who witnesses media violence behaves aggressively. So, how do we explain the connections between violence in the media and aggression?

Go to

http://www.thomsonedu.com/psychology/rathus

for an interactive version of this review.

Personality and Emotional Development

In the early childhood years, children's personalities start becoming more defined. Their sense of self—who they are and how they feel about themselves—continues to develop and becomes more complex. They begin to acquire a sense of their own abilities and their increasing mastery of the environment. As they move out into the world, they also face new experiences that may cause them to feel fearful and anxious. Let's explore some of these facets of personality and emotional development.

The Self

The sense of self, or the **self-concept,** emerges gradually during infancy. Infants and toddlers visually begin to recognize themselves and differentiate from other individuals such as their parents.

Question: How does the self develop during early childhood? In the preschool years, children continue to develop their sense of self. Almost as soon as they begin to speak, they describe themselves in terms of certain categories, such as age groupings (baby, child, adult) and sex (girl, boy). These self-definitions that refer to concrete external traits have been called the **categorical self.**

Children as young as 3 years are able to describe themselves in terms of behaviors and internal states that appear to occur frequently and are fairly stable over time (Eder, 1989, 1990). For example, in response to the question "How do you feel when you're scared?" young children frequently respond, "Usually like running away" (Eder, 1989). Or, in answer to the question "How do you usually act around grown-ups?" a typical response might be, "I mostly been good with grown-ups." Thus, even preschoolers seem to understand that they have stable characteristics that endure over time.

One aspect of the self-concept is **self-esteem,** the value or worth that people attach to themselves. Children who have a good opinion of themselves during the preschool years are more likely to show secure attachment and have parents who are attentive to their needs (Booth-LaForce et al., 2006; Patterson & Bigler, 2006). They also are more likely to engage in prosocial behavior (Salmivalli et al., 2005).

Preschool children begin to make evaluative judgments about two different aspects of themselves by the age of 4 (Harter & Pike, 1984). One is their cognitive and physical competence (e.g., being good at puzzles, counting, swinging, tying shoes), and the second is their social acceptance by peers and parents (e.g., having lots of friends, being read to by Mom) (Clark & Symons, 2004; Piek et al., 2006). But preschoolers do not yet make a clear distinction between different areas of competence. For example, a child of this age is not likely to report being good in school but poor in physical skills. One is either "good at doing things" or one is not (Harter & Pike, 1984).

self-concept One's impression of oneself; self-awareness.

categorical self Definitions of the self that refer to concrete external traits.

self-esteem The sense of value, or worth, that people attach to themselves.

During middle childhood, personality traits become increasingly important in children's self-definitions. Children then are also able to make judgments about their self-worth in many different areas of competence, behavioral conduct, appearance, and social relations.

Initiative versus Guilt

As preschool children continue to develop a separate sense of themselves, they increasingly move out into the world and take the initiative in learning new skills. Erik Erikson (1963) refers to these early childhood years as the stage of initiative versus guilt.

Children in this stage strive to achieve independence from their parents and master adult behaviors. They are curious, try new things, and test themselves. These qualities are illustrated in the following account of a day in the life of a 5-year-old:

> In a single day, he decided to see how high he could build his blocks, invented a game that consisted of seeing who could jump the highest on his parents' bed, and led the family to a new movie containing a great deal of action and violence.

> —Crain (2000)

During these years, children learn that not all their plans, dreams, and fantasies can be realized. Adults prohibit children from doing certain things, and children begin to internalize these adult rules. Fear of violating the rules may cause the child to feel guilty and may curtail efforts to master new skills. Parents can help children develop and maintain a healthy sense of initiative by encouraging their attempts to learn and explore and by not being unduly critical and punitive.

Fears: The Horrors of Early Childhood

In Erik Erikson's view, fear of violating parental prohibitions can be a powerful force in the life of a young child. *Question: What sorts of fears do children have in the early years?*

Both the frequency and the content of fears change as children move from infancy into the preschool years. The number of fears seems to peak between 2½ and 4 years and then taper off (Miller et al., 1990b).

The preschool period is marked by a decline in fears of loud noises, falling, sudden movement, and strangers. **Truth or Fiction Revisited:** Fear of social disapproval is not the most common fear among preschoolers. Preschoolers are most likely to have fears that revolve around animals, imaginary creatures, the dark, and personal safety (Field, 2006; Muris et al., 2003). The fantasies of young children frequently involve stories they are told and media imagery. Frightening images of imaginary creatures can persist. Many young children are reluctant to have the lights turned off at night for fear that these creatures may harm them in the dark. Imaginary creatures also threaten personal safety.

But real objects and situations also cause many children to fear for their personal safety, such as lightning, thunder and other loud noises, the dark, high places, sharp objects and being cut, blood, unfamiliar people, strange people, stinging and crawling insects, and other animals.

During middle childhood, children's fears become more realistic. They become less fearful of imaginary creatures, but fears of bodily harm and injury remain fairly common. Children grow more fearful of failure and criticism in school and in social relationships (Ollendick & King, 1991).

Girls report more fears and higher levels of anxiety than boys (Ollendick et al., 1991; Weems et al., 1999). Whether these findings reflect actual differences in fears and anxieties or differences in the willingness of girls and boys to report "weaknesses" is a matter of debate.

A Closer Look

Helping Children Cope with Fears

A number of methods have been developed to help children cope with fears. Professionals who work with children today are most likely to use such behavior modification methods as desensitization, operant conditioning, and participant modeling (Gordon et al., 2007). Each method is based on principles of learning.

Desensitization

Desensitization exposes children gradually to the sources of their fears while they are engaging in behavior that is incompatible with fear (Gordon et al., 2007). Fear includes bodily responses such as rapid heart rate and respiration rate. Thus, doing things that reduce the heart and respiration rates is incompatible with fear.

In a classic study, Mary Cover Jones (1924) used a form of desensitization along with counterconditioning to eliminate a fear of rabbits in a 2-year-old boy named Peter. Desensitization consisted of bringing a rabbit gradually closer to Peter. Fear was counterconditioned in that as the rabbit was being brought closer, the boy was experiencing pleasure from munching away merrily on candy and cookies. Peter, to be sure, cast a wary eye in the rabbit's direction, but he continued to eat. Jones suspected that if she brought the rabbit too close too quickly, the cookies left on Peter's plate and those already eaten might have decorated the walls. But gradually the animal could be brought nearer without upsetting the boy. Eventually, Peter could eat and touch the rabbit at the same time. Jones gave the child a treat. Other methods of relaxing the child are having the child play with a game or favorite toy and asking the child to talk about a favorite book or TV hero.

Operant Conditioning

In operant conditioning, children are guided into desirable behaviors and then reinforced for engaging in them. In using behavior modification in the classroom, good behavior is reinforced and misbehavior is ignored.

Parents and other adults use operant techniques all the time. They may teach children how to draw letters of the alphabet by guiding their hand and saying "Good!" when the desired result is obtained. When children fear touching a dog, parents frequently take their hands and guide them physically in petting the animal. Then they say something reinforcing, such as "Look at that big girl/boy petting that doggy!" or "Isn't the puppy nice and soft?" (Ollendick & Seligman, 2006).

Participant Modeling

In participant modeling, children first observe live models or filmed or taped models (ideally, children similar in age) engage in the behavior that evokes fear. Then they imitate the behavior of the models. In an often-cited experiment on participant modeling, Albert Bandura and his colleagues (1969) found that participant modeling helped people who were afraid of snakes. ● Figure 10.3 shows children and adults in the Bandura study who imitated unafraid models.

Reflect: How can you apply the methods discussed in this feature to a possible "grown-up" fear you might have?

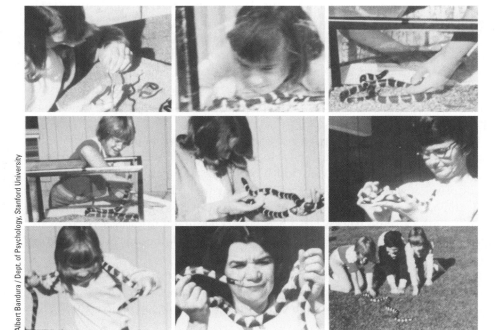

Albert Bandura / Dept. of Psychology, Stanford University

● **Figure 10.3**
Participant Modeling

Participant modeling helps children overcome fears through principles of observational learning. In these photos, children with a fear of snakes observe, then imitate, models who are unafraid. Parents often try to convince children that something tastes good by eating it in front of them and saying "Mmm!"

Active Review

14. Self-definitions that refer to concrete external traits are called the _____ self.
15. Self-_____ is the value or worth that people attach to themselves.
16. Children who are _____ attached tend to have high self-esteem.
17. Erikson referred to early childhood as the stage of _____ versus guilt.
18. Early childhood fears tend to revolve around personal _____.

19. (Boys or Girls?) report more fears and higher levels of anxiety.

Reflect & Relate: Do you remember any fears from early childhood? Have they faded over the years?

Go to

http://www.thomsonedu.com/psychology/rathus
for an interactive version of this review.

Development of Gender Roles and Sex Differences

> I am woman, hear me roar . . . I am strong
> I am invincible
> I am woman

These lyrics are from the song "I Am Woman" by Helen Reddy and Ray Burton. They capture the attention because they run counter to the **stereotype** of the woman as vulnerable and in need of the protection of a man. The stereotype of the vulnerable woman, as with all stereotypes, is a fixed, oversimplified, and often distorted idea about a group of people, in this case, women. The stereotype of the chivalrous, protective man is also a stereotype. *Questions: What are stereotypes and gender roles? How do they develop?*

Cultural stereotypes of males and females involve broad expectations of behavior that we call **gender roles.** In our culture, the feminine gender-role stereotype includes such traits as dependence, gentleness, helpfulness, warmth, emotionality, submissiveness, and home orientation. The masculine gender-role stereotype includes aggressiveness, self-confidence, independence, competitiveness, and competence in business, math, and science (Miller et al., 2006).

Gender-role stereotypes appear to develop through a series of stages. First, children learn to label the sexes. At about 2 to 2½ years of age, they become quite accurate in identifying pictures of girls and boys (Fagot & Leinbach, 1993). By age 3, they display knowledge of gender stereotypes for toys, clothing, work, and activities (Campbell et al., 2004). For example, children of this age generally agree that boys play with cars and trucks, help their fathers, and tend to hit others. They also agree that girls play with dolls, help their mothers, and do not hit others (Cherney et al., 2006).

Showing distress apparently becomes gender typed so that preschoolers judge it to be acceptable for girls. One study found that preschool boys but not girls were rejected by their peers when they showed distress (Walter & LaFreniere, 2000). The

stereotype A fixed, conventional idea about a group.

gender role A complex cluster of traits and behaviors that are considered stereotypical of females and males.

same study found that peers rejected preschoolers of both sexes when they displayed too much anger.

Children become increasingly traditional in their stereotyping of activities, occupational roles, and personality traits between the ages of 3 and 9 or 10 (Miller et al., 2006). For example, traits such as "cruel" and "repairs broken things" are viewed as masculine, and traits such as "often is afraid" and "cooks and bakes" are seen as feminine. A study of 55 middle-class, primarily European American children, age 39–84 months, found that they considered men to be more competent in traditionally masculine-typed occupations (such as occupations in science and transportation) and women to be more competent in traditionally feminine-typed occupations (such as nursing and teaching) (Levy et al., 2000). The children equated competence with income: They believed that men earned more money in the masculine-typed jobs but that women earned more in the feminine-typed jobs.

Stereotyping levels off or declines beyond the preschool years (Martin & Ruble, 2004). Older children and adolescents apparently become somewhat more flexible in their perceptions of males and females. They retain the broad stereotypes but also perceive similarities between the sexes and recognize that there are individual differences. They are more capable of recognizing the arbitrary aspects of gender categories and more willing to try behaviors that typify the other sex.

Children and adolescents show some chauvinism by perceiving their own sex in a somewhat better light. For example, girls perceive other girls as nicer, more hardworking, and less selfish than boys. Boys, on the other hand, think that they are nicer, more hardworking, and less selfish than girls (Matlin, 2008; Miller et al., 2006).

Sex Differences

Clearly, females and males are anatomically different. And according to the gender-role stereotypes we have just examined, people believe that females and males also differ in their behaviors, personality characteristics, and abilities. *Question: How different are females and males in terms of cognitive and social and emotional development?*

Sex differences in infancy are small and rather inconsistent. In this chapter, we have reviewed sex differences during early childhood. Young girls and boys display some differences in their choices of toys and play activities. Boys engage in more rough-and-tumble play and also are more aggressive. Girls tend to show more empathy and to report more fears. Girls show greater verbal ability than boys, whereas boys show greater visual–spatial ability than girls. *Question: What are the origins of sex differences in behavior?* Different views have been proposed.

Theories of the Development of Sex Differences

Like mother, like daughter; like father, like son—at least often, if not always. Why is it that little girls (often) grow up to behave according to the cultural stereotypes of what it means to be female? Why is it that little boys (often) grow up to behave like male stereotypes? Let's have a look at various explanations of the development of sex differences.

The Roles of Evolution and Heredity

According to evolutionary psychologists, sex differences were fashioned by natural selection in response to problems in adaptation that were repeatedly encountered by humans over thousands of generations (Buss & Duntley, 2006; Geary, 2006). The story of the survival of our ancient ancestors is now etched in our genes. Genes that bestow attributes that increase an organism's chances of surviving to produce viable offspring are most likely to be transmitted to future generations. We thus possess the genetic codes for traits that helped our ancestors survive and reproduce. These traits include structural sex differences, such as those found in the brain, and differences in body chemistry, such as hormones.

Consider a sex difference. Males tend to place relatively more emphasis on physical appearance in mate selection than females do, whereas females tend to place relatively more emphasis on personal factors such as financial status and reliability (Buss, 2000; Schmitt, 2003). Why? Evolutionary psychologists believe that evolutionary forces favor the survival of women who seek status in their mates and men who seek physical allure because these preferences provide reproductive advantages. Some physical features such as cleanliness, good complexion, clear eyes, strong teeth and healthy hair, firm muscle tone, and a steady gait are found to be universally appealing to both males and females (Buss, 1999). Perhaps such traits have value as markers of better reproductive potential in prospective mates. According to the "parental investment model," a woman's appeal is more strongly connected with her age and health, both of which are markers of reproductive capacity. The value of men as reproducers, however, is more intertwined with factors that contribute to a stable environment for child rearing, such as social standing and reliability. For such reasons, these qualities may have grown relatively more alluring to women over the millennia (Brase, 2006).

This theory is largely speculative, however, and not fully consistent with all the evidence. Women, like men, are attracted to physically appealing partners, and women tend to marry men similar to them in physical attractiveness and socioeconomic standing.

But evolution has also led to the development of the human brain. As we see in the next section, the organization of the brain apparently plays a role in gender typing.

Organization of the Brain

The organization of the brain is largely genetically determined, and it at least in part involves prenatal exposure to sex hormones (Collins et al., 2000; Maccoby, 2000). The hemispheres of the brain are specialized to perform certain functions. In most people, the left hemisphere is more involved in language skills, whereas the right hemisphere is specialized to carry out visual–spatial tasks.

Both males and females have a left hemisphere and a right hemisphere. They also share other structures in the brain, but the question is whether they use them in quite the same way. Consider the hippocampus, a brain structure that is involved in the formation of memories and the relay of incoming sensory information to other parts of the brain (Ohnishi et al., 2006). Matthias Riepe and his colleagues (Grön et al., 2000) have studied the ways in which humans and rats use the hippocampus when they are navigating mazes. Males use the hippocampus in both hemispheres when they are navigating (Grön et al., 2000). Women, however, rely on the hippocampus in the right hemisphere in concert with the right prefrontal cortex, an area of the brain that evaluates information and makes plans. Researchers have also found that females tend to rely on landmarks when they are finding their way ("Go a block past Ollie's Noodle Shop, turn left, and go to the corner past Café Lalo"). Men rely more on geometry, as in finding one's position in terms of coordinates or on a map ("You're on the corner of Eleventh Avenue and 57th Street, and you want to get to Seventh Avenue and 55th Street,[2] so . . .) (Grön et al., 2000). Riepe and colleagues (Grön et al., 2000) speculated that a female's prefrontal activity represents the conscious effort to keep landmarks in mind. The "purer" hippocampal activity in males might represent a more geometric approach.

Some psychological activities, such as the understanding and production of language, are regulated by structures in the left hemisphere, particularly in Broca's area

---

[2]This is the location of the Carnegie Deli in New York. Cholesterol shmolesterol. You live just once. Go. Enjoy.

and Wernicke's area. But emotional and aesthetic responses, along with some other psychological activities, are more or less regulated in the right hemisphere. Brain-imaging research suggests that the left and right hemispheres of males may be more specialized than those of females (Shaywitz & Shaywitz, 2003). For example, if you damage the left hemisphere of a man's brain, you may cause greater language difficulties than if you cause similar damage in a woman. The right hemisphere is thought to be relatively more involved in spatial relations tasks, and damage in this hemisphere is more costly to a male's spatial-relations skills than to a female's.

If the brain hemispheres of women "get along better" than those of men—that is, if they better share the regulation of various cognitive activities—we may have an explanation of why women frequently outperform men in language tasks that involve some spatial organization, such as spelling, reading, and enunciation. Yet men, with more specialized spatial-relations skills, could be expected to generally outperform women at visualizing objects in space and reading maps.

Sex Hormones

Sex hormones and other chemical substances stoke the prenatal differentiation of sex organs. Toward the end of the embryonic stage, androgens—male sex hormones—are sculpting male genital organs. These chemicals may also "masculinize" or "feminize" the brain; in other words, they may give rise to behavioral tendencies that are consistent with gender-role stereotypes (Cohen-Bendahan et al., 2004; Pei et al., 2006).

Let us also consider psychological views of the development of sex differences.

Lessons in Observation
Gender

 To watch this video, visit the book companion website. You can also answer the questions and e-mail your responses to your professor.

When asked "What doll takes care of the babies?" children typically respond in a stereotypical manner by pointing to the female doll.

Learning Objectives

- At what age do children begin expressing stereotypical ideas about gender?
- What is the difference between gender identity and gender role?
- At what age do children seem to first understand that their own sex will remain stable?
- Are preschool children flexible or inflexible when it comes to their ideas concerning gender-typed behavior?

Applied Lesson

Describe the concepts of gender identity, gender stability, and gender constancy. How do they develop, according to Kohlberg? Does research support Kohlberg's view of when children should show preferences for gender-typed toys and activities?

Critical Thinking

If a child is reared without gender-typed toys in the household or if the child's parents avoid giving the child gender-typed messages about what kinds of behaviors are appropriate, how might that child's views on gender differ from those of his or her classmates? Are classmates likely to respond flexibly to that child's views of gender?

Social Cognitive Theory

Social cognitive theorists attempt to straddle the gulf between behaviorism and cognitive perspectives on human development. As such, they pay attention both to the roles of rewards and punishments (reinforcement) in gender typing and to the ways in which children learn from observing others and then decide what behaviors are appropriate for them. Children learn much about what society considers "masculine" or "feminine" by observing and imitating models of the same sex. These models may be their parents, other adults, other children, even characters in electronic media such as TV and video games.

The importance of observational learning was shown in a classic experiment conducted by Kay Bussey and Albert Bandura (1984). In this study, children obtained information on how society categorizes behavior patterns by observing how often they were performed either by men or by women. While children of ages 2 to 5 observed them, female and male adult role models exhibited different behavior patterns, such as choosing a blue or a green hat, marching or walking across a room, and repeating different words. Then the children were given a chance to imitate the models. Girls were twice as likely to imitate the woman's behavior as the man's, and boys were twice as likely to imitate the man's behaviors as the woman's.

Socialization also plays a role in gender typing. Parents, teachers, other adults— even other children—provide children with information about the gender-typed behaviors they are expected to display (Sabattini & Leaper, 2004). Children are rewarded with smiles and respect and companionship when they display "gender-appropriate" behavior. Children are punished (with frowns and "yucks" and loss of friends) when they display behavior considered inappropriate for their sex.

Boys are encouraged to be independent, whereas girls are more likely to be restricted and given help. Boys are allowed to roam farther from home at an earlier age and are more likely to be left unsupervised after school (Miller et al., 2006).

Fathers are more likely than mothers to communicate norms for gender-typed behaviors to their children (Miller et al., 2006). Mothers are usually less demanding. Fathers tend to encourage their sons to develop instrumental behavior (i.e., behavior that gets things done or accomplishes something) and their daughters to develop warm, nurturant behavior. Fathers are likely to cuddle daughters. By contrast, they are likely to toss their sons into the air and use hearty language with them, such as "How're yuh doin', Tiger?" and "Hey you, get your keister over here." Being a nontraditionalist, I would toss my young daughters into the air, which raised objections from relatives who criticized me for being too rough. This criticism, of course, led me to modify my behavior. I learned to toss my daughters into the air when the relatives were not around.

Acquiring Gender Roles

What psychological factors contribute to the acquisition of gender roles? Psychoanalytic theory focuses on the concept of identification. Social cognitive theory focuses on imitation of the behavior patterns of same-sex adults and reinforcement by parents and peers.

© Sylvie Villeger/Photo Researchers, Inc.

© Kathy Sloane/Photo Researchers, Inc.

Nature and Gender Typing

Deals with the roles of evolution, heredity, and biology in gender typing.

Perspective	Key Points	Comments
Evolution and heredity	Psychological sex differences were fashioned by natural selection in response to challenges that humans faced repeatedly over thousands of generations.	Evolutionary theorists believe that sex differences in aggression are natural. They suggest that a woman's allure is strongly connected with her age and health, which are markers of reproductive capacity, but the value of men as reproducers is also connected with factors that create a stable environment for child rearing.
Organization of the brain	The hemispheres of the brain are more specialized in males than in females.	Sex differences in brain organization might explain why women tend to excel in language skills and men in visual–spatial tasks.
Sex hormones	Sex hormones may prenatally "masculinize" or "feminize" the brain by creating predispositions consistent with gender roles.	Male rats are generally superior to females in maze-learning ability, a task that requires spatial skills. Aggressiveness appears to be connected with testosterone.

© Sylvie Villeger/Photo Researchers, Inc.

© Kathy Sloane/Photo Researchers, Inc.

Nurture and Gender Typing

Deals with theories in psychology—for example, learning theory, and cognitive theory—and related research.

Perspective	Key Points	Comments
Social cognitive theory	Children learn what is masculine or feminine by observational learning.	Parents and others tend to reinforce children for gender-appropriate behavior.
Cognitive-developmental theory	Gender typing is connected with the development of the concepts of gender identity, gender stability, and gender constancy.	Research evidence shows that children develop gender-typed preferences and behaviors before development of gender stability and gender constancy.
Gender-schema theory	Cultures tend to organize social life around polarized gender roles. Children accept these scripts and try to behave in accord with them.	Research evidence suggests that polarized female–male scripts pervade our culture. For example, children tend to distort their memories to conform to the gender schema.

Primary schoolchildren show less stereotyping if their mothers frequently engage in traditionally "masculine" household and child-care tasks such as yard work, washing the car, taking children to ball games, or assembling toys (Powlishta, 2004). Many daughters have mothers who serve as career-minded role models. Maternal employment is associated with less polarized gender-role concepts for girls and boys (Sabattini & Leaper, 2004; Powlishta, 2004). The daughters of employed women also have higher educational and career aspirations than daughters of unemployed women, and they are more likely to choose careers that are nontraditional for women.

Social cognitive theory has helped outline the ways in which rewards, punishments, and modeling foster gender-typed behavior. But how do rewards and punishment influence behavior? Do reinforcers mechanically increase the frequency of behavior, or, as suggested by cognitive theories, do they provide us with concepts that in turn guide our behavior? Let's consider two cognitive approaches to gender typing that address these matters: cognitive-developmental theory and gender-schema theory.

Cognitive-Developmental Theory

Lawrence Kohlberg (1966) proposed a cognitive-developmental view of gender typing. According to this perspective, children play an active role in gender typing (Martin & Ruble, 2004). They form concepts about gender and then fit their behavior to the concepts. These developments occur in stages and are entwined with general cognitive development.

According to Kohlberg, gender typing involves the emergence of three concepts: gender identity, gender stability, and gender constancy. The first step in gender typing is attaining **gender identity.** Gender identity is the knowledge that one is male or female. At 2 years, most children can say whether they are boys or girls. By the age of 3, many children can discriminate anatomic sex differences (Campbell et al., 2004; Ruble et al., 2006).

At around age 4 or 5, most children develop the concept of **gender stability,** according to Kohlberg. They recognize that people retain their sexes for a lifetime. Girls no longer believe that they can grow up to be daddies, and boys no longer think that they can become mommies. **Truth or Fiction Revisited:** Because most 2½-year-olds have not developed gender stability, a girl of this age may know that she is a girl but think that she can grow up to be a daddy.

By the age of 5 to 7 years, Kohlberg believes that most children develop the more sophisticated concept of **gender constancy.** Children with gender constancy recognize that sex does not change, even if people modify their dress or behavior. A woman who cuts her hair short remains a woman. A man who dons an apron and cooks dinner remains a man.

We could relabel gender constancy "conservation of gender," highlighting the theoretical debt to Jean Piaget. Indeed, researchers have found that the development of gender constancy is related to the development of conservation (de Lisi & Gallagher, 1991). According to cognitive-developmental theory, once children have established concepts of gender stability and constancy, they seek to behave in ways that are consistent with their sex (Martin & Ruble, 2004).

Cross-cultural studies in the United States, Samoa, Nepal, Belize, and Kenya (Munroe et al., 1984) have found that the concepts of gender identity, gender stability, and gender constancy emerge in the order predicted by Kohlberg (Leonard & Archer, 1989). Nevertheless, children may achieve gender constancy earlier than Kohlberg stated. Many 3- and 4-year-olds show some understanding of the concept (Leonard & Archer, 1989).

Kohlberg's theory also has difficulty accounting for the age at which gender-typed play emerges. Girls show preferences for dolls and soft toys and boys for hard

gender identity Knowledge that one is female or male. Also, the name of the first stage in Kohlberg's cognitive-developmental theory of the assumption of gender roles.

gender stability The concept that one's sex is a permanent feature.

gender constancy The concept that one's sex remains the same despite superficial changes in appearance or behavior.

transportation toys by the age of 1½ to 3 (Alexander, 2003; Campbell et al., 2004; Powlishta, 2004). At this age, children are likely to have a sense of gender identity, but gender stability and gender constancy remain a year or two away.

Gender-Schema Theory

Gender-schema theory proposes that children use sex as one way of organizing their perceptions of the world (Campbell et al., 2004; Martin & Ruble, 2004). A gender schema is a cluster of concepts about male and female physical traits, behaviors, and personality traits. For example, consider the dimension of strength–weakness. Children learn that strength is linked to the male gender-role stereotype and weakness to the female stereotype. They also learn that some dimensions, such as strength–weakness, are more relevant to one gender than the other—in this case, to males. A boy will learn that the strength he displays in weight training or wrestling affects the way others perceive him. But most girls do not find this trait to be important to others, unless they are competing in gymnastics, tennis, swimming, or other sports. Even so, boys are expected to compete in these sports and girls are not. A girl is likely to find that her gentleness and neatness are more important in the eyes of others than her strength.

From the viewpoint of gender-schema theory, gender identity alone can inspire "gender-appropriate" behavior (Ruble et al., 2006). As soon as children understand the labels "girl" and "boy," they seek information concerning gender-typed traits and try to live up to them. A boy may fight back when provoked because boys are expected to do so. A girl may be gentle and kind because that is expected of girls. Both boys' and girls' self-esteem will depend on how they measure up to the gender schema.

Studies indicate that children do possess information according to a gender schema. For example, boys show better memory for "masculine" toys, activities, and occupations, whereas girls show better memory for "feminine" toys, activities, and occupations (Martin & Ruble, 2004). However, gender-schema theory does not answer the question of whether biological forces also play a role in gender typing.

Psychological Androgyny

Let's be aboveboard about it. I have made several subtle suggestions about being male and about being female in this chapter. I have acknowledged that there is probably something biological involved in it, including brain organization and baths in bodily fluids that are brimming with sex hormones. But I have probably also suggested that we may put too much stock in what is "masculine" and what is "feminine" and that we may often do boys and girls more harm than good when we urge them to adhere to strict cultural stereotypes.

Cultural stereotypes tend to polarize females and males. They tend to push females and males to the imagined far ends of a continuum of gender-role traits (Rathus et al., 2008). It is common to label people as masculine or feminine. It is also common to assume that the more feminine people are, the less masculine they are, and vice versa. That is, the female U.S. Marines helicopter pilot usually is not conceptualized as wearing lipstick or baking. The tough male business executive is not usually conceptualized as changing diapers and playing peek-a-boo. An "emotional" boy who also shows the "feminine" traits of nurturance and tenderness is probably thought of as less masculine than other boys. Outspoken, competitive girls are likely to be seen not only as masculine but also as unfeminine.

However, the traits that supposedly characterize masculinity and femininity can be found within the same individual. That is, people (male or female) who obtain high scores on measures of masculine traits on personality tests can also score high on feminine traits. *Question: What is psychological androgyny?* People with both stereotypical feminine and masculine traits are termed **psychologically androgynous**

gender-schema theory The view that one's knowledge of the gender schema in one's society (the behavior patterns that are considered appropriate for men and women) guides one's assumption of gender-typed preferences and behavior patterns.

psychological androgyny Possession of both stereotypical feminine and masculine traits.

(from the Greek roots *andr,* meaning man, and *gyne,* meaning woman). People who are high in stereotypical masculine traits only are typed as masculine. People who are high in stereotypical feminine traits only are typed as feminine. People who show neither strong feminine nor masculine traits are termed undifferentiated (Bem, 1993).

Some psychologists suggest that it is worthwhile to promote psychological androgyny in children because they will then possess both the feminine and masculine traits that are valued in our culture. A good deal of evidence suggests that androgynous children and adolescents are relatively well adjusted, apparently because they can summon a wider range of traits to meet the challenges in their lives (Lefkowitz & Zeldow, 2006). For example, compared with their masculine, feminine, or undifferentiated peers, androgynous children and adolescents have better social relations, superior adjustment, greater creativity (Norlander et al., 2000), and more willingness to pursue occupations stereotyped as "belonging" to the other sex (Hebert, 2000).

The changes in physical, cognitive, social, and emotional development reviewed in these last three chapters lay the groundwork for the next major period in development: the middle childhood years. We explore those years in the next three chapters, beginning with physical development in Chapter 11.

Active Review

20. Cultural stereotypes of males and females involve broad expectations for behavior that are called gender _____.
21. The organization of the brain involves prenatal exposure to _____ hormones.
22. Brain imaging suggests that the hemispheres of the brain are more specialized in (Males or Females?).
23. (Mothers or Fathers?) are more likely to communicate norms for gender-typed behaviors to children.
24. Kohlberg proposes that the emergence of three concepts guides gender typing: gender identity, gender stability, and gender _____.

25. Gender-_____ theory proposes that children blend their self-concepts with the gender schema of their culture.

Reflect & Relate: Do you see yourself as being traditionally feminine, traditionally masculine, or psychologically androgynous? Have the gender roles and stereotypes of our culture created opportunities or conflicts for you? Explain.

Go to

http://www.thomsonedu.com/psychology/rathus

for an interactive version of this review.

1. **What are the dimensions of child rearing?**

Parental approaches to child rearing can be classified according to the independent dimensions of warmth–coldness and restrictiveness–permissiveness. Consistent control and firm enforcement of rules can have positive consequences for the child.

2. **What techniques do parents use to restrict their children's behavior?**

Parents tend to use inductive methods, power assertion, and withdrawal of love to enforce rules. Inductive methods use "reasoning," or explaining why one sort of behavior is good and another is not.

3. **What parenting styles are involved in the transmission of values and standards?**

The main methods are authoritative, authoritarian, and permissive. Authoritative parents are restrictive but warm and tend to have the most competent and achievement-oriented children. Authoritarian parents are restrictive and cold. The sons of authoritarian parents tend to be hostile and defiant; daughters are low in independence. Children of neglectful parents show the least competence and maturity.

4. **How do the situation and the child influence parenting styles?**

Parents tend to prefer power-assertive techniques when they believe that children understand the rules they have violated and are capable of acting appropriately. Stress contributes to the use of power assertion.

5. **How do siblings influence social and emotional development in early childhood?**

Siblings provide caregiving, emotional support, advice, role models, social interaction, restrictions, and cognitive stimulation. However, they are also sources of conflict, control, and competition. Younger siblings usually imitate older siblings.

6. **What does the research say about the effects of being a firstborn or an only child?**

Firstborn and only children are generally more highly motivated to achieve, more cooperative, more helpful, more adult oriented, and less aggressive. Later-born children tend to be more aggressive, have lower self-esteem, and have greater social skills with peers.

7. **How do peers influence social and emotional development in early childhood?**

Children learn social skills—such as sharing, helping, taking turns, and coping with conflict—from peers. Peers foster development of physical and cognitive skills and provide emotional support. Preschoolers' friendships are characterized by shared activities and feelings of attachment.

8. **What do developmentalists know about child's play?**

Play is meaningful, pleasurable, and internally motivated and develops motor, social, and cognitive skills. It may help children deal with conflict and anxiety. Parten followed the development of six types of play among 2–5-year-olds: unoccupied play, solitary play, onlooker play, parallel play, associative play, and cooperative play.

9. **Are there boys' toys and girls' toys?**

It seems so. Children show preferences for gender-stereotyped toys by 15 to 30 months of age. Boys' toys commonly include transportation toys (cars and trucks) and weapons; girls' toys more often include dolls. Boys in early childhood prefer vigorous outdoor activities and rough-and-tumble play. Girls are more likely to engage in arts and crafts. Preferences for toys may involve the interaction of biological factors and socialization.

10.	**Why do children choose to associate with peers of their own sex?**	Preschool children generally prefer playmates of their own sex partly because of shared interest in activities. Boys' play is more oriented toward dominance, aggression, and rough play.
11.	**How does prosocial behavior develop?**	Prosocial behavior—altruism—begins to develop in the first year, when children begin to share. Development of prosocial behavior is linked to the development of empathy and perspective taking. Girls show more empathy than boys do.
12.	**How does aggression develop?**	The aggression of preschoolers is frequently instrumental or possession oriented. By age 6 or 7, aggression becomes hostile and person oriented. Aggressive behavior appears to be generally stable and predictive of problems in adulthood.
13.	**What causes aggression in children?**	Genetic factors may be involved in aggressive behavior. Genes may be expressed in part through the male sex hormone testosterone. Impulsive and relatively fearless children are more likely to be aggressive. Aggressive boys are more likely than non-aggressive boys to incorrectly assume that other children mean them ill. Social cognitive theory suggests that children become aggressive as a result of frustration, reinforcement, and observational learning. Aggressive children are often rejected by less aggressive peers. Children who are physically punished are more likely to behave aggressively. Observing aggressive behavior teaches aggressive skills, disinhibits the child, and habituates children to violence.
14.	**How does the self develop during early childhood?**	Self-definitions that refer to concrete external traits are called the categorical self. Children as young as 3 years can describe themselves in terms of characteristic behaviors and internal states. Secure attachment and competence contribute to the development of self-esteem.
15.	**What sorts of fears do children have in the early years?**	Preschoolers are most likely to fear animals, imaginary creatures, and the dark; the theme involves threats to personal safety. Girls report more fears than boys do.
16.	**What are stereotypes and gender roles? How do they develop?**	A stereotype is a fixed conventional idea about a group. Females are stereotyped as dependent, gentle, and home oriented. Males are stereotyped as aggressive, self-confident, and independent. Cultural expectations of females and males are called gender roles.
17.	**How different are females and males in terms of cognitive and social and emotional development?**	Males tend to excel in math and spatial-relations skills, whereas girls tend to excel in verbal skills. Stereotypical gender preferences for toys and play activities are in evidence at an early age. Males are more aggressive and more interested in sex than females. The size and origins of all these sex differences is under debate.
18.	**What are the origins of sex differences in behavior?**	Testosterone may specialize the hemispheres of the brain, more so in males than in females, explaining why females excel in verbal skills that require some spatial organization, such as reading. Males might be better at specialized spatial-relations tasks. Male sex hormones are connected with greater maze-learning ability in rats and with aggressiveness. Social cognitive theorists explain the development of gender-typed behavior in terms of observational learning and socialization. According to Kohlberg's

cognitive-developmental theory, gender-typing involves the emergence of three concepts: gender identity, gender stability, and gender constancy. According to gender-schema theory, preschoolers attempt to conform to the cultural gender schema.

19. What is psychological androgyny?

People with both stereotypical feminine and masculine traits are said to be psychologically androgynous. Theorists differ as to whether it is beneficial to promote psychological androgyny.

Key Terms

inductive, 333
authoritative, 334
authoritarian, 335
permissive–indulgent, 335
rejecting–neglecting, 335
individualist, 339
collectivist, 339
regression, 339
sibling rivalry, 339

peers, 341
dramatic play, 344
nonsocial play, 344
social play, 345
prosocial behavior, 347
empathy, 348
disinhibit, 351
self-concept, 355
categorical self, 355

self-esteem, 355
stereotype, 358
gender role, 358
gender identity, 364
gender stability, 364
gender constancy, 364
gender-schema theory, 365
psychological androgyny, 365

Active Learning Resources

Childhood & Adolescence Book Companion Website

http://www.thomsonedu.com/psychology/rathus

Visit your book companion website where you will find more resources to help you study. There you will find interactive versions of your book features, including the Lessons in Observation video, Active Review sections, and the Truth or Fiction feature. In addition, the companion website contains quizzing, flash cards, and a pronunciation glossary.

Thomson NOW! is an easy-to-use online resource that helps you study in less time to get the grade you want—NOW.

http://www.thomsonedu.com/login

Need help studying? This site is your one-stop study shop. Take a Pre-Test and ThomsonNOW will generate a Personalized Study Plan based on your test results. The Study Plan will identify the topics you need to review and direct you to online resources to help you master those topics. You can then take a Post-Test to determine the concepts you have mastered and what you still need to work on.

11 Middle Childhood:
Physical Development

Truth or Fiction?

T F Children outgrow "baby fat." p. 374

T F The typical American child is exposed to about 10,000 food commercials each year. p. 375

T F Most American children are physically fit. p. 380

T F Hyperactivity is caused by chemical food additives. p. 384

T F Stimulants are often used to treat children who are already hyperactive. p. 386

T F Some children who are intelligent and provided with enriched home environments cannot learn how to read or do simple math problems. p. 386

Preview

Growth Patterns
Height and Weight
Nutrition and Growth
Sex Similarities and Differences in
    Physical Growth
Overweight in Children

A Closer Look: Helping Overweight Children
    Manage Their Weight

Motor Development
Gross Motor Skills
Fine Motor Skills
Sex Similarities and Differences in
    Motor Development
Exercise and Fitness

Children with Disabilities
Attention-Deficit/Hyperactivity Disorder
    (ADHD)

Developing in a World of Diversity:
    African American Youth and ADHD

Learning Disabilities
Educating Children with Disabilities

© Lori Adamski-Peek/Jupiterimages

Go to

http://www.thomsonedu.com/psychology/rathus
for an interactive version of this "Truth or Fiction" feature.

t is 6-year old Jessica's first day of school. During recess, she runs to the climbing apparatus in the schoolyard and climbs to the top. As she reaches the top, she announces to the other children, "I'm coming down." She then walks to the parallel bars, goes halfway across, lets go, and tries again.

Steve and Mike are 8-year-olds. They are riding their bikes up and down the street. Steve tries riding with no hands on the handlebars. Mike starts riding fast, standing up on the pedals. Steve shouts, "Boy, you're going to break your neck!" (adapted from Rowen, 1973).

Middle childhood is a time for learning many new motor skills. Success in both gross and fine motor skills reflects children's increasing physical maturity, their opportunities to learn, and personality factors such as their persistence and self-confidence. Competence in motor skills enhances children's self-esteem and their acceptance by their peers.

In this chapter, we examine physical and motor development during middle childhood. We also discuss children with certain disabilities.

Growth Patterns

Question: What patterns of growth occur in middle childhood? Gains in height and weight are fairly steady throughout middle childhood. But notable variations in growth patterns also occur from child to child.

Height and Weight

Following the growth trends begun in early childhood, boys and girls continue to gain a little over 2 inches in height per year during the middle childhood years. This pattern of gradual gains does not vary significantly until children reach the adolescent **growth spurt** (see ● Figure 11.1). The average gain in weight between the ages of 6 and 12 is about 5 to 7 pounds a year. During these years, children continue to become less stocky and more slender (Kuczmarski et al., 2000).

Most deviations from these average height and weight figures are quite normal. Individual differences are more marked in middle childhood than they were earlier. For example, most 3-year-olds are within 8 to 10 pounds and 4 inches of one another. But by the age of 10, children's weights may vary by as much as 30 to 35 pounds, and their heights may vary by as much as 6 inches.

Nutrition and Growth

In middle childhood, average body weight doubles. Children also expend a good deal of energy as they engage in physical activity and play. To fuel this growth and activity, children need to eat more than they did in the preschool years. The average 4- to 6-year-old needs 1,400 to 1,800 calories per day. But the average 7- to 10-year-old requires 2,000 calories a day (Ekvall, 1993a).

Nutrition involves much more than calories, as we will see in the section on childhood obesity. The U.S. government has a food pyramid that suggests that it is healthful to eat fruits and vegetables, fish, poultry (without skin), and whole grains and to limit intake of fats, sugar, and starches. However, the food offered to children in school and elsewhere tends to be heavy on sugar, animal fats, and salt (Bauer et al., 2004). In addition, food portions have grown over the past couple of decades, particularly for salty snacks, desserts, soft drinks, fruit drinks, french fries, hamburgers, cheeseburgers, and Mexican food (Nielsen & Popkin, 2003). The largest portions are eaten at fast-food restaurants.

growth spurt A period during which growth advances at a dramatically rapid rate compared with other periods.

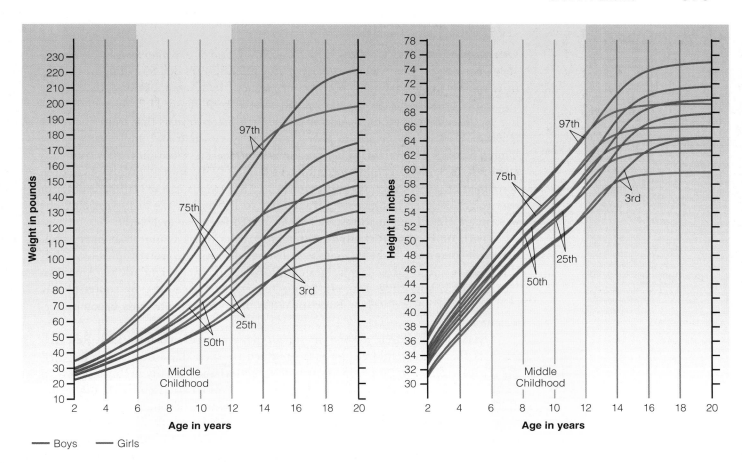

— Boys — Girls

● **Figure 11.1**   Growth Curves for Height and Weight

Gains in height and weight are fairly steady during middle childhood. Boys continue to be slightly heavier and taller than girls through 9 or 10 years of age. Girls then begin their adolescent growth spurt and surpass boys in height and weight until about age 13 or 14.

Source: Kuczmarski et al. (2000, Figures 9–12).

Nutrition and social class are also connected. Consider two studies with African American mothers and daughters. Daughters living at the poverty line were likely to be fed diets high in fats and fast foods (Miklos et al., 2004). Middle-class mothers, however, were concerned about the weight of their daughters and encouraged physical activity as a means of weight control. The mothers also tended to limit consumption of snack foods and sugar-laden carbonated beverages. Instead, they encouraged their daughters to drink water (V. J. Thompson et al., 2003).

Sex Similarities and Differences in Physical Growth

Figure 11.1 also reveals that boys continue to be slightly heavier and taller than girls through the age of 9 or 10. Girls then begin their adolescent growth spurt and surpass boys in height and weight until about age 13 or 14. At that time, boys are approaching the peak of their adolescent growth spurt, and they become taller and heavier than girls (Malina & Bouchard, 1991).

The steady gain in height and weight during middle childhood is paralleled by an increase in muscular strength for both girls and boys (Malina & Bouchard, 1991). The relative proportion of muscle and fatty tissue is about the same for boys and girls in early middle childhood. But this begins to change at about age 11, as males develop relatively more muscle tissue and females develop more fatty tissue (Michael, 1990).

Overweight in Children

Questions: How many children in the United States are overweight? Why are they overweight? The American Heart Association (2007) defines being overweight in terms not only of weight, but also in terms of body composition—that is, the amount of muscle and fatty tissue. As you can see in ● Figure 11.2, research including the three largest ethnic groups in the United States reveals that from one in six (16% to 17%) to about one in four (about 25%) children and adolescents in the United States is overweight. When the American Heart Association (2007) compares all groups of American children combined from the 1970s with all groups of children combined of the 2000s, it finds that for 6- to 11-year-olds, the overall percentage of overweight children has increased from 4.0% to 17.5%. For 12- to 19-year-olds, the percentage of overweight adolescents has increased from 6% to 17%.

Truth or Fiction Revisited: Although parents often assume that heavy children will "outgrow" "baby fat"—especially once they hit the growth spurt of adolescence—it is not so. Most overweight children become overweight adults (American Heart Association, 2007; Daniels, 2006; Tercyak & Tyc, 2006). By contrast, only about 40% of normal-weight boys and 20% of normal-weight girls become overweight adults.

Overweight children, despite the stereotype, are usually far from jolly. Research suggests that heavy children are often rejected by their peers or a source of derision (Latner & Schwartz, 2005; Storch et al., 2007). They usually perform poorly in sports, which can provide a source of prestige for slimmer children (Kirkcaldy et al., 2002). As overweight children approach adolescence, they become even less popular, because they are less likely to be found sexually attractive. It is no surprise, then, that overweight children have poorer body images than children of normal weight (Storch et al., 2007). Moreover, overweight adolescents are more likely to be depressed and anxious than peers who are normal in weight (Kirkcaldy et al., 2002).

Children who are overweight are also at greater risk of encountering a number of physical health problems, in childhood and later in life (American Heart Association, 2007; Daniels, 2006). Among these are high blood pressure, hardening of the arteries (atherosclerosis), type 2 diabetes, fatty liver disease, ovary disorders, and abnormal breathing patterns during sleep. Being overweight in childhood can accelerate the development of heart disease, which can lead to heart attacks or stroke in adulthood. The dramatically increased prevalence of overweight in childhood might even reverse the contemporary increase in life expectancy, such that overweight youth lead less

● **Figure 11.2**

Percent of Children (Ages 6–11) and Adolescents (Ages 12–19) Who Are Overweight, According to the American Heart Association (AHA)

In arriving at these figures, the AHA considered both body weight and body composition (amount of muscle and fat tissue).

Source: American Heart Association (2007).

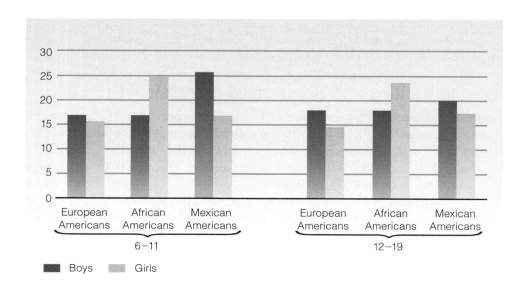

healthy and shorter lives than their parents, which as Daniels (2006) notes, would be the first reversal in lifespan in modern life.

Causes of Overweight

Why are so many children overweight? Is it simply a matter of eating too much? We will see that what might seem simple is actually quite complex.

Being overweight runs in families (Baker et al., 2000; Treuth et al., 2004). Research provides convincing evidence that heredity plays a role. Some people, for example, apparently inherit a tendency to burn up extra calories, whereas others inherit a tendency to turn their extra calories into fat (Kolata, 2007). A classic study showed that identical twins have a similar body weight in adulthood whether they had been reared together or apart (Stunkard et al., 1990). Childhood experiences appeared to have little effect on adult weight.

Weight has also been related to the amount of fat cells, or **adipose tissue,** that we have, and we may have some tendency to inherit different numbers of fat cells. The hunger drive is connected with the quantity of fat accumulated in these cells. The blood-sugar level is relatively high after one has eaten; then it drops as time elapses. As the blood-sugar level declines, the well of fat in fat cells is tapped to nourish the person, and the cells shrivel up. Eventually—and in some cases, "eventually" happens sooner than we might like!—the hypothalamus learns of the deficit and stirs the hunger drive (Woods & Seeley, 2002).

Children who have more fat cells than other children feel hungry sooner, even if they are the same is weight. Perhaps the possession of more fat cells means that more signals are being transmitted to the hypothalamus in the brain. Children (and adults) who are overweight and those who were once overweight usually have more fat cells than individuals who have weighed less. This abundance is no blessing. Overweight in childhood may cause adolescents or adult dieters to feel persistent hunger, even after they have leveled off at a weight they prefer (Guerdjikova et al., 2007).

The environment also influences weight. Family, peers, and other environmental factors play roles in children's eating habits (Bauer et al., 2004; Moens et al., 2007). Overweight parents, for example, may serve as examples of poor exercise habits, encourage overeating, and keep unhealthful foods in the home.

Watching television also affects children's weight (Schumacher & Queen, 2007). Children who watch television extensively during the middle childhood years are more likely to become overweight as adolescents than children who do not watch as extensively (Schumacher & Queen, 2007). The influence of TV watching is at least threefold (Stephenson & Banet-Weiser, 2007). First, children tend to consume snacks while watching. Second, television bombards children with commercials for fattening foods, such as candy and potato chips. Third, watching television is a sedentary activity. We burn fewer calories sitting than engaging in physical activity. **Truth or Fiction Revisited:** It is true that American children are exposed to about 10,000 food commercials per year. The bulk of them are for fast foods such as Burger King and Pizza Hut, highly sweetened cereals, soft drinks, and candy bars (Goossens et al., 2007; Theim et al., 2007).

Stressors and emotional reactions can also promp children to eat (Schumacher & Queen, 2007). Children may eat in response to bickering in the home, parental divorce, or the birth of a sibling. Family celebrations and arguments are quite different, but both can lead to overeating or breaking a diet. Efforts to control eating may also be hampered by anxiety or depression (Goossens et al., 2007; Guerdjikova et al., 2007). The rule of thumb seems to be this: If life is awful, try chocolate (or french fries, or pizza, or whatever).

For some suggestions on how parents can help their children (and themselves) lose weight, see the nearby "A Closer Look" feature "Helping Overweight Children Manage Their Weight."

Overweight in Childhood
Like mother, like daughter? Weight problems run in families, but environmental as well as genetic factors appear to be involved.

adipose tissue Fat.

A CLOSER LOOK

Helping Overweight Children Manage Their Weight

Health-conscious parents not only want to be slimmer themselves but are also more aware of the health benefits their children gain by avoiding being overweight. However, losing weight is a difficult problem in self-control for children and adults alike. Nevertheless, childhood is the optimal time to prevent or reverse obesity because it is easiest to promote a lifetime pattern of healthful behaviors during childhood (Blom-Hoffman et al., 2006; Schumacher & Queen, 2007).

Cognitive behavioral methods show promise in helping children lose weight (American Heart Association, 2007; Johnston & Steele, 2007; Wadden & Stunkard, 2002) by (1) improving nutritional knowledge, (2) reducing calories, (3) introducing exercise, and (4) modifying behavior. Behavioral methods involve tracking the child's calorie intake and weight, keeping the child away from temptations, setting a good example, and systematically using praise and other rewards. The most successful weight-loss programs for children combine exercise, decreased caloric intake, behavior modification, and emotional support from parents. Here are some suggestions from the literature:

- Teach children about nutrition: calories, protein, vitamins, minerals, fiber, food groups, and so on. Indicate which foods may be eaten in nearly unlimited quantities (e.g., green vegetables) and which foods should be eaten only sparingly (cakes, cookies, soft drinks sweetened with sugar, and so on). Check out the "Traffic Light Diet" (● Figure 11.3).

Physical Activity, Weight, and Fitness
Get kids away from those TV sets! One way parents can motivate their children to engage in regular physical activity is to find time for family outdoor activities that promote weight control and fitness.

- Do not insist that the entire family sit down at the same time for a large meal. Allow your child to eat only when hungry. This practice will break the tyranny of the clock, the expectation that he or she must be hungry because it is noon or 6 p.m.
- Substitute low-calorie foods for high-calorie foods. Calories translate into pounds.
- Do not push your child to "finish the plate." Allow children to stop eating when they feel full.
- Prepare low-calorie snacks for your child to eat throughout the day. Children who feel deprived and desperate for food may go on a binge.
- Do not cook, eat, or display fattening foods when the child is at home. The sight and aroma of such foods can be tantalizing.
- Involve the child in more activities. When children are busy, they are less likely to think about food. (And physical activity burns calories.)
- Do not take your child food shopping, or, if you do, try to avoid the market aisles with ice cream, cake, and candy.
- Ask relatives and friends not to offer fattening treats when you visit.
- Do not allow snacking in front of the TV set or while playing, reading, or engaging in any other activity. Allowing children to snack while watching TV makes eating a mindless habit.
- Involve the child in calorie-burning exercise, such as swimming or prolonged bicycle riding. Exercise will burn calories, increase the child's feelings of competence and self-esteem, improve cardiovascular condition, and, possibly, promote lifetime exercise habits.
- Reward the child for steps in the right direction, such as eating less or exercising more. Praise is a powerful reward, but children also respond to tangible rewards such as a new toy.
- Do not assume that it is a catastrophe if the child slips and goes on a binge. Talk over what triggered the binge with the child to avert similar problems in the future. Remind the child that tomorrow is a new day and a new start.
- If you and your children are overweight, consider losing weight together. It is more effective for overweight children and their parents to diet and exercise together than for children to go it alone.

Reflect:

- You believe that a friend's or relative's child is dangerously obese, but the parent thinks it's normal or just "baby fat." What do you do?
- Imagine yourself about to visit a relative or friend whose self-esteem is wrapped up in spreading appealing but fattening food around during visits. How can you prevent your children from overeating? Must you stay home or go somewhere else?
- You are concerned about your child's weight and learn that he or she has been sneaking "forbidden" foods. What do you do?

● **Figure 11.3**   The Traffic Light Diet

Johnston and Steele (2007) have shown that the Traffic Light Diet can help children manage their weight. Children (or adults using the diet) may eat unlimited quantities of green foods, which consist mainly of vegetables (without butter or salad dressing) and fruit. They may use reasonable amounts of low-fat (preferably nonfat) milk, roasted or baked poultry (but not the skin), fish, pasta, whole-grain cereals and baked goods (without the butter or margarine), beans, nuts, and small quantities of relatively low-fat cuts of meat (pork is lower in fat than beef). Vegetable oils (such as olive oil) are amber foods whose fat content is high in calories but not otherwise harmful to the cardiovascular system. Red foods are to be eaten in relatively small quantities by children, and among adolescents and adults who are trying to lose weight, they should be eaten rarely or in *very* small amounts; they consist of animal fats, cream, full-fat cheeses, butter, margarine, mayonnaise, and the like.

Active Review

1. Gains in height and weight are generally (Abrupt or Steady?) throughout middle childhood.
2. Children gain a little over _____ inches in height per year during middle childhood.
3. They gain about _____ pounds a year.
4. (Boys or Girls?) are slightly heavier and taller through the age of 9 or 10.
5. Boys begin to become more muscular than girls at about the age of _____ .
6. About _____% of American children are overweight.
7. Children (Do or Do not?) tend to outgrow "baby fat."

8. Being overweight (Does or Does not?) run in families.

Reflect & Relate: How were overweight children treated by their peers in your elementary school? Were you sensitive to these children's feelings, or were you part of the problem?

Go to

http://www.thomsonedu.com/psychology/rathus

for an interactive version of this review.

Motor Development

Question: What changes in motor development occur in middle childhood? The school years are marked by increases in the child's speed, strength, agility, and balance (Abdelaziz et al., 2001; Loovis & Butterfield, 2000). These developments, in turn, lead to more skillful performance of motor activities, such as skipping.

Gross Motor Skills

Throughout middle childhood, children show steady improvement in their ability to perform various gross motor skills (Abdelaziz et al., 2001). School-age children are usually eager to participate in group games and athletic activities that require the movement of large muscles, such as catching and throwing balls. As seen in Concept Review 11.1, children are hopping, jumping, and climbing by age 6 or so; by age 6 or 7, they are usually capable of pedaling and balancing on a bicycle. By the ages of 8 to 10, children are showing the balance, coordination, and strength that allow them to engage in gymnastics and team sports.

During these years, the muscles are growing stronger, and the pathways that connect the cerebellum to the cortex are becoming increasingly myelinated. Experience also plays an indispensable role in refining many sensorimotor abilities, especially at championship levels, but individual differences that seem inborn are also present. Some people, for example, have better visual acuity or better depth perception than others. For such reasons, they will have an edge in playing the outfield or hitting a golf ball.

reaction time The amount of time required to respond to a stimulus.

One of the most important factors in athletic performance is **reaction time,** or the amount of time required to respond to a stimulus. Reaction time is basic to the child's timing of a swing of the bat to meet the ball. Reaction time is also basic to adjusting to a fly ball or hitting a tennis ball. It is also involved in children's responses to cars and other (sometimes deadly) obstacles when they are riding their bicycles or running down the street.

Reaction time gradually improves (i.e., decreases) from early childhood to about age 18 (Abdelaziz et al., 2001; Karatekin et al., 2007). However, individual differences can be large (Largo et al., 2001). Reaction time begins to increase again in the adult years. Even so, 75-year-olds still outperform children. Baseball and volleyball may be "child's play," but, everything else being equal, adults will respond to the ball more quickly.

Fine Motor Skills

By the age of 6 to 7 years, children can usually tie their shoelaces and hold their pencils as adults do (see Concept Review 11.1). Their abilities to fasten buttons, zip zippers, brush teeth, wash themselves, coordinate a knife and fork, and use chopsticks all develop during the early school years and improve during childhood (Abdelaziz et al., 2001; Beilei et al., 2002).

Concept Review 11.1   Development of Motor Skills during Middle Childhood

Age	Skills
Gross Motor Skills	
6 years	• Hops, jumps, climbs
7 years	• Balances on and pedals a bicycle
8 years	• Has good body balance
9 years	• Engages in vigorous bodily activities, especially team sports such as baseball, football, volleyball, and basketball
10 years	• Balances on one foot for 15 seconds; catches a fly ball
12 years	• Displays some awkwardness as a result of asynchronous bone and muscle development

© David Fischer/Getty Images

Fine Motor Skills	
6–7 years	• Ties shoelaces • Throws ball by using wrist and finger release • Holds pencil with fingertips • Follows simple mazes • May be able to hit a ball with a bat
8–9 years	• Spaces words when writing • Writes and prints accurately and neatly • Copies a diamond shape correctly • Swings a hammer well • Sews and knits • Shows good hand–eye coordination

© Monika Graff/The Image Works

Sex Similarities and Differences in Motor Development

Question: Are there sex differences in motor skills? Throughout the middle years, boys and girls perform similarly in most motor activities. Boys show slightly greater overall strength and, in particular, more forearm strength, which aids them in swinging a bat or throwing a ball (Butterfield & Loovis, 1993).

Girls, on the other hand, show somewhat greater limb coordination and overall flexibility, which is valuable in dancing, balancing, and gymnastics (Abdelaziz et al., 2001; Cratty, 1986). Girls with a certain type of physique seem particularly well suited to gymnastics. Those who are short, lean, and small boned make the best gymnasts, according to Olympic coaches, because they displace gravity most effectively, which may explain why female gymnasts are considered old for the sport by the time they reach their late teens. By then, they have often grown taller and their body contours have filled out (Cumming et al., 2005; Scanlan et al., 2005).

At puberty, sex differences in motor performance favoring boys become progressively greater (Smoll & Schultz, 1990). What factors might account for the development of sex differences in physical performance? The slight sex differences in motor performance before puberty apparently cannot be attributed to biological factors (Thomas & French, 1985). (The one exception may be throwing, a skill in which boys excel from an early age.) Boys are more likely than girls to receive encouragement, support, and opportunities for participation in sports (Geary, 1998). Even during the preschool years, parents emphasize physical activity in boys more than in girls. By middle childhood, boys are involved in competitive games and in games of longer duration more so than girls. They also engage in more vigorous activity on average than girls (A. M. Thompson et al., 2003).

At puberty, when boys begin to excel in such areas as running, the long jump, sit-ups, and grip strength, boys' greater size and strength confer a biological advantage. But some environmental factors that operated in middle childhood may exert even greater importance in puberty. "Tomboy" behavior in girls is less socially accepted in adolescence than it was in middle childhood. Therefore, girls may become less interested in participating in athletic activities and may be less motivated to do well in the ones in which they do engage (Geary, 1998; Vu et al., 2006). By the ages of 12 and 13, girls are less likely than boys to perceive themselves as competent (Whitehead & Corbin, 1991), and self-perception of competence predicts participation in sports (Papaioannou et al., 2006).

In any event, physical activity decreases with age between middle childhood and adolescence in both sexes (R. A. Thompson et al., 2003). Physical activities become increasingly stereotyped by children as being masculine (e.g., football) or feminine (e.g., dance) (Meaney et al., 2002).

Exercise and Fitness

The health benefits of exercise for both adults and children are well known. Exercise reduces the risk of heart disease, stroke, diabetes, and certain forms of cancer (Atkinson & Davenne, 2007; Daubenmier et al., 2007). Exercise confers psychological benefits as well. Physically active adolescents have a better self-image and better coping skills than those who are inactive (Kirkcaldy et al., 2002).

Questions: Are children in the United States physically fit? If not, why not? American adults are becoming more conscientious about exercising and staying fit. **Truth or Fiction Revisited:** However, most children in the United States are not physically fit. A majority of American children do not meet the standards set by the President's Council on Physical Fitness (Schumacher & Queen, 2007).

What are some possible reasons for this decline in fitness? Again, one obvious culprit is watching television. Students who watch relatively little television have less body fat and are more physically fit than those who watch for several hours per day (Schumacher & Queen, 2007).

Cardiac and muscular fitness, both in childhood and adulthood, is developed by participation in continuous exercise such as running, walking quickly, swimming laps, bicycling, or jumping rope for intervals of several minutes at a time. However, schools and parents tend to focus on sports such as baseball and football, which are less apt to promote fitness (Schumacher & Queen, 2007).

Children with high levels of physical activity are more likely to have school officials and parents who encourage their children to exercise and who actively exercise themselves (Schumacher & Queen, 2007). How, then, can more children be motivated to engage in regular physical activity? Here are some ideas for parents:

- Engage in family outdoor activities that promote fitness: walking, swimming, bicycling, skating.
- Reduce the amount of time spent watching television.
- Encourage outdoor play during daylight hours after school.
- Do not assume that your child gets sufficient exercise by participating in a team sport. Many team sports involve long periods of inactivity.

Organized sports for children are enormously popular, but many children lose their enthusiasm and drop out. Participation in sports declines as middle childhood progresses (Schumacher & Queen, 2007). Why? Sometimes children are pushed too hard, too early, or too quickly by parents or coaches. If competition is stressed, children may feel frustrated or inferior; they are sometimes injured. Hence, parents are advised not to place excessive demands for performance on their children. Let them progress at their own pace. Encourage them to focus on the fun and health benefits of physical activity and sports, not on winning.

Active Review

9. During middle childhood, children show (Abrupt or Steady?) improvement in gross motor skills.
10. By the age of about _____, children show the balance, coordination, and strength that allow them to engage in gymnastics and team sports.
11. Reaction time gradually (Increases or Decreases?) from early childhood to about age 18.
12. (Boys or Girls?) tend to show greater overall strength.
13. (Boys or Girls?) show somewhat greater coordination and flexibility.
14. Most children in the United States tend to be physically (Fit or Unfit?).

Reflect & Relate: When did you become "good at" things such as riding a bicycle, skating, or team sports? Did these activities provide an opportunity for fulfillment and social approval for you, or were they a source of anxiety? Did you approach these activities with pleasure, or did you shy away from them? Explain.

Go to

http://www.thomsonedu.com/psychology/rathus

for an interactive version of this review.

Children with Disabilities

Certain disabilities of childhood are most apt to be noticed in the middle childhood years, when the child enters school. The school setting requires that a child sit still, pay attention, and master a number of academic skills. But some children have difficulty with one or more of these demands. In this section, we focus on children with various disabilities. ■ Table 11.1 highlights the types of disabilities that can affect a child's functioning, especially in school. Let us consider attention-deficit/hyperactivity disorder and learning disabilities in greater depth.

Attention-Deficit/Hyperactivity Disorder (ADHD)

Nine-year-old Eddie is a problem in class. His teacher complains that he is so restless and fidgety that the rest of the class cannot concentrate on their work. He hardly ever sits still. He is in constant motion, roaming the classroom, talking to other children while they are working. He has been suspended repeatedly for outrageous behavior, most recently swinging from a fluorescent light fixture and unable to get himself down. His mother reports that Eddie has been a problem since he was a toddler. By the age of 3, he had become unbearably restless and demanding. He has never needed much sleep and always awakened before anyone else in the family, making his way downstairs and wrecking things in the living room and kitchen. Once, at the age of 4, he unlocked the front door and wandered into traffic, but was rescued by a passerby.

Psychological testing shows Eddie to be average in academic ability but to have a "virtually nonexistent" attention span. He shows no interest in television or in games or toys that require some concentration. He is unpopular

■ **Table 11.1** Types of Disabilities

Overall intellectual functioning	• Mental retardation (Chapter 12)
Learning disabilities*	• Reading disability (dyslexia) (this chapter)
	• Mathematics disability (dyscalculia) (this chapter)
	• Disorder of written expression
Speech disorders	• Articulation disorder
	• Voice disorders
	• Fluency disorders
Physical disabilities	• Visual impairment
	• Hearing impairment
	• Paralysis
Social and emotional disorders	• Attention-deficit/hyperactivity disorder (this chapter)
	• Autism spectrum disorders (Chapter 7)
	• Conduct disorders (Chapter 13)
	• Childhood depression (Chapter 13)
	• Childhood anxiety (Chapter 13)

* The American Psychiatric Association (2000) uses the term *learning disorder* rather than *learning disability*. Most educators appear to prefer the term *learning disability*.

with peers and prefers to ride his bike alone or to play with his dog. He has become disobedient at home and at school and has stolen small amounts of money from his parents and classmates.

Eddie has been treated with methylphenidate (Ritalin), but it was discontinued because it had no effect on his disobedience and stealing. However, it did seem to reduce his restlessness and increase his attention span at school.

—Adapted from Spitzer et al., 2002

Many parents think that their children do not pay enough attention to them, that they tend to run around as the whim strikes and to do things in their own way. Some inattention, especially at early ages, is to be expected. *Question: How does run-of-the-mill failure to "listen" to adults differ from attention-deficit/hyperactivity disorder?* In **attention-deficit/hyperactivity disorder (ADHD),** the child shows developmentally inappropriate or excessive inattention, impulsivity, and **hyperactivity** (Nigg et al., 2006; Weisler & Sussman, 2007). A more complete list of problems is shown in ■ Table 11.2. The degree of hyperactive behavior is crucial, because many normal children are labeled overactive and fidgety from time to time. In fact,

attention-deficit/hyperactivity disorder (ADHD) A behavior disorder characterized by excessive inattention, impulsiveness, and hyperactivity.

hyperactivity Excessive restlessness and overactivity; one of the primary characteristics of attention-deficit/hyperactivity disorder (ADHD). Not to be confused with misbehavior or with normal high-activity levels that occur during childhood.

■ Table 11.2 Symptoms of Attention-Deficit/Hyperactivity Disorder (ADHD)

Kind of Problem	Specific Patterns of Behavior
Lack of attention	• Fails to attend to details or makes careless errors in schoolwork, and so on • Has difficulty sustaining attention in schoolwork or play activities • Does not appear to pay attention to what is being said • Fails to follow through on instructions or to finish work • Has trouble organizing work and other activities • Avoids work or activities that require sustained attention • Loses work tools (e.g., pencils, books, assignments, toys) • Becomes readily distracted • Is forgetful in daily activities
Hyperactivity	• Fidgets with hands or feet or squirms in his or her seat • Leaves seat in situations such as the classroom in which remaining seated is required • Constantly runs around or climbs on things; "running like a motor" • Has difficulty playing quietly • Shows excessive motor activity when asleep • Talks excessively
Impulsivity	• Often acts without thinking • Shifts from activity to activity • Cannot organize tasks or work • Requires constant supervision • Often "calls out" in class • Does not wait his or her turn in line, games, and so on

Source: Adapted from American Psychiatric Association (2000).

A Boy with Attention-Deficit/ Hyperactivity Disorder
Hyperactive children are continually on the go, as if their "motors" are constantly running. The psychological disorder we refer to as hyperactivity is not to be confused with the normal high energy levels of children. However, it is sometimes—*sometimes*—difficult to tell where one ends and the other begins.

if talking too much were the sole criterion for ADHD, the label would have applied to many of us.

The onset of ADHD occurs by age 7. According to the American Psychiatric Association (2000), the behavior pattern must have persisted for at least 6 months for the diagnosis to be made. The hyperactivity and restlessness of children with ADHD impair their ability to function in school. They simply cannot sit still. They also have difficulty getting along with others. Their disruptive and noncompliant behavior often elicits punishment from parents. ADHD is quite common. It is diagnosed in about 1% to 5% of school-age children and is one of the most common causes of childhood referrals to mental health clinics. ADHD is many times more common in boys than in girls.

Some psychologists and educators argue that ADHD is often "overdiagnosed" (Weisler & Sussman, 2007). That is, many children who do not toe the line in school tend to be diagnosed with ADHD and are medicated to encourage more acceptable behavior. Research also suggests that professionals who diagnose children with ADHD tend to be "suggestible." That is, they are more likely to diagnose children with the disorder when other sources of information—for example, from teachers and parents—say the children do not adequately control their behavior (Reddy & De Thomas, 2007; Wiesler & Sussman, 2007).

Causes of ADHD

Question: What are the causes of ADHD? Because ADHD is in part characterized by excessive motor activity, many theorists focus on possible physical causes. For one thing, ADHD tends to run in families, for both girls and boys (Faraone et al., 2000). Therefore, some researchers suggest there may be a genetic component to the disorder (Thapar et al., 2007; Walitza et al., 2006). If so, that genetic component might involve the brain messenger dopamine (Mazei-Robison et al., 2005; Walitza et al., 2006). Brain-imaging studies support the probability that many genes are involved and that they affect the brain's use of dopamine (Walitza et al., 2006).

ADHD is also found to coexist with other psychological disorders and problems, ranging from oppositional defiant disorder and anxiety disorders to mood disorders and even tics (Biederman et al., 2007; Hasler et al., 2007). Studies in brain imaging have found differences in the brain chemistry of children with ADHD and ADHD plus other disorders such as serious mood disorders, leading to the prospect that different causes and treatments will be discovered for various groups of children with ADHD.

In the 1970s, it was widely believed—because of anecdotal evidence presented by Benjamin Feingold—that artificial food colorings and (benzoate) food preservatives were largely responsible for hyperactivity. Feingold then introduced what became dubbed the "Feingold diet," which removed such chemicals from foods and, according to Feingold and a few researchers, reduced hyperactivity in children who used the diet. **Truth or Fiction Revisited:** However, over the years, studies in the use of the Feingold diet have yielded conflicting results, and researchers now generally agree that food coloring and preservatives have not been shown to cause the ADHD epidemic (Cruz & Bahna, 2006; Eigenmann & Haenggeli, 2004).

Joel T. Nigg (2001; Nigg et al., 2006) notes that children with ADHD do not *inhibit,* or control, impulses that most children can control. But Nigg argues that "inhibition" is defined differently by different theorists. Nigg (2001, Nigg et al., 2006) distinguishes between inhibition that is under the executive control of the brain—a sort of cognitive–neurological inhibition—and inhibition that is normally motivated by emotions such as anxiety and fear (e.g., anxiety about disappointing a teacher or fear of earning poor grades). Nigg argues that ADHD is unlikely to reflect failure to respond to feelings of anxiety or fear. He believes that the disorder is more

Developing in a World of Diversity

African American Youth and ADHD

The diagnosis and treatment of attention-deficit/hyperactivity disorder (ADHD) have come under scrutiny in the media and in medical circles, but as is often the case with medical concerns that become public issues, the focus has been almost exclusively on European American middle-class children (Hervey-Jumper et al., 2006).

African American children also suffer from ADHD, but cultural issues make diagnosis and treatment of the disorder challenging in these children, according to psychiatrist Gail Mattox (American Psychiatric Association, 2001). Although African American children respond to treatment as well as European American children do (Hervey-Jumper et al., 2006), European American children displaying comparable symptoms receive medications for ADHD at twice the rate of African American children.

Speaking at the 30th anniversary conference of the Black Psychia-

trists of America, Mattox emphasized that a lack of "culturally competent providers" is one obstacle preventing African American children from getting optimal care for ADHD. Another challenge is poverty. Moreover, a substantial number are in the juvenile justice or child welfare systems, where the personnel change often and "inadequate medical care and diagnoses" are a fact of life.

Clinicians assessing or treating these youngsters must be aware of cultural considerations if their services are to be effective. For one thing, teachers are more likely to diagnose African American children as hyperactive than European American children when the children display essentially the same behavior (Epstein et al., 2005). For another, African American parents may be less informed about ADHD than their European American counterparts and are more likely to attribute ADHD symptoms to other causes such as sugar intake. In addition, school officials are more likely to as-

sign African American children to special-education classes than they are European American children, and class placement is "the only educational resource used" to address many African American children's ADHD (Bailey & Owens, 2005). But proper treatment might allow them to remain in their regular classes. Special-education placements often go unchallenged by African American parents because they may be less aware of their rights regarding school decisions and because they face limited access to other potentially useful services in their communities.

■ Table 11.3 reveals the results of a Harris Poll on barriers that prevent African American, European American, and Latino and Latina American children from getting treatment for ADHD.

Reflect: *Check out Table 11.3. How would you say the three groups are alike in the barriers they perceive? How do they seem to differ?*

■ **Table 11.3** Barriers That Prevent Parents from Obtaining Treatment for ADHD for Their Children

Barrier	Latino and Latina Americans (%)	African Americans (%)	European Americans (%)
Concern that the child will be "labeled"	51	57	52
Lack of information about ADHD	57	58	51
Concern that treatment will be based on the child's racial or ethnic background	19	36	13
Language barriers between parent or child and health care professional	32	28	23
Cost of treatment	53	52	47

Source: Adapted from Taylor & Leitman (2003).

likely due to a lack of executive control of the brain but admits that the precise nature of this control—its exact neurological aspects—remains poorly understood.

Treatment and Outcome

Truth or Fiction Revisited: Stimulants such as Ritalin are often used to treat hyperactive children. In fact, they are the most widespread treatment for ADHD. *Question: Why are children with ADHD treated with stimulants?* It may seem ironic that stimulants are used with children who are already overly active. The rationale is that the activity of the hyperactive child stems from inability of the cerebral cortex to inhibit more primitive areas of the brain (Hazell, 2007; Reiff & Mansoor, 2007).

The stimulants that are used block the "reuptake"—that is, the reabsorption—of two brain chemicals: dopamine and noradrenaline. Keeping more of these brain chemicals active stimulates the cerebral cortex. Because the cerebral cortex contains the "executive center" of the brain—the part of the brain that makes decisions and plans—the chemicals also have the effect of helping the cerebral cortex control more primitive areas of the brain. It is of interest that another stimulant, caffeine, the stimulant found in coffee, tea, colas, and chocolate (yes, chocolate), also helps children control hyperactivity (Leon, 2000; Rezvani & Levin, 2001).

Stimulants help children with ADHD increase their attention span, improve their cognitive and academic performance, and reduce their disruptive, annoying, and aggressive behavior (Posey et al., 2007). But the use of stimulants is controversial. Some critics argue that stimulants suppress gains in height and weight, do not contribute to academic gains, and lose effectiveness over time. Another concern is that stimulants are overused or misused in an attempt to control normal high-activity levels of children—especially boys in middle childhood—at home or in the classroom. Supporters of stimulant treatment argue that many ADHD children are helped by medication. They counter that the suppression of growth appears to be related to the dosage of the drug and that low doses seem to be about as effective as large doses (Evans et al., 2001).

Cognitive behavioral therapy (CBT) also shows some promise in treating children with ADHD. CBT attempts to increase the child's self-control and problem-solving abilities through modeling, role playing, and self-instruction. A Spanish study taught many children with ADHD to "stop and think" before giving in to angry impulses and behaving aggressively (Miranda & Presentacion, 2000). However, the Multimodal Treatment Study sponsored by the National Institute of Mental Health found that stimulant medication was more effective than cognitive behavioral therapy (Greene & Ablon, 2001; Whalen, 2001). Stephen Hinshaw (2006) argues that CBT for children should use clear rewards and punishments, and they should involve parents and teachers. James Waxmonsky (2005) suggests that children may fare better with medication, whereas adolescents and adults with ADHD may profit more from CBT.

Many but not all children "outgrow" ADHD. Longitudinal studies have found that at least two-thirds of children with ADHD continue to have problems in attention, conduct, hyperactivity, or learning in adolescence and adulthood (Barkley, 2004; Nigg et al., 2004).

Learning Disabilities

Nelson Rockefeller served as vice president of the United States under Gerald Ford. He was intelligent and well educated. Yet despite the best of tutors, he could never master reading. Rockefeller suffered from **dyslexia. Truth or Fiction Revisited:** It is true that some children who are intelligent and who are provided with enriched home environments cannot learn how to read or do simple math problems. Many such children have learning disabilities.

stimulants Drugs that increase the activity of the nervous system.

dyslexia A reading disorder characterized by problems such as letter reversals, mirror reading, slow reading, and reduced comprehension (from the Greek roots *dys,* meaning "bad," and *lexikon,* meaning "of words").

Question: What are learning disabilities? Dyslexia is one type of **learning disability.** The term *learning disabilities* refers to a group of disorders characterized by inadequate development of specific academic, language, and speech skills (see Concept Review 11.2). Learning-disabled children may show problems in math, writing, or reading. Some have difficulties in articulating sounds of speech or in understanding spoken language. Others have problems in motor coordination. Children are usually considered to have a learning disability when they are performing below the level expected for their age and level of intelligence and when there is no evidence of other handicaps such as vision or hearing problems, mental retardation, or socioeconomic disadvantage (Joshi, 2003; Lyon et al., 2003). However, some psychologists and educators argue that too much emphasis is placed on the discrepancy between intelligence and reading achievement (Fiorello et al., 2007; Vellutino et al., 2004).

Children with learning disabilities frequently have other problems as well. They are more likely than other children to have ADHD (Schulte-Körne et al., 2006), and, as they mature, they are more likely than other adolescents or adults to develop schizophrenia (Maneschi et al., 2006). They do not communicate as well with their

learning disabilities A group of disorders characterized by inadequate development of specific academic, language, and speech skills.

Concept Review 11.2   Types of Learning Disabilities

Reading Disability (Dyslexia)

- As measured by a standardized test that is given individually, the child's ability to read (accuracy or comprehension) is substantially less than what one would expect considering his or her age, level of intelligence, and educational experiences.
- The reading disorder materially interferes with the child's academic achievement or daily living.
- If there is also a sensory or perceptual defect, the reading problems are worse than one would expect with it.

Mathematics Disability (Dyscalculia)

- As measured by a standardized test that is given individually, the child's mathematical ability is substantially less than what one would expect considering his or her age, level of intelligence, and educational experiences.
- The mathematics disorder materially interferes with the child's academic achievement or daily living.
- If there is also a sensory or perceptual defect, the problems in mathematics are worse than one would expect with it.

Disorder of Written Expression

- As measured by assessment of functioning or by a standardized test that is given individually, the child's writing ability is substantially less than what one would expect considering his or her age, level of intelligence, and educational experiences.
- The problems in writing grammatically correct sentences and organized paragraphs materially interfere with the child's academic achievement or daily living.
- If there is also a sensory or perceptual defect, the problems in writing are worse than one would expect with it.

Source: Adapted from American Psychiatric Association (2000).

Note: The American Psychiatric Association uses the term *learning disorder* rather than *learning disability.* However, most educators appear to prefer the term *learning disability.*

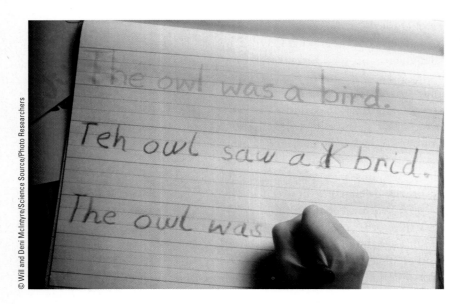

● **Figure 11.4**   Writing Sample of a Dyslexic Child

Dyslexic children have trouble perceiving letters in their correct orientation. They may perceive letters upside down (confusing *w* with *m*) or reversed (confusing *b* with *d*). This perceptual difficulty may lead to rotations or reversals in their writing, as shown here.

peers, have poorer social skills, show more behavior problems in the classroom, and are more likely to experience emotional problems (Frith, 2001; Lyon et al., 2003).

Learning disabilities most often persist through life. But with early recognition and appropriate remediation, many individuals can learn to overcome or compensate for their learning disability (Vellutino et al., 2004).

It has been estimated that dyslexia affects anywhere from 5% to 17.5% of American children (Shaywitz, 1998). Most studies show that dyslexia is much more common in boys than in girls. ● Figure 11.4 is a writing sample from a dyslexic child.

In childhood, treatment of dyslexia focuses on remediation (Bakker, 2006; Tijms, 2007). Children are given highly structured exercises to help them become aware of how to blend sounds to form words, such as identifying word pairs that rhyme and do not rhyme. Later in life, the focus tends to be on accommodation rather than on remediation. For example, college students with dyslexia may be given extra time to do the reading involved in taking tests. Interestingly, college students with dyslexia are frequently excellent at word recognition. Even so, they continue to show problems in decoding new words.

Origins of Dyslexia

Question: What are the origins of dyslexia? Current views of dyslexia focus on the ways in which sensory and neurological problems may contribute to reading problems we find in dyslexic individuals, but first let us note that genetic factors appear to be involved in dyslexia. Dyslexia runs in families. It has been estimated that 25% to 65% of children who have one dyslexic parent are dyslexic themselves (Fernandez & State, 2004; Plomin & Walker, 2003). About 40% of the siblings of children with dyslexia are also dyslexic.

Genetic factors may give rise to neurological problems. The problems can involve "faulty wiring" or circulation problems in the left hemisphere of the brain, which is usually involved in language functions (Arduini et al., 2006; Grigorenko, 2007). The circulation problems would result in less oxygen than is desirable. A part of the brain called the angular gyrus lies in the left hemisphere between the visual cortex and Wernicke's area. The angular gyrus "translates" visual information, such as written words, into auditory information (sounds) and sends it on to Wernicke's area. Problems in the angular gyrus may give rise to reading problems because it becomes difficult for the reader to associate letters with sounds (Greigorenko, 2007; Shaywitz et al., 2006b). For example, we develop habits of seeing an *f* or *aph* or *agh* and saying or hearing an *f* sound in our brains. Dyslexic individuals find it more difficult to go from the visual stimulus to the correct sound.

Some researchers report evidence that dyslexic children have difficulty controlling their eye movements (Boden & Giaschi, 2007), but most researchers today focus on dyslexic individuals' "phonological processing," that is, the ways in which they make, or do not make, sense of sounds. It was once thought that dyslexic children hear as well as other children do, but now it seems that they may not discriminate sounds as accurately as other children do (Halliday & Bishop, 2006). As a result, *b*'s and *d*'s and *p*'s, for example, may have been hard to tell apart at times, creating confusion that impaired reading ability (Boada & Pennington, 2006; Shaywitz et al., 2006a).

We also have the **double-deficit hypothesis** of dyslexia, which suggests that dyslexic children have neurologically based deficits both in *phonological processing* and in *naming speed.* (Sawyer, 2006; Vukovic & Siegel, 2006). Therefore, not only do they have difficulty sounding out a *b* as a *b;* it also takes them longer than other children to name or identify a *b* when they attempt to do so.

Educating Children with Disabilities

Special educational programs have been created to meet the needs of schoolchildren with mild to moderate disabilities. These disabilities include learning disabilities, emotional disturbance, mild mental retardation, and physical disabilities such as blindness, deafness, or paralysis. *Question: Should children with learning disabilities be placed in regular classrooms (i.e., should they be "mainstreamed")?* Evidence is mixed on whether placing disabled children in separate classes can also stigmatize them and segregate them from other children. Special-needs classes also negatively influence teacher expectations. Neither the teacher nor the students themselves come to expect very much. This negative expectation becomes a self-fulfilling prophecy, and the exceptional students' achievements suffer.

Mainstreaming is intended to counter the negative effects of special-needs classes. In mainstreaming, disabled children are placed in regular classrooms that have been adapted to their needs. Most students with mild learning disabilities spend most of their school day in regular classrooms (Soan & Tod, 2006).

Although the goals of mainstreaming are laudable, observations of the results are mixed. Some studies indicate that disabled children may achieve more when they are mainstreamed (e.g., Fergusson, 2007). But other studies suggest that many disabled children do not fare well in regular classrooms (Frostad & Pijl, 2007). Rather than inspiring them to greater achievements, regular classrooms can be overwhelming for many disabled students.

High-quality teaching methods are needed for children with learning disabilities. For example, in an experiment on instructing children with learning disabilities,

double-deficit hypothesis The theory of dyslexia which suggests that dyslexic children have biological deficits in two areas *phonological processing* (interpreting sounds) and in *naming speed* (for example, identifying letters such as *b* versus *d,* or *w* versus *m*).

mainstreaming Placing disabled children in classrooms with nondisabled children.

Mainstreaming

Today, most students with mild disabilities spend at least part of their school day in regular classrooms. The goals of mainstreaming include providing broader educational opportunities for disabled students and fostering interactions with nondisabled children.

Alice Wilder and Joanna Williams (2001) recruited 91 students (59 boys and 32 girls) from special-education classrooms in New York City. The city Board of Education had certified the students as being learning disabled. Most children had obtained IQ scores of at least 85. The study attempted to determine whether special instruction could help the students pick out the themes in stories. A story was read aloud, and students were then asked to consider questions, such as the following:

> Who was the main character?
> What was his or her problem?
> What did he or she do?
> What happened at the end of the story?
> Was what happened good or bad?
> Why was it good or bad?

Students receiving this form of instruction were more capable of identifying the themes and applying them to everyday life than children who received more traditional instruction. The investigators concluded that this sort of "theme identification" program enables children with severe learning disabilities to profit from instruction that is geared toward abstract thinking and understanding. Perhaps we can generalize to note that these results seem to be underscoring that "good teaching helps," often, if not always. (Why isn't this kind of teaching "traditional instruction"?)

Perhaps any method that carefully assesses the child's skills, identifies deficits, and creates and follows precise plans for remediating these deficits can be of help. Having said that, it seems that no method identified to date provides children with the levels of skills that so many children apply with ease. But reading and other academic skills are important in everyday life in our society, and any advance would appear to be better than none.

Our examination of educational programs for children with disabilities leads us next into an investigation of cognitive development in middle childhood and the conditions that influence it. We address this topic in Chapter 12.

Active Review

15. Children with _____ (ADHD) show developmentally inappropriate or excessive inattention, impulsivity, and hyperactivity.

16. ADHD is more common among (Boys or Girls?).

17. ADHD (Does or Does not?) tend to run in families.

18. Children with ADHD are likely to be treated with (Stimulants or Tranquilizers?).

19. Learning _____ are a group of disorders characterized by inadequate development of specific academic, language, and speech skills.

20. Difficulty learning to read is called _____.

21. Current views of dyslexia focus on the ways that _____ problems contribute to the perceptual problems we find in dyslexic children.

22. Dyslexia (Does or Does not?) tend to run in families.

Reflect & Relate: Did you know any children with disabilities who were "mainstreamed" in your classes? How were they treated by other students? How were they treated by teachers? Do you believe that mainstreaming was helpful for them?

Go to

http://www.thomsonedu.com/psychology/rathus

for an interactive version of this review.

1. What patterns of growth occur in middle childhood?

Children tend to gain a little over 2 inches in height and 5 to 7 pounds in weight per year during middle childhood. Children become more slender. Boys are slightly heavier and taller than girls through the ages of 9 or 10, when girls begin the adolescent growth spurt. At around age 11, boys develop relatively more muscle tissue and females develop more fatty tissue.

2. How many children in the United States are overweight? Why are they overweight?

About one-sixth of American children are overweight, and the prevalence of being overweight has been increasing. Overweight children usually do not "outgrow" "baby fat." During childhood, heavy children are often rejected by their peers. Heredity plays a role in being overweight. Children with high numbers of fat cells feel food deprived sooner than other children. Overweight parents may encourage overeating by keeping fattening foods in the home. Sedentary habits also foster being overweight.

3. What changes in motor development occur in middle childhood?

Middle childhood is marked by increases in speed, strength, agility, and balance. Children show regular improvement in gross motor skills and are often eager to participate in athletic activities, such as ball games that require movement of large muscles. Muscles grow stronger and pathways that connect the cerebellum to the cortex become more myelinated. Reaction time gradually decreases. Fine motor skills also improve, with 6- to 7-year-olds tying shoelaces and holding pencils as adults do.

4. Are there sex differences in motor skills?

Boys have slightly greater overall strength, whereas girls have better coordination and flexibility, which is valuable in dancing, balancing, and gymnastics. Boys generally receive more encouragement than girls to excel in athletics.

5. Are children in the United States physically fit? If not, why not?

Most children in the United States are not physically fit. One reason is the amount of time spent watching television.

6. How does run-of-the-mill failure to "listen" to adults differ from attention-deficit/hyperactivity disorder?

Attention-deficit/hyperactivity disorder (ADHD) involves lack of attention, impulsivity, and hyperactivity. ADHD impairs children's ability to function in school. ADHD tends to be overdiagnosed and overmedicated.

7. What are the causes of ADHD?

ADHD runs in families and coexists with other problems. Abnormalities may suggest brain damage. Children with ADHD do not inhibit impulses that most children control, suggesting poor executive control in the brain.

8. Why are children with ADHD treated with stimulants?

Stimulants are used to stimulate the cerebral cortex to inhibit more primitive areas of the brain. Stimulants increase the attention span and academic performance of children with ADHD, but there are side effects and the medications may be used too often. Cognitive behavioral therapy can also help teach children self-control.

9. What are learning disabilities?

Learning disabilities are characterized by inadequate development of specific academic, language, and speech skills. Children may be diagnosed with a learning disability when their performance is below that expected for their age and level of intelligence. Learning disabilities tend to persist.

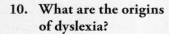

10. What are the origins of dyslexia?

Current views of dyslexia focus on the ways that neurological problems may contribute to perceptual problems. Genetic factors appear to be involved, because dyslexia runs in families. The double-deficit hypothesis suggests that dyslexic children have neurologically based deficits in phonological processing and in naming speed.

11. Should children with learning disabilities be placed in regular classrooms (i.e., should they be "mainstreamed")?

Research evidence on this question is mixed. Some studies suggest that disabled children achieve more when they are mainstreamed. Other studies suggest that many disabled children find regular classrooms overwhelming.

Key Terms

growth spurt, 372
adipose tissue, 375
reaction time, 378
attention-deficit/hyperactivity
     disorder (ADHD), 383

hyperactivity, 383
stimulants, 386
dyslexia, 386
learning disabilities, 387

double-deficit hypothesis, 389
mainstreaming, 389

Active Learning Resources

Childhood & Adolescence Book Companion Website
http://www.thomsonedu.com/psychology/rathus

Visit your book companion website where you will find more resources to help you study. There you will find interactive versions of your book features, including the Lessons in Observation video, Active Review sections, and the Truth or Fiction feature. In addition, the companion website contains quizzing, flash cards, and a pronunciation glossary.

Thomson NOW! is an easy-to-use online resource that helps you study in less time to get the grade you want—NOW.
http://www.thomsonedu.com/login

Need help studying? This site is your one-stop study shop. Take a Pre-Test and ThomsonNOW will generate a Personalized Study Plan based on your test results. The Study Plan will identify the topics you need to review and direct you to online resources to help you master those topics. You can then take a Post-Test to determine the concepts you have mastered and what you still need to work on.

12 Middle Childhood:
Cognitive Development

Truth or Fiction?

T F Don't try the "Yes, but" defense with a 5-year-old. If you did it, you're guilty, even if it was an accident. p. 402

T F Memorizing the alphabet requires that children keep 26 chunks of information in mind at once. p. 409

T F An IQ is a score on a test. p. 416

T F Two children can answer exactly the same items on an intelligence test correctly, yet one can be above average in intelligence and the other below average. p. 419

T F Highly intelligent children are creative. p. 426

T F Adopted children are more similar in intelligence to their adoptive parents than to their biological parents. p. 428

T F Bilingual children encounter more academic problems than children who speak only one language. p. 434

© Howard Kingsnorth/Getty Images

Preview

Piaget: The Concrete-Operational Stage
Conservation

Lessons in Observation: Piaget's Concrete-Operational Stage

Transitivity
Class Inclusion
Applications of Piaget's Theory to Education
Evaluation of Piaget's Theory

Moral Development: The Child as Juror
Piaget's Theory of Moral Development
Kohlberg's Theory of Moral Development

Information Processing: Learning, Remembering, Problem Solving
Development of Selective Attention
Developments in the Storage and Retrieval of Information
Development of Recall Memory
Development of Metacognition and Metamemory

A Closer Look: Children's Eyewitness Testimony

Intellectual Development, Creativity, and Achievement
Theories of Intelligence
Measurement of Intellectual Development

A Closer Look: Emotional Intelligence and Social Intelligence?

Patterns of Intellectual Development
Differences in Intellectual Development
Creativity and Intellectual Development

Developing in a World of Diversity: Socioeconomic and Ethnic Differences in IQ

Determinants of Intellectual Development

Language Development and Literacy
Vocabulary and Grammar
Reading Skills and Literacy
Methods of Teaching Reading
Diversity of Children's Linguistic Experiences in the United States: Ebonics and Bilingualism

Go to

http://www.thomsonedu.com/psychology/rathus
for an interactive version of this "Truth or Fiction" feature.

id you hear the one about the judge who pounded her gavel and yelled, "Order! Order in the court!"? "A hamburger and French fries, Your Honor," responded the defendant. Or how about this one? "I saw a man-eating lion at the zoo." "Big deal! I saw a man eating snails at a restaurant." Or how about, "Make me a glass of chocolate milk!"? "Poof! You're a glass of chocolate milk." These children's jokes are based on ambiguities in the meanings of words and phrases. Most 7-year-olds will find the joke about order in the court funny and can recognize that the word order has more than one meaning. The jokes about the man-eating lion and chocolate milk will strike most children as funny at about the age of 11, when they can understand ambiguities in grammatical structure.

Children make enormous strides in their cognitive development during the middle childhood years. Their thought processes and language become more logical and more complex. In this chapter, we follow the course of cognitive development in middle childhood. First, we continue our discussion of Piaget's cognitive-developmental view from Chapter 9. We then consider the information-processing approach that has been stimulated by our experience with the computer. We next explore the development of intelligence, ways of measuring it, and the roles of heredity and environment in shaping it. Finally, we turn to the development of language.

Piaget: The Concrete-Operational Stage

According to Jean Piaget, the typical child is entering the stage of **concrete operations** by the age of 7. ***Question: What is meant by the stage of concrete operations?*** In the stage of concrete operations, which lasts until about the age of 12, children show the beginnings of the capacity for adult logic. However, their thought processes, or operations, generally involve tangible objects rather than abstract ideas, which is why we refer to their thinking as "concrete."

The thinking of the concrete-operational child is characterized by **reversibility** and flexibility. Consider adding the numbers 2 and 3 to get 5. Adding is an operation. The operation is reversible in that the child can then subtract 2 from 5 to get 3. There is flexibility in that the child can also subtract 3 from 5 to get the number 2. To the concrete-operational child, adding and subtracting are not simply rote activities. The concrete-operational child recognizes that there are relationships among numbers, that operations can be carried out according to rules. This understanding lends concrete-operational thought flexibility and reversibility.

Concrete-operational children are less egocentric than other children. Their abilities to take on the roles of others and to view the world and themselves from other peoples' perspectives are greatly expanded. They recognize that people see things in different ways because of different situations and different sets of values.

Compared with preoperational children, who can focus on only one dimension of a problem at a time, concrete-operational children can engage in **decentration.** That is, they can focus on multiple parts of a problem at once. Decentration has implications for conservation and other intellectual undertakings.

Conservation

Concrete-operational children show understanding of the laws of conservation. The 7-year-old girl in ● Figure 12.1 would say that the flattened ball still has the same amount of clay. If asked why, she might reply, "Because you can roll it up again like the other one." This answer shows reversibility.

concrete operations The third stage in Piaget's scheme, characterized by flexible, reversible thought concerning tangible objects and events.

reversibility According to Piaget, recognition that processes can be undone, leaving things as they were before. Reversibility is a factor in conservation of the properties of substances.

decentration Simultaneous focusing (centering) on more than one aspect or dimension of a problem or situation.

● Figure 12.1
Conservation of Mass

This girl is in the concrete-operational stage of cognitive development. She has rolled two clay balls. In the photo on the left, she agrees that both have the same amount (mass) of clay. In the photo on the right, she (gleefully) flattens one clay ball. When asked whether the two pieces still have the same amount of clay, she says yes.

Lessons in Observation
Piaget's Concrete-Operational Stage

 To watch this video, visit the book companion website. You can also answer the questions and e-mail your responses to your professor.

Children in Piaget's concrete-operational stage can not only understand that both glasses contain the same amount of water no matter what the shape of the glass is but can also explain why.

Learning Objectives

■ What is the concrete-operational stage of cognitive development?
■ How do conservation tasks help illustrate whether or not a child has reached the concrete-operational stage?
■ What is the difference between logical and intuitive approaches to problem solving?
■ How is reversibility related to ability to engage in concrete operations?

Applied Lesson

Imagine that you are showing a preoperational child 100 rolls of 100 pennies each and a $100 bill. You ask the child which is more money. What do you think the child will say? Why? Now imagine that you ask the same question of a concrete-operational child. Would you expect the same answer? Why or why not? Now do some thinking of your own. Which is less expensive: a $3,000 computer or a $12,000 car? Explain your answer in as much detail as you like.

Critical Thinking

Recall the video you watched in Chapter 9, "Piaget's Preoperational Stage." Describe the differences in reasoning between the younger children in Chapter 9 and the children in this chapter. How has the reasoning of the children in this chapter advanced over that of the children shown in the video that accompanies Chapter 9?

Judy Allen-Newberry

The concrete-operational girl knows that objects can have several properties or dimensions. Things that are tall can also be heavy or light. Things that are red can also be round or square, or thick or thin. Knowledge of this principle allows the girl to decenter and to avoid focusing on only the diameter of the clay pancake. By attending to both the height and the width of the clay, she recognizes that the loss in height compensates for the gain in width.

Children do not necessarily develop conservation in all kinds of tasks simultaneously. Conservation of mass usually develops first, followed by conservation of weight and conservation of volume. Piaget theorized that the gains of the concrete-operational stage are so tied to specific events that achievement in one area does not necessarily transfer to achievement in another.

Transitivity

Question of the day: If your parents are older than you are and you are older than your children, are your parents older than your children? (How do you know?)

We have posed some tough questions in this book, but the one about your parents is a real ogre. The answer, of course, is yes. But how did you arrive at this answer? If you said yes simply on the basis of knowing that your parents are older than your children (e.g., 58 and 56 compared with 5 and 3), your answer did not require concrete-operational thought. One aspect of concrete-operational is the principle of **transitivity:** If A exceeds B in some property (say, age or height) and if B exceeds C, then A must also exceed C.

Researchers can assess whether or not children understand the principle of transitivity by asking them to place objects in a series, or order, according to some property or trait, such as lining up one's family members according to age, height, or weight. Placing objects in a series is termed **seriation.** Let's consider some examples with preoperational and concrete-operational children.

Piaget frequently assessed children's abilities at seriation by asking them to place 10 sticks in order of size. Children who are 4 to 5 years of age usually place the sticks in a random sequence, or in small groups, as in small, medium, or large. Six- to 7-year-old children, who are in transition between the preoperational and concrete-operational stages, may arrive at proper sequences. However, they usually do so by trial and error, rearranging their series a number of times. In other words, they are capable of comparing two sticks and deciding that one is longer than the other, but their overall perspective seems limited to the pair they are comparing at the time and does not seem to encompass the entire array.

But consider the approach of 7- and 8-year-olds who are capable of concrete operations. They go about the task systematically, usually without error. For the 10 sticks, they look over the array, then select either the longest or shortest and place it at the point from which they will build their series. Then they select the next longest (or shortest) and continue in this fashion until the task is complete.

Knowledge of the principle of transitivity allows concrete-operational children to go about their task unerringly. They realize that if stick A is longer than stick B and stick B is longer than stick C, then stick A is also longer than stick C. After putting stick C in place, they need not double-check in hope that it will be shorter than stick A; they know it will be.

Concrete-operational children also have the decentration capacity to allow them to seriate in two dimensions at once. Consider a seriation task used by Piaget and his longtime colleague Barbel Inhelder. In this test, children are given 49 leaves and asked to classify them according to size and brightness (from small to large and from dark to light) (see ● Figure 12.2). As the grid is completed from left to right, the leaves become lighter. As it is filled in from top to bottom, the leaves become larger.

transitivity The principle that if A is greater than B in a property and B is greater than C, then A is greater than C.

seriation Placing objects in an order or series according to a property or trait.

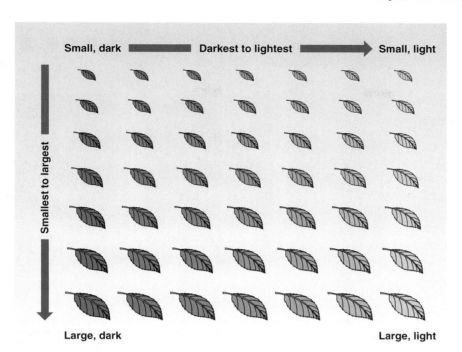

● **Figure 12.2** A Grid for Demonstrating the Development of Seriation

To classify these 49 leaves, children must be able to focus on two dimensions at once: size and lightness. They must also recognize that if quantity A exceeds quantity B and quantity B exceeds quantity C, then quantity A must also exceed quantity C. This relationship is called the *principle of transitivity*.

Preoperational 6-year-olds can usually order the leaves according to size or brightness, but not both simultaneously. But concrete-operational children of age 7 or 8 can work with both dimensions at once and fill in the grid properly.

A number of researchers have argued that children can seriate earlier than Piaget believed and that Piaget's results reflected the demand characteristics of his experiments (Blevins-Knabe, 1987; Siegler & Alibali, 2005). This may be so, but the sequence of developments in seriation and transitivity seems to have been captured fairly well by Piaget.

Class Inclusion

Another example of an operation is **class inclusion,** which we learned about in Chapter 9. In the example in Chapter 9 (see page 302), a 4-year-old was shown pictures of four cats and six dogs. When asked whether there were more dogs or more animals, she said more dogs. This preoperational child apparently could not focus on the two subclasses (dogs, cats) and the larger subclass (animals) at the same time. But concrete-operational children can focus on two dimensions (in this case, classes and subclasses) at the same time. Therefore, they are more likely to answer the question about the dogs and the animals correctly (Chapman & McBride, 1992). But their thought remains concrete in that they will give you the correct answer if you ask them about dogs and animals (or daffodils and flowers) but not if you attempt to phrase the question in terms of abstract symbols, such as A, B_1, and B_2. As with other areas of cognitive development, researchers have taken issue with Piaget's views of the ages at which class-inclusion skills develop. They have argued that language continues to pose hazards for the children being tested. Aspects of concrete-operational thinking are summarized in Concept Review 12.1.

Applications of Piaget's Theory to Education

Question: Can we apply Piaget's theory of cognitive development to educational practices? It seems that we can (Crain, 2000). Piaget pointed out some applications himself. First, Piaget believed that learning involves active discovery. Therefore,

class inclusion The principle that one category or class of things includes several subclasses.

Concept Review 12.1   Aspects of Concrete-Operational Thinking

Conservation

Concrete-operational children show conservation of mass and number.

As you may remember the girl on the right shows conservation of the mass of the clay. Refer back to Figure 9.3 (p. 301), showing the experiment using pennies to test conservation of number. A concrete-operational child will conserve number and say that both panels have the same number of pennies. Preoperational children will say that the wider row has "more."

| Child is shown two rows of pennies. | Experimenter moves pennies in one row. |

Seriation

A concrete-operational child understands the principle of transitivity (if A > B, and B > C, then A > C).

Therefore, the child can place the sticks in order from longest to shortest.

Class Inclusion

Here are 10 animals, including 6 dogs. When asked whether there are more dogs or animals, the preoperational child, focusing on one aspect of the problem at a time, may see that there are more dogs than cats and say, "Dogs." The concrete-operational child is more likely to recognize that the class "animals" includes both "dogs" and "cats" and thus will answer, "animals."

teachers should not simply try to impose knowledge on the child but instead should find interesting and stimulating materials. Second, instruction should be geared to the child's level of development. When teaching a concrete-operational child about fractions, for example, the teacher should not only lecture but should also allow the child to divide concrete objects into parts. Third, Piaget believed that learning to take into account the perspectives of others is a key ingredient in the development of both cognition and morality. Accordingly, he thought that teachers should promote group discussions and interactions among their students.

Evaluation of Piaget's Theory

Although Piaget's theory has led many psychologists to recast their concepts of children, it has also met with criticism on several grounds. As noted in Chapters 6 and 9, some researchers have shown that Piaget underestimated children's abilities. Modified task demands suggest that children are capable of conservation and other concrete-operational tasks earlier than Piaget believed. Cognitive skills may develop more independently and continuously than Piaget thought, not in stages. For example, conservation does not arrive all at once. Children develop conservation for mass, weight, and volume at different ages. The onset of conservation can be seen in terms of the gradual accumulation of problem-solving abilities instead of in terms of suddenly changing cognitive structures (Flavell et al., 2002). However, the sequences of development—which are at the core of Piaget's theory—continue to appear to remain the same. In sum, Piaget's theoretical edifice has been rocked, but it has not been dashed to rubble.

In the next section, we revisit Piaget and examine his views on children's decisions about right and wrong. Then we consider the views of Lawrence Kohlberg on the same topic.

Active Review

1. Concrete-operational children are (More or Less?) egocentric than preoperational children.
2. The principle of _____ holds that if A exceeds B and B exceeds C, then A must exceed C.
3. Class _____ involves the ability to recognize that one class of things (A) can include subclasses (B₁ and B₂).

Reflect & Relate: George becomes angry that Delores wants to break off the relationship and beats her so badly that she must remain in the hospital for 6 months. Gus makes a mistake at the nuclear energy plant where he works, causing a nuclear accident in which a great deal of radiation is released, killing 300 people within a week and shortening the lives of more than 1 million people because of cancer. Which person has done something naughtier, George or Gus? Explain your viewpoint. (Now you are ready to read the next section.)

Go to

http://www.thomsonedu.com/psychology/rathus

for an interactive version of this review.

Moral Development: The Child as Juror

Moral development is a complex issue with both cognitive and behavioral aspects. On a cognitive level, moral development concerns the basis on which children make judgments that an act is right or wrong. In this section, we examine the contributions of Jean Piaget and Lawrence Kohlberg to our understanding of children's moral development.

Piaget and Kohlberg argued that moral reasoning undergoes the same cognitive-developmental pattern around the world. The moral considerations that children weigh at a given age are likely to reflect the values of the social and cultural settings in which they are being reared. However, moral reasoning is also theorized to reflect the orderly unfolding of cognitive processes (Krebs & Denton, 2006; Lapsley, 2006). Moral reasoning is related to the child's overall cognitive development. *Question: How does Piaget view the development of moral reasoning?*

Piaget's Theory of Moral Development

For years, Piaget observed children playing games such as marbles and making judgments on the seriousness of the wrongdoing of characters in stories. On the basis of these observations, he concluded that children's moral judgments develop in two major overlapping stages: moral realism and autonomous morality (Piaget, 1932).

The Stage of Moral Realism

The first stage is usually referred to as the stage of **moral realism,** or of **objective morality.** During this stage, which emerges at about the age of 5, children consider behavior to be correct when it conforms to authority or to the rules of the game. When asked why something should be done in a certain way, the 5-year-old may answer "Because that's the way to do it" or "Because my Mommy says so."

At about the age of 5, children perceive rules as embedded in the structure of things. Rules, to them, reflect ultimate reality, hence the term *moral realism*. Rules and right and wrong are seen as absolute. They are not seen as deriving from people to meet social needs.

Another consequence of viewing rules as embedded in the fabric of the world is **immanent justice,** or automatic retribution. Thinking that negative experiences are punishment for prior misdeeds, even when realistic causal links are absent, is what is meant by immanent justice reasoning (Callan et al., 2006). Five- or 6-year-old children who lie or steal usually believe that they will be found out or at least punished for their acts. If they trip and scrape their knees, they may assume that this accident represents punishment for a transgression.

Truth or Fiction Revisited: It is true that you are guilty in the eyes of a 5-year-old even if your behavior was an accident. Preoperational children tend to focus on only one dimension at a time. Therefore, they judge the wrongness of an act only in terms of the amount of damage done, not in terms of the intentions of the wrongdoer. Children in the stage of moral realism are tough jurors indeed. They do not excuse the person who harms by accident. As an illustration, consider children's response to Piaget's story about the broken cups. Piaget told children a story in which one child breaks 15 cups accidentally and another child breaks one cup deliberately. Which child is naughtiest? Which should be punished most? Children in the stage of moral realism typically say that the child who did the most damage is the naughtiest and should be punished most. The amount of damage is more important than the child's intentions (Piaget, 1932).

The Stage of Autonomous Morality

Piaget found that when children reach the ages of 9 to 11, they begin to show **autonomous morality.** Their moral judgments tend to become more autonomous, or self-governed. Children come to view social rules as arbitrary agreements that can be changed. Children no longer automatically view obedience to authority figures as right. They realize that circumstances can require breaking rules.

Children who show autonomous morality are capable of flexible operational thought. They can focus simultaneously on multiple dimensions, so they consider not only social rules but also the motives of the wrongdoer.

moral realism According to Piaget, the stage during which children judge acts as moral when they conform to authority or to the rules of the game. Morality at this stage is perceived as embedded in the structure of the universe.

objective morality The perception of morality as objective, that is, as existing outside the cognitive functioning of people; a characteristic of Piaget's stage of moral realism.

immanent justice The view that retribution for wrongdoing is a direct consequence of the wrongdoing, reflective of the belief that morality is embedded within the structure of the universe.

autonomous morality The second stage in Piaget's cognitive-developmental theory of moral development. In this stage, children base moral judgments on the intentions of the wrongdoer and on the amount of damage done. Social rules are viewed as agreements that can be changed.

Children in this stage also show a greater capacity to take the point of view of others, to empathize with them. Decentration and increased empathy prompt children to weigh the intentions of the wrongdoer more heavily than the amount of damage done. The child who broke one cup deliberately may be seen as deserving of more punishment than the child who broke 15 cups accidentally. Children become capable of considering mitigating circumstances. Accidents are less likely to be considered crimes.

Piaget assumed that autonomous morality usually develops as a result of cooperative peer relationships. But he also believed that parents could help foster autonomous morality by creating egalitarian relationships with their children and explaining the reasons for social rules. As we see in the next section, knowledge of social rules is also a key factor in Kohlberg's theory of moral development.

Moral Realism

It looks bad, but Mom asked her to find the car keys. Mom wasn't thinking of having her go through her purse, however. If she breaks things or drops them on the floor in the effort, is she being "bad"? Children in the stage of moral realism might well say yes because they focus on the damage done, not on the intentions of the wrongdoer.

Kohlberg's Theory of Moral Development

Question: What is Kohlberg's theory of moral development? Kohlberg (1981, 1985) advanced the cognitive-developmental theory of moral development by elaborating on the kinds of information children use and on the complexities of moral reasoning. Before we discuss Kohlberg's views, read the tale that Kohlberg used in his research and answer the questions that follow.

> In Europe, a woman was near death from a special kind of cancer. There was one drug that the doctors thought might save her. It was a form of radium that a druggist in the same town had recently discovered. The drug was expensive to make, but the druggist was charging 10 times what the drug cost him to make. He paid $200 for the radium and charged $2,000 for a small dose of the drug. The sick woman's husband, Heinz, went to everyone he knew to borrow the money, but he could only get together about $1,000 which was half of what it cost. He told the druggist that his wife was dying and asked him to sell it cheaper or let him pay later. But the druggist said: "No, I discovered the drug and I'm going to make money from it." So Heinz got desperate and broke into the man's store to steal the drug for his wife.
>
> —Kohlberg (1969)

Kohlberg emphasized the importance of being able to view the moral world from the perspective of another person (Krebs & Denton, 2005). Look at this situation from Heinz's perspective. What do you think? Should Heinz have tried to steal the drug? Was he right or wrong? As you can see from ■ Table 12.1, the issue is more complicated than a simple yes or no. Heinz is caught in a moral dilemma in which legal or social rules (in this case, laws against stealing) are pitted against a strong human need (Heinz's desire to save his wife). According to Kohlberg's theory, children

■ **Table 12.1** Kohlberg's Levels and Stages of Moral Development

Stage of Development	Examples of Moral Reasoning That Support Heinz's Stealing the Drug	Examples of Moral Reasoning That Oppose Heinz's Stealing the Drug
Level I: Preconventional—Typically Begins in Early Childhood[a]		
Stage 1: Judgments guided by obedience and the prospect of punishment (the consequences of the behavior)	It is not wrong to take the drug. Heinz did try to pay the druggist for it, and it is only worth $200, not $2,000.	Taking things without paying is wrong because it is against the law. Heinz will get caught and go to jail.
Stage 2: Naively egoistic, instrumental orientation (things are right when they satisfy people's needs)	Heinz ought to take the drug because his wife really needs it. He can always pay the druggist back.	Heinz should not take the drug. If he gets caught and winds up in jail, it won't do his wife any good.
Level II: Conventional—Typically Begins in Middle Childhood		
Stage 3: Good-boy/good-girl orientation (moral behavior helps others and is socially approved)	Stealing is a crime, so it is bad, but Heinz should take the drug to save his wife or else people would blame him for letting her die.	Stealing is a crime. Heinz should not just take the drug because his family will be dishonored and they will blame him.
Stage 4: Law-and-order orientation (moral behavior is doing one's duty and showing respect for authority)	Heinz must take the drug to do his duty to save his wife. Eventually, he has to pay the druggist for it, however.	If we all took the law into our own hands, civilization would fall apart, so Heinz should not steal the drug.
Level III: Postconventional—Typically Begins in Adolescence[b]		
Stage 5: Contractual, legalistic orientation (one must weigh pressing human needs against society's need to maintain social order)	This thing is complicated because society has a right to maintain law and order, but Heinz has to take the drug to save his wife.	I can see why Heinz feels he has to take the drug, but laws exist for the benefit of society as a whole and cannot simply be cast aside.
Stage 6: Universal ethical principles orientation (people must follow universal ethical principles and their own conscience, even if it means breaking the law)	In this case, the law comes into conflict with the principle of the sanctity of human life. Heinz must take the drug because his wife's life is more important than the law.	If Heinz truly believes that stealing the drug is worse than letting his wife die, he should not take it. People have to make sacrifices to do what they think is right.

[a] Tends to be used less often in middle childhood.

[b] May not develop at all.

and adults arrive at yes or no answers for different reasons. These reasons can be classified according to the level of moral development they reflect.

Children (and adults) are faced with many moral dilemmas. Consider cheating in school. When children fear failing a test, they may be tempted to cheat. Different children may decide not to cheat for different reasons. One child may simply fear getting caught. A second child may decide that it is more important to live up to her moral principles than to get the highest possible grade. In each case, the child's decision is not to cheat. However, the cognitive processes behind each decision reflect different levels of reasoning.

As a stage theorist, Kohlberg argued that the developmental stages of moral reasoning follow the same sequence in all children. Children progress at different rates, and not all children (or adults) reach the highest stage. But children must experience Stage 1 before they enter Stage 2, and so on. According to Kohlberg, there are three levels of moral development and two stages within each level.

Let us return to Heinz and see how responses to the questions we have posed can reflect different levels and stages of moral development.

The Preconventional Level

In the **preconventional level,** children base their moral judgments on the consequences of their behavior. For instance, Stage 1 is oriented toward obedience and punishment. Good behavior means being obedient, which allows one to avoid punishment. According to Stage 1 reasoning, Heinz could be urged to steal the drug because he did ask to pay for it first. But he could also be urged not to steal the drug so that he will not be sent to jail (see Table 12.1).

In Stage 2, good behavior allows people to satisfy their own needs and, perhaps, the needs of others. A Stage 2 reason for stealing the drug is that Heinz's wife needs it. Therefore, stealing the drug—the only way of attaining it—is not wrong. A Stage 2 reason for not stealing the drug would be that Heinz's wife might die even if he does so. Thus, he might wind up in jail needlessly.

In a study of American children age 7 through 16, Kohlberg (1963) found that Stage 1 and 2 types of moral judgments were offered most frequently by 7- and 10-year-olds. There was a steep falling off of Stage 1 and 2 judgments after age 10.

The Conventional Level

In the **conventional level** of moral reasoning, right and wrong are judged by conformity to conventional (family, religious, societal) standards of right and wrong. According to the Stage 3 "good-boy/good-girl orientation," it is good to meet the needs and expectations of others. Moral behavior is what is "normal," what the majority does. From the Stage 3 perspective, Heinz should steal the drug because that is what a "good husband" would do. It is "natural" or "normal" to try to help one's wife. Or Heinz should not steal the drug because "good people do not steal." Stage 3 judgments also focus on the role of sympathy, the importance of doing what will make someone else feel good or better.

In Stage 4, moral judgments are based on rules that maintain the social order. Showing respect for authority and duty is valued highly. From this perspective, one could argue that Heinz must steal the drug, because it is his duty to save his wife. He would pay the druggist when he could. Or one could argue that Heinz should not steal the drug, because he would be breaking the law. He might also be contributing to the breakdown of the social order. Many people do not develop beyond the conventional level.

Kohlberg (1963) found that Stage 3 and 4 types of judgments emerge during middle childhood. They are all but absent among 7-year-olds. However, they are reported by about 20% of 10-year-olds (and by higher percentages of adolescents).

preconventional level According to Kohlberg, a period during which moral judgments are based largely on expectations of rewards or punishments.

conventional level According to Kohlberg, a period during which moral judgments largely reflect social rules and conventions.

The Postconventional Level

In the **postconventional level,** moral reasoning is based on the person's own moral standards. If this level of reasoning develops at all, it is found among adolescents and adults (see Table 12.1).

Active Review

4. Piaget believed that children's moral judgments develop in two stages: moral realism and _____ morality.
5. Preoperational children judge the wrongness of an act in terms of (The amount of damage done or The intentions of the wrongdoer?).
6. In Kohlberg's _____ level, children base their moral judgments on the consequences of their behavior.
7. In the _____ level, right and wrong are judged by conformity to conventional (family, religious, societal) standards of right and wrong.

Reflect & Relate: Do you believe that Heinz should have taken the drug without paying? Why or why not? What does your reasoning suggest about your level of moral development?

Go to

http://www.thomsonedu.com/psychology/rathus

for an interactive version of this review.

Information Processing: Learning, Remembering, Problem Solving

Question: What is the difference between Piaget's view of cognitive development and the information-processing approach? Whereas Piaget looked on children as budding scientists, psychologists who view cognitive development in terms of **information processing** see children (and adults) as somewhat akin to computers. Children, like computers, attain information (input) from the environment, store it, retrieve it, manipulate it, and then respond to it overtly (output). One goal of the information-processing approach is to learn how children store, retrieve, and manipulate information, how their "mental programs" develop. Information-processing theorists also study the development of children's strategies for processing information (Bjorklund & Rosenblum, 2001; Pressley & Hilden, 2006).

Although something may be gained from thinking of children in terms of computers, children, of course, are not computers. Children are self-aware and capable of creativity and intuition.

Key elements in information processing include the following:

- Development of selective attention: development of children's abilities to focus on the elements of a problem and find solutions
- Development of capacity for storage and retrieval of information: development of the capacity of memory and of children's understanding of the processes of memory and how to strengthen and use memory
- Development of strategies for processing information: development of ability to solve problems as, for example, by finding the correct formula and applying it

postconventional level
According to Kohlberg, a period during which moral judgments are derived from moral principles and people look to themselves to set moral standards.

information processing
The view in which cognitive processes are compared to the functions of computers. The theory deals with the input, storage, retrieval, manipulation, and output of information. The focus is on the development of children's strategies for solving problems, or their "mental programs."

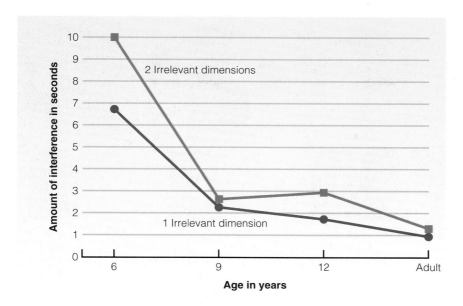

● **Figure 12.3**
Development of the Ability to Ignore Distractions

Strutt and his colleagues demonstrated how the ability to ignore distractions develops during middle childhood. The effect of irrelevant dimensions on sorting speed was determined by subtracting the speed of the sort in the no-irrelevant-dimension condition from the speed of the other two conditions. As shown here, irrelevant information interfered with sorting ability for all age groups, but older children were less affected than younger ones.

Strutt et al. (1975).

Development of Selective Attention

A key cognitive process is the ability to pay attention to relevant features of a task. The ability to focus one's attention and screen out distractions advances steadily through middle childhood (Rubia et al., 2006). Preoperational children engaged in problem solving tend to focus (or center) their attention on one element of the problem at a time, which is a major reason that they lack conservation. Concrete-operational children, by contrast, can attend to multiple aspects of the problem at once, permitting them to conserve number, volume, and so on.

An experiment illustrates how selective attention and the ability to ignore distractions develop during middle childhood. The researchers (Strutt et al., 1975) asked children between 6 and 12 years of age to sort a deck of cards as quickly as possible on the basis of the figures depicted on each card (e.g., circle versus square). In one condition, only the relevant dimension (i.e., form) was shown on each card. In another condition, a dimension not relevant to the sorting also was present (e.g., a horizontal or vertical line in the figure). In a third condition, two irrelevant dimensions were present (e.g., a star above or below the figure, in addition to a horizontal or vertical line in the figure). As seen in ● Figure 12.3, the irrelevant information interfered with sorting ability for all age groups, but older children were much less affected than younger children. In the next section, we learn more about how children gain the ability to store and retrieve information.

Developments in the Storage and Retrieval of Information

Question: What is meant by the term memory? Keep in mind that the word **memory** is not a scientific term, even though psychologists and other scientists may use it for the sake of convenience. Psychologists usually use the term to refer to the processes of storing and retrieving information. Many but not all psychologists divide memory functioning into three major processes or structures: sensory memory, working memory (short-term memory), and long-term memory (● Figure 12.4).

Sensory Memory

When we look at an object and then blink our eyes, the visual impression of the object lasts for a fraction of a second in what is called **sensory memory,** or the **sensory register.** Then the "trace" of the stimulus decays. The concept of sensory memory applies

memory The processes by which we store and retrieve information.

sensory memory The structure of memory first encountered by sensory input. Information is maintained in sensory memory for only a fraction of a second.

sensory register Another term for sensory memory.

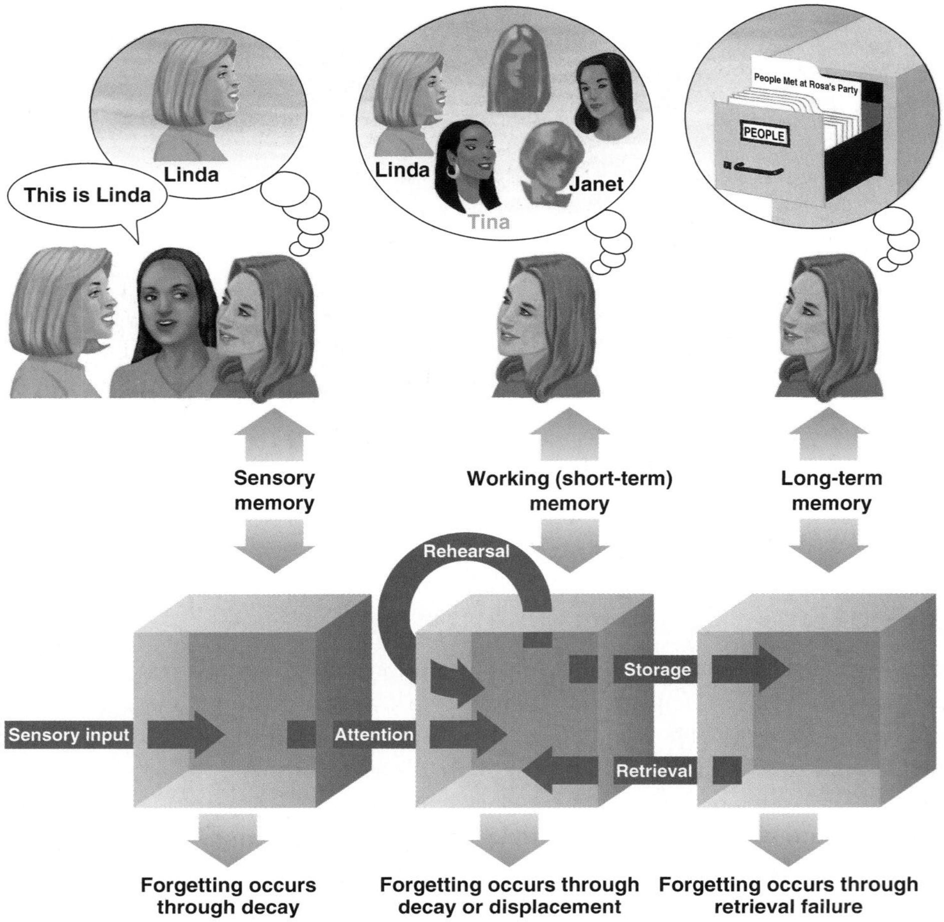

● Figure 12.4
The Structure of Memory

Many psychologists divide memory into three processes or "structures." Sensory information enters the registers of sensory memory, where memory traces are held briefly before decaying. If we attend to the information, much of it is transferred to working memory (also called short-term memory), where it may decay or be displaced if it is not transferred to long-term memory. We usually use rehearsal (repetition) or elaborative strategies to transfer memories to long-term memory. Once in long-term memory, memories can be retrieved through appropriate search strategies. But if information is organized poorly or if we cannot find cues to retrieve it, it may be "lost" for all practical purposes.

See your student companion website for an interactive version of Figure 12.4.

working memory The structure of memory that can hold a sensory stimulus for up to 30 seconds after the trace decays. Also called *short-term memory*.

encode To transform sensory input into a form that is more readily processed.

rehearse Repeat.

to all the senses. For example, when we are introduced to somebody, the trace of the sound of the name also decays, but as we see in the next section, we can maintain the name in memory by focusing on it.

Working Memory (Short-Term Memory)

When children focus their attention on a stimulus in the sensory register, it tends to be retained in **working memory** (also called *short-term memory*) for up to 30 seconds after the trace of the stimulus decays. Ability to maintain information in short-term memory depends on cognitive strategies and on basic capacity to continue to perceive a vanished stimulus. Memory function in middle childhood seems largely adult-like in organization and strategies and shows only gradual improvement in a quantitative sense through early adolescence (Alloway et al., 2004; Archibald & Gathercole, 2006).

Auditory stimuli can be maintained longer in short-term memory than can visual stimuli. For this reason, one strategy for promoting memory is to **encode** visual stimuli as sounds, or auditory stimulation. Then the sounds can be repeated out loud or mentally. For example, in Figure 12.4, mentally repeating the sound of Linda's name helps the other girl remember it. That is, the sounds can be **rehearsed**.

Capacity of Short-Term Memory
The basic capacity of the short-term memory can be described in terms of the number of "bits" or chunks of information that can be kept in memory at once. To remember a new phone number, for example, one must keep seven chunks of information in short-term memory simultaneously; that is, one must rehearse them consecutively.

Classic research shows that the typical adult can keep about seven chunks of information—plus or minus two—in short-term memory at a time (Miller, 1956).

As measured by the ability to recall digits, the typical 5- to 6-year-old can work on two chunks of information at a time. The ability to recall a series of digits improves throughout middle childhood, and adolescents can keep about seven chunks of information in short-term memory at the same time (Chen & Cowan, 2005; Towse & Cowan, 2005; Gathercole et al., 2004b).

The information-processing view focuses on children's capacity for memory and their use of cognitive strategies, such as the way in which they focus their attention (Gathercole et al., 2004a, 2004b). Certain Piagetian tasks require several cognitive strategies instead of one. Young children frequently fail at such tasks because they cannot simultaneously hold many pieces of information in their short-term memories. Put another way, preschoolers can solve problems that have only one or two steps, whereas older children can retain information from earlier steps as they proceed to subsequent steps.

But how do young children remember the alphabet, which is 26 chunks of information? **Truth or Fiction Revisited:** It is not true that learning the alphabet requires keeping 26 chunks of information in mind at once. Children usually learn the alphabet by **rote learning**, simple associative learning based on repetition. After the alphabet is repeated many, many times, M triggers the letter N, N triggers O, and so on. The typical 3-year-old who has learned the alphabet by rote will not be able to answer the question "What letter comes after N?" However, if you recite "H, I, J, K, L, M, N" with the child and then pause, the child is likely to say, "O, P." The 3-year-old probably will not realize that he or she can find the answer by using the cognitive strategy of reciting the alphabet, but many 5- or 6-year-olds will.

Long-Term Memory

Think of **long-term memory** as a vast storehouse of information containing names, dates, places, what Johnny did to you in second grade, what Alyssa said about you when you were 12. Long-term memories may last days, years, or, for practical purposes, a lifetime.

Questions: How much information can be stored in long-term memory? How is it "filed"? There is no known limit to the amount of information that can be stored in long-term memory. From time to time, it may seem that we have forgotten, or lost, a long-term memory, such as the names of elementary or high school classmates. But it is more likely that we simply cannot find the proper cues to help us retrieve the information. It is "lost" in the same way as when we misplace an object but know that it is still in the house. It remains there somewhere for the finding.

How is information transferred from short-term memory to long-term memory? Rehearsal is one method. Older children are more likely than younger children to use rehearsal (Cowan et al., 2003; Saito & Miyake, 2004; Towse & Cowan, 2005). But pure rehearsal, with no attempt to make information meaningful by linking it to past learning, is no guarantee that the information will be stored permanently.

A more effective method than simple rehearsal is to purposefully relate new material to well-known information. Relating new material to well-known material is known as an **elaborative strategy** (Siegler & Alibali, 2005). English teachers encourage children to use new vocabulary words in sentences to help them remember them. This is an example of an elaborative strategy. In this way, children are building extended **semantic codes** that will help them retrieve the words' meanings in the future.

Before we proceed to the next section, here's a question for you. Which of the following words is spelled correctly: *retreival* or *retrieval*? The spellings sound alike, so an acoustic code for reconstructing the correct spelling would not be of help. But a semantic code, such as the spelling rule "*i* before *e* except after *c*," would allow you to reconstruct the correct spelling: retrieval. That is why children are taught rules and principles. Of course, whether these rules are retrieved in the appropriate situation is another issue.

rote learning Learning by repetition.

long-term memory The memory structure capable of relatively permanent storage of information.

elaborative strategy A method for increasing retention of new information by relating it to well-known information.

semantic code A code based on the meaning of information.

Organization in Long-Term Memory

As children's knowledge of concepts advances, the storehouse of their long-term memory becomes gradually organized according to categories. Preschoolers tend to organize their memories by grouping objects that share the same function (Lucariello et al., 2004; Towse, 2003). "Toast" may be grouped with "peanut butter sandwich," because both are edible. Only during the early elementary school years are toast and peanut butter likely to be joined under the concept of food.

When items are correctly categorized in long-term memory, children are more likely to recall accurate information about them. For instance, do you "remember" whether whales breathe underwater? If you did not know that whales are mammals or if you knew nothing about mammals, a correct answer might depend on some remote instance of rote learning. If children have incorrectly classified whales as fish, they might search their "memories" and construct the incorrect answer that whales breathe underwater. Correct categorization, in sum, expands children's knowledge and allows them to retrieve information more readily.

But it has also been shown that when the knowledge of children in a particular area surpasses that of adults, the children show superior capacity to store and retrieve related information. For example, chess experts are superior to amateurs at remembering where chess pieces had been placed on the board (Gobet & Simon, 2000; Saariluoma, 2001). This finding may not surprise you, until you learn that in these studies, the experts were 8- to 12-year-old children and the amateurs were adults.

Development of Recall Memory

Recall memory involves retrieval of information from memory. As children develop, their capacity for recalling information increases (Gathercole et al., 2004a, 2004b). Improvement in memory is linked to their ability to quickly process (i.e., scan and categorize) information. Children's memory is a good overall indicator of their cognitive ability (Towse & Cowan, 2005).

In an experiment on categorization and memory, researchers placed objects that fell into four categories (furniture, clothing, tools, fruit) on a table before second- and fourth-graders (Hasselhorn, 1992). The children were allowed 3 minutes to arrange the pictures as they wished and to remember as many as they could. Fourth-graders were more likely to categorize, and recall, the pictures than second-graders.

Research also reveals that children are more likely to accurately recall information when they are strongly motivated to do so (Roebers et al., 2001). Fear of poor grades can encourage recall even in middle childhood. The promise of rewards also helps.

Development of Metacognition and Metamemory

Question: What do children understand about the functioning of their cognitive processes and, more particularly, their memory? Children's knowledge and control of their cognitive abilities is termed **metacognition**. The development of metacognition is shown by the ability to formulate problems, awareness of the processes required to solve a problem, activation of cognitive strategies, maintaining focus on the problem, and checking answers.

When a sixth-grader decides which homework assignments to do first, memorizes the state capitals for tomorrow's test, and then tests herself to see which ones she needs to study more, she is displaying metacognition. Teaching students metacognitive skills improves their performance in reading and other areas of education (Flavell et al., 2002; Stright et al., 2001).

Metamemory is one aspect of metacognition. It more specifically refers to children's awareness of the functioning of their memory. Older children show greater

metacognition Awareness of and control of one's cognitive abilities, as shown by the intentional use of cognitive strategies in solving problems.

metamemory Knowledge of the functions and processes involved in one's storage and retrieval of information (memory), as shown by use of cognitive strategies to retain information.

insight into how memory works (Towse & Cowan, 2005). For example, young elementary school students frequently announce that they have memorized educational materials before they have actually done so. Older students are more likely to accurately assess their knowledge (Paris & Winograd, 1990). As a result, older children store and retrieve information more effectively than younger children (Siegler & Alibali, 2005).

Older children also show more knowledge of strategies that can be used to facilitate memory. Preschoolers will usually use rehearsal if someone else suggests that they do, but not until about the age of 6 or 7 do children use rehearsal on their own (Flavell et al., 2002). Older elementary school children also become better at adapting their memory strategies to fit the characteristics of the task at hand (Siegler & Alibali, 2005; Towse et al., 2002).

As children develop, they also are more likely to use selective rehearsal to remember important information. That is, they exclude the meaningless mass of perceptions milling about them by confining rehearsal to what they are trying to remember. Selectivity in rehearsal is found more often among adults than among 10-year-olds (Karatekin, 2004).

If you are trying to remember a new phone number, you would know to rehearse it several times or to write it down before setting out to do math problems. However, 5-year-olds, asked whether it would make a difference if they jotted the number down before or after doing the math problems, do not reliably report that doing the problems first would matter. Ten-year-olds, however, are aware that new mental activities (the math problems) can interfere with old ones (memorizing the telephone number) and usually suggest jotting the number down before doing the math problems.

Your metamemory is advanced to the point, of course, where you recognize that it would be poor judgment to read this book while watching *General Hospital* or fantasizing about your next vacation, isn't it?

We have seen that children's memory improves throughout middle childhood. But how good is the memory of children for observed or experienced events? For a discussion of this controversial issue, turn to the nearby "A Closer Look" feature.

Active Review

8. Ability to screen out distractions (Increases or Decreases?) through middle childhood.
9. When children focus on stimuli, they can keep them in _____ memory for about 30 seconds.
10. Children can remember visual stimuli longer when they _____ it as sounds.
11. Repetition of sounds or other stimuli is known as _____ learning.
12. _____ rehearsal is relation of new information to things that are already known.
13. _____ refers to children's awareness of the functioning of their memory processes.

Reflect & Relate: How is information transferred from short-term memory to long-term memory? How is the process analogous to placing information in a computer's "memory" into a computer's "storage" device? What happens if you forget to "save" information in the computer's memory?

Go to

http://www.thomsonedu.com/psychology/rathus

for an interactive version of this review.

A CLOSER LOOK

Children's Eyewitness Testimony

Jean Piaget distinctly "remembered" an attempt to kidnap him from his baby carriage as he was being wheeled along the Champs Élysées. He recalled the excited throng, the abrasions on the face of the nurse who rescued him, the police officer's white baton, and the flight of the assailant. Although they were graphic, Piaget's memories were false. Years later, the nurse admitted that she had made up the tale.

Children are often called on to testify about events they have seen or experienced, often involving child abuse (Koriat et al., 2001). But how reliable is children's testimony?

Even preschoolers can recall and describe personally experienced events, although the accounts may be sketchy (Bruck et al., 2006; Roebers & Schneider, 2002). However, there are many individual differences. Consequently, the child witness is typically asked questions to prompt information. But such questions may be "leading," that is, they may suggest an answer. For example, "What happened at school?" is not a leading question, but "Did your teacher touch you?" is.

Can children's testimony be distorted by leading questions? It appears that by the age of 10 or 11, children are no more suggestible than adults, but younger children are more likely to be misled (Bruck et al., 2006; Krackow & Lynn, 2003).

One hotly debated question is whether children can be led into making false reports of abuse (Krackow & Lynn, 2003). There is no simple answer to this question, as illustrated by a study carried out by Gail Goodman and her colleagues (Goodman & Clarke-Stewart, 1991). They interviewed 5- and 7-year-old girls following a routine medical checkup that included genital and anal exams for half the girls. Most of the children who experienced genital and anal touching failed to mention it

How Reliable Is Children's Eyewitness Testimony?
This question remains hotly debated. By age 10 or 11, children may be no more suggestible than adults. The findings for younger children are inconsistent, however.

Glow Images/Alamy

when simply asked what happened during the exam. But when asked specific leading questions ("Did the doctor touch you there?"), 31 of 36 girls mentioned the experience. Of the 36 girls who did not have genital and anal exams, none reported any such experience when asked what happened during the exam. When asked the leading questions, three falsely reported being touched in these areas, illustrating the dilemma faced by investigators of sexual abuse. Although children may not reveal genital contact until specifically asked, asking may influence some children to give a false report.

Research indicates that repeated questioning may lead children to make up events that never happened to them (Roebers & Schneider, 2002). In one study, preschoolers were questioned each week for 11 weeks about events that either had or had not happened to them (Ceci, 1993). By the 11th week, 58% of the children reported at least one false event as true.

What, then, are investigators to do when the only witnesses to criminal events are children? Maggie Bruck and her colleagues (2006) recommended that interviewers avoid leading or suggestive questions to minimize influencing the child's response. It might also be useful to ask the child whether he or she actually saw what happened or merely heard about it. Young children do not always make this distinction by themselves.

Reflect:

- There are problems in children's eyewitness testimony. What would be lost if we did not allow children's eyewitness testimony? Give examples.

Intellectual Development, Creativity, and Achievement

At an early age, we gain impressions of how intelligent we are compared with other family members and schoolmates. We think of some people as having more **intelligence** than others. We associate intelligence with academic success, advancement on the job, and appropriate social behavior.

Question: What is intelligence? Despite our sense of familiarity with the concept of intelligence, intelligence cannot be seen, touched, or measured physically. For this reason, intelligence is subject to various interpretations. Theories about intelligence are some of the most controversial issues in psychology today.

Psychologists generally distinguish between **achievement** and intelligence. Achievement is what a child has learned, the knowledge and skills that have been gained by experience. Achievement involves specific content areas such as English, history, and math. Educators and psychologists use achievement tests to measure what children have learned in academic areas. The strong relationship between achievement and experience seems obvious. We are not surprised to find that a student who has taken Spanish but not French does better on a Spanish achievement test than on a French achievement test.

The meaning of *intelligence* is more difficult to pin down (Cornoldi, 2006; Fuster, 2005; Sternberg et al., 2005). Most psychologists would agree that intelligence provides the cognitive basis for academic achievement. Intelligence is usually perceived as a child's underlying competence or *learning ability,* whereas achievement involves a child's acquired competencies or *performance.* Most psychologists also would agree that many of the competencies underlying intelligence manifest themselves during middle childhood, when most children are first exposed to formal schooling. Psychologists disagree, however, about the nature and origins of a child's underlying competence or learning ability.

Theories of Intelligence

Let's consider some theoretical approaches to intelligence. Then we see how researchers and practitioners actually assess intellectual functioning.

Factor Theories

Many investigators have viewed intelligence as consisting of one or more major mental abilities, or **factors.** *Question: What are "factor theories" of intelligence?* In 1904, British psychologist Charles Spearman suggested that the various behaviors we consider intelligent have a common, underlying factor: *g,* or "general intelligence." He thought that *g* represented broad reasoning and problem-solving abilities. He supported this view by noting that people who excel in one area generally show the capacity to excel in others. But he also noted that even the most capable people seem more capable in some areas—perhaps in music or business or poetry—than in others. For this reason, he also suggested that *s,* or specific capacities, accounts for a number of individual abilities (Lubinski, 2004).

This view seems to make sense. Most of us know children who are good at math but poor in English and vice versa. Nonetheless, some link—*g*—seems to connect different mental abilities. Few if any people surpass 99% of the population in one mental ability, yet are surpassed by 80% to 90% of the population in other abilities.

To test his views, Spearman developed **factor analysis**, a statistical technique that allows researchers to determine which items on tests seem to be measuring the same things. Researchers continue to find a key role for *g* in performance on many intelligence tests. Some (e.g., Jackson & Rushton, 2006) claim that *g* underlies scores

intelligence A complex and controversial concept, defined by David Wechsler as the "capacity . . . to understand the world [and the] resourcefulness to cope with its challenges." Intelligence implies the capacity to make adaptive choices (from the Latin *inter*, meaning "among," and *legere*, meaning "to choose").

achievement That which is attained by one's efforts and presumed to be made possible by one's abilities.

factor A condition or quality that brings about a result; in this case, "intelligent" behavior. A cluster of related items, such as those found on an intelligence or personality test.

factor analysis A statistical technique that allows researchers to determine the relationships among a large number of items, such as test items.

● **Figure 12.5**
Sternberg's Triarchic Theory of Intelligence

Robert Sternberg views intelligence as three-pronged: as having analytical, creative, and practical aspects.

Analytical intelligence
(academic ability)
Abilities to solve problems, compare and contrast, judge, evaluate, and criticize

Creative intelligence
(creativity and insight)
Abilities to invent, discover, suppose, and theorize

Practical intelligence
("street smarts")
Abilities to adapt to the demands of one's environment and apply knowledge in practical situations

on the verbal and quantitative Scholastic Achievement Tests (SATs), although we can also note that it would be absurd to argue that education has nothing to do with SAT scores. A number of researchers (e.g., Colom et al., 2003; Saggino et al., 2006) claim to have found evidence that connects *g* with *working memory,* that is, the ability to keep various elements of a problem in mind at once. Contemporary psychologists continue to speak of the extent to which a particular test of intellectual ability measures *g* (Lubinski, 2006).

American psychologist Louis Thurstone (1938) used factor analysis and concluded that intelligence consists of several specific factors, which he termed *primary mental abilities,* including visual–spatial abilities, perceptual speed, numerical ability, the ability to learn the meanings of words, ability to bring to mind the right word rapidly, and ability to reason. Thurstone believed that these factors were somewhat independent; therefore, we might be able to rapidly develop lists of words that rhyme but might not be particularly able to solve math problems.

The Triarchic Theory of Intelligence

Psychologist Robert Sternberg (Sternberg, 2000; Sternberg & The Rainbow Project, 2006) constructed a three-pronged, or **triarchic,** theory of intelligence, which is similar to a view proposed by the Greek philosopher Aristotle (Tigner & Tigner, 2000). *Question: What is Sternberg's triarchic model of intelligence?* The three prongs of Sternberg's theory are *analytical intelligence, creative intelligence,* and *practical intelligence* (see ● Figure 12.5).

Analytical intelligence is academic ability. It enables us to solve problems and acquire new knowledge. Creative intelligence is defined by the abilities to cope with novel situations and to profit from experience. Creativity allows us to relate novel situations to familiar situations (i.e., to perceive similarities and differences) and fosters adaptation. Both Aristotle and Sternberg speak of practical intelligence, or "street smarts." Practical intelligence enables people to adapt to the demands of their environment, including the social environment. Psychologists who believe that creativity is separate from analytical intelligence (academic ability) find only small to moderate relationships between academic ability and creativity (Kim, 2005). However, to Sternberg, creativity is a basic facet of intelligence.

The Theory of Multiple Intelligences

Psychologist Howard Gardner (1983, 2006), like Sternberg, believes that intelligence—or intelligences—reflects more than academic ability. *Question: What is meant by multiple intelligences?* Gardner refers to each kind of intelligence in his theory as "an intelligence" because the kinds differ in quality (see ● Figure 12.6). He also believes that each intelligence is based in a different part of the brain.

triarchic Governed by three. Descriptive of Sternberg's view that intellectual functioning has three aspects: analytical intelligence, creative intelligence, and practical intelligence.

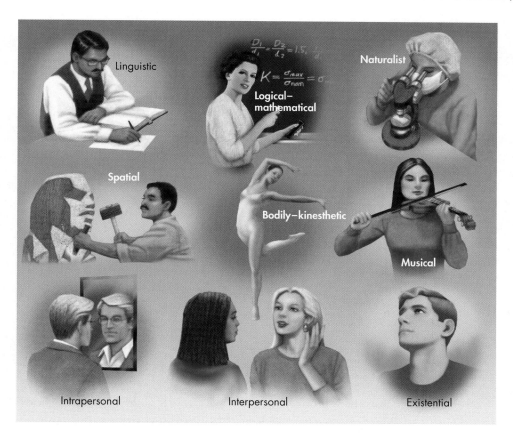

Gardner's Theory of Multiple Intelligences

Howard Gardner argued that there are many intelligences, not just one, including bodily talents as expressed through dancing or gymnastics. Each "intelligence" is presumed to have its neurological base in a different part of the brain. Each is an inborn talent that must be developed through educational experiences if it is to be expressed.

Three of Gardner's intelligences are familiar enough: verbal ability, logical–mathematical reasoning, and spatial intelligence (visual–spatial skills). But Gardner also includes bodily–kinesthetic intelligence (as shown by dancers and gymnasts), musical intelligence, interpersonal intelligence (as shown by empathy and ability to relate to others), and personal knowledge (self-insight). Occasionally, individuals show great "intelligence" in one area, such as the genius of the young Mozart with the piano or the island girl who can navigate her small boat to hundreds of islands by observing the changing patterns of the stars, without notable abilities in others. Gardner (2001) recently added "naturalist intelligence" and "existential intelligence." Naturalist intelligence refers to the ability to look at natural events, such as various kinds of animals and plants or the stars above, and develop insights into their nature and the laws that govern their behavior. Existential intelligence involves dealing with the larger philosophical issues of life. According to Gardner, one can compose symphonies or advance mathematical theory yet be average in, say, language and personal skills. (Are not some academic "geniuses" foolish in their personal lives?)

Critics of Gardner's view agree that people function more intelligently in some areas of life than others. They also agree that many people have special talents, such as bodily–kinesthetic talents, even if their overall intelligence is average. But they question whether such special talents are "intelligences" (Neisser et al., 1996). Language skills, reasoning ability, and ability to solve math problems seem to be more closely related than musical or gymnastic talent to what most people mean by intelligence.

The various theories of intelligence are reviewed in Concept Review 12.2. We do not yet have the final word on the nature of intelligence, but I would like to share with you David Wechsler's definition of intelligence. Wechsler is the originator of the most widely used series of contemporary intelligence tests, and he defined intelligence as the "capacity of an individual to understand the world [and the] resourcefulness to cope with its challenges" (Wechsler, 1975, p. 139). To Wechsler, intelligence involves accurate representation of the world and effective problem solving (adapting to one's

Concept Review 12.2   Theories of Intelligence

Theory	Basic Information	Comments
General versus specific factors (main proponent: Charles Spearman) Archives of the History of American Psychology—The University of Akron	• Spearman created factor analysis to study intelligence • Strong evidence for general factor (*g*) in intelligence • *s* factors are specific abilities, skills, talents	• Concept of *g* remains in use to-day—a century later
Primary mental abilities (proponent: Louis Thurstone) © George Skadding/ Getty Images	• Used factor analysis • Found many "primary" abilities • All abilities/factors academically oriented	• Other researchers (e.g., Guilford) claim to have found hundreds of factors • The more factors claimed, the more they overlap
Triarchic theory (proponent: Robert Sternberg) Courtesy of Robert Sternberg	• Intelligence as three-pronged—with analytical, creative, and prac-tical components • Analytical intelligence analogous to academic ability	• Coincides with views of Aristotle • Critics do not view creativity as a component of intelligence
Multiple intelligences (proponent: Howard Gardner) © 2003 J. Gardner	• Theorized distinct "intelligences" • Includes academic intelligences, personal and social intelligences, talents, and philosophical intelligences • Theorizes different bases in brain for different intelligences	• Continues to expand number of "intelligences" • Critics see little value to theorizing "intelligences" rather than aspects of intelligence • Most critics consider musical and bodily skills to be special talents, not "intelligences"

environment, profiting from experience, selecting the appropriate formulas and strat-egies, and so on).

Measurement of Intellectual Development

There may be disagreements about the nature of intelligence, but thousands of intel-ligence tests are administered by psychologists and educators every day.

The Stanford–Binet Intelligence Scale (SBIS) and the Wechsler scales for pre-school children, school-age children, and adults are the most widely used and well-respected intelligence tests. The SBIS and Wechsler scales yield scores called **intelli-gence quotients (IQs)**. **Truth or Fiction Revisited:** An IQ is in fact a score on a test.

intelligence quotient (IQ) (1) Originally, a ratio obtained by dividing a child's score (or "mental age") on an intel-ligence test by his or her chronological age. (2) In general, a score on an intelli-gence test.

A CLOSER LOOK

Emotional Intelligence and Social Intelligence?

Psychologists Peter Salovey and John Mayer developed the theory of emotional intelligence, which was popularized by *New York Times* writer Daniel Goleman (1995). The theory holds that social and emotional skills are a form of intelligence, just as academic skills are (Barchard & Hakstian, 2004; Mayer et al., 2004; Salovey & Pizarro, 2003). Emotional intelligence bears resemblance to two of Gardner's intelligences: awareness of one's inner feelings and sensitivity to the feelings of others. It also involves recognition and control of one's feelings.

The theory suggests that self-awareness and social awareness are best learned during childhood. Failure to develop emotional intelligence is connected with childhood depression and aggression. Moreover, childhood experiences may even mold the brain's emotional responses to life's challenges. Therefore, it is useful for schools to teach skills related to emotional intelligence as well as academic ability. "I can foresee a day," wrote Goleman (1995), "when education will routinely include [teaching] essential human competencies such as self-awareness, self-control and empathy, and the arts of listening, resolving conflicts and cooperation."

No one argues that self-awareness, self-control, empathy, and cooperation are unimportant. But critics argue that schools may not have the time to teach these skills. Psychologist Robert McCall (1997) wrote, "There are so many hours in a day, and one of the characteristics of American schools is we've saddled them with teaching driver's education, sex education, drug education and other skills, to the point that we don't spend as much time on academics as other countries do. There may be consequences for that."

Is emotional intelligence a form of intelligence? Psychologist Ulric Neisser (1997) wrote, "The skills that Goleman describes . . . are certainly important for determining life outcomes, but nothing is to be gained by calling them forms of intelligence."

Ten years later, Goleman stirred the controversy anew by returning with another best-seller, *Social Intelligence* (2006). This time around, Goleman described how an American commander prevented a confrontation between his troops and an Iraqi mob by ordering the troops to point their rifles at the ground and smile. Although there was a language barrier, the aiming of the weapons downward and the smiles were a form of universal language that was understood by the Iraqis who then smiled back. Conflict was avoided. According to Goleman, the commander had shown social intelligence: the ability to read the Iraqi's social concerns and the ability to solve the social problem by coming up with a useful social response. Social intelligence, like emotional intelligence, also corresponds to Gardner's intelligences, and critics ask whether it brings anything new to the table (Landy, 2006).

Goleman (and Gardner before him) suggests that we may be genetically "prewired" to connect with other people. But some people are better at it than others. Nevertheless, we can all work at developing social intelligence by trying to understanding other people's feelings, seeing things from their points of view, and observing their facial expressions and their tones of voices. The purpose of social intelligence, as Goleman sees it, is not to manipulate other people, but rather to understand them, feel what they are feeling, and develop mutually nourishing relationships with them. Children can be encouraged to develop social intelligence by being asked what their classmates and friends might be thinking in certain situations and to interpret their facial expressions. Parents and teachers can give children practice solving social problems and conflicts in nonaggressive ways.

Reflect:

- Do you think that the concepts of emotional intelligence and social intelligence add anything to Howard Gardner's views? Explain.
- Do emotional intelligence and social intelligence seem like kinds of intelligence to you or like something else? Explain.
- You tell someone "I don't think there's any such thing as social intelligence" and the other person says, "Oh, you don't think it's important to understand how other people feel?" How do you respond?

The concept of intelligence per se is more difficult to define. The SBIS and Wechsler scales have been carefully developed and revised over the years. Each of them has been used to make vital educational decisions about children. In many cases, children whose test scores fall below or above certain scores are placed in special classes for mentally retarded or gifted children.

It must be noted just as emphatically that each test has been accused of discriminating against ethnic minorities (such as African American children and Latino and Latina American children), the foreign-born, and the children of socially and economically disadvantaged people (Harris et al., 2003; Maynard et al., 2005). Because of the controversy surrounding IQ tests, important decisions about children should not be made on the basis of a single test score. Decisions about children should be made on the basis of a battery of tests given by a qualified psychologist in the student's native language, and in consultation with the student's family, teachers, and, when appropriate, social agencies.

Question: What is the Stanford–Binet Intelligence Scale (SBIS)?

The Stanford–Binet Intelligence Scale

The SBIS originated in the work of Frenchmen Alfred Binet and Theodore Simon about a century ago. The French public school system sought an instrument to identify children who were unlikely to profit from the regular classroom so that they could receive special attention. The Binet–Simon scale came into use in 1905. Since then, it has undergone revision and refinement.

Binet assumed that intelligence increased with age. Therefore, older children should get more items right. Thus, Binet arranged a series of questions in order of difficulty, from easier to harder. Items that were answered correctly by about 60% of the children at a given age level were considered to reflect intellectual functioning at that age. It was also required that the questions be answered correctly by fewer children who were a year younger and by a greater number of children who were a year older.

The Binet–Simon scale yielded a score called a **mental age (MA)**. The MA shows the intellectual level at which a child is functioning. A child with an MA of 6 is functioning, intellectually, like the average 6-year-old child. In taking the test, children earned months of credit for each correct answer. Their MA was determined by adding the months of credit they attained.

Louis Terman adapted the Binet–Simon scale for use with American children. Because Terman carried out his work at Stanford University, he renamed the test the Stanford–Binet Intelligence Scale. The first version of the SBIS was published in 1916. The SBIS yielded an intelligence quotient, or IQ, rather than an MA. The SBIS today can be used with children from the age of 2 onward up to adults. ■ Table 12.2 shows the kinds of items that define typical performance at various ages.

The IQ states the relationship between a child's mental age and his or her actual or **chronological age (CA).** The ratio reflects that the same MA score has different meanings for children of different ages. That is, an MA of 8 is an above-average score for a 6-year-old but a below-average score for a 10-year-old.

The IQ is computed by the formula

$$IQ = \frac{\text{Mental Age (MA)}}{\text{Chronological Age (CA)}} \times 100$$

mental age (MA) The accumulated months of credit that a person earns on the Stanford–Binet Intelligence Scale.

chronological age (CA) A person's age.

According to this formula, a child with an MA of 6 and a CA of 6 would have an IQ of 100. Children who can handle intellectual problems and older children will have IQs above 100. For instance, an 8-year-old who does as well on the SBIS as the average 10-year-old will attain an IQ of 125. Children who do not answer as many items correctly as other children of their age will attain MAs that are lower than their CAs. Their IQ scores will be below 100.

■ **Table 12.2** Items Similar to Those on the Stanford–Binet Intelligence Scale

Age	Item
2 years	1. Children show knowledge of basic vocabulary words by identifying parts of a doll, such as the mouth, ears, and hair.
	2. Children show counting and spatial skills along with visual–motor coordination by building a tower of four blocks to match a model.
4 years	1. Children show word fluency and categorical thinking by filling in the missing words when they are asked questions such as "Father is a man; mother is a _____?" and "Hamburgers are hot; ice cream is _____?"
	2. Children show comprehension by answering correctly when they are asked questions such as "Why do people have automobiles?" and "Why do people have medicine?"
9 years	1. Children can point out verbal absurdities, as in this question: "In an old cemetery, scientists unearthed a skull which they think was that of George Washington when he was only 5 years of age. What is silly about that?"
	2. Children display fluency with words, as shown by answering questions such as "Can you tell me a number that rhymes with snore?" and "Can you tell me a color that rhymes with glue?"
Adult	1. Adults show knowledge of the meanings of words and conceptual thinking by correctly explaining the differences between word pairs such as "sickness and misery," "house and home," and "integrity and prestige."
	2. Adults show spatial skills by correctly answering questions such as "If a car turned to the right to head north, in what direction was it heading before it turned?"

Truth or Fiction Revisited: It is true that two children can answer exactly the same items on an intelligence test correctly, yet one can be above average in intelligence and the other below average. When we consider each child's chronological age, we see that the younger of the two children obtains a higher intelligence test score.

Today, IQ scores on the SBIS are derived by comparing children's and adults' performances with those of other people of the same age. People who get more items correct than average attain IQ scores above 100, and people who answer fewer items correctly attain scores below 100. But again, if two children answer exactly the same items correctly, the younger of the two will obtain the higher score.

Question: How do the Wechsler scales differ from the Stanford–Binet test?

The Wechsler Scales

David Wechsler (1975) developed a series of scales for use with school-age children (Wechsler Intelligence Scale for Children; WISC), younger children (Wechsler Preschool and Primary Scale of Intelligence; WPPSI), and adults (Wechsler Adult Intelligence Scale; WAIS). These tests have been repeatedly revised. For example, the current version of the WISC is the WISC–IV, and it is available both in Spanish and English.

The Wechsler scales group test questions into subtests (such as those shown in ■ Table 12.3). Each subtest measures a different intellectual task. For this reason, the test compares a person's performance on one type of task (such as defining words)

■ **Table 12.3** Kinds of Items Found on Wechsler's Intelligence Scales

Verbal Items	Nonverbal–Performance Items
Information: "What is the capital of the United States?" "Who was Shakespeare?"	Picture completion: Pointing to the missing part of a picture.
Comprehension: "Why do we have ZIP codes?" "What does 'A stitch in time saves 9' mean?"	Picture arrangement: Arranging cartoon pictures in sequence so that they tell a meaningful story.
Arithmetic: "If 3 candy bars cost 25 cents, how much will 18 candy bars cost?"	Block design: Copying pictures of geometric designs using multicolored blocks.
Similarities: "How are good and bad alike?" "How are peanut butter and jelly alike?"	Object assembly: Putting pieces of a puzzle together so that they form a meaningful object.
Vocabulary: "What does canal mean?"	Coding: Rapid scanning and drawing of symbols that are associated with numbers.
Digit span: Repeating a series of numbers, presented by the examiner, forward and backward.	Mazes: Using a pencil to trace the correct route from a starting point to home.

Note: Items for verbal subtests are similar but not identical to actual test items on the Wechsler intelligence scales.

with another (such as using blocks to construct geometric designs). The Wechsler scales thus suggest children's strengths and weaknesses and provide overall measures of intellectual functioning.

Wechsler described some subtests as measuring verbal tasks and others as assessing performance tasks. In general, verbal subtests require knowledge of verbal concepts, whereas performance subtests (see ● Figure 12.7) require familiarity with spatial-relations concepts. Wechsler's scales permit the computation of verbal and performance IQs. Nontechnically oriented college students often obtain higher verbal than performance IQs.

● Figure 12.8 indicates the labels that Wechsler assigned to various IQ scores and the approximate percentages of the population who attain IQ scores at those levels. As you can see, most children's IQ scores cluster around the average. Only about 5% of the population have IQ scores above 130 or below 70.

Question: Many psychologists and educators consider standard intelligence tests to be culturally biased. What is that controversy about?

The Testing Controversy

I was almost one of the testing casualties. At 15 I earned an IQ test score of 82, three points above the track of the special education class. Based on this score, my counselor suggested that I take up brick-laying because I was "good with my hands." My low IQ, however, did not allow me to see that as desirable.

—Williams (1974, p. 32)

This ironic testimony, offered by African American psychologist Robert Williams, echoes the sentiments of many psychologists. Most psychologists and educational specialists consider intelligence tests to be at least somewhat biased against African Americans and members of lower social classes (Snyderman & Rothman, 1990). To fill in a bit more historical background, let's note that during the 1920s, intel-

Picture arrangement

These pictures tell a story, but they are in the wrong order. Put them in the right order so that they tell a story.

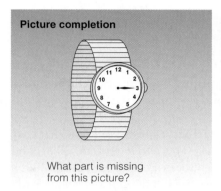

Picture completion

What part is missing from this picture?

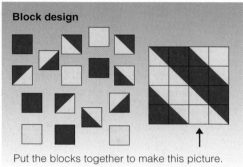

Block design

Put the blocks together to make this picture.

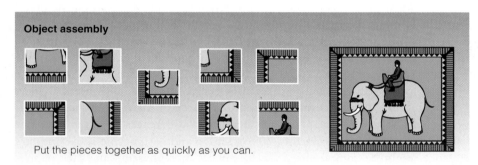

Object assembly

Put the pieces together as quickly as you can.

● **Figure 12.7**
Performance Items on an Intelligence Test

This figure shows a number of items that resemble those found on the Wechsler Intelligence Scale for Children.

See your student companion website for an interactive version of Figure 12.7.

ligence tests were used to prevent many Europeans and others from immigrating to the United States. For example, testing pioneer H. H. Goddard assessed 178 newly arrived immigrants at Ellis Island and claimed that most of the Hungarians, Italians, and Russians were "feeble-minded." It was apparently of little concern to Goddard that these immigrants, by and large, did not understand English, the language in

● **Figure 12.8**
Variations in IQ Scores

IQ scores vary according to a bell-shaped, or "normal," curve. Scores tend to bunch around the central score (100) and then to decrease in frequency as they move upward and downward.

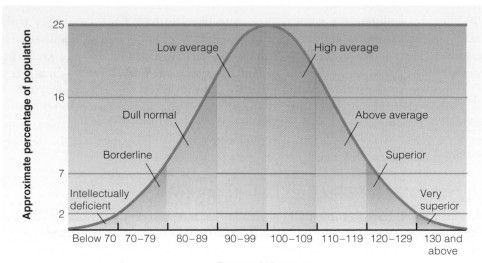

Approximate percentage of population

25 — 16 — 7 — 2

Low average   High average
Dull normal   Above average
Borderline   Superior
Intellectually deficient   Very superior

Below 70 70–79 80–89 90–99 100–109 110–119 120–129 130 and above

Range of IQ scores

● **Figure 12.9**   Sample Items from Cattell's Culture-Fair Intelligence Test

Culture-fair tests attempt to exclude items that discriminate on the basis of cultural background rather than intelligence.

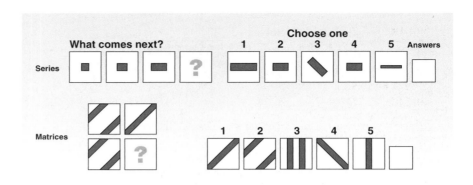

which the tests were administered! Because of a history of abuse of intelligence testing, some states have outlawed the use of IQ tests as the sole standard for placing children in special-education classes.

On the other hand, supporters of standard intelligence tests point out that they appear to do a good job of measuring Spearman's *g* (Frey & Detterman, 2004) and cognitive skills that are valued in modern high-tech societies (Maynard et al., 2005). The vocabulary and arithmetic subtests on the Wechsler scales, for example, clearly reflect achievement in language arts and computational ability. Although the broad types of achievement measured by these tests reflect intelligence, they might also reflect cultural familiarity with the concepts required to answer questions correctly. In particular, the tests seem to reflect middle-class European American culture in the United States (Maynard et al., 2005; Okazaki & Sue, 2000).

If scoring well on intelligence tests requires a certain type of cultural experience, the tests are said to have a **cultural bias.** Children reared in African American neighborhoods could be at a disadvantage, not because of differences in intelligence but because of cultural differences (Helms, 2006). Latino and Latina American children's performance might be compromised by differences in motivation and lack of self-confidence on intelligence tests (Stevens et al., 2006). For this reason, psychologists have tried to construct **culture-free** or culture-fair intelligence tests.

Some tests do not rely on expressive language at all. For example, Raymond Cattell's (1949) Culture-Fair Intelligence Test evaluates reasoning ability through the child's comprehension of the rules that govern a progression of geometric designs, as shown in ● Figure 12.9.

Unfortunately, culture-free tests have not lived up to their promise. First, middle-class children still outperform lower-class children on them (Rushton et al., 2003). Middle-class children, for example, are more likely to have basic familiarity with materials such as blocks and pencils and paper. They are more likely than disadvantaged children to have arranged blocks into various designs (a practice relevant to the Cattell test). Second, culture-free tests do not predict academic success as well as other intelligence tests, and scholastic aptitude remains the central concern of educators.

Might there be no such thing as a culture-free intelligence test? Motivation to do well, for example, might be a cultural factor. Because of lifestyle differences, some children from low-income families in the United States might not share the motivation of middle-class children to succeed on tests (Keogh & Whyte, 2006).

Patterns of Intellectual Development

Sometimes you have to run rapidly to stay in the same place, at least in terms of taking intelligence tests. That is, the "average" taker of an intelligence test obtains an IQ score of 100. However, as childhood progresses that person must answer more questions correctly to obtain the same score. Even though his or her intelligence is "devel-

cultural bias A factor hypothesized to be present in intelligence tests that provides an advantage for test takers from certain cultural or ethnic backgrounds but that does not reflect true intelligence.

culture-free Descriptive of a test in which cultural biases have been removed. On such a test, test takers from different cultural backgrounds would have an equal opportunity to earn scores that reflect their true abilities.

oping" at a typical pace, he or she continues to obtain the same score. *Question: Putting test scores aside, how does intelligence develop?*

Rapid advances in intellectual functioning occur during childhood. Within a few years, children gain the ability to symbolize experiences and manipulate symbols to solve increasingly complex problems. Their vocabularies leap, and their sentences become more complex. Their thought processes become increasingly logical and abstract, and they gain the capacity to focus on two or more aspects of a problem at once.

Intellectual growth seems to occur in at least two major spurts. The first growth spurt occurs at about the age of 6. This spurt coincides with entry into a school system and also with the shift from preoperational to concrete-operational thought. The school experience may begin to help crystallize intellectual functioning at this time. The second spurt occurs at about age 10 or 11.

Once they reach middle childhood, however, children appear to undergo relatively more stable patterns of gains in intellectual functioning, although there are still spurts (Deary et al., 2004). As a result, intelligence tests gain greater predictive power. In a classic study by Marjorie Honzik and her colleagues (1948), intelligence test scores taken at the age of 9 correlated strongly (+0.90) with scores at the age of 10 and more moderately (+0.76) with scores at the age of 18. Testing at age 11 even shows a moderate to high relationship with scores at the age of 77 (Deary et al., 2004).

Despite the increased predictive power of intelligence tests during middle childhood, individual differences exist. In the classic Fels Longitudinal Study (see ● Figure 12.10), two groups of children (Groups 1 and 3) made reasonably consistent gains in intelligence test scores between the ages of 10 and 17, whereas three groups showed declines. Group 4, children who had shown the most intellectual promise at age 10, went on to show the most precipitous decline, although they still wound up in the highest 2% to 3% of the population (McCall et al., 1973). Many factors influence changes in intelligence test scores, including changes in the child's home environment, social and economic circumstances, educational experiences, even B vitamins such as folic acid (Deary et al., 2004).

Although intelligence test scores change throughout childhood, many children show reasonably consistent patterns of below-average or above-average performance. In the next section, we discuss children who show consistent patterns of extreme scores, low and high.

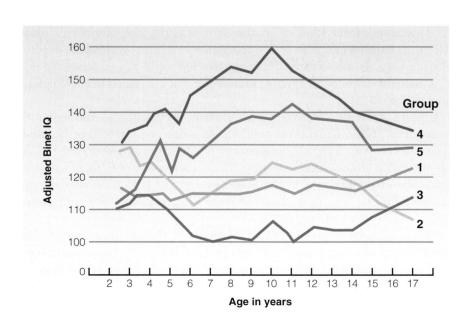

● **Figure 12.10** Five Patterns of Change in IQ Scores for Children in the Fels Longitudinal Study

In the Fels Longitudinal Study, IQ scores remained stable between the ages of 2½ and 17 for only one of five groups, Group 1.

Source: McCall et al. (1973).

Differences in Intellectual Development

The average IQ score in the United States is close to 100. About half the children in the United States attain IQ scores in the broad average range from 90 to 110 (see Figure 12.8). Nearly 95% attain scores between 70 and 130. But what of the other 5%? Children who attain IQ scores below 70 are generally labeled "intellectually deficient" or "mentally retarded." Children who attain scores of 130 or above are usually labeled "gifted." These labels—these verbal markers of extreme individual differences—lead to certain expectations of children. Ironically, the labels can place heavy burdens on children and parents.

Mental Retardation

Question: What is mental retardation? According to the American Association on Intellectual and Developmental Disabilities (AAIDD, 2007), "Mental retardation is a disability characterized by significant limitations both in intellectual functioning and in adaptive behavior as expressed in conceptual, social, and practical adaptive skills." Mental retardation involves an IQ score of no more than 70 to 75.

Most of the children (more than 80%) who are retarded are mildly retarded. Mildly retarded children, as the term implies, are the most capable of adjusting to the demands of educational institutions and, eventually, to society at large. Many mildly retarded children are mainstreamed in regular classrooms, as opposed to being placed in special-needs classes.

Children with Down syndrome are most likely to fall within the moderately retarded range. Moderately retarded children can learn to speak, dress, feed, and clean themselves, and, eventually, engage in useful work under supportive conditions, as in a sheltered workshop. However, they usually do not acquire skills in reading and arithmetic. Severely and profoundly retarded children may not acquire speech and self-help skills and may remain highly dependent on others for survival throughout their lives.

What causes retardation? Some of the causes of retardation are biological. Retardation, for example, can stem from chromosomal abnormalities, such as Down syndrome; genetic disorders, such as phenylketonuria (PKU); and brain damage (AAIDD, 2007). Brain damage can have many origins, including accidents during childhood and problems during pregnancy. For example, maternal alcohol abuse, malnutrition, or diseases during pregnancy can lead to retardation in the fetus.

There is also **cultural–familial retardation,** in which the child is biologically normal but does not develop age-appropriate behaviors at the normal pace because of social isolation of one kind or another. For example, the later-born children of impoverished families may have little opportunity to interact with adults or play with stimulating toys. As a result, they may not develop sophisticated language skills or the motivation to acquire the kinds of knowledge that are valued in a technologically oriented society.

Naturally, we wish to encourage all children to develop to the maximum of their capacities, including retarded children. As a rule of thumb, keep in mind that IQs are scores on tests. They are not perfectly reliable, meaning that they can and do change somewhat from testing to testing. Thus, it is important to focus on children's current levels of achievement in the academic and self-help skills that we wish to impart; by doing so, we can try to build these skills gradually and coherently, step by step.

Children with cultural–familial retardation can change dramatically when we provide enriched learning experiences, especially at early ages. Head Start programs, for example, have enabled children at cultural–familial risk to function at above-average levels.

cultural–familial retardation Substandard intellectual performance that is presumed to stem from lack of opportunity to acquire the knowledge and skills considered important within a cultural setting.

Giftedness

Question: What does it mean to be gifted? Giftedness involves more than excellence on the tasks provided by standard intelligence tests. In determining who is gifted, most educators include children who have outstanding abilities; are capable of high performance in a specific academic area, such as language or mathematics; or who show creativity, leadership, distinction in the visual or performing arts, or bodily talents, as in gymnastics and dancing. Sternberg (2007) presents a "WICS" model of giftedness, which is a play on the letters in the WISC–IV. Sternberg describes giftedness as involving wisdom, intelligence, and creativity synthesized (assembled together). He claims that giftedness basically involves expertise. In gifted children, it involves expertise in development.

Question: What are the socioeconomic and ethnic differences in intelligence? As you can see in the nearby "Developing in a World of Diversity" feature, there are also socioeconomic and ethnic differences in IQ.

Creativity and Intellectual Development

Question: What is creativity? To illustrate something about the nature of creativity, let me ask you a rather ordinary question: What does the word *duck* mean? Now let me ask you a somewhat more interesting question: How many meanings can you find for the word *duck*? Arriving at a single correct answer to the question might earn you points on an intelligence test. Generating many answers to the question, as we will see, may be a sign of creativity as well as of the knowledge of the meaning of words.

Creativity is the ability to do things that are novel and useful (Sternberg, 2007). Creative children and adults can solve problems to which there are no preexisting solutions, no tried and tested formulas (Mumford, 2003; Simonton, 2006). Creative children share a number of qualities (Milgram & Livne, 2006; Sternberg, 2006; Sternberg & Lubart, 1995, 1996):

- They take chances. (They may use sentence fragments in essays, and they may color outside the lines in their coloring books.)
- They refuse to accept limitations and try to do the impossible.
- They appreciate art and music (which sometimes leaves them out among their peers).
- They use the materials around them to make unique things.
- They challenge social norms. (Creative children are often independent and nonconformist, but independence and nonconformity do not necessarily make a child creative. Creative children may be at odds with their teachers because of their independent views. Faced with the task of managing large classes, teachers often fall into preferences for quiet, submissive, "good" children.)
- They take unpopular stands (which sometimes gives them the appearance of being oppositional, when they are expressing their genuine ideas and feelings).
- They examine ideas that other people accept at face value. (They come home and say, "_____ said that yada yada. What's that all about?")

A professor of mine once remarked that there is nothing new under the sun, only new combinations of existing elements. Many psychologists agree. They see creativity as the ability to make unusual, sometimes remote, associations to the elements of a problem to generate new combinations. An essential aspect of a creative response is the leap from the elements of the problem to the novel solution. A predictable solution is not creative, even if it is hard to reach.

creativity The ability to generate novel solutions to problems. A trait characterized by flexibility, ingenuity, and originality.

Question: What is the relationship between creativity and intelligence? The answer to this question depends on how one defines intelligence. If one accepts Sternberg's model, creativity is one of three aspects of intelligence (along with analytical thinking and practical intelligence). From this perspective, creativity overlaps with intelligence. **Truth or Fiction Revisited:** However, otherwise it is not necessarily true that highly intelligent children are creative.

Some scientists argue that creativity and innovation require high levels of general intelligence (Heilman et al., 2003), but the tests we use to measure intelligence and creativity tend to show only a moderate relationship between global intelligence test scores and measures of creativity (Simonton, 2006; Sternberg & Williams, 1997). In terms of Gardner's theory of multiple intelligences, we can note that some children who have only average intellectual ability in some areas, such as logical analysis, can excel in areas that are considered more creative, such as music or art.

convergent thinking A thought process that attempts to focus in on the single best solution to a problem.

Children mainly use convergent thinking to arrive at the correct answers on intelligence tests. In **convergent thinking,** thought is limited to present facts; the problem solver narrows his or her thinking to find the best solution. (A child uses convergent thinking to arrive at the right answer to a multiple-choice question or to a question on an intelligence test.)

Developing in a World of Diversity

Socioeconomic and Ethnic Differences in IQ

What is your own ethnic background? Are there any stereotypes about how people from your ethnic background perform in school or on IQ tests? If so, what is your reaction to these stereotypes? Why?

Research suggests that differences in IQ exist between socioeconomic and ethnic groups. Lower-class American children obtain IQ scores some 10 to 15 points lower than those obtained by middle- and upper-class children. African American children tend to obtain IQ scores some 15 points lower than those obtained by their European American peers (Neisser et al., 1996). Latino and Latina American and Native American children also tend to score below the norms for European Americans (Neisser et al., 1996).

Several studies of IQ have confused social class with ethnicity because larger proportions of African Americans, Latino and Latina Americans, and Native Americans have lower socioeconomic status (Neisser et al., 1996). When we limit our observations to particular ethnic groups, we still find an effect for social class. That is, middle-class European Americans outscore lower-class

Who's Smart?
Asian children and Asian American children frequently outscore other American children on intelligence tests. Can we attribute the difference to genetic factors or to Asian parents' emphasis on acquiring cognitive skills?

European Americans. Middle-class African Americans, Latino and Latina Americans, and Native Americans also outscore their less affluent counterparts.

Research has also suggested possible cognitive differences between Asians and Caucasians. Youth of Asian descent, for example, frequently outscore youth of European backgrounds on achievement tests in math and science, including the math portion of the SAT (Dandy & Nettelbeck, 2002; Stevenson et al., 1993). Asian Americans are more likely than European Americans, African Americans, and Latino and Latina Americans to graduate from high school and complete college (Sue & Okazaki, 1990). Asian Americans are highly overrepresented in competitive U.S. colleges and universities.

Attributions for success may also be involved. Research shows that Asian students and their mothers

Creative thinking tends to be divergent rather than convergent (Vartanian et al., 2003). In **divergent thinking,** the child associates freely to the elements of the problem, allowing "leads" to run a nearly limitless course. (Children use divergent thinking when they are trying to generate ideas to answer an essay question or to find keywords to search on the Internet.) Tests of creativity determine how flexible, fluent, and original a person's thinking is. Here, for example, is an item from a test used to measure associative ability, a factor in creativity (Getzels & Jackson, 1962): "Write as many meanings as you can for each of the following words: (a) duck; (b) sack; (c) pitch; (d) fair." Those who write several meanings for each word, rather than only one, are rated as potentially more creative.

Another measure of creativity might ask children to produce as many words as possible that begin with T and end with N within a minute. Still another item might give people a minute to classify a list of names in as many ways as possible. In how many ways can you classify the following group of names?

Martha   Paul   Jeffry   Sally   Pablo   Joan

Sometimes, arriving at the right answer involves both divergent and convergent thinking. When presented with a problem, a child may first use divergent thinking to generate many possible solutions to the problem. Convergent thinking may then be used to select likely solutions and reject others.

divergent thinking
A thought process that attempts to generate multiple solutions to problems. Free and fluent association to the elements of a problem.

(continued)

tend to attribute academic successes to hard work (Randel et al., 2000). American mothers, in contrast, are more likely to attribute children's academic successes to "natural" ability (Basic Behavioral Science Task Force, 1996). Asians are more likely to believe that they can work to make good scores happen.

Stanley Sue and Sumie Okazaki (1990) argue that because Asian Americans have been discriminated against in blue-collar careers, they have come to emphasize the value of education. This finding also holds true in Australia (Dandy & Nettelbeck, 2002). In Japan, emphasis on succeeding through hard work is illustrated by the increasing popularity of cram schools, or *juku,* which prepare Japanese children for entrance exams to private schools and colleges (Ruiz & Tanaka, 2001). More than half of all Japanese schoolchildren are enrolled in these schools, which meet after the regular school day is

over. Looking to other environmental factors, Laurence Steinberg and his colleagues (1996) claimed that parental encouragement and supervision in combination with peer support for academic achievement partially explain the superior performances of European Americans and Asian Americans compared with African Americans and Latino and Latina Americans.

Psychologist Richard Nisbett (2005) argues that continuing to believe that European Americans are superior to African Americans in intelligence ignores evidence about the alterability of African American children's IQ scores by early education programs and the results of adoptee studies. Robert Sternberg and his colleagues (2005) argue that as long as there remains a dispute as to what intelligence *is,* the attempt to relate intelligence to ethnicity makes no sense.

Reflect:
• *In my classes, many European American students are willing to believe that they are smarter than African American students for genetic reasons. However, they believe that if Asian students are smarter than they are, it is because the Asian students work harder. How would you explain that difference?*

• *If one ethnic group is smarter, on average, than another, does that make them "better"?*

• *To say that one ethnic group is genetically smarter than another, do we have to be able to point to the genes that are responsible? Explain.*

• *Do you think we should be conducting research into the relationships between ethnicity and intelligence? Explain.*

Intelligence tests such as the Stanford–Binet and Wechsler scales require children to focus in on the single right answer. On intelligence tests, ingenious responses that differ from the designated answers are marked wrong. Tests of creativity, by contrast, are oriented toward determining how flexible and fluent one's thinking can be. Such tests include items such as suggesting improvements or unusual uses for a familiar toy or object, naming things that belong in the same class, producing words similar in meaning, and writing different endings for a story.

Determinants of Intellectual Development

Questions: What are the roles of nature (heredity) and nurture (environmental influences) on the development of intelligence? No research strategy for attempting to ferret out genetic and environmental determinants of IQ is flawless (McLafferty, 2006; Moore, 2007). Still, a number of ingenious approaches have been devised. The evidence provided through these approaches is instructive.

Genetic Influences

Various strategies have been devised for research into genetic factors, including kinship studies and studies of adopted children.

If heredity is involved in human intelligence, closely related people ought to have more similar IQs than distantly related or unrelated people, even when they are reared separately. ● Figure 12.11 shows the averaged results of more than 100 studies of IQ and heredity in human beings (T. J. Bouchard et al., 1990). The IQ scores of identical (monozygotic; MZ) twins are more alike than the scores for any other pairs, even when the twins have been reared apart. The average correlation for MZ twins reared together is +0.85; for those reared apart, it is +0.67. Correlations between the IQ scores of fraternal (dizygotic; DZ) twins, siblings, and parents and children are generally comparable, as is their degree of genetic relationship. The correlations tend to vary from about +0.40 to +0.59. Correlations between the IQ scores of children and their natural parents (+0.48) are higher than those between children and adoptive parents (+0.18). **Truth or Fiction Revisited:** Actually, adopted children are more similar in intelligence to their biological parents than to their adoptive parents, which is suggestive of the role of genetic factors in intellectual functioning.

All in all, studies suggest that the **heritability** of intelligence is between 40% and 60% (T. J. Bouchard et al., 1990; Neisser et al., 1996). In other words, about

heritability The degree to which the variations in a trait from one person to another can be attributed to, or explained by, genetic factors.

● **Figure 12.11**
Findings of Studies of the Relationship Between IQ Scores and Heredity

The data are a composite of studies summarized in *Science* magazine (T. J. Bouchard et al., 1990). By and large, correlations grow stronger for persons who are more closely related. Persons reared together or living together have more similar IQ scores than persons reared or living apart. Such findings support both genetic and environmental hypotheses of the origins of intelligence.

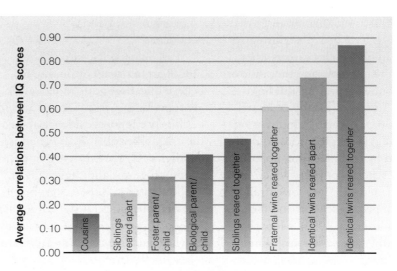

half the variations (the technical term is *variance*) in IQ scores can be accounted for by heredity. It is not the same as saying that you inherited about half of your intelligence. The implication of such a statement would be that you "got" the other half of your intelligence somewhere else. Rather, it means that about half of the difference between your IQ score and the IQ scores of other people can be explained in terms of genetic factors.

Let's return to Figure 12.11 for a moment. Note that genetic pairs (such as MZ twins) reared together show higher correlations between IQ scores than similar genetic pairs (such as other MZ twins) who were reared apart. This finding holds for MZ twins, siblings, parents, children, and unrelated people. For this reason, the same group of studies that suggests that heredity plays a role in determining IQ scores also suggests that the environment plays a role.

When children are separated from their biological parents at early ages, one can argue that strong relationships between their IQ scores and those of their natural parents reflect genetic influences. Strong relationships between their IQs and those of their adoptive parents, on the other hand, might reflect environmental influences. Classic projects involving adopted children in Colorado, Texas, and Minnesota (Coon et al., 1990; Scarr, 1993; Turkheimer, 1991) have found a stronger relationship between the IQ scores of adopted children and their biological parents than between the IQ scores of adopted children and their adoptive parents.

These studies, then, also point to a genetic influence on intelligence. Nevertheless, the environment also has an effect.

Environmental Influences

Studies of environmental influences on IQ use several research strategies, including discovering situational factors that affect IQ scores, exploring children's abilities to rebound from early deprivation, and exploring the effects of positive early environments.

In some cases, we need look no further than the testing situation to explain some of the discrepancy between the IQ scores of middle-class children and those of children from economically disadvantaged backgrounds. In one study (Zigler et al., 1982), the examiner simply made children as comfortable as possible during the test. Rather than being cold and impartial, the examiner was warm and friendly, and care was taken to see that the children understood the directions. As a result, the children's test anxiety was markedly reduced and their IQ scores were 6 points higher than those for a control group treated in a more indifferent manner. Disadvantaged children made relatively greater gains from the procedure. By doing nothing more than making testing conditions more optimal for all children, we can narrow the IQ gap between low-income and middle-class children.

Stereotype vulnerability is another aspect of the testing situation, and it also affects test scores. For example, African American and Latino and Latina American children may carry an extra burden on intelligence tests (Inzlicht & Good, 2006). They may worry that they risk confirming their group's negative stereotype by doing poorly. Their concern may create anxiety, which can distract them from the questions, hurting their scores.

In Chapter 7, we discussed a longitudinal study of retarded orphanage children that provided striking evidence that children can recover from early deprivation. In the orphanage, 19-month-old children were placed with surrogate mothers who provided a great deal of intellectual and social stimulation. Four years later, the children showed dramatic gains in IQ scores.

Children whose parents are responsive and provide appropriate play materials and varied experiences during the early years attain higher IQ and achievement test scores (Bradley, 2006). Graduates of Head Start and other preschool programs show significant gains in later educational outcomes (Phillips & Styfco, 2007).

Although kinship studies and studies of adoptees suggest that there is a genetic influence on intelligence, they also suggest a role for environmental influences. For example, an analysis of a large number of twin and kinship studies showed that the older twins and other siblings become, the less alike they are on various measures of intelligence and personality (McCartney et al., 1990). This finding appears to be due to increasing exposure to different environments and experiences outside the family.

Studies of adopted children also indicate the importance of environment. African American children who were adopted during the first year by European American parents who were above average in income and education showed IQ scores that were 15 to 25 points higher than those attained by African American children reared by their biological parents (Scarr & Weinberg, 1976). The adopted children's average IQ scores, about 106, remained somewhat below those of their adoptive parents' natural children, about 117 (Scarr & Weinberg, 1977). Even so, the adoptive early environment closed a good deal of the IQ gap. Many psychologists believe that heredity and environment interact to influence intelligence (Lubinski & Benbow, 2000; Winner, 2000). An impoverished environment may prevent some children from living up to their potential. An enriched environment may encourage others to realize their potential, minimizing possible differences in heredity.

Perhaps we need not be concerned with how much of a person's IQ is due to heredity and how much is due to environmental influences. Psychology has traditionally supported the dignity of the individual. It might be more appropriate for us to try to identify children of all races whose environments place them at high risk for failure and to do what we can to enrich them.

Active Review

14. Spearman suggested that the behaviors we consider intelligent have a common factor, which he labeled _____.

15. Gardner argues for the existence of _____ intelligences, each of which is based in a different area of the brain.

16. The IQ states the relationship between a child's _____ age and chronological age.

17. The Wechsler scales have subtests that assess _____ tasks and performance tasks.

18. If scoring well on an IQ test requires a certain type of cultural experience, the tests are said to have a cultural _____.

19. The first spurt in intellectual growth occurs at about the age of _____.

20. Lower-class children in the United States obtain IQ scores some _____ points lower than those obtained by middle- and upper-class children.

21. Children tend to use (Convergent or Divergent?) thinking when they are thinking creatively.

22. Studies find that there is a stronger relationship between the IQ scores of adopted children and their (Adoptive or Biological?) parents than between the IQ scores of adopted children and their (Adoptive or Biological?) parents.

Reflect & Relate: As you look back on your own childhood, can you point to any kinds of family or educational experiences that seem to have had an effect on your intellectual development? Would you say that your background, overall, was deprived or enriched? In what ways?

Go to

http://www.thomsonedu.com/psychology/rathus

for an interactive version of this review.

Language Development and Literacy

Question: How does language develop in middle childhood? Children's ability to understand and use language becomes increasingly sophisticated in middle childhood. Children learn to read as well. Many children are exposed to a variety of linguistic experiences other than standard English, and these experiences have important ramifications for language development. In this section, we examine each of these topics.

Vocabulary and Grammar

By the age of 6, the child's vocabulary has expanded to 10,000 words, give or take a few thousand. By 7 to 9 years of age, most children realize that words can have different meanings, and they become entertained by riddles and jokes that require semantic sophistication. (Remember the jokes at the beginning of the chapter?) By the age of 8 or 9, children are able to form "tag questions," in which the question is tagged on to the end of a declarative sentence (Weckerly et al., 2004). "You want more ice cream, don't you?" and "You're sick, aren't you?" are examples of tag questions.

Children also make subtle advances in articulation and in the capacity to use complex grammar. For example, preschool-age children have difficulty understanding passive sentences such as "The truck was hit by the car," but children in the middle years have less difficulty interpreting the meanings of passive sentences (Aschermann et al., 2004).

During these years, children develop the ability to use connectives, as illustrated by the sentence "I'll eat my spinach, but I don't want to." They also learn to form indirect object–direct object constructions (e.g., "She showed her sister the toy").

Reading Skills and Literacy

In many ways, reading is a key to unlocking the benefits society has to offer. Good readers find endless pleasure in literature, reading and rereading favorite poetic passages. Reading makes textbook learning possible. Reading also permits us to identify subway stops, to consider the contents of food packages, to assemble barbecue grills and children's swing sets, and to learn how to use a microcomputer.

As you can see in ■ Table 12.4, millions of people around the world are not literate and therefore cannot enjoy many of the benefits of contemporary knowledge

■ **Table 12.4** Literacy Rates of 15- to 24-Year-Olds, 2000–2004

Region/Nation	Total	Men	Women
Europe	99.4	99.4	99.3
Northern Africa	78.5	84.1	72.5
Sub-Saharan Africa	76.6	81.0	72.3
Latin America and the Caribbean	94.7	94.2	95.2
Eastern Asia	98.9	99.2	98.6
Southern Asia	72.3	81.5	62.5
Southeastern Asia	95.4	96.0	94.9
United States	97.0	97.0	97.0
Western Asia	85.6	84.4	78.1

Sources: Central Intelligence Agency (2004) and United Nations Statistics Division (2004).

Reading
Children who read at home during the school years show better reading skills in school and more positive attitudes toward reading.

and society. Even in the United States, millions of people cannot read or write even brief sentences, and the problem is most severe among recent immigrants. According to the U.S. Bureau of Labor Statistics (U.S. Department of Labor, 2004), more than 280,000 teachers are working to teach people, age 15 to 25, to read. Most Americans, fortunately, learn to read when they enter school. *Question: What cognitive skills are involved in reading?*

Integration of Auditory and Visual Information

Reading is a complex process that depends on perceptual, cognitive, and linguistic processes (Smolka & Eviatar, 2006). It relies on skills in the integration of visual and auditory information. Accurate awareness of the sounds in the child's language is an extremely important factor in subsequent reading achievement (Caravolas & Bruck, 2000; Dufva et al., 2001). Reading also requires the ability to make basic visual discriminations (Levinthal & Lleras, 2007). In reading, for example, children must "mind their *p*'s and *q*'s." That is, to recognize letters, children must be able to perceive the visual differences between letters such as *b* and *d* and *p* and *q*.

During the preschool years, neurological maturation and experience combine to allow most children to make visual discriminations between different letters with relative ease. Those children who can recognize and name the letters of the alphabet by kindergarten age are better readers in the early school grades (Siegler & Alibali, 2005).

How do children become familiar with their own written languages? More and more today, American children are being exposed to TV programs such as *Sesame Street,* but these are relatively recent educational innovations. Children are also exposed to books, street signs, names of stores and restaurants, and the writing on packages, especially at the supermarket. Some children, of course, have more books in the home than others do. Children from affluent homes where books and other sources of stimulation are plentiful learn to read more readily than children from impoverished homes. But regardless of income level, reading storybooks with parents in the preschool years helps prepare a child for reading (Dockett et al., 2006; Raikes et al., 2006). Children who read at home during the school years also show better reading skills in school and more positive attitudes toward reading.

Methods of Teaching Reading

When they read, children integrate visual and auditory information (they associate what they see with sounds), whether they are reading by the word-recognition method or the phonetic method. If they are using the **word-recognition method,** they must be able to associate visual stimuli such as *cat* and *Robert* with the sound combinations that produce the spoken words "cat" and "Robert." This capacity is usually acquired by rote learning, or extensive repetition.

In the **phonetic method,** children first learn to associate written letters and letter combinations (such as *ph* or *sh*) with the sounds they are meant to indicate. Then they sound out words from left to right, decoding them. The phonetic method has the obvious advantage of giving children skills that they can use to decode (read) new words (Bastien-Toniazzo & Jullien, 2001; Murray, 2006). However, some children learn more rapidly at early ages through the word-recognition method. The phonetic method can also slow them down when it comes to familiar words. Most children and adults, in fact, tend to read familiar words by the word-recognition method (regardless of the method of their original training) and to make some effort to sound out new words.

Which method is superior? A controversy rages over the issue, and we cannot resolve it here. But let us note that some words in English can be read only by the

word-recognition method A method for learning to read in which children come to recognize words through repeated exposure to them.

phonetic method A method for learning to read in which children decode the sounds of words based on their knowledge of the sounds of letters and letter combinations.

word-recognition method. For example, consider the words *one* and *two.* This method is useful when it comes to words such as *danger, stop, poison,* and the child's name, because it helps provide children with a basic **sight vocabulary.** But decoding skills must be acquired so that children can read new words on their own.

Diversity of Children's Linguistic Experiences in the United States: Ebonics and Bilingualism

Some children in the United States are exposed to nonstandard English. Others are exposed to English plus a second language. Let's explore their linguistic experiences.

Ebonics

Question: What is Ebonics? The term *Ebonics* is derived from the words *ebony* and *phonics.* It was coined by the African American psychologist Robert Williams. Ebonics was previously called Black Vernacular English or Black Dialect (Fasold, 2006).

Ebonics has taken hold most strongly in working-class African American neighborhoods. According to linguists, Ebonics is rooted in the remnants of the West African dialects used by slaves. It reflects attempts by the slaves, who were denied formal education, to imitate the speech of the dominant European American culture. Some observers believe that Ebonics uses verbs haphazardly, downgrading standard English. As a result, some school systems react to the concept of Ebonics with contempt, which is hurtful to the child who speaks Ebonics. Other observers say that Ebonics has different grammatical rules than standard English but that the rules are consistent and allow for complex thought (Fasold, 2006).

"To Be or Not to Be": Use of Verbs in Ebonics
The use of verbs is different in Ebonics and standard English (Bohn, 2003). For example, the Ebonics usage "She-ah touch us" corresponds to the standard English "She will touch us." The Ebonics "He be gone" is the equivalent of the standard English "He has been gone for a long while." "He gone" is the same as "He is not here right now" in standard English.

Consider the rules in Ebonics that govern the use of the verb *to be.* In standard English, *be* is part of the infinitive form of the verb and is used to form the future tense, as in "I'll be angry tomorrow." Thus, "I *be* angry" is incorrect. But in Ebonics, *be* refers to a continuing state of being. The Ebonics sentence "I be angry" is the same as the standard English "I have been angry for a while" and is grammatically correct.

Ebonics leaves out forms of *to be* in cases in which standard English would use a contraction. For example, the standard "She's the one I'm talking about" could be "She the one I talking about" in Ebonics. Ebonics also often drops *-ed* from the past tense and lacks the possessive *'s.*

"Not to Be or Not to Be Nothing": Negation in Ebonics
Consider the sentence "I don't want no trouble," which is, of course, commendable. Middle-class European American children would be corrected for using double negation (*don't* along with *no*) and would be encouraged to say "I don't want *any* trouble." Yet double negation is acceptable in Ebonics (Pinker, 1994).

Some African American children are bicultural and bilingual (Delpit, 2006; Rickford, 2006). They function competently within the dominant culture in the United States and among groups of people from their own ethnic background. They use standard English in a conference with their teacher or in a job interview, but switch to Ebonics with their friends.

© Tony Freeman/PhotoEdit

Ebonics in the Classroom
Ebonics is spoken by many African American children. The major differences between Ebonics and standard English lie in the use of verbs.

sight vocabulary Words that are immediately recognized on the basis of familiarity with their overall shapes, rather than decoded.

Bilingualism: Linguistic Perspectives on the World

Most people throughout the world speak two or more languages. Most countries have minority populations whose languages differ from the national tongue. Nearly all Europeans are taught English and the languages of neighboring nations. Consider the Netherlands. There, Dutch is the native tongue, but all children are also taught French, German, and English and are expected to become fluent in each of them.

In 2000, approximately 47 million Americans spoke a language other than English at home (Shin & Bruno, 2003; see ■ Table 12.5). Spanish, Chinese, Korean, or Russian is spoken in the home and, perhaps, the neighborhood. *Question: What does research reveal about the advantages and disadvantages of bilingualism?*

Truth or Fiction Revisited: It is not true that bilingual children encounter more academic problems than children who speak only one language. Nevertheless, a century ago it was widely believed that children reared in bilingual homes were retarded in their cognitive and language development. The theory was that mental capacity is limited, so people who store two linguistic systems are crowding their mental abilities. It is true that there is some "mixing" of languages by bilingual children (Gonzalez, 2005), but they can generally separate the two languages from an early age. At least half the children in the United States who speak Spanish in the home are proficient in both languages (Shin & Bruno, 2003). In fact, many children who speak Spanish in the home and English in school come to prefer to read in English because they are taught to read in English (Brenneman et al., 2007).

■ **Table 12.5** Languages Most Often Spoken at Home According to English Ability for Population 5 Years of Age and Above

Language Spoken at Home	Total	English-Speaking Ability (Percents)			
		Very Well	Well	Not Well	Not at All
Spanish	28,101,052	51.1%	20.1%	18.0%	9.9%
Chinese	2,022,143	42.3%	29.4%	20.2%	8.0%
French	1,643,838	74.8%	16.4%	8.4%	0.5%
German	1,382,613	78.1%	15.9%	5.8%	0.3%
Tagalog	1,224,241	67.6%	25.4%	6.5%	0.4%
Vietnamese	1,009,627	33.9%	33.7%	26.8%	5.5%
Italian	1,008,370	69.5%	19.4%	9.8%	1.2%
Korean	894,063	40.4%	30.0%	25.5%	4.0%
Russian	706,242	43.2%	29.6%	21.2%	6.2%
Polish	667,414	58.1%	25.1%	14.2%	2.6%
Arabic	614,582	65.6%	22.8%	9.5%	2.0%
Portuguese	564,630	56.8%	22.2%	16.0%	5.0%
Japanese	477,997	50.6%	30.7%	17.6%	1.2%
French Creole	453,368	54.2%	26.9%	15.7%	3.2%
Greek	365,436	71.9%	17.8%	9.1%	1.2%
Hindi	317,057	77.3%	16.4%	5.3%	1.0%
Persian	312,085	63.5%	22.7%	10.6%	3.3%
Urdu	262,900	68.5%	21.6%	7.9%	2.0%

Source: Adapted from U.S. Census Bureau (2007).

Moreover, analysis of older studies in bilingualism shows that the observed bilingual children often lived in poor families and received little education (Gonzalez, 2005). Yet these bilingual children were compared with middle-class monolingual children. In addition, achievement and intelligence tests were conducted in the monolingual child's language, which was the second language of the bilingual child. Lack of education and inadequate testing methods, rather than bilingualism per se, accounted for the apparent differences in achievement and intelligence.

Today most linguists consider it advantageous for children to be **bilingual**. Knowledge of more than one language expands children's awareness of different cultures and broadens their perspectives (Macrory, 2006). There is evidence that bilingualism contributes to the complexity of the child's cognitive processes (Bialystok & Craik, 2007; Gort, 2006). For example, bilingual children are more likely to understand that the symbols used in language are arbitrary. Monolingual children are more likely to think erroneously that the word *dog* is somehow intertwined with the nature of the beast. Bilingual children therefore have somewhat more cognitive flexibility.

Richard Levine/Alamy

Bilingualism

Most people throughout the world speak two or more languages. It was once thought that children reared in bilingual homes were retarded in their cognitive and language development, but today most linguists consider it advantageous for children to be bilingual.

bilingual Using or capable of using two languages with nearly equal or equal facility.

Active Review

23. Reading relies on skills in the integration of _____ and auditory information.
24. In using the _____ method of reading, children associate written letters and letter combinations (such as *ph* or *sh*) with the sounds they indicate.
25. Bilingual children generally (Can or Cannot?) separate the two languages at an early age.
26. Today most linguists consider it a(n) (Advantage or Disadvantage?) to be bilingual.

Reflect & Relate: Did you grow up speaking a language other than English in the home? If so, what special opportunities and problems were connected with the experience?

Go to

http://www.thomsonedu.com/psychology/rathus

for an interactive version of this review.

1. **What is meant by the stage of concrete operations?**

In the stage of concrete operations, children begin to show the capacity for adult logic with tangible objects. Concrete-operational thinking is characterized by reversibility, flexibility, and decentration. Concrete-operational children show understanding of conservation, transitivity, and class inclusion.

2. **Can we apply Piaget's theory of cognitive development to educational practices?**

Piaget believed that learning involves active discovery. Thus, teachers should not impose knowledge on the child but find materials to interest and stimulate the child. Instruction should be geared to the child's level of development.

3. **How does Piaget view the development of moral reasoning?**

Piaget theorized two stages of moral development: moral realism and autonomous morality. The earlier stage emerges at about the age of 5 and judges behavior as right when it conforms to rules. Five-year-olds see rules as embedded in the structure of things and believe in immanent justice. Preoperational children focus on one dimension at a time; for example, they focus on the amount of damage and not the intentions of the wrongdoer. Children begin to show autonomous morality in middle childhood. At that time, they view social rules as agreements that can be changed.

4. **What is Kohlberg's theory of moral development?**

Kohlberg believed that there are three levels of moral development and two stages within each level. In the preconventional level, children base moral judgments on the consequences of behavior. In the conventional level, right and wrong are judged by conformity to conventional standards. In the postconventional level, moral reasoning is based on one's own values.

5. **What is the difference between Piaget's view of cognitive development and the information-processing approach?**

Information-processing theorists aim to learn how children store, retrieve, and manipulate information, how their "mental programs" develop. One key cognitive process is selective attention—attending to the relevant features of a task—which advances steadily through middle childhood.

6. **What is meant by the term *memory*?**

Memory refers to the storage and retrieval of information. Many psychologists divide memory functioning into three major processes: sensory memory, working memory, and long-term memory. Maintenance of information in working memory depends on cognitive strategies such as encoding and rehearsing stimuli. Older children process information more efficiently.

7. **How much information can be stored in long-term memory? How is it "filed"?**

There is no known limit to the capacity of long-term memory. Information is transferred from short-term memory to long-term memory by rehearsal and elaboration. Children organize their long-term memory into categories. Correct categorization expands knowledge and allows for efficient retrieval.

8. **What do children understand about the functioning of their cognitive processes and, more particularly, their memory?**

Awareness and conscious control of cognitive abilities is termed metacognition, as evidenced by ability to formulate problems, awareness of how to solve them, use of rules and strategies, ability to remain focused, and ability to check answers. Metamemory refers to children's awareness of the workings of their memory. By age 6 or 7, children know to use rehearsal to remember things.

9. **What is intelligence?**

Intelligence provides the basis for academic achievement. It is a child's underlying competence or learning ability.

10. **What are "factor theories" of intelligence?**

Spearman suggested that the behaviors we consider intelligent have a common, underlying factor: *g*. But *s*, or specific capacities, accounts for some individual abilities. Thurstone used factor analysis to define several primary mental abilities.

11. **What is Sternberg's triarchic model of intelligence?**

Sternberg proposes a three-pronged theory of intelligence, including analytical intelligence (academic ability), creative intelligence, and practical intelligence ("street smarts").

12. **What is meant by *multiple intelligences*?**

Gardner believes that people have multiple "intelligences," each of which is based in a different part of the brain. Some of these—verbal ability, logical–mathematical reasoning, and spatial intelligence—involve academic ability. Others—for example, bodily–kinesthetic intelligence, musical intelligence, interpersonal intelligence, and personal knowledge—strike other psychologists as special talents or other skills.

13. **What is the Stanford–Binet Intelligence Scale (SBIS)?**

The SBIS assumes that intelligence increases with age, so older children must answer more items correctly than younger children to obtain a comparable score, which Binet referred to as a mental age (MA). A comparison of a child's mental age with his or her chronological age (CA)—(MA/CA) multiplied by 100—yields an intelligence quotient (IQ). The average IQ score is defined as 100.

14. **How do the Wechsler scales differ from the Stanford–Binet test?**

The Wechsler scales group test questions into subtests that measure different types of intellectual tasks. Some tasks are mainly verbal, whereas others rely more on spatial-relations skills. Wechsler innovated a deviation IQ.

15. **Many psychologists and educators consider standard intelligence tests to be culturally biased. What is that controversy about?**

Most psychologists and educational specialists believe that intelligence tests are at least somewhat biased against African Americans and members of lower social classes. In addition to underlying competence, the tests reflect knowledge of the language and culture in which the test is administered along with motivation to succeed on them.

16. **Putting test scores aside, how does intelligence develop?**

During middle childhood, thought processes become more logical and abstract. Children gain the capacity to focus on two or more aspects of a problem at once. The first intellectual spurt occurs at about the age of 6 and coincides with entry into school. The second spurt occurs at age 10 or 11. Intelligence tests gain greater predictive power during middle childhood.

17. **What is mental retardation?**

Mental retardation refers to limitations in intellectual functioning that are characterized by an IQ score of no more than 70 to 75. Some causes of retardation are biological, but there is also cultural–familial retardation.

18. **What does it mean to be gifted?**

Giftedness involves outstanding abilities, high performance in a specific academic area, such as language or mathematics, or leadership, distinction in the arts, or bodily talents. Gifted children tend to be successful as adults.

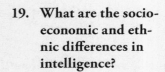

19. **What are the socio-economic and ethnic differences in intelligence?**

Lower-class children in the United States obtain lower IQ scores than more affluent children. Children from most ethnic minority groups obtain IQ scores below those obtained by European Americans. But Asian Americans tend to outscore European Americans.

20. **What is creativity?**

Creativity is the ability to do things that are novel and useful. Creative children take chances, refuse to accept limitations, and appreciate art and music.

21. **What is the relationship between creativity and intelligence?**

The relationship between intelligence test scores and measures of creativity are only moderate. Children mainly use convergent thinking to arrive at the correct answers on intelligence tests. Creative thinking tends to be divergent rather than convergent.

22. **What are the roles of nature (heredity) and nurture (environmental influences) on the development of intelligence?**

The closer the relationship between people, the more alike their IQ scores. The IQ scores of adopted children are more like those of their biological parents than those of their adoptive parents. Research also finds situational influences on IQ scores, including motivation, familiarity with testing materials, and the effects of enriched environments.

23. **How does language develop in middle childhood?**

In middle childhood, language use becomes more sophisticated, including understanding that words can have multiple meanings. There are advances in articulation and use of grammar.

24. **What cognitive skills are involved in reading?**

Reading relies on skills in the integration of visual and auditory information. During the preschool years, neurological maturation and experience combine to allow most children to make visual discriminations between letters with relative ease.

25. **What is Ebonics?**

Ebonics derives from the words ebony and phonics and refers to what was previously called Black Vernacular English. Ebonics has different grammatical rules than standard English, but the rules are consistent and allow for complex thought.

26. **What does research reveal about the advantages and disadvantages of bilingualism?**

Research shows that children can generally separate two languages from an early age and that most Americans who first spoke another language in the home also speak English well. Knowledge of more than one language expands children's knowledge of different cultures.

Key Terms

concrete operations, 396
reversibility, 396
decentration, 396
transitivity, 398
seriation, 398
class inclusion, 399
moral realism, 402

objective morality, 402
immanent justice, 402
autonomous morality, 402
preconventional level, 405
conventional level, 405
postconventional level, 406
information processing, 406

memory, 407
sensory memory, 407
sensory register, 407
working memory, 408
encode, 408
rehearse, 408
rote learning, 409

long-term memory, 409
elaborative strategy, 409
semantic code, 409
metacognition, 410
metamemory, 410
intelligence, 413
achievement, 413
factor, 413

factor analysis, 413
triarchic, 414
intelligence quotient (IQ), 416
mental age (MA), 418
chronological age (CA), 418
cultural bias, 422
culture-free, 422
cultural–familial retardation, 424

creativity, 425
convergent thinking, 426
divergent thinking, 427
heritability, 428
word-recognition method, 432
phonetic method, 432
sight vocabulary, 433
bilingual, 435

Active Learning Resources

Childhood & Adolescence Book Companion Website

http://www.thomsonedu.com/psychology/rathus

Visit your book companion website where you will find more resources to help you study. There you will find interactive versions of your book features, including the Lessons in Observation video, Active Review sections, and the Truth or Fiction feature. In addition, the companion website contains quizzing, flash cards, and a pronunciation glossary.

Thomson NOW! is an easy-to-use online resource that helps you study in less time to get the grade you want—NOW.

http://www.thomsonedu.com/login

Need help studying? This site is your one-stop study shop. Take a Pre-Test and ThomsonNOW will generate a Personalized Study Plan based on your test results. The Study Plan will identify the topics you need to review and direct you to online resources to help you master those topics. You can then take a Post-Test to determine the concepts you have mastered and what you still need to work on.

13

Middle Childhood:
Social and Emotional Development

Truth or Fiction?

T F Children's self-esteem tends to rise in middle childhood. p. 446

T F Parents who are in conflict should stay together "for the sake of the children." p. 454

T F The daughters of employed women are more achievement oriented and set higher career goals for themselves than the daughters of unemployed women. p. 455

T F In middle childhood, popular children tend to be attractive and relatively mature for their age. p. 456

T F Teachers who have higher expectations of students may elicit greater achievements from them. p. 462

T F Some children—like some adults—blame themselves for all the problems in their lives, whether they deserve the blame or not. p. 467

T F It is better for children with school phobia to remain at home until the origins of the problem are uncovered and resolved. p. 470

Preview

Theories of Social and Emotional Development in Middle Childhood
Psychoanalytic Theory
Social Cognitive Theory
Cognitive-Developmental Theory and Social Cognition
Development of the Self-Concept in Middle Childhood
Lessons in Observation: Self-Concept

The Family
Parent–Child Relationships
Lesbian and Gay Parents
A Closer Look: How to Answer a 7-Year-Old's Questions about—Gulp—Sex
Generation X or Generation Ex? What Happens to Children Whose Parents Get Divorced?
The Effects of Maternal Employment

Peer Relationships
Peers as Socialization Influences
Peer Acceptance and Rejection
Development of Friendships

The School
Entry into School: Getting to Know You
A Closer Look: Bullying: An Epidemic of Misbehavior and Fear
The School Environment: Setting the Stage for Success, or . . .
Teachers: Setting Limits, Making Demands, Communicating Values, and—Oh, Yes—Teaching

Social and Emotional Problems
Conduct Disorders
Childhood Depression
Childhood Anxiety
Developing in a World of Diversity: Problems? No Problem. (For Some Children)

Ariel Skelley/Getty Images

 Go to

http://www.thomsonedu.com/psychology/rathus
for an interactive version of this "Truth or Fiction" feature.

college student taking a child development course had the following conversation with a 9-year-old girl named Karen:

Student: Karen, how was school today?
Karen: Oh, it was all right. I don't like it a lot.
Student: How come?
Karen: Sara and Becky won't talk to me. I told Sara I thought her dress was very pretty, and she pushed me out of the way. That made me so mad.
Student: That wasn't nice of them.
Karen: No one is nice except for Amy. At least she talks to me.

Here is part of a conversation between a different college student and her 9-year-old cousin Sue:

Sue: My girl friend Heather in school has the same glasses as you. My girl friend, no, not my girl friend—my friend—my friend picked them up yesterday from the doctor, and she wore them today.
Student: What do you mean—not your girl friend, but your friend? Is there a difference?
Sue: Yeah, my friend. 'Cause Wendy is my girl friend.
Student: But what's the difference between Heather, your friend, and Wendy, your girl friend?
Sue: Well, Wendy is my best friend, so she's my girl friend. Heather isn't my best friend, so she's just a friend.

—Adapted from Rowen (1973)

In the years between 6 and 12, the child's social world expands. As illustrated by the remarks of these 9-year-old girls, peers take on greater importance and friendships deepen (Hamm, 2000). Entry into school exposes the child to the influence of teachers and to a new peer group. Relationships with parents change as children develop greater independence. Some children will face adjustments resulting from the divorce and remarriage of parents. During these years, major advances occur in children's ability to understand themselves. Their knowledge of social relationships and their skill in developing such relationships increase as well (Collins, 1984; Davis, 2001). Some children, unfortunately, develop problems during these years, although some are able to cope with life's stresses better than others.

In this chapter, we discuss each of these areas. First, we examine major theories of social and emotional development in the middle years. Next we examine the development of self-concept and the development of relationships with parents and peers. Then we turn to the influences of the school. Finally, we look at some of the social and emotional problems that can arise in middle childhood.

Theories of Social and Emotional Development in Middle Childhood

Question: What are some features of social and emotional development in middle childhood? The major theories of personality have had less to say about this age group than about the other periods of childhood and adolescence. Nevertheless, common threads emerge. They include the development of skills, the importance of interpersonal relationships, and the expansion of self-understanding.

Psychoanalytic Theory

According to Sigmund Freud, children in the middle years are in the **latency stage.** Freud believed that sexual feelings remain repressed (unconscious) during this period. Children use this period to focus on developing intellectual, social, and other culturally valued skills.

Erik Erikson, like Freud, sees the major developmental task of middle childhood as the acquisition of cognitive and social skills. Erikson labels this stage **industry versus inferiority.** Children who are able to master the various tasks and challenges of the middle years develop a sense of industry or competence. Children who have difficulties in school or with peer relationships may develop a sense of inferiority.

Development of Skills
According to psychoanalytic theory, the major development task of middle childhood is to acquire cognitive, social, physical, and other culturally valued skills. Children who develop valued skills tend to have high self-esteem and to be admired by peers.

Social Cognitive Theory

Social cognitive theory focuses on the continued importance of rewards and modeling in middle childhood. During these years, children depend less on external rewards and punishments and increasingly regulate their own behavior (Crain, 2000).

How do children acquire moral and social standards for judging their own behavior? One mechanism is direct reward and punishment. For example, parents may praise a child when she shares her toys with her younger brother. In time, she incorporates the importance of sharing into her own value system.

Another mechanism for acquiring self-evaluative standards is modeling. Children in the middle years are exposed to an increasing variety of models. Not only parents but also teachers, other adults, peers, and symbolic models (such as TV characters or the heroine in a story) can serve as influential models (Anderson et al., 2007; Bandura, 2002; Oates & Messer, 2007).

Cognitive-Developmental Theory and Social Cognition

Cognitive-developmental theory stresses the importance of the child's growing cognitive capacities. According to Jean Piaget, middle childhood coincides with the stage of concrete operations and is partly characterized by a decline in egocentrism and an expansion of the capacity to view the world and oneself from other people's perspectives. This cognitive advance not only enhances the child's intellectual functioning but also has a major effect on the child's social relationships (Mischo, 2004; Zan & Hildebrandt, 2003).

Question: What is the relationship between social cognition and perspective taking? **Social cognition** refers to the development of children's knowledge about the social world. It focuses on the child's understanding of the relationship between the self and others. A key aspect of the development of social cognition is the ability to assume the role or perspective of another person. Robert Selman and his colleagues (Selman, 1980; Selman & Dray, 2006) devised a method to study the development of perspective-taking skills in childhood. Selman (1980, p. 36) presented children with a social dilemma such as the following:

> Holly is an 8-year-old girl who likes to climb trees. She is the best tree climber in the neighborhood. One day while climbing down from a tall tree, she falls off the bottom branch but does not hurt herself. Her father sees her fall. He

latency stage In psychoanalytic theory, the fourth stage of psychosexual development, characterized by repression of sexual impulses and development of skills.

industry versus inferiority The fourth stage of psychosocial development in Erikson's theory, occurring in middle childhood. Mastery of tasks leads to a sense of industry, whereas failure produces feelings of inferiority.

social cognition Development of children's understanding of the relationship between the self and others.

■ **Table 13.1** Levels of Perspective Taking

Level	Approximate Age (Years)	What Happens
0	3–6	Children are egocentric and do not realize that other people have perspectives different from their own. A child of this age will typically say that Holly will save the kitten because she likes kittens and that her father will be happy because he likes kittens too. The child assumes that everyone feels as she does.
1	5–9[a]	Children understand that people in different situations may have different perspectives. The child still assumes that only one perspective is "right." A child might say that Holly's father would be angry if he did not know why she climbed the tree. But if she told him why, he would understand. The child recognizes that the father's perspective may differ from Holly's because of lack of information. But once he has the information, he will assume the "right" (i.e., Holly's) perspective.
2	7–12[a]	The child understands that people may think or feel differently because they have different values or ideas. The child also recognizes that others are capable of understanding the child's own perspective. Therefore, the child is better able to anticipate reactions of others. The typical child of this age might say that Holly knows that her father will understand why she climbed the tree and that he therefore will not punish her.
3	10–15[a]	The child finally realizes that both she and another person can consider each other's point of view at the same time. The child may say something similar to this reasoning: Holly's father will think that Holly shouldn't have climbed the tree. But now that he has heard her side of the story, he would feel that she was doing what she thought was right. Holly realizes that her father will consider how she felt.
4	12 and above[a]	The child realizes that mutual perspective taking does not always lead to agreement. The perspectives of the larger social group also must be considered. A child of this age might say that society expects children to obey their parents and therefore that Holly should realize why her father might punish her.

Source: Selman (1976).

[a]Ages may overlap.

is upset and asks her to promise not to climb trees any more. Holly promises. Later that day, Holly and her friends meet Sean. Sean's kitten is caught up in a tree and can't get down. Something has to be done right away, or the kitten may fall. Holly is the only one who climbs trees well enough to reach the kitten and get it down, but she remembers her promise to her father.

The children then were asked a series of questions designed to test their ability to take the role of another person (e.g., "How will Holly's father feel if he finds out she climbed the tree?"). Based on the children's responses to these questions, Selman (1976) described five levels of perspective-taking skills in childhood (see ■ Table 13.1).

Research supports Selman's developmental progression in perspective taking (De Lisi, 2005; Mischo, 2005; Nakkula & Nikitopoulos, 2001). Children with better perspective-taking skills tend to be more skilled at negotiating and peer relations (Fitzgerald & White, 2003; Selman & Dray, 2006; Strough et al., 2001).

Development of the Self-Concept in Middle Childhood

Question: How does the self-concept develop during middle childhood? In early childhood, children's self-concepts, or self-definitions, focus on concrete external traits, such as appearance, activities, and living situations. But as children undergo the cognitive developments of middle childhood, their more abstract internal traits, or personality characteristics, begin to play a role in their self-definition. Social relationships and group memberships take on significance (Damon, 2000; Harter, 2006; Thompson, 2006).

An investigative method called the Twenty Statements Test bears out this progression and also highlights the relationships between the self-concept and general cognitive development. According to this method, children are given a sheet of paper with the question "Who am I?" and 20 spaces in which to write answers. Consider the answers of a 9-year-old boy and an 11-year-old girl:

The nine-year-old boy: My name is Bruce C. I have brown eyes. I have brown hair. I have brown eyebrows. I'm 9 years old. I LOVE? sports. I have 7 people in my family. I have great? eye site. I have lots! of friends. I live on 1923 Pinecrest Drive. I'm going on 10 in September. I'm a boy. I have a uncle that is almost 7 feet tall. My school is Pinecrest. My teacher is Mrs. V. I play hockey! I'm also the smartest boy in the class. I LOVE! food. I love fresh air. I LOVE school.

The eleven-year-old girl: My name is A. I'm a human being. I'm a girl. I'm a truthful person. I'm not pretty. I do so-so in my studies. I'm a very good cellist. I'm a very good pianist. I'm a little bit tall for my age. I like several boys. I like several girls. I'm old fashioned. I play tennis. I am a very good musician. I try to be helpful. I'm always ready to be friends with anybody. Mostly I'm good, but I lose my temper. I'm not well liked by some girls and boys. I don't know if boys like me or not.

—Montemayor & Eisen (1977, pp. 317–318)

Only the 9-year-old lists his age and address, discusses his family, and focuses on physical traits, such as eye color, in his self-definition. The 9-year-old mentions his likes, which can be considered rudimentary psychological traits, but they are tied to the concrete, as would be expected of a concrete-operational child.

The 9- and 11-year-olds both list their competencies. The 11-year-old's struggle to bolster her self-esteem—her insistence on her musical abilities despite her qualms about her attractiveness—shows a greater concern with internal traits, psychological characteristics, and social relationships.

Research also finds that females are somewhat more likely than males to define themselves in terms of the groups to which they belong (Madson & Trafimow, 2001). A Chinese study found that children with siblings are more likely than only children to define themselves in terms of group membership (Wang et al., 1998).

Self-Esteem

One of the most critical aspects of self-concept is **self-esteem,** the value or worth that people attach to themselves. A positive self-image is crucial to psychological adjustment in children and adults (Chen et al., 2001; Feinberg et al., 2000). *Question: How does self-esteem develop during middle childhood?*

As children enter middle childhood, their self-concepts become more differentiated and they are able to evaluate their self-worth in many different areas (Tassi et al., 2001). Preschoolers do not generally make a clear distinction between different areas of competence. They are either "good at doing things" or not. At one time, it was

self-esteem The sense of value or worth that people attach to themselves.

Zigy Kaluzny/Getty Images

Authoritative Parenting and Self-Esteem

Research suggests that parental demands for mature behavior, imposition of restrictions, and warmth help children develop behavior patterns that are connected with self-esteem.

assumed that before age 8, children could differentiate between only two broad facets of self-concept. One involved general competence and the other, social acceptance (Harter, 2006). It was also believed that an overall, or general, self-concept did not emerge until the age of 8. But research indicates that even as early as 5 to 7 years of age, children are able to make judgments about their performance in seven different areas: physical ability, physical appearance, peer relationships, parent relationships, reading, mathematics, and general school performance. They also display an overall, or general, self-concept (Harter, 2006).

Truth or Fiction Revisited: Children's self-esteem actually declines throughout middle childhood, reaching a low point at about age 12 or 13. Then it increases during adolescence (Harter, 2006). What accounts for the decline? Because young children are egocentric, their initial self-concepts may be unrealistic. As children become older, they compare themselves with other children and adjust their self-concepts. For most children, the comparison results in a more critical self-appraisal and the consequent decline in self-esteem.

Do girls or boys have a more favorable self-image? The answer depends on the area (Quatman & Watson, 2001). Girls tend to have more positive self-concepts regarding reading, general academics, and helping others than boys do, whereas boys tend to have more positive self-concepts in math, physical ability, and physical appearance (Jacobs et al., 2005; Wang, 2005). Cross-cultural studies in China (Dai, 2001), Finland (Lepola et al., 2000), and Germany (Tiedemann, 2000) also find that girls tend to have higher self-concepts in writing and that boys tend to have higher self-concepts in math.

Why do girls and boys differ in their self-concepts? Socialization and gender stereotypes appear to affect the way females and males react to their achievements. For example, girls predict that they will do better on tasks that are labeled "feminine," and boys predict better performance for themselves when tasks are labeled "masculine" (Jacobs et al., 2005; Rathus et al., 2008).

Authoritative parenting apparently contributes to children's self-esteem (Baumrind, 1991a, 1991b; Linares et al., 2002; Supple & Small, 2006). Children with a favorable self-image tend to have parents who are restrictive, involved, and loving. Children with low self-esteem are more likely to have authoritarian or rejecting–neglecting parents.

High self-esteem in children is related to their closeness to parents, especially as found in father–son and mother–daughter relationships (Fenzel, 2000). Close relationships between parents are also associated with positive self-concepts in children (DeHart et al., 2006; Maejima & Oguchi, 2001).

Peers play a role in children's self-esteem (Nesdale & Lambert, 2007). Social acceptance by peers is related to self-perceived competence in academic, social, and athletic domains (Laireiter & Lager, 2006). Parents and classmates have an equally strong effect on children's sense of self-worth in the middle years. Friends and teachers have relatively less influence in shaping self-esteem, but are also important (Harter, 2006).

Self-esteem appears to have a genetic component, which would contribute to its stability. A Japanese study found that that the concordance (agreement) rate for self-esteem is higher among identical (MZ) twins than for fraternal (DZ) twins (Kamakura et al., 2007). A longitudinal British study found that both genetic and environmental factors appeared to contribute to the stability of children's self-esteem (Neiss et al., 2006). Most children will encounter failure, but high self-esteem may contribute to the belief that they can master adversity. Low self-esteem may become a self-fulfilling prophecy: Children with low self-esteem may not carve out much to boast about.

Learned Helplessness

One outcome of low self-esteem in academics is known as **learned helplessness.** *Question: What is learned helplessness, and how does it develop in middle childhood?* Learned helplessness refers to an acquired belief that one is unable to obtain the rewards that one seeks. "Helpless" children tend to quit following failure, whereas children who believe in their own ability tend to persist in their efforts or change their strategies (Zimmerman, 2000). One reason for this difference is that helpless children believe that success is due more to ability than to effort and they have little ability in a particular area. Consequently, persisting in the face of failure seems futile (Bandura et al., 2001; Sutherland et al., 2004). "Helpless" children typically perform more poorly in school and on standardized tests of intelligence and achievement than other children (Goldstein & Brooks, 2005).

Sex Differences in Learned Helplessness

It is unclear whether girls or boys exhibit more learned helplessness in middle childhood (Boggiano & Barrett, 1991; Valas, 2001). But a sex difference does emerge in mathematics (Simpkins et al., 2006). Researchers have found that even when girls are performing as well as boys in math and science, they have less confidence in their ability (Anderman et al., 2001). Why? Parents' expectations that children will do well (or poorly) in a given area influence both the children's self-perceptions and their performance. Parents tend to hold the stereotyped view that girls have less math ability than boys. This viewpoint is true regardless of their own daughter's actual performance in math. Because of lower parental expectations, girls may shy away from math and not develop their math skills as much as boys do (Simpkins et al., 2006). Here we have an example of the self-fulfilling prophecy.

learned helplessness An acquired (hence, learned) belief that one is unable to control one's environment.

Lessons in Observation
Self-Concept

To watch this video, visit the book companion website. You can also answer the questions and e-mail your responses to your professor.

At age 4½, Christopher describes himself by listing objects and possessions in his house.

Learning Objectives

- What is a self-concept?
- How does the self-concept develop over time?
- When do children begin to incorporate personal traits into their self-descriptions?

Applied Lesson

How would you describe yourself? What information do you choose to include? Why?

Critical Thinking

You cannot see or touch a self-concept. How do researchers study the self-concept? Are you satisfied with their methods? Why or why not?

Active Review

1. Erikson labels middle childhood the stage of _____ versus inferiority.
2. According to Piaget, middle childhood coincides with the stage of _____ operations.
3. A key aspect of the development of social cognition is the ability to take the _____ of another person.
4. Children's self-esteem (Increases or Decreases?) during middle childhood.
5. (Authoritarian or Authoritative?) parenting contributes to high self-esteem in children.

Reflect & Relate: Are you "responsible" for your own self-esteem, or does your self-esteem generally vary with the opinion that others have of you? Why is this question important?

Go to

http://www.thomsonedu.com/psychology/rathus

for an interactive version of this review.

The Family

Question: What kinds of influences are exerted by the family during middle childhood? In middle childhood, the family continues to play a key role in socializing the child, even though peers, teachers, and other outsiders begin to play a greater role (Harter, 2006; Thompson, 2006). In this section, we look at developments in parent–child relationships during the middle years. We also consider the effects of different family environments: the family environment provided by lesbian and gay parents and the experience of living in families with varying marital arrangements. We also consider the effects of maternal employment.

Parent–Child Relationships

Parent–child interactions focus on some new concerns during the middle childhood years. They include school-related matters, assignment of chores, and peer activities (Collins et al., 2003).

During the middle years, parents do less monitoring of children's activities and provide less direct feedback than they did in the preschool years. In middle childhood, children do more monitoring of their own behavior. Although the parents still retain control over the child, control is gradually transferred from parent to child, a process known as **coregulation** (Maccoby, 2002; Wahler et al., 2001). Children no longer need to be constantly reminded of do's and dont's as they begin to internalize the standards of their parents.

Children and parents spend less time together in middle childhood than in the preschool years. But as in early childhood, children spend more of this time with their mothers than with their fathers (Russell & Russell, 1987). Mothers' interactions with school-age children continue to revolve around caregiving and household tasks, whereas fathers are relatively more involved in recreational activities, when they are involved, especially with sons. But here, too, mothers may actually spend more time (Wolfenden & Holt, 2005).

coregulation A gradual transferring of control from parent to child, beginning in middle childhood.

In the later years of middle childhood (ages 10 to 12), children evaluate their parents more critically than they do in the early years (Reid et al., 1990). This shift in perception may reflect the child's developing cognitive ability to view relationships in more complex ways (Selman & Dray, 2006). But throughout middle childhood, children rate their parents as their best source of emotional support, rating them more highly than friends (Cowan & Cowan, 2005; Katz et al., 2005). And emotional support is more valuable than economics in middle childhood (Santinello & Vieno, 2002).

Lesbian and Gay Parents

"Where did you get that beautiful necklace?" I asked the little girl in the pediatrician's office.

"From my Moms," she answered. It turned out that her family consisted of two women, each of whom had a biological child, one girl and one boy. *Question: What are the effects of having lesbian or gay parents?*

Research on **lesbian** and **gay** parenting has fallen into two general categories: the general adjustment of children and whether the children of lesbian and gay parents are more likely than other children to be lesbian or gay themselves. Research by Charlotte Patterson (2006) has generally found that the psychological adjustment of children of lesbian and gay parents—whether conceived by intercourse or donor insemination, or adopted—is comparable to that of children of heterosexual parents. Patterson and others (Wainright et al., 2004) have concluded that despite the stigma attached to homosexuality, lesbians and gay men frequently create and sustain positive family relationships.

Now let's consider the sexual orientation of the children of lesbian and gay parents. In doing so, we begin a generation back with the research of psychiatrist

lesbian A female who is interested romantically and sexually in other females.

gay A male who is interested romantically and sexually in other males. (Also used more broadly to refer to both lesbians and gay males.)

A Closer Look

How to Answer a 7-Year-Old's Questions about—Gulp—Sex

Daddy, where do babies come from?
Why are you asking me? Ask your mother.

Most children do not find it easy to talk to parents about sex. Only about one-quarter of the children in a national survey had done so (National Campaign to Prevent Teenage Pregnancy, 2003). Children usually find it easier to approach their mothers than their fathers (Guttmacher Institute, 2007).

Yet most children are curious about where babies come from, about how girls and boys differ, and the like. Adults who avoid these issues convey their own uneasiness about sex and may teach children that sex is something to be ashamed of.

Adults need not be sex experts to talk to their children about sex. They can surf the Internet to fill gaps in knowledge or to find books written for parents to read to children. They can admit they do not know all the answers.

Here are some pointers (Rathus et al., 2008):

- Be approachable. Be willing to discuss sex.
- Provide accurate information. The 6-year-old who wants to know where babies mature within the mother should not be told "in Mommy's tummy." It's wrong and isn't cute; the "tummy" is where food is digested. The child may worry that the baby is going to be digested. The child should be told, instead, "In Mommy's uterus" and be shown diagrams if he or she wants specifics.
- Teach children the correct names of their sex organs and that the "dirty words" others use to refer to the sex organs are not acceptable in most social settings. Avoid using silly words like "pee pee" or "private parts" to describe sex organs.

Reflect: Why do you think parents are reluctant to use anatomically correct words for sex organs when they are talking with their young children?

Richard Green. In a classic study, Green (1978) observed 37 children and young adults, age 3 to 20 years old, who were being reared—or had been reared—by lesbians or **transsexuals.** All but one of the children reported or recalled preferences for toys, clothing, and friends (male or female) that were typical for their sex and age. All the 13 older children who reported sexual fantasies or sexual behavior were heterosexually oriented. In a subsequent study, Green and his colleagues (1986) compared the children of European American mothers who were currently single, 50 of whom were lesbians and 40 of whom were heterosexual. Boys from the two groups showed no significant differences in intelligence test scores, sexual orientation, gender-role preferences, relationships with family and peer groups, and adjustment to life with a single parent. Girls showed slight differences, including somewhat more flexibility in gender roles. Green concluded that the mother's sexual orientation had no connection with parental fitness. A study by Patterson and her colleagues (Brodzinsky et al., 2002) suggested that many adoption agencies now agree with Green's conclusions.

Another review by Patterson (2003) addressed the personal and social development of children with lesbian and gay parents. Patterson found that the sexual orientation of the children was generally heterosexual. When parents had gotten divorced and created families with same-sex partners because of their sexual orientations, their children experienced a period of adjustment that entailed some difficulties, as do children when heterosexual parents get divorced. Children who are adopted by lesbian or gay parents tend to be well adjusted. The point here—reinforcing Green's findings—is that wanting the child is more important to the child's adjustment than the sexual orientation of the parents.

Generation X or Generation Ex? What Happens to Children Whose Parents Get Divorced?

To many in the United States, the 2000s are the period of "Generation X." However, it may be more accurate to think of our time as that of "Generation Ex," that is, a generation characterized by ex-wives and ex-husbands. Their children are also a part of Generation Ex, which is large and growing continuously. More than 1 million American children each year experience the divorce of their parents (U.S. Bureau of the Census, 2004). Nearly 40% of European American children and 75% of African American children in the United States who are born to married parents will spend at least part of their childhoods in single-parent families as a result of divorce (Marsiglio, 2004).

Question: What are the effects of divorce on the children? Divorce may be tough on parents; it can be even tougher on children (Amato, 2006; Rogers, 2004). The automatic aspects of family life cease being automatic. No longer do children eat with both parents. No longer do they go to ball games, the movies, or Disneyland with both of them. No longer do they curl up with them on the sofa to watch TV. No longer do they kiss both at bedtime. The parents are now often supporting two households, resulting in fewer resources for the children (Tashiro et al., 2006). Children lose other things besides family life. Sometimes the losses are minor, but many children who live with their mothers scrape by—or fail to scrape by—at the poverty level or below. Some children move from spacious houses into cramped apartments or from a desirable neighborhood to one where they are afraid to walk the streets. The mother who was once available may become an occasional visitor, spending more time at work and placing the kids in day care for extended periods.

In considering the effects of divorce on family members—both children and adults—Paul Amato (2006) suggests that researchers consider whether the effects are due to divorce or to "selection factors." For example, are the effects on children due to divorce per se, to marital conflict, to inadequate parental problem-solving ability,

transsexual A person who would prefer to be a person of the other sex and who may undergo hormone treatments, cosmetic surgery, or both to achieve the appearance of being a member of the other sex.

or to changes in financial status? Also, do children undergo a temporary crisis and gradually adjust, or do stressors persist indefinitely? For example, 3 years after the divorce, feelings of sadness, shock, disbelief, and desire for parental reunion tend to decline, but even 10 years later, children tend to retain anger toward the parent they hold responsible for the breakup.

Parents who get divorced are often in conflict about many things, and one of them typically involves how to rear the children (Amato, 2006). Because the children often hear their parents fighting over child rearing, the children may come to blame themselves for the split. Young children, who are less experienced than adolescents, are more likely to blame themselves. Young children also worry more about uncharted territory and the details of life after the breakup. Adolescents are relatively more independent and have some power to control their day-to-day lives.

Most children live with their mothers after a divorce (Amato, 2006; Ulloa & Ulibarri, 2004). Some fathers remain fully devoted to their children despite the split, but others tend to spend less time with their children as time goes on. This pattern is especially common when fathers create other families, such that the children of their new partners are competing with their biological children. Not only does the drop-off in paternal attention deprive children of activities and social interactions, but it also saps their self-esteem: "Why doesn't Daddy love me anymore? What's wrong with me?"

There is no question that divorce has challenging effects on children. The children of divorce are more likely to have conduct disorders, lower self-esteem, drug abuse, and poor grades in school (Amato, 2006; Adamsons & Pasley, 2006). Their physical health may decline, at least temporarily (Troxel & Matthews, 2004). There are individual differences, but, by and large, the fallout for children is worst during the first year after the breakup. Children tend to rebound after a couple of years or so (Malone et al., 2004).

A parental breakup is connected with a decline in the quality of parenting. A longitudinal study by E. Mavis Hetherington and her colleagues (Hetherington, 2006; Hetherington et al., 1989) tracked the adjustment of children who were 4 years old at the time of the divorce; the follow-ups occurred 2 months, 1 year, 2 years, and 6 years after the divorce. The investigators found that the organization of family life deteriorates. The family is more likely to eat meals pickup style, as opposed to sitting

© Royalty-Free/CORBIS

Generation Ex: Ex-Husband, Ex-Wife, Ex-Family, Ex-Security

Nearly half of American marriages end in divorce, and divorce turns life topsy-turvy for children. Younger children tend to erroneously blame themselves for the dissolution of the family, but children in middle childhood come to see things more accurately. Children of divorce tend to develop problems, many of which fade as time passes. Should parents in conflict stay together for the sake of the children? The answer seems to be that the children will not be better off if the parents continue to fight in front of them.

together. Children are less likely to get to school or to sleep on schedule. Divorced mothers have a more difficult time setting limits and enforcing restrictions on sons' behavior. Divorced parents are significantly less likely to show the authoritative behaviors that foster competence. They make fewer demands for mature behavior, communicate less, and show less nurturance and warmth. Their disciplinary methods become inconsistent.

Cross-cultural studies show that children of divorce in other cultures experience problems similar to those experienced by children in the United States (Boey et al., 2003). A study in China matched 58 children of divorce with 116 children from intact families according to sex, age, and social class. Children of divorce were more likely than the other children to make somatic complaints ("My stomach hurts," "I feel nauseous"), demonstrate lower social competence, and behave aggressively (Liu et al., 2000a). Another Chinese study found that divorce impairs the quality of parent–child relationships, interferes with concern over the children's education, and creates financial woes (Sun, 2001). A third Chinese study showed that divorce compromises the academic and social functioning of both Chinese and American children (Zhou et al., 2001).

A study of children and their mothers in Botswana, Africa, had similar results (Maundeni, 2000). Divorce led to economic hardship for most mothers and children. Lack of money made some children feel inferior to other children. Financial worries and feelings of resentment and betrayal led to social and emotional problems among both children and mothers.

Back to the United States: Boys seem to have a harder time than girls coping with divorce, and they take a longer time to recover (Grych, 2005; Malone et al., 2004). In the Hetherington study, boys whose parents were divorced showed more social, academic, and conduct problems than boys whose parents were married. These problems sometimes persisted for 6 years. Girls, by contrast, tended to regain functioning within 2 years.

K. Alison Clarke-Stewart and her colleagues (2000) compared the well-being of children in families headed by a separated or divorced mother with the well-being of about 170 children reared in intact families. As a group, the children who were being reared in two-parent families exhibited fewer problematic behaviors, more social skills, and higher IQ test scores. They were more securely attached to their mothers. But then the researchers factored in the mother's level of education, her socioeconomic status, and her psychological well-being. Somewhat surprisingly, the differences between the children in the two groups (one-parent versus intact families) almost vanished. The researchers concluded that at least in this study, it was not the parental breakup per se that caused the problems among the children. Instead, the difficulties were connected with the mother's psychological status (such as feelings of depression), income, and level of education. Other research confirms that maternal depression following divorce contributes to adjustment problems in the children (Hammen, 2003).

By and large, research shows that the following sources of support help children cope with divorce: social support from the immediate family, support from the extended family, support of friends, membership in a religious community, communication among family members, and financial security (Greeff & Van Der Merwe, 2004; Rogers, 2004).

Some children of divorce profit from psychological treatment (Bonkowski, 2005). Many programs include parents. The usefulness of a program that includes the mother was studied with 240 children, age 9 to 12 (Wolchik et al., 2000). The program addressed the quality of the mother–child relationship, ways of disciplining the child, ways of coping with interparental conflict, and the nature of the father–child relationship. Children were also helped to handle stressors (by thinking of them as difficult but not impossible) and to not blame themselves. Children's adjustment showed improvement at completion of the program and at a 6-month follow-up.

Life in Stepfamilies: His, Hers, Theirs, and . . .

Most divorced people remarry, usually while the children are young. More than one in three American children will spend part of his or her childhood in a stepfamily (U.S. Bureau of the Census, 2004).

The rule of thumb about the effects of living in stepfamilies is that there is no rule of thumb. Living in a stepfamily may have no measurable psychological effects (Coleman et al., 2000). Stepparents may claim stepchildren as their own (Marsiglio, 2004). There are also some risks to living in stepfamilies. Stepchildren appear to be at greater risk of being physically abused by stepparents than by biological parents (Adler-Baeder, 2006). Infanticide (killing infants) is a rarity in the United States, but the crime occurs 60 times as often in stepfamilies as in families with biological kinship (Daly & Wilson, 2000). There is a significantly higher incidence—by a factor of eight—of sexual abuse by stepparents than natural parents.

Why do we find these risks in stepfamilies? According to evolutionary psychologists, people often behave as though they want their genes to flourish in the next generation. Thus, it could be that stepparents are less devoted to rearing other people's children. They may even see "foreign" children as competitors for resources for their own children. Or a stepfather may see a woman's possession of children by another man as lessening her capacity to bear and rear his children (Brody, 1998). Evolutionary psychologists then often stray into research that describes how dominant males in many species do away with the offspring of females that have been sired by other males. (I'm not going there.)

"All Right, We Fight—Should We Remain Married 'for the Sake of the Children'?"

Questions: What is best for the children? Should parents who bicker remain together for their children's sake? Let's have it out at once. I am going to address this issue from a psychological perspective only. Many readers believe—for moral reasons—that marriage and family life must be permanent, no matter what. Readers will have to consider the moral aspects of divorce in the light of their own value systems.

So—from a purely psychological perspective—what should bickering parents do? The answer seems to depend largely on how they behave in front of the children. Research shows that parental bickering—especially severe fighting—is linked to the same kinds of problems that children experience when their parents get separated or divorced (Furstenberg & Kiernan, 2001; Troxel & Matthews, 2004). Moreover, when children are exposed to adult or marital conflict, they display a biological "alarm reaction": their heart rate, blood pressure, and sweating rise sharply (El-Sheikh, 2007; El-Sheikh & Harger, 2001). The bodily response is stronger yet when children blame themselves for parental conflict, as is common among younger children.

One study analyzed data from 727 children, age 4 to 9 years, from intact families and followed them 6 years later, when many of the families had undergone separation or divorce (Morrison & Coiro, 1999). Both separation and divorce were associated with increases in behavior problems in children, regardless of the amount of conflict between the parents. However, in the marriages that remained intact, high levels of marital conflict were associated with yet more behavior problems in the children. The message? Although separation and divorce are connected with adjustment problems in children, the outcome can be worse for children when conflicted parents stay together.

Because of the stresses experienced by children caught up in marital conflict, Hetherington and her colleagues suggest that divorce can be a positive alternative to harmful family functioning (Hetherington, 1989; Wallerstein et al., 2005). **Truth or Fiction Revisited:** From a psychological perspective, when bickering parents stay together "for the sake of the children," the children encounter stress.

The Effects of Maternal Employment

Why is this section labeled "The Effects of Maternal Employment"? Why not "Parental Employment" or "Paternal Employment"? Perhaps because of the traditional role of women as homemakers.

Even so, the past half-century has witnessed one of the most dramatic social changes in the history of the United States. Mothers are entering the labor force in record numbers. A half-century ago, most women remained in the home, but today, nearly three out of four married mothers of children under age 18 are employed, as are four out of five divorced, separated, or widowed mothers (U.S. Bureau of the Census, 2007). Family lifestyles have changed as more women combine maternal and occupational roles. *Question: What are the effects of maternal employment on children?* Do problems arise when mother is not available for round-the-clock love and attention?

Many psychologists and educators—and lay commentators—have been concerned about the effects of maternal employment on children. Part of the brouhaha has been based on traditionalist, moralistic values which argue that the mother ought to remain in the home. But concern has also been based on research findings that suggest that maternal employment (and nonmaternal care) have some negative effects on children (Belsky, 2006a).

One common belief is that Mom being in the workforce rather than in the home leads to delinquency. Researchers using data on 707 adolescents, age 12 to 14, from the National Longitudinal Survey of Youth examined whether the occupational status of a mother was connected with delinquent behavior (Vander Ven et al., 2001; Vander Ven & Cullen, 2004). They found that maternal employment per se made relatively little or no difference, but there was a slight indirect effect in that deviant behavior was connected with lack of supervision. The issue, then, would seem to be for the parents to ensure that children receive adequate supervision regardless of who—Mom or Dad or both—is on the job.

We can see that this issue is gender biased in the sense that the evidence suggests that *paternal* employment is potentially as harmful as *maternal* employment. Yet, who argues that fathers rather than mothers should remain in the home to ward off problems related to poor supervision? After all, the father is the traditional breadwinner and the mother is the traditional homemaker.

Political and moral arguments aside, there is little evidence that maternal employment harms children. Elizabeth Harvey (1999) and other researchers (Han et al., 2001) have examined data from the National Longitudinal Survey of Youth on the effects of early parental employment on children. The effects were minimal. Neither the timing nor the continuity of early maternal employment was consistently related to children's development. Harvey did find that working a greater number of hours was linked with slightly lower scores on measures of cognitive development through the age of 9 and with slightly lower academic achievement scores before the age of 7. However, there was no connection between maternal employment and children's conduct disorders, compliance, or self-esteem. And now for the pluses: Harvey found that early parental employment was beneficial for single mothers and lower-income

What Are the Effects of Maternal Employment?
Let's be honest here. Why doesn't the caption read: "What are the effects of parental employment?" The answer is that the vestiges of sexism run rampant in society. When things go wrong with children in families in which both parents must work—or choose to work—the tendency remains to blame the mother. However, research shows that maternal employment is actually connected with few problems with children; it is also connected with more egalitarian attitudes. (Go, Mom!)

families. Why? It brought in cash, and increasing family income has positive effects on children's development. (Is anyone surprised?)

There are other family benefits for maternal employment. Maternal employment appears to benefit school-age children, especially daughters, by fostering greater independence, emotional maturity, and higher achievement orientation (Hangal & Aminabhavi, 2007). **Truth or Fiction Revisited:** Daughters of employed women are more achievement oriented and do set higher career goals for themselves than daughters of nonworking women. A Canadian study found that children whose mothers were employed tended to be more prosocial and less anxious than other children (Nomaguchi, 2006). Both the sons and daughters of employed women appear to be more flexible in their gender-role stereotypes (Wright & Young, 1998). For example, sons of working women are more helpful with housework. Of course, these same findings will be considered challenging to men who wish to enforce traditional gender roles that oppress females.

There are other interesting findings on maternal employment. For example, Lois Hoffman and Lise Youngblade (1998) studied a sample of 365 mothers of third- and fourth-graders in an industrialized midwestern city. They discovered that working-class full-time homemakers were more likely to be depressed than employed mothers. Feelings of depression were related to permissive and authoritarian parenting styles, suggesting that many financially stressed homemakers do not have the emotional resources to give their children the best possible rearing. Among middle-class mothers, employment was not related to mood or style of parenting. Greater family financial resources apparently lift the mood. (Again: Is anybody surprised?)

A study of 116 urban Japanese women with children in the second grade also looked at the effects of maternal employment from the perspective of the mother. It found that the most satisfied women were those with more children but who were highly committed to their roles in the workforce, and, in case that were not enough, who felt that they were doing an excellent job as mothers (Holloway et al., 2006).

Active Review

6. During the middle years, parents do (More or Less?) monitoring of children's activities and provide less direct feedback than they did in the preschool years.

7. The children of lesbian and gay parents are most likely to be (Heterosexual or Homosexual?) in their sexual orientation.

8. Children of divorce most often experience (Upward or Downward?) movement in financial status.

9. Most children of divorce live with their (Mothers or Fathers?).

10. (Boys or Girls?) seem to have a harder time coping with divorce.

11. Research suggests that children are more likely to engage in delinquent behavior as a result of (Maternal employment or Lack of supervision?).

Reflect & Relate: Have you known children whose families have undergone divorce? What were (or *are*) the effects on the children?

Go to

http://www.thomsonedu.com/psychology/rathus

for an interactive version of this review.

Peer Relationships

Families exert the most powerful influences on a child during his or her first few years. But as children move into middle childhood, their activities and interests become directed farther away from home. *Question: What is the influence of peers during middle childhood?* Peers take on increasing importance in middle childhood. Let us explore the ways in which peers socialize one another. Then we examine factors in peer acceptance and rejection. Finally, we see how friendships develop.

Peers as Socialization Influences

Peer relationships are a major part of growing up. Peers exert powerful socialization influences and pressures to conform (Hanlon et al., 2004; Keddie, 2004). Even highly involved parents can only provide children with experience relating to adults. Children profit from experience relating to peers because peers have interests and skills that reflect being part of the same generation as the child. Peers differ as individuals, however. For all these reasons, peer experiences broaden children (Molinari & Corsaro, 2000).

Peers guide children and afford practice in sharing and cooperating, in relating to leaders, and in coping with aggressive impulses, including their own. Peers can be important confidants (Dunn et al., 2001). Peers, like parents, help children learn what types of impulses—affectionate, aggressive, and so on—they can safely express and with whom. Children who are at odds with their parents can turn to peers as sounding boards. They can compare feelings and experiences they would not bring up in the home. When children share troubling ideas and experiences with peers, they often learn that friends have similar concerns. They realize that they are normal and not alone (Barry & Wentzel, 2006; Wentzel et al., 2004).

Peer Acceptance and Rejection

Acceptance or rejection by peers is of major importance in childhood because problems with peers affect adjustment later on (Wentzel et al., 2004). What are the characteristics of popular and rejected children?

Truth or Fiction Revisited: Popular children tend to be attractive and relatively mature for their age, although attractiveness seems to be more important for girls than for boys (Langlois et al., 2000). Socially speaking, popular children are friendly, nurturant, cooperative, helpful, and socially skillful (Chen et al., 2001; Xie et al., 2006). Popular children have higher self-esteem than other children, which tends to reflect success in academics or valued extracurricular activities such as sports (Chen et al., 2001). Later-born children are more likely to be popular than firstborns, perhaps because they tend to be more sociable (Beck et al., 2006).

Children who show behavioral and learning problems, who are aggressive, and who disrupt group activities are more likely to be rejected by peers (Boivin et al., 2005). However, aggressive children who are also highly popular may be excused for their aggressive ways (A. J. Rose et al., 2004). Moreover, aggressive children are more likely to seek out aggressive friends (A. J. Rose et al., 2004).

© Nancy Richmond/The Image Works

Peer Rejection

Few things are as painful as rejection by one's peers in middle childhood. Children may be rejected if they look unusual or unattractive, lack valued skills, or are aggressive.

Although pressure to conform to group norms and standards can be powerful, most rejected children do not shape up. Instead, they tend to remain lonely—on the fringes of the group (Wentzel et al., 2004). Fortunately, training in social skills seems to help increase children's popularity (Cashwell et al., 2001; Webster-Stratton et al., 2001b).

Development of Friendships

Question: How do children's concepts of friendship develop? In the preschool years and early years of middle childhood, friendships are based on geographic closeness or proximity. Friendships are relatively superficial; they are quickly formed and easily broken. What matters are activity levels, shared activities, and who has the swing set or sandbox. Children through the age of 7 usually report that their friends are the children with whom they share activities (Berndt, 2004; Berndt & Perry, 1986; Gleason et al., 2005). There is little reference to friends' traits.

Between the ages of 8 and 11, children show increased recognition of the importance of friends meeting each other's needs and possessing desirable traits (Zarbatany et al., 2000, 2004). Children at these ages are more likely to say that friends are nice to one another and share interests as well as things. During these years, children increasingly pick friends who are similar to themselves in behavior and personality. Trustworthiness, mutual understanding, and a willingness to share personal information characterize friendships in middle childhood and beyond (Hamm, 2000; Rotenberg et al., 2004). Girls tend to develop closer friendships than boys (Zarbatany et al., 2000). Girls are more likely to seek confidants, girls with whom they can share their inmost feelings.

Robert Selman (1980) described five stages in children's changing concepts of friendship (see ■ Table 13.2). The stages correspond to the five levels of perspective-taking skills discussed earlier in the chapter.

Friends behave differently with each other than they do with other children. School-age friends are more verbal, attentive, expressive, relaxed, and mutually responsive to each other during play than are children who are only acquaintances (Cleary et al., 2002). Cooperation occurs more readily between friends than between other groupings, as might be expected. But intense competition can also occur among friends, especially among boys (Hartup, 1993). When conflicts occur between friends, they tend to be less intense and are resolved in ways that maintain positive social interaction (Hartup, 1993; Wojslawowicz Bowker et al., 2006).

In one study, 696 fourth- and fifth-grade children responded to 30 hypothetical situations involving conflict with a friend (Rose & Asher, 1999). It was found that those children who responded to conflict by seeking revenge were least likely to have friendships or close friendships. Sex differences were also found. Girls were generally more interested in resolving conflicts than boys were.

Children in middle childhood typically will tell you that they have more than one "best" friend (Berndt et al., 1989). One study found that 9-year-olds reported having an average of four best friends (Lewis & Feiring, 1989). Best friends tend to be more alike than other friends.

In middle childhood, boys tend to play in larger groups than girls. Children's friendships are almost exclusively with others of the same sex, continuing the trend of sex segregation (Hartup, 1993).

Colorblind/Getty Images

Friendship, Friendship . . . A Perfect "Blendship"?
Children's concepts of friendship develop over time. In middle childhood, friendship is generally seen in terms of what children do for each other. These children are beginning to value loyalty and intimacy.

■ **Table 13.2** Stages in Children's Concepts of Friendship

Stage	Name	Approximate Age (Years)	What Happens
0	Momentary physical interaction	3–6	Children remain egocentric and unable to take one another's point of view. Thus, their concept of a friend is one who likes to play with the same things they do and who lives nearby.
1	One-way assistance	5–9[a]	Children realize that their friends may have different thoughts and feelings than they do, but they place their own desires first. They view a friend as someone who does what they want.
2	Fair-weather cooperation	7–12[a]	Friends are viewed as doing things for one another (reciprocity), but the focus remains on each individual's self-interest rather than on the relationship per se.
3	Intimate and mutual sharing	10–15[a]	The focus is on the relationship itself, rather than on the individuals separately. The function of friendship is viewed as mutual support over a long period of time, rather than concern about a given activity or self-interest.
4	Autonomous interdependence	12 and above[a]	Children (adolescents, and adults) understand that friendships grow and change as people change. They realize that they may need different friends to satisfy different personal and social needs.

Source: Selman (1980).

[a]Ages may overlap

During middle childhood, contact with members of the other sex is strongly discouraged by peers. For example, a study of European American, African American, Latino and Latina American, and Native American 10- and 11-year-olds found that those who crossed the "sex boundary" were especially unpopular with their peers (Sroufe et al., 1993).

Active Review

12. As children move into middle childhood, their activities and interests become directed (Closer to or Farther away from?) the home.

13. Popular children tend to be attractive and relatively (Mature or Immature?) for their age.

14. (Firstborn or Later-born?) children are more likely to be popular.

15. During middle childhood, contact with members of the other sex is (Encouraged or Discouraged?) by peers.

Reflect & Relate: What do you look for in a friend? What "stage" are you in, according to Table 13.2?

Go to

http://www.thomsonedu.com/psychology/rathus

for an interactive version of this review.

The School

Question: What are the effects of the school on children's social and emotional development? The school exerts a powerful influence on many aspects of the child's development. Schools, like parents, set limits on behavior, make demands for mature behavior, attempt to communicate, and are oriented toward nurturing positive physical, social, and cognitive development. The schools, like parents, have a direct influence on children's IQ scores, achievement motivation, and career aspirations (Aber et al., 2007; Woolfolk, 2008). As in the family, schools influence social and moral development (Aber et al., 2007; Killen & Smetana, 2006).

Schools are also competitive environments, and children who do too well—and students who do not do well enough—can suffer from the resentment or the low opinion of others. An Italian study placed 178 male and 182 female 8- to 9-year-old elementary school students in competitive situations (Tassi et al., 2001). It was found that when the students were given the task of trying to outperform one another, competition led to social rejection by students' peers. On the other hand, when the students were simply asked to do the best they could, high rates of success led to admiration by one's peers.

In this section, we consider children's transition to school and then examine the effects of the school environment and of teachers.

Entry into School: Getting to Know You

An increasing number of children attend preschool. About half have had some type of formal prekindergarten experience, often part-time (Slavin, 2006; Woolfolk, 2008). But most children first experience full-time schooling when they enter kindergarten or first grade. Children must master many new tasks when they start school. They will have to meet new academic challenges, learn new school and teacher expectations, and fit into a new peer group. They must learn to accept extended separation from parents and develop increased attention, self-control, and self-help skills.

What happens to children during the transition from home or preschool to elementary school may be critical for the eventual success or failure of their educational experience, particularly for low-income children. Families of children living in poverty may be less able to supply both the material and emotional supports that help the child adjust successfully to school (Slavin, 2006; Woolfolk, 2008).

How well prepared are children to enter school? Discussions of school readiness must consider at least three critical factors:

1. The diversity and inequity of children's early life experiences
2. Individual differences in young children's development and learning
3. The degree to which schools establish reasonable and appropriate expectations of children's capabilities when they enter school

Unfortunately, some children enter school less well prepared than others. In one survey, 7,000 American kindergarten teachers reported that more than one-third of their students began school unprepared to learn (Chira, 1991). Nearly half the teachers thought that children entered school less ready to learn than had children 5 years earlier. Most of the teachers said that children often lacked the language skills needed to succeed. This report and others (Slavin, 2006; Woolfolk, 2008) concluded that poor health care and nutrition and lack of adequate stimulation and support by parents place many children at risk for academic failure even before they enter school.

A study by the U.S. Department of Education concluded that schools could do a better job of easing the transition to kindergarten (Love et al., 1992). The researchers surveyed schools in 1,003 school districts and also visited 8 schools. The average school reported that between 10% and 20% of incoming kindergartners had difficulty adjusting to kindergarten. Adjusting to the academic demands of school was reported to be the area of greatest difficulty. Children whose families were low in socioeconomic status had a more difficult time adjusting than other children, particularly in academics. Children who enter school with deficits in language and math skills generally continue to show deficits in these areas during at least the first years of school (Slavin, 2006; Woolfolk, 2008).

The School Environment: Setting the Stage for Success, or . . .

*Question: **What are the characteristics of a good school?*** Research summaries (Slavin, 2006; Woolfolk, 2008) indicate that an effective school has the following characteristics:

- An active, energetic principal
- An atmosphere that is orderly but not oppressive
- Empowerment of teachers; that is, teachers participating in decision making
- Teachers who have high expectations that children will learn
- A curriculum that emphasizes academics
- Frequent assessment of student performance

A Closer Look

Bullying: An Epidemic of Misbehavior and Fear

Nine-year-old Stephanie did not want to go to school. As with many other children who refuse to go to school, she showed anxiety at the thought of leaving home. But Stephanie was not experiencing separation anxiety from her family. It turns out that she had gotten into a disagreement with Susan, and Susan had told her she would beat her mercilessly if she showed up at school again. To highlight her warning, Susan had shoved Stephanie across the hall.

Stephanie was a victim of bullying. Susan was a bully. Stephanie did not know it, but there was something of an irony. Susan was also bullied from time to time by a couple of girls at school.

Was there something unusual about all this bullying? Not really. Boys are more likely than girls to be bullies, but many girls engage in bullying (Batsche & Porter, 2006; Li, 2006, 2007; Perren & Alsaker, 2006). All in all, it is estimated that 10% of students have been exposed to extreme bullying and that 70% to 75% of students overall have been bullied (Li, 2006, 2007).

Bullying has devastating effects on the school atmosphere. It transforms the perception of school from a safe place into a violent place (Batsche & Porter, 2006; Perren & Alsaker, 2006). Bullying also impairs adjustment to middle school, where bullying is sometimes carried out by older children against younger children (Perren & Alsaker, 2006; Scheithauer, et al., 2006). It especially impairs adjustment for children who speak another language in the home, who tend to be picked on more often (Yu et al., 2003).

Many but not all bullies have some things in common. For one thing, their achievement tends to be lower than average, such that peer approval (or deference from peers) might be more important to them than academics (Batsche & Porter, 2006; Perren & Alsaker, 2006. Bullies are more likely to come from homes of lower socioeconomic status (Perren & Alsaker, 2006; Pereira et al., 2004). Many of these homes are characterized by violence between parents (Baldry, 2003; Batsche & Porter, 2006).

Numerous studies have also investigated the personalities of bullies. One study compared middle-school bullies to matched controls (Coolidge et al., 2004). Bullying was associated with more frequent diagnoses of conduct disorder, oppositional defiant disorder, attention-deficit/hyperactivity disorder, and depression. Bullies were also more likely to have personality problems, such as assuming that others were predisposed to harming them. They also showed more problems in impulse control.

Cyberbullying

Some children are bullied electronically, not in person. They receive threatening messages from fellow students by means of computers, cell phones, or personal digital assistants (PDAs) (Patchin & Hinduja, 2006). This phenomenon is referred to as *cyberbullying*. Although

- Empowerment of students; that is, students participating in setting goals, making classroom decisions, and engaging in cooperative learning activities with other students

Certain aspects of the school environment are important as well. One key factor is class size. Smaller classes permit students to receive more individual attention and to express their ideas more often (Slavin, 2006). Smaller classes lead to increased achievement in mathematics and reading in the early primary grades. Smaller classes are particularly useful in teaching the "basics"—reading, writing, and arithmetic—to elementary school students at risk for academic failure (Slavin, 2006; Woolfolk, 2008).

Teachers: Setting Limits, Making Demands, Communicating Values, and—Oh, Yes—Teaching

The influence of the schools is mainly due to teachers. Teachers, like parents, set limits, make demands, communicate values, and foster development. Teacher–student relationships are more limited than parent–child relationships, but teachers still have the opportunity to serve as powerful role models and dispensers of rein-

Bullying

For victims of bullying the school can become a violent place rather than a safe one. Although many schools and families try to control bullying, much of it goes unreported.

© Bill Bachmann/Rainbow

cyberbullying might seem to provide a "comfortable" distance between the bully and the victim, its effects can be devastating, and perhaps as devastating, as those of in-person bullying. Cases of severe anxiety, including school phobia and refusal, depression, lowered self-esteem, and even the occasional suicide, have been reported (S. P. Thomas, 2006). As with other forms of bullying, the majority of cyberbullies are male, and most victims do not report the incidents (Li, 2006, 2007).

Is there a "cure" for bullying? School systems and families have a stake in controlling bullying, and sometimes setting strict limits on bullies is of help. But, as noted, much—or most—bullying goes unreported, sometimes because children are embarrassed to admit they are being bullied, sometimes because they fear retaliation by the bully (Li, 2006, 2007). Many children simply learn to accommodate or avoid bullies until they are out of school (Hunter & Boyle, 2004). Then they go their separate ways.

Reflect:
- Were you ever bullied in school? If so, how did you handle it?
- What should teachers and school official do about bullies?
- What should parents tell their children about bullies?

forcement. After all, children spend several hours each weekday in the presence of teachers.

Teacher Influences on Student Performance

Many aspects of teacher behavior are related to student achievement (Slavin, 2006). Achievement is enhanced when teachers expect students to master the curriculum, allocate most of the available time to academic activities, and manage the classroom environment effectively. Students learn more in classes when actively instructed or supervised by teachers than when working on their own. The most effective teachers ask questions, give personalized feedback, and provide opportunities for drill and practice, as opposed to straight lecturing.

Student achievement also is linked to the emotional climate of the classroom (Slavin, 2006). Students do not do as well when teachers rely heavily on criticism, ridicule, threats, or punishment. Achievement is high in classrooms with a pleasant, friendly atmosphere but not in classrooms with extreme teacher warmth.

Teacher Expectations

There is a saying that "You find what you're looking for." Consider the so-called **Pygmalion effect** in education. In Greek mythology, the amorous sculptor Pygmalion breathed life into a beautiful statue he had carved. Similarly, in the musical *My Fair Lady,* a reworking of the Pygmalion legend, Henry Higgins fashions a great lady from the lower-class Eliza Doolittle.

Teachers also try to bring out positive traits they believe dwell within their students. **Truth or Fiction Revisited:** A classic experiment by Robert Rosenthal and Lenore Jacobson (1968) suggested that teacher expectations can become **self-fulfilling prophecies.** As reported in the classic *Pygmalion in the Classroom,* Rosenthal and Jacobson (1968) first gave students a battery of psychological tests. Then they informed teachers that a handful of the students, although average in performance to date, were about to blossom forth intellectually in the current school year.

Now, in fact, the tests had indicated nothing in particular about the "chosen" children. These children had been selected at random. The purpose of the experiment was to determine whether changing teacher expectations could affect student performance. As it happened, the identified children made significant gains in intelligence test scores.

In subsequent research, however, results have been mixed. Some studies have found support for the Pygmalion effect (Madon et al., 2001; Sarrazin et al., 2005a, 2005b). Others have not. A review of 18 such experiments found that the Pygmalion effect was most pronounced when the procedure for informing teachers of the potential in the target student had greatest credibility (Raudenbusch, 1984). A fair conclusion would seem to be that teacher expectations sometimes, but not always, affect students' motivation, self-esteem, expectations for success, and achievement.

These findings have serious implications for children from ethnic minority and low-income families. There is some indication that teachers expect less academically from children in these groups (Slavin, 2006; Woolfolk, 2008). Teachers with lower expectations for certain children may spend less time encouraging and interacting with them.

What are some of the ways that teachers can help motivate all students to do their best? Anita Woolfolk (2008) suggests the following:

- Make the classroom and the lesson interesting and inviting.
- Ensure that students can profit from social interaction.
- Make the classroom a safe and pleasant place.
- Recognize that students' backgrounds can give rise to diverse patterns of needs.

Pygmalion effect A self-fulfilling prophecy; an expectation that is confirmed because of the behavior of those who hold the expectation.

self-fulfilling prophecy An event that occurs because of the behavior of those who expect it to occur.

- Help students take appropriate responsibility for their successes and failures.
- Encourage students to perceive the links between their own efforts and their achievements.
- Help students set attainable short-term goals.

Sexism in the Classroom

Although girls were systematically excluded from formal education for centuries, today we might not expect to find **sexism** among teachers. Teachers, after all, are generally well educated. They are also trained to be fair minded and sensitive to the needs of their young charges in today's changing society.

However, we may not have heard the last of sexism in our schools. According to a classic review of more than 1,000 research publications about girls and education, girls are treated unequally by their teachers, their male peers, and the school curriculum (American Association of University Women, 1992). The reviewers concluded:

- Many teachers pay less attention to girls than boys, especially in math, science, and technology classes.
- Many girls are subjected to **sexual harassment**—unwelcome verbal or physical conduct of a sexual nature—from male classmates, and many teachers minimize the harmfulness of harassment and ignore it.
- Some school textbooks still stereotype or ignore women, more often portraying males as the shakers and movers in the world.

Waiting to Be Called On
Who is the teacher most likely to call on? Some studies say that teachers may favor the boy and call on him before the girl, especially in math, science, and technology classes.

In a widely cited study, Myra Sadker and David Sadker (1994; Sadker & Silber, 2007) observed students in fourth-, sixth-, and eighth-grade classes in four states and in the District of Columbia. Teachers and students were European American and African American, urban, suburban, and rural. In almost all cases, the findings were depressingly similar. Boys generally dominated classroom communication, whether the subject was math (a traditionally "masculine" area) or language arts (a traditionally "feminine" area). Despite the stereotype that girls are more likely to talk or even chatter, boys were eight times more likely than girls to call out answers without raising their hands. So far, it could be said, we have evidence of a sex difference, but not of sexism. However, teachers were less than impartial in responding to boys and girls when they called out. Teachers, male and female, were significantly more likely to accept calling out from boys. Girls were significantly more likely, as the song goes, to receive "teachers' dirty looks" or to be reminded that they should raise their hands and wait to be called on. Boys, it appears, are expected to be impetuous, but girls are reprimanded for "unladylike behavior." Sad to say, until they saw videotapes of themselves, the teachers generally were unaware that they were treating girls and boys differently.

Other observers note that primary and secondary teachers tend to give more attention to boys than to girls, especially in math and technology courses (Bell & Norwood, 2007; Crocco & Libresco, 2007; Koch, 2007). They call on boys more often, ask them more questions, talk to and listen to them more, give them lengthier directions, and praise and criticize them more often.

The irony is that our educational system has been responsible for lifting many generations of the downtrodden into the mainstream of American life (Sadker & Zittleman, 2007). Unfortunately, the system may be doing more to encourage development of academic skills—especially skills needed in our new technological age—in boys than in girls.

sexism Discrimination or bias against people based on their sex.

sexual harassment Unwelcome verbal or physical conduct of a sexual nature.

Active Review

16. Children whose families are (High or Low?) in socioeconomic status have a more difficult time adjusting to school.
17. (Smaller or Larger?) classes facilitate learning during middle childhood.
18. An experiment by Rosenthal and Jacobson suggests that teacher expectations can become _____ prophecies.
19. (Boys or Girls?) tend to be favored by teachers in the classroom.

Reflect & Relate: Do you remember what it was like to enter school at kindergarten or first grade? Did you experience some adjustment problems? What were they?

Go to

http://www.thomsonedu.com/psychology/rathus
for an interactive version of this review.

Social and Emotional Problems

Millions of children in the United States suffer from emotional or behavioral problems that could profit from professional treatment. But most of them are unlikely to receive help. What are some of the more common psychological problems of middle childhood? In previous chapters, we examined attention-deficit/hyperactivity disorder (ADHD) and learning disabilities. Here, we focus on those problems more likely to emerge during middle childhood: conduct disorders, depression, and anxiety. We use the terminology in the Diagnostic and Statistical Manual (DSM) of the American Psychiatric Association (2000) because it is the most widely used index of psychological disorders.

Conduct Disorders

> David is a 16-year-old high school dropout. He has just been arrested for the third time in 2 years for stealing video equipment and computers from people's homes. Acting alone, David was caught in each case when he tried to sell the stolen items. In describing his actions in each crime, David expressed defiance and showed a lack of remorse. In fact, he bragged about how often he had gotten away with similar crimes.
>
> —Adapted from Halgin & Whitbourne (1993, p. 335)

David has a **conduct disorder**. *Questions: What are conduct disorders? What can we do about them?* Children with conduct disorders, like David, persistently break rules or violate the rights of others. They exhibit behaviors such as lying, stealing, fire setting, truancy, cruelty to animals, and fighting (American Psychiatric Association, 2000). To receive this diagnosis, children must engage in the behavior pattern for at least 6 months. Conduct disorders typically emerge by 8 years of age and are much more prevalent in boys than in girls (Nock et al., 2006).

Children with conduct disorders are often involved in sexual activity before puberty and smoke, drink, and abuse other substances (American Psychiatric Associ-

conduct disorders Disorders marked by persistent breaking of the rules and violations of the rights of others.

ation, 2000). They have a low tolerance for frustration and may have temper flare-ups. They tend to blame other people for their scrapes. They believe that they are misunderstood and treated unfairly. Academic achievement is usually below grade level, but intelligence is usually at least average. Many children with conduct disorders also are diagnosed with ADHD (Chronis et al., 2007; Drabick et al., 2004).

Origins of Conduct Disorders

Conduct disorders may have a genetic component (Scourfield et al., 2004). They are more likely to be found among the biological parents than the adoptive parents of adopted children with such problems (Langbehn & Cadoret, 2001). Other contributors include antisocial family members, deviant peers, inconsistent discipline, parental insensitivity to the child's behavior, physical punishment, and family stress (Black, 2007; Jaffee et al., 2006).

A study of 123 African American boys and girls pointed toward the relationships between parental discipline, parental monitoring, and conduct problems (Kilgore et al., 2000). The researchers found that coercive parental discipline and poor parental monitoring at the age of 4½ were reliable predictors of conduct problems for boys and girls at the age of 6. The families were poor, and the parents had no choice but to send the children to schools with many peers with conduct disorders. However, once socioeconomic status and school choice were taken into account, parental discipline and monitoring were the strongest predictors of conduct disorders. The findings are consistent with research on European American more advantaged boys, which suggests that family processes are stronger predictors of conduct disorders than ethnicity.

Treatment of Conduct Disorders

The treatment of conduct disorders is challenging, but it would seem that cognitive-behavioral techniques involving parent training hold promise (Cavell, 2001; Kazdin, 2000; Sukhodolsky et al., 2005). Children with conduct disorders profit from interventions in which their behavior is monitored closely, there are consequences (such as time-outs) for unacceptable behavior, physical punishment is avoided, and positive social behavior is rewarded. That is, rather than just targeting noncompliant behavior, it is useful to attend to children when they are behaving properly and to reward them for doing so (Cavell, 2001).

Other approaches include teaching aggressive children methods for coping with feelings of anger that will not violate the rights of others. One promising cognitive-behavioral method teaches children social skills and how to use problem solving to manage interpersonal conflicts (Webster-Stratton et al., 2001b). Desirable social skills include asking other children to stop annoying behavior rather than hitting them. Children are also taught to "stop and think" before engaging in aggressive behavior. They are encouraged to consider the outcomes of their behavior and find acceptable ways to reach their goals.

Childhood Depression

Kristin, an 11-year-old, feels "nothing is working out for me." For the past year, she has been failing in school, although she previously had been a B student. She has trouble sleeping, feels tired all the time, and has started refusing to go to school. She cries easily and thinks her peers are making fun of her because she is "ugly and stupid." Her mother recently found a note written by Kristin that said she wanted to jump in front of a car "to end my misery."

—Adapted from Weller & Weller (1991, p. 655)

Childhood is the happiest time of life, correct? Not necessarily. Many children are happy enough, protected by their parents and unencumbered by adult responsibilities. From the perspective of aging adults, their bodies seem made of rubber and free of aches. Their energy is apparently boundless.

Yet many children, like Kristin, are depressed. ***Questions: What is depression? What can we do about it?*** Depressed children may feel sad, blue, down in the dumps. They may show poor appetite, insomnia, lack of energy and inactivity, loss of self-esteem, difficulty concentrating, loss of interest in people and activities they usually enjoy, crying, feelings of hopelessness and helplessness, and thoughts of suicide (American Psychiatric Association, 2000).

But many children do not recognize depression in themselves until the age of 7 or so. Part of the problem is cognitive developmental. The capacity for concrete operations apparently contributes to children's abilities to perceive internal feeling states (Glasberg & Aboud, 1982).

When children cannot report their feelings, depression is inferred from behavior. Depressed children in middle childhood engage in less social activity and have poorer social skills than peers (American Psychiatric Association, 2000). In some cases, childhood depression is "masked" by conduct disorders, physical complaints, academic problems, and anxiety.

It has been estimated that between 5% and 9% of children are seriously depressed in any given year (American Psychiatric Association, 2000). Depression occurs equally often in girls and boys during childhood but is more common among women later in life. Depressed children frequently continue to have depressive episodes as adolescents and adults.

Childhood Depression
Depressed children may complain of poor appetite, insomnia, lack of energy, difficulty concentrating, loss of interest in other people and activities they used to like, and feelings of worthlessness. But many depressed children do not recognize feelings of sadness. In some cases, childhood depression is "masked" by physical complaints, academic problems, anxiety, and even conduct disorders.

Origins of Depression

The origins of depression are complex and varied. Psychological and biological explanations have been proposed.

Some social cognitive theorists explain depression in terms of relationships between competencies (knowledge and skills) and feelings of self-esteem. Children who gain academic, social, and other competencies usually have high self-esteem. Perceived low levels of competence are linked to helplessness, low self-esteem, and depression. Longitudinal studies of primary schoolchildren have found that problems in academics, socializing, physical appearance, and sports can predict feelings of depression (Cole et al., 2001; Kistner, 2006). Conversely, self-perceived competence in these areas is negatively related to feelings of depression (Cole et al., 2001). That is, competence appears to "protect" children from depression. Children who have not developed competencies because of lack of opportunity, inconsistent parental reinforcement, and so on may develop feelings of helplessness and hopelessness. Similarly, stressful life events, daily hassles, and poor problem-solving ability can give rise to feelings of helplessness and hopelessness that trigger depression (Reinecke & DuBois, 2001).

In contrast, social support and self-confidence tend to protect children from depression. Some competent children might not credit themselves because of excessive parental expectations. Or children may be perfectionistic themselves. Perfectionistic children may be depressed because they cannot meet their own standards.

Children in elementary school are likely to be depressed because of situational stresses, such as family problems. Among middle schoolers, however, we find cognitive contributors to depression. For example, a study of 582 Chinese children from Hong Kong secondary schools found that cognitive distortions, such as minimizing accomplishments and blowing problems out of proportion, were associated with feelings of depression (Leung & Poon, 2001). A European study found that ruminating about problems (going over them again and again—and again), blaming oneself for things that are not one's fault, and blowing problems out of proportion are linked with depression (Garnefski et al., 2001).

A tendency to blame oneself (an internal attribution) or others (an external attribution) is called a child's **attributional style.** Certain attributional styles can contribute to helplessness and hopelessness and hence to depression (Kagan et al., 2004; Runyon & Kenny, 2002).

Truth or Fiction Revisited: It is true that some children blame themselves for all the problems in their lives, whether they deserve the blame or not. Research shows that children who are depressed are more likely to attribute the causes of their failures to internal, stable, and global factors, factors they are relatively helpless to change (Lewinsohn et al., 2000b). Helplessness triggers depression. Consider the case of two children who do poorly on a math test. John thinks, "I'm a jerk! I'm just no good in math! I'll never learn." Jim thinks, "That test was tougher than I thought it would be. I'll have to work harder next time." John is perceiving the problem as global (he's "a jerk") and stable (he'll "never learn"). Jim perceives the problem as specific rather than global (related to the type of math test the teacher makes up) and as unstable rather than stable (he can change the results by working harder). In effect, John thinks "It's me" (an internal attribution). By contrast, Jim thinks "It's the test" (an external attribution). Depressed children tend to explain negative events in terms of internal, stable, and global causes. As a result, they, like John, are more likely than Jim to be depressed.

There is also evidence of genetic factors in depression (Cryan & Slattery, 2007; Kendler et al., 2007; Orstavik et al., 2007). For example, the children of depressed parents are at greater risk for depression and other disorders (Jang et al., 2004; Korszun et al., 2004). A Norwegian study of 2,794 twins estimated that the heritability of depression in females was 49% and 25% in males (Orstavik et al., 2007). On a neurological level, evidence suggests that depressed children (and adults) "underutilize" the neurotransmitter **serotonin** (Vitiello, 2006). Learned helplessness is linked to lower serotonin levels in the brains of humans and rats (Joca et al., 2006; Wu et al., 1999).

Treatment of Depression

Parents and teachers can do a good deal to alleviate relatively mild feelings of depression among children. They can involve children in enjoyable activities, encourage the development of skills, offer praise when appropriate, and point out when children are being too hard on themselves. But if feelings of depression persist, treatment is called for.

Psychotherapy for depression tends to be mainly cognitive-behavioral these days, and it is often straightforward. Children (and adolescents) are encouraged to do enjoyable things and build social skills. They are made aware of their tendencies to minimize their accomplishments, catastrophize their problems, and overly blame themselves for shortcomings (e.g., Ellis & Dryden, 1996).

We noted that many depressed children underutilize the neurotransmitter serotonin. Antidepressant medication (selective serotonin reuptake inhibitors, or SSRIs), such as Luvox, Prozac, and Zoloft, increase the action of serotonin in the brain and are sometimes used to treat childhood depression. Studies of their effectiveness yield a mixed review, ranging from something like "deadly dangerous" to "often effective" (Vitiello, 2006). Although SSRIs are often effective, the Food and Drug Administration has warned that there may be a link between their use and suicidal thinking in children (Harris, 2004).

Childhood depression is frequently accompanied by anxiety (Kendler et al., 2007; Masi et al., 2004), as we see in the next section. Social and emotional problems that tend to emerge in middle childhood are summarized in Concept Review 13.1.

attributional style The way in which one is disposed toward interpreting outcomes (successes or failures), as in tending to place blame or responsibility on oneself or on external factors.

serotonin A neurotransmitter that is involved in mood disorders such as depression.

Concept Review 13.1   Social and Emotional Problems That May Emerge During Middle Childhood

Problem	Behavior Patterns	Comments
Conduct disorders 	• Precocious sexual activity, substance abuse • Truancy, stealing, lying, and aggression	• More common in boys • Child blames others for problems • Probably connected with genetic factors • Other contributors—antisocial family members, deviant peers, inconsistent discipline, physical punishment, family stress • Tends to be stable throughout adolescence and into adulthood • Frequently accompanied by ADHD
Childhood depression 	• Feelings of sadness, poor appetite, insomnia, lack of energy and inactivity, loss of self-esteem, difficulty concentrating, loss of interest in people and activities, crying, feelings of hopelessness and helplessness, and thoughts of suicide • Can be masked by conduct disorders, physical complaints, academic problems, and anxiety	• Occurs about equally in both sexes • Connected with lack of competencies (knowledge and skills) • Connected with situational stresses, such as divorce • Connected with feelings of helplessness and hopelessness • Connected with cognitive factors such as perfectionism, rumination, minimization of achievements, blowing problems out of proportion, and a negative attributional style—internal, stable, and global attributions for failures • Possibly connected with genetic factors • Connected with "underutilization" of the neurotransmitter serotonin • Frequently accompanied by anxiety
Childhood anxiety: • Phobias (e.g., separation anxiety disorder, stage fright, school phobia) • Panic disorder • Generalized anxiety disorder	• Obsessive–compulsive disorder • Stress disorders • Persistent, excessive worrying • Fear of the worst happening • Anxiety inappropriate for child's developmental level • Physical symptoms such as stomachaches, nausea, and vomiting • Nightmares • Concerns about death and dying	• More common in girls • Genetic factors implicated • Frequently develops after stressful life events, such as divorce, illness, death of relative or pet, or change of schools or homes • Often overlaps with—but not the same as—school refusal • Frequently accompanied by depression

generalized anxiety disorder (GAD) An anxiety disorder in which anxiety appears to be present continuously and is unrelated to the situation.

Childhood Anxiety

Children show many kinds of anxiety disorders, and these disorders are accompanied by depression in 50% to 60% of children (Kendler et al., 2007; Masi et al., 2004). Yet many children show anxiety disorders, such as **generalized anxiety disorder (GAD),** in the absence of depression (Kearney & Bensaheb, 2007). Other anxiety disorders shown by children include **phobias** such as **separation anxiety disorder (SAD)** and stage fright (Beidel & Turner, 2007).

A cross-cultural study compared anxiety disorders in 862 German children and 975 Japanese children between the ages of 8 and 12 (Essau et al., 2004). The German children were significantly more likely to report generalized anxiety, separation anxiety, social phobias, and **obsessive-compulsive disorder (OCD).** The Japanese children were more likely to report physical complaints and phobias in the realm of bodily injury. In both nations, girls were more likely than boys to report anxieties.

Separation Anxiety Disorder

It is normal for children to show anxiety when they are separated from their caregivers. Separation anxiety is a normal feature of the child–caregiver relationship and begins during the first year. But the sense of security that is usually provided by bonds of attachment encourages children to explore their environments and become progressively independent of caregivers. *Question: What is separation anxiety disorder?*

Separation anxiety disorder affects an estimated 4% to 5% of children and young adolescents (American Psychiatric Association, 2000; Shear et al., 2006). The disorder occurs most often in girls and is often associated with school refusal. It also frequently occurs together with social anxiety (Ferdinand et al., 2006). The disorder may persist into adulthood, leading to an exaggerated concern about the well-being of one's children and spouse and difficulty tolerating any separation from them.

SAD is diagnosed when separation anxiety is persistent and excessive, when it is inappropriate for the child's developmental level, and when it interferes with the activities or development tasks, the most important of which is attending school. Six-year-olds ought to be able to enter first grade without anxiety-related nausea and vomiting and without dread that they or their parents will come to harm. Children with SAD tend to cling to their parents and follow them around the house. They may voice concerns about death and dying and insist that someone stay with them while they are falling asleep. They may complain of nightmares, stomachaches, and nausea and vomiting on school days. They may plead with their parents not to leave the house, or they may throw tantrums.

SAD may occur before middle childhood, preventing adjustment to day care or nursery school. In adolescence, refusal to attend school is often connected with academic and social problems, in which cases the label of SAD would not apply. SAD usually becomes a significant problem in middle childhood because that is when children are expected to adjust to school. The disorder may persist into adulthood, leading to an exaggerated concern about the well-being of one's children and spouse and difficulty tolerating any separation from them.

SAD frequently develops after a stressful life event, such as illness, the death of a relative or pet, or a change of schools or homes. Alison's problems followed the death of her grandmother:

> Alison's grandmother died when Alison was 7 years old. Her parents decided to permit her request to view her grandmother in the open coffin. Alison took a tentative glance from her father's arms across the room, then asked to be taken out of the room. Her 5-year-old sister took a leisurely close-up look, with no apparent distress.
>
> Alison had been concerned about death for two or three years by this time, but her grandmother's passing brought on a new flurry of questions: "Will I die?" "Does everybody die?" and so on. Her parents tried to reassure her by saying, "Grandma was very, very old, and she also had a heart condition. You are very young and in perfect health. You have many, many years before you have to start thinking about death."
>
> Alison also could not be alone in any room in her house. She pulled one of her parents or her sister along with her everywhere she went. She also

phobia An irrational, excessive fear that interferes with one's functioning.

separation anxiety disorder (SAD) An extreme form of otherwise normal separation anxiety that is characterized by anxiety about separating from parents; SAD often takes the form of refusal to go to school.

obsessive-compulsive disorder (OCD) An anxiety disorder characterized by obsessions (recurring thoughts or images that seem beyond control) and compulsions (irresistible urges to repeat an act, such as hand washing or checking that one has put one's homework in one's backpack).

reported nightmares about her grandmother and, within a couple of days, insisted on sleeping in the same room with her parents. Fortunately, Alison's fears did not extend to school. Her teacher reported that Alison spent some time talking about her grandmother, but her academic performance was apparently unimpaired.

Alison's parents decided to allow Alison time to "get over" the loss. Alison gradually talked less and less about death, and by the time 3 months had passed, she was able to go into any room in her house by herself. She wanted to continue to sleep in her parents' bedroom, however. So her parents "made a deal" with her. They would put off the return to her own bedroom until the school year had ended (a month away), if Alison would agree to return to her own bed at that time. As a further incentive, a parent would remain with her until she fell asleep for the first month. Alison overcame the anxiety problem in this fashion with no additional delays.

—Author's files

© Sean Cayton/The Image Works

Separation Anxiety

School phobia is often a form of separation anxiety. This boy is afraid to be separated from his mother. He imagines that something terrible will happen to her (or to him) when they are apart. Many mornings he complains of a tummy ache or of being too tired to go to school.

Separation Anxiety Disorder, School Phobia, and School Refusal

Question: What are the connections between separation anxiety disorder, school phobia, and school refusal? SAD is similar to but not the same as school phobia. SAD is an extreme form of separation anxiety. It is characterized by anxiety about separating from parents and may be expressed as **school phobia**—which means fear of school—or of refusal to go to school (which can be based on fear or other factors). Separation anxiety—fear—is not behind all instances of school refusal (Bernstein & Layne, 2006). Some children refuse school because they perceive it as unpleasant, unsatisfying, or hostile, and sometimes it is. Some children are concerned about doing poorly in school or being asked to answer questions in class (in which case, they might be suffering from the social phobia of stage fright). High parental expectations to perform may heighten concern. Other children may refuse school because of problems with classmates (Ishikawa et al., 2003).

Question: What can we do about school phobia or school refusal?

Treatment of School Phobia or School Refusal

Truth or Fiction Revisited: It is usually not better for children with school phobia to remain at home until the origins of the problem are uncovered and resolved. A phobia is an irrational or overblown fear, a fear out of proportion to any danger in the situation. Therefore, one need not protect the child from school phobia. Most professionals agree that the first rule in the treatment of school phobia is: Get the child back into school. The second rule is: Get the child back into school. The third rule . . . Even without investigating the "meanings" of the child's refusal to attend school, many of the "symptoms" of the disorder disappear once the child is back in school on a regular basis.

Put it this way: There is nothing wrong with trying to understand why a child refuses to attend school. Knowledge of the reasons for refusal can help parents and educators devise strategies for assisting the child to adjust. But should such understanding precede insistence that the child return to school? Perhaps not. Here are some things parents can do to get a child back into school:

school phobia Fear of attending school, marked by extreme anxiety at leaving parents.

- Do not give in to the child's demands to stay home. If the child complains of being tired or ill, tell the child he or she may feel better at school and can rest there if necessary.
- Discuss the problem with the child's teacher, principal, and school nurse. (Gain the cooperation of school professionals.)
- If there is a specific school-related problem, such as an overly strict teacher, help the child find ways to handle the situation. (Finding ways to handle such problems can be accomplished while the child is in school. Not all such problems need be ironed out before the child returns to school.)
- Reward the child for attending school. (Yes, parents shouldn't "have to" reward children for "normal" behavior, but do you want the child in school or not?)

What if these measures don't work? How do professionals help? A variety of therapeutic approaches have been tried, and it would appear that cognitive-behavioral approaches are the most effective (Kendall et al., 2004; Turner, 2006; Valderhaug et al., 2004). One cognitive-behavioral method is counterconditioning to reduce the child's fear. (As described in Chapter 10, Mary Cover Jones used counterconditioning to reduce Peter's fear of rabbits.) Other cognitive-behavioral methods include systematic desensitization, modeling, cognitive restructuring, and the shaping and rewarding of school attendance.

When possible, the children's parents are taught to apply cognitive-behavioral methods. One study assessed the effectiveness of so-called family-based group cognitive-behavioral treatment (FGCBT) for anxious children (Shortt et al., 2001). It included 71 children between the ages of 6 and 10 who were diagnosed with SAD, generalized anxiety (anxiety that persisted throughout the day), or social phobia (e.g., stage fright). The children and their families were assigned at random to FGCBT or to a 10-week waiting list ("We'll get to you in 10 weeks"), which was the control group. The effectiveness of the treatment was evaluated after treatment and at a 12-month follow-up. The researchers found that nearly 70% of the children who had completed FGCBT were no longer diagnosable with anxiety disorders, compared with 6% of the children on the waiting list. Even at the 12-month follow-up, 68% of children remained diagnosis free.

Antidepressant medication has been used—often in conjunction with cognitive-behavioral methods—with a good deal of success (Murphy et al., 2000; Pine et al., 2001; Walkup et al., 2001). Antidepressants can have side effects, however, such as abdominal discomfort (Burke & Baker, 2001). Moreover, some professionals fear that they can trigger suicidal thoughts in children (Mosholder, 2004). However, drugs in themselves do not teach children how to cope with situations. Many health professionals suggest that the drugs—in this case, antidepressants—are best used only when psychological treatments have proven to be ineffective (Masi et al., 2001).

Daniel Pine and his colleagues (2001) reported a study on the treatment of 128 anxious children, age 6 to 17 years. Like those children in the Shortt study, they were diagnosed with a social phobia (such as stage fright), SAD, or GAD. All the children had received psychological treatment for 3 weeks without improvement. The children were assigned at random to receive an antidepressant (fluvoxamine) or a placebo (a "sugar pill") for 8 weeks. Neither the children, their parents, their teachers, nor the researchers knew which child had received which treatment. After 8 weeks, the children's anxiety was evaluated. Forty-eight of 63 children (76%) who had received the antidepressant improved significantly, compared with 19 of 65 children (29%) who had received the placebo.

It seems unfortunate to depart middle childhood following a discussion of social and emotional problems. Most children in developed nations come through middle childhood quite well, in good shape for the challenges and dramas of adolescence.

Perhaps all children encounter some stress. But some children bear a heavy burden. The cumulative effect of stressors such as poverty, parental discord, or abuse or neglect places children at high risk of maladjustment. But some children are more resilient than others. They adapt and thrive despite stress (Haeffel & Grigorenko, 2007; Kim-Cohen, 2007). How do resilient children differ from those who are more vulnerable to stress? Two key factors appear to be the child's personality and social support.

Personality Characteristics

Genetics and temperament may play key roles in children's resilience (Bartels & Hudziak, 2007; Rutter, 2006b). At 1 year of age, resilient children are securely attached to their mothers. At age 2, they are independent and easygoing, even if they are abused or neglected. Not only is the easygoing child less likely to be the target of negative behavior from parents, but he or she is also better able to cope with stress. By 3½ years of age, they are cheerful, persistent, flexible, and capable of seeking help from adults. In middle childhood, they distance themselves from turmoil and show independence. They believe that they can make good things happen (Griffin et al., 2001; Sandler, 2001).

Social Support

Support from others—parents, grandparents, siblings, peers, or teachers—helps children cope with stress (Davies & Windle, 2001; Greeff & Van Der Merwe, 2004; Kim-Cohen, 2007). Social support is particularly important for children who live in poverty. Children from ethnic minority groups and from families headed by single mothers are especially likely to be poor. Nearly 35 million Americans live in poverty, and most of them are children (U.S. Bureau of the Census, 2007). African Americans and Latino and Latina Americans are "overrepresented" in the statistics, with more than 20% of each group living in poverty. By contrast, only about 7.5% of European Americans and 11% of Asian Americans live in poverty. But here's a startler: Five times as many households headed by single women live in poverty as households headed by a married couple.

Yet many poor children from ethnic minority groups have extended families that include grandparents who live with them or nearby. Extended families provide economic, social, and emotional support for children (Barrow et al., 2007; Cooper & Crosnoe, 2007). Grandmothers, in particular, play a key role. Extended families enable single mothers to attend school or work and increase the quality of child care (Barrow et al., 2007; Cooper & Crosnoe, 2007).

The message is that many, many children do well despite adversity. In fact, Ann Masten (2001) characterized such an outcome as somewhat "ordinary." Hey, kids: Just do it!

Active Review

20. Conduct disorders are more likely to be found among the (Biological or Adoptive?) parents of adopted children with conduct disorders.

21. Self-perceived competence appears to (Protect children from or Make children vulnerable to?) feelings of depression.

22. Depressed children tend to (Underutilize or Overutilize?) the neurotransmitter serotonin in the brain.

23. Separation _____ disorder is similar to but not exactly the same as school phobia.

24. Separation anxiety (Is or Is not?) behind all instances of school refusal.

Reflect & Relate: Have you known children with conduct disorders, depression, or separation anxiety disorder (or school phobia)? Do you have any thoughts about the origins of the problems? Were the problems treated? What happened to the children?

Go to

http://www.thomsonedu.com/psychology/rathus

for an interactive version of this review.

RECITE: *An Active Summary*

1. **What are some features of social and emotional development in middle childhood?**

   Social development in middle childhood involves the development of skills, changes in interpersonal relationships, and the expansion of self-understanding. Freud viewed the period as the latency stage; Erikson saw it as the stage of industry versus inferiority. Social cognitive theorists note that children now depend less on external rewards and punishments and increasingly regulate their own behavior. Cognitive-developmental theory notes that concrete operations enhance social development.

2. **What is the relationship between social cognition and perspective taking?**

   In middle childhood, children become more capable of taking the role or perspective of another person. Selman theorizes that children move from egocentricity to seeing the world through the eyes of others in five stages.

3. **How does the self-concept develop during middle childhood?**

   In early childhood, children's self-concepts focus on concrete external traits. In middle childhood, children begin to include abstract internal traits. Social relationships and group membership assume importance.

4. **How does self-esteem develop during middle childhood?**

   In middle childhood, competence and social acceptance contribute to self-esteem, but self-esteem tends to decline because the self-concept becomes more realistic. Authoritative parenting fosters self-esteem.

5. **What is learned helplessness, and how does it develop in middle childhood?**

   Learned helplessness is the acquired belief that one cannot obtain rewards. "Helpless" children tend not to persist in the face of failure. Girls tend to feel more helpless in math than boys do, largely because of gender-role expectations.

6. **What kinds of influences are exerted by the family during middle childhood?**

   In middle childhood, the family continues to play a key role in socialization. Parent–child interactions focus on school-related issues, chores, and peers. Parents do less monitoring of children; "coregulation" develops.

7. **What are the effects of having lesbian or gay parents?**

   Children of lesbian and gay parents by and large develop as well as children of heterosexual parents. The sexual orientation of these children is generally heterosexual.

8. **What are the effects of divorce on the children?**

   Divorce disrupts children's lives and usually lowers the family's financial status. Children are likely to greet divorce with sadness, shock, and disbelief. Children of divorce fare better when parents cooperate on child rearing. Children's adjustment is related to the mother's coping ability.

9. **What is best for the children? Should parents who bicker remain together for their children's sake?**

   In terms of the child's psychological adjustment, the answer seems to be not necessarily. Children appear to suffer as much from marital conflict as from divorce per se.

10. **What are the effects of maternal employment on children?**

    Having both parents in the workforce may be related to relative lack of supervision. However, there is little evidence that maternal employment harms children. Maternal employment fosters greater independence and flexibility in gender-role stereotypes.

11. What is the influence of peers during middle childhood?

Peers take on increasing importance and exert pressure to conform. Peer experiences also broaden children. Peers afford practice in social skills, sharing, relating to leaders, and coping with aggressive impulses. Popular children tend to be attractive and mature for their age.

12. How do children's concepts of friendship develop?

Early in middle childhood, friendships are based on proximity. Between the ages of 8 and 11, children become more aware of the value of friends as meeting each other's needs and having traits such as loyalty. At this age, peers tend to discourage contact with members of the other sex.

13. What are the effects of the school on children's social and emotional development?

Schools make demands for mature behavior and nurture positive physical, social, and cognitive development. Readiness for school is related to children's early life experiences, individual differences in development and learning, and the schools' expectations.

14. What are the characteristics of a good school?

An effective school has an energetic principal, an orderly atmosphere, empowerment of teachers and students, high expectations for children, and solid academics. Teachers' expectations can become self-fulfilling prophecies. Many girls suffer from sexism and sexual harassment in school. Math and science are generally stereotyped as masculine, and language arts as feminine.

15. What are conduct disorders? What can we do about them?

Children with conduct disorders persistently break rules or violate the rights of others. There may be a genetic component to such disorders, but sociopathic models in the family, deviant peers, and inconsistent discipline all contribute. Parental training in cognitive-behavioral methods holds promise for treating these disorders.

16. What is depression? What can we do about it?

Depressed children tend to complain of poor appetite, insomnia, lack of energy, and feelings of worthlessness. Depressed children tend to blame themselves excessively for shortcomings. Psychotherapy tends to make children aware of their tendencies to minimize their accomplishments and overly blame themselves for shortcomings. Antidepressants are sometimes helpful but controversial.

17. What is separation anxiety disorder?

Separation anxiety disorder (SAD) is diagnosed when separation anxiety is persistent and excessive and interferes with daily life. Children with SAD tend to cling to parents and may refuse to attend school.

18. What are the connections between separation anxiety disorder, school phobia, and school refusal?

SAD is an extreme form of otherwise normal separation anxiety and may take the form of school phobia. But children can refuse school for other reasons, including finding school to be unpleasant or hostile.

19. What can we do about school phobia or school refusal?

The most important aspect of treatment is to insist that the child attend school. Cognitive-behavioral therapy and medicine may also be of use.

Key Terms

latency stage, 443
industry versus inferiority, 443
social cognition, 443
self-esteem, 445
learned helplessness, 447
coregulation, 448
lesbian, 449
gay, 449

transsexual, 450
Pygmalion effect, 462
self-fulfilling prophecy, 462
sexism, 463
sexual harassment, 463
conduct disorders, 464
attributional style, 467
serotonin, 467

generalized anxiety disorder
    (GAD), 468
phobia, 469
separation anxiety disorder
    (SAD), 469
obsessive-compulsive disorder
    (OCD), 469
school phobia, 470

Active Learning Resources

Childhood & Adolescence Book Companion Website
http://www.thomsonedu.com/psychology/rathus

Visit your book companion website where you will find more resources to help you study. There you will find interactive versions of your book features, including the Lessons in Observation video, Active Review sections, and the Truth or Fiction feature. In addition, the companion website contains quizzing, flash cards, and a pronunciation glossary.

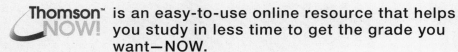

is an easy-to-use online resource that helps you study in less time to get the grade you want—NOW.

http://www.thomsonedu.com/login

Need help studying? This site is your one-stop study shop. Take a Pre-Test and ThomsonNOW will generate a Personalized Study Plan based on your test results. The Study Plan will identify the topics you need to review and direct you to online resources to help you master those topics. You can then take a Post-Test to determine the concepts you have mastered and what you still need to work on.

14 Adolescence:
Physical Development

Truth or Fiction?

T F American adolescents are growing taller than their parents. p. 481

T F Girls are fertile immediately after their first menstrual period. p. 485

T F Boys and girls who mature early have higher self-esteem than those who mature late. p. 488

T F Most adolescents in the United States are unaware of the risks of HIV/AIDS. p. 491

T F Substance abuse is the leading cause of death among male adolescents in the United States. p. 497

T F You can never be too rich or too thin. p. 498

T F Some college women control their weight by going on cycles of binge eating followed by self-induced vomiting. p. 501

T F Substance use and abuse is on the rise among high school students. p. 507

T F Substance abuse is highest among African American and Latino American high school students. p. 509

Preview

Puberty: The Biological Eruption
The Adolescent Growth Spurt: Changed Forever
Pubertal Changes in Boys
Pubertal Changes in Girls
Early versus Late Maturers: Does It Matter When You Arrive, as Long as You Do?
Body Image in Adolescence

Emerging Sexuality and the Risks of Sexually Transmitted Infections
HIV/AIDS
Risk Factors
Prevention of Sexually Transmitted Infections

A Closer Look: Preventing HIV/AIDS and Other STIs: It's More than Safe(r) Sex

Health in Adolescence
Risk Taking in Adolescence
Nutrition: An Abundance of Food
An Abundance of Eating Disorders: When Dieting Turns Deadly
Substance Abuse and Dependence: Where Does It Begin? Where Does It End?

Developing in a World of Diversity: Sex, College Plans, Ethnicity, and Substance Abuse

Go to

http://www.thomsonedu.com/psychology/rathus
for an interactive version of this "Truth or Fiction" feature.

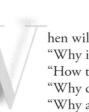

"hen will it happen?"

"Why is my voice acting so funny?"

"How tall will I be?"

"Why do I get pimples?"

"Why am I getting hairy?"

"Why is mine not like his?"

"What's happening to me?"

Perhaps no other period of life is as exciting—and as bewildering—as adolescence. Except for infancy, more changes occur during adolescence than during any other time of life.

In our society, adolescents are "neither fish nor fowl," as the saying goes, neither children nor adults. Adolescents may be old enough to reproduce and may be as large as their parents, yet they are required to remain in school through age 16, they may not be allowed to get drivers' licenses until they are 16 or 17, and they cannot attend R-rated films unless accompanied by an adult. Given the restrictions placed on adolescents, their growing yearning for independence, and a sex drive heightened by high levels of sex hormones, it is not surprising that adolescents occasionally are in conflict with their parents.

The capacity to think abstractly and hypothetically emerges during the teenage years. This ability gives rise to a stream of seemingly endless "Who am I?" questions, as adolescents search for a sense of identity and ponder the possible directions their adult lives may take.

Question: What is adolescence? Adolescence is a transitional period between childhood and adulthood, a coming of age. A century ago, most children in the United States assumed adult responsibilities early. Adolescence began to emerge as a distinct stage of development between childhood and adulthood when the demands of an increasingly complex society required a longer period of education and delayed entry into the labor force. It is no longer easy for American adolescents to know when they have made the transition to adulthood. One legally becomes an adult at different ages, depending on whether one is enlisting in the armed services, buying a drink, driving a car, voting, or getting married.

The idea that adolescence is an important and separate developmental stage was proposed by G. Stanley Hall (1904), an early American psychologist. Hall believed that adolescence is marked by intense turmoil. He used the German term *Sturm und Drang* ("storm and stress") to refer to the conflicts and stresses of adolescence. According to Hall, adolescents swing back and forth between happiness and sadness, overconfidence and self-doubt, dependence and independence. Hall believed that adolescent mood swings and conflicts with parents are a necessary part of growing up. He thought that children have to rebel against their parents and their parents' values to make the transition to adulthood.

Sigmund Freud (1964 [1933]) placed relatively little emphasis on adolescence, because he believed that the first 5 years of life are the most critical. According to Freud, we enter the **genital stage** of psychosexual development at puberty. Sexual feelings are initially aimed at the parent of the other sex, but they become transferred, or displaced, onto other adults or adolescents of the other sex. Anna Freud (1969), Freud's daughter, saw adolescence as a turbulent period resulting from an increase in the sex drive. The adolescent tries to keep surging sexual impulses in check and redirects them from the parents to more acceptable outlets. The result is unpredictable behavior, defiance of parents, confusion, and mood swings. Anna Freud, like G. Stanley Hall, believed that adolescent turmoil is a part of normal development.

But adolescence need not be a time of "storm and stress." Contemporary theorists no longer see adolescent storm and stress as inevitable (Smetana, 2005; Susman & Rogol, 2004). Instead, they see adolescence as a period when biological, cognitive, social, and emotional functioning are reorganized.

genital stage In psychoanalytic theory, the fifth and final stage of psychosexual development in which gratification is attained through sexual intercourse with an individual of the other sex.

Some theorists even argue that the concept of adolescence as a period of storm and stress marginalizes adolescents (Susman & Rogol, 2004). Seeing young people as "troubled" or "troubling" encourages adults to eye them warily and to not take their problems seriously. It is more useful to try to understand adolescents' problems and find ways of helping them cope.

Even if adolescence does not necessarily involve storm and stress, adolescents face the challenge of adapting to numerous biological, cognitive, and social and emotional changes. In this chapter, we focus on the biological and physical changes of adolescence. Let us begin—as adolescence begins—with puberty. *Questions: What is puberty? What happens during puberty?*

Puberty: The Biological Eruption

Puberty is a stage of development characterized by reaching sexual maturity and the ability to reproduce. The onset of adolescence coincides with the advent of puberty. Puberty, however, is a biological concept, whereas adolescence is a psychosocial concept with biological correlates.

Puberty is controlled by a complex **feedback loop** involving the **hypothalamus, pituitary gland,** gonads—ovaries in females and testes in males—and hormones. The hypothalamus sends signals to the pituitary gland, which, in turn, releases hormones that control physical growth and the functioning of the gonads. The gonads respond to pituitary hormones by increasing their production of sex hormones (androgens and estrogens). The sex hormones further stimulate the hypothalamus, thus perpetuating the feedback loop.

The sex hormones also trigger the development of both the primary and secondary sex characteristics. The **primary sex characteristics** are the structures that make reproduction possible. In girls, these structures are the ovaries, vagina, uterus, and fallopian tubes. In boys, they are the penis, testes, prostate gland, and seminal vesicles. The **secondary sex characteristics** are physical indicators of sexual maturation that do not involve the reproductive structures. They include breast development, deepening of the voice, and the appearance of facial, pubic, and underarm hair. Let us now explore the physical changes of puberty, starting with the growth spurt and then examining other pubertal changes in boys and girls involving the primary and secondary sex characteristics. *Question: What happens during the adolescent growth spurt?*

The Adolescent Growth Spurt: Changed Forever

The stable growth patterns in height and weight that characterize early and middle childhood come to an abrupt end with the adolescent growth spurt. Girls start to spurt in height sooner than boys, at an average age of a little more than 10. Boys start to spurt about 2 years later, at an average age of about 12. Girls and boys reach their periods of peak growth in height about 2 years after the growth spurt begins, at about 12 and 14 years, respectively (see ● Figure 14.1). The spurt in height for both girls and boys continues for about another 2 years at a gradually declining pace. Boys grow more than girls do during their spurt, averaging nearly 4 inches per year during the fastest year of the spurt compared with slightly more than 3 inches per year for girls. Overall, boys add an average of 14½ inches to their height during the spurt and girls add a little more than 13 inches (Tanner, 1991a).

Adolescents begin to spurt in weight about half a year after they begin to spurt in height. The period of peak growth in weight occurs about a year and a half after the onset of the spurt. As is the case with height, the growth spurt in weight then continues for a little more than 2 years for both girls and boys. As you can see in

Is Adolescence a Period of Storm and Stress? Research challenges the view that "storm and stress" are either normal or beneficial for adolescents. Neither violent mood swings nor deep-rooted parental conflicts appear inevitable, and most teenagers report feeling happy with their lives.

puberty The biological stage of development characterized by changes that lead to reproductive capacity. Puberty signals the beginning of adolescence.

feedback loop A system in which glands regulate each other's functioning through a series of hormonal messages.

hypothalamus A pea-sized structure above the pituitary gland that is involved in the regulation of body temperature, motivation (e.g., hunger, thirst, sex), and emotion.

pituitary gland The body's "master gland," which is located in the lower central part of the brain and which secretes many hormones essential to development, such as oxytocin, prolactin, and growth hormone.

primary sex characteristics The structures that make reproduction possible.

secondary sex characteristics Physical indicators of sexual maturation—such as changes to the voice and growth of bodily hair—that do not directly involve reproductive structures.

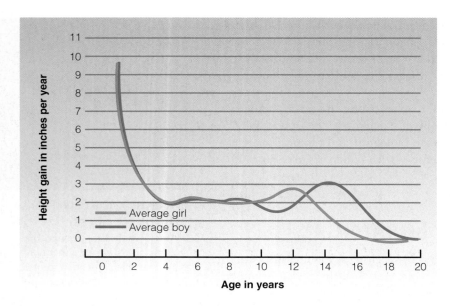

● **Figure 14.1** Spurts in Growth

Girls begin the adolescent growth spurt about 2 years earlier than boys. Girls and boys reach their periods of peak growth about 2 years after the spurt begins, at about 12 and 14 years, respectively.

● Figure 14.2, girls are taller and heavier than boys from about age 9 or 10 until about age 13 or 14 because their growth spurt occurs earlier. Once boys begin their growth spurt, they catch up with girls and eventually become taller and heavier.

Because the spurt in weight lags the spurt in height, many adolescents are relatively slender compared with their preadolescent and postadolescent stature. However, adolescents tend to eat enormous quantities of food to fuel their growth spurts. Active 14- and 15-year-old boys may consume 3,000 to 4,000 calories a day without becoming obese. If they were to eat this much 20 years later, they might gain upward of 100 pounds per year. It's little wonder that adults fighting the dismal battle of the bulge stare at adolescents in amazement as they inhale pizza for lunch and go out later for burgers and fries!

Girls' and boys' body shapes begin to differ in adolescence. For one thing, boys' shoulders become broader than those of girls, whereas the hip dimensions of both sexes do not differ much. Thus, girls have relatively broader hips compared with their shoulders, whereas the opposite is true for boys. A girl's body shape is also more rounded than that of a boy because, during puberty, girls gain almost twice as much fatty tissue as boys do. Boys, on the other hand, gain twice as much muscle tissue as girls do. Thus, a larger proportion of a male's body weight is composed of his muscle mass, whereas a relatively larger part of a female's body weight is composed of fatty tissue.

Individual Differences in the Growth Spurt

The figures given in this discussion are averages. Few of us begin or end our growth spurts right on the mark. Children who spurt earlier are likely to wind up with somewhat shorter legs and longer torsos, whereas children who spurt late are somewhat longer legged. However, there are no significant differences between early and late spurters in the total height attained at maturity (Peeters et al., 2005; Tanner, 1991a).

Regardless of the age at which the growth spurt begins, there is a moderate to high correlation between a child's height at the onset of adolescence and at maturity (Tanner, 1989). Are there exceptions? Of course. However, everything else being equal, a tall child has a reasonable expectation of becoming a tall adult, and similarly for a small child.

Asynchronous Growth: On Being Gawky

Adolescents are often referred to as awkward and gawky. A major reason for this is **asynchronous growth**, when different parts of the body grow at different rates. In an exception to the principle of proximodistal growth, the hands and feet mature before the arms and legs do. As a consequence, adolescent girls and boys may complain of big hands or feet. And, in an apparent reversal of the cephalocaudal growth trend, legs reach their peak growth before the shoulders and chest. In other words, boys stop growing out of their pants about a year before they stop growing out of their jackets (Tanner, 1989).

asynchronous growth Imbalanced growth, such as the growth that occurs during the early part of adolescence and causes many adolescents to appear gawky.

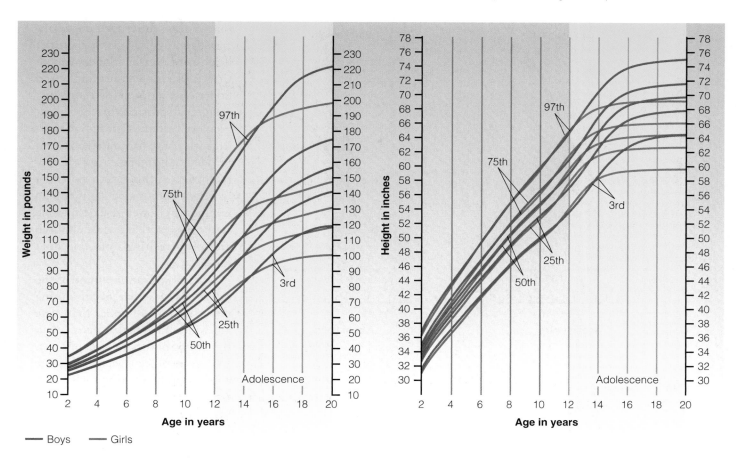

● **Figure 14.2** Growth Curves for Height and Weight

Girls are taller and heavier than boys from about age 9 or 10 until about age 13 because their growth spurt occurs earlier. Once boys begin their growth spurt, they catch up with girls and eventually become taller and heavier.

Source: Kuczmarski et al. (2000, Figures 9–12).

The Secular Trend in Growth

During the past century, children in the Western world have grown dramatically more rapidly and have wound up taller than children from earlier times (Sun et al., 2005). This historical trend toward increasing adult height, which also has been accompanied by an earlier onset of puberty, is known as the **secular trend.** ● Figure 14.3 shows that Swedish boys and girls grew more rapidly in 1938 and 1968 than they did in 1883 and ended up several inches taller. At the age of 15, the boys were more than 6 inches taller and the girls were more than 3 inches taller, on average, than their counterparts from the previous century (Tanner, 1989). The occurrence of a secular trend in height and also in weight has been documented in nearly all European countries and the United States.

    Truth or Fiction Revisited: It turns out that children from middle- and upper-class families in industrialized countries, including the United States, have now stopped growing taller, whereas their poorer counterparts continue to make gains in height from generation to generation (Tanner, 1989). Why?

    Nutrition apparently plays an important role. U.S. government surveys have shown that children from middle- and upper-class families are taller and heavier than their age-mates from lower-class families. But these data in themselves are not very convincing. For example, it could be argued that genetic factors provide advantages

secular trend A historical trend toward increasing adult height and earlier puberty.

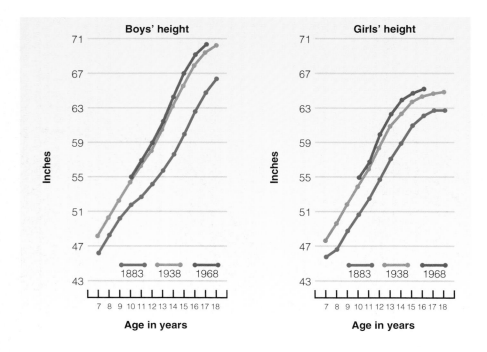

● Figure 14.3
Are We Still Growing
Taller than Our Parents?

Twentieth-century children grew more rapidly and grew taller than children in preceding centuries. However, it seems that children from affluent families are no longer growing taller than their parents. But children from the lower part of the socioeconomic spectrum are still doing so.

Source: Tanner (1989).

larynx The part of the throat that contains the vocal cords.

semen The fluid that contains sperm and substances that nourish and help transport sperm.

that increase the chances for financial gain as well as for greater height and weight. But remember that children from the middle- and upper-class portion of the socioeconomic spectrum are no longer growing taller. Perhaps Americans who have had nutritional and medical advantages have simply reached their full genetic potential in height. Continued gains among families of lower socioeconomic status suggest that poorer children are still benefiting from improved nutrition.

We now examine some of the other changes that occur during puberty. You will notice that there are wide individual differences in the timing of the events of puberty. In a group of teenagers of the same age and sex, you may well find some who have completed puberty, others who have not even started, and others who are somewhere in between.

Pubertal Changes in Boys

At puberty, the pituitary gland stimulates the testes to increase their output of testosterone, leading to further development of the male genitals. The first visible sign of puberty is accelerated growth of the testes, which begins at an average age of about 11½, although a range of ages of plus or minus 2 years is considered perfectly normal. Testicular growth further accelerates testosterone production and other pubertal changes. The penis begins a spurt of accelerated growth about a year later, and still later, pubic hair begins a growth spurt.

Underarm hair appears at about age 15. Facial hair is at first a fuzz on the upper lip. An actual beard does not develop for another 2 to 3 years, and only half of American boys shave (of necessity) by 17. The beard and chest hair continue to develop past the age of 20.

At 14 or 15, the voice deepens because of growth of the "voice box," or **larynx**, and the lengthening of the vocal cords. The developmental process is gradual, and adolescent boys sometimes encounter an embarrassing cracking of the voice.

Testosterone also triggers the development of acne, which afflicts between 75% and 90% of adolescents (Goldstein, 2004). Severe acne is manifested by multiple pimples and blackheads on the face, chest, and back. Although boys are more prone to acne than girls, we cannot say that girls suffer less from it. In our society, a smooth complexion has a higher value for girls than for boys, and girls with acne that boys would consider mild may suffer terribly.

Males are capable of producing erections in early infancy (and some male babies are born with erections), but the phenomenon is not frequent until age 13 or 14. Adolescent males may experience unwanted and unprovoked erections. Many boys worry that they will be caught with erections when walking between classes or when asked to stand before the class. The organs that produce **semen** grow rapidly, and boys typically ejaculate seminal fluid by age 13 or 14—about 1½ years after the penis begins its growth spurt—although here, too, there is much individual variation. About a year later they begin to have **nocturnal emissions,** also called wet dreams because of the myth that emissions accompany erotic dreams. However, nocturnal emissions and erotic dreams need not coincide. Mature sperm are found in ejaculatory emissions by about the age of 15. And so ejaculation is not adequate evidence of reproductive capacity. Ejaculatory ability in boys usually precedes the presence of mature sperm by at least a year.

Nearly half of all boys experience enlargement of the breasts, or **gynecomastia,** which usually declines in a year or two. Gynecomastia stems from the small amount of female sex hormones secreted by the testes. When gynecomastia persists or becomes distressful, it can be treated with drugs, such as tamoxifen (Derman et al., 2003). Some males choose surgery.

At age 20 or 21, men stop growing taller because testosterone causes **epiphyseal closure,** which prevents the long bones from making further gains in length. And so, puberty for males draws to a close. The changes of puberty in males are summarized in Concept Review 14.1.

nocturnal emission Emission of seminal fluid while asleep.

gynecomastia Enlargement of breast tissue in males.

epiphyseal closure The process by which the cartilage that separates the long end (epiphysis) of a bone from the main part of the bone turns to bone.

Concept Review 14.1 — Stages of Pubertal Development in Males

Age of Onset (Years)	Characteristics
Between 9 and 15	• Testicles begin to grow. • Skin of the scrotum becomes redder and coarser. • Straight pubic hairs begin to appear at the base of the penis. • Muscle mass develops, and the boy begins to grow taller. • Areola (the dark area around the nipple) grows larger and darker.
Between 11 and 16	• Penis begins to grow longer. • Testicles and scrotum continue to grow. • Pubic hair becomes coarser and more curled and spreads to cover the area between the legs. • Body gains in height. • Shoulders broaden. • Hips narrow. • Larynx enlarges, and voice deepens. • Sparse facial and underarm hair appears.
Between 11 and 17	• Penis begins to increase in circumference as well as in length (although more slowly). • Testicles continue to increase in size. • Texture of the pubic hair becomes more adult-like. • Growth of facial and underarm hair increases. • First ejaculation occurs. • Gynecomastia occurs in nearly half of all boys. • Increased skin oils may produce acne.
Between 14 and 18	• Body nears final adult height, genitals achieve adult shape and size, pubic hair spreads to thighs and upward toward the belly. • Chest hair appears. • Facial hair reaches full growth. • Further increases in height, body hair, and muscle growth and strength may continue into the early 20s.

Source: From *The Kinsey Institute New Report on Sex,* 1990, pp. 272–273. Reprinted by permission of The Kinsey Institute for Research in Sex, Gender, and Reproduction, Inc.
Note: This review is a general guideline. Changes may appear sooner or later than shown and do not always appear in the indicated sequence.

Pubertal Changes in Girls

In girls, the pituitary gland signals the ovaries to vastly increase estrogen production at puberty. Estrogen may stimulate the growth of breast tissue ("breast buds") as early as the ages of 8 or 9, but the breasts usually begin to enlarge during the 10th year. The development of fatty tissue and ducts elevates the areas of the breasts surrounding the nipples and causes the nipples themselves to protrude. The breasts typically reach full size in about 3 years, but the **mammary glands** do not mature fully until a woman has a baby.

Estrogen also promotes the growth of the fatty and supporting tissue in the hips and buttocks, which, along with the widening of the pelvis, causes the hips to become rounded. Growth of fatty deposits and connective tissue varies considerably. For this reason, development of breasts and hips differs.

Beginning at about the age of 11, girls' adrenal glands produce small amounts of androgens that, along with estrogen, stimulate the growth of pubic and underarm hair. Excessive androgen production can darken or increase the amount of facial hair. Androgens and estrogen have other functions as well.

Estrogen causes the **labia,** vagina, and uterus to develop during puberty, and androgens cause the **clitoris** to develop. The vaginal lining varies in thickness according to the amount of estrogen in the bloodstream.

Estrogen typically brakes the female growth spurt some years before testosterone brakes that of males. Girls deficient in estrogen during their late teens may grow quite tall, but most girls reach their heights because of normal, genetically determined variations.

Menarche

Menarche (first menstruation) commonly occurs between the ages of 11 and 14. But it is quite normal for menarche to occur as early as age 9 or as late as age 16 (Capron et al., 2007; Mendle et al., 2006). In the middle 1800s, European girls first menstruated at about the age of 16, as shown in ● Figure 14.4. During the past century and a half, however, the processes of puberty have occurred at progressively earlier ages in Western nations, an example of the secular trend in development. By the 1960s, the

mammary glands Glands that secrete milk.

labia The major and minor lips of the female genitalia.

clitoris A female sex organ that is highly sensitive to sexual stimulation but not directly involved in reproduction.

menarche The onset of menstruation.

● **Figure 14.4** The Decline in Age at Menarche

The age at menarche has been declining since the mid-1800s among girls in Western nations, apparently because of improved nutrition and health care. Menarche may be triggered by the accumulation of a critical percentage of body fat.

Source: Tanner (1989).

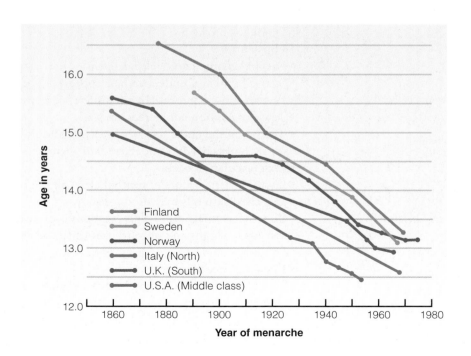

average age of menarche in the United States had plummeted to its current figure of 12½ (Tanner, 1991b).

No single theory of the onset of puberty has found wide acceptance. In any event, the average age of the advent of puberty for girls and boys appears to have leveled off in recent years. The precipitous drop suggested in Figure 14.4 seems to have come to an end.

What accounts for the earlier age of puberty? One hypothesis is that girls must reach a certain body weight to trigger pubertal changes such as menarche. Body fat could trigger the changes because fat cells secrete the protein leptin. Leptin would then signal the brain to secrete a cascade of hormones that raise estrogen levels in the body. Menarche comes later to girls who have a lower percentage of body fat, such as those with eating disorders or athletes (Bosi & de Oliveira, 2006; Frisch, 1997).

The average body weight for triggering menarche depends on the girl's height. For girls who are 5 feet to 5½ feet tall, the average triggering weight is between 97 and 114 pounds (Frisch, 1991). Today's children are larger than the children of the early 20th century, probably because of improved nutrition and health care. It seems that the age threshold for reaching menarche may have been attained because the average age has leveled off in recent years.

Hormonal Regulation of the Menstrual Cycle

Testosterone levels remain fairly stable in boys, although they decline gradually in adulthood. However, estrogen and progesterone levels vary markedly and regulate the menstrual cycle. Following menstruation—the sloughing off of the endometrium— estrogen levels increase, leading once more to the growth of endometrial tissue. **Truth or Fiction Revisited:** It is usually not true that girls can become pregnant after they have their first menstrual period. Girls usually don't begin to ovulate until 12 to 18 months after menarche. A ripe ovum is released by the ovary when estrogen reaches peak blood levels. Then the inner lining of the uterus thickens in response to the secretion of progesterone. In this way, it gains the capacity to support an embryo if fertilization should occur. If the ovum is not fertilized, estrogen and progesterone levels drop suddenly, triggering menstruation once again.

The average menstrual cycle is 28 days, but variation between girls and in the same girl is common. Girls' cycles are often irregular for a few years after menarche but later tend to assume patterns that are reasonably regular. Most menstrual cycles during the first 2 years or so after menarche occur without ovulation having taken place. But keep in mind that in any given individual cycle, an ovum may be produced, making pregnancy possible. So it is possible to become pregnant shortly after the onset of menarche.

The Psychological Impact of Menarche

In different times, in different places, menarche has had different meanings. The Manus of New Guinea greet menarche with elaborate ceremony (Golub, 1992). The other girls of the village sleep in the menstruating girl's hut. They feast and have parties. In the West, menstruation has historically received a mixed response. The menstrual flow itself has generally been seen, erroneously, as polluting, and the frequent discomforts of menstruation have led many menstruating women to be stereotyped as irrational (Rathus et al., 2008). Menarche itself has generally been perceived as the event in which a girl suddenly develops into a woman, but because of taboos and prejudice against menstruating women, girls historically matured in ignorance of menarche.

Girls' attitudes toward menarche reflect their level of education as well as certain physical realities. A Hong Kong study of 1,573 Chinese high school students found a mixed response to the onset of menstruation (Tang et al., 2003). The average age of menarche was 11.67 years. Although most of the girls reported that menstruation was annoying (it involved some discomfort for them, along with the need to dispose of the menstrual flow), two in three reported feeling more "grown up" and four in ten felt that they had become more feminine. Girls who felt positively about menarche were more likely to be educationally prepared to welcome it as a natural event, have a positive body image, and reject traditional negative attitudes.

Most American girls currently receive advance information about menstruation, not only from family and girlfriends but also from school health classes. The old horror stories are pretty much gone, at least in mainstream society (Gillooly, 2004). However, most girls experience at least some menstrual discomfort and need to discreetly dispose of the menstrual flow (Costos et al., 2002; Rathus et al., 2008). Most girls can separate pride in "becoming women" from the realities of some discomfort and the fact that menarche usually means that the girl will not be growing much taller, because of the braking effects of estrogen. The changes of puberty in females are summarized in Concept Review 14.2.

Concept Review 14.2 Stages of Pubertal Development in Females

Age of Onset (Years)	Characteristics
Between 8 and 11	• Pituitary hormones stimulate ovaries to increase production of estrogen. • Internal reproductive organs begin to grow.
Between 9 and 15	• First the areola and then the breasts increase in size and become more rounded. • Pubic hair becomes darker and coarser. • Growth in height continues. • Body fat rounds body contours. • A normal vaginal discharge becomes noticeable. • Sweat and oil glands increase in activity, and acne may appear. • Internal and external reproductive organs and genitals grow, making the vagina longer and the labia more pronounced.
Between 10 and 16	• Areola and nipples grow, often forming a second mound sticking out from the rounded breast mound. • Pubic hair begins to grow in a triangular shape and to cover the center of the pubic area. • Underarm hair appears. • Menarche occurs. • Internal reproductive organs continue to develop. • Ovaries may begin to release mature eggs capable of being fertilized. • Growth in height slows.
Between 12 and 19	• Breasts near adult size and shape. • Pubic hair fully covers the pubic area and spreads to the top of the thighs. • Voice may deepen slightly (but not as much as in males). • Menstrual cycles become more regular. • Further changes in body shape may occur into the early 20s.

Source: From *The Kinsey Institute New Report on Sex,* 1990, pp. 264–265. Reprinted by permission of The Kinsey Institute for Research in Sex, Gender, and Reproduction, Inc.
Note: This review is a general guideline. Changes may appear sooner or later than shown and do not always appear in the indicated sequence

Early versus Late Maturers:
Does It Matter When You Arrive, as Long as You Do?

I remember Al from my high school days. When Al entered the ninth grade, he was all of 14, but he was also about 6 feet 3 inches tall, with broad shoulders and arms thick with muscle. His face was cut from rock, and his beard was already dark. Al paraded down the hallways with an entourage of male and female admirers. When there were shrieks of anticipation, you could bet that Al was coming around the corner. Al was given a wide berth in the boys' room. He would have to lean back when he combed his waxed hair up and back; otherwise, his head would be too high for the mirror. At that age, my friends and I liked to tell ourselves that Al was not all that bright. (This stereotype is unfounded, as we will see.) Nevertheless, my friends and I were envious of Al.

Al had arrived. Al had matured early, and he had experienced the positive aspects of maturing early. What causes some children to mature earlier or later than others? Genetic, dietary, and health factors all seem to influence the timing of puberty. And one controversial new theory suggests that childhood stress may trigger early puberty in girls. ***Question: What are the effects of early or late maturation on adolescents?***

Early and Late Maturation in Boys

Research findings about boys who mature early are mixed, but the weight of the evidence suggests that the effects of early maturation are generally positive (Graber et al., 2004; Weichold et al., 2003). Late-maturing boys may feel conspicuous because they are among the last of their peers to lose their childhood appearance.

Early-maturing boys tend to be more popular than their late-maturing peers and more likely to be leaders in school (Ge et al., 2001b; Graber et al., 2004; Weichold et al., 2003). Early-maturing boys in general are also more poised, relaxed, and good-natured. Their edge in sports and the admiration of their peers heighten their sense of self-worth. Some studies have suggested that the stereotype of the mature tough-looking boy as dumb is just that, a stereotype.

On the negative side, early maturation is associated with greater risks of aggression and delinquency (Lynne et al., 2007) and abuse of alcohol and other drugs (Costello et al., 2007). Early maturation may also hit some boys before they are psy-

© Ellen Senisi/The Image Works

Early and Late Maturation in Boys
The effects of early maturation in boys are generally positive. Late-maturing boys may feel conspicuous because they are among the last of their peers to lose their childhood appearance.

chologically prepared to live up to the expectations of those who admire their new bodies. Coaches may expect too much of them in sports, and peers may want them to fight their battles for them (Ge et al., 2001b; O'Sullivan et al., 2000). Sexual opportunities may create demands before they know how to respond to them (Lam et al., 2002). Some early maturers may therefore worry about living up to the expectations of others.

Late maturers have the "advantage" of avoiding these early pressures. They are not rushed into maturity. On the other hand, late-maturing boys often feel dominated by early-maturing boys. They have been found to be more dependent and insecure. Although they are smaller and weaker than early maturers, they may be more likely to get involved in disruptive behavior and substance abuse (Ge et al., 2003; Graber et al., 2004; Weichold et al., 2003).

But there are individual differences. Although some late maturers appear to fight their physical status and get into trouble, others adjust and find acceptance through academic achievement, music, clubs, and other activities. The benefits of early maturation appear to be greatest among lower-income adolescents, because physical prowess is valued more highly among these youngsters. Middle- and upper-income adolescents also are likely to place more value on the types of achievements—academic and so on—available to late-maturing boys (Graber et al., 2004; Weichold et al., 2003).

Early and Late Maturation in Girls

The situation is somewhat reversed for girls. Whereas early maturation poses distinct advantages for boys, the picture is more mixed for girls. Adolescents tend to be concerned if they differ from their peers. **Truth or Fiction Revisited:** Although boys who mature early usually have higher self-esteem than those who mature late, the same may not hold true for girls. Early-maturing girls may feel awkward, because they are among the first of their peers to begin the physical changes of puberty. They outgrow not only their late-maturing female counterparts but also their male age-mates. With their tallness and their developing breasts, they become conspicuous. Boys of their age may tease them about their breasts and their height. Tall girls of dating age frequently find that shorter boys are reluctant to approach them or be seen with them. Some tall girls walk with a slight hunch, as if trying to minimize their height. All in all, early-maturing girls are at greater risk for a host of psychological problems and substance abuse than girls who mature later on (Ge et al., 2003; Hayward, 2003; Kaltiala-Heino et al., 2003; Lynne et al., 2007).

Many girls who mature early have a poorer body image than those who mature later (Williams & Currie, 2000). These negative feelings are more pronounced for girls who are in elementary school, where they are conspicuous, but less pronounced in high school, where others are catching up.

Adolescent girls are quite concerned about their body shapes. Early maturers who are taller and heavier than other girls their age do not conform to the current cultural emphasis on thinness. Thus, they have more negative feelings about their bodies. Early maturation in girls is associated with a variety of other problems. Early-maturing girls obtain lower grades in school and have more conduct problems, a greater incidence of substance abuse, and a higher incidence of emotional disturbance, including depression (Lanza & Collins, 2002; Stice et al., 2001). They are literally larger targets for deviant peer pressure (Lanza & Collins, 2002). They initiate sexual activity earlier (Lam et al., 2002). They become involved with older girls and boys. Their concern about their body shape also appears to heighten the risk of developing eating disorders (Kaltiala-Heino et al., 2001; Striegel-Moore et al., 2003).

The parents of early-maturing girls may increase their vigilance and restrictiveness. Increased restrictiveness can lead to new child–parent conflicts. A study of 302 African American adolescent–mother pairs found that mothers of early-maturing daughters had more heated discussions with them than with later-maturing daughters (Sagrestano et al., 1999). Girls who mature early are also at greater risk of sexual abuse (Romans et al., 2001; Vigil et al., 2005). The early-maturing girl can thus be a target of inappropriate parental attention and develop severe conflicts about her body as a result.

Body Image in Adolescence

Our body image refers to how physically attractive we perceive ourselves to be and to how we feel about our body. Adolescents are quite concerned about their physical appearance, particularly in early adolescence when the rapid physical changes of puberty are occurring (Jones & Crawford, 2006; Stanford & McCabe, 2005).

Question: How do adolescents feel about their bodies? By the age of 18, girls and boys are more satisfied with their bodies than they were in the earlier teen years (Eisenberg et al., 2006). A 5-year longitudinal study investigated the relationship between body image and depressed mood in 645 adolescents at ages 13, 15, and 18 (Holsen et al., 2001). On average, girls reported having a more negative body image and feeling more depressed about their bodies at all three ages. Dissatisfaction with body image led to feelings of depression among both sexes (Paxton et al., 2006). Adolescent females in our society tend to be more preoccupied with body weight and slimness than adolescent males (Paxton et al., 2006). Compared with females, however, many adolescent males want to put weight on and build their muscle mass (Jones & Crawford, 2006; Stanford & McCabe, 2005). Compared with adolescent boys, adolescent girls have a less positive body image and are more dissatisfied with their weight; the majority of girls are likely to be dieting or to have been on diets (Jones & Crawford, 2006). And girls are more likely to suffer from eating disorders, as we see later in the chapter.

© Rod Morato/Getty Images

Body Image
Adolescent females in our society are much more preoccupied with appearance, body weight, and slimness than are adolescent males. Why?

Active Review

1. G. Stanley Hall proposed that adolescence is a period of storm and _____.
2. Puberty is controlled by a _____ loop involving hormones.
3. The gonads produce _____ hormones (androgens and estrogens).
4. Girls begin their _____ spurt in height at about 10, and boys spurt about 2 years later.
5. _____ growth may produce gawkiness in adolescents.
6. Males stop growing taller because testosterone causes _____ closure.
7. _____ brakes the female growth spurt.

8. (Boys or Girls?) are more likely to benefit from early maturation.
9. (Boys or Girls?) are more likely to have a positive body image.

Reflect & Relate: Was your adolescence a period of storm and stress? If so, what factors contributed to the turbulence?

Go to

http://www.thomsonedu.com/psychology/rathus
for an interactive version of this review.

Emerging Sexuality and the Risks of Sexually Transmitted Infections

In an episode of the TV series *Growing Pains,* an adolescent was referred to as a "hormone with feet." As we noted in our discussion of puberty, many or most adolescents are preoccupied with sex to some degree. These preoccupations are fueled by a powerful sex drive. And many or most adolescents are not quite sure about what to do with these pressing urges. Should they masturbate? Should they pet? Should they engage in sexual intercourse? Parents and sex educators often say no, or wait. Yet it can seem that "Everyone's doing it." In Chapter 16, we will discuss various sexual outlets and sexual orientation. Here, we focus on the risks of sexually transmitted infections.

Given a body that is suddenly sexually mature, a high sex drive, vulnerability to peer pressure, and limited experience in handling temptation, teenagers are at particular risk for sexually transmitted infections (STIs). Sexually active adolescents have higher rates of STIs than any other age group. Each year, an estimated 2.5 million adolescents—one of every six—contracts a sexually transmitted infection (Centers for Disease Control and Prevention, 2006). *Question: What kinds of sexually transmitted infections are there?* Chlamydia (a bacterial infection of the vagina or urinary tract that can result in sterility) is the most commonly occurring STI in adolescents, followed by gonorrhea, genital warts, genital herpes, syphilis, and **HIV/AIDS.** Because of its lethality, HIV/AIDS tends to capture most of the headlines. However, other STIs are more widespread, and some of them can also be deadly.

Nearly 2.8 million new chlamydia infections occur each year (Centers for Disease Control and Prevention, 2006). The incidence of chlamydia infections is especially high among teenagers and college students (Centers for Disease Control and Prevention, 2006). Chlamydia is a major cause of pelvic inflammatory disease (PID), which often leads to infertility.

HIV/AIDS HIV stands for human immunodeficiency virus, the virus that causes AIDS. AIDS stands for acquired immunodeficiency syndrome, a condition that cripples the body's immune system, making the person vulnerable to diseases that would not otherwise be as threatening.

Each year in the United States, there are about 1 million new infections with the human papilloma virus (HPV), which causes genital warts and is associated with cervical cancer (Centers for Disease Control and Prevention, 2006). A vaccine is available that prevents most young women from being infected with HPV and is best administered before they become sexually active (Pichichero, 2006). It is estimated that more than half of the sexually active adolescent women in some cities in the United States are infected with HPV. Genital warts may appear in visible areas of the skin, but most appear in areas that cannot be seen, such as on the cervix in women or in the urethra in men. Women who initiate sexual intercourse before the age of 18 and who have many sex partners are particularly susceptible to infection. Fortunately, most healthy young women clear these infections on their own.

HIV/AIDS

HIV/AIDS is the most devastating of STIs; if left untreated, it is lethal. And the long-term prospects of those who do receive treatment remain unknown. HIV—the virus that causes AIDS—is spreading rapidly around the world, and, by the end of the 20th century, it had infected nearly 39 million people worldwide (UNAIDS, 2006). Young gay males and homeless and runaway youths have elevated risk for HIV/AIDS. Anal intercourse is a likely route of transmission of HIV and is often practiced by gay males (see ■ Table 14.1). Homeless and runaway adolescents are likely to engage in unprotected sex with several partners. Injecting drugs is another risk factor for HIV/AIDS because sharing needles with infected individuals can transmit HIV.

Women account for a minority of cases of HIV/AIDS in the United States but are more likely than males to be infected with HIV in many places around the world. A United Nations study in Europe, Africa, and Southeast Asia has found that sexually active teenage girls have higher rates of HIV infection than older women or young men (UNAIDS, 2006). A number of erroneous assumptions about HIV/AIDS have had a disproportionately negative effect on women. They include the notions that HIV/AIDS is primarily a disease of gay men and people who inject drugs and that it is difficult to contract HIV/AIDS through male–female sexual intercourse. However, the primary mode of HIV transmission worldwide is male–female intercourse. Among American women, male–female intercourse is the major source of infection by HIV.

Truth or Fiction Revisited: Studies regarding knowledge, attitudes, and beliefs about HIV/AIDS find that even children in the early school years are aware of HIV/AIDS. Nearly all high school students know that HIV/AIDS is transmitted by sexual intercourse, but about half do not modify their sexual practices as a result of fear of the disease (Santelli et al., 2000). Adolescents often deny the threat of HIV/

■ **Table 14.1** U.S. Adolescents and Adults with AIDS; Number of Cases by Exposure Category

Exposure Category	Male	Female	Total
Men who have sex with men	441,380	—	441,380
Injecting drug use	176,162	72,651	248,813
Men who have sex with men and inject drugs	64,833	—	64,833
Male–female sex	59,939	99,175	159,114
Other	14,085	6,636	20,721
Totals	756,399	178,463	934,862

Source: Centers for Disease Control and Prevention (2005).

■ **Table 14.2** Percentage of Adolescents Who Have Engaged in Vaginal Intercourse, According to the National Survey of Family Growth

Age	15	16	17	18	19	20–21	22–24
Male	25	37	46	62	69	85	89
Female	26	40	49	70	77	81	92

Source: Mosher et al. (2005, figures 2 and 3).

What Is the Risk of Their Contracting a Sexually Transmitted Infection? Young people generally know of the risks of HIV/AIDS, but knowledge of risks does not always translate into behavior. Young people have heard of chlamydia and of genital warts, but they tend to underestimate the effects of these STIs.

AIDS to them. As one high school girl said, "I can't believe that anyone I would have sex with would be infected." Guess what: Some are.

Risk Factors

Adolescents often take risks, with harmful consequences for their health and well-being. **Question: *What factors place adolescents at risk for contracting STIs?***

First, and most obvious, is sexual activity itself. As you can see in ■ Table 14.2, a U.S. government survey found that the percentage of adolescents who engage in sexual intercourse increases dramatically between the ages of 15 to 18. At the age of 15, about one adolescent in four has engaged in sexual intercourse, but the number has surged to two out of three by the age of 18.

A second risk factor for contracting STIs is sex with multiple partners. About one in five high school students engages in sex with four or more different partners (Dailard, 2001; Spitalnick et al., 2007).

A third factor is failure to use condoms. In recent surveys, the majority of sexually active adolescents reported not using condoms or using them inconsistently (Dailard, 2001; Parkes et al., 2007; Spitalnick et al., 2007).

A fourth factor is drug abuse (UNAIDS, 2006). Adolescents who abuse drugs are also more likely to engage in other risky behaviors, such as sex without condoms (Appel et al., 2006; Abbey et al., 2006; Parkes et al., 2007).

The causes, methods of transmission, symptoms, and treatment—where it exists—of sexually transmitted infections (STIs) are described in ■ Table 14.3 (pages 494–495).

Prevention of Sexually Transmitted Infections

Question: *Given the threat of HIV/AIDS and other STIs, what can be done to prevent STIs?* Prevention and education are the primary weapons against STIs (UNAIDS, 2006). Adolescents need to learn about the transmission, symptoms, and consequences of STIs. They need to learn about "safer sex" techniques, including abstinence, and, if they are sexually active, the use of condoms. Educating young people to use condoms is associated with lower levels of infection (Wingood et al., 2006). (See the nearby "A Closer Look" feature on preventing HIV/AIDS and other STIs.)

But knowledge alone may not change behavior. For example, many female adolescents lack power in their relationships. Males are likely to pressure them into unwanted or unprotected sexual relations (Wingood et al., 2006). Other goals of educational programs should include enhancing the adolescent's sense of control over the prevention of AIDS and modifying behavior associated with being infected with HIV. As with programs designed to prevent substance abuse, the development of effective decision-making and social skills may be critical in programs designed to prevent STIs (UNAIDS, 2006).

A Closer Look

Preventing HIV/AIDS and Other STIs: It's More than Safe(r) Sex

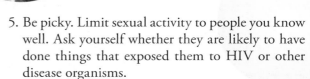

How does one protect oneself from being infected with a sexually transmitted infection (STI)? Because discussing STIs with a partner can be such a daunting task, some people wing it. They admit that they just hope for the best. But even if they do bring up the topic, they need to recognize that many people—perhaps most people—do not know whether they are infected with an STI, especially the organisms that cause chlamydia, gonorrhea, and AIDS. In any event, putting blinders on is not the answer to STIs:

What can we do to prevent STIs? A number of things:

1. Use sex education in the schools.
2. Keep the prevalence and harmful nature of STIs in mind. Many young people try not to think about the threats posed by STIs. Don't play the dangerous game that involves pretending (especially in the heat of passion) that they do not exist.
3. Just say no; that is, remain abstinent. One way of curtailing the transmission of infections is abstinence. But what does abstinence mean? Is it limited to avoiding sexual intercourse with another person? Hugging, kissing, and petting (without contacting semen or vaginal fluids) are usually safe, although readers may argue about whether these behaviors are consistent with the definition of abstinence.
4. Limit yourself to a monogamous relationship with a partner who is not infected. It is safe to engage in sexual intercourse in a monogamous relationship with a person who does not have an STI. The question is, can you be certain that your partner is free of STIs and faithful?

Adolescents who are unwilling to abstain from sexual intercourse or to limit themselves to one partner can still do things to make sex safer, if not perfectly safe:

5. Be picky. Limit sexual activity to people you know well. Ask yourself whether they are likely to have done things that exposed them to HIV or other disease organisms.
6. Check out your partner's genitals. Examine them for unpleasant odors, discharges, blisters, rashes, warts, and lice during foreplay. These signs are possible symptoms of STIs.
7. Wash the genitals. Washing yourself beforehand helps protect your partner. Washing with soap and water afterward may kill or remove some pathogens. Urinating afterward might be of some help, particularly to men, because the acidity of urine can kill some disease organisms in the urethra.
8. Use latex condoms, which protect partners from exchanging infected bodily fluids.
9. Talk to a doctor. Use of antibiotics and antiviral medications after unprotected sex can guard against some bacterial and viral infections, even HIV. Check with a doctor *immediately* if you think you might have been exposed to an STI.
10. Have regular medical checkups to learn about disorders whose symptoms might go unnoticed.

Reflect:
- How can shyness endanger your health in relation to STIs?
- Why do women need a certain degree of power in their relationships to protect themselves from STIs?
- Do some research: What is the difference between being *exposed to HIV* and being *infected by HIV?* Why should you visit a doctor as soon as possible if you suspect you might have been exposed to HIV?

■ **Table 14.3** Overview of Sexually Transmitted infections (STIs)

STI and Cause	Transmission	Symptoms	Diagnosis	Treatment
Bacterial vaginosis: *Gardnerella vaginalis* bacterium and other bacteria	• Overgrowth of organisms in vagina • Allergic reactions • Sexual contact	• In women, may be symptom-free or there may be a thin, foul-smelling vaginal discharge, irritation of genitals, and mild pain during urination • In men, may be symptom-free or burning or painful urination, and slight discharge	• Culture and examination of bacterium	• Oral treatment with metronidazole (Flagyl)
Candidiasis (moniliasis, thrush, "yeast infection"): caused by *Candida albicans,* a yeast-like fungus	• Overgrowth of fungus in the vagina • Sexual contact • Sharing a washcloth or towel with an infected person	• In women, vulval itching; discharge; soreness or swelling of genital tissues. • In men, itching and burning on urination, or inflammation of the penis	• Diagnosis usually made on basis of symptoms	• Vaginal suppositories, creams, or tablets containing miconazole, clotrimazole, or teraconazole • Keeping infected area dry
Chlamydia and nongonococcal urethritis (NGU): caused by *Chlamydia trachomatous* bacterium in women and by several bacteria in men, including *Ureaplasma urealycticum*	• Vaginal, oral, or anal sexual activity • Transmitted to the eye by touching one's eyes after touching the genitals of an infected partner • To newborns passing through the birth canal of an infected mother	• In women, may be symptom-free or there may be frequent and painful urination, lower abdominal pain and inflammation, and vaginal discharge • In men, may be symptom-free or there may be burning or painful urination, and slight penile discharge • Sore throat may follow oral-genital contact	• The Abbott Testpack analyzes a cervical smear in women • In men, an extract of fluid from the penis is analyzed	• Antibiotics
Genital herpes: caused by Herpes simplex virus–type 2 (HSV-2)	• Vaginal, oral, or anal sexual activity • Most contagious during active outbreaks of the disease, but may be transmitted at any time	• Painful, reddish bumps around the genitals, thigh, or buttocks • Bumps become blisters or sores that fill with pus and break, shedding viral particles • Burning urination, fever, aches and pains, swollen glands, and vaginal discharge possible	• Clinical inspection of sores • Culture and examination of fluid drawn from sore	• Antiviral drugs may provide relief and help with healing but are not cures • Counseling and support groups may be of help
Gonorrhea ("clap," "drip": Gonococcus bacterium (*Neisseria gonorrhoeae*)	• Vaginal, oral, or anal sexual activity • To newborns passing through the birth canal of an infected mother	• In men, yellowish, thick discharge, burning urination • In women, may be symptom-free or there may be increased vaginal discharge, burning urination, irregular menstruation	• Clinical inspection • Culture of sample discharge	• Antibiotics

■ Table 14.3 (continued)

STI and Cause	Transmission	Symptoms	Diagnosis	Treatment
HIV/AIDS: Acronym for human immunodeficiency virus, the cause of acquired immunodeficiency syndrome	• Vaginal or anal sexual intercourse • Infusion with contaminated blood by needle sharing or from mother to baby during childbirth • Breast-feeding	• Usually symptom-free for many years • Flu-like symptoms • Chronically swollen lymph nodes, fever, weight loss, fatigue, diarrhea • Lethal "opportunistic infections"	• Blood, saliva, or urine tests detect HIV antibodies in the bloodstream • Other tests confirm the presence of the virus (HIV) itself	• There is no cure for HIV/AIDS • Highly active antiviral therapy (HAART), a "cocktail" of antiviral drugs, is prolonging life in many people living with HIV/AIDS
HPV/genital warts (venereal warts): caused by human papilloma virus (HPV)	• Sexual contact • Contact with infected towels or clothing	• Painless warts resembling cauliflowers on the genitals or anus or in the rectum • Associated with cervical cancer in women	• Clinical inspection	• A vaccine can prevent most young women from being infected with HPV • Warts can be removed by freezing, podophyllin, burning, and surgery
Oral herpes: caused by Herpes simplex virus–type 1 (HSV-1)	• Touching, kissing, sexual contact with sores or blisters • Sharing cups, towels • Toilet seats	• Cold sores or fever blisters on the lips, mouth, or throat • Sores on the genitals (from oral-genital contact)	• Clinical inspection	• Over-the-counter lip balms, cold-sore medications; but check with your physician.
Pubic lice ("crabs"): *Pthirus pubis* (an insect, not a crab)	• Sexual contact • Contact with an infested towel, sheet, or toilet seat	• Intense itching in pubic area and other hairy regions to which lice can attach	• Clinical examination	• Drugs containing pyrethrins or piperonal butoxide (e.g., NIX, A200, RID, Triple X)
Syphilis: *Treponema pallidum*	• Vaginal, oral, or anal sexual activity • Touching an infectious chancre • Can be congenital	• Hard, round painless chancre or sore appears at site of infection within 2 to 4 weeks • May progress through additional stages if left untreated • Potentially lethal	• Clinical examination or examination of fluid from a chancre • Blood test (the VDRL)	• Antibiotics
Trichomoniasis ("trich"): caused by *Trichomonas vaginalis,* a protozoan (one-celled animal)	• Almost always transmitted sexually	• In women, may be symptom-free or there may be a foamy, yellowish, odorous vaginal discharge; itching or burning in genital region • Men are usually symptom-free but may experience mild burning urination	• Microscopic examination of vaginal secretions • Examination of a culture of a sample of vaginal secretions (preferred)	• Metronidazole (Flagyl)

Active Review

10. _____ is the most common sexually transmitted infection in adolescents.
11. Infection by _____ is linked to development of cancer of the cervix.
12. HIV is the virus that causes _____.
13. A (Minority or Majority?) of sexually active adolescents use condoms consistently.

Reflect & Relate: Do you—or did you—know any adolescents who contracted STIs? How? Were they aware at the time of the existence of the STIs and how they are transmitted? Have these STIs caused problems for those who were infected? Explain.

Go to

http://www.thomsonedu.com/psychology/rathus

for an interactive version of this review.

Health in Adolescence

Adolescents are young and growing. Most seem sturdy. Injuries tend to heal quickly. *Question: How healthy are American adolescents?* The good news is that most American adolescents are healthy. Few are chronically ill or miss school. However, about 18% of the nation's adolescents have at least one serious health problem (Bloom et al., 2006). In fact, American teenagers may be less healthy than their parents were at the same age.

Drinking and Driving: A Deadly Mix

The majority of adolescent deaths are due to accidents, most of them involving motor vehicles. Alcohol often is involved in accidental deaths.

Risk Taking in Adolescence

The reason that adolescents may be less healthy than their parents were at the same age is not an increase in the incidence of infectious diseases or other physical illnesses. Rather, the causes are external and rooted in lifestyle and risky behavior: excessive drinking, substance abuse, reckless driving, violence, disordered eating behavior, and, as we have seen, unprotected sexual activity (Bloom et al., 2006). Let us consider the causes of death in adolescence and then turn to the remaining two major health problems faced by teens: eating disorders and substance abuse. The third major health problem facing teens, sexually transmitted infections (STIs), was discussed in the previous section.

Causes of Death

Although adolescents are healthy as a group, a number of them die. *Questions: What are the causes of death among adolescents?* Death rates are low in adolescence, although they are higher for older adolescents than for younger ones. For example, each year about twice as many 15- to 17-year-olds as 12- to 14-year-olds die (Centers for Disease Control and Prevention, 2005). Death rates are nearly twice as great for male adolescents as for female adolescents. A major reason for this discrepancy is that males are more likely to take risks that end in death as a result of accidents, suicide, or homicide (Centers for Disease Control and Prevention, 2005). These three causes of death account for the great majority of all adolescent deaths. **Truth or Fiction Revisited:** It is not true that substance abuse is the leading cause of death among male adolescents in the United States.

Sixty percent of adolescent deaths are due to accidents, and most of these involve motor vehicles (Centers for Disease Control and Prevention, 2005). Alcohol often is involved in accidental deaths. Alcohol-related motor vehicle accidents are the leading cause of death for 15- to 24-year-olds. Alcohol frequently is implicated in other causes of accidental death or injury, including drowning and falling (Centers for Disease Control and Prevention, 2005).

Adolescents who are poor and who live in urban areas of high population density have the greatest risk of death by homicide (Centers for Disease Control and Prevention, 2005). African American adolescents are more likely than European American adolescents to fit this description. Therefore, it is not surprising that the homicide rate is greater among African American adolescents (see ● Figure 14.5).

Homicide is the leading cause of death in 15- to 19-year-old African American males, whereas accidents are the major cause of death for European American teens (Centers for Disease Control and Prevention, 2005). African American adolescents, age 15 to 19, are nearly 10 times as likely as their European American age-mates to be murdered. Females are not exempt from this pattern. African American females, age 15 to 19, are more than five times as likely as their European American counterparts to be victims of homicide. The figures for Latino and Latina American adolescents are lower than those for African American youth but higher than those for European Americans (Centers for Disease Control and Prevention, 2005).

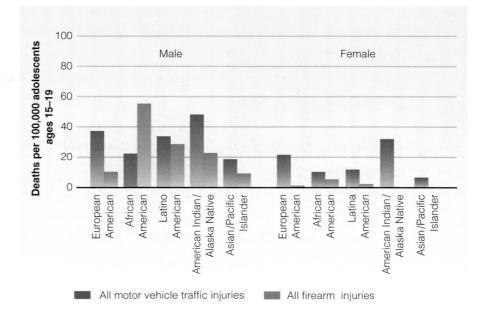

● **Figure 14.5**
Injury Death Rates among Adolescents Ages 15–19 by Sex, Ethnicity, and Type of Injury, 2002

Note: There were too few firearm deaths to calculate a reliable rate for American Indian/Alaska Native females and Asian/Pacific Islander females.

Source: Centers for Disease Control and Prevention (2005).

Nutrition: An Abundance of Food

Physical growth occurs more rapidly in the adolescent years than at any other time after birth, with the exception of the first year of life. *Questions: What are the nutritional needs of adolescents? What do adolescents actually eat?* To fuel the adolescent growth spurt, the average girl, depending on activity level, needs to consume 1,800 to 2,400 calories per day and the average boy needs 2,200 to 3,200 calories (USDA, 2005). The nutritional needs of adolescents vary according to their stage of pubertal development. For example, at the peak of their growth spurt, adolescents use twice as much calcium, iron, zinc, magnesium, and nitrogen as they do during the other years of adolescence (USDA, 2005). Calcium intake is particularly important for females to build up their bone density and help prevent **osteoporosis**, a progressive loss of bone, later in life. Osteoporosis affects millions of women, particularly after **menopause.** But most teenagers—both girls and boys—do not consume enough calcium. Adolescents also are likely to obtain less vitamin A, thiamine, and iron but more fat, sugar, protein, and sodium than recommended (USDA, 2005).

osteoporosis A condition involving progressive loss of bone tissue.

menopause The cessation of menstruation, typically occurring between ages 48 and 52.

**Nutritional Needs—
Or Should We Say Habits—
of Adolescents**
Teenagers require lots of calories to fuel the adolescent growth spurt. They may consume large amounts of fast food and junk food, which is high in calories and fat but not always very nutritious.

One reason for adolescents' nutritional deficits is irregular eating patterns. Breakfast is often skipped, especially by girls who are watching their weight (Niemeier et al., 2006). Teenagers are more likely to miss meals or eat away from home than they were in childhood (Thompson et al., 2004). They may consume large amounts of fast food and junk food, which is high in fat and calories but not very nutritious (Niemeier et al., 2006). Junk food is connected with being overweight, and being overweight in adolescence can lead to chronic illness and earlier death in adulthood, even for teens who later lose weight (Niemeier et al., 2006). Overweight adolescents are more likely than adolescents of normal weight to incur heart disease, strokes, and cancer as adults (USDA, 2005).

An Abundance of Eating Disorders: When Dieting Turns Deadly

The American ideal has slimmed down to where most American females of "average" weight (we are not talking here about those who are overweight!) are dissatisfied with the size and shape of their bodies (Paxton et al., 2005; Striegel-Moore et al., 2003). The wealthier your family, the more unhappy you are likely to be with your body (Polivy et al., 2005). Perhaps, then, it is no surprise that dieting has become the normal way of eating for most U.S. adolescent females (Polivy et al., 2005)! Plumpness has been valued in many preliterate societies, and Western paintings of previous centuries suggest that there was a time when physically well-rounded women were the ideal. But in contemporary Western culture, slim is in (Polivy et al., 2005).

Adolescents are highly concerned about their bodies. Puberty brings rapid changes, and adolescents wonder what they will look like once the flood of hormones has ebbed. In Chapter 15, we will see that adolescents also tend to think that others are paying a great deal of attention to their appearance. Because of cultural emphasis on slimness and the psychology of the adolescent, adolescents—especially girls—are highly vulnerable to eating disorders. ***Question: What are eating disorders?*** The eating disorders of *anorexia nervosa* and *bulimia nervosa* are characterized by gross disturbances in patterns of eating.

Anorexia Nervosa

All right: More adolescent girls diet than not. What's wrong with that? After all, there's the saying "You can never be too rich or too thin." **Truth or Fiction Revisited:** Most teens are not worried about a fat bank account, but one can certainly be too skinny, as in **anorexia nervosa.** Anorexia nervosa is a life-threatening eating disorder characterized by extreme fear of being too heavy, dramatic weight loss, a distorted body image, and resistance to eating enough to reach or maintain a healthful weight. Note the case of Rachel:

> I wanted to be a runner. Runners were thin and I attributed this to dieting, not training. So I began restricting my diet: No butter, red meat, pork, dessert, candy, or snacking. If I ate any of the forbidden items, I obsessed about it and felt guilty for days.
>
> As a high school freshman, I wanted to run with the fastest girls so I trained hard, really hard, and ate less. Lunch was lettuce sandwiches, carrots, and an apple. By my senior year, I was number three on the team and lunch was a bagel and an orange.
>
> I maintained a rigid schedule—running cross country and track, having a seat on student council, volunteering, and maintaining a 3.9 GPA

anorexia nervosa An eating disorder characterized by irrational fear of weight gain, distorted body image, and severe weight loss.

throughout high school—while starving myself (1,000 calories per day), trying to attain the impossible perfection I thought couldn't be far away if I only slimmed down a little bit more.

Several teammates were concerned, but I shrugged them off saying family members were tall and slender; I was a health nut, I didn't like fatty foods; I was a vegetarian; I didn't like sweets; I wasn't hungry; I wasn't starving.

A psychiatrist didn't help at all. I went in, sat on the couch, and told her what she wanted to hear: I would eat more, run less, stop restricting myself, and quit obsessing about being thin. I was very good at knowing exactly what to tell others.

I dropped 10 pounds my freshman year—from 125 to 115 pounds. I was five feet, eight inches tall and wore a size five. I hated my body so I starved myself and ran like a mad woman. In quiet moments, I was sad and worried about what might be going on inside me.

I was already taking birth control to regain my menstrual cycle; my weight was 15% below what was recommended for my height; I was always cold; I had chest pains and an irregular heartbeat; my hair was limp and broke off; my skin was colorless.

It wasn't until I came to the University of Iowa and joined the varsity women's cross country team that I began to see what I was doing to myself. A teammate had an eating problem. Every time I saw her, I felt sick to my stomach. She had sunken cheeks, eyes so big they swallowed her face. She was an excellent student and a college-level varsity athlete. Many people wondered at her determination, but I understood. She used the same excuses I did.

For one sick instant, I wondered if I would be happier if I were that thin. That is when I started to realize I was slowly killing myself.

At the urging of my coach, I saw the team nutritionist who recommended a psychiatrist who felt no pity for me and made me take a brutally honest look at who I was and why I was starving myself. She didn't accept any of my excuses. She helped me realize that there are other things to think about besides food and body image. About this time I decided to quit the cross country team. The pressure I felt to be thin and competition at the college level were too much when I needed to focus on getting well.

After two months of therapy, my weight had dropped again. I'm not sure how far because I refused to step on a scale, but my size five pants were falling off. My psychiatrist required weekly weigh-ins.

I wasn't putting into practice any of the things my nutritionist and counselor suggested. They told me that if I wanted to have children someday I needed to eat. They warned me of osteoporosis at age 30. Then my psychiatrist scared me to death. She told me I needed to start eating more or I would be checked into the hospital and hooked up to an IV. That would put me on the same level as my Iowa teammate. I had looked at her with such horror and never realized that I was in the same position.

My psychiatrist asked how my family would feel if they had to visit me in the hospital because I refused to eat. It was enough to make me think hard the next time I went through the food service lines.

Of course, I didn't get better the next day. But it was a step in the right direction. It's taken me three years to get where I am now. At five foot, eight and three-fourth inches (I even grew as I got healthier) and 145 pounds, I look and feel healthier, have better eating and exercise habits, and I don't obsess about food as much as I used to. On rare occasions, I think about controlling my food intake. My eating disorder will haunt me for the rest of my life. If I'm not careful, it could creep back.

An Adolescent with Anorexia Nervosa

Anorexia nervosa is a life-threatening eating disorder in which an individual—most often an adolescent or young adult female—has a distorted body image and consequently refuses to eat. She may lose 25% of her body weight in a year and impair the health of nearly all her bodily systems.

Rachel, like other people with anorexia nervosa, weighed less than 85% of her desirable body weight, and "desirable" body weights are already too slender for many individuals. Anorexia nervosa afflicts males as well as females, but females with eating disorders outnumber males. Most studies put the female-to-male ratio at 10 to 1 or greater, but some find a smaller sex difference (Kjelsås et al., 2004; Striegel-Moore & Cachelin, 2001). By and large, anorexia nervosa afflicts women during adolescence and young adulthood (Polivy et al., 2005). The typical person with anorexia is a young European American female of higher socioeconomic status (Striegel-Moore et al, 2003). Affluent females have greater access to fitness centers and health clubs and are more likely to read the magazines that idealize slender bodies and shop in the boutiques that cater to females with svelte figures. All in all, they are regularly confronted with unrealistically high standards of slimness that make them extremely unhappy with their own physiques (Forbush et al., 2007). We know that the incidences of anorexia nervosa and bulimia nervosa have increased markedly in recent years.

Females with anorexia nervosa can drop 25% or more of their weight within a year. Severe weight loss triggers abnormalities in the endocrine system (i.e., with hormones) that prevent ovulation (Nielsen & Palmer, 2003). General health declines. Nearly every system in the body is affected. There are problems with the respiratory system (Forman-Hoffman et al., 2006) and with the cardiovascular system (Katzman, 2005). Females with anorexia are at risk for premature development of osteoporosis, a condition characterized by loss of bone density that usually afflicts people in late adulthood (Katzman, 2005). Given these problems, it is not surprising that the mortality rate for anorexic females is approximately 4% to 5%.

In one common pattern, the girl sees that she has gained some weight after menarche, and she resolves that she must lose it. But even after the weight is gone, she maintains her pattern of dieting and, in many cases, exercises at a fever pitch (Shroff et al., 2006). This pattern continues as she plunges toward her desirable weight—according to weight charts—and even after those who care about her tell her that she is becoming all skin and bones. Denial is a huge part of anorexia nervosa. Anorexic girls deny they are losing too much weight. They deny any health problems, pointing to their feverish exercise routines as evidence. Distortion of the body image is a major feature of the disorder. Others see anorexic females as skin and bones, whereas anorexic women fix their gaze in the mirror and believe that they are looking at a body that is too heavy.

Bulimia Nervosa

Bulimia nervosa is sort of a companion disorder to anorexia nervosa, as we see in the case of Nicole:

> Nicole awakens in her cold dark room and already wishes it was time to go back to bed. She dreads the thought of going through this day, which will be like so many others in her recent past. She asks herself the question every morning, "Will I be able to make it through the day without being totally obsessed by thoughts of food, or will I blow it again and spend the day [binge eating]"? She tells herself that today she will begin a new life, today she will start to live like a normal human being. However, she is not at all convinced that the choice is hers.
>
> —Boskind-White & White (1983, p. 29)

So, does Nicole begin a new life today? No. Despite her pledge to herself, Nicole begins the day with eggs and toast, butter included. Then she downs cookies; bagels smothered with cream cheese, butter, and jelly; doughnuts; candy bars; bowlfuls of cereal and milk—all in less than an hour. When her body cries "No more!" she turns to the next step: purging. Purging also is a routine. In the bathroom, she ties back her hair. She runs the shower to mask noise, drinks some water, and makes herself throw everything up. Afterward she makes another pledge to herself: "Starting tomorrow, I'm going to change." Will she change? In truth, she doubts it.

Bulimia nervosa, Nicole's eating disorder, is symptomized by recurrent cycles of binge eating and purging. Binge eating often follows on the heels of food restriction, that is, dieting (Williams, 2004). There are various methods of purging. Nicole vomited. Other avenues include strict dieting or fasting, laxatives, and demanding, prolonged exercise regimes. Individuals with eating disorders, such as Rachel and Nicole, tend to be perfectionistic about their bodies. They will not settle for less than their idealized body shape and weight (Kaye et al., 2004). Bulimia, like anorexia, is connected with irregular menstrual cycles (Edler et al., 2007).

Bulimia nervosa, like anorexia nervosa, tends to afflict women during adolescence and young adulthood (Nolen-Hoeksema et al., 2007). **Truth or Fiction Revisited:** It is true that some college women—and other young women—control their weight by going on cycles of binge eating followed by self-induced vomiting. Eating disorders are upsetting and dangerous in themselves, of course, but they also are connected with depression (Nolen-Hoeksema et al., 2007). *Question: What are the origins of eating disorders?*

Perspectives on Eating Disorders

Health professionals have done a great deal of research into the origins of eating disorders. Yet they will be the first to admit that many questions about these disorders remain unanswered (Polivy et al., 2005).

According to some psychoanalysts, anorexia nervosa may symbolize a young woman's efforts to cope with sexual fears, especially the possibility of becoming pregnant. They interpret the female's behavior as an attempt to regress to prepubescence. Anorexia nervosa prevents some adolescents from separating from their families and assuming adult responsibilities. Their breasts and hips flatten once more because of the loss of fatty tissue. In the adolescent's fantasies, perhaps, she remains a sexually undifferentiated child.

Many parents are obsessed with encouraging their children—especially their infants—to eat adequately. Thus, some observers suggest that children may refuse to eat as a way of battling with their parents. ("You have to eat something!" "I'm not hungry!") It often seems that warfare does occur in the families of adolescents with eating disorders. Parents in such families are often unhappy and have their own issues with eating and dieting. They also "act out" against their daughters, letting them know that they consider them unattractive and, before the development of the eating disorder, letting them know that they think they should lose weight (Hanna & Bond, 2006).

A particularly disturbing risk factor for eating disorders in adolescent females is a history of child abuse, particularly sexual abuse (Corstorphine et al., 2007). One study found a history of childhood sexual abuse in about half of women with bulimia nervosa, as opposed to a rate of about 7% among women without the disorder (Deep et al., 1999). Another study compared 45 pairs of sisters, one of whom was diagnosed with anorexia nervosa (Karwautz et al., 2001). Those with anorexia were significantly more likely to be exposed to high parental expectations and to sexual abuse.

Certainly young women have a very slender social ideal set before them in women such as Paris Hilton. Miss America, the annually renewed American role model, has also been slenderizing across the years. The pageant began in 1922. Over the past 80 years, the winner has added only 2% in height but has lost 12 pounds in weight. In the early days of the 1920s, Miss America's weight relative to her height yielded

bulimia nervosa An eating disorder characterized by cycles of binge eating and vomiting as a means of controlling weight gain.

a body mass index (BMI[1]) of 20 to 25, which is considered normal by the World Health Organization (WHO). The WHO labels people as malnourished when their BMIs are lower than 18.5. However, recent Miss Americas come in at a BMI near 17 (Rubinstein & Caballero, 2000). So Miss America adds to the woes of "normal" young women and even to those of young women who hover near the WHO "malnourished" borderline. As the cultural ideal slenderizes, women with desirable body weights, according to the health charts, feel overweight, and overweight women feel gargantuan (Winzelberg et al., 2000).

Many individuals with eating disorders, such as Rachel, are involved in activities that demand weight limits, such as dancing, acting, and modeling (Ravaldi et al., 2003). Gym enthusiasts and male wrestlers also feel the pressure to stay within an "acceptable" weight range (Ravaldi et al., 2003). Men, like women, experience pressure to create an ideal body, one with power in the upper torso and a trim abdomen.

Eating disorders tend to run in families, which raises the possibility of genetic involvement (Bellodi et al., 2001; Kaye et al., 2004; Speranza et al., 2001). Genetic factors do not directly cause eating disorders, but they appear to involve obsessionistic and perfectionistic personality traits (Kaye et al., 2004). In a society in which so much attention is focused on the ideal of the slender body, these personality traits encourage dieting (Wade et al., 2000). Anorexia also often co-occurs with depression (Lewinsohn et al., 2000b; Wade et al., 2000). Perfectionistic people are likely to be disappointed in themselves, giving rise to feelings of depression. But it may also be that both anorexia and depression share genetic factors. Genetically inspired perfectionism, cultural emphasis on slimness, self-absorption, and family conflict may create a recipe for development of eating disorders (Kaye et al., 2004).

Treatment and Prevention

Treatment of eating disorders—particularly anorexia nervosa—is a great challenge. The disorders are connected with serious health problems, and the low weight of individuals with anorexia is often life-threatening. Some adolescent girls are admitted to the hospital for treatment against their will (Brunner et al., 2005). Denial is a feature of anorexia nervosa, and many girls do not recognize—or do not admit—that they have a problem. When the individual with anorexia does not—or cannot—eat adequately through the mouth, measures such as nasogastric (tube) feeding may be used.

Antidepressants are frequently used in the treatment of eating disorders (Grilo et al., 2005; Walsh et al., 2006). Eating disorders are frequently accompanied by depression, and it may be that the common culprit in eating disorders and depression is a lower than normal level of the neurotransmitter serotonin. Antidepressants such as Prozac and Zoloft enhance the activity of serotonin in the brain, often increasing food intake in anorexic individuals and decreasing binge eating in bulimic people. In one study, 10 of 11 anorexic females showed significant weight gain after 14 weeks of treatment with an antidepressant, and they maintained the gain at a 64-week follow-up (Santonastaso et al., 2001). They were also evaluated as being significantly less depressed and perfectionistic. Other researchers combine antidepressants with nutritional supplements (Barbarich et al., 2004).

Because family problems are commonly connected with eating disorders, family therapy is often used to treat these disorders (Fishman, 2006; Lock et al., 2006). Family therapy has positive outcomes in many cases, but it is not an appropriate setting for dealing with childhood sexual abuse.

---

[1]You can calculate your body mass index as follows. Write down your weight in pounds. Multiply it by 703. Divide the product by your height in inches squared. For example, if you weigh 160 lbs and are 5 feet 8 inches tall, your BMI is $(160 \times 703)/68^2$, or 24.33. A BMI of more than 25 is defined as overweight.

Cognitive-behavioral therapy has been used to help anorexic and bulimic individuals challenge their perfectionism and distorted body images. It has also been used to systematically reinforce appropriate eating behavior. But let's remember that all this is connected with cultural attitudes that idealize excessive thinness. "Prevention" will have to address cultural values as well as potential problems in individual adolescents.

Substance Abuse and Dependence: Where Does It Begin? Where Does It End?

Think of the United States as a cafeteria with brightly colored drugs glimmering on the shelves and in the trays. In almost any high school in any part of the country, adolescents will tell you that drugs are available. In fact, so will many middle schoolers. And so will some elementary school children. Credit adolescents who do not use drugs. They generally refuse them as a matter of choice, not because of lack of supply. The drugs are there, and some of the most harmful drugs are perfectly legal, at least for adults.

Children and adolescents use drugs not only to cope with medical problems but also to deal with daily tensions, run-of-the-mill depression, even boredom. Many adolescents use drugs for the same reasons that adults do, but they also use them because they are imitating peers or rebelling against parents who beg them not to (Costello, 2007). They use drugs to experience pleasure, to deaden pain, and to earn prestige among peers.

Adolescents frequently get involved with drugs that cripple their ability to attend school or to pay attention when they do. Alcohol and other drugs are also linked with reckless, sometimes deadly, behavior (Centers for Disease Control and Prevention, 2005). Alcohol is the BDOC—the Big Drug on Campus. It is the most widely used substance in high schools and on college campuses (Johnston et al., 2006b). Marijuana is no slacker either. Nearly half of high school students have tried it before they graduate (Johnston et al., 2006b).

Where does the use of a drug or substance end and substance abuse begin? *Questions: What is substance abuse? What is substance dependence?* According to the American Psychiatric Association (2000), **substance abuse** is the ongoing use of a substance despite the social, occupational, psychological, or physical problems it causes. When adolescents miss school or fail to complete assignments because they are intoxicated or "sleeping it off," they are abusing alcohol. The amount they drink is not the issue; the problem is the role that the substance plays in their lives.

Substance dependence is more serious than substance abuse. An adolescent who is dependent on a substance loses control over using it and may organize his or her life around getting the substance and using it. Substance dependence also changes the body. Having it in one's body becomes the norm so that the adolescent may experience tolerance, withdrawal symptoms, or both. **Tolerance** develops as the body becomes habituated to the substance; as a result, the adolescent has to use progressively higher doses to achieve the same effects. A number of substances are physically addictive, so when the addicted adolescent stops using it or lowers the dosage, characteristic withdrawal symptoms occur; this addiction is also known as **abstinence syndrome.** When addicted individuals lower their intake of alcohol, they may experience symptoms such as tremors (shakes), high blood pressure, rapid heart and pulse rate, anxiety, restlessness, and weakness. Many adolescents who begin to use substances such as alcohol for pleasure wind up using them to escape the abstinence syndrome.

Why, you might wonder, are psychologists and educators so concerned about substance abuse? It is not just a moral issue. Drugs are not "bad" simply because they

© Michael Siluk/The Image Works

Substance Use and Abuse
It is important to distinguish between the use and abuse of substances. Many adolescents occasionally experiment with substances such as alcohol and marijuana.

substance abuse A persistent pattern of use of a substance characterized by frequent intoxication and impairment of physical, social, or emotional well-being.

substance dependence A persistent pattern of use of a substance that is accompanied by physiological addiction.

tolerance Habituation to a drug such that increasingly higher doses are needed to achieve similar effects.

abstinence syndrome A characteristic cluster of symptoms that results from a sudden decrease in the level of usage of a substance.

are illegal. Children and adolescents are not advised to avoid them simply because they are under age. Drugs can have serious harmful effects on health. Consider the effects of some depressants, stimulants, and hallucinogenics.

Effects of Depressants

Question: What are the effects of depressants? All depressants slow the activity of the nervous system. Beyond that, they have different cognitive and biological effects. Depressants include alcohol, narcotics derived from the opium poppy (heroin, morphine, and the like), and **sedatives** (such as barbiturates and methaqualone).

Alcohol lessens inhibitions so that drinkers may do things when drinking that they would otherwise resist (Bartholow et al., 2006; Donohue et al., 2007). Ingesting five or more drinks in a row—that is, *binge drinking*—is connected with bad grades and risky behavior, including risky (unprotected, promiscuous) sex, acts of aggression, and accidents (Birch et al., 2007; Keller et al., 2007). Small amounts of alcohol can be stimulating, but high doses have a sedative effect, which is why alcohol is labeled a depressant. Alcohol is also an intoxicant: It distorts perceptions, impairs concentration, hinders coordination, and slurs the speech. The media pay more attention to deaths resulting from heroin and cocaine overdoses, but hundreds of college students die each year from causes related to drinking, including accidents and overdoses (Centers for Disease Control and Prevention, 2005). (Yes, a person can die from drinking too much at one time.)

Adolescent drinking often leads to drinking as an adult, and chronic drinking can lead to serious physical disorders such as cirrhosis or cancer of the liver. Chronic heavy drinking has been linked to cardiovascular disorders. Heavy drinking increases the risk of breast cancer among women and may harm the embryo if she is pregnant (Rathus et al., 2008).

Heroin is a depressant that is derived from the opium poppy. Like morphine and other opioids, its major medical use is relief from pain. But it also can provide a euphoric "rush," which is why many experimenters are tempted to use it again. Heroin is addictive, and regular users develop tolerance.

Barbiturates are depressants with various legitimate medical uses, such as relief from pain, anxiety, and tension and treatment of insomnia, high blood pressure, and epilepsy, but people can become rapidly dependent on them. These drugs are used illegally by adolescents because of their relaxing effects and their ability to produce a mild euphoria. Depressants have additive effects; therefore, mixing barbiturates and other depressants is risky.

Effects of Stimulants

Question: What are the effects of stimulants? Using stimulants is like stepping on the body's accelerator pedal. Stimulants speed up the heartbeat and other bodily functions. They can also keep people awake and alert, but at the expense of some wear and tear. Nicotine, cocaine, and amphetamines are the most commonly used stimulants.

Nicotine is found in cigars, cigarettes, and chewing tobacco. Nicotine causes the release of the hormone adrenaline, which ramps up the heart, disrupts its rhythm, and causes the liver to pour sugar into the blood. Nicotine, like other stimulants, also raises the rate at which the body burns calories and lowers the appetite, so some adolescents smoke as a means of weight control (Anzengruber et al., 2006; Copeland et al., 2006). Nicotine is also the chemical that addicts people to tobacco (Nonnemaker & Homsi, 2007). The abstinence syndrome from nicotine includes symptoms such as drowsiness and loss of energy (the stimulant is gone, after all), palpitations of the heart (irregular heartbeats), sweating, tremors, lightheadedness and dizziness, insomnia, headaches, and digestive problems (irregular bowel movements and cramps). Nearly 450,000 Americans die from smoking-related problems each year (American

sedatives Drugs that soothe or quiet restlessness or agitation.

Lung Association, 2007). Cigarette smoke contains carbon monoxide, which causes shortness of breath, and hydrocarbons ("tars"), which are responsible for most respiratory diseases and cases of lung cancer (American Lung Association, 2007). Pregnant smokers increase the risk of miscarriage, stillbirths, preterm births, and low-birth-weight babies (American Lung Association, 2007).

The stimulant cocaine produces feelings of euphoria, relieves pain, boosts self-confidence, and reduces the appetite. Cocaine has biological as well as psychological effects: It accelerates the heart rate, spikes the blood pressure, constricts the arteries of the heart, and thickens the blood, a combination of effects that can cause cardiovascular and respiratory collapse (Mitchell, 2006). Cocaine has caused the deaths of several young athletes who used it to boost performance and confidence. Because cocaine is a stimulant, overdoses can cause restlessness, insomnia, and tremors.

Amphetamines are widely known to students as enablers of all-night cram sessions. Many dieters rely on them to reduce their appetites. Tolerance for amphetamines develops rapidly, and adolescents can become dependent on them, especially when they use them to self-medicate themselves for depression. Regular use of the powerful amphetamine called methamphetamine may be physically addictive (Jonkman, 2006; Shen et al., 2007), but the extent to which amphetamines cause physical addiction has been a subject of controversy. High doses of amphetamines, as with high doses of cocaine, can cause restlessness and insomnia, irritability, and loss of appetite.

Effects of Hallucinogenics

Question: What are the effects of hallucinogenics? **Hallucinogenics** give rise to perceptual distortions called hallucinations. The hallucinator may believe that the hallucination cannot be real, yet it assaults the senses so strongly that it is confused with reality. Marijuana, Ecstasy, LSD, and PCP are examples of hallucinogenic drugs.

Marijuana is derived from the *Cannabis sativa* plant. It is typically smoked, although it can be eaten. Many adolescents report that marijuana helps them relax and elevates their mood. Adolescents who use marijuana report greater sensory awareness, self-insight, creativity, and empathy for other people's feelings. Smokers become highly attuned to bodily sensations, especially their heartbeat, which tends to accelerate. They experience visual and other hallucinations, as in time seeming to slow down so that a song might seem to go on indefinitely. But strong intoxication can disorient and frighten some smokers.

Marijuana carries a number of health risks. It impairs the perceptual–motor coordination used in driving, for example. It impairs short-term memory and slows learning (Egerton et al., 2006; Lamers et al., 2006). Although it causes positive mood changes in many people, some experience anxiety and confusion (Bonn-Miller et al., 2007). Users can become psychologically dependent on marijuana, and research also suggests that regular users can experience withdrawal, which is a sign of physical addiction (Budney et al., 2007).

Ecstasy—also known as MDMA (an abbreviation for its chemical formula)—is a popular "party drug" or "club drug." Its chemical formula has similarities both to amphetamines, the stimulants, and mescaline, a hallucinogenic drug (Lamers et al., 2006). As a result, Ecstasy gives users the boost of a stimulant, making them somewhat more alert and suffusing them with feelings of elation and self-confidence. As a mild hallucinogenic, it also removes users a bit from reality. The combination appears to free them to some degree from inhibitions and cognitive awareness of the possible consequences of risky behavior, such as unprotected sex. Ecstasy can

© Tom & Dee Ann McCarthy/CORBIS

Which Adolescents Are Most Likely to Smoke?

Over the past 30 years, the percentage of twelfth-graders who disapprove of smoking a pack a day has increased from two out of three to more than four out of five (see Table 14.6). It is encouraging news (see Table 14.7) that only 10% or 11% of twelfth-graders who plan to attend college for 4 years or more now smoke daily; however, about twice as many have used cigarettes at least once within the past 30 days, so the threat of greater usage remains. And, of course, smoking is more common among seniors with lesser plans for college and, likely, for high school dropouts.

hallucinogenics Drugs that give rise to hallucinations.

■ **Table 14.4** Drugs and Their Effects

Drug	Type	How Taken	Desired Effects	Tolerance	Abstinence Syndrome	Side Effects
Alcohol	Depressant	By mouth	Relaxation, euphoria, lowered inhibitions	Yes	Yes	Impaired coordination, poor judgment, hangover[a]
Heroin	Depressant	Injected, smoked, by mouth	Relaxation, euphoria, relief from anxiety and pain	Yes	Yes	Impaired coordination and mental functioning, drowsiness, lethargy[a]
Barbiturates and Methaqualone	Depressants	By mouth, injected	Relaxation, sleep, euphoria, lowered inhibitions	Yes	Yes	Impaired coordination and mental functioning, drowsiness, lethargy[a]
Amphetamines	Stimulants	By mouth, injected	Alertness, euphoria	Yes	?	Restlessness, loss of appetite, psychotic symptoms
Cocaine	Stimulant	By mouth, snorted, injected	Euphoria, self-confidence	Yes	Yes	Restlessness, loss of appetite, convulsions, strokes, psychotic symptoms
Nicotine (cigarettes)	Stimulant	By tobacco (smoked, chewed, or sniffed)	Relaxation, stimulation, weight control	Yes	Yes	Cancer, heart disease, lung and respiratory diseases
Marijuana	Hallucinogenic	Smoked, by mouth	Relaxation, perceptual distortions, enhancement of experience	[b]	[b]	Impaired coordination, learning, respiratory problems, panic
MDMA (Ecstasy)	Stimulant/ hallucinogenic	By mouth	Alertness, self-confidence, hallucinations	?	?	Impaired memory, increased heart rate, anxiety, confusion, possible depression
LSD, PCP	Hallucinogenic	By mouth	Perceptual distortions, vivid hallucinations	Yes	No	Impaired coordination, psychotic symptoms, panic

[a]Overdose can result in death.

[b]Recent research suggests the answer is yes, although some might consider the "jury to still be out."

also impair working memory (not helpful in studying), increase anxiety, and lead to depression (Lamers et al., 2006).

LSD is the acronym for lysergic acid diethylamide, another hallucinogenic drug. Regular use of hallucinogenics can cause psychological dependence and tolerance, but people are not known to become physically addicted to them. High doses can impair coordination and judgment (driving while using hallucinogenic drugs poses grave risks), change the mood, and cause hallucinations and paranoid delusions (belief that one is in danger or being observed or followed).

Various drugs and their effects are summarized in ■ Table 14.4.

Prevalence of Substance Abuse

Truth or Fiction Revisited: Substance use and abuse among high school students seems to be experiencing a slight decline in the early years of the 21st century. Ongoing surveys of high school students by the Institute of Social Research at the University of Michigan find that use of illicit drugs by eighth- through twelfth-graders has generally declined over the past few decades (Johnston et al., 2006a).

Question: How widespread is substance abuse among adolescents? ■ Table 14.5 compares self-reported substance abuse in 1996 with that in 2006 for eighth-, tenth-, and twelfth-graders. There was a decline in the use of (any) illicit drug from about 31% to 21% among eighth-graders during this decade, and from about 45% to 35% among tenth-graders. (Note that experience with drugs increased with age in both years.) But there was something of a catch-up effect by twelfth grade, with about 51% of twelfth-graders having used an illicit drug in 1996 as compared with 48% in 2006.

The incidence of use of some drugs was relatively high: alcohol, cigarettes (nicotine is actually the drug in cigarettes), and marijuana. Some drugs have been used by fewer than 10% of students: MDMA, cocaine, LSD, steroids, PCP, and heroin. Perhaps the most heartening news in the survey results is that messages about the dan-

■ **Table 14.5** Trends in Lifetime Use of Various Drugs for Eighth-, Tenth-, and Twelfth-Graders, 1996 versus 2006 (Percents)

	1996	2006		1996	2006
Any illicit drug			**MDMA (Ecstasy)**		
8th grade	31.2%	20.9%	8th grade	3.4	2.5
10th grade	45.4	36.1	10th grade	5.6	4.5
12th grade	50.8	48.2	12th grade	6.1	6.5
Alcohol			**Cocaine**		
8th grade	55.3	40.56	8th grade	4.5	3.4
10th grade	71.8	61.5	10th grade	6.5	4.8
12th grade	79.2	72.7	12th grade	7.1	8.5
Cigarettes			**LSD**		
8th grade	49.2	24.6	8th grade	5.1	1.6
10th grade	61.2	36.1	10th grade	9.4	2.7
12th grade	63.5	47.1	12th grade	12.6	3.3
Marijuana			**Steroids**		
8th grade	23.1	15.7	8th grade	1.8	1.6
10th grade	39.8	31.8	10th grade	1.8	1.8
12th grade	44.9	42.3	12th grade	1.9	1.7
Amphetamines			**PCP**		
8th grade	13.5	7.3	8th grade	—	—
10th grade	17.7	11.2	10th grade	—	—
12th grade	15.3	12.4	12th grade	4.0	2.2
Inhalants			**Heroin**		
8th grade	21.2	16.1	8th grade	2.4	1.4
10th grade	19.3	13.3	10th grade	2.1	1.4
12th grade	16.6	11.1	12th grade	1.8	1.4
Barbiturates					
8th grade	—	—			
10th grade	—	—			
12th grade	7.6	10.2			

Source: Johnston et al. (2006b, table 1).

gers of cigarette smoking have apparently been getting through to youngsters; only one-quarter of eighth-graders report that they have ever used cigarettes.

Less than 2% of high school students report they have used steroids. Steroids, which build muscle mass, are typically used by boys to improve their athletic performance, although some users also want to improve their physical appearance.

Students' Attitudes Toward Drugs

The University of Michigan researchers have also tracked the extent to which high school students disapprove of drug use over the past generation. ***Question: How many adolescents disapprove of use of drugs?*** ■ Table 14.6 shows the percentage of high school seniors who disapproved of various kinds of drug use in the year 1976 and 30 years later in 2006. In most cases, the table compares the disapproval rating for drugs that are used experimentally ("once or twice") or regularly. In general, students of both eras are more likely to disapprove of regular drug use than experimental drug use. For example, about half of students disapprove of use of marijuana on an experimental basis (47% in 1975 and 53% in 2003), but the disapproval rate for regular smoking

■ **Table 14.6** Disapproval of Drug Use by Twelfth-Graders, 1976 versus 2006

Do you disapprove of people (who are 18 or older) doing each of the following?	Percent Disapproving, Class of 1976	Percent Disapproving, Class of 2006
Try marijuana once or twice	38.4%	55.6%
Smoke marijuana regularly	69.5	82.2
Try LSD once or twice	84.6	88
Take LSD regularly	95.3	95.9
Try MDMA (Ecstasy) one or twice	—	89
Try cocaine once or twice	82.4	89.1
Take cocaine regularly	93.9	96.1
Try crack once or twice	—	88.8
Take crack regularly	—	93.8
Try heroin once or twice	92.6	93.8
Take heroin regularly	97.5	96.9
Try amphetamines once or twice	75.1	86.3
Take amphetamines regularly	92.8	95.3
Try barbiturates once or twice	81.3	85.3
Take barbiturates regularly	93.6	95.1
Try one or two drinks of an alcoholic beverage (beer, wine, liquor)	18.2	29
Take one or two drinks nearly every day	68.9	72.8
Take four or five drinks nearly every day	90.7	90.6
Have five or more drinks once or twice each weekend	58.6	68.5
Smoke one or more packs of cigarettes per day	65.9	81.5
Take steroids	—	89.4

Source: Johnston et al. (2006b, table 10).

of marijuana rises to 72% in 1975 and 79% in 2003. The discrepancy between disapproval for experimental and regular use of alcohol is most noticeable. Only a minority—although a growing minority—of high school seniors (18% in 1976 and 29% in 2006) disapproved of trying a drink or two. However, most seniors in both eras disapproved of daily drinking and of weekend binge drinking. Overall, disapproval ratings are somewhat higher in 2006 than in 1976. Perhaps antidrug messages have been having an effect. The percentage of students who disapproved of experimenting with heroin and cocaine or using them regularly was high in both eras. All in all, high school seniors are least likely to be concerned about trying a drink or two.

Factors in Substance Abuse and Dependence

Question: What factors are associated with substance abuse and dependence?
Adolescents often become involved with substance abuse and dependence through experimental use (Commission on Adolescent Substance and Alcohol Abuse, 2005; Costello, 2007). Some are conforming to peer pressure; acceptance by peers means doing what the peers do. Some are rebelling against moral or social constraints. Others are in it for the experience. Of these, some are simply curious; they want to see what effects the drugs will have. Others are trying to escape from boredom or from

Developing in a World of Diversity

Sex, College Plans, Ethnicity, and Substance Abuse

There is quite some diversity in the prevalence of substance abuse among adolescents. The Institute of Social Research at the University of Michigan has regularly asked high school seniors whether they have used various substances within the past year (the annual prevalence) and a variety of questions in the cases of alcohol and cigarettes. ■ Table 14.7 shows the self-reported behavior of the class of 2005, broken down according to the sex of the student, the college plans of the student, and the ethnicity or ancestry of the student. Ethnicity is limited to European Americans, African American, and Latino and Latina Americans because even though several thousand students were surveyed, the researchers were not satisfied that they had sufficient samples to report on Asian Americans and Native Americans.

For every substance shown in Table 14.7 and for every situation described, adolescent males are more likely than adolescent females to have used or abused the substance. This finding holds for widely abused substances such as alcohol and marijuana, and for relatively rarely used substances such as heroin and crack. Table 14.7 also reveals that plans to complete 4 years of college appear to have a restraining effect on substance abuse. In every category, seniors who anticipate at least 4 more years of schooling are less likely than seniors who plan no further schooling or less than 4 years of further schooling to engage in substance abuse.

Now consider the three ethnic groups studied by the researchers. **Truth or Fiction Revisited:** Substance abuse is highest among European American twelfth-graders. Which ethnic group is least likely to report substance abuse?

Reflect:
- *Why do you think that adolescent males are more likely than adolescent females to report engaging in substance abuse?*
- *Why do you think that plans to attend college for 4 years might have a restraining effect on substance abuse among twelfth-graders?*
- *Are you surprised by the relationship between substance abuse and ethnicity shown in Table 14.7? Why or why not?*
- *Is it possible that the worst adolescent substance abusers were not in the group sampled by the Institute for Social Research? Explain.*
- *Can you think of any reasons adolescents in the sample might have been motivated to misrepresent their behavior? Explain.*

■ **Table 14.7** Twelfth-graders' Prevalence of Use of Various Licit and Illicit Drugs According to Sex, College Plans, and Ethnicity—Year 2005 (in Percents)

		Sex		College Plans		Ethnicity		
PART A: ANNUAL PREVALENCES (ANY USE IN PAST YEAR)								
Drug	Total	Male	Female	Plan to Complete No College or Less Than 4 Years	Plan to Complete 4 Years of College	European American	African American	Latino or Latina American
Any illicit drug	38.4%	42.1%	34.5%	46.5%	36.1%	41.6%	29.0%	34.5%
Marijuana	33.6	37.6	29.6	41.3	31.5	36.6	26.3	29.6
Inhalants	5.0	6.2	4.1	7.3	4.6	5.1	1.9	5.3
LSD	1.8	2.7	0.9	3.4	1.3	2.2	0.7	1.7
MDMA (Ecstasy)	3.0	3.3	2.7	3.7	2.8	3.9	1.4	3.0
Cocaine	5.1	5.8	4.2	7.5	4.4	5.6	1.2	6.2
Crack	1.9	2.2	1.6	3.4	1.6	2.1	0.9	3.1
Heroin	0.8	1.2	0.5	1.8	0.6	0.7	0.8	1.3
Amphetamines	8.6	9.1	7.9	11.5	7.8	11.0	2.4	6.7
Barbiturates	7.2	7.7	6.6	10.7	6.3	7.9	2.6	5.8
Steroids	1.5	2.6	0.4	2.1	1.2	2.1	1.6	2.0
PART B: PREVALENCES AS SHOWN								
Alcohol—any use in past 30 days	47%	50.7%	43.3%	52.8%	45.5%	52.3%	29.0%	43.3%
Alcohol—been drunk in past 30 days	30.2	33.6	26.4	34.3	28.5	36.5	15.4	22.2
Alcohol—had 5 or more drinks in a row in past 2 weeks	27.1	32.6	21.6	34.3	25.1	32.5	11.3	23.9
Cigarettes—any use in past 30 days	23.2	24.8	20.7	34.8	20.0	27.6	10.7	17.1
Cigarettes—daily use in past 30 days	13.6	14.6	11.9	24.9	10.5	17.1	5.6	7.7

Source: Johnstonet al. (2006a).

the pressures of school or the neighborhood. Some, of course, are looking for pleasure or excitement. Some youngsters are imitating what they see their own parents doing.

Social cognitive theorists suggest that children and adolescents usually try drugs because someone has recommended them or because they have observed someone else using them. But whether or not they continue to use the drug depends on factors such as whether use is reinforced by peer approval. The drug can also be reinforcing by enhancing the user's mood or by reducing unpleasant emotions such as anxiety and tension. For individuals who are addicted, the prevention of the abstinence syndrome is reinforcing. Carrying the substance and obtaining a "rainy day" supply are reinforcing because the child or adolescent does not have to worry about being caught short.

Why, you may wonder, do children and adolescents use drugs when their health education courses inform them that they are harmful? Do they not believe their teachers? Some do; some don't. But the reinforcement value of the substances occurs now, today. The harmful effects are frequently long term, or theoretical.

Associating with peers who use drugs and who tolerate drug use is one of the strongest predictors of adolescent drug use and abuse (Costello, 2007). Children are highly vulnerable to peer pressure in the early teen years. If they are closely involved with a drug-abusing group, they may feel pressured to join in. Adolescents who are extensively involved with peers, especially to the exclusion of their families, are at greater risk for drug use.

Parenting styles play a role. Having open lines of communication with a parent helps inhibit drug use. The authoritative pattern of child rearing appears to protect children from substance abuse (Dorius et al., 2004; Patock-Peckham & Morgan-Lopez, 2006). Heavy drug use is most likely to occur in families with permissive or neglecting–rejecting parenting styles.

Adolescent drug users often experience school problems. They do poorly in school, and their academic motivation is low (Dunn & Mezzich, 2007). Certain psychological characteristics are associated with drug use, including anxiety and depression, antisocial behavior, and low self-esteem (Donohue et al., 2006; Gau et al., 2007).

Biological factors are apparently involved in determining which experimenters will continue to use a drug and which will not. Children may inherit genetic predispositions toward abuse of specific substances, including depressants, stimulants, and hallucinogenics (Gelernter et al., 2007; Lynskey et al., 2007; Redgrave et al., 2007). For example, the biological children of alcoholics who are reared by adoptive parents are more likely to abuse alcohol than are the biological children of the adoptive parents.

Treatment and Prevention

Question: How can we treat and prevent substance abuse? Health professionals, educators, police departments, and laypeople have devised many approaches to the prevention and treatment of substance abuse and dependence among adolescents. However, treatment has been a frustrating endeavor, and it is not clear which approaches are most effective. In many cases, adolescents with drug dependence really do not want to discontinue the substances they are abusing. Many are referred to treatment by parents or school systems, but they deny the negative effect of drugs on their lives. They may belong to a peer group that frowns on prevention or treatment programs (Lochman et al., 2007). When addicted adolescents come for treatment, helping them through a withdrawal syndrome may be straightforward enough. But once their bodies no longer require the substance to feel "normal," they may return to the social milieu that fosters substance abuse and be unable to find strong reasons for living a life without drugs (Lochman et al., 2007). The problem of returning to abuse and dependence following treatment—that is, the problem of relapse—can thus be more troublesome than the problems involved in initial treatment (Anderson et al., 2007; Sussman et al., 2006).

Many adolescents with substance abuse problems also have psychological disorders or serious family problems. When treatment programs focus only on substance abuse and do little to treat the psychological disorder or relationships in the family, the outcome of treatment tends to suffer (Sussman et al., 2006).

The ability of teenagers to deal with the physical changes of adolescence and to engage in health-promoting behaviors depends in part on their growing cognitive abilities. We examine development in that area in Chapter 15.

Active Review

14. Death rates are greater for (Male or Female?) adolescents.
15. Most adolescent deaths are due to _____.
16. _____ is a life-threatening eating disorder characterized by intense fear of being overweight, a distorted body image, and refusal to eat.
17. Bulimia nervosa is characterized by recurrent cycles of binge eating followed by _____.
18. Anorexia nervosa and bulimia nervosa (Do or Do not?) tend to run in families.
19. Eating disorders are connected with traits such as _____.
20. Substance _____ is the repeated use of a substance even though it is causing or compounding social, occupational, psychological, or physical problems.
21. Substance dependence is characterized by loss of control over the substance, tolerance, and a(n) _____ syndrome.

22. _____ is the most commonly used substance by adolescents.
23. _____ is the agent that creates physiological dependence on tobacco.
24. High school seniors are more likely to disapprove of (Experimental or Regular?) drug use.

Reflect & Relate: How widespread were eating disorders and substance abuse in your own high school? Did you notice sex differences in the rates of these two problems? How did these problems begin? What are some ways in which parents and educators might help adolescents avoid them?

Go to

http://www.thomsonedu.com/psychology/rathus
for an interactive version of this review.

1. What is adolescence?

Adolescence is a transitional period between childhood and adulthood. G. Stanley Hall believed that adolescence is marked by "storm and stress." Current views challenge the idea that storm and stress are normal or beneficial.

2. What is puberty? What happens during puberty?

Puberty is a stage of physical development that is characterized by reaching sexual maturity. Puberty is controlled by a feedback loop involving glands. Sex hormones trigger the development of primary and secondary sex characteristics.

3. What happens during the adolescent growth spurt?

Girls spurt sooner than boys. Boys tend to spurt up to 4 inches per year, and girls, up to 3 inches per year. During their growth spurts, boys catch up with girls and grow taller and heavier. Boys' shoulders become broader, and girls develop broader and rounder hips. More of a male's body weight is made of muscle. Adolescents may look gawky because of asynchronous growth. Boys typically ejaculate by age 13 or 14. Female sex hormones regulate the menstrual cycle.

4. What are the effects of early or late maturation on adolescents?

The effects of early maturation are generally positive for boys and often negative for girls. Early-maturing boys tend to be more popular. Early-maturing girls become conspicuous, often leading to sexual approaches, deviant behavior, and a poor body image.

5. How do adolescents feel about their bodies?

Girls are generally more dissatisfied with their bodies than boys are. By age 18, dissatisfaction tends to decline.

6. What kinds of sexually transmitted infections are there?

Sexually transmitted infections (STIs) include bacterial infections such as chlamydia, gonorrhea, and syphilis; viral infections such as HIV/AIDS, HPV, and genital herpes; and some others.

7. What factors place adolescents at risk for contracting STIs?

The factors include sexual activity with multiple partners and without condoms, and substance abuse. Sharing hypodermic needles with an infected person can also transmit HIV.

8. Given the threat of HIV/AIDS and other STIs, what can be done to prevent STIs?

Prevention involves education about STIs, along with advice concerning abstinence or "safer sex."

9. How healthy are American dolescents?

Most American adolescents are healthy, but about one in five has a serious health problem. Most adolescent health problems stem from their lifestyle.

10. What are the causes of death among adolescents?

Death rates are greater for older adolescents and for male adolescents. Accidents, suicide, and homicide account for about three in four deaths among adolescents.

11. What are the nutritional needs of adolescents? What do adolescents actually eat?

The average girl needs about 2,200 calories per day, and the average boy needs about 3,000 calories. Adolescents need high quantities of elements such as calcium, iron, zinc, magnesium, and nitrogen. Adolescents usually need more vitamins than they take in but less sugar, fat, protein, and sodium.

12.	**What are eating disorders?**	Eating disorders include anorexia nervosa and bulimia nervosa. Anorexia nervosa is characterized by fear of being overweight, a distorted body image, and refusal to eat. Bulimia nervosa is characterized by recurrent cycles of binge eating followed by purging. Eating disorders mainly afflict females.
13.	**What are the origins of eating disorders?**	Some psychoanalysts suggest that anorexia represents efforts to remain prepubescent. One risk factor for eating disorders in adolescent females is a history of child abuse. Eating disorders may develop because of fear of gaining weight resulting from cultural idealization of the slim female. Genetic factors may connect eating disorders with perfectionistic personality styles.
14.	**What is substance abuse? What is substance dependence?**	Substance abuse is use of a substance despite the social, occupational, psychological, or physical problems. Substance dependence is characterized by loss of control over the substance and is typified by tolerance and withdrawal symptoms.
15.	**What are the effects of depressants?**	Depressants are addictive substances that slow the activity of the nervous system. Alcohol lowers inhibitions, relaxes, and intoxicates. Heroin can provide a strong euphoric "rush." Barbiturates relieve anxiety and tension.
16.	**What are the effects of stimulants?**	Stimulants accelerate the heartbeat and other bodily functions and depress the appetite. Nicotine is the stimulant in tobacco. The stimulant cocaine produces euphoria and bolsters self-confidence, but it occasionally causes respiratory and cardiovascular collapse. Some adolescents use amphetamines to remain awake for cram sessions.
17.	**What are the effects of hallucinogenics?**	Hallucinogenics give rise to perceptual distortions called hallucinations. Marijuana helps some adolescents relax and elevates the mood, but it impairs perceptual–motor coordination and short-term memory. LSD ("acid") produces vivid hallucinations.
18.	**How widespread is substance abuse among adolescents?**	About half of high school seniors have tried illicit drugs. Marijuana use seems to have stabilized or slightly declined. Most students have tried alcohol, and many use it regularly. About 30% of high school seniors have engaged in binge drinking.
19.	**How many adolescents disapprove of use of drugs?**	Adolescents are more likely to disapprove of regular or excessive drug use than experimental drug use. Most high school seniors disapprove of regular use of LSD, cocaine, crack, heroin, amphetamines, barbiturates, and smoking.
20.	**What factors are associated with substance abuse and dependence?**	Substance abuse and dependence usually begin with experimental use in adolescence. Adolescents may experiment because of curiosity, conformity to peer pressure, parental use, rebelliousness, and a desire to escape from boredom or pressure and to seek excitement or pleasure. Some individuals may also have a genetic predisposition toward dependence on certain substances.
21.	**How can we treat and prevent substance abuse?**	It may be relatively simple to help an adolescent through an abstinence syndrome (the process is called detoxification); it is more difficult to prevent relapse.

Key Terms

genital stage, 478
puberty, 479
feedback loop, 479
hypothalamus, 479
pituitary gland, 479
primary sex characteristics, 479
secondary sex characteristics, 479
asynchronous growth, 480
secular trend, 481
larynx, 482

semen, 482
nocturnal emission, 483
gynecomastia, 483
epiphyseal closure, 483
mammary glands, 484
labia, 484
clitoris, 484
menarche, 484
HIV/AIDS, 490
osteoporosis, 497

menopause, 497
anorexia nervosa, 498
bulimia nervosa, 501
substance abuse, 503
substance dependence, 503
tolerance, 503
abstinence syndrome, 503
sedatives, 504
hallucinogenics, 505

Active Learning Resources

Childhood & Adolescence Book Companion Website

http://www.thomsonedu.com/psychology/rathus

Visit your book companion website where you will find more resources to help you study. There you will find interactive versions of your book features, including the Lessons in Observation video, Active Review sections, and the Truth or Fiction feature. In addition, the companion website contains quizzing, flash cards, and a pronunciation glossary.

 is an easy-to-use online resource that helps you study in less time to get the grade you want—NOW.

http://www.thomsonedu.com/login

Need help studying? This site is your one-stop study shop. Take a Pre-Test and ThomsonNOW will generate a Personalized Study Plan based on your test results. The Study Plan will identify the topics you need to review and direct you to online resources to help you master those topics. You can then take a Post-Test to determine the concepts you have mastered and what you still need to work on.

15

Adolescence:
Cognitive Development

Truth or Fiction?

T F Many adolescents see themselves as being on stage. p. 523

T F It is normal for male adolescents to think of themselves as action heroes and to act as though they are made of steel. p. 523

T F Adolescent boys outperform adolescent girls in mathematics. p. 526

T F Most adolescents make moral decisions based on their own ethical principles and may choose to disobey the laws of the land if they conflict with their principles. p. 529

T F The transition from elementary school is more difficult for boys than for girls. p. 533

T F Adolescents who work after school obtain lower grades. p. 540

Preview

The Adolescent in Thought: My, My, How "Formal"
Piaget's Stage of Formal Operations

Lessons in Observation: Piaget's Formal Operational Stage: Abstraction and Hypothetical Propositions

A Closer Look: The Puzzle and the Pendulum

Adolescent Egocentrism: Center Stage
Sex Differences in Cognitive Abilities

The Adolescent in Judgment: Moral Development
The Postconventional Level
Moral Behavior and Moral Reasoning: Is There a Relationship?

Developing in a World of Diversity: Cross-Cultural and Sex Differences in Moral Development

The Adolescent in School
Making the Transition from Elementary School
Dropping Out of School

A Closer Look: Beyond the Classroom: How Parents Can Help Teenagers Improve Their Academic Performance

The Adolescent at Work: Career Development and Work Experience
Career Development
Adolescents in the Workforce

Developing in a World of Diversity: Ethnic Identity and Gender in Career Self-Efficacy Expectancies

Go to

http://www.thomsonedu.com/psychology/rathus
for an interactive version of this "Truth or Fiction" feature.

I am a college student of extremely modest means. Some crazy psychologist interested in something called "formal operational thought" has just promised to pay me $20 if I can make a coherent logical argument for the proposition that the federal government should under no circumstances ever give or lend more to needy college students. Now what could people who believe that possibly say by way of supporting that argument? Well, I suppose they *could* offer this line of reasoning . . .

—Flavell et al. (2002)

This "college student of extremely modest means" is thinking like an adolescent, quite differently from an elementary school child and differently from most middle-school children. Children in the concrete-operational stage are bound by the facts as they are. They are not given to hypothetical thinking, to speculation about what might be. They are mainly stuck in what is. But the adolescent, like the adult, can ponder abstract ideas and see the world as it could be. Our "college student of extremely modest means" recognizes that a person can find arguments for causes in which he or she does not believe.

In this chapter, we learn about cognitive development in adolescence. We focus first on aspects of intellectual development, including Piaget's stage of formal operations, adolescent egocentrism, and sex differences. We then turn to moral development, focusing on the views of Kohlberg and Gilligan. We conclude with a look at some areas that are strongly tied to cognitive development: school, vocational development, and work experience.

The Adolescent in Thought: My, My, How "Formal"

The growing intellectual capabilities of adolescents change the way they approach the world. The cognitive changes of adolescence influence how adolescents view themselves and their families and friends and how they deal with broader social and moral questions. *Question: What is cognitive development during adolescence like, according to Piaget's stage of formal operations?*

Piaget's Stage of Formal Operations

The stage of **formal operations** is the top level in Jean Piaget's theory. Children or adolescents in this stage have reached cognitive maturity, even if some rough edges remain. Yet for many children in developed nations, the stage of formal operations can begin quite early, at about the time of puberty, 11 or 12 years old. But some children reach this stage somewhat later, and some not at all. Piaget describes the accomplishments of the stage of formal operations in terms of the individual's increased ability to classify objects and ideas, engage in logical thought, and hypothesize, just as researchers make hypotheses in their investigations. The adolescent in the stage of formal operations can think about abstract ideas and about concrete objects. The adolescent can group and classify symbols, statements, and even theories, just as we classify certain views of child development as psychoanalytic theories, learning theories, or socio-

Formal Operations
The ability to deal with the abstract and the hypothetical and the capacity to engage in deductive reasoning are the key features of formal-operational thought. Formal-operational thinking allows adolescents to engage in scientific reasoning.

cultural theories, even if they differ quite a bit in their particulars. Formal operations are flexible and reversible. Adolescents are thus capable of following and formulating arguments from their premises to their conclusions and back once more, even if they do not believe in them. Hypothetical thinking, the use of symbols to represent other symbols, and deductive reasoning allow the adolescent to more fully comprehend the real world and to play with the world that dwells within the mind alone.

Hypothetical Thinking

In formal-operational thought, children—or, should we say, adolescents?—discover the concept of "what might be" rather than "what is." Adolescents can project themselves into situations that transcend their immediate experience, and, for this reason, they may become wrapped up in lengthy fantasies. Many adolescents can explore endless corridors of the mind, perceiving what would happen as one decision leads to another point where a choice presents itself—and then still another decision is

formal operations The fourth stage in Piaget's cognitive-developmental theory, characterized by the capacity for flexible, reversible operations concerning abstract ideas and concepts, such as symbols, statements, and theories.

Lessons in Observation

Piaget's Formal Operational Stage: Abstraction and Hypothetical Propositions

 To watch this video, visit the book companion website. You can also answer the questions and e-mail your responses to your professor.

Learning Objectives

- What is Piaget's stage of formal operations?
- What is hypothetical reasoning?
- How do preadolescents and adolescents tend to differ in the ways in which they answer hypothetical questions?

Applied Lesson

How has your own ability to reason hypothetically changed as you have matured? Do you reason at different levels in different kinds of situations?

Critical Thinking

Explain the different ways in which preadolescents and adolescents address the question "What if people had no thumbs?" Describe how these different answers illustrate the idea of Piaget's stage of formal operations.

Researchers asked children and adolescents of different ages, "What if people had no thumbs?" Formal-operational adolescents, such as the young man on the top, can mentally picture the situation and answer hypothetically, contrasting it with reality. The younger boy on the bottom still answers in terms of his own reality and has difficulty hypothesizing a world without thumbs.

made. Adolescents become aware that situations can have different outcomes. They can think ahead, systematically trying out various possibilities in their minds.

You may think of scientists as people in white lab coats, with advanced degrees and a devotion to exploring uncharted territory. And some are like that, of course. But many more wear blue jeans and experiment with their hair and ways of relating to people whom they find attractive. Many adolescents in the stage of formal operations consider themselves disinterested in science, yet they conduct research daily to see whether their hypotheses about themselves and their friends and teachers are correct. These explorations are not laboratory experiments that involve calipers or Bunsen burners. It is more common for adolescents to explore uncharted territory by trying on different clothes and "attitudes" to see which work best for them.

Adolescents, who can look ahead to multiple outcomes, may also see many possibilities for themselves. Some recognize that they can, to a large extent, fashion themselves according to their own images of what they are capable of becoming. In terms of career decisions, the wealth of possible directions leads some adolescents to experience anxiety about whether they will pick the career that really is them and to experience a sense of loss about the possibility that they may be able to choose only one.

This capacity to look ahead, to fashion futures, also frequently leads to **utopian** thinking. Just as adolescents can foresee many possibilities for themselves, they can also imagine different outcomes for suffering humanity. "What if" thinking enables adolescents to fashion schemes for putting an end to hunger, disease, and international strife.

A Mammal That Requires Some Deductive Reasoning!

The Australian duck-billed platypus has a bill like, well, a duck rather than a warm, furry nose. It is also hairless and reproduces by laying eggs. However, formal-operational thought—and another fact—allow us to deduce that the platypus is a mammal. How? Like this: Premise: All animals that feed their young with breast milk are mammals. Observation: Platypuses feed their young with breast milk. Conclusion: Therefore, platypuses are mammals.

utopian Referring to an ideal vision of society.

Sophisticated Use of Symbols

Children in elementary school can understand what is meant by abstract symbols such as 1 and 2. They can also perform operations in which numbers are manipulated—added, subtracted, and so on. But now consider x, that unknown (and sometimes elusive) quantity in algebra. This x may be a familiar letter of the alphabet, but its designation as a symbol for an unknown quantity is a formal abstract operation. One symbol (an x) is being made to stand for something just as abstract (the unknown). Children up to the age of 11 or 12 or so usually cannot fully understand this concept, even if they can be taught the mechanics of solving for x in simple equations. But older, formal-operational children show a sophisticated grasp of the nature of symbols. They can grasp intuitively what is meant by x. Formal-operational children, or adolescents, can perform mental operations with symbols that stand for nothing in their own experience.

These symbols include those used in geometry. Adolescents work with points that have no dimensions, lines that have no width and that are infinite in length, and circles that are perfectly round, even though they may never find them in nature. Ability to manipulate these symbols will eventually permit them to do work in theoretical physics or math or to obtain jobs in engineering or architecture. They learn to apply symbols to the world of tangible objects and materials.

Formal-operational individuals can also understand, appreciate, and sometimes produce metaphors. Metaphors are figures of speech in which words or phrases that ordinarily signify one thing are applied to another. We find metaphor in literature, but consider how everyday figures of speech enhance our experience: *squeezing* out a living, *basking in the sunshine* of fame or glory, *hanging by a thread, jumping* to conclusions, and so on.

A CLOSER LOOK

The Puzzle and the Pendulum

If you hang a weight from a string and set it swinging back and forth, you have a pendulum. Bärbel Inhelder and Jean Piaget (1959) used a pendulum to explore ways in which children of different ages go about solving problems.

The researchers showed children several pendulums, with different lengths of string and with different weights at their ends, as in ● Figure 15.1. They attached the strings to rods and sent the weights swinging. They dropped the weights from various heights and pushed them with different amounts of force. The question they posed—the puzzle—was, What determines how fast the pendulum will swing back and forth?

The researchers had varied four factors:

1. The amount of weight
2. The length of the string
3. The height from which the weight was released
4. The force with which the weight was pushed

The answer lies either in one of these factors or in some combination of them. That is, one factor, two factors, three factors, or all four factors could determine the speed of the pendulum.

One could try to solve this problem by deduction based on principles of physics, and experienced physicists might prefer a deductive, mathematical approach. However, one can also solve the problem by trying out each possible combination of factors and observing the results. This strategy is an empirical approach. Because children (and most adults) are not physicists, they will usually take the empirical approach.

Of the children observed by Inhelder and Piaget, those between the ages of 8 and 13 could not arrive at the correct answer. The fault lay largely in their approach, which was only partly systematic. They made some effort to account for the various factors but did not control carefully for every possibility. For example, one child compared a pendulum with a light weight and a short string to a pendulum with a heavy weight and a long string.

The 14- and 15-year-olds generally sat back and reflected before doing anything. Then, in contrast to the younger children, who haphazardly varied several factors at once, the older children tried to exclude each factor

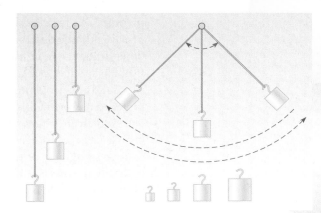

● **Figure 15.1   The Pendulum Problem**

What determines how fast the pendulum will swing back and forth? The amount of weight? The length of the string? The height from which the weight is released? The force with which the weight is pushed? A combination of the above? Formal-operational children attempt to exclude each factor systematically.

systematically. You could say that they used the "process of elimination," as we often do with multiple-choice tests. Not all the 14- and 15-year-olds solved the problem, but as a group, their approach was more advanced and more likely to succeed.

According to Inhelder and Piaget, the approach of the 14- and 15-year-olds typified formal-operational thought. The approach of the 8- to 13-year-olds typified concrete-operational thought. As with many other aspects of Piaget's views and methods, we have to be flexible about Piaget's age estimates for ability to solve the problem. Robert Siegler and his associates (1973), for example, were able to train 10-year-olds to approach the problem systematically and isolate the correct answer (drum roll!): the length of the string. Thus, education and training can influence the development of cognitive skills.

Reflect: How did the adolescents in the study use an empirical approach to determine which factor controlled the speed of the pendulum?

The moral judgments of many adolescents and adults are based on formal-operational thought. That is, they derive their judgments about what is right and wrong in specific situations by reasoning deductively from general moral principles. Their capacity for decentration also allows them to take a broad view of the situation. They can focus on many aspects of a situation at once in making judgments and solving moral dilemmas.

Enhanced cognitive abilities can backfire when adolescents adamantly advance their religious, political, and social ideas without recognition of the subtleties and practical issues that might give pause to adults. For example, let's begin with the premise, "Industries should not be allowed to pollute the environment." We then discover that Industry A pollutes the environment. An adolescent may argue to shut down Industry A, at least until it stops polluting. The logic is reasonable and the goal is noble enough, but Industry A may be indispensable to the nation at large, or many thousands of people may be put out of work if it is shut down. Other people might prefer to seek some kind of compromise.

Adolescents' new intellectual powers often present them with what seem to be crystal-clear solutions to the world's problems, and they may become intolerant of the relative stodginess of their parents. Their utopian images of how to reform the world make them unsympathetic to their parents' earthbound pursuit of a livelihood and other mundane matters.

Reevaluation of Piaget's Theory

Piaget's account of formal operations has received quite a bit of support. There appears to be little question that unique changes do occur in the nature of reasoning between preadolescence and adolescence (U. Mueller et al., 1999, 2001). For example, research strongly supports Piaget's view that the capacity to reason deductively does not emerge until adolescence (U. Mueller et al., 1999, 2001).

But note that formal-operational thought is not a universal step in cognitive development. The ability to solve abstract problems, such as those found in algebra and the pendulum problem, is more likely to be developed in technologically oriented Western societies or in major cities than in less well developed areas or nations (Flavell et al., 2002; Siegler & Alibali, 2005). Moreover, formal-operational thought may occur later than Piaget thought, if at all. For example, many early adolescents (ages 13 to 16) still perform better on concrete problems than on abstract ones (Markovitz & Vachon, 1990). Reviews of the literature suggest that formal-operational thought is found among only 40% to 60% of first-year college students (Flavell et al., 2002; Siegler & Alibali, 2005). Also, the same individual may do well on one type of formal-operational task and poorly on another. We are more likely to use formal-operational thought in our own academic specialties. Some of us are formal operational in math or science but not in the study of literature, and vice versa. Piaget (1972) recognized that adolescents may not always demonstrate formal-operational thought because they are unfamiliar with a particular task.

Adolescent Egocentrism: Center Stage

Did you think that egocentrism was limited to the thought of preschool children, who show difficulty taking the perspective of other people in the three-mountains test? Wrong. Yes, teenagers are capable of hypothetical thinking, and they can argue for causes in which they do not believe (if you pay them enough to do so). However, they also can show a somewhat different brand of egocentrism in a number of ways. Adolescents comprehend the ideas of other people, but have difficulty sorting out those things that concern other people from the things that concern themselves. *Question: How is adolescent egocentrism shown in the* **imaginary audience** *and in the* **personal fable***?*

The Imaginary Audience

Many adolescents fantasize about becoming rock stars or movie stars who are adored by millions. The concept of the **imaginary audience** achieves part of that fantasy, sort of. It places the adolescent on stage, surrounded by critics, however, more than by admirers. Adolescents assume that other people are concerned with their appearance and behavior, more so than they really are (Bell & Bromnick, 2003; Elkind, 1967, 1985; Flavell et al., 2002; Vartanian, 2001). **Truth or Fiction Revisited:** Thus, it is true that adolescents generally see themselves as being on stage, with countless eyes peering in on them. This self-perception may account for the common adolescent intense desire for privacy. The concept of the imaginary audience helps explain why teenagers are so preoccupied with their appearance. It helps explain why the mirror is the constant companion of the teenager, who grooms endlessly, searches out every facial blemish, and agonizes over every zit. Being caught up with the mirror seems to peak sometime during eighth grade and declines over the remainder of adolescence.

The Imaginary Audience
Adolescents tend to feel that other people are continuously scrutinizing their appearance and behavior, which may explain why so many adolescents worry about every facial blemish and spend long hours grooming.

Whereas some researchers view the emergence of the imaginary audience purely in cognitive-developmental terms, others believe that many adolescents are responding to increased social scrutiny (Bell & Bromnick, 2003; Kelly et al., 2002). One research group attributes the imaginary audience more to social anxiety than to cognitive development (Kelly et al., 2002).

The Personal Fable

Spider-Man and the Fantastic Four: Stand aside! Because of the **personal fable**, many adolescents become action heroes, at least in their own minds. If the imaginary audience puts adolescents on stage, the personal fable justifies being there. The personal fable, another aspect of adolescent egocentrism, is the belief that one's thoughts and emotions are special and unique (Aalsma et al., 2006). It also refers to the common adolescent belief that one is all but invulnerable, like Superman or Superwoman. **Truth or Fiction Revisited:** It is normal for male adolescents to think of themselves as action heroes and to act as though they are made of steel.

The personal fable is connected with such behaviors as showing off and risk taking (Omori & Ingersoll, 2005). Many adolescents assume that they can smoke with impunity. Cancer? "It can't happen to me." They drive recklessly. They engage in spontaneous unprotected sexual activity, assuming that sexually transmitted infections (STIs) and unwanted pregnancies happen to other people, not to them. Ronald King (2000), of the HIV Community Coalition of Washington, D.C., put it this way: "All youth—rich, poor, black, white—have this sense of invincibility, invulnerability." Adolescents are more likely than their parents to minimize their assessment of risks (Berger et al., 2005; Nowinski, 2007).

The specialness and uniqueness of the adolescent experience? Many adolescents believe that their parents and other adults—even their peers—could never feel what they are feeling or know the depth of their passions. "You just don't understand me!" claims the adolescent. But, at least often enough, we do.

Sex Differences in Cognitive Abilities

Although females and males do not differ noticeably in overall intelligence, beginning in childhood sex differences appear in certain cognitive abilities (Johnson & Bouchard, 2007). ***Question: What are the sex differences in cognitive abilities?***

imaginary audience The belief that others around us are as concerned with our thoughts and behaviors as we are; one aspect of adolescent egocentrism.

personal fable The belief that our feelings and ideas are special and unique and that we are invulnerable; one aspect of adolescent egocentrism.

Females are somewhat superior to males in verbal ability. Males, on the other hand, seem somewhat superior in visual–spatial skills. The picture for mathematics ability is more complex, with females excelling in some areas and males excelling in others. Let's take a closer look at these sex differences.

Verbal Ability

Verbal abilities include a large number of language skills, such as reading, spelling, grammar, oral comprehension, and word fluency. As a group, females surpass males in verbal ability (Halpern, 2003, 2004). These differences show up early. Girls seem to acquire language faster than boys. They make more prelinguistic vocalizations, utter their first word sooner, and develop larger vocabularies. Boys in the United States are more likely than girls to be dyslexic (Halpern, 2003, 2004). They also are more likely to have other reading problems, such as reading below grade level.

Why do females excel in verbal abilities? For one thing, parents talk more to their infant daughters than to their infant sons (see Chapter 7). This encouragement of verbal interaction may be connected with girls' relative verbal precocity. Because of this early language advantage, girls may rely more on verbal skills to interact with people, thus furthering their abilities in this area (Halpern & LaMay, 2000). How do we account for sex differences in reading? Biological factors such as the organization of the brain may play a role, but do not discount cultural factors. One issue is whether a culture stamps reading as a gender-neutral, masculine, or feminine activity (Goldstein, 2005). Consider Nigeria and England. Reading is looked on as a masculine activity in these nations, and boys traditionally surpass girls in reading ability (and other academic skills). In the United States and Canada, however, reading tends to be stereotyped as feminine, and girls tend to excel in reading in these nations. People of all ages and all cultures tend to apply themselves more diligently to pursuits that they believe are "meant" for them, whether it is the life of the nomad, ballet, ice hockey, or reading.

Visual–Spatial Ability

Visual–spatial ability refers to the ability to visualize objects or shapes and to mentally manipulate and rotate them. As you can imagine, this ability is important in such fields as art, architecture, and engineering. Boys begin to outperform girls on many types of visual–spatial tasks starting at age 8 or 9, and the difference persists into adulthood (Ecuyer-Dab & Robert, 2004; Johnson & Bouchard, 2007; Parsons et al., 2004). The sex difference is particularly notable on mental rotation tasks (see ● Figure 15.2), which require imagining how objects will look if they are rotated in space (Delgado & Prieto, 2004).

What is the basis for the sex difference in visual–spatial skills? A number of biological and environmental explanations have been offered. One biological theory that has received some attention is that visual–spatial ability is influenced by sex-linked recessive genes on the X sex chromosome. But this theory has not been supported by research (Halpern & LaMay, 2000).

Some researchers link visual–spatial performance to evolutionary theory and sex hormones. For example, male humans, as with many other male mammals, have a larger "home range." It may be related to a genetic tendency to create and defend a territory; and the size of the home range is connected with spatial ability (Ecuyer-Dab & Robert, 2004). Also, high levels of prenatal androgens have been linked to better performance on visual–spatial and arithmetic tasks among 4- and 6-year-old girls (Finegan et al., 1992; Jacklin et al., 1988). One study (Kimura & Hampson, 1992) found that women performed better on visual–spatial tasks when their estrogen levels were low than when their estrogen levels were high. (By contrast, they were better at tasks involving verbal skills when estrogen levels were high.)

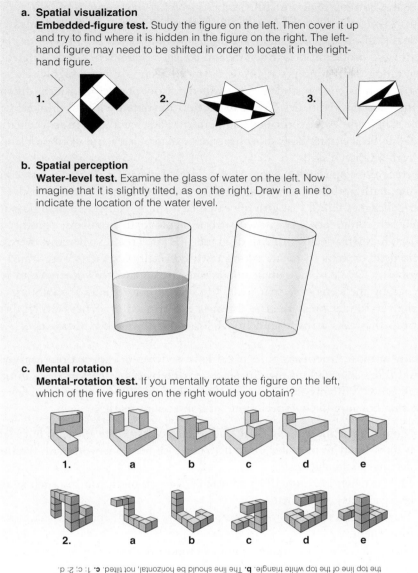

a. Spatial visualization
Embedded-figure test. Study the figure on the left. Then cover it up and try to find where it is hidden in the figure on the right. The left-hand figure may need to be shifted in order to locate it in the right-hand figure.

b. Spatial perception
Water-level test. Examine the glass of water on the left. Now imagine that it is slightly tilted, as on the right. Draw in a line to indicate the location of the water level.

c. Mental rotation
Mental-rotation test. If you mentally rotate the figure on the left, which of the five figures on the right would you obtain?

Answers: a. 1: Orient the pattern as if it were a tilted capital M, with the left portion along the top of the white triangle. 2: This pattern fits along the right sides of the two black triangles on the left. 3: Rotate this figure about 100° to the right, so that it forms a Z, with the top line coinciding with the top line of the top white triangle. **b.** The line should be horizontal, not tilted. **c.** 1: c; 2: d.

● **Figure 15.2**
Examples of Tests Used to Measure Visual–Spatial Ability

No sex differences are found on the spatial visualization tasks in part (a). Boys do somewhat better than girls on the tasks measuring spatial perception in part (b). The sex difference is greatest on the mental rotation tasks in part (c). What are some possible reasons for these differences?

See your student companion website for an interactive version of Figure 15.2.

One environmental theory is that gender stereotypes influence the spatial experiences of children. Gender-stereotyped "boys' toys," such as blocks, Legos, and Erector sets, provide more practice with spatial skills than gender-stereotyped "girls' toys." Boys are also more likely to engage in sports, which involve moving balls and other objects through space. Boys are allowed to travel farther from home than girls are, providing greater opportunities for exploration and a greater "home range" (Halpern, 2004). It is no secret that participation in spatially related activities is associated with better performance on visual–spatial tasks.

Mathematical Ability

Male adolescents generally outperform females in mathematics (Collaer & Hill, 2006; Halpern, 2004), and research suggests that visual–spatial skills—which are frequently superior among males—are connected with performance in the areas of geometry and word problems (Delgado & Prieto, 2004). Until recently, reviewers of the research on sex differences in math concluded that sex differences appear in adolescence, but in a review of 100 studies involving more than 3 million individuals, Janet Hyde and her colleagues (1990) found a slight superiority for girls in computational skills in the elementary and middle-school years. Boys began to perform better in word problems in high school and college. There were no sex differences in understanding math concepts at any age. Among groups of more highly selected individuals, such as college students or mathematically precocious youth, differences were larger and favored males. **Truth or Fiction Revisited:** Critical thinkers will see that the statement "Adolescent boys outperform adolescent girls in mathematics" is too broad to be accurate. Boys show superiority in geometry and word problems, but not in computational skills.

There is also some evidence that adolescent males may fare better at tasks, such as confusing math problems, that challenge their ability to cope. Carol Dweck (2007) and her colleagues found that girls appeared to be more vulnerable than boys to losing their self-confidence when faced with difficult math problems. Another study found that mathematically gifted sixth-grade girls fared poorly when they were overly perfectionistic or anxious about taking tests, especially tests that were timed (Tsui & Maziocco, 2007). Many female adolescents are apparently vulnerable to feeling threatened by the stereotype that males are better than females at math, especially when they are under pressure. The threat is experienced as anxiety which distracts them from the tasks at hand and impairs their performance (Muzzatti & Agnoli, 2007).

Many or most Americans quite unfairly have different expectations for boys and girls, and these expectations may increase sex differences in performance in mathematics (Ceci & Williams, 2007; Eccles, 2007; Halpern, 2006). Let us list a few of the reasons that boys are likely to feel more "at home" with math:

- Mom may be more likely than Dad to help Missy write an essay, but Dad is more likely to be called on to help her with her homework with fractions, decimals, and algebra.
- Male teachers are more likely to teach advanced math courses, such as algebra, geometry, and calculus.
- Teachers tend to spend more time with boys in math and to expect more from them.
- Girls receive less encouragement and support than boys from parents and peers for studying math.
- Parents are more likely to buy math and science books for boys than girls.

Given such experiences with math, we should not be surprised that:

- By junior high school, boys see themselves as being better in math than girls, even when their skills are identical.
- By junior high school, students perceive math as being part of the male domain.
- By junior high school, boys are more likely to perceive math as playing a useful role in their lives.
- Girls are more likely than boys to experience math anxiety.
- High school and college women take fewer math courses than males do and are less likely to pursue careers in math or related fields, even when they excel in them.

What, then, shall we conclude about sex differences in cognitive abilities? First, it appears that girls show greater verbal ability than boys do but that boys show greater visual–spatial and math skills (Bailey, 2003; Halpern 2004). However, sex differences in cognitive skills are group differences, not individual differences. That is, the difference in, say, reading skills between a male who reads well and a male who is dyslexic

■ **Table 15.1** Women as a Percentage of College Students Receiving Bachelor's Degrees in the Sciences

Field	1971	2002
Biology	29%	61%
Chemistry	18	48
Computer Science	14	28
Engineering	1	19
Geology	11	45
Mathematics	38	47
Physics	7	23

Source: Cox & Alm (2005, February 25).

is greater than the average group sex difference in reading ability. Moreover, despite group differences, millions of females exceed the average American male in math and visual–spatial skills. Similarly, despite group differences, millions of males exceed the average American female in writing, spelling, and articulation. Hundreds of thousands of American women perform well in domains that had once been considered masculine, such as medicine and law.

While scholars sit around and debate sex differences in intellectual functioning, women are voting on the issue by flooding many fields once populated almost exclusively by men (Eccles, 2007; Halpern, 2006, 2007). ■ Table 15.1 and ● Figure 15.3 show that women are tossing these stereotypes out the window by entering the sciences and professional fields ranging from business to law to medicine in increasing numbers.

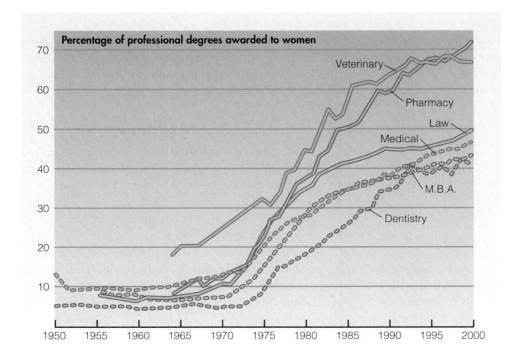

● **Figure 15.3**
Women Flood Professions Once Populated Almost Exclusively by Men

Active Review

1. The stage of _____ operations is the final stage in Piaget's scheme.
2. Adolescent _____ is connected with the concepts of the imaginary audience and the personal fable.
3. Females are somewhat (Superior or Inferior?) to males in verbal ability.
4. Males are somewhat (Superior or Inferior?) to females in visual–spatial ability.
5. Research links _____ hormones to visual–spatial performance.

Reflect & Relate: Did you have a strong need for privacy when you were an adolescent? If so, do you recall why? Can you explain this need in cognitive-developmental terms?

Go to

http://www.psychology.thomson.com/rathus

for an interactive version of this review.

The Adolescent in Judgment: Moral Development

Moral development in adolescence is a complex issue, with cognitive and behavioral aspects. As noted in Chapter 12, children in early childhood tend to view right and wrong in terms of rewards and punishments. Lawrence Kohlberg referred to such judgments as *preconventional*. ***Question: What are Kohlberg's views on moral reasoning in adolescence?*** In middle childhood, *conventional* thought tends to emerge, and children usually begin to judge right and wrong in terms of social conventions, rules, and laws (see Table 12.1 on page 406). In adolescence, many—not all—individuals become capable of formal-operational thinking, which allows them to derive conclusions about what they should do in various situations by reasoning from ethical principles. And many of these individuals engage in *postconventional* moral reasoning. They *deduce* proper behavior just as they might deduce that a platypus is a mammal because platypuses feed their young with breast milk (see page 520).

postconventional level According to Kohlberg, a period during which moral judgments are derived from moral principles and people look to themselves to set moral standards.

The Postconventional Level

In the **postconventional level**, moral reasoning is based on the person's own moral standards. Consider the case of Heinz (● Figure 15.4). Moral judgments are derived from personal values, not from conventional standards or authority figures. In the contractual, legalistic orientation of Stage 5, it is recognized that laws stem from agreed-on procedures and that many rights have great value and should not be violated (see ■ Table 15.2). But under exceptional circumstances, such as in the case of Heinz, laws cannot bind the individual. A Stage 5 reason for stealing the drug might be that it is the right thing to do, even though it is illegal. Conversely, it

● Figure 15.4   The Case of Heinz

In Europe a woman was near death from a special kind of cancer. There was one drug that the doctors thought might save her. It was a form of radium that a druggist in the same town had recently discovered. The drug was expensive to make, but the druggist was charging 10 times what the drug cost him to make. He paid $200 for the radium and charged $2,000 for a small dose of the drug. The sick woman's husband, Heinz, went to everyone he knew to borrow the money, but he could only get together about $1,000 which was half of what it cost. He told the druggist that his wife was dying and asked him to sell it cheaper or let him pay later. But the druggist said: "No, I discovered the drug and I'm going to make money from it." So Heinz got desperate and broke into the man's store to steal the drug for his wife. *Kohlberg (1969).*

■ **Table 15.2** Kohlberg's Postconventional Level of Moral Development

Stage	Examples of Moral Reasoning That Support Heinz's Stealing the Drug	Examples of Moral Reasoning That Oppose Heinz's Stealing the Drug
Stage 5: *Contractual, legalistic orientation:* One must weigh pressing human needs against society's need to maintain social order.	This thing is complicated because society has a right to maintain law and order, but Heinz has to take the drug to save his wife.	I can see why Heinz feels he has to take the drug, but laws exist for the benefit of society as a whole and cannot simply be cast aside.
Stage 6: *Universal ethical principles orientation:* People must follow universal ethical principles and their own conscience, even if it means breaking the law.	In this case, the law comes into conflict with the principle of the sanctity of human life. Heinz must take the drug because his wife's life is more important than the law.	If Heinz truly believes that stealing the drug is worse than letting his wife die, he should not take it. People have to make sacrifices to do what they think is right.

could be argued that if everyone in need broke the law, the legal system and the social contract would be destroyed.

Stage 6 thinking relies on supposed universal ethical principles, such as those of human life, individual dignity, justice, and **reciprocity**. Behavior that is consistent with these principles is considered right. If a law is seen as unjust or contradicts the right of the individual, it is wrong to obey it.

In the case of Heinz, it could be argued from the perspective of Stage 6 that the principle of preserving life takes precedence over laws prohibiting stealing. Therefore, it is morally necessary for Heinz to steal the drug, even if he must go to jail. Note that it could also be asserted, from the principled orientation, that if Heinz finds the social contract or the law to be the highest principle, he must remain within the law, despite the consequences.

Stage 5 and 6 moral judgments were virtually absent among the 7- and 10-year-olds in Kohlberg's (1963) sample of American children. They increased in frequency during the early and middle teens. By age 16, Stage 5 reasoning was shown by about 20% of adolescents and Stage 6 reasoning was demonstrated by about 5% of adolescents. However, Stage 3 and 4 judgments were made more frequently at all ages—7 through 16—studied by Kohlberg and other investigators (Colby et al., 1983; Commons et al., 2006; Rest, 1983) (see ● Figure 15.5). **Truth or Fiction Revisited:** It is not true that most adolescents make moral decisions based on their own ethical principles. Postconventional moral reasoning appears in adolescence *if it appears at all, but most adolescents reason at lower levels.*

Moral Behavior and Moral Reasoning: Is There a Relationship?

Is there a relationship between moral cognitive development and moral behavior? Are individuals whose moral judgments are more mature more likely to engage in moral behavior? The answer seems to be yes; many studies have found positive relationships between a person's level of moral development and his or her behavior (Cheung et al., 2001; Emler et al., 2007; Greenberg, 2002).

Individuals whose moral reasoning is at Stage 2 cheat, steal, and engage in other problem behaviors more often than peers whose moral reasoning is at higher stages (Greenberg, 2002; Richards et al., 1992). Adolescents with higher levels of moral reasoning are more likely to exhibit moral behavior, including altruistic behavior (D. Hart et al., 2003; Maclean et al., 2004).

© Bettmann/CORBIS

Postconventional Thought
Rosa Parks smiles in this photo taken on December 21, 1956, after the U.S. Supreme Court banned segregation on city public transit. On December 1 of the previous year, Ms. Parks energized the civil rights movement with a simple act of unlawful protest: She refused to surrender her seat on a public bus to a European American man. In her own words, "I did not get on the bus to get arrested. I got on the bus to go home." Nevertheless, Parks's own postconventional thinking—her own sense of what was right and wrong—took precedence over the law at the time.

reciprocity The principle that actions have mutual effects and that people depend on one another to treat each other morally.

● **Figure 15.5** Age and Type of Moral Judgment

The incidence of preconventional reasoning declines from greater than 90% of moral statements at age 7 to less than 20% of moral statements at age 16. Conventional moral statements increase with age between the ages of 7 and 13 but then level off to account for 50% to 60% of moral statements at ages 13 and 16. Postconventional moral statements are all but absent at ages 7 and 10 but account for about 20% to 25% of moral statements at ages 13 and 16.

Source: Kohlberg (1963).

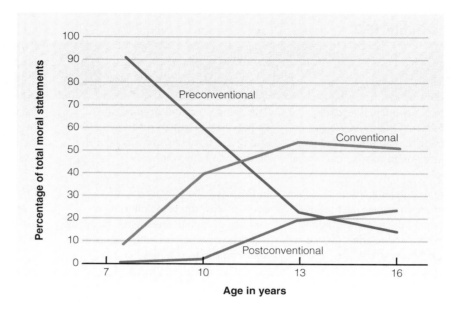

Experiments also have been conducted in the hope of advancing moral reasoning as a way of decreasing immoral behavior (Palmer, 2005). A number of studies have found that group discussion of moral dilemmas elevates delinquents' level of moral reasoning (Smetana, 1990). Is moral behavior affected as well? In one study, discussions of moral dilemmas improved moral reasoning and reduced incidents of, for example, school tardiness, behavior referrals, and police and court contacts among adolescents with behavioral problems (Arbuthnot & Gordon, 1988).

Evaluation of Kohlberg's Theory

Despite a number of challenges, evidence appears to continue to support Kohlberg's view that the moral judgments of children develop in an upward sequence (Boom et al., 2007), even though most children do not reach postconventional thought. Postconventional thought, when it is found, first occurs during adolescence.

Why doesn't postconventional moral reasoning appear until age 13 or so? A number of studies suggest that formal-operational thinking is a prerequisite and that education is likely to play a role (Boom et al., 2007; Patenaude et al., 2003). Postconventional reasoning appears to require the capacities to understand abstract moral principles and to empathize with the views and feelings of others. However, neither formal-operational thought nor education guarantees the development of postconventional moral judgments.

Kohlberg believed that the stages of moral development follow the unfolding of innate sequences and are therefore universal. But he may have underestimated the influence of social, cultural, and educational institutions (Dawson, 2002; Nucci, 2002). Parents are also important. Inductive disciplinary methods, including discussions of the feelings of others, advance moral reasoning (Dawson, 2002; Eisenberg & Valiente, 2002; Palmer & Hollin, 2001).

Postconventional thinking is all but absent in developing societies and is infrequent in the United States (Commons et al., 2006; Snarey, 1994). Perhaps postconventional reasoning reflects Kohlberg's personal ideals and not a natural, universal stage of development (Helwig, 2006). Stage 6 reasoning is based on the acceptance of supposedly universal ethical principles. The principles of freedom, justice, equality, tolerance, integrity, and reverence for

Parents Influence Children's Moral Development
Parents help advance their children's moral development when they discuss moral dilemmas with them. Most adolescents respect their parents' views.

Developing in a World of Diversity

Cross-Cultural and Sex Differences in Moral Development

Cultural background is a powerful shaper of moral reasoning. Kohlberg found postconventional thinking among a minority of American adolescents, and it was all but absent among adolescents in villages in Mexico, Taiwan, Turkey (Kohlberg, 1969), and the Bahamas (White et al., 1978). Reviews of the literature conclude that postconventional reasoning is more likely to be found in urban cultural groups and in middle-class populations but that it is rarely seen in traditional folk cultures (Boom et al., 2007; Dawson, 2002; Snarey, 1994).

Another cross-cultural study indicates that the moral reasoning of children from Western industrialized countries such as Germany, Poland, and Italy is similar to that of American children from urban areas (Boehnke et al., 1989). On the other hand, the moral reasoning of American children and Israeli city children is more self-oriented and less oriented to the needs of others than the reasoning of Israeli kibbutz children (Eisenberg et al., 1990). These differences are consistent with the differences in the children's social environments. The kibbutz is a collective farm community that emphasizes cooperative relationships and a communal philosophy.

A similar pattern has been found in comparisons of middle-class American and Hindu Indian children and adults. Hindu Indians are more likely to show a caring orientation in making moral judgments, whereas Americans more often demonstrate a justice orientation. These findings are consistent with the greater emphasis that Hindu Indian culture puts on the importance of taking responsibility for others (Miller, 1994; Miller & Bersoff, 1992).

Sex Differences in Moral Development: Justice versus Caring?

Some researchers claim that males reason at higher levels of moral development than females in terms of responses to Heinz's dilemma. For example, Kohlberg and Kramer (1969) reported that the average stage of moral development for men was Stage 4, which emphasizes justice, law, and order. The average stage for women was reported to be Stage 3, which emphasizes caring and concern for others.

Carol Gilligan (Gilligan, 1977, 1982; Gilligan & Attanucci, 1988) argues that this sex difference reflects patterns of socialization. Gilligan provides two examples of responses to Heinz's dilemma. Eleven-year-old Jake views the dilemma as a math problem. He sets up an equation showing that life has greater value than property. Heinz should thus steal the drug. Eleven-year-old Amy, on the other hand, notes that stealing the drug and letting Heinz's wife die would both be wrong. Amy searches for alternatives, such as getting a loan, stating that it would profit Heinz's wife little if he went to jail and was no longer around to help her.

Although Gilligan sees Amy's pattern of reasoning as being as sophisticated as Jake's, it would be rated as showing a lower level of moral development in Kohlberg's system. Gilligan asserts that Amy, like other girls, has been socialized into focusing on the needs of others and foregoing simplistic judgments of right and wrong. Jake, by contrast, has been socialized into making judgments based on logic. To him, clear-cut conclusions are to be derived from a set of premises. Amy was aware of the logical considerations that struck Jake, but she processed them as one source of information, not as the sole source. It is ironic that Amy's empathy, a trait that has "defined the 'goodness' of women," marks Amy "as deficient in moral development" (Gilligan, 1982, p. 18).

Kohlberg, Gilligan, and other researchers tend to agree that in making moral judgments, females are more likely to show a caring orientation, whereas males are more likely to assume a justice orientation (Jorgensen, 2006). But there remains a dispute as to whether this difference means that girls reason at a lower level than boys do (Jorgensen, 2006; Knox et al., 2004). Kohlberg, by the way, viewed Gilligan's ideas as an extension of his own views, not as a repudiation of them, and Gilligan largely supported Kohlberg's stage theory and his claim of its universality (Jorgensen, 2006).

Reflect:

- *Why would Kohlberg be interested in whether or not moral development in foreign countries follows the pattern he found in the United States?*
- *How would you describe Carol Gilligan's criticisms of Lawrence Kohlberg's theory of moral development? For example, does she consider the theory to be completely invalid? Explain.*

human life have high appeal for most American adolescents who are reared to idealize these principles.

As we look around the world—and at many of the horrors of the unfolding 21st century—we find that principles such as freedom and tolerance of differences are not universally admired. They may reflect Western cultural influences more than the cognitive development of the child. In many cultures, to be honest about it, violation of the dominant religious tradition is a capital offense and freedom to worship—or the freedom not to worship—is unheard of. In his later years, Kohlberg (1985) dropped Stage 6 reasoning from his theory in recognition of these problems.

Finally, we must recognize that Kohlberg's view of moral reasoning and moral development is not the only one, and that as time goes on, it is possible that Kohlberg's views may be of little more than historic interest (Krebs & Denton, 2006; Lapsley, 2006). But as is the case with Jean Piaget, we are not there yet.

Active Review

6. In Kohlberg's _____ level, moral reasoning is based on the person's own moral standards.
7. Many studies have found (Positive or Negative?) relationships between the child's level of moral development and moral behavior.

Reflect & Relate: What is your stage of moral development, according to Kohlberg? How do you know? How do you feel about it?

Go to

http://www.psychology.thomson.com/rathus
for an interactive version of this review.

The Adolescent in School

How can we emphasize the importance of the school to the development of the adolescent? Adolescents are highly influenced by the opinions of their peers and their teachers. Their self-esteem rises or falls consistently with the pillars of their skills. *Question: How do adolescents make the transition from elementary school to middle, junior high, or high school?*

Making the Transition from Elementary School

Students make at least one and sometimes two transitions to a new school before they complete high school. Think back to your own school days. Did you spend the years from kindergarten to eighth grade in one building and then move on to high school? Did you instead attend elementary school through sixth grade and then go to junior high for grades 7–9 before starting high school? Or did you complete grades kindergarten through grades 4 or 5 in one school, then attend a middle school for grades 5 or 6 to 8, and then move on to high school for grades 9–12? (This last scenario has become the most common pattern in recent years.)

The transition to middle, junior high, or high school generally involves a shift from a smaller neighborhood elementary school with self-contained classrooms to a larger, more impersonal setting with many more students and with different teachers for different classes. These changes may not fit very well with the developmental needs of early adolescents. For example, adolescents express a desire for increased autonomy, yet teachers in junior high typically allow less student input and exert more behavioral control than teachers in elementary school (Tobbell, 2003). Moreover, in the shift to the new school, students move from being the "top dog" (i.e., the oldest and most experienced students) to being the "bottom dog." These changes are not the only ones facing the early adolescent. Many youngsters also are going through the early stages of pubertal development at about the same time they move to a new school.

How well do students adjust to the transition to a new school? Much of the research has examined children's experiences as they move from elementary school to junior high school. The transition to the new school setting often is accompanied by a decline in grades and in participation in school activities. Students may also experience a drop in self-esteem and an increase in psychological distress (Rudolph & Flynn, 2007; Tobbell, 2003). A German study found a connection between the adolescent's psychological adjustment and his or her grades by the end of the first year in high school (Ball et al., 2006).

Truth or Fiction Revisited: The transition from elementary school appears to be more difficult for girls than for boys. In one study, girls who switched to a junior high for seventh grade showed a decrease in self-esteem, whereas girls who stayed in their kindergarten through eighth-grade school did not. Boys' self-esteem did not change when they switched to junior high (Simmons & Blyth, 1987). The difference may reflect that fact that girls are more likely to be undergoing puberty at about this time. Girls at this age are also likely to earn the attention of boys in higher grades, whereas younger boys are not likely to be of much interest to older girls. Girls experience major life changes, and children who experience several life changes at once find it more difficult to adjust to a new school (Tobbell, 2003).

But transition need not be that stressful. Students who are in greater control of their lives tend to do better with the transition (Rudolph et al., 2001). Elementary and middle schools can help ease the transition to high school. For example, one longitudinal study followed the progress of students who received a 2-year social decision-making and problem-solving program in elementary school. When followed in high school 4 to 6 years later, these students showed higher levels of prosocial behavior and fewer conduct problems than students who had not been in the program (Elias et al., 1991). Some middle schools create a more intimate, caring atmosphere by, for instance, establishing smaller schools within the school building. Others have "bridge programs" during the summer between middle school and high school. The programs introduce students to the new school culture and strengthen their academic skills.

Dropping Out of School

School is a key path to success in our society, but not all adolescents complete high school. *Questions: What are the consequences of dropping out of school? Why do adolescents drop out?*

The Transition from Elementary School
The transition to junior high or high school is not always easy. The transition coincides with the biological forces of puberty and concerns about how one will turn out—physically, that is. It is not surprising that some children experience a decline in grades and self-esteem.

Are These Adolescents on the Path to Dropping out of School?
The consequences of dropping out of school can be harsh. High school dropouts earn less and are more likely to be unemployed than students who stay in school. Programs have been developed to prevent dropping out, but potential dropouts must first be identified.

Completing high school is one of the most critical developmental tasks facing adolescents. The consequences of dropping out can be grim indeed. High school dropouts are more likely to be unemployed (Wald & Losen, 2007). They make lower salaries. Research suggests that each year of education, from grade school through graduate school, adds about 16% to an individual's lifetime earnings (Passell, 1992). (This finding is a good incentive for you not only to complete college but also to consider graduate work!) Dropouts are also more likely to show problem behaviors, including delinquency, criminal behavior, and substance abuse (Donovan & Wells, 2007; Wald & Losen, 2007). However, it is sometimes difficult to disentangle the consequences of dropping out from its causes. A pattern of delinquent behavior, for example, might precede as well as follow dropping out.

Who Drops Out?

It is difficult to estimate the magnitude of the school dropout problem, because states use different reporting systems and most do not track those who quit after eighth grade. Overall, about 15% of males, age 18 to 24, and 12% of females in the same age group have dropped out of high school (National Center for Education Statistics, 2007). However, dropout rates vary considerably from ethnic group to ethnic group. ■ Table 15.3 shows dropout rates for various racial and ethnic groups for tenth-

■ **Table 15.3**   Dropout Rates and Distribution of 15- through 24-Year-Olds Who Dropped Out of Grades 10–12, According to Various Background Characteristics

Characteristic	Dropout Rate (percent)	Number of Dropouts (thousands)	Population Enrolled (thousands)	Percent of all Dropouts
Total	3.8	414	10,870	100.0
Sex				
Male	4.2	233	5,515	56.3
Female	3.4	181	5,355	43.7
Race/ethnicity				
European American	2.8	196	6,897	47.3
African American	7.3	112	1,538	27.2
Latino and Latina American	5.0	86	1,717	20.8
Asian/Pacific Islander	1.6	6	411	1.5
More than one race	4.9	12	241	2.9
Family income				
Low income	8.9	137	1,544	33.1
Middle income	3.8	228	5,990	55.2
High income	1.5	49	3,326	11.7
Age				
15–16	2.1	72	3,347	17.4
17	2.4	93	3,797	22.5
18	3.9	105	2,693	25.3
19	9.1	64	702	15.4
20–24	24.4	81	331	19.5

Source: National Center for Education Statistics (2007, June; table 1).

through twelfth-graders as reported by the National Center for Education Statistics (2007). The reported dropout rate was highest for African Americans, at 7.3%. That rate was followed by Latino and Latina Americans at 5%. European Americans dropped out at a reported rate of 2.8%. Students from lower-income backgrounds and older students were more likely to drop out. The higher dropout rates for children from African American and Latino and Latina American minority groups are linked to the lower socioeconomic status of their families. Children from lower-income households have higher dropout rates (Suh et al., 2007). When income levels are held constant, racial and ethnic differences in school dropout rates are reduced (National Center for Education Statistics, 2007).

Excessive school absence and reading below grade level are two of the earliest and strongest predictors of school dropout (Lever et al., 2004). Other risk factors include low grades, poor problem-solving ability, low self-esteem, problems with teachers,

A CLOSER LOOK

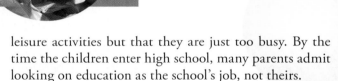

Beyond the Classroom: How Parents Can Help Teenagers Improve Their Academic Performance

Some adolescents profit more from education than others. Why do some adolescents perform better than others in the classroom? Certainly intelligence plays a role. So does the adequacy of the school and the teachers. Surveys of high school students suggest that the behavior and attitudes of parents and teenagers play key roles as well (Bacete & Remirez, 2001; Steinberg, 1996). One study, by psychologist Laurence Steinberg and his colleagues, cut across the ethnic spectrum. It included 20,000 African American, Asian American, Latino and Latina American, and European American students from California and Wisconsin; the investigation is recounted in Steinberg's 1996 book, *Beyond the Classroom.*

One problem that is connected with poor school performance is that many parents, according to Steinberg, are "disconnected" from their children's lives. Note some of his findings:

- Half the students said it would not upset their parents if they brought home grades of C or worse.
- Forty percent of students said that their parents never attended school functions.
- One-third of the students said that their parents did not even know how they were doing in school.
- One-third of the students said that they primarily spent the day "goofing off" with their friends.
- Only one-third of the students said that they had daily conversations with their parents.

Steinberg and his co-researchers, Bradford Brown and Sanford Dornbusch, also looked at the situation from the parents' point of view. Many parents said that they would like to be involved in their children's school and leisure activities but that they are just too busy. By the time the children enter high school, many parents admit looking on education as the school's job, not theirs.

So what can parents do to help their teenagers improve their academic performance? It turns out to be pretty simple. Steinberg makes some recommendations. First and foremost, parents need to be more involved with their teenagers. For example, parents can

- Communicate regularly with their teenagers about school and personal matters
- Use consistent discipline (as opposed to being dictatorial or too permissive)
- Regularly attend school functions
- Consult with their children's teachers and follow through on their suggestions

Parents may also have to contend with their teenagers' peers. Although some teenagers encourage others to do well in school, Steinberg (1996) found that many peers have a harmful effect on grades. For example, nearly one in five said that he or she did not do as well as possible for fear of earning the disapproval of peers! Parents may effectively deal with fear of peer disapproval by encouraging their children to focus on their long-term goals, such as a career or college, and reminding them that their current group of peers may not be playing much of a role in their future lives.

Reflect: Why may helping their adolescents in school set many parents on a collision course with their children's friends?

dissatisfaction with school, substance abuse, being old for one's grade level, and being male (Christenson & Thurlow, 2004; South et al., 2007). Adolescents who adopt adult roles early, especially marrying at a young age or becoming a parent, are also more likely to drop out (Bohon et al., 2007). Students from low-income households, large urban areas, and the West and South are at greater risk (National Center for Education Statistics, 2007). But not all dropouts come from low-income families. Middle-class youth who feel bored with school, alienated, or strongly pressured to succeed also are at risk (Battin-Pearson et al., 2000; Lee & Burkam, 2003).

Preventing Dropping Out

Many programs have been developed to prevent school dropout. Successful programs have some common characteristics (Bost & Riccomini, 2006; Lever et al., 2004; Reschly & Christenson, 2006):

- Early preschool interventions (such as Head Start)
- Identification and monitoring of high-risk students throughout the school years
- Small class size, individualized instruction, and counseling
- Vocational components that link learning and community work experiences
- Involvement of families or community organizations
- Positive school climate
- Clear and reasonable educational goals (if you don't know where you're going, how you get there isn't very important), student accountability for behavior, and motivational systems that involve penalties and rewards

Most intervention efforts are usually not introduced until students are on the verge of dropping out—when it is usually too late.

Active Review

8. Teachers in junior high typically exert (More or Less?) behavioral control than teachers in elementary school.

9. Students undergoing the transition from elementary school are more likely to experience a (Rise or Drop?) in self-esteem.

10. (Boys or Girls?) appear to be more negatively affected by the junior high transition.

11. High school dropouts are (More or Less?) likely to be unemployed as adults.

12. (Boys or Girls?) are more likely to drop out of high school.

Reflect & Relate: Do you know people who dropped out of high school? Why did they drop out? What were the consequences of dropping out?

Go to

http://www.psychology.thomson.com/rathus
for an interactive version of this review.

The Adolescent at Work: Career Development and Work Experience

Deciding what job or career we will pursue after completion of school is one of the most important choices we make. *Question: How do adolescents make career choices?*

Career Development

When I was a child, I wanted to be an astronaut or an explorer. I became a psychologist and author. My daughter Allyn wanted to be a rock star. Now she is a college graduate in musical theater and has not given up on the possibility of becoming a rock star.

My course of career development is more typical than Allyn's, or at least it is so far. Children's career aspirations may not be practical at first. They become increasingly realistic—and often more conventional—as children mature and gain experience. In adolescence, ideas about the kind of work one wants to do tend to become more firmly established, or crystallized, but a particular occupation may not be chosen until the college years or afterward (Rottinghaus et al., 2003; Sullivan & Hansen, 2004).

A Social-Cognitive Perspective

From a social-cognitive perspective, many factors influence an adolescent's choice of a career (Hartman & Betz, 2007; Lent et al., 2007; Navarro et al., 2007), including his or her

- Competencies: his or her knowledge or skills
- "Encoding strategies": his or her way of viewing a career, or himself or herself in relation to a career
- Expectancies: his or her expectations as to what will happen in a given career, including **self-efficacy expectations**—that is, his or her beliefs that he or she will be able to handle the tasks in a given career

Sometimes we plan our careers, based on our perceived abilities and personality traits (Rottinghaus et al., 2003; Skorikov, 2007). Sometimes our early work experiences help point us in certain directions (Creed et al., 2007).

Holland's Career Typology

Psychologists have devised approaches to matching personality traits with careers to predict adjustment in a given career. John Holland's (1997) RIASEC method, as used in his Vocational Preference Inventory, matches six personality types to various kinds of careers: realistic, investigative, artistic, social, enterprising, and conventional (see ● Figure 15.6 on page 539). Within each "type" of career, some are more sophisticated than others and require more education and training.

- Realistic people, according to Holland, are concrete in thinking. They are mechanically oriented. They tend to be best adjusted in occupations that involve motor activity. Examples of such occupations include unskilled labor, such as attending gas stations; farming; and the skilled trades, such as auto repairs, electrical work, plumbing, or construction work.
- Investigative people are abstract in their thinking. They are creative and tend to be introverted but open to new experience. They tend to do well in college and university teaching and in research positions.
- Artistic people also tend to be creative and open to new experience. As a group, they are emotional, interested in the emotional life, and intuitive. They tend to be happiest in the visual and the performing arts.
- Socially oriented people tend to be outgoing (extraverted) and concerned for social welfare. They often are agreeable and have a need for affiliation. They gravitate toward occupations in teaching (kindergarten through high school), counseling, and social work.
- Enterprising people tend to be adventurous. They tend to be outgoing and dominant. They gravitate toward industrial roles that involve leadership and planning. They climb the ladder in government and social organizations.

self-efficacy expectations
One's beliefs that he or she can handle the requirements of a situation.

- Conventional people thrive on routine. They are not particularly imaginative. They have needs for order, self-control, and social approval. They gravitate toward occupations in banking, accounting, clerical work, and the military.

Many people combine several of these vocational types (Darcy & Tracey, 2007; Nauta, 2007). A copywriter in an advertising agency might be both artistic and enterprising. Clinical and counseling psychologists tend to be investigative, artistic, and socially oriented. Military people and beauticians tend to be realistic and conventional. But military leaders who plan major operations and form governments are also enterprising; and individuals who create new hair styles and fashions are also artistic. Holland's Vocational Preference Inventory assesses these personality types, as do various vocational tests that are used in high schools and colleges.

All in all, more than 20,000 occupations are found in *The Dictionary of Occupational Titles*, which is compiled by the U.S. Department of Labor. But most young people choose from a relatively small range of occupations on the basis of their personalities, experiences, and opportunities (Arbona, 2005; Laplan, 2004). Many fall into jobs that are offered to them or follow career paths that are blazed by parents or role models in the community (Laplan, 2004; Nauta, 2007).

Adolescents in the Workforce

Kimberly, age 16, has a job at a fast-food restaurant located in the suburb of a midwestern city. She has already saved $1,000 toward a car and a stereo by working at the restaurant after school and on weekends. Kimberly is worried because her state legislature is considering regulations that would cut back the number of hours she is allowed to work.

Developing in a World of Diversity

Ethnic Identity and Gender in Career Self-Efficacy Expectancies

Our ethnic identity can play a key role in our ideas as to what is available to us. One study explored the effects of ethnic identity and attitudes toward roles on the early career decision-making in a sample of ninth-grade African American and Latina adolescents (Gushue & Whitson, 2006). It was found that girls with stronger ethnic identities and nontraditional attitudes toward gender roles also had higher self-efficacy expectancies or self-confidence that she would be able to handle the tasks involved in career decision making, such as accurately assessing her skills and abilities, gathering information

about careers, selecting career and educational goals, and making appropriate plans to meet those goals.

A second study confirmed the importance of a strong ethnic identity to feelings of self-efficacy in career decision making among female African American adolescents (Rollins & Valdez, 2006). This study also found that African American girls had higher career self-efficacy than African American boys, perhaps because they were relatively less likely to find themselves victimized by discrimination.

Research by Albert Bandura and his colleagues (2001) suggested that

adolescent girls who have more confidence in their ability to function in the business world—that is, higher self-efficacy expectations—are more likely to select nontraditional careers. Intellectually gifted girls are more likely than their less gifted peers to break out of the shackles of traditional career expectations (Mendez, 2000).

Reflect: *Why do you think ethnic identity might be related to career self-efficacy expectations among African American adolescent girls?*

C

These people have clerical or numerical skills. They like to work with data, to carry out other people's directions, or to carry things out in detail.

R

These people have mechanical or athletic abilities. They like to work with machines and tools, to be outdoors, or to work with animals or plants.

I

These people like to learn new things. They enjoy investigating and solving problems and advancing knowledge.

E

These people like to work with people. They like to lead and influence others for economic or organizational gains.

S

This group enjoys working with people. They like to help others, including the sick. They enjoy informing and enlightening people.

A

This group is highly imaginative and creative. They enjoy working in unstructured situations. They are artistic and innovative.

● **Figure 15.6**   Assessing an Adolescent's Career Type by Attending a "Job Fair"

Adolescents can be given insight into where they might fit in the career world by picturing themselves at a job fair such as the one pictured here. Students and employers have a chat. As time passes, they discover mutual interests and begin to collect in groups accordingly. Adolescents can consider the types of people in the six groups by reading the descriptions for each. Then they can ask themselves, "Which group would I most like to join?" What does their answer suggest about the career choices that might be of greatest interest to them?

Life experiences help shape vocational development. One life experience that is common among American teenagers is holding a job. ***Questions: How many American adolescents hold jobs? What are the pros and cons of adolescents working?***

Prevalence of Adolescent Employment

Chances are that you did hold a job. About half of all high school sophomores, two-thirds of juniors, and almost three-fourths of seniors have a job during the school year (Bachman et al., 2003). Girls and boys are equally likely to be employed, but boys work more hours (Staff et al., 2004).

Millions of adolescents between the ages of 14 to 18 are legally employed. But perhaps another 2 to 3 million are working illegally (Bachman et al., 2003; Holloway,

2004). Some of these teenagers are paid in cash so that their employers can avoid paying taxes or minimum wages. Others work too many hours, work late hours on school nights, or work at hazardous jobs. Some are younger than 14 and are too young to be legally employed except on farms.

Adolescent employment rates show ethnic and social-class differences (Bachman et al., 2003). European American teenagers are twice as likely to be employed as teenagers from ethnic minority groups, for example. In past years, teenagers from poorer households were more likely to work to help support the family. Nowadays, adolescent employment is more common among middle-class youth. This change may be partly because middle-class families are more likely to live near locations, such as suburban shopping malls, that are fertile sources of jobs for teenagers. But employed lower-income adolescents work longer hours than working middle-class teens do (Bachman et al., 2003).

Pros and Cons of Adolescent Employment

The potential benefits of adolescent employment include developing a sense of responsibility, self-reliance, and discipline; learning to appreciate the value of money and education; acquiring positive work habits and values; and enhancing occupational aspirations (Porfeli, 2007). On the other hand, the meaning of work for adolescents—at least for middle-class adolescents—seems to have changed. Most adolescents who work do not do so to help support their families or to put money away for college. Although adolescents of lower socioeconomic status work mainly to supplement the family income (Leventhal et al., 2001), most middle-class adolescents use their income for personal purchases, such as clothing, iPods, CDs, DVDs, gear, and car payments (Bachman et al., 2003). The proportion of earnings devoted to family expenses or put away for college is small.

Then, too, most working adolescents are in jobs with low pay, high turnover, little authority, and little chance for advancement. They typically perform simple, repetitive tasks requiring no special skills (Staff et al., 2004). Some question the benefits of such jobs.

Truth or Fiction Revisited: Adolescents who work after school, as a group, do obtain lower grades. Therefore, teenage employment may be harmful. Students who work lengthy hours—more than 11 to 13 hours per week—report lower grades, higher rates of drug and alcohol use, more delinquent behavior, lower self-esteem, and higher levels of psychological problems than students who do not work or who work only a few hours (Brandstätter & Farthofer, 2003; Holloway, 2004; Quirk et al., 2001). Grades and time spent on homework drop for students who work long hours. Adolescents who work longer hours also spend less time in family activities, are monitored less by their parents, and are granted more freedom with day-to-day decisions (Oettinger, 1999; Singh, 1998; Singh & Ozturk, 2000).

Perhaps the most prudent course is for parents and educators to limit the number of hours adolescents work. Some are tightening their regulations on the number of hours teenagers can work during the school year.

Throughout this chapter, we have seen that the intellectual, moral, and vocational development of adolescents is influenced by parents and peers. Adolescents' relationships with family and friends, along with other aspects of their social and emotional development, are the topic of the final chapter.

© David Young-Wolff/PhotoEdit

Teenagers and Work

What are the pros and cons of part-time employment during high school?

Active Review

13. Children's career aspirations become increasingly _____ as they mature and gain experience.

14. Career choices of males and females are still to some degree influenced by traditional _____ -role stereotypes.

15. An adolescent's career self-_____ expectations are his or her beliefs that he or she will be able to handle the tasks in a given career.

16. The (Majority or Minority?) of high school students have a job during the school year.

Reflect: When you were in high school, did you have a job after school or on weekends? What were the effects of working on your grades, your social life, and your social maturation?

Go to

http://www.psychology.thomson.com/rathus
for an interactive version of this review.

RECITE: *An Active Summary*™

1. What is cognitive development during adolescence like, according to Piaget's stage of formal operations?

In Western societies, formal operational thought begins at about the time of puberty. The major achievements of the stage involve classification, logical thought (deductive reasoning), and the ability to hypothesize. Adolescents can project themselves into situations that transcend their experience and become wrapped up in fantasies.

2. How is adolescent egocentrism shown in the *imaginary audience* and in the *personal fable*?

The imaginary audience concept is the belief that others around us are concerned with our thoughts and behaviors, giving rise to the desire for privacy. The personal fable is the belief that our feelings and ideas are special and that we are invulnerable, which may underlie adolescent risk taking.

3. What are the sex differences in cognitive abilities?

Females tend to excel in verbal ability. Males tend to excel in visual–spatial ability and math. Boys are more likely than girls to have reading problems. Sex differences in visual–spatial skills have been linked to biological factors and to gender stereotypes.

4. What are Kohlberg's views on moral reasoning in adolescence?

In the postconventional level, according to Kohlberg, moral reasoning is based on the person's own moral standards.

5. How do adolescents make the transition from elementary school to middle, junior high, or high school?

The transition to middle, junior high, or high school generally involves a shift from a smaller neighborhood elementary school to a larger, more impersonal setting. The transition is often accompanied by a decline in grades and a drop in self-esteem.

6. What are the consequences of dropping out of school? Why do adolescents drop out?

High school dropouts are more likely to be unemployed and earn lower salaries. Dropouts are more likely to show delinquent behaviors. Truancy and reading below grade level predict school dropout.

7. How do adolescents make career choices?

Children's career aspirations are often not practical at first but become increasingly realistic as children mature and gain experience. Factors that influence choice of a career include abilities and personality traits.

8. How many American adolescents hold jobs? What are the pros and cons of adolescents working?

More than half of high school students hold part-time jobs during the school year. The benefits of adolescent employment include developing a sense of responsibility, self-reliance, and discipline, and learning to appreciate the value of money and education. But students who work also report lower grades and other problems.

Key Terms

formal operations, 519
utopian, 520
imaginary audience, 522

personal fable, 522
postconventional level, 528

reciprocity, 529
self-efficacy expectations, 537

Active Learning Resources

Childhood & Adolescence Book Companion Website
http://www.thomsonedu.com/psychology/rathus

Visit your book companion website where you will find more resources to help you study. There you will find interactive versions of your book features, including the Lessons in Observation video, Active Review sections, and the Truth or Fiction feature. In addition, the companion website contains quizzing, flash cards, and a pronunciation glossary.

 **is an easy-to-use online resource that helps you study in less time to get the grade you want—NOW.**

http://www.thomsonedu.com/login

Need help studying? This site is your one-stop study shop. Take a Pre-Test and ThomsonNOW will generate a Personalized Study Plan based on your test results. The Study Plan will identify the topics you need to review and direct you to online resources to help you master those topics. You can then take a Post-Test to determine the concepts you have mastered and what you still need to work on.

16 Adolescence:
Social and Emotional Development

Truth or Fiction?

T F Many adolescents imitate their peers' clothing, speech, hairstyles, and ideals. p. 547

T F American adolescent males are more concerned about occupational choices than American adolescent females are. p. 552

T F Adolescents are in a constant state of rebellion against their parents. p. 554

T F Most adolescents' friends are "bad influences." p. 558

T F Petting is practically universal among American adolescents. p. 562

T F About 800,000 American teenagers become pregnant each year. p. 565

T F Only a minority of American adolescents engage in delinquent behavior. p. 568

T F Suicide is the leading cause of death among American adolescents. p. 572

T F Adolescents reach adulthood at age 21. p. 576

Preview

Development of Identity and the Self-Concept: "Who Am I?" (and Who Else?)
Erikson's View of Identity Development
"Identity Statuses": Searching for the Self, Making a Commitment
Ethnicity and Development of Identity
Sex and Development of Identity
Development of the Self-Concept in Adolescence
Self-Esteem in Adolescence: Bottoming? Rising?

Relationships with Parents and Peers
Relationships with Parents
Relationships with Peers

Sexuality: When? What? (How?) Who? Where? and Why?—Not to Mention, "Should I?"
Masturbation
Sexual Orientation
Male–Female Sexual Behavior
Teenage Pregnancy

A Closer Look: What Parents Want from Sex Education Courses

Juvenile Delinquency
Ethnicity, Sex, and Juvenile Delinquency
Who Are the Delinquents? What Are They Like?
Prevention and Treatment of Juvenile Delinquency

Suicide: When the Adolescent Has Nothing—Except Everything—to Lose
Risk Factors for Suicide
Ethnicity, Sex, and Suicide

A Closer Look: Warning Signs of Suicide

Epilogue: Emerging Adulthood—Bridging Adolescence and the Life Beyond

Go to

http://www.thomsonedu.com/psychology/rathus
for an interactive version of this "Truth or Fiction" feature.

hat am I like as a person? Complicated! I'm sensitive, friendly and outgoing, though I can also be shy, self-conscious, and even obnoxious. I'd like to be friendly and tolerant all of the time. That's the kind of person I want to be, and I'm disappointed when I'm not. I'm responsible, even studious every now and then, but on the other hand I'm a goof-off too, because if you're too studious, you won't be popular. I'm a pretty cheerful person, especially with my friends, where I can even get rowdy. But I'm usually pretty stressed-out at home, or sarcastic, since my parents are always on my case. They expect me to get all A's. It's not fair! I worry about how I probably should get better grades. But I'd be mortified in the eyes of my friends. Sometimes I feel phony, especially around boys. Say I think some guy might be interested in asking me out. I try to act different, like Madonna. I'll be flirtatious and fun-loving. And then everybody else is looking at me like they think I'm totally weird! Then I get self-conscious and embarrassed and become radically introverted, and I don't know who I really am! But I don't really care what they think anyway. I just want to know what my close friends think. I can be my true self with my close friends. I can't be my real self with my parents. They don't understand me. They treat me like I'm still a kid. That gets confusing, though. I mean, which am I, a kid or an adult? It's scary, too, because I don't have any idea what I want to be when I grow up. I mean, I have lots of ideas. My friend Sheryl and I talk about whether we'll be teachers, or lawyers, veterinarians, maybe mothers. I know I don't want to be a waitress or a secretary. But how do you decide all of this? I mean, I think about it a lot, but I can't resolve it.

—Adapted from Harter (1990, pp. 352–353)

This self-description of a 15-year-old girl illustrates a key aspect of the adolescent years: the search for an answer to the question "Who am I?" She is struggling to reconcile contradictory traits and behaviors to determine the "real me." She is preoccupied not only with her present self but also with what she wants to become. What were your concerns at this age?

In this chapter, we explore social and emotional development in adolescence. We begin with the formation of identity and related changes in self-concept and self-esteem. We consider adolescents' relationships with their parents and their peers. We consider the emergence of sexual behaviors and attitudes and focus on the issue of teenage pregnancy. We address the problems of juvenile delinquency and suicide. Then, as we bring our present voyage to a close, we explore what some developmentalists consider a new stage in human development: emerging adulthood.

Development of Identity and the Self-Concept: "Who Am I?" (and Who Else?)

Adolescence is a key period in the lifelong process of defining just who we are—and who we are not. In this section, we examine Erikson's influential theory of identity development in adolescence. We then turn to Marcia's identity statuses. Next, we consider sex and cultural perspectives on identity development. Finally, we look at the development of self-concept and self-esteem during adolescence.

Erikson's View of Identity Development

Question: What does Erikson have to say about the development of identity during adolescence? Erik Erikson's fifth stage of psychosocial development is called identity versus identity diffusion. The primary task of this stage is for adolescents to develop **ego identity**: a sense of who they are and what they stand for. Individuals are faced with making choices about their future occupation, their ideological view of the world (including political and religious beliefs), and gender roles. The ability to engage in formal-operational thinking helps adolescents make these choices. Because thought is no longer tied to concrete experience, adolescents can weigh the options available to them, even though they may not have directly experienced them (Roeser et al., 2006; Schwartz, 2001).

An important aspect of identity development is what Erikson (1968) referred to as a **psychological moratorium**: a sort of time-out during which adolescents experiment with different roles, values, beliefs, and relationships. During the moratorium, adolescents undergo an **identity crisis** in which they examine their values and make decisions about their life roles. Should they attend college? What career should they pursue? Should they become sexually active? With whom? Adolescents in developed nations may feel overwhelmed by the options before them and by the need to make choices that will narrow their future alternatives (Crain, 2000).

On the other hand, as noted by Jennifer Pastor and her colleagues (2007), adolescent girls of color who live in the inner city are unlikely to have the choices available that Erikson was theorizing about. They may become sexually active due to local custom and peer pressure at early ages. College may be out of the question. Occupational choices may be severely limited. For indigent adolescent girls of color, the Eriksonian developmental sequence is a distant dream.

Truth or Fiction Revisited: In their search for identity, many—certainly not all—adolescents join "in" groups, slavishly imitating their peers' clothing, speech, hairstyles, ideals, and MP3 players. They may become intolerant of outsiders (Erikson, 1963). Those who successfully resolve their identity crisis develop a strong sense of who they are and what they stand for. Those who fail to resolve the crisis may continue to be intolerant of people who are different and continue to blindly follow people who adhere to convention.

"Identity Statuses": Searching for the Self, Making a Commitment

Building on Erikson's approach, James Marcia (1991) theorized four identity statuses. *Question: What are Marcia's "identity statuses"?* The statuses represent the four possible combinations of the dimensions of exploration and commitment that Erikson believed were critical to the development of identity (Schwartz, 2001) (see Concept Review 16.1). **Exploration** involves active questioning and searching among alternatives in the quest to establish goals, values, or beliefs. **Commitment** is a stable investment in one's goals, values, or beliefs.

Identity diffusion is the least developmentally advanced status. This category includes individuals who neither have commitments nor are trying to form them (Berzonsky, 2005; Berzonsky & Kuk, 2005). This stage is often characteristic of primary school and early high school children. Older adolescents who remain diffused may drift through life in a carefree, uninvolved way or they may be unhappy and lonely. Some diffused individuals are apathetic and adopt an "I don't care" attitude. Others are angry, alienated, and rebellious and may reject socially approved goals, values, and beliefs (Kroger, 2003; Snarey & Bell, 2003).

ego identity According to Erikson, one's sense of who one is and what one stands for.

psychological moratorium A time-out period when adolescents experiment with different roles, values, beliefs, and relationships.

identity crisis A turning point in development during which one examines one's values and makes decisions about life roles.

exploration Active questioning and searching among alternatives in the quest to establish goals, values, or beliefs.

commitment A stable investment in one's goals, values, or beliefs.

identity diffusion An identity status that characterizes those who have no commitments and who are not in the process of exploring alternatives.

Concept Review 16.1   The Four Identity Statuses of James Marcia

Commitment	Exploration	
	Yes	**No**
Yes	**Identity Achievement** • Most developed in terms of identity • Has experienced a period of exploration • Has developed commitments • Has a sense of personal well-being, high self-esteem, and self-acceptance • Cognitively flexible • Sets goals and works toward achieving them	**Foreclosure** • Has commitments without considering alternatives • Commitments based on identification with parents, teachers, or other authority figures • Often authoritarian and inflexible
No	**Moratorium** • Actively exploring alternatives • Attempting to make choices with regard to occupation, ideological beliefs, and so on • Often anxious and intense • Ambivalent feelings toward parents and authority figures	**Identity Diffusion** • Least developed in terms of identity • Lacks commitments • Not trying to form commitments • May be carefree and uninvolved or unhappy and lonely • May be angry, alienated, rebellious

© Jeff Greenberg/PhotoEdit

What Is the Identity Status of These Adolescents?

foreclosure An identity status that characterizes those who have made commitments without considering alternatives.

In the **foreclosure** status, individuals make commitments without ever seriously considering alternatives. These commitments usually are established early in life and often are based on identification with parents, teachers, or religious leaders who have made a strong impression on the child. For example, a college student may unquestioningly prepare for a career that has been chosen for him by his parents. In other cases, the adolescent may uncritically adopt the lifestyle of a religious cult or extremist political group, as we see in so-called closed-minded fundamentalists (Saroglou &

Galand, 2004). Foreclosed individuals are authoritarian and inflexible (Saroglou & Galand, 2004).

The **moratorium** status refers to a person who is actively exploring alternatives in an attempt to make choices with regard to occupation, ideological beliefs, and so on (Akman, 2007; Snarey & Bell, 2003). Such individuals are often anxious and intense as they struggle to work toward commitment (Kroger, 2003).

Identity achievement refers to those who have experienced a period of exploration and have developed relatively firm commitments. Individuals who have achieved a clear sense of identity show a number of strengths. They have a sense of personal well-being in the form of high self-esteem and self-acceptance. As opposed to foreclosed individuals, those who achieve identity are cognitively flexible and capable of reason. They are able to set goals and work toward achieving them (Adams et al., 2006).

Development of Identity Statuses

Before high school, children show little interest in questions related to identity. Most of them are either in identity diffusion or foreclosure statuses. During the high school and college years, adolescents increasingly move from the diffusion and foreclosure statuses to the moratorium and achievement statuses (Kroger, 2003; Snarey & Bell, 2003). The greatest gains in identity formation occur in college (Adams et al., 2006; Berzonsky & Kuk, 2005). College students are exposed to a broad spectrum of lifestyles, belief systems, and career choices. These experiences spur consideration of identity issues. Are you one of the college students who have changed majors once or twice (or more)? If so, you have most likely experienced the moratorium identity status, which is common among college students. You should be comforted by the results of studies that show that college seniors have a stronger sense of identity than first-year students. The identity commitments of older students are likely to result from successfully resolving crises experienced during the moratorium (Lewis, 2003).

Ethnicity and Development of Identity

Question: What are the connections between ethnicity and other sociocultural factors—such as sex—and identity? The connection between ethnicity and identity had a special significance during journalist Don Terry's childhood:

> When I was a kid growing up in Chicago, I used to do anything I could to put off going to bed. One of my favorite delaying tactics was to engage my mother in a discussion about the important questions of the day, questions my friends and I had debated in the backyards of our neighborhood that afternoon—like Who did God root for, the Cubs or the White Sox? (The correct answer was, and still is, the White Sox.)
>
> Then one night I remember asking my mother something I had been wondering for a long time. "Mom," I asked, "What am I?"
>
> "You're my darling Donny," she said.
>
> "I know. But what else am I?"
>
> "You're a precious little boy who someday will grow up to be a wonderful, handsome man."
>
> "What I mean is, you're white and Dad's black, so what does that make me?"
>
> "Oh, I see," she said. "Well, you're half-black and you're half-white, so you're the best of both worlds."
>
> The next day, I told my friends that I was neither black nor white. "I'm the best of both worlds," I announced proudly.
>
> Man, you're crazy," one of the backyard boys said. "You're not even the best of your family. Your sister is. That girl is fine."

moratorium An identity status that characterizes those who are actively exploring alternatives in an attempt to form an identity.

identity achievement An identity status that characterizes those who have explored alternatives and have developed commitments.

For much of my life, I've tried to believe my mother. Having grown up in a family of blacks and whites, I'd long thought I saw race more clearly than most people. I appreciated being able to get close to both worlds, something few ever do. It was like having a secret knowledge.

And yet I've also known from an early age that things were more complicated than my mother made them out to be. Our country, from its very beginnings, has been obsessed with determining who is white and who is black. Our history has been shaped by that disheartening question. To be both black and white, then, is to do nothing less than confound national consciousness.

—Terry (2000)

To be both black and white—African American and European American—can also confound or confuse the consciousness of the individual (Schiff & O'Neill, 2007; Shih et al., 2007). Don Terry's mother had once been married to a European American, and Don had European American brothers. His experiences of the next several years reveal his efforts to come to grips with a nation that saw him as African American, not half and half. He chronicles his experiences with prejudice, even within his own family, and how he eventually embraced blackness—as a shield and a cause.

I signed up for a course on black nationalism. The decision was one of the most important developments of my life. Black studies saved me. It gave me a sense of discovery both academically and personally. Black studies helped me find an identity. As important, it helped me for the first time to understand my father's anger.

—Terry (2000)

Being African American, Asian American, European American, Latino or Latina American, Native American, or a combination of these is part of the self-identity of the individual. So is one's sex—being male or being female. So is one's religion, whether Christian, Hindu, Jewish, or any of the hundreds of other religions we find in the United States.

The development of self-identity is a key task for all American adolescents. The task is more complex for adolescents who are members of ethnic minority groups (Pastor et al., 2007; Phinney, 2006; Phinney & Ong, 2007). Adolescents who belong to the dominant culture—in this country, European Americans of Christian, especially Protestant, heritage—are usually faced with assimilating one set of cultural values into their identities. However, adolescents who belong to ethnic minority groups, such as African Americans and Jewish Americans, confront two sets of cultural values: the values of the dominant culture and those of their particular ethnic group (Phinney & Alipuria, 2006). If the cultural values conflict, the adolescent needs to sort out the values that are most meaningful to him or her and incorporate them into his or her identity. Some adolescents do it cafeteria style; they take a little bit of this and a little bit of that. For example, a young Catholic woman may decide to use artificial means of birth control even though doing so conflicts with her religion's teachings. Methods of birth control are well publicized in the culture at large, and the woman may decide to use them, although she may not tell her priest or her family.

Another problem in forging a sense of identity is that adolescents from ethnic minority groups often experience prejudice and discrimination. Their cultural heroes may be ignored. A relative scarcity of successful role models can be a problem, particularly for youth who live in poverty (Pastor et al., 2007). Identifying too strongly with the dominant culture may lead to rejection by the minority group. On the other hand, rejecting the dominant culture's values for those of the minority group may limit opportunities for advancement in the larger society. Biracial adolescents—those with parents from two different racial or ethnic groups—wrestle not only with these issues but also with issues relating to their dual cultural heritage (Phinney & Alipuria, 2006).

Many adolescents from ethnic minority groups have fewer educational and career opportunities than those from the dominant culture (Pastor et al., 2007). If one cannot expect a future, why explore one's options? Some adolescents from ethnic minority groups—Latino and Latina Americans, African Americans, and Native Americans—foreclose earlier on identity issues than do their European American peers. Others are actively engaged in the search for identity (Pastor et al., 2007; Phinney & Alipuria, 2006). Adolescents from ethnic minority groups may develop strategies for handling conflicting cultural demands such as those we find in the following comment:

> Being invited to someone's house, I have to change my ways of how I act at home, because of culture differences. I would have to follow what they do. . . . I am used to it now, switching off between the two. It is not difficult.
>
> —Phinney & Rosenthal (1992)

Question: Are there stages in developing an ethnic identity? Some researchers hypothesize three stages in the development of **ethnic identity** (Phinney, 2006; Umaña-Taylor et al., 2004). The first is **unexamined ethnic identity**. It is similar to Marcia's ego identity statuses of diffusion or foreclosure. In some cases, the early adolescent has not given much thought to ethnic identity issues (diffusion). In other instances, the young adolescent may have adopted an identity either with the dominant group or with the minority group based on societal or parental values but without much exploration or thought. This stage represents a foreclosed status. In the second stage, the adolescent embarks on an **ethnic identity search**. This second stage, similar to Marcia's moratorium, may be based on some incident that makes the adolescent aware of her ethnicity. During this stage, the adolescent may explore her ethnic culture, intensely participating in cultural events, reading, and talking to others. In the third stage, individuals have an **achieved ethnic identity** that involves a clear, confident acceptance of oneself as a member of one's ethnic group.

As minority youth move through adolescence, they are increasingly likely to explore their own ethnicity and to acquire an achieved ethnic identity. For example, only about one-third of African American eighth-graders were found to show evidence of ethnic identity search, compared with half of African American tenth-graders (Phinney, 1989). A longitudinal study (Phinney & Chavira, 1992) found movement from lower to higher stages of ethnic identity between 16 and 19 years of age. And college undergraduates show higher levels of ethnic identity achievement than eleventh- or twelfth-graders (Phinney, 1992).

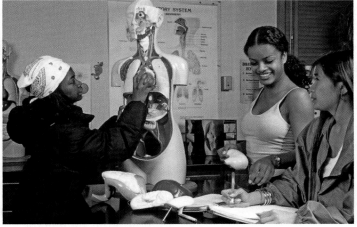

How Does Ethnic Identity Develop?
According to Phinney, adolescents undergo a three-stage process of the development of ethnic identity: unexamined ethnic identity, ethnic identity search, and achieved ethnic identity. Adolescents from ethnic minority groups may be faced with conflicting values: those of their ethnic group and those of the dominant culture.

ethnic identity A sense of belonging to an ethnic group.

unexamined ethnic identity The first stage of ethnic identity development; similar to the diffusion or foreclosure identity statuses.

ethnic identity search The second stage of ethnic identity development; similar to the moratorium identity status.

achieved ethnic identity The final stage of ethnic identity development; similar to the identity achievement status.

Sex and Development of Identity

And what of sex? ***Question: Does the development of ego identity differ in males and females?*** Erikson believed that there were sex differences in the development of identity, and his views reflected the times in which he wrote. Identity development relates both to relationships and occupational choice, among other matters. Erikson (1968, 1975; Anthis et al., 2004) assumed that relationships were more important to women's development of identity, whereas occupational and ideological matters were relatively more important to men's. He believed that a young woman's identity was intimately bound up with her roles as wife and mother. Erikson, like most thinkers of his day, saw a woman's primary roles as related to her home life. In sum, it was normal for men to develop their identities before they developed (meaningful) intimate relationships. But women might develop their identities simultaneously with the development of intimate relationships.

However, the evidence from numerous studies suggests that females approach identity formation in a manner that is comparable to that of males (Murray, 1998; Phinney, 2006). In one study, both men and women claimed that the interpersonal area was the most important (Bilsker et al., 1988). **Truth or Fiction Revisited:** Other studies find that adolescent females and males are both concerned about occupational choices, but that females are more likely to integrate occupational and family plans (Berzonsky, 2004). This sex difference may persist because females continue to assume primary responsibility for child rearing, even though most women are employed outside the home (Anthis et al., 2004).

What about the timing of identity development in women and men? Both begin identity formation in adolescence. Those women who have uninterrupted careers, like men, tend to complete the task of identity achievement in late adolescence. Women who are full-time homemakers or who defer employment until their children are in school are more likely to develop a strong sense of personal identity after their children reach school age (Anthis, 2006; Anthis et al., 2004).

Development of the Self-Concept in Adolescence

The adolescent preoccupation with developing a sense of identity is part of a broader process of redefining the way adolescents view themselves. *Question: How does the self-concept develop during adolescence?* Before adolescence, children describe themselves primarily in terms of their physical characteristics and their actions. As they approach adolescence, children begin to incorporate psychological characteristics and social relationships into their self-descriptions. Adolescents tend to describe themselves in terms of distinct and enduring personality traits (Damon, 1991).

The self-concept also becomes more differentiated; adolescents add more categories to their self-description. Also, self-descriptions begin to vary according to adolescents' social roles. Like the 15-year-old at the beginning of the chapter, adolescents may describe themselves as anxious or sarcastic with parents but as caring, talkative, and cheerful with friends. Such contradictions and conflicts in self-description reach their peak at about age 14 and then begin to decline in later adolescence (Harter & Monsour, 1992). The more advanced formal-operational skills of the older adolescent allow her to integrate the many apparently contradictory elements of the self. For example, the older adolescent might say: "I'm very adaptable. When I'm around my friends, who think that what I say is important, I'm very talkative; but around my family, I'm quiet because they're not interested enough to really listen to me" (Damon, 1991, p. 988).

© SW Productions/Jupiterimages

Development of Self-Esteem during Adolescence

Self-esteem tends to dip during early adolescence as young people face the differences between their real self and their ideal self. However, self-esteem tends to improve with emotional support from family and peers.

Self-Esteem in Adolescence: Bottoming? Rising?

Question: What happens to self-esteem during adolescence? **Self-esteem** tends to decline as the child progresses from middle childhood to about the age of 12 or 13 (Harter & Whitesell, 2003). What might account for the drop-off? The growing cognitive maturity of young adolescents makes them increasingly and painfully aware of the disparity between their ideal self and their real self. The sense of discrepancy between the real self and ideal self is especially great in the area of physical appearance.

Physical appearance contributes more to the development of self-esteem during adolescence than any other characteristic (Durkin et al., 2007; Seidah & Bouffard, 2007). Boys might fantasize they would like to have the physiques of the warriors they see in video games or in the media (Konijn et al., 2007). Most girls want to be thin, thin, thin (O'Dea, 2006).

After hitting a low point at about age 12 or 13, self-esteem gradually improves throughout adolescence (Harter & Whitesell, 2003). Perhaps adolescents adjust their notions of the ideal self to better reflect reality. Also, as adolescents develop academic, physical, and social skills, they may gradually grow less self-critical (Shirk et al., 2003).

For most adolescents, low self-esteem produces temporary discomfort (Harter & Whitesell, 2003). For others, low self-esteem has serious psychological and behavioral consequences. For example, low self-esteem is often found in teenagers who are depressed or suicidal (Shirk et al., 2003).

Emotional support from parents and peers is important in the development of self-esteem during adolescence. Adolescents who feel that they are highly regarded by family and friends are more likely to have positive feelings about themselves than are those who feel they are lacking such support (Costigan et al., 2007; Soenens et al., 2007). In early adolescence, support from parents is equally as important as peer support. By late adolescence, peer support carries more weight.

self-esteem The sense of value or worth that people attach to themselves.

Active Review

1. Erikson's fifth (adolescent) stage of psychosocial development is called _____ versus identity diffusion.
2. Erikson defined a psychological _____ as a time-out during which adolescents experiment with different roles, values, beliefs, and relationships.
3. According to Marcia, identity _____ refers to adolescents who have experienced a period of exploration and developed relatively firm commitments.

4. Girls generally show (Higher or Lower?) self-esteem than boys during adolescence.

Reflect & Relate: Does your ethnic background play an important role in your self-identity? Explain.

Go to

http://www.psychology.thomson.com/rathus

for an interactive version of this review.

Relationships with Parents and Peers

Adolescents coping with the task of establishing a sense of identity and direction in their lives are heavily influenced by both their parents and peers. *Question: How do relationships with one's parents and peers change during the course of the teenage years?*

Relationships with Parents

During adolescence, children spend much less time with their parents than they did during childhood. In one study, children ranging in age from 9 to 15 years carried electronic pagers for a week and reported what they were doing each time they were signaled by the pagers (Larson & Richards, 1991). The amount of time spent with family dramatically declined as the age of the children increased. The 15-year-olds spent half as much time with their families as the 9-year-olds. For older boys, the time with family was replaced by time spent alone, whereas older girls spent more time alone or with friends.

Adolescents continue to interact more with their mothers than with their fathers, continuing the pattern begun in childhood. Teenagers engage in more conflicts with their mothers, but they also view their mothers as being more supportive, as knowing them better, and as being more likely to accept the teenager's opinions (Costigan et al., 2007; Sheeber et al., 2007). Adverse relationships with fathers are often associated with depression in adolescents (Sheeber et al., 2007). On the other hand, good relations with fathers strongly contribute to the psychological well-being of adolescents (Flouri & Buchanan, 2003).

The decrease in time spent with family may reflect the adolescents' striving to become more independent from their parents. A certain degree of distancing from parents may be adaptive for adolescents as they engage in the tasks of forming relationships outside the family and entering adulthood. But greater independence does not mean that adolescents become emotionally detached from their mothers and fathers. Adolescents continue to maintain a great deal of love, loyalty, and respect for their parents (Collins & Laursen, 2006). And adolescents who feel close to their parents are more likely to show greater self-reliance and independence, higher self-esteem, better school performance, and fewer psychological and social problems (Costigan et al., 2007; Flouri & Buchanan, 2003).

The relationship between parents and teens is not always rosy, of course. Early adolescence, in particular, is characterized by increased bickering and disagreements and by a decrease in shared activities and in expressions of affection (Smetana et al., 2003, 2006).

Conflict is greatest during puberty and declines in later adolescence (Smetana et al., 2003, 2006). Conflicts typically center on the everyday details of family life, such as chores, homework, curfews, personal appearance, finances, and dating. Conflicts may arise in these areas because adolescents believe that personal issues—such as choice of clothes and friends—that were previously controlled by parents should now come under the control of the adolescent (Costigan et al., 2007; Smetana et al., 2006). But parents, especially mothers, continue to believe that they should retain control in most areas, such as encouraging adolescents to do their homework and clean their rooms. And so conflicts arise. As adolescents get older, however, they and their parents are more likely to compromise (Smetana et al., 2003, 2006). On the other hand, parents and adolescents are usually quite similar in their values and beliefs regarding social, political, religious, and economic issues (Collins & Laursen, 2006). Even though the notion of a generation gap between adolescents and their parents may persist as a popular stereotype, there is little evidence to support it. **Truth or Fiction Revisited:** Adolescents are not in a constant state of rebellion against their parents.

During adolescence, most teenagers and their parents establish a balance between adolescent independence and continued family connectedness. Although some conflict is inevitable, it usually is not severe (Smetana et al., 2006). As adolescents grow older, parents are more likely to relax controls and are less likely to use punishment (Smetana et al., 2006). Although parent–child relationships change, most adolescents feel that they are close to and get along with their parents, even though they may develop a less idealized view of them (Collins & Laursen, 2006).

© David Young-Wolff/PhotoEdit

What Happens to Relationships with Parents during Adolescence?

Parent–adolescent relationships become redefined during adolescence, as most adolescents strive for independence. There are often conflicts about choice of friends and clothing and how and where adolescents spend their time. But despite conflict, most adolescents continue to love and respect their parents.

Parenting Styles

Children's development is affected by the degree to which their parents show warmth and set limits on the child's behavior. Differences in parenting styles continue to influence the development of adolescents as well (Collins & Laursen, 2006; Costigan et al., 2007). Adolescents from authoritative homes—whose parents are willing to exert control and explain the reasons for doing so—show more competent behavior than any other group of teenagers. They are more self-reliant, do better in school, have better mental health, and show the lowest incidence of psychological problems and misconduct, including drug use.

Relationships with Peers

The transition from childhood to adolescence is accompanied by a shift in the relative importance of parents and peers. Although relationships with parents generally remain positive, the role of peers as a source of activities, influence, and support increases markedly during the teen years. For example, parents are perceived as the most frequent providers of social and emotional support by fourth-graders. But by seventh grade, friends of the same sex are seen to be as supportive as parents. And by tenth grade, same-sex friends are viewed as providing more support than parents (Furman & Buhrmester, 1992).

Friendships in Adolescence

Friendships occupy an increasingly important place in the lives of adolescents. Adolescents have more friends than younger children do (Feiring & Lewis, 1991). Most adolescents have one or two "best friends" and several good friends. Teenagers see their friends frequently, usually several hours a day (Hartup, 1993). And when teenagers are not with their friends, you can often find them talking with each other on the phone. In fact, I frequently warned my children that I would take them in for major surgery—telephonectomy—unless they got the phones out of their ears by themselves. The warning went unheard (because the children were on the phone). I therefore solved the problem by having a separate line installed for the children and investing heavily in the local telephone company.

Friendships in adolescence differ in important ways from the friendships of childhood. For one thing, adolescents are much more likely to stress the importance of acceptance, intimate self-disclosure, and mutual understanding in their friendships (González et al., 2004). For example, one eighth-grade girl described her best friend this way: "I can tell her things and she helps me talk. And she doesn't laugh at me if I do something weird—she accepts me for who I am" (Berndt & Perry, 1990, p. 269). Second, adolescents stress loyalty and trustworthiness as important aspects of friendship more than younger children do (González et al., 2004; Rotenberg et al., 2004). For example, they may say that a friend will "stick up for you in a fight" and will not "talk about you behind your back." Finally, adolescents are more likely than younger children to share with friends and are less likely to compete with them.

Adolescents and their friends are similar in many respects. They typically are the same age and the same race. They almost always are the same sex. Even though romantic attachments increase during the teen years, most adolescents still choose members of their own sex as best friends (Hartup, 1993). Friends are likely to share certain behavioral similarities. They often are alike in their school attitudes, educational aspirations, and school achievement. Friends also tend to have similar attitudes about drinking, drug use, and sexual activity (Hartup, 1993; Youniss & Haynie, 1992).

Friendship contributes to a positive self-concept and psychological adjustment. Adolescents who have a close friend have higher self-esteem than adolescents who do not. Teenagers who have intimate friendships also are more likely to show advanced

Development of Friendship in Adolescence

Adolescents tend to spend more time with their friends than with their families. They look for one or more close friends, or confidants. They also tend to belong to cliques and crowds. All these relationships serve different but overlapping functions.

stages of identity development (Berndt, 1992; Bukowski et al., 1993b). These relationships have been found for both European American and African American youth (Savin-Williams & Berndt, 1990).

Ethnicity, Sex, and Adolescent Friendships

I always notice one thing when I walk through the commons at my high school: The whites are on one side of the room, and the blacks are on the other. When I have to walk through the "black" side to get to class, the black students just quietly ignore me and look in the other direction, and I do the same. But there's one who sometimes catches my eye, and I can't help feel awkward when I see him. He was a close friend from childhood. Ten years ago, we played catch in our backyards, went bike riding, and slept over at one another's houses. By the fifth grade, we went to movies and amusement parks and bunked together at summer camp. We're both juniors now at the same high school. We usually don't say anything when we see each other, except maybe a polite "Hi." Since entering high school, we haven't shared a single class or sport. It's as if fate has kept us apart, though, more likely, it's peer pressure.

—Adapted from Jarvis (1993, p. 14)

Children are more likely to choose friends from their own ethnic group than from others (Hamm, 2000). This pattern strengthens in adolescence (Hartup, 1993). Adolescents from ethnic minority groups grow aware of the differences between their culture and the dominant culture. Peers from their own ethnic group provide a sense of camaraderie that reduces the pain of feeling isolated from the dominant culture (Spencer et al., 1990).

One study compared friendship patterns of African American and European American adolescents who attended an integrated junior high school (DuBois & Hirsch, 1990). More than 80% of the students of both ethnic groups reported having a school friend of the other ethnicity, but only 28% of the students saw such a friend frequently outside school. African American youths were almost twice as likely as European American youths to see a friend of another ethnicity outside school. Children who lived in integrated as opposed to segregated neighborhoods were more likely to see a friend of another ethnicity outside the school setting.

Sex differences relating to peer intimacy and support were found for European American students but not for African American students. European American girls reported talking more with friends about personal problems and reported that their friends were more available for help than did European American boys (Hartup, 1993; Youniss & Haynie, 1992). But African American girls and boys reported the same degree of intimacy and support in their friendships. How can these differences be explained? The researchers suggest that the African American students may have faced ethnicity-related stressors in their school, which was integrated but predominantly European American. To cope more effectively, both girls and boys may have relied heavily on the support of their peers.

Intimacy and closeness appear to be more central to the friendships of girls than of boys both in childhood and in adolescence (Berndt & Perry, 1990; Schraf & Hertz-Lazarowitz, 2003). Both female and male adolescents describe girls' friendships as more intimate than boys' friendships (Hartup, 1993). Girls spend more time with their friends than boys do (Schraf & Hertz-Lazarowitz, 2003). Adolescent girls view close friendships as more important than adolescent boys do, and they report putting more effort into improving the depth and quality of the relationship. Adolescent and adult females also are generally more likely than males to disclose secrets, personal problems, thoughts, and feelings to their friends (Dindia & Allen, 1992; Schraf & Hertz-Lazarowitz, 2003). Males, however, may be more likely to disclose information about their sex lives (Chiou & Wan, 2006).

Friendship networks among girls are smaller and more exclusive than friendship networks among boys (Schraf & Hertz-Lazarowitz, 2003). That is, girls tend to have one or two close friends, whereas boys tend to congregate in larger, less intimate groups. The activities of girls' and boys' friendship networks differ as well. Girls are more likely to engage in unstructured activities such as talking and listening to music. Boys, on the other hand, are more likely to engage in organized group activities, games, and sports.

Peer Groups

In addition to forming close friendships, most adolescents also belong to one or more larger peer groups. *Question: What kinds of adolescent peer groups are there?* Such groups include *cliques* and *crowds* (Henzi et al., 2007; Palla et al., 2007). **Cliques** consist of five to ten individuals who hang around together and share activities and confidences. **Crowds** are larger groups who may or may not spend much time together and are identified by the particular activities or attitudes of the group. Crowds are usually given labels by other adolescents. Think back on your high school days. Different groups of individuals are commonly given labels such as "jocks," "brains," "druggies," "nerds," and so on. The most negatively labeled groups ("druggies," "rejects," and so on) show higher levels of alcohol and drug use, delinquency, and depression than other groups.

Adolescent peer groups differ from childhood peer groups. For one thing, the time spent with peers increases. High school students spend more than half their time with peers and only about 15% of their time with parents or other adults (Halpern, 2005; Staff et al., 2004). Korean and Japanese students spend significantly more time than their European and American peers on homework and in preparation for college entrance exams (Halpern, 2005).

A second difference between adolescent and childhood peer groups is that adolescent peer groups function with less adult guidance or control (Staff et al., 2004). Childhood peer groups stay closer to home, under the watchful eye of parents. Adolescent peer groups are more likely to congregate in settings with less adult supervision (the school) or with no supervision.

A third change in adolescent peer groups is the addition of peers of the other sex, which sharply contrasts with the sex segregation of childhood peer groups (Staff et al., 2004). Association with peers of the other sex may lead to dating and romantic relationships.

Dating and Romantic Relationships

Question: When do romantic relationships develop? Romantic relationships begin to appear during early and middle adolescence, and most adolescents start dating or going out by the time they graduate from high school (Florsheim, 2003). The development of dating typically takes the following sequence: putting oneself in situations where peers of the other sex probably will be present (e.g., hanging out at the mall), group activities including peers of the other sex (e.g., school dances or parties), group dating (e.g., joining a mixed-sex group at the movies), and then traditional two-person dating (Connolly et al., 2004).

clique A group of five to ten individuals who hang around together and who share activities and confidences.

crowd A large, loosely organized group of people who may or may not spend much time together and who are identified by the activities of the group.

Dating serves a number of important functions. First and foremost, people date to have fun. High school students rate time spent with a person of the other sex as the time when they are happiest (Csikszentmihalyi & Larson, 1984). Dating, especially in early adolescence, also serves to enhance prestige with one's peers. Dating gives adolescents additional experiences in learning to relate positively to different people. Finally, dating provides preparation for adult courtship activities (Florsheim, 2003).

Dating relationships tend to be casual and short-lived in early adolescence. In late adolescence, relationships tend to become more stable and committed (Connolly et al., 2000). It is therefore not surprising that 18-year-olds are more likely than 15-year-olds to mention love, trust, and commitment when describing their romantic relationships (Feiring, 1993).

Peer Influence

Parents often worry that their teenage children will fall in with the wrong crowd and be persuaded by their peers to engage in behaviors that are self-destructive or go against the parents' wishes (Brown et al., 1993). How much influence do peers have on each other? Does peer pressure cause adolescents to adopt behaviors and attitudes of which their parents disapprove? Peer pressure actually is fairly weak in early adolescence. It peaks during midadolescence and declines in late adolescence, after about age 17 (Brown et al., 1993; Reis & Youniss, 2004).

Why do peers increase in influence during adolescence? One suggestion is that peers provide a standard by which adolescents measure their behavior as they begin to develop independence from the family (Foster-Clark & Blyth, 1991). Another reason is that peers provide social, emotional, and practical support in times of trouble (Kirchler et al., 1991; Pombeni et al., 1990).

It was once the conventional wisdom that peer influence and parental influence were in conflict, with peers exerting pressure on adolescents to engage in negative behaviors such as alcohol and drug use. Research paints a more complex picture. For one thing, we have seen that adolescents often maintain close and warm relationships with their parents. **Truth or Fiction Revisited:** It is not true that most adolescents' friends are bad influences. Parents and peers usually are complementary rather than competing influences on teenagers (Brown et al., 1993; Reis & Youniss, 2004).

Parents and peers also seem to exert influence in somewhat different domains. Adolescents are more likely to conform to peer standards in matters pertaining to style and taste, such as clothing, hairstyles, speech patterns, and music (Camarena, 1991). They are much more likely to agree with their parents on many serious issues, such as moral principles and future educational and career goals (Savin-Williams & Berndt, 1990).

Adolescents influence each other both positively and negatively. In many cases, peer pressure to finish high school and achieve academically can be stronger than pressures to engage in areas of misconduct, such as drug use, sexual activity, and minor delinquency (Brown et al., 1993). Moreover, at least in this experiment, teenagers were less inclined to follow peer pressure to engage in antisocial activity than in a neutral activity.

A 10-year study of 20,000 ninth- through twelfth-graders also found that some adolescents encourage one another to do well in school (Steinberg, 1996). Yet more often than not, adolescents discouraged one another from doing well or from doing *too* well. One in five reported not trying to perform as well as possible for fear of earning the disapproval of peers. Then, too, half reported that they never discussed schoolwork and grades with their friends.

It is true that adolescents who smoke, drink, use drugs, and engage in sexual activity often have friends who also engage in these behaviors. But we must keep in mind that adolescents tend to choose friends and peers who are similar to them to begin with. Peers reinforce behavior patterns and predispositions that may have existed before the individual joined the group. That is true for positive behaviors, such as academic achievement, as well as for negative behaviors, such as drug use (Brown, 1990).

A number of other factors affect the susceptibility of adolescents to peer influence. One of these is sex. Girls appear to be slightly more concerned with peer acceptance than boys, but boys are more likely than girls to conform to pressures to engage in misconduct (Camarena, 1991; Foster-Clark & Blyth, 1991). Parenting style also is related to susceptibility to peer pressure. Authoritative parenting appears to discourage negative peer influence, whereas authoritarian and permissive parenting seem to encourage it (Foster-Clark & Blyth, 1991; Fuligni & Eccles, 1993).

Active Review

5. Adolescents interact more with their (Mothers or Fathers?).
6. Adolescents generally (Do or Do not?) love and respect their parents.
7. The role of peers (Increases or Decreases?) markedly from childhood to adolescence.
8. Children are more likely to choose friends from (Their own or Other?) ethnic groups.

Reflect & Relate: How did your relationships with family members change during adolescence? Did you make the changes or simply respond to them? Were the changes for the better or for the worse? Explain.

Go to

http://www.psychology.thomson.com/rathus

for an interactive version of this review.

Sexuality: When? What? (How?) Who? Where? and Why?— Not to Mention, "Should I?"

My first sexual experience occurred in a car after the high school junior prom. We were both virgins, very uncertain but very much in love. We had been going together since eighth grade. The experience was somewhat painful. I remember wondering if I would look different to my mother the next day. I guess I didn't because nothing was said.

Because of the flood of sex hormones, many or most adolescents experience a powerful sex drive. In addition, they are bombarded with sexual messages in the media, including scantily clad hip-grinding, crotch-grabbing pop stars; print ads for barely there underwear; and countless articles on "How to tell if your boyfriend has been (whatever)" and "The 10 things that will drive your girlfriend wild." Teenagers are strongly motivated to follow the crowd, yet they are also influenced by the views of their parents and teachers. So what is a teen to do? What do American teens do? *Question: What are some patterns of sexual behavior in adolescence?*

Sexual activity in adolescence can take many forms. In this section, we consider masturbation, homosexuality, heterosexuality, and use of contraceptives.

Masturbation

Masturbation, or sexual self-stimulation, is the most common sexual outlet in adolescents. Even before children conceive of sexual experiences with others, they may learn that touching their own genitals can produce pleasure.

Surveys indicate that most adolescents masturbate at some time. The well-known Kinsey studies, published in the mid-20th century (Kinsey et al., 1948, 1953), suggested that masturbation was nearly universal among male adolescents but less common among adolescent females. This sex difference is confirmed in nearly every survey (Baumeister et al., 2001; Larsson & Svedin, 2002). Boys who masturbate may do so several times a week, on average, many times more often than girls who masturbate. It is unclear whether this sex difference reflects a stronger sex drive in boys (Peplau, 2003), greater social constraints on girls (Pinkerton et al., 2002), or both. Not surprisingly, (inaccurate) beliefs that masturbation is harmful and guilt about masturbation tend to lessen the incidence of masturbation (Ortega et al., 2005).

Sexual Orientation

Most people, including the great majority of adolescents, have a heterosexual orientation. That is, they are sexually attracted to and interested in forming romantic relationships with people of the other sex. However, some people have a **homosexual** orientation. That is, they are attracted to and interested in forming romantic relationships with people of their own sex. Males with a homosexual orientation are referred to as *gay males*. Females with a homosexual orientation are referred to as *lesbians*. However, males and females with a homosexual orientation are sometimes categorized together as "gay people," or "gays." *Bisexual* people are attracted to both females and males.

The concept of *sexual orientation* is not to be confused with *sexual activity*. For example, engaging in sexual activity with people of one's own sex does not necessarily mean that one has a homosexual orientation. Sexual activity between males sometimes reflects limited sexual opportunities.

According to Ritch Savin-Williams and Lisa Diamond (2000, 2004; Savin-Williams, 2007), the development of sexual identity in gay males and lesbians involves several facets: attraction to members of the same sex, self-labeling as gay or lesbian, sexual contact with members of the same sex, and eventual disclosure of one's sexual orientation to other people. However, Diamond's (2006) ongoing study of young "sexual minority women" revealed that many maintain some attraction to males. By and large, Savin-Williams and Diamond found a 10-year gap between initial attraction to members of one's own sex, which tended to occur at about the age of 8 or 9, and disclosure of one's orientation to other people, which usually occurred at about age 18. On the other hand, some gay males and lesbians never disclose their sexual orientations to certain people, such as their parents. Some keep their orientation hidden for a lifetime (Rathus et al., 2008).

masturbation Sexual self-stimulation.

homosexual Referring to an erotic orientation toward members of one's own sex.

Development of a Gay Male or Lesbian Sexual Orientation Students at the Stratford (Connecticut) High School get together weekly after classes to talk about sexuality and anti-gay bigotry. Many gay males and lesbians become aware of their sexual orientations during adolescence but fear coming out because of societal pressures. These types of classes try to help create a more positive environment for gay and lesbian students.

Coming Out

The process of "coming out"—that is, accepting one's homosexual orientation and declaring it to others—may be a long and painful struggle (Bagley & D'Augelli, 2000; Crockett & Silbereisen, 2000). Gay adolescents may be ostracized and rejected by family and friends. Depression and suicide rates are higher among gay youth than among heterosexual adolescents. It has been estimated that as many as one in three gay, lesbian, or bisexual adolescents has attempted suicide (Ciro et al., 2005; Hershberger & D'Augelli, 2000). Homosexual adolescents often engage in substance abuse, run away from home, and do poorly in school (Russell, 2006). These factors also heighten the risk of suicide among gay, lesbian, and bisexual adolescents (Ciro et al., 2005; Hershberger & D'Augelli, 2000).

"Coming out to others" sometimes means an open declaration to the world. More often, an adolescent feels more comfortable telling a couple of close friends than his or her parents. Before they inform family members, gay adolescents often anticipate their family's negative reactions, including denial, anger, and rejection (Bagley & D'Augelli, 2000). Yet some families are more accepting. Perhaps they had suspicions and prepared themselves for the news. Then, too, many families are initially rejecting but often eventually come to at least grudging acceptance that an adolescent is gay.

The Origins of Sexual Orientation

Surveys find that about 3% of males and 2% of females in the United States identify themselves as being gay, although larger percentages of adolescents have had sexual experiences with people of their own sex (Laumann et al., 1994). Theories of the origins of sexual orientation look both at nature and nurture—the biological makeup of the individual and environmental influences. Several theories bridge the two. *Question: What do we know about the origins of gay male and lesbian sexual orientations?*

Learning theorists look for the roles of factors such as reinforcement and observational learning. From this perspective, reinforcement of sexual behavior with members of one's own sex—as in reaching orgasm with them when members of the other sex are unavailable—might affect one's sexual orientation. Similarly, childhood sexual abuse by someone of the same sex could lead to fantasies about sex with people of one's own sex and affect sexual orientation. Observation of others engaged in enjoyable male–male or female–female sexual encounters could also affect the development of sexual orientation. But critics point out that most individuals become aware of their sexual orientation before they experience sexual contacts with other people of either sex (Laumann et al., 1994; Savin-Williams, 2007; Savin-Williams & Diamond, 2004). Moreover, in a society that largely condemns homosexuality, young people are unlikely to believe that a homosexual orientation will have positive effects for them.

Although gay people are less likely than heterosexual people to have children, sexual orientation nevertheless tends to run in families. There is some evidence for genetic factors in sexual orientation (Hyde, 2005; Kohl, 2007; Sefcek et al., 2007). One study found that 22% of the brothers of 51 gay men were gay or bisexual, although one would expect to find only 3% of the brothers to also be gay if the relationship were just coincidental (Pillard & Weinrich, 1986). Twin studies support a role for genetics. About 52% of identical (monozygotic) twin pairs are "concordant" (in agreement) for a gay male sexual orientation, compared with 22% for fraternal (dizygotic) twins (Bailey & Pillard, 1991). Monozygotic twins fully share their genetic heritage, whereas dizygotic twins, like other pairs of siblings, have a 50% overlap.

Sex hormones promote the development of male and female sex organs and regulate the menstrual cycle. They also have both activating and organizing effects on sexual behavior. That is, they fuel the sex drive and affect *whom* one will find to be sexually attractive. Sex hormones are thus likely candidates for influencing the development of sexual orientation (Lalumière et al., 2000).

It has been demonstrated repeatedly that sex hormones predispose lower animals, such as rats, to stereotypical masculine or feminine mating patterns. Does that mean that gay males and lesbians differ from heterosexuals in their levels of sex hormones? Among gay male and lesbian adolescents and adults, the answer is apparently not. Sexual orientation has not been reliably connected with adolescent or adult levels of sex hormones (Gooren, 2006). But sex hormones may influence the developing human embryo and fetus (Dessens et al., 1999; Friedman & Downey, 2001).

We have to conclude by confessing that much about the development of sexual orientation remains speculative. There are possible roles for prenatal exposure to certain hormones. Exposure to these hormones, in turn, may be related to genetic factors. Even the possibility that childhood experiences play a role has not been ruled out. But the interactions among these factors largely remain a mystery. Nor is there reason to believe that the development of sexual orientation must follow the same path in everyone.

Male–Female Sexual Behavior

Adolescents today start dating and going out earlier than in past generations. Teens who date earlier are more likely to engage in sexual activity during high school (Guttmacher Institute, 2007). Teens who initiate sexual activity earlier are also less likely to use contraception and more likely to become pregnant. But early dating does not always lead to early sex, and early sex does not always lead to unwanted pregnancies. Still, some young women find their options in adulthood restricted by a chain of events that began in early adolescence.

Truth or Fiction Revisited: It is true that petting is practically universal among American adolescents and has been for many generations. Adolescents use petting to express affection, satisfy their curiosities, heighten their sexual arousal, and reach orgasm while avoiding pregnancy and maintaining virginity. Many adolescents do not see themselves as having sex if they stop short of vaginal intercourse. Girls are more likely than boys to be coerced into petting and to feel guilty about it (Larsson & Svedin, 2002).

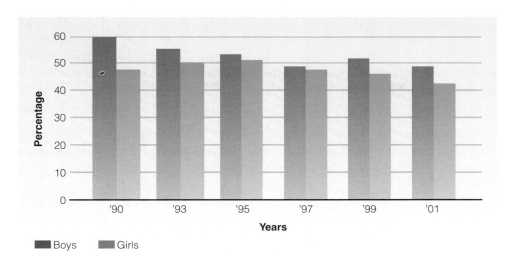

● **Figure 16.1**

Percentage of Students in Grades 9–12 Who Report Ever Having Had Sexual Intercourse

Despite a gradual decline in the incidence of sexual intercourse since the early 1990s, the incidence of high school students who have engaged in sexual intercourse remains between 40% and 50%, with boys reporting a higher incidence than girls.

Sources: Centers for Disease Control and Prevention, the Alan Guttmacher Institute, and the Child Trends Databank, as reported in the *New York Times*, March 7, 2004. Reprinted by permission of the New York Times Co.

The incidence of oral sex increases with age. According to a survey by the Centers for Disease Control and Prevention, 42% of girls of ages 15 to 17 reported engaging in oral sex compared with 72% of girls aged 18 to 19 (Mosher et al., 2005). Among adolescents who have not engaged in sexual intercourse, the lowest rates of oral sex (about 19%) were for adolescents who cited moral or religious reasons for abstaining from sexual intercourse. Some adolescent couples use oral sex as a means of preventing pregnancy.

Surveys show that since the early 1990s, the percentage of high school students who have engaged in sexual intercourse has been gradually declining (see ● Figure 16.1). Nevertheless, between 40% and 50% of high school students have had sexual intercourse, and male high school students are somewhat more likely than girls to be sexually active. The incidences of kissing, "making out," oral sex, and sexual intercourse all increase with age.

Most teenagers do not plan their first sexual experience. Rather, they perceive it as simply happening to them (Browning et al., 2000; O'Donnell et al., 2003). *Question: Why do some teenagers initiate sexual activity at an early age, whereas others wait until later?* Let us consider some determinants of early sexual behavior.

Effects of Puberty

The hormonal changes of puberty probably are partly responsible for the onset of sexual activity. In boys, levels of testosterone are associated with sexual behavior. In girls, however, testosterone levels are linked to sexual interests but not to sexual behavior. Social factors may therefore play a greater role in regulating sexual behavior in girls than in boys (Browning et al., 2000; O'Donnell et al., 2003).

The physical changes associated with puberty also may serve as a trigger for the onset of sexual activity. For example, the development of secondary sex characteristics such as breasts in girls and muscles and deep voices in boys may make them more sexually attractive. Early-maturing girls are more likely to have older friends, which may draw them into early sexual relationships.

Parental Influences

Teenagers who have close relationships with their parents are less likely to initiate sexual activity at an early age (Bynum, 2007; DiIorio et al., 2007; Ohalete, 2007). Adolescents who communicate well with their parents also delay the onset of sexual activity (Aspy et al., 2007; National Campaign to Prevent Teen Pregnancy, 2003). If these youngsters do have sexual intercourse, they are more likely to use birth control and to have fewer sexual partners (Aspy et al., 2007; National Campaign to Prevent Teen Pregnancy, 2003).

The double standard of sexuality in our society—that premarital sexual activity is acceptable for boys but not for girls—seems to influence the way in which parental communication affects sexual behavior in teenagers. The message for daughters appears to be "Don't do it," whereas the message for sons is "It's okay to do it as long as you take precautions."

Peer Influences

Peers also play an important role in determining the sexual behavior of adolescents. One of the most powerful predictors of sexual activity for both female and male adolescents is the sexual activity of their best friends (Dishion & Stormshak, 2007; O'Donnell et al., 2003).

When teenagers are asked why they do not wait to have sexual intercourse until they are older, the main reason reported is usually peer pressure (O'Donnell et al., 2003). Peers, especially those of the same sex, also serve as a key source of sex education for adolescents. Adolescents report that they are somewhat more likely to receive information about sex from friends and media sources—TV shows, films, magazines, and the Internet—than from sex education classes or their parents (Kaiser Family Foundation et al., 2003).

Teenage Pregnancy

The title of this section is "loaded." It suggests that there is a problem with teenage pregnancy. So let's toss in a couple of caveats at the beginning. First, throughout most of history, even most of the history of the United States, girls were first becoming pregnant in their teens. Second, throughout most cultures in the world today, girls are first becoming pregnant in their teens (Save the Children, 2004b). Why, then, do we bother with a section on this topic? The answer is that in the United States today, nine in ten adolescents who become pregnant do so accidentally and without committed partners (America's Children, 2007). Most young women in developed nations defer pregnancy until after they have completed some or all of their education. Many defer pregnancy until they are well into their careers and in their late 20s, their 30s, even their 40s. So it is in our place and time that we have a topic called "Teenage Pregnancy," implying that there might be a problem with it.

Question: In this cultural setting, why do teenage girls become pregnant? There are many, many reasons. For one thing, adolescent girls typically get little advice in school or at home about how to deal with boys' sexual advances. Another reason is failure to use contraception. Some initiate sex at very early ages, when they are least likely to use contraception (Buston et al., 2007). Many adolescent girls, especially younger adolescents, do not have access to contraceptive devices. Among those who do, fewer than half use them reliably (Buston et al., 2007).

Some teenage girls purposefully get pregnant to try to force their partners to make a commitment to them. Some are rebelling against their parents or the moral standards of their communities. But most girls are impregnated because they and their partners do not know as much about reproduction and contraception as they think they do or because they miscalculate the odds of getting pregnant (Buston et al., 2007). Even those who have been to all the sex education classes and who have access to family planning clinics slip up now and then, especially if their partners push them or do not want to use condoms. ● Figure 16.2 shows that the percentage of sexually active high school students who use condoms reliably has been increasing

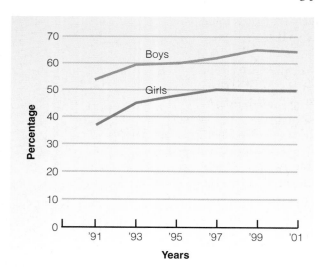

● **Figure 16.2**

Percentage of Sexually Active Students in Grades 9–12 Who Report Using a Condom the Last Time They Had Sexual Intercourse

Sources: Centers for Disease Control and Prevention, the Alan Guttmacher Institute, and the Child Trends Databank, as reported in the *New York Times*, March 7, 2004. Reprinted by permission of the New York Times Co.

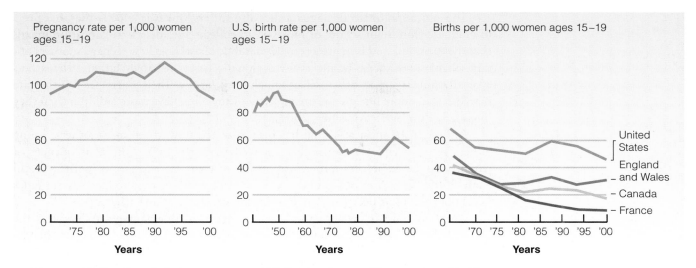

● Figure 16.3 Trends in Pregnancy and Birthrates Among Women, Age 15–19, in the United States and Other Developed Nations

Sources: Centers for Disease Control and Prevention, the Alan Guttmacher Institute, and the Child Trends Databank, as reported in the *New York Times*, March 7, 2004. Reprinted by permission of the New York Times Co.

since the early 1990s, but even so, we seem to be leveling off at an unacceptable 50% for girls and 65% for boys.

Truth or Fiction Revisited: For all these reasons, it is true that about 800,000 teenage girls in the United States are impregnated each year. The pregnancies result in about half a million births (see ● Figure 16.3). However large this number may sound, 10 to 20 years ago, about 1 million girls were getting pregnant each year. The drop-off may reflect findings that sexual activity among teenagers has leveled off (Figure 16.1) and that relatively more adolescents are using contraception consistently (Figure 16.2). Researchers at the Centers for Disease Control and Prevention attribute the drop-off in careless sex to educational efforts by schools, the media, religious institutions, and communities (America's Children, 2007).

Nearly half of pregnant teenagers will get an abortion. Most others will become single mothers. Pregnancy rates are higher among adolescents of lower socioeconomic status and among those from ethnic minority groups (America's Children, 2007). As shown in Figure 16.3, however, the number of births per 1,000 adolescents, age 15–19, remains higher in the United States than in other developed nations.

Consequences of Teenage Pregnancy

Question: What are the consequences of teenage pregnancy? Again, some caveats: The outcome of teenage pregnancies for young women who want their babies and have the resources to nurture them are generally good (Rathus et al., 2008). Females tend to be healthy in late adolescence, and again—historically speaking—people might wonder why we raise this issue at all.

We raise it because the medical, social, and economic costs of *unplanned* or *unwanted* pregnancies among adolescents are enormous both to the mothers and to the children. The problems begin with the pregnancy itself. Adolescent mothers are more likely to experience medical complications during the months of pregnancy and their labor is likely to be prolonged. The babies are at greater risk of being premature and of low birth weight (Mathews & MacDorman, 2007). These medical problems are not necessarily because of the age of the mother but rather because teenage mothers—especially those who dwell at the lower end of the socioeconomic spectrum—are less likely to have access to prenatal care or to obtain adequate nutrition.

The education of the teenage mother also suffers. She is less likely than her peers to graduate from high school or move on to college. Her deficit in education means that she earns less and is in greater need of public assistance. Few teenage mothers obtain reliable assistance—financial or emotional—from the babies' fathers. The fathers typically cannot support themselves, much less a family. Their marriages—if they are married—are more likely to be unstable, and they often have more children than they intended (Bunting & McAuley, 2004).

Although the most attention has been directed toward teenage mothers, young fathers bear an equal responsibility for teenage pregnancies. The consequences of parenthood for adolescent fathers are similar to those for adolescent mothers (Kalil et al., 2005; Quinlivan & Condon, 2005). Teenage fathers tend to have lower grades in school than their peers, and they enter the workforce at an earlier age.

Children born to teenage mothers also are at a disadvantage. As early as the pre-school years, they show lower levels of cognitive functioning and more behav-

A Closer Look

What Parents Want from Sex Education Courses

Not so many years ago, clashes over sex education focused on parents who were concerned that schools were teaching about sex at all. However, a survey conducted by NPR/Kaiser/Harvard (2004) found that the overwhelming majority of parents now want schools to provide sex education. ■ Table 16.1 shows that parents almost universally want their children to be taught about sexually transmitted infections and how to talk to their parents about sex. Most parents would also like their children to be encouraged to wait to have sex until they are older. And a majority want discussions to cover avoiding pregnancy, abortion, even sexual orientation. Smaller majorities—but majorities nonetheless—think that school discussions of oral sex and of how to get birth control pills without parental permission are appropriate topics. The conflicts that remain are likely to break out in the latter areas, but apparently not when debating whether to discuss STIs and even the mechanics of reproduction.

Reflect: What is your view concerning covering each of the following subjects in high school sex education programs? Explain.

• Abortion methods
• How to obtain methods of contraception without parental permission
• How to use condoms

What Parents Want in Sex Education Courses
American parents overwhelmingly favor sex education. Nearly all want these courses to educate about sexually transmitted infections, and majorities want the courses to cover abortion and sexual orientation. However, there are concerns about how these topics are covered.

ioral and emotional problems. Boys appear to be more affected than girls. By adolescence, offspring of teenage mothers are doing more poorly in school, and they are more likely to become teenage parents themselves (Coley & Chase-Lansdale, 1998). Again, these problems seem to result not from the mother's age but from the socially and economically deprived environments in which teen mothers and their children often live.

Preventing Teenage Pregnancy

The past several decades have seen a dramatic increase in programs to help prevent teenage pregnancies. Prevention efforts include educating teenagers about sexuality and contraception and providing contraceptive and family planning services (Santelli

■ Table 16.1 Sex Education in America: What to Teach About Sex

Topic	TOTAL APPROPRIATE	Middle School	High School	Both	NOT APPROPRIATE
STIs other than HIV/AIDS	99	9	15	75	1
HIV/AIDS	98	9	11	78	1
How to talk with parents about sex	97	12	8	77	2
Basics of how babies are made	96	14	13	69	3
Waiting to have intercourse until older	95	10	12	73	4
How to get tested for HIV and other STIs	94	5	33	56	4
Birth control	94	8	29	57	5
How to deal with the emotional issues and consequences of being sexually active	94	7	23	64	5
Waiting to have sexual Intercourse until married	93	8	13	72	7
How to talk with a girlfriend/boyfriend about "how far to go" sexually	92	6	23	63	6
How to make responsible sexual choices based on individual values	91	9	21	61	8
How to use and where to get contraceptives	86	5	37	44	12
Abortion	85	5	30	50	13
How to put on a condom	83	5	38	40	15
Masturbation	77	8	22	47	19
Homosexuality and sexual orientation	73	5	24	44	25
Oral sex	72	4	29	39	27
That teens can obtain birth control pills from family planning clinics and doctors without permission from a parent	71	3	40	28	28

Note: Don't know/refused responses are not shown.

et al., 2003). An overwhelming majority of American parents want their children to have sex education in the public schools. The nearby "A Closer Look" feature specifies what parents would like to see covered in sex education.

How successful are sex education programs? The better programs increase students' knowledge about sexuality. Despite fears that sex education will increase sexual activity in teenagers, some programs seem to delay the onset of sexual activity (Bennett & Assefi, 2005; Santelli et al., 2003). Among teenagers who already are sexually active, sex education is associated with the increased use of effective contraception.

School-based clinics that distribute contraceptives and contraceptive information to students have been established in some school districts, and not without controversy. In high schools that have such clinics, birthrates often drop significantly (Blake et al., 2003). Whether or not school-based programs distribute contraceptives or contraceptive information, a federally funded multiyear study by the nonpartisan Mathematica Policy Research corporation of Princeton, New Jersey, found that abstinence-only programs have no effect on teenage pregnancy rates (Trenholm et al., 2007). Put it this way: Abstinence works. However, teaching nothing but abstinence in sex education has been shown to be useless (Trenholm et al., 2007).

Active Review

9. _____ is the most common sexual outlet in adolescents.
10. A _____ orientation is defined as being attracted to and interested in forming romantic relationships with people of one's own sex.
11. It is believed that prenatal exposure to sex _____ may play a key role in sexual orientation.
12. Teenagers who have close relationships with their parents are (More or Less?) likely to initiate sexual activity at an early age.
13. The top reason usually given by adolescents for why they did not wait to have sexual intercourse is _____ pressure.

Reflect & Relate: How important a part of your adolescence (or that of your peers) was sexuality? Did any of your peers experience problems related to their sexuality during adolescence? Did they resolve these problems? If so, how?

Go to

http://www.psychology.thomson.com/rathus

for an interactive version of this review.

Juvenile Delinquency

Did you ever commit a delinquent act in your teen years? If you said yes, then you are like most adolescents. The great majority of adolescents have done something against the law, whether it is underage smoking, drinking, or something like petty theft. **Truth or Fiction Revisited:** Therefore, it is not true that only a minority of American adolescents engage in delinquent behavior.

Question: What is juvenile delinquency? The term **juvenile delinquency**, however, tends to be used more specifically in reference to children or adolescents who engage in illegal activities and come into contact with the criminal justice system (Bishop, 2005; Snyder & Sickmund, 2006). At the most extreme end, juvenile

juvenile delinquency Conduct in a child or adolescent characterized by illegal activities.

delinquency includes serious behaviors such as homicide, rape, and robbery, which are considered criminal acts at any age. Less serious offenses, such as truancy, underage drinking, running away from home, and sexual promiscuity, are considered illegal only when performed by minors. Hence, these activities are termed **status offenses**.

Antisocial and criminal behaviors show a dramatic increase in many societies during adolescence and then taper off during adulthood. For example, about four in ten serious crimes in the United States are committed by individuals under the age of 21, and about three in ten are committed by adolescents under the age of 18 (Snyder & Sickmund, 2006).

Many delinquent acts do not result in arrest or conviction. And when adolescents are arrested, their cases may be disposed of informally, such as by referral to a mental health agency, without the juvenile's being formally declared delinquent in a juvenile court (Snyder & Sickmund, 2006).

Juvenile Delinquency
Most adolescents have engaged in some sort of illegal behavior, but most are not "processed" by the juvenile justice system.

Ethnicity, Sex, and Juvenile Delinquency

African American adolescents are more likely to be arrested than European American adolescents. For example, African American youths constitute about 13% of the adolescent population in the United States but about one-fourth of the juvenile arrests and about one-half of those arrested for violent crimes (Snyder & Sickmund, 2006). ● Figure 16.4 shows that in the year 2002, the delinquency case rate for African American youngsters was 94 per 1,000, or more than twice as many as for European American youngsters (44 per 1,000).

In an article titled "The Role of Race and Ethnicity in Juvenile Justice Processing," criminologist Donna Bishop (2005) notes that there are a couple of possible explanations for the European American–African American difference. The *differential offending hypothesis* suggests that there are actual racial differences in the incidence and seriousness of delinquent behavior. The *differential treatment hypothesis* suggests that African American and European American youth probably do not behave all that differently, but are treated differently—intentionally or accidentally—by the juvenile justice system. In other words, "the system" expects worse behavior from African American youngsters, so it polices them more actively and cracks down on them more harshly. One result of differential treatment is that African American adolescents are likely to have much more interaction with the juvenile justice system and thus more likely to come to develop the self-concept of being offenders or criminals— outside the system, outside the mainstream.

Economic and family factors are also connected with racial and ethnic differences in juvenile offending. As you see in ● Figure 16.5, African American (and Latino and Latina American) children and adolescents are three times as likely as European American youth to be living in poverty (Snyder & Sickmund, 2006). Moreover, as you see in ● Figure 16.6, African American children are less likely than European American (or Latino and Latina American) children to be living with both of their

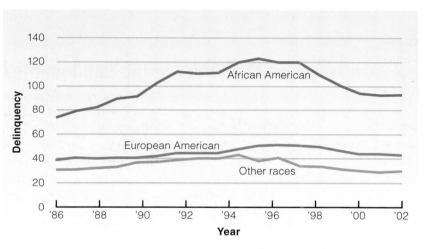

● **Figure 16.4**
The Delinquency Case Rate per 1,000 Juveniles

status offenses Offenses considered illegal only when performed by minors, such as truancy and underage drinking.

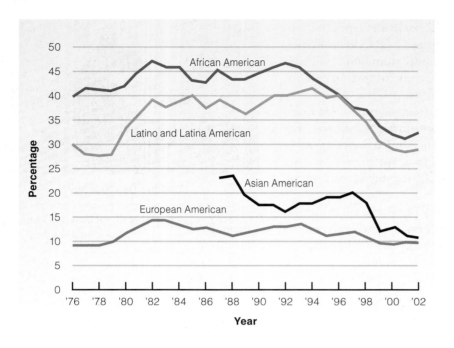

biological parents, regardless of whether or not their parents are married (Snyder & Sickmund, 2006). In other words, biological parents who are living together without being married are included in the 38%. We cannot say that poverty *causes* delinquency or that a broken family *causes* delinquency, but, statistically speaking, poverty and broken families appear to be risk factors.

Question: What are the sex differences in delinquent behavior? Boys are much more likely than girls to engage in delinquent behavior, especially in crimes of violence (see ■ Table 16.2). On the other hand, girls are more likely to commit status offenses such as truancy or running away (not shown in the table; Snyder & Sickmund, 2006).

● **Figure 16.5**
Percentage of Americans under the Age of 18 Who Are Living in Poverty

In 2002, Black juveniles and Hispanic juveniles were more than three times as likely to live in poverty as non-Hispanic white juveniles.

Who Are the Delinquents? What Are They Like?

Question: Who is most likely to engage in delinquent behavior? Many risk factors are associated with juvenile delinquency, but the direction and timing of these factors is not always clear-cut. For example, poor school performance is related to delinquency (Vermeiren et al., 2004). But does school failure lead to delinquency, or is delinquency the cause of the school failure?

Even if the causal paths are less than clear, a number of factors are associated with delinquency. Children who show aggressive, antisocial, and hyperactive behavior at an early age are more likely to show delinquent behavior in adolescence (Baron et al., 2007; Pardini et al., 2006). Delinquency also is associated with having a lower verbal IQ, immature moral reasoning, low self-esteem, feelings of alienation, and impulsivity (Lynam et al., 2007). Other personal factors include little interest in school, early substance abuse, early sexuality, and delinquent friends (Ruchkin & Vermeiren, 2006). On a cognitive level, aggressive delinquents tend to approve of violence as a way of dealing with social provocations and to misinterpret other people's intentions as hostile when they are not (Calvete, 2007).

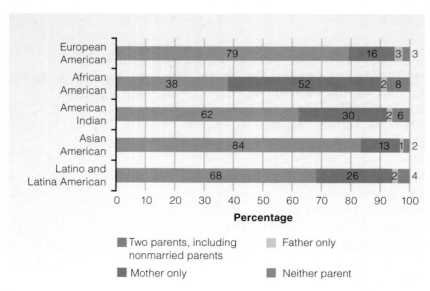

● **Figure 16.6**
Living Arrangements of Children According to Race and Ethnicity

Source: Snyder & Sickmund (2006, p. 11).

Family factors also are powerful predictors of delinquent behavior. The families of juvenile delinquents often are characterized by lax and ineffective discipline, low levels of affection, and high levels of family conflict, physical abuse, severe parental punishment, and neglect (Snyder & Sickmund, 2006; Vermeiren et al., 2004). The parents and siblings of juvenile delinquents frequently have engaged in antisocial, deviant, or criminal behavior themselves (Snyder & Sickmund, 2006). Delinquents are also more likely to live in neighborhoods in which they themselves are likely to have been victimized, giving rise to the belief that crime is "normal" in a statistical sense, and giving rise to feelings of anger (Hay & Evans, 2006). Moreover, when youth in such situations are tempted by opportunities to victimize others they are unlikely to be restrained by considerations such as what a criminal record might do to their chances of being admitted to Yale and to their career aspirations of becoming physicians or attorneys (Baron et al., 2007; Ratcliffe, 2006). These constraints are as unlikely to enter their minds as the realities are to enter their lives.

Prenatal smoking (by the mother!) is another interesting risk factor for juvenile delinquency. Lauren Wakschlag and her colleagues (2006) compared boys in the Pittsburgh Youth Study whose mothers smoked when they were in utero with boys whose mothers had not smoked. The sons of the smokers were significantly more likely to develop a combination of conduct disorder and attention deficit/hyperactivity disorder (ADHD) in early grades and to have an earlier onset of delinquent behavior when compared with the other boys. The authors admit that they cannot precisely define the role of prenatal smoking in children's behavioral problems, but it seems to be another risk factor or marker.

Prevention and Treatment of Juvenile Delinquency

Many approaches have been tried to prevent delinquent behavior or to deal with it early. One type of approach focuses on the individual adolescent offender. Such programs may provide training in moral reasoning, social skills, problem-solving skills, or a combination of these skills. These programs focus on individual offenders rather than on the larger social systems in which juvenile delinquents are embedded, and results are mixed at best (A. Roberts, 2007; Webb, 2007). Moreover, delinquents are individuals with individual problems and situations, and it is not possible to meaningfully generalize to the effects of a treatment method on delinquency per se (Zonnevylle-Bender et al., 2007). Also, delinquency is crime, not illness. Therefore, the concept of treatment may very well be misplaced.

Another approach tries to deal with various social systems, such as the family, peer groups, school, or community (Aber et al., 2007; A. Roberts, 2007). Examples of such interventions are family therapy approaches; school-based strategies involving teams of students, parents, teachers, and staff; and various community- and neighborhood-based programs. These broader multisystem approaches appear to be more successful in reducing problem behaviors and improving family relations of delinquent adolescents (Welsh & Farrington, 2007a, 2007b).

One other promising approach starts with the very young child and is aimed at promoting a host of positive child outcomes, not just delinquency prevention. This approach consists of the early childhood intervention programs, such as Head Start. The preschoolers who participated in several of these programs have been tracked longitudinally through adolescence. These follow-ups show several encouraging outcomes, including reductions in aggressive and delinquent behavior (Aber et al., 2007).

■ **Table 16.2** Proportion of Juvenile Offenses Committed by Females

Offense	Female Proportion (Percent)
Crimes Against People	28%
Homicide	13
Forcible rape	3
Robbery	9
Assault	26–32
Crimes Against Property	26
Burglary	10
Larceny–theft	38
Motor vehicle theft	23
Arson	13
Vandalism	16
Trespassing	19
Drug law violation	18
Public order offense	28
Obstruction of justice	29
Disorderly conduct	33
Weapons offense	14
Liquor law violation	32
Nonviolent sex offense	19
TOTAL DELINQUENCY	26%

Source: Adapted from Snyder & Sickmund (2006, p. 160).

Active Review

14. Offenses that are illegal only when performed by minors are called _____ offenses.
15. Boys are (More or Less?) likely than girls to engage in most delinquent behaviors.
16. Children who show aggressive, antisocial, and hyperactive behavior at an early age are (More or Less?) likely to show delinquent behavior in adolescence.

Reflect & Relate: Were there any juvenile delinquents in your high school? What behavior patterns led to the label? What happened to them? Do you know what they are doing now?

Go to

http://www.psychology.thomson.com/rathus

for an interactive version of this review.

Suicide: When the Adolescent Has Nothing—Except Everything—to Lose

Adolescence is such an exciting time of life. For many, the future is filled with promise. Many count the days until they graduate high school, until they enter college. Many enjoy thrilling fantasies of what might be.

And then there are those who take their own lives. **_Questions: How many adolescents commit suicide? Why do they do so?_** **Truth or Fiction Revisited:** Suicide is the third leading cause of death among adolescents (National Center for Injury Prevention and Control, 2007). Since 1960, the suicide rate has more than tripled for young people, age 15 to 24. About 1 to 2 American adolescents in 10,000 commit suicide each year. About 1 in 10 has attempted suicide at least once. What prompts young people to take their own lives? Who is most at risk?

Risk Factors for Suicide

Most suicides among adolescents and adults are linked to feelings of depression and hopelessness (Cheng & Chan, 2007; National Center for Injury Prevention and Control, 2007; Wong et al., 2007). Jill Rathus—who has presented me with grandchildren and research articles—and her colleagues (Miller, Rathus, & Linehan, 2007; Rathus & Miller, 2002) have found that suicidal adolescents experience four areas of psychological problems: (1) confusion about the self, (2) impulsiveness, (3) emotional instability, and (4) interpersonal problems. Some suicidal teenagers are highly achieving, rigid perfectionists who have set impossibly high expectations for themselves (Miller et al., 2000; Wu et al., 2001). Many teenagers throw themselves into feelings of depression and hopelessness by comparing themselves negatively with others, even when the comparisons are inappropriate. ("Yes, you didn't get into Harvard, but you did get into the University of California at Irvine, and it's a great school.")

Adolescent suicide attempts are more common after stressful life events, especially events that entail loss of social support, as in the death of a parent or friend, breaking up with a boyfriend or girlfriend, or a family member leaving home (Cooper et al., 2002). Other contributors to suicidal behavior include concerns over sexuality, pressures to achieve in school, problems at home, and substance abuse (Conner & Goldston, 2007; Cuellar & Curry, 2007). It is not always a stressful event itself that precipitates suicide but the adolescent's anxiety or fear of being "found out" for something, such as failing a course or getting arrested (Cooper et al., 2002). Young people contemplating suicide are less likely to find productive ways of changing the stressful situation.

Suicide tends to run in families (National Center for Injury Prevention and Control, 2007). Many suicide attempters have family members with serious psychological problems, and many have family members who have taken their lives. How do we account for the correlation? Do genetic factors play a role, possibly leading to psychological disorders, such as depression, that are connected with suicide? Could it be that a socially impoverished family environment infuses several family members with feelings of hopelessness? Or does the suicide of one family member simply give others the idea that suicide is the way in which one manages problems? Perhaps these possibilities and others—such as poor problem-solving ability—form a complex web of contributing factors.

- Belief that it is acceptable to kill oneself (Joe et al., 2007)
- Drug abuse and other kinds of delinquency (Cuellar & Curry, 2007; Garlow et al., 2007; Thompson et al., 2007)
- Victimization by bullying (Klomek et al., 2007)
- Extensive body piercing (Suris et al., 2007)
- Stress (Cheng & Chan, 2007)
- Hostility (Dervic et al., 2007)
- Depression and other psychological disorders (Klomek et al., 2007; Libal, 2007; Smarty & Findling, 2007)
- Heavy smoking (Riala et al., 2007)
- Low self-esteem (Wong et al., 2007)
- Increasing age from 11 to 21 (Conner & Goldston, 2007)

Ethnicity, Sex, and Suicide

Rates of suicide and suicide attempts vary among different ethnic groups. Native American and Latino and Latina teenagers have the highest suicide rates, in part because of the stresses to which they are exposed, in part because of their lack of access to health care (Duarté-Vélez & Bernal, 2007; Freedenthal, 2007; National Center for Injury Prevention and Control, 2007). European Americans are next. African American teens are least likely to attempt suicide or to think about it. However, African American adolescents are only 65% as likely as European American adolescents to contact health professionals when they are considering suicide (Freedenthal, 2007).

About three times as many adolescent females as males attempt suicide, but about four times as many males complete a suicide (National Center for Injury Prevention and Control, 2007). Males are apparently more likely to "succeed" at suicide—if this can be called "success"—because of the methods they choose. Males are more likely to use more rapid and lethal methods such as shooting themselves, whereas females are more likely to overdose on drugs like tranquilizers or sleeping pills (National Center for Injury Prevention & Control, 2007). Females often do not take enough of these chemicals to kill themselves. It also takes time for them to work, providing an opportunity for other people to intervene before they die.

The nearby "A Closer Look" feature describes some of the warning signs of suicide and some things you can do if you notice them in a friend or family member.

A CLOSER LOOK

Warning Signs of Suicide

Most young people who commit suicide send out signals about their intentions (National Center for Injury Prevention and Control, 2007). Sad to say, these signals often are overlooked or unrecognized. Sometime adolescents do not receive help until they attempt suicide, and sometimes not even then. Here are some clues that a teenager may be at risk:

- Changes in eating and sleeping patterns
- Difficulty concentrating on schoolwork with a decline in grades and attendance
- Loss of interest in previously enjoyed activities and relationships
- Giving away prized possessions
- Complaints about physical problems when no medical basis can be found
- Personality or mood changes
- Talking or writing about death or dying
- Abuse of drugs or alcohol
- Availability of a handgun
- A precipitating event such as an argument with parents, a broken romantic relationship, academic difficulties, loss of a friend, or trouble with the law
- Knowing or hearing about another teenager who has committed suicide
- Threatening or attempting to commit suicide

Here are some things you can do if you notice one or more of these warning signs (Buda, 2007; Crawford et al., 2007; Lewis, 2007; Rodgers et al., 2007):

- Make an appointment for the adolescent with a helping professional, or suggest that the adolescent go with you right now to get professional help.
- Draw the adolescent out. Ask questions such as "What's going on?" "Where do you hurt?" and "What would you like to see happen?" Such questions may encourage the expression of frustrated needs and provide some relief.
- Be empathetic. Show that you understand how upset the adolescent is.
- Suggest that actions other than suicide might solve the problem, even if they are not apparent at the time.
- Ask how the adolescent intends to commit suicide. Adolescents with concrete plans and an available weapon

Adolescents May Have "So Much to Live for," But . . .
Suicide is a key cause of death for adolescents. When adolescents experience conflicts and dips in self-esteem, when they have failed at something, when they fear they will be found out for something, their thoughts may turn to suicide. How can you determine whether an adolescent is considering suicide? What can you do about it?

are at greater risk. Ask if you might hold on to the weapon for a while. Sometimes the adolescent says yes.
- Extract a promise that the adolescent will not commit suicide before seeing you again. Arrange a concrete time and place to meet. Get professional help as soon as you are apart.

Reflect:

- Would you feel flustered or resentful if an adolescent told you that he or she is thinking about committing suicide? (Many people do.) Explain.
- Do you know anybody right now who is thinking about committing suicide? Do you think you should do anything about it? Explain.
- Do you think people have the right to commit suicide? Why or why not?

Active Review

17. Suicide is a (Rare or Common?) cause of death among older teenagers.
18. Most suicides among adolescents and adults are linked to feelings of _____.
19. Suicide (Does or Does not?) tend to run in families.

Reflect & Relate: Do you know anyone who has committed suicide or thought about committing suicide? What pressures or disappointments was the person experiencing at the time? Did anybody intervene? How?

Go to

http://www.psychology.thomson.com/rathus

for an interactive version of this review.

Epilogue: Emerging Adulthood—Bridging Adolescence and the Life Beyond

When our mothers were our age, they were engaged. They at least had some idea what they were going to do with their lives. I, on the other hand, will have a dual degree in majors that are ambiguous at best and impractical at worst (English and political science), no ring on my finger and no idea who I am, much less what I want to do. Under duress, I will admit that this is a pretty exciting time. Sometimes, when I look out across the wide expanse that is my future, I can see beyond the void. I realize that having nothing ahead to count on means I now have to count on myself; that having no direction means forging one of my own.

—Kristen, age 22 (Page, 1999, pp. 18, 20)

Well, Kristen has some work to do: She needs to forge her own direction. Just think: What if Kristen had been born into the caste system of old England or India, into a traditional Islamic society, or into the United States of the 1950s, where the TV sitcom *Father Knows Best* was perennially in the top 10? Kristen would have had a sense of direction, that's certain. But, of course, it would have been the sense of direction society or tradition created for her, not her own.

But Kristen was not born into any of these societies. She was born into the open and challenging United States of the current generation. She has the freedom to become whatever the interaction of her genetic heritage and her educational and social opportunities will enable her to become, and the opportunities are many. With freedom comes the need to make choices. When we need to make choices, we profit from information. Kristen is in the process of accumulating information about herself and about the world outside. According to psychologist Jeffrey Arnett (2007), she is in *emerging adulthood*. In earlier days, adolescents made a transition, for better or worse, directly into adulthood. Now many of them—especially those in affluent nations with abundant opportunities—spend time in what some theorists think of as a new period of development roughly spanning the ages of 18 to 25.

"Emerging Adulthood": A New Stage of Development in Developed Nations

Some researchers suggest that affluent societies like ours have spawned a new stage of development, emerging adulthood, which involves an extended period of self-exploration, during which one remains financially dependent.

© Tom Stewart/CORBIS

Question: How do we define adulthood? There's a question. Legally, adulthood has many ages, depending on what you want to do. The age of consent to marry varies from state to state, but in general, marriage is permitted in the teens. The age for drinking legally is 21. The age for driving varies. By and large, however, adulthood is usually defined in terms of what people do rather than how old they are. **Truth or Fiction Revisited:** Adolescents do not necessarily reach adulthood at age 21. Over the years, marriage has been a key criterion for people who write about human development (Carroll et al., 2007). Other criteria include holding a full-time job and living independently (not with one's parents). Today, the transition to adulthood is mainly marked by adjustment issues, such as deciding on ones values and beliefs, accepting self-responsibility, becoming financially independent, and establishing an equal relationship with one's parents (Arnett, 2007; Gottlieb et al., 2007). Marriage is no longer necessarily a crucial marker for entering adulthood (Gottlieb et al., 2007).

Adulthood itself has been divided into stages, and the first of these, young adulthood, has been largely seen as the period of life when people focus on establishing their careers or pathways in life. It has been acknowledged that the transition to adulthood could be slow or piecemeal, with many individuals in their late teens and early 20s remaining dependent on their parents and reluctant or unable to make enduring commitments, in terms of either identity formation or the development of intimate relationships. The question is whether we can speak of the existence of another stage of development, one that bridges adolescence and young adulthood. A number of developmental theorists, including Arnett (2007), believe that we can. ***Question: What is "emerging adulthood"?***

Emerging adulthood is theorized to be a distinct period of development that is found in societies that allow young people an extended opportunity to explore their roles in life. They tend to be affluent societies, such as those found in developed nations, our own among them. Parents in the United States are often affluent enough to continue to support their children throughout college and in graduate school. When parents cannot do the job, the government often steps in to help, for example, through student loans. These supports allow young people the luxury of sorting out identity issues and creating meaningful life plans, even if some still do not know where they are going after they graduate from college. Should they know who they are and what they are doing by the age of 21 or 22? Are they spoiled? The answers are value judgments that may or may not be on the mark. But let us note that many adults change their careers several times, partly because they did not sort out who they were and where they were going at an early age. On the other hand, even in the United States, many people cannot obtain the supports necessary for sojourning in emerging adulthood.

Arnett (2007) summarizes the kinds of social and technological influences that have spurred the rise of emerging adulthood:

- The changes from a manufacturing-based economy to an information-based economy increased the need for advanced education and training.
- The advent of the birth control pill made it possible for late adolescents to become sexually active without becoming pregnant.
- Increased social acceptance of premarital sex and cohabitation weakened the traditional connection between marriage and the onset of sexual activity; therefore, the median ages of beginning marriage and parenthood rose into the middle to late 20s.
- The period of life from the late teens through the mid-20s became, for many in the developed world, a period of advanced self-development and of gradually laying a foundation for "adulthood."

Erik Erikson (1968) did not use the term *emerging adulthood*, but he did recognize that developed nations tend to elongate the period of adolescence. Erikson used the term *moratorium* to describe the extended quest for identity among people who dwell in adolescence. Erikson and other theorists also believed that it was more meaningful for the individual to take the voyage to identity rather than foreclose it by adopting the viewpoints of other people. Although there are pluses to taking time to formulate one's identity, there are downsides. For example, remaining dependent on parents can compromise an individual's self-esteem. Taking out loans for graduate school means that there is more to pay back; many individuals mortgage their own lives as they invest in their futures. Women who focus on their educations and their careers may marry later and bear children later. Although many people appreciate children more when they bear them later in life, they also become less fertile as the years wend their ways, and they may find themselves in a race with their "biological clock."

Young people in the United States seem to be generally aware of the issues involved in defining the transition from adolescence to adulthood. Arnett (2000) reported what individuals in their late teens and early 20s say when they are asked whether they think they have become adults. About three in five say something like, "In some respects yes and in other respects no." Many think that they have developed beyond the conflicts and exploratory voyages of adolescence, but they may have not yet obtained the ability to assume the financial and interpersonal responsibilities they associate with adulthood.

And then, of course, there are those who remain adolescents forever.

Active Review

20. Historically speaking, _____ has been an important standard in determining whether or not one has reached adulthood.

21. Today, the criteria of holding a full-time _____ and a residence separate from one's parents are also applied.

22. _____ adulthood is a hypothesized period of development that spans the ages of 18 through 25 and exists in societies that permit young people extended periods of independent role exploration.

Reflect & Relate: Do you see yourself as an adolescent, an emerging adult, or an adult? What standards are you using in defining yourself?

Go to

http://www.psychology.thomson.com/rathus

for an interactive version of this review.

RECITE: *An Active Summary*

1. What does Erikson have to say about the development of identity during adolescence?

Erikson's adolescent stage of psychosocial development is identity versus identity diffusion. The primary task of this stage is for adolescents to develop a sense of who they are and what they stand for.

2. What are Marcia's "identity statuses"?

The identity statuses represent the four combinations of the dimensions of exploration and commitment: identity diffusion, foreclosure, moratorium, and identity achievement.

3. What are the connections between ethnicity and other sociocultural factors—such as sex—and identity?

Development of identity is more complicated for adolescents who belong to ethnic minority groups. Youth from minority groups are faced with two sets of cultural values and may need to reconcile and incorporate elements of both.

4. Are there stages in developing an ethnic identity—that is, a sense of belonging to an ethnic group?

Researchers propose a three-stage model of the development of ethnic identity: unexamined ethnic identity, an ethnic identity search, and an achieved ethnic identity. As minority youth move through adolescence, they are increasingly likely to explore and achieve ethnic identity.

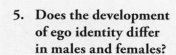

5. Does the development of ego identity differ in males and females?	Erikson proposed that interpersonal relationships are more important to women's identity than occupational and ideological issues, bur research suggests that U.S. adolescent females and males are equally concerned about careers.
6. How does the self-concept develop during adolescence?	Adolescents incorporate psychological traits and social relationships into their self-descriptions.
7. What happens to self-esteem during adolescence?	Self-esteem tends to decline as the child progresses from middle childhood into early adolescence, perhaps because of increasing recognition of the disparity between the ideal self and the real self. Then self-esteem gradually improves.
8. Are there ethnic differences in the development of self-esteem during adolescence?	Minority youth often suffer prejudice and discrimination, and one might therefore expect that their self-esteem might be diminished. However, research shows that the self-concepts and self-esteem of minority youth are as positive as or more positive than those of European American youth.
9. Are there sex differences in self-esteem during adolescence?	As a group, adolescent girls show lower self-esteem than boys. One reason for the sex difference may involve the physical changes of adolescence, which are related to physical appearance, a factor that is relatively more important for girls. Another factor may be sexism—that is, the negative messages that many girls receive in school.
10. How do relationships with one's parents and peers change during the course of the teenage years?	During adolescence, children spend much less time with parents than during childhood. Although adolescents become more independent of their parents, they generally continue to love and respect them. The role of peers increases markedly during the teen years. Adolescents are more likely than younger children to stress intimate self-disclosure and mutual understanding in friendships.
11. What kinds of adolescent peer groups are there?	The two major types of peer groups are cliques and crowds. Adolescent peer groups also include peers of the other sex.
12. When do romantic relationships develop?	Romantic relationships begin to appear during early and middle adolescence. Dating is a source of fun, it enhances prestige, and it provides experience in relationships. Dating is also a preparation for adult courtship.
13. What are some patterns of sexual behavior in adolescence?	Masturbation is the most common sexual outlet in adolescents. Some adolescents have a homosexual orientation. The process of "coming out" may be a long and painful struggle.
14. What do we know about the origins of gay male and lesbian sexual orientations?	From a learning theory point of view, early reinforcement of sexual behavior influences sexual orientation. Researchers have found evidence for genetic and hormonal factors in sexual orientation.
15. Why do some teenagers initiate sexual activity at an early age, whereas others wait until later?	Early onset of puberty is connected with earlier sexual activity. Adolescents who have close relationships with parents are less likely to initiate sexual activity early. Peer pressure is a powerful contributor to sexual activity.

16.	**In this cultural setting, why do teenage girls become pregnant?**	Many girls who become pregnant receive little advice about how to resist sexual advances. Most of them do not have access to contraception. Most misunderstand reproduction or miscalculate the odds of conception.
17.	**What are the consequences of teenage pregnancy?**	Teenage mothers are more likely to have medical complications during pregnancy and birth, largely because of inadequate medical care. The babies are more likely to be premature and to have low birth weight. Teenage mothers have a lower standard of living and a greater need for public assistance. Their children have more academic and emotional problems.
18.	**What is juvenile delinquency?**	Juvenile delinquency refers to illegal activities committed by a child or adolescent. Behaviors, such as drinking, that are considered illegal when performed by minors are called status offenses.
19.	**What are the sex differences in delinquent behavior?**	Boys are more likely than girls to engage in most delinquent behaviors. Boys are more apt to commit crimes of violence, whereas girls are more likely to commit status offenses.
20.	**Who is most likely to engage in delinquent behavior?**	Risk factors associated with juvenile delinquency include poor school performance, delinquent friends, early aggressive or hyperactive behavior, substance abuse, low verbal IQ, low self-esteem, impulsivity, and immature moral reasoning. The parents and siblings of delinquents have frequently engaged in antisocial behavior themselves.
21.	**How many adolescents commit suicide? Why do they do so?**	Suicide is the third or fourth leading cause of death among older teenagers. Most suicides among adolescents and adults are linked to stress, feelings of depression, identity problems, impulsivity, and social problems. Girls are more likely to attempt suicide, whereas boys are more likely to "succeed."
22.	**How do we define *adulthood?***	Historically, marriage has been an important criterion in defining adulthood. Today, the focus is more on holding a full-time occupation and maintaining a separate residence.
23.	**What is "emerging adulthood"?**	Emerging adulthood is a period of development, spanning the ages of 18 to 25, in which young people engage in extended role exploration. Emerging adulthood can occur in affluent societies that grant young people the luxury of developing their identities and their life plans.

Key Terms

ego identity, 547
psychological moratorium, 547
identity crisis, 547
exploration, 547
commitment, 547
identity diffusion, 547
foreclosure, 548

moratorium, 549
identity achievement, 549
ethnic identity, 551
unexamined ethnic identity, 551
ethnic identity search, 551
achieved ethnic identity, 551
self-esteem, 553

clique, 557
crowd, 557
masturbation, 560
homosexual, 560
juvenile delinquency, 568
status offenses, 569

Active Learning Resources

Childhood & Adolescence Book Companion Website
http://www.thomsonedu.com/psychology/rathus

Visit your book companion website where you will find more resources to help you study. There you will find interactive versions of your book features, including the Lessons in Observation video, Active Review sections, and the Truth or Fiction feature. In addition, the companion website contains quizzing, flash cards, and a pronunciation glossary.

 **is an easy-to-use online resource that helps you study in less time to get the grade you want—NOW.**

http://www.thomsonedu.com/login

Need help studying? This site is your one-stop study shop. Take a Pre-Test and ThomsonNOW will generate a Personalized Study Plan based on your test results. The Study Plan will identify the topics you need to review and direct you to online resources to help you master those topics. You can then take a Post-Test to determine the concepts you have mastered and what you still need to work on.

Answers to Active Reviews

Chapter 1
1. Puberty
2. Development
3. Theories
4. Freud
5. Eight
6. Operant
7. Piaget
8. Processing
9. Ecological
10. Sociocultural
11. Nature
12. Discontinuous
13. Hypothesis
14. Naturalistic
15. Case
16. Cause
17. Control
18. Longitudinal
19. Sectional

Chapter 2
1. Chromosomes
2. Deoxyribonucleic
3. Mitosis
4. Meiosis
5. Monozygotic, identical
6. Dizygotic, fraternal
7. Carriers
8. Down syndrome
9. Recessive
10. Sickle-cell
11. Amniocentesis
12. Ultrasound
13. Genotype
14. Phenotype
15. 50
16. Monozygotic, identical
17. Dizygotic, fraternal
18. Conception, fertilization
19. Fallopian
20. Sperm
21. Ovulate

Chapter 3
1. Blastocyst
2. Trophoblast
3. Implantation
4. Amniotic
5. Proximodistal
6. Outer
7. Females
8. Placenta
9. Umbilical cord
10. Maturation
11. Thirteenth
12. Fourth
13. Neural
14. Teratogens
15. Can
16. Blood
17. Rh
18. DES
19. Marijuana
20. Fetal
21. Oxygen
22. Slow

Chapter 4
1. Braxton-Hicks
2. Amniotic
3. Dilated
4. Transition
5. Umbilical
6. Placenta
7. General
8. Epidural, spinal
9. Lamaze
10. Cesarean section, C-section
11. Oxygen
12. Preterm
13. Birth weight
14. Helpful
15. Majority
16. Estrogen
17. Does not
18. Apgar
19. Rooting
20. Nearsighted
21. Do
22. Smaller
23. Sudden infant death syndrome (SIDS)

Chapter 5
1. Head, brain
2. Proximodistal
3. Five
4. Positive
5. Canalization
6. Antibodies
7. Neurons
8. Axon
9. 70
10. Cerebellum
11. One
12. Ulnar
13. Visual
14. Sit up, crawl
15. Increase
16. Experience, practice, nurture
17. Did not
18. Real
19. Edges
20. Cliff
21. 2–3
22. Greater
23. Capture
24. Nurture

Chapter 6
1. Schemas
2. Assimilate
3. Sensorimotor
4. Circular
5. Secondary
6. Tertiary
7. Permanence
8. Information
9. Memory
10. Deferred
11. Motor
12. Neurological
13. Visual
14. Babbling
15. Referential
16. Overextension
17. Holophrases
18. The same
19. Learning
20. Psycholinguistic
21. Acquisition
22. Left
23. Wernicke's

Chapter 7
1. Attachment
2. Strange situation
3. Insecure
4. Explore
5. Indiscriminate
6. Behavioral, behaviorist, learning
7. Contact
8. Fixed
9. Avoided
10. Withdrawal
11. Neglect
12. Autism, autism spectrum disorders
13. Majority
14. Higher
15. More
16. Excitement
17. Majority
18. Referencing
19. Regulation
20. Concept
21. Temperament
22. Slow
23. 12 to 18

Chapter 8
1. 2 to 3
2. 4 to 6
3. Brain
4. Myelination
5. Cerebellum
6. Right
7. Right
8. Plasticity
9. Girls
10. Boys
11. Decrease
12. Boys
13. Higher
14. Decreases
15. Unintentional injuries, accidents
16. Lead
17. 10
18. Sleep terrors
19. Sleep walking
20. Does
21. Boys
22. Constipation

Chapter 9
1. Symbolic, pretend
2. Operations
3. Egocentric
4. Animistic
5. Transductive
6. Conservation
7. One
8. Scaffolding
9. Responsive
10. Home environment
11. Can
12. Less
13. More

14. False
15. Senses
16. Recognition
17. Autobiographical, episodic
18. Better
19. Positively
20. Rehearsal, rote rehearsal, rote learning
21. Mapping
22. Whole
23. One
24. Contrast
25. Inner

Chapter 10
1. Restrictiveness–permissiveness
2. Inductive
3. Authoritative
4. Authoritarian
5. Firstborn
6. Solitary
7. Associative
8. Same
9. Altruism
10. Reject
11. Testosterone
12. Social cognitive, social learning
13. Disinhibit
14. Categorical
15. Esteem
16. Securely
17. Initiative
18. Safety
19. Girls
20. Roles, role stereotypes
21. Sex
22. Males
23. Fathers
24. Constancy
25. Schema

Chapter 11
1. Steady
2. 2
3. 5 to 7
4. Boys
5. 11
6. 25

7. Do not
8. Does
9. Steady
10. 8 to 10
11. Decreases
12. Boys
13. Girls
14. Unfit
15. Attention-deficit/hyperactivity disorder
16. Boys
17. Does
18. Stimulants
19. Disabilities, disorders
20. Dyslexia
21. Neurological
22. Does

Chapter 12
1. Less
2. Transitivity
3. Inclusion
4. Autonomous
5. The amount of damage done
6. Preconventional
7. Conventional
8. Increases
9. Working, short-term
10. Encode, rehearse
11. Rote
12. Elaborative
13. Metamemory
14. *g*
15. Multiple
16. Mental
17. Verbal
18. Bias
19. 6
20. 10 to 15
21. Divergent
22. Biological, Adoptive
23. Visual
24. Phonetic
25. Can
26. Advantage

Chapter 13
1. Industry
2. Concrete
3. Perspective, viewpoint

4. Decreases
5. Authoritative
6. Less
7. Heterosexual
8. Downward
9. Mothers
10. Boys
11. Lack of supervision
12. Farther away from
13. Mature
14. Later-born
15. Discouraged
16. Low
17. Smaller
18. Self-fulfilling
19. Boys
20. Biological
21. Protect children from
22. Underutilize
23. Anxiety
24. Is not

Chapter 14
1. Stress
2. Feedback
3. Sex
4. Growth
5. Asynchronous
6. Epiphyseal
7. Estrogen
8. Boys
9. Boys
10. Chlamydia
11. Human papillomavirus (HPV or genital warts)
12. Acquired immunodeficiency syndrome, AIDS
13. Minority
14. Male
15. Accidents
16. Anorexia nervosa
17. Purging
18. Do
19. Perfectionism, obsessiveness, depression
20. Abuse

21. Abstinence, withdrawal
22. Alcohol
23. Nicotine
24. Regular

Chapter 15
1. Formal
2. Egocentrism
3. Superior
4. Superior
5. Sex
6. Postconventional
7. Positive
8. More
9. Drop
10. Girls
11. More
12. Boys
13. Realistic, practical, conventional
14. Gender
15. Efficacy
16. Majority

Chapter 16
1. Identity, ego identity
2. Moratorium
3. Achievement
4. Lower
5. Mothers
6. Do
7. Increases
8. Their own
9. Masturbation
10. Homosexual, gay male or lesbian
11. Hormones
12. Less
13. Peer
14. Status
15. More
16. More
17. Common
18. Depression, helplessness, hopelessness
19. Does
20. Marriage
21. Job
22. Emerging

Glossary

abstinence syndrome: A characteristic cluster of symptoms that results from a sudden decrease in the level of usage of a substance.

accommodation: According to Piaget, the modification of existing schemes so as to incorporate new events or knowledge.

achieved ethnic identity: The final stage of ethnic identity development; similar to the identity achievement status.

achievement: That which is attained by one's efforts and presumed to be made possible by one's abilities.

adaptation: According to Piaget, the interaction between the organism and the environment. It consists of two processes: assimilation and accommodation.

adipose tissue: Fat.

adrenaline: A hormone that generally arouses the body, increasing the heart and respiration rates.

allele: A member of a pair of genes.

alpha-fetoprotein (AFP) assay: A blood test that assesses the mother's blood level of alpha-fetoprotein, a substance that is linked with fetal neural tube defects.

ambivalent/resistant attachment: A type of insecure attachment characterized by severe distress at the leave-takings of and ambivalent behavior at reunions with an attachment figure.

American Sign Language (ASL): The communication of meaning through the use of symbols that are formed by moving the hands and arms. The language used by some deaf people.

amniocentesis: (AM-nee-oh-sent-TEE-sis) A procedure for drawing and examining fetal cells sloughed off into amniotic fluid to determine the presence of various disorders.

amniotic fluid: Fluid within the amniotic sac that suspends and protects the fetus.

amniotic sac: The sac containing the fetus.

amplitude: Height. The higher the amplitude of sound waves, the louder they are.

androgens: Male sex hormones (from roots meaning "giving birth to men").

anesthetics: Agents that produce partial or total loss of the sense of pain (from Greek roots meaning "without feeling").

animism: The attribution of life and intentionality to inanimate objects.

anorexia nervosa: An eating disorder characterized by irrational fear of weight gain, distorted body image, and severe weight loss.

anoxia: A condition characterized by lack of oxygen.

Apgar scale: A measure of a newborn's health that assesses appearance, pulse, grimace, activity level, and respiratory effort.

aphasia: A disruption in the ability to understand or produce language.

apnea: (AP-nee-uh) Temporary suspension of breathing (from the Greek *a-*, meaning "without," and *pnoie*, meaning "wind").

appearance–reality distinction: The difference between real events on the one hand and mental events, fantasies, and misleading appearances on the other hand.

artificial insemination: Injection of sperm into the uterus to fertilize an ovum.

artificialism: The belief that environmental features were made by people.

assimilation: According to Piaget, the incorporation of new events or knowledge into existing schemes.

asynchronous growth: Imbalanced growth, such as the growth that occurs during the early part of adolescence and causes many adolescents to appear gawky.

attachment: An affectional bond between individuals characterized by a seeking of closeness or contact and a show of distress upon separation.

attachment-in-the-making phase: The second phase in the development of attachment, occurring at 3 or 4 months of age and characterized by preference for familiar figures.

attention-deficit/hyperactivity disorder (ADHD): A behavior disorder characterized by excessive inattention, impulsiveness, and hyperactivity.

attributional style: The way in which one is disposed toward interpreting outcomes (successes or failures), as in tending to place blame or responsibility on oneself or on external factors.

authoritarian: A child-rearing style in which parents demand submission and obedience from their children but are not very communicative and warm.

authoritative: A child-rearing style in which parents are restrictive and demanding yet communicative and warm.

autism: A developmental disorder characterized by failure to relate to others, communication problems, intolerance of change, and ritualistic behavior.

autism spectrum disorders (ASDs): Developmental disorders—including autism, Asperger's syndrome, Rett's disorder, and childhood disintegrative disorder—that are characterized by impairment in communication skills, social interactions, and repetitive, stereotyped behavior. Also referred to as pervasive developmental disorders.

autobiographical memory: The memory of specific episodes or events.

autonomous morality: The second stage in Piaget's cognitive-developmental theory of moral development. In this stage, children base moral judgments on the intentions of the wrongdoer and on the amount of damage done. Social rules are viewed as agreements that can be changed.

autosome: A member of a pair of chromosomes (with the exception of sex chromosomes).

avoidant attachment: A type of insecure attachment characterized by apparent indifference to the leave-takings of and reunions with an attachment figure.

axon: A long, thin part of a neuron that transmits impulses to other neurons through small branching structures called axon terminals.

babbling: The child's first vocalizations that have the sounds of speech.

Babinski reflex: A reflex in which infants fan their toes when the undersides of their feet are stroked.

bed-wetting: Failure to control the bladder during the night. (Frequently used interchangeably with enuresis, although bed-wetting refers to the behavior itself and enuresis is a diagnostic category, related to the age of the child.)

behavior modification: The systematic application of principles of learning to change problem behaviors or encourage desired behaviors.

behaviorism: John B. Watson's view that a science or theory of development must study observable behavior only and investigate relationships between stimuli and responses.

bilingual: Using or capable of using two languages with nearly equal or equal facility.

blastocyst: A stage within the germinal period of prenatal development in which the zygote has the form of a sphere of cells surrounding a cavity of fluid.

bonding: The process of forming bonds of attachment between parent and child.

Braxton-Hicks contractions: The first, usually painless, contractions of childbirth.

Brazelton Neonatal Behavioral Assessment Scale: A measure of a newborn's motor behavior, response to stress, adaptive behavior, and control over physiological state.

breech presentation: A position in which the fetus enters the birth canal buttocks first.

Broca's aphasia: A form of aphasia caused by damage to Broca's area and characterized by slow, laborious speech.

bulimia nervosa: An eating disorder characterized by cycles of binge eating and vomiting as a means of controlling weight gain.

canalization: The tendency of growth rates to return to genetically determined patterns after undergoing environmentally induced change.

carrier: A person who carries and transmits characteristics but does not exhibit them.

case study: A carefully drawn biography of the life of an individual.

categorical self: Definitions of the self that refer to concrete external traits.

centration: Focusing on one dimension of a situation while ignoring others.

cephalocaudal: From head to tail.

cerebellum: (ser-uh-BEH-lum) The part of the hindbrain involved in muscle coordination and balance.

cerebrum: (seh-REE-brum) The large mass of the forebrain, which consists of two hemispheres.

cesarean section: A method of childbirth in which the neonate is delivered through a surgical incision in the mother's abdomen. (Also spelled Caesarean.)

child: A person undergoing the period of development from infancy through puberty.

chorionic villus sampling: (CORE-ee-AH-nick VILL-us) A method for the prenatal detection of genetic abnormalities that samples the membrane enveloping the amniotic sac and fetus.

chromosomes: Rod-shaped structures composed of genes that are found within the nuclei of cells.

chronological age (CA): A person's age.

chronosystem: The environmental changes that occur over time and have an effect on the child (from the Greek *chronos*, meaning "time").

class inclusion: The principle that one category or class of things can include several subclasses.

classical conditioning: A simple form of learning in which one stimulus comes to bring forth the response usually brought forth by a second stimulus by being paired repeatedly with the second stimulus.

clear-cut-attachment phase: The third phase in the development of attachment, occurring at 6 or 7 months of age and characterized by intensified dependence on the primary caregiver.

clique: A group of five to ten individuals who hang around together and who share activities and confidences.

clitoris: A female sex organ that is highly sensitive to sexual stimulation but not directly involved in reproduction.

cognitive-developmental theory: The stage theory that holds that the child's abilities to mentally represent the world and solve problems unfold as a result of the interaction of experience and the maturation of neurological structures.

cohort effect: Similarities in behavior among a group of peers that stem from the fact that group members are approximately of the same age. (A possible source of misleading information in cross-sectional research.)

collectivist: A person who defines herself or himself in terms of relationships to other people and groups and gives priority to group goals.

commitment: A stable investment in one's goals, values, or beliefs.

conception: The union of a sperm cell and an ovum that occurs when the chromosomes of each of these cells combine to form 23 new pairs.

concrete operations: The third stage in Piaget's scheme, characterized by flexible, reversible thought concerning tangible objects and events.

conditioned response (CR): A learned response to a previously neutral stimulus.

conditioned stimulus (CS): A previously neutral stimulus that elicits a response because it has been paired repeatedly with a stimulus that already elicited that response.

conduct disorders: Disorders marked by persistent breaking of the rules and violations of the rights of others.

cones: In the eye, cone-shaped receptors of light that transmit sensations of color.

congenital: Present at birth; resulting from the prenatal environment.

conservation: In cognitive psychology, the principle that properties of substances such as weight and mass remain the same (are conserved) when superficial characteristics such as their shapes or arrangement are changed.

contact comfort: The pleasure derived from physical contact with another; a hypothesized need or drive for physical contact with another.

contrast assumption: The assumption that objects have only one label. Also known as the mutual exclusivity assumption (if a word means one thing, it cannot mean another).

control group: A group made up of subjects in an experiment who do not receive the treatment but for whom all other conditions are comparable to those of subjects in the experimental group.

conventional level: According to Kohlberg, a period during which moral judgments largely reflect social rules and conventions.

convergence: The inward movement of the eyes as they focus on an object that is drawing nearer.

convergent thinking: A thought process that attempts to focus in on the single best solution to a problem.

cooing: Prelinguistic, articulated vowel-like sounds that appear to reflect feelings of positive excitement.

coregulation: A gradual transferring of control from parent to child, beginning in middle childhood.

corpus callosum: The thick bundle of nerve fibers that connects the left and right hemispheres of the brain.

correlation coefficient: A number ranging from $+1.00$ to -1.00 that expresses the direction (positive or negative) and strength of the relationship between two variables.

creativity: The ability to generate novel solutions to problems. A trait characterized by flexibility, ingenuity, and originality.

critical period: A period of development during which a releasing stimulus can elicit a fixed action pattern (FAP). In other usage, a period during which an embryo is particularly vulnerable to a certain teratogen.

cross-sectional research: The study of developmental processes by taking measures of children of different age groups at the same time.

cross-sequential research: An approach that combines the longitudinal and cross-sectional methods by following individuals of different ages for abbreviated periods of time.

crowd: A large, loosely organized group of people who may or may not spend much time together and who are identified by the activities of the group.

cultural bias: A factor hypothesized to be present in intelligence tests that provides an advantage for test takers from certain cultural or ethnic backgrounds but that does not reflect true intelligence.

cultural–familial retardation: Substandard intellectual performance that is presumed to stem from lack of opportunity to acquire the knowledge and skills considered important within a cultural setting.

culture-free: Descriptive of a test in which cultural biases have been removed. On such a test, test takers from different cultural backgrounds would have an equal opportunity to earn scores that reflect their true abilities.

cystic fibrosis: A fatal genetic disorder in which mucus obstructs the lungs and pancreas.

decentration: Simultaneous focusing (centering) on more than one aspect or dimension of a problem or situation.

deep structure: The underlying meaning of a sentence.

deferred imitation: The imitation of people and events that occurred hours, days, or weeks in the past.

dendrites: The rootlike parts of a neuron that receive impulses from other neurons (from the Greek *dendron*, meaning "tree" and referring to the branching appearance of dendrites).

deoxyribonucleic acid (DNA): Genetic material that takes the form of a double helix composed of phosphates, sugars, and bases.

dependent variable: A measure of an assumed effect of an independent variable.

DES: Abbreviation for diethylstilbestrol, a powerful estrogen that has been linked to cancer in the reproductive organs of children of women who used the hormone when pregnant.

design stage: A stage in drawing in which children begin to combine shapes.

development: The processes by which organisms unfold features and traits, grow, and become more complex and specialized in structure and function.

differential emotions theory: Izard's view that the major emotions are distinct at birth but emerge gradually in accord with maturation and the child's developing needs

differentiation: The processes by which behaviors and physical structures become more specialized.

dilate: To make wider or larger.

disinhibit: To stimulate a response that has been suppressed (inhibited) by showing a model engaging in that response without aversive consequences.

disorganized–disoriented attachment: A type of insecure attachment characterized by dazed and contradictory behaviors toward an attachment figure.

divergent thinking: A thought process that attempts to generate multiple solutions to problems. Free and fluent association to the elements of a problem.

dizygotic (DZ) twins: Twins that derive from two zygotes; fraternal twins.

dominant trait: A trait that is expressed.

donor IVF: The transfer of a donor's ovum, fertilized in a laboratory dish, to the uterus of another woman.

double-deficit hypothesis: The theory of dyslexia which suggests that dyslexic children have biological deficits in two areas phonological processing (interpreting sounds) and in naming speed (for example, identifying letters such as b versus d, or w versus m).

Down syndrome: A chromosomal abnormality characterized by mental retardation and caused by an extra chromosome in the 21st pair.

dramatic play: Play in which children enact social roles; made possible by the attainment of symbolic thought. A form of pretend play.

dyslexia: A reading disorder characterized by problems such as letter reversals, mirror reading, slow reading, and reduced comprehension (from the Greek roots *dys*, meaning "bad," and *lexikon*, meaning "of words").

echolalia: The automatic repetition of sounds or words.

ecological systems theory: The view that explains child development in terms of the reciprocal influences between children and the settings that make up their environment.

ecology: The branch of biology that deals with the relationships between living organisms and their environment.

ectoderm: The outermost cell layer of the newly formed embryo from which the skin and nervous system develop.

efface: To rub out or wipe out; to become thin.

ego identity: According to Erikson, one's sense of who one is and what one stands for.

egocentrism: Putting oneself at the center of things such that one is unable to perceive the world from another person's point of view.

elaborative strategy: A method for increasing retention of new information by relating it to well-known information.

electroencephalograph (EEG): An instrument that measures electrical activity of the brain.

elicit: (ee-LISS-it) To bring forth; evoke.

embryonic disk: The platelike inner part of the blastocyst that differentiates into the ectoderm, mesoderm, and endoderm of the embryo.

embryonic stage: The stage of prenatal development that lasts from implantation through the eighth week of pregnancy; it is characterized by the development of the major organ systems.

embryonic transplant: The transfer of an embryo from the uterus of one woman to that of another.

emotion: A state of feeling that has physiological, situational, and cognitive components.

emotional regulation: Techniques for controlling one's emotional states.

empathy: Ability to share another person's feelings.

empirical: Based on observation and experimentation.

encode: To transform sensory input into a form that is more readily processed.

encopresis: Failure to control the bowels once the normal age for bowel control has been reached. Also called soiling.

endoderm: The inner layer of the embryo from which the lungs and digestive system develop.

endometriosis: (end-oh-me-tree-OH-sis) Inflammation of endometrial tissue sloughed off into the abdominal cavity rather than out of the body during menstruation; the condition is characterized by abdominal pain and sometimes infertility.

endometrium: The inner lining of the uterus.

enuresis: (en-you-REE-sis) Failure to control the bladder (urination) once the normal age for control has been reached.

epiphyseal closure: The process by which the cartilage that separates the long end (epiphysis) of a bone from the main part of the bone turns to bone.

episiotomy: (ih-pee-zee-AH-tuh-mee) A surgical incision in the area between the birth canal and the anus that widens the vaginal opening, preventing random tearing during childbirth.

equilibration: The creation of an equilibrium, or balance, between assimilation and accommodation as a way of incorporating new events or knowledge.

estrogen: A female sex hormone produced mainly by the ovaries.

ethnic groups: Groups of people distinguished by cultural heritage, race, language, and common history.

ethnic identity: A sense of belonging to an ethnic group.

ethnic identity search: The second stage of ethnic identity development; similar to the moratorium identity status.

ethologist: A scientist who studies the behavior patterns that are characteristic of various species.

ethology: The study of behaviors that are specific to a species.

exosystem: Community institutions and settings that indirectly influence the child, such as the school board and the parents' workplaces (from the Greek *exo*, meaning "outside").

experiment: A method of scientific investigation that seeks to discover cause-and-effect relationships by introducing independent variables and observing their effects on dependent variables.

experimental group: A group made up of subjects who receive a treatment in an experiment.

exploration: Active questioning and searching among alternatives in the quest to establish goals, values, or beliefs.

expressive language style: Use of language primarily as a means for engaging in social interaction.

expressive vocabulary: The sum total of the words that one can use in the production of language.

extinction: The decrease and eventual disappearance of a response in the absence of reinforcement.

factor: A condition or quality that brings about a result; in this case, "intelligent" behavior. A cluster of related items, such as those found on an intelligence or personality test.

factor analysis: A statistical technique that allows researchers to determine the relationships among a large number of items, such as test items.

failure to thrive (FTT): A disorder of impaired growth in infancy and early childhood characterized by failure to gain weight within normal limits.

fallopian tube: A tube through which ova travel from an ovary to the uterus.

fast mapping: A process of quickly determining a word's meaning, which facilitates children's vocabulary development.

feedback loop: A system in which glands regulate each other's functioning through a series of hormonal messages.

fetal alcohol effect (FAE): A cluster of symptoms less severe than those of fetal alcohol syndrome shown by children of women who drank moderately during pregnancy.

fetal alcohol syndrome (FAS): A cluster of symptoms shown by children of women who drank heavily during pregnancy, including characteristic facial features and mental retardation.

fetal monitoring: The use of instruments to track the heart rate and oxygen levels of the fetus during childbirth.

fetal stage: The stage of development that lasts from the beginning of the ninth week of pregnancy through birth; it is characterized by gains in size and weight and by maturation of the organ systems.

fine motor skills: Skills employing the small muscles used in manipulation, such as those in the fingers.

fixed action pattern (FAP): An instinct; a stereotyped behavior pattern that is characteristic of a species and is triggered by a releasing stimulus.

forceps: A curved instrument that fits around the head of the baby and permits it to be pulled through the birth canal.

foreclosure: An identity status that characterizes those who have made commitments without considering alternatives.

formal operations: The fourth stage in Piaget's cognitive-developmental theory, characterized by the capacity for flexible, reversible operations concerning abstract ideas and concepts, such as symbols, statements, and theories.

gay: A male who is interested romantically and sexually in other males. (Also used more broadly to refer to both lesbians and gay males.)

gender: The psychological state of being female or being male, as influenced by cultural concepts of gender-appropriate behavior. Compare and contrast the concept of gender with anatomic sex, which is based on the physical differences between females and males.

gender constancy: The concept that one's sex remains the same despite superficial changes in appearance or behavior.

gender identity: Knowledge that one is female or male. Also, the name of the first stage in Kohlberg's cognitive-developmental theory of the assumption of gender roles.

gender role: A complex cluster of traits and behaviors that are considered stereotypical of females and males.

gender stability: The concept that one's sex is a permanent feature.

gender-schema theory: The view that one's knowledge of the gender schema in one's society (the behavior patterns that are considered appropriate for men and women) guides one's assumption of gender-typed preferences and behavior patterns.

gene: The basic unit of heredity. Genes are composed of deoxyribonucleic acid (DNA).

general anesthesia: The process of eliminating pain by putting the person to sleep.

generalized anxiety disorder (GAD): An anxiety disorder in which anxiety appears to be present continuously and is unrelated to the situation.

genetic counseling: Advice concerning the probabilities that a couple's children will show genetic abnormalities.

genetics: The branch of biology that studies heredity.

genital stage: In psychoanalytic theory, the fifth and final stage of psychosexual development in which gratification is attained through sexual intercourse with an individual of the other sex.

genotype: The genetic form or constitution of a person as determined by heredity.

germinal stage: The period of development between conception and the implantation of the embryo.

goodness of fit: Agreement between the parents' expectations of or demands on the child and the child's temperamental characteristics.

grasping reflex: A reflex in which infants grasp objects that cause pressure against the palms.

gross motor skills: Skills employing the large muscles used in locomotion.

growth: The processes by which organisms increase in size, weight, strength, and other traits as they develop.

growth spur: A period during which growth advances at a dramatically rapid rate compared with other periods.

gynecomastia: Enlargement of breast tissue in males.

habituation: A process in which one becomes used to and therefore pays less attention to a repeated stimulus.

hallucinogenics: Drugs that give rise to hallucinations.

handedness: The tendency to prefer using the left or right hand in writing and other activities.

hemophilia: (he-moe-FEEL-yuh) A genetic disorder in which blood does not clot properly.

heredity: The transmission of traits and characteristics from parent to child by means of genes.

heritability: The degree to which the variations in a trait from one person to another can be attributed to, or explained by, genetic factors.

heterozygous: Having two different alleles.

HIV/AIDS: HIV stands for a virus, the human immunodeficiency virus, which cripples the body's immune system. AIDS stands for acquired immunodeficiency syndrome. HIV is a sexually transmitted infection that can also be transmitted in other ways, such as sharing needles when shooting up drugs. AIDS is caused by HIV and describes the body's state when the immune system is weakened to the point where it is vulnerable to a variety of diseases that would otherwise be fought off.

holophrase: A single word that is used to express complex meanings.

homosexual: Referring to an erotic orientation toward members of one's own sex.

homozygous: Having two identical alleles.

hue: Color.

Huntington's disease: A fatal genetic neurologic disorder whose onset is in middle age.

hyaluronidase: (high-al-you-RON-uh-dace) An enzyme that briefly thins the zona pellucida, enabling a single sperm cell to penetrate. (From roots referring to a "substance that breaks down a glasslike fluid.")

hyperactivity: Excessive restlessness and overactivity; one of the primary characteristics of attention-deficit/hyperactivity disorder (ADHD). Not to be confused with misbehavior or with normal high-activity levels that occur during childhood.

hypothalamus: A pea-sized structure above the pituitary gland that is involved in the regulation of body temperature, motivation (e.g., hunger, thirst, sex), and emotion.

hypothesis: (high-POTH-uh-sis) A Greek word meaning "groundwork" or "foundation" that has come to mean a specific statement about behavior that is tested by research.

hypoxia: A condition characterized by less oxygen than is required.

identity achievement: An identity status that characterizes those who have explored alternatives and have developed commitments.

identity crisis: A turning point in development during which one examines one's values and makes decisions about life roles.

identity crisis: According to Erikson, a period of inner conflict during which one examines one's values and makes decisions about one's life roles.

identity diffusion: An identity status that characterizes those who have no commitments and who are not in the process of exploring alternatives.

imaginary audience: The belief that others around us are as concerned with our thoughts and behaviors as we are; one aspect of adolescent egocentrism.

immanent justice: The view that retribution for wrongdoing is a direct consequence of the wrongdoing, reflective of the belief that morality is embedded within the structure of the universe.

imprinting: The process by which some animals exhibit the fixed action pattern (FAP) of attachment in response to a releasing stimulus. The FAP occurs during a critical period and is difficult to modify.

in vitro fertilization: (VEE-tro) Fertilization of an ovum in a laboratory dish.

incubator: A heated, protective container in which premature infants are kept.

independent variable: A condition in a scientific study that is manipulated (changed) so that its effects can be observed.

indiscriminate attachment: The display of attachment behaviors toward any person.

individualist: A person who defines herself or himself in terms of personal traits and gives priority to her or his own goals.

inductive: Characteristic of disciplinary methods, such as reasoning, that attempt to foster an understanding of the principles behind parental demands.

industry versus inferiority: The fourth stage of psychosocial development in Erikson's theory, occurring in middle childhood. Mastery of tasks leads to a sense of industry, whereas failure produces feelings of inferiority.

infancy: The period of very early childhood, characterized by lack of complex speech; the first 2 years after birth.

information processing: The view in which cognitive processes are compared to the functions of computers. The theory deals with the input, storage, retrieval, manipulation, and output of information. The focus is on the development of children's strategies for solving problems, or their "mental programs."

initial-preattachment phase: The first phase in the formation of bonds of attachment, lasting from birth to about 3 months of age and characterized by indiscriminate attachment.

inner speech: Vygotsky's concept of the ultimate binding of language and thought. Inner speech originates in vocalizations that may regulate the child's behavior and become internalized by age 6 or 7.

insomnia: One or more sleep problems including falling asleep, difficulty remaining asleep during the night, and waking early.

intelligence: A complex and controversial concept, defined by David Wechsler as the "capacity . . . to understand the world [and the] resourcefulness to cope with its challenges." Intelligence implies the capacity to make adaptive choices (from the Latin *inter*, meaning "among," and *legere*, meaning "to choose").

intelligence quotient (IQ): (1) Originally, a ratio obtained by dividing a child's score (or "mental age") on an intelligence test by his or her chronological age. (2) In general, a score on an intelligence test.

intensity: Brightness.

intonation: The use of pitches of varying levels to help communicate meaning.

irreversibility: Lack of recognition that actions can be reversed.

juvenile delinquency: Conduct in a child or adolescent characterized by illegal activities.

Klinefelter syndrome: A chromosomal disorder found among males that is caused by an extra X sex chromosome and that is characterized by infertility and mild mental retardation.

labia: The major and minor lips of the female genitalia.

Lamaze method: A childbirth method in which women are educated about childbirth, learn to relax and breathe in patterns that conserve energy and lessen pain, and have a coach (usually the father) present during childbirth. Also called prepared childbirth.

language acquisition device (LAD): In psycholinguistic theory, neural "prewiring" that facilitates the child's learning of grammar.

lanugo: (luh-NOO-go) Fine, downy hair that covers much of the body of the neonate, especially preterm babies.

larynx: The part of the throat that contains the vocal cords.

latency stage: In psychoanalytic theory, the fourth stage of psychosexual development, characterized by repression of sexual impulses and development of skills.

learned helplessness: An acquired (hence, learned) belief that one is unable to control one's environment.

learning disabilities: A group of disorders characterized by inadequate development of specific academic, language, and speech skills.

lesbian: A female who is interested romantically and sexually in other females.

life crisis: An internal conflict that attends each stage of psychosocial development. Positive resolution of early life crises sets the stage for positive resolution of subsequent life crises.

local anesthetic: A method that reduces pain in an area of the body.

locomotion: Movement from one place to another.

longitudinal research: The study of developmental processes by taking repeated measures of the same group of children at various stages of development.

long-term memory: The memory structure capable of relatively permanent storage of information.

macrosystem: The basic institutions and ideologies that influence the child, such as the American ideals of freedom of expression and equality under the law (from the Greek *makros*, meaning "long" or "enlarged").

mainstreaming: Placing disabled children in classrooms with nondisabled children.

mammary glands: Glands that secrete milk.

masturbation: Sexual self-stimulation.

maturation: The unfolding of genetically determined traits, structures, and functions.

mean length of utterance (MLU): The average number of morphemes used in an utterance.

medulla: A part of the brain stem that regulates vital and automatic functions such as breathing and the sleep–wake cycle.

meiosis: The form of cell division in which each pair of chromosomes splits so that one member of each pair moves to the new cell. As a result, each new cell has 23 chromosomes.

memory: The processes by which we store and retrieve information.

menarche: The onset of menstruation.

menopause: The cessation of menstruation, typically occurring between ages 48 and 52.

mental age (MA): The accumulated months of credit that a person earns on the Stanford–Binet Intelligence Scale.

mental representations: The mental forms that a real object or event can take, which may differ from one another. (Successful problem solving is aided by accurate mental representation of the elements of the problem.)

mesoderm: The central layer of the embryo from which the bones and muscles develop.

mesosystem: The interlocking settings that influence the child, such as the interaction of the school and the larger community when children are taken on field trips (from the Greek *mesos*, meaning "middle").

metacognition: Awareness of and control of one's cognitive abilities, as shown by the intentional use of cognitive strategies in solving problems.

metamemory: Knowledge of the functions and processes involved in one's storage and retrieval of information (memory), as shown by use of cognitive strategies to retain information.

microsystem: The immediate settings with which the child interacts, such as the home, the school, and one's peers (from the Greek *mikros*, meaning "small").

midwife: An individual who helps women in childbirth (from Old English roots meaning "with woman").

mitosis: The form of cell division in which each chromosome splits lengthwise to double in number. Half of each chromosome combines with chemicals to retake its original form and then moves to the new cell.

models: In learning theory, those whose behaviors are imitated by others.

monozygotic (MZ) twins: Twins that derive from a single zygote that has split into two; identical twins. Each MZ twin carries the same genetic code.

moral realism: According to Piaget, the stage during which children judge acts as moral when they conform to authority or to the rules of the game. Morality at this stage is perceived as embedded in the structure of the universe.

moratorium: An identity status that characterizes those who are actively exploring alternatives in an attempt to form an identity.

Moro reflex: A reflex in which infants arch their back, fling out their arms and legs, and draw them back toward the chest in response to a sudden change in position.

morpheme: The smallest unit of meaning in a language.

motility: Self-propulsion.

motor development: The development of the capacity for movement, particularly that made possible by changes in the nervous system and the muscles.

multifactorial problems: Problems that stem from the interaction of heredity and environmental factors.

multiple sclerosis: A disorder in which myelin is replaced by hard fibrous tissue that impedes neural transmission.

muscular dystrophy: (DIS-truh-fee) A chronic disease characterized by a progressive wasting away of the muscles.

mutation: A sudden variation in a heritable characteristic, as by an accident that affects the composition of genes.

mutism: Inability or refusal to speak.

myelin sheath: (MY-uh-lin) A fatty, whitish substance that encases and insulates neurons, permitting more rapid transmission of neural impulses.

myelination: The process by which axons are coated with myelin.

natural childbirth: A method of childbirth in which women use no anesthesia and are educated about childbirth and strategies for coping with discomfort.

naturalistic observation: A method of scientific observation in which children (and others) are observed in their natural environments.

nature: The processes within an organism that guide that organism to develop according to its genetic code.

negative correlation: A relationship between two variables in which one variable increases as the other variable decreases.

negative reinforcer: A reinforcer that, when removed, increases the frequency of a response.

neonate: A newborn child (from the Greek *neos*, meaning "new," and the Latin *natus*, meaning "born").

nerves: Bundles of axons from many neurons.

neural: Of the nervous system.

neural tube: A hollowed-out area in the blastocyst from which the nervous system develops.

neurons: Nerve cells; cells found in the nervous system that transmit messages.

neuroticism: A personality trait characterized by anxiety and emotional instability.

neurotransmitter: A chemical substance that enables the transmission of neural impulses from one neuron to another.

nightmares: Frightening dreams that occur during REM sleep, often in the morning hours.

nocturnal emission: Emission of seminal fluid while asleep.

non-rapid-eye-movement (non-REM) sleep: Periods of sleep during which we are unlikely to dream.

nonsocial play: Forms of play (solitary play or onlooker play) in which play is not influenced by the play of nearby children.

nurture: The processes external to an organism that nourish it as it develops according to its genetic code or that cause it to swerve from its genetically programmed course. Environmental factors that influence development.

object permanence: Recognition that objects continue to exist even when they are not seen.

objective morality: The perception of morality as objective, that is, as existing outside the cognitive functioning of people; a characteristic of Piaget's stage of moral realism.

observational learning: The acquisition of expectations and skills by means of observing others.

obsessive-compulsive disorder (OCD): An anxiety disorder characterized by obsessions (recurring thoughts or images that seems beyond control) and compulsions (irresistible urges to repeat an act, such as hand washing or checking that one has put one's homework in one's backpack).

operant conditioning: A simple form of learning in which an organism learns to engage in behavior that is reinforced.

operations: Flexible, reversible mental manipulations of objects, in which objects can be mentally transformed and then returned to their original states.

oral rehydration therapy: A treatment involving administration of a salt and sugar solution to a child who is dehydrated from diarrhea.

osteoporosis: A condition involving progressive loss of bone tissue.

overextension: Use of words in situations in which their meanings become extended or inappropriate.

overregularization: The application of regular grammatical rules for forming inflections (e.g., past tense and plurals) to irregular verbs and nouns.

ovulation: The releasing of an ovum from an ovary.

oxytocin: (ok-see-TOE-sin) A pituitary hormone that stimulates labor contractions (from the Greek *oxys*, meaning "quick," and *tokos*, meaning "birth").

pacifier: An artificial nipple, teething ring, or similar device that, when sucked, soothes babies.

peers: Children of the same age. (More generally, people of similar background and social standing.)

pelvic inflammatory disease (PID): An infection of the abdominal region that may have various causes and that may impair fertility.

perception: The process by which sensations are organized into a mental map of the world.

perceptual constancy: The tendency to perceive objects as the same even though sensations produced by them may differ when, for example, they differ in position or distance.

permissive–indulgent: A child-rearing style in which parents are not controlling and restrictive but are warm.

personal fable: The belief that our feelings and ideas are special and unique and that we are invulnerable; one aspect of adolescent egocentrism.

personality: An individual's distinctive ways of responding to people and events.

phenotype: The actual form or constitution of a person as determined by heredity and environmental factors.

phenylketonuria (PKU): (fee-nill-key-toe-NOOR-ee-uh) A genetic abnormality in which phenylalanine builds up and causes mental retardation.

phobia: An irrational, excessive fear that interferes with one's functioning.

phonetic method: A method for learning to read in which children decode the sounds of words based on their knowledge of the sounds of letters and letter combinations.

pictorial stage: A stage in drawing attained between ages 4 and 5 in which designs begin to resemble recognizable objects.

pincer grasp: The use of the opposing thumb to grasp objects between the thumb and other fingers.

pitch: The highness or lowness of a sound, as determined by the frequency of sound waves.

pituitary gland: The body's "master gland," which is located in the lower central part of the brain and which secretes many hormones essential to development, such as oxytocin, prolactin, and growth hormone.

PKU: See Phenylketonuria.

placement stage: An early stage in drawing, usually found among 2-year-olds, in which children place their scribbles in various locations on the page (such as in the middle or near a border).

placenta: (pluh-SEN-tuh) An organ connected to the uterine wall and to the fetus by the umbilical cord. The placenta serves as a relay station between mother and fetus for the exchange of nutrients and wastes.

plasticity: The tendency of new parts of the brain to take up the functions of injured parts.

polygenic: Resulting from many genes.

positive correlation: A relationship between two variables in which one variable increases as the other variable increases.

positive reinforcer: A reinforcer that, when applied, increases the frequency of a response.

postconventional level: According to Kohlberg, a period during which moral judgments are derived from moral principles and people look to themselves to set moral standards.

postpartum depression (PPD): Severe, prolonged depression that afflicts 10–20% of women after delivery and that is characterized by sadness, apathy, and feelings of worthlessness.

postpartum period: The period that immediately follows childbirth.

pragmatics: The practical aspects of communication, such as adaptation of language to fit the social situation.

precausal: A type of thought in which natural cause-and-effect relationships are attributed to will and other preoperational concepts. (For example, the sun sets because it is tired.)

preconventional level: According to Kohlberg, a period during which moral judgments are based largely on expectations of rewards or punishments.

prelinguistic: Referring to vocalizations made by the infant before the development of language. (In language, words symbolize objects and events.)

premature: Born before the full term of gestation. Also referred to as preterm.

prenatal period: The period of development from conception to birth. (From roots meaning "prior to birth.")

preoperational stage: The second stage in Piaget's scheme, characterized by inflexible and irreversible mental manipulation of symbols.

preterm: Born at or before completion of 37 weeks of gestation.

primary circular reactions: The repetition of actions that first occurred by chance and that focus on the infant's own body.

primary sex characteristics: The structures that make reproduction possible.

progestin: A hormone used to maintain pregnancy that can cause masculinization of the fetus.

prosocial behavior: Behavior intended to benefit another without expectation of reward.

prostaglandins: (pross-tuh-GLAN-dins) Hormones that stimulate uterine contractions.

proximodistal: From the inner part (or axis) of the body outward.

psycholinguistic theory: The view that language learning involves an interaction between environmental influences and an inborn tendency to acquire language. The emphasis is on the inborn tendency.

psychological androgyny: Possession of both stereotypical feminine and masculine traits.

psychological moratorium: A time-out period when adolescents experiment with different roles, values, beliefs, and relationships.

psychosexual development: In psychoanalytic theory, the process by which libidinal energy is expressed through different erogenous zones during different stages of development.

psychosocial development: Erikson's theory, which emphasizes the importance of social relationships and conscious choice throughout the eight stages of development.

puberty: The biological stage of development characterized by changes that lead to reproductive capacity. Puberty signals the beginning of adolescence.

punishment: An unpleasant stimulus that suppresses behavior.

Pygmalion effect: A self-fulfilling prophecy; an expectation that is confirmed because of the behavior of those who hold the expectation.

rapid-eye-movement (REM) sleep: A period of sleep during which we are likely to dream, as indicated by rapid eye movements.

reaction range: The variability in the expression of inherited traits as they are influenced by environmental factors.

reaction time: The amount of time required to respond to a stimulus.

recall: A memory task in which the individual must reproduce material from memory without any cues.

receptive vocabulary: The sum total of the words whose meanings one understands.

recessive trait: A trait that is not expressed when the gene or genes involved have been paired with dominant genes. Recessive traits are transmitted to future generations and expressed if they are paired with other recessive genes.

reciprocity: The principle that actions have mutual effects and that people depend on one another to treat each other morally.

recognition: A memory task in which the individual indicates whether presented information has been experienced previously.

referential language style: Use of language primarily as a means for labeling objects.

reflex: An unlearned, stereotypical response to a stimulus.

regression: A return to behaviors characteristic of earlier stages of development.

rehearse: Repeat.

reinforcement: The process of providing stimuli following a response, which has the effect of increasing the frequency of the response.

rejecting–neglecting: A child-rearing style in which parents are neither restrictive and controlling nor supportive and responsive.

releasing stimulus: A stimulus that elicits a fixed action pattern (FAP).

respiratory distress syndrome: A cluster of breathing problems, including weak and irregular breathing, to which preterm babies are particularly prone.

reversibility: According to Piaget, recognition that processes can be undone, leaving things as they were before. Reversibility is a factor in conservation of the properties of substances.

Rh incompatibility: A condition in which antibodies produced by the mother are transmitted to the child, possibly causing brain damage or death.

rods: In the eye, rod-shaped receptors of light that are sensitive to intensity only. Rods permit black-and-white vision.

rooting reflex: A reflex in which infants turn their mouths and heads in the direction of a stroking of their cheek or the corner of their mouth.

rote learning: Learning by repetition.

rough-and-tumble play: Play fighting and chasing.

rubella: A viral infection that can cause retardation and heart disease in the embryo. Also called German measles.

saturation: Richness or purity of a color.

scaffolding: Vygotsky's term for temporary cognitive structures or methods of solving problems that help the child as he or she learns to function independently.

scheme: According to Piaget, an action pattern or mental structure that is involved in the acquisition and organization of knowledge.

schizophrenia: A severe psychological disorder characterized by disturbances in thought and language, perception and attention, motor activity, and mood and by withdrawal and absorption in daydreams or fantasy.

school phobia: Fear of attending school, marked by extreme anxiety at leaving parents.

scripts: Abstract generalized accounts of familiar repeated events.

secondary circular reactions: The repetition of actions that produce an effect on the environment.

secondary sex characteristics: Physical indicators of sexual maturation—such as changes to the voice and growth of bodily hair—that do not directly involve reproductive structures.

secular trend: A historical trend toward increasing adult height and earlier puberty.

secure attachment: A type of attachment characterized by mild distress at leave-takings, seeking nearness to an attachment figure, and being readily soothed by the figure.

sedatives: Drugs that soothe or quiet restlessness or agitation.

self-concept: One's impression of oneself; self-awareness.

self-efficacy expectations: One's beliefs that he or she can handle the requirements of a situation.

self-esteem: The sense of value or worth that people attach to themselves.

self-fulfilling prophecy: An event that occurs because of the behavior of those who expect it to occur.

semantic code: A code based on the meaning of information.

semen: The fluid that contains sperm and substances that nourish and help transport sperm.

sensation: The stimulation of sensory organs such as the eyes, ears, and skin and the transmission of sensory information to the brain.

sensitive period: In linguistic theory, the period from about 18 months to puberty when the brain is thought to be especially capable of learning language because of its plasticity.

sensory memory: The structure of memory first encountered by sensory input. Information is maintained in sensory memory for only a fraction of a second.

sensory register: Another term for sensory memory.

separation anxiety: Fear of being separated from a target of attachment, usually a primary caregiver.

separation anxiety disorder (SAD): An extreme form of otherwise normal separation anxiety that is characterized by anxiety about separating from parents; SAD often takes the form of refusal to go to school.

separation–individuation: The child's increasing sense of becoming separate from and independent of the mother.

seriation: Placing objects in an order or series according to a property or trait.

serotonin: A naturally occurring brain chemical that is involved in transmission of messages from one brain cell to another, the responsiveness of the medulla, emotional responses such as depression, and motivational responses such as hunger.

sex chromosome: A chromosome in the shape of a Y (male) or X (female) that determines the sex of the child.

sexism: Discrimination or bias against people based on their sex.

sex-linked chromosomal abnormalities: Abnormalities that are transmitted from generation to generation, carried by a sex chromosome, usually an X sex chromosome.

sex-linked genetic abnormalities: Abnormalities resulting from genes that are found on the X sex chromosome. They are more likely to be shown by male offspring (who do not have an opposing gene from a second X chromosome) than by female offspring.

sexual harassment: Unwelcome verbal or physical conduct of a sexual nature.

shape constancy: The tendency to perceive objects as being the same shape even though the shapes of their retinal images may differ when the objects are viewed from different positions.

shape stage: A stage in drawing, attained by age 3, in which children draw basic shapes such as circles, squares, triangles, crosses, X's and odd shapes.

shaping: A procedure for teaching complex behavior patterns by means of reinforcing small steps toward the target behavior.

sibling rivalry: Jealousy or rivalry among brothers and sisters.

sickle-cell anemia: A genetic disorder that decreases the blood's capacity to carry oxygen.

SIDS: See Sudden infant death syndrome.

sight vocabulary: Words that are immediately recognized on the basis of familiarity with their overall shapes, rather than decoded.

size constancy: The tendency to perceive objects as being the same size even though the sizes of their retinal images may differ as a result of distance.

sleep terrors: Frightening dreamlike experiences that occur during the deepest stage of non-REM sleep, shortly after the child has gone to sleep.

small for dates: Descriptive of neonates who are unusually small for their age.

social cognition: Development of children's understanding of the relationship between the self and others.

social cognitive theory: A cognitively oriented learning theory that emphasizes observational learning in the determining of behavior.

social play: Play in which children interact with and are influenced by the play of others. Examples are parallel play, associative play, and cooperative play.

social referencing: Using another person's reaction to a situation to form one's own assessment of it.

social smile: A smile that occurs in response to a human voice or face.

socialization: A process in which children are encouraged to adopt socially desirable behavior patterns through a system of guidance, rewards, and punishments.

somnambulism: Sleep walking (from the Latin *somnus*, meaning "sleep," and *ambulare*, meaning "to walk").

sonogram: A procedure for using ultrasonic sound waves to create a picture of an embryo or fetus.

spina bifida: A neural tube defect that causes abnormalities of the brain and spine.

spontaneous abortion: Unplanned, accidental abortion.

stage theory: A theory of development characterized by hypothesizing the existence of distinct periods of life. Stages follow one another in an orderly sequence.

standardized test: A test of some ability or trait in which an individual's score is compared to the scores of a group of similar individuals.

status offenses: Offenses considered illegal only when performed by minors, such as truancy and underage drinking.

stepping reflex: A reflex in which infants take steps when held under the arms and leaned forward so that the feet press against the ground.

stereotype: A fixed, conventional idea about a group.

stillbirth: The birth of a dead fetus.

stimulants: Drugs that increase the activity of the nervous system.

stimulus: A change in the environment that leads to a change in behavior.

stranger anxiety: A fear of unfamiliar people that emerges between 6 and 9 months of age. Also called fear of strangers.

substance abuse: A persistent pattern of use of a substance characterized by frequent intoxication and impairment of physical, social, or emotional well-being.

substance dependence: A persistent pattern of use of a substance that is accompanied by physiological addiction.

sudden infant death syndrome (SIDS): The death, while sleeping, of apparently healthy babies who stop breathing for unknown medical reasons. Also called crib death.

surface structure: The superficial grammatical construction of a sentence.

surrogate mother: A woman who is artificially inseminated and carries to term a child who is then given to another woman, typically the spouse of the sperm donor.

symbolic play: Play in which children make believe that objects and toys are other than what they are. Also called pretend play.

syntax: The rules in a language for placing words in proper order to form meaningful sentences (from the Latin *syntaxis*, meaning "joining together").

syphilis: A sexually transmitted infection that, in advanced stages, can attack major organ systems.

Tay-Sachs disease: A fatal genetic neurological disorder.

telegraphic speech: Type of speech in which only the essential words are used.

temperament: Individual differences in styles of reaction that are present early in life.

teratogens: Environmental influences or agents that can damage the embryo or fetus (from the Greek *teras*, meaning "monster").

term: A set period of time, such as the typical period of time between conception and the birth of a baby.

tertiary circular reactions: The purposeful adaptation of established schemes to new situations.

testosterone: A male sex hormone—a steroid—that is produced by the testes and that promotes growth of male sexual characteristics and sperm.

thalidomide: A sedative used in the 1960s that has been linked to birth defects, especially deformed or absent limbs.

theory: A formulation of relationships underlying observed events. A theory involves assumptions and logically derived explanations and predictions.

theory of mind: A commonsense understanding of how the mind works.

time lag: The study of developmental processes by taking measures of children of the same age group at different times.

time out: A behavior-modification technique in which a child who misbehaves is temporarily placed in a drab, restrictive environment in which reinforcement is unavailable.

toddler: A child who walks with short, uncertain steps. Toddlerhood lasts from about 18 to 30 months of age, thereby bridging infancy and early childhood.

tolerance: Habituation to a drug such that increasingly higher doses are needed to achieve similar effects.

tonic-neck reflex: A reflex in which infants turn their head to one side, extend their arm and leg on that side, and flex their limbs on the opposite side. Also known as the "fencing position."

toxemia: A life-threatening disease that can afflict pregnant women; it is characterized by high blood pressure.

track: Follow.

tranquilizer: A drug that reduces feelings of anxiety and tension.

transductive reasoning: Reasoning from the specific to the specific. (In deductive reasoning, one reasons from the general to the specific; in inductive reasoning, one reasons from the specific to the general.)

transition: The initial movement of the head of the fetus into the birth canal.

transitional object: A soft, cuddly object often carried to bed by a child to ease the separation from parents.

transitivity: The principle that if A is greater than B in a property and B is greater than C, then A is greater than C.

transsexual: A person who would prefer to be a person of the other sex and who may undergo hormone treatments, cosmetic surgery, or both to achieve the appearance of being a member of the other sex.

treatment: In an experiment, a condition received by subjects so that its effects may be observed.

triarchic: Governed by three. Descriptive of Sternberg's view that intellectual functioning has three aspects: analytical intelligence, creative intelligence, and practical intelligence.

trophoblast: The outer part of the blastocyst from which the amniotic sac, placenta, and umbilical cord develop.

Turner syndrome: A chromosomal disorder found among females that is caused by having a single X sex chromosome and is characterized by infertility.

ulnar grasp: A method of grasping objects in which the fingers close somewhat clumsily against the palm.

ultrasound: Sound waves too high in pitch to be sensed by the human ear.

umbilical cord: A tube that connects the fetus to the placenta.

unconditioned response (UCR): An unlearned response. A response to an unconditioned stimulus.

unconditioned stimulus (UCS): A stimulus that elicits a response from an organism without learning.

unconscious: In psychoanalytic theory, not available to awareness by simple focusing of attention.

unexamined ethnic identity: The first stage of ethnic identity development; similar to the diffusion or foreclosure identity statuses.

uterus: The hollow organ within females in which the embryo and fetus develop.

utopian: Referring to an ideal vision of society.

vacuum extraction tube: An instrument that uses suction to pull the baby through the birth canal.

variables: Quantities that can vary from child to child or from occasion to occasion, such as height, weight, intelligence, and attention span.

vernix: An oily white substance that coats the skin of the neonate, especially preterm babies.

visual accommodation: The automatic adjustments made by the lenses of the eyes to bring objects into focus.

visual acuity: Keenness or sharpness of vision.

visual recognition memory: The kind of memory shown in an infant's ability to discriminate previously seen objects from novel objects.

Wernicke's aphasia: A form of aphasia caused by damage to Wernicke's area and characterized by impaired comprehension of speech and difficulty in attempting to produce the right word.

whole-object assumption: The assumption that words refer to whole objects and not to their component parts or characteristics.

word-recognition method: A method for learning to read in which children come to recognize words through repeated exposure to them.

working memory: The structure of memory that can hold a sensory stimulus for up to 30 seconds after the trace decays. Also called short-term memory.

zona pellucida: (pell-LOOSE-see-duh) A gelatinous layer that surrounds an ovum. (From roots referring to a "zone through which light can shine.")

zone of proximal development (ZPD): Vygotsky's term for the situation in which a child carries out tasks with the help of someone who is more skilled, frequently an adult who represents the culture in which the child develops.

zygote: A new cell formed from the union of a sperm and an ovum (egg cell); a fertilized egg.

References

AAIDD. (2007). American Association on Intellectual and Developmental Disabilities. Available at www.aamr.org. Accessed May 24, 2007.

Aalsma, M. C., Lapsley, D. K., & Flannery, D. J. (2006). Personal fables, narcissism, and adolescent adjustment. *Psychology in the Schools, 43*(4), 481–491.

Abbey, A., Saenz, C., Buck, P. O., Parkhill, M. R., & Hayman, L. W. Jr. (2006). The effects of acute alcohol consumption, cognitive reserve, partner risk, and gender on sexual decision making. *Journal of Studies on Alcohol, 67*(1), 113–121.

Abdelaziz, Y. E., Harb, A. H., & Hisham, N. (2001). *Textbook of Clinical Pediatrics.* Philadelphia: Lippincott Williams & Wilkins.

Abe-Kim, J., Okazaki, S., & Goto, S. G. (2001). Unidimensional versus multidimensional approaches to the assessment of acculturation for Asian American populations. *Cultural Diversity and Ethnic Minority Psychology, 7*(3), 232–246.

Abelev, M., & Markman, E. (2006). Young children's understanding of multiple object identity: Appearance, pretense and function. *Developmental Science, 9*(6), 590–596.

Aber, J. L., Bishop-Josef, S. J., Jones, S. M., McLearn, K. T., & Phillips, D. A. (Eds.). (2007). *Child development and social policy: Knowledge for action. APA Decade of Behavior volumes.* Washington, DC: American Psychological Association.

Abravanel, E., & DeYong, N. G. (1991). Does object modeling elicit imitative-like gestures from young infants? *Journal of Experimental Child Psychology, 52*, 22–40.

Adams, G. R., Berzonsky, M. D., & Keating, L. (2006). Psychosocial resources in first-year university students: The role of identity processes and social relationships. *Journal of Youth and Adolescence, 35*(1), 81–91.

Adamsons, K., & Pasley, K. (2006). Coparenting following divorce and relationship dissolution. In M. A. Fine & J. H. Harvey (Eds.), *Handbook of divorce and relationship dissolution* (pp. 241–261). Mahwah, NJ: Erlbaum.

Adler, J., & Starr, M. (1992, August 10). Flying high now. *Newsweek,* pp. 20–21.

Adler-Baeder, F. (2006). What do we know about the physical abuse of stepchildren? A review of the literature. *Journal of Divorce & Remarriage, 44*(3–4), 67–81.

Adolph, K. E. (2000). Specificity of learning: Why infants fall over a veritable cliff. *Psychological Science, 11*(4), 290–295.

Adolph, K. E., & Berger, S. E. (2005). Physical and motor development. In M. H. Bornstein & M. E. Lamb (Eds.), *Developmental science:*

An advanced textbook (5th ed.) (pp. 223–281). Hillsdale, NJ: Erlbaum.

Adolph, K. E., Vereijken, B., & Shrout, P. E. (2003). What changes in infant walking and why. *Child Development, 74*(2), 475–497.

Agency for Healthcare Research and Quality. (2004, April). Chronic illnesses. In *Child Health Research Findings,* Program Brief, AHRQ Publication 04-P011. Rockville, MD: Agency for Healthcare Research and Quality. Available at http://www.ahrq.gov/research/childfind/chfchrn.htm.

Aguiar, A., & Baillargeon, R. (1999). 2.5-month-old infants' reasoning about when objects should and should not be occluded. *Cognitive Psychology, 39*(2), 116–157.

Aguiar, A., & Baillargeon, R. (2002). Developments in young infants' reasoning about occluded objects. *Cognitive Psychology, 45*(2), 267–336.

Ainsworth, M. D. S. (1967). *Infancy in Uganda: Infant care and the growth of love.* Baltimore: Johns Hopkins University Press.

Ainsworth, M. D. S. (1989). Attachments beyond infancy. *American Psychologist, 44,* 709–716.

Ainsworth, M. D. S., Blehar, M. C., Waters, E., & Wall, S. (1978). *Patterns of attachment: A psychological study of the Strange Situation.* Hillsdale, NJ: Erlbaum.

Ainsworth, M. D. S., & Bowlby, J. (1991). An ethological approach to personality development. *American Psychologist, 46*(4), 333–341.

Akman, Y. (2007). Identity status of Turkish university students in relation to their evaluation of family problems. *Social Behavior and Personality, 35*(1), 79–88.

Alexander, G. M. (2003). An evolutionary perspective of sex-typed toy preferences: Pink, blue, and the brain. *Archives of Sexual Behavior, 32*(1), 7–14.

Alfirevic, Z., Sundberg, K., & Brigham, S. (2003). Amniocentesis and chorionic villus sampling for prenatal diagnosis. *Cochrane Database of Systematic Reviews,* DOI: 10.1002/14651858.CD003252.

Allen, M. C., & Alexander, G. R. (1990). Gross motor milestones in preterm infants: Correction for degree of prematurity. *Journal of Pediatrics, 116,* 955–959.

Alloway, T. P., Gathercole, S. E., Willis, C., & Adams, A. (2004). A structural analysis of working memory and related cognitive skills in young children. *Journal of Experimental Child Psychology, 87*(2), 85–106.

Als, H., et al. (2003). A three-center, randomized, controlled trial of individualized developmental care for very low birth weight

preterm infants: Medical, neurodevelopmental, parenting, and caregiving effects. *Journal of Developmental and Behavioral Pediatrics, 24*(6), 399–408.

Amato, P. R. (2006). Marital discord, divorce, and children's well-being: Results from a 20-year longitudinal study of two generations. In A. Clarke-Stewart & J. Dunn (Eds.), *Families count: Effects on child and adolescent development. The Jacobs Foundation series on adolescence* (pp. 179–202). New York: Cambridge University Press.

America's Children. (2007). Centers for Disease Control and Prevention. National Center for Health Statistics. Childstats.gov. *America's children: Key national indicators of well-being, 2007.* Adolescent births. Indicator Fam6: Birth Rates for Females Ages 15–17 by Race and Hispanic Origin, 1980–2005. Available at http://www.childstats.gov/americaschildren/famsoc6.asp.

American Academy of Family Physicians. (2006, November 1). Nutrition in toddlers. *American Family Physician, 74*(9). Available at http://www.aafp.org/afp/20061101/1527.html.

American Academy of Pediatrics. (2007, February 7). *A woman's guide to breastfeeding.* Available at http://www.aap.org/family/brstguid.htm.

American Association of University Women. (1992). *How schools shortchange women: The AAUW report.* Washington, DC: AAUW Educational Foundation.

American Fertility Association. (2007). Available at http://www.theafa.org/fertility/malefactor/index.html. Accessed February 6, 2007.

American Heart Association. (2007). Overweight in children. Available at http://www.americanheart.org/presenter.jhtml?identifier=4670. Accessed May 18, 2007.

American Lung Association. (2007). Various fact sheets. Available at http://www.lungusa.org/. Accessed June 24–July 5, 2007.

American Psychiatric Association. (2000). *Diagnostic and statistical manual of mental disorders (DSM–IV–TR).* Washington, DC: Author.

American Psychiatric Association. (2001, May 18). African-American youngsters inadequately treated for ADHD. *Psychiatric News, 36*(10), 17. Also available at http://pn.psychiatryonline.org/cgi/content/full/36/10/17-a.

American Psychologist. (2006). Gold medal award for life achievement in the science of psychology: Albert Bandura. *American Psychologist, 61*(5), 405–407.

Ammaniti, M., Speranza, A. M., & Fedele, S. (2005). Attachment in infancy and in early and late childhood: A longitudinal study. In K. A Kerns & R. A. Richardson (Eds.), *Attachment in middle childhood* (pp. 115–136). New York: Guilford.

Ances, B. M. (2002). New concerns about thalidomide. *Obstetrics & Gynecology, 99,* 125–128.

Anderman, E. M., et al. (2001). Learning to value mathematics and reading: Relations to mastery and performance-oriented instructional practices. *Contemporary Educational Psychology, 26*(1), 76–95.

Anderson, C. A., & Dill, K. E. (2000). Video games and aggressive thoughts, feelings, and behavior in the laboratory and in life. *Journal of Personality and Social Psychology, 78*(4), 772–790.

Anderson, C. A., Gentile, D. A., & Buckley, K. E. (2007). *Violent video game effects on children and adolescents: Theory, research, and public policy.* New York: Oxford University Press.

Anderson, K. G., Ramo, D. E., Schulte, M. T., Cummins, K., & Brown, S. A. (2007). Substance use treatment outcomes for youth: Integrating personal and environmental predictors. *Drug and Alcohol Dependence, 88*(1), 42–48.

Andreou, G., Krommydas, G., Gourgoulianis, K. I., Karapetsas, A., & Molyvdas, P. A. (2002). Handedness, asthma, and allergic disorders: Is there an association? *Psychology, Health, and Medicine, 7*(1), 53–60.

Angier, N. (2007, June 12). Sleek, fast, and focused: The cells that make dad dad. *New York Times,* pp. F1, F6.

Annett, M. (1999). Left-handedness as a function of sex, maternal versus paternal inheritance, and report bias. *Behavior Genetics, 29*(2), 103–114.

Annett, M., & Moran, P. (2006). Schizotypy is increased in mixed-handers, especially right-handed writers who use the left hand for primary actions. *Schizophrenia Research, 81*(2–3), 239–246.

Anthis, K. (2006). Possible selves in the lives of adult women: A short-term longitudinal study. In C. Dunkel & J. Kerpelman (Eds.), *Possible selves: Theory, research and applications* (pp. 123–140). Hauppauge, NY: Nova Science Publishers.

Anthis, K. S., Dunkel, C. S., & Anderson, B. (2004). Gender and identity status differences in late adolescents' possible selves. *Journal of Adolescence, 27*(2), 147–152.

Anzengruber, D., et al. (2006). Smoking in eating disorders. *Eating Behaviors, 7*(4), 291–299.

Appel, P. W., Piculell, R., Jansky, H. K., & Griffy, K. (2006). Assessing alcohol and other drug problems (AOD) among sexually transmitted disease (STD) clinic patients with a modified CAGE-A: Implications for AOD intervention services and STD prevention. *American Journal of Drug and Alcohol Abuse, 32*(2), 225–236.

Arbona, C. (2005). Promoting the career development and academic achievement of at-risk youth: College access programs. In S. D. Brown & R. W. Lent. (Eds.), *Career development and counseling: Putting theory and research to work* (pp. 525–550). Hoboken, NJ: Wiley.

Arbuthnot, J., & Gordon, D. A. (1988). Crime and cognition: Community applications of sociomoral reasoning development. *Criminal Justice and Behavior, 15*(3), 379–393.

Archer, J. (2006). Testosterone and human aggression: An evaluation of the challenge hypothesis. *Neuroscience & Biobehavioral Reviews, 30*(3), 319–345.

Archibald, L. M. D., & Gathercole, S. E. (2006). Short-term memory and working memory in specific language impairment. In T. P. Alloway & S. E. Gathercole (Eds.), *Working memory and neurodevelopmental disorders* (pp. 139–160). New York: Psychology Press.

Arduini, R. G., Capellini, S. A., & Ciasca, S. M. (2006). Comparative study of the neuropsychological and neuroimaging evaluations in children with dyslexia. *Arquivos de Neuro-Psiquiatría, 64*(2-B), 369–375.

Arija, V., et al. (2006). Nutritional status and performance in test of verbal and non-verbal intelligence in 6-year-old children. *Intelligence, 34*(2), 141–149.

Arnett, J. J. (2000). Emerging adulthood. *American Psychologist, 55*(5), 469–480.

Arnett, J. J. (2007). Socialization in emerging adulthood: From the family to the wider world, from socialization to self-socialization. In J. E. Grusec & P. D. Hastings (Eds.), *Handbook of socialization: Theory and research* (pp. 208–231). New York: Guilford.

Arnon, S., et al. (2006). Live music is beneficial to preterm infants in the neonatal intensive care unit environment. *Birth: Issues in Perinatal Care, 33*(2), 131–136.

Arriaga, P., Esteves, F., Carneiro, P., & Monteiro, M. B. (2006). Violent computer games and their effects on state hostility and physiological arousal. *Aggressive Behavior, 32*(4), 358–371.

Aschermann, E., Gülzow, I., & Wendt, D. (2004). Differences in the comprehension of passive voice in German- and English-speaking children. *Swiss Journal of Psychology, 63*(4), 235–245.

Ash, D. (2004). Reflective scientific sense-making dialogue in two languages: The science in the dialogue and the dialogue in the science. *Science Education, 88*(6), 855–884.

Aslin, R. N., & Schlaggar, B. L. (2006). Is myelination the precipitating neural event for language development in infants and toddlers? *Neurology, 66*(3), 304–305.

Aspy, C. B., et al. (2007). Parental communication and youth sexual behaviour. *Journal of Adolescence, 30*(3), 449–466.

Atkinson, G., & Davenne, D. (2007). Relationships between sleep, physical activity and human health. *Physiology & Behavior, 90*(2–3), 229–235.

August, D., Carlo, M., Dressler, C., & Snow, C. (2005). The critical role of vocabulary development for English language learners. *Learning Disabilities Research & Practice, 20*(1), 50–57.

Ayyash-Abdo, H. (2001). Individualism and collectivism: The case of Lebanon. *Social Behavior and Personality, 29*(5), 503–518.

Azar, B. (1998). What predicts which foods we eat? A genetic disposition for certain tastes may affect people's food preferences. *APA Monitor, 29,* 1.

Bacete, F. G., & Remirez, J. R. (2001). Family and personal correlates of academic achievement. *Psychological Reports, 88*(2), 533–547.

Bachman, J. G., Safron, D. J., Sy, S. R., & Schulenberg, J. E. (2003). Wishing to work: New perspectives on how adolescents' part-time work intensity is linked to educational disengagement, substance use, and other problem behaviours. *International Journal of Behavioral Development, 27*(4), 301–315.

Bagley, C., & D'Augelli, A. R. (2000). Suicidal behaviour in gay, lesbian, and bisexual youth. *British Medical Journal, 320,* 1617–1618.

Bailey, J. M. (2003). *The man who would be queen: The science of gender-bending and transsexualism.* Washington, DC: Joseph Henry Press.

Bailey, J. M., & Pillard, R. C. (1991). A genetic study of male sexual orientation. *Archives of General Psychiatry, 48,* 1089–1096.

Bailey, R. K., & Owens, D. L. (2005). Overcoming challenges in the diagnosis and treatment of attention-deficit/hyperactivity disorder in African Americans. *Journal of the National Medical Association, 97*(10, Suppl), S5–S10.

Baillargeon, R. (1987). Object permanence in 3½- and 4½-month-old infants. *Developmental Psychology, 23,* 655–664.

Bakalar, N. (2005, November 22). Premature births increase along with C-sections. *New York Times,* p. F8.

Baker, C. W., Whisman, M. A., & Brownell, K. D. (2000). Studying intergenerational transmission of eating attitudes and behaviors: Methodological and conceptual questions. *Health Psychology, 19*(4), 376–381.

Bakker, D. J. (2006). Treatment of developmental dyslexia: A review. *Pediatric Rehabilitation, 9*(1), 3–13.

Baldry, A. C. (2003). Bullying in schools and exposure to domestic violence. *Child Abuse and Neglect, 27*(7), 713–732.

Ball, H. L. (2006). Parent–infant bed-sharing behavior. *Human Nature, 17*(3), 301–318.

Ball, J., Lohaus, A., & Miebach, C. (2006). Psychological adjustment and school achievement during transition from elementary to secondary school. *Zeitschrift für Entwicklungspsychologie und Pädagogische Psychologie, 38*(3), 101–109.

Balluz, L. S., et al. (2000). Vitamin and mineral supplement use in the United States: Results from the Third National Health and Nutrition Examination Survey. *Archives of Family Medicine, 9,* 258.

Bandura, A. (1986). *Social foundations of thought and action: A social-cognitive theory.* Englewood Cliffs, NJ: Prentice Hall.

Bandura, A. (2002). Social cognitive theory in cultural context. *Applied Psychology: An International Review, 51*(2), 269–290.

Bandura, A. (2006a). Going global with social cognitive theory: From prospect to paydirt. In S. I. Donaldson, D. E. Berger, & K. Pezdek (Eds.), *Applied psychology: New frontiers and rewarding careers* (pp. 53–79). Hillsdale, NJ: Lawrence Erlbaum Associates Publishers.

Bandura, A. (2006b). Toward a psychology of human agency. *Perspectives on Psychological Science, 1*(2), 164–180.

Bandura, A., Barbaranelli, C., Vittorio Caprara, G., & Pastorelli, C. (2001). Self-efficacy beliefs as shapers of children's aspirations and career trajectories. *Child Development, 72*(1), 187–206.

Bandura, A., Blanchard, E. B., & Ritter, B. (1969). The relative efficacy of desensitization and modeling approaches for inducing behavioral, affective, and cognitive changes. *Journal of Personality and Social Psychology, 13,* 173–199.

Bandura, A., Ross, S. A., & Ross, D. (1963). Imitation of film-mediated aggressive models. *Journal of Abnormal and Social Psychology, 66,* 3–11.

Barbarich, N. C., et al. (2004). Use of nutritional supplements to increase the efficacy of fluoxetine in the treatment of anorexia nervosa. *International Journal of Eating Disorders, 35*(1), 10–15.

Barchard, K. A., & Hakstian, A. R. (2004). The nature and measurement of emotional intelligence abilities: Basic dimensions and their relationships with other cognitive abilities and personality variables. *Educational & Psychological Measurement, 64*(3), 437–462.

Bard, C., Hay, L., & Fleury, M. (1990). Timing and accuracy of visually directed movements in children: Control of direction and amplitude components. *Journal of Experimental Child Psychology, 50,* 102–118.

Barkley, R. A. (2004). Adolescents with attention-deficit/hyperactivity disorder: An overview of empirically based treatments. *Journal of Psychiatric Practice, 10*(1), 39–56.

Baron, S. W., Forde, D. R., & Kay, F. M. (2007). Self-control, risky lifestyles, and situation: The role of opportunity and context in the general theory. *Journal of Criminal Justice, 35*(2), 119–136.

Barr, R. G., Paterson, J. A., MacMartin, L. M., Lehtonen, L., & Young, S. N. (2005). Prolonged and unsoothable crying bouts in infants with and without colic. *Journal of Developmental & Behavioral Pediatrics, 26*(1), 14–23.

Barr, R., Rovee-Collier, C., & Campanella, J. (2005). Retrieval protracts deferred imitation by 6-month-olds. *Infancy, 7*(3), 263–283.

Barrile, M., Armstrong, E. S., & Bower, T. G. R. (1999). Novelty and frequency as determinants of newborn preference. *Developmental Science, 2*(1), 47–52.

Barrow, F. H., Armstrong, M. I., Vargo, A., & Boothroyd, R. A. (2007). Understanding the findings of resilience-related research for fostering the development of African American adolescents. *Child and Adolescent Psychiatric Clinics of North America, 16*(2), 393–413.

Barry, C. M., & Wentzel, K. R. (2006). Friend influence on prosocial behavior: The role of motivational factors and friendship characteristics. *Developmental Psychology, 42*(1), 153–163.

Bartels, M., & Hudziak, J. J. (2007). Genetically informative designs in the study of resilience in developmental psychopathology. *Child and Adolescent Psychiatric Clinics of North America, 16*(2), 323–339.

Barth, J., & Call, J. (2006). Tracking the displacement of objects: A series of tasks with great apes (*Pan troglodytes, Pan paniscus, Gorilla gorilla,* and *Pongo pygmaeus*) and young children (*Homo sapiens*). *Journal of Experimental Psychology: Animal Behavior Processes, 32*(3), 239–252.

Bartholow, B. D., Dicter, C. L., & Sestir, M. A. (2006). Stereotype activation and control of race bias: Cognitive control of inhibition and its impairment by alcohol. *Journal of Personality and Social Psychology, 90*(2), 272–287.

Bartzokis, G. (2004). Age-related myelin breakdown: A developmental model of cognitive decline and Alzheimer's disease. *Neurobiology of Aging, 25*(1), 5–18.

Basic Behavioral Science Task Force of the National Advisory Mental Health Council. (1996). Basic behavioral science research for mental health: Sociocultural and environmental practices. *American Psychologist, 51,* 722–731.

Bastien-Toniazzo, M., & Jullien, S. (2001). Nature and importance of the logographic phase in learning to read. *Reading and Writing, 14*(1–2), 119–143.

Batsche, G. M., & Porter, L. J. (2006). Bullying. In G. G. Bear & K. M. Minke (Eds.), *Children's needs III: Development, prevention, and intervention* (pp. 135–148). Washington, DC: National Association of School Psychologists.

Bauer, K. W., Yang, Y. W., & Austin, S. B. (2004). "How can we stay healthy when you're throwing all of this in front of us?" Findings from focus groups and interviews in middle schools on environmental influences on nutrition and physical activity. *Health Education and Behavior, 31*(1), 33–46.

Bauer, P. J., & Mandler, J. M. (1990). Remembering what happened next: Very young children's recall of event sequences. In R. Fivush & J. A. Hudson (Eds.), *Knowing and remembering in young children.* Cambridge: Cambridge University Press.

Bauman, M. L., Anderson, G., Perry, E., & Ray, M. (2006). Neuroanatomical and neurochemical studies of the autistic brain: Current thought and future directions. In S. O. Moldin & J. L. R. Rubenstein (Eds.), *Understanding autism: From basic neuroscience to treatment* (pp. 303–322). Boca Raton, FL: CRC Press.

Baumeister, R. F., Catanese, K. R., & Vohs, K. D. (2001). Is there a gender difference in strength of sex drive? Theoretical views, conceptual distinctions, and a review of relevant evidence. *Personality and Social Psychology Review, 5*(3), 242–273.

Baumrind, D. (1989). Rearing competent children. In W. Damon (Ed.), *Child development today and tomorrow.* San Francisco: Jossey-Bass.

Baumrind, D. (1991a). The influence of parenting style on adolescent competence and substance use. *Journal of Early Adolescence, 11,* 56–95.

Baumrind, D. (1991b). Parenting styles and adolescent development. In J. Brooks-Gunn, R. Lerner, & A. C. Petersen (Eds.), *Encyclopedia of adolescence.* New York: Garland.

Baumrind, D. (2005). Taking a stand in a morally pluralistic society: Constructive obedience and responsible dissent in moral/character education. In L. Nucci (Ed.), *Conflict, contradiction, and contrarian elements in moral development and education* (pp. 21–50). Mahwah, NJ: Erlbaum.

Bayoumi, R. A., et al. (2006). The genetic basis of inherited primary nocturnal enuresis: A UAE study. *Journal of Psychosomatic Research, 61*(3), 317–320.

Bearce, K. H., & Rovee-Collier, C. (2006). Repeated priming increases memory accessibility in infants. *Journal of Experimental Child Psychology, 93*(4), 357–376.

Beck, E., Burnet, K. L., & Vosper, J. (2006). Birth-order effects on facets of extraversion. *Personality and Individual Differences, 40*(5), 953–959.

Beer, J. M., & Horn, J. M. (2000). The influence of rearing order on personality development within two adoption cohorts. *Journal of Personality, 68*(4), 789–819.

Behrman, R. E., Kliegman, R. M., & Jenson, H. B. (2000). *Nelson review of pediatrics* (2nd ed.). Philadelphia: W. B. Saunders.

Beidel, D. C., & Turner, S. M. (2007). Clinical presentation of social anxiety disorder in children and adolescents. In D. C. Beidel & S. M. Turner (Eds.), *Shy children, phobic adults: Nature and treatment of social anxiety disorders* (2nd ed.) (pp. 47–80). Washington, DC: American Psychological Association.

Beilei, L., Lei, L., Qi, D., & von Hofsten, C. (2002). The development of fine motor skills and their relations to children's academic achievement. *Acta Psychologica Sinica, 34*(5), 494–499.

Bell, J. H., & Bromnick, R. D. (2003). The social reality of the imaginary audience: A ground theory approach. *Adolescence, 38*(150), 205–219.

Bell, K. N., & Norwood, K. (2007). Gender equity intersects with mathematics and technology: Problem-solving education for changing times. In D. M. Sadker & E. S. Silber (Eds.), *Gender in the classroom: Foundations, skills, methods, and strategies across the curriculum* (pp. 225–258). Mahwah, NJ: Erlbaum.

Bellodi, L., et al. (2001). Morbidity risk for obsessive-compulsive spectrum disorders in first-degree relatives of patients with eating disorders. *American Journal of Psychiatry, 158,* 563–569.

Belmonte, M. K., & Carper, R. A. (2006). Monozygotic twins with Asperger syndrome: Differences in behaviour reflect variations in brain structure and function. *Brain and Cognition, 61*(1), 110–121.

Belsky, J. (1990a). Developmental risks associated with infant day care: Attachment insecurity, noncompliance and aggression? In S. Cherazi (Ed.), *Psychosocial issues in day care.* New York: American Psychiatric Press.

Belsky, J. (1990b). The "effects" of infant day care reconsidered. In N. Fox & G. G. Fein (Eds.), *Infant day care: The current debate.* Norwood, NJ: Ablex.

Belsky, J. (2001). Emanuel Miller Lecture: Developmental risks (still) associated with early child care. *Journal of Child Psychology and Psychiatry and Allied Disciplines, 42*(7), 845–859.

Belsky, J. (2006a). Determinants and consequences of infant–parent attachment. In L. Balter & C. S. Tamis-LeMonda (Eds.), *Child psychology: A handbook of contemporary issues* (2nd ed.) (pp. 53–77). New York: Psychology Press.

Belsky, J. (2006b). Early child care and early child development: Major findings of the NICHD Study of Early Child Care. *European Journal of Developmental Psychology, 3*(1), 95–110.

Belsky, J., et al. (2007). Are there long-term effects of early child care? *Child Development, 78*(2), 681–701.

Bem, S. L. (1983). Gender schema theory and its implications for child development: Raising gender-aschematic children in a gender-schematic society. *Signs, 8,* 598–616.

Bem, S. L. (1989). Genital knowledge and gender constancy in preschool children. *Child Development, 60,* 649–662.

Bem, S. L. (1993). *The lenses of gender.* New Haven, CT: Yale University Press.

Bender, H. L., et al. (2007). Use of harsh physical discipline and developmental outcomes in adolescence. *Development and Psychopathology, 19*(1) 227–242.

Bendersky, M., Bennett, D., & Lewis, M. (2006). Aggression at age 5 as a function of prenatal exposure to cocaine, gender, and environmental risk. *Journal of Pediatric Psychology, 31*(1), 71–84.

Bennett, D. S., Bendersky, M., & Lewis, M. (2004). On specifying specificity: Facial expressions at 4 months. *Infancy, 6*(3), 425–429.

Bennett, S. E., & Assefi, N. P. (2005). School-based teenage pregnancy prevention programs: A systematic review of randomized controlled trials. *Journal of Adolescent Health, 36*(1), 72–81.

Benoit, D., & Coolbear, J. (2004). Disorders of attachment and failure to thrive. In L. Atkinson & S. Goldberg (Eds.), *Attachment issues in psychopathology and intervention* (pp. 49–64). Hillsdale, NJ: Erlbaum.

Berg, C. J., Chang, J., Callaghan, W. M., & Whitehead, S. J. (2003). Pregnancy-related mortality in the United States, 1991–1997. *Obstetrics and Gynecology, 101,* 289–296.

Berger, L. E., Jodl, K. M., Allen, J. P., McElhaney, K. B., & Kuperminc, G. P.(2005). When adolescents disagree with others about their symptoms: Differences in attachment organization as an explanation of discrepancies between adolescent, parent, and peer reports of behavior problems. *Development and Psychopathology, 17*(2), 509–528.

Berko, J. (1958). The child's learning of English morphology. *Word, 14,* 150–177.

Berndt, T. J. (1992). Friendship and friends' influence in adolescence. *Current Directions in Psychological Science, 1,* 156–159.

Berndt, T. J. (2004). Friendship and three A's (aggression, adjustment, and attachment). *Journal of Experimental Child Psychology, 88*(1), 1–4.

Berndt, T. J., Miller, K. E., & Park, K. E. (1989). Adolescents' perceptions of friends and parents' influence on aspects of their school adjustment. *Journal of Early Adolescence, 9,* 419–435.

Berndt, T. J., & Perry, T. B. (1986). Children's perceptions of friendships as supportive relationships. *Developmental Psychology, 22,* 640–648.

Berndt, T. J., & Perry, T. B. (1990). Distinctive features and effects of early adolescent friendships. In R. Montemayor, G. R. Adams, & T. P. Gullotta (Eds.), *From childhood to adolescence: A transitional period?* Newbury Park, CA: Sage.

Bernstein, G. A., & Layne, A. E. (2006). Separation anxiety disorder and generalized anxiety disorder. In M. K. Dulcan & J. M. Wiener, (Eds.), *Essentials of child and adolescent psychiatry* (pp. 415–439). Washington, DC: American Psychiatric Publishing.

Bernstein, I. M., et al. (2005). Maternal smoking and its association with birth weight. *Obstetrics & Gynecology, 106,* 986–991.

Berry, J. W., & Triandis, H. C. (2006). Culture. In K. Pawlik & G. d'Ydewalle (Eds.), *Psychological concepts: An international historical perspective* (pp. 47–62). Hove, England: Psychology Press/Taylor & Francis.

Bertenthal, B. I., & Campos, J. J. (1990). A systems approach to the organizing effects of self-produced locomotion during infancy. In C. Rovee-Collier & L. Lipsitt (Eds.), *Advances in infancy research,* Vol. 6. Norwood, NJ: Ablex.

Berzonsky, M. D. (2004). Identity style, parental authority, and identity commitment. *Journal of Youth and Adolescence, 33*(3), 213–220.

Berzonsky, M. D. (2005). Ego identity: A personal standpoint in a postmodern world. *Identity, 5*(2), 125–136.

Berzonsky, M. D., & Kuk, L. S. (2005). Identity style, psychosocial maturity, and academic performance. *Personality and Individual Differences, 39*(1), 235–247.

Bhutta, A. T., Cleves, M. A., Casey, P. H., Cradock, M. M., & Anand, K. J. S. (2002). Cognitive and behavioral outcomes of school-aged children who were born preterm: A meta-analysis. *Journal of the American Medical Association, 288,* 728–737.

Bialystock, E., & Senman, L. (2004). Executive processes in appearance–reality tasks: The role of inhibition of attention and symbolic representation. *Child Development, 75*(2), 562–579.

Bialystok, E. K., & Craik, F. I. M. (2007). Bilingualism and naming: Implications for cognitive assessment. *Journal of the International Neuropsychological Society, 13*(2), 209–211.

Biederman, J., et al. (2007). Effect of comorbid symptoms of oppositional defiant disorder on responses to atomoxetine in children with ADHD: A meta-analysis of controlled clinical trial data. *Psychopharmacology, 190*(1), 31–41.

Bilsker, D., Schiedel, D., & Marcia, J. E. (1988). Sex differences in identity status. *Sex Roles, 18,* 231–236.

Birch, C. D., Stewart, S. H., & Brown, C. G. (2007). Exploring differential patterns of situational risk for binge eating and heavy drinking. *Addictive Behaviors, 32*(3), 433–448.

Birch, L. L., Gunder, L., Grimm-Thomas, K., & Laing, D. G. (1998). Infants' consumption of a new food enhances acceptance of similar foods. *Appetite, 30*(3), 283–295.

Bird, A., Reese, E., & Tripp, G. (2006). Parent-child talk about past emotional events: Associations with child temperament and goodness-of-fit. *Journal of Cognition and Development, 7*(2), 189–210.

Bishop, D. M. (2005). The role of race and ethnicity in juvenile justice processing. In D. F. Hawkins & K. Kempf-Leonard (Eds.), *Our children, their children: Confronting racial and ethnic differences in American juvenile justice* (pp. 23–82). The John D. and Catherine T. MacArthur foundation series on mental health and development. Research network on adolescent development and juvenile justice. Chicago: University of Chicago Press.

Bjorklund, D. F., & Rosenblum, K. E. (2001). Children's use of multiple and variable addition strategies in a game context. *Developmental Science, 4*(2), 184–194.

Black, D. W. (2007). Antisocial personality disorder, conduct disorder, and psychopathy. In J. E. Grant, & M. N. Potenza. (Eds.). *Textbook of men's mental health.* (pp. 143–170). Washington, DC: American Psychiatric Publishing, Inc.

Blake, S. M., Ledsky, R., Goodenow, C., Sawyer, R., Lohrmann, D., & Windsor, R. (2003). Condom availability programs in Massachusetts high schools: Relationships with condom use and sexual behavior. *American Journal of Public Health, 93,* 955–962.

Blanchette, N., Smith, M. L., Fernandes-Penney, A., King, S., & Read, S. (2001). Cognitive and motor development in children with vertically transmitted HIV infection. *Brain and Cognition, 46*(1–2), 50–53.

Blass, E. M., & Camp, C. A. (2003). Changing determinants in 6- to 12-week-old human infants. *Developmental Psychobiology, 42*(3), 312–316.

Blevins-Knabe, B. (1987). Development of the ability to insert into a series. *Journal of Genetic Psychology, 148,* 427–441.

Bloch, M., Rotenberg, N., Koren, D., & Ehud, K. (2006). Risk factors for early postpartum depressive symptoms. *General Hospital Psychiatry, 28*(1), 3–8.

Blom-Hoffman, J., George, J. B., & Franko, D. L. (2006). Childhood overweight. In G. G. Bear & K. M. Minke (Eds.), *Children's needs III: Development, prevention, and intervention* (pp. 989–1000). Washington, DC: National Association of School Psychologists.

Bloom, B., Dey, A. N., & Freeman, G. (2006). Summary health statistics for U.S. children: National Health Interview Survey, 2005. *National Center for Health Statistics, Vital Health Stat 10*(231).

Bloom, L. (1998). Language acquisition in its developmental context. In W. Damon (Ed.), *Handbook of child psychology* (5th ed.), Vol. 2. New York: Wiley.

Bloom, P. (2002). Mind reading, communication, and the learning of names for things. *Mind and Language, 17*(1–2), 37–54.

Boada, R., & Pennington, B. F. (2006). Deficient implicit phonological representations in children with dyslexia. *Journal of Experimental Child Psychology, 95*(3), 153–193.

Boccia, M., & Campos, J. J. (1989). Maternal emotional signals, social referencing, and infants' reactions to strangers. In N. Eisenberg (Ed.), *New directions for child development,* No. 44, *Empathy and related emotional responses.* San Francisco: Jossey-Bass.

Boden, C., & Giaschi, D. (2007). M-stream deficits and reading-related visual processes in developmental dyslexia. *Psychological Bulletin, 133*(2), 346–366.

Boehnke, K., Silbreisen, R. K., Eisenberg, N., Reykowski, J., & Palmonari, A. (1989). The development of prosocial motivation: A cross-national study. *Journal of Cross-Cultural Psychology, 20,* 219–243.

Boey, C. C. M., Omar, A., & Phillips, J. A. (2003). Correlation among academic performance, recurrent abdominal pain and other factors in year-6 urban primary-school children in Malaysia. *Journal of Paediatrics and Child Health, 39*(5), 352–357.

Boggiano, A. K., & Barrett, M. (1991). Strategies to motivate helpless and mastery-oriented children: The effect of gender-based expectancies. *Sex Roles, 25,* 487–510.

Bohannon, J. N., III, & Stanowicz, L. (1988). The issue of negative evidence: Adult responses to children's language errors. *Developmental Psychology, 24,* 684–689.

Bohn, A. P. (2003). Familiar voices: Using Ebonics communication techniques in the primary classroom. *Urban Education, 38*(6), 688–707.

Bohon, C., Garber, J., & Horowitz, J. L. (2007). Predicting school dropout and adolescent sexual behavior in offspring of depressed and nondepressed mothers. *Journal of the American Academy of Child & Adolescent Psychiatry, 46*(1), 15–24.

Boivin, M., Vitaro, F., & Poulin, F. (2005). Peer relationships and the development of aggressive behavior in early childhood. In R. E. Tremblay, W. W. Hartup, & J. Archer (Eds.), *Developmental origins of aggression* (pp. 376–397). New York: Guilford.

Boman, U. W., Hanson, C., Hjelmquist, E., & Möller, A. (2006). Personality traits in women with Turner syndrome. *Scandinavian Journal of Psychology, 47*(3), 219–223.

Bonkowski, S. (2005). Group work with children of divorce. In G. L. Greif & P. H. Ephross (Eds.), *Group work with populations at risk* (2nd ed.) (pp. 135–145). New York: Oxford University Press.

Bonn-Miller, M. O., Zvolensky, M. J., & Bernstein, A. (2007). Marijuana use motives: Concurrent relations to frequency of past 30-day use and anxiety sensitivity among young adult marijuana smokers. *Addictive Behaviors, 32*(1) 49–62.

Boom, J., Wouters, H., & Keller, M. (2007). A cross-cultural validation of stage development: A Rasch re-analysis of longitudinal socio-moral reasoning data. *Cognitive Development, 22*(2), 213–229.

Booth, A., Johnson, D. R., Granger, D. A., Crouter, A. C., & McHale, S. (2003). Testosterone and child and adolescent adjustment: The moderating role of parent–child relationships. *Developmental Psychology, 39*(1), 85–98.

Booth-LaForce, C., et al. (2006). Attachment, self-worth, and peer-group functioning in middle childhood. *Attachment & Human Development, 8*(4), 309–325.

Bosi, M,. L. & de Oliveira, F. P. (2006). Bulimic behavior in adolescent athletes. In P. I. Swain (Ed.), *New developments in eating disorders research.* (pp. 123–133). Hauppauge, NY: Nova Science Publishers.

Boskind-White, M., & White, W. C. (1983). *Bulimarexia: The binge/purge cycle.* New York: Norton.

Bost, L. W., & Riccomini, P. J (2006). Effective instruction: An inconspicuous strategy for dropout prevention. *Remedial and Special Education, 27*(5), 301–311.

Bouchard, C., et al. (1990). The response to long-term overfeeding in identical twins. *New England Journal of Medicine, 322,* 1477–1482.

Bouchard, T. J., Jr., & Loehlin, J. C. (2001). Genes, evolution, and personality. *Behavior Genetics, 31*(3), 243–273.

Bouchard, T. J., Jr., Lykken, D. T., McGue, M., Segal, N. L., & Tellegen, A. (1990). Sources of human psychological differences: The Minnesota study of twins reared apart. *Science, 250,* 223–228.

Bouldin, P., & Pratt, C. (1999). Characteristics of preschool and school-age children with imaginary companions. *Journal of Genetic Psychology, 160*(4), 397–410.

Bower, T. G. R. (1974). *Development in infancy.* San Francisco: W. H. Freeman.

Bowlby, J. (1988). *A secure base.* New York: Basic Books.

Boysson-Bardies, B. de, & Halle, P. A. (1994). Speech development: Contributions of cross-linguistic studies. In A. Vyt et al. (Eds.), *Early child development in the French tradition: Contributions from current research.* Hillsdale, NJ: Erlbaum.

Bradley, R. H. (2006). The home environment. In N. F. Watt et al. (Eds.), *The crisis in youth mental health: Critical issues and effective programs,* Vol. 4, *Early intervention programs and policies, Child psychology and mental health* (pp. 89–120). Westport, CT: Praeger/Greenwood.

Bradley, R. H., Caldwell, B. M., & Corwyn, R. F. (2003). The child care HOME inventories: Assessing the quality of family child care homes. *Early Childhood Research Quarterly, 18*(3), 294–309.

Bradley, R. H., & Corwyn, R. F. (2006). The family environment. In L. Balter & C. S. Tamis-LeMonda (Eds.), *Child psychology: A handbook of contemporary issues* (2nd ed.) (pp. 493–520). New York: Psychology Press.

Bramlett, M. D., & Mosher, W. D. (2002). *Cohabitation, marriage, divorce, and remarriage.* National Center for Health Statistics, Vital Health Statistics, 23(22). Available at http://www.cdc.gov/nchs/data/series/sr_23/sr23_022.pdf.

Branco, J. C., & Lourenço, O. (2004). Cognitive and linguistic aspects in 5- to 6-year-olds' class-inclusion reasoning. *Psicologia Educação Cultura, 8*(2), 427–445.

Brandstätter, H., & Farthofer, A. (2003). Influence of part-time work on university students' academic performance. *Zeitschrift für Arbeits- und Organisationspsychologie, 47*(3), 134–145.

Brandtjen, H., & Verny, T (2001). Short and long term effects on infants and toddlers in full time daycare centers. *Journal of Prenatal & Perinatal Psychology & Health, 15*(4), 239–286.

Brase, G. L. (2006). Cues of parental investment as a factor in attractiveness. *Evolution and Human Behavior, 27*(2), 145–157.

Braza, F., et al. (2000). Efecto de los hermanos en la flexibilidad de comportamiento de ninos preescolares. *Revista Mexicana de Psicologia, 17*(2), 181–190.

Brazier, A., & Rowlands, C. (2006). PKU in the family: Working together. *Clinical Child Psychology and Psychiatry, 11*(3), 483–488.

Breastfeeding. (2006). Centers for Disease Control and Prevention. Department of Health and Human Services. Available at http://www.cdc.gov/breastfeeding/faq/index.htm. Accessed July 16, 2007.

Bremner, A., & Bryant, P. (2001). The effect of spatial cues on infants' responses in the AB task, with and without a hidden object. *Developmental Science, 4*(4), 408–415.

Brenneman, M. H., Morris, R. D., & Israelian, M. (2007). Language preference and its relationship with reading skills in English and Spanish. *Psychology in the Schools, 44*(2), 171–181.

Bretherton, I., Golby, B., & Halvorsen, C. (1993, March). *Fathers as attachment and caregiving figures.* Paper presented at the meeting of the Society for Research in Child Development, New Orleans, LA.

Bridges, K. (1932). Emotional development in early infancy. *Child Development, 3,* 324–341.

Briones, T. L., Klintsova, A. Y., & Greenough, W. T. (2004). Stability of synaptic plasticity in the adult rat visual cortex induced by complex environment exposure. *Brain Research, 1018*(1), 130–135.

"British study finds leukemia risk in children of A-plant workers." (1990, February 18). *New York Times,* p. A27.

Brody, J. E. (1998, February 10). Genetic ties may be factor in violence in stepfamilies. *New York Times,* pp. F1, F4.

Brody, L. R., Zelazo, P. R., & Chaika, H. (1984). Habituation–dishabituation to speech in the neonate. *Developmental Psychology, 20,* 114–119.

Brodzinsky, D. M., Patterson, C. J., & Vaziri, M. (2002). Adoption agency perspectives on lesbian and gay prospective parents: A national study. *Adoption Quarterly, 5*(3), 5–23.

Bronfenbrenner, U. (1973). The dream of the kibbutz. In *Readings in human development.* Guilford, CT: Dushkin.

Bronfenbrenner, U., & Morris, P. A. (2006). The bioecological model of human development. In R. M. Lerner & W. Damon (Eds.), *Handbook of child psychology* (6th ed.), Vol. 1, *Theoretical models of human development* (pp. 793–828). Hoboken, NJ: Wiley.

Bronson, G. W. (1990). Changes in infants' visual scanning across the 2- to 14-week age period. *Journal of Experimental Child Psychology, 49,* 101–125.

Bronson, G. W. (1991). Infant differences in rate of visual encoding. *Child Development, 62,* 44–54.

Bronson, G. W. (1997). The growth of visual capacity: Evidence from infant scanning patterns. *Advances in Infancy Research, 11,* 109–141.

Brown, A. M. (1990). Development of visual sensitivity to light and color vision in human infants: A critical review. *Vision Research, 30,* 1159–1188.

Brown, B. B., Mounts, N., Lamborn, S. D., & Steinberg, L. (1993). Parenting practices and peer group affiliation in adolescence. *Child Development, 64,* 467–482.

Brown, R. (1973). *A first language: The early stages.* Cambridge, MA: Harvard University Press.

Brown, R. (1977). Introduction. In C. A. Snow & C. Ferguson (Eds.), *Talking to children.* New York: Cambridge University Press.

Brownell, C. A., & Carriger, M. S. (1990). Changes in cooperation and self-other differentiation during the second year. *Child Development, 61,* 1164–1174.

Browning, J. R., Hatfield, E., Kessler, D., & Levine, T. (2000). Sexual motives, gender, and sexual behavior. *Archives of Sexual Behavior, 29*(2), 135–153.

Bruck, M., Ceci, S. J., & Principe, G. F. (2006). The child and the law. In K. Renninger I. E.

Sigel, W. Damon, & R. M. Lerner (Eds.), *Handbook of child psychology* (6th ed.), Vol. 4, *Child psychology in practice* (pp. 776–816). Hoboken, NJ: Wiley.

Brunner, R., Parzer, P., & Resch, F. (2005). Involuntary hospitalization of patients with anorexia nervosa: Clinical issues and empirical findings. *Fortschritte der Neurologie, Psychiatrie, 73*(1), 9–15.

Bryden, P. J., Bruyn, J., & Fletcher, P. (2005). Handedness and health: An examination of the association between different handedness classifications and health disorders. *Laterality: Asymmetries of Body, Brain and Cognition, 10*(5), 429–440.

Buckley, K. E., & Anderson, C. A. (2006). A theoretical model of the effects and consequences of playing video games. In P. Vorderer & J. Bryant (Eds.), *Playing video games: Motives, responses, and consequences* (pp. 363–378). Mahwah, NJ: Erlbaum.

Buda, B. (2007). The science of suicide prevention. *Crisis: The Journal of Crisis Intervention and Suicide Prevention, 28*(1), 51–52.

Budney, A. J., Vandrey, R. G., Hughes, J. R., Moore, B. A., & Bahrenburg, B. (2007). Oral delta-9-tetrahydrocannabinol suppresses cannabis withdrawal symptoms. *Drug and Alcohol Dependence, 86*(1), 22–29.

Bugental, D. B., & Happaney, K. (2004). Predicting infant maltreatment in low-income families: The interactive effects of maternal attributions and child status at birth. *Developmental Psychology, 40*(2), 234–243.

Bukowski, W. M., Gauze, C., Hoza, B., & Newcomb, A. F. (1993a). Differences and consistency between same-sex and other-sex peer relationships during early adolescence. *Developmental Psychology, 29,* 255–263.

Bukowski, W. M., Hoza, B., & Boivin, M. (1993b). Popularity, friendship, and emotional adjustment during early adolescence. In B. Laursen (Ed.), *New directions in child development,* No. 60, *Close friendships in adolescence.* San Francisco: Jossey-Bass.

Bunikowski, R., et al. (1998). Neurodevelopmental outcome after prenatal exposure to opiates. *European Journal of Pediatrics, 157*(9), 724–730.

Bunting, L., & McAuley, C. (2004). Teenage pregnancy and motherhood: The contribution of support. *Child and Family Social Work, 9*(2), 207–215.

Burke, J. M., & Baker, R. C. (2001). Is fluvoxamine safe and effective for treating anxiety disorders in children? *Journal of Family Practice, 50*(8), 719.

Bushman, B. J. (1998). Priming effects of media violence on the accessibility of aggressive constructs in memory. *Personality and Social Psychology Bulletin, 24*(5), 537–545.

Bushnell, E. W. (1993, June). *A dual-processing approach to cross-modal matching: Implications for development.* Paper presented at the Society for Research in Child Development, New Orleans, LA.

Bushnell, I. W. R. (2001). Mother's face recognition in newborn infants: Learning and memory. *Infant and Child Development, 10*(1–2), 67–74.

Buss, D., & Duntley, J. D. (2006). The evolution of aggression. In M. Schaller, J. A. Simpson, & D. T. Kenrick (Eds.), *Evolution and social psychology: Frontiers of social psychology* (pp. 263–285). Madison, CT: Psychosocial Press.

Buss, D. M. (1999). Adaptive individual differences revisited. *Journal of Personality, 67*(2), 259–264.

Buss, D. M. (2000). The evolution of happiness. *American Psychologist, 55,* 15–23.

Bussey, K., & Bandura, A. (1984). Influence of gender constancy and social power on sex-linked modeling. *Journal of Personality and Social Psychology, 47,* 1292–1302.

Buston, K., Williamson, L., & Hart, G. (2007). Young women under 16 years with experience of sexual intercourse: Who becomes pregnant? *Journal of Epidemiology & Community Health, 61*(3) 221–225.

Butterfield, S. A., & Loovis, E. M. (1993). Influence of age, sex, balance, and sport participation on development of throwing by children in grades K–8. *Perceptual and Motor Skills, 76,* 459–464.

Butterworth, G., Verweij, E., & Hopkins, B. (1997). The development of prehension in infants: Halverson revisited. *British Journal of Developmental Psychology, 15*(2), 223–236.

Buxhoeveden, D. P., Hasselrot, U., Buxhoeveden, N. E., Booze, R. M., & Mactutus, C. F. (2006). Microanatomy in 21 day rat brains exposed prenatally to cocaine. *International Journal of Developmental Neuroscience, 24*(5), 335–341

Bynum, M. S. (2007). African American mother–daughter communication about sex and daughters' sexual behavior: Does college racial composition make a difference? *Cultural Diversity & Ethnic Minority Psychology, 13*(2), 151–160.

Cabeza, R., Locantore, J. K., & Anderson, N. D. (2003). Lateralization of prefrontal activity during episodic memory retrieval: Evidence for the production-monitoring hypothesis. *Journal of Cognitive Neuroscience, 15*(2), 249–259.

Cairns, R. B., & Cairns, B. D. (1991). Social cognition and social networks: A developmental perspective. In D. J. Pepler & K. H. Rubin (Eds.), *The development and treatment of childhood aggression.* Hillsdale, NJ: Erlbaum.

Call, J. (2001). Object permanence in orangutans (*Pongo pygmaeus*), chimpanzees (*Pan troglodytes*), and children (*Homo sapiens*). *Journal of Comparative Psychology, 115*(2), 159–171.

Callan, M. J., Ellard, J. H., & Nicol, J. E. (2006). The belief in a just world and immanent justice reasoning in adults. *Personality and Social Psychology Bulletin, 32*(12), 1646–1658.

Calvert, S. L., & Kotler, J. A. (2003). Lessons from children's television: The impact of the Children's Television Act on children's learning. *Journal of Applied Developmental Psychology, 24*(3), 275–335.

Calvete, E. (2007). Justification of violence beliefs and social problem-solving as mediators between maltreatment and behavior problems in adolescents. *The Spanish Journal of Psychology, 10*(1), 131–140.

Camarena, P. M. (1991). Conformity in adolescence. In R. M. Lerner, A. C. Petersen & J. Brooks-Gunn (Eds.), *Encyclopedia of Adolescence.* New York: Garland.

Campanella, J., & Rovee-Collier, C. (2005). Latent learning and deferred imitation at 3 months. *Infancy, 7*(3), 243–262.

Campbell, A., Shirley, L., & Caygill, L. (2002). Sex-typed preferences in three domains: Do two-year-olds need cognitive variables? *British Journal of Psychology, 93*(2), 203–217.

Campbell, A., Shirley, L., Heywood, C., & Crook, C. (2000). Infants' visual preference for sex-congruent babies, children, toys and activities: A longitudinal study. *British Journal of Developmental Psychology, 18*(4), 479–498.

Campbell, D. A., Lake, M. F. Falk, M., & Backstrand, J. R. (2006). A randomized control trial of continuous support in labor by a lay doula. *Journal of Obstetric, Gynecologic, and Neonatal Nursing, 35*(4), 456–464.

Campbell, D. W., & Eaton, W. O. (1999). Sex differences in the activity level of infants. *Infant and Child Development, 8*(1), 1–17.

Campbell, D. W., Eaton, W. O., & McKeen, N. A. (2002). Motor activity level and behavioural control in young children. *International Journal of Behavioral Development, 26*(4), 289–296.

Campbell, J. O., Bliven, T. D., Silver, M. M., Snyder, K. J., & Spear, L. P. (2000). Effects of prenatal cocaine on behavioral adaptation to chronic stress in adult rats. *Neurotoxicology and Teratology, 22*(6), 845–850.

Campbell, S. B. (1990). *Behavior problems in preschool children: Clinical and developmental issues.* New York: Guilford.

Campbell, S. B., et al. (2004). The course of maternal depressive symptoms and maternal sensitivity as predictors of attachment security at 36 months. *Development and Psychopathology, 16*(2), 231–252.

Campos, J. J., Hiatt, S., Ramsey, D., Henderson, C., & Svejda, M. (1978). The emergence of fear on the visual cliff. In M. Lewis & L. Rosenblum (Eds.), *The origins of affect.* New York: Plenum.

Campos, J. J., Langer, A., & Krowitz, A. (1970). Cardiac responses on the visual cliff in pre-locomotor human infants. *Science, 170,* 196–197.

Candy, T. R., Crowell, J. A., & Banks, M. S. (1998). Optical, receptoral, and retinal constraints on foveal and peripheral vision in the human neonate. *Vision Research, 38*(24), 3857–3870.

Canitano, R. (2007). Epilepsy in autism spectrum disorders. *European Child & Adolescent Psychiatry, 16*(1), 61–66.

Canton, D. A. (2005). Black fathers in contemporary American society: Strengths, weaknesses, and strategies for change. *Sex Roles, 52*(9–10), 715–716.

Caplan, M., Vespo, J., Pedersen, J., & Hale, D. F. (1991). Conflict and its resolution in small groups of one and two-year-olds. *Child Development, 62,* 1513–1524.

Caplan, P. J., & Larkin, J. (1991). The anatomy of dominance and self-protection. *American Psychologist, 46,* 536.

Capron, C., Thérond, C., & Duyme, M. (2007). Brief report: Effect of menarcheal status and family structure on depressive symptoms and emotional/behavioural problems in young adolescent girls. *Journal of Adolescence, 30*(1), 175–179.

Caravolas, M., & Bruck, M. (2000). Vowel categorization skill and its relationship to early literacy skills among first-grade Quebec-French children. *Journal of Experimental Child Psychology, 76*(3), 190–221.

Carey, B. (2007a, March 26). Poor behavior is linked to time in day care. *New York Times online.*

Carey, B. (2007b, June 22). Research finds firstborns gain the higher I.Q. *The New York Times online.*

Carlo, G., Knight, G. P., Eisenberg, N., & Rotenberg, K. (1991). Cognitive processes and prosocial behaviors among children: The role of affective attributions and reconciliations. *Developmental Psychology, 27, 456–461.*

Caron, A. J., Caron, R. F., & Carlson, V. R. (1979). Infant perception of the invariant shape of objects varying in slant. *Child Development, 50,* 716–721.

Carroll, J. S., et al. (2007). So close, yet so far away: The impact of varying marital horizons on emerging adulthood. *Journal of Adolescent Research, 22*(3), 219–247.

Carver, L. J., & Vaccaro, B. G. (2007). 12-month-old infants allocate increased neural resources to stimuli associated with negative adult emotion. *Developmental Psychology, 43*(1), 54–69.

Casas, J. F., et al. (2006). Early parenting and children's relational and physical aggression in the preschool and home contexts. *Journal of Applied Developmental Psychology, 27*(3), 209–227.

Cashwell, T. H., Skinner, C. H., & Smith, E. S. (2001). Increasing second-grade students' reports of peers' prosocial behaviors via direct instruction, group reinforcement, and progress feedback: A replication and extension. *Education and Treatment of Children, 24*(2), 161–175.

Cassia, V. M., Simion, F., & Umilta, C. (2001). Face preference at birth: The role of an orienting mechanism. *Developmental Science, 4*(1), 101–108.

Caton, D., et al. (2002). Anesthesia for childbirth: Controversy and change. *American Journal of Obstetrics & Gynecology, 186*(5), S25–S30.

Cattell, R. B. (1949). *The culture-fair intelligence test.* Champaign, IL: Institute for Personality and Ability Testing.

Caulfield, R. (2000). Beneficial effects of tactile stimulation on early development. *Early Childhood Education Journal, 27*(4), 255–257.

Cavallini, A., et al. (2002). Visual acuity in the first two years of life in healthy term newborns: An experience with the Teller Acuity Cards. *Functional Neurology: New Trends in Adaptive and Behavioral Disorders, 17*(2), 87–92.

Cavell, T. A. (2001). Updating our approach to parent training. I. The case against targeting noncompliance. *Clinical Psychology: Science and Practice, 8*(3), 299–318.

Ceci, S. J. (1993, August). *Cognitive and social factors in children's testimony.* Master lecture presented at the meeting of the American Psychological Association, Toronto.

Ceci, S. J., & Williams, W. M. (Eds.). *Why aren't more women in science: Top researchers debate the evidence.* Washington, DC: American Psychological Association.

Centers for Disease Control and Prevention. (2001, December 3). *Sexually transmitted disease surveillance 2000.* Atlanta, GA: Division of STD Prevention, National Center for HIV, STD, and TB Prevention.

Centers for Disease Control and Prevention. (2002a). *Laboratory guidelines screening tests to detect* Chlamydia trachomatis *and* Neisseria gonorrhoeae *infections.* Atlanta, GA: Division of Sexually Transmitted Diseases, National Center for HIV, STD, and TB Prevention. Available at http://www .cdc.gov/STD/ LabGuidelines/default.htm.

Centers for Disease Control and Prevention. (2002b). Cited in J. E. Brody (2002, January 1), What women must know about fertility, *New York Times,* F6.

Centers for Disease Control and Prevention. (2004). *DES update: Health care providers.* Available at http://www.cdc.gov/ des/hcp/ index.html. Accessed May 4, 2004.

Centers for Disease Control and Prevention. (2005). DES Update: For Consumers. Available at http://www.cdc.gov/DES/consumers/ index.html.

Centers for Disease Control and Prevention. (2005). National Center for Health Statistics. *America's children, 2005. America's children: Key national indicators of well-being 2005.* Childstats.gov. Available at http://www .childstats.gov/amchildren05/hea8.asp.

Centers for Disease Control and Prevention. (2006a). HIV/AIDS Surveillance Report, 2005, v. 17. Atlanta: U.S. Department of Health and Human Services, Centers for Disease Control and Prevention. Available at http://www.cdc.gov/hiv/topics/surveillance/ resources/reports/.

Centers for Disease Control and Prevention. (2006b). National Center for Health Statistics. *America's Children in Brief: Key National Indicators of Well-Being, 2006.* Available at www .childstats.gov/americaschildren/tables/pop6a .asp. Accessed May 11, 2007.

Centers for Disease Control and Prevention. (2007a). Coverage estimates for school entry vaccinations: 2005–2006 school year. National Immunization Program. Available at http://www2.cdc.gov/nip/schoolsurv/ nationalAvg.asp.

Centers for Disease Control and Prevention. (2007b, January 10). Ten things you need to know about immunizations. Department of Health and Human Services. Available at http://www.cdc.gov/nip/publications/ fs/gen/shouldknow.htm. Accessed May 6, 2007.

Central Intelligence Agency. (2004, September 17). *The World Factbook.* Available at http://www.cia.gov/cia/publications/ factbook/geos/us.html#People.

Cernoch, J., & Porter, R. (1985). Recognition of maternal axillary odors by infants. *Child Development, 56,* 1593–1598.

Chance, S. E., Brown, R. T., Dabbs, J. M., Jr., & Casey, R. (2000). Testosterone, intelligence and behavior disorders in young boys. *Personality and Individual Differences, 28*(3) 437–445.

Chang, L., Schwartz, D., Dodge, K., & McBride-Chang, C. (2003). Harsh parenting in relation to child emotion regulation and aggression. *Journal of Family Psychology, 17*(4), 598–606.

Chapman, M., & McBride, M. C. (1992). Beyond competence and performance: Children's class inclusion strategies, superordinate class cues, and verbal justifications. *Developmental Psychology, 28,* 319–327.

Chaudhry, V., et al. (2002). Thalidomide-induced neuropathy. *Neurology, 59*(12), 1872–1875.

Chelonis, J. J., Gillam, M. P., & Paule, M. G. (2003). The effects of prenatal cocaine exposure on reversal learning using a simple visual discrimination task in rhesus monkeys. *Neurotoxicology and Teratology, 25*(4), 437–446.

Chen, X., Chen, H., & Kaspar, V. (2001). Group social functioning and individual socioemotional and school adjustment in Chinese children. *Merrill–Palmer Quarterly, 47*(2), 264–299.

Chen, Z., & Cowan, N. (2005). Chunk limits and length limits in immediate recall: A reconciliation. *Journal of Experimental Psychology: Learning, Memory, and Cognition, 31*(6), 1235–1249.

Cheng, S-T., & Chan, A. C. M. (2007). Multiple pathways from stress to suicidality and the protective effect of social support in Hong Kong adolescents. *Suicide and Life-Threatening Behavior, 37*(2), 187–196.

Cherney, I. D., Harper, H. J., & Winter, J. A. (2006). Nouveaux jouets: Ce que les enfants identifient comme "jouets de garcons" et "jouets de filles." *Enfance, 58*(3), 266–282.

Chess, S., & Thomas, A. (1984). *Origins and evolution of behavior disorders: From infancy to early adult life.* New York: Brunner/ Mazel.

Chess, S., & Thomas, A. (1991). Temperament. In M. Lewis (Ed.), *Child and adolescent psychiatry: A comprehensive textbook.* Baltimore: Williams & Wilkins.

Cheung, C., Chan, W., Lee, T., Liu, S., & Leung, K. (2001). Structure of moral consciousness and moral intentions among youth in Hong Kong. *International Journal of Adolescence and Youth, 9*(2–3), 83–116.

Chiou, W-B, & Wan, C-S. (2006). Sexual self-disclosure in cyberspace among Taiwanese adolescents: Gender differences and the interplay of cyberspace and real life. *CyberPsychology & Behavior, 9*(1), 46–53.

Chira, S. (1991, December 8). Report says too many aren't ready for school. *New York Times,* p. B18.

Chomsky, N. (1988). *Language and problems of knowledge.* Cambridge, MA: MIT Press.

Chomsky, N. (1990). On the nature, use, and acquisition of language. In W. G. Lycan (Ed.), *Mind and cognition.* Oxford: Blackwell.

Chou, T-L., et al. (2006). Developmental and skill effects on the neural correlates of semantic processing to visually presented words. *Human Brain Mapping, 27*(11), 915–924.

Christenson, S. L., & Thurlow, M. L. (2004). School dropouts: Prevention considerations, interventions, and challenges. *Current Directions in Psychological Science, 13*(1), 36–39.

Christian, P., et al. (2003). Effects of alternative maternal micronutrient supplements on low birth weight in rural Nepal: Double blind randomised community trial. *British Medical Journal, 326,* 571.

Christophersen, E. R., & Mortweet, S. L. (2003). Establishing bedtime. In E. R. Christophersen & S. L. Mortweet (Eds.), *Parenting that works: Building skills that last a lifetime* (pp. 209–228). Washington, DC: American Psychological Association.

Chronis, A. M., et al. (2007). Maternal depression and early positive parenting predict future conduct problems in young children with attention-deficit/hyperactivity disorder. *Developmental Psychology, 43*(1), 70–82.

Cicchetti, D., Rogosch, F. A., & Toth, S. L. (2006). Fostering secure attachment in infants in maltreating families through preventive interventions. *Development and Psychopathology, 18*(3), 623–649.

Ciro, D., et al. (2005). Lesbian, gay, bisexual, sexual-orientation questioning adolescents seeking mental health services: Risk factors, worries, and desire to talk about them. *Social Work in Mental Health, 3*(3), 213–234.

Clancy, B., & Finlay, B. (2001). Neural correlates of early language learning. In M. Tomasello & E. Bates (Eds.), *Language development: The essential readings.* Malden, MA: Blackwell.

Clark, E. V. (1973). What's in a word? On the child's acquisition of semantics in his first language. In E. Moore (Ed.), *Cognitive development and the acquisition of language.* New York: Academic Press.

Clark, E. V. (1975). Knowledge, context, and strategy in the acquisition of meaning. In D. P. Date (Ed.), *Georgetown University roundtable on language and linguistics.* Washington, DC: Georgetown University Press.

Clark, J. (2005). Sibling relationships: Theory and issues for practice. *Child & Family Social Work, 10*(1), 90–91.

Clark, K. E., & Ladd, G. W. (2000). Connectedness and autonomy support in parent–child relationships: Links to children's socio-emotional orientation and peer relationships. *Developmental Psychology, 36*(4), 485–498.

Clark, R. (1983). *Family life and school achievement: Why poor black children succeed or fail.* Chicago: University of Chicago Press.

Clark, S. E., & Symons, D. K. (2000). A longitudinal study of Q-sort attachment security and self-processes at age 5. *Infant and Child Development, 9*(2), 91–104.

Clarke-Stewart, K. A. (1998). Reading with children. *Journal of Applied Developmental Psychology, 19*(1), 1–14.

Clarke-Stewart, K. A., & Beck, R. J. (1999). Maternal scaffolding and children's narrative retelling of a movie story. *Early Childhood Research Quarterly, 14*(3), 409–434.

Clarke-Stewart, K. A., Vandell, D. L., McCartney, K., Owen, M. T., & Booth, C. (2000). Effects of parental separation and divorce on very young children. *Journal of Family Psychology, 14*(2), 304–326.

Clayton, R., & Crosby, R. A. (2006) Measurement in health promotion. In R. A. Crosby, R. J. DiClemente, & L. F. Salazar (Eds.), *Research methods in health promotion* (pp. 229–259). San Francisco: Jossey-Bass.

Cleary, D. J., Ray, G. E., LoBello, S. G., & Zachar, P. (2002). Children's perceptions of close peer relationships: Quality, congruence

and meta-perceptions. *Child Study Journal, 32*(3), 179–192.

Clode, D. (2006). Review of A left-hand turn around the world: Chasing the mystery and meaning of all things southpaw. *Laterality: Asymmetries of Body, Brain and Cognition, 11*(6) 580–581.

Cnattingius, S. (2004). The epidemiology of smoking during pregnancy: Smoking prevalence, maternal characteristics, and pregnancy outcomes. *Nicotine & Tobacco Research, 6*(Supp. l2), S125–S140.

Cnattingius, S., et al. (2000). Caffeine intake and the risk of first-trimester spontaneous abortion. *New England Journal of Medicine, 343*(25), 1839–1845.

Cohen, D. (Ed.). (2006). *The development of play.* New York: Routledge.

Cohen, E., & Feig, C. (2003, July 22). Delivery debate: Vaginal or C-section? More women are selecting surgery without a medical reason. Available at http://www.CNN.com.

Cohen, L. S., et al. (2006). Relapse of major depression during pregnancy in women who maintain or discontinue antidepressant treatment. *Journal of the American Medical Association, 295*(5), 499–507.

Cohen-Bendahan, C. C. C., Buitelaar, J. K., van Goozen, S. H. M., & Cohen-Kettenis, P. T. (2004). Prenatal exposure to testosterone and functional cerebral lateralization: A study in same-sex and opposite-sex twin girls. *Psychoneuroendocrinology, 29*(7), 911–916.

Cohen-Bendahan, C. C. C., Buitelaar, J. K., van Goozen, S. H. M., Orlebeke, J. F., & Cohen-Kettenis, P. T. (2005). Is there an effect of prenatal testosterone on aggression and other behavioral traits? A study comparing same-sex and opposite-sex twin girls. *Hormones and Behavior, 47*(2), 230–237.

Colby, A., Kohlberg, L. G., J., & Lieberman, M. (1983). A longitudinal study of moral judgment. *Monographs of the Society for Research in Child Development, 48*(4, Serial No. 200).

Cole, C., et al. (2003). The educational impact of Rechov Sumsum/Shara'a Simsim: A Sesame Street television series to promote respect and understanding among children living in Israel, the West Bank, and Gaza. *International Journal of Behavioral Development, 27*(5), 409–422.

Cole, D. A., Jacquez, F. M., & Maschman, T. L. (2001). Social origins of depressive cognitions: A longitudinal study of self-perceived competence in children. *Cognitive Therapy and Research, 25*(4), 377–395.

Coleman, P. K. (2003). Perceptions of parent–child attachment, social self-efficacy, and peer relationships in middle childhood. *Infant and Child Development, 12*(4), 351–368.

Coley, J. D. (1993, March). *Parental feedback to child labeling as input to conceptual development.* Paper presented at the meeting of the

Society for Research in Child Development, New Orleans, LA.

Coley, R. L., & Chase-Lansdale, P. L. (1998). Adolescent pregnancy and parenthood: Recent evidence and future directions. *American Psychologist, 53*(2), 152–166.

Collaer, M. L., & Hill, E. M. (2006). Large sex difference in adolescents on a timed line judgment task: Attentional contributors and task relationship to mathematics. *Perception, 35*(4), 561–572.

Collins, W. A. (1984). Conclusion: The status of basic research on middle childhood. In W. A. Collins (Ed.), *Development during middle childhood: The years from six to twelve.* Washington, DC: National Academy Press.

Collins, W. A., & Laursen, B. (2006). Parent–adolescent relationships. In P. Noller & J. A. Feeney (Eds.), *Close relationships: Functions, forms and processes* (pp. 111–125). Hove, England: Psychology Press/Taylor & Francis.

Collins, W. A., Maccoby, E. E., Steinberg, L., Hetherington, E. M., & Bornstein, M. H. (2000). Contemporary research on parenting: The case for nature and nurture. *American Psychologist, 55*(2), 218–232.

Collins, W. A., Maccoby, E. E., Steinberg, L., Hetherington, E. M., & Bornstein, M. H. (2003). Contemporary research on parenting: The case for nature and nurture. In M. E. Hertzig & E. A. Farber (Eds.), *Annual progress in child psychiatry and child development: 2000–2001* (pp. 125–153). New York: Brunner-Routledge.

Colom, R., Flores-Mendoza, C., & Rebollo, I. (2003). Working memory and intelligence. *Personality and Individual Differences, 34*(1), 33–39.

Colombo, J. (1993). *Infant cognition.* Newbury Park, CA: Sage.

Colwell, M. J., & Lindsey, E. W. (2005). Preschool children's pretend and physical play and sex of play partner: Connections to peer competence. *Sex Roles, 52*(7–8), 497–509.

Commission on Adolescent Substance and Alcohol Abuse. (2005). Prevention of substance use disorders. In D. L. Evans et al. (Eds.), *Treating and preventing adolescent mental health disorders: What we know and what we don't know: A research agenda for improving the mental health of our youth* (pp. 411–426). New York: Oxford University Press.

Commons, M. L., Galaz-Fontes, J. F., & Morse, S. J. (2006). Leadership, cross-cultural contact, socio-economic status, and formal operational reasoning about moral dilemmas among Mexican non-literate adults and high school students. *Journal of Moral Education, 35*(2), 247–267

Conner, K. R., & Goldston, D. B. (2007). Rates of suicide among males increase steadily from age 11 to 21: Developmental framework and outline for prevention. *Aggression and Violent Behavior, 12*(2), 193–207.

Connolly, J., Craig, W., Goldberg, A., & Pepler, D. (2004). Mixed-gender groups, dating, and romantic relationships in early adolescence. *Journal of Research on Adolescence, 14*(2), 185–207.

Connolly, J., Furman, W., & Konarski, R. (2000). The role of peers in the emergence of heterosexual romantic relationships in adolescence. *Child Development, 71*(5), 1395–1408.

Connor, J. R. (2004). Myelin breakdown in Alzheimer's disease: A commentary. *Neurobiology of Aging, 25*(1), 45–47.

Connor, M. E. (2006). Walking the walk: Community programs that work. In M. E. Connor & J. L. White (Eds.), *Black fathers: An invisible presence in America* (pp. 257–267). Mahwah, NJ: Erlbaum.

Connor, P. D., Sampson, P. D., Streissguth, A. P., Bookstein, F. L., & Barr, H. M. (2006). Effects of prenatal alcohol exposure on fine motor coordination and balance: A study of two adult samples. *Neuropsychologia, 44*(5), 744–751.

Constantine, M. G. (2007). Racial microaggressions against African American clients in cross-racial counseling relationships. *Journal of Counseling Psychology, 54*(1), 1–16.

Constantino, J. N., et al. (2006). Autistic social impairment in the siblings of children with pervasive developmental disorders. *American Journal of Psychiatry, 163*(2), 294–296.

Coolidge, F. L., DenBoer, J. W., & Segal, D. L. (2004). Personality and neuropsychological correlates of bullying behavior. *Personality and Individual Differences, 36*(7), 1559–1569.

Coon, H., Fulker, D. W., & DeFries, J. C. (1990). Home environment and cognitive ability of 7-year-old children in the Colorado adoption project: Genetic and environmental etiologies. *Developmental Psychology, 26*, 459–468.

Cooper, C. E., & Crosnoe, R. (2007). The engagement in schooling of economically disadvantaged parents and children. *Youth & Society, 38*(3), 372–391.

Cooper, J., Appleby, L., & Amos, T. (2002). Life events preceding suicide by young people. *Social Psychiatry and Psychiatric Epidemiology, 37*(6), 271–275.

Coovadia, H. (2004). Antiretroviral agents: How best to protect infants from HIV and save their mothers from AIDS. *New England Journal of Medicine, 351*(3), 289–292.

Copeland, A. L., Martin, P. D., Geiselman, P. J., Rash, C. J., & Kendzor, D. E. (2006). Smoking cessation for weight-concerned women: Group vs. individually tailored, dietary, and weight-control follow-up sessions. *Addictive Behaviors, 31*(1), 115–127.

Coplan, R. J., Rubin, K. H., Fox, N. A., Calkins, S. D., & Stewart, S. L. (1994). Being alone, playing alone, and acting alone: Distinguishing among reticence, and passive-, and active-solitude in young children. *Child Development, 65,* 129–137.

Corbett, S. S., & Drewett, R. F. (2004). To what extent is failure to thrive in infancy associated with poorer cognitive development? A review and meta-analysis. *Journal of Child Psychology and Psychiatry, 45*(3), 641–654.

Coren, S. (1992). *The left-hander syndrome.* New York: Free Press.

Cornoldi, C. (2006). The contribution of cognitive psychology to the study of human intelligence. *European Journal of Cognitive Psychology, 18*(1), 1–17.

Cornwell, A. A., C., & Feigenbaum, P. (2006). Sleep biological rhythms in normal infants and those at high risk for SIDS. *Chronobiology International, 23*(5), 935–961.

Corstorphine, E., Waller, G., Lawson, R., & Ganis, C. (2007). Trauma and multi-impulsivity in the eating disorders. *Eating Behaviors, 8*(1), 23–30.

Costello, E. J. (2007). Psychiatric predictors of adolescent and young adult drug use and abuse. *Drug and Alcohol Dependence, 88,* S1–S3.

Costello, E. J., Sung, M., Worthman, C., & Angold, A. (2007). Pubertal maturation and the development of alcohol use and abuse. *Drug and Alcohol Dependence, 88,* S50–S59.

Costigan, C. L., Cauce, A. M., & Etchison, K. (2007). Changes in African American mother–daughter relationships during adolescence: Conflict, autonomy, and warmth. In B. J. R. Leadbeater & N. Way (Eds.), *Urban girls revisited: Building strengths* (pp. 177–201). New York: New York University Press.

Costos, D., Ackerman, R., & Paradis, L. (2002). Recollections of menarche: Communication between mothers and daughters regarding menstruation. *Sex Roles, 46*(1–2), 49–59.

Cotton, S., & Richdale, A. (2006). Brief report: Parental descriptions of sleep problems in children with autism, Down syndrome, and Prader-Willi syndrome. *Research in Developmental Disabilities, 27*(2), 151–161.

Courage, M. L., Howe, M. L., & Squires, S. E. (2004). Individual differences in 3.5-montholds' visual attention: What do they predict at 1 year? *Infant Behavior and Development, 27*(1), 19–30.

Cowan, N., et al. (2003). Children's working-memory processes: A response-timing analysis. *Journal of Experimental Psychology: General, 132*(1), 113–132.

Cowan, P. A., & Cowan, C. P. (2005). Five-domain models: Putting it all together. In P. A. Cowan, C. P. Cowan, J. C. Ablow, V. K. Johnson, & J. R. Measelle (Eds.), *The family context of parenting in children's adaptation to elementary school, Monographs in parenting series* (pp. 315–333). Mahwah, NJ: Erlbaum.

Cox, W. M., & Alm, R. (2005, February 25). Scientists are made, not born. *New York Times online.*

Crain, W. C. (2000). *Theories of development: Concepts and applications* (4th ed.). Englewood Cliffs, NJ: Prentice Hall.

Cratty, B. (1986). *Perceptual and motor development in infants and children* (3rd ed.). Englewood Cliffs, NJ: Prentice Hall.

Crawford, M. J., Thomas, O., Khan, N., & Kulinskaya, E. (2007). Psychosocial interventions following self-harm. Systematic review of their efficacy in preventing suicide. *British Journal of Psychiatry, 190*(1), 11–17.

Creed, P. A., Patton, W., & Prideaux, L-A. (2007). Predicting change over time in career planning and career exploration for high school students. *Journal of Adolescence, 30*(3), 377–392.

Crittenden, P. M., & Ainsworth, M. D. S. (1989). Child maltreatment and attachment theory. In D. Cicchetti & V. Carlson (Eds.), *Child maltreatment: Theory and research on the causes and consequences of child abuse and neglect.* Cambridge: Cambridge University Press.

Crocco, M. S., & Libresco, A. S. (2007). Citizenship education for the 21st century—A gender inclusive approach to social studies. In D. M. Sadker & E. S. Silber (Eds.), *Gender in the classroom: Foundations, skills, methods, and strategies across the curriculum* (pp. 119–164). Mahwah, NJ: Erlbaum.

Crockett, L. J., & Silbereisen, R. K. (Eds.). (2000). *Negotiating adolescence in times of social change.* Cambridge: Cambridge University Press.

Crombie, G., & Desjardins, M. J. (1993, March). *Predictors of gender: The relative importance of children's play, games, and personality characteristics.* Paper presented at the meeting of the Society for Research in Child Development, New Orleans, LA.

Crook, C. K., & Lipsitt, L. P. (1976). Neonatal nutritive sucking: Effects of taste stimulation upon sucking rhythm and heart rate. *Child Development, 47,* 518–522.

Crowther, C., et al. (2006). Neonatal respiratory distress syndrome after repeat exposure to antenatal corticosteroids: A randomised control trial. *Lancet, 367*(9526), 1913–1919.

Cruz, N. V., & Bahna, S. L. (2006). Do foods or additives cause behavior disorders? *Psychiatric Annals, 36*(10), 724–732.

Cryan, J. F., & Slattery, D. A. (2007). Animal models of mood disorders: Recent developments. *Current Opinion in Psychiatry, 20*(1), 1–7.

Csikszentmihalyi, M., & Larson, R. (1984). *Being adolescent.* New York: Basic Books.

Cuellar, J., & Curry, T. R. (2007). The prevalence and comorbidity between delinquency, drug abuse, suicide attempts, physical and sexual abuse, and self-mutilation among delinquent Hispanic females. *Hispanic Journal of Behavioral Sciences, 29*(1), 68–82.

Culebras, A. (2005). Sleep and neuromuscular disorders. *Neurologic Clinics, 23*(4), 1209–1223.

Cumming, S. P., Eisenmann, J. C., Smoll, F. L., Smith, R. E., & Malina, R. M. (2005). Body size and perceptions of coaching behaviors by adolescent female athletes. *Psychology of Sport and Exercise, 6*(6), 693–705.

Cunningham, R. L., & McGinnis, M. Y. (2007). Factors influencing aggression toward females by male rats exposed to anabolic androgenic steroids during puberty. *Hormones and Behavior, 51*(1), 135–141.

Curtner-Smith, M. E. (2000). Mechanisms by which family processes contribute to school-age boy's bullying. *Child Study Journal, 30*(3), 169–186.

Cystic Fibrosis Foundation. (2007). Available at www.cff.org. Accessed February 23, 2007.

Dai, D. Y. (2001). A comparison of gender differences in academic self-concept and motivation between high-ability and average Chinese adolescents. *Journal of Secondary Gifted Education, 13*(1), 22–32.

Dailard, C. (2001, February). *Sex education: Politicians, parents, teachers and teens.* Guttmacher Report on Public Policy. New York: Alan Guttmacher Institute.

Daly, M., & Wilson, M. (2000). Genetic ties may be factor in violence in stepfamilies. *American Psychologist, 55*(6), 679–680.

Daman-Wasserman, M., Brennan, B., Radcliffe, F., Prigot, J., & Fagen, J. (2006). Auditory-visual context and memory retrieval in 3-month-old infants. *Infancy, 10*(3) 201–220.

Damon, W. (1991). Adolescent self-concept. In R. M. Lerner, A. C. Petersen, & J. Brooks-Gunn (Eds.), *Encyclopedia of adolescence.* New York: Garland.

Damon, W. (2000). Setting the stage for the development of wisdom: Self-understanding and moral identity during adolescence. In W. S. Brown (Ed.), *Understanding wisdom: Sources, science, and society* (pp. 339–360). Philadelphia: Templeton Foundation Press.

Dandy, J., & Nettelbeck, T. (2002). The relationship between IQ, homework, aspirations and academic achievement for Chinese, Vietnamese and Anglo-Celtic Australian school children. *Educational Psychology, 22*(3), 267–276.

Dane, S., & Erzurumluoglu, A. (2003). Sex and handedness differences in eye–hand visual reaction times in handball players. *International Journal of Neuroscience, 113*(7), 923–929.

Dang-Vu, T. T., Desseilles, M., Peigneux, P., & Maquet, P. (2006). A role for sleep in brain plasticity. *Pediatric Rehabilitation, 19*(2) 98–118.

Daniels, S. R. (2006). The consequences of childhood overweight and obesity. *The Future of Children, 16*(1), 47–67.

Darcy, M. U. A., & Tracey, T. J. G. (2007). Circumplex structure of Holland's RIASEC interests across gender and time. *Journal of Counseling Psychology, 54*(1), 17–31.

Daubenmier, J. J., et al. (2007). The contribution of changes in diet, exercise, and stress management to changes in coronary risk in women and men in the Multisite Cardiac Lifestyle Intervention Program. *Annals of Behavioral Medicine, 33*(1), 57–68.

Davies, P. T., & Windle, M. (2001). Interparental discord and adolescent adjustment trajectories: The potentiating and protective role of intrapersonal attributes. *Child Development, 72*(4), 1163–1178.

Davis, A. (1991). Piaget, teachers and education: Into the 1990s. In P. Light, S. Sheldon, & M. Woodhead (Eds.), *Learning to think.* New York: Routledge.

Davis, H. A. (2001). The quality and impact of relationships between elementary school students and teachers. *Contemporary Educational Psychology, 26*(4), 431–453.

Davis, L., Edwards, H., Mohay, H., & Wollin, J. (2003). The impact of very premature birth on the psychological health of mothers. *Early Human Development, 73*(1–2), 61–70.

Davis, S. R., Davison, S. L., Donath, S., & Bell, R. J. (2005). Circulating androgen levels and self-reported sexual function in women. *Journal of the American Medical Association, 294*(1), 91–96.

Dawson, T. L. (2002). New tools, new insights: Kohlberg's moral judgement stages revisited. *International Journal of Behavioral Development, 26*(2), 154–166.

Day, N. L., Goldschmidt, L., & Thomas, C. A. (2006). Prenatal marijuana exposure contributes to the prediction of marijuana use at age 14. *Addiction, 101*(9), 1313–1322.

De Haan, M., & Groen, M. (2006). Neural bases of infants' processing of social information in faces. In P. J. Marshall & N. A. Fox (Eds.), *The development of social engagement: Neurobiological perspectives. Series in affective science* (pp. 46–80). New York: Oxford University Press.

De Lisi, R. (2005). A lifetime of work using a developmental theory to enhance the lives of children and adolescents. *Journal of Applied Developmental Psychology, 26*(1), 107–110.

de Lisi, R., & Gallagher, A. M. (1991). Understanding of gender stability and constancy in Argentinean children. *Merrill-Palmer Quarterly, 37*(3), 483–502.

de Oliveira, F. S., Viana, M. R., Antoniolli, A. R., & Marchioro, M. (2001). Differential effects of lead and zinc on inhibitory avoidance learning in mice. *Brazilian Journal of Medical and Biological Research, 34*(1), 117–120.

de Villiers, J. G., & de Villiers, P. A. (1999). Language development. In M. H. Bornstein & M. E. Lamb (Eds.), *Developmental psychology: An advanced textbook* (4th ed.) (pp. 313–373). Mahwah, NJ: Erlbaum.

de Vries, J. I. P., & Hopkins, B. (2005). Fetal movements and postures: What do they mean for postnatal development? In B. Hopkins & S. P. Johnson (Eds.), *Prenatal development of postnatal functions. Advances in infancy research* (pp. 177–219). Westport, CT: Praeger Publishers/Greenwood.

Deary, I. J., Whiteman, M. C., Starr, J. M., Whalley, L. J., & Fox, H. C. (2004). The impact of childhood intelligence on later life: Following up the Scottish mental surveys of 1932 and 1947. *Journal of Personality and Social Psychology, 86*(1), 130–147.

DeCasper, A. J., & Fifer, W. P. (1980). Of human bonding: Newborns prefer their mothers' voices. *Science, 208,* 1174–1176.

DeCasper, A. J., & Prescott, P. A. (1984). Human newborns' perception of male voices: Preference, discrimination, and reinforcing value. *Developmental Psychobiology, 17,* 481–491.

DeCasper, A. J., & Spence, M. J. (1986). Prenatal maternal speech influences newborns' perception of speech sounds. *Infant Behavior and Development, 9,* 133–150.

DeCasper, A. J., & Spence, M. J. (1991). Auditorily mediated behavior during the perinatal period: A cognitive view. In M. J. Weiss & P. R. Zelazo (Eds.), *Infant attention* (pp. 142–176). Norwood, NJ: Ablex.

Deep, A. L., et al. (1999). Sexual abuse in eating disorder subtypes and control women: The role of comorbid substance dependence in bulimia nervosa. *International Journal of Eating Disorders, 25*(1), 1–10.

Dehaene-Lambertz, G., Pena, M., Christophe, A., & Landrieu, P. (2004). Phoneme perception in a neonate with a left sylvian infarct. *Brain and Language, 88*(1), 26–38.

DeHart, T., Pelham, B. W., & Tennen, H. (2006). What lies beneath: Parenting style and implicit self-esteem. *Journal of Experimental Social Psychology, 42*(1), 1–17.

Delaney-Black, V., et al. (2004). Prenatal cocaine: Quantity of exposure and gender influences on school-age behavior. *Developmental and Behavioral Pediatrics, 25*(4), 254–263.

Delgado, A. R., & Prieto, G. (2004). Cognitive mediators and sex-related differences in mathematics. *Intelligence, 32*(1), 25–32.

DeLoache, J. S. (2002). The symbol-mindedness of young children. In W. Hartup & R. A. Weinberg (Eds.), *Child psychology in retrospect and prospect: In celebration of the 75th anniversary of the Institute of Child Development* (pp. 73–101). Mahwah, NJ: Erlbaum.

DeLoache, J. S., Cassidy, D. J., & Brown, A. L. (1985). Precursors of mnemonic strategies in very young children's memory. *Child Development, 56,* 125–137.

Delpit, L. (2006). What should teachers do? Ebonics and culturally responsive instruction. In S. J. Nero (Ed.), *Dialects, Englishes, creoles, and education* (pp. 93–101). Mahwah, NJ: Erlbaum.

DeMarie, D., Miller, P. H., Ferron, J., & Cunningham, W. R. (2004). Path analysis tests of theoretical models of children's memory performance. *Journal of Cognition and Development, 5*(4), 461–492.

Dennis, W. (1960). Causes of retardation among institutional children: Iran. *Journal of Genetic Psychology, 96,* 47–59.

Dennis, W., & Dennis, M. G. (1940). The effect of cradling practices upon the onset of walking in Hopi children. *Journal of Genetic Psychology, 56,* 77–86.

Derman, O., Kanbur, N. O., & Kutluk, T. (2003). Tamoxifen treatment for pubertal gynecomastia. *International Journal of Adolescent Medicine and Health, 15*(4), 359–363.

Dervic, K., Grunebaum, M. F., Burke, A. K., Mann, J. J., & Oquendo, M. A. (2007). Cluster C personality disorders in major depressive episodes: The relationship between hostility and suicidal behavior. *Archives of Suicide Research, 11*(1), 83–90.

Dessens, A. B., et al. (1999). Prenatal exposure to anticonvulsants and psychosexual development. *Archives of Sexual Behavior, 28*(1), 31–44.

Dezoete, J. A., MacArthur, B. A., & Tuck, B. (2003). Prediction of Bayley and Stanford–Binet scores with a group of very low birthweight children. *Child: Care, Health and Development, 29*(5), 367–372.

Diamond, L. M. (2006). What we got wrong about sexual identity development: Unexpected findings from a longitudinal study of young women. In A. M. Omoto & H. S. Kurtzman (Eds.), *Sexual orientation and mental health: Examining identity and development in lesbian, gay, and bisexual people* (pp. 73–94). *Contemporary perspectives on lesbian, gay, and bisexual psychology.* Washington, DC: American Psychological Association.

Dieterich, S. E., Hebert, H. M., Landry, S. H., Swank, P. R., & Smith, K. E. (2004). Maternal and child characteristics that influence the growth of daily living skills from infancy to school age in preterm and term children. *Early Education and Development, 15*(3), 283–303.

DiIorio, C., McCarty, F., Denzmore, P., & Landis, A. (2007). The moderating influence of mother–adolescent discussion on early and middle African-American adolescent sexual behavior. *Research in Nursing & Health, 30*(2), 193–202.

DiLalla, D. L., Gottesman, I. I., Carey, G., & Bouchard, T. J., Jr. (1999). Heritability of MMPI Harris–Lingoes and Subtle–Obvious subscales in twins reared apart. *Assessment, 6*(4), 353–366.

Dindia, K., & Allen, M. (1992). Sex differences in self-disclosure: A meta-analysis. *Psychological Bulletin, 112,* 106–124.

Ding, Q. J., & Hesketh, T. (2006). Family size, fertility preferences, and sex ratio in China in the era of the one child family policy: Results from National Family Planning and Reproductive Health Survey. *British Medical Journal, 333*(7564), 371–373.

Dishion, T. J., & Stormshak, E. A. (2007a). Child and adolescent intervention groups. In T. J. Dishion & E. A. Stormshak (Eds.), *Intervening in children's lives: An ecological, family-centered approach to mental health care* (pp. 201–215). Washington, DC: American Psychological Association.

Dishion, T. J., & Stormshak, E. A. (2007b). Family and peer social interaction. In T. J. Dishion & E. A. Stormshak. (Eds.), *Intervening in children's lives: An ecological, family-centered approach to mental health care* (pp. 31–48). Washington, DC: American Psychological Association.

Dobbinson, S., Perkins, M., & Boucher, J. (2003). The interactional significance of formulas in autistic language. *Clinical Linguistics and Phonetics, 17*(4–5), 299–307.

Dockett, S., Perry, B., & Whitton, D. (2006). Picture storybooks and starting school. *Early Child Development and Care, 76*(8), 835–848.

Dodge, K. A., Laird, R., Lochman, J. E., Zelli, A., & Conduct Problems Prevention Research Group U.S. (2002). Multidimensional latent-construct analysis of children's social information processing patterns: Correlations with aggressive behavior problems. *Psychological Assessment, 14*(1), 60–73.

Dogil, G., et al. (2002). The speaking brain: A tutorial introduction to fMRI experiments in the production of speech, prosody, and syntax. *Journal of Neurolinguistics, 15*(1), 59–90.

Dollfus, S., et al. (2005). Atypical hemispheric specialization for language in right-handed schizophrenia patients. *Biological Psychiatry, 57*(9), 1020–1028.

Dombrowski, M. A. S., et al. (2000). Kangaroo skin-to-skin care for premature twins and their adolescent parents. *American Journal of Maternal/Child Nursing, 25*(2), 92–94.

Donaldson, M. (1979). *Children's minds.* New York: Norton.

Donohue, B. C., Karmely, J., & Strada, M. J. (2006). Alcohol and drug abuse. In M. Hersen (Ed.), *Clinician's handbook of child behavioral assessment* (pp. 337–375). San Diego, CA: Elsevier Academic Press.

Donohue, K. F., Curtin, J. J., Patrick, C. J., & Lang, A. R. (2007). Intoxication level and emotional response. *Emotion, 7*(1), 103–112.

Donovan, D. M., & Wells, E. A. (2007). "Tweaking 12-Step": The potential role of 12-Step self-help group involvement in metham-

phetamine recovery. *Addiction, 102*(Suppl. 1), 121–129 .

Dorius, C. J., Bahr, S. J., Hoffmann, J. P., & Harmon, E. L. (2004). Parenting practices as moderators of the relationship between peers and adolescent marijuana use. *Journal of Marriage and Family, 66*(1), 163–178.

Dorling, J., et al. (2006). Data collection from very low birthweight infants in a geographical region: Methods, costs, and trends in mortality, admission rates, and resource utilisation over a five–year period. *Early Human Development, 82*(2), 117–124.

Downey, D. B. (2001). Number of siblings and intellectual development: The resource dilution explanation. *American Psychologist, 56*(6/7), 497–504.

Drabick, D. A. G., Gadow, K. D., Carlson, G. A., & Bromet, E. J. (2004). ODD and ADHD symptoms in Ukrainian children: External validators and comorbidity. *Journal of the American Academy of Child and Adolescent Psychiatry. 43*(6), 735–743.

Drasgow, E., Halle, J. W., & Phillips, B. (2001). Effects of different social partners on the discriminated requesting of a young child with autism and severe language delays. *Research in Developmental Disabilities, 22*(2), 125–139.

Drewett, R., Blair, P., Emmett, P., Emond, A., & The ALSPAC Study Team. (2004). Failure to thrive in the term and preterm infants of mothers depressed in the postnatal period: A population-based birth cohort study. *Journal of Child Psychology and Psychiatry and Allied Disciplines, 45*(2), 359–366.

Drewett, R. F., Corbett, S. S., & Wright, C. M. (2006). Physical and emotional development, appetite and body image in adolescents who failed to thrive as infants. *Journal of Child Psychology and Psychiatry, 47*(5), 524–531.

Du Rocher Schudlich, T. D., Shamir, H., & Cummings, E. M. (2004). Marital conflict, children's representations of family relationships, and children's dispositions towards peer conflict strategies. *Social Development, 13*(2), 171–192.

Duarté-Vélez, Y. M., & Bernal, G. (2007). Suicide behavior among Latino and Latina adolescents: Conceptual and methodological issues. *Death Studies, 31*(5) 425–455.

DuBois, D. L., & Hirsch, B. J. (1990). School and neighborhood friendship patterns of blacks and whites in early adolescence. *Child Development, 61,* 524–536.

Dufva, M., Niemi, P., & Voeten, M. J. M. (2001). The role of phonological memory, word recognition, and comprehension skills in reading development: From preschool to grade 2. *Reading and Writing, 14*(1–2), 91–117.

Duggan, A., et al. (2004). Evaluating a statewide home visiting program to prevent child abuse in at-risk families of newborns: Fathers' participation and outcomes. *Child Maltreat-*

ment: *Journal of the American Professional Society on the Abuse of Children, 9*(1), 3–17.

Dunn, J., Davies, L. C., O'Connor, T. G., & Sturgess, W. (2001). Family lives and friendships: The perspectives of children in step-, single-parent, and nonstep families. *Journal of Family Psychology, 15*(2), 272–287.

Dunn, J., & Hughes, C. (2001). "I got some swords and you're dead!": Violent fantasy, antisocial behavior, friendship, and moral sensibility in young children. *Child Development, 72*(2), 491–505.

Dunn, M. G., & Mezzich, A. C. (2007). Development in childhood and adolescence: Implications for prevention research and practice. In P. Tolan, J. Szapocznik, & S. Sambrano (Eds.), *Preventing youth substance abuse: Science-based programs for children and adolescents* (pp. 21–40). Washington, DC: American Psychological Association.

Durkin, S. J., Paxton, S. J., & Sorbello, M. (2007). An integrative model of the impact of exposure to idealized female images on adolescent girls' body satisfaction. *Journal of Applied Social Psychology, 37*(5), 1092–1117.

Dweck, C. S. (2007). Is math a gift? Beliefs that put females at risk. In S. J. Ceci & W. M. Williams (Eds.), *Why aren't more women in science: Top researchers debate the evidence* (pp. 47–55). Washington, DC: American Psychological Association.

Dyer, S., & Moneta, G. B. (2006). Frequency of parallel, associative, and co-operative play in British children of different socioeconomic status. *Social Behavior and Personality, 34*(5), 587–592.

Dykman, R. A., Casey, P. H., Ackerman, P. T., & McPherson, W. B. (2001). Behavioral and cognitive status in school-aged children with a history of failure to thrive during early childhood. *Clinical Pediatrics, 40*(2), 63–70.

East, C. E., Chan, F. Y., Brennecke, S. P., King, J. F., & Colditz, P. B. (2006). Women's evaluations of their experience in a multicenter randomized controlled trial of intrapartum fetal pulse oximetry (The FOREMOST Trial). *Birth: Issues in Perinatal Care, 33*(2), 101–109.

Eaton, W. O., McKeen, N. A., & Campbell, D. W. (2001). The waxing and waning of movement: Implications for psychological development. *Developmental Review, 21*(2), 205–223.

Eaton, W. O., & Yu, A. P. (1989). Are sex differences in child motor activity a function of sex differences in maturational status? *Child Development, 60,* 1005–1011.

Eberhardy, F. (1967). The view from "the couch." *Journal of Child Psychological Psychiatry, 8,* 257–263.

Eccles, J. S. (2007). Where are all the women? Gender differences in participation in physical science and engineering. In S. J. Ceci & W. M. Williams (Eds.), *Why aren't more women in science: Top researchers debate the evidence* (pp. 199–210). Washington, DC: American Psychological Association.

Eccles, J. S., et al. (2000). Gender-role socialization in the family: A longitudinal approach. In T. Eckes & H. M. Trautner (Eds.), *The developmental social psychology of gender* (pp. 333–360). Mahwah, NJ: Erlbaum.

Eckenrode, J., Laird, M., & Doris, J. (1993). School performance and disciplinary problems among abused and neglected children. *Developmental Psychology, 29,* 53–62.

Eckerman, C. O., Hsu, H.-C., Molitor, A., Leung, E. H. L., & Goldstein, R. F. (1999). Infant arousal in an en-face exchange with a new partner: Effects of prematurity and perinatal biological risk. *Developmental Psychology, 35*(1), 282–293.

Ecuyer-Dab, I., & Robert, M. (2004). Spatial ability and home-range size: Examining the relationship in Western men and women (*Homo sapiens*). *Journal of Comparative Psychology, 118*(2), 217–231.

Eddy, J. M., & Chamberlain, P. (2000). Family management and deviant peer association as mediators of the impact of treatment condition on youth antisocial behavior. *Journal of Consulting and Clinical Psychology, 68*(5), 857–863.

Eddy, J. M., Leve, L. D., & Fagot, B. I. (2001). Coercive family processes: A replication and extension of Patterson's Coercion Model. *Aggressive Behavior, 27*(1), 14–25.

Eder, R. A. (1989). The emergent personologist: The structure and content of 3½-, 5½-, and 7½-year-olds' concepts of themselves and other persons. *Child Development, 60,* 1218–1228.

Eder, R. A. (1990). Uncovering young children's psychological selves: Individual and developmental differences. *Child Development, 61,* 849–863.

Edler, C., Lipson, S. F., & Keel, P. K. (2007). Ovarian hormones and binge eating in bulimia nervosa. *Psychological Medicine, 37*(1), 131–141.

Edwards, V. J., Holden, G. W., Felitti, V. J., & Anda, R. F. (2003). Relationship between multiple forms of childhood maltreatment and adult mental health in community respondents: Results from the Adverse Childhood Experiences study. *American Journal of Psychiatry, 160*(8), 1453–1460.

Egeland, B., Jacobvitz, D., & Sroufe, L. A. (1988). Breaking the cycle of abuse. *Child Development, 59,* 1080–1088.

Egeland, B., & Sroufe, L. A. (1981). Attachment and early maltreatment. *Child Development, 52,* 44–52.

Egerton, A., Allison, C., Brett, R. R., & Pratt, J. A. (2006). Cannabinoids and prefrontal cortical function: Insights from preclinical studies. *Neuroscience & Biobehavioral Reviews, 30*(5), 680–695.

Eigenmann, P. A., & Haenggeli, C. A. (2004). Food colourings and preservatives—allergy and hyperactivity. *Lancet, 364*(9437), 823–824.

Eimas, P. D., Sigueland, E. R., Juscyk, P., & Vigorito, J. (1971). Speech perception in infants. *Science, 171,* 303–306.

Eisenberg, M. E., Neumark-Sztainer, D., & Paxton, S. J. (2006). Five-year change in body satisfaction among adolescents. *Journal of Psychosomatic Research, 61*(4), 521–527.

Eisenberg, N., Hertz-Lazarowitz, R., & Fuchs, I. (1990). Prosocial moral judgment in Israeli kibbutz and city children: A longitudinal study. *Merrill–Palmer Quarterly, 36,* 273–285.

Eisenberg, N., & Valiente, C. (2002). Parenting and children's prosocial and moral development. In M. H. Bornstein (Ed.), *Handbook of parenting,* Vol. 5, *Practical issues in parenting* (2nd ed.) (pp. 111–142). Mahwah, NJ: Erlbaum.

Eisenberg, N., Wolchik, S. A., Goldberg, L., & Engel, I. (1992). Parental values, reinforcement, and young children's prosocial behavior: A longitudinal study. *Journal of Genetic Psychology, 153*(1), 19–36.

Eisner, E. W. (1990). The role of art and play in children's cognitive development. In E. Klugman & S. Smilansky (Eds.), *Children's play and learning: Perspectives and policy implications.* New York: Teachers College Press.

Ekvall, S. W. (Ed.). (1993a). *Pediatric nutrition in chronic diseases and developmental disorders: Prevention, assessment, and treatment.* New York: Oxford.

Elias, M. J., Gara, M. A., Schuyler, T. F., Brandon-Muller, L. R., & Sayette, M. A. (1991). The promotion of social competence: Longitudinal study of a preventative school-based program. *American Journal of Orthopsychiatry, 61,* 409–417.

Elkind, D. (1967). Egocentrism in adolescence. *Child Development, 38,* 1025–1034.

Elkind, D. (1985). Egocentrism redux. *Developmental Review, 5,* 218–226.

Elkind, D. (2007). *The power of play: How spontaneous imaginative activities lead to happier, healthier children.* Cambridge, MA: Da Capo Press.

Ellis, A., & Dryden, W. (1996). *The practice of rational emotive behavior therapy.* New York: Springer.

Else-Quest, N. M., Hyde, J. S., Goldsmith, H. H., & Van Hulle, C. A. (2006). Gender differences in temperament: A meta-analysis. *Psychological Bulletin, 132*(1), 33–72.

El-Sheikh, M. (2007). Children's skin conductance level and reactivity: Are these measures stable over time and across tasks? *Developmental Psychobiology, 49*(2), 180–186.

El-Sheikh, M., & Harger, J. (2001). Appraisals of marital conflict and children's adjustment, health, and physiological reactivity. *Developmental Psychology, 37*(6), 875–885.

Eltzschig, H., Lieberman, E., & Camann, W. (2003). Regional anesthesia and analgesia for labor and delivery. *New England Journal of Medicine, 348*(4), 319–332.

Emde, R. N., Gaensbauer, T. J., & Harmon, R. J. (1976). *Emotional expression in infancy: A biobehavioral study.* New York: International Universities Press.

Emler, N., Tarry, H., & St. James, A. (2007). Post-conventional moral reasoning and reputation. *Journal of Research in Personality, 41*(1), 76–89.

Environmental Protection Agency. (2007, February 20). Lead in paint, dust, and soil. Available at http://www.epa.gov/lead/pubs/leadinfo.htm#checking. Accessed May 7, 2007.

Epstein, J. N. et al. (2005). The role of children's ethnicity in the relationship between teacher ratings of attention-deficit/hyperactivity disorder and observed classroom behavior. *Journal of Consulting and Clinical Psychology, 73*(3), 424–434.

Erikson, E. H. (1963). *Childhood and society.* New York: Norton.

Erikson, E. H. (1968). *Identity: Youth and crisis.* New York: Norton.

Erikson, E. H. (1975). *Life history and the historical moment.* New York: Norton.

Eron, L. D. (1982). Parent–child interaction, television violence, and aggression of children. *American Psychologist, 37,* 197–211.

Eron, L. D. (1993). Cited in T. DeAngelis (1993), It's baaack: TV violence, concern for kid viewers, *APA Monitor, 24*(8), 16.

Eron, L. D., Huesmann, L. R., & Zelli, A. (1991). The role of parental variables in the learning of aggression. In D. J. Pepler & K. H. Rubin (Eds.), *The development and treatment of childhood aggression.* Hillsdale, NJ: Erlbaum.

Ertem, I. O., Leventhal, J. M., & Dobbs, S. (2000). Intergenerational continuity of child physical abuse: How good is the evidence? *Lancet, 356,* 814–819.

Essau, C. A., Sakano, Y., Ishikawa, S., & Sasagawa, S. (2004). Anxiety symptoms in Japanese and in German children. *Behaviour Research and Therapy, 42*(5), 601–612.

Evans, S. W., et al. (2001). Dose–response effects of methylphenidate on ecologically valid measures of academic performance and classroom behavior in adolescents with ADHD. *Experimental and Clinical Psychopharmacology, 9*(2), 163–175.

Fabricius, W. V., & Cavalier, L. (1989). The role of causal theories about memory in young children's memory strategy choice. *Child Development, 60,* 298–308.

Fagot, B. I. (1990). A longitudinal study of gender segregation: Infancy to preschool. In F. F. Strayer (Ed.), *Social interaction and behavioral development during early childhood.* Montreal: La Maison D'Ethologie de Montreal.

Fagot, B. I., & Hagan, R. (1991). Observations of parent reactions to sex-stereotyped behaviors: Age and sex effects. *Child Development, 62,* 617–628.

Fagot, B. I., & Leinbach, M. D. (1993). Gender-role development in young children: From discrimination to labeling. *Developmental Review, 13,* 205–224.

Fagot, B. I., Rodgers, C. S., & Leinbach, M. D. (2000). Theories of gender socialization. In T. Eckes & H. M. Trautner (Eds.), *The developmental social psychology of gender* (pp. 65–89). Mahwah, NJ: Erlbaum.

Fantz, R. L. (1961). The origin of form perception. *Scientific American, 204,* 66–72.

Fantz, R. L., Fagan, J. F., III, & Miranda, S. B. (1975). Early visual selectivity. In L. B. Cohen & P. Salapatek (Eds.), *Infant perception: From sensation to cognition,* Vol. 1. New York: Academic Press.

Faraone, S. V., et al. (2000). Family study of girls with attention deficit hyperactivity disorder. *American Journal of Psychiatry, 157*(7), 1077–1083.

Farmer, A., Elkin, A., & McGuffin, P. (2007). The genetics of bipolar affective disorder. *Current Opinion in Psychiatry, 20*(1), 8–12.

Fasold, R. W. (2006). Ebonic need not be English. In H. Luria, D. M. Seymour, & T. Smoke (Eds.), *Language and linguistics in context: Readings and applications for teachers* (pp. 191–196). Mahwah, NJ: Erlbaum.

Feijó, L., et al. (2006). Mothers' depressed mood and anxiety levels are reduced after massaging their preterm infants. *Infant Behavior & Development, 29*(3), 476–480.

Feinberg, M. E., Neiderhiser, J. M., Howe, G., & Hetherington, E. M. (2001). Adolescent, parent, and observer perceptions of parenting: Genetic and environmental influences on shared and distinct perceptions. *Child Development, 72*(4), 1266–1284.

Feinberg, M. E., Neiderhiser, J. M., Simmens, S., Reiss, D., & Hetherington, E. M. (2000). Sibling comparison of differential parental treatment in adolescence: Gender, self-esteem, and emotionality as mediators of the parenting-adjustment association. *Child Development, 71*(6), 1611–1628.

Feiring, C. (1993, March). *Developing concepts of romance from 15 to 18 years.* Paper presented at the meeting of the Society for Research in Child Development, New Orleans, LA.

Feiring, C., & Lewis, M. (1991). The transition from middle to early adolescence: Sex differences in the social network and perceived self-competence. *Sex Roles, 24,* 489–509.

Feldman, R., & Masalha, S. (2007). The role of culture in moderating the links between early ecological risk and young children's adaptation. *Development and Psychopathology, 19*(1), 1–21.

Fenzel, L. M. (2000). Prospective study of changes in global self-worth and strain during the transition to middle school. *Journal of Early Adolescence, 20*(1), 93–116.

Ferdinand, R. F., Bongersa, I. L., van der Ende, J., van Gastela, W., Tick, N., Utens, E. et al. (2006). Distinctions between separation anxiety and social anxiety in children and adolescents. *Behaviour Research and Therapy, 44,* 1523–1535.

Fergusson, A. (2007). What successful teachers do in inclusive classrooms: Research-based teaching strategies that help special learners succeed. *European Journal of Special Needs Education, 22*(1), 108–110.

Fernandez, T., & State, M. (2004). Genetics and genomics of neurobehavioral disorders. *Journal of the American Academy of Child Psychiatry, 43*(3), 370–371.

Fernandez-Twinn, D. S., & Ozanne, S. E. (2006). Mechanisms by which poor early growth programs type-2 diabetes, obesity and the metabolic syndrome. *Physiology & Behavior, 88*(3), 234–243.

Féron, J., Gentaz, E., & Streri, A. (2006). Evidence of amodal representation of small numbers across visuo-tactile modalities in 5-month-old infants. *Cognitive Development, 21*(2), 81–92.

Festini, F., et al. (22 August 2006). The open problems of China's One-Child Family Policy: Men surplus and support of the elders. Available at www.bmj.com.

Fetrick, A., Christensen, M., & Mitchell, C. (2003). Does public health nurse home visitation make a difference in the health outcomes of pregnant clients and their offspring? *Public Health Nursing, 20*(3), 184–189.

Field, A. P. (2006). The behavioral inhibition system and the verbal information pathway to children's fears. *Journal of Abnormal Psychology, 115*(4), 742–752.

Field, T. (1999). Sucking and massage therapy reduce stress during infancy. In M. Lewis & D. Ramsay (Eds.), *Soothing and stress* (pp. 157–169). Hillsdale, NJ: Erlbaum .

Field, T., Hernandez-Reif, M., Feijo, L., & Freedman, J. (2006). Prenatal, perinatal and neonatal stimulation: A survey of neonatal nurseries. *Infant Behavior & Development, 29*(1), 24–31.

Finegan, J. K., Niccols, G. A., & Sitarenios, G. (1992). Relations between prenatal testosterone levels and cognitive abilities at 4 years. *Developmental Psychology, 28,* 1075–1089.

Finkelhor, D., Cross, T. P., & Cantor, E. N. (2005a). The justice system for juvenile victims: A comprehensive model of case flow. *Trauma, Violence, & Abuse, 6*(2), 83–102.

Finkelhor, D., Ormrod, R., Turner, H., & Hamby, S. L. (2005b). The victimization of children and youth: A comprehensive, national survey. *Child Maltreatment: Journal of* the American Professional Society on the Abuse of Children, 10(1), 5–25.

Fiorello, C. A., et al. (2007). Interpreting intelligence test results for children with disabilities: Is global intelligence relevant? Applied Neuropsychology, 14(1), 2–12.

Fisch, S. M. (2004). Children's learning from educational television: Sesame Street and beyond. Mahwah, NJ: Erlbaum.

Fiset, S., & Doré, F. Y. (2006). Duration of cats' (Felis catus) working memory for disappearing objects. Animal Cognition, 9(1), 62–70.

Fishman, H. C. (2006). Juvenile anorexia nervosa: Family therapy's natural niche. Journal of Marital & Family Therapy, 32(4), 505–514.

Fitzgerald, D. P., & White, K. J. (2003). Linking children's social worlds: Perspective-taking in parent–child and peer contexts. Social Behavior and Personality, 31(5), 509–522.

Fitzgerald, H. E., et al. (1991). The organization of lateralized behavior during infancy. In H. E. Fitzgerald, B. M. Lester, & M. W. Yogman (Eds.), Theory and research in behavioral pediatrics. New York: Plenum.

Fivush, R. (2002). Scripts, schemas, and memory of trauma. In N. L. Stein et al. (Eds.), Representation, memory, and development: Essays in honor of Jean Mandler (pp. 53–74). Mahwah, NJ: Erlbaum.

Fivush, R., & Hammond, N. R. (1990). Autobiographical memory across the preschool years: Toward reconceptualizing childhood amnesia. In R. Fivush & J. A. Hudson (Eds.), Knowing and remembering in young children. Cambridge: Cambridge University Press.

Fivush, R., Kuebli, J., & Clubb, P. A. (1992). The structure of events and event representations: A developmental analysis. Child Development, 63, 188–201.

Fivush, R., Sales, J, M., Goldberg, A., Bahrick, L., & Parker, J. (2004). Weathering the storm: Children's long-term recall of Hurricane Andrew. Memory, 12(1), 104–118.

Flavell, J. H. (1993). Young children's understanding of thinking and consciousness. Current Directions in Psychological Science, 2, 40–43.

Flavell, J. H., Miller, P. H., & Miller, S. A. (2002). Cognitive development (4th ed.). Upper Saddle River, NJ: Prentice Hall.

Florsheim, P. (Ed.). (2003). Adolescent romantic relations and sexual behavior: Theory, research, and practical implications. Mahwah, NJ: Erlbaum.

Flouri, E., & Buchanan, A. (2003). The role of father involvement and mother involvement in adolescents' psychological well-being. British Journal of Social Work, 33(3), 399–406.

Floyd, R. L., O'Connor, M. J., Sokol, R. J., Bertrand, J., & Cordero, F. F. (2005). Recognition and prevention of fetal alcohol syndrome. Obstetrics & Gynecology, 106, 1059–1064.

Flynn, E., O'Malley, C., & Wood, D. (2004). A longitudinal, microgenetic study of the emergence of false belief understanding and inhibition skills. Developmental Science, 7(1), 103–115.

Focus on Fertility. (2007). Available at http://www.focusonfertility.org. Accessed February 6, 2007.

Foley, G. M. (2006). Self and social–emotional development in infancy: A descriptive synthesis. In G. M. Foley & J. D. Hochman (Eds.), Mental health in early intervention: Achieving unity in principles and practice (pp. 139–173). Baltimore: Paul H. Brookes.

Fontaine, A-M. (2005). Écologie développementale des premières interactions entre enfants: Effet des matériels de jeu. Enfance, 57(2), 137–154.

Food and Drug Administration. (2004, July 20). Decreasing the chance of birth defects. Available at http://www.fda.gov/ fdac/features/996_bd.html.

Forbush, K., Heatherton, T. F., & Keel, P. K. (2007). Relationships between perfectionism and specific disordered eating behaviors. International Journal of Eating Disorders, 40(1), 37–41.

Forman-Hoffman, V. L., Ruffin, T., & Schultz, S. K. (2006). Basal metabolic rate in anorexia nervosa patients: Using appropriate predictive equations during the refeeding process. Annals of Clinical Psychiatry, 18(2), 123–127.

Fortier, J. C., Carson, V. B., Will, S., & Shubkagel, B. L. (1991). Adjustment to a newborn: Sibling preparation makes a difference. Journal of Obstetric, Gynecologic, and Neonatal Nursing, 20, 73–79.

Foster-Clark, F. S., & Blyth, D. A. (1991). Peer relations and influences. In R. M. Lerner, A. C. Petersen, & J. Brooks-Gunn (Eds.), Encyclopedia of adolescence. New York: Garland.

Fouad, N. A., & Arredondo, P. (2007). Implications for Psychologists as Researchers. In N. A. Fouad & P. Arredondo (Eds.), Becoming culturally oriented: Practical advice for psychologists and educators (pp. 81–93). Washington, DC: American Psychological Association.

Franklin, A., Pilling, M., & Davies, I. (2005). The nature of infant color categorization: Evidence from eye movements on a target detection task. Journal of Experimental Child Psychology, 91(3), 227–248.

Freedenthal, S. (2007). Racial disparities in mental health service use by adolescents who thought about or attempted suicide. Suicide and Life-Threatening Behavior, 37(1), 22–34.

Freeman, M. S., Spence, M. J., and Oliphant, C. M. (1993, June). Newborns prefer their mothers' low-pass filtered voices over other female filtered voices. Paper presented at the meeting of the American Psychological Society, Chicago.

French, D. C., Rianasari, M., Pidada, S., Nelwan, P., & Buhrmester, D. (2001). Social support of Indonesian and U.S. children and adolescents by family members and friends. Merrill–Palmer Quarterly, 47(3), 377–394.

Frerichs, L., Andsager, J. L., Campo, S., Aquilino, M., & Dyer, C. S. (2006). Framing breastfeeding and formula-feeding messages in popular U.S. magazines. Women & Health, 44(1), 95–118.

Frey, M. C., & Detterman, D. K. (2004). Scholastic assessment or g? The relationship between the scholastic assessment test and general cognitive ability. Psychological Science, 15(6), 373–378.

Fried, P. A., & Smith, A. M. (2001). A literature review of the consequences of prenatal marijuana exposure: An emerging theme of a deficiency in aspects of executive function. Neurotoxicology and Teratology, 23(1), 1–11.

Friedman, R. C., & Downey, J. I. (2001). The Oedipus complex and male homosexuality. In P. Hartocollis (Ed.), Mankind's Oedipal destiny: Libidinal and aggressive aspects of sexuality (pp. 113–138). Madison, CT: International Universities Press.

Frisch, R. (1997). Speech reported in N. Angier (1997), Chemical tied to fat control could help trigger puberty, New York Times, pp. C1, C3.

Frith, U. (2001). What framework should we use for understanding developmental disorders? Developmental Neuropsychology, 20(2), 555–563.

Frodi, A. M. (1985). When empathy fails: Infant crying and child abuse. In B. M. Lester & C. F. Z. Boukydis (Eds.), Infant crying. New York: Plenum.

Fromkin, V., et al. (2004).The development of language in Genie: A case of language acquisition beyond the "critical period." New York: Psychology Press.

Frostad, P., & Pijl, S. J. (2007). Does being friendly help in making friends? The relation between the social position and social skills of pupils with special needs in mainstream education. European Journal of Special Needs Education, 22(1), 15–30.

Fry, D. P. (2005). Rough-and-tumble social play in humans. In A. D. Pellegrini & P. K. Smith (Eds.), The nature of play: Great apes and humans (pp. 54–85). New York: Guilford Press.

Fu, J. H., Chiu, C., Morris, M. W., & Young, M. J. (2007). Spontaneous inferences from cultural cues: Varying responses of cultural insiders and outsiders. Journal of Cross-Cultural Psychology, 38(1), 58–75.

Fuligni, A. J., & Eccles, J. S. (1993). Perceived parent–child relationships and early adolescents' orientation toward peers. Developmental Psychology, 29, 622–632.

Funk, J. B., Buchman, D., Myers, M., & Jenks, J. (2000, August 7). Asking the right *question in research on violent electronic games.* Paper presented at the annual meeting of the American Psychological Association, Washington, DC.

Furman, W., & Buhrmester, D. (1992). Age and sex differences in perceptions of networks of personal relationships. *Child Development, 63,* 103–115.

Furman, W., Rahe, D., & Hartup, W. W. (1979). Social rehabilitation of low-interactive preschool children by peer intervention. *Child Development, 50,* 915–922.

Furstenberg, F. F., & Kiernan, K. E. (2001). Delayed parental divorce: How much do children benefit? *Journal of Marriage and the Family, 63*(2), 446–457.

Fuster, J. M. (2005). The cortical substrate of general intelligence. *Cortex, 41*(2), 228–229.

Gabriel, M., Taylor, C., & Burhans, L. (2003). In utero cocaine, discriminative avoidance learning with low-salient stimuli, and learning-related neuronal activity in rabbits (*Oryctolagus cuniculus*). *Behavioral Neuroscience, 117*(5), 912–926.

Ganesh, M. P., & Magdalin, S. (2007). Perceived problems and academic stress in children of disrupted and non-disrupted families. Journal *of the Indian Academy of Applied Psychology, 33*(1), 53–59.

Gao, F., Levine, S. C., & Huttenlocher, J. (2000). What do infants know about continuous quantity? *Journal of Experimental Child Psychology, 77*(1), 20–29.

Garber, H. L. (1988). *The Milwaukee Project: Preventing mental retardation in children at risk.* Washington, DC: American Association on Mental Retardation.

Garcia-Coll, C. T. (1990). Developmental outcome of minority infants: A process-oriented look into our beginnings. *Child Development, 61,* 270–289.

Gardner, H. (1983). *Frames of mind: The theory of multiple intelligences.* New York: Basic Books.

Gardner, H. (2001, April 5). Multiple intelligence. *New York Times,* p. A20.

Gardner, H. (2006). *The development and education of the mind: The selected works of Howard Gardner.* Philadelphia: Routledge/Taylor & Francis.

Garlow, S. J., Purselle, D. C., & Heninger, M. (2007). Cocaine and alcohol use preceding suicide in African American and White adolescents. *Journal of Psychiatric Research, 41*(6), 530–536.

Garnefski, N., Kraaij, V., & Spinhoven, P. (2001). De relatie tussen cognitieve copingstrategieen en symptomen van depressie, angst en suiecidaliteit. *Gedrag and Gezondheid: Tijdschrift voor Psychologie and Gezondheid, 29*(3), 148–158.

Gartstein, M. A., Slobodskaya, H. R., & Kinsht, I. A. (2003). Cross-cultural differences in temperament in the first year of life: United States of America (U.S.) and Russia. *International Journal of Behavioral Development, 27*(4), 316–328.

Garvey, C. (1990). *Developing child.* Cambridge, MA: Harvard University Press.

Gathercole, S. E., Pickering, S. J., Ambridge, B., & Wearing, H. (2004a). The structure of working memory from 4 to 15 years of age. *Developmental Psychology, 40*(2), 177–190.

Gathercole, S. E., Pickering, S. J., Knight, C., & Stegmann, Z. (2004b). Working memory skills and educational attainment: Evidence from national curriculum assessments at 7 and 14 years of age. *Applied Cognitive Psychology, 18*(1), 1–16.

Gau, S. S. F., et al. (2007). Psychiatric and psychosocial predictors of substance use disorders among adolescents. Longitudinal study. *British Journal of Psychiatry, 190*(1), 42–48.

Gavin, N. I., et al. (2005). Perinatal depression: A systematic review of prevalence and incidence. *Obstetrics & Gynecology, 106,* 1071–1083.

Ge, X., Conger, R. D., & Elder, G. H., Jr. (2001b). The relation between puberty and psychological distress in adolescent boys. *Journal of Research on Adolescence, 11*(1), 49–70.

Ge, X., et al. (2003). It's about timing and change: Pubertal transition effects on symptoms of major depression among African American youths. *Developmental Psychology, 39*(3), 430–439.

Geary, D. C. (1998). *Male, female: The evolution of human sex differences.* Washington, DC: American Psychological Association.

Geary, D. C. (2006). Sex differences in social behavior and cognition: Utility of sexual selection for hypothesis generation. *Hormones and Behavior, 49*(3), 273–275.

Gelernter, J., et al. (2007). Genomewide linkage scan for nicotine dependence: Identification of a chromosome 5 risk locus. *Biological Psychiatry, 61*(1), 119–126.

Geller, P. A., Kerns, D., & Klier, C. M. (2004). Anxiety following miscarriage and the subsequent pregnancy: A review of the literature and future directions. *Journal of Psychosomatic Research, 56*(1), 35–45.

Gelman, S. A., & Kremer, K. E. (1991). Understanding natural cause: Children's explanations of how objects and their properties originate. *Child Development, 62,* 396–414.

Georgiades, S., et al. (2007). Structure of the autism symptom phenotype: A proposed multidimensional model. *Journal of the American Academy of Child & Adolescent Psychiatry, 46*(2), 188–196.

Geschwind, D. H. (2000). Interview cited in D. E. Rosenbaum (2000, May 16), On left-handedness, its causes and costs, *New York Times,* pp. F1, F6.

Gesell, A. (1928). *Infancy and human growth.* New York: Macmillan.

Gesell, A. (1929). Maturation and infant behavior patterns. *Psychological Review, 36,* 307–319.

Getzels, J. W., & Jackson, P. W. (1962). *Creativity and intelligence.* New York: Wiley.

Gevers Deynoot-Schaub, M. J., & Riksen-Walraven, J. M. (2006). Peer contacts of 15-month-olds in childcare: Links with child temperament, parent–child interaction and quality of childcare. *Social Development, 15*(4), 709–729.

Ghetti, S., & Alexander, K. W. (2004). "If it happened, I would remember it": Strategic use of event memorability in the rejection of false autobiographical events. *Child Development, 75*(2), 542–561.

Gibson, E. J. (1969). *Principles of perceptual learning and development.* New York: Appleton-Century-Crofts.

Gibson, E. J. (1991). *An odyssey in learning and perception.* Cambridge, MA: MIT Press.

Gibson, E. J., & Walk, R. D. (1960). The visual cliff. *Scientific American, 202,* 64–71.

Gilligan, C. (1977). In a different voice: Women's conceptions of self and morality. *Harvard Educational Review, 47,* 481–517.

Gilligan, C. (1982). *In a different voice.* Cambridge, MA: Harvard University Press.

Gilligan, C., & Attanucci, J. (1988). Two moral orientations: Gender differences and similarities. *Merrill–Palmer Quarterly, 34,* 223–237.

Gillooly, J. B. (2004). Making menarche positive and powerful for both mother and daughter. *Women & Therapy, 27*(3–4), 23–35.

Giussani, D. A. (2006). Prenatal hypoxia: Relevance to developmental origins of health and disease. In P. Gluckman & M. Hanson (Eds.), *Developmental origins of health and disease* (pp. 178–190). New York: Cambridge University Press.

Glasberg, R., & Aboud, F. (1982). Keeping one's distance from sadness: Children's self-reports of emotional experience. *Developmental Psychology, 18,* 287–293.

Gleason, T. R. (2002). Social provisions of real and imaginary relationships in early childhood. *Developmental Psychology, 38*(6), 979–992.

Gleason, T. R. (2004). Imaginary companions and peer acceptance. *International Journal of Behavioral Development, 28*(3), 204–209.

Gleason, T. R., Gower, A. L., Hohmann, L. M., & Gleason, T. C. (2005). Temperament and friendship in preschool-aged children. *International Journal of Behavioral Development, 29*(4), 336–344.

Gleason, T. R., & Hohmann, L. M. (2006). Concepts of real and imaginary friendships in early childhood. *Social Development, 15*(1), 128–144.

Gleason, T. R., Sebanc, A. M., & Hartup, W. W. (2003). Imaginary companions of preschool children. In M. E. Hertzig & E. A. Farber (Eds.), *Annual progress in child* psychiatry and child development: 2000–2001 (pp. 101–121). New York: Brunner-Routledge.

Gobet, F., & Simon, H. A. (2000). Five seconds or sixty? Presentation time in expert memory. *Cognitive Science, 24*(4), 651–682.

Goel, P., Radotra, A., Singh, I., Aggarwal, A., & Dua, D. (2004). Effects of passive smoking on outcome in pregnancy. *Journal of Postgraduate Medicine, 50*(1), 12-16.

Gogate, L. J., Bahrick, L. E., & Watson, J. D. (2000). A study of multimodal motherese: The role of temporal synchrony between verbal labels and gestures. *Child Development, 71*(4), 878–894.

Golan, H., & Huleihel, M. (2006). The effect of prenatal hypoxia on brain development: Short- and long-term consequences demonstrated in rodent models. *Developmental Science, 9*(4), 338–349.

Goldberg, J, Holtz, D., Hyslop, T., & Tolosa, J. E. (2002). Has the use of routine episiotomy decreased? Examination of episiotomy rates from 1983 to 2000. *Obstetrics and Gynecology, 99*(3), 395–400.

Goldschmidt, L., Day, N. L., & Richardson, G. A. (2000). Effects of prenatal marijuana exposure on child behavior problems at age 10. *Neurotoxicology and Teratology, 22*(3), 325–336.

Goldsmith, H. H., et al. (2003). Part III: Genetics and development. In R. J. Davidson et al. (Eds.), *Handbook of affective sciences.* London: Oxford University Press.

Goldstein, E. B. (2005). *Cognitive psychology: Connecting mind, research, and everyday experience.* Belmont, CA: Wadsworth.

Goldstein, S., & Brooks, R. B. (2005). *Handbook of resilience in children.* New York: Kluwer Academic/Plenum.

Goleman, D. J. (1995). *Emotional intelligence.* New York: Bantam Books.

Goleman, D. P. (2006). *Social intelligence.* New York: Bantam Books.

Golub, S. (1992). *Periods: From menarche to menopause.* Newbury Park, CA: Sage.

Gonzalez, V. (2005). Cultural, linguistic, and socioeconomic factors influencing monolingual and bilingual children's cognitive development. In V. Gonzalez & J. Tinajero (Eds.), *Review of research and practice,* Vol. 3 (pp. 67–104). Mahwah, NJ: Erlbaum.

González, Y. S., Moreno, D. S., & Schneider, B. H. (2004). Friendship expectations of early adolescents in Cuba and Canada. *Journal of Cross-Cultural Psychology, 35*(4), 436–445.

Goodman, G. S., & Clarke-Stewart, A. (1991). Suggestibility in children's testimony: Implications for sexual abuse investigations. In J. Doris (Ed.), *The suggestibility of children's recollections.* Washington, DC: American Psychological Association.

Goodman, G. S., Rudy, L., Bottoms, B. L., & Aman, C. (1990). Children's concerns and memory: Issues of ecological validity in the study of children's eyewitness testimony. In R. Fivush & J. A. Hudson (Eds.), *Knowing and remembering in young children.* Cambridge: Cambridge University Press.

Gooren, L. (2006). The biology of human psychosexual differentiation. *Hormones and Behavior, 50*(4), 589–601.

Goossens, L., Braet, C., & Decaluwé, V. (2007). Loss of control over eating in obese youngsters. *Behaviour Research and Therapy, 45*(1), 1–9.

Gopnik, A., & Meltzoff, A. N. (1992). Categorization and naming: Basic-level sorting in eighteen-month-olds and its relation to language. *Child Development, 63,* 1091–1103.

Gopnik, A., & Slaughter, V. (1991). Young children's understanding of changes in their mental states. *Child Development, 62,* 98–110.

Gordon, J., King, N. J., Gullone, E., Muris, P., & Ollendick, T. H. (2007). Treatment of children's nighttime fears: The need for a modern randomised controlled trial. *Clinical Psychology Review, 27*(1), 98–113.

Gormally, S., et al. (2001). Contact and nutrient caregiving effects on newborn infant pain responses. *Developmental Medicine and Child Neurology, 43*(1), 28–38.

Gort, M. (2006). Strategic codeswitching, interliteracy, and other phenomena of emergent bilingual writing: Lessons from first grade dual language classrooms. *Journal of Early Childhood Literacy, 6*(3), 323–354.

Gottfried, G. M., Hickling, A. K., Totten, L. R., Mkroyan, A., & Reisz, A. (2003). To be or not to be a galaprock: Preschoolers' intuitions about the importance of knowledge and action for pretending. *British Journal of Developmental Psychology, 21*(3), 397–414.

Gottlieb, B. H., Still, E., & Newby-Clark, I. R. (2007). Types and precipitants of growth and decline in emerging adulthood. *Journal of Adolescent Research, 22*(2), 132–155.

Gowers, S. G., & Bryan, C. (2005). Families of children with a mental disorder. In N. Sartorius et al. (Eds.), *Families and mental disorders: From burden to empowerment* (pp. 127–159). Hoboken, NJ: John Wiley & Sons Ltd.

Graber, J. A., Seeley, J. R., Brooks-Gunn, J., & Lewinsohn, P. M. (2004). Is pubertal timing associated with psychopathology in young adulthood? *Journal of the American Academy of Child and Adolescent Psychiatry, 43*(6), 718–726.

Graffy, J., Taylor, J., Williams, A., & Eldridge, S. (2004). Randomised controlled trial of support from volunteer counsellors for mothers considering breast feeding. *British Medical Journal, 328*(7430), 26–29.

Granot, D., & Mayseless, O. (2001). Attachment security and adjustment to school in middle childhood. *International Journal of Behavioral Development, 25*(6), 530–541.

Greco, C., Rovee-Collier, C., Hayne, H., Griesler, P., & Early, L. (1986). Ontogeny of early event memory: II. Encoding and retrieval by 2- and 3-month-olds. *Infant Behavior and Development, 9,* 461–472.

Greeff, A. P., & Van Der Merwe, S. (2004). Variables associated with resilience in divorced families. *Social Indicators Research, 68*(1), 59–75.

Green, J. A., Jones, L. E., & Gustafson, G. E. (1987). Perception of cries by parents and nonparents: Relation to cry acoustics. *Developmental Psychology, 23,* 370–382.

Green, R. (1978). Sexual identity of 37 children raised by homosexual or transsexual parents. *American Journal of Psychiatry, 135,* 692–697.

Green, R., Mandel, J. B., Hotvedt, M. E., Gray, J., & Smith, L. (1986). Lesbian mothers and their children: A comparison with solo parent heterosexual mothers and their children. *Archives of Sexual Behavior, 15,* 167–184.

Greenberg, J. (2002). Who stole the money, and when? Individual and situational determinants of employee theft. *Organizational Behavior and Human Decision Processes. 89*(1), 985–1003.

Greene, R. W., & Ablon, J. S. (2001). What does the MTA study tell us about effective psychosocial treatment for ADHD? *Journal of Clinical Child Psychology, 30*(1), 114–121.

Greene, S. M., Anderson, E. R., Doyle, E. A., Riedelbach, H., & Bear, G. G. (2006). Divorce. In K. M. Minke (Ed.), *Children's needs III: Development, prevention, and intervention* (pp. 745–757). Bethesda, MD: National Association of School Psychologists.

Greenough, W. T., Black, J. E., & Wallace, C. S. (2002). Experience and brain development. In M. H. Johnson, Y. Munakata, & R. O. Gilmore (Eds.), *Brain development and cognition: A reader* (2nd ed.) (pp. 186–216). Malden, MA: Blackwell.

Griffin, K. W., Scheier, L. M., Botvin, G. J., & Diaz, T. (2001). Protective role of personal competence skills in adolescent substance use: Psychological well-being as a mediating factor. *Psychology of Addictive Behaviors, 15*(3), 194–203.

Grigorenko, E. L. (2007). Triangulating developmental dyslexia: Behavior, brain, and genes. In D. Coch, G. Dawson, & K. W. Fischer. (Eds.). *Human behavior, learning, and the developing brain: Atypical development.* (pp. 117–144). New York: Guilford.

Grilo, C. M., Masheb, R. M., & Wilson, G. T. (2005). Efficacy of cognitive behavioral therapy and fluoxetine for the treatment of binge eating disorder: A randomized double-blind placebo-controlled comparison. *Biological Psychiatry, 57*(3), 301–309.

Grindrod, C. M., & Baum, S. R. (2005). Hemispheric contributions to lexical ambiguity resolution in a discourse context: Evidence from individuals with unilateral left and right hemisphere lesions. *Brain and Cognition, 57*(1), 70–83.

Grolnick, W. S., McMenamy, J. M., & Kurowski, C. O. (2006). Emotional self-regulation in infancy and toddlerhood. In L. Balter & C. S. Tamis-LeMonda (Eds.), *Child psychology: A handbook of contemporary issues* (2nd ed.) (pp. 3–25). New York: Psychology Press.

Grön, G., Wunderlich, A. P., Spitzer, M., Tomczak, R., & Riepe, M. W. (2000). Brain activation during human navigation: Gender-different neural networks as substrate of performance. *Nature Neuroscience, 3*(4), 404–408.

Grossmann, K., et al. (2002). The uniqueness of the child–father attachment relationship: Fathers' sensitive and challenging play as a pivotal variable in a 16-year longitudinal study. *Social Development, 11*(3), 307–331.

Grusec, J. E. (1991). Socializing concern for others in the home. *Developmental Psychology, 27,* 338–342.

Grusec, J. E. (2002). Parenting socialization and children's acquisition of values. In M. H. Bornstein (Ed.), *Handbook of parenting* (2nd ed.), Vol. 5, *Practical issues in parenting* (pp. 143–167). Mahwah, NJ: Erlbaum.

Grusec, J. E. (2006). The development of moral behavior and conscience from a socialization perspective. In M. Killen & J. G. Smetana (Eds.), *Handbook of moral development* (pp. 243–265). Mahwah, NJ: Erlbaum.

Grusec, J. E., Goodnow, J. J., & Kuczynski, L. (2000). New directions in analyses of parenting contributions to children's acquisition of values. *Child Development, 71*(1), 205–211.

Grusec, J. E., & Lytton, H. (1988). *Social development: History, theory, and research.* New York: Springer-Verlag.

Grych, J. H. (2005). Interparental conflict as a risk factor for child maladjustment: Implications for the development of prevention programs. *Family Court Review, 43*(1), 97–108.

Guerdjikova, A. I., McElroy, S. L., Kotwal, R., Stanford, K., & Keck Jr., P. E. (2007). Psychiatric and metabolic characteristics of childhood versus adult-onset obesity in patients seeking weight management. *Eating Behaviors, 8*(2), 266–276.

Guerin, D. W., Gottfried, A. W., & Thomas, C. W. (1997). Difficult temperament and behaviour problems: A longitudinal study from 1.5 to 12 years. *International Journal of Behavioral Development, 21*(1), 71–90.

Guerrero, M. C. M., & Villamil, O. S. (2000). Activating the ZPD: Mutual scaffolding in L2 peer revision. *Modern Language Journal, 84*(1), 51–68.

Guerrini, I., Thomson, A. D., & Gurling, H. D. (2007). The importance of alcohol misuse, malnutrition and genetic susceptibility on

brain growth and plasticity. *Neuroscience & Biobehavioral Reviews, 31*(2), 212–220

Güntürkün, O. (2006). Letters on nature and nurture. In P. B. Baltes et al. (Eds.), *Lifespan development and the brain: The perspective of biocultural co-constructivism* (pp. 379–397). New York: Cambridge University Press.

Gushue, G. V., & Whitson, M. L. (2006). The relationship of ethnic identity and gender role attitudes to the development of career choice goals among black and Latina girls. *Journal of Counseling Psychology, 53*(3), 379–385.

Gutknecht, L. (2001). Full-genome scans with autistic disorder: A review. *Behavior Genetics, 31*(1), 113–123.

Guttmacher Institute. (2007, June 8). Available at http://www.guttmacher.org/.

Guzikowski, W. (2006). Doula—a new model of delivery (continuous, nonprofessional care during the delivery). *Ceska Gynekologie, 71*(2), 103–105.

Haapasalo, J., & Moilanen, J. (2004). Official and self-reported childhood abuse and adult crime of young offenders. *Criminal Justice and Behavior, 31*(2), 127–149.

Haden, C. A., Ornstein, P. A., Eckerman, C. O., & Didow, S. M. (2001). Mother–child conversational interactions as events unfold: Linkages to subsequent remembering. *Child Development, 72*(4), 1016–1031.

Haeffel, G. J., & Grigorenko, E. L. (2007). Cognitive vulnerability to depression Exploring risk and resilience. *Child and Adolescent Psychiatric Clinics of North America, 16*(2), 435–448.

Haith, M. M. (1966). The response of the human newborn to visual movement. *Journal of Experimental Child Psychology, 3,* 235–243.

Haith, M. M. (1979). Visual cognition in early infancy. In R. B. Kearsly & I. E. Sigel (Eds.), *Infants at risk: Assessment of cognitive functioning.* Hillsdale, NJ: Erlbaum.

Haith, M. M. (1990). Progress in the understanding of sensory and perceptual processes in early infancy. *Merrill–Palmer Quarterly, 36,* 1–26.

Haith, M. M. (1998). Who put the cog in infant cognition? Is rich interpretation too costly? *Infant Behavior and Development, 21*(2), 167–179.

Hala, S., Hug, S., & Henderson, A. (2003). Executive function and false-belief understanding in preschool children: Two tasks are harder than one. *Journal of Cognition and Development, 4*(3), 275–298.

Halgin, R. P., & Whitbourne, S. K. (1993). *Abnormal psychology.* Fort Worth, TX: Harcourt Brace Jovanovich.

Halliday, L. F., & Bishop, D. V. M. (2006). Auditory frequency discrimination in children with dyslexia. *Journal of Research in Reading, 29*(2), 213–228.

Halpern, D. F. (2003). Sex differences in cognitive abilities. *Applied Cognitive Psychology, 17*(3), 375–376.

Halpern, D. F. (2004). A cognitive-process taxonomy for sex differences in cognitive abilities. *Current Directions in Psychological Science, 13*(4), 135–139.

Halpern, D. F. (2006). Girls and academic success: Changing patterns of academic achievement. In J. Worell & C. D. Goodheart (Eds.), *Handbook of girls' and women's psychological health: Gender and well-being across the lifespan* (pp. 272–282). Oxford series in clinical psychology. New York: Oxford University Press.

Halpern, D. F. (2007). Science, sex, and good sense: Why women are underrepresented in some areas of science and math. In S. J. Ceci & W. M. Williams (Eds.), *Why aren't more women in science: Top researchers debate the evidence* (pp. 121–130). Washington, DC: American Psychological Association.

Halpern, D. F., & LaMay, M. L. (2000). The smarter sex: A critical review of sex differences in intelligence. *Educational Psychology Review, 12*(2), 229–246.

Halpern, R. (2005). Book Review: Examining adolescent leisure time across cultures: New Directions for Child and Adolescent Development, No. 99. *Journal of Adolescent Research, 20*(4), 524–525.

Hamm, J. V. (2000). Do birds of a feather flock together? The variable bases for African American, Asian American, and European American adolescents' selection of similar friends. *Developmental Psychology, 36*(2), 209–219.

Hammen, C. (2003). Social stress and women's risk for recurrent depression. *Archives of Women's Mental Health, 6*(1), 9–13.

Han, W., Waldfogel, J., & Brooks-Gunn, J. (2001). The effects of early maternal employment on later cognitive and behavioral outcomes. *Journal of Marriage and the Family, 63*(2), 336–354.

Hangal, S., & Aminabhavi, V. A. (2007). Self-concept, emotional maturity, and achievement motivation of the adolescent children of employed mothers and homemakers. *Journal of the Indian Academy of Applied Psychology, 33*(1), 103–110.

Hanlon, T. E., Bateman, R. W., Simon, B. D., O'Grady, K. E., & Carswell, S. B. (2004). Antecedents and correlates of deviant activity in urban youth manifesting behavioral problems. *Journal of Primary Prevention, 24*(3), 285–309.

Hanna, A. C., & Bond, M. J. (2006). Relationships between family conflict, perceived maternal verbal messages, and daughters' disturbed eating symptomatology. *Appetite, 47*(2), 205–211.

Hannon, P., Bowen, D. J., Moinpour, C. M., & McLerran, D. F. (2003). Correlations in perceived food use between the family food preparer and their spouses and children. *Appetite, 40*(1), 77–83.

Hannon, P., Willis, S. K., Bishop-Townsend, V., Martinez, I. M., & Scrimshaw, S. C. (2000).

African-American and Latina adolescent mothers' infant feeding decisions and breast-feeding practices: A qualitative study. *Journal of Adolescent Health, 26*(6), 399–407.

Harding, J. E., & McCowan, L. M. E. (2003). Perinatal predictors of growth patterns to 18 months in children born small for gestational age. *Early Human Development, 74*(1), 13–26.

Harel, J., & Scher, A. (2003). Insufficient responsiveness in ambivalent mother–infant relationships: Contextual and affective aspects. *Infant Behavior and Development, 26*(3), 371–383.

Harlow, H. F., & Harlow, M. K. (1966). Learning to love. *American Scientist, 54,* 244–272.

Harlow, H. F., Harlow, M. K., & Suomi, S. J. (1971). From thought to therapy: Lessons from a primate laboratory. *American Scientist, 59,* 538–549.

Harris, D. L., Brown, E., Marriott, C., Whittall, S., & Harmer, S. (1991). Monsters, ghosts, and witches: Testing the limits of the fantasy–reality distinction in young children. *British Journal of Developmental Psychology, 9,* 105–123.

Harris, G. (2004, September 14). *FDA links drugs to being suicidal.* Available at http://www.nytimes.com.

Harris, J. G., Tulsky, D. S., & Schultheis, M. T. (2003). Assessment of the non-native English speaker: Assimilating history and research findings to guide clinical practice. In D. S. Tulsky et al. (Eds.), *Clinical interpretation of the WAIS–III and WMS–III* (pp. 343–390). San Diego: Academic Press.

Harris, J. R. (2007, March 26). To the editor: Day care and a child's behavior. *New York Times online.*

Harris, S. R., Megens, A. M., Backman, C. L., & Hayes, V. E. (2005). Stability of the Bayley II Scales of Infant Development in a sample of low-risk and high-risk infants. *Developmental Medicine & Child Neurology, 47*(12), 820–823.

Hart, D., Burock, D., London, B., & Atkins, R. (2003). Prosocial tendencies, antisocial behavior, and moral development. In A. Slater & G. Bremner (Eds.), *An introduction to developmental psychology* (pp. 334–356). Malden, MA: Blackwell.

Hart, S. J., Davenport, M. L., Hooper, S. R., & Belger, A. (2006). Visuospatial executive function in Turner syndrome: Functional MRI and neurocognitive findings. *Brain: A Journal of Neurology, 129*(5), May, 1125–1136.

Harter, S. (1990). Self and identity development. In S. S. Feldman & G. R. Elliott (Eds.), *At the threshold: The developing adolescent.* Cambridge, MA: Harvard University Press.

Harter, S. (2006). The Self. In K. A. Renninger, I. E. Sigel, W. Damon, & R. M. Lerner

(Eds.), *Handbook of child psychology* (6th ed.), Vol. 4, *Child psychology in practice* (pp. 505–570). Hoboken, NJ: Wiley.

Harter, S., & Monsour, A. (1992). Developmental analysis of conflict caused by opposing attributes in the adolescent self-portrait. *Developmental Psychology, 28,* 251–260.

Harter, S., & Pike, R. (1984). The pictorial scale of perceived competence and social acceptance for young children. *Child Development, 55,* 1969–1982.

Harter, S., & Whitesell, N. R. (2003). Beyond the debate: Why some adolescents report stable self-worth over time and situation, whereas others report changes in self-worth. *Journal of Personality, 71*(6), 1027–1058.

Hartman, R. O., & Betz, N. E. (2007). The five-factor model and career self-efficacy: General and domain-specific relationships. *Journal of Career Assessment, 15*(2), 145–161.

Hartup, W. W. (1983). The peer system. In P. H. Mussen (Ed.), *Handbook of child psychology,* Vol. 4, *Socialization, personality, and social development.* New York: Wiley.

Harvey, E. (1999). Short-term and long-term effects of early parental employment on children of the National Longitudinal Survey of Youth. *Developmental Psychology, 35*(2), 445–459.

Hasler, G., et al. (2007). Familiality of factor analysis-derived YBOCS dimensions in OCD-affected sibling pairs from the OCD Collaborative Genetics Study. *Biological Psychiatry, 61*(5), 617–625.

Hasselhorn, M. (1992). Task dependency and the role of typicality and metamemory in the development of an organizational strategy. *Child Development, 63,* 202–214.

Hastings, P. D., Zahn-Waxler, C., Robinson, J., Usher, B., & Bridges, D. (2000). The development of concern for others in children with behavior problems. *Developmental Psychology, 36*(5), 531–546.

Hatcher, R. A., et al. (Eds.). (2007). *Contraceptive technologies* (18th rev. ed.). New York: Ardent Media.

Haugaard, J. J. (2000). The challenge of defining child sexual abuse. *American Psychologist, 55*(9), 1036–1039.

Hawkins, S. S., & Law, C. (2006). A review of risk factors for overweight in preschool children: A policy perspective. *International Journal of Pediatric Obesity, 1*(4), 195–209.

Hay, C., & Evans, M. M. (2006). Violent victimization and involvement in delinquency: Examining predictions from general strain theory. *Journal of Criminal Justice, 34*(3), 261–274.

Hay, D. F., Payne, A., & Chadwick, A. (2004). Peer relations in childhood. *Journal of Child Psychology and Psychiatry. 45*(1), 84–108.

Hayne, H., & Fagen, J. W. (Eds.). (2003). *Progress in infancy research,* Vol. 3. Mahwah, NJ: Erlbaum.

Hayward, C. (Ed.). (2003). *Gender differences at puberty.* New York: Cambridge University Press.

Hazell, P. (2007). Drug therapy for attention-deficit/hyperactivity disorder-like symptoms in autistic disorder. *Journal of Paediatrics and Child Health, 43*(1–2), 19–24.

Healy, M. D., & Ellis, B. J. (2007). Birth order, conscientiousness, and openness to experience Tests of the family-niche model of personality using a within-family methodology. *Evolution and Human Behavior, 28*(1), 55–59.

Hebert, T. P. (2000). Gifted males pursuing careers in elementary education: Factors that influence a belief in self. *Journal for the Education of the Gifted, 24*(1), 7–45.

Heilman, K. M., Nadeau, S. E., & Beversdorf, D. O. (2003). Creative innovation: Possible brain mechanisms. *Neurocase, 9*(5), 369–379.

Heim, C., et al. (2000). Pituitary–adrenal and autonomic responses to stress in women after sexual and physical abuse in childhood. *Journal of the American Medical Association, 284,* 592–597.

Heimann, M., et al. (2006). Exploring the relation between memory, gestural communication, and the emergence of language in infancy: A longitudinal study. *Infant and Child Development, 15*(3), 233–249.

Heindel, J. J., & Lawler, C. (2006) Role of exposure to environmental chemicals in developmental origins of health and disease. In P. Gluckman & M. Hanson (Eds.), *Developmental origins of health and disease* (pp. 82–97). New York: Cambridge University Press.

Helms, J. E. (2006). Fairness is not validity or cultural bias in racial-group assessment: A quantitative perspective. *American Psychologist, 61*(8), 845–859.

Helwig, C. C. (2006). Rights, civil liberties, and democracy across cultures. In M. Killen & J. G. Smetana (Eds.), *Handbook of moral development* (pp. 185–210). Mahwah, NJ: Erlbaum.

Henry, D., et al. (2000). Normative influences on aggression in urban elementary school classrooms. *American Journal of Community Psychology, 28*(1) 59–81.

Hensch, T. K. (2003). Controlling the critical period. *Neuroscience Research, 47*(1), 17–22.

Henzi, S. P., et al. (2007). Look who's talking: developmental trends in the size of conversational cliques. *Evolution and Human Behavior, 28*(1), 66–74.

Hepper, P. G., Shahidullah, S., & White, R. (1990, October 4). Origins of fetal handedness. *Nature, 347,* 431.

Hershberger, S. L., & D'Augelli, A. R. (2000). Issues in counseling lesbian, gay, and bisexual adolescents. In R. M. Perez, K. A. De-Bord, & K. J. Bieschke (Eds.), *Handbook of counseling and psychotherapy with lesbian, gay, and bisexual clients* (pp. 225–247). Washington, DC: American Psychological Association.

Hertenstein, M. J., & Campos, J. J. (2004). The retention effects of an adult's emotional displays on infant behavior. *Child Development, 75*(2), 595–613.

Hervey-Jumper, H., Douyon, K., & Franco, K. N. (2006). Deficits in diagnosis, treatment and continuity of care in African-American children and adolescents with ADHD. *Journal of the National Medical Association, 98*(2), 233–238.

Hesketh, T., & Xing, Z. W. (2006). Abnormal sex ratios in human populations: Causes and consequences. *Proceedings of the National Academy of Sciences, 103,* 13271–13275.

Hetherington, E. M. (1989). Coping with family transition: Winners, losers, and survivors. *Child Development, 60,* 1–14.

Hetherington, E. M. (2006). The influence of conflict, marital problem solving and parenting on children's adjustment in nondivorced, divorced and remarried families. In A. Clarke-Stewart & J. Dunn (Eds.), *Families count: Effects on child and adolescent development, The Jacobs Foundation series on adolescence* (pp. 203–237). Cambridge, UK: Cambridge University Press.

Hetherington, E. M., et al. (1992). *Coping with marital transitions.* Monographs of the Society for Research in Child Development, 57(2–3, ser. 227).

Hetherington, E. M., Stanley-Hagan, M., & Anderson, E. R. (1989). Marital transitions: A child's perspective. *American Psychologist, 44,* 303–312.

Hickling, A. K., & Wellman, H. M. (2001). The emergence of children's causal explanations and theories: Evidence from everyday conversation. *Developmental Psychology, 37*(5), 668–683.

Hicks, B. M., et al. (2007). Genes mediate the association between P3 amplitude and externalizing disorders. *Psychophysiology, 44*(1), 98–105.

Hill, S. E., & Flom, R. (2007). 18- and 24-month-olds' discrimination of gender-consistent and inconsistent activities. *Infant Behavior & Development, 30*(1) 168–173.

Hill, S. Y., et al., (2007). Cerebellar volume in offspring from multiplex alcohol dependence families. *Biological Psychiatry, 61*(1), 41–47.

Hindley, C. B., Filliozat, A. M., Klackenberg, G., Nicolet-Neister, D., & Sand, E. A. (1966). Differences in age of walking for five European longitudinal samples. *Human Biology, 38,* 364–379.

Hindmarsh, G. J., O'Callaghan, M. J., Mohay, H. A., & Rogers, Y. M. (2000). Gender differences in cognitive abilities at 2 years in ELBW infants. *Early Human Development, 60*(2), 115–122.

Hines, D. A., & Finkelhor, D. (2007). Statutory sex crime relationships between juveniles and adults: A review of social scientific re-search. *Aggression and Violent Behavior, 12*(3), 300–314.

Hinojosa, T., Sheu, C., & Michel, G. F. (2003). Infant hand-use preferences for grasping objects contributes to the development of a hand-use preference for manipulating objects. *Developmental Psychobiology, 43*(4), 328–334.

Hinshaw, S. P. (2006). Treatment for children and adolescents with attention-deficit/hyper-activity disorder. In P. C. Kendall (Ed.), *Child and adolescent therapy: Cognitive-behavioral procedures* (3rd ed.) (pp. 82–113). New York: Guilford.

Ho, A., Todd, R. D., & Constantino, J. N. (2005). Autistic traits in twins vs. non-twins-A preliminary study. *Journal of Autism and Developmental Disorders, 35*(1), 129–133.

Hoegh, D. G., & Bourgeois, M. J. (2002). Prelude and postlude to the self: Correlates of achieved identity. *Youth and Society, 33*(4), 573–594.

Hoff, E. (2006). Language experience and language milestones during early childhood. In K. McCartney & D. Phillips (Eds.), *Blackwell handbook of early childhood development., Blackwell handbooks of developmental psychology* (pp. 233–251). Malden, MA: Blackwell.

Hoff, E. V. (2005). A friend living inside me—The forms and functions of imaginary companions. *Imagination, Cognition and Personality, 24*(2), 151–189.

Hoffman, L. W., & Youngblade, L. M. (1998). Maternal employment, morale, and parenting style: Social class comparisons. *Journal of Applied Developmental Psychology, 19*(3), 389–413.

Hogan, A. M., de Haan, M., Datta, A., & Kirkham, F. J. (2006). Hypoxia: An acute, intermittent and chronic challenge to cognitive development. *Developmental Science, 9*(4), 335–337.

Hogan, A. M., Kirkham, F. J., Isaacs, E. B., Wade, A. M., & Vargha-Khadem, F. (2005). Intellectual decline in children with moyamoya and sickle cell anaemia. *Developmental Medicine & Child Neurology, 47*(12), 824–829.

Holland, J. J. (2000, July 25). *Groups link media to child violence.* Available at http://www .ap.org/.

Holland, J. L. (1997). *Making vocational choices: A theory of vocational personalities and work environments* (3rd ed.). Odessa, FL: Psychological Assessment Resources.

Holliday, R. E. (2003). Reducing misinformation effects in children with cognitive interviews: Dissociating recollection and familiarity. *Child Development, 74*(3), 728–751.

Holloway, J. H. (2004). *Part-time work and student achievement.* Alexandria VA: Association for Supervision and Curriculum Development. Available at http://www.ascd .org/publications/ed_lead/200104/ holloway.html.

Holloway, S. D., Suzuki, S., Yamamoto, Y., & Mindnich, J. D. (2006). Relation of maternal role concepts to parenting, employment choices, and life satisfaction among Japanese women. *Sex Roles, 54*(3–4), 235–249.

Holsen, I., Kraft, P., & Roysamb, E. (2001). The relationship between body image and depressed mood in adolescence: A 5-year longitudinal panel study. *Journal of Health Psychology, 6*(6), 613–627.

Homer, B. D., & Nelson, K. (2005). Seeing objects as symbols and symbols as objects: Language and the development of dual representation. In B. D. Homer & C. S. Tamis-LeMonda (Eds.), *The development of social cognition and communication* (pp. 29–52). Mahwah, NJ: Erlbaum.

Honein, M. A., Paulozzi, L. J., Mathews, T. J., Erickson, J. D., & Wong, L. C. (2001). Impact of folic acid fortification of the U.S. food supply on the occurrence of neural tube defects. *Journal of the American Medical Association, 285*(23), 2981–2986.

Honzik, M. P., Macfarlane, J. W., & Allen, L. (1948). The stability of mental test performance between two and eighteen years. *Journal of Experimental Education, 17,* 309–324.

Hopkins, W. D., Dahl, J. F., & Pilcher, D. (2001). Genetic influence on the expression of hand preferences in chimpanzees (*Pan troglodytes*): Evidence in support of the right-shift theory and developmental instability. *Psychological Science, 12*(4), 299–303.

Hopkins-Golightly, T., Raz, S., & Sander, C. J. (2003). Influence of slight to moderate risk for birth hypoxia on acquisition of cognitive and language function in the preterm infant: A cross-sectional comparison with preterm-birth controls. *Neuropsychology, 17*(1), 3–13.

Hossain, M., Chetana, M., & Devi, P. U. (2005). Late effect of prenatal irradiation on the hippocampal histology and brain weight in adult mice. *International Journal of Developmental Neuroscience, 23*(4), 307–313.

Howe, M. L. (2006). Developmentally invariant dissociations in children's true and false memories: Not all relatedness is created equal. *Child Development, 77*(4), 1112–1123.

Hoy, E. A., & McClure, B. G. (2000). Preschool experience: A facilitator of very low birthweight infants' development? *Infant Mental Health Journal, 21*(6), 481–494.

Huber, J., Darling, S., Park, K., & Soliman, K. F. A. (2001). Altered responsiveness to stress and NMDA following prenatal exposure to cocaine. *Physiology and Behavior, 72*(1–2), 181–188.

Hudson, J. A. (1990). The emergence of autobiographical memory in mother–child conversation. In R. Fivush & J. A. Hudson (Eds.), *Knowing and remembering in young children.* Cambridge: Cambridge University Press.

Hudziak, J. J. (2001). Latent class analysis of ADHD and comorbid symptoms in a population sample of adolescent female twins. *Journal of Child Psychology and Psychiatry and Allied Disciplines, 42*(7), 933–942.

Huesmann, L. R., Dubow, E. F., Eron, L. D., & Boxer, P. (2006). Middle childhood family contextual factors as predictors of adult outcomes. In A. C. Huston & M. N. Ripke (Eds.), *Middle Childhood: Contexts of Development.* Cambridge, UK: Cambridge University Press.

Huestis, M. A., et al. (2002). Drug abuse's smallest victims: in utero drug exposure. *Forensic Science International, 128*(2), 20.

Huizink, A. C., & Mulder, E. J. H. (2006). Maternal smoking, drinking or cannabis use during pregnancy and neurobehavioral and cognitive functioning in human offspring. *Neuroscience & Biobehavioral Reviews, 30*(1), 24–41.

Hunt, C. E., & Hauck, F. R. (2006). Sudden infant death syndrome. *Canadian Medical Association Journal, 174*(13), 1861–1869.

Hunter, B. C., & Sahler, O. J. Z. (2006). Music for very young ears. *Birth: Issues in Perinatal Care, 33*(2), 137–138.

Hunter, S. C., & Boyle, J. M. E. (2004). Appraisal and coping strategy use in victims of school bullying. *British Journal of Educational Psychology, 74*(1), 83–107.

Hur, Y. (2005). Genetic and environmental influences on self-concept in female preadolescent twins: Comparison of Minnesota and Seoul data. *Twin Research and Human Genetics, 8*(4), 291–299.

Hurd, Y. L., et al. (2005). Marijuana impairs growth in mid–gestation fetuses. *Neurotoxicology and Teratology, 27*(2), 221–229.

Hyde, J. S. (2005). The genetics of sexual orientation. In J. S. Hyde (Ed.), *Biological substrates of human sexuality* (pp. 9–20). Washington, DC: American Psychological Association.

Hyde, J. S., Fennema, E., & Lamon, S. J. (1990). Gender differences in mathematics performance: A meta-analysis. *Psychological Bulletin, 107,* 139–155.

Hynes, M., Sheik, M., Wilson, H. G., & Spiegel, P. (2002). Reproductive health indicators and outcomes among refugee and internally displaced persons in postemergency phase camps. *Journal of the American Medical Association, 288,* 595–603.

Hyson, M., Copple, C., & Jones, J. (2006). Early childhood development and education. In K. A. Renninger, I. E. Sigel, W. Damon, & R. M. Lerner (Eds.), *Handbook of child psychology* (6th ed.), Vol. 4, *Child psychology in practice* (pp. 3–47). Hoboken, NJ: Wiley.

IJzendoorn, M. H. van, & Hubbard, F. O. A. (2000). Are infant crying and maternal responsiveness during the first year related to infant–mother attachment at 15 months? *Attachment and Human Development, 2*(3), 371–391.

IJzendoorn, M. H. van, & Juffer, F. (2006). The Emanuel Miller Memorial Lecture 2006: Adoption as intervention. Meta-analytic evidence for massive catch-up and plasticity in physical, socio-emotional, and cognitive development. *Journal of Child Psychology and Psychiatry, 47*(12), 1228–1245.

IJzendoorn, M. H. van, Moran, G., Belsky, J., Pederson, D., Bakermans-Kranenburg, M. J., & Kneppers, K. (2000). The similarity of siblings' attachments to their mother. *Child Development, 71*(4), 1086–1098.

Ikeda, K., Koga, A., & Minami, S. (2006). Evaluation of a cure process during alarm treatment for nocturnal enuresis. *Journal of Clinical Psychology, 62*(10), 1245–1257.

Infant and Toddler Nutrition. (2007, April 10). National Institutes of Health, Department of Health and Human Services. Available at http://www.nlm.nih.gov/medlineplus/infantandtoddlernutrition.html.

Inhelder, B., & Piaget, J. (1959). *The early growth of logic in the child: Classification and seriation.* New York: Harper & Row.

Inzlicht, M., & Good, C. (2006). How environments can threaten academic performance, self-knowledge, and sense of belonging. In S. Levin & C. van Laar (Eds.), *Stigma and group inequality: Social psychological perspectives. The Claremont symposium on Applied Social Psychology* (pp. 129–150). Mahwah, NJ: Erlbaum.

Ishikawa, S., Oota, R., & Sakano, Y. (2003). The relationship between anxiety disorders tendencies and subjective school maladjustment in childhood. *Japanese Journal of Counseling Science, 36*(3), 264–271.

Izard, C. E. (1983). *Maximally discriminative facial movement scoring system.* Newark, DE: University of Delaware Instructional Resources Center.

Izard, C. E. (2004). The generality–specificity issue in infants' emotion responses: A comment on Bennett, Bendersky, and Lewis (2002). *Infancy, 6*(3), 417–423.

Izard, C. E., Hembree, E. A., & Huebner, R. R. (1987). Infants' emotion expressions to acute pain: Developmental change and stability of individual differences. *Developmental Psychology, 23,* 105–113.

Izard, C. E., & Malatesta, C. Z. (1987). Perspectives on emotional development. I. Differential emotions theory of early emotional development. In J. D. Osofsky (Ed.), *Handbook of infant development* (2nd ed.). New York: Wiley.

Izard, C. E., Youngstrom, E. A., Fine, S. E., Mostow, A. J., & Trentacosta, C. J. (2006). Emotions and developmental psychopathology. In D. Cicchetti & D. J. Cohen (Eds.), *Developmental psychopathology,* Vol. 1, *Theory and method* (2nd ed.) (pp. 244–292). Hoboken, NJ: Wiley.

Jacklin, C. N., & McBride-Chang, C. (1991). The effects of feminist scholarship on developmental psychology. *Psychology of Women Quarterly, 15,* 549–556.

Jacklin, C. N., Wilcox, K. T., & Maccoby, E. E. (1988). Neonatal sex-steroid hormones and cognitive abilities at six years. *Developmental Psychobiology, 21,* 567–574.

Jackson, D. N., & Rushton, J. P. (2006). Males have greater g: Sex differences in general mental ability from 100,000 17- to 18-year-olds on the Scholastic Assessment Test. *Intelligence, 34*(5), 479–486.

Jacobs, D. M., Levy, G., & Marder, K. (2006). Dementia in Parkinson's disease, Huntington's disease, and related disorders. In M. J. Farah & T. E. Feinberg (Eds.), *Patient-based approaches to cognitive neuroscience* (2nd ed.) (pp. 381–395). Cambridge, MA: MIT Press.

Jacobs, J. E., Davis-Kean, P., Bleeker, M., Eccles, J. S., & Malanchuk, O. (2005). "I can, but I don't want to": The impact of parents, interests, and activities on gender differences in math. In A. M. Gallagher & J. C. Kaufman (Eds.), *Gender differences in mathematics: An integrative psychological approach* (pp. 246–263). New York: Cambridge University Press.

Jacobson, J. L., Jacobson, S. W., Padgett, R. J., Brumitt, G. A., & Billings, R. L. (1992). Effects of prenatal PCB exposure on cognitive processing efficiency and sustained attention. *Developmental Psychology, 28,* 297–306.

Jacobson, P. F., & Schwartz, R. G. (2005). English past tense use in bilingual children with language impairment. *American Journal of Speech-Language Pathology, 14*(4), 313–323.

Jaffee, S. R., Belsky, J., Harrington, H. L., Caspi, A., & Moffitt, T. E. (2006). When parents have a history of conduct disorder: How is the caregiving environment affected? *Journal of Abnormal Psychology, 115*(2), 309–319.

Jago, R., Baranowski, T., Baranowski, J. C., Thompson, D., & Greaves, K. A. (2005). BMI from 3–6 y of age is predicted by TV viewing and physical activity, not diet. *International Journal of Obesity, 29*(6), 557–564.

James, W. 1890. *The principles of psychology.* Mineola, NY: Dover (Reprint publisher).

Jamieson, S., & Marshall, W. L. (2000). Attachment styles and violence in child molesters. *Journal of Sexual Aggression, 5*(2), 88–98.

Jang, K. L., Livesley, W. J., Taylor, S., Stein, M. B., & Moon, E. C. (2004). Heritability of individual depressive symptoms. *Journal of Affective Disorders, 80*(2–3), 125–133.

Jarvis, B. (1993, May 3). Against the great divide. *Newsweek,* p. 14.

Javo, C., Ronning, J. A., & Heyerdahl, S. (2004). Child-rearing in an indigenous Sami population in Norway: A cross-cultural comparison of parental attitudes and expectations. *Scandinavian Journal of Psychology, 45*(1), 67–78.

Jeng, S.-F., Yau, K.-I. T., Liao, H.-F., Chen, L.-C., & Chen, P.-S. (2000). Prognostic factors for walking attainment in very lowbirthweight preterm infants. *Early Human Development, 59*(3), 159–173.

Jiang, J., et al. (2006). Risk factors for overweight in 2- to 6-year-old children in Beijing, China. *International Journal of Pediatric Obesity, 1*(2), 103–108.

Joca, S. R. L., Zanelati, T., & Guimaraes, F. S. (2006). Post-stress facilitation of serotonergic, but not noradrenergic, neurotransmission in the dorsal hippocampus prevents learned helplessness development in rats. *Brain Research, 1087*(1), 67–74.

Joe, S., Romer, D., & Jamieson, P. (2007). Suicide acceptability is related to suicide planning in U.S. adolescents and young adults. *Suicide and Life-Threatening Behavior, 37*(2), 165–178.

Johnson, C. M. (1991). Infant and toddler sleep: A telephone survey of parents in one community. *Developmental and Behavioral Pediatrics, 12,* 108–114.

Johnson, W., & Bouchard, T. J., Jr., (2007). Sex differences in mental abilities: g masks the dimensions on which they lie. *Intelligence, 35*(1), 23–39.

Johnson, W., Emde, R. N., Pannabecker, B., Stenberg, C., & Davis, M. (1982). Maternal perception of infant emotion from birth to 18 months. *Infant Behavior and Development, 5,* 313–322.

Johnson, W., & Krueger, R. F. (2006). How money buys happiness: Genetic and environmental processes linking finances and life satisfaction. *Journal of Personality and Social Psychology, 90*(4), 680–691.

Johnson, W., McGue, M., Krueger, R. F., & Bouchard, T. J., Jr. (2004). Marriage and personality: A genetic analysis. *Journal of Personality and Social Psychology, 86*(2), 285–294.

Johnston, C. A., & Steele, R. G. (2007). Treatment of pediatric overweight: An examination of feasibility and effectiveness in an applied clinical setting. *Journal of Pediatric Psychology, 32*(1), 106–110.

Johnston, L. D., O'Malley, P. M., & Bachman, J. G. (2006a). Demographic subgroup trends for various licit and illicit drugs 1975–2005. *Monitoring the Future occasional paper 63.* Ann Arbor: University of Michigan Institute for Social Research.

Johnston, L. D., O'Malley, P. M., Bachman, J. G., & Schulenberg, J. E. (2006b). *Monitoring the Future National Results on Adolescent Drug Use. Overview of Key Findings, 2006.* Bethesda, MD: National Institute on Drug Abuse. U.S. Department of Health and Human Services.

Johnston, L. D., O'Malley, P. M., Bachman, J. G. & Schulenberg, J. E. (December 21, 2006). *Teen drug use continues down in 2006, particularly among older teens; but use of prescription-type drugs remains high.* University of Michigan News and Information Services: Ann Arbor, MI. Available at www.monitoringthefuture.org. Accessed February 25, 2007.

Jones, D. C., & Crawford, J. K. (2006). The peer appearance culture during adolescence: Gender and body mass variations. *Journal of Youth and Adolescence, 35*(2), 257–269.

Jones, D. C., Swift, D. J., & Johnson, M. A. (1988). Nondeliberate memory for a novel event among preschoolers. *Developmental Psychology, 24,* 641–645.

Jones, M. C. (1924). Elimination of children's fears. *Journal of Experimental Psychology, 7,* 381–390.

Jones, S. S., & Hong, H-W. (2005). How some infant smiles get made. *Infant Behavior & Development, 28*(2), 194–205.

Jonkman, S. (2006). Sensitization facilitates habit formation: Implications for addiction. *Journal of Neuroscience, 26*(28), 7319–7320.

Jorgensen, G. (2006). Kohlberg and Gilligan: Duet or duel? *Journal of Moral Education, 35*(2), 179–196.

Joshi, P. T., Salpekar, J. A., & Daniolos, P. T. (2006). Physical and sexual abuse of children. In M. K. Dulcan & J. M. Wiener (Eds.), *Essentials of child and adolescent psychiatry* (pp. 595–620). Washington, DC: American Psychiatric Publishing.

Joshi, R. M. (2003). Misconceptions about the assessment and diagnosis of reading disability. *Reading Psychology, 24*(3–4), 247–266.

Kagan, J., & Klein, R. E. (1973). Cross-cultural perspectives on early development. *American Psychologist, 28,* 947–961.

Kagan, L. J., MacLeod, A. K., & Pote, H. L. (2004). Accessibility of causal explanations for future positive and negative events in adolescents with anxiety and depression. *Clinical Psychology and Psychotherapy, 11*(3), 177–186.

Kaiser Family Foundation, Holt, T., Greene, L., & Davis, J. (2003). *National Survey of Adolescents and Young Adults: Sexual health knowledge, attitudes, and experiences.* Menlo Park, CA: Henry J. Kaiser Family Foundation.

Kalil, A., Ziol-Guest, K. M., & Coley, R. L. (2005). Perceptions of father involvement patterns in teenage-mother families: Predictors and links to mothers' psychological adjustment. *Family Relations, 54*(2), 197–211.

Kaltiala-Heino, R., Marttunen, M., Rantanen, P., & Rimpelä, M. (2003). Early puberty is associated with mental health problems in middle adolescence. *Social Science and Medicine, 57*(6), 1055–1064.

Kaltiala-Heino, R., Rimpelae, M., Rissanen, A., & Rantanen, P. (2001). Early puberty and early sexual activity are associated with bu-

limic-type eating pathology in middle adolescence. *Journal of Adolescent Health, 28*(4), 346–352.

Kamakura, T., Ando, J., & Ono, Y. (2007). Genetic and environmental effects of stability and change in self-esteem during adolescence. *Personality and Individual Differences, 42*(1), 181–190.

Kaminski, R. A., & Stormshak, E. A. (2007). Project STAR: Early intervention with preschool children and families for the prevention of substance abuse. In P. Tolan, J. Szapocznik, & S. Sambrano (Eds.), *Preventing youth substance abuse: Science-based programs for children and adolescents* (pp. 89–109). Washington, DC: American Psychological Association.

Kanevsky, L., & Geake, J. (2004). Inside the zone of proximal development: Validating a multifactor model of learning potential with gifted students and their peers. *Journal for the Education of the Gifted, 28*(2), 182–217.

Karapetsas, A., & Kantas, A. (1991). Visuomotor organization in the child: A neuropsychological approach. *Perceptual and Motor Skills, 72,* 211–217.

Karatekin, C. (2004). Development of attentional allocation in the dual task paradigm. *International Journal of Psychophysiology, 52*(1), 7–21.

Karatekin, C., Marcus, D. J., & White, T. (2007). Oculomotor and manual indexes of incidental and intentional spatial sequence learning during middle childhood and adolescence. *Journal of Experimental Child Psychology, 96*(2), 107–130.

Karavasilis, L., Doyle, A. B., & Markiewicz, D. (2003). Associations between parenting style and attachment to mother in middle childhood and adolescence. *International Journal of Behavioral Development, 27*(2), 153–164.

Karwautz, A., et al. (2001). Individual-specific risk factors for anorexia nervosa: A pilot study using a discordant sister-pair design. *Psychological Medicine, 31*(2), 317–329.

Katz, R., Lowenstein, A., Phillips, J., & Daatland, S. O. (2005). Theorizing intergenerational family relations: Solidarity, conflict, and ambivalence in cross-national contexts. In V. L. Bengtson et al. (Eds.), *Sourcebook of family theory & research* (pp. 393–420). Thousand Oaks, CA: Sage.

Katzman, D. K. (2005). Medical complications in adolescents with anorexia nervosa: A review of the literature. *International Journal of Eating Disorders, 37*(Suppl), S52–S59.

Kaufman, J., & Zigler, E. (1992). The prevention of child maltreatment: Programming, research, and policy. In D. J. Willis, E. W. Holden, & M. Rosenberg (Eds.), *Prevention of child maltreatment: Developmental and ecological perspectives.* New York: Wiley.

Kavanaugh, R. D. (2006). Pretend play. In B. Spodek & O. N. Saracho (Eds.), *Handbook of research on the education of young children* (2nd ed.) (pp. 269–278). Mahwah, NJ: Erlbaum.

Kavcic, T., & Zupancic, M. (2005). Sibling relationship in early/middle childhood: Trait- and dyad-centered approach. *Studia Psychologica, 47*(3), 179–197.

Kaye, W. H., et al. (2004). Genetic analysis of bulimia nervosa: Methods and sample description. *International Journal of Eating Disorders, 35*(4), 556–570.

Kazdin, A. E. (2000). Treatments for aggressive and antisocial children. *Child and Adolescent Psychiatric Clinics of North America, 9*(4), 841–858.

Kazui, M., Endo, T., Tanaka, A., Sakagami, H., & Suganuma, M. (2000). Intergenerational transmission of attachment: Japanese mother–child dyads. *Japanese Journal of Educational Psychology, 48*(3), 323–332.

Kearney, C. A., & Bensaheb, A. (2007). Assessing anxiety disorders in children and adolescents. In S. R. Smith & L. Handler (Eds.), *The clinical assessment of children and adolescents: A practitioner's handbook* (pp. 467–483). Mahwah, NJ: Erlbaum.

Keddie, A. (2004). Research with young children: The use of an affinity group approach to explore the social dynamics of peer culture. *British Journal of Sociology of Education, 25*(1), 35–51.

Keen, D., Rodger, S., Doussin, K., & Braithwaite, M. (2007). A pilot study of the effects of a social-pragmatic intervention on the communication and symbolic play of children with autism. *Autism, 11*(1), 63–71.

Keenan, P. A., & Soleymani, R. M. (2001). Gonadal steroids and cognition. In R. E. Tarter et al. (Eds.), *Medical neuropsychology: Clinical issues in neuropsychology* (2nd ed.) (pp. 181–197). Dordrecht, Netherlands: Kluwer Academic.

Keller, H., et al. (2006). Cultural models, socialization goals, and parenting ethnotheories: A multicultural analysis. *Journal of Cross-Cultural Psychology, 37*(2), 155–172.

Keller, H., Kärtner, J., Borke, J., Yovsi, R., & Kleis, A. (2005). Parenting styles and the development of the categorical self: A longitudinal study on mirror self-recognition in Cameroonian Nso and German families. *International Journal of Behavioral Development, 29*(6), 496–504.

Keller, S., Maddock, J. E., Laforge, R. G., Velicer, W. F., & Basler, H-D. (2007). Binge drinking and health behavior in medical students. *Addictive Behaviors, 32*(3), 505–515.

Kellman, P. J., & Arterberry, M. E. (2006). Infant visual perception. In D. Kuhn et al. (Eds.), *Handbook of child psychology: Vol. 2, Cognition, perception, and language* (6th ed.) (pp. 109–160). Hoboken, NJ: Wiley.

Kellogg, R. (1959). *What children scribble and why.* Oxford: National Press.

Kellogg, R. (1970). Understanding children's art. In P. Cramer (Ed.), *Readings in developmental psychology today.* Del Mar, CA: CRM.

Kelly, K. M., Jones, W. H., & Adams, J. M. (2002). Using the Imaginary Audience Scale as a measure of social anxiety in young adults. *Educational and Psychological Measurement, 62*(5), 896–914.

Kelly, Y., Sacker, A., Schoon, I., & Nazroo, J. (2006). Ethnic differences in achievement of developmental milestones by 9 months of age: The Millenium Cohort Study. *Developmental Medicine & Child Neurology, 48*(10), 825–830.

Kempes, M., Matthys, W., de Vries, H., & van Engeland, H. (2005). Reactive and proactive aggression in children: A review of theory, findings and the relevance for child and adolescent psychiatry. *European Child & Adolescent Psychiatry, 14*(1), 11–19.

Kendall, P. C., Safford, S., Flannery-Schroeder, E., & Webb, A. (2004). Child anxiety treatment: outcomes in adolescence and impact on substance use and depression at 7.4-year follow-up. *Journal of Consulting and Clinical Psychology, 72,* 276–287.

Kendler, K. S., Gardner, C. O., Gatz, M., & Pedersen, N. L. (2007). The sources of comorbidity between major depression and generalized anxiety disorder in a Swedish national twin sample. *Psychological Medicine, 37*(3), 453–462.

Keogh, A. F., & Whyte, J. (2006). Exploring children's concepts of intelligence through ethnographic methods. *Irish Journal of Psychology, 27*(1–2), 69–78.

Kerns, K. A., Abraham, M. M., Schlegelmilch, A., & Morgan, T. A. (2007). Mother–child attachment in later middle childhood: Assessment approaches and associations with mood and emotion regulation. *Attachment & Human Development, 9*(1), 33–53.

Kerr, D. C. R., Lopez, N. L., Olson, S. L., & Sameroff, A. J. (2004). Parental discipline and externalizing behavior problems in early childhood: The roles of moral regulation and child gender. *Journal of Abnormal Child Psychology, 32*(4), 369–383.

Kidd, E., & Bavin, E. L. (2007). Lexical and referential influences on on-line spoken language comprehension: A comparison of adults and primary-school-age children. *First Language, 27*(1), 29–52.

Kilgore, K., Snyder, J., & Lentz, C. (2000). The contribution of parental discipline, parental monitoring, and school risk to early-onset conduct problems in African American boys and girls. *Developmental Psychology, 36*(6), 835–845.

Killen, M., & Smetana, J. G. (Eds.). (2006). *Handbook of moral development.* Mahwah, NJ: Erlbaum.

Kim, J-Y., McHale, S. M., Osgood, D. W., & Crouter, A. C. (2006). Longitudinal course and family correlates of sibling relationships from childhood through adolescence. *Child Development, 77*(6), 1746–1761.

Kim, K. H. (2005). Can only intelligent people be creative? A meta-analysis. *Journal of Secondary Gifted Education, 16*(2–3), 57–66.

Kim-Cohen, J. (2007). Resilience and developmental psychopathology. *Child and Adolescent Psychiatric Clinics of North America, 16*(2), 271–283.

Kimura, D., & Hampson, E. (1992). Neural and hormonal mechanisms mediating sex differences in cognition. In P. A. Vernon (Ed.), *Biological approaches to the study of human intelligence.* Norwood, NJ: Ablex.

King, L. A., Scollon, C. K., Ramsey, C., & Williams, T. (2000). Stories of life transition: Subjective well-being and ego development in parents of children with Down syndrome. *Journal of Research in Personality, 34*(4), 509–536.

King, R. (2000). Interview comments in L. Frazier (2000, July 16), The new face of HIV is young, black, *Washington Post,* p. C01.

Kinsbourne, M. (2003). The corpus callosum equilibrates the cerebral hemispheres. In E. Zaidel & M. Iacoboni (Eds.), *The parallel brain: The cognitive neuroscience of the corpus callosum* (pp. 271–281). Cambridge, MA: MIT Press.

Kinsey, A. C., Pomeroy, W. B., & Martin, C. E. (1948). *Sexual behavior in the human male.* Philadelphia: W. B. Saunders.

Kinsey, A. C., Pomeroy, W. B., Martin, C. E., & Gebhard, P. H. (1953). *Sexual behavior in the human female.* Philadelphia: W. B. Saunders.

Kirchler, E., Pombeni, M. L., & Palmonari, A. (1991). Sweet sixteen . . . Adolescents' problems and the peer group as source of support. *European Journal of Psychology of Education, 6,* 393–410.

Kirkcaldy, B. D., Shephard, R. J., & Siefen, R. G. (2002). The relationship between physical activity and self-image and problem behaviour among adolescents. *Social Psychiatry and Psychiatric Epidemiology, 37*(11), 544–550.

Kistner, J. (2006). Children's peer acceptance, perceived acceptance, and risk for depression. In T. E. Joiner, J. S. Brown, & J. Kistner (Eds.), *The interpersonal, cognitive, and social nature of depression* (pp. 1–21). Mahwah, NJ: Erlbaum.

Kjelsås, E., Bjornstrom, C., & Götestam, K. G. (2004). Prevalence of eating disorders in female and male adolescents (14–15 years). *Eating Behaviors, 5*(1), 13–25.

Klaus, M., & Kennell, J. (1976). *Maternal–infant bonding.* St. Louis: C. V. Mosby.

Klaus, M. H., & Kennell, J. H. (1978). Parent-to-infant attachment. In J. H. Stevens Jr.

& M. Mathews (Eds.), *Mother/child, father/child relationships*. Washington, DC: National Association for the Education of Young Children.

Klein, P. J., & Meltzoff, A. N. (1999). Long-term memory, forgetting and deferred imitation in 12-month-old infants. *Developmental Science, 2*(1), 102–113.

Klier, C. M. (2006). Mother–infant bonding disorders in patients with postnatal depression: The Postpartum Bonding Questionnaire in clinical practice. *Archives of Women's Mental Health, 9*(5), 289–291.

Klintsova, A. Y., & Greenough, W. T. (1999). Synaptic plasticity in cortical systems. *Current Opinion in Neurobiology, 9*(2), 203–208.

Klomek, A. B., et al. (2007). Bullying, depression, and suicidality in adolescents. *Journal of the American Academy of Child & Adolescent Psychiatry, 46*(1), 40–49.

Knaak, S. (2005). Breast-feeding, bottle-feeding and Dr. Spock: The shifting context of choice. *Canadian Review of Sociology and Anthropology, 42*(2), 197–216.

Knafo, A., & Plomin, R. (2006a). Parental discipline and affection and children's prosocial behavior: Genetic and environmental links. *Journal of Personality and Social Psychology, 90*(1), 147–164.

Knafo, A., & Plomin, R. (2006b). Prosocial behavior from early to middle childhood: Genetic and environmental influences on stability and change. *Developmental Psychology, 42*(5), 771–786.

Knox, P. L., Fagley, N. S., & Miller, P. M. (2004). Care and justice moral orientation among African American college students. *Journal of Adult Development, 11*(1), 41–45.

Kobayashi-Winata, H., & Power, T. G. (1989). Childrearing and compliance: Japanese and American families in Houston. *Journal of Cross-Cultural Psychology, 20,* 333–356.

Koch, J. (2007). A gender inclusive approach to science education. In D. M. Sadker & E. S. Silber (Eds.), *Gender in the classroom: Foundations, skills, methods, and strategies across the curriculum* (pp. 205–223). Mahwah, NJ: Erlbaum.

Kochanska, G. (2001). Emotional development in children with different attachment histories: The first three years. *Child Development, 72*(2), 474–490.

Kochanska, G., Coy, K. C., Murray, K. T. (2001). The development of self-regulation in the first four years of life. *Child Development, 72*(4), 1091–1111.

Kogan, M. D., et al. (2000). Trends in twin birth outcomes and prenatal care utilization in the United States, 1981–1997. *Journal of the American Medical Association, 284*(3), 335–341.

Kohl, C. (2004). Postpartum psychoses: Closer to schizophrenia or the affective spectrum? *Current Opinion in Psychiatry, 17*(2), 87–90.

Kohl, J. V. (2007). The mind's eyes: Human pheromones, neuroscience, and male sexual preferences. *Journal of Psychology & Human Sexuality, 18*(4), 313–369.

Kohlberg, L. (1963). Moral development and identification. In H. W. Stevenson (Ed.), *Child psychology: 62nd yearbook of the National Society for the Study of Education.* Chicago: University of Chicago Press.

Kohlberg, L. (1966). Cognitive stages and preschool education. *Human Development, 9,* 5–17.

Kohlberg, L. (1969). Stage and sequence: The cognitive-developmental approach to socialization. In D. A. Goslin (Ed.), *Handbook of socialization theory and research.* Chicago: Rand McNally.

Kohlberg, L. (1981). *The meaning and measurement of moral development.* Worcester, MA: Clark University Press.

Kohlberg, L. (1985). *The psychology of moral development.* San Francisco: Harper & Row.

Kohlberg, L., & Kramer, R. (1969). Continuities and discontinuities in childhood and adult moral development. *Human Development, 12,* 93–120.

Kohyama, J., Shiiki, T., Ohinata-Sugimoto, J., & Hasegawa, T. (2002). Potentially harmful sleep habits of 3-year-old children in Japan. *Journal of Developmental and Behavioral Pediatrics, 23*(2), 67–70.

Kolata, G. (2007, May 8). Genes take charge, and diets fall by the wayside. *New York Times online.*

Kolb, B., & Gibb, R. (2007). Brain plasticity and recovery from early cortical injury. *Developmental Psychobiology, 49*(2), 107–118.

Konijn, E. A., Bijvank, M. N., & Bushman, B. J. (2007). I wish I were a warrior: The role of wishful identification in the effects of violent video games on aggression in adolescent boys. *Developmental Psychology, 43*(4), 1038–1044.

Konner, M. J. (1977). Infancy among the Kalahari San. In P. H. Leiderman, S. R. Tulkin, & A. Rosenfeld (Eds.), *Culture and infancy: Variations in the human experience.* New York: Academic Press.

Koopmans-van Beinum, F. J., Clement, C. J., & van den Dikkenberg-Pot, I. (2001). Babbling and the lack of auditory speech perception: A matter of coordination? *Developmental Science, 4*(1), 61–70.

Kopp, C. B. (1989). Regulation of distress and negative emotions: A developmental view. *Developmental Psychology, 25,* 343–354.

Koriat, A., Goldsmith, M., Schneider, W., & Nakash-Dura, M. (2001). The credibility of children's testimony: Can children control the accuracy of their memory reports? *Journal of Experimental Child Psychology, 79*(4), 405–437.

Korszun, A., et al. (2004). Familiality of symptom dimensions in depression. *Archives of General Psychiatry, 61*(5), 468–474.

Krackow, E., & Lynn, S. J. (2003). Is there touch in the game of Twister? The effects of innocuous touch and suggestive questions on children's eyewitness memory. *Law and Human Behavior, 27*(6), 589–604.

Krebs, D. L., & Denton, K. (2005). Toward a more pragmatic approach to morality: A critical evaluation of Kohlberg's model. *Psychological Review, 112*(3), 629–649.

Krebs, D. L., & Denton, K. (2006). Explanatory limitations of cognitive-developmental approaches to morality. *Psychological Review. 113*(3), 672–675.

Krippner, S., & McIntyre, T. (Eds.). (2003). *The psychological impact of war trauma on civilians: An international perspective.* Westport, CT: Praeger/Greenwood.

Kristensen, P., & Bjerkedal, T. (2007). Explaining the relation between birth order and intelligence. *Science, 313*(5832), 1717.

Kroeger, K. A., & Nelson, W. M., III. (2006). A language programme to increase the verbal production of a child dually diagnosed with Down syndrome and autism. *Journal of Intellectual Disability Research, 50*(2), 101–108.

Kroger, J. (2003). Identity development during adolescence. In G. R. Adams & M. D. Berzonsky (Ed.), *Blackwell handbook of adolescence* (pp. 205–226). Malden, MA: Blackwell.

Krojgaard, P. (2005). Continuity and discontinuity in developmental psychology. *Psyke & Logos, 26*(2), 377–394.

Krueger, C., Holditch-Davis, D., Quint, S., & DeCasper, A. (2004). Recurring auditory experience in the 28- to 34-week-old fetus. *Infant Behavior & Development, 27*(4), 537–543.

Kuczaj, S. A., II (1982). On the nature of syntactic development. In S. A. Kuczaj II (Ed.), *Language development,* Vol. 1, *Syntax and semantics.* Hillsdale, NJ: Erlbaum.

Kuczmarski, R. J., et al. (2000, December 4). *CDC growth charts: United States.* Advance Data from Vital and Health Statistics, No. 314. Hyattsville, MD: National Center for Health Statistics.

Kuhl, P. K., et al. (1997). Cross-language analysis of phonetic units in language addressed to infants. *Science, 277*(5326), 684–686.

Kuhl, P. K., et al. (2006). Infants show a facilitation effect for native language phonetic perception between 6 and 12 months. *Developmental Science, 9*(2) F13–F21.

Kuhn, D. (2007). Editorial. *Cognitive Development, 22*(1), 1–2.

Kulp, J. (2007, March 27). To the editor: Day care and a child's behavior. *New York Times online.*

Kundanis, R., & Massaro, D. W. (2004). Televisual media for children are more interactive. *American Journal of Psychology, 117*(4), 643–648.

Kwok, H. W. M. (2003). Psychopharmacology in autism spectrum disorders. *Current Opinion in Psychiatry, 16*(5), 529–534.

Labrell, F., & Ubersfeld, G. (2004). Parental verbal strategies and children's capacities at 3 and 5 years during a memory task. *European Journal of Psychology of Education, 19*(2), 189–202.

Lai, H-L., et al. (2006). Randomized controlled trial of music during kangaroo care on maternal state anxiety and preterm infants' responses. *International Journal of Nursing Studies, 43*(2), 139–146.

Lai, T. J., Guo, Y. I., Guo, N.-W., & Hsu, C. C. (2001). Effect of prenatal exposure to polychlorinated biphenyls on cognitive development in children: A longitudinal study in Taiwan. *British Journal of Psychiatry, 178*(Suppl. 40), S49–S52.

Laireiter, A-R., & Lager, C. (2006). Soziales Netzwerk, soziale Unterstützung und soziale Kompetenz bei Kindern. *Zeitschrift für Entwicklungspsychologie und Pädagogische Psychologie, 38*(2), 69–78.

Lalumière, M. L., Blanchard, R., & Zucker, K. J. (2000). Sexual orientation and handedness in men and women: A meta-analysis. *Psychological Bulletin, 126*(4), 575–592.

Lam, K. S. L., Aman, M. G., & Arnold, L. E. (2006). Neurochemical correlates of autistic disorder: A review of the literature. *Research in Developmental Disabilities, 27*(3), 254–289.

Lam, T. H., Shi, H. J., Ho, L. M., Stewart, S. M., & Fan, S. (2002). Timing of pubertal maturation and heterosexual behavior among Hong Kong Chinese adolescents. *Archives of Sexual Behavior, 31*(4), 359–366.

Lamaze, F. (1981). *Painless childbirth.* New York: Simon & Schuster.

Lamb, M. E., & Ahnert, L. (2006). Nonparental child care: Context, concepts, correlates, and consequences. In K. A. Renninger, I. E. Sigel, W. Damon, & R. M. Lerner (Eds.), *Handbook of child psychology* (6th ed.), Vol. 4, *Child psychology in practice* (pp. 950–1016). Hoboken, NJ: Wiley.

Lamb, M. E., Sternberg, K. J., & Prodromidis, M. (1992b). Nonmaternal care and the security of infant–mother attachment: A reanalysis of the data. *Infant Behavior and Development, 15,* 71–83.

Lamers, C. T. J., Bechara, A., Rizzo, M., & Ramaekers, J. G. (2006). Cognitive function and mood in MDMA/THC users, THC users and non-drug using controls. *Journal of Psychopharmacology, 20*(2), 302–311.

Lampel, J., & Honig, B. (2006). Let the children play: Muppets in the middle of the Middle East. In J. Lampel, J. Shamsie, & T. K. Lant (Eds.), *Strategic perspectives on entertainment and media.* Mahwah, NJ: Erlbaum.

Lampl, M., Veldhuis, J. D., & Johnson, M. L. (1992). Saltation and stasis: A model of human growth. *Science, 258,* 801–803.

Landy, F. J. (2006).The long, frustrating, and fruitless search for social intelligence: A cautionary tale. In K. R. Murphy (Ed.), *A critique of emotional intelligence: What are the problems and how can they be fixed?* (pp. 81–123). Mahwah, NJ: Erlbaum.

Langbehn, D. R., & Cadoret, R. J. (2001). The adult antisocial syndrome with and without antecedent conduct disorder: Comparisons from an adoption study. *Comprehensive Psychiatry, 42*(4), 272–282.

Lange, G., & Pierce, S. H. (1992). Memory-strategy learning and maintenance in preschool children. *Developmental Psychology, 28,* 453–462.

Langlois, J. H., et al. (2000). Maxims or myths of beauty? A meta-analytic and theoretical review. *Psychological Bulletin, 126*(3), 390–423.

Lansford, J. E., Malone, P. S., Castellino, D. R., Dodge, K. A., Pettit, G. S., & Bates, J. E. (2006). Trajectories of internalizing, externalizing, and grades for children who have and have not experienced their parents' divorce or separation. *Journal of Family Psychology. 20*(2), 292–301.

Lantolf, J. P., & Thorne, S. L. (2007). Sociocultural theory and second language learning. In B. VanPatten & J. Williams (Eds.), *Theories in second language acquisition: An introduction* (pp. 201–224). Mahwah, NJ: Erlbaum.

Lanza, S. T., & Collins, L. M. (2002). Pubertal timing and the onset of substance use in females during early adolescence. *Prevention Science, 3*(1), 69–82.

Laplan, R. T. (2004). *Career development across the K-16 years: Bridging the present to satisfying and successful futures.* Alexandria, VA: American Counseling Association.

LaPointe, L. L. (Ed.). (2005). Feral children. *Journal of Medical Speech-Language Pathology, 13*(1), vii–ix.

Lapsley, D. K. (2006). Moral stage theory. In K. Killen & J. G. Smetana (Eds.), *Handbook of moral development* (pp. 37–66). Mahwah, NJ: Erlbaum.

Largo, R. H., et al. (2001). Neuromotor development from 5 to 18 years. Part 1: Timed performance. *Developmental Medicine and Child Neurology, 43*(7), 436–443.

Larroque, B., et al. (2005). Temperament at 9 months of very preterm infants born at less than 29 weeks' gestation: The Epipage study. *Journal of Developmental & Behavioral Pediatrics, 26*(1), 48–55.

Larson, R., & Richards, M. H. (1991). Daily companionship in late childhood and early adolescence: Changing developmental contexts. *Child Development, 62,* 284–300.

Larsson, I., & Svedin, C. (2002). Experiences in childhood: Young adults' recollections. *Archives of Sexual Behavior, 31*(3), 263–273.

Latham, G. P., & Budworth, M.-H. (2007). The study of work motivation in the 20th century. In L. L. Koppes, (Ed.), *Historical perspectives in industrial and organizational psychology* (pp. 353–381). Mahwah, NJ: Erlbaum.

Latner, J. D., & Schwartz, M. B. (2005). Weight bias in a child's world. In K. D. Brownell et al. (Eds.), *Weight bias: Nature, consequences, and remedies* (pp. 54–67). New York: Guilford.

Lau, A. S., Litrownik, A. J., Newton, R. R., Black, M. M., & Everson, M. D. (2006). Factors affecting the link between physical discipline and child externalizing problems in Black and White families. *Journal of Community Psychology, 34*(1), 89–103.

Laumann, E. O., Gagnon, J. H., Michael, R. T., & Michaels, S. (1994). *The social organization of sexuality.* Chicago: University of Chicago Press.

Laurendeau, M., & Pinard, A. (1970). *The development of the concept of space in the child.* New York: International Universities Press.

Lawrence, J. M., et al. (2003). Design and evaluation of interventions promoting periconceptional multivitamin use. *American Journal of Preventive Medicine, 25*(1), 17–24.

Lawson, K., & Ruff, H. A. (2004). Early focused attention predicts outcome for children born prematurely. *Journal of Developmental & Behavioral Pediatrics, 25*(6), 399–406.

Leaper, C. (2002). Parenting girls and boys. In M. H. Bornstein (Ed.), *Handbook of parenting* (2nd ed.), Vol. 1, *Children and parenting* (pp. 189–225). Mahwah, NJ: Erlbaum.

Lecanuet, J-P., Granier-Deferre, C., & DeCasper, A. (2005). Are we expecting too much from prenatal sensory experiences? In B. Hopkins & S. P Johnson (Eds.), *Prenatal development of postnatal functions. Advances in infancy research* (pp. 31–49). Westport, CT: Praeger Publishers/Greenwood.

Lecanuet, J. P., Graniere-Deferre, C., Jacquet, A.-Y., & DeCasper, A. J. (2000). Fetal discrimination of low-pitched musical notes. *Developmental Psychobiology, 36*(1), 29–39.

Lederman, N. M. (2007, March 27). To the editor: Day care and a child's Behavior. *New York Times online.*

Lee, V. E., & Burkam, D. T. (2003). Dropping out of high school: The role of school organization and structure. *American Educational Research Journal, 40*(2), 353–393.

Leerkes, E. M., & Crockenberg, S. C. (2006). Antecedents of mothers' emotional and cognitive responses to infant distress: The role of family, mother, and infant characteristics. *Infant Mental Health Journal, 27*(4), 405–428.

Lefkowitz, E. S., & Zeldow, P. B. (2006). Masculinity and femininity predict optimal mental health: A belated test of the androgyny hypothesis. *Journal of Personality Assessment, 87*(1), 95–101.

Legro, R. S., et al. (2007). Clomiphene, metformin, or both for infertility in the polycystic ovary syndrome. *New England Journal of Medicine, 356*(6), 551–566.

Lejeune, C., et al. (2006). Prospective multicenter observational study of 260 infants born to 259 opiate-dependent mothers on methadone or high-dose buprenorphine substitution. *Drug and Alcohol Dependence, 82*(3), 250–257.

Lengua, L., J., Honorado, E., & Bush, N. R. (2007). Contextual risk and parenting as predictors of effortful control and social competence in preschool children. *Journal of Applied Developmental Psychology, 28*(1), 40–55.

Lenneberg, E. H. (1967). *Biological foundations of language.* New York: Wiley.

Lent, R. W., Singley, D., Sheu, H.-B., Schmidt, J. A., & Schmidt, L. C. (2007). Relation of social-cognitive factors to academic satisfaction in engineering students. *Journal of Career Assessment, 15*(1), 87–97.

Leon, M. R. (2000). Effects of caffeine on cognitive, psychomotor, and affective performance of children with attention-deficit/hyperactivity disorder. *Journal of Attention Disorders, 4*(1) 27–47.

Leon, V. (2001). *Uppity women of the New World.* Berkeley, CA: Conari Press.

Leonard, S. P., & Archer, J. (1989). A naturalistic investigation of gender constancy in three- to four-year-old children. *British Journal of Developmental Psychology, 7,* 341–346.

Leonardo, E. D., & Hen, R. (2006). Genetics of affective and anxiety disorders. *Annual Review of Psychology. 57,* 117–137.

Lepola, J., Vaurus, M., & Maeki, H. (2000). Gender differences in the development of academic self-concept of attainment from the 2nd to the 6th grade: Relations with achievement and perceived motivational orientation. *Psychology: The Journal of the Hellenic Psychological Society, 7*(3), 290–308.

Letourneau, E. J., Schoenwald, S. K., & Sheidow, A. J. (2004). Children and adolescents with sexual behavior problems. *Child Maltreatment: Journal of the American Professional Society on the Abuse of Children, 9*(1), 49–61.

Leung, C., McBride-Chang, C., & Lai, B. (2004). Relations among maternal parenting style, academic competence, and life satisfaction in Chinese early adolescents. *Journal of Early Adolescence, 24*(2), 113–143.

Leventhal, T., Graber, J. A., & Brooks-Gunn, J. (2001). Adolescent transitions to young adulthood: Antecedents, correlates, and consequences of adolescent employment. *Journal of Research on Adolescence, 11*(3), 297–323.

Lever, N., et al. (2004). A drop-out prevention program for high-risk inner-city youth. *Behavior Modification, 28*(4), 513–527.

Levinthal, B. R., & Lleras, A. (2007). The unique contributions of retinal size and perceived size on change detection. *Visual Cognition, 15*(1), 101–105.

Levitt, M. J., Weber, R. A., Clark, M. C., & McDonnell, P. (1985). Reciprocity of exchange in toddler sharing behavior. *Developmental Psychology, 21,* 122–123.

Levy, G. D., Sadovsky, A. L., & Troseth, G. L. (2000). Aspects of young children's perceptions of gender-typed occupations. *Sex Roles, 42*(11–12), 993–1006.

Lewinsohn, P. M., Rohde, P., Seeley, J. R., Klein, D. N., & Gotlib, I. H. (2000b). Natural course of adolescent major depressive disorder in a community sample: Predictors of recurrence in young adults. *American Journal of Psychiatry, 157,* 1584–1591.

Lewis, B. A., et al. (2004). Four-year language outcomes of children exposed to cocaine in utero. *Neurotoxicology and Teratology, 26*(5), 617–627.

Lewis, H. L. (2003). Differences in ego identity among college students across age, ethnicity, and gender. *Identity, 3*(2), 159–189.

Lewis, L. M. (2007). No-harm contracts: A review of what we know. *Suicide and Life-Threatening Behavior, 37*(1), 50–57.

Lewis, M., & Feiring, C. (1989). Early predictors of childhood friendship. In T. J. Berndt & G. W. Ladd (Eds.), *Peer relationships in child development.* New York: Wiley.

Li, J. (2004).Gender inequality, family planning, and maternal and child care in a rural Chinese county. *Social Science & Medicine, 59,* 659–708.

Li, Q. (2006). Cyberbullying in schools: A research of gender differences. *School Psychology International, 27*(2), 157–170.

Li, Q. (2007). New bottle but old wine: A research of cyberbullying in schools. *Computers in Human Behavior, 23*(4), 1777–1791.

Libal, J. (2007). *Antidepressants and suicide: When treatment kills.* Broomall, PA: Mason Crest Publishers.

Lickliter, R. (2001). The dynamics of language development: From perception to comprehension. *Developmental Science, 4*(1), 21–23.

Lim, M. M., et al. (2004). Enhanced partner preference in a promiscuous species by manipulating the expression of a single gene. *Nature, 429*(6993), 754–757.

Lim, M. M., & Young, L. J. (2006). Neuropeptidergic regulation of affiliative behavior and social bonding in animals. *Hormones and Behavior, 50*(4), 506–517.

Linares, M C. C., García, P., & Santiago, L. J. (2002). Parenting styles and adolescents' psychosocial competence. *Anuario de Psicología, 33*(1), 79–95.

Linebarger, D. L., & Walker, D. (2005). Infants' and toddlers' television viewing and language outcomes. *American Behavioral Scientist, 48*(5), 624–645.

Lins-Dyer, M. T., & Nucci, L. (2007). The impact of social class and social cognitive domain on northeastern Brazilian mothers' and daughters' conceptions of parental control. *International Journal of Behavioral Development, 31*(2), 105–114.

Lipman, E. L. et al. (2006). Testing effectiveness of a community-based aggression man-

agement program for children 7 to 11 years old and their families. *Journal of the American Academy of Child & Adolescent Psychiatry, 45*(9), 1085–1093.

Lipsitt, L. P. (2002). Early experience and behavior in the baby of the twenty-first century. In J. Gomes-Pedro et al. (Eds.), *The infant and family in the twenty-first century* (pp. 55–78). London: Brunner-Routledge.

Lipsitt, L. P. (2003). Crib death: A biobehavioral phenomenon? *Current Directions in Psychological Science, 12*(5), 164–170.

Liu, X., et al. (2000a). Behavioral and emotional problems in Chinese children of divorced parents. *Journal of the American Academy of Child and Adolescent Psychiatry, 39*(7), 896–903.

Liu, X., Sun, Z., Uchiyama, M., Li, Y., & Okawa, M. (2000b). Attaining nocturnal urinary control, nocturnal enuresis, and behavioral problems in Chinese children aged 6 through 16 years. *Journal of the American Academy of Child and Adolescent Psychiatry, 39*(12), 1557–1564.

Lo, J. C. (2003). Patients' attitudes vs. physicians' determination: Implications for cesarean sections. *Social Science and Medicine, 57*(1), 91–96.

Lochman, J. E., Wells, K. C., & Murray, M. (2007). The Coping Power Program: Preventive intervention at the middle school transition. In P. Tolan, J. Szapocznik, & S. Sambrano, (Eds.), *Preventing youth substance abuse: Science-based programs for children and adolescents* (pp. 185–210). Washington, DC: American Psychological Association.

Lock, J., Couturier, J., & Agras, W. S. (2006). Comparison of long-term outcomes in adolescents with anorexia nervosa treated with family therapy. *Journal of the American Academy of Child & Adolescent Psychiatry, 45*(6), 666–672.

Loovis, E. M., & Butterfield, S. A. (2000). Influence of age, sex, and balance on mature skipping by children in grades K–8. *Perceptual and Motor Skills, 90*(3), 974–978.

Lorenz, K. (1962). *King Solomon's ring.* London: Methuen.

Lorenz, K. (1981). *The foundations of ethology.* New York: Springer-Verlag.

Lovaas, O. I. (1977). *The autistic child: Language development through behavior modification.* New York: Halstead Press.

Lovaas, O. I., Smith, T., & McEachin, J. J. (1989). Clarifying comments on the young autism study: Reply to Schapler, Short, and Mesibov. *Journal of Consulting and Clinical Psychology, 57,* 165–167.

Love, J. M., Logue, M. E., Trudeau, J. V., & Thayer, K. (1992). *Transitions to kindergarten in American schools.* Portsmouth, NH: RMC Research Corp.

Lubinski, D. (2004). Introduction to the Special Section on Cognitive Abilities: 100 Years

After Spearman's (1904) "'General Intelligence,' Objectively Determined and Measured." *Journal of Personality and Social Psychology, 86*(1), 96–111.

Lubinski, D. (2006). Ability tests. In M. Eid & E. Diener (Eds.), *Handbook of multimethod measurement in psychology* (pp. 101–114). Washington, DC: American Psychological Association.

Lubinski, D., & Benbow, C. P. (2000). States of excellence. *American Psychologist, 55,* 137–150.

Lucariello, J. M., Hudson, J. A., Fivush, R., & Bauer, P. J. (Eds.). (2004). *The development of the mediated mind: Sociocultural context and cognitive development.* Mahwah, NJ: Erlbaum.

Luciano, M., Kirk, K. M., Heath, A. C., & Martin, N. G. (2005). The genetics of tea and coffee drinking and preference for source of caffeine in a large community sample of Australian twins. *Addiction, 100*(10), 1510–1517.

Lueng, W. L., & Poon, M. W. L. (2001). Dysfunctional schemas and cognitive distortions in psychopathology: A test of the specificity hypothesis. *Journal of Child Psychology and Psychiatry and Allied Disciplines, 42*(6), 755–765.

Lugo, J. N. Jr., Wilson, M. A., & Kelly, S. J. (2006). Perinatal ethanol exposure alters met-enkephalin levels of male and female rats. *Neurotoxicology and Teratology, 28*(2), 238–244.

Luster, T., & Dubow, E. (1992). Home environment and maternal intelligence as predictors of verbal intelligence: A comparison of preschool and school-age children. *Merrill–Palmer Quarterly, 38,* 151–173.

Lykken, D. T. (2006a). In C. J. Patrick (Ed.), *Psychopathic personality: The scope of the problem* (pp. 3–13). New York: Guilford.

Lykken, D. T. (2006b). The mechanism of emergenesis. *Genes, Brain & Behavior, 5*(4), 306–310.

Lykken, D. T., & Csikszentmihalyi, M. (2001). Happiness: Stuck with what you've got? *Psychologist, 14*(9), 470–472.

Lynam, D. R., Caspi, A., Moffitt, T. E., Loeber, R., & Stouthamer-Loeber, M. (2007). Longitudinal evidence that psychopathy scores in early adolescence predict adult psychopathy. *Journal of Abnormal Psychology, 116*(1), 155–165.

Lynne, S. D., Graber, J. A., Nichols, T. R., Brooks-Gunn, J., & Botvin, G. J. (2007). Links between pubertal timing, peer influences, and externalizing behaviors among urban students followed through middle school. *Journal of Adolescent Health, 40*(2), 181.e7–181.e13.

Lynskey, M. T., et al. (2007). Stimulant use and symptoms of abuse/dependence: Epidemiology and associations with cannabis use—A twin study. *Drug and Alcohol Dependence, 86*(2–3) 147–153.

Lyon, G. R., Shaywitz, S. E., & Shaywitz, B. A. (2003). A definition of dyslexia. *Annals of Dyslexia, 53,* 1–14.

Lytle, D. E. (Ed.). (2003). *Play and educational theory and practice.* Westport, CT: Praeger/Greenwood.

Maccoby, E. E. (1990a). Gender and relationships: A developmental account. *American Psychologist, 45,* 513–520.

Maccoby, E. E. (1990b). The role of gender identity and gender constancy in sex-differentiated development. In D. Schrader (Ed.), *New directions for child development, no. 47, The legacy of Lawrence Kohlberg.* San Francisco: Jossey-Bass.

Maccoby, E. E. (1991). Gender and relationships: A reprise. *American Psychologist, 46,* 538–539.

Maccoby, E. E. (2000). Perspectives on gender development. *International Journal of Behavioral Development, 24*(4), 398–406.

Maccoby, E. E. (2002). Parenting effects: Issues and controversies. In J. G. Borkowski et al. (Eds.), *Parenting and the child's world: Influences on academic, intellectual, and social-emotional development* (pp. 35–46). Mahwah, NJ: Erlbaum.

Maccoby, E. E., & Jacklin, C. N. (1974). *The psychology of sex differences.* Stanford, CA: Stanford University Press.

Macfarlane, A. (1975). Olfaction in the development of social preferences in the human neonate. In M. A. Hofer (Ed.), *Parent–infant interaction.* Amsterdam: Elsevier.

Macfarlane, A. (1977). *The psychology of childbirth.* Cambridge, MA: Harvard University Press.

Mackic-Magyar, J., & McCracken, J. (2004). Review of autism spectrum disorders: A research review for practitioners. *Journal of Child and Adolescent Psychopharmacology, 14*(1), 17–18.

Mackner, L. M., Black, M. M., & Starr, R. H., Jr. (2003). Cognitive development of children in poverty with failure to thrive: A prospective study through age 6. *Journal of Child Psychology and Psychiatry and Allied Disciplines, 44*(5), 743–751.

Maclean, A. M., Walker, L. J., & Matsuba, M. K. (2004). Transcendence and the moral self: Identity integration, religion, and moral life. *Journal for the Scientific Study of Religion, 43*(3), 429–437.

Macrory, G. (2006). Bilingual language development: What do early years practitioners need to know? *Early Years: An International Journal of Research and Development, 26*(2), 159–169.

Madon, S., et al. (2001). Am I as you see me or do you see me as I am? Self-fulfilling prophecies and self-verification. *Personality and Social Psychology Bulletin, 27*(9), 1214–1224.

Madson, L., & Trafimow, D. (2001). Gender comparisons in the private, collective, and allocentric selves. *Journal of Social Psychology, 141*(4), 551–559.

Maejima, K., & Oguchi, T. (2001). The effect of marital discord on children's self-esteem, emotionality, and aggression. *Japanese Journal of Family Psychology, 15*(1), 45–56.

Magnusson, C. (2001). Adolescent girls' sexual attitudes and opposite-sex relation in 1970 and in 1996. *Journal of Adolescent Health, 28*(3), 242–252.

Mahler, M. S., Pine, F., & Bergman, A. (1975). *The psychological birth of the human infant: Symbiosis and individuation.* New York: Basic Books.

Maimburg, R. D., & Væth, M. (2006). Perinatal risk factors and infantile autism. *Acta Psychiatrica Scandinavica, 114*(4), 257–264.

Malina, R. M., & Bouchard, C. (1991). *Growth, maturation, and physical activity.* Champaign, IL: Human Kinetics Academic.

Malinosky-Rummell, R., & Hansen, D. H. (1993). Long-term consequences of childhood physical abuse. *Psychological Bulletin, 114,* 68–79.

Malone, P. S., et al. (2004). Divorce and child behavior problems: Applying latent change score models to life event data. *Structural Equation Modeling, 11*(3), 401–423.

Maluccio, A. N., & Ainsworth, F. (2003). Drug use by parents: A challenge for family reunification practice. *Children and Youth Services Review, 25*(7), 511–533.

Mandler, J. M. (1990). Recall and its verbal expression. In R. Fivush & J. A. Hudson (Eds.), *Knowing and remembering in young children.* Cambridge: Cambridge University Press.

Maneschi, M. L., Maddalena, F., & Bersani, G. (2006). The role of genetic factors in developmental dyslexia. Convergence between schizophrenia and other psychiatric disorders. *Rivista di Psichiatria, 41*(2), 81–92.

Mangelsdorf, S. C. (1992). Developmental changes in infant–stranger interaction. *Infant Behavior and Development, 15,* 191–208.

Maratsos, M. P. (2007). Commentary. *Monographs of the Society for Research in Child Development, 72*(1), 121–126.

Marcia, J. E. (1991). Identity and self-development. In R. M. Lerner, A. C. Petersen, & J. Brooks-Gunn (Eds.), *Encyclopedia of adolescence.* New York: Garland.

Marcovitch, S., & Zelazo, P. D. (2006). The influence of number of A trials on 2-year-olds' behavior in two A-not-B-type search tasks: A test of the hierarchical competing systems model. *Journal of Cognition and Development, 7*(4), 477–501.

Marcovitch, S., Zelazo, P. D., & Schmuckler, M. A. (2002). The effect of the number of A trials on performance on the A-not-B task. *Infancy, 3*(4), 519–529.

Marean, G. C., Werner, L. A., & Kuhl, P. K. (1992). Vowel categorization by very young infants. *Developmental Psychology, 28,* 396–405.

Markova, G., & Legerstee, M. (2006). Contingency, imitation, and affect sharing: Foundations of infants' social awareness. *Developmental Psychology, 42*(1), 132–141.

Markovitz, H., & Vachon, R. (1990). Conditional reasoning, representation, and level of abstraction. *Developmental Psychology, 26,* 942–951.

Markus, H., & Kitayama, S. (1991). Culture and the self. *Psychological Review, 98*(2), 224–253.

Marlier, L., & Schaal, B. (2005). Human newborns prefer human milk: Conspecific milk odor is attractive without postnatal exposure. *Child Development, 76*(1), 155–168.

Marsiglio, W. (2004). When stepfathers claim stepchildren: A conceptual analysis. *Journal of Marriage and Family, 66*(1), 22–39.

Martin, C. L., & Ruble, D. (2004). Children's search for gender cues: Cognitive perspectives on gender development. *Current Directions in Psychological Science, 13*(2), 67–70.

Martin, C. L., Ruble, D. N., & Szkrybalo, J. (2002). Cognitive theories of early gender development. *Psychological Bulletin, 128*(6), 903–933.

Martínez, I., Musitu, G., Garcia, J. F., & Camino, L. (2003). A cross-cultural analysis of the effects of family socialization on self-concept: Spain and Brazil. *Psicologia Educaçáo Cultura, 7*(2), 239–259.

Masataka, N. (1998). Perception of motherese in Japanese sign language by 6-month-old hearing infants. *Developmental Psychology, 34*(2), 241–246.

Masi, G., et al. (2004). Generalized anxiety disorder in referred children and adolescents. *Journal of the American Academy of Child and Adolescent Psychiatry. 43*(6), 752–760.

Masi, G., Mucci, M., & Millepiedi, S. (2001). Separation anxiety disorder in children and adolescents: Epidemiology, diagnosis, and management. *CNS Drugs, 15*(2), 93–104.

Massaro, A. N., Rothbaum, R., & Aly, H. (2006). Fetal brain development: The role of maternal nutrition, exposures and behaviors. *Journal of Pediatric Neurology, 4*(1), 1–9.

Masten, A. S. (2001). Ordinary magic: Resilience processes in development. *American Psychologist, 56*(3), 227–238.

Maternity Center Association. (2004, April). *What every pregnant woman needs to know about cesarean section.* New York: MCA.

Mathews, T.J., & MacDorman, M.F. (2007). Infant mortality statistics from the 2004 period linked birth/infant death data set. *National Vital Statistics Reports, 55* (14). Hyattsville, MD: National Center for Health Statistics.

Matlin, M. W. (2008). *The psychology of women* (8th ed.). Belmont, CA: Thomson/Wadsworth.

Matthews, J. (1990). Drawing and individual development. In R. M. Thomas (Ed.), *The encyclopedia of human development and education: Theory, research, and studies.* Oxford: Pergamon.

Maundeni, T. (2000). The consequences of parental separation and divorce for the economic, social and emotional circumstances of children in Botswana. *Childhood: A Global Journal of Child Research, 7*(2), 213–223.

Maurer, D. M., Lewis, T, L., Brent, H. P., & Levin, A. V. (1999). Rapid improvement in the acuity of infants after visual input. *Science, 286*(5437), 108–110.

Maurer, D. M., & Maurer, C. E. (1976, October). Newborn babies see better than you think. *Psychology Today,* pp. 85–88.

Mayer, J. D., Salovey, P., & Caruso, D. R. (2004). Emotional intelligence: Theory, findings, and implications. *Psychological Inquiry, 15*(3), 197–215.

Maynard, A. E., Subrahmanyam, K., & Greenfield, P. M. (2005). Technology and the development of intelligence: From the loom to the computer. In R. J. Sternberg & D. D. Preiss (Eds.), *Intelligence and technology: The impact of tools on the nature and development of human abilities. The educational psychology series* (pp. 29–53). Mahwah, NJ: Erlbaum.

Mazei-Robison, M. S., Couch, R. S., Shelton, R. C., Stein, M. A., & Blakely, R. D. (2005). Sequence variation in the human dopamine transporter gene in children with attention deficit hyperactivity disorder. *Neuropharmacology, 49*(6), 724–736.

McCall, R. (1997). Cited in S. Sleek, Can "emo-tional intelligence" be taught in today's schools? *APA Monitor, 28*(6), 25.

McCall, R. B., Applebaum, M. I., & Hogarty, P. S. (1973). *Developmental changes in mental performance.* Monographs of the Society for Research in Child Development, 38(3, ser. 150).

McCartney, K., Harris, M. J., & Bernjeri, F. (1990). Growing up and growing apart: A developmental meta-analysis of twin studies. *Psychological Bulletin, 107,* 226–237.

McCartney, K., Owen, M. T., Booth, C. L., Clarke-Stewart, K. A., & Vandell, D. L. (2004). Testing a maternal attachment model of behavior problems in early childhood. *Journal of Child Psychology and Psychiatry, 45*(4), 765–778.

McClellan, J. M., & Werry, J. S. (2003). Evidence-based treatments in child and adolescent psychiatry: An inventory. *Journal of the American Academy of Child and Adolescent Psychiatry, 42*(12), 1388–1400.

McCoy, R. C., et al. (2004). Frequency of bed sharing and its relationship to breastfeeding. *Journal of Developmental & Behavioral Pediatrics, 25*(3), 141–149.

McCrae, R. R., et al. (2000). Nature over nurture: Temperament, personality, and life span development. *Journal of Personality and Social Psychology, 78*(1), 173–186.

McCrink, K., & Wynn, K. (2004). Large-number addition and subtraction by 9-month-old infants. *Psychological Science, 15*(11), 776–781.

McCune, L. (1993). The development of play as the development of consciousness. In M. H. Bornstein & A. W. O'Reilly (Eds.), *New directions for child development,* No. 59, *The role of play in the development of thought.* San Francisco: Jossey-Bass.

McDevitt, T. M., & Ormrod, J. E. (2002). *Child development and education.* Upper Saddle River, NJ: Prentice Hall.

McDonough, L. (2002). Basic-level nouns: First learned but misunderstood. *Journal of Child Language, 29*(2), 357–377.

McEachin, J. J., Smith, T., & Lovaas, O. I. (1993). Long-term outcome for children with autism who received early intensive behavioral treatment. *Journal of Mental Retardation, 97,* 359–372.

McEwan, M. H., Dihoff, R. E., & Brosvic, G. M. (1991). Early infant crawling experience is reflected in later motor skill development. *Perceptual and Motor Skills, 72,* 75–79.

McGlaughlin, A., & Grayson, A. (2001). Crying in the first year of infancy: Patterns and prevalence. *Journal of Reproductive and Infant Psychology, 19*(1), 47–59.

McGrath, M., et al. (2005). Early precursors of low attention and hyperactivity in a preterm sample at age four. *Issues in Comprehensive Pediatric Nursing, 28*(1), 1–15.

McGuinness, D. (1990). Behavioral tempo in preschool boys and girls. *Learning and Individual Differences, 2,* 315–325.

McHale, S. M., Kim, J.-Y., & Whiteman, S. D. (2006). Sibling relationships in childhood and adolescence. In P. Noller & J. A. Feeney (Eds.), *Close relationships: Functions, forms and processes* (pp. 127–149). New York: Psychology Press/Taylor & Francis.

McIlvane, W. J., & Dube, W. V. (2003). Stimulus control topography coherence theory: Foundations and extensions. *Behavior Analyst, 26*(2), 195–213.

McLafferty, C. L. Jr. (2006). Examining unproven assumptions of Galton's nature–nurture paradigm. *American Psychologist, 61*(2), 177–178.

McMahon, T. J., & Spector, A. Z. (2007). Fathering and the mental health of men. In J. E. Grant & M. N. Potenza (Eds.), *Textbook of men's mental health* (pp. 259–282). Washington, DC: American Psychiatric Publishing.

McManus, C. (2003). Right hand, left hand: The origins of asymmetry in brains, bodies, atoms and cultures. *Cortex, 39*(2), 348–350.

McManus, I. C., et al. (1988). The development of handedness in children. *British Journal of Developmental Psychology, 6,* 257–273.

Meaney, K. S., Dornier, L. A., & Owens, M. S. (2002). Sex-role stereotyping for selected sport and physical activities across age groups. *Perceptual and Motor Skills, 94*(3), 743–749.

Meier, B. P., Robinson, M. D., & Wilkowski, B. M. (2006). Turning the other cheek: Agreeableness and the regulation of aggression-related primes. *Psychological Science, 17*(2), 136–142.

Meijer, J., & Elshout, J. J. (2001). The predictive and discriminant validity of the zone of proximal development. *British Journal of Educational Psychology, 71*(1), 93–113.

Meldrum, M, L. (2003). A capsule history of pain management. *Journal of the American Medical Association, 290,* 2470–2475.

Mellon, M. W. (2006). Enuresis and encopresis. In G. G.Bea, & K. M. Minke (Eds.), *Children's needs III: Development, prevention, and intervention* (pp. 1041–1053). Washington, DC: National Association of School Psychologists.

Mellon, M. W., & Houts, A. C. (2006). Nocturnal enuresis. In J. E. Fisher & W. T. O'Donohue (Eds.), *Practitioner's guide to evidence-based psychotherapy* (pp. 432–441). New York: Springer Science + Business Media.

Meltzoff, A. N., & Prinz, W. (Eds.). (2002). *The imitative mind: Development, evolution, and brain bases.* New York: Cambridge University Press.

Mendez, L. M. R. (2000). Gender roles and achievement-related choices: A comparison of early adolescent girls in gifted and general education programs. *Journal for the Education of the Gifted, 24*(2), 149–169.

Mendle, J., et al. (2006). Family structure and age at menarche: A children-of-twins approach. *Developmental Psychology, 42*(3), 533–542.

Mennella, J. A. (2001). Regulation of milk intake after exposure to alcohol in mothers' milk. *Alcoholism: Clinical and Experimental Research, 25*(4), 590–593.

Mennella, J. A., & Beauchamp, G. K. (2002). Flavor experiences during formula feeding are related to preferences during childhood. *Early Human Development, 68*(2), 71–82.

Mennella, J. A., Kennedy, J. M., & Beauchamp, G. K. (2006). Vegetable acceptance by infants: Effect of formula flavors. *Early Human Development, 82*(7), 463–468.

Merrill, L. L., Crouch, J. L., Thomsen, C. J., & Guimond, J. M. (2004). Risk for intimate partner violence and child physical abuse: Psychosocial characteristics of multi-risk male and female Navy recruits. *Child Maltreatment: Journal of the American Professional Society on the Abuse of Children, 9*(1), 18–29.

Mesich, H. M. (2005). Mother–infant co-sleeping: Understanding the debate and maximizing infant safety. *MCN: The American Journal of Maternal/Child Nursing, 30*(1), 30–37.

Mesman, J., Bongers, I. L., & Koot, H. M. (2001). Preschool developmental pathways to preadolescent internalizing and externalizing problems. *Journal of Child Psychology and Psychiatry and Allied Disciplines, 42*(5), 679–689.

Metcalfe, J. S., et al. (2005). Development of somatosensory-motor integration: An event-related analysis of infant posture in the first year of independent walking. *Developmental Psychobiology, 46*(1), 19–35.

Metzger, K. L., et al. (2007). Effects of nicotine vary across two auditory evoked potentials in the mouse. *Biological Psychiatry, 61*(1), 23–30.

Meyer, S. L., Murphy, C. M., Cascardi, M., & Birns, B. (1991). Gender and relationships: Beyond the peer group. *American Psychologist, 46,* 537.

Meyer, S., & Shore, C. (2001). Children's understanding of dreams as mental states. *Dreaming, 11*(4), 179–194.

Mezzacappa, E. S., Kelsey, R. M., & Katkin, E. S. (2005). Breast feeding, bottle feeding, and maternal autonomic responses to stress. *Journal of Psychosomatic Research, 58*(4), 351–365.

Michael, E. D. (1990). Physical development and fitness. In R. M. Thomas (Ed.), *The encyclopedia of human development and education: Theory, research, and studies.* Oxford: Pergamon.

Miklos, E. A., Brahler, C. J., Baer, J. T., & Dolan, P. (2004). Dietary deficiencies and excesses: A sample of African American mothers and daughters eligible for nutrition assistance programs. *Family and Community Health, 27*(2), 123–129.

Mikulincer, M., & Shaver, P. R. (2001). Attachment theory and intergroup bias: Evidence that priming the secure base schema attenuates negative reactions to out-groups. *Journal of Personality and Social Psychology, 81*(1), 97–115.

Milgram, R. M., & Livne, N. L. (2006). Research on creativity in Israel: A chronicle of theoretical and empirical development. In J. C. Kaufman & R. J. Sternberg (Eds.), *The international handbook of creativity* (pp. 307–336). New York: Cambridge University Press.

Millar, W. S. (1990). Span of integration for delayed-reward contingency learning in 6- to 8-month-old infants. In A. Diamond (Ed.), *The development and neural bases of higher cognitive functions.* New York: New York Academy of Sciences.

Miller, A. L., Rathus, J. H., & Linehan, M. M. (2007). *Dialectical behavior therapy with suicidal adolescents.* New York: Guilford.

Miller, A. L., Wyman, S. E., Huppert, J. D., Glassman, S. L., & Rathus, J. H. (2000). Analysis of behavioral skills utilized by suicidal adolescents receiving dialectical behavior therapy. *Cognitive and Behavioral Practice, 7*(2), 183–187.

Miller, C. F., Trautner, H. M., & Ruble, D. N. (2006). The role of gender stereotypes in children's preferences and behavior. In L. Balter & C. S. Tamis-LeMonda (Eds.), *Child psychology: A handbook of contemporary issues* (2nd ed.) (pp. 293–323). New York: Psychology Press.

Miller, G. A. (1956). The magical number seven, plus or minus two: Some limits on our capacity to process information. *Psychological Review, 63,* 81–97.

Miller, J. G. (1994). Cultural diversity in the morality of caring: Individually-oriented versus duty-based interpersonal moral codes. *Cross-Cultural Research, 28,* 3–39.

Miller, J. G., & Bersoff, D. M. (1992). Culture and moral judgment: How are conflicts between justice and interpersonal responsibilities resolved? *Journal of Personality and Social Psychology, 62,* 541–554.

Miller, R. (2005). Overcoming violence against women and girls: The international campaign to eradicate a worldwide problem. *Culture, Health & Sexuality, 7*(5), 519–521.

Miller, S. M., Boyer, B. A., & Rodoletz, M. (1990b). Anxiety in children: Nature and development. In M. Lewis & S. M. Miller (Eds.), *Handbook of developmental psychopathology.* New York: Plenum.

Miranda, A., & Presentacion, M. J. (2000). Efectos de un tratamiento cognitivo-conductual en ninos con trastorno por deficit de atencion con hiperactividad, agresivos y no agresivos: Cambio clinicamente significativo. *Infancia y Aprendizaje, 92,* 51–70.

Miscarriage. (2007, January 11). Available at http://www.nlm.nih.gov/medlineplus/ency/article/001488.htm. Accessed February 23, 2007.

Mischo, C. (2004). Fördert Gruppendiskussion die Perspektiven-Koordination? *Zeitschrift für Entwicklungspsychologie und Pädagogische Psychologie, 36*(1), 30–37.

Mischo, C. (2005). Promoting perspective coordination by dilemma discussion. The effectiveness of classroom group discussion on interpersonal negotiation strategies of 12-year-old students. *Social Psychology of Education, 8*(1), 41–63.

Mitchell, A. L. (2006). Medical consequences of cocaine. *Journal of Addictions Nursing, 17*(4), 249.

Moens, E., Braet, C., & Soetens, B. (2007). Observation of family functioning at mealtime: A comparison between families of children with and without overweight. *Journal of Pediatric Psychology, 32*(1), 52–63.

Molenda-Figueira, H. A., et al. (2006). Nuclear receptor coactivators function in estrogen receptor- and progestin receptor-dependent aspects of sexual behavior in female rats. *Hormones and Behavior, 50*(3), 383–392.

Molfese, V. J., DiLalla, L. F., & Bunce, D. (1997). Prediction of the intelligence test scores of 3- to 8-year-old children by home environment, socioeconomic status, and biomedical risks. *Merrill–Palmer Quarterly, 43*(2), 219–234.

Molinari, L., & Corsaro, W. A. (2000). Le relazioni amicali nella scuola dell'infanzia e nella scuola elementare: Uno studio longitudinale. *Eta Evolutiva, 67,* 40–51.

Moller, L. C., Hymel, S., & Rubin, K. H. (1992). Sex typing in play and popularity in middle childhood. *Sex Roles, 26,* 331–353.

Montemayor, R., & Eisen, M. (1977). The development of self-conceptions from childhood to adolescence. *Developmental Psychology, 13,* 314–319.

Moore, D. S. (2007). A very little bit of knowledge: Re-evaluating the meaning of the heritability of IQ. *Human Development, 49*(6), 347–353.

Moore, L. L., et al. (1991). Influence of parents' physical activity levels on activity levels of young children. *Journal of Pediatrics, 118,* 215–219.

Morelli, G. A., Oppenheim, D., Rogoff, B., & Goldsmith, D. (1992). Cultural variation in infants' sleeping arrangements: Questions of independence. *Developmental Psychology, 28,* 604–613.

Moreno, M., Trigo, J. M., Escuredo, L., Rodriguez de Fonseca, F., & Navarro, M. (2003). Perinatal exposure to Delta-sup-9 tetrahydrocannabinol increases presynaptic dopamine D-sub-2 receptor sensitivity: A behavioral study in rats. *Pharmacology, Biochemistry and Behavior, 75*(3), 565–575.

Morley, J. E., & Perry, H. M., III (2003). Androgens and women at the menopause and beyond. *Journals of Gerontology, Series A: Biological Sciences and Medical Sciences, 58A*(5), 409–416.

Morrell, J., & Steele, H. (2003). The role of attachment security, temperament, maternal perception, and care-giving behavior in persistent infant sleeping problems. *Infant Mental Health Journal, 24*(5), 447–468.

Morrison, D. R., & Coiro, M. J. (1999). Parental conflict and marital disruption: Do children benefit when high-conflict marriages are dissolved? *Journal of Marriage and the Family, 61*(3), 626–637.

Morton, S. M. B. (2006). Maternal nutrition and fetal growth and development. In

P. Gluckman & M. Hanson (Eds.), *Developmental origins of health and disease.* (pp. 98–129). New York: Cambridge University Press.

Moses, L. J., & Flavell, J. H. (1990). Inferring false beliefs from actions and reactions. *Child Development, 61,* 929–945.

Mosher, W. D., Chandra, A., & Jones, J. (2005). *Sexual behavior and selected health measures: men and women 1–B 44 years of age, United States, 2002. Advance data from vital and health statistics.* Centers for Disease Control and Prevention. National Center for Health Statistics, Number 362, Figures 2 and 3.

Mosholder, A. D. (2004). Cited in G. Harris (2004, September 24), *Warning called likely on drug risk for suicide.* Available at http://www.nytimes.com.

Mueller, R., Pierce, K., Ambrose, J. B., Allen, G., & Courchesne, E. (2001). Atypical patterns of cerebral motor activation in autism: A functional magnetic resonance study. *Biological Psychiatry, 49*(8) 665–676.

Mueller, U., Overton, W. F., & Reene, K. (2001). Development of conditional reasoning: A longitudinal study. *Journal of Cognition and Development, 2*(1), 27–49.

Mueller, U., Sokol, B., & Overton, W. F. (1999). Developmental sequences in class reasoning and propositional reasoning. *Journal of Experimental Child Psychology, 74*(2), 69–106.

Muir, D. W., & Hains, S. M. J. (1993). Infant sensitivity to perturbations in adult facial, vocal, tactile, and contingent stimulation during face-to-face interactions. In B. de Boysson-Bardies, S. de Schonen, P. W. Jusczyk, P. F. MacNeilage, & J. Morton (Eds.), *Changes in speech and face processing in infancy: A glimpse at developmental mechanisms of cognition.* Dordrecht, Netherlands: Kluwer Academic.

Muir, G. D. (2000). Early ontogeny of locomotor behaviour: A comparison between altricial and precocial animals. *Brain Research Bulletin, 53*(5), 719–726.

Mumford, M. D. (2003). Where have we been, where have we going? Taking stock in creativity research. *Creativity Research Journal, 15*(2–3), 107–120.

Munroe, R. H., Shimmin, H. S., & Munroe, R. L. (1984). Gender role understanding and sex role preference in four cultures. *Developmental Psychology, 20,* 673–682.

Murata, A., & Fuson, K. (2006). Teaching as assisting individual constructive paths within an interdependent class learning zone: Japanese first graders learning to add using 10. *Journal for Research in Mathematics Education, 37*(5), 421–456.

Muris, P., Bodden, D., Merckelbach, H., Ollendick, T. H., & King, N. (2003). Fear of the beast: A prospective study on the effects of negative information on childhood fear. *Behaviour Research and Therapy, 41*(2), 195–208.

Murphy, T. K., Bengtson, M. A., Tan, J. Y., Carbonell, E., & Levin, G. M. (2000). Selective serotonin reuptake inhibitors in the treatment of paediatric anxiety disorders: A review. *International Clinical Psychopharmacology, 15*(Suppl. 2), S47–S63.

Murray, B. (1998). Survey reveals concerns of today's girls. *APA Monitor, 29*(10).

Murray, B. A. (2006). Hunting the elusive phoneme: A phoneme-direct model for learning phoneme awareness. In K. A. Dougherty Stahl & M. C. McKenna (Eds.), *Reading research at work: Foundations of effective practice* (pp. 114–125). New York: Guilford.

Muzzatti, B., & Agnoli, F. (2007). Gender and mathematics: Attitudes and stereotype threat susceptibility in Italian children. *Developmental Psychology, 43*(3), 747–759.

Nadeau, L., et al. (2003). Extremely premature and very low birthweight infants: A double hazard population? *Social Development, 12*(2), 235–248.

Nagin, D. S., & Tremblay, R. E. (2001). Parental and early childhood predictors of persistent physical aggression in boys from kindergarten to high school. *Archives of General Psychiatry, 58*(4), 389–394.

Nakkula, M. J., & Nikitopoulos, C. E. (2001). Negotiation training and interpersonal development: An exploratory study of early adolescents in Argentina. *Adolescence, 36*(141), 1–20.

National Campaign to Prevent Teen Pregnancy. (2003, September 30). *Teens say parents most influence their sexual decisions: New polling data and "Tips for Parents" released.* Available at http://www.teenpregnancy.org/about/announcements/pr/2003/release9_30 _03.asp.

National Center for Children in Poverty. (2004). Low-income children in the United States (2004). Available at http://cpmcnet.columbia.edu/dept/nccp/.

National Center for Education Statistics. (2007, June). Dropout rates in the United States: 2005. Available at http://nces.ed.gov/pubs2007/dropout05/. Accessed July 20, 2007.

National Center for Injury Prevention and Control, Office of Statistics and Programming, Centers for Disease Control and Prevention. (2007a, March 29). National Center for Health Statistics (NCHS), National Vital Statistics System. Accessed May 7, 2007. Available at http://webappa.cdc.gov/cgi-bin/broker.exe.

National Center for Injury Prevention and Control. (2007b, July 11). Suicide: Fact sheet. Available at http://www.cdc.gov/ncipc/factsheets/suifacts.htm.

National Guideline Clearinghouse. (2007). Use of clomiphene citrate in women. Available at http://www.guideline.gov/summary/summary.aspx?ss=15&doc_id=4843&nbr=3484. Last updated January 29, 2007. Accessed February 6, 2007.

National Institutes of Health. (2002). Available at http://cerhr.niehs.nih.gov/genpub/topics/vitamin_a-ccae.html.

National Sleep Foundation. (2007). Children's sleep habits. Available at http://www.sleepfoundation.org/site/c.huIXKjM0IxF/b.2453615/apps/nl/content3.asp?content_id={5239AA1B-DB37-42DA-B1ED-436FA086D3AC}&notoc=1.

Natsopoulos, D., Kiosseoglou, G., & Xeromeritou, A. (1992). Handedness and spatial ability in children: Further support for Geschwind's hypothesis of "pathology of superiority" and for Annett's theory of intelligence. *Genetic, Social, and General Psychology Monographs, 118*(1) 103–126.

Nauta, M. M. (2007). Career interests, self-efficacy, and personality as antecedents of career exploration. *Journal of Career Assessment, 15*(2), 162–180.

Navarro, R. L., Flores, L. Y., & Worthington, R. L. (2007). Mexican American middle school students' goal intentions in mathematics and science: A test of social cognitive career theory. *Journal of Counseling Psychology, 54*(3), 320–335.

Nazzi, T., & Gopnik, A. (2000). A shift in children's use of perceptual and causal cues to categorization. *Developmental Science, 3*(4), 389–396.

Nduati, R., et al. (2000). Effect of breastfeeding and formula feeding on transmission of HIV-1. *Journal of the American Medical Association, 283,* 1167–1174.

Needlman, R. (2001). *Understanding encopresis (fecal soiling).* America Online, AOL Parenting. Available at http://www.aol.com.

Neiss, M. B., Sedikides, C., & Stevenson, J. (2006). Genetic influences on level and stability of self-esteem. *Self and Identity, 5*(3), 247–266.

Neisser, U. (1997). Interview comments in S. Sleek (1997), Can "emotional intelligence" be taught in today's schools? *APA Monitor, 28*(6), 25.

Neisser, U., et al. (1996). Intelligence: Knowns and unknowns. *American Psychologist, 51,* 77–101.

Nelson, C. A., de Haan, M., & Thomas, K. M. (2006). Neuroscience of cognitive development: The role of experience and the developing brain. Hoboken, NJ: Wiley.

Nelson, C. A., & Luciana, M. (Eds.). (2001). *Handbook of developmental cognitive neuroscience.* Cambridge, MA: MIT Press.

Nelson, C. A., & Ludemann, P. M. (1989). Past, current, and future trends in infant face perception research. *Canadian Journal of Psychology, 43,* 183–198.

Nelson, K. (1973). *Structure and strategy in learning to talk.* Monographs for the Society for Research in Child Development, 38(1–2, ser. 149).

Nelson, K. (1981). Individual differences in language development: Implications for development of language. *Developmental Psychology, 17,* 170–187.

Nelson, K. (1990). Remembering, forgetting, and childhood amnesia. In R. Fivush & J. A. Hudson (Eds.), *Knowing and remembering in young children.* Cambridge: Cambridge University Press.

Nelson, K. (1993). Events, narratives, memory: What develops? In C. A. Nelson (Ed.), *Minnesota symposia on child psychology,* Vol. 26, *Memory and affect in development.* Hillsdale, NJ: Erlbaum.

Nelson, K. (2005). Cognitive functions of language in early childhood. In B. D. Homer & C. S. Tamis-LeMonda (Eds.), *The development of social cognition and communication* (pp. 7–28). Mahwah, NJ: Erlbaum.

Nelson, K. (2006). Advances in pragmatic developmental theory: The case of language acquisition. *Human Development, 49*(3), 184–188.

Nelson, K., & Fivush, R. (2004). The emergence of autobiographical memory: A social cultural developmental theory. *Psychological Review, 111*(2), 486–511.

Nerum, H., Halvorsen, L., Sorlie, T., & Oian, P. (2006). Maternal request for cesarean section due to fear of birth: Can it be changed through crisis-oriented counseling? *Birth: Issues in Perinatal Care, 33*(3), 221–228.

Nesdale, D., & Lambert, A. (2007). Effects of experimentally manipulated peer rejection on children's negative affect, self-esteem, and maladaptive social behavior. *International Journal of Behavioral Development, 31*(2), 115–122.

Newburn-Cook, C. V., et al. (2002). Where and to what extent is prevention of low birth weight possible? *Western Journal of Nursing Research, 24*(8), 887–904.

Newman, R., Ratner, N. B., Jusczyk, A. M., Jusczyk, P. W., & Dow, K. A. (2006). Infants' early ability to segment the conversational speech signal predicts later language development: A retrospective analysis. *Developmental Psychology, 42*(4), 643–655.

Newport, D. J., Heim, C., Bonsall, R., Miller, A. H., & Nemeroff, C. B. (2004). Pituitary–adrenal responses to standard and low-dose dexamethasone suppression tests in adult survivors of child abuse. *Biological Psychiatry, 55*(1), 10–20.

Newport, E. L. (1992, June). *Critical periods and creolization: Effects of maturational state and input on the acquisition of language.* Paper presented at the meeting of American Psychological Society, San Diego, CA.

Nielsen, S., & Palmer, B. (2003). Diagnosing eating disorders: AN, BN, and the others. *Acta Psychiatrica Scandinavica, 108*(3), 161–162.

Nielsen, S. J., & Popkin, B. M. (2003). Patterns and trends in food portion sizes, 1977–1998. *Journal of the American Medical Association, 289*(4), 450–453.

Niemeier, H. M., Raynor, H. A., Lloyd-Richardson, E. E., Rogers, M. L., & Wing, R. R. (2006). Fast food consumption and breakfast skipping: Predictors of weight gain from adolescence to adulthood in a nationally representative sample. *Journal of Adolescent Health, 39*(6), 842–849.

Nigg, J. T. (2001). Is ADHD a disinhibitory disorder? *Psychological Bulletin, 127*(5), 571–598.

Nigg, J. T., Goldsmith, H. H., & Sachek, J. (2004). Temperament and attention deficit hyperactivity disorder: The development of a multiple pathway model. *Journal of Clinical Child and Adolescent Psychology, 33*(1), 42–53.

Nigg, J. T., Hinshaw, S. P., & Huang-Pollock, C. (2006). Disorders of attention and impulse regulation. In D. Cicchetti & D. J. Cohen (Eds.), *Developmental psychopathology,* Vol. 3, *Risk, disorder, and adaptation* (2nd ed.) (pp. 358–403). Hoboken, NJ: Wiley.

Nisbett, R. E. (2005). Heredity, environment, and race differences in IQ: A commentary on Rushton and Jensen (2005). *Psychology, Public Policy, and Law, 11*(2), 302–310.

Nock, M. K., Kazdin, A. E., Hiripi, E., & Kessler, R. C. (2006). Prevalence, subtypes, and correlates of DSM-IV conduct disorder in the National Comorbidity Survey Replication. *Psychological Medicine, 36,* 699–710.

Nolen-Hoeksema, S., Stice, E., Wade, E., & Bohon, C. (2007). Reciprocal relations between rumination and bulimic, substance abuse, and depressive symptoms in female adolescents. *Journal of Abnormal Psychology, 116*(1), 198–207.

Noll, J. G., Trickett, P. K., & Putnam, F. W. (2000). Social network constellation and sexuality of sexually abused and comparison girls in childhood and adolescence. *Child Maltreatment: Journal of the American Professional Society on the Abuse of Children, 5*(4), 323–337.

Nomaguchi, K. M. (2006). Maternal employment, nonparental care, mother–child interactions, and child outcomes during preschool years. *Journal of Marriage and Family, 68*(5), 1341–1369.

Nonaka, A. M. (2004). The forgotten endangered languages: Lessons on the importance of remembering from Thailand's Ban Khor Sign Language. *Language in Society, 33*(5), 737–767.

Nonnemaker, J. M., & Homsi, G. (2007). Measurement properties of the Fagerström Test for nicotine dependence adapted for use in an adolescent sample. *Addictive Behaviors, 32*(1), 181–186.

Norlander, T., Erixon, A., & Archer, T. (2000). Psychological androgyny and creativity: Dynamics of gender-role and personality trait. *Social Behavior and Personality, 28*(5), 423–435.

Nowinski, J. (2007). *The identity trap: Saving our teens from themselves.* New York: AMACOM.

NPR/Kaiser/Harvard. (2004). Sex Education in America. General Public/Parents Survey. A National Public Radio/Kaiser Family Foundation/Harvard University John F. Kennedy School of Government Poll. Available at http://www.npr.org/templates/story/story.php?storyId=1622610.

Nucci, L. P. (2002). The development of moral reasoning. In U. Goswami (Ed.), *Blackwell handbook of childhood cognitive development* (pp. 303–325). Malden, MA: Blackwell.

Nyunt, A., et al. (2005). Androgen status in healthy premenopausal women with loss of libido. *Journal of Sex & Marital Therapy, 31*(1), 73–80.

O'Boyle, M. W., & Benbow, C. P. (1990). Handedness and its relationship to ability and talent. In S. Coren (Ed.), *Left-handedness: Behavior implications and anomalies.* Amsterdam: North-Holland.

O'Dea, J. A. (2006). Self-concept, self-esteem and body weight in adolescent females: A three-year longitudinal study. *Journal of Health Psychology, 11*(4), 599–611.

O'Donnell, L., et al. (2003). Long-term influence of sexual norms and attitudes on timing of sexual initiation among urban minority youth. *Journal of School Health, 23*(2), 68–75.

O'Keeffe, M. J., O'Callaghan, M., Williams, G. M., Najman, J. M., & Bor, W. (2003). Learning, cognitive, and attentional problems in adolescents born small for gestational age. *Pediatrics, 112*(2), 301–307.

O'Neill, D. K., & Chong, S. C. F. (2001). Preschool children's difficulty understanding the types of information obtained through the five senses. *Child Development, 72*(3), 803–815.

O'Neill, D. K., & Gopnik, A. (1991). Young children's ability to identify the sources of their beliefs. *Developmental Psychology, 27*, 390–397.

O'Shea, R. P., & Corballis, P. M. (2005). Binocular rivalry in the divided brain. In D. Alais & R. Blake (Eds.), *Binocular rivalry.* (pp. 301–315). Cambridge, MA: MIT Press.

O'Sullivan, L. F., Meyer-Bahlburg, H. F. L., & Watkins, B. X. (2000). Social cognitions associated with pubertal development in a sample of urban, low-income, African-American and Latina girls and mothers. *Journal of Adolescent Health, 27*(4), 227–235.

Oates, J., & Messer, D. (2007). Growing up with TV. *The Psychologist, 20*(1), 30–32.

Oettinger, G. (1999). Does high school employment affect high school academic performance? *Industrial and Labor Relations Review, 53*(1), 136–151.

Office of National Statistics. (2006). Available at http://www.multiplebirths.org.uk/media.asp. Accessed February 6, 2007.

Ogunfowora, O. B., Olanrewaju, D. M., & Akenzua, G. I. (2005). A comparative study of academic achievement of children with sickle cell anemia and their healthy siblings. *Journal of the National Medical Association, 97*(3), 405–408.

Ohalete, N. (2007). Adolescent sexual debut: A case for studying African American father–adolescent reproductive health communication. *Journal of Black Studies, 37*(5), 737–752.

Ohnishi, T., Matsuda, H., Hirakata, M., & Ugawa, Y. (2006). Navigation ability dependent neural activation in the human brain: An fMRI study. *Neuroscience Research, 55*(4), 361–369.

Okazaki, S., & Sue, S. (2000). Implications of test revisions for assessment with Asian Americans. *Psychological Assessment, 12*(3), 272–280.

Ollendick, T. H., Hagopian, L. P., & Huntzinger, R. M. (1991). Cognitive-behavior therapy with nighttime fearful children. *Journal of Behavioral Therapy and Experimental Psychiatry, 22*, 113–121.

Ollendick, T. H., & King, N. J. (1991). Origins of childhood fears: An evaluation of Rachman's theory of teen-acquisition. *Behavior Research and Therapy, 29*, 117–123.

Ollendick, T. H., & Seligman, L. D. (2006). Anxiety disorders. In C. Gillberg, R. Harrington, & H.-C. Steinhausen (Eds.), *A clinician's handbook of child and adolescent psychiatry* (pp. 144–187). New York: Cambridge University Press.

Oller, D. K. (2000). *The emergence of the speech capacity.* Mahwah, NJ: Erlbaum.

Olson, S. L., Bates, J. E., Sandy, J. M., & Lanthier, R. (2000). Early developmental precursors of externalizing behavior in middle childhood and adolescence. *Journal of Abnormal Child Psychology, 28*(2), 119–133.

Olson, S. L., Kashiwagi, K., & Crystal, D. (2001). Concepts of adaptive and maladaptive child behavior: A comparison of U.S. and Japanese mothers of preschool-age children. *Journal of Cross-Cultural Psychology, 32*(1), 43–57.

Omori, M., & Ingersoll, G. M. (2005). Health-endangering behaviours among Japanese college students: A test of psychosocial model of risk-taking behaviours. *Journal of Adolescence, 28*(1), 17–33.

Örnkloo, H., & von Hofsten, C. (2007). Fitting objects into holes: On the development of spatial cognition skills. *Developmental Psychology, 43*(2), 404–416.

Ornoy, A. (2002). The effects of alcohol and illicit drugs on the human embryo and fetus. *Israel Journal of Psychiatry and Related Sciences, 39*(2), 120–132.

Orstavik, R. E., Kendler, K. S., Czajkowski, N., Tambs, K., & Reichborn-Kjennerud, T. (2007). Genetic and environmental contributions to depressive personality disorder in a population-based sample of Norwegian twins. *Journal of Affective Disorders, 99*(1–3), 181–189.

Ortega, V., Ojeda, P., Sutil, F., & Sierra, J. C. (2005). Culpabilidad sexual en adolescentes: Estudio de algunos factores relacionados. *Anales de Psicología, 21*(2), 268–275.

Ostatnikova, D., et al. (2002). Biological aspects of intellectual giftedness. *Studia Psychologica, 44*(1), 3–13.

Ouellette, G. P. (2006). What's meaning got to do with it: The role of vocabulary in word reading and reading comprehension. *Journal of Educational Psychology, 98*(3), 554–566.

Oztop, E., Kawato, M., & Arbib, M. (2006) Mirror neurons and imitation: A computationally guided review. *Neural Networks, 19*(3), 254–271.

Paavola, L., Kemppinen, K., Kumpulainen, K., Moilanen, I., & Ebeling, H. (2006). Maternal sensitivity, infant co-operation and early linguistic development: Some predictive relations. *European Journal of Developmental Psychology, 3*(1), 13–30.

Page, K. (1999, May 16). The graduate. *Washington Post Magazine, 152*, 18, 20.

Palla, G., Barabási, A-L., & Vicsek, T. (2007). Quantifying social group evolution. *Nature, 446*(7136), 664–667.

Palmer, E. J. (2005). The relationship between moral reasoning and aggression, and the implications for practice. *Psychology, Crime & Law, 11*(4), 353–361.

Palmer, E. J., & Hollin, C. R. (2001). Sociomoral reasoning, perceptions of parenting and self-reported delinquency in adolescents. *Applied Cognitive Psychology, 15*(1), 85–100.

Palmer, E. L. (2003). Realities and challenges in the rapidly changing televisual media landscape. In E. L. Palmer & B. M. Young (Eds.), *The faces of televisual media: Teaching, violence, selling to children* (2nd ed.) (pp. 361–377). Mahwah, NJ: Erlbaum.

Pancsofar, N., & Vernon-Feagans, L. (2006). Mother and father language input to young children: Contributions to later language development. *Journal of Applied Developmental Psychology, 27*(6), 571–587.

Papaioannou, A., Bebetsos, E., Theodorakis, Y., Christodoulidis, T., & Kouli, O. (2006). Causal relationships of sport and exercise involvement with goal orientations, perceived competence and intrinsic motivation in physical education: A longitudinal study. *Journal of Sports Sciences, 24*(4), 367–382.

Pardini, D., Obradovic, J., & Loeber, R. (2006). Interpersonal callousness, hyperactivity/impulsivity, inattention, and conduct problems as precursors to delinquency persistence in boys: A comparison of three grade-based cohorts. *Journal of Clinical Child and Adolescent Psychology, 35*(1), 46–59.

Paris, S. G., & Winograd, P. (1990). How metacognition can promote academic learning and instruction. In B. F. Jones & L. Idol (Eds.), *Dimensions of thinking and cognitive instruction.* Hillsdale, NJ: Erlbaum.

Park, K. A., Lay, K., & Ramsay, L. (1993). Individual differences and developmental changes in preschoolers' friendships. *Developmental Psychology, 29,* 264–270.

Parke, R. D., & Buriel, R. (2006). Socialization in the family: Ethnic and ecological perspectives. In N. Eisenberg, W. Damon, & R. M. Lerner (Eds.), *Handbook of child psychology* (6th ed.), *Vol. 3, Social, emotional, and personality development* (pp. 429–504). Hoboken, NJ: Wiley.

Parkes, A., Wight, D., Henderson, M., & Hart, G. (2007). Explaining Associations between Adolescent Substance Use and Condom Use. *Journal of Adolescent Health, 40*(2), 180.e1–180.e18.

Parks, P., & Bradley, R. (1991). The interaction of home environment features and their relation to infant competence. *Infant Mental Health Journal, 12,* 3–16.

Parsons, T. D., et al. (2004). Sex differences in mental rotation and spatial rotation in a virtual environment. *Neuropsychologia, 42*(4), 555–562.

Parten, M. B. (1932). Social participation among preschool children. *Journal of Abnormal and Social Psychology, 27,* 243–269.

Pascual-Leone, J. (2000). Reflections on working memory: Are the two models complementary? *Journal of Experimental Child Psychology, 77*(2), 138–154.

Passell, P. (1992, August 9). Twins study shows school is a sound investment. *New York Times,* p. A14.

Pastor, J., et al. (2007). Makin' homes: An urban girl thing. In B. J. R. Leadbeater & N. Way (Eds.), *Urban girls revisited: Building strengths* (pp. 75–96). New York: New York University Press.

Patchin, J. W., & Hinduja, S. (2006). Bullies move beyond the schoolyard: A preliminary look at cyberbullying. *Youth Violence and Juvenile Justice, 4*(2), 148–169.

Patenaude, J., Niyonsenga, T., & Fafard, D. (2003). Changes in students' moral development during medical school: A cohort study. *Canadian Medical Association Journal, 168*(7), 840–844.

Paterson, D. S., et al. (2006). Multiple serotonergic brainstem abnormalities in sudden infant death syndrome. *Journal of the American Medical Association, 296,* 2124–2132.

Patock-Peckham, J. A., & Morgan-Lopez, A. A. (2006). College drinking behaviors: Mediational links between parenting styles, impulse control, and alcohol-related outcomes. *Psychology of Addictive Behaviors, 20*(2), 117–125.

Patterson, C. J. (2003). Children of lesbian and gay parents. In L. D. Garnets & D. C. Kimmel (Eds.), *Psychological perspectives on lesbian, gay, and bisexual experiences* (2nd ed.) (pp. 497–548). New York: Columbia University Press.

Patterson, C. J. (2006). Children of lesbian and gay parents. *Current Directions in Psychological Science, 15*(5), 241–244.

Patterson, G. R. (2005). The next generation of PMTO models. *The Behavior Therapist, 28*(2), 27–33.

Patterson, M. M., & Bigler, R. S. (2006). Preschool children's attention to environmental messages about groups: Social categorization and the origins of intergroup bias. *Child Development, 77*(4), 847–860.

Pauli-Pott, U., Mertesacker, B., & Beckmann, D. (2003). Ein Fragebogen zur Erfassung des frühkindlichen Temperaments im Elternurteil. *Zeitschrift für Kinder- und Jugendpsychiatrie und Psychotherapie, 31*(2), 99–110.

Paulussen-Hoogeboom, M. C., Stams, G. J. J. M., Hermanns, J. M. A., & Peetsma, T. T. D. (2007). Child negative emotionality and parenting from infancy to preschool: A meta-analytic review. *Developmental Psychology, 43*(2), 438–453.

Paus, T., et al. (1999). Structural maturation of neural pathways in children and adolescents: In vivo study. *Science, 283*(5409), 1908–1911.

Paxton, S. J., Neumark-Sztainer, D., Hannan, P. J., & Eisenberg, M. E. (2006). Body dissatisfaction prospectively predicts depressive mood and low self-esteem in adolescent girls and boys. *Journal of Clinical Child and Adolescent Psychology, 35*(4), 539–549.

Paxton, S. J., Norris, M., Wertheim, E. H., Durkin, S. J., & Anderson, J. (2005). Body dissatisfaction, dating, and importance of thinness to attractiveness in adolescent girls. *Sex Roles, 53*(9–10), 663–675.

Peeters, M. W., et al. (2005). Genetic and environmental causes of tracking in explosive strength during adolescence. *Behavior Genetics, 35*(5), 551–563.

Pei, M., Matsuda, K., Sakamoto, H., & Kawata, M. (2006). Intrauterine proximity to male fetuses affects the morphology of the sexually dimorphic nucleus of the preoptic area in the adult rat brain. *European Journal of Neuroscience, 23*(5), 1234–1240.

Pelligrini, A. D. (1990). Elementary school children's playground behavior: Implications for children's social-cognitive development. *Children's Environments Quarterly, 7,* 8–16.

Pelphrey, K. A., et al. (2004). Development of visuospatial short-term memory in the second half of the first year. *Developmental Psychology, 40*(5), 836–851.

Pemberton, E. F. (1990). Systematic errors in children's drawings. *Cognitive Development, 5,* 395–404.

Penn, H. E. (2006). Neurobiological correlates of autism: A review of recent research. *Child Neuropsychology, 12*(1), 57–79.

Penza, K. M., Heim, C., & Nemeroff, C. B. (2006). Trauma and depression. In C. L. M. Keyes & S. H. Goodman (Eds.), *Women and depression: A handbook for the social, behavioral, and biomedical sciences* (pp. 360–381). New York: Cambridge University Press.

Peplau, L. A. (2003). Human sexuality: How do men and women differ? *Current Directions in Psychological Science, 12*(2), 37–40.

Pereira, B., Mendonça, D., Neto, C., Valente, L., & Smith, P. K. (2004). Bullying in Portuguese schools. *School Psychology International, 25*(2), 241–254.

Perren, S., & Alsaker, F. D. (2006). Social behavior and peer relationships of victims, bully-victims, and bullies in kindergarten. *Journal of Child Psychology and Psychiatry, 47*(1), 45–57.

Persson, G. E. B. (2005). Developmental perspectives on prosocial and aggressive motives in preschoolers' peer interactions. *International Journal of Behavioral Development, 29*(1), 80–91.

Petersen, & J. Brooks-Gunn (Eds.), *Encyclopedia of adolescence.* New York: Garland.

Philip, J., et al. (2004). Late first-trimester invasive prenatal diagnostic results of an international randomized trial. *Obstetrics & Gynecology, 103*(6), 1164–1173.

Phillips, A. S., & Phillips, C. R. (2000). Birth-order differences in self-attributions for achievement. *Journal of Individual Psychology, 56*(4), 474–480.

Phillips, D. A., & Styfco, S. J. (2007). Child development research and public policy: Triumphs and setbacks on the way to maturity. In J. L. Aber et al. (Eds.), *Child development and social policy: Knowledge for action. APA Decade of Behavior volumes* (pp. 11–27). Washington, DC: American Psychological Association.

Phinney, J. S. (1989). Stages of ethnic identity in minority group adolescents. *Journal of Early Adolescence, 9,* 34–49.

Phinney, J. S. (1992). The multigroup ethnic identity measure: A new scale for use with adolescents and young adults with diverse groups. *Journal of Adolescent Research, 12,* 156–176.

Phinney, J. S. (2006). Ethnic identity exploration in emerging adulthood. In J. J. Arnett & J. L. Tanner (Eds.), *Emerging adults in America: Coming of age in the 21st century* (pp. 117–134). Washington, DC: American Psychological Association.

Phinney, J. S., & Alipuria, L. L. (2006). Multiple social categorization and identity among multiracial, multiethnic, and multicultural individuals: Processes and implications. In R. J. Crisp & M. Hewstone (Eds.), *Multiple social categorization: Processes, models and applications* (pp. 211–238). New York: Psychology Press.

Phinney, J. S., & Chavira, P. (1992). Ethnic identity and self-esteem: An exploratory longitudinal study. *Journal of Adolescence, 15,* 1–11.

Phinney, J. S., & Ong, A. D. (2007). Conceptualization and measurement of ethnic identity: Current status and future directions. *Journal of Counseling Psychology, 54*(3), 271–281.

Phinney, J. S., & Rosenthal, D. A. (1992). Ethnic identity in adolescence: Process, context, and outcome. In G. R. Adams, T. P. Gullotta, & R. Montemayor (Eds.), *Adolescent identity formation.* Newbury Park, CA: Sage.

Phipps, M. G., Blume, J. D., & DeMonner, S. M. (2002). Young maternal age associated with increased risk of postneonatal death. *Obstetrics and Gynecology, 100,* 481–486.

Piaget, J. (1932). *The moral judgment of the child.* London: Kegan Paul.

Piaget, J. (1962). *Play, dreams, and imitation in childhood.* New York: Norton. (Originally published in 1946.)

Piaget, J. (1963). *The origins of intelligence in children.* New York: Norton. (Originally published in 1936.)

Piaget, J. (1967). In D. Elkind (Ed.), *Six psychological studies.* New York: Random House. (Originally published in 1964.)

Piaget, J. (1972). Intellectual evolution from adolescence to adulthood. *Human Development, 15,* 1–12.

Piaget, J. (1976). *The grasp of consciousness: Action and concept in the young child.* Cambridge, MA: Harvard University Press.

Pichichero, M. E. (2006). Prevention of cervical cancer through vaccination of adolescents. *Clinical Pediatrics, 45*(5), 393–398.

Piek, J. P. (2006). *Infant motor development.* Champaign, IL: Human Kinetics.

Piek, J. P., Baynam, G. B., & Barrett, N. C. (2006). The relationship between fine and gross motor ability, self-perceptions and self-worth in children and adolescents. *Human Movement Science, 25*(1), 65–75.

Pierce, K. M., & Vandell, D. L. (2006). Child care. In G. G. Bear & K. M. Minke (Eds.), *Children's needs III: Development, prevention, and intervention* (pp. 721–732). Washington, DC: National Association of School Psychologists.

Pillard, R. C., & Weinrich, J. D. (1986). Evidence of familial nature of male homosexuality. *Archives of Sexual Behavior, 43,* 808–812.

Pine, D. S., et al. (2001). Fluvoxamine for the treatment of anxiety disorders in children and adolescents. *New England Journal of Medicine, 344*(17), 1279–1285.

Pine, K. J., & Nash, A. (2002). Dear Santa: The effects of television advertising on young

children. *International Journal of Behavioral Development, 26*(6), 529–539.

Pinker, S. (1994). *The language instinct.* New York: William Morrow.

Pinker, S., & Jackendoff, R. (2005). The faculty of language: What's special about it? *Cognition, 95*(2), 201–236.

Pinkerton, S. D., Bogart, L. M., Cecil, H., & Abramson, P. R. (2002). Factors associated with masturbation in collegiate sample. *Journal of Psychology & Human Sexuality, 14*(2–3), 103–121.

Plomin, R. (2000). Behavioural genetics in the 21st century. *International Journal of Behavioral Development, 24*(1), 30–34.

Plomin, R. (2001). Genetic factors contributing to learning and language delays and disabilities. *Child and Adolescent Psychiatric Clinics of North America, 10*(2), 259–277.

Plomin, R. (Ed.). (2002). *Behavioral genetics in the postgenomic era.* Washington, DC: American Psychological Association.

Plomin, R., Owen, M. J., & McGuffin, P. (1994). The genetic basis of complex human behaviors. *Science, 264,* 1733–1739.

Plomin, R., & Walker, S. O. (2003). Genetics and educational psychology. *British Journal of Educational Psychology, 73*(1), 3–14.

Polivy, J., Herman, C. P., & Boivin, M. (2005). Eating disorders. In J. E. Maddux & B. A. Winstead (Eds.), *Psychopathology: Foundations for a contemporary understanding* (pp. 229–254). Mahwah, NJ: Erlbaum.

Pollock, B., Prior, H., & Güntürkün, O. (2000). Development of object permanence in food-storing magpies (*Pica pica*). *Journal of Comparative Psychology, 114*(2), 148–157.

Pombeni, M. L., Kirchler, E., & Palmonari, A. (1990). Identification with peers as a strategy to muddle through the troubles of the adolescent years. *Journal of Adolescence, 13,* 351–369.

Ponnappa, B. C., & Rubin, E. (2000). Modeling alcohol's effects on organs in animal models. *Alcohol Research and Health, 24*(2), 93–104.

Pope, H. G., Kouri, E. M., & Hudson, J. I. (2000). Effects of supraphysiologic doses of testosterone on mood and aggression in normal men: A randomized controlled trial. *Archives of General Psychiatry, 57,* 133–140.

Popma, A., et al. (2007). Cortisol moderates the relationship between testosterone and aggression in delinquent male adolescents. *Biological Psychiatry, 61*(3), 405–411.

Porfeli, E. J. (2007). Work values system development during adolescence. *Journal of Vocational Behavior, 70*(1), 42–60.

Porter, R. H., Makin, J. W., Davis, L. B., & Christensen, K. M. (1992). Breast-fed infants respond to olfactory cues from their own mother and unfamiliar lactating females. *Infant Behavior and Development, 15,* 85–93.

Posey, D. J., et al. (2007). Positive effects of methylphenidate on inattention and hyperactivity in pervasive developmental disorders: An analysis of secondary measures. *Biological Psychiatry, 61*(4), 538–544.

Posner, M. I., & Rothbart, M. K. (2007). *Relating brain and mind. Educating the human brain.* Washington, DC: American Psychological Association.

Potts, M. (2006). China's one child policy. *British Medical Journal, 333,* 361–362.

Power, T. G., Kobayashi-Winata, H., & Kelley, M. L. (1992). Childrearing patterns in Japan and the United States: A cluster analytic study. *International Journal of Behavioral Development, 15,* 185–205.

Powlishta, K. K. (2004). Gender as a social category: Intergroup processes and gender-role development. In M. Bennett & F. Sani (Eds.), *The development of the social self* (pp. 103–133). New York: Psychology Press.

Powlishta, K. K., Sen, M. G., Serbin, L. A., Poulin-Dubois, D., & Eichstedt, J. A. (2001). From infancy through middle childhood: The role of cognitive and social factors in becoming gendered. In R. K. Unger (Ed.), *Handbook of the psychology of women and gender* (pp. 116–132). New York: Wiley.

Prato-Previde, E., Fallani, G., & Valsecchi, P. (2006). Gender differences in owners interacting with pet dogs: An observational study. *Ethology, 112*(1), 64–73.

Pratt, C., & Bryant, P. (1990). Young children understand that looking leads to knowing (so long as they are looking into a single barrel). *Child Development, 61,* 973–982.

Press, A. (1992, August 10). Old too soon, wise too late? *Newsweek,* pp. 22–25.

Pressley, M., & Hilden, K. (2006). Cognitive strategies. In D. Kuhn, R. S. Siegler, W. Damon, & R. M. Lerner (Eds.), *Handbook of child psychology* (6th ed.), Vol. 2, *Cognition, perception, and language* (pp. 511–556). Hoboken, NJ: Wiley.

Priner, R., Freeman, S., Perez, R., & Sohmer, H. (2003). The neonate has a temporary conductive hearing loss due to fluid in the middle ear. *Audiology & Neurotology, 8*(2), 100–110.

Provence, S., & Lipton, R. C. (1962). *Infants in institutions.* New York: International Universities Press.

Pryce, C. R., Bettschen, D., Bahr, N. I., & Feldon, J. (2001). Comparison of the effects of infant handling, isolation, and nonhandling on acoustic startle, prepulse inhibition, locomotion, and HPA activity in the adult rat. *Behavioral Neuroscience, 115*(1), 71–83.

Pugh, K. R., et al. (2000). The angular gyrus in developmental dyslexia: Task-specific differences in functional connectivity within posterior cortex. *Psychological Science, 11*(1), 51–56.

Pujol, J., et al. (2006). Myelination of language-related areas in the developing brain. *Neurology, 66*(3), 339–343.

Pulverman, R., Hirsh-Pasek, K., Golinkoff, R. M., Pruden, S., & Salkind, S. J. (2006). Conceptual foundations for verb learning: Celebrating the event. In K. Hirsh-Pasek & R. M. Golinkoff (Eds.), *Action meets word: How children learn verbs* (pp. 134–159). New York: Oxford University Press.

Quatman, T., & Watson, C. M. (2001). Gender differences in adolescent self-esteem: An exploration of domains. *Journal of Genetic Psychology, 162*(1), 93–117.

Quinlivan, J. A., & Condon, J. (2005). Anxiety and depression in fathers in teenage pregnancy. *Australian and New Zealand Journal of Psychiatry, 39*(10), 915–920.

Quintana, S. M. (1998). Children's developmental understanding of ethnicity and race. *Applied and Preventive Psychology, 7*(1), 27–45.

Quintana, S. M., et al. (2006). Race, ethnicity, and culture in child development: Contemporary research and future directions. *Child Development, 77*(5), 1129–1141.

Quirk, K. J., Keith, T. Z., & Quirk, J. T. (2001). Employment during high school and student achievement: Longitudinal analysis of national data. *Journal of Educational Research, 95*(1), 4–10.

Rabasca, L. (2000). Pre-empting racism. *Monitor on Psychology, 31*(11), 60.

Rabinowitz, F. M., Howe, M. L., & Saunders, K. (2002). Age, memory load, and individual differences in working memory as determinants of class-inclusion reasoning. *Journal of Experimental Child Psychology, 81*(2), 157–193.

Raikes, H., et al. (2006). Mother–child bookreading in low-income families: Correlates and outcomes during the first three years of life. *Child Development, 77*(4), 924–953.

Rakison, D. H., & Oakes, L. M. (Eds.). (2003). *Early category and concept development: Making sense of the blooming, buzzing confusion.* London: Oxford University Press.

Ramey, C. T., Campbell, F. A., & Ramey, S. L. (1999). Early intervention: Successful pathways to improving intellectual development. *Developmental Neuropsychology, 16*(3) 385–392.

Ramsey, J. L., Langlois, J. H., Hoss, R. A., Rubenstein, A. J., & Griffin, A. M. (2004). Origins of a stereotype: Categorization of facial attractiveness by 6-month-old infants. *Developmental Science, 7*(2), 201–211.

Randel, B., Stevenson, H. W., & Witruk, E. (2000). Attitudes, beliefs, and mathematics achievement of German and Japanese high school students. *International Journal of Behavioral Development, 24*(2), 190–198.

Rapin, I. (1997). Autism. *New England Journal of Medicine, 337*, 97–104.

Ratcliffe, J. H. (2006). A temporal constraint theory to explain opportunity-based spatial offending patterns. *Journal of Research in Crime and Delinquency, 43*(3), 261–291.

Rathus, J. H., & Miller, A. L. (2002). Dialectical Behavior Therapy adapted for suicidal adolescents. *Suicide and Life-Threatening Behavior, 32*(2), 146–157.

Rathus, S. A., Nevid, J. S., & Fichner-Rathus, L. (2008). *Human sexuality in a world of diversity* (7th ed.). Boston: Allyn & Bacon.

Raudenbusch, S. W. (1984). Magnitude of teacher expectancy effects on pupil IQ as a function of credibility of expectancy induction: A synthesis from 18 experiments. *Journal of Experimental Psychology, 76*, 85–97.

Ravaldi, C., et al. (2003). Eating disorders and body image disturbances among ballet dancers, gymnasium users, and body builders. *Psychopathology, 36*(5), 247–254.

Rebar, R. W., & DeCherney, A. H. (2004). Assisted reproductive technology in the United States. *New England Journal of Medicine, 350*(16), 1603–1604.

Reddy, L. A., & De Thomas, C. (2007). Assessment of attention-deficit/hyperactivity disorder with children. In S. R. Smith & L. Handler (Eds.), *The clinical assessment of children and adolescents: A practitioner's handbook* (pp. 365–387). Mahwah, NJ: Erlbaum.

Redgrave, G. W., Coughlin, J. W., Heinberg, L. J., & Guarda, A. S. (2007). First-degree relative history of alcoholism in eating disorder inpatients: Relationship to eating and substance use psychopathology. *Eating Behaviors, 8*(1), 15–22.

Reef, S., Zimmerman-Swain, L., & Coronado, V. (2004). Disease description: Rubella is a viral illness caused by a togavirus of the genus *Rubivirus.* Available at http://www.cdc.gov/nip/diseases/rubella/default.htm.

Rees, S., Harding, R., & Inder, T. (2006). The developmental environment and the origins of neurological disorders. In P. Gluckman & M. Hanson (Eds.), *Developmental origins of health and disease* (pp. 379–391). New York: Cambridge University Press.

Reid, M., Ramey, S. L., & Burchinal, M. (1990). Dialogues with children about their families. In I. Bretherton & M. Watson (Eds.), *New directions for child development,* no. 48, *Children's perspectives on their families.* San Francisco: Jossey-Bass.

Reiff, M. I., & Mansoor, E. (2007). Journal article reviews: Attention-deficit/hyperactivity disorder. *Journal of Developmental & Behavioral Pediatrics, 28*(1), 71–72.

Reijneveld, S. A., et al. (2004). Infant crying and abuse. *Lancet, 364*(9442), 1340–1342.

Reinecke, M. A., & DuBois, D. L. (2001). Socioenvironmental and cognitive risk and resources: Relations to mood and suicidality among inpatient adolescents. *Journal of Cognitive Psychotherapy, 15*(3), 195–222.

Reis, O., & Youniss, J. (2004). Patterns in identity change and development in relationships with mothers and friends. *Journal of Adolescent Research, 19*(1), 31–44.

Reschly, A., & Christenson, S. L. (2006). School completion. In G. G. Bear & K. M. Minke (Eds.), *Children's needs III: Development, prevention, and intervention* (pp. 103–113). Washington, DC: National Association of School Psychologists.

Rest, J. R. (1983). Morality. In P. H. Mussen (Ed.), *Handbook of child psychology,* Vol. 3, *Cognitive development.* New York: Wiley.

Rezvani, A. H., & Levin, E. D. (2001). Cognitive effects of nicotine. *Biological Psychiatry, 49*(3), 258–267.

Rheingold, H. L., Gewirtz, J. L., & Ross, H. W. (1959). Social conditioning of vocalizations in the infant. *Journal of Comparative and Physiological Psychology, 52,* 68–73.

Riala, K., et al. (2007). Heavy daily smoking among under 18-year-old psychiatric inpatients is associated with increased risk for suicide attempts. *European Psychiatry, 22*(4), 219–222.

Rice, C. (2007). Prevalence of autism spectrum disorders—Autism and Developmental Disabilities Monitoring Network, 14 Sites, United States. *Morbidity and Mortality Weekly Report, 56*(SS01), 12–28.

Richards, H. C., Bear, G. G., Stewart, A. L., & Norman, A. D. (1992). Moral reasoning and classroom conduct: Evidence of a curvilinear relationship. *Merrill–Palmer Quarterly, 38,* 176–190.

Richler, J., et al. (2006). Is there a "regressive phenotype" of autism spectrum disorder associated with the measles-mumps-rubella vaccine? A CPEA study. *Journal of Autism and Developmental Disorders, 36*(3), 299–316.

Rickford, J. R. (2006). Linguistics, education, and the Ebonics firestorm. In S. J. Nero (Ed.), *Dialects, Englishes, creoles, and education* (pp. 71–92). Mahwah, NJ: Erlbaum.

Riley, B., & Kendler, K. S. (2005). Genetics of schizophrenia: Linkage and association studies. In K. S. Kendler & L. J. Eaves (Eds.), *Psychiatric genetics, Review of psychiatry series, 24*(1) (pp. 95–140). Washington, DC: American Psychiatric Publishing, Inc.

Rizzolatti, G., Fadiga, L., Fogassi, L., & Gallese, V. (2002). From mirror neurons to imitation: Facts and speculations. In A. N. Meltzoff & W. Prinz (Eds.), *The imitative mind: Development, evolution, and brain bases.* New York: Cambridge University Press.

Roberts, A. R. (Ed.). (2007). Prologue. *Victims & Offenders, 2*(2) 103–104.

Robins Wahlin, T., Lundin, A., & Dear, K. (2007). Early cognitive deficits in Swedish gene carriers of Huntington's disease. *Neuropsychology, 21*(1), 31–44.

Robinson, J. R., Drotar, D., & Boutry, M. (2001). Problem-solving abilities among mothers of infants with failure to thrive. *Journal of Pediatric Psychology, 26*(1), 21–32.

Robles de Medina, P. G., Visser, G. H. A., Huizink, A. C., Buitelaar, J. K., & Mulder,

E. J. H. (2003). Fetal behaviour does not differ between boys and girls. *Early Human Development, 73*(1–2), 17–26.

Rodgers, P. L., Sudak, H. S., Silverman, M. M., & Litts, D. A. (2007). Evidence-Based Practices Project for suicide prevention. *Suicide and Life-Threatening Behavior, 37*(2), 154–164.

Roebers, C. M., Moga, N., & Schneider, W. (2001). The role of accuracy motivation on children's and adults' event recall. *Journal of Experimental Child Psychology, 78*(4), 313–329.

Roebers, C. M., & Schneider, W. (2002). Stability and consistency of children's event recall. *Cognitive Development, 17*(1), 1085–1103.

Roelofs, J., Meesters, C., Ter Huurne, M., Bamelis, L., & Muris, P. (2006). On the links between attachment style, parental rearing behaviors, and internalizing and externalizing problems in non-clinical children. *Journal of Child and Family Studies, 15*(3), 331–344.

Roeser, R. W., Peck, S. C., & Nasir, N. S. (2006). Self and identity processes in school motivation, learning, and achievement. In P. A. Alexander & P. H. Winne (Eds.), *Handbook of educational psychology* (pp. 391–424). Mahwah, NJ: Erlbaum.

Roffwarg, H. P., Muzio, J. N., & Dement, W. C. (1966). Ontogenetic development of the human sleep–dream cycle. *Science, 152,* 604–619.

Rogers, K. N. (2004). A theoretical review of risk and protective factors related to post-divorce adjustment in young children. *Journal of Divorce and Remarriage, 40*(3–4), 135–147.

Rogoff, B., & Mistry, J. (1990). The social and functional context of children's remembering. In R. Fivush & J. A. Hudson (Eds.), *Knowing and remembering in young children.* Cambridge: Cambridge University Press.

Rogowski, J. A., et al. (2004). Indirect vs. direct hospital quality indicators for very low-birth-weight infants. *Journal of the American Medical Association, 291,* 202–209.

Rollins, V. B., & Valdez, J. N. (2006). Perceived racism and career self-efficacy in African American adolescents. *Journal of Black Psychology, 32*(2), 176–198.

Romans, S. E., Gendall, K. A., Martin, J. L., & Mullen, P. E. (2001). Child sexual abuse and later disordered eating: A New Zealand epidemiological study. *International Journal of Eating Disorders, 29*(4), 380–392.

Ronald, A., et al. (2006). Genetic heterogeneity between the three components of the autism spectrum: A twin study. *Journal of the American Academy of Child & Adolescent Psychiatry, 45*(6), 691–699.

Roncesvalles, M. N., Schmitz, C., Zedka, M., Assaiante, C., & Woollacott, M. (2005). From egocentric to exocentric spatial orientation: Development of posture control in bi-

manual and trunk inclination tasks. *Journal of Motor Behavior, 37*(5), 404–416.

Rondal, J. A., & Ling, L. (2006). Neurobehavioral specificity in Down's Syndrome. *Revista de Logopedia, Foniatría y Audiología, 26*(1), 12–19.

Roopnarine, J. L., Krishnakumar, A., Metindogan, A., & Evans, M. (2006). Links between parenting styles, parent–child academic interaction, parent–school interaction, and early academic skills and social behaviors in young children of English-speaking Caribbean immigrants. *Early Childhood Research Quarterly, 21*(2), 238–252.

Rose, A. J., & Asher, S. R. (1999). Children's goals and strategies in response to conflicts within a friendship. *Developmental Psychology, 35*(1), 69–79.

Rose, A. J., Swenson, L. P., & Carlson, W. (2004). Friendships of aggressive youth: Considering the influences of being disliked and of being perceived as popular. *Journal of Experimental Child Psychology, 88*(1), 25–45.

Rose, S. A., Feldman, J. F., & Jankowski, J. J. (2001). Visual short-term memory in the first year of life: Capacity and recency effects. *Developmental Psychology, 37*(4), 539–549.

Rose, S. A., Feldman, J. F., & Jankowski, J. J. (2004). Infant visual recognition memory. *Developmental Review, 24*(1), 74–100.

Rose, S. A., Feldman, J. F., & Jankowski, J. J. (2005). The structure of infant cognition at 1 year. *Intelligence, 33*(3), 231–250.

Rose, S. A., Feldman, J. F., & Wallace, I. F. (1992). Infant information processing in relation to six-year cognitive outcomes. *Child Development, 63,* 1126–1141.

Rosen, H. J., Ojemann, J. G., Ollinger, J. M., & Petersen, S. E. (2000). Comparison of brain activation during word retrieval done silently and aloud using fMRI. *Brain and Cognition, 42*(2), 201–217.

Rosenbaum, D. E. (2000, May 16). On left-handedness, its causes, and costs. *New York Times,* pp. F1, F6.

Rosenstein, D., & Oster, H. (1988). Differential facial responses to four basic tastes. *Child Development, 59,* 1555–1568.

Rosenthal, R., & Jacobson, L. (1968). *Pygmalion in the classroom.* New York: Holt, Rinehart & Winston.

Ross, G., Kagan, J., Zelazo, P., & Kotelchuck, M. (1975). Separation protest in infants in home and laboratory. *Developmental Psychology, 11,* 256–257.

Ross, H., Ross, M., Stein, N., & Trabasso, T. (2006). How siblings resolve their conflicts: The importance of first offers, planning, and limited opposition. *Child Development. 77*(6) 1730–1745.

Rotenberg, K. J., et al. (2004). Cross-sectional and longitudinal relations among peer-reported trustworthiness, social relationships, and psychological adjustment in children and

early adolescents from the United Kingdom and Canada. *Journal of Experimental Child Psychology, 88*(1), 46–67.

Roth, T. L., Wilson, D. A., & Sullivan, R. M. (2004). Neurobehavioral development of infant learning and memory: Implications for infant attachment. In P. J. B. Slater et al. (Eds.), *Advances in the study of behavior, 34* (pp. 103–133). New York: Elsevier Academic Press.

Rothbart, M. K., Ellis, L. K., & Posner, M. I. (2004). Temperament and self-regulation. In R. F. Baumeister & K. D. Vohs (Eds.), *Handbook of self-regulation: Research, theory, and applications.* New York: Guilford.

Rothbart, M. K., & Sheese, B. E. (2007). Temperament and emotion regulation. In J. J. Gross (Ed.), *Handbook of emotion regulation* (pp. 331–350). New York: Guilford.

Rothrauff, T., Middlemiss, W., & Jacobson, L. (2004). Comparison of American and Austrian infants' and toddlers' sleep habits: A retrospective, exploratory study. *North American Journal of Psychology, 6*(1), 125–144.

Rottinghaus, P. J., Betz, N. E., & Borgen, F. H. (2003). Validity of parallel measures of vocational interests and confidence. *Journal of Career Assessment, 11*(4), 355–378.

Roulet-Perez, E., & Deonna, T. (2006). Autism, epilepsy, and EEG epileptiform activity. In R. Tuchman & I. Rapin (Eds.), *Autism: A neurological disorder of early brain development* (pp. 174–188). *International review of child neurology.* London: Mac Keith Press.

Rovee-Collier, C. (1993). The capacity for long-term memory in infancy. *Current Directions in Psychological Science, 2,* 130–135.

Rowen, B. (1973). *The children we see.* New York: Holt, Rinehart & Winston.

Royal Australasian College of Physicians, Paediatrics & Child Health Division. (2006). Management of procedure-related pain in neonates. *Journal of Paediatrics and Child Health, 42*(Supp. l1), S31–S39.

Rubia, K., et al. (2006). Progressive increase of frontostriatal brain activation from childhood to adulthood during event-related tasks of cognitive control. *Human Brain Mapping, 27*(12), 973–993.

Rubin, K. H., Bukowski, W. M., & Parker, J. G. (2006). Peer interactions, relationships, and groups. In N. Eisenberg, W. Damon, & R. M. Lerner (Eds.), *Handbook of child psychology* (6th ed.), Vol. 3, *Social, emotional, and personality development* (pp. 571–645). Hoboken, NJ: Wiley.

Rubinstein, S., & Caballero, B. (2000). Is Miss America an undernourished role model? *Journal of the American Medical Association, 283*(12), 1569.

Ruble, D. N., Martin, C. L., & Berenbaum, S. A. (2006). Gender development. In N. Eisenberg, W. Damon, & R. M. Lerner (Eds.), *Handbook of child psychology* (6th ed.),

Vol. 3, *Social, emotional, and personality development.* (pp. 858–932). Hoboken, NJ: Wiley.

Ruchkin, V., & Vermeiren, R. (2006). Juvenile justice. *Child and Adolescent Psychiatric Clinics of North America, 15*(2), xix–xxii.

Rudolph, K. D., & Flynn, M. (2007). Childhood adversity and youth depression: Influence of gender and pubertal status. *Development and Psychopathology, 19*(2), 497–521.

Rudolph, K. D., Lambert, S. F., Clark, A. G., & Kurlakowsky, K. D. (2001). Negotiating the transition to middle school: The role of self-regulatory processes. *Child Development, 72*(3), 929–946.

Rudy, D., & Grusec, J. E. (2006). Authoritarian parenting in individualist and collectivist groups: Associations with maternal emotion and cognition and children's self-esteem. *Journal of Family Psychology, 20*(1), 68–78.

Ruiz, F., & Tanaka, K. (2001). The *ijime* phenomenon and Japan: Overarching considerations for cross-cultural studies. *Psychologia: An International Journal of Psychology in the Orient, 44*(2), 128–138.

Rumbold, A. R., et al. (2006). Vitamins C and E and the risks of preeclampsia and perinatal complications. *New England Journal of Medicine, 354,* 1796–1806.

Runyon, M. K., & Kenny, M. C. (2002). Relationship of attributional style, depression, and posttrauma distress among children who suffered physical or sexual abuse. *Child Maltreatment: Journal of the American Professional Society on the Abuse of Children, 7*(3), 254–264.

Rushton, J. P., Skuy, M., & Fridjhon, P. (2003). Performance on Raven's Advanced Progressive Matrices by African, East Indian, and White engineering students in South Africa. *Intelligence, 31*(2), 123–137.

Russ, S. W. (2006). Pretend play, affect, and creativity. In P. Locher, C. Martindale, & L. Dorfman (Eds.), *New directions in aesthetics, creativity and the arts, Foundations and frontiers in aesthetics* (pp. 239–250). Amityville, NY: Baywood.

Russell, G., & Russell, A. (1987). Mother–child and father–child relationships in middle childhood. *Child Development, 58,* 1573–1585.

Russell, S.T. (2006). Substance use and abuse and mental health among sexual-minority youths: Evidence from add health. In A. M. Omoto & H. S. Kurtzman (Eds.), *Sexual orientation and mental health: Examining identity and development in lesbian, gay, and bisexual people* (pp. 13–35). Washington, DC: American Psychological Association.

Rutter, M. (2006a). The promotion of resilience in the face of adversity. In A. Clarke-Stewart & J. Dunn (Eds.), *Families count: Effects on child and adolescent development. The Jacobs Foundation series on adolescence* (pp. 26–52). New York: Cambridge University Press.

Rutter, M. (2006b). The psychological effects of early institutional rearing. In P. J. Marshall & N. A.Fox (Eds.), *The development of social engagement: Neurobiological perspectives. Series in affective science* (pp. 355–391). New York: Oxford University Press.

Saariluoma, P. (2001). Chess and content-oriented psychology of thinking. *Psicologica, 22*(1), 143–164.

Saaristo-Helin, K., Savinainen-Makkonen, T., & Kunnari, S. (2006). The phonological mean length of utterance: Methodological challenges from a crosslinguistic perspective. *Journal of Child Language, 33*(1), 179–190.

Sabattini, L., & Leaper, C. (2004). The relation between mothers' and fathers' parenting styles and their division of labor in the home: Young adults' retrospective reports. *Sex Roles, 50*(3–4), 217–225.

Sadker, D. M., & Silber, E. S. (Eds.) (2007). *Gender in the classroom: Foundations, skills, methods, and methods across the curriculum.* Mahwah, NJ: Erlbaum.

Sadker, D. M., & Zittleman, K. (2007). Practical strategies for detecting and correcting gender bias in your classroom. In D. M. Sadker & E. S. Silber (Eds.), *Gender in the classroom: Foundations, skills, methods, and strategies across the curriculum* (pp. 259–275). Mahwah, NJ: Erlbaum.

Sadker, M., & Sadker, D. (1994). *Failing at fairness: How America's schools cheat girls.* New York: Scribners.

Sadler, T. W. (Ed.). (2005). Abstracts of papers presented at the thirty-fifth annual meeting the Japanese Teratology Society, Tokyo, Japan. *Teratology, 52*(4), b1–b51.

Saffran, J. R., Werker, J. F., & Werner, L. A. (2006). The infant's auditory world: Hearing, speech, and the beginnings of language. In D. Kuhn, R. S. Siegler, W. Damon, & R. M. Lerner (Eds.), *Handbook of child psychology,* Vol. 2, *Cognition, perception, and language* (6th ed.) (pp. 58–108). Hoboken, NJ: Wiley.

Saggino, A., Perfetti, B., Spitoni, G., & Galati, G. (2006). Fluid intelligence and executive functions: New perspectives. In L. V. Wesley (Ed.), *Intelligence: New research* (pp. 1–22). Hauppauge, NY: Nova Science Publishers.

Sagrestano, L. M., McCormick, S. H., Paikoff, R. L., & Holmbeck, G. N. (1999). Pubertal development and parent–child conflict in low-income, urban, African American adolescents. *Journal of Research on Adolescence 9*(1), 85–107.

Saigal, S., et al. (2006). Transition of extremely low-birth-weight infants from adolescence to young adulthood: Comparison with normal birth-weight controls. *Journal of the American Medical Association, 295*(6), 667–675.

Saiki, J., & Miyatsuji, H. (2007). Feature binding in visual working memory evaluated by type identification paradigm. *Cognition, 102*(1), 49–83.

Saito, S., & Miyake, A. (2004). On the nature of forgetting and the processing–storage relationship in reading span performance. *Journal of Memory and Language, 50*(4), 425–443.

Salapatek, P. (1975). Pattern perception in early infancy. In L. B. Cohen & P. Salapatek (Eds.), *Infant perception: From sensation to cognition.* New York: Academic Press.

Sales, J. M., Fivush, R., & Peterson, C. (2003). Parental reminiscing about positive and negative events. *Journal of Cognition and Development, 4*(2), 185–209.

Salmivalli, C., Ojanen, T., Haanpää, J., & Peets, K. (2005). "I'm OK but you're not" and other peer-relational schemas: Explaining individual differences in children's social goals. *Developmental Psychology, 41*(2), 363–375.

Salovey, P., & Pizarro, D. A. (2003). The value of emotional intelligence. In R. J. Sternberg et al. (Eds.), *Models of intelligence: International perspectives* (pp. 263–278). Washington, DC: American Psychological Association.

Salzarulo, P., & Ficca, G. (Eds.). (2002). *Awakening and sleep–wake cycle across development.* Amsterdam: John Benjamins.

Sandler, I. (2001). Quality and ecology of adversity as common mechanisms of risk and resilience. *American Journal of Community Psychology, 29*(1), 19–61.

Santelli, J. S., et al. (2003). Reproductive health in school-based health centers: Findings from the 1998–99 census of school-based health centers. *Journal of Adolescent Health, 32*(6), 443–451.

Santelli, J. S., Lindberg, J. D., Abma, J., Mc-Neely, C. S., & Resnick, M. (2000). Adolescent sexual behavior: Estimates and trends from four nationally representative surveys. *Family Planning Perspectives, 32*(4), 156–165, 194.

Santinello, M., & Vieno, A. (2002). The influence of economic and social support on preadolescents' disorders. *Bollettino di Psicologia Applicata, 238,* 33–42.

Santonastaso, P., Friederici, S., & Favaro, A. (2001). Sertraline in the treatment of restricting anorexia nervosa: An open controlled trial. *Journal of Child and Adolescent Psychopharmacology, 11*(2), 143–150.

Santos, D. C. C., Gabbard, C., & Goncalves, V. M. G. (2000). Motor development during the first 6 months: The case of Brazilian infants. *Infant and Child Development, 9*(3), 161–166.

Saroglou, V., & Galand, P. (2004). Identities, values, and religion: A study among Muslim, other immigrant, and native Belgian young adults after the 9/11 attacks. *Identity, 4*(2), 97–132.

Sarrazin, P., Trouilloud, D., & Bois, J. (2005a). Attentes du superviseur et performance sportive du pratiquant. Amplitude et fonctionnement de l'effet Pygmalion en contexte sportif. *Bulletin de Psychologie, 58*(1), 63–68.

Sarrazin, P., Trouilloud, D., Tessier, D., Chanal, J., & Bois, J. (2005b). Attentes de motivation et comportements différenciés de l'enseignant d'éducation physique et sportive à l'égard de ses élèves: une étude en contexte naturel d'enseignement. *Revue Européenne de Psychologie Appliquée, 55*(2), 111–120.

Saudino, K. J., & Eaton, W. O. (1993, March). *Genetic influences on activity level. II. An analysis of continuity and change from infancy to early childhood.* Paper presented at the meeting of the Society for Research in Child Development, New Orleans, LA.

Saunders, K. W. (2003). Regulating youth access to violent video games. *Law Review–Michigan State University, 51*(70).

Save the Children. (2004b). *State of the world's mothers 2004.* Available at http://www.savethechildren.org/mothers/report_2004/index.asp. Accessed June 2004.

Savin-Williams, R. C. (2007). Girl-on-girl sexuality. In B. J. R. Leadbeater & N. Way (Eds.), *Urban girls revisited: Building strengths* (pp. 301–318). New York: New York University Press.

Savin-Williams, R. C., & Berndt, T. (1990). Friendship and peer relations. In S. S. Feldman & G. R. Elliott (Eds.), *At the threshold: The developing adolescent.* Cambridge, MA: Harvard University Press.

Savin-Williams, R. C., & Diamond, L. M. (2000). Sexual identity trajectories among sexual-minority youths: Gender comparisons. *Archives of Sexual Behavior, 29*(6), 607–627.

Savin-Williams, R. C., & Diamond, L. M. (2004). Sex. In R. M. Lerner & L. Steinberg (Eds.), *Handbook of adolescent psychology* (2nd ed.) (pp. 189–231). Hoboken, NJ: Wiley.

Sawyer, D. J. (2006). Dyslexia: A generation of inquiry. *Topics in Language Disorders, 26*(2), 95–109.

Saywitz, K. J., Mannarino, A. P., Berliner, L., & Cohen, J. A. (2000). Treatment for sexually abused children and adolescents. *American Psychologist, 55*(9), 1040–1049.

Scanlan, T. K., Babkes, M. L., & Scanlan, L. A. (2005). Participation in sport: A developmental glimpse at emotion. In J. L. Mahoney, R. W. Larson, & J. S. Eccles. (Eds.). *Organized activities as contexts of development: Extracurricular activities, after-school and community programs.* (pp. 275–309). Mahwah, NJ: Erlbaum.

Scarr, S. (1993, March). *IQ correlations among members of transracial adoptive families.* Paper presented at the meeting of the Society for Research in Child Development, New Orleans, LA.

Scarr, S., & Weinberg, R. A. (1976). IQ test performance of black children adopted by white families. *American Psychologist, 31,* 726–739.

Scarr, S., & Weinburg, R. A. (1977). Intellectual similarities within families of both adopted and biological children. *Intelligence, 1,* 170–191.

Schaffer, H. R., & Emerson, P. E. (1964). *The development of social attachments in infancy.* Monographs of the Society for Research in Child Development, *29*(94).

Scharf, M., Shulman, S., & Avigad-Spitz, L. (2005). Sibling relationships in emerging adulthood and in adolescence. *Journal of Adolescent Research, 20*(1), 64–90.

Scheithauer, H., Hayer, T., Petermann, F., & Jugert, G. (2006). Physical, verbal, and relational forms of bullying among German students: Age trends, gender differences, and correlates. *Aggressive Behavior, 32*(3), 261–275.

Scheres, A., & Castellanos, F. X. (2003). Assessment and treatment of childhood problems, 2nd ed.: A clinician's guide. *Psychological Medicine, 33*(8), 1487–1488.

Schiff, B., & O'Neill, T. (2007). The relational emplotment of mixed racial identity. In R. Josselson, A. Lieblich, & D. P. McAdams (Eds.), *The meaning of others: Narrative studies of relationships* (pp. 143–163). Washington, DC: American Psychological Association.

Schmitt, D. P. (2003). Universal sex differences in the desire for sexual variety: Tests from 52 nations, 6 continents, and 13 islands. *Journal of Personality and Social Psychology, 85*(1), 85–104.

Schonfeld, A. M., Mattson, S. N., & Riley, E. P. (2005). Moral maturity and delinquency after prenatal alcohol exposure. *Journal of Studies on Alcohol, 66*(4), 545–554.

Schoppe-Sullivan, S. J., Mangelsdorf, S. C., Brown, G. L., & Sokolowski, M. S. (2007). Goodness-of-fit in family context: Infant temperament, marital quality, and early coparenting behavior. *Infant Behavior & Development, 30*(1), 82–96.

Schraf, M., & Hertz-Lazarowitz, R. (2003). Social networks in the school context: Effects of culture and gender. *Journal of Social and Personal Relationships, 20*(6), 843–858.

Schuetze, P., Lawton, D., & Eiden, R. D. (2006). Prenatal cocaine exposure and infant sleep at 7 months of age: The influence of the caregiving environment. *Infant Mental Health Journal, 27*(4), 383–404.

Schuetze, P., & Zeskind, P. S. (2001). Relations between women's depressive symptoms and perceptions of infant distress signals varying in pitch. *Infancy, 2*(4), 483–499.

Schuetze, P., Zeskind, P. S., & Eiden, R. D. (2003). The perceptions of infant distress signals varying in pitch by cocaine-using mothers. *Infancy, 4*(1), 65–83.

Schulte-Körne, G., Warnke, A., & Remschmidt, H. (2006). Genetics of dyslexia. *Zeitschrift für Kinder- und Jugendpsychiatrie und Psychotherapie, 34*(6), 435–444.

Schultz, D., & Shaw, D. S. (2003). Boys' maladaptive social information processing, family emotional climate, and pathways to early conduct problems. *Social Development, 12*(3), 440–460.

Schultz, D. P., & Schultz, S. E. (2008). A history of modern psychology (9th Ed.). Belmont, CA: Thomson/Wadsworth.

Schumacher, D., & Queen, J. A. (2007). *Overcoming obesity in childhood and adolescence: A guide for school leaders.* Thousand Oaks, CA: Corwin Press.

Schwartz, S. J. (2001). The evolution of Eriksonian and neo-Eriksonian identity theory and research: A review and integration. *Identity, 1*(1), 7–58.

Schwartz, T. H., Haglund, M. M., Lettich, E., & Ojemann, G. A. (2000). Asymmetry of neuronal activity during extracellular microelectrode recording from left and right human temporal lobe neocortex during rhyming and line-matching. *Journal of Cognitive Neuroscience, 12*(5), 803–812.

Schweinhart, L. J., & Weikart, D. P. (Eds.). (1993). *Significant benefits: The High/Scope Perry Preschool Study through age 27.* Ypsilanti, MI: High/Scope Press.

Scott, J. R. (2006). Preventing eclampsia. *Obstetrics & Gynecology, 108,* 824–825.

Scourfield, J., Van den Bree, M., Martin, N., & McGuffin, P. (2004). Conduct problems in children and adolescents: A twin study. *Archives of General Psychiatry, 61,* 489–496.

Secker-Walker, R. H., & Vacek, P. M. (2003). Relationships between cigarette smoking during pregnancy, gestational age, maternal weight gain, and infant birthweight. *Addictive Behaviors, 28*(1), 55–66.

Sefcek, J. A., Brumbach, B. H., Vasquez, G., & Miller, G. F. (2007). The evolutionary psychology of human mate choice: How ecology, genes, fertility, and fashion influence mating strategies. *Journal of Psychology & Human Sexuality, 18*(2–3) 125–182.

Seidah, A., & Bouffard, T. (2007). Being proud of oneself as a person or being proud of one's physical appearance: What matters for feeling well in adolescence? *Social Behavior and Personality, 35*(2), 255–268.

Selman, R. L. (1976). Social-cognitive understanding. In T. Lickona (Ed.), *Moral development and behavior: Theory, research, and social issues.* New York: Holt, Rinehart & Winston.

Selman, R. L. (1980). *The growth of interpersonal understanding: Developmental and clinical analysis.* New York: Academic Press.

Selman, R. L., & Dray, A. J. (2006). Risk and prevention. In K. A. Renninger, I. E. Sigel, W. Damon, & R. M. Lerner (Eds.), *Handbook of child psychology* (6th ed.), Vol. 4, *Child psychology in practice* (pp. 378–419). Hoboken, NJ: Wiley.

Serbin, L. A., Poulin-Dubois, D., Colburne, K. A., Sen, M. G., & Eichstedt, J. A. (2001).

Gender stereotyping in infancy: Visual preferences for and knowledge of gender-stereotyped toys in the second year. *International Journal of Behavioral Development, 25*(1), 7–15.

Shaw, G. M., Velie, E. M., & Schaffer, D. (1996). Risk of neural tube defect–affected pregnancies among obese women. *Journal of the American Medical Association, 275,* 1093–1096.

Shaywitz, B. A., Lyon, G. R., & Shaywitz, S. E. (2006a). The role of functional magnetic resonance imaging in understanding reading and dyslexia. *Developmental Neuropsychology, 30*(1), 613–632.

Shaywitz, S. E. (1998). Dyslexia. *New England Journal of Medicine, 338,* 307–312.

Shaywitz, S. E., Mody, M., & Shaywitz, B. A. (2006b). Neural mechanisms in dyslexia. *Current Directions in Psychological Science, 15*(6), 278–281.

Shaywitz, S. E., & Shaywitz, B. A. (2003). Neurobiological indices of dyslexia. In H. L. Swanson et al. (Eds.), *Handbook of learning disabilities* (pp. 514–531). New York: Guilford.

Shear, K., Jin, R., Ruscio, A. M., Walters, E. E., & Kessler, R. C. (2006). Prevalence and correlates of estimated DSM-IV child and adult separation anxiety disorder in the National Comorbidity Survey Replication. *American Journal of Psychiatry 163,* 1074–1083.

Sheeber, L. B., Davis, B., Leve, C., Hops, H., & Tildesley, E. (2007). Adolescents' relationships with their mothers and fathers: Associations with depressive disorder and subdiagnostic symptomatology. *Journal of Abnormal Psychology, 116*(1), 144–154.

Shen, R-Y, Choong, K-C, & Thompson, A. C. (2007). Long-term reduction in ventral tegmental area dopamine neuron population activity following repeated stimulant or ethanol treatment. *Biological Psychiatry, 61*(1), 93–100.

Shenal, B. V., & Harrison, D. W. (2003). Investigation of the laterality of hostility, cardiovascular regulation, and auditory recognition. *International Journal of Neuroscience, 113*(2), 205–222.

Sherry, J. L., Lucas, K., Greenberg, B. S., & Lachlan, K. (2006). Video game uses and gratifications as predicators of use and game preference. In P. Vorderer & J. Bryant (Eds.), *Playing video games: Motives, responses, and consequences* (pp. 213–224). Mahwah, NJ: Erlbaum .

Sherwin-White, S. (2006). The social toddler: Promoting positive behaviour. *Infant Observation, 9*(1), 95–97.

Shevell, T., et al. (2005). Assisted reproductive technology and pregnancy outcome. *Obstetrics & Gynecology, 106,* 1039–1045.

Shih, M., Bonam, C., Sanchez, D., & Peck, C. (2007). The social construction of race: Biracial identity and vulnerability to stereotypes. *Cultural Diversity & Ethnic Minority Psychology, 13*(2), 125–133.

Shin, H. B., & Bruno, R. (2003, October). *Language use and English speaking ability: 2000.* Washington, DC: U.S. Bureau of the Census.

Shirk, S., Burwell, R., & Harter, S. (2003). Strategies to modify low self-esteem in adolescents. In M. A. Reinecke et al. (Eds.), *Cognitive therapy with children and adolescents: A casebook for clinical practice* (2nd ed.) (pp. 189–213). New York: Guilford.

Shonk, S. M., & Cicchetti, D. (2001). Maltreatment, competency deficits, and risk for academic and behavioral maladjustment. *Developmental Psychology, 37*(1), 3–17.

Shortt, A. L., Barrett, P. M., & Fox, T. L. (2001). Evaluating the FRIENDS Program: A cognitive-behavioral group treatment for anxious children and their parents. *Journal of Clinical Child Psychology, 30*(4), 525–535.

Shroff, H., et al. Features associated with excessive exercise in women with eating disorders. *International Journal of Eating Disorders, 39*(6), 454–461.

Shute, B., & Wheldall, K. (1999). Fundamental frequency and temporal modifications in the speech of British fathers to their children. *Educational Psychology, 19*(2), 221–233.

Shute, B., & Wheldall, K. (2001). How do grandmothers speak to their grandchildren? Fundamental frequency and temporal modifications in the speech of British grandmothers to their grandchildren. *Educational Psychology, 21*(4), 493–503.

SIDS Network. (2001, May 14). Available at http://www.sids-network.org.

Siegel, L. S. (1992). Infant motor, cognitive, and language behaviors as predictors of achievement at school age. In C. Rovee-Collier & L. P. Lipsitt (Eds.), *Advances in infancy research,* Vol. 7. Norwood, NJ: Ablex.

Siegler, R. S., & Alibali, M. W. (2005). *Children's thinking* (4th ed.). Upper Saddle River, NJ: Prentice Hall.

Siegler, R. S., Liebert, D. E., & Liebert, R. M. (1973). Inhelder and Piaget's pendulum problem: Teaching pre-adolescents to act as scientists. *Developmental Psychology, 9,* 97–101.

Signorello, L. B., & McLaughlin, J. K. (2004). Maternal caffeine consumption and spontaneous abortion: A review of the epidemiologic evidence. *Epidemiology, 15*(2), 229–239.

Silbereisen, R. K. (2006). Development and ecological context: History of the psychological science in a personal view and experience—An interview with Urie Bronfenbrenner. *Psychologie in Erziehung und Unterricht, 53*(1), 241–249.

Sim, T. N., & Ong, L. P. (2005). Parent physical punishment and child aggression in a Singapore Chinese preschool. *Journal of Marriage and Family, 67*(1), 85–99.

Simion, F., Cassia, V. M., Turati, C., & Valenza, E. (2001). The origins of face perception: Specific versus nonspecific mechanisms. *Infant and Child Development, 10*(1–2), 59–65.

Simmons, R. G., & Blyth, D. A. (1987). *Moving into adolescence: The impact of pubertal change and school context.* Hawthorne, NY: Aldine deGruyter.

Simonelli, A., Monti, F., & Magalotti, D. (2005). The complex phenomenon of failure to thrive: Medical, psychological and relational-affective aspects. *Psicologia Clinica dello Sviluppo, 9*(2), 183–212.

Simonton, D. K. (2006). Creativity around the world in 80 ways … but with one destination. In J. C. Kaufman & R. Sternberg (Eds.), *The international handbook of creativity* (pp. 490–496). New York: Cambridge University Press.

Simpkins, S. D., Fredricks, J. A., Davis-Kean, P. E., & Eccles, J. S. (2006). Healthy mind, healthy habits: The influence of activity involvement in middle childhood. In A. C. Huston & M. N. Ripke (Eds.), *Developmental contexts in middle childhood: Bridges to adolescence and adulthood. Cambridge studies in social and emotional development* (pp. 283–302). New York: Cambridge University Press.

Simpson, J. L. (2000, June 1). *Invasive diagnostic procedures for prenatal genetic diagnosis.* Journal Watch Women's Health. Available at http://womenshealth.jwatch.org.

Singer, L. T., et al. (2005). Prenatal cocaine exposure and infant cognition. *Infant Behavior & Development, 28*(4), 431–444.

Singh, K. (1998). Part-time employment in high school and its effect on academic achievement. *Journal of Educational Research, 91*(3), 131–139.

Singh, K., & Ozturk, M. (2000). Effect of part-time work on high school mathematics and science course taking. *Journal of Educational Research, 91*(2), 67–74.

Sirrs, S. M., et al. (2007). Normal-appearing white matter in patients with phenylketonuria: Water content, myelin water fraction, and metabolite concentrations. *Radiology, 242,* 236–243.

Skeels, H. M. (1966). *Adult status of children with contrasting early life experiences: A follow-up study.* Monographs of the Society for Research in Child Development, 31(3, ser. 105).

Skinner, B. F. (1957). *Verbal behavior.* New York: Appleton.

Skinner, B. F. (1983). *A matter of consequences.* New York: Knopf.

Skoczenski, A. M. (2002). Limitations on visual sensitivity during infancy: Contrast sensitivity, vernier acuity, and orientation processing. In J. W. Fagen & H. Hayne (Eds.), *Progress in infancy research,* Vol. 2. Mahwah, NJ: Erlbaum.

Skorikov, V. (2007). Continuity in adolescent career preparation and its effects on adjustment. *Journal of Vocational Behavior, 70*(1), 8–24.

Slater, A. (2000). Visual perception in the young infant: Early organization and rapid learning. In D. Muir & A. Slater (Eds.), *Infant development: The essential readings.* Malden, MA: Blackwell.

Slater, A., Mattock, A., & Brown, E. (1990). Size constancy at birth: Newborn infants' responses to retinal and real size. *Journal of Experimental Child Psychology, 49,* 314–322.

Slavin, R. E. (2006). *Educational psychology: Theory and practice* (8th ed.). Boston: Allyn & Bacon.

Sloan, S., Sneddon, H., Stewart, M., & Iwaniec, D. (2006). Breast is best? Reasons why mothers decide to breastfeed or bottlefeed their babies and factors influencing the duration of breastfeeding. *Child Care in Practice, 12*(3), 283–297.

Slobin, D. I. (2001). Form/function relations: How do children find out what they are? In M. Tomasello & E. Bates (Eds.), *Language development: The essential readings.* Malden, MA: Blackwell.

Small, M. Y. (1990). *Cognitive development.* San Diego: Harcourt Brace Jovanovich.

Smarty, S., & Findling, R. L. (2007). Psychopharmacology of pediatric bipolar disorder: A review. *Psychopharmacology, 191*(1), 39–54.

Smetana, J. G. (1990). Morality and conduct disorders. In M. Lewis & S. M. Miller (Eds.), *Handbook of developmental psychopathology.* New York: Plenum.

Smetana, J. G. (2005). Adolescent–parent conflict: Resistance and subversion as developmental process. In L. Nucci (Ed), *Conflict, contradiction, and contrarian elements in moral development and education* (pp. 69–91). Mahwah, NJ: Erlbaum.

Smetana, J. G., Campione-Barr, N., & Metzger, A. (2006). Adolescent development in interpersonal and societal contexts. *Annual Review of Psychology, 57,* 255–284.

Smetana, J. G., Daddis, C., & Chuang, S. S. (2003). "Clean your room!" A longitudinal investigation of adolescent–parent conflict and conflict resolution in middle-class African American families. *Journal of Adolescent Research, 18*(6), 631–650.

Smiley, P. A., & Johnson, R. S. (2006). Self-referring terms, event transitivity and development of self. *Cognitive Development, 21*(3), 266–284.

Smith, C. L., Calkins, S. D., Keane, S. P., Anastopoulos, A. D., & Shelton, T. L. (2004). Predicting stability and change in toddler behavior problems: Contributions of maternal behavior and child gender. *Developmental Psychology, 40*(1), 29–42.

Smith, P. K. (1979). The ontogeny of fear in children. In W. Sluckin (Ed.), *Fears in animals and man.* London: Van Nostrand Reinhold.

Smith, P. K. (2005). Play: Types and functions in human development. In B. J. Ellis & D. F. Bjorklund (Eds.), *Origins of the social mind: Evolutionary psychology and child development* (pp. 271–291). New York: Guilford Press.

Smolka, E., & Eviatar, Z. (2006). Phonological and orthographic visual word recognition in the two cerebral hemispheres: Evidence from Hebrew. Cognitive *Neuropsychology, 23*(6), 972–989.

Smoll, F. L., & Schultz, R. W. (1990). Quantifying gender differences in physical performance: A developmental perspective. *Developmental Psychology, 26,* 360–369.

Snarey, J. R. (1994). Cross-cultural universality of social-moral development: A critical review of Kohlbergian research. In B. Puka (Ed.), *New research in moral development* (pp. 268–298). New York: Garland.

Snarey, J. R., & Bell, D. (2003). Distinguishing structural and functional models of human development. *Identity, 3*(3), 221–230.

Snedeker, J., Geren, J., & Shafto, C. L. (2007). Starting over: International adoption as a natural experiment in language development. *Psychological Science, 18*(1), 79–87.

Snegovskikh, V., Park, J. S., & Norwitz, E. R. (2006). Endocrinology of parturition. *Endocrinology and Metabolism Clinics of North America, 35*(1), 173–191.

Snow, C. (2006). Cross-cutting themes and future research directions. In D. August & T. Shanahan (Eds.), *Developing literacy in second-language learners: Report of the National Literacy Panel on Language-Minority Children and Youth* (pp. 631–651). Mahwah, NJ: Erlbaum.

Snyder, H. M., & Sickmund, M. (2006). *Juvenile offenders and victims: 2006 national report.* Washington, DC: U.S. Department of Justice, Office of Justice Programs, Office of Juvenile Justice and Delinquency Prevention.

Snyderman, M., & Rothman, S. (1990). *The IQ controversy.* New Brunswick, NJ: Transaction.

Soan, S., & Tod, J. (2006). Review of dyslexia. *European Journal of Special Needs Education, 21*(3), 354–356.

Sodian, B., Taylor, C., Harris, P. L., & Perner, J. (1991). Early deception and the child's theory of mind: False trails and genuine markers. *Child Development, 62,* 468–483.

Soenens, B., et al. (2007). Conceptualizing parental autonomy support: Adolescent perceptions of promotion of independence versus promotion of volitional functioning. *Developmental Psychology, 43*(3), 633–646.

Sommer, I. E. C., Ramsey, N. F., Mandl, R. C. W., & Kahn, R. S. (2002). Language lateralization in monozygotic twin pairs concordant and discordant for handedness. *Brain, 125*(12), 2710–2718.

Sontag, L. W., & Richards, T. W. (1938). *Studies in fetal behavior: Fetal heart rate as a behav-ioral indicator.* Child Development Monographs, *3*(4).

Sorce, J., Emde, R. N., Campos, J. J., Klinnert, M. D. (2000). Maternal emotional signaling: Its effect on the visual cliff behavior of 1-year-olds. In D. Muir & A. Slater, (Eds.), *Infant development: The essential readings. Essential readings in developmental psychology* (pp. 282–292). Malden, MA: Blackwell.

South, S. J., Haynie, D. L., & Bose, S. (2007). Student mobility and school dropout. *Social Science Research, 36*(1), 68–94.

Spelke, E. S., & Owsley, C. (1979). Inter-modal exploration and knowledge in infancy. *Infant Behavior and Development, 2,* 13–27.

Spencer, M. B., Dornbusch, S. M., & Mont-Reynaud, R. (1990). Challenges in studying minority youth. In S. S. Feldman & G. R. Elliott (Eds.), *At the threshold: The developing adolescent.* Cambridge, MA: Harvard University Press.

Spencer, N. (2006). Explaining the social gradient in smoking in pregnancy: Early life course accumulation and cross-sectional clustering of social risk exposures in the 1958 British national cohort. *Social Science & Medicine, 62*(5), 1250–1259.

Speranza, M., et al. (2001). Obsessive compulsive disorders in eating disorders. *Eating Behaviors, 2*(3), 193–207.

Spieker, S., Nelson, D., DeKlyen, M., & Staerkel, F. (2005). Enhancing early attachments in the context of Early Head Start: Can programs emphasizing family support improve rates of secure infant–mother attachments in low-income families? In L. J. Berlin, Y. Ziv, L. Amaya-Jackson, & M. T. Greenberg (Eds.), *Enhancing early attachments: Theory, research, intervention, and policy. Duke series in child development and public policy* (pp. 250–275). New York: Guilford.

Spieker, S. J., et al. (2003). Joint influence of child care and infant attachment security for cognitive and language outcomes of low-income toddlers. *Infant Behavior and Development, 26*(3), 326–344.

Spitalnick, J. S., et al. (2007). Brief report: Sexual sensation seeking and its relationship to risky sexual behaviour among African-American adolescent females. *Journal of Adolescence, 30*(1), 165–173.

Spitz, R. A. (1965). *The first year of life: A psychoanalytic study of normal and deviant object relations.* New York: International Universities Press.

Spitzer, R. L., Gibbon, M., Skodol, A. E., Williams, J. B. W., & First, M. B. (2002). *DSM–IV–TR casebook.* Washington, D.C.: American Psychiatric Press.

Sroufe, L. A. (1979). Socioemotional development. In J. Osofsky (Ed.), *Handbook of infant development.* New York: Wiley.

Sroufe, L. A. (1998). Cited in S. Blakeslee (1998, August 4), Re-evaluating significance of baby's bond with mother, *New York Times*, pp. F1, F2.

Sroufe, L. A. (2005). Attachment and development: A prospective, longitudinal study from birth to adulthood. *Attachment & Human Development, 7*(4), 349–367.

Sroufe, L. A., Bennett, C., Englund, M., Urban, J., & Shulman, S. (1993). The significance of gender boundaries in pre-adolescence: Contemporary correlates and antecedents of boundary violation and maintenance. *Child Development, 64,* 455–466.

Sroufe, L. A., Waters, E., & Matas, L. (1974). Contextual determinants of infant affectional response. In M. Lewis & L. Rosenblum (Eds.), *The origins of fear.* New York: Wiley.

Staff, J., Mortimer, J. T., & Uggen, C. (2004). Work and leisure in adolescence. In Lerner, R. M., & Steinberg, L. (Eds.), *Handbook of adolescent psychology* (2nd ed.) (pp. 429–450). Hoboken, NJ: Wiley.

Stagnitti, K., Unsworth, C., & Rodger, S. (2000). Development of an assessment to identify play behaviours that discriminate between the play of typical preschoolers and preschoolers with pre-academic problems. *Canadian Journal of Occupational Therapy, 67*(5), 291–303.

Stahmer, A. C., Ingersoll, B., & Koegel, R. L. (2004). Inclusive programming for toddlers autism spectrum disorders: Outcomes from the Children's Toddler School. *Journal of Positive Behavior Interventions, 6*(2), 67–82.

Stams, G. J. M., Juffer, F., & IJzendoorn, M. H. van (2002). Maternal sensitivity, infant attachment, and temperament in early childhood predict adjustment in middle childhood: The case of adopted children and their biologically unrelated parents. *Developmental Psychology, 38*(5), 806–821.

Stanford, J. N., & McCabe, M. P. (2005). Sociocultural influences on adolescent boys' body image and body change strategies. *Body Image, 2*(2), 105–113.

Stankoff, B., et al. (2006). Imaging of CNS myelin by positron-emission tomography. *Proceedings of the National Academy of Sciences of the United States of America, 103*(24), 9304–9309.

Stanley, C., Murray, L., & Stein, A. (2004). The effect of postnatal depression on mother–infant interaction, infant response to the still-face perturbation, and performance on an instrumental learning task. *Development and Psychopathology, 16*(1), 1–18.

Stanwood, G. D., Washington, R. A., & Levitt, P. (2001). Identification of a sensitive period of prenatal cocaine exposure that alters the development of the anterior cingulate cortex. *Cerebral Cortex, 11*(5), 430–440.

Stauffacher, K., & DeHart, G. B. (2006). Crossing social contexts: Relational aggression between siblings and friends during early and middle childhood. *Journal of Applied Developmental Psychology, 27*(3), 228–240.

Steele, H. (2005). Editorial. *Attachment & Human Development, 7*(4), 345.

Steele, M., Hodges, J., Kaniuk, J., Hillman, S., & Henderson, K. (2003). Attachment representations and adoption: Associations between maternal states of mind and emotion narratives in previously maltreated children. *Journal of Child Psychotherapy, 29*(2), 187–205.

Steinberg, L. (1996). *Beyond the classroom: Why school reform has failed and what parents need to do.* New York: Simon & Schuster.

Steinberg, L., Brown, B. B., & Dornbusch, S. M. (1996). Ethnicity and adolescent achievement. *American Educator, 20*(2), 28–35.

Stemberger, J. P. (2004). Phonological priming and irregular past. *Journal of Memory and Language, 50*(1), 82–95.

Stephenson, R. H., & Banet-Weiser, S. (2007). Super-sized kids: Obesity, children, moral panic, and the media. In J. A. Bryant (Ed.), *The children's television community* (pp. 277–291). Mahwah, NJ Erlbaum.

Sternberg, R. J. (2000). In search of the zipperump-a-zoo. *Psychologist, 13*(5), 250–255.

Sternberg, R. J. (2006). The nature of creativity. *Creativity Research Journal, 18*(1), 87–98.

Sternberg, R. J. (2007). A systems model of leadership: WICS. *American Psychologist, 62*(1), 34–42.

Sternberg, R. J., Grigorenko, E. L., & Kidd, K. K. (2005). Intelligence, race, and genetics. *American Psychologist, 60*(1), 46–59.

Sternberg, R. J., & Lubart, T. I. (1995). *Defying the crowd: Cultivating creativity in a culture of conformity.* New York: Free Press.

Sternberg, R. J., & Lubart, T. I. (1996). Investing in creativity. *American Psychologist, 51,* 677–688.

Sternberg, R. J., & The Rainbow Project Collaborators. (2006). The Rainbow Project: Enhancing the SAT through assessments of analytical, practical, and creative skills. *Intelligence, 34*(4), 321–350.

Sternberg, R. J., & Williams, W. M. (1997). Does the Graduate Record Examination predict meaningful success in the graduate training of psychologists? *American Psychologist, 52,* 630–641.

Stevens, B., et al. (2005). Consistent management of repeated procedural pain with sucrose in preterm neonates: Is it effective and safe for repeated use over time? *Clinical Journal of Pain, 21*(6), 543–548.

Stevens, T., Olivárez, Jr., A., & Hamman, D. (2006). The role of cognition, motivation, and emotion in explaining the mathematics achievement gap between Hispanic and White students. *Hispanic Journal of Behavioral Sciences, 28*(2), 161–186.

Stevenson, H. W., Chen, C., & Lee, S. (1993). Mathematics achievement of Chinese, Japanese, and American children: Ten years later. *Science, 259,* 53–58.

Stevenson, J. (1992). Evidence for a genetic etiology in hyperactivity in children. *Behavior Genetics, 22,* 337–344.

Steward, D. K. (2001). Behavioral characteristics of infants with nonorganic failure to thrive during a play interaction. *American Journal of Maternal/Child Nursing, 26*(2), 79–85.

Stifter, C. A., & Wiggins, C. N. (2004). Assessment of disturbances in emotion Regulation and temperament. In R. DelCarmen-Wiggins & A. Carter (Eds.), *Handbook of infant, toddler, and preschool mental health assessment* (pp. 79–103). New York: Oxford University Press.

Stipek, D., & Hakuta, K. (2007). Strategies to ensure that no child starts from behind. In J. L. Aber et al. (Eds.), *Child development and social policy: Knowledge for action, APA Decade of Behavior volumes* (pp. 129–145). Washington, DC: American Psychological Association.

Stipek, D., Recchia, S., & McClintic, S. (1992). *Self-evaluation in young children.* Monographs of the Society for Research in Child Development, 57(1, ser. 226).

Stoel-Gammon, C. (2002). Intervocalic consonants in the speech of typically developing children: Emergence and early use. *Clinical Linguistics and Phonetics, 16*(3), 155–168.

Storch, E. A., et al. (2007). Peer victimization, psychosocial adjustment, and physical activity in overweight and at-risk-for-overweight youth. *Journal of Pediatric Psychology, 32*(1), 80–89.

Stores, G., & Wiggs, L. (Eds.). (2001). *Sleep disturbance in children and adolescents with disorders of development: Its significance and management.* New York: Cambridge University Press.

Straus, M. A. (1995). Cited in C. Collins (1995, May 11), Spanking is becoming the new don't, *New York Times,* p. C8.

Straus, M. A. (2000). Corporal punishment and primary prevention of physical abuse. *Child Abuse and Neglect, 24*(9), 1109–1114.

Straus, M. A., & Field, C. J. (2003). Psychological aggression by American parents: National data on prevalence, chronicity, and severity. *Journal of Marriage and Family, 65*(4), 795–808.

Straus, M. A., & Gelles, R. J. (1990). Societal change and change in family violence from 1975 to 1985 as revealed by two national surveys. In M. A. Straus & R. J. Gelles (Eds.), *Physical violence in American families.* New Brunswick, NJ: Transaction.

Straus, M. A., & Stewart, J. H. (1999). Corporal punishment by American parents: National data on prevalence, chronicity, severity, and duration, in relation to child and family characteristics. *Clinical Child and Family Psychology Review, 2*(2), 55–70.

Strayer, F. F. (1990). The social ecology of toddler play groups and the origins of gender discrimination. In F. F. Strayer (Ed.), *Social interaction and behavioral development during early childhood.* Montreal: La Maison D'Ethologie de Montreal.

Strayer, J., & Roberts, W. (2004). Children's anger, emotional expressiveness, and empathy: Relations with parents' empathy, emotional expressiveness, and parenting practices. *Social Development, 13*(2), 229–254.

Streri, A. (2002). Hand preference in 4-month-old infants: Global or local processing of objects in the haptic mode. *Current Psychology Letters: Behaviour, Brain and Cognition, 7,* 39–50.

Striegel-Moore, R. H., & Cachelin, F. M. (2001). Etiology of eating disorders in women. *Counseling Psychologist, 29*(5), 635–661.

Striegel-Moore, R. H., et al. (2003). Eating disorders in White and Black women. *American Journal of Psychiatry, 160*(7), 1326–1331.

Stright, A. D., Neitzel, C., Sears, K. G., & Hoke-Sinex, L. (2001). Instruction begins in the home: Relations between parental instruction and children's self-regulation in the classroom. *Journal of Educational Psychology, 93*(3), 456–466.

Strock, M. (2004). *Autism spectrum disorders (pervasive developmental disorders).* NIH Publication NIH-04–5511. Bethesda, MD: National Institute of Mental Health, National Institutes of Health, U.S. Department of Health and Human Services. Available at http://www.nimh.nih.gov/publicat/autism.cfm.

Strohner, H., & Nelson, K. E. (1974). The young child's development of sentence comprehension: Influence of event probability, nonverbal context, syntactic form, and strategies. *Child Development, 45,* 567–576.

Strough, J., Berg, C. A., & Meegan, S. P. (2001). Friendship and gender differences in task and social interpretations of peer collaborative problem solving. *Social Development, 10*(1), 1–22.

Strutt, G. F., Anderson, D. R., & Well, A. D. (1975). A developmental study of the effects of irrelevant information on speeded classification. *Journal of Experimental Child Psychology, 20,* 127–135.

Stunkard, A. J., Harris, J. R., Pedersen, N. I., & McClearn, G. E. (1990). The body-mass index of twins who have been reared apart. *New England Journal of Medicine, 322,* 1483–1487.

Sue, S., & Okazaki, S. (1990). Asian-American educational achievements. *American Psychologist, 45,* 913–920.

Suh, S., Suh, J., & Houston, I. (2007). Predictors of categorical at-risk high school drop-

outs. *Journal of Counseling & Development.. 85*(2), 196–203.

Suizzo, M-A. (2004). French and American mothers' childrearing beliefs: Stimulating, responding, and long-term goals. *Journal of Cross-Cultural Psychology, 35*(5), 606–626.

Sukhodolsky, D. G., Golub, A., Stone, E. C., & Orban, L. (2005). Dismantling anger control training for children: A randomized pilot study of social problem-solving versus social skills training components. *Behavior Therapy, 36,* 15–23.

Sullivan, B. A., & Hansen, J. C. (2004). Mapping associations between interests and personality: Toward a conceptual understanding of individual differences in vocational behavior. *Journal of Counseling Psychology, 51*(3), 287–298.

Sulloway, F. J. (2007). Birth order and intelligence. *Science, 316*(5832), 1711–1712.

Sullum, J. (2007, January 25). 10 million missing Chinese girls? *Reason online.* Available at http://www.reason.com/blog/show/118311.html.

Sumner, C. R., Schuh, K. J., Sutton, V. K., Lipetz, R., & Kelsey, D. K. (2006). Placebo-controlled study of the effects of atomoxetine on bladder control in children with nocturnal enuresis. *Journal of Child and Adolescent Psychopharmacology, 16*(6), 699–711

Sun, S. S., et al. (2005). Is sexual maturity occurring earlier among U.S. children? *Journal of Adolescent Health, 37*(5), 345–355.

Sun, Y. (2001). Family environment and adolescents' well-being before and after parents' marital disruption: A longitudinal analysis. *Journal of Marriage and Family, 63*(3), 697–713.

Suomi, S. J. (2005). Mother–infant attachment, peer relationships, and the development of social networks in rhesus monkeys. *Human Development, 48*(1–2), 67–79.

Suomi, S. J., Harlow, H. F., & McKinney, W. T. (1972). Monkey psychiatrists. *American Journal of Psychiatry, 128,* 927–932.

Supple, A. J., & Small, S. A. (2006). The influence of parental support, knowledge, and authoritative parenting on Hmong and European American adolescent development. *Journal of Family Issues, 27*(9), 1214–1232.

Suris, J-C., Jeannin, A., Chossis, I., & Michaud, P-A. (2007). Piercing among adolescents: Body art as risk marker—A population-based survey. *Journal of Family Practice, 56*(2), 126–130.

Susman, E. J., & Rogol, A. (2004). Puberty and psychological development. In R. M. Lerner & L. Steinberg (Eds.), *Handbook of adolescent psychology* (2nd ed.) (pp. 15–44). Hoboken, NJ: Wiley.

Sussman, S., Skara, S., & Ames, S. L. (2006). Substance abuse among adolescents. In T. G. Plante (Ed.), *Mental disorders of the new mil-

lennium: Public and social problems (Vol. 2)* (pp. 127–169). Westport, CT: Praeger Publishers/Greenwood.

Sutherland, K. S., Singh, N. N., Conroy, M., & Stichter, J. P. (2004). Learned helplessness and students with emotional or behavioral disorders: Deprivation in the classroom. *Behavioral Disorders, 29*(2), 169–181.

Sylva, K., et al. (2007). Curricular quality and day-to-day learning activities in pre-school. *International Journal of Early Years Education, 15*(1), 49–65.

Szaflarski, J. P., et al. (2006). A longitudinal functional magnetic resonance imaging study of language development in children 5 to 11 years old. *Annals of Neurology, 59*(5), 796–807.

Takahashi, K. (1990). Are the key assumptions of the "Strange Situation" procedure universal? A view from Japanese research. *Human Development, 33,* 23–30.

Takahashi, M., & Sugiyama, M. (2003). Improvement and prevention of misbehavior in a junior high school student: An analysis of behavioral contingency and change of stimulus function in a social setting. *Japanese Journal of Counseling Science, 36*(2), 165–174.

Tallandini, M. A., & Valentini, P. (1991). Symbolic prototypes in children's drawings of schools. *Journal of Genetic Psychology, 152,* 179–190.

Tamis-LeMonda, C. S., Bornstein, M. H., & Baumwell, L. (2001). Maternal responsiveness and children's achievement of language milestones. *Child Development, 72*(3), 748–767.

Tamis-LeMonda, C. S., Cristofaro, T. N., Rodriguez, E. T., & Bornstein, M. H. (2006). Early language development: Social influences in the first years of life. In L. Balter & C. S. Tamis-LeMonda (Eds.), *Child psychology: A handbook of contemporary issues* (2nd ed.) (pp. 79–108). New York: Psychology Press.

Tan, G. (1999). Perceptions of multiculturalism and intent to stay in school among Mexican American students. *Journal of Research and Development in Education, 33*(1), 1–14.

Tang, C. S., Yeung, D. Y., & Lee, A. M. (2003). Psychosocial correlates of emotional responses to menarche among Chinese adolescent girls. *Journal of Adolescent Health. 33*(3), 193–201.

Tanner, J. M. (1989). *Fetus into man: Physical growth from conception to maturity.* Cambridge, MA: Harvard University Press.

Tapper, K., & Boulton, M. J. (2004). Sex differences in levels of physical, verbal, and indirect aggression amongst primary school children and their associations with beliefs about aggression. *Aggressive Behavior, 30*(2), 123–145.

Tardif, T., et al. (2005). Preschoolers' understanding of knowing-that and knowing-how in the United States and Hong Kong. *Developmental Psychology, 41*(3), 562–573.

Tashiro, T., Frazier, P., & Berman, M. (2006). Stress-related growth following divorce and relationship dissolution. In M. A. Fine & J. H. Harvey (Eds.), *Handbook of divorce and relationship dissolution* (pp. 361–384). Mahwah, NJ: Erlbaum.

Tassi, F., Schneider, B. H., & Richard, J. F. (2001). Competitive behavior at school in relation to social competence and incompetence in middle childhood. *Revue Internationale de Psychologie Sociale, 14*(2), 165–184.

Taylor, B. (2006). Vaccines and the changing epidemiology of autism. *Child: Care, Health and Development, 32*(5), 511–519.

Taylor, C. (2007). To the editor: Day care and a child's behavior. *New York Times online.*

Taylor, H., & Leitman, R. (Eds.). (2003, April 29). Barriers to the diagnosis and treatment of attention deficit hyperactivity disorder (ADHD) among African American and Hispanic children: The Harris Poll. *Health Care News*, p. 2. Available at http://www.harrisinteractive.com/news/ newsletters/healthnews/HI_HealthCare News2003Vol3_Iss07.pdf.

Taylor, H. G., Minich, N. M., Klein, N., & Hack, M. (2004). Longitudinal outcomes of very low birth weight: Neuropsychological findings. *Journal of the International Neuropsychological Society, 10*(2), 149–163.

Taylor, M. (1999). *Imaginary companions and the children who create them.* London: Oxford University Press.

Taylor, M., & Hort, B. (1990). Can children be trained in making the distinction Tehrani, J. A., & Mednick, S. A. (2000). Genetic factors and criminal behavior. *Federal Probation, 64*(2), 24–27.

Tercyak, K. P., & Tyc, V. L. (2006). Opportunities and challenges in the prevention and control of cancer and other chronic diseases: Children's diet and nutrition and weight and physical activity. *Journal of Pediatric Psychology, 31*(8), 750–763.

Terry, D. (2000, July 16). *Getting under my skin.* Available at http://www.nytimes.com.

Thapar, A., Langley, K., Asherson, P., & Gill, M. (2007). Gene-Environment interplay in attention-deficit hyperactivity disorder and the importance of a developmental perspective. *British Journal of Psychiatry, 190*(1), 1–3.

Theim, K. R., et al. (2007). Children's descriptions of the foods consumed during loss of control eating episodes. *Eating Behaviors, 8*(2), 258–265.

Theimer, C. E., Killen, M., & Stangor, C. (2001). Young children's evaluations of exclusion in gender-stereotypic peer contexts. *Developmental Psychology, 37*(1), 18–27.

Thelen, E. (2000). Motor development as foundation and future of developmental psychology. *International Journal of Behavioral Development, 24*(4), 385–397.

Thierry, A. G. M., Huisman, E. B., Martin, E., & Nadal, D. (2005). Diffusion tensor imaging in progressive multifocal leukoencephalopathy: Early predictor for demyelination? *American Journal of Neuroradiology, 26*, 2153–2156

Thomas, A., & Chess, S. (1989). Temperament and personality. In G. A. Kohnstamm, J. E. Bates, & M. K. Rothbart (Eds.), *Temperament in childhood.* Chichester, England: Wiley.

Thomas, D. E., et al. (2006). The impact of classroom aggression on the development of aggressive behavior problems in children. *Development and Psychopathology, 18*(2), 471–487.

Thomas, J. R., & French, K. E. (1985). Gender differences across age in motor performance: A meta-analysis. *Psychological Bulletin, 98*, 260–282.

Thomas, S. P. (Ed.). (2006). From the editor—The phenomenon of cyberbullying. *Issues in Mental Health Nursing, 27*(10), 1015–1016.

Thompson, A. M., Baxter-Jones, A. D. G., Mirwald, R. L., & Bailey, D. A. (2003). Comparison of physical activity in male and female children: Does maturation matter? *Medicine and Science in Sports and Exercise. 35*(10), 1684–1690.

Thompson, B. L., Levitt, P., & Stanwood, G. D. (2005). Prenatal cocaine exposure specifically alters spontaneous alternation behavior. *Behavioural Brain Research, 164*(1), 107–116.

Thompson, M. P., Ho, C-H., & Kingree, J. B. (2007). Prospective associations between delinquency and suicidal behaviors in a nationally representative sample. *Journal of Adolescent Health, 40*(3), 232–237.

Thompson, O. M., et al. (2004). Food purchased away from home as a predictor of change in BMI *z*-score among girls. *International Journal of Obesity and Related Metabolic Disorders, 28*(2), 282–289.

Thompson, R. A. (2006). The development of the person: Social understanding, relationships, conscience, self. In N. Eisenberg, W. Damon, & R. M. Lerner (Eds.), *Handbook of child psychology* (6th ed.), Vol. 3, *Social, emotional, and personality development* (pp. 24–98). Hoboken, NJ: Wiley.

Thompson, R. A., Easterbrooks, M. A., & Padilla-Walker, L. M. (2003). Social and emotional development in infancy. In R. M. Lerner et al. (Eds.), *Handbook of psychology: Developmental psychology.* New York: Wiley.

Thompson, R. A., & Limber, S. P. (1990). "Social anxiety" in infancy: Stranger and separation reactions. In H. Leitenberg (Ed.), *Handbook of social and evaluation anxiety.* New York: Plenum.

Thompson, R. A., & Meyer, S. (2007). Socialization of emotion regulation in the family. In J. J. Gross (Ed.), *Handbook of emotion regulation* (pp. 249–268). New York: Guilford.

Thompson, V. J., et al. (2003). Influences on diet and physical activity among middle-class African-American 8- to 10-year old girls at risk of becoming obese. *Journal of Nutrition Education and Behavior, 35*(3), 115–123.

Thurstone, L. L. (1938). *Primary mental abilities.* Psychometric Monographs, 1.

Thyssen, S. (2003). Child culture, play, and child development. *Early Child Development and Care, 173*(6), 589–612.

Tiedemann, J. (2000). Parents' gender stereotypes and teachers' beliefs as predictors of children's concept of their mathematical ability in elementary school. *Journal of Educational Psychology, 92*(1), 144–151.

Tigner, R. B., & Tigner, S. S. (2000). Triarchic theories of intelligence: Aristotle and Sternberg. *History of Psychology, 3*(2), 168–176.

Tijms, J. (2007). The development of reading accuracy and reading rate during treatment of dyslexia. *Educational Psychology, 27*(2), 273–294.

Timmerman, L. M. (2006). Family care versus day care: Effects on children. In B. M. Gayle et al. (Eds.), *Classroom communication and instructional processes: Advances through meta-analysis* (pp. 245–260). Mahwah, NJ: Erlbaum.

Tobbell, J. (2003). Students' experiences of the transition from primary to secondary school. *Educational and Child Psychology, 20*(4), 4–14.

Torres, L., & Rollock, D. (2007). Acculturation and depression among Hispanics: The moderating effect of intercultural competence. *Cultural Diversity & Ethnic Minority Psychology, 13*(1), 10–17.

Towse, J. (2003). Lifespan development of human memory. *Quarterly Journal of Experimental Psychology: Human Experimental Psychology, 56A*(7), 1244–1246.

Towse, J., & Cowan, N. (2005). Working memory and its relevance for cognitive development. In W. Schneider, R. Schumann-Hengsteler, & B. Sodian (Eds.), *Young children's cognitive development: Interrelationships among executive functioning, working memory, verbal ability, and theory of mind* (pp. 9–37). Mahwah, NJ: Erlbaum.

Towse, J. N., Hitch, G. J., & Hutton, U. (2002). On the nature of the relationship between processing activity and item retention in children. *Journal of Experimental Child Psychology, 82*(2), 156–184.

Trainor, L. J., & Desjardins, R. N. (2002). Pitch characteristics of infant-directed speech affect infants' ability to discriminate vowels. *Psychonomic Bulletin & Review, 9*(2), 335–340.

Trehub, S. E., & Hannon, E. E. (2006). Infant music perception: Domain-general or domain-specific mechanisms? *Cognition, 100*(1), 73–99.

Trenholm, C., et al. (2007). *Impacts of four Title V, Section 510 abstinence education programs.*

Final report. Submitted to U.S.D.H.H.S., Office of the Assistant Secretary for Planning and Evaluation. Submitted by Mathematica Policy Research, Inc. Contract No.: HHS 100-98-0010. Available at http://www .mathematica-mpr.com/publications/PDFs/ impactabstinence.pdf.

Treuth, M. S., Butte, N. F., Adolph, A. L., & Puyau, M. R. (2004). A longitudinal study of fitness and activity in girls predisposed to obesity. *Medicine and Science in Sports and Exercise, 36*(2), 198–204.

Trevarthen, C. (2003). Conversations with a two-month-old. In J. Raphael-Leff (Ed.), *Parent–infant psychodynamics: Wild things, mirrors, and ghosts*. London: Whurr.

Triandis, H. C. (2005). Issues in individualism and collectivism research. In R. M. Sorrentino, D. Cohen, J. M. Olson, & M. P. Zanna (Eds.), *Cultural and social behavior: The Ontario Symposium,* Vol. 10 (pp. 207–225). Mahwah, NJ: Erlbaum.

Troxel, W. M., & Matthews, K. A. (2004). What are the costs of marital conflict and dissolution to children's physical health? *Clinical Child and Family Psychology Review, 7*(1), 29–57.

Tsui, J. M., & Maziocco, M. M. M. (2007). Effects of math anxiety and perfectionism on timed versus untimed math testing in mathematically gifted sixth graders. *Roeper Review, 29*(2), 132–139.

Tsuneishi, S., & Casaer, P. (2000). Effects of preterm extrauterine visual experience on the development of the human visual system: A flash VEP study. *Developmental Medicine and Child Neurology, 42*(10), 663–668.

Turkheimer, E. (1991). Individual and group differences in adoption studies of IQ. *Psychological Bulletin, 110,* 392–405.

Turner, C. M. (2006). Cognitive-behavioural theory and therapy for obsessive-compulsive disorder in children and adolescents: Current status and future directions. *Clinical Psychology Review, 26,* 912–938.

U.S. Bureau of the Census. (2004). *Statistical abstract of the United States* (124th ed.). Washington, DC: U.S. Government Printing Office.

U.S. Bureau of the Census. (2006). *Statistical abstract of the United States* (126th ed.). Washington, DC: U.S. Government Printing Office.

U.S. Bureau of the Census. (2007). *Statistical abstract of the United States* (127th ed.). Washington, DC: U.S. Government Printing Office.

U.S. Department of Health and Human Services. (2004). *Child abuse and neglect fatalities: Statistics and interventions-Child maltreatment 2002*. Available at http:// nccanch.acf.hhs. gov/pubs/factsheets/fatality.cfm.

U.S. Department of Labor, Bureau of Labor Statistics. (2004). *Teachers: Adult literacy and remedial and self-enrichment education.* Available at http://www.bls.gov/oco/ocos064 .htm.

Ullman, S. E. (2007). Relationship to perpetrator, disclosure, social reactions, and PTSD symptoms in child sexual abuse survivors. *Journal of Child Sexual Abuse, 16*(1), 19–36.

Ulloa, E. C., & Ulibarri, M. D. (2004). Man and wife in America: A history. *Archives of Sexual Behavior, 33*(3), 313–315.

Umaña-Taylor, A. J., Yazedjian, A., & Bámaca-Gómez, M. (2004). Developing the ethnic identity scale using Eriksonian and social identity perspectives. *Identity, 4*(1), 9–38.

Umek, L. M., Podlesek, A., & Fekonja, U. (2005). Assessing the home literacy environment: Relationships to child language comprehension and expression. *European Journal of Psychological Assessment, 21*(4), 271–281.

UNAIDS. (2006). *Report on the global AIDS epidemic: Executive summary.* Joint United Nations Programme on HIV/AIDS (UNAIDS). UNAIDS. 20 Avenue Appia. CH-1211. Geneva 27 Switzerland.

UNICEF. (2006). *The state of the world's children: 2007*. New York: United Nations.

United Nations Statistics Division. (2004, March). *UNESCO: World and Regional Trends,* Table 8. Available at http:// millenniumindicators.un.org/unsd/ mi/mi_worldregn.asp.

USDA. (2005). *Adequate nutrients within calorie needs. Dietary guidelines for Americans.* U.S. Department of Agriculture. Available at http://www.health.gov/dietaryguidelines/ dga2005/document/html/chapter2.htm.

Uylings, H. B. M. (2006). Development of the human cortex and the concept of "critical" or "sensitive" periods. *Language Learning, 56*(Suppl. 1), 59–90.

Valas, H. (2001). Learned helplessness and psychological adjustment: Effects of age, gender, and academic achievement. *Scandinavian Journal of Educational Research, 45*(1), 71–90.

Valderhaug, R., Götestam, K. G., & Larsson, B. (2004). Clinicians' views on management of obsessive-compulsive disorders in children and adolescents. *Nordic Journal of Psychiatry, 58*(2), 125–132.

Valentino, K., Cicchetti, D., Toth, S. L., & Rogosch, F. A. (2006). Mother–child play and emerging social behaviors among infants from maltreating families. *Developmental Psychology, 42*(3), 474–485.

Valkenburg, P. M., & Buijzen, M. (2005). Identifying determinants of young children's brand awareness: Television, parents, and peers. *Journal of Applied Developmental Psychology, 26*(4), 456–468.

van Rijn, S., Swaab, H., Aleman, A., & Kahn, R. S. (2006). X chromosomal effects on social cognitive processing and emotion regulation: A study with Klinefelter men (47,XXY). *Schizophrenia Research, 84*(2–3), 194–203.

Vander Ven, T., & Cullen, F. T. (2004). The impact of maternal employment on serious youth crime: Does the quality of working conditions matter? *Crime & Delinquency, 50*(2), 272–291.

Vander Ven, T. M., Cullen, F. T., Carrozza, M. A., & Wright, J. P. (2001). Home alone: The impact of maternal employment on delinquency. *Social Problems, 48*(2), 236–257.

Vartanian, L. R. (2001). Adolescents' reactions to hypothetical peer group conversations: Evidence for an imaginary audience. *Adolescence, 36*(142), 347–380.

Vartanian, O., Martindale, C., & Kwiatkowski, J. (2003). Creativity and inductive reasoning: The relationship between divergent thinking and performance on Wason's 2-4-6 task. *Quarterly Journal of Experimental Psychology: Human Experimental Psychology. 56A*(4), 641–655.

Vellutino, F. R., Fletcher, J. M., Snowling, M. J., & Scanlon, D. M. (2004). Specific reading disability (dyslexia): What have we learned in the past four decades? *Journal of Child Psychology and Psychiatry, 45*(1), 2–40.

Veríssimo, M., & Salvaterra, F. (2006). Maternal secure-base scripts and children's attachment security in an adopted sample. *Attachment & Human Development, 8*(3), 261–273.

Vermeiren, R., Bogaerts, J., Ruchkin, V., Deboutte, D., & Schwab-Stone, M. (2004). Subtypes of self-esteem and self-concept in adolescent violent and property offenders. *Journal of Child Psychology and Psychiatry, 45*(2), 405–411.

Vigil, J. M., Geary, D. C., & Byrd-Craven, J. (2005). A life history assessment of early childhood sexual abuse in women. *Developmental Psychology, 41*(3), 553–561.

Villani, S. (2001). Impact of media on children and adolescents: A 10-year review of the research. *Journal of the American Academy of Child and Adolescent Psychiatry, 40*(4), 392–401.

Virji-Babul, N., Kerns, K., Zhou, E., Kapur, A., & Shiffrar, M. (2006). Perceptual-motor deficits in children with Down syndrome: Implications for intervention. *Down Syndrome: Research & Practice, 10*(2), 74–82.

Visscher, W. A., Feder, M., Burns, A. M., Brady, T. M., & Bray, R. M. (2003). The impact of smoking and other substance use by urban women on the birthweight of their infants. *Substance Use and Misuse, 38*(8), 1063–1093.

Vitaro, F., Brendgen, M., & Barker, E. D. (2006). Subtypes of aggressive behaviors: A developmental perspective. *International Journal of Behavioral Development, 30*(1), 12–19.

Vitiello, B. (Ed.). (2006). Guest editorial: Selective serotonin reuptake inhibitors (SSRIs) in children and adolescents. *Journal of Child and Adolescent Psychopharmacology, 16*(1–2), 7–9.

Volkmar, F. R. (2001). Pharmacological interventions in autism: Theoretical and practical issues. *Journal of Clinical Child Psychology, 30*(1), 80–87.

Volkova, A., Trehub, S. E., & Schellenberg, E. G. (2006). Infants' memory for musical performances. *Developmental Science, 9*(6), 583–589.

Volling, B. L. (2001). Early attachment relationships as predictors of preschool children's emotion regulation with a distressed sibling. *Early Education and Development, 12*(2), 185–207.

Volling, B. L. (2003). Sibling relationships. In M. H. Bornstein et al. (Eds.), *Well-being: Positive development across the life course* (pp. 205–220). Mahwah, NJ: Erlbaum.

Volterra, M. C., Caselli, O., Capirci, E., & Pizzuto, E. (2004). Gesture and the emergence and development of language. In M. Tomasello & D. I. Slobin (Eds.), *Beyond nature–nurture.* Mahwah, NJ. Erlbaum.

von Gontard, A. (2006). Elimination disorders: Enuresis and encopresis. In C. Gillberg, R. Harrington, & H.-C.Steinhausen, (Eds.), *A clinician's handbook of child and adolescent psychiatry* (pp. 625–654). New York: Cambridge University Press.

von Gontard, A., Freitag, C. M., Seifen, S., Pukrop, R., & Röhling, D. (2006). Neuromotor development in nocturnal enuresis. *Developmental Medicine & Child Neurology, 48*(9), 744–750.

Vu, M. B., Murrie, D., Gonzalez, V., & Jobe, J. B. (2006). Listening to girls and boys talk about girls' physical activity behaviors. *Health Education & Behavior, 33*(1), 81–96.

Vukovic, R. K., & Siegel, L. S. (2006). The double-deficit hypothesis: A comprehensive analysis of the evidence. *Journal of Learning Disabilities, 39*(1), 25–47.

Vurpillot, E. (1968). The development of scanning strategies and their relation to visual differentiation. *Journal of Experimental Child Psychology, 6,* 632–650.

Vygotsky, L. (1978). *Mind in society: The development of higher psychological processes.* Cambridge, MA: Harvard University Press.

Vygotsky, L. S. (1962). *Thought and language.* Cambridge, MA: MIT Press.

Wachs, T. D. (2006). The nature, etiology, and consequences of individual differences in temperament. In L. Balter & C. S. Tamis-LeMonda (Eds.), *Child psychology: A handbook of contemporary issues* (2nd ed.) (pp. 27–52). New York: Psychology Press.

Wadden, T. A., & Stunkard, A. J. (Eds.). (2002). *Handbook of obesity treatment.* New York: Guilford.

Wade, T. D., Bulik, C. M., Neale, M., & Kendler, K. S. (2000). Anorexia nervosa and major depression: Shared genetic and environmental risk factors. *American Journal of Psychiatry, 157,* 469–471.

Wahler, R. G., Herring, M., & Edwards, M. (2001). Coregulation of balance between children's prosocial approaches and acts of compliance: A pathway to mother–child cooperation? *Journal of Clinical Child Psychology, 30*(4), 473–478.

Wainright, J. L., Russell, S. T., & Patterson, C. J. (2004). Psychosocial adjustment, school outcomes, and romantic relationships of adolescents with same-sex parents. *Child Development, 75*(6), 1886–1898.

Wakschlag, L. S., Pickett, K. E., Kasza, K. E., & Loeber, R. (2006). Is prenatal smoking associated with a developmental pattern of conduct problems in young boys? *Journal of the American Academy of Child & Adolescent Psychiatry, 45*(4), 461–467.

Wald, J., & Losen, D. J. (2007). Out of sight: The journey through the school-to-prison pipeline. In S. Books (Ed.), *Invisible children in the society and its schools* (3rd ed.) (pp. 23–37). Mahwah, NJ: Erlbaum.

Walitza, S., et al. 2006). Genetic and neuroimaging studies in attention deficit hyperactivity disorder. *Nervenheilkunde: Zeitschrift für interdisziplinaere Fortbildung, 25*(6), 421–429.

Walkup, J. T., et al. (2001). Fluvoxamine for the treatment of anxiety disorders in children and adolescents. *New England Journal of Medicine, 344*(17), 1279–1285.

Waller, M. R., & Swisher, R. (2006). Fathers' risk factors in fragile families: Implications for "healthy" relationships and father involvement. *Social Problems, 53*(3), 392–420.

Wallerstein, J., Lewis, J., Blakeslee, S., Hetherington, E. M., & Kelly, J. (2005). Issue 17: Is divorce always detrimental to children? In R. P. Halgin (Ed.), *Taking sides: Clashing views on controversial issues in abnormal psychology* (3rd ed.) (pp. 298–321). New York: McGraw-Hill.

Walsh, B. T., et al. (2006). Fluoxetine after weight restoration in anorexia nervosa: A randomized controlled trial. *Journal of the American Medical Association, 295*(22), 2605–2612.

Walter, J. L., & LaFreniere, P. J. (2000). A naturalistic study of affective expression, social competence, and sociometric status in preschoolers. *Early Education and Development, 11*(1), 109–122.

Walther, F. J., Ouden, A. L. den, & Verloove-Vanhorick, S. P. (2000). Looking back in time: Outcome of a national cohort of very preterm infants born in The Netherlands in 1983. *Early Human Development, 59*(3), 175–191.

Wang, L. (2005). Correlations between self-esteem and life satisfaction in elementary school students. *Chinese Mental Health Journal, 19*(11), 745–749.

Wang, Q., Leichtman, M. D., & White, S. H. (1998). Childhood memory and self-description in young Chinese adults: The impact of growing up an only child. *Cognition, 69*(1), 73–103.

Wang, S.-H., Baillargeon, R., & Paterson, S. (2005). Detecting continuity violations in infancy: A new account and new evidence from covering and tube events. *Cognition, 95*(2), 129–173.

Wang, X., Dow-Edwards, D., Anderson, V., Minkoff, H., & Hurd, Y. L. (2004). In utero marijuana exposure associated with abnormal amygdala dopamine d-sub-2 gene expression in the human fetus. *Biological Psychiatry, 56*(12), 909–915.

Ware, E. A., Uttal, D. H., Wetter, E. K., & DeLoache, J. S. (2006). Young children make scale errors when playing with dolls. *Developmental Science, 9*(1), 40–45.

Washburn, D. A. (Ed.). (2007). *Primate perspectives on behavior and cognition.* Washington, DC: American Psychological Association.

Wasserman, G. A., et al. (2000). Yugoslavia Prospective Lead Study: Contributions of prenatal and postnatal lead exposure to early intelligence. *Neurotoxicology and Teratology, 22*(6), 811–818.

Watson, J. B. (1924). *Behaviorism.* New York: Norton.

Waxman, S. R., & Lidz, J. L. (2006). Early word learning. In D. Kuhn, R. S. Siegler, W. Damon, & R. M. Lerner (Eds.), *Handbook of child psychology* (6th ed.), Vol. 2, *Cognition, perception, and language* (pp. 299–335). Hoboken, NJ: Wiley.

Waxmonsky, J. G. (2005). Nonstimulant therapies for attention-deficit hyperactivity disorder (ADHD) in children and adults. *Essential Psychopharmacology, 6*(5), 262–276.

Webb, P. (2007). Review of Juvenile delinquency: Prevention, assessment, and intervention. *Youth Violence and Juvenile Justice, 5*(2), 211–214.

Weber, R., Ritterfeld, U., & Mathiak, K. (2006). Does playing violent video games induce aggression? Empirical evidence of a functional magnetic resonance imaging study. *Media Psychology, 8*(1), 39–60.

Webster-Stratton, C., & Reid, M. J. (2007). Incredible Years. Parents and Teachers Training Series: A Head Start partnership to promote social competence and prevent conduct problems. In P. Tolan, J. Szapocznik, & W. Sambrano (Eds.), *Preventing youth substance abuse: Science-based programs for chil-*

dren and adolescents (pp. 67–88). Washington, DC: American Psychological Association.

Webster-Stratton, C., Reid, J., & Hammond, M. (2001b). Social skills and problem-solving training for children with early-onset conduct problems: Who benefits? *Journal of Child Psychology and Psychiatry and Allied Disciplines, 42*(7), 943–952.

Wechsler, D. (1975). Intelligence defined and undefined: A relativistic appraisal. *American Psychologist, 30,* 135–139.

Weckerly, J., Wulfeck, B., & Reilly, J. (2004). The development of morphosyntactic ability in atypical populations: The acquisition of tag questions in children with early focal lesions and children with specific-language impairment. *Brain and Language, 88*(2), 190–201.

Weems, C. F., Silverman, W. K., Saavedra, L. M., Pina, A. A., & Lumpkin, P. W. (1999). The discrimination of children's phobias using the Revised Fear Survey Schedule for Children. *Journal of Child Psychology and Psychiatry, 40*(6), 941–952.

Weichold, K., Silbereisen, R. K., & Schmitt-Rodermund, E. (2003). Short-term and long-term consequences of early versus late physical maturation in adolescents. In C. Hayward (Ed.), *Gender differences at puberty* (pp. 241–276). New York: Cambridge University Press.

Weinberg, R. A. (2004). The infant and the family in the twenty-first century. *Journal of the American Academy of Child and Adolescent Psychiatry, 43*(1), 115–116.

Weiner, T. S., & Adolph, K. E. (1993, March). *Toddler's perception of slant vs. slope height for descending slopes.* Paper presented at the meeting of the Society for Research in Child Development, New Orleans, LA.

Weisler, R. H., & Sussman, N. (2007). Treatment of attention-deficit/hyperactivity disorder. *Primary Psychiatry, 14*(1), 39–42.

Weller, E. B., & Weller, R. A. (1991). Mood disorders. In M. Lewis (Ed.), *Child and adolescent psychiatry: A comprehensive textbook.* Baltimore: Williams & Wilkins.

Wellman, H. M. (2002). Understanding the psychological world: Developing a theory of mind. In U. Goswami (Ed.), *Blackwell handbook of childhood cognitive development* (pp. 167–187). Malden, MA: Blackwell.

Wellman, H. M., Cross, D., & Bartsch, K. (1986). *Infant search and object permanence: A meta-analysis of the A-not-B error.* Monographs of the Society for Research in Child Development, 5(3, ser. 214).

Wellman, H. M., Fang, F., Liu, D., Zhu, L., & Liu, G. (2006). Scaling of theory-of-mind understandings in Chinese children. *Psychological Science, 17*(12), 1075–1081.

Welsh, B. C., & Farrington, D. P. (2007a). Saving children from a life of crime: Toward a national strategy for early prevention. *Victims & Offenders, 2*(1), 1–20.

Welsh, B. C., & Farrington, D. P. (Eds.). (2007b). Early prevention of delinquency and later criminal offending: An introduction. *Victims & Offenders, 2*(2), 105–107.

Wennergren, A.-C., & Rönnerman, K. (2006). The relation between tools used in action research and the zone of proximal development. *Educational Action Research, 14*(4), 547–568.

Wentworth, N., Benson, J. B., & Haith, M. M. (2000). The development of infants' reaches for stationary and moving targets. *Child Development, 71*(3), 576–601.

Wentzel, K. R., Barry, C. M., & Caldwell, K. A. (2004). Friendships in middle school: Influences on motivation and school adjustment. *Journal of Educational Psychology, 96*(2), 195–203.

Weppelman, T. L., Bostow, A., Schiffer, R., Elbert-Perez, E., & Newman, R. S. (2003). Children's use of the prosodic characteristics of infant-directed speech. *Language and Communication, 23*(1), 63–80.

Werker, J. F. (1989). Becoming a native listener. *American Scientist, 77,* 54–59.

Werker, J. F., & Desjardins, R. N. (2001). Listening to speech in the 1st year of life. In M. Tomasello & E. Bates (Eds.), *Language development: The essential readings.* Malden, MA: Blackwell.

Werker, J. F., et al. (2007). Infant-directed speech supports phonetic category learning in English and Japanese. *Cognition, 103*(1), 147–162.

Werker, J. F., & Tees, R. C. (2005). Speech perception as a window for understanding plasticity and commitment in language systems of the brain. *Developmental Psychobiology, 46*(3), 233–234.

Werner, E. E. (1988). A cross-cultural perspective on infancy. *Journal of Cross-Cultural Psychology, 19,* 96–113.

Werner, L. A., & Bernstein, I. L. (2001). Development of the auditory, gustatory, olfactory, and somatosensory systems. In E. B. Goldstein (Ed.), *Blackwell handbook of perception., Handbook of experimental psychology series* (pp. 669–708). Boston: Blackwell.

Whalen, C. K. (2001). ADHD treatment in the 21st Century: Pushing the envelope. *Journal of Clinical Child Psychology, 30*(1), 136–140.

Whitall, J. (1991). The developmental effect of concurrent cognitive and locomotor skills: Time-sharing from a dynamical perspective. *Journal of Experimental Child Psychology, 51,* 245–266.

White, C. B., Bushnell, N., & Regnemer, J. L. (1978). Moral development in Bahamian school children: A three-year examination of Kohlberg's stages of moral development. *Developmental Psychology, 14,* 58–65.

White, J. W., & Smith, P. H. (2004). Sexual assault perpetration and reperpetration: From adolescence to young adulthood. *Criminal Justice and Behavior, 31*(2), 182–202.

Whitehead, B. D., & Popenoe, D. (2006) *The state of our unions: The social health of marriage in America.* New Brunswick, NJ: Rutgers University. Available at http://marriage.rutgers.edu/Publications/Print/PrintSOOU2006.htm.

Whitehead, J. R., & Corbin, C. B. (1991). Effects of fitness test type, teacher, and gender on exercise intrinsic motivation and physical self-worth. *Journal of School Health, 61,* 11–16.

Whitehouse, E. M. (2006). Poverty. In G. G. Bear & K. M. Minke (Eds.), *Children's needs III: Development, prevention, and intervention* (pp. 835–845). Washington, DC: National Association of School Psychologists.

Whiting, B. B., & Edwards, C. P. (1988). *Children of different worlds.* Cambridge, MA: Harvard University Press.

Wilder, A. A., & Williams, J. P. (2001). Students with severe learning disabilities can learn higher order comprehension skills. *Journal of Educational Psychology, 93*(2), 268–278.

Williams, J. M., & Currie, C. (2000). Self-esteem and physical development in early adolescence: Pubertal timing and body image. *Journal of Early Adolescence, 20*(2), 129–149.

Williams, M. S. (2004). The psychology of eating. *Psychology and Health, 19*(4), 541–542.

Williams, R. L. (1974, May). Scientific racism and IQ: The silent mugging of the black community. *Psychology Today,* p. 32.

Wilson, E. O. (2004). *On Human Nature.* Cambridge, MA: Harvard University Press.

Wilson, P. (2004). A preliminary investigation of an early intervention program: Examining the intervention effectiveness of the Bracken Concept Development Program and the Bracken Basic Concept Scale–Revised with Head Start students. *Psychology in the Schools, 41*(3), 301–311.

Wingood, G. M., et al. (2006). Efficacy of an HIV prevention program among female adolescents experiencing gender-based violence. *American Journal of Public Health, 96*(6), 1085–1090.

Winner, E. (2000). The origins and ends of giftedness. *American Psychologist, 55,* 159–169.

Winzelberg, A. J., et al. (2000). Effectiveness of an Internet-based program for reducing risk factors for eating disorders. *Journal of Consulting and Clinical Psychology, 68,* 346–350.

Witherington, D. C., Campos, J. J., Anderson, D. I., Lejeune, L., & Seah, E. (2005). Avoidance of heights on the visual cliff in newly walking infants. *Infancy, 7*(3), 285–298.

Wocadlo, C., & Rieger, I. (2006). Educational and therapeutic resource dependency at early school-age in children who were born very preterm. *Early Human Development, 82*(1), 29–37.

Wodrich, D. L. (2006). Sex chromosome anomalies. In L. Phelps (Ed.), *Chronic health-related disorders in children: Collaborative medical and psychoeducational interventions* (pp. 253–270). Washington, DC: American Psychological Association.

Wojslawowicz Bowker, J. C., Rubin, K. H., Burgess, K. B., Booth-Laforce, C., & Rose-Krasnor, L. (2006). Behavioral characteristics associated with stable and fluid best friendship patterns in middle childhood. *Merrill-Palmer Quarterly, 52*(4), 671–693.

Wolchik, S. A., et al. (2000). An experimental evaluation of theory-based mother and mother–child programs for children of divorce. *Journal of Consulting and Clinical Psychology, 68*(5), 853–856.

Wolf, A., & Lozoff, B. (1989). Object attachment, thumbsucking, and the passage to sleep. *Journal of the American Academy of Child and Adolescent Psychiatry, 28,* 287–292.

Wolfenden, L. E., & Holt, N. L. (2005). Talent development in elite junior tennis: Perceptions of players, parents, and coaches. *Journal of Applied Sport Psychology, 17*(2), 108–126.

Wong, S. S., Ang, R. P., & Huan, V. S. (2007). Externalizing problems, internalizing problems, and suicidal ideation in Singaporean adolescents: Sex differences. *Current Psychology: Developmental, Learning, Personality, Social, 25*(4), 231–244.

Woods, S. C., & Seeley, R. J. (2002). Hunger and energy homeostasis. In H. Pashler & R. Gallistel (Eds.), *Steven's handbook of experimental psychology* (3rd ed.), Vol. 3, *Learning, motivation, and emotion* (pp. 633–668). Hoboken, NJ: Wiley.

Woolfolk, A. (2008). *Educational psychology, Active learning edition* (10th ed.). Boston: Allyn & Bacon.

Worell, J., & Goodheart, C. D. (Eds.), (2006). *Handbook of girls' and women's psychological health: Gender and well-being across the lifespan.* New York: Oxford University Press.

World Health Organization. (2003). *Training in the management of severe malnutrition.* Geneva: World Health Organization Department of Nutrition for Health and Development. Available at http://www .who.int/nut/ documents/manage_severe _malnutrition_ training_fly_eng.pdf.

World Health Organization. (2004, March 3). *Alleviating protein-energy malnutrition.* Available at http://www.who.int/nut/ pem.htm.

Wozniak, J. R., & Lim, K. O. (2006). Advances in white matter imaging: A review of in vivo magnetic resonance methodologies and their applicability to the study of development and aging. *Neuroscience & Biobehavioral Reviews, 30*(6), 762–774.

Wright, C., & Birks, E. (2000). Risk factors for failure to thrive: A population-based survey. *Child: Care, Health, and Development, 26*(1), 5–16.

Wright, D. W., & Young, R. (1998). The effects of family structure and maternal employment on the development of gender-related attitudes among men and women. *Journal of Family Issues, 19*(3), 300–314.

Wu, J., et al. (1999). Serotonin and learned helplessness: A regional study of 5-HTsub(1A), 5-HT-sub(2A) receptors and the serotonin transport site in rat brain. *Journal of Psychiatric Research, 33*(1), 17–22.

Wu, P., et al. (2001). Factors associated with use of mental health services for depression by children and adolescents. *Psychiatric Services, 52*(2), 189–195.

Wulff, K., & Siegmund, R. (2001). Circadian and ultradian time patterns in human behaviour. Part 1: Activity monitoring of families from prepartum to postpartum. *Biological Rhythm Research, 31*(5), 581–602.

Wynn, K. (1992, August 27). Addition and subtraction by human infants. *Nature, 358,* 749–750.

Wynn, K. (2002). Do infants have numerical expectations or just perceptual preferences?: Comment. *Developmental Science, 5*(2), 207–209.

Xie, H. L., Yan, B., Signe M., Hutchins, B. C., & Cairns, B. D. (2006). What makes a girl (or a boy) popular (or unpopular)? African American Children's perceptions and developmental differences. *Developmental Psychology, 42*(4), 599–612.

Yamada, H., et al. (2000). A milestone for normal development of the infantile brain detected by functional MRI. *Neurology, 55*(2), 218–223.

Yarrow, L. J., & Goodwin, M. S. (1973). The immediate impact of separation: Reactions of infants to a change in mother figures. In L. J. Stone, H. T. Smith, & L. B. Murphy (Eds.), *The competent infant: Research and commentary.* New York: Basic Books.

Yarrow, L. J., Goodwin, M. S., Manheimer, H., & Milowe, I. D. (1971, March). *Infant experiences and cognitive and personality development at ten years.* Paper presented at the meeting of the American Orthopsychiatric Association, Washington, DC.

Yokota, F., & Thompson, K. M. (2000). Violence in G-rated animated films. *Journal of the American Medical Association, 283,* 2716–2720.

Young, D. (2006). Review of Breastfeeding handbook for physicians. *Birth: Issues in Perinatal Care, 33*(3), 260–261.

Youniss, J., & Haynie, D. L. (1992). Friendship in adolescence. *Developmental and Behavioral Pediatrics, 13,* 59–66.

Zajonc, R. B. (2001). The family dynamics of intellectual development. *American Psychologist, 56*(6/7), 490–496.

Zajonc, R. B., & Mullally, P. R. (1997). Birth order: Reconciling conflicting effects. *American Psychologist, 52*(7), 685–699.

Zan, B., & Hildebrandt, C. (2003). First graders' interpersonal understanding during cooperative and competitive games. *Early Education and Development, 14*(4), 397–410.

Zarbatany, L., Conley, R., & Pepper, S. (2004). Personality and gender differences in friendship needs and experiences in preadolescence and young adulthood. *International Journal of Behavioral Development, 28*(4), 299–310.

Zarbatany, L., McDougall, P., & Hymel, S. (2000). Gender-differentiated experience in the peer culture: Links to intimacy in preadolescence. *Social Development, 9*(1), 62–79.

Zeifman, D. M. (2004). Acoustic features of infant crying related to intended caregiving intervention. *Infant and Child Development, 13*(2), 111–122.

Zelazo, P. R. (1998). McGraw and the development of unaided walking. *Developmental Review, 18*(4), 449–471.

Zheng, S., & Colombo, J. (1989). Sibling configuration and gender differences in preschool social participation. *Journal of Genetic Psychology, 150,* 45–50.

Zhou, Z., Bray, M. A., Kehle, T. J., & Xin, T. (2001). Similarity of deleterious effects of divorce on Chinese and American children. *School Psychology International, 22*(3), 357–363.

Zhu, W. X. (2003). The one child family policy. *Archives of Disease in Childhood, 88,* 463–464.

Zigler, E., Abelson, W. D., Trickett, P. K., & Seitz, V. (1982). Is an intervention program necessary in order to improve economically disadvantaged children's IQ scores? *Child Development, 53,* 340–348.

Zigler, E., & Styfco, S. J. (2001). Extended childhood intervention prepares children for school and beyond. *Journal of the American Medical Association, 285*(18), 2378–2380.

Zimmerman, A. W., Connors, S. L., & Pardo-Villamizar, C. A. (2006). Neuroimmunology and neurotransmitters in autism. In R. Tuchman & I. Rapin (Eds.), *Autism: A neurological disorder of early brain development* (pp. 141–159). *International Review of Child Neurology.* London: Mac Keith Press.

Zimmerman, B. J. (2000). Self-efficacy: An essential motive to learn. *Contemporary Educational Psychology, 25*(1), 82–91.

Zimmermann, P., Maier, M. A., Winter, M., & Grossmann, K. E. (2001). Attachment and adolescents' emotion regulation during a joint problem-solving task with a friend. *International Journal of Behavioral Development, 25*(4), 331–343.

Ziv, M., & Frye, D. (2003). The relation between desire and false belief in children's theory of mind: No satisfaction? *Developmental Psychology, 39*(5), 859–876.

Zonnevylle-Bender, M. J. S., Matthys, W., Van De Wiel, N. M. H., & Lochman, J. E. (2007). Preventive effects of treatment of disruptive behavior disorder in middle childhood on substance use and delinquent behavior. *Journal of the American Academy of Child & Adolescent Psychiatry,*

Zweigenhaft, R. L., & Von Ammon, J. (2000). Birth order and civil disobedience: A test of Sulloway's "born to rebel" hypothesis. *Journal of Social Psychology, 140*(5), 624–627.

Name Index

Aalsma, M. C., 523
Abbey, A., 492
Abdelaziz, Y. E., 378, 379, 380
Abe-Kim, J., 338
Abelev, M., 314
Aber, J. L., 459, 571
Ablon, J., 386
Aboud, F., 466
Abravanel, E., 199
Adams, G. R., 549
Adamsons, K., 451
Adler-Baeder, F., 453
Adolph, K. E., 88, 168, 170, 173–74
Agnoli, F., 526
Aguiar, A., 192, 194
Ahnert, L., 244
Ainsworth, F., 236
Ainsworth, M., 222, 226, 227, 228–29, 236
Akman, Y., 549
Alabali, M. W., 20
Alexander, G. M., 365
Alexander, G. R., 169
Alexander, K. W., 317
Alfirevic, Z., 59
Alibali, M. W., 188, 195, 198, 399, 409, 411, 432, 522
Alipuria, L. L., 550, 551
Allen, M., 557
Allen, M. C., 169
Alloway, T. P., 408
Als, H., 127
Alsaker, F. D., 460
Amato, P. R., 450, 451
American Academy of Family Physicians, 276, 277
American Academy of Pediatrics, 158, 159
American Association of University Women, 463
American Association on Intellectual and Developmental Disabilities, 424
American Fertility Association, 53, 66
American Heart Association, 374, 376
American Lung Association, 504–5
American Psychiatric Association, 127, 128, 287, 384, 385, 464, 466, 469, 503
America's Children, 564, 565
Aminabhavi, V. A., 455
Ammaniti, M., 225, 226
Ances, B. M., 98
Anderman, E. M., 447

Anderson, C. A., 353, 354, 512
Anderson, K. G., 443
Andreou, G., 274
Angier, N., 65
Annett, M., 274
Anthis, K., 551, 552
Anzengruber, D., 504
Appel, P. W., 492
Arbona, C., 538
Arbuthnot, J., 530
Archer, J., 22, 350, 364
Archibald, L. M. D., 408
Arduini, R. G., 388
Arija, V., 157
Arnett, J., 575, 576, 577
Arnon, S., 126
Arredondo, P., 25
Arriaga, P., 353
Arterberry, M. E., 135, 136, 137
Aschermann, E., 431
Ash, D., 25
Asher, S. R., 457
Aslin, R. N., 163
Aspy, C. B., 563
Assefi, N. P., 568
August, D., 211
Ayyash-Abdo, H., 338
Azar, B., 178

Bacete, F. G., 535
Bachman, J. G., 539, 540
Bagley, C., 560
Bahna, S. L., 384
Bailey, J. M., 526
Bailey, R. K., 385
Baillargeon, R., 192, 194
Bakalar, N., 120
Baker, C. W., 375
Baker, R. C., 471
Bakker, D. J., 388
Baldry, A. C., 460
Ball, H. L., 285, 533
Balluz, L. S., 94
Bandura, A., 17, 32, 346, 351, 352, 357, 362, 443, 538
Banet-Weiser, S., 375
Barbarich, N. C., 502
Barchard, K. A., 417
Barkley, R. A., 386
Baron, S. W., 570, 571
Barr, R. G., 142
Barrett, M., 447
Barrile, M., 175

Barrow, F. H., 472
Barry, C. M., 456
Bartels, M., 472
Barth, J., 192, 196
Bartholow, B. D., 504
Bartzokis, G., 163
Basic Behavioral Science Task Force, 427
Bastien-Toniazzo, M., 432
Batsche, G. M., 460
Bauer, K. W., 375
Bauer, P. J., 316
Baum, S. R., 268
Bauman, M. L., 242
Baumeister, R. F., 560
Baumrind, D., 332, 334, 335, 446
Bavin, E. L., 212
Bayley, N., 200
Bayoumi, R. A., 289
Bearce, K. H., 198
Beauchamp, G. K., 177
Beck, E., 340, 456
Beck, R., 306
Beer, J. M., 340
Beidel, D .C., 469
Beilei, L., 379
Bell, D., 547, 549
Bell, J. H., 523
Bell, K. N., 463
Bellodi, L., 502
Belmonte, M. K., 62
Belsky, J., 222, 223, 224, 225, 244, 245, 246, 454
Bem, S. L., 366
Benbow, C. P., 274, 275, 430
Bender, H. L., 332, 333
Bendersky, M., 354
Bennett, S. E., 568
Benoit, D., 157
Bensaheb, A., 468
Berg, C. J., 104
Berger, L. E., 523
Berger, S. E., 88, 168, 170, 173
Berko, J., 323
Bernal, G., 573
Berndt, T. J., 457, 555, 556, 558
Bernstein, G. A., 470
Bernstein, I. L., 137, 138
Bernstein, I. M., 101
Berry, J. W., 338
Bertenthal, B. I., 173
Berzonsky, M. D., 547, 549, 552
Betz, N. E., 537
Bhutta, A. T., 94

Bialystok, E., 314, 435
Biederman, J., 384
Bigler, R. S., 355
Birch, C. D., 504
Birch, L., 178
Bird, A., 256
Birks, E., 157
Bishop, D. M., 568, 569
Bishop, D. V. M., 389
Bjerkedal, T., 340
Bjorklund, D. F., 406
Black, D. W., 465
Blake, S. M., 568
Blanchette, N., 164
Blass, E. M., 138
Blevins-Knabe, B., 399
Bloch, M., 128
Blom-Hoffman, J., 376
Bloom, B., 214, 496
Bloom, L., 203
Bloom, P., 320, 321
Blyth, D. A., 533, 558, 559
Boada, R., 389
Boccia, M., 251
Boden, C., 388
Boehnke, K., 531
Boey, C. C. M., 452
Boggiano, A. K., 447
Bohannon, J. N., III, 211
Bohn, A. P., 433
Bohon, C., 536
Boivin, M., 456
Boman, U. W., 56
Bond, M. J., 501
Bonkowski, S., 452
Bonn-Miller, M. O., 505
Boom, J., 530, 531
Booth, A., 350
Booth-LaForce, C., 355
Bosi, M. L., 485
Boskind-White, M., 500
Bost, L. W., 536
Bouchard, C., 373
Bouchard, T. J., Jr., 62, 63, 428, 523, 524
Bouffard, T., 553
Bouldin, P., 340
Boulton, M. J., 349, 350
Bourgeois, M. J., 13
Bower, T., 174
Bowlby, J., 222, 227, 228–29
Boyle, J. M. E., 461
Bradley, R. H., 306, 307, 429
Bramlett, M. D., 342
Branco, J. c., 302
Brändstatter, H., 540
Brandtjen, H., 244
Brase, G. L., 360

Braza, F., 340
Brazier, A., 57
Breastfeeding, 161
Bremner, A., 193
Brenneman, M. H., 434
Bretherton, I., 251
Bridges, K., 248
Briones, T. L., 166
Brody, J. E., 137, 453
Brodzinsky, D. M., 450
Bromnick, R. D., 523
Bronfenbrenner, U., 22, 23, 24, 32
Bronson, G. W., 172, 173
Brooks, R. B., 447
Brown, B. B., 558, 559
Brown, R., 208, 209, 211
Brownell, C. A., 253
Browning, J. R., 563
Bruck, M., 412, 432
Brunner, R., 502
Bruno, R., 434
Bryan, C., 53
Bryant, P., 193, 314
Bryden, P. J., 274
Buchanan, A., 554
Buckley, K. E., 353
Buda, B., 574
Budney, A. J., 505
Budworth, M.-H., 340
Bugental, D. B., 126, 236
Buhrmester, D., 555
Buijzen, M., 316
Bukowski, W. M., 347, 556
Bunikowski, R., 98
Bunting, L., 566
Buriel, R., 337
Burke, J. M., 471
Bushman, B. J., 352
Bushnell, E. W., 178
Bushnell, I. W. R., 172
Buss, D., 350, 359, 360
Bussey, K., 346, 362
Buston, K., 564
Butterfield, S. A., 378, 380
Butterworth, G., 167
Buxhoeveden, D. P., 100
Bynum, M. S., 563

Cabeza, R., 268
Caesar, P., 166
Cairns, B. D., 351
Cairns, R. B., 351
Caldwell, B. M., 306
Call, J., 192, 196
Callan, M. J., 402
Calvert, S. L., 309
Calvete, E., 570

Camarena, P. M., 558, 559
Camp, C. A., 138
Campanella, J., 198
Campbell, A., 100, 253, 257, 346
Campbell, D. A., 119
Campbell, D. W., 270, 272
Campbell, S. B., 332, 339, 358, 364, 365
Campos, J., 173, 251
Candy, T. R., 135
Canitano, R., 242
Canton, D. A., 342
Caplan, M., 349
Caplan, P. J., 272, 347
Capron, C., 484
Caravolas, M., 432
Cardoret, R. J., 465
Carey, B., 244, 245, 340
Carlo, G., 348
Caron, A. J., 175
Carper, R. A., 62
Carriger, M. S., 253
Carroll, J. S., 576
Carver, L., 251
Casas, J. F., 336
Cashwell, T. H., 457
Cassia, V. M., 172
Castellanos, F. X., 287
Caton, D., 118
Cattell, R., 422
Caulfield, R., 127
Cavalier, L., 319
Cavallini, A., 171
Cavell, T. A., 465
Ceci, S. J., 412, 526
Centers for Disease Control and Prevention, 95, 96, 98, 342, 490, 491, 496, 497, 503, 504
Cernoch, J., 138, 198
Chan, A. C. M., 572, 573
Chance, S. E., 350
Chang, L., 354
Chapman, M., 399
Chase-Lansdale, P. L., 567
Chaudhry, V., 98
Chavira, P., 551
Chelonis, J. J., 100
Chen, X., 445, 456
Chen, Z., 409
Cheng, S.-T., 572, 573
Cherney, I. D., 358
Chess, S., 254, 256
Cheung, C., 529
Chiou, W.-B., 557
Chira, S., 459
Chong, S. C. F., 314
Chou, T.-L., 267
Christenson, S. L., 536

Christian, P., 94
Christophersen, E. R., 284, 286
Chronis, A. M., 465
Cicchetti, D., 224, 235
Ciro, D., 560
Clancy, B., 213, 214, 215
Clark, E., 208
Clark, J., 337
Clark, K. E., 349
Clark, R., 324
Clark, S. E., 355
Clarke-Stewart, K. A., 306, 412, 452
Clayton, R., 131
Cleary, D. J., 457
Cnattingius, S., 101, 102
Cohen, D., 128, 314
Cohen, E., 120
Cohen-Bendahan, C. C. C., 350, 361
Coiro, M. J., 453
Colby, A., 529
Cole, C., 310, 466
Coleman, P. K., 224, 453
Coley, J. D., 211, 567
Collaer, M. L., 525
Collins, L. M., 488
Collins, W. A., 360, 442, 448, 554, 555
Colom, R., 414
Colombo, J., 201, 345
Colwell, M. J., 271
Commission on Adolescent Substance
    and Alcohol Abuse, 509
Commons, M. L., 529, 530
Condon, J., 566
Conner, K. R., 573
Connolly, J., 557, 558
Connor, J. R., 163, 342
Connor, M. E., 100
Constantine, M. G., 27
Constantino, J. N., 241, 242
Cooke, 277
Coolbear, J., 157
Coolidge, F. L., 460
Coon, H., 429
Cooper, C. E., 472
Cooper, J., 572–73
Coovadia, H., 96, 97, 120
Copeland, A. L., 504
Coplan, R. J., 346
Corballis, P. M., 268
Corbett, S. S., 157
Corbin, C. B., 380
Coren, S., 275
Cornoldi, C., 413
Cornwell, A. A. C., 140
Corsaro, W. A., 456
Corstorphine, E., 501
Corwyn, R. F., 306, 307

Costello, E. J., 487, 503, 509, 511
Costigan, C. L., 553, 554, 555
Costos, D., 486
Cotton, S., 285
Courage, M. L., 201
Cowan, C. P., 449
Cowan, N., 409, 410, 411
Cowan, P. A., 449
Craik, F. I. M., 435
Crain, W. C., 19, 299, 325, 356, 399,
    443, 547
Cratty, B., 380
Crawford, J. K., 489
Crawford, M. J., 574
Creed, P. A., 537
Crittenden, P. M., 236
Crocco, M. S., 463
Crockenberg, S. C., 130
Crockett, L. J., 560
Crombie, G., 346, 347
Crook, C. K., 138
Crosby, R. A., 131
Crosnoe, R., 472
Crowther, C., 125
Cruz, N. V., 384
Cryan, J. F., 467
Csikszentmihalyi, M., 62, 558
Cuellar, J., 573
Culebras, A., 157
Cullen, F. T., 454
Cumming, S. P., 380
Cunningham, R. L., 350
Currie, C., 488
Curry, T. R., 573
Cystic Fibrosis Foundation, 57

Dai, D. Y., 446
Dailard, C., 492
Daly, M., 453
Daman-Wasserman, M., 198
Damon, W., 445, 552
Dandy, J., 426, 427
Dane, S., 275
Dang-Vu, T. T., 142
Daniels, S. R., 374, 375
Darcy, M. U. A., 538
D'Augelli, A. R., 560
Davies, P. T., 472
Davis, A., 104
Davis, H. A., 442
Davis, L., 126
Davis, S. R., 22
Dawson, T. L., 530, 531
Day, N. L., 99
De Boysson-Bardies, B., 203
De Haan, M., 172
De Lisi, R., 444

De Oliveira, F. P., 103, 485
De Thomas, C., 384
De Villiers, J. G., 206
De Villiers, P. A., 206
De Vries, J. I. P., 89
Deary, I. J., 423
DeCasper, A., 87, 137, 139, 198
DeCherney, A. H., 66
Dehaene-Lambertz, G., 137, 214
DeHart, G. B., 351, 446
Delaney-Black, V., 99
Delgado, A. R., 524, 525
DeLoache, J. S., 315, 318
Delpit, L., 433
DeMarie, D., 319
Dennis, M., 169
Dennis, W., 169, 170
Denton, K., 402, 403, 532
Deonna, T., 242
Derman, O., 483
Dervic, K., 573
Desjardins, M. J., 346, 347
Desjardins, R. N., 212, 213
Dessens, A. B., 562
Detterman, D. K., 422
DeYong, N. G., 199
Dezoete, J. A., 201
Diamond, L., 560, 561
Dieterich, S. E., 126
DiIorio, C., 563
DiLalla, D. L., 63
Dill, K. E., 354
Dindia, K., 557
Ding, Q. J., 70
Dishion, T. J., 341, 564
Dobbinson, S., 241
Dockett, S., 432
Dogil, G., 214
Dollfus, S., 274
Dombrowski, M. A. S., 127
Donaldson, M., 302
Donohue, B. C., 511
Donohue, K. F., 504
Donovan, D. M., 534
Doré, F. Y., 192
Dorius, C. J., 511
Dorling, J., 123
Downey, D. B., 340, 341
Downey, J. I., 562
Drabick, D. A. G., 465
Drasgow, E., 243
Dray, A. J., 443, 444, 449
Drewett, R. F., 157
Dryden, W., 467
Du Rocher Schudlich, T. D., 341
Duarté-Vélez, Y. M., 573
DuBois, D. L., 466, 556

Dubow, E., 307
Duggan, A., 238
Dunn, J., 297, 456
Dunn, M. G., 511
Duntley, J. D., 350, 359
Durkin, S. J., 553
Dweck, C., 526
Dyer, S., 345
Dykman, R. A., 157

East, C. E., 120
Eaton, W. O., 270, 272
Eberhardy, F., 241
Eccles, J. S., 258, 526, 527, 559
Eckenrode, J., 235
Eckerman, C. O., 126
Ecuyer-Dab, I., 524
Eddy, J. M., 351
Eder, R. A., 355
Edler, C., 501
Edwards, C. P., 271, 349
Edwards, V. J., 234
Egeland, B., 225, 236
Egerton, A., 505
Eigenmann, P. A., 384
Eimas, P. D., 176
Eisen, M., 445
Eisenberg, M. E., 489, 531
Eisenberg, N., 530
Eisner, E. W., 273
Ekvall, S. W., 372
El-Sheikh, M., 453
Elias, M. J., 533
Elkind, D., 205, 344, 523
Ellis, A., 467
Ellis, B., 340
Else-Quest, N. M., 346
Elshout, J. J., 25
Eltzschig, H., 118
Emde, R. N., 227
Emler, N., 529
Epstein, J. N., 385
Erikson, E., 11, 226, 356, 547, 551
Eron, L. D., 349, 351, 354
Ertem, I. O., 236
Erzurumluoglu, A., 275
Essau, C. A., 469
Evans, M. M., 571
Evans, S. W., 386

Fabricius, W. V., 319
Fagen, J. W., 198
Fagot, B. I., 258, 347, 358
Fantz, R., 135, 172
Faraone, S. V., 384
Farmer, A., 48
Farrington, D. P., 571

Farthofer, A., 540
Fasold, R. W., 433
Feig, C., 120
Feigenbaum, P., 140
Feijó, L., 126
Feinberg, M. E., 333, 445
Feiring, C., 457, 555, 558
Feldman, R., 296
Fenzel, L. M., 446
Ferdinand, R. F., 469
Fergusson, A., 389
Fernandez, T., 388
Fernandez-Twinn, D. S., 93
Féron, J., 178
Festini, F., 70
Fetrick, A., 159
Ficca, G., 140, 141
Field, A. P., 126, 143, 356
Field, C. J., 233
Fifer, W., 87, 139, 198
Findling, R. L., 573
Finegan, J. K., 524
Finkelhor, D., 234
Finlay, B., 213, 214, 215
Fiorello, C. A., 387
Fisch, S. M., 309, 310
Fiset, S., 192
Fishman, H. C., 502
Fitzgerald, D. P., 444
Fitzgerald, H. E., 274
Fivush, R., 316, 317, 318
Flavell, J. H., 20, 188, 313, 314, 401, 410, 411, 518, 522, 523
Flom, R., 257
Florsheim, P., 557, 558
Flouri, E., 554
Floyd, R. L., 100
Flynn, E., 314
Flynn, M., 533
Focus on Fertility, 67
Foley, G. M., 253
Fontaine, A.-M., 341
Food and Drug Administration, 96
Forbush, K., 500
Forman-Hoffman, V. L., 500
Fortier, J. C., 339
Foster-Clark, F. S., 558, 559
Fouad, N. A., 25
Franklin, A., 137
Freedenthal, S., 573
Freeman, M. S., 137
French, D. C., 338
French, K. E., 380
Frerichs, L., 158
Freud, A., 478
Freud, S., 478
Frey, M. C., 422

Fried, P. A., 99
Friedman, R. C., 562
Frisch, R., 485
Frith, U., 388
Frodi, A. M., 236
Fromkin, V., 215
Frostad, P., 389
Fry, D. P., 271
Frye, D., 314
Fu, J. H., 27
Fuligni, A. J., 559
Funk, J. B., 354
Furman, W., 231, 555
Furstenberg, F. F., 453
Fuster, J. M., 413

Gabriel, M., 100
Galand, P., 549
Ganesh, M. P., 231
Gao, F., 197
Garcia, J., 207
Garcia, P., 178
Garcia-Coll, C. T., 169
Gardner, H., 414, 415, 416
Garlow, S. J., 573
Garnefski, N., 467
Garvey, C., 347
Gathercole, S. E., 408, 409, 410
Gau, S. S. F., 511
Gavin, N. I., 128
Ge, X., 487, 488
Geake, J., 25
Geary, D. C., 22, 359, 380
Gelernter, J., 511
Geller, P. A., 80
Gelman, S. A., 304
Georgiades, S., 241
Geschwind, D. H., 275
Gesell, A., 8, 169
Getzels, J. W., 427
Gevers Deynoot-Schaub, M. J., 341
Ghetti, S., 317
Giaschi, D., 388
Gibb, R., 268
Gibson, E., 173, 179
Gilligan, C., 531
Gillooly, J. B., 486
Giussani, D. A., 93
Glasberg, R., 466
Gleason, T. R., 297, 341, 343, 457
Gobet, F., 410
Goel, P., 102
Gogate, L. J., 212
Golan, H., 122
Goldberg, J., 115
Goldschmidt, L., 99
Goldsmith, H. H., 254

Goldstein, E. B., 482
Goldstein, S., 447, 524
Goldston, D. B., 573
Goleman, D., 417
Golub, S., 485
Gonzalez, V., 434, 435, 555
Good, C., 429
Goodheart, C. D., 258
Goodman, G. S., 318, 412
Goodwin, M. S., 232
Gooren, L., 562
Goossens, L., 375
Gopnik, A., 314, 324
Gordon, D. A., 530
Gordon, J., 357
Gormally, S., 142
Gort, M., 435
Gottfried, G. M., 299
Gottlieb, B. H., 576
Gowers, S. G., 53
Graber, J. A., 487, 488
Graffy, J., 159
Granot, D., 224
Grayson, A., 143
Greco, C., 198
Greeff, A. P., 452, 472
Green, R., 450
Greenberg, J., 529
Greene, R. W., 35, 386
Greenough, W. T., 166, 180
Griffin, K. W., 472
Grigorenko. E. L., 388, 472
Grilo, C. M., 502
Grindrod, C. M., 268
Groen, M., 172
Grolnick, W. S., 252
Grön, G., 360
Grossmann, K., 225
Grusec, J. E., 333, 334, 335, 336, 341, 348
Grych, J. H., 452
Guerdjikova, A. I., 375
Guerin, D. W., 255
Guerrero, M. C. M., 25
Guerrini, I., 93, 100, 166
Güntürkün, O., 165
Gushue, G. V., 538
Gutknecht, L., 242
Guttmacher Institute, 449, 562
Guzikowski, W., 119

Haapasalo, J., 235
Haden, C. A., 306
Haeffel, G. J., 472
Haenggeli, C. A., 384
Hagan, B. I., 347
Hagan, R., 347

Hains, S. M. J., 172
Haith, M. M., 136, 167, 171, 173, 179
Hakstian, A. R., 417
Hakuta, K., 308, 309
Hala, S., 314
Halgin, R. P., 464
Hall, G. S., 478
Halle, P. A., 203
Halliday, L. F., 389
Halpern, D. F., 524, 525, 526, 527, 557
Hamm, J. V., 442, 457, 556
Hammen, C., 452
Hammond, N. R., 316, 318
Hampson, E., 524
Han, W., 454
Hangal, S., 455
Hanlon, T. E., 456
Hanna, A. C., 501
Hannon, E. E., 137, 159, 277
Hansen, D. H., 235
Hansen, J. C., 537
Happaney, K., 126, 236
Harding, J. E., 157
Harel, J., 224
Harger, J., 453
Harlow, H. F., 227, 231
Harlow, M. K., 227
Harris, D. L., 314
Harris, G., 467
Harris, J. G., 418
Harris, J. R., 245
Harris, S. R., 201
Harrison, D. W., 268
Hart, D., 56, 529
Harter, S., 355, 445, 446, 448, 546, 552, 553
Hartman, R. O., 537
Hartup, W. W., 349, 457, 555, 556, 557
Harvey, E., 454
Hasler, G., 384
Hasselhorn, M., 410
Hastings, P. D., 348, 350
Hatcher, R. A., 67
Hauck, F. R., 144
Haugaard, J. J., 234
Hawkins, S. S., 310
Hay, C., 571
Hay, D. F., 347
Hayne, H., 198
Haynie, D. L., 555, 556
Hayward, C., 488
Hazell, P., 386
Healy, M. D., 340
Hebert, T. P., 366
Heim, C., 237

Heimann, M., 202
Heindel, J. J., 103
Helms, J. E., 422
Helwig, C. C., 530
Hen, R., 48
Henry, D., 349, 351
Henzi, S. P., 557
Hepper, P. G., 276
Hershberger, S. L., 560
Hertenstein, M. J., 251
Hertz-Lazarowitz, R., 556, 557
Hervey-Jumper, H., 385
Hesketh, T., 70
Hetherington, E. M., 35, 37, 451, 454
Hickling, A. K., 304
Hicks, B. M., 350
Hildebrandt, C., 443
Hilden, K., 406
Hill, E. M., 525
Hill, S. E., 48, 257
Hindley, C. B., 169
Hindmarsh, G. J., 123
Hinduja, S., 460
Hines, D. A., 234
Hinojosa, T., 274
Hinshaw, S., 386
Hirsch, B. J., 556
Ho, A., 242
Hoegh, D. G., 13
Hoff, E., 205, 206, 207, 208, 297
Hoffman, L., 455
Hogan, A. M., 57, 122
Hohmann, L. M., 341, 343
Holland, J. J., 352, 354, 537
Holliday, R. E., 316
Hollin, C. R., 530
Holloway, J. H., 455, 539, 540
Holsen, I., 489
Holt, N. L., 448
Homer, B. D., 320, 321, 324
Homsi, G., 504
Honein, M. A., 94
Hong, H.-W., 227
Honig, B., 310
Hopkins, B., 89
Hopkins, W. D., 276
Hopkins-Golightly, T., 122
Horn, J. M., 340
Hort, B., 314
Hossain, M., 103
Houts, A. C., 287, 289
Howe, M. L., 319
Hoy, E. A., 123
Hubbard, F. O. A., 143, 222
Huber, J., 100
Hudson, J. A., 318
Hudziak, J. J., 472

Huesmann, L. R., 16, 307
Huestis, M. A., 99
Hughes, C., 297
Huizink, A. C., 99
Huleihel, M., 122
Hunt, C. E., 144
Hunter, B. C., 126
Hunter, S. C., 461
Hur, Y., 62
Hurd, Y. L., 98
Hyde, J., 526
Hyde, J. S., 562
Hynes, M., 94
Hyson, M., 309

Ijzendoorn, M. H. van, 143, 157, 222, 224
Ikeda, K., 288
Infant and Toddler Nutrition, 158
Ingersoll, G. M., 523
International Human Genome Sequencing Consortium, 48
Inzlicht, M., 429
Ishikawa, S., 470
Izard, C., 248, 249

Jackendoff, Ray, 214
Jacklin, C. N., 257, 524
Jackson, D. N., 413
Jackson, P. W., 427
Jacobs, D. M., 57
Jacobs, J. E., 446
Jacobson, J. L., 103
Jacobson, L., 462
Jacobson, P. F., 321
Jaffee, S. R., 465
Jago, R., 310
James, William, 134
Jamieson, S., 238
Jang, K. L., 467
Jarvis, B., 556
Javo, C., 285
Jeng, S.-F., 123
Jiang, J., 310
Joca, S. R. L., 467
Joe, S., 573
Johnson, C. M., 285
Johnson, R. S., 253
Johnson, W., 48, 62, 249, 523, 524
Johnston, C. A., 376
Johnston, L. D., 100, 503, 507
Jones, D. C., 316, 317, 489
Jones, M. C., 357
Jones, S. S., 227
Jonkman, S., 505
Jorgensen, G., 531
Joshi, P. T., 234, 236, 238, 387

Juffer, F., 157
Jullien, S., 432

Kagan, J., 233
Kagan, L. J., 467
Kaiser Family Foundation, 564
Kalil, A., 566
Kaltiala-Heino, R., 488
Kamakura, T., 446
Kaminski, R. A., 22, 23
Kanevsky, L., 25
Kantas, A., 274
Karapetsas, A., 274
Karatekin, C., 379, 411
Karavasilis, L., 225, 226
Karwautz, A., 501
Katzman, D. K., 500
Kaufman, J., 236
Kavanaugh, R. D., 341, 344
Kavcic, T., 339
Kaye, W. H., 501, 502
Kazdin, A. E., 465
Kazui, M., 224
Kearney, C. A., 468
Keddie, A., 456
Keen, D., 296
Keenan, P. A., 98
Keller, H., 253, 338
Keller, S., 504
Kellman, P. J., 135, 136, 137
Kellogg, R., 273
Kelly, K. M., 523
Kelly, Y., 169
Kempes, M., 350
Kendall, P. C., 471
Kendler, K. S., 48, 467, 468
Kennell, J. H., 129
Kenny, M. C., 467
Keogh, A. F., 422
Kerns, K. A., 224
Kerr, D. C. R., 333
Kidd, E., 212
Kiernan, K. E., 453
Kilgore, K., 465
Killen, M., 459
Kim, J.-Y., 337
Kim, K. H., 414
Kim-Cohen, J., 472
Kimura, D., 524
King, L, A., 53
King, N. J., 356
King, R., 523
Kinsbourne, M., 268
Kinsey, A. C., 560
Kirchler, E., 558
Kirkcaldy, B. D., 374, 380
Kistner, J., 466

Klaus, M. H., 130
Klein, P. J., 198
Klein, R. E., 233
Klier, C. M., 129
Klintsova, A. Y., 166
Klomek, A. B., 573
Knaak, S., 158
Knafo, A., 48, 348, 349
Knox, P. L., 531
Kobayashi-Winata, H., 338
Koch, J., 463
Kochanska, G., 249, 334
Kogan, M. D., 123
Kohl, C., 128, 562
Kohlberg, L., 364, 403, 405, 529, 531, 532
Kohyama, J., 284
Kolata, G., 375
Kolb, B., 268
Konner, M. J., 24
Koopmans van Beinum, F. J., 203
Kopp, C., 252
Koriat, A., 412
Korszun, A., 467
Kotler, J. A., 309
Krackow, E., 412
Kramer, R., 531
Krebs, D. L., 402, 403, 532
Kremer, K. E., 304
Krippner, S., 284
Kristensen, P., 340
Kroeger, K. A., 211
Kroger, J., 547, 549
Krojgaard, P., 195
Krueger, R. F., 48, 87
Kuczaj, S. A., II, 210
Kuczmarski, R. J., 153, 266, 372
Kuhl, P. K., 176
Kuhn, D., 195
Kuk, L. S., 547, 549
Kulp, J., 245
Kundanis, R., 310
Kwok, H. W. M., 243

Labrell, F., 318
Ladd, G. W., 349
Laflamme, 225
LaFreniere, P. J., 349, 351, 358
Lager, C., 446
Lai, H.-L., 103, 126
Laireiter, A.-R., 446
Lalumière, M. L., 562
Lam, K. S., 242
Lam, T. H., 488
LaMay, M. L., 524
Lamb, M. E., 225, 244
Lambert, A., 446

Lamers, C. T. J., 505, 506
Lampel, J., 310
Lampl, M., 155
Landy, F. J., 417
Langbehn, D. R., 465
Lange, G., 319
Langlois, J. H., 456
Lansford, J. E., 35
Lantolf, J. P., 306
Lanza, S. T., 488
Laplan, R. T., 538
LaPointe, L. L., 215
Lapsley, D. K., 402, 532
Largo, R. H., 379
Larkin, J., 272, 347
Larroque, B., 126
Larson, R., 554, 558
Larsson, I., 560, 562
Latham, G. P., 340
Latner, J. D., 374
Lau, A. S., 333
Laumann, E. O., 560, 561
Laurendeau, M., 298
Laursen, B., 554, 555
Law, C., 310
Lawler, C., 103
Lawrence, J. M., 94
Lawson, K., 126
Layne, A. E., 470
Leaper, C., 362, 364
Lecanuet, J.-P., 87
Lederman, N. M., 245
Leerkes, E. M., 130
Lefkowitz, E. S., 366
Legerstee, M., 348
Legro, R. S., 67
Leinbach, M. D., 358
Lejeune, C., 98
Lengua, L. J., 306
Lent, R. W., 537
Leon, M. R., 27, 386
Leonard, S. P., 364
Leonardo, E. D., 48
Letourneau, E. J., 234, 235
Leung, C., 333
Leung, W. L., 466
Leventhal, T., 540
Lever, N., 535, 536
Levin, E. D., 386
Levinthal, B. R., 432
Levitt, M. J., 349
Levy, G. D., 359
Lewinsohn, P. M., 467, 502
Lewis, B. A., 99
Lewis, H. L., 549
Lewis, L. M., 574
Lewis, M., 457, 555

Li, J., 70, 460, 461
Libal, J., 573
Libresco, A. S., 463
Lickliter, R., 205
Lidz, J. L., 320, 321, 324
Lim, K. O., 165
Lim, M. M., 129
Limber, S. P., 251
Linares, M. C. C., 446
Lindsey, E. W., 271
Linebarger, D. L., 310
Linehan, M. M., 572
Ling, L., 53
Lins-Dyer, M. T., 338
Lipman, E. L., 336
Lipsitt, L. P., 138, 139, 143, 144
Lipton, R. C., 232
Liu, X., 287, 452
Livne, N. L., 425
Lleras, A., 432
Lo, J. C., 120
Lochman, J. E., 511
Lock, J., 502
Loehlin, J. C., 62
Loovis, E. M., 378, 380
Lorenz, K., 228
Losen, D. J., 534
Lourenço, O., 302
Lovaas, O. I., 242, 243
Love, J. M., 459
Lozoff, B., 285
Lubart, T. I., 425
Lubinski, D., 413, 414, 430
Lucariello, J. M., 410
Luciana, M., 267
Luciano, M., 62
Ludemann, P. M., 172
Lugo, J. N., Jr., 101
Luster, T., 307
Lykken, D., 62, 63, 350
Lynam, D. R., 570
Lynn, S. J., 412
Lynne, S. D., 487, 488
Lynskey, M. T., 511
Lyon, G. R., 387
Lytle, D. E., 296

Maccoby, E. E., 257, 272, 347, 360, 448
MacDorman, M. F., 565
Macfarlane, A., 137
Mackic-Magyar, J., 241, 242
Mackner, L. M., 157
Maclean, A. M., 529
Macrory, G., 435
Madon, S., 462
Madson, L., 445
Maejima, K., 446

Magdalin, S., 231
Mahler, M., 253
Maimburg, R. D., 242
Malatesta, C. Z., 249
Malina, R. M., 373
Malinosky-Rummell, R., 235
Malone, P. S., 451, 452
Maluccio, A. N., 236
Mandler, J. M., 316, 318
Maneschi, M. L., 387
Mangelsdorf, S. C., 251
Mansoor, E., 386
Maratsos, M. P., 195
Marcia, J., 547
Marcovitch, S., 193
Marean, G. C., 177
Markman, E., 314
Markova, G., 348
Markovitz, H., 522
Marlier, L., 161
Marshall, W. L., 238
Marsiglio, W., 450, 453
Martin, C. L., 258, 317, 346, 359, 364, 365
Martínez, I., 333
Masalha, S., 296
Masataka, N., 212
Masi, G., 467, 468, 471
Massaro, A. N., 166
Massaro, D. W., 310
Masten, A., 472
Maternity Center Association, 120
Mathews, T. J., 565
Matlin, M. W., 257, 258, 359
Matthews, J., 274, 453
Matthews, K. A., 451
Maundeni, T., 452
Maurer, C. E., 135
Maurer, D. M., 135, 181
Mayer, J. D., 417
Maynard, A. E., 418, 422
Mayseless, O., 224
Mazei-Robison, M. S., 384
Maziocco, M. M. M., 526
McAuley, C., 566
McBride, M. C., 399
McCabe, M. P., 489
McCall, R., 417, 423
McCartney, K., 222, 223, 224, 430
McClellan, J. M., 243
McClure, B. G., 123
McCowan, L. M. E., 157
McCoy, R. C., 285
McCracken, J., 241, 242
McCrae, R. R., 62
McCrink, K., 197
McCune, L., 297

McDevitt, T. M., 269
McDonough, L., 208
McEachin, J. J., 243
McEwan, M. H., 270
McGinnis, M. Y., 350
McGlaughlin, A., 143
McGrath, M., 126
McGuinness, D., 272
McHale, S. M., 336, 337
McIntyre, T., 284
McLafferty, C. L., Jr., 428
McLaughlin, J., 101
McMahon, T. J., 342
McManus, C., 274, 275
Meaney, K. S., 380
Mednick, S., 350
Meier, B. P., 352
Meijer, J., 25
Meldrum, M. L., 119
Mellon, M. W., 287, 289
Meltzoff, A. N., 195, 196, 198, 199, 324
Mendez, L. M. R., 538
Mendle, J., 484
Mennella, J. A., 177
Merrill, L. L., 236
Mesman, J., 349
Messer, D., 443
Metcalfe, J. S., 169
Metzger, K. L., 48
Meyer, S., 252, 272, 299
Mezzacappa, E. S., 161
Mezzich, A. C., 511
Michael, E. D., 373
Miklos, E. A., 373
Mikulincer, M., 223
Milgram, R. M., 425
Millar, W. S., 139
Miller, A. L., 572
Miller, C. F., 358, 359, 362
Miller, G. A., 408
Miller, R., 235
Miller, S. M., 356
Miranda, A., 386
Miscarriage, 80
Mischo, C., 443, 444
Mistry, J., 318
Mitchell, A. L., 505
Miyake, A., 409
Miyatsuji, H., 192
Moens, E., 375
Moilanen, J., 235
Molenda-Figueira, H. A., 98
Molfese, V. J., 307
Molinari, L., 456
Moller, L. C., 272
Mollnow, 103
Moneta, G. B., 345

Monsour, A., 552
Montemayor, R., 445
Moore, D. S., 428
Moore, L. L., 271
Moore, M. K., 195
Moran, P., 274
Morelli, G. A., 284, 285
Moreno, M., 99
Morgan-Lopez, A. A., 511
Morley, J. E., 83
Morrell, J., 225
Morris, P. A., 22, 23, 32
Morrison, D. R., 453
Morton, S. M. B., 93
Mortweet, S. L., 284, 286
Moses, L., 313
Mosher, W. D., 342, 563
Mosholder, A. D., 471
Mueller, R., 242
Mueller, U., 522
Muir, D. W., 172
Muir, G. D., 169
Mulder, E. J. H., 99
Mullally, P. R., 340
Mumford, M. D., 425
Munroe, R. H., 364
Muris, P., 356
Murphy, T. K., 471
Murray, B., 552
Murray, B. A., 432
Muzzatti, B., 526

Nadeau, L., 123
Nagin, D. S., 349
Nakkula, M. J., 444
Nash, A., 310
National Campaign to Prevent Teenage
    Pregnancy, 449, 563
National Center for Children in Poverty,
    158
National Center for Education Statistics,
    534, 535, 536
National Center for Injury Prevention
    and Control, 283, 572, 573, 574
National Guideline Clearinghouse, 51
National Institutes of Health, 98
National Sleep Foundation, 284
Natsopoulos, D., 275
Nauta, M. M., 538
Navarro, R. L., 537
Nazzi, T., 324
Nduati, R., 96
Needlman, R., 289
Neisser, U.l, 415, 417, 426, 428
Nelson, C. A., 172, 267, 268
Nelson, K., 206, 208, 211, 316, 317, 318,
    320, 321, 323, 324

Nelson, W. M., III, 211
Nerum, H., 120
Nesdale, D., 446
Nettelbeck, T., 426, 427
Newburn-Cook, C. V., 101
Newman, R., 200, 205
Newport, D. J., 237
Newport, E. L., 215
Nielsen, S., 372, 500
Niemeier, H. M., 498
Nigg, J. T., 383, 384, 386
Nikitopoulos, C. E., 444
Nisbett, R., 427
Nock, M. K., 464
Nolen-Hoeksema, S., 501
Noll, J. G., 235
Nomaguchi, K. M., 455
Nonaka, A. M., 212
Nonnemaker, J. M., 504
Norlander, T., 366
Norwood, K., 463
Nowinski, J., 523
Nucci, L. P., 530
Nyunt, A., 84

Oakes, L. M., 324
Oates, J., 443
O'Boyle, M. W., 274, 275
O'Dea, J. A., 553
O'Donnell, L., 563, 564
Oettinger, G., 540
Office of National Statistics, 51
Oguchi, T., 446
Ogunfowora, O. B., 57
Ohalete, N., 563
Ohnishi, T., 360
Okazaki, S., 422, 426, 427
O'Keefe, M. J., 123
Ollendick, T. H., 356, 357
Oller, D. K., 203
Olson, S. L., 348, 349
Omori, M., 523
O'Neill, D., 314
O'Neill, T., 550
Ong, A. D., 550
Ong, L. P., 16
Ormrod, J. E., 269
Örnkloo, H., 257
Ornoy, A., 101
Orstavik, R. E., 467
Ortega, V., 560
O'Shea, R. P., 268
Ostatnikova, D., 274
Oster, H., 138
O'Sullivan, L. F., 488
Ouellette, G. P., 205
Owens, D. L., 385

Owsley, C., 176
Ozanne, S. E., 93
Oztop, E., 199
Ozturk, M., 540

Paavola, L., 297
Page, K., 575
Palmer, B., 309, 310, 500
Palmer, E. J., 530
Pancsofar, N., 208
Papaioannou, A., 380
Pardini, D., 570
Paris, S. G., 411
Park, K. A., 341
Parke, R. D., 337
Parkes, A., 492
Parks, P., 307
Parsons, T. D., 524
Parten, M., 344
Pascual-Leone, J., 198
Pasley, K., 451
Passell, P., 534
Pastor, J., 547, 550, 551
Patchin, J. W., 460
Patenaude, J., 530
Paterson, D. S., 144
Patock-Peckham, J. A., 511
Patterson, C., 449, 450
Patterson, G., 351
Patterson, M. M., 355
Pauli-Pott, U., 255
Paulussen-Hoogeboom, M. C., 333, 334
Paus, T., 267
Paxton, S. J., 489, 498
Peeters, M. W., 480
Pei, M., 361
Pelligrini, A. D., 272
Pelphrey, K. A., 198
Pemberton, E. F., 274
Penn, H. E., 242
Pennington, B. F., 389
Penza, K. M., 237
Peplau, L. A., 560
Perren, S., 460
Perry, H. M., III, 83
Perry, T. B., 457, 555, 556
Persson, G. E. B., 349
Phillips, A. S., 340
Phillips, C. R., 340
Phillips, D. A., 429
Phinney, J. S., 550, 551, 552
Phipps, M. G., 104
Piaget, J., 19, 188, 190, 191, 192, 193,
    296, 299, 302, 324, 344, 402, 521,
    522
Pichichero, M. E., 491
Piek, J. P., 167, 355

Pierce, K. M., 244
Pierce, S. H., 319
Pijl, S. J., 389
Pike, R., 355
Pillard, R. C., 562
Pinard, A., 298
Pine, D. S., 471
Pine, K. J., 310
Pinker, S., 213, 214, 433
Pinkerton, S. D., 560
Pizarro, D. A., 417
Plomin, R., 48, 62, 242, 254, 348, 349,
    388
Polivy, J., 498, 501
Pollock, B., 196
Pombeni, M. L., 558
Ponnappa, B. C., 101
Poon, M. W. L., 466
Pope, H. G., 350
Popenoe, D., 342
Popkin, B. M., 372
Popma, A., 350
Porfeli, E. J., 540
Porter, R., 138, 198
Porter, R. H., 138
Posey, D. J., 386
Posner, M. I., 165
Potts, M., 70
Power, T. G., 338
Powlishta, K. K., 258, 364, 365
Prato-Previde, E., 212
Pratt, C., 314, 340
Prescott, P. A., 87, 137
Presentacion, M. J., 386
Pressley, M., 406
Prieto, G., 524, 525
Priner, R., 137
Prinz, W., 198, 199
Provence, S., 232
Pryce, C. R., 169
Pugh, K. R., 215
Pujol, J., 163

Quatman, T., 446
Queen, J. A., 375, 376, 380, 381
Quinlivan, J. A., 566
Quintana, S. M., 303
Quirk, K. J., 540

Rabasca, L., 303
Rabinowitz, F. M., 302
Raikes, H., 432
Rainbow Project, The, 414
Rakison, D. H., 324
Ramey, C. T., 93
Ramsey, J. L., 172
Randel, B., 427

Rapin, I., 243
Ratcliffe, J. H., 571
Rathus, J. H., 96, 365, 446, 449, 485,
    486, 504, 560, 565, 572
Raudenbusch, S. W., 462
Ravaldi, C., 502
Rebar, R. W., 66
Reddy, L. A., 384
Redgrave, G. W., 511
Reef, S., 96
Rees, S., 122
Reid, M., 449
Reid, M. J., 309
Reiff, M. I., 386
Reijneveld, S. A., 142, 143
Reinecke, M. A., 466
Reis, O., 558
Remirez, J. R., 535
Reschly, A., 536
Rest, J. R., 529
Rezvani, A. H., 386
Rheingold, H. L., 15
Riala, K., 573
Riccomini, P., 536
Richards, M. H., 554
Richards, T. W., 87
Richdale, A., 285
Richler, J., 242
Rickford, J. R., 433
Rieger, I., 123
Riksen-Walraven, J. M., 341
Riley, B., 48
Rizzolatti, G., 198, 199
Robert, M., 524
Roberts, A., 571
Roberts, W., 348, 349
Robins Wahlin, T., 57
Robinson, J. R., 157
Robles de Medina, P. G., 89
Rodgers, P. L., 574
Roebers, C. M., 410, 412
Roelofs, J., 354
Roeser, R. W., 547
Rogers, K. N., 450, 452
Rogoff, B., 318
Rogol, A., 478, 479
Rollack, D., 27
Rollins, V. B., 538
Romans, S. E., 489
Ronald, A., 62
Roncesvalles, M. N., 169
Rondal, J. A., 53
Rönnerman, K., 306
Roopnarine, J. L., 334
Rose, A. J., 456, 457
Rose, S. A., 198, 200, 202
Rosen, H. J., 214

Rosenblum, K. E., 406
Rosenstein, D., 138
Rosenthal, D. A., 551
Rosenthal, R., 462
Ross, G., 225
Ross, H. W., 225
Rotenberg, K. J., 457, 555
Roth, T. L., 87
Rothbart, M. K., 165, 251, 252, 255
Rothman, S., 420
Rothrauff, T., 285
Rottinghaus, P. J., 537
Roulet-Perez, E., 242
Rovee-Collier, C., 198
Rowen, B., 372, 442
Rowlands, C., 57
Royal Australasian College of Physicians, 139
Rubia, K., 407
Rubin, E., 101
Rubin, K. H., 341, 343
Ruble, D., 317, 346, 359, 364, 365
Ruchkin, V., 570
Rudolph, K. D., 533
Rudy, D., 333, 334, 335
Ruff, H. A., 126
Ruiz, F., 427
Rumbold, A. R., 96
Runyon, M. K., 467
Rushton, J. P., 413, 422
Russ, S. W., 297
Russell, A., 448
Russell, G., 448
Russell, S. T., 560
Rutter, M., 233, 472

Saariluoma, P., 410
Saaristo-Helin, K., 208
Sabattini, L., 362, 364
Sadker, D. M., 463
Sadler, T. W., 103
Saffran, J. R., 175
Saggino, A., 414
Sagrestano, L. M., 489
Sahler, O. J. Z., 126
Saigal, S., 125
Saiki, J., 192
Saito, S., 409
Sales, J. M., 317
Salmivalli, C., 355
Salovey, P., 417
Salvaterra, F., 226, 229
Salzarulo, P., 140, 141
Sandler, I., 472
Santelli, J. S., 491, 567–68
Santinello, M., 449
Santonastaso, P., 502

Santos, D. C. C., 167
Saroglou, V., 548–49
Sarrazin, P., 462
Saudino, K. J., 272
Saunders, 353
Save the Children, 104, 121, 564
Savin-Williams, R. C., 556, 558, 560, 561
Sawyer, D. J., 389
Saywitz, K. J., 235
Scanlan, T. K., 380
Scarr, S., 429, 430
Schaal, B., 161
Scharf, M., 337
Scheithauer, H., 460
Scher, A., 224
Scheres, A., 287
Schiff, B., 550
Schlaggar, B. L., 163
Schmitt, D. P., 360
Schneider, W., 412
Schonfeld, A. M., 100
Schoppe-Sullivan, S. J., 255, 256
Schraf, M., 556, 557
Schuetze, P., 99, 236
Schulte-Körne, G., 387
Schultz, D. P., 10, 18
Schultz, R. W., 380
Schultz, S. E., 10, 18
Schumacher, D., 375, 376, 380, 381
Schwartz, M. B., 374
Schwartz, R. G., 321
Schwartz, S. J., 547
Schwartz, T. H., 214
Schweinhart, L. J., 309
Scott, J. R., 96
Scourfield, J., 465
Secker-Walker, R. H., 102
Seeley, R. J., 375
Sefcek, J. A., 562
Seidah, A., 553
Seligman, L. D., 357
Selman, R., 443, 444, 449, 457
Senman, L., 314
Serbin, L. A., 257, 346
Sharon, 315
Shaver, P. R., 223
Shaw, G. M., 93
Shaywitz, B. A., 361, 388
Shaywitz, S. E., 361
Shear, K., 469
Sheeber, L. B., 554
Sheese, B. E., 251, 252
Shen, R.-Y., 505
Shenal, B. V., 268
Sherry, J. L., 353
Sherwin-White, S., 341

Shevell, T., 67
Shih, M., 550
Shin, H. B., 434
Shirk, S., 553
Shonk, S. M., 235
Shore, C., 299
Shortt, A. L., 471
Shroff, H., 500
Sickmund, M., 342, 568, 569, 570
SIDS Network, 144
Siegel, L. S., 201, 389
Siegler, R. S., 20, 188, 195, 198, 399, 409, 411, 432, 521, 522
Siegmund, R., 140
Signorello, L., 101
Silber, E. S., 463
Silbereisen, R. K., 23, 560
Sim, T. N., 16
Simion, F., 172
Simmons, R. G., 533
Simon, H. A., 410
Simonelli, A., 157
Simonton, D. K., 426
Simpkins, S. D., 447
Simpson, J. L., 59
Singer, L. T., 99
Singh, K., 540
Sirrs, S. M., 164
Skeels, H. M., 233
Skinner, B. F., 210
Skoczenski, A. M., 171
Skorikov, V., 537
Slater, A., 174
Slattery, D. A., 467
Slaughter, V., 314
Slavin, R. E., 459, 460, 461, 462
Sloan, S., 158, 159
Slobin, D. I., 209, 211
Small, M. Y., 319
Small, S. A., 446
Smarty, S., 573
Smetana, J. G., 459, 478, 530, 554
Smiley, P. A., 253
Smith, A. M., 99
Smith, C. L., 254
Smith, P. H., 236
Smith, P. K., 250, 271
Smoll, F. L., 380
Snarey, J. R., 530, 531, 547, 549
Snedeker, J., 212
Snegovskikh, V., 113
Snow, C., 215
Snyder, H. M., 342, 568, 569, 570
Snyderman, M., 420
Soan, S., 389
Sodian, B., 313
Soleymani, R. M., 98

Sommer, I. E. C., 276
Sontag, L. W., 87
Sorce, J., 173
Spearman, C., 416
Spector, A. Z., 342
Spelke, E. S., 176
Spence, M. J., 87, 139, 198
Spencer, M. B., 102
Speranza, M., 502
Spieker, S., 223, 224
Spitalnick, J. S., 492
Spitz, R., 231
Spitzer, R. L., 383
Sroufe, L. A., 223, 225, 248, 251, 458
Staff, J., 539, 540, 557
Stagnitti, K., 297
Stanford, J. N., 489
Stankoff, B., 164
Stanley, C., 128
Stanowicz, L., 211
Stanwood, G. D., 100
State, M., 388
Stauffacher, K., 351
Steele, H., 223, 224, 225
Steele, R. G., 376
Steinberg, L., 427, 535, 558
Stemberger, J. P., 321, 322
Stephenson, R. H., 375
Sternberg, R. J., 413, 414, 416, 425, 427
Stevens, B., 143
Stevens, T., 422
Steward, D. K., 157
Stewart, J. H., 233, 234
Stice, E., 488
Stifter, C. A., 254
Stipek, D., 253, 308, 309
Stoel-Gammon, C., 205
Storch, E. A., 374
Stores, G., 286
Stormshak, E. A., 22, 23, 341, 564
Straus, M. A., 233, 234, 236
Strayer, F. F., 347, 349
Strayer, J., 348
Striegel-Moore, R. H., 488, 498, 500
Stright, A. D., 410
Strohner, H., 323
Strough, J., 444
Strutt, G. F., 407
Stunkard, A. J., 375, 376
Styfco, S. J., 309, 429
Sue, S., 422, 426, 427
Suh, S., 535
Suizzo, M.-A., 338
Sukhodolsky, D. G., 465
Sullivan, B. A., 537
Sulloway, F. J., 340
Sullum, J., 70

Sun, S. S., 452, 481
Suomi, S. J., 231
Supple, A. J., 446
Suris, J.-C., 573
Susman, E. J., 478, 479
Sussman, N., 383, 384, 512
Svedin, C., 560, 562
Swisher, R., 342
Sylva, K., 306
Symons, D. K., 355
Szaflarski, J. P., 268

Takahashi, K., 285
Talladini, M. A., 274
Tamis-LeMonda, C. S., 205, 207, 208, 209, 210, 212, 213, 319, 321, 323
Tan, G., 23
Tanaka, K., 427
Tang, C. S., 485
Tanner, J. M., 155, 266, 479, 480, 481, 485
Tapper, K., 349, 350
Tardif, T., 313
Tashiro, T., 450
Tassi, F., 445, 459
Taylor, B., 242
Taylor, C., 245
Taylor, H. G., 123
Taylor, M., 297, 314
Tees, R. C., 215
Tehrani, J., 350
Tercyak, K. P., 374
Terry, D., 549–50
Theim, K. R., 375
Theimer, C. E., 347
Thierry, A. G. M., 164
Thomas, A., 254, 256
Thomas, D. E., 351
Thomas, J. R., 380
Thomas, S. P., 461
Thompson, A. M., 380
Thompson, B. L., 100
Thompson, K. M., 352
Thompson, M. P., 573
Thompson, O. M., 498
Thompson, R. A., 225, 251, 252, 380, 445, 448
Thompson, V. J., 373
Thorne, S. L., 306
Thurlow, M. L., 536
Thurstone, L., 414, 416
Thyssen, S., 297
Tigner, R. B., 414
Tigner, S. S., 414
Tijms, J., 388
Timmerman, L. M., 244
Tobbell, J., 533

Tod, J., 389
Torres, L., 27
Towse, J., 409, 410, 411
Tracey, T. J. G., 538
Trafimow, D., 445
Traindis, H. C., 338
Trainor, L. J., 212
Trehub, S. E., 137
Tremblay, R. E., 349
Trenholm, C., 568
Treuth, M. S., 375
Trevarthen, C., 212, 213
Troxel, W. M., 451, 453
Tsui, J. M., 526
Tsuneishi, S., 166
Turkheimer, E., 429
Turner, C. M., 471
Turner, S. M., 469
Tyc, V. L., 374

U. S. Bureau of the Census, 450, 453, 454, 472
U. S. Department of Agriculture, 497, 498
U. S. Department of Health and Human Services, 234
U. S. Department of Labor, 432
Ubersfeld, G., 318
Ulibarri, M. D., 451
Ullman, S. E., 235
Ulloa, E. C., 451
Umek, L. M., 25
UNAIDS, 161, 491, 492, 493
UNICEF, 280, 281
Uylings, H. B. M., 215

Vaccaro, B., 251
Vacek, P. M., 102
Vachon, R., 522
Valderhaug, R., 471
Valdez, J. N., 538
Valentini, P., 274
Valentino, K., 341
Valiente, C., 530
Valkenburg, P. M., 316
Van Der Merwe, S., 452, 472
Van Rijn, S., 56
Vandell, D. L., 244
Vander Ven, T., 454
Vartanian, L. R., 427, 523
Væth, M., 242
Vellutino, F. R., 387, 388
Verissimo, M., 226, 229
Vermeiren, R., 570
Verny, T., 244
Vieno, A., 449
Villamil, O. S., 25

Villani, S., 351, 352
Virji-Babul, N., 53
Visscher, W. A., 98
Vitaro, F., 350
Vitiello, B., 467
Volkmar, F. R., 243
Volkova, A., 137
Volling, B. L., 252, 337, 339
Volterra, M. C., 205, 214
Von Ammon, J., 340
Von Gontard, A., 287, 288, 289
Von Hofsten, C., 257
Vorhees, 103
Vu, M. B., 380
Vukovic, R. K., 389
Vurpillot, E., 268
Vygotsky, L., 25, 325

Wachs, T. D., 254, 255
Wadden, T. A., 376
Wade, T. D., 502
Wahler, R. G., 448
Wainright, J. L., 449
Wakschlag, L., 571
Wald, J., 534
Walitza, S., 384
Walk, R., 173
Walker, D., 310
Walker, S. O., 388
Walkup, J. T., 471
Waller, M. R., 342
Wallerstein, J., 454
Walsh, B. T., 502
Walter, J. L., 349, 351, 358
Walther, F. J., 123
Wan, C.-S., 557
Wang, L., 99, 194, 195
Wang, Q., 445
Ware, E. A., 315
Washburn, D. A., 21
Wasserman, G. A., 103
Watson, C. M., 446
Watson, J. B., 8
Waxman, S. R., 320, 321, 324
Waxmonsky, J., 386
Webb, P., 571
Weber, R., 353
Webster-Stratton, C., 309, 457, 465
Wechsler, D., 415, 419

Weckerly, J., 431
Weems, C. F., 356
Weichold, K., 487, 488
Weikart, D. P., 309
Weinberg, R. A., 430
Weinrich, J. D., 562
Weisler, R. H., 383, 384
Weller, E. B., 465
Weller, R. A., 465
Wellman, H. M., 194, 304, 313, 314
Wells, E. A., 534
Welsh, B. C., 571
Wennergren, A.-C., 306
Wentworth, N., 167
Wentzel, K. R., 456, 457
Weppelman, T. L., 212, 213
Werker, J. F., 176, 213, 215
Werner, E. E., 195, 227
Werner, L. A., 137, 138
Werry, J. S., 243
Whalen, C. K., 386
Whitbourne, S. K., 464
White, C. B., 531
White, J. W., 236
White, K., 444
White, W. C., 500
Whitehead, B. D., 342
Whitehead, J. R., 380
Whitehouse, E. M., 308
Whitesell, N. R., 552, 553
Whiting, B. B., 271, 349
Whitson, M. L., 538
Whyte, J., 422
Wiggins, C. N., 254
Wiggs, L., 286
Wilder, A., 390
Williams, J., 390
Williams, J. M., 488
Williams, M. S., 501
Williams, R., 420
Williams, W. M., 426, 526
Willinger, 144
Wilson, E. O., 308, 350
Wilson, M., 453
Windle, M., 472
Wingood, G. M., 492
Winograd, P., 411
Winzelberg, A. J., 502
Witherington, D. C., 173

Wocadlo, C., 123
Wodrich, D. L., 53, 56
Wojslawowicz Bowker, J. C., 457
Wolchik, S. A., 452
Wolf, A., 285
Wolfenden, L. E., 448
Wong, S. S., 572, 573
Woods, S. C., 375
Woolfolk, A., 459, 460, 461, 462
Worell, J., 258
World Health Organization, 160
Wozniak, J. R., 165
Wright, C., 157
Wright, D. W., 455
Wu, J., 467
Wulff, K., 140
Wynn, K., 197

Xie, H. L., 456
Xing, Z. W., 70

Yarrow, L., 232
Yokota, F., 352
Young, D., 285
Young, L. J., 129
Young, R., 455
Youngblade, L., 455
Youniss, J., 555, 556, 558
Yu, A. P., 272, 460

Zajonc, R. B., 340
Zan, B., 443
Zarbatany, L., 457
Zeifman, D. M., 142, 143
Zelazo, P. R., 170, 193
Zeldow, P. B., 366
Zeskind, P. S., 236
Zheng, S., 345
Zhou, Z., 452
Zigler, E., 236, 309, 429
Zimmerman, A. W., 242, 447
Zimmerman, P., 252
Zittleman, K., 463
Ziv, M., 314
Zonnevylle-Bender, M. J. S., 571
Zupancic, M., 339
Zweigenhaft, R. L., 340

Subject Index

abortion
    sex selection and, 70
    spontaneous, 65, 80
abstinence syndrome, 503
abuse, child. *See* child abuse
acceptance, peer, 456–457
accidents in preschoolers', 281–283
accommodation
    cognitive development, 19, 188
    visual, 136
accutane, *105*
achieved ethnic identity, 551
active-passive controversy, 31–32
    perceptual development and, 178–180
acuity, visual, 134–136, 171
adaptation, 19
ADHD. *See* attention-deficit/
    hyperactivity disorder
adipose tissue, 375
adolescence
    body image in, 489
    bridging adulthood and, 575–577
    career development during, 537–538
    dating and romantic relationships in, 557–558
    death rates, 496–497
    defined, 478–479
    dropping out of school, 533–536, *534*
    early versus late maturers in, 487–489
    eating disorders in, 498–503
    egocentrism in, 522–523
    employment during, 536–540
    formal operational stage, 518–522
    gender differences in cognitive abilities in, 523–527
    growth spurt, 479–482, *480, 481*
    HIV/AIDS and, 491–493, *495*
    hypothetical thinking in, 519–520
    identity development in, 546–553
    imaginary audience in, 522, 523
    intellectual processes, 518–527
    juvenile delinquency and, 568–572
    mathematical ability in, 525–527
    menarche in, 484–486
    moral development in, 528–532, *529, 530*
    nutrition in, 497–498
    peer influence on, 558–559
    peer relationships, *458,* 555–559
    personal fable in, 522, 523
    pubertal changes in boys, 482–483, *483*
    pubertal changes in girls, 484–486, *486*
    relationships with parents, 553–555
    risk taking in, 496–497, 523
    school and, 532–536
    self-concept in, 552
    self-esteem in, 552–553, 555–556
    sexual orientation, 560–562
    sexuality, 490–496, 559–568
    smoking by, 504–505
    sophisticated use of symbols in, 520, 522
    substance abuse by, 503–512
    suicide and, 572–575
    verbal ability in, 524
    visual-spatial ability in, 524–525, *525*
adoption, 69, *69*
    attachment and, 232–233
    studies, 63
adrenaline, 104
adulthood, emerging, 575–577
African Americans
    adolescent friendships, 556–557
    attention-deficit/hyperactivity disorder and, 385
    biracial, 549–551
    career self-efficacy expectations and, 538
    conduct disorders and, 465
    early maturation in, 488–489
    ebonics and, 433–435
    ethnic identity and, 549–551
    fathers, 342, *343*
    homicide and, 497
    intelligence testing, 420–422, 426
    juvenile delinquency and, 569–570
    substance abuse and, 509
aggression, *33*
    in early childhood, 349–354
    media influence on, 351–354
    theories of, 350–355
    violent video games and, 353
alcohol use
    by adolescents, 504, *506*
    during pregnancy, 5, *100,* 100–101, *105,* 177–178
alpha-fetoprotein assay, 61
ambivalent/resistant attachment, 223
American Psychological Association, 39–40
American Sign Language, 206–207, 216
amniocentesis, 58, *59,* 64
amniotic fluid, 84, 112
amniotic sac, 84, 112
amphetamines, *506*

anal stage in psychosexual development, 10, *12*
androgens, 82–84
androgyny, psychological, 365–366
anemia, 158
anesthesia, *105,* 117–118
animism, 299, *300*
anorexia nervosa, 498–500
anoxia, 122
antibiotics, 98
antidepressants, 467, 471, 502
anxiety
    childhood, *468,* 468–471
    enuresis and, 289
    separation, 222, 469–470
    stranger, 250–251
Apgar scores, 115, 130–131
aphasia, 214
appearance-reality distinction, 314–315
artificial insemination, 68
artificialism, 299, *300*
Asian Americans, 426–427, 509
Asperger's disorder, 240
aspirin, *105*
assimilation, 19, 188
associative play, *345*
asynchronous growth, 480
attachment
    ambivalent/resistant, 223
    autism spectrum disorders and, 240–243
    avoidant, 223
    child abuse and neglect effects on, 233–239
    contact comfort and, 227, *228,* 229, *230*
    critical period, 228, 229
    day care effect on, 244–248
    defined, 222
    disorganized-disoriented, 223
    emotional development and, 248–252
    emotional regulation and, 251–252
    establishing, 224–225
    ethological view of, 227–229, *230*
    failure, 229–243
    to fathers, 225
    patterns, 222–224
    releasing stimuli and, 227, 229
    secure, 222–224
    separation anxiety and, 222
    social deprivation and, 231–233
    social referencing and, 251
    stability of, 225–226

attachment (*continued*)
  stages of, 226
  stranger anxiety and, 250–251
  theories of, 226–229, *230*
attachment-in-the-making phase, 226
attention, selective, 407
attention-deficit/hyperactivity disorder, 382–386, *383*
attributional style, 467
audience, imaginary, 522, 523
authoritarian parenting, 335
authoritative parenting, 333, 334, 446
autism spectrum disorders, 5, 62, 240–241
  causes of, 242
  characteristics of, 240–241
  treatment of, 242–243
autobiographical memory, 317–318
autonomous morality, 402–403
autonomy versus shame and doubt in psychosocial development, *12*
autosomes, 49
avoidant attachment, 223
axons, 162, *163*

babbling, 203, 205
babinski reflex, 133
baby blues, 128–129
bacterial vaginosis, *494*
Baley Scales of Infant Development, *200*, 200–201, *201*
Bandura, Albert, *17, 28*
barbiturates, 504, *506*
bed-wetting, 287–289
behavior
  modification, 13
  moral, 529–532
  of parents towards boys versus girls, 258
  prosocial, 347–349
behaviorism, 8, 13–17
  attachment and, 227, *230*
bendectin, *105*
bilingualism, 433–435
Binet, Alfred, 7
biological factors in aggression, 350
biological perspective on child development, 21–22, *29*
biracial children, 549–551
birth
  order, 340–341
  rates, 90–92
blastocysts, 78–79
blood tests, 60
body image in adolescence, 489
  eating disorders and, 498–503
body proportions, 156, *156*

bonding, postpartum, 129–130
bottle feeding, 158–161
boys. *See* gender
brain
  anatomy, *164,* 164–165
  development, 266–268
  nature versus nurture in development of, 165–166
  nervous system and, 162–164
  organization and gender, 360–361, *363*
  plasticity, 268
  right versus left, 268
  structures involved in language, 214–215, *215*
  vision and, 267–268
Braxton-Hicks contractions, 112
Brazelton Neonatal Behavioral Assessment Scale, 131
breast feeding, 158–161
breech presentation, 122
Bridges's and Sroufe's theory of emotional development, 248–249
Broca's aphasia, 215, *215*
Broca's area, 214–215
Bronfenbrenner, Urie, 22, 32
bulimia nervosa, 500–501
bullying, 460–461

caffeine, 101, *105*
cancer, 491
candidiasis, *494*
carbamazepine, *105*
career development, 537–538
career typology, 537–538, *539*
carriers, gene, 51–52
case studies, 34–35
catch-up growth, 157
categorical self, 355
causality and preoperational children, 298–299, 304, *305*
cell division, 49–50
centration, 300–301
cephalocaudal development, 80, 152–153, *154*
cerebellum, 164, *164*
cerebrum, *164,* 164–165
cervix, 113
  cancer of, 491
cesarean section, 119–120
child abuse, 5
  attachment and, 233–239
  causes of, 235–238
  effects of, 234–235
  psychological disorders in adulthood and, 237
  sexual, 234, 235, 239

in stepfamilies, 453
techniques for dealing with, 238–239
child development
  controversies in, 30–32
  development of, 6–7
  ecological perspective on, 22–24
  how to study, 32–40
  optimizing conditions of, 6
  pioneers in study of, 7
  reasons for studying, 5–6
  terms, 4–5
  theories, 8–30
child labor laws, 7, *7*
childbirth
  anesthesia during, 117–118
  centers, 121
  cesarean section, 119–120
  countdown to, 112–113
  first stage, 113–114
  home, 121
  labor and, 112–113
  methods, 117–121
  midwives and, 117, 120–121
  postpartum period, 127–130
  prepared, 118–119
  problems, 122–127
  second stage, *114,* 114–116
  third stage, 116
childhood disintegrative disorder, 240
china, 70, *71*
chlamydia, 490, *494*
chorionic villus sampling, 58–59
chromosomes, 48–49, *50*
  abnormalities, 53–56, *54, 61*
  sex, 49
chronological age, 418
chronosystems, 23, *23*
cigarettes, 101–102, *105*
class inclusion, 301–302, 399, *400*
classical conditioning, 13–14, 139
classical music and fetal development, 87–88
clear-cut-attachment phase, 226
cliques, 557
clitoris, 484
cocaine, 99–100, *506*
codes, semantic, 409
coefficients, correlation, 35
cognitive behavioral therapy, 386, 471, 503
cognitive development, 18–21, *28*
  adolescent, 523–527
  appearance-reality distinction in, 314–315
  attachment and, 227, *230*
  class inclusion in, 301–302, 399, *400*
  concrete-operational stage, 396–401

conservation in, 300, *301,* 396–398, *400*

early childhood education and, 308–309

factors in, 306–312

false beliefs and, *313,* 313–314

HOME inventory, 306–307, *307*

individual differences in intelligence among infants and, 200–202

information processing, 198–199

language and, 324–325

memory development in, 315–319, 406–412

metacognition and metamemory, 410–412

object permanence and, 192–195

origins of knowledge and, 314

play and, 344

preoperational stage, *20,* 296–305

scaffolding in, 25, 306

sensorimotor stage, *20,* 188–192

seriation in, 398, *399, 400*

television and, 309–312

theory of mind and, 312–315

transitivity in, 398–399

visual recognition memory and, 201–202

zone of proximal development in, 25, 306

See also language development

cognitive factors in aggression, 350

cognitive-developmental theory, 18–20

gender differences and, *363,* 364–365

middle childhood and, 443–444

cohort effect, 38, *38*

collectivism, 338, *339*

color perception in neonates, 136

comfort, contact, 227, *228,* 229, *230*

coming out, 561

commercials, television, 310, 311

commitment and identity, 547

conception. *See* pregnancy

concrete-operational stage in cognitive development, *20,* 396–401

conditioned response, 13, 14

conditioned stimulus, 13, 14

conditioning

classic, 13–16, 139

operant, 14, 15, 139, 357

conduct disorders, 464–465, *468*

congenital syphilis, 95, *105*

conservation in cognitive development, 300, *301,* 396–398, *400*

constancy, gender, 364

constructive play, 344

contact comfort, 227, *228, 229, 230*

continuity-discontinuity controversy, 31

contraceptives, *564, 566, 567,* 568

contractions, 112–116

Braxton-Hicks, 112

contrast assumption, 321

control groups, 36

controversies in child development, 30–32

conventional level of moral development, *404,* 405

convergence, visual, 136, *136*

cooing, 205

Cooley's anemia, 55

cooperative play, *345*

coordination of secondary schemes, 191, *191*

coregulation, 448

correlations, positive and negative, 35

couch-potato effect of television, 310

crawling, 168, *169*

creativity

intellectual development and, 425–428

triarchic theory of, 414

crime, 497, 568–572

crises, identity, 11, 547

critical period of life and attachment, 228, 229

cross-sectional research, 37, *38,* 38–39

cross-sequential research, 39, *39*

crowds, 557

crying, neonate, 142–143

cultural bias in intelligence testing, 420–422

cultural-familial retardation, 424

cyberbullying, 460–461

cystic fibrosis, *54, 57*

Darwin, Charles, 7, 21

dating, 557–558

day care, 244–248

deaths, adolescent, 496–497

decentration, 396

deep structure of language, 214

deferred imitation, 195

dendrites, 162, *163*

densensitization, 357

deoxyribonucleic acid (DNA), 48–49, *49*

dependent variables in experiments, 36

depressant drugs, 504, *506*

depression

childhood, 465–468, *468,* 471

postpartum, 128–129

suicide and, 572–575

deprivation, social, 231–233

depth perception, 173–174

DES, 98, *105*

diarrhea, 280, 281

diethylstilbestrol, 98, *105*

differential emotions theory, 248

differentiation, 153, *154*

difficult temperaments, 254–256

diffusion, identity, 547, *548*

dilation, cervical, 113

dimensions of child rearing, 332–334

disabilities

attention-deficit/hyperactivity disorder, 382–386, *383*

autism spectrum disorders, 5, 62, 240–243

education of children with, 389–390

learning, 386–389

mental retardation, 424

in middle childhood, 382–390

types of, *382*

See also disorders

disinhibition and aggression, 352

disorders

anxiety, 222, 250–251, 289, *468,* 468–471

conduct, 464–465, *468*

eating, 498–503

phobia, 469, 470–471

of written expression, *387*

See also disabilities

disorganized-disoriented attachment, 223

divergent thinking, 427

diversity

African American youth and ADHD, 385

babbling, 203

career self-efficacy expectations and, 538

child development theories and, 24, 25–27

development of concepts of ethnicity and race, 303

gender differences in activity levels, 272

individualism, collectivism, and patterns of child rearing, 338, *339*

macrosystems and, 24

maternal and infant mortality, 124, *125*

missing American fathers, 342

moral development and, 531

population growth and, 90–92

protein-energy malnutrition and, 160

sex, college plans, ethnicity, and substance abuse, 509

sex selection practices, 70, *71*

sleeping arrangements, 285

socioeconomic and ethnic differences in IQ, 426

stress and, 472

diversity (*continued*)
two-word sentences and, 211
See also ethnicity and culture
divorce, 450–454
dizygotic twins, 50–51, 62–63
DNA. *See* deoxyribonucleic acid (DNA)
dominant and recessive traits, 51–53
donor IVF, 68
double-deficit hypothesis, 389
down syndrome, 5, *54, 56,* 64
chromosomal abnormality, 53
dramatic play, 344
drawings, children's, *273,* 273–274
dreams, 299
dropouts, school, 533–536, *534*
drugs
abuse and sexually transmitted
infections, 492
antidepressant, 467, 471, 502
depressant, 504, *506*
effects of various, 504–505, *506*
hallucinogenic, 505–506, *506*
stimulant, 504–505, *506*
students' attitudes toward, 508–509
tolerance, 503
for treating ADHD, 386
used during pregnancy, 97–102, *105,*
177–178
See also substance abuse
Duchenne muscular dystrophy, *55,* 58
dyscalculia, *387*
dyslexia, 5, 386, *387, 388,* 388–389

early childhood
accidents in, 281–283
aggression in, 349–355
appearance-reality distinction in,
314–315
bed-wetting by, 287–289
brain development, 266–269
causality and, 298–299, 304, *305*
confusion of mental and physical
events in, 299, *305*
dimensions of child rearing and,
332–334
drawings, *273,* 273–274
eating patterns, 277–278, *278*
education, 308–309
egocentrism in, 298, *300,* 304, *305*
elimination disorders in, 287–289
empathy in, 348
false beliefs in, *313,* 313–314
fears in, 356–358
fine motor skills, *272,* 272–273
focus on one dimension at a time in,
300–302, *305*
gender role development in, 358–366

grammar development, 321–323
gross motor skills, 269–270, *271*
handedness in, 274–276
health and illness, 278–283
immunizations, *279,* 280, *280, 281*
influence of siblings on, 336–341
language development, 319–325, *320*
major illnesses in, 280–281
memory development, 315–319
minor illnesses in, 280
motor development, 269–276
nutrition, 276–278
origins of knowledge in, 314
parenting styles in, 334–336
peer relationships in, 341, 343, *458*
personality and emotional development in, 355–366
perspective taking in, 348
physical activity, 270–272
physical growth, 266, *267*
play in, 296–298, 344–347
pragmatics in language development,
323–324
preoperational stage, *20,* 296–305
prosocial behavior in, 347–349
the self in, 355–356
sleep needs, 283–286
social behaviors in, 344–355
television and, 309–312
theory of mind, 313–315
vocabulary development, 319–321
easy temperaments, 254–256
eating disorders, 498–503
eating patterns, preschoolers', 277–278,
278
ebonics, 433–435
echolalia, 205
ecological perspective on child
development, 22–24, *29*
Ecstasy, 505, *506*
ectoderm, 80
education
applications of Piaget's theory to,
399–401
of children with disabilities,
389–390
early childhood, 308–309
environment, 459–463
gender and, 27
Head Start, 308–309
mathematics, 526–527
middle childhood, 399–401
reading, 432–433
school refusal and, 470–471
sex, 566, *567*
sexism in, 463
teachers and, 461–463

television, 309–310
See also schools
effacement, cervical, 113
ego identity, 547
ego integrity versus despair in
psychosocial development, *12*
egocentrism
in adolescence, 522–523
in early childhood, 298, *300,* 304,
305
elaborative strategy, 409
elementary school, 532–533
elicitation of response, 13
elimination disorders in preschoolers,
287–289
embryonic disk, 79
embryonic stage, 80–85
amniotic sac, 84
development phases, *81*
placenta, 84–85
sexual differentiation in, *82–83,*
82–84
embryonic transplant, 68
emerging adulthood, 575–577
emotional development
attachment and, 248–252
in early childhood, 355–366
in middle childhood, 448
emotional intelligence, 417
empathy, 348, 403
employment
adolescent, 536–540
career development and, 537–538
of children, 7, *7*
maternal, 454–455
encoding, 408
encopresis, 289
endoderm, 80
endometriosis, 67
endometrium, 64
enuresis, 287–289
environment
cognitive development and, 306–307,
429–430
school, 460–463
environmental influences on prenatal
development
drug, 97–102
hazards, 102–104
nutrition, 93–94
temperament and, 255–256
teratogens, 94–97
epiphyseal closure, 483
episiotomy, 113, 115–116
equilibration, 19
Erikson, Erik, *11,* 11–13, *28,* 547, 577
establishing attachment, 224–225

estrogen, 56, 484
ethical considerations in child
    development research, 39–40
ethnic groups and child development
    theories, 25–27
ethnic identity, 551
ethnicity and culture
    attention-deficit/hyperactivity
        disorder and, 385
    biracial children and, 549–551
    chromosomal abnormalities and,
        53–56, *54, 61*
    conduct disorders and, 465
    development of concepts of, 303
    friendship patterns and, 556–557
    HIV/AIDS and, 96
    identity development and, 549–551
    intelligence and, 420–422, 426–427,
        429
    juvenile delinquency and, *569,*
        569–570, *570*
    missing American fathers and, 342
    moral development and, 531
    overweight and, *374*
    school dropout rates and, *534,*
        534–536
    substance abuse and, 509
    suicide and, 573
    See also diversity
ethnology, 21–22
ethological view of attachment, 227–229,
    230
European Americans
    adolescent friendships, 556–557
    biracial, 549–551
evolutionary theory
    of aggression, 350
    of sex differences, 359–360, *363*
exercise. *See* physical activity
exosystems, 22–23, *23*
experiments, 36–37
exploration and identity, 547, *548*
expressive language style, 208
expressive vocabulary, 205
extinction and behavior, 14, 211
eyewitness testimony by children, 412

fables, personal, 522, 523
factor analysis, 413–414, *416*
factor theories of intelligence, 413–414
failure to thrive, 156–157, 158
fallopian tubes, 64, 65, *66,* 68
false beliefs, *313,* 313–314
families
    divorce and, 450–454
    of juvenile delinquents, 569–571,
        570

lesbian and gay, 449–450
    parent-child relationships in,
        448–449
    step-, 453
    See also parenting
fast-mapping, 320
fathers
    adolescent relationships with, 554
    attachment of children to, 225
    conception and, 64, 65–66, *66,*
        66–67
    divorced, 450–453
    gender role development and,
        362–364
    missing American, 342, *343*
    See also parenting
fears
    in early childhood, 356–358
    of strangers, 250–251
feedback loops, 479
Fels Longitudinal Study, 37
fertility, 66–69
    age and, 104
    rates, 90–92
fetal alcohol effect, 101
fetal alcohol syndrome, 5, *100,* 100–101
fetal monitoring, 113
fetal movements, 88–89
fetal stage, 85–89, *86–87*
    fetal movements during, 88–89
fine motor skills
    drawing and, *273,* 273–274
    early childhood, *272,* 272–273
    handedness and, 274–276
    middle childhood, 379, *379*
fixed action patterns, 21
    attachment and, 227–228
forceps, 113
foreclosure, identity, *548,* 548–549
formal games, 344
formal operational stage in cognitive
    development, *20,* 518–522
foster parents, 232
Freud, Sigmund, 7, 9–11, *10, 12,* 21, *28*
    See also psychoanalytic perspective on
        child development
friendships
    adolescent, *458,* 555–557
    in early childhood, 341, 343, *458*
    in middle childhood, 457–458, *458*
    patterns and ethnicity and sex,
        556–557
functional play, 344

games, formal, 344
gathering information, 34–35
gay parents, 449–450

gender
    body image and, 489
    brain organization and, 360–361, *363*
    cognitive-developmental theory of,
        363, 364–365
    constancy, 364
    differences development theories,
        359–365
    differences in activity levels, 272
    differences in cognitive abilities,
        523–527
    differences in learned helplessness,
        447
    differences in physical growth, 373
    differences in play, 346–347, 525
    early and late maturation and,
        487–489
    eating disorders and, 498–503
    friendship patterns and, 556–557
    human diversity and, 27
    identity, 364
    identity development and, 551–552
    juvenile delinquency and, 570, *571*
    mathematical ability and, 525–527
    moral development and, 531
    psychological androgyny and,
        365–366
    pubertal changes and, 482–483, *483,*
        484–486, *486*
    roles, 5, 38–39, 358–366
    -schema theory, *363,* 365
    selection, 69, 70, *71*
    sex hormones and, 361, *363*
    similarities and differences in motor
        development, 380
    social cognitive theory and, 362–364,
        363
    stereotypes, 358, 365–366
    suicide and, 573
    temperament and, 256–258
    verbal ability and, 524
    visual-spatial ability and, 524–525,
        525
general anesthesia, 117
generalized anxiety disorder, 468–469
Generation X, 450
generativity versus stagnation in
    psychosocial development, *12*
genes, 48–49
genetics
    abnormalities, 56–58
    chromosomal abnormalities and,
        53–56, *54*
    counseling and prenatal testing,
        58–61, 64
    DNA in, 48–49
    dominant and recessive traits, 51–53

genetics (*continued*)
of identical and fraternal twins,
50–51, 62–63
intelligence and, *428,* 428–429
mitosis and meiosis in, 49–50, *50*
mutations, 49
sex-linked abnormalities, 57–58
genital herpes, 490, *494*
genital stage, 478
genital stage in psychosexual
development, 10, *12*
genital warts, 490, 491, *495*
genotypes, 62
germinal stage, 78–80
Gesell, Arnold, 7
giftedness, 425
girls. *See* gender
gonorrhea, 490, *494*
goodness of fit between environment and
temperament, 255–256
grammar development, 321–323, 431
grasping reflex, 133, *133*
gross motor skills
early childhood, 269–270, *270, 271*
middle childhood, 378–379, *379*
growth. *See* physical growth and
development
gynecomastia, 483

habituation
aggression and, 354
hearing and, 176
Hall, G. Stanley, 7
hallucinogenics, 505–506, *506*
handedness, 274–276
Harlow's view of attachment, 227
Head Start, 308–309, 536
health and illness
in adolescence, 496–512
overweight and, 374–375
preschoolers', 278–283
hearing
development, 175–177
neonate, 137
heavy metal exposure during pregnancy,
102–103, *105*
height and weight growth, 5
adolescence, 479–482, *480, 481*
early childhood, 266, *267*
infants, 153–156, *155*
middle childhood, 372, *373*
helplessness, learned, 447
hemophilia, *55, 57*
heredity
chromosomal abnormalities and,
53–56, *54*
chromosomes and genes in, 48–49
dominant and recessive traits in,
51–53

environment versus, 30–31, 61–63
genetic abnormalities and, 56–58
genetic counseling and prenatal
testing and, 58–61, 64
identical and fraternal twins and,
50–51, 62–63
intelligence and, *428,* 428–429
mitosis and meiosis in, 49–50, *50*
sex differences and, 359–360, *363*
heritability of intelligence, *428,* 428–429
heroin, 98, *506*
Hindu Indians, 531
history of child development field, 6–7
HIV/AIDS
adolescents and, 491–493, *495*
breastfeeding and, 161
cesarean section and, 120
defined, 490
prenatal development and, 96, 97,
105
holophrases, 209
home births, 121
HOME inventory, 306–307, *307*
homicide, 497
homosexual orientation, 449–450,
560–562
hormones
menstrual cycle regulation, 485–486
prescription, 98
Horney, Karen, 11, *11*
human papilloma virus, 491, *495*
Huntington's disease, *55, 57*
hyaluronidase, 66
hyperactivity, 383, *383*
hypothalamus, 479
hypotheses, 33
hypothetical thinking, 519–520
hypoxia, 122

identical and fraternal twins, 50–51
identity
achievement, *548,* 549
crises, 11, 547
development in adolescents,
546–553
diffusion, 547, *548*
ego, 547
ethnic, 551
ethnicity and development of,
549–551
gender, 364
versus role diffusion in psychosocial
development, *12*
sex and development of, 551–552
statuses, 547–549, *548*
imaginary audiences, 522, 523
imitation
deferred, 195

infants, 198–199, *199*
language development and, 210
immanent justice, 402
immunizations, *279,* 280, *280, 281*
imprinting and smiling, 227–229
in vitro fertilization, 68
inclusion, class, 301–302, 399, *400*
increased arousal and aggression, 352
incubators, infant, 126
independent variables in experiments, 36
India, 70
individualism, 338, *339*
inductive methods in parenting,
333–334
Industrial Revolution, the, 7
industry versus inferiority in psychosocial
development, *12,* 443
infanticide, 70, 453
infants
attachment phases, 226
body proportions, 156, *156*
brain development in, 162–166
breast feeding versus bottle feeding,
158–161
cephalocaudal development, 80,
152–162, *154*
differentiation, 153, *154*
early vocalizations, 203–205
failure to thrive in, 156–157, 158
growth patterns in height and weight,
153–156, *155*
hearing, 137, 175–177
individual differences in intelligence
among, 200–202
language development in, 203–216
memory, 198
Motherese and, 212–213
motor development, 166–170
nutrition, 157–162
proximodistal development, 153, *154*
social smiles, 227
temperaments, 254–258
vision, 134–136, 171–174
See also neonates
infections
prenatal development and, 95–96
sexually transmitted, 490–496
infertility, 66–69
age and, 104
information gathering, 34–35
information processing in middle
childhood, 406–412
information-processing theory, 20–21,
29, 198–199
initial-preattachment phase, 226
initiative versus guilt in psychosocial
development, *12,* 356
inner speech, 325

insemination, artificial, 68
insomnia, 286
intelligence
      creativity and, 425–428
      development determinants, 428–430
      development patterns, 422–423
      differences among infants, 200–202
      factor theories of, 413–414
      giftedness and, 425
      heredity and, *428*, 428–429
      measurement of, 416–422, *421, 422,*
            428
      mental retardation and, 424
      multiple, 414–416, *415, 416*
      race and, 420–422, 426–427, 429
      socioeconomic differences and,
            426–427
      theories of, 413–416, *416*
      triarchic theory of, 414, *416*
interactionist view on language develop-
      ment and cognition, 324–325
interest level and memory, 317
intervention programs for preterm in-
      fants, 126–127, *127*
intimacy versus isolation in psychosocial
      development, *12*
invention of new means through mental
      combinations, 192
irreversibility, 301
Izard's theory of emotional development,
      249, *249*

Japan, 338, *339,* 455
justice, immanent, 402
juvenile delinquency, 568–572, *569,*
      570

kindergarten, 459–460
kinship studies, 62–63, 430, 562
Klinefelter syndrome, *54,* 56
knowledge, origins of, 314
Kohlberg's theory of moral development,
      403–405
!Kung people, 24

labia, 484
labor and childbirth, 112–115
Lamaze method, 118–119
language acquisition device, 214
language development
      babbling in, 203, 205
      bilingualism and, 433–435
      brain structures involved in, 214–215
      cognition and, 324–325
      early childhood, 319–325, *320*
      early vocalizations in, 203–205
      ebonics in, 433–435

egocentrism and, 304
grammar in, 321–323, 431
imitation and, 210
inner speech, 325
literacy and, 431–435
Motherese in, 212–213
nature and, 213–216
nurture and, 210–213
pragmatics in, 323–324
psycholinguistic theory in, 214
reinforcement and, 210–213
sensitive period in, 215–216
sentence development in, 208–209
sign language and, 206–207
symbols in, 520, 522
theories of, 209–216
vocabulary development in, 205–208,
      319–321, 431
See also cognitive development
lanugo, 123–124, *124*
larynx, 482
latency stage, 443
latency stage in psychosexual develop-
      ment, 10, *12*
Latino and Latina Americans
      career self-efficacy expectations and,
            538
      fathers, 342, *343*
      intelligence and, 426
      substance abuse by, 509
      suicide among, 573
lead exposure and poisoning, 102–103,
      105, 281, 282
learned helplessness, 447
learning
      aggression and social, 350–351
      disabilities, 386–389
      in middle childhood, 406–412
      by neonates, 139
      observational, 17
      perspective on child development,
            13–18, *28*
      rote, 409
left brain, 268
left-handedness, 274–276
lesbian parents, 449–450
life crises, 11
literacy and language development,
      431–435
local anesthetics, 118
Locke, John, 6–7
locomotion development, 167–169
longitudinal research, 37–39, *38*
long-term memory, 409–410
Lorenz, Konrad, 21
low-birth-weight infants, 122–127
LSD, 506, *506*

macrosystems, 23, *23*
mainstreaming, 389, *389*
malnutrition, protein-energy, 160
mammary glands, 484
marijuana, 98–99, *105, 506*
masturbation, 560
maternal employment, 454–455
mathematical ability and gender,
      525–527
mathematics disability, *387*
maturation, 8
MDMA, 505, *506*
mean length of utterance, 208–209
measurement of intellectual development,
      416–422, 428, *525*
media influence
      on aggression, 311, 351–354
      on sexuality, 559–560, 564
medulla, 144–145, 164, *164*
meiosis and mitosis, 49–50
memory
      autobiographical, 317–318
      in early childhood, 315–319
      factors influencing, 317–318
      infants', 198
      interest level and, 317
      long-term, 409–410
      measurement, 318
      in middle childhood, 406–412
      recall, 315–316, *316,* 410
      rehearsal and, 318, 408
      retrieval cues, 317–318
      scripts, 316–318
      sensory, 407–408
      short-term, 408–409
      strategies, 318–319
      structure of, *408*
      testimony by children and, 412
      types of, 317
      visual recognition, 201–202, 315–316,
            316
      working, 408–409
menarche, 484–486
Mendelian genetics, 51
menopause, 497
mental age, 418
mental blinders, 300–302
mental representations, 314
mental retardation, 424
mercury exposure, 103, *105*
mesoderm, 81
mesosystems, 22, *23*
metacognition and metamemory,
      410–412
metamemory and metacognition,
      410–412
metaphors, 520, 522

methadone, 98
methaqualone, *506*
microsystems, 22, *23*
Middle Ages, the, 6
middle childhood
    childhood depression, 465–468
    concrete-operational stage, 396–401
    conduct disorders in, 464–465
    conservation in, 396–398, *400*
    creativity in, 425–428
    disabilities and, 382–390
    education in, 399–401
    exercise and fitness in, 380–381
    fine motor skills, 379, *379*
    gross motor skills, 378–379, *379*
    growth patterns, 372–378
    information processing in, 406–412
    intellectual development in, 422–430
    language development and literacy in,
        431–435
    moral development in, 401–406
    nutrition, 372–373
    overweight in, 374–378
    peer relationships in, 456–458, *458*
    school and, 459–464, 532–533
    selective attention in, 407
    self-concept in, 445–448
    self-definition in, 356
    self-esteem in, 445–446
    sex differences in play in, 346
    sex similarities and differences in
        motor development in, 380
    social and emotional problems in,
        464–472, *468*
    theories of intelligence and, 413–416
    theories of social and emotional devel-
        opment in, 442–448
    transitivity in, 398–399
midwives, 117, 120–121
miscarriage, 80, 98
mitosis and meiosis, 49–50, *50*
modeling, participant, 357
monitoring, fetal, 113
monkeys and attachment, *228,* 229, 231,
    231
monozygotic twins, 50–51, 62–63
moral development
    in adolescence, 528–532, *529, 530*
    diversity and, 531
    in middle childhood, 401–406
moral realism, 402
morality
    autonomous, 402–403
    objective, 402
moro reflex, *132,* 132–133
morphemes, 208–209
mortality, maternal and infant, 124, *125*

motherese, 212–213
mothers
    divorced, 450–453
    employed, 454–455
    gender role development and,
        362–364
    stress and prenatal development, 104
    teenage, 564–568
    See also parenting
motility, sperm, 66–67
motor development, 4
    early childhood, 269–276, *270*
    fine motor skills, *272,* 272–276, *273,*
        379, *379*
    gender similarities and differences in,
        380
    gross, 269–276, *270,* 378–379, *379*
    infants, 166–170
    middle childhood, 378–379
Müllerian inhibiting substance, 83
multifactorial problems, 53
multiple intelligences, theory of,
    414–416, *415, 416*
multiple sclerosis, 164
muscular dystrophy, *55, 58*
mutations, genetic, 49
myelin, *163,* 163–164

National Institute of Child Health and
    Human Development, 244, 246
Native Americans, 509, 573
natural childbirth, 118
naturalistic observation, 33, 34
nature-nurture controversy, 30–31,
    61–63
    brain development and, 165–166
    language development and, 210–216
    motor development and, 169–170
    in perceptual development, 180–181
negative correlations, 35
negative reinforcers, 14, 15–16
neglect and attachment, 233–239
neonates, 78, 113
    Babinski reflex, 133
    bonding with, 129–130
    characteristics of, 130–145
    crying by, 142–143
    grasping reflex, 133, *133*
    health assessment of, 115, 130–131
    hearing, 137
    learning capabilities, 139
    Moro reflex, *132,* 132–133
    preterm and low-birth-weight,
        122–127
    reflexes, 131–134, *189,* 190
    rooting reflex, 132, *132*
    sensory capabilities of, 134–139

    sleeping and waking patterns,
        139–142
    smell sense in, 137–138
    soothing, 143
    stages of attachment, 226
    stepping reflex, 133, *133*
    sudden infant death syndrome and, 5,
        143–145
    taste sense in, 138
    tonic-neck reflex, 133, *134*
    touch and pain sense in, 138–139
    vision, 134–136
    See also infants
nervous system development, 162–166
neural tube
    defects, *55*
    development, 80
neurons, 162–164, *163*
neurotransmitters, 163
newborns. *See* neonates
nightmares, 284, 286
nocturnal emissions, 483
nongonococcal urethritis, *494*
non-REM sleep, 140–142
nonsocial play, 344–345, *345,*
    345–346
nutrition
    adolescent, 497–498
    eating disorders and, 498–503
    middle childhood, 372–373
    overweight and, 374–378
    physical growth and development and,
        157–162
    prenatal development and, 93–94
    preschooler, 276–278, *278*

Oberlin College, 27
object permanence, 192–195, 196
objective morality, 402
observation
    concrete-operational stage, 397
    formal operational stage, 519
    gender differences, 361
    gross and fine motor skills, 275
    learning and aggression, 352
    naturalistic, 33, 34
    preoperational stage, 302
    self-concept, 447
observational learning, 17
onlooker play, *345*
operant conditioning, 14, 15, 139, 357
operations by preoperational children,
    297–298
opiates, *105*
oral herpes, *495*
oral rehydration therapy, 281
oral sex, 563

oral stage in psychosexual development, 10, *12*

origins of knowledge, 314

osteoporosis, 497

ova, 64, 65, *65, 66*, 67

overextension, 208

overregularization, 321–323

overweight in children, 374–378

ovulation, 51

oxygen deprivation during childbirth, 122

oxytocin, 113, 129

parallel play, *345*

parenting
  authoritarian, 335
  authoritative, 333, 334, 446
  dimensions of child rearing and, 332–334
  inductive techniques, 333–334
  influences on sexual activity by adolescents, 563–564
  lesbian and gay, 449–450
  parent-child relationships and, 448–449, 553–555
  permissive, 333, 335
  power-assertive methods in, 334
  restrictiveness-permissiveness in, 333
  styles, 334–336, 349, 451–452, 555
  substance abuse by adolescents and, 511
  warmth-coldness in, 332–333
  withdrawal of love and, 334
  See also families; fathers; mothers

participant modeling, 357

passive sentences, 323

patterns of attachment, 222–224

patterns of eating, preschoolers', 277–278, *278*

patterns of intellectual development, 422–423

Pavlov, Ivan, *28*

PCBs, 103, *105*

PCP, *506*

peer relationships
  adolescent, *458*, 555–559
  in early childhood, 341, 343, *458*
  in middle childhood, 456–458, *458*
  sexual behavior and, 564

pelvic inflammatory disease, 67, 490

pendulum problem, 521

perceptual constancy, 174

peripheral vision, 171

permissive parenting, 333, 335

personal fables, 522, 523

personality development, 252
  in early childhood, 355–366

self-concept in, 253–254
  temperament and, 254–256

perspective taking, 348, 444, *444*

phallic stage in psychosexual development, 10, *12*

phenotypes, 62

phenylketonuria (PKU), 5, *55*, 56–57

phobias, 469, 470–471

phonetic method in reading instruction, 432–433

physical activity
  in early childhood, 270–272
  in middle childhood, 380–381
  prenatal, *118*
  television and, 310
  weight control and, 376

physical growth and development
  adolescence, 479–482, *480, 481*
  brain and nervous system, 162–166, 266–268
  cephalocaudal, 80, 152–153
  early childhood, 266, *267*
  height and weight, 5, 153–156, *155*, 266, *267*, 372, *373*
  middle childhood, 372–378, *373*
  motor, 4, 166–170, 269–276
  nutrition and, 157–162, 372–373
  sensory and perceptual, 171–181
  sequences, 152–153
  sex similarities and differences in, 373

Piaget, Jean, 7, *18*, 18–20, *28*
  applications to education, 399–401
  concrete-operational stage, 396–401
  evaluation of, 302–304, 401
  formal operations stage, 518–522
  pendulum problem, 521
  preoperational stage, *20*, 296–305
  on sensorimotor development, 193, 195–196
  theory of moral development in, 402–403

pictorial stage in drawing, 273

pincer grasp, 167, *167*

pituitary gland, 479

placement stage in drawing, 272, 273

placenta, 79, 84–85

plasticity of the brain, 268

play
  cognitive development and, 344
  constructive, 344
  dramatic, 344
  formal games, 344
  functional, 344
  gender differences in, 346–347, 525
  nonsocial, 344–346, *345*
  social, *345*, 345–346

symbolic, 296–297, *297*, 344
  types of, 344–346

polychlorinated biphenyls, 103, *105*

polygenic traits, 48

positive correlations, 35

positive reinforcers, 14, 15–16

postconventional level of moral development, *404*, 406, 528–529

postpartum depression, 128–129

postpartum period, 127–130

power-assertive methods in parenting, 334

pragmatics, 323–324

preconventional level of moral development, *404*, 405

pregnancy, teenage, 564–568

pregnancy and conception, 4
  implantation period, 80
  infertility and, 66–69
  ova in, 64, *65, 66*, 67
  ovarian cycle and, *79*
  sperm cells and, 64, 65–66, *66*, 66–67
  teenage, 564–568
  See also prenatal period

preimplantation genetic diagnosis, 69

premature birth, 96

prenatal period, the
  defined, 4
  drugs used during, 97–102, *105*, 177–178
  embryonic stage, 80–85
  environmental influences on, 93–106
  fetal stage, 85–89
  germinal stage, 78–80
  maternal stress during, 104
  nutrition, 93–94
  parents' age and, 104
  sex selection, 69, 70, *71*
  sexually transmitted infections and, 95–96
  teratogens, 94–97
  testing and genetic counseling, 58–61, 64
  weight gain, 94
  See also pregnancy and conception

preoperational stage in cognitive development, *20*
  appearance-reality distinction in, 314–315
  causality in, 298–299, *300*, 304, *305*
  confusion of mental and physical events, 299, *305*
  egocentrism in, 298, *300*, 304, *305*
  evaluation of, 302–304
  focus on one dimension at a time in, 300–302, *305*

preoperational stage in cognitive development (*continued*)
    symbolic play, 296–297, *297*
    symbolic thought, 296, *305*
    transformers of the mind, 297–298
prepared childbirth, 118–119
preschool, 459
preschoolers. *See* early childhood
pretend play, 296–297, *297*
preterm infants, 122–127
prevention
    academic problems, 535
    accident, 281–283
    eating disorders, 502–503
    juvenile delinquency, 571
    school drop out, 536
    sexually transmitted infections, 492–493
    substance abuse, 511–512
primary circular reactions, *190,* 190–191
primary sex characteristics, 479
priming of aggressive thoughts and memories, 352
problem solving in middle childhood, 406–412
progestin, 98, *105*
prosocial behavior, 347–349
prostaglandins, 113
protein-energy malnutrition, 160
proximodistal development, 80, 153, *154*
psychoanalytic perspective on child development, 9–13, *28*
    adolescence and, 478
    attachment and, 227, *230*
    middle childhood and, 443
    self-concept in, 253–254
psycholinguistic theory, 214
psychological androgyny, 365–366
psychological disorders and child abuse, 237
psychological impact of menarche, 485–486
psychological moratorium, 547, *548,* 549
psychosexual development, 9–11, *12, 28*
psychosocial development, 10, 11–13, *28,* 356, 443
psychotherapy, 467
puberty
    changes in boys, 482–483, *483*
    changes in girls, 484–486, *486*
    growth spurt during, 479–482
    sexual activity onset and, 563
pubic lice, *495*

publishing findings of studies, 33
punishments, 14, 16
pygmalion effect, 462

questions asking by preschoolers, 323

race. *See* ethnicity and culture
radiation exposure, 103–104, *105*
random assignments in experiments, 36–37
reaction range, 61–62
reaction time, 378–379
reading
    disability (*See* dyslexia)
    methods of teaching, 432–433
    skills and literacy, 431–432
realism, moral, 402
reasoning
    moral, 528–532
    transductive, 299
recall memory, 315–316, *316,* 410
receptive vocabulary, 205
recessive and dominant traits, 51–53
reciprocity, 529
recognition tasks, 315–316, *316*
referencing, social, 251
referential language style, 208
reflexes, neonate, 131–134, *189,* 190
register, sensory, 407–408
regression, 339
regulation, emotional, 251–252
rehearsal and memory, 318, 408
reinforcement, 14, 15–16
    attachment and, 227
    language development and, 210–213
rejecting-neglecting parenting, 333
rejection, peer, 456–457
releasing stimuli and attachment, 227, 229
REM sleep, 140–142
research
    cross-sectional, 37, *38,* 38–39
    cross-sequential, 39, *39*
    longitudinal, 37–39, *38*
    questions, 33
respiratory distress syndrome, 124, 125
restrictiveness-permissiveness in parenting, 333
retardation, mental, 424
retrieval cues, 317–318, 407–410
Rett's disorder, 240
reversibility in concrete-operational stage, 396
rh incompatibility, 96–97, *105*
right brain, 268
right-handedness, 274–276
risk taking in adolescence, 496–497, 523

rivalry, sibling, 339
romantic relationships among adolescents, 557–558
rooting reflex, 132, *132*
rote learning, 409
Rousseau, Jean-Jacques, 6–7
rubella, 96, *105*

scaffolding, 25, 306
schemes in cognitive-developmental theory, 18–19, 191, *191*
schizophrenia, 122
schools
    adolescents and, 532–536
    dropouts, 533–536, *534*
    elementary, 532–533
    refusal, 470–471
    structure in middle childhood, 459–463, 532–533
    See also education
scientific method, 32–34, *33*
scripts, memory, 316–318
secondary circular reactions, 191, *191*
secondary sex characteristics, 479
secure attachment, 222–224
sedatives, 504
selective attention, 407
selective reinforcement, 211
self, the, 355–356
self-concept
    in adolescence, 552
    in middle childhood, 445–448
    personality development and, 253–254
self-efficacy expectations, 537
self-esteem, 355, 445–446
    in adolescence, 552–553, 555–556
self-fulfilling prophecies, 462
semantic codes, 409
semen, 482–483
sensitive period in language development, 215–216
sensorimotor stage in cognitive development, *20,* 188–192
    object permanence and, 192–195, 196
sensory and perceptual development
    active-passive controversy in, 178–180
    coordination of senses and, 177–178
    hearing, 137, 175–177
    nature and nurture in, 180–181
    in neonates, 134–139
    vision, 134–136, 171–174
sensory memory, 407–408
sentence development, 208–209
separation anxiety, 222, 469–470
separation-individuation, 253–254
seriation, 398, *399, 400*

serotonin, 145, 467
Sesame Street, 309–310
sex
    children's questions about, 449
    chromosomes, 49
    differences (*See* gender)
    education, 566, *567*
    identity development and, 551–552
    -linked chromosomal abnormalities, 53–56
    -linked genetic abnormalities, 57–58
    oral, 563
    selection, 69, 70, *71*
sex hormones
    gender differences in, 361, *363*
    and sexual differentiation in embryos, *82–83,* 82–84
    sexual orientation and, 562
sexism in the classroom, 463
sexual abuse of children, 234, 235, 239
sexual harassment, 463
sexual orientation
    of adolescents, 560–562
    of parents, 449–450
sexuality, adolescent
    influences on, 559–560
    male-female sexual behavior in, 562–564
    masturbation in, 560
    sexually transmitted infections and, 490–496
    teenage pregnancy and, 564–568
sexually transmitted infections
    adolescents and, 490–496
    prenatal development and, 95–96
shape constancy, 174, 175
shape stage in drawing, 273
shaping
    behavior, 16
    vocabulary, 211
short-term memory, 408–409
siblings
    adjusting to birth of, 337, 339
    attachment to mothers, 224
    birth order and, 340–341
    influence in early childhood, 336–339
    intelligence and, *428,* 430
    rivalry, 339
sickle-cell anemia, *55, 57*
sight vocabulary, 433
sign language, 206–207, 216
Simon, Theodore, 7
size constancy, 174
Skinner, B. F., *14, 28*
sleep
    cross-cultural diversity in arrangements for, 285

disorders, 284, 286
    divorce and, 452
    insomnia, 286
    preschoolers and, 283–286
    terrors, 284, 286
    and waking patterns in neonates, 139–142
    walking, 286
slow to warm up temperaments, 254–256
small for dates infants, 122–123
smell sense in neonates, 137–138
smiling and imprinting, 227–229
smoking
    by adolescents, 504–505, *506*
    during pregnancy, 101–102, *105*
Snellen chart, *134,* 134–135
social and emotional development
    dimensions of child rearing and, 332–334
    divorce and, 450–453
    gay and lesbian parents and, 449–450
    influence of siblings on, 336–341
    maternal employment and, 454–455
    in middle childhood, 442–448
    parenting styles and, 334–336
    peer relationships in, 341, 343
    problems in middle childhood, 464–472, *468*
social cognitive theory, 17–18, *28*
    day care and, 244–248
    gender differences and, 362–364, *363*
    middle childhood and, 443
    substance abuse and, 511
social deprivation and attachment, 231–233
social intelligence, 417
social learning and aggression, 350–351
social play, *345,* 345–346
social referencing, 251
social smiles, infant, 227
socialization, 16, 456
Society for Research in Child Development, 39–40
sociocultural perspective on child development, 24–27, *29*
socioeconomic differences
    in growth, 482
    in intelligence, 426–427
    teenage pregnancy and, 565
solitary play, *345*
somnambulism, 286
sonograms, 59–60, *60*
soothing neonates, 143
speech, inner, 325
sperm cells, 64, 65–66, *66,* 66–67
spina bifida, 58, 61
spontaneous abortion, 65, 80

stability
    attachment, 225–226
    temperament, 255
stage theory, 9–10
stages of attachment, 226
stages of childbirth
    first, 113–114
    second, *114,* 114–116
    third, 116
standardized tests, 34, 35
    intelligence, 416–422, 428
Stanford-Binet Intelligence Scale, 418–419, *419,* 428
status offenses, 569
statuses, identity, 547–549, *548*
stepfamilies, 453
stepping reflex, 133, *133*
stereotypes, gender, 358, 365–366
stillbirth, 93
stimulant drugs, 504–505, *506*
stimulus and behavior, 13, 227
strangers, fear of, 250–251
streptomycin, *105*
stress
    child abuse and, 236
    in child adjusting to birth of a sibling, 337, 339
    child vulnerability to, 472
    divorce and, 453–454
    maternal, 104
study of child development
    adoption and, 63
    correlation in, 35–36
    day care and, 244–246
    ethical considerations, 39–40
    experiments in, 36–37
    information gathering, 34–35
    kinship, 62–63
    longitudinal research in, 37–39
    scientific method in, 32–34
    social deprivation, 231–233
substance abuse
    by adolescents, 503–512
    depressants, 504, *506*
    factors in, 509–511
    prenatal development and, 97–102, *105*
    prevalence of, 507–508, *510*
    prevention, 511–512
    race and, 509
    stimulants, 504–505, *506*
    students' attitudes toward, 508–509
    treatment, 511–512
    See also drugs
Sudden infant death syndrome (SIDS), 5, 143–145
suicide, 572–575

surface structure of language, 214
surrogate mothers, 68–69
symbolic play, 296–297, *297,* 344
symbolic thought, 296
symbols, abstract, 520, 522
syphilis, 490, *495*
    congenital, 95, *105*

taste sense in neonates, 138
Tay-Sachs disease, *55,* 57
teachers, 461–463
teenage pregnancy, 564–568
telegraphing ideas, 208–209, 216
television
    cognitive development and, 309–312
    weight control and, 376
temperament, 254–256
teratogens and prenatal development,
    94–97
Terman Studies of Genius, 37, 38
terrors, sleep, 284, 286
tertiary circular reactions, 191–192, *192*
testimony by children, eyewitness, 412
testosterone
    in adolescence, 482, 485
    in embryos, 82–83
    Klinefelter syndrome and, 56
tests, standardized, 34, 35
tetracycline, *105*
thalassemia, *55*
thalidomide, 98, *105*
theories of aggression, 350–354
theories of attachment, 226–229, *230*
theories of child development
    biological perspective, 21–22, *29*
    cognitive, 18–21, *28,* 188–195
    diversity and, 24, 25–27
    ecological perspective, 22–24, *29*
    learning perspective, 13–18, *28*
    psychoanalytic, 9–13, *28*
    purpose of, 8–9
    sociocultural perspective, 24–27, *29*
theory of mind, 312–315
thinking
    divergent, 427
    hypothetical, 519–520
    utopian, 520
time out punishment, 16
time-lag comparisons, 39, *39*

Tinbergen, Niko, 21
toddlers, 168, *169*
    language development in, 205–207
    peer relationships, 341
toilet training, 287, *287*
tolerance, drug, 503
tonic-neck reflex, 133, *134*
touch and pain sense in neonates,
    138–139
toxemia, 96
tranquilizers, 117
transductive reasoning, 299
transformers of the mind, 297–298
transition, labor, 114
transitional objects and sleep, 284
transitivity, 398–399
transsexuals, 450
treatment
    ADHD, 386
    autism spectrum disorders, 242–243
    conduct disorders, 465
    depression, 467
    eating disorders, 502–503
    experiments, 36
    juvenile delinquency, 571
    sexually transmitted infections,
        494–495
    substance abuse, 511–512
triarchic theory of intelligence, 414, *416*
trichomoniasis, *495*
trophoblast, 79
trust versus mistrust in psychosocial
    development, *12*
Turner syndrome, *54,* 56
twins, 50–51, 62–63, *428,* 430, 562
two-word sentences, 209, 211
typology, career, 537–538, *539*

ulnar grasp, 167
ultrasound, 59–60, *60*
umbilical cord, 79, *116,* 122
unconditioned response, 13
unconditioned stimulus, 13
unconscious, the, 10
unoccupied play, *345*
utopian thinking, 520

vaccines, *279,* 280, *280, 281*
vacuum extraction tube, 113

vagina, 484
vaginosis, bacterial, *494*
vasopressin, 129
verbal ability in adolescents, 524
vernix, 123–124, *124*
video games, violent, 353
violence in the media, 311, 351–354
vision
    brain development and, 267–268
    depth perception in, 173–174
    development, 171–174
    neonate, 134–136
    peripheral, 171
visual accommodation, 136
visual acuity, 134–136, 171
visual recognition memory, 201–202,
    315–316, *316*
visual-spatial ability in adolescents,
    524–525, *525*
vitamins, 98, *105*
vocabulary development, 205–208,
    319–321, 431
Vygotsky, Lev Semenovich, 24, 25, *25,*
    29

walking, sleep, 286
warmth-coldness of parents, 332–333
Watson, John B., 7, 8, *13,* 13–14, *28*
Wechsler Scales, 419–420, *420,* 428
Wernicke's aphasia, 215, *215*
whole-object assumption, 320
withdrawal of love by parents, 334
word-recognition method in reading
    instruction, 432–433
working memory, 408–409
written expression, disorder of, *387*

XXX syndrome, *54*
XYY syndrome, *54*

zinc exposure, *105*
zona pellucida, 66
zone of proximal development, 25, 306
zygotes, 64